# THE PENGUIN HISTORY OF AUSTRALIAN CRICKET

1-12-09

Dear Stripy John,

We hope this book will help you to play better.

Love

Adrienne and Michael

VIKING

Published by the Penguin Group
Penguin Group (Australia)
250 Camberwell Road, Camberwell, Victoria 3124, Australia
(a division of Pearson Australia Group Pty Ltd)
Penguin Group (USA) Inc.
375 Hudson Street, New York, New York 10014, USA
Penguin Group (Canada)
90 Eglinton Avenue East, Suite 700, Toronto, Canada ON M4P 2Y3
(a division of Pearson Penguin Canada Inc.)
Penguin Books Ltd
80 Strand, London WC2R 0RL England
Penguin Ireland
25 St Stephen's Green, Dublin 2, Ireland
(a division of Penguin Books Ltd)
Penguin Books India Pvt Ltd
11 Community Centre, Panchsheel Park, New Delhi – 110 017, India
Penguin Group (NZ)
67 Apollo Drive, Rosedale, North Shore 0632, New Zealand
(a division of Pearson New Zealand Ltd)
Penguin Books (South Africa) (Pty) Ltd
24 Sturdee Avenue, Rosebank, Johannesburg 2196, South Africa

Penguin Books Ltd, Registered Offices: 80 Strand, London, WC2R 0RL, England

First published by André Deutsch Ltd 1993
Second edition published by Carlton Books Ltd 2003
This revised edition first published by Carlton Books Ltd 2008
This revised edition published by Penguin Group (Australia) 2008

1 3 5 7 9 10 8 6 4 2



Typeset by SX Composing Ltd, Essex
Printed by Mackays, UK

National Library of Australia
Cataloguing-in-Publication data:

Harte, Chris
The Penguin history of Australian cricket.
Rev. and updated ed.
Includes index.
ISBN 9780670072873 (pbk.)
1. Cricket – Australia – History. I. Whimpress, Bernard, 1948–. II. Title.

796.3580994

penguin.com.au

# THE PENGUIN HISTORY OF AUSTRALIAN CRICKET

**CHRIS HARTE**
**with Bernard Whimpress**

**REVISED and UPDATED**

**Introduction by**
**RICHIE BENAUD**

VIKING
*an imprint of*
PENGUIN BOOKS

*Cricket books by the same author*

The Fight for the Ashes, 1982–83
Cricket Rebels
The History of the Sheffield Shield
Cricket Safari
Seven Tests
Two Tours and a Pollock
SACA: The History of the South Australian Cricket Association
Cricket Indulgence
Reminiscences of a Sportswriter

# Introduction

## by Richie Benaud

Australian cricket is different. The club with which I played cricket at grade level in Sydney, Central Cumberland, originally the Parramatta club but sometimes known as Cumberland and now again as Parramatta, was a focal point of cricket in the early days of the Colony and I grew up with a love of the written word of cricket history.

Like any other Australian youngster living in a country area, I watched matches between adjoining towns and played on antbed or polished concrete pitches then, when moving to Sydney, I played 'Test' matches on dirt pitches in a paddock and on concrete pitches, sometimes with a type of matting over them, in an open park. Rarely though did I play on turf, and this has always been one of the big differences between Australian cricket and English cricket. That need not come as a shock but it should be borne in mind when reading anything conected with the game which has been part of Australian culture for a little less than two hundred years.

The emphasis was on rough facilities and cricket played in the early days in a harsh outback. From those areas come some of the greatest cricketers ever to appear at International level, cricketers who followed on from the standards set by W. L. Murdoch's team in 1882.

It was not a matter of living in the past because I have long held the belief that, as we approach the twenty-first century, thc players are every bit as good or better than those who went before them. It is very important though, that occurrences prior to this modern era should be correctly recorded and this should be done in a fashion which the reader will find fulfilling. It is essential in modern times, with the emphasis on television and videotape libraries of history, that the written word should not be discarded.

It was time for the history of Australian cricket to be updated and for further research to be done on matters which for many years have been lacking in some detail.

A wise choice has been made in asking Chris Harte to do the job because few pay more attention to detail or have the ability to find new aspects of a subject where, at first glance, the facts might appear to have been exhausted.

There are many these days who are more interested in matters other than history, but I have always been fascinated by the history of cricket. The story of that first Australian victory in England in 1882 made nerve-tingling reading for me as a youngster, and it hasn't changed these days when again I browse through the *Bell's Life* account of that wonderful tour. For an Australian team to have pulled off the stunning victory assumes pride of place with me in the whole of Australian cricket history.

The prime requirement of a book of this kind is accuracy and Chris Harte is accurate. Another requirement is to probe and he does that well, so well that some of his research has produced new information about various aspects of Australian cricket. No game contains more good or ill fortune than cricket and Mr Harte has had the good fortune to find this new material and we are all in his debt.

The saga of Bill McElhone and Ernie Bean is one which has been mentioned in early histories but not in the fascinating detail shown here, and any modern history must include the arrival of World Series Cricket and the changed structure of the game in Australia. Australian cricket has gone through some turbulent times over the period from 1803 to 1993 and Chris Harte has caught my attention by chronicling matters of which previously I had no knowledge.

From what is written in the following pages, it seems we should await with great anticipation the details of the finale of World Series Cricket and how the agreement between the Australian Cricket Board and World Series Cricket was signed. That will be no more intriguing than the indication that there were reasons Sir Donald Bradman decided not to renominate for his administrative position in cricket in the aftermath of the final agreement.

The 'Gabba Test of 1963, where Ian Meckiff was no-balled, was the last time I captained Australia. It also appears now to have been a match which followed on discussions about Ian at an Australian Board of Control meeting prior to the Test against South Africa. This is interesting enough but, even more so, is that fact that, astonishingly, a legal opinion was obtained.

I knew about Sir Donald Bradman addressing the Australian players prior to the Tied Test in Brisbane because I was there, and I was also at the Melbourne Cricket Ground when 90,800 spectators paid £18,000 at the turnstiles. I'd forgotten until reminded in these pages what innovative methods they used to protect the cash!

There is no doubt about the turbulent nature of the early days when interstate matches were played and rivalry was intense. It may surprise that such rivalry could exist in a young country, but I suppose there is comparison possible with the feeling between Yorkshire and Lancashire and similar happenings in other countries.

The New South Wales–Victoria matches in which I played in the period from 1948 to 1964 were, on many occasions, tougher than Test cricket.

This is probably because the first mainland intercolonial match in Australia was between these two States and the accounts of the game lend weight to the suggestion that, from 1856, rivalry between Victoria and NSW has sometimes been as intense as the rivalry between Australia and England for the Ashes.

Some books tracing the history of a sport or other aspects of life can vary between being interesting and dry as the dust which adorns their jackets. This *History of Australian Cricket* is factual and lively in style, and I am delighted to have the privilege of offering an Introduction to a book which will assume a very important part of the total history of the game.

RICHIE BENAUD
1993

# Contents


| | | |
|---|---|---|
| Introduction by Richie Benaud | | v |
| *List of Illustrations* | | *xi* |
| *Author's Preface and Acknowledgements* | | xiii |
| 1 | Colonial Days | 1 |
| 2 | Intercolonial Visits | 32 |
| 3 | Early Tours | 58 |
| 4 | The Game Develops | 80 |
| 5 | Overseas | 99 |
| 6 | Ashes to Ashes | 115 |
| 7 | Disagreements | 132 |
| 8 | Revival with Lord Sheffield | 150 |
| 9 | The Australasian Cricket Council | 178 |
| 10 | The Decline of Player Power | 202 |
| 11 | Triangular Troubles | 242 |
| 12 | War and the AIF | 259 |
| 13 | Armstrong and 1921 | 273 |
| 14 | Sport and Politics | 283 |
| 15 | The Changing of the Guard | 298 |
| 16 | The Bradman Factor | 318 |
| 17 | Bodyline: Causes and Effects, 1932–34 | 339 |
| 18 | A Feast of runs and crowds | 359 |
| 19 | 'No-one remembers us now' | 384 |
| 20 | Resumption | 392 |
| 21 | Bradman and after, 1948–51 | 404 |
| 22 | Board Matters | 417 |

| | | |
|---|---|---|
| 23 | The 1950s – Cricket in the Doldrums | 432 |
| 24 | Cricket in Controversy | 450 |
| 25 | The Benaud Years | 472 |
| 26 | Educating the Board | 492 |
| 27 | Sponsorship and the World XI | 520 |
| 28 | Disciplinary Problems | 542 |
| 29 | Test Match Pay | 557 |
| 30 | WSC v. the Board | 579 |
| 31 | The Rapprochement | 606 |
| 32 | Politicking | 630 |
| 33 | Official and Unofficial | 649 |
| 34 | The Crowds decline | 666 |
| 35 | 'The Nervous Nineties' | 679 |
| 36 | The Fifth World Cup | 698 |
| 37 | The Story So Far | 705 |
| 38 | That Ball – The End of the Border Years | 715 |
| 39 | The Taylor Era | 724 |
| 40 | Waugh Time | 740 |
| 41 | Eighth World Cup and Waugh's End | 755 |
| 42 | Ponting at the Helm | 764 |
| 43 | A New Game? | 787 |

| | | |
|---|---|---|
| Appendix A | Australian Test averages (to March 2008) | 795 |
| Appendix B | Pura Cup Winners (formerly Sheffield Shield) | 822 |
| Appendix C | Australian Limited-over averages | 823 |
| Appendix D | Select Bibliography | 832 |

Index 841

# Illustrations

The old Albert Ground in Redfern, Sydney, 1874; twenty-two of South Australia play W.G. Grace's team, 26 March 1874

Charles Lawrence and a group of old cricketers, c. 1890; scoreboard of NSW's big defeat of South Australia, 1900–01; Australia v. England, third Test, January 1902

Clem Hill; Victor Trumper; Montague Noble; the 1902 team to England

Warren Bardsley strikes out for Australia v. South Africa, May 27, 1912; the 1912 Australian team to England

George Giffen in 1918, aged 59; Trumper in his late years; Giffen's 'early risers'

Warwick Armstrong; Charlie McCartney; Armstrong leads out his team, 1921

The 1926 Australians; scoreboard of Victoria's record total of 1,107

A gathering of old cricketers, 1929; the Australian team of 1930 arrives at Dover

Third 'Bodyline' Test at Adelaide Oval; Woodfull struck; Oldfield hit on head

Woodfull and Ponsford; Bradman; Richardson; Grimmett

The Australian and England teams being photographed, 1938; relaxation at golf – Ted White, Don Bradman, Ernie McCormick and Bill Jeanes

Bradman batting in 1948; Syd Webb, Syd Smith and Aubrey Oxlade, 1952

Keith Miller; the 1953 team at Worcester

The Australian team for the fourth Test against West Indies, 1960–61; Mackay and Kline in their last-wicket stand

Benaud bowling at Lord's in 1961; Davidson bowling against MCC on the same tour

South Australia celebrate winning the Sheffield Shield, 1963–64; Bobby Simpson, captain of the 1964 Australians, batting in the opening match in England

Bobby Simpson and Bill Lawry, openers and successive captains; Board of Control meeting in 1969

Ian Chappell; Chappell's team at Edgbaston, 1975

Dennis Lillee; Jeff Thomson

Greg Chappell batting, 1977; (*below*) his team for the Centenary Test tour of England, 1980

The WACA ground at Perth – John Inverarity stand unveiling of the Clarrie Grimmett Stone, with Len Darling, Bill O'Reilly, Sir Donald Bradman

Sir Donald Bradman at the opening of the Bradman Stand, Adelaide Oval, January 1990; Allan Border, whose 1989 side brought home the Ashes; Marsh and Taylor, 301 for no wicket

That ball! Shane Warne dimisses Gatting, 1993; Merv 'the Swerve' Hughes

Allan Border v. South Africa, 1994; Michael Clarke celebrates his century on debut, v. India, Bangalore, 2004

Mark Taylor shoulders arms v. Pakistan, 1998; Mark Waugh and Warne 'fess up, 1998

Mark Waugh and Darren Lehmann in World Cup Final, 1999; Warne traps England's Marcus Trescothick, The Oval, 2005

Michael Hussey, a prolific run scorer from the start of his Test career; Glenn McGrath catches Michael Vaughan, Adelaide, 2002

Adam Gilchrist set a new template for wicket-keeper/batsmen; World Cup celebrations, 2003

Stuart Clark, part of the new breed of Australian pace men; Justin Langer, McGrath and Warne say goodbye to Test cricket, 2007

Matthew Hayden, top run-scorer at the 2007 World Cup; Glenn McGrath bows out of international cricket with the World Cup, 2007

*Acknowledgements for the illustrations are given in the captions to the pictures. The authors and the publishers would like particularly to acknowledge the illustrations that have been taken from* True to the Blue: A History of the New South Wales Association *by Philip Derriman, published by Richard Smart Publishing (1985). Where no source is mentioned the copyright is the author's. Colour section supplied by Getty Images.*

# Preface to the Third Edition

It was a great pleasure to bring this book up to date for a second time, but the last five years seem to have passed as swiftly as yesterday. Well, they do until one realises how much cricket Australia has packed into that time: 56 Test matches in 20 series; 24 limited-over international series including a World Cup and two Champions Trophies; and now the new game, Twenty20, which has been fitted into an already bursting schedule.

Australia has maintained its ascendancy but there have been occasional dips as well as peaks. The main dip was losing the best Test series ever – the Ashes of 2005 – although most pundits felt it was good for the game. Minor slips were posting a then world-record one-day international score of 434 for four at Johannesburg in 2006, but losing by one wicket off the final ball; and losing five successive ODI matches in a row entering the 2007 World Cup. The peaks were winning the Border-Gavaskar trophy in India in 2004, the first series victory on the subcontinent since 1969; exacting enormous revenge by beating England 5-0 in the 2006-07 Ashes series; dominating the 2007 World Cup without losing a game; and establishing a second 16-game winning streak in Test matches from December 2005 to January 2008.

In one sense Australian cricket has been stable with leadership of the Test team passing seamlessly to Ricky Ponting upon Steve Waugh's retirement in 2004, so that Ponting has led his country in both major forms of the game since 2004. In another it has been innovative with winter Test matches staged at Darwin and Cairns in 2003 and 2004, bringing the current total of Australian Test venues to eight.

Inevitably players' careers draw to a close and Australia has lost several cricketing giants – Steve Waugh, Glenn McGrath, Shane Warne (although he tantalises about returning) and Adam Gilchrist – along with brilliant performers such as Damien Martyn, Justin Langer, Jason Gillespie and Stuart MacGill. Australian cricketing stocks are strong, if not as deep as in 2003, and I look forward to our sides continuing to play fine cricket in a changing world in the years ahead.

Bernard Whimpress
Adelaide, June 2008

# Author's Preface and Acknowledgements

It all started in a taxi in late 1976. One the way home from an evening's imbibing, two Australian historians, Richard Cashman and Michael McKernan, fell into conversation regarding the public lack of knowledge on the history of sport. They came to the conclusion that a conference on the subject would be a good idea.

They thought what they were doing was unique, as indeed it was in Australian terms. But they were unaware that, four years earlier, in 1972, the North American Society for Sports History had started, with a foundation convention a year later.

The University of New South Wales supported the idea of an Australian conference, and this was held in July 1977. Suddenly, from out of the closet came academics and historians who, according to Cashman, 'declared that they "would really have liked to have written this history years ago"' or saying 'This is really what I want to work on . . . and now feel more justified in doing so'. Cashman himself added that 'it was certainly an exhilarating and encouraging experience to find that so many shared this perspective'. Conferences were held in 1979 and 1981 without any formal basis, while in England, Richard Cox had founded the British Society of Sports History in 1982.

The 1983 Australian conference was originally scheduled for Canberra until the Melbourne Cricket Club made an offer to stage the gathering. This was a significant watershed for the sports history movement which not only found a suitable home outside academe, at the Melbourne Cricket Ground itself, but offered the opportunity to invite journalists, active sports persons and club officials.

It was discovered at Melbourne that there was a wider audience for sports history than ever imagined. The papers presented varied in quality but the atmosphere was stimulating. It was the first time I had met such a wide group of people with the same interests as myself and with such a high level of debate. At that meeting we launched the Australian Society for Sports History (ASSH).

From then until my return to live in England in late 1990, I was deeply involved in an organisation with which it was a privilege to be associated. They taught me so much and, from the likes of Richard Cashman, Wray Vamplew, Richard Stremski, Max Howell, Ian Jobling, John O'Hara and others came a completely revisionist attitude towards the writing and research of Australian sport.

To the expert and aficionado the quality of Australian cricket publications had nose-dived in the 1960s and 1970s to become little more than 'pot-boilers'. Maybe one or two – but no more – stood out from the pack but even then their works were of the old-style English 'jolly good show, old chaps'. They told 'super-duper' stories of Don Bradman, were sad about anti-establishment characters such as Sid Barnes, and looked upon the four-yearly cycle of visits from English teams as the social and sporting occasion of the time.

To my mind, and I know there are many who agree with me, the formation of ASSH was the catalyst in the writing on Australian sport. No longer did the reader only have obsequious publications full of mythology to read but slowly and surely came histories and biographies which told the truth: warts and all. Now we could read and learn more about our favoured sport. Australian Rules football had Stremski's magnificent work on Collingwood; Vamplew's was on professionalism in sport; Colin Tatz on Aborigines; O'Hara on gaming and betting, Geoff Lawrence and David Rowe on commercialisation, and Bob Stewart on football.

Cricket saw the emergence of writers of skill who cleared away so much of the fantasy created by those who only knew how to wriye for a quick dollar. Without doubt Cashman started the ball rolling. His *Patron, Players and the Crowd: The Phenomenon of Indian Cricket* (1980) showed us what he could do but it was his first Australian work *'Ave A Go, Yer Mug!* (1984) followed immediately by *Australian Cricket Crowds: The Attendance Cycle* (1984) which opened the eyes of us stagnant beings. Cashman's objectivity and Vamplew's gentle prodding made me realise some of the faults in my own initial major cricketing effort, *The Fight for the Ashes 1982–83*.

Two friends, alas no longer with us, showed me the untouched treasures which lay in the files of cricket bodies throughout Australia. My first serious venture, *The History of the Sheffield*

*Shield*, gained information and detail which had not been published before. Even in 1985 the realisation dawned that the true history of Ausralian cricket had yet to be written. What lay in dusty, unloved, occasionally rotting files around the continent was very special. Regrettably, many were to be destroyed before I could read them.

As I was distracted with tour books and *The History of the South Australian Cricket Association* so more ASSH influenced works were seeing the light of day. Ric Sissons with his *The Players, A social history of the professional cricketer*; Cashman's biography of Fred Spofforth; Brian Stoddart on Saturday afternoon fever, Martin Sharp with cricket and rugby in late-nineteenth century Sydney; Max Howell with various books on Queensland sport; John Daly's various works, and especially *Elysian Fields*. It was a heady time in Australian sports writing with the biennial conferences getting bigger and better each time.

Then, out of the blue, came a telephone call from the librarian of the Melbourne Cricket Club, Rex Harcourt. Names were being suggested for this book and would I care to discuss the matter. Indeed I would, and after taking guidance from my mentors the processes leading up to an agreement were put into action. That all took place in July 1988, and for the best part of the following year I researched around the sporting archives of Australia in parallel with finishing another book and editing two professional journals.

Towards the end of 1989 a message left on my answering machine sent me scurrying to the palatial home of a cricket identity. He knew of my work and felt, somewhat strongly, that this history should reflect the truth as best it could. He asked me to look in some trunks. What was there was staggering and forms a large part of this work. Checking what I [had] read was difficult as many people were dead and others very reluctant to say too much – even of incidents long ago.

The freemasonry of Australian cricket has been somewhat breached by my efforts but there is far more work for future historians to do. My colleagues at ASSH have helped me through some very trying times during the writing of this work and I publicly thank them for the strength they gave me. There may be those in authority in the Australian game who will try and denigrate my words. Be assured, this is only the tip of a very large iceberg

When it came to making a list of the individuals who had helped me with this book it read like a 'Who's Who' of cricket. Therefore I feel it wise just to thank all of those people and to say how grateful I am for them for their time and effort.

This work has been researched in Australia, England, New Zealand and South Africa, and contains the benefit of over one hundred interviews recorded on both audio and video cassette. I now possess a splendid oral-history library.

Papers on sections of this book have been presented at Sports History conferences in Australia, Canada, England and the United States with the professional critiques and analysis being of enormous assistance for the final draft.

My wish is that the efforts of my work prove to be a catalyst amongst current and future cricket historians. Considerable research still needs to be undertaken on many aspects of Australia's cricket life. I hope this book can provide the inspiration needed.

# 1

# Colonial Days

### *Introduction*

Australia's national heroes have, in the main, been connected with sport. The country can relate to a Don Bradman more than to any politician; to a Dawn Fraser rather than to an artist; to athletes, swimmers, boxers, footballers of varying codes and even to a racehorse such as Phar Lap. Yet cricket is the only major *national* sport of the Australian continent.

When one looks for a national identity it could be said that the vast outback, or the surf, or even the goldfields contributed most to the search. Australian nationalism, however, really came of age when the first English cricket touring team arrived in late 1861 and from then on Australian sporting heroes have abounded in the minds of the nation.

The new world was now challenging the old. Not immediately on an equal footing of course. The colonials knew they were deficient and that they had to learn from their famous visitors. The attitudes they expressed were those of humility and deference, but the Australians did learn – and they learnt quickly.

### *New South Wales*

When Arthur Phillip sailed from Portsmouth in May 1787 to become the first Governor of the new land, his eleven ships carried over a thousand convicts and new settlers. By then the game of cricket had become established in many parts of the old country where, that same year, the Marylebone Cricket Club was founded and Thomas Lord took over his first ground. It is more than likely, therefore, that those early arrivals in Australia had played a type of cricket as part of their recreation. Both convict and soldier could well have improvised to provide themselves with bats, balls and stumps in the characteristic, resourceful way of pioneers.

For the first sixteen years of the life of European-ruled Australia, British ships came and went, many of them bringing their cargoes of misery to the new shores; but there is no report, not even in church records, of cricket being played in what was then called Sydney Town.

However, not long after Governor King took over at the beginning of the nineteenth century, he gave authority for the first newspaper to be printed. *The Sydney Gazette and New South Wales Advertiser* first appeared on 5 March 1803 and ten months later, on 8 January 1804, it reported on a game of cricket played by the officers and crew of HMS *Calcutta* on a cleared piece of land which is now known as Hyde Park: 'The late intense weather has been very favourable to the amateurs of cricket who have scarce lost a day for the last month. The frequent immoderate heat might have been considered inimical to the amusement, but was productive of the very opposite consequences, as the state of the atmosphere might always regulate the portions of exercise necessary to the ends of this laborious diversion was originally intended to answer.'

Alas, no scores were given by the paper which concerned itself mainly with government notices and cases in the courts.

The game was crude, as would be expected, and according to brief reports in the following years, cricket was played as a recreation with no thought of competition. Bats were heavy and used as bludgeons, wickets were roughly hewn and overs consisted of four deliveries.

The next reference in *The Gazette* came seven years later when the convict editor George Howe wrote on 28 April 1810: 'Monday last being Easter Monday, a fair commenced on the Cricket Ground, to which a sort of popular acquiescence has given the appellation of St George's Fields.'

The area was known by various names such as 'The Common', 'Racecourse', 'Exercising Ground', 'Phillip's Common' and others with 'St George's Fields' being in use for a short time in 1810 before 'Hyde Park' became officially sanctioned.

Then, on 5 October 1811, *The Gazette* published a government decree which outlined the boundaries of Sydney Common. This area included what would later become Moore Park and the Sydney Cricket Ground.

References to the game in those formative years are sketchy, but in 1821 Governor Macquarie was recorded 'as ordering bats from His Majesty's Lumber Yard for his son Lachlan, then a student at the Reverend Thomas Reddall's school at Macquarie Fields.' At this stage, though, horse racing was the most popular sport in the colony.

The real pioneers of cricket in Australia, however, were the British Army regiments and the New South Wales Army Corps who played the game regularly during the 1820s. A press report in *The Australian* on 9 August 1826 referred to a match held two days earlier on the 'Hyde Park ground'. After the match, presumably a scratch affair, the players suggested forming 'The Australian Cricket Club'. The same paper stated on 3 January 1827 that: 'The Australian Cricket Club had their periodical meeting on New Year's Day'. After 'some good playing', club members dined together. *The Sydney Gazette* of 12 January stated that 'the Members of the Cricket Club played a grand match at Hyde Park yesterday'. Another paper, *The Monitor*, sceptical about whether the Australian Cricket Club, or ACC, constituted a real club, argued on 1 January 1827 'that a few mechanics of Sydney got together on New Year's Day and attempted to play a few games at cricket, but their mode of handling their bats and balls was most unskilful, and worse playing was never witnessed either in England or the Colony'.

One crucial problem facing the ACC was to find an opponent. The Windsor Cricket Club, which was in existence at the beginning of 1827 and may even have been founded before the ACC, was reported to have declined to play the ACC and seems to have folded soon afterwards. A group of cricketers formed a club at Campbelltown in 1827 but this too seems to have collapsed quickly.

The lack of competition appears to be the main reason why there is no reference to cricket in the Sydney press for more than two years from 1 March 1827. Then *The Australian* of 16 September 1829 provided details of a new club, The Sydney Club, formed to take on the ACC and based on a paddock, the other side of the turnpike on the road west to Parramatta and the Blue Mountains, probably on the site of what is now the Central Station. The new club included a number of established Sydney merchants among its batsmen: Spyer, Paul, Levey and Mitchell. However, the new club was ejected from government-owned land in October 1829 and soon collapsed.

Fortunately yet another club had sprung up at Campbelltown and the ACC defeated them at Hyde Park on 25 January 1830. Although no details are known of the scores this is the first game of interclub competition in Sydney, let alone Australia. After the match victors and vanquished sat down to a substantial supper at 'Mr Hill's house of good cheer', probably the Wheelwrights Arms, kept by the ACC player David Hill. The Secretary of the ACC was directed to write to his counterpart to arrange a return match for fifty guineas but, like with so many others, there was no further mention of this Campbelltown Club. The problem of raising stake money of such magnitude seems to explain why there were so few interclub games in the 1830s and why so many clubs literally went into liquidation. ACC members continued to practise regularly at Hyde Park on Mondays.

The big games of 1830 were not between the emerging clubs but between 'Military' and 'Civilians'. As a result of a challenge from eleven from all Sydney, for £20 a side, matches were played on 26 February before several hundred spectators and on 23 March before an 'immense concourse'. The 'Civilians', referred to in some reports as 'Natives' since eight of the side were 'Currency lads' (i.e. colonial born), won both games. The bulk of the 'Civilians' came from the ACC.

The men of the British regiments were still the mainstay of the game in the central Sydney area. The 'Military' team of February 1830 were soldiers of the 57th (West Middlesex) Regiment. The story put about in later years of a 'Military Club' is quite incorrect, according to James Scott who chronicled much on the game in his book *Early Cricket in Sydney*. Scott's records, now in the library of the New South Wales Cricket Association, give no indication of any military club in the 1830s but they detail when various regiments organised teams. Between 1832 and 1835 the teams which played were made up from two regiments: the 17th and 39th (1832), and the 4th and 17th (1835).

The 1832 match, played on 7 May, aroused such interest amongst the population 'that an estimated two thousand attended', and 'more than £300 was said to have changed hands'. This match was also the first in which a complete scorecard was published (although the figures do not add up and 'not outs' are not given). A return match a fortnight later was equally well attended, and a third match followed between a 'Combined Military' and 'Civilians', most of whom again came from the Australian Cricket Club.

**39th REGIMENT**

| First Innings | | Second Innings | |
|---|---|---|---|
| Cowell, c Barker | 6 | c Conn | 0 |
| Hopewell, b Stafford | 12 | b Carnell | 0 |
| Lieut. G.C. Borough, b Stafford | 6 | c Webb | 2 |
| Gambler, b Carnell | 4 | b Carnell | 7 |
| Hyam, b Carnell | 2 | c Carnell | 0 |
| Upton, b Stafford | 0 | b Stafford | 2 |
| Hines, c Carnell | 3 | c Conn | 12 |
| Wren, b Stafford | 1 | b Carnell | 2 |
| Westbrook, c Turner | 20 | b Carnell | 5 |
| Osborne, b Stafford | 0 | b Stafford | 8 |
| Minahan | 0 | b Stafford | 1 |
| Bye | 1 | | 1 |
| **Total** | **55** | | **40** |

**17th REGIMENT**

| First Innings | | Second Innings | |
|---|---|---|---|
| Stafford, b Gambler | 20 | b Hopewell | 9 |
| Carnell, b Gambler | 6 | b Gambler | 4 |
| D. Conn, b Hopewell | 6 | b Gambler | 5 |
| J. Conn, b Hopewell | 2 | b Gambler | 8 |
| Arnold, c Upton | 0 | | |
| Donnelly, b Gambler | 4 | b Hopewell | 1 |
| Webb, c Borough | 7 | b Gambler | 0 |
| Turner, c Hopewell | 1 | b Gambler | 18 |
| Barker, b Gambler | 0 | | |
| Reeder, b Gambler | 0 | | |
| Lieut. W.R. Ball, b Gambler | 0 | | |
| Byes | 1 | | 5 |
| **Total** | **47** | | **50** |

Clubs were now starting to spring up all around the Sydney area. The Amateur Cricket Club (also known as Marylebone) was formed on 4 September 1832, followed by another Campbelltown club on 15 October, and then a short-lived club at Penrith.

Innkeepers played a prominent role in early club cricket – John Beeson was Treasurer of the Amateurs and Edward Flood a key figure for the Australian Cricket Club. When the Amateurs first played the ACC they had four innkeepers in their side and the ACC two, while another two players were probably brothers of innkeepers. Given that there were few other suitable public meeting places a pub was almost essential for club meetings and dinners, especially as a match was often played for a dinner. Publicans chipped in a little extra for the stake money which could vary from twenty to fifty guineas and provided the initial deposit (£5 for this game) to bind the match.

The first match between the ACC and the Amateurs took place on 15 October 1832 for a stake of £20. It was keenly contested. The Amateurs were successful, but there was a dispute after one of the ACC batsmen had been dismissed: 'one of the Amateurs challenged to fight for it, and this created a disturbance which well nigh terminated the game altogether'. Two subsequent matches between these clubs, on 29 October 1832 and 1 January 1833 for stakes of £30 and £50 respectively, were both won comfortably by the ACC, who, by 1832–33, had established themselves as a successful and well organised club, a position which they maintained for the next two decades. Although the bulk of the members were 'Currency Lads', the ACC could also boast men of status and influence. A British-born solicitor, Francis Stephen, who became joint editor of *The Australian* on 3 May 1833, came from a prominent colonial family. The Club was bolstered by the arrival in Sydney in October 1832 of the Hardy brothers, John and William, sons of Admiral Hardy. The former, a Cambridge 'Blue' of 1829, found that his round-arm bowling was regarded as unfair, it not being accepted in Australia until 1843 when Robert Still's action was allowed, although even then not universally approved. John Hardy became editor of *The Australian* in November 1834. He, along with his brother and John Rickards, son of a merchant who became a wholesale importer and haberdasher, were men of professional status and education who played alongside less privileged figures such as the self-made publican and 'original club member', Edward Flood. Born in Sydney in 1805, Flood was the illegitimate son of an Irish convict who was to become a successful and prominent builder, pastoralist*

*A pastoralist denotes a person who has obtained a large amount of good quality grazing land for use by cattle or, as in Flood's case, sheep. He also became an umpire after ceasing to play.

and politician after he retired from playing cricket in 1837. Another notable player was Edward William Gregory. He was an infant when his parents arrived in the colony in 1814, but after his mother died in 1819, Gregory's father returned to England leaving him and his two brothers in the Male Orphan Institute. Edward, initially a tradesman, later became a master at Cape's Grammar School. He had seven sons, three of whom (Fred, Walter and Albert) played club cricket, but David, Charles, Edward and Arthur also represented New South Wales.

After internal wranglings the Australian Cricket Club reappeared in time to play the Union Club on 28 December 1837. Other clubs at this time were coming and going: the Union Club lasted four seasons (1836–40), the Prince Albert Club one season (1840–41) and the Royal Victoria five (1839–45). Only with the formation of the Currency Club in 1843–44 – which included William Tunks, Harry Hilliard and John McKone – did a rival club of substance emerge. However, by 1850 its best players had moved over to the reformed Amateur Cricket Club, now known permanently as the Marylebone Club.

The Australian Cricket Club – one of whose members, William Still, is credited with being the first man in the country to wear pads and gloves – was so strong in 1841–42 that it took on 'The Colony' (i.e., all the other clubs) and won two out of the three games. The Club did a considerable amount of work to consolidate the game in country areas and in the 1844–45 season won matches home and away against Maitland.

Maitland was one of the earliest country towns to organise cricket. Around the same time clubs were emerging in Bathurst, Morpeth, Raymond Terrace and Parramatta. The game was growing in popularity, and many new clubs were being formed. One club in particular, the Albert Club, which started in 1852, contained then, and in later times, many of the finest players in the colony: Dave Gregory, Fred Spofforth, Ned Sheridan, Alick and Charles Bannerman, William Caffyn (the English tourist of 1861–62 and 1863–64), Edwin Evans, Ned Gregory, Frank Iredale, Charles Lawrence (also an English tourist of 1861–62 whom the Albert Club engaged as their coach), Hugh Massie, Harry Moses, W. L. 'Billy' Murdoch and Nat Thomson.

The Albert Club was instrumental in bringing a measure of discipline into the game. They published printed rules and distributed them; their administrators ran a tight ship whereas other clubs were lax; the players were told what, and what not, to wear, and the club had its own distinguishing colours.

In 1854 two major NSW towns formed their first cricket clubs: Newcastle, on the coast north of Sydney, and Albury, astride the

River Murray in the south, on the present-day border with Victoria.

In Newcastle the first organised matches were played in the grounds of the Mental Hospital, later at the Police Barracks. Those early participants were mainly officers and men of the NSW Army Corps and a few local enthusiasts. Newcastle's lead was followed by Wallsend, Wickham, Lambton and Hamilton from surrounding areas. Competitive matches were played on St John's Green (now Centennial Park) with schoolboy games taking place on Prosser's Paddock. One of the ambitions of any early Newcastle player was to hit a ball over the adjoining Wharf Road and into the harbour.

In 1863, with the formation of five further clubs, the need for new grounds became urgent. The Newcastle Club was fortunate in electing E. C. Merewether as its president (a position he held for twenty-eight years) for he was an influential figure in the city and head of a major land-holding company. In 1864 he granted the club a lengthy lease on company land that was soon transformed into the Newcastle Cricket Ground, which today is a regular first-class venue.

Just outside Newcastle, in Wallsend, in the 1868–69 season, Michael Curry, playing for a visiting Tom Wills XI against a William Ross' XI (actually a twelve-a-side fixture), became the first bowler in Australia to take twenty wickets in a match.

As the game spread through the colony of New South Wales the northern areas were organising themselves into a group. In July 1861 a team representing the Richmond area – mainly from the towns of Casino and Lismore – travelled to Grafton to play a side from Clarence, and emerged victors by seven runs. A return match was organised which *The Casino-Kyogle Courier* reported on 6 September 1861:

> The Clarence team left Grafton on September 3, starting for Richmond to gain lost honours. . . . They were confronted by rapid creeks to pass, muddy roads and jaded horses to spur onward, yet the gallant few surmounted them. Once at their destination all their troubles were soon forgotten, festivity upon festivity was held in honour of the visitors.

Clarence won this return encounter by six wickets, and in so doing cemented the base for the Far North Coast contests in NSW which still continue today.

It was at Casino in May 1869 that a match was arranged between 'Single Men' and 'Married Men'. The day was warm and the beer flowed freely. *The Courier* reported two days later: 'The day passed off very pleasantly save one incident which reflected upon the person chiefly concerned in anything but a creditable manner . . . the incident will probably appear in the Casino police records.' The 'incident' was the first recorded report of a 'streaker' on an Australian cricket field.

The southern part of New South Wales saw cricket clubs and associations formed with each passing year. The Albury Club toured the local area for matches, playing on both sides of the border. Further west at Deniliquin the first recorded match on 17 August 1860 saw the town defeat Morago by 59 runs. At a club meeting on 7 September 1860 it was agreed 'that Deniliquin members should report for training at six o'clock every Friday morning'!

As the 1860s moved on, and towns were springing up on both sides of the Great Dividing Range (the Blue Mountains), so cricket became established in the main towns: not only Bathurst but also Dubbo, Tamworth, Yass, Nowra, Cowra, Moree, Glen Innes and even on the far western borders at Wentworth.

But the most progress was being made in Sydney itself. As older clubs died (such as The Australian Cricket Club in 1867–68) so the Albert Club became the prototype of the new era. It was organised along commercial lines and committed to regular interclub competition. The Alberts boasted ninety-three registered players by 1859, and they continued to grow. The benefit showed when, on 29 October 1864, the Albert Ground at Redfern was officially opened. It was the first enclosed ground with a permanent grandstand and, in 1871, major games were transferred there because it alone had the facility to collect gate-money.

Following a dispute over umpiring in February 1863 no intercolonial matches were arranged for the following two seasons, but this enabled the two strongest clubs in NSW and Victoria, the Albert CC and the Melbourne CC, to challenge one another. The first match took place in Melbourne from 26–29 December 1863 when the Albert Club won by an innings and four runs.

The return fixture took place fourteen months later when the Melbourne Cricket Club sent a much stronger team to Sydney. Honour was restored for the visitors who won by an innings and 59 runs. (Scorecards, see page 000).

These matches were more than adequate replacements for the intercolonial fixtures and deserve to have been awarded first-class status. The majority of the players in the Albert Club had represented the colony and the strength and depth of the club was reflected in their overall results.

In 1875 the Albert Club toured Tasmania. They defeated Southern Tasmania, in Hobart, by eight wickets; drew against Northern Tasmania in Launceston (Nat Thomson 6/41 and 6/50), and rounded off the visit by beating a Combined Tasmania side by 126 runs (Fred Spofforth 8/48 and 6/3).

By this time the game was well established in New South Wales, and other successful sides were growing in Sydney. Clubs such as National, Belvidere, Carlton and University were producing top players and large scores were being made. Batting, indeed, was beginning to dominate. For example, in 1875, in a match between Ulster and Macquarie at Moore Park, Ulster batted for four successive Saturday afternoons and scored 1238 (J.Flynn 249, G.Mullens 247, M.Brereton 186, J.White 178, H.Brown 147, T.Flynn 94) with sundries (extras) exceeding one hundred.

## *Victoria*

The formation of the game in Victoria took place along much firmer guidelines than in the much earlier case in New South Wales (Victoria remained officially part of the NSW colony, until 1851). Within three years of settlement in Victoria, on 15 November 1838, five gentlemen sat down and drew up a document to form the Melbourne Cricket Club.

As in New South Wales, racing had been the first sport in the new colony with a meeting taking place in March 1838 organised by Robert Russell, a thirty-year-old surveyor who drew up the plans for Melbourne itself and laid it out in a precise system of rectangles. Russell initially suggested there should be a village cricket club for the gentlemen of the colony and from that idea the club was formed.

Originally subscriptions were to be 'half a guinea', but this was soon changed to one guinea so as to attract the right quality of people. The original signatories were F. A. Powlett, A. M. Mundy, C. F. Mundy, G. B. Smyth and Robert Russell himself. They all paid their one guinea and on the same day the first secretary D.G.McArthur, bought two bats, balls and stumps at a cost of £2-0s-3d. Cricket equipment at that time was very limited and poor in quality. Bats and balls were roughly hewn, while stumps were made from the ti ti tree which grew along the banks of the Yarra River in an area called the West Melbourne swamp.

The founders were all influential figures in the new colony. Powlett, the club's first president, was Crown Land Commissioner of the Western Division of Port Phillip Settlement and the initial magistrate for the colony; Russell, as a surveyor, had drawn up the plans for Melbourne under the instructions of Governor Bourke; the Mundys ran the Melbourne Insurance Company while Smyth, then an army captain, later became a captain of Melbourne's Mounted Police.

A week later, on 22 November, the first recorded match in Victoria took place between Melbourne Cricket Club and the Military on a site which is now the heart of the city centre between William and Lonsdale Streets. *The Port Phillip Gazette* described it as one of the most 'beautiful pleasure grounds around this fast rising town', and added:

> During the week, arrangements had been made by the Gentlemen civilians of the district to play a match of cricket against the Military. Captain Smyth with the enthusiasm natural to him, and desirous of forwarding everything either really beneficial or of useful amusement, joined by many of those who had retired from the Service but whose hearts are still with it, mustered on the ground a company with which they would have attempted a more stirring contest. It was a heart-enlivening sight to witness from an adjacent hill the ground as it was laid out. Camps pitched, banners tastefully arranged and the all-enlivening smiles of beauty that would have graced a far-famed tournament of the olden times, formed a scene we trust often to witness.
>
> At twelve precisely a signal called the players to their post, when the game commenced, the Military taking first innings. We have not the particulars of the game before us and can therefore but briefly notice those who particularly distinguished themselves. After a duration of some hours, the match concluded by a triumph on the part of the civilians. Mr Powlett's and Mr McArthur's bowling, and Mr Russell's batting, attracted universal applause. On the whole the game was played with an esprit de corps, a judgment, and an activity that a first-rate club in England might not have been ashamed to boast.

After the Melbourne Cricket Club the next known organised club in Victoria was the Melbourne Union, which comprised people mainly from retail business or tradesmen. On 12 January 1839 the two teams met, the Union winning by a large margin. A week later Powlett scored 120, the first century in the colony, as Melbourne CC turned the tables. The Union's star player was Thomas Halfpenny, a tradesman, who was a hard-hitting batsman and more than competent wicketkeeper.

Two clubs could not play against each other indefinitely, so it was decided to play themed matches such as 'Marrieds' against 'Singles', 'Smokers' against 'Non-Smokers' and even 'Whiskers' against 'Clean Shaven'. However, a third club was formed in 1841–42 at Brighton, on a ground which 'a couple of years previously had been more or less a camping ground for the blacks'. The Brighton team proved so strong that the Melbourne club did not gain one victory from 1842–45.

After the club had been formed at Brighton, it was followed by others: Williamstown, whose life is unbroken since 1852, Richmond, Collingwood, East Melbourne, South Melbourne and St Kilda. Even in country areas there were strong teams at Ballarat, Bendigo and Castlemaine.

The Brighton Club was a formidable side particularly because it possessed in Frederick Coleman the first round-arm bowler in the colony, or more properly speaking, the district of Port Phillip.

Round-arm bowling at that time meant that the raising of the hand or arm above the level of the shoulder received a call of 'no-ball'. Coleman, however, mastered his art and was always considered a fair bowler. Brighton also 'possessed in Brown one of the hardest hitters of the day, and as there were no boundaries all hits were run out, a drive for nine was not of infrequent occurrence'.

On the other side of Port Phillip Bay was Geelong (more commonly known then as Corio). The first recorded cricket match took place in 1840 with the first club formed the following year at the Retreat Inn at South Geelong. Supported by publican Joseph Griffin the aim of the club was to 'pit themselves against the Gentlemen of Melbourne'. Matches tended to be various intra-club combinations with a popular fixture being between 'the bricklayers and the carpenters, all of Geelong'.

In April 1845 a team from Geelong visited Melbourne with honours going to the visitors after three games. In 1847 the Melbourne Cricket Club team sailed for eight hours on the steamer *Asphrasia* so that they could start a match against Geelong at noon. The Geelong (or Corio) Club players travelled in the same manner for the return match the following week.

The Melbourne CC moved in 1848 to a new ground on the south side of the Yarra River at Emerald Hill, now known as South Melbourne. It was the paddock where John Fawkner, twelve years earlier, had first grown wheat in the colony. The Melbourne secretary, George Cavenagh, petitioned the Governor for the land and was granted ten acres. Immediately the club erected a wooden booth, somewhat of an improvement on the tent it had on its original site. A four-rail fence was erected at a cost of just over £30, while part of the ground was turfed for a little under £25. Members were, however, asked to pay their subscriptions in advance in order to finance these developments. On 18 November 1848 a match took place between 'eleven natives of Europe' and a team of Australian-born called 'Eleven New Hollanders'. The local-born triumphed, 59 and 42 to 25 and 75, so winning by one run.

It came, therefore, as all the more of a shock when the club heard that a railway line was going to be built from the centre of Melbourne to Sandridge (now Port Melbourne) and that the track would pass straight across the centre of the ground. Governor La Trobe offered the club two alternative sites – the current one, and the one now occupied by the Richmond Club. On 23 September 1853 the Melbourne CC committee were granted a ten-acre site, which could be enclosed, 'under permissive occupancy for five years'. All of 1854 was devoted to clearing the site, it being clear from the Melbourne club records that from the start the committee had one aim in mind: to make the Melbourne ground the finest in all the colonies.

As the area was being turfed and trees chopped down in preparation for the new season, immigrants were pouring into the area at a rate of 3,000 a week. The gold rush was on inland and organised cricket stumbled whilst many men went off to try and earn their fortune.

The goldrush, however, created some cricket memories for many, and one – 'An Old Fogey', he called himself – wrote of a cricket match on 'the diggings' in 1853:

> Well, one night as we sat round the camp fire talking about one thing and another, the subject of cricket cropped up. Amongst those present were men who had been at Oxford and at Cambridge, and gradually these worked themselves almost into a white heat over the cricket merits of their respective Universities. The upshot of it all was that a match was arranged to be played between teams to be called the Dark Blue and the Light Blue, these names being chosen at the express wish of the 'varsity men. Some difficulty was experienced in procuring the necessary materials. Stumps were easily made; but it took some time to form bats, and even when these were ready for use it could not be said that we were wielders of the willow, for in the absence of more suitable wood, we had to make our bats of iron bark. So far so good. But though stumps and bats are all very well, they are of little use without a ball, and to get one was the great desideratum.
>
> At length . . . a man was found with a good sized solid india-rubber ball in his possession. This was duly secured, and all preliminaries having been settled, the match was set to commence next day on a level spot about a mile from the town. It was found on picking sides that we could only muster six men each; but our hearts and souls were in the match, just as if we had the orthodox eleven, and had played on soft and velvety turf instead of white and flint-like ground. The occasion was observed a special holiday, and when the teams reached the convincing* ground a goodly company had assembled, composed for the most part of diggers, who rigged out as they were in suits of all sorts of styles and colours, caused the scene to be a picturesque one. I played with the Dark Blues, and having won the toss we went to the wickets. I remember well the

*Local parlance for 'getting a result'.

enthusiastic burst of applause the diggers gave when our first two men opened the proceedings. The applause, however, had hardly died away when two wickets were down for nothing and who that saw it could forget the subdued and crestfallen look of the two batsmen, who a few minutes previously had gone forth from the tent with faces glowing with confidence and hope. The next two carried the score to 20 or thereabouts. One of them, a fellow called Barney, who in his huge boots, his broad-brimmed hat and jet black flowing beard, looked more like a bandit than a cricketer, was a tremendous slogger, and created quite a sensation by his mighty smiting. Barney at length fell, and I then went in and managed to knock up a few. Our innings closed for 43, a party by the name of Johnson heading the list with 19, and if he did not play quite according to Fuller Pilch, his comrades and the crowd by their hearty cheers showed that they thought quite as much of him as if he had so played.

During luncheon, which took place shortly after the close of our innings, the wagering of the partisans of the respective sides went on at a great rate, and lots of good-humoured chaff was indulged in. By and bye our opponents started their innings, and opened very well, 10 runs quickly going down on the score sheet, or rather the inside cover of a novel, which served for scoring purposes, and which, by the way, being still in my possession, has enabled me to give the details of this match of many years ago. The score was 15, with no wickets down, when I determined to try underhand lobs. The first ball was hit for 5, the biggest hit of the match, but the second, to my delight, secured a wicket, and the score was 20 for one out only. Without any alteration of the score two wickets fell, and our supporters began to gain heart again. An old Cantab was next and by as correct play as could be shown on our peculiar wicket, he increased the score to 35. Here a crisis occurred. One of the batsmen, not the Cantab, you may be sure, was very eager in backing up, and once when at my end he overshot the mark before the ball was delivered, and I, turning suddenly, knocked the stumps flying, while the batsman was fully a foot out of his ground. The umpire of course gave him out, and the batsman made tracks for the tent. The crowd, however, shouted out 'swindle', and several stopped the batsman and told him to go back. The hum of voices soon swelled into a deafening roar. Oh! what a row, what a rumpus, what a rioting it was to be sure. After a lengthy explanation, it was admitted by all that the player was out. Then the wild excitement died gradually away; the game was resumed, and harmony and pleasantness reigned once more. The last two of our opponents were now in, and we worked our level best to get them out.

When only three runs short of our score, one of the batsmen

made a good hit. They ran one, and the fielder fumbling the ball, the crowd yelled 'go again'. So they did, but the fielder recovering the ball splendidly, made a flying shot, and knocked a stump clean out of the ground, with the batsman a yard or so out of his crease. Thus the match ended in our favour by two runs. The successful fielder was rushed by our supporters, and borne shoulder high to the tent, to the tune of some triumphant march whistled by certain of the diggers. In the evening, we had our supper, for which in terms of agreement the losers had to pay.

The gold seekers gradually drifted back to Melbourne from the diggings and in four months the Melbourne CC gained two hundred new members. Cricket was gaining strength with various types of competitions in force for club championships.

An Australian Cricket Club had been formed in October 1850 with its base at the White Hart Hotel at the top of Bourke Street in Melbourne, but it had only a short life. The South Melbourne Cricket Club was founded in 1853 but early records of the club are hard to find.

On 23 January 1854 W. S. Woolcott wrote to the Colonial Secretary on the letter heading of the newspaper *The Express*:

> At a meeting held by a few gentlemen at my house at Richmond it was resolved that a cricket club, to be called the Richmond Cricket Club, should be formed. It was further resolved as a preliminary step that your permission should, if possible, be obtained to allow the club to practise on the Government paddock at Wellington Parade until such time as the club could obtain suitable ground, and as the treasurer, I have been requested to seek that permission from you. Will you kindly accord it for the remainder of the season? Before the commencement of the next we hope to be provided with a ground of our own.

A week later the necessary permission was granted. The following year, on 25 October, the secretary of the Richmond Cricket Club, Joseph Rhodes, wrote again to the Colonial Office informing them that the club's headquarters were at the Royal Hotel, Punt Road, Richmond, and asked if they could use the site opposite the hotel as their ground. After an inspection was made by the Commission of Crown Lands the club was granted the site on 18 November 1855, a ground it still holds. Twelve months earlier Richmond's nextdoor neighbour, the Melbourne Cricket Club, had held their first match on their new ground.

The following year, 1855, saw the formation of the St Kilda Cricket

Club. The area had its social problems at the time: transport was poor, drainage was virtually non-existent and bushrangers were active 'on the road from Melbourne' which was a little over two miles away. The first site for the club was Albert Park (then called Home Park) which was swampy and contained numerous wild-fowl. Pigs were kept next door to the ground and this caused a few problems on hot days! On 19 April 1855, therefore, the St Kilda secretary, Elmslie Stephen, wrote to the Surveyor-General asking permission to use an eight-acre site bounded by Queen's Road, Fitzroy Street, 'and the lagoon' (now known as Albert Park Lake). Despite opposition from officials of the Lands Department, the request was agreed to early in 1856 and, other than some minor site boundary changes, the Junction Oval today is the same area as originally granted.

The first grandstand was quickly purchased – it being from the site of the old Elsternwick Racecourse – and by the end of 1856 the club boasted a membership of 158. Its president was Sir George Stephens, a well-known lawyer and the first Australian commoner knighted by Queen Victoria after she ascended the throne in 1837.

In 1857 the club conceived the idea of seeking Royal patronage and requested Queen Victoria to permit them to call themselves 'The Royal Cricket Club of Victoria'. The Governor of Victoria, Sir Henry Barkly, wrote to his superior in London, the Secretary of State for the Colonies (Lord Stanley), saying:

> My Lord, I should scarcely have ventured, even in the routine of the Colonial Regulations, to trouble Your Lordship with the enclosed application from the St Kilda Cricket Club praying for the Queen's patronage, had I not been informed by Sir George Stephens that the duplicate was sent direct to the Colonial Office by the last mail. Among the national institutions which the Australian Colonists have transplanted to these shores, the game of cricket takes high rank, the deepest interest is excited by the matches annually between the rival clubs of Melbourne, Sydney and Hobart, even the sittings of the Legislature giving way on such occasions. The club established in the suburban municipality of St Kilda includes, I believe, some of our best players, but as I am not cognisant of the special grounds on which it now aspires to a distinction which assuredly will not be enjoyed without jealousy, I must leave the petition to speak for itself on the subject.

Sir Henry's doubts were supported in London and the request was refused. The fact that Sir Henry himself was president of the Richmond Cricket Club at the time was presumably considered irrelevant.

Also around this time a number of clubs had appeared, all of whom used either Carlton Gardens or Royal Park as their grounds. A University club was in existence in 1855 with Judge (later Sir Redmond) Barry as president and they played on a ground at the back of Melbourne University where the Colleges stand today. There was also a Royal Park Club and a Carlton Tradesmen Club. Then towards the end of the 1850s came a very strong North Melbourne Club who played a number of matches against the various schools.

In 1857, four students from Scotch College – Tom and Charley Dight, and John and Fred Moody – formed the Abbotsford Cricket Club at Dight's Paddock in Abbotsford. Their first match was against Williamstown Alliance, followed by fixtures against Royal Park and the Press Cricket Club. In 1860 Abbotsford changed its name to the East Melbourne Cricket Club and was granted a piece of land opposite the Melbourne CC ground.

Out of Melbourne, in what today are suburbs, grew a number of other clubs. Warrandyte Cricket Club was founded in 1855 and the following year was granted perpetual use of the Recreation Ground. This helped to bring about a growth of the game in the area to the east of Melbourne, with clubs springing up such as Anderson's Creek, Caledonia, Ringwood, Lilydale, Eltham, Kangaroo Grounds, Panton Hills, Christmas Hills, Croydon and West End Brewery.

Ballarat and Bendigo were great centres of the game and, as the railways spread, metropolitan clubs regularly toured country districts. Places as distant (153 miles) as Wangaratta, in the far north-east of the colony, and Sale in the wilds of Gippsland, were visited. (Gippsland bounds the coast of Victoria and the mountains from a distance of 60 to 250 miles east of Melbourne.) Other towns which boasted clubs in the late 1850s and early 1860s were Colac, Wahgunyah, Beechworth, Ararat, Hamilton, Camperdown, Warrnambool, Benalla and Castlemaine.

Back in 1852, at Easter, a team from Adelaide had travelled to Melbourne to play a match on the old Emerald Hill ground. The progress of the game had been slow in South Australia and *The Argus* reported:

> That the match was not finished, when time was called, was a godsend to the Adelaidians, who would in all probability have been soundly beaten if it had been played out, the scores to the Melbournites for two innings being so large as almost to preclude hope for the other side, even had they played their second innings. We may mention that Mr Fook's wicket-keeping was clever and that the fielding of Messrs Cary and Dicker was very much admired.

Although mainland intercolonial matches had started in 1856, the game was still finding its feet on a domestic level. Attempts were made, unsuccessfully, to form a Victorian Cricketers Association. At this period, indeed, players would change clubs regularly during the season. The star of the Melbourne team was Thomas Wentworth Wills. He was a third-generation Australian – a rarity then – and had been sent to Rugby School in England from 1852–55. He became the school rugby and cricket captain and received regular cricket coaching from John Lillywhite. Wills was an outstanding round-arm bowler and an excellent fielder. He made appearances in 1856 for both Kent and the Marylebone Cricket Club, and also for Cambridge University against Oxford. At the end of the year he returned to Australia.

The lack of fitness among Victoria's leading cricketers so shocked Wills – he blaming their inactive lives during the winter – that he, and his cousin Colden Harrison, invented Australian Rules football as a new sport for the colonies.

Those early years of cricket in Victoria showed above all else a colony in which life was relatively orderly. The game grew naturally, with one interesting suggestion coming from Sir George Stephens in 1859 when, at a meeting of club representatives, he tried to introduce a motion calling on 'a cricket congress of the Australian Colonies'. But he was ruled out of order.

Official records started in 1860–61 with Richmond as the premier team, but the honours for subsequent years mainly went to Melbourne CC and East Melbourne both of whom built up strong sides. There was also a Challenge Cup in the 1860s, presented by the Hon. George Coppin, president of the Richmond Club.

The era saw clubs formed which are still active today. The sub-district club Camberwell played its first match in March 1864 against Hawthorn United; Carlton was in being for the 1860–61 season, although a player dispute saw them fold, then return phoenix-like soon afterwards. They obtained their ground at Princes Park on 12 May 1865 and have played there ever since. J. C. Brodie in his *Victorian Cricketer's Guide*, the first of many short-lived cricket annuals which appeared in 1861, summed up the prevailing view of the game in Melbourne:

> Many persons may argue that the rifle movement provides sufficient incentive to exercise of an equally improving kind, so far as the individual man is concerned, and more important as regards our community or our nation. However pointed this reasoning may in these eventful times be, yet it cannot carry sufficient weight to cause the rifle even now to supersede the bat altogether. But, supposing the necessity for universal arming to arise, still cricket may

be made one of the most useful auxiliaries to martial exercise and development, inasmuch as many of the requisite qualities of the soldier are created, and all of them fostered, in the cricket field. A keen eye, a steady hand, a stout heart, strong limbs with activity, coolness and precision, alike produce the soldier and the cricketer. Therefore, it is to be hoped that those in command of the various volunteer corps throughout the Colony will show some forbearance to those members who, having become somewhat proficient in drill, desire to vary their exercise by occasional indulgence in the manly game of cricket. What outdoor exercise so congenial to the refined mind, what better adapted for the muscular development of the body, what more exhilarating to the spirits, or more conducive to health, than the noble game of cricket?

### *Tasmania*

The first decade of the nineteenth century saw settlements established at two centres in Tasmania. In the south, Hobart was founded in 1803 while, in the north the following year, Launceston became a reality on the banks of the Tamar River. From these settlements two quite separate cricket areas developed. Hobart became the capital of what was then still Van Diemen's Land, but any political dominance over the north did not extend to cricket. Travel between the two towns was difficult and teams from the mainland always found it easier to get to Launceston than take the longer journey to Hobart.

The earliest report of a game on the island came from the colony's chaplain at Hobart, Reverend Robert Knopwood, who stated that 'crickett was a popular pastime in the hot weather that prevailed in late December 1814'. Knopwood's diaries contain several references to the game which was well established in the south by 1820. Likewise, in the north, as *The Hobart Town Gazette* recorded on Saturday 4 January 1817: 'The Christmas Holidays throughout the Colony have been spent with the utmost conviviality by the young folks. Dancing and cricketing was in full perfection at Port Dalrymple [the first settlement made in northern Tasmania more or less where Launceston now stands], no accident occurred there, excepting a lea board making its exit and the village lawyer being deprived of following his profession for a few days by an unfortunate catastrophe which darkened his eyesight.'

Although a number of the free-settlers in Hobart would have played the game of cricket before arriving in Tasmania, it was not until 1825 that the Plymouth-born publican Joseph Bowden organised the first recorded match in the town. After much discussion he promoted a match early in the year between a team of free-settlers and troops from the local garrison on a site which is now directly in the heart of

Hobart's retail district. The military 'won by fifteen runs in a keenly-fought but primitive game'. The following season on Easter Monday, Bowden staged another game, this time with a stake of fifty guineas. According to his advertisement, free colonists from the English counties of Sussex and Kent, impregnated with cricket lore, were to battle with 'the choice of the whole island'. The only known result of this match was the arrest of a convict posing as a casual spectator.

For the next six years there were probably a number of games in Hobart – all records having been lost – for two clubs, the 'Cricketer's Club' and 'Union Club', were both formed and subsequently dissolved. Organised cricket came into being on 27 October 1832 with the founding of the Hobart Town Cricket Club. Although Bowden's name does not appear among those who sponsored the venture, the new club was granted, by Governor Arthur, tenancy of its own ground at the site of the now disused railway station. The first match was played on 1 January 1833 but nothing more of importance took place until 19 January 1835 when a fixture was played against a combined team of the visiting HMS *Hyacinth* and the locally based 21st Regiment. The game lasted for five hours and 'was to be a trial of strength with no betting'.

Batting first, Hobart Town scored 83 (Smith 21, John Marshall 13, Blackwood seven wickets) to which the so-styled United Services replied with 39 (Marshall seven wickets). After a break, and with the band playing continually, Hobart Town made 84 (Roper 46). Needing 129 for victory, United Services crumbled for 21 (Marshall five wickets) to lose to the home side by 107 runs.

The hero of the day was forty-year-old John Marshall who scored 13 and 10 and took twelve wickets. His display caused him to become known as the 'Champion Cricketer of Hobart Town', a status he retained for another twenty years. Marshall, a heavy man, bearded and brawny like the traditional blacksmith, was born in England in 1795. He made his first-class debut at the age of fifty-six and played for the following three seasons for his colony against a Victorian side.

The United Services match stirred the Hobart Club into arranging matches the following month against Carlton, a settlement twelve miles out of town. The Carlton team contained an aboriginal player called Shiney who made three ducks in his four visits to the crease. Hobart won both matches but an internal row saw the club splitting into factions at an acrimonious meeting on 14 February 1835. Several players, including Marshall, formed the Derwent Cricket Club and, the following day in a grudge match, Derwent defeated Hobart in a single-wicket contest.

In its early stages the Derwent club had as a member the Hon.

John Elliott who was a nephew of Governor Franklin. This 'official' sanction increased the players' stature within the town.

In February 1839, a team led by Marshall won a challenge cup by defeating a side captained by James Fisher by the then incredible margin of an innings and 32 runs.

Although other teams were now being formed in the colony – the strong side at Sorell getting some challenges but their distance of forty miles from Hobart being considered too far to visit by many – some of the best games were intra-club clashes. On 1 February 1840 the Derwent Club announced that 'a great cricket match would be played that day' and that £100 was at stake. Twenty-two players formed Elliott's XI which challenged Marshall's XI and it was a history-making day for Henry Wade who scored the first century in Hobart cricket. It must have been an innings of high class for Wade had to face the bowling of Marshall at his best. The scores were: Elliott's XI 89 (Wade 27) and 162 (Wade 101, Fisher 23) defeated Marshall's XI 100 (Marshall 30) and 86 by 65 runs.

Unfortunately for Wade his century was not the first in the colony, for a few days earlier Emmett had made an unbeaten 137 for South Esk against Launceston. In the north, cricket had been played for many years but not on an organised basis. For example, on 11 May 1833 *The Launceston Examiner* reported: 'Notwithstanding the appearance of the weather was uninviting it was numerously attended. The several games were well contested and kept up with spirit until sundown. We congratulate our fellow-townsmen upon the establishment of a club, composed as it is of the most respectable inhabitants of the country, and founded upon the rules and regulations of the first cricket clubs in England.'

Then on 14 December 1833, the same paper said: 'We understand that a cricket match will be played by twenty two of the commoners of Launceston on 26th December for fifty sovereigns. It will take place on the Government Green, and it is anticipated to afford much play. We heartily recommend to the support of every well-wisher on the Colony this manly game, and trust that at a meeting which will be held at the Launceston Hotel on Monday 23rd December at half past six o'clock pm it will be shown by a liberal countenance on it.'

The Launceston Cricket Club was founded in November 1838, but for the next three seasons played only intra-club matches such as Married versus Singles, and Lefthanders versus Righthanders. Official rules were not drawn up until 11 September 1841 after which the club was properly constituted.

The *Cornwall Chronicle* on Saturday 27 November 1841 then gave news of 'the first match between the Launceston and Tamar Clubs which was played on Tuesday last on the racecourse.' The scores given were: Launceston 61 (E. Green 26*, W. Baldwin five wickets) and 73 (W. Baldwin seven wickets) lost to Tamar 107 (W. Clarke 52, W. Henty six wickets) and 28 for two by eight wickets.

The big matches of the 1840s were between Launceston and the Cornwall Club. On 12 January 1843 a tied match was played by the teams (Launceston 35 and 33; Cornwall 40 and 28) but the result was disputed, so a replay took place on 9 January 1844 which Cornwall won by 51 runs.

In 1844 the 96th Regiment, having arrived in Hobart for a five-year posting, soon formed the Garrison Club which played regular matches, occasionally combining with Derwent to play fixtures against country clubs.

Cricket grew on the island but both North and South remained largely ignorant of each other's progress. Launceston had, in fact, forged ahead of any of the Hobart clubs and in 1850 issued a challenge to the Melbourne Cricket Club to visit for a match. Through various inefficiencies the invitation did not reach the Melbourne CC in time, the upshot being that the Launceston Club then challenged the Derwent Club in a North versus South contest. The match took place at Oatlands (nearly halfway between Hobart and Launceston) on 23 April 1850 with Launceston 40 (Clarke 13, Brown five wickets) and 37, defeating Derwent 36 (Orford 17) and 29 (Orford 12) by 12 runs.

These matches continued for the next 126 years – until Tasmania entered the Sheffield Shield competition – and remained the principal proving ground for aspiring cricketers; while the first intercolonial fixture in Tasmania took place in 1851. Clubs grew in and around the two main towns and also on the north-west coast. Parochial problems persisted, however, and each area tended to raise its standards without any help from the others. Regrettably this situation still exists today.

## *South Australia*

From the earliest days of colonial settlement cricket was an integral part of life in South Australia. The Adelaide Cricket Club was founded in 1839 – the same year as Adelaide gained city status – and other clubs in the city soon followed. Then, as agricultural settlement expanded and mining towns grew up, cricket spread into the country areas of the colony and into the majority of its newly-evolving communities.

Cricket equipment was known to be aboard the initial settlement ship *Buffalo*, which landed settlers at Holdfast Bay on 28 December 1836, but the first known reference to any game was in the infant

* As is usual in cricket scores, an asterisk denotes 'not out'.

newspaper *The Gazette* which carried an advertisement on 3 November 1838 announcing that patrons of the London Tavern in Adelaide were desirous of forming a club to play 'that old English and manly game of cricket'.

The game was played on any flat ground which could be found. Three perfect sites were located in easy reach of Adelaide: one being 'on the parklands just north of where King William Road passes to North Adelaide' – this being near to, but not on the site of the present Adelaide Oval. Another site was at the far north-west corner of the parklands at Thebarton, and the third on the east parklands.

A number of minor clubs sprang up in the early 1840s including Thebarton and Walkerville. Other teams known to exist were in Willunga, Morphett Vale, Echunga, Hahndorf and in close city villages such as Klemzig and Mackgill (Magill). As areas opened up, clubs were formed in the Clare Valley, Yorke Peninsula and in the South-East, some three hundred miles from Adelaide.

In mid-1846 the man who would be cricket's catalyst in South Australia arrived from England. John Collard Cocker was thirty-one, having been born on a farm near Thurnham, Kent, a village on the Pilgrims' Way. He was an average cricketer who was a right-handed batsman, and bowled lobs. He played for the Leeds club in Kent, some four miles south of his home, and represented West Kent in occasional matches.

On 30 November 1846 Thebarton challenged Walkerville to a match. Stakes were set at 'a guinea a bat', the daily newspaper *The Register* endorsed the game as 'healthful and gentlemanly', and the fixture, played at Hindmarsh, attracted a large attendance. John Cocker was in the Walkerville team. He took nine wickets in the match with his right-arm lobs and scored 32 in his team's second innings.

A month earlier Cocker had purchased a hotel in Lower North Adelaide and called it The Kentish Arms. Situated on the corner of Stanley Street and East Pallant Street, the hotel was adjacent to the north-eastern parklands which surround the city. Cocker then founded the Kent and Sussex Cricket Club, who played their matches on a site now mainly occupied by olive trees.

Walter Andrews, who became secretary of the Adelaide Cricket Club and Registrar-General in the colony, arrived from Western Australia in 1847 and later noted: 'John Cocker was the central figure in the game, and was by far the best player'.

In January 1853 a group of players formed a club at Marryatville under the guiding hand of John Hunter. They called themselves The Union Cricket Club and soon had forty members. But according to James Scandrett writing three years later:

> Since the Union Club was established it has passed through many changes, the most trying time for its existence being when the gold diggings in Victoria were at their most alluring [1853–55] at which time cricketing in Adelaide was virtually suspended. However, the Union Club has since rallied and is now strong as regards playing members. But we have to regret a great want of interest on the part of the general members who seem to think that if they play now and then in a match it is all that is required of them, forgetting the saying 'practice makes perfect'. The Union Club has been very successful during this past season (1856–57) having played five matches, winning four. Two games were against the Adelaide Club and three with the South Australian Club.

Of all the clubs, it was the South Australian which became the most influential in the colony. It contained names of players such as Cope, Cussen, Dutton, Freeling, French, Fullarton, Giles, Gooch, Goode, Jamieson, Maddock, May, O'Halloran, Peryman, Sanderson, Scott, Smith (later Sir Edwin), Vautin, Wright and Wyatt.

In 1856–57 William Fullarton top-scored for the South Australians with 66 runs in the season from four matches, which did not compare too well with Tom Baker of Union who made 143 in five matches. Maddock of the South Australians took 27 wickets compared to 36 by W. Hall of Union.

John Cocker moved to the South Australian Club for the 1857–58 season, making no impact with the bat and in bowling taking only 5 for 42 in his two matches. In November 1858 the Universal Cricket Club was founded with thirty-two members and John Barrow as the first president. Their first match, against the South Australians, resulted in a heavy defeat.

Cricket was declining in popularity that season, but received an impetus when on 25–26 February 1859 a match was played between elevens of British and Colonial-taught players. The success of this match raised interest although as William Fullarton reported at the time: 'There are many ardent lovers of the game in Adelaide, however the clubs do have reason to complain as they receive little or no support from the most influential class of the community'.

Fullarton continued: 'The clubs number so few playing members that frequently they survive only a few seasons. The South Australian Club is an exception to the general rule, and it has been kept up more by the zeal of its members than by its strength.'

The 1858–59 season saw a number of new clubs emerge besides Universal. They included Munno Para – said to be strong enough to rival any other club – Woodville, Macclesfield, Strathalbyn and one from the Morphett Vale area. Schools were also introducing the game with St Peters College and Whinham College leading the way.

On 2 March 1859, *The Register* said in an editorial:

> A nation indicates its character by its sports. The noble game of cricket occupies a high if not the highest place . . . It is calculated to exert a beneficial influence on any community where it is played and more importantly, cricket is a manly, scientific, sober and salubrious sport. It has the advantage of bringing about a great amount of union between different classes in the community, blending merchants with the nobility, tradesman with artisan, in the same nervous trial of skill.

It was as though Mr Fullarton and the editor had got together to spell it out clearly to the South Australian community. Be that as it may, by the following season the Governor was giving vice-regal patronage to club matches and the young ladies of the city were taking such an interest in the South Australian Club that it is recorded; 'a bevy of the fair ones worked the colours of the club into a beautiful pennant which Lady MacDonnell, wife of the Governor, duly presented to the recipients'.

Not long after *The Register*'s editorial, a dinner was held in the Kent Town Hotel – the licensee of which was the cricketer James Chittleborough – on 6 July 1859. The vice-president of the Universal Cricket Club, G.W. Hawkes, proposed a toast to the game of cricket which possessed, he said, 'advantages for society in forming a social intercourse between men of all classes'. Two days later *The Register* highlighted the speech.

In the late 1890s Chittleborough reflected wistfully on such nights to Clarence Moody: 'The speech-making and drinking were kept up until the small hours. Fancy the leading cricketers of today indulging like that!'

The game now started to advance in leaps and bounds. The United Tradesmen Club was formed in 1861 by William Botten, who was landlord of the Lord Melbourne Hotel in Melbourne Street, Lower North Adelaide, a street parallel to the one where John Cocker had his hotel. The two old friends played against each other's teams on Good Friday 1861 for a wager of supper. Botten's team won by seven runs and the supper was held at Cocker's Kentish Arms Hotel. William Bundy presided, and before the evening broke up, Botten's club was formally created.

The evolution of this team, along with the new Eastern Suburbans side, eventually saw the growth of cricket in the area until, in 1865, the Norwood Club (now East Torrens) was formed. North Adelaide (now Prospect) came into existence in 1860, followed by Hindmarsh (now West Torrens) in 1862, Albert in 1863, Kent in 1866, Kensington in 1869, and South Adelaide in 1870.

A most important early decision was one made by the committee of the South Australian Club. In 1865 they secured a lease at a peppercorn rental from the Corporation of the City of Adelaide for six acres on the parklands just north of the River Torrens on the western side of King William Road, where the Adelaide Oval now is. The land was fenced and John Cocker, as the only man with sufficient knowledge, was asked to prepare a pitch.

Outside the Adelaide area approximately ninety clubs were known to exist by 1870, situated mainly in the oldest-settled areas in the Adelaide hills and extending northward to the Clare Valley. The game was also strong on the Yorke Peninsula, around the copper mining towns of Moonta, Kadina and Wallaroo whose settlers were generally of Cornish descent; but the country areas tended to play amongst themselves – along the usual lines of Married versus Single, British versus Colonial, and Shopkeepers versus Farmers – because distances were too great to travel.

### *Queensland*

There was no separate colony of Queensland until 10 December 1859, when the colony was separated off from New South Wales. Until then the area in its south-eastern corner had been the only part of the future Queensland in which the game of cricket had been recorded. In particular the towns of Brisbane, Ipswich and Toowoomba had matches noted by local newspapers prior to 1850.

Following an unsuccessful effort to make a penal colony in the area now occupied by Brisbane, free settlement started in what was called Moreton Bay in 1842. Two years later, on 18 April 1844, *The Sydney Morning Herald* published a report from Moreton Bay:

> The lovers of the manly and exhilarating game of cricket, will soon have an opportunity of displaying their prowess, a club having been formed at South Brisbane designated as the Albion Cricket Club. Mr D. Bunten of the Woolpack Inn, acting as treasurer, and Mr John Payne, secretary, and Messrs Hopkins, Smith, Mather, and Love, as a committee, for carrying the arrangements into effect. Parties are admitted members by paying a small fee to the secretary, and the field operations will commence so soon as the bats, ball and stumps are received from Sydney.

By 1846 there were two main districts in the area: Brisbane, and Darling Downs. Intense rivalry existed between the town people and country folk whenever they competed. Cricket was played in quite primitive conditions, unlike the development of the game in other colonies at that time. It was said: 'Interest may have been high but standards were low. Cricket matches were often largely an excuse for "nobblerising"* . . . The players' equipment was primitive, balls and bats being costly to import and colonial substitutes deficient in craftsmanship. The game was generally played barefoot . . . and was decidedly colonial, agricultural and uncouth.'

In the second issue of *The Moreton Bay Courier* on Saturday 27 June 1846 an article appeared headed 'Cricket': 'As a finale to the amusement of raceweek, a challenge from eleven of the working men of Brisbane to play an equal number of gentlemen, for five pounds ten shillings a side, was accepted by the latter and the match came off on the terrace leading to the Government Gardens.'

The gentlemen won easily, the workers handed over the winnings and arrangements were made for a similar match to take place the following year.

Interest in cricket was maintained in the Brisbane area for, on 28 August 1847, *The Moreton Bay Courier* published an article entitled 'Hints to Cricketers' which detailed the fundamental laws of the game. On 18 October 1848 *The Courier* referred to a cricket club being established in Ipswich with its first match 'commencing on Monday last, 13 October'. The club had twenty members who 'when sufficiently practised intend challenging the Brisbane club'.

Further inland, Drayton, an outer suburb of Toowoomba on the Darling Downs, held a race meeting which finished early on 14 May 1850. It was decided by those present to 'get up a cricket match for the afternoon of the two following days between eleven squatters and eleven Draytonians'. The Squatters 40 (Bell 7) and 48 (Wiggins 13) defeated Drayton 24 and 21 by 43 runs. Newspaper reports say that 'Knights took twelve wickets for Drayton . . . Sir Arthur Hodgson took eight wickets'.

This rather casual game aroused much interest when the news reached Ipswich, for the club then issued a challenge to the Squatters which called for a match to be played at Ipswich on Friday 14 June for 'either the championship or a sum of money to be named on Thursday 13th at not later than 9pm at the Queen's Arms'. The game was a very close encounter, with Ipswich 66 (Goode 14, Byrnes 11) and 68 (Wilkinson 12, Warren 20*) defeating the Squatters 69 (Burgoyne 23, R. Thelwell 16) and 59 (Burgoyne 25, Walker 11) by six runs.

A few days later *The Courier* bemoaned how 'insufficient players were available in Brisbane to play against the Squatters' in a fixture which had been scheduled for the Ipswich Racecourse. The last report of the Squatters team was on 17 December 1850 when *The Courier* reported on the planned Christmas sports at Drayton

*Old Australian slang for 'boozing'.

saying 'the Squatters are to have a cricket match . . . and a pigeon match'.

Following this initial burst of enthusiasm, interest in cricket seems to have waned; but no doubt there were games which went unreported for certainly cricket was being played at Ipswich during the 1854–55 season.

The next cricket club to have its formation noted was the Ipswich Cricket Club, since the earlier club seems to have failed. The local newspaper *The North Australian* made a series of references to the club during the final six weeks of 1857. The paper reported that a meeting was held on 10 November 1857 at the Old Court House, with C. S. Warry in the chair to form a club 'to be governed by the same rules as the New South Wales Club'. The entrance fee was to be half-a-guinea and monthly payments would be half-a-crown. By the end of the month there were eighteen members and they issued a challenge to the Stanley Cricket Club in Brisbane.

No match took place but, on 24 March 1859, the North Australian Cricket Club was formed in Ipswich and they issued a challenge to the Brisbane-based Moreton Bay Club when it was formed in mid-May 1859. The challenge was accepted and the Moreton Bay officials were authorised 'to invite non-members to play in the forthcoming match, with powers to guarantee their expenses, if they shall deem such a course expedient'. The team eventually comprised doctors, solicitors and various professional men plus a cobbler, James Bolger, an underarm bowler who was also highly regarded for his wicketkeeping.

It was decided to play two matches on a home and away basis, with the first fixture taking place on the North Ipswich cricket ground on 11 June 1859. The Ipswich team, playing under the banner of the North Australian Cricket Club, was full of 'accountants, tellers and ledger-keepers from the classic cricket recruiting grounds of Launceston [Tasmania] and Maitland [NSW]'. The match saw North Australian 99 (Glassford 39, Bryant 20) and 53 (Slack 12, Maughan 12*) defeat Moreton Bay 65 (Cannan 14) and 44 (Bolger 11, Cronk 10) by 43 runs.

The return match took place over two days on 29 July and 4 August 1859 at North Quay, Brisbane. *The Courier* said:

> The people of Brisbane made a holiday of the occasion and it was quite cheery to witness the interest manifested. A tent was erected for the comfort of lady patrons and each team was nationally picturesque, the Brisbane players sporting white shirts and blue caps, the Ipswich players red shirts containing colours so popular in the Crimean War, red, white and blue.'

The North Australian team won the toss and put Moreton Bay into bat. Each side had one innings each on the first day, and when play resumed the following Saturday, James Bolger, opening the innings for the home side, scored the first century recorded in Queensland. The scores were: Moreton Bay 97 (Cronk 26) and 204 (Bolger 118, Birley 30, Shaw 29, Bryant seven wickets) defeated North Australian 115 (Maughan 34) and 134 (Bryant 29, Maughan 25) by 51 runs. Bolger's innings took three and a half hours as he 'stood in the hot sun'. *The Courier* added, 'he succumbed to fatigue and was bowled by Bryant'. Spectators surrounded Bolger as he walked from the wicket and carried him to the tent 'where he might refresh himself and gain some repose'.

A third, and deciding, match played on 30 November saw Moreton Bay 87 and 91 (Bolger 47*) defeat North Australian 64 and 81 (Maughan 34) by 33 runs.

Clubs were now springing up in the country too. Dalby had a club in 1859, Maryborough in 1861, Bowen and Rockhampton 1862, Gayndah, Biggenden and Nanago in 1864. In Brisbane a match took place on 13 March 1861 between North Brisbane and South Brisbane at Green Hills. Although some careful organisation was evident in the arrangement of matches, a formal Association was needed.

On 23 December 1861 a meeting, called to form a cricket association, ended up creating a Brisbane Cricket Club, a somewhat confusing title as a club already existed bearing that name. The meeting was inconclusive and the idea of an association soon dropped from sight, but cricket spread up and down the long Queensland coastline. Many of the towns could only be reached by boat and teams visiting in this way were guaranteed special hospitality by welcoming populations. At Bowen, which is credited with staging the first match in northern Queensland, the local club played a team from the crew of the survey ship *Pioneer* in 1862. *The Port Denison Times* reported on a game in 1863 with the crew of the *Salamander*. When Rockhampton played its first match on 24 May 1862 the hosts, the Central Queensland Cricket Club, called themselves 'Australia' and their visitors, 'The World'.

In Brisbane, the Albert and Victoria clubs were formed and, after the first intercolonial clash with New South Wales in June 1864, Queensland gained a professional coach when James Moore accepted the position, based with the Brisbane Cricket Club 'for £2 a week'.

Standards now started to improve dramatically. Country teams were more prepared to travel as communications became easier. Maryborough went to Rockhampton; the I Zingari Club of Warwick visited Brisbane, and all over the colony cricket was becoming organised.

One benefit to the game was the number of children of colonists who returned home after having been to England to complete the education at Oxford or Cambridge universities. By 1876, in the Mackay area alone, there were no fewer than seven sugar planters who had played first-class cricket for one of the universities.

## *Western Australia*

The first sixty years of the colony of Western Australia was insignificant in a cricketing sense. Perth was founded in 1829, but it could have been on the other side of the world as far as the rest of Australia was concerned: the only connecting link was by sea.

The first reference to cricket was made in the *Perth Gazette* on 5 April 1835: 'The mechanics engaged in building the Commissariat Store hereby challenge those employed in erecting the Government House to play them one or more games in cricket on any terms which may be agreed upon. For particulars apply to B. von Bibra.'

There were no takers to the first challenge which was reissued six days later, and accepted; but no record exists of either the scores or the result of the match.

On 13 April the *Perth Gazette* noted with approval the progress of the game: 'This manly exercise has been started with some spirit within the last fortnight in Perth, and we understand a club is likely also to be formed at Guildford. The Perth Club at present consists of about twenty-two members.'

A fortnight later the *Perth Gazette* reported a response from the Perth Club which stated 'that on Easter Eve we played the Guildford Club at Perth and beat them by forty runs'.

In May 1846, the Tradesmen Club issued a challenge to the Perth Club. It was an important match, not least for being the first for which full scores were kept. The slow-growing population of just over 4,500 people needed good entertainment and the *Perth Gazette* reported:

> We have seldom seen any of our public amusements so well attended. In fact, everyone was there. The day was cool, but the ground horribly dusty and a brisk breeze having set in from the north-west, the clouds of dust were stifling. At 9.30 the umpires commenced to pitch the wickets and at 10.20 the first ball was bowled. Throughout the innings the bowling was admirable, chiefly being of the 'slow school', but not less dangerous than the rapid play of some modern artists. As the scores show the incautious or hasty player had no chance, but so wary were the strikers in most cases that sometimes three overs were called without a notch. In general the batting was good. There was a visible want of practice in most of the men on both sides, but there was sometimes some exquisite play. In fielding, the Club men had it hollow. In short, on reconsidering

. ‸ matter, we think the Tradesmen showed the best bowlers, .o the best fielders, and if there be any difference in the batting .nything, it is very slight – we think it is in favour of the Club. ıt ıs worthy of note that throughout the match not a wide ball was scored.

The scores were: Tradesmen 38 (E. King 18*, Harris five wickets) and 26 (C. King 11, Harris six wickets) lost to Perth Cricket Club 45 (Steele 10, C. King nine wickets) and 21 for five, by five wickets. An interesting point was that the Tradesmen player Hall was given out 'touched ball', the first recording of this mode of dismissal in Australian cricket. A return match five days later saw Perth record another victory, this time by 26 runs.

The 51st Regiment, based in Perth, played on a regular basis – their players having been weaned on the game in England – and matches took place against teams from the numerous ships which visited the town. The Regimental side accepted as many challenges as they could and it is reported they 'played in Bunbury, York, Toodyay, Northam and (what is now known as) Busselton'. Other fixtures took place in Albany and Geraldton along the coastline.

The Perth Club had its first real taste of a challenge when the newly formed Fremantle Cricket Club visited Perth on 11 November 1852. *The Gazette* reported 'that the match was played on the park', an area now known as the Esplanade.

By now the separate centres of Perth and Fremantle were growing rapidly, and both were aiming to become the capital of the colony. Therefore the challenge match took on special significance. Reports on the day stated 'that the boundaries were marked by small red flags'. A marquee was erected so that the ladies present could dine in private during the lunch break; a pastrycook 'constantly perambulated the ground', and also 'the band played throughout the day'. The match saw Fremantle score 62 and 42, so losing to Perth, 61 and 45 for seven, by three wickets.

The two newspaper reporters present devoted most of their space to the prominent people at the game, the standard of catering of Messrs Condron and Toovey, and the large number of people who had travelled from Fremantle.

The return match took place fifteen days later on 26 November on a sandy pitch in scrubland on the shores of the Swan estuary, a short distance outside Fremantle. This time Fremantle were victorious, scoring 40 and 46 for three in reply to Perth's 48 and 37. So were born the 'Tests' which were to be played between the two sides for the following fifty years.

In December 1862 the Fremantle Cricket Club left on their first tour, taking the cutter *Wild Wave* to Bunbury. Many of the players suffered sea-sickness during the voyage south but recovered on arrival. The ground on which the contest took place was reported as being far better than any other in the colony, lying on an open plain between the town and the sea.

Fremantle's aim of establishing the town as the principal centre of the colony prompted local cricket officials to try and obtain a good cricket ground. They were able to persuade the government to prepare and level a piece of ground which was far superior to any previously used and which became known as Fremantle Green. The first match was played there in November 1867 and put the locals one up on Perth which had yet to create a proper cricket ground.

In 1869 the officers and crew of HMS *Galatea* played on the ground in the presence of the Duke of Edinburgh, after which the Duke 'partook of refreshments at the residence of the harbour master'; but although many such social contests took place, the standard was not high, as the scores indicate. By 1875 there was still only one club in Perth and the Recreation Ground, on which matches were played, was often used for other purposes, sometimes even as a scratch match was going on.

On 14 January 1876, on Fremantle Green, the Port team played against officers and men from the visiting HMS *Sapphire*. This saw not only the first century recorded in Western Australia but two in the one innings when Port scored 260, with G. Parker reaching 106, followed shortly afterwards by C. Hanham with 102. On 30 January 1878 *The West Australian* reported on the annual meeting of the Perth Cricket Club when 'a resolution was made to improve the lot of the cricketer by pushing for a decent ground on which to play'. The club was prepared to finance improvements for themselves but they did not have control over the area they wished to develop.

Five weeks later, on 6 March 1878, the Perth Union and Perth clubs decided to amalgamate to form the Metropolitan Cricket Club which, it was hoped, would consolidate the best cricketing talent available.

Easter 1884 saw Albany send a team to Fremantle to play the other teams in the colony. Several good players were in the party including George Bailey, the manager of the Union Bank in Albany, who, when playing in Tasmania had been selected to tour England with the 1878 Australians.

The following year, 1885, saw the goldrush to the Kimberley area which brought many new settlers to Perth. Many of them who had cricketing backgrounds were quickly drafted into teams of newly formed clubs. By the end of the year the formation of a Cricket Association was being considered, and only eight years further on Western Australia played in its initial first-class match.

# 2

# Intercolonial Visits

From the time of Australia's initial first-class match, which took place in Launceston in 1851, through to the advent of the Sheffield Shield competition in 1892, a total of 153 first-class matches were played in Australia. Of these, 76 were intercolonial fixtures, the rest being against English touring teams, the Australia XI, and other occasional groupings. In addition there were numerous 'odds' matches, sixteen of which were intercolonial, in which teams varied in size from fourteen to twenty-two. There were, however, other matches mainly concerning the Melbourne and the East Melbourne Cricket Clubs, which should have been granted first-class status.*

The first contests between the colonies were great occasions, very colourful and never seeming to lack controversy. Australia's first such match, which started on Wednesday 11 February 1851, was typical.

After the misunderstandings of April 1850, when the Victorian team failed to arrive in Launceston for a scheduled fixture, more watertight arrangements had been made. The Victorians arrived early on 9 February 1851. They were then given two days of lavish hospitality following which the match took place with 'upwards of a thousand people assembled to witness the historic moment' and the town reportedly deserted. The team selected to represent Van Diemen's Land (as Tasmania was called until 1855) reflected the benefit of the North versus South match played the previous April when the Victorians failed to turn up. The

*The precise definition of a first-class match did not come about until a meeting at Lord's in 1947. The defining of all matches actually took place in Upminster, Essex, in 1981.

For Australia it was agreed (though I differ in opinion) that only interstate or intercolonial fixtures were to receive first-class internal status. The committee refused to acknowledge palpably first-class games played by the Melbourne Cricket Club – who were stronger than Marylebone – and the East Melbourne Club which was the Victorian Cricket Association under another name.

In the case of the Tasmania v. Victoria match at Launceston in 1851, the players at the time knew they were participating in the colony's (i.e. Australia) first *intercolonial* fixture.

Launceston selectors had no hesitation in inviting Hobart players to join the team.

The Tasmanian captain, John Marshall, sent Victoria in to bat, and the initial ball of Australian first-class cricket was delivered by the slow bowler, William Henty. A Sussex-born man, Henty served as Colonial Secretary in Tasmania from 1857–62 before returning to England. Henty's bowling partner was Robert McDowall, from Yorkshire, and they bowled unchanged as Victoria made 82. In reply Tasmania's opening pair of Gervase du Croz and John Marshall put on 45 before Marshall was dismissed. After a mid-innings slump Tasmania reached 104, an invaluable lead of 22 runs. Du Croz, with 27, held Tasmania together in what would be his only match for his adopted colony. London born, he played for the Launceston club and died four years later 'due to inflammation of the bowel' when only thirty-five years old.

Late on the first day Victoria's second innings was in ruins, having reached only 57, and that due to a splendid effort from Thomas Hamilton who made 35. Needing just 36 to win, Tasmania were in serious trouble at 15 for six when the umpires prudently ended the day's play in fading light.

Big hitting by Tom Tabart the following day, after he had been dropped early on, turned the tide and Tasmania won by three wickets. *The Cornwall Chronicle* reported that 'the game throughout was marked by the most gentlemanly feeling and good humour and reflects a great credit upon all'. The newspaper also commented on the behaviour of the crowd, noting that 'the spectators refrained from clapping or shouting on the fall of a rival wicket or a rare stroke from their own'.

The Victorians were accompanied on their visit by a large number of supporters and their Tasmanian hosts had great delight in organising a public ball on the Thursday night at the Cornwall Hotel 'where over 350 people attended'. They danced the night away until at 4.30am, the visitors 'were warned it was time to depart'.

Before the Victorians left, however, arrangements were made for a return match to be played in Melbourne the following season. This match began on 29 March 1852 on the Melbourne Cricket Club's South Yarra ground at Emerald Hill. The élite of Melbourne watched the game as Victoria, batting first, scored 80 (Hamilton 42) to which Tasmania replied with 65, batting one man short due to 'Maddox being incapacitated by a severe knock on the shin'. Victoria consolidated their lead by scoring 127, and by the second morning the home side had won by 61 runs.

Although a deciding match was played in Launceston in March 1854 – which Tasmania (97 and 35 for 2) won by defeating Victoria (80 and

50) by eight wickets – the Victorians were definite that it would be the last meeting between the colonies for some time. As businessmen and only amateur cricketers they objected to having to leave their occupations for over a fortnight for a trip which, by sea, was about 400 miles and even nowadays takes thirteen hours on the ferry.

Although a contest had taken place between eleven Melbourne gentlemen and eleven gentlemen from Adelaide in 1852, the first intercolonial match between *mainland* colonies did not take place until 26 March 1856 when New South Wales took the field on Melbourne Cricket Ground. An advertisement had been placed in the *Melbourne Argus* challenging any team in the Australian colonies to play the Melbourne Cricket Club. In taking up the challenge the NSW team spurned the offer of £200-a-side, preferring to play for the honour of the game. Both teams fielded with their boots off, some even in bare feet because the ground was devoid of grass. The first day's play was summarised in two sentences in the *Argus*, which stated that before play began betting was 3 to 2 on Victoria.

The batting surface was so rough that any batsman who made double figures was heroic. There was argument about procedures, such as who should bat first, what the umpires should wear, whether different pitches should be used for each innings, and whether the scorers should sit together, but finally these matters were settled. Sargeant and Mather went to the wicket for Victoria, and Gilbert bowled the first ball for NSW. Sargeant drove it for two – the first runs between Victoria and New South Wales.

Victoria's poor fielding allowed NSW to score 76 in reply to their own first innings of 63. Gate money on the first day was £60-5s-0d. McKone took 5 for 11 off 52 balls in Victoria's second innings, which ended at only 28. NSW lost seven wickets in making the 15 runs they required for victory.

However, the visit south had been a financial disaster for NSW. William Tunks, who put the team together, collected money from various sources to try and cover expenses: he added also money of his own, and then persuaded Richard Driver, a barrister, to join the team initially as their umpire. Driver put in £60 to make sure that the visit took place. It involved, of course, considerable distance. The sea journey is 770 miles from Melbourne to Sydney and in the 1850s could take three to five days.

But New South Wales had won and the members of the team were hailed as conquering heroes on their return home. The NSW 'Inter-Colonial Committee', as they titled themselves, met to consider another match against Victoria, and were in favour also of trying to form a full Cricket Association. This meeting was held at James Cunningham's hotel at the corner of King and Castlereagh

Streets. Among those present were William Tunks, who was made Honorary Treasurer; Joe Clayton, Honorary Secretary; and George Gilbert, Captain.

The Governor of NSW, Sir William Denison, was appointed President and, despite a protest from the curator of the Botanic Gardens, the site selected for the match was The Domain, a part of the Botanic Gardens in central Sydney which has always been used for recreation. A concession was obtained from the government to allow the city corporation carts to tip loads of soil on to the lower side to level the ground. The date of the match was to be 14–15 January 1857.

George Gilbert, who had played in England for the Gentlemen against the Players in 1851, was a controversial figure. One critic wrote that 'his batting was very effective, but wanting in finish and he would do more if not so fond of cutting to leg. His fielding is good and would be rendered more elegant if he curbed his sometimes too exuberant spirits for the "cabbage tree mob's" gratification.'

On Gilbert's leadership qualities, the same critic wrote 'he placed his men well, but we consider it was throwing away a chance not having a wicketkeeper'. In 1857 the NSW team had only Sadler at long-stop, whilst the Victorians had both a wicketkeeper and a long-stop.

On the first day of the 'grand match' the crowd was estimated at 'around ten thousand', with a third-day figure given as 'about fifteen thousand'. His Excellency the Governor was present and was entertained before the match by the band of the 11th Regiment. The crowd included Members of Parliament and other notable gentlemen of the city, along with representatives of the theatrical world and, according to *Bell's Life*, 'fair ladies mustered in such force to illuminate with their sunny smiles and bright eyes the sombre "phisogs" of the "nobler sex".'

*Bell's Life* also commented on 'the persevering effort of a great many individuals who, despite the great activity of the police to restrain them, insisted upon continually annoying the scorers by standing in front of their tent and shouting absurd applause with stentorian lungs'.

Before the match started it was agreed that the bowlers be restricted to round-arm or under-arm actions and that overs would be of four balls, as was normal then. Betting was 5 to 4 on the Victorians and they were backed in Sydney and Melbourne 'to the tune of some four or five thousand pounds'. Even *The Sydney Morning Herald* reported hearing of a bet of £1600 to £1000 on. After the first day's play both sides had completed one innings and NSW, who batted first, led by 80 to 63. Despite some fine bowling by the Victorians, particularly Tom Wills who took 6/25 and 4/40, NSW won by 65 runs on the second day.

In those days there was no score board but *The Sydney Morning*

*Herald* explained how Mr Taylor of *Bradshaw's Guide* was able to keep spectators in touch with the progress of the game: 'Information as to the names of the players, the state of the game etc., was afforded the public very rapidly, he having placed a small printing press on the ground, by means of which cards were struck off at the fall of each wicket, giving the latest state of the game.'

The 'grand match' aroused interest and excitement among the cricketers of Sydney. The NSW Cricket Association, although not officially recognised until 1859, was conceived at this moment while around the city and in the suburbs new clubs were being formed.

So by now, in a matter of seven cricket seasons, there had been five full intercolonial matches. The following year, 1857–58, saw three further fixtures take place. In the first, in Melbourne, Victoria gained what was then considered an overwhelming victory by 171 runs. The game was notable in Australian cricket history for the fact that George Gilbert of NSW took a hat-trick, the first such feat in first-class fixtures. The following month Victoria travelled to Tasmania to play matches in both Launceston and Hobart.

On the island, John Marshall had finally retired from playing cricket. He was approaching sixty years of age but still had enough drive and ability to unite cricketers from Tasmania's two major centres. During the four years' break between contests, however, Victoria had begun to outpace Tasmania in both the general and cricketing senses. The influx of migrants from the old country, mainly due to the attraction of the goldfields, brought Victoria (and the other mainland colonies) men well versed in the skills of cricket. Also, the start of the Victoria/New South Wales clashes had taken public interest away from regular contact with Tasmania and as a consequence the game on the island began to drop in standard.

The Launceston Cricket Club, by far the most dominant in the north of the island, organised a match against a Victorian team – selected by the Melbourne Cricket Club – which started on 26 February 1858. Naturally, players from the south were also chosen so that the team was representative, but Tasmania, batting first, could only score 33 runs of which 14 were sundries. Gideon Elliott, who opened the bowling with Tom Wills, had the amazing analysis of 19 overs, 17 maidens, 2 runs and 9 wickets. Victoria replied with 115 – three players passing twenty – and on the second day won by an innings and 20 runs.

Elliott's success was due to his using a bowling style, fast round-arm, which was not practised with any degree of skill in Tasmania. Under-arm slow bowling was still the generally accepted style in club matches for the island's cricketers had ignored the type of bowling which had been legal in England for the previous thirty years. In short, just as Tasmania was becoming used to round-arm, so over-arm bowling was being accepted elsewhere, although the NSW/ Victoria match of January 1857 had also not allowed over-arm bowling.

After playing a scratch match in Launceston due to the early finish of the main game, the Victorian cricketers headed for Hobart. It was to be the town's first intercolonial fixture and from early morning on 4 March a stream of visitors poured in to watch the contest.

The composition of the Victorian team showed exactly the path cricket was taking in the colony, nine being English born while the tenth, Tom Wills the captain, had been to Cambridge and played for the University. None of the players had taken part in any of the three earlier fixtures against Tasmania, whereas many of the home team were the regulars from the early 1850s.

For instance John Tabart, who played in all the matches for Tasmania in the 1850s, was the Council Clerk at Oatlands in the midlands of the island. It was unlikely therefore that he could have been aware of the progress of the game, particularly the changing bowling actions. This would apply equally to his amateur colleagues.

The Hobart match started at 11 am with 'about five thousand present'. Victoria batted first and reached 78 of which George Marshall contributed 32. This excited the crowd who had read in the newspapers that the Victorian team 'were on a par with the leading English counties'. Tasmania replied with 51 which exceeded all local expectations. Then came the crunch as Victoria scored 67 and set Tasmania 95 runs to win.

The target did not initially appear to be beyond Tasmania, but they failed miserably. Wills and Elliott dismissed the home team for just 25 runs, Elliott taking 4/6, giving him 7/25 in the match, with Wills getting 5/10 and match figures of 11/35. The conclusion agreed by both sides was that a break should take place in their contests for a few more years, to allow Tasmanian cricket to catch up with that in the other colonies.

Important moves were now afoot in Sydney to bring organisation to the game and put the 'Inter-Colonial Committee' on a structured basis. An advertisement, which appeared in *The Sydney Morning Herald* on 27 April 1859, invited secretaries of cricket clubs in Sydney to meet 'for the purpose of forming an Association'. The purpose of the Association, said the advertisement, was to 'have the management of affairs in which the clubs generally are concerned and take immediate steps to adopt those means best calculated to improve the cricket players of this colony'.

The last few words summed up why it was considered necessary to organise the game more efficiently in Sydney. On 20–22 January 1859, when NSW had met Victoria again on the Domain in Sydney and lost by two wickets, it was felt that forming an association would help to raise the standard of cricket and enable Victoria to be beaten.

The club secretaries met on 3 May, agreed to form an association, and decided to send delegates to a meeting on 3 June. For some reason this meeting did not take place, and the next move took place on 2 November 1859 when club representatives met to plan for the forthcoming fixture against Victoria.

Three days later *Bell's Life* reported: 'After some deliberation it was decided to appoint a Cricketing Association, to whom the management of these intercolonial contests shall be confided in future'.

William Tunks and Richard Driver were then appointed joint secretaries with a brief to bring the association into existence, and on 13 December 1859 *The Sydney Morning Herald* contained an advertisement 'summoning cricketers to a meeting of the Cricketing Association' at 4 pm that day on the ground at the Domain. Surprisingly neither Driver nor Tunks turned up, which caused *The Sydney Morning Herald* the next day to say 'owing to the non-appearance of either of the secretaries at which considerable disapprobation was expressed, the business did not commence till some time afterwards'. Twenty-five people were present and they elected a 'number of gentlemen'. Joseph Clayton was elected Treasurer and the absent joint secretaries were retained. John Kinloch, secretary of the University Club, submitted a set of rules which were agreed to after some amendment.

Nine months later, on 18 September 1860, a proper constitution was published in *The Sydney Morning Herald*. Under these rules the Association was to be controlled by a president, four vice-presidents, a treasurer and a secretary; membership was to be open to eligible people on payment of an annual subscription, and was to be run by a management committee which would meet monthly.

On 16 November 1860 a meeting of the Association elected office-bearers. A prominent Sydney lawyer and politician, J. B. Darvall, became president; John Fairfax, Richard Jones, William Tunks and Captain Ward were vice-presidents, with Joseph Clayton taking the secretary's role. The Governor, Sir William Denison, agreed to be patron. The New South Wales Cricket Association was now up and running.

After the initial England tour of Australia in 1861–62 under H. H Stephenson, New South Wales was strengthened by the inclusion of Charles Lawrence, the England, Surrey and Middlesex all-rounder, who took over as NSW captain in 1862–63. As cricket was becoming more popular so crowds were increasing, particularly for the now traditional 'grudge' matches between the colonies.

The 5 February 1863 match started quietly enough with New South

Wales scoring 108, and in reply Victoria reached 76. On the second day the Victorian bowler John Conway struck Sydney Jones, the NSW batsman, on the leg with a fast delivery. Jones needed a runner and continued to hobble around in considerable pain. When Jones wandered out of his crease, George Marshall took off the bails and appealed for a run-out. Richard Driver, the NSW appointed umpire, turned down the appeal saying that he had already called 'over'. However, the Victorian umpire, J. A. Smith, disagreed and gave Jones out. A long argument followed which concluded with the Victoria players walking off the ground and returning to their hotel.

After tempers had cooled the next day, nine of the Victorians returned to the Domain to continue the match and they immediately withdrew their appeal against Jones. However, George Marshall, William Greaves and Umpire Smith caught the next ship back to Melbourne. NSW won by 84 runs, and the Sydney newspapers claimed that the loss of Marshall and Greaves did not affect the result.

George Marshall thought otherwise and on return to Melbourne gave his version of events to *The Argus*:

> The ball went through to the longstop and was returned to me. Jones, in attempting to regain his equilibrium, drew one foot over the crease and I put down the wicket and threw the ball up. While the ball was in the air, the Sydney umpire called 'Over', and on my appealing to our umpire, Jones was given out. The consequence was that a scene ensued which I am happy to say is never witnessed out of Sydney. The mob refused to let Jones retire, or Thomson to come in, although the Sydney captain, Lawrence, ordered it, and we were all compelled to leave the ground. Wills was struck a severe blow in the face by a cowardly vagabond, and Huddlestone and Hope were both struck by heavy sticks from behind. I was bullied and threatened not only at the ground but even at my hotel, where a deputation waited on me with the avowed purpose of assaulting me.

Marshall said that he withdrew from the game in fairness to those who had subscribed the money to send the team to Sydney. He also added some fairly strong comments on the behaviour of the NSWCA committeemen. Tom Wills added fuel to the fire by writing to *The Sydney Morning Herald*. The real culprit in his view was the former New South Wales captain, George Gilbert, who had 'aroused the mob' when he came out from the NSW tent shouting 'Go back, go back' to Jones.

Letters went back and forth between Sydney and Melbourne. Letters appeared in newspapers, each side condemning the other. On 23 February 1863 the NSWCA set up a sub-committee of investigation and wrote to the Victorian Intercolonial Match Committee inviting them to join in. The result of all the fuss was a gap of two seasons in meetings between the colonies.

A United Victorian Cricketers' Association had been formed in 1860 with the object of providing relief for former cricketers who, from old age or accident, might be unable to provide for themselves or their families. It had no real control over the game in Melbourne, neither had the Victorian Cricketers' Association which was formed, on 10 October 1864, in the wake of the Sydney affair.

The new body had five objectives: the resumption of the matches against New South Wales; the control and management of all future intercolonial and international fixtures; the settlement of any disputes which might arise; to interpret any of the Laws of the game; and to establish a committee to take the initiative in all matters pertaining to cricket in Victoria. The president was W. C. Haines, a trustee of the Melbourne Cricket Club who had been the first Premier of Victoria, appointed in 1856; the secretary was M. E. O'Brien and the treasurer Richard Wardill. The committee of nine included William Hammersley, James Brodie and Donald Campbell. Since membership was to be on an individual basis, the organisation was not an Association of clubs, and therein lay its weakness.

*Bell's Life in Victoria* reported on 4 November 1865 'that the Victorian Cricketers' Association (VCA) had arrived at an agreement with the Melbourne Cricket Club whereby it rented the club's grounds on the basis of [the Melbourne CC] receiving 15% of nett profits out of the first £300 and 30% on any greater nett profits'.

Alas, no papers survive of the original VCA and it is not known how it folded or in what circumstances. It is clear from other records, however, that it was not in existence in 1869. Not until 1875 would another such body be formed.

The established New South Wales Cricket Association now started to look further afield for matches. They had some formidable players to choose from, particularly those of the Albert and Warwick clubs. The latter could boast the Gregory brothers, Dave and Ned; the Bannerman brothers, Charles and Alick; and W. L. 'Billy' Murdoch. Charles Lawrence, who had stayed behind after H. H. Stephenson's tour, was joined three years later by Billy Caffyn who, after the 1863–64 English visit, had coached for a season in Melbourne before being lured to Sydney.

In February 1863 the Brisbane Club suggested that a New South Wales team should visit Brisbane to play a representative Queensland side. The offer was accepted. However, before the home team could even consider any type of success they had to prepare themselves, for the previous season the Queenslanders had been unable to raise a 'twenty-two' to play against the touring Englishmen. Team trials started early in 1864 with matches taking place on 17 and 24 January between the two strongest clubs, Brisbane United and Victoria. Then, on 12 February, Ipswich travelled to play Victoria 'on the ground near the reservoir'. It was not only in Brisbane and Ipswich that team trials were taking place. On 2 April Toowoomba hosted a team from Dalby and 9 May saw Ipswich take on Brisbane.

The final preliminary match took place on 14 May 1864 when Ipswich travelled to Brisbane and played a tied game. Then on 21 May, the all-important final trial took place when 'A Brisbane XI' played '22 other players' on what *The Courier* called 'the new ground' at Green Hills.

The NSW team, captained by Charles Lawrence, travelled by sea from Sydney and arrived in a very wet Brisbane. But luckily *The Courier* was able to report:

> The rain having ceased on Thursday night and the great exertions which had been made by the secretary and the members of the Queensland intercolonial match committee, giving promise of, at all events, a dry wicket, it was arranged that the contending parties should meet at the trysting place.

The newspapers talked at length about the weather prospects, the fact that the pitch 'was damp and spongy', and that the bowlers would require 'a plentiful supply of sawdust'.

The first session of play on 3 June 1864 was for barely three-quarters of an hour before 'the players and their friends assembled together . . . and partook of an excellent lunch provided by Messrs Stewart and Shaw'. As lunch was ending so the Governor and Lady Bowen arrived somewhat unexpectedly. Word soon got around town about Vice-Regal support for the match so that, 'prior to their arrival on the ground the attendance was very slack, but as the day advanced so the number of spectators increased'.

The Governor departed during the afternoon but Lady Bowen stayed until close of play which meant that all other ladies had to stay as well 'accompanied by the Colonial Secretary, Attorney-General and several other members of the Legislature'.

New South Wales batted first and scored 32 (T. Foden 6/16, E. Shaw 4/15) and 145 (J. Clarke 42, C. Lawrence 28) to defeat twenty-two of Queensland 45 (C. Lawrence 14/25, N. Thomson 7/9) and 49 (J. Bolger 26*, J. Moore 11/14, N. Thomson 7/25) by 83 runs. The match finished at 12.30 pm on the fourth day and, after a lengthy lunch, 'a single-wicket match was played between two of the Sydney side and six Queenslanders'. The visitors won this game as well.

The match aroused a great deal of enthusiasm for the game in Brisbane, but the grounds were poor, finances were difficult to balance, the players were crude in their technique and overall the game in Queensland was still very much in its infancy. Although a Queensland Cricket Association had been spoken about, it would be another eleven years before any action was taken. However the Brisbane Club did engage the colony's first professional coach when they persuaded Jemmy Moore, a NSW player, to take up the position.

Moore immediately improved the quality of play. This was shown in the trial matches played before the return contest against NSW in Sydney. Moore organised a match on 25 February 1865 which saw a 'Queensland 1st XI' play 'The Next XVI'. He made sure that nine such fixtures took place with the final one being an eleven-a-side Brisbane versus Country match, with the result that eight country players were signed up for city clubs.

Queensland's second intercolonial fixture started on the Albert Ground in Sydney on 15 April 1865 with W. G. Macnish winning the toss for the visitors and electing to bat. After four days play, Twenty-Two of Queensland 50 (J. Moore 14, N. Thomson 16/16) and 41 (C. Lawrence 12/24) lost to NSW 195 (W. Caffyn 55, G. Gilbert 20) by an innings and 104 runs.

The Queensland selection committee sent a telegram to the NSWCA 'expressing dissatisfaction at Caffyn being chosen 'but adding that they would 'not raise any further objections' if he did play. It was felt, correctly, that a player of Caffyn's ability would be of too much benefit to NSW.

The day after the main match had finished, 19 April, eleven of the Queensland team played a NSW second eleven scoring 26 and 45 to 85, so recording another loss, this time by an innings and 14 runs. The following week the whole Twenty-Two of Queensland played the Toxteth Park Cricket Club – and lost again.

Another match was planned for Brisbane for April 1866 but it never took place, and ten years went by before the teams met again. Yet *The Courier* reported on how much the players felt they had learned by their visit to Sydney, particularly 'the experience of playing with Lawrence, Caffyn and Thomson'.

The growing organisation of Australian cricket now moved to Tasmania where, on 1 February 1866, the Southern Tasmanian Cricket Association (STCA) was formed. Old records show that William Hogg was elected chairman, Thomas Whitesides as secretary, and Cecil Perry as treasurer. The main clubs involved were Derwent, Break o'Day and Wellington.

The first annual meeting took place on 8 October 1867 at the Bird-in-Hand Hotel in Hobart (subsequently the Grand Lodge Room of the Odd Fellows' Hall for the reason that, as the Governor had become Patron, you could not expect him to chair the AGM in a pub!) and it reported on three matches played against Victoria in the preceding year.

The Victorians had agreed to travel to Tasmania to play matches in Launceston (which they won by an innings and 25 runs) and Hobart (Tasmania victorious by 18 runs) in February 1866 on two conditions. The first was that Tasmania would play sixteen-a-side as even teams would show an imbalance in skill; secondly that a team would visit Melbourne in January 1867 so that Victoria could recoup its financial losses.

From 1865–66 to 1871–72, Australian first-class cricket saw only the colonial matches between Victoria and New South Wales, except for three one-sided contests between Victoria and Tasmania. Following Tasmania's win in an odds-match in January 1868 at Hobart, however, the STCA pushed for a match on equal terms. The Launceston Cricket Club was reluctant to share the Association's view that 'a hollow victory with sixteen men was infinitely preferable to a fearful drubbing with eleven men'. Victoria agreed with the Launceston view, but when only eleven men arrived in Melbourne in February 1869 the hosts were presented with a *fait accompli*. Yet the Tasmanians, with four of their top cricketers not available for the trip, should have chosen a better moment for a show of bravado. Dismissed for 18 in their first innings, they could only watch as Victoria finished the first day at 265 for six. By mid-afternoon the following day, Victoria had won by an innings and 260 runs.

After the final 'odds' match in Launceston in March 1870, the sides contested on level terms twice in the next three years but after that they did not meet again until January 1889.

Australian cricket mythology records that the Norwood Cricket Club Secretary, Yorke Sparks, was the brains behind the formation of the South Australian Cricketing Association (SACA) in 1871. He was, in fact, only the 'front man' with the strings being pulled from, of all places, Government House.

Sir James Fergusson had been appointed Governor of South Australia in 1869. On his arrival in Adelaide he brought with him from England a number of his family including his younger brother Adam.

At this point Sparks had visited Melbourne when he took time to inspect the ground of the Melbourne Cricket Club. He saw how the Melbourne CC maintained the area and how the necessary funds were obtained. The ground at the time was in the process of being redesigned by Robert Bagot (who had also designed the Flemington Racecourse).

Sparks was struck by what he saw. Bagot had altered the shape of the ground from a square with rounded edges to a perfect oval. He put drainage pipes underneath the surface, then replanted and returfed the whole area. Bagot had the help of Baron von Mueller (who created Melbourne's Botanic Gardens). He now gave four hundred choice trees for planting between the inner and outer fences. Bagot's 1869 plans show a raised wicket area sloping gently down towards the boundaries.

Sparks returned to Adelaide and, with the backing of the Norwood club, approached the North Adelaide and Kent clubs with a proposal to form a proper cricket ground. He failed to get their support, so on behalf of his own club he issued the following circular, which was dated 19 November 1869:

> I beg to inform you that an effort is now being made to form a Central Cricket Ground similar to those at present existing in the sister colonies, the want of which has hitherto acted very prejudicially against the success of the game here and as the Corporation has granted a suitable plot of ground it is proposed to have it grassed, levelled, fenced, and surrounded by a belt of shrubs, trees, etc., so as to render it both serviceable and ornamental and a place of pleasant resort. As the achievement of this object will necessarily incur a large expenditure, the committee have thought it desirable to appeal to the admirers and patrons of manly sports for assistance. May I have the pleasure of including your name in the list of subscribers?

Sparks followed this ten days later with a lengthy letter to Adelaide's morning newspaper *The Register* in which he advocated using the proposed ground not only for cricket but a variety of sports, particularly athletics and croquet.

The appeal raised £150 and initial works were started on the ground of the South Australian Cricket Club which, with minor boundary changes, is now the Adelaide Oval. The work cost £200 and various methods were used to try to raise funds to meet the deficiency. These all failed, particularly as the Adelaide City Council refused to allow for admission charges to be made for club matches.

During this time cricketers from other clubs were discussing the idea that the ground should be taken over by an organisation who could obtain a lease from the Council.

Sparks once again became the public face for these ideas and, on

14 February 1871, published another letter in *The Register* advocating the formation of a controlling representative body. *The Register* was again used as a sounding board on 10 March when William Whitridge suggested forming an Association with the definite object of raising £200 and taking over the arrangements for organising proposed intercolonial matches.

Behind the scenes, Adam Fergusson was speaking to the important people involved in the running of the five major clubs of the time – Kent, North Adelaide, Norwood, the South Australian from the city, and Gawler from the country. The obvious club to make a move to form an Association was Norwood, the top club of the colony. At their end-of-season committee meeting held on 9 May 1871 at the Criterion Hotel in King William Street, Adelaide, the Norwood Club members authorised their newly elected secretary, John Pickering (he had taken over that night from John Hill, father of future Australian captain Clem Hill), 'to communicate with the secretaries of the South Australian, Kent, North Adelaide and Gawler Cricket Clubs with a view of obtaining their sanction to place their names to an advertisement calling a meeting to discuss the desirability of forming a Cricketing Association in South Australia'.

Great interest was shown in the proposal, helped along by Whitridge who was not only a journalist for *The Register* but whose editor was his father, W. W. R. Whitridge. The letters column of the newspaper carried supporting views under various guises, but in fact they were written by Adam Fergusson.

Pickering sent a circular letter to as many influential people in the colony as he could, requesting their attendance and interest in the proposal. He had also foreseen the need to have a set of rules as guidance and on 19 May had received the Melbourne Cricket Club's details from their secretary, W. H. Handfield. He encouraged Pickering to get them adopted at the first meeting, which is what happened.

Adam Fergusson chaired the meeting at which sixty-three people were present. The motion to form an Association was passed unanimously. Then the meeting decided to define the objects of the new body which were:

> To prepare and keep in order a central cricket ground, with all necessary requirements, and stimulate their improvement in the interests of the game, and to make arrangements for occasional intercolonial matches.

A fortnight later a formal structure was organised. The Governor accepted the position of President and donated five guineas to SACA funds. Adam Fergusson was elected chairman along with a committee of fifteen representatives, three from each of the five major clubs.

John Darling, MP (father of Joe, another future Australian captain), pushed through a Bill in the Colonial Parliament in September 1871 formally to create the Adelaide Oval, after which work started on trying to bring the ground up to an acceptable playing standard.

The first time South Australia was called upon to provide players for a representative team, they were still five years away from their initial first-class match, whereas Victoria, New South Wales and Tasmania all possessed experienced cricketers. It was the idea of a Victorian, Hon. George Coppin – MP, theatre entrepreneur and president of the Richmond Cricket Club – to organise a match in Melbourne in December 1872 which saw Victoria play a 'Combination Team'. This team of thirteen players consisted of seven players from NSW with three each from South Australia and Tasmania.

The match started on Boxing Day and almost immediately a sensation occurred when Combination opening bowler, Dave Gregory, was no-balled for throwing by the umpire, George Curtis. However, the game continued with little further fuss with the visitors winning by five wickets late on the third day. The scores were: Victoria 136 (S. Cosstick 36, B. B. Cooper 29, W. W. Gaggin 27) and 89 (J. Coates 7-39) lost to Combination Team 113 (S. Cosstick 9/61) and 113 for seven (J. L. A. Arthur 34*, E. J. Gregory 27) by five wickets.

This match was regarded as first-class even though the sides were not equal. With Victoria not having lost a game against New South Wales since December 1866, the stage had been reached when it appeared that no side could match Victoria on even terms. In order to arrange the match, George Coppin had organised a team which was of at least equal ability to Victoria and so he gave the opposing side an odds advantage, which in reality it did not need.

Victoria followed this match by a visit to Sydney to defeat NSW by 24 runs on the Albert Ground and a week later they won in Launceston by seven wickets against Tasmania. There then followed a twenty-one-month gap before the next first-class match took place, when NSW were victorious in Melbourne at the end of December 1874.

However, a month earlier, Victoria had visited Adelaide to play an odds match against South Australia – the first meeting between the two colonies. The match had been two years in the making and Adelaide had prepared itself well to receive their honoured guests, offering various 'entertainments' from a Town Hall reception through to a visit to 'Mr Hardy's vineyard'.

The Victorian side to play in Adelaide was a strong one. Nine of their players had already appeared in first-class matches, and two of them, Tom Horan and Harry Boyle, would eventually play in a total of twenty-seven Tests against England. Joseph Phillips (Victoria) and

Alex Lungley (SA) were the respective captains, and just after 1 pm on Saturday 7 November 1874 the initial match between the two colonies got under way when Andrew Scott sent down the first delivery to the Irishman William Gaggin. Victoria made 92 runs from the same number of four-ball overs – fifty of which were maidens – with Gaggin top-scoring with 22, and Scott claiming 5/28. The South Australians gained a first innings lead of 17 on the second day, when the visitors' second innings had reached a precarious 36 for seven wickets. Charles Allee and Michael Murphy, however, saw the Victorians to 98. Needing 82 runs to win, South Australia fell to the cunning round-arm bowling of Tom Horan and Victoria ended up victors by 14 runs.

With the public taking obvious objection to the two-shilling admittance charge, an attendance of around 2,500 saw the takings reach only £285, far short of the South Australians' expectations. The players, however, enjoyed the experience and *The Register* reported that, while the caterer was preparing lunch on the second day, 'some half a dozen sturdy men of the teams got between the shafts, while an equal number added their extra weight to the roller, and the pitch was rolled ready for the resumption of the game'.

Before the match SACA had received a shock when they were sent a letter from the local champion all-rounder, Tom Cole, asking to be paid £5 for playing in the match, 'in order to cover his expenses'. The Committee met and discussed this, finally offering Cole £2-2s-0d 'to cover any actual loss'. Cole refused and was dropped from the team.

The time was now considered ripe in Melbourne to make a more serious attempt to form a Victorian Cricketers' Association. The efforts of the preceding fifteen years had failed for different reasons, so on 22 September 1875 the Melbourne, East Melbourne and South Melbourne clubs joined forces. The man who planned the meeting was Augustus Robinson, originally from South Australia, currently secretary of the Melbourne CC and later to become involved in New South Wales cricket. Historians have grossly underestimated Robinson's role in the early development of South Australian and Victorian cricket associations and his critical involvement in 1892 over the Sheffield Shield.

Robinson called the September meeting and the VCA was formed with six delegates – two from each club. Along with Robinson from Melbourne CC was William Handfield who became the first VCA secretary. From South Melbourne came John Conway, the Victorian captain who was to leave his mark on Australian cricket, and William Bunting, the club secretary. East Melbourne provided Dan Wilkie, an under-arm bowler with a fearsome moustache who played for Victoria from 1865 for ten years, and Owen Williams, a club stalwart who died under mysterious circumstances in Ceylon during the first world war.

Donald McArthur was appointed president of the VCA, a far

cry from his position as the first secretary of the Melbourne CC thirty-seven years earlier. The treasurer came from the Civil Service Club when Harry Shelton accepted the committee's offer, and a match committee of Conway, Wilkie and Tom Kelly (of Melbourne) was appointed. Soon after its formation, the VCA expanded to include the Richmond, Hotham (now North Melbourne), Carlton, St. Kilda, and Civil Service Clubs. Civil Service disbanded at the end of the 1878–79 season when the VCA dissolved itself and immediately reformed under a new constitution. Hotham then withdrew but other clubs quickly took their places such as Kew, Williamstown, Bendigo and Ballarat.

In Queensland, in the ten years since New South Wales had last entertained Queensland in Sydney in 1865, new clubs had been formed and the standard generally improved. Negotiations between the NSWCA and a Brisbane Intercolonial Match Committee resulted in three games being arranged for December 1875 and January 1876. All matches would be odds games, with the important one starting first on 27 December on a ground in the suburb of Hamilton, which lies between the city of Brisbane and Eagle Farm Racecourse. There 'Eighteen of Queensland' took on a 'NSW Eleven' with the visitors having in their side the twenty-one-year-old Alick Bannerman and the seventeen-year-old Tom Garrett.

The match was a triumph for Queensland who won their first intercolonial fixture against a NSW side who were by no means lacking in skill even though they were a Second Eleven as the first team was playing in Melbourne. Their first innings put the home team in a very advantageous position and allowed room for a second-innings collapse. The scores: Eighteen of Queensland 121 (W. Sheehan 20, Millar 18) and 47 (E. Banbury 10) defeated NSW 48 (A. Geary 11) and 51 (A. Bannerman 10*) by 69 runs.

The attendance on the first day was over 3,000 but, according to *The Courier*, 'owing to bad management the supply of drink of all kinds gave out quite early and even water was not procurable at threepence a glass, until some people found the Chinaman's Well (forty foot deep) under Sutherland Hill'.

The NSW side then went to Warwick to play an I Zingari Eighteen followed by a return to the city to take on Eighteen of Brisbane. NSW won both matches by an innings.

The poor management of the game could clearly not be tolerated. Just after the departure of the NSW team a letter appeared in *The Courier* of 21 January 1876 in which the writer suggested 'that the secretaries of the different clubs be asked to meet at an early date for the purpose of forming a Cricket Association'. Early in February

*The Courier* published an article which suggested 'that public opinion was obviously taking an interest in cricket affairs'. On 25 February the Intercolonial Match Committee met and passed a motion which said, 'before winding up, the committee instructed the secretary to call a meeting of all interested in cricket for the purpose of forming a Cricket Association in Brisbane'. Matters then started to move. In early March the Albert Cricket Club named five delegates for the Association, and during the month the Stanley, Milton, Eagle Farm, Shaws, Police and G.P.O. Clubs followed suit.

A meeting of 'interested persons' held at the Royal Hotel, Brisbane, in mid-March 1876 resolved that – 'This meeting is of the opinion that it is desirable that a Cricket Association be at once formed in Brisbane, such Association to be called "The Queensland Cricket Association".' The first president was appointed, Sir Maurice O'Connell (a grandson of Governor Bligh) and a vice-president was the eminent jurist Sir Samuel Walker Griffith.

The first general meeting after the Association's formation was held on 5 April at the Australian Hotel when John Gaul was elected secretary and William Parker as treasurer. The meeting also elected a committee to draw up a code of rules and then made the quite extraordinary decision, after a lengthy discussion, to allow 'House Clubs' – a club on an estate but without a formal constitution – as members of the Association. This idea was a throwback to the Country House matches in England enjoyed by those who had returned 'home' to finish their education. Luckily for the QCA this idea never took hold.

On 4 May 1876 another QCA meeting was held, this time at the Brisbane School of Arts. William Parker, of the Stanley Club, was in the chair and for a man of only twenty-nine did extremely well in controlling a very vocal gathering. The minutes read:

> The minutes of the previous meeting were read but not confirmed, as some of the delegates present objected to the rules being passed by the former meeting (held on 13 April), and they thought that the meeting was for the purpose of reconsidering the rules.

Two days later *The Courier* reported that 'after considerable discussion, the chairman, on being told that a number of delegates would leave the room if consideration of the rules was not allowed to proceed, put the matter to the meeting, which decided in favour of reconsideration'. After two of the proposed rules were passed, a stormy discussion arose on the third. Over an hour later a resolution was carried which called for a Special General Meeting to adopt the rules and John Gaul, the secretary, even younger than Parker at twenty-two years of age, was given the onerous task of calling and preparing the meeting. As a recompense the final item on the night's agenda was to present Gaul with a bat 'for his services in connection with the recent intercolonial match'.

Gaul not only quietened down the club delegates, he made them see reason over the rules. The SGM held on 11 May smoothed over the cracks and a united QCA emerged. More clubs now joined, including Aubigny (Toowoomba); Blackall (South Brisbane), Richmond (New Farm), Toowoomba, Waratah (Brisbane), I Zingari (Warwick) and country clubs in Laidley and Gatton. These clubs also took a role in expanding the game, visiting country centres either by boat or stage-coach and playing at Tweed River, Nerang, Coomera, Tallebudgera and even as far north as Cooktown.

John Conway, the Victorian captain, summed up 'Cricket in Queensland' in his *Australian Cricketer's Annual, 1876–77*:

> This Colony, being the youngest of the Australian group, it naturally follows that cricket there is in a corresponding stated infancy. Still though little is known outside its boundaries of its capabilities in this department, it actually possesses a good deal of talent, which, if concentrated would give it a foremost position. At present, this talent is scattered over a large area, and is generally of a nomadic character, being embodied largely in the persons of ex-University and Public School men, who have migrated hence from England in search of Colonial experience and fortune. Amongst the ranks of squatters there are many first-class cricketers, and around Mackay there are no less than seven sugar planters who have at one time or other figured in Oxford or Cambridge Elevens! In Rockhampton and further north, little is heard of local cricket, the extremely high latitude having evidently an exhausting effect and proving detrimental to active outdoor exercise.

By this time New South Wales and Victoria were playing home and away matches each season, except in 1876 –77 when the Englishmen were touring. South Australia had played an odds match in Adelaide against Victoria in February 1876 and had won by an innings and 77 runs.

A number of matches played around this time were first-class in all but name. One was South Australia's match against the East Melbourne Club at Easter 1877 in Adelaide. The SACA had decided at their February 1877 committee meeting to invite EMCC to play on equal terms. The reasoning behind this move was to test the ability of the South Australian players. Sixteen of the twenty-two players were, or were to become, first-class players and three would represent their country.

Saturday 31 March saw the debut of George Giffen who was just four days past his eighteenth birthday. Giffen, who top-scored in both South Australian innings with 16 and 14, met for the first time two Victorian players with whom he would tour overseas: Tom Horan and Harry Boyle.

The match started promptly at 11.45 am with Toms umpiring for the home side, and Budd for the visitors. Dan Wilkie won the toss and put South Australia in to bat with 2,500 spectators scattered around the ground. The home side was dismissed in the forty-fourth over for just 56, Boyle taking 5/18. When East Melbourne batted they had escape after escape as the home team's fielding went from bad to worse. Then Will Whitridge was called for throwing by Harry Budd. Many contended that Whitridge's round-arm bowling caused him to throw a number of his deliveries, but ranks closed when a Victorian umpire dared to question the action of one of the colony's top cricketers. The newspapers had a field day, dragging the controversy out for some months. Whitridge, incidentally, was never called again for throwing and, after a close examination later in the month by the England captain James Lillywhite, his action was said 'to be perfectly fair'.

East Melbourne completed their first innings on Easter Monday totalling 89. South Australia reached only 65 in their second attempt and eventually lost the match by eight wickets.

Aware of the success of coaches in Melbourne and Sydney, the SACA decided to hold a special public meeting on Thursday 12 April 1877 at which the SACA chairman, Edward Ashwin, accepted the motion: 'That this Association empowers the committee to engage a coach from England'.

This worried SACA committee members who were negotiating, through their former assistant secretary Augustus Robinson who now lived in Victoria, with Ben Terry, the Melbourne Cricket Club coach, who had just umpired the first two Test matches.

Terry was offered the position but he turned it down in mid-July. Then the committee wrote to James Lillywhite in England asking for help, the result being a most successful five-year agreement with the Sussex all-rounder, Jesse Hide.

However, twelve months before Hide's arrival in November 1878, South Australia had played their initial first-class match. Charles Leader, their secretary, had informed the SACA committee on 15 October 1877 of a letter received from Archibald Godden, secretary of the Queen and Albert Cricket Association of Port Adelaide. The letter told of an impending visit by a Tasmanian team to celebrate the opening of Alberton Oval. Would SACA care to help defray their costs by arranging to play Tasmania in a match on the Adelaide Oval? The Association agreed generous terms, and the match was scheduled for 10–13 November 1877.

Unbeknown to anyone in South Australia, the Tasmanian visit would cause ructions in cricket on the island for the following two seasons, mainly due to parochial feuding between the Northern and Southern Associations over the Launceston player, James Ferguson.

The Tasmanians arrived in Adelaide without Ferguson who had travelled with them as far as Melbourne and, with the prior permission of his Association, had stayed in Victoria to conduct some business. Alas, no-one had passed this information on to the captain, William Walker, who took Ferguson's absence as a flagrant breach of team discipline. Ferguson joined the team at Port Adelaide on the first morning of the two-day match, 8 November. Walker refused to let Ferguson play, so he joined the 150 spectators present in watching the Tasmanians field. The following day some three hundred paid to see the game which resulted in a large financial loss to the Q & A, to be added to which was the £500 spent on erecting a new 250-seat stand especially for the match.

At Adelaide Oval the following morning the South Australian captain, Charles Gibbs, won the toss and elected to bat. In front of 1,500 spectators, King was bowled without scoring in Bayly's first over, after which Lucas and Giffen had a half-century partnership. During the afternoon the Tasmanian bowler William Birch (who had taken 3/13 in seven overs) retired injured and, only after representation from the rest of the team, did Walker allow Ferguson to take his place. Ferguson was also allowed to bat in both of Tasmania's innings, becoming one of those rare players who batted in a first-class match as a substitute.

South Australia won a one-sided match on the second afternoon by an innings and 13 runs, with John Bevan taking 6/23 and 8/36 in his only first-class match before leaving the colony to take up a position with the Melbourne Cricket Club. Not until March 1989 would Tasmania record a victory against South Australia.

After the match SACA sent a cheque to the Q & A Association for £89 6s 8d, followed two months later by a donation of £15 15s. 0d. to help them out of debt. Not only was it a generous gesture but it also showed that SACA were now in a position, when necessary, to come to the aid of minor Associations.

As for Tasmanian cricket at home, the development was continuing. Back in 1874 the Albert Club of Sydney had played matches in Hobart and Launceston, winning by eight and seven wickets respectively. In November 1875, Tasmania paid their first visit to New South Wales for the return match and were beaten by 126 runs. While in Sydney they accepted a challenge to play the Bathurst Cricket Club, and in century-plus heat won by 51 runs.

Following the Adelaide trip, Tasmanian cricket received a boost in January 1879 when a New Zealand team from Canterbury called in at Hobart on their way home from a short tour of the Australian mainland. The Southern Tasmanian team batted first in the single innings match scoring 87, William Walker 27, with the Kiwis in reply 56 without loss until pacebowler Henry Bailey took charge. He claimed 7/22 as only 25 further runs were added so that the Tasmanians were victorious by just six runs.

This win boosted the confidence of the islanders to visit Melbourne again in December 1879. They obtained a match against East Melbourne who were, at the time, a very strong team comprising eight first-class players, three of whom would play Test cricket. East Melbourne batted first with Harry Musgrove soon out, bowled by Boddam for five. Then the run-riot began: William Gaggin 100, his maiden century; Donald Campbell, former Oxford University player, 94; Harry Boyle 70; Charlie Allee 64; Gideon Elliott 49; and at the end, unbeaten on 250, Tom Horan had created an Australian individual record score. The East Melbourne total of 742 was then a new world record having beaten the Royal Artillery's 724 for eight made against the Engineers in England. Henry Bailey took his solitary wicket with the last ball of the match, which was also the second delivery of his 148th four-ball over. A commentator at the time wrote: 'It was computed that H. V. Bailey, a fast bowler who took a long run, must have run nearly seven miles in the two days – a wonderful performance'. The East Melbourne innings lasted both days, and when the time came for the Tasmanians to bat they conceded the match and returned home.

The next overseas side to tour Australia (apart from tours by English teams which are described in the following chapter) were the same New Zealanders from Canterbury. They played seven fixtures between 27 December 1878 and 23 January 1879, with three wins and four defeats.

The first match, in Ballarat, started immediately on their arrival in the town. 'The Canterbury players were tired with their exertions after their travels,' the *Ballarat Courier* reported; 'and bowling and fielding were below their usual standard.' Nielsen won the toss for the visitors and elected to bat with Ollivier top-scoring with 31 in their total of 131. Ballarat replied with 42 and, following-on, reached 135, Nettle 32. Canterbury were winners by eight wickets. But it was a different matter when they played the Melbourne Cricket Club on the Melbourne Cricket Ground in the game which started on 4 January 1879. Melbourne had in their side George Alexander of the Australian team as well as first-class players in the Jamaican-born wicketkeeper George Gibson, the future Test player Percy McDonnell, the former Tasmanian John Tennent, Test representative Thomas Kelly, professional player Frederick McEvoy, and umpires George McShane and George Coulthard, and another future Test player in Thomas Kendall. Only McGrimmon and McKinnon were pure club players.

The visitors were overwhelmed as the Melbourne CC opened with 142, Alexander 77, to Canterbury's 87, Kendall 5-33. In the second innings Tennent made 75 and Kendall 54 not out in 236 which left Canterbury to score a virtually impossible 292 to win. The visitors slid from 59 without loss to 123 all out as Alexander took 9-50 from 28 overs of his fast round-arm.

Twelve days later South Melbourne won by an innings and 93 runs at Albert Park with the left-hander, Frederick Baker, scoring 105 for the home team and so recording the only century scored against the visitors on tour. The destroyer of the Canterbury side was William Cooper whose leg-breaks claimed 8-35 and 3-40.

Then came the match of the tour against an East Melbourne side which had not been beaten for three seasons. The home line-up was a virtual 'Who's Who' of Victorian cricket at the time: Groube, Horan, Campbell, Hastings, Allee, Musgrove, Boyle, Goldsmith, Trapp, Dobson and Passfield.

East Melbourne were five-to-one favourites in the pre-match betting especially as they had four current Australian Test players in their side. Then came the unexpected as Bill and Charlie Frith, along with John Lee, had East Melbourne 78 for seven until Goldsmith and Trapp pulled their side around to 188. Canterbury passed this total with only five wickets down by stumps on the first day, and went on to a lead of 82. East Melbourne in reply slid to 58 for five until Harry Boyle (40), Harry Musgrove (33) and Charlie Allee (25) stopped the rot. After a final fling from Bill Frith, who finished with 6/69, Canterbury were left to score 99 for victory in exactly 75 minutes. Within that time East Melbourne sent down 32 four-ball overs without success as the visitors recorded an historic win by ten wickets.

But the tour was a financial disaster, and money had to be sent from Christchurch before the visitors could play the rest of their matches. While they were playing the Bohemians on the Melbourne Cricket Ground – on a pitch already used for several days for the recent England versus Australia Test match – the Canterbury team's home body passed a motion dissociating itself from the tourists.

The Bohemians won easily by eight wickets and, although defeating Richmond two days later by the same amount, the Canterbury team left the mainland in debt.

The following year saw East Melbourne tour Tasmania to record a victory in Launceston and suffer a three-run deficit in Hobart. Victoria and South Australia met for the first time on even terms and started playing annually. English sides were now touring regularly, but the game was strongest only in New South Wales, Victoria and South Australia. The Cricket Associations of all three colonies, now well established, brought stability and an organised structure to the game.

There was still, however, a need for higher standards in the other colonies and, to this end, two important tours took place in the latter part of the 1883–84 season. In May 1883 the Canterbury Cricket Association issued an invitation to Tasmania to tour during the latter part of the following season. This was a surprising move as it had been expected that the invitation, when issued, would have gone to the Melbourne Cricket Club.

The Tasmanians originally intended that the team would be equally shared between Hobart and Launceston, but two factors upset the balance. The first was that, owing to the parlous state of the Tasmanian Cricket Association's finances (the debt for the season having been reduced only to £751-5s-1d), each player had to pay his own way. The other was the difficulty that some players had in obtaining leave from their jobs. Four had to decline invitations for this reason alone, and by the time the final twelve set sail on 24 January 1884, only three came from Launceston. The Annual Report of the TCA presented on 1 October 1884 said: 'Your committee undertook to send a team to New Zealand but declined to take any responsibility beyond making the necessary arrangements for the trip. The players having agreed to defray their own expenses.'

The steamship *Manapouri* transported the team across the Tasman Sea in four days to land at The Bluff, just south of Invercargill. A proposed match in the southern city was postponed due to rain, so the Tasmanians took a train to Dunedin where they were due to play Otago. The new ground at Carisbrook had been under water owing to tremendous rain, and one and a half days of pumping by the local fire brigade were needed for a start to be made on 1 February 1884. It was, naturally, a low-scoring match as Tasmania 40 (H. McNeil 6/25) and 47 (C. Frith 5/8) lost to Otago 65 (L.M. Harris 41*, T. Kendall 7/24) and 24 for two, by eight wickets. To make matters worse for the tourists, their dressing-room was ransacked and a total of £10 stolen.

More rain saw a delayed start to the next match against Canterbury at Lancaster Park, Christchurch. It was here that the Tasmanians really started to show some skill and class. Vere Harris (years later to play for Western Australia) scored 60 in Tasmania's first innings of 226 with the local paper stating: 'Harris's innings stands out as one of the best innings seen for some time – his cutting being a treat to witness and his leg hitting well timed and safe'. Canterbury eventually won by one wicket late on the third day but the visitors' ability was a surprising revelation to their hosts.

A two-day game at Ashburton against eighteen locals was easily dispensed with after which the return match with Otago was drawn. Further matches took place in Timaru (won by nine wickets), Christchurch where Canterbury won the return by six runs, and Invercargill (drawn) before the Tasmanians boarded their ship for a storm-tossed journey back to Hobart. This tour was Tasmania's only overseas venture and, it could be said to mark a peak in the varying ups and downs of cricket on the island.

The other major tour of the 1883–84 season saw New South Wales play Queensland three times during the month of April 1884. Although the visitors were a privately organised team and not an official representative side, the patronage of the NSWCA was good enough for the Queenslanders.

The first match, which took place at Eagle Farm Racecourse on 12 and 14 April saw Fifteen of Queensland 122 (J.Ashby 27) and 68 (C. Nettle 23) defeat NSW 78 (P. Marr 50, A. Laing 5/4) and 39 by 73 runs much to the pleasure of Queensland's sole selector, J.V. Francis, who had been criticised for his choice of players. *The Courier* reported on, 'the remarkably good fielding' of the Queensland team, and later added: 'The easy and unexpected victory of the Queenslanders will doubtless give a great impetus to cricket in Brisbane.'

A return match was started two days later on the Queens Park ground (in what is now Brisbane's Botanical Gardens) and resulted in Queensland 118 (Wearne 43, Downes 7/46) beating NSW 33 (Perkins 5/19, Wearne 4/13) and 68 (Silvester 4/11) by an innings and 17 runs.

So keen were the Queenslanders to prove their worth that they hastily arranged an eleven-a-side match for the next day, 17 April. They lost by eight wickets but the enthusiasm generated by these three contests was soon noticeable throughout the colony.

The Queensland Cricket Association felt that they should keep up the momentum and, two days later, arranged a match for City against Country which drew a large crowd at Toowoomba. The Association was now composed of all the top teams from Brisbane, namely Alberts, Bowen Hills, Carlton, Brisbane, Stanleys, Toombul, Union and National Bank. From the regions came Limestone (Ipswich), One Mile (Gympie), Roma, Southport, Toowoomba United, and West End (Ipswich).

There were now only to be three further important intercolonial matches against odds until Queensland obtained first-class status.

In early 1889 New South Wales won by four wickets at the Albert Sports Ground and the following month Victoria played in a drawn match. The final fixture of Fifteen of Queensland against Eleven of NSW was played in Sydney in March 1890 when NSW won by an innings and 111 runs.

The game was now developing so rapidly in Queensland, as well as elsewhere in Australia, that the end of odds matches, or other uneven contests, can be seen to mark the conclusion of the learning side of cricket in the north-east part of the continent. From now on, most intercolonial fixtures would be contested on an even basis.

Australia was a part of the British Empire where new ideas and practices, symbolising the bond to England, were readily grasped. To play each other on an even basis, as in the old country, was each colony's aim. Queensland did not take long in attaining these heights.

# 3

# Early Tours

Although first-class cricket was played between Victoria and Tasmania as early as 1851, the date that marks the beginning of the major intercolonial contests was 26 March 1856.

This also marked the first epoch in Australian cricket; and the second can be said to begin on 1 January 1862, when an English side opened its first tour of the Colonies.

The Englishmen's welcome was beyond expectation. At the time virtually the whole population of Australia (i.e., 98 per cent) was Anglo-Celtic. They were either born in, or were descendants of migrants from England, Ireland, Scotland and Wales.

Pro-Imperial sentiment was particularly strong in the colonial middle class which drew its greatest proportion from England and Scotland. When an indigenous nationalism began to emerge from the beginning of the 1860s, it was not in any sense anti-British; rather it was expressed in terms of Anglo-Australian ideals. These suggested that Australians – particularly from the middle classes – viewed themselves as dual citizens, as much British as Australian. Even now, at the beginning of the twenty-first century, large pockets of Australians, particularly in Queensland, still look on themselves in this light; but back in the 1860s all but a few saw themselves as citizens of both a particular nation and a wider empire. In the minds of many there was no clear distinction between an Englishman, a Scot or an Australian. The common reference to Britain as 'home' underlined the strength of the British attachment, with 'home' being seen as culturally superior.

The first stirrings of nationalism in Australia were hesitant and tentative and, it can be argued, the game of cricket had much to do with the emergence of a nation from its 'mother's' apron- strings.

As the most English of English games, cricket was thought to express imperial ideas and the concept of a cultural bond better than any other sport. With these associations, cricket was the favoured middle-class team sport in Australia for much of the nineteenth century and it became a significant element in the development of Australian nationalism.

The growth of the game between 1850 and 1875 was remarkable.

Prior to 1850, horse-racing had occupied seventy per cent of the recreation time of the peoples of the various colonies. In twenty-five years this recreation time declined to twenty per cent, while participation in or just watching cricket rose from negligible proportions to over one in three of the population.

The game had boomed from the time of the first mainland intercolonial fixture in 1856. The crowds that flocked to the various matches in Melbourne and Sydney found new heroes to idolise. Such a hero was Tom Wills. In the second, or return, match against NSW in 1857 Wills became a Victorian hero by taking 6/28 in the first innings and 4/40 in the second. He was to have a profound influence on Australian sport.

His father, Horace Spencer Wills, had settled at Ararat in the Western districts of Victoria in 1839. These offer the richest grazing and growing soils in Australia, and he became a wealthy man. In 1852 he was able to send Tom 'home' to England to be educated at Rugby School. Wills was captain of both cricket and football at Rugby and, on going to Cambridge University, was considered one of the most promising young cricketers in England.

When he returned to Victoria in December 1856 he proceeded to win back his colony's reputation at cricket, so much so that, by 1860, Victoria's score against NSW was three matches to two.

In one match Victoria's score reached 238, a massive total for the times with Wills, the hero, making 61 not out. The initial first-class century in Australia was still seventeen years in the future.

Wills followed his batting performance by taking 5/25 and 3/34 as his side ran on to victory.

In that year his father sold his property at Ararat and bought a station near Moreton Bay (Brisbane) in Queensland. Tom Wills, his father, family and employees took ten months to get to their new property having driven 10,000 sheep with them.

Horace Wills, on arrival, made a monumental error of judgment. He assumed that the Moreton Bay Aboriginals would be as friendly as those he had left behind in Victoria. They were completely the opposite, being wild and uncontrollable.

The great quantities of provisions which the Wills family had brought with them fascinated the tribesmen. On 17 October 1861, only seven weeks after the family had arrived, and choosing their time carefully – the hottest time of day when all the station hands were sleeping in the sub-tropical heat - the Aboriginals attacked. It came as a complete surprise and all nineteen people on the station were butchered. It was the worst Aboriginal massacre in Australian history. The camp was ransacked, everything being wrecked.

The revenge of the local white settlers was awful with whole Aboriginal tribes – many of them innocent – being slaughtered.

Tom Wills was the only surviving member of his family for, at the time, he was on his way to his new home having collected a dray which had broken down two days' journey from the station.

He stayed in the area for three more years before returning to Melbourne where he played against the second visiting team from England in 1864.

Wills' value to cricket in Australia is beyond estimation. In the years prior to, and after, his return from the north he was the 'W. G. Grace' of the colonies.

A year after his remarkable debut for Victoria, it had been Tom Wills' skill which enabled Victoria to gain their revenge over NSW in Melbourne by the (then) massive margin of 171 runs. Wills took eight wickets and top-scored with an unbeaten 49. Wills dominated the next two matches in the series, taking 5/24 and 6/25 in 1859, followed by 6/23 and 3/16 in 1860.

On his return from Queensland Wills continued to be a match-winner. He was widely known for his coaching ability and acted professionally in this role for many years. His first-class record is not an accurate reflection of his skills. From 1854–75, in 32 games, he scored 602 runs at an average of 12.28 with a highest score of 58. In bowling he collected 130 wickets at 10.07, including taking five or more wickets in an innings on fourteen occasions – quite remarkable for those times.

The idea of bringing a team of cricketers from England to Australia was first thought up by Felix Spiers and Christopher Pond.

Spiers owned the Royal Hotel in Melbourne's Bourke Street and Pond the Piazza Hotel on the corner with King Street. They jointly owned the fashionable Café de Paris, also in Bourke Street, and were trying to find ways in which they could promote both their establishments and their catering business.

They had thought at one time of bringing out to Australia various people of note, including the writer Charles Dickens. However, Pond was on friendly terms with two of the founder members of the old Royal Park Cricket Club (now known as Carlton) – George Gibson and Thomas Moody.

It was they who put the idea into Pond's head – and he later convinced Spiers – that as cricket was so popular, attracting enormous crowds, why did he not promote a cricket team?

The proposition appealed to both men who, after a lot of discussion, decided to invite a group of English cricketers to tour southern Australia. When they put the idea to a few business friends, however, they were ridiculed, for the scheme was clearly a huge financial risk.

But profits were there to be made and, even after convincing a number of people to share the burden of putting £7000 up front, they decided to take on all of the risk themselves. With the technical backing of the impresario George Coppin, Spiers and Pond arranged to send one of his agents, William Mallam, to England to organise a team of twelve players. They would be paid all first-class travelling expenses and £150 for the tour.

Mallam arrived in England to find that the two great teams of the time 'The All-England Eleven' and 'The United All-England Eleven' had both split up and become 'Players of the North' and 'Players of the South'.

Mallam made his way to Aston Park, Birmingham, where the two sides were playing each other – having first sought the advice of the Surrey County Cricket Club secretary, William Burrup. He was invited to a dinner put on for the two teams at the Hen and Chickens Hotel, and it was there that he outlined the proposal for the tour of Australia.

George Parr, captain of the Northern team and former captain of the old All-England Eleven, along with most of his team felt that the terms offered by Mallam were inadequate. Parr had, in late 1859, taken charge of the first tour overseas by an English side when they spent nine weeks in North America. From his experiences then, a potential seven months away from home seemed worth far more than £150.

Undaunted, Mallam spoke again with Burrup and then with Heathfield Stephenson, the Surrey captain. The end-result was a team comprising seven Surrey players, two from Yorkshire and one each from Kent, Middlesex and Sussex.

However, as ten of the top players of the time had refused Stephenson's invitation – Anderson, Caesar, Carpenter, Daft, Grundy, Hayward, Jackson, Lockyer, Parr and Willsher – the party was not the strongest England had to offer. Nevertheless it was a good enough group of players to challenge Australia at that time.

George Wells, the Sussex all-rounder, accompanied by his wife, left England before the rest of the party who departed from Liverpool on the SS *Great Britain* on 20 October 1861. The voyage took until 24 December and although the ship sailed through calm seas, many of the players found the time tedious.

As was the regular practice at that time, the ship had its own newspaper, *The Cabinet*, which was edited by one Alexander Reid and published weekly. His edition of 9 November 1861 carried a story on 'Our Distinguished Passengers' which was no doubt aided by William Mallam giving some background detail to the tour. Reid's report began:

A brief sketch of those of our fellow passengers who have left their native land and crossed the ocean to maintain the honour of England in the cricket field, and on whom all eyes will be centred both in England and at the Antipodes, cannot fail to be interesting to our readers. We need not say that we refer to the Eleven of All-England. . . .

Reid then went on to portray the individual players, including the following:

STEPHENSON, HEATHFIELD HARMAN: Born at Esher, Surrey, member of the A.E.E., and captain of the Australian team, is one of the best cricketers of the day, and for his gentlemanly demeanour and partiality among the 'profession' is much respected. His wicket-keeping is splendid, equalling anyone's; as a hitter, he is unquestionably very scientific; and his bowling is the most difficult in England, his pace being fast with a peculiar delivery.

CAFFYN, WILLIAM: Born Reigate, Surrey, member of the A.E.E., and on the committee. His services to his country as well as for England, are most invaluable, being both first-rate as a bat and bowler, which high position he has held for some years.

MORTLOCK, WILLIAM: Born at Kennington, Surrey, member of the U.A.E.E. According to his performances, he is unquestionably the best long-stop in England. He has also a commanding style of batting, and generally scores well, being steady and persevering.

GRIFFITH, GEORGE: Born at Ripley, Surrey, member of the U.A.E.E. A most terrific left-hand hitter; no one can excel his brilliant hitting when the ground is suitable for the purpose. He is a good left-hand fast bowler, and a splendid slip.

LAWRENCE, CHARLES: Born at Hoxton, Middlesex, captain of the A.E.I.A. A good cricketer all round, first-rate bat, and a good field.

WELLS, GEORGE (gone): Born London, Middlesex. A good cricketer all round, being a splendid bat, a first-rate bowler and a capital point. Is a member of the U.A.E.E.

Reid's account continued:

There can be no doubt that the English cricketers left their homes with the respect and good wishes of all who knew them.

> And how could it be otherwise? Are not the names of Stephenson and Caffyn, Mortlock and Griffith, familiar as household words, and is not this a sufficient guarantee of the confidence and respect which they enjoyed in their native land? . . .
>
> And, as to the future, we have it from the public voice of Australia, that whenever the Eleven may arrive, they 'may rest assured that they will receive a welcome which will prove to them that Victoria has not degenerated from the parent stock in her notions of hospitality'. In connection with this subject, it may be satisfactory to some of our readers to know . . . [that] Melbourne contains twenty-one clubs, each enjoying a large share of public patronage. Of the 'up country' clubs, the following may be selected as claiming special notice: Ballarat, Bendigo, Beechworth, Tarrangower and Creswick. Ballarat, being the largest inland town in the colony, has five clubs, the largest of which is the Ballarat club, numbering about 200 members, and possessing a pleasantly situated ground, about a mile from the township, equal to any in the colony.

In his penultimate edition, after the cricketers had left the ship at Sandridge (now Port Melbourne), Reid wrote as follows:

> The landing of the Eleven was, of course, an event of itself. So soon as the vessel was telegraphed off Cape Otway the excitement, we learn by the Melbourne press, was great among all classes, and it culminated on her appearance off Sandridge on Tuesday morning. By that time Sandridge had put out all its bunting, and one indefatigable gentleman had even improvised a triumphal arch – not a triumph in itself – while the ships in the Bay were gay with colours. The debarkation of the Eleven was not to take place, however, until the same hour of the clock. On board the steamer therefore, the men remained, in company with Mr Mallam. To those who paid an early visit to the ship, they were easily distinguishable from the rest of the passengers by the distinctive hat of grey felt and blue ribbon which some liberal hatter of Liverpool had presented to them just before their departure.
>
> In due time the committee were brought to the *Great Britain* – the introductory speech of Mr Rusden, and Mr Stephenson's short, sharp decisive reply, were completed – the cricketers, committee, and sundries were on board the little *Lioness* and the railway pier, upon which a population seemed to have suddenly grown, was reached. There was much excitement, which expressed itself in vociferous cheers, and in rushing after the 'lions' as they made for the Pier Hotel. The number of people who congregated outside this

place during the while it contained the cricketing champions could not have mustered less than four or five thousand. Loud cries were raised by these outsiders, the purport of which was understood to be that the knights of the blue ribbon should make their appearance upon the balcony. This request was complied with, and the cheering recommenced. Cheers were given for the Eleven, or Twelve it might be for Wells, the Yorkshire pioneer, had rejoined his friends of the bat, and had donned likewise a grey felt hat with blue ribbon. Cheers were given for Mr Mallam, the agent who had shepherded them on their way, and cheers again for Messrs Spiers and Pond, who were conspicuous among the throng. More cheers, as the newcomers climbed to the top of a gay coach drawn by eight handsome greys; more cheers as they dashed along the Sandridge road; and then Sandridge seemed to take unto itself low-backed cars and railway trains, and to melt into Melbourne.

Although it was Christmas Eve, the crowd which greeted the team on their arrival at the Café de Paris was viewed by the *Melbourne Herald* as: 'There had been no welcome like it since the Athenians arrived in Corinth'.

The entertainment was lavish and hardly a day went by on the tour in which a champagne breakfast did not take place. But enthusiastic as the crowds may have been, the players still had to practise. The venues were meant to be secret but they were soon found at either the Richmond or St Kilda grounds.

For the first match, scheduled for 1 January 1862 on the Melbourne Cricket Ground, twenty-two of Victoria were originally selected but Stephenson argued that, as his players had still not recovered fully from their journey, could this figure not be reduced to fifteen? In the end eighteen was agreed.

Before the match the Melbourne Cricket Club took the opportunity to issue the following information to local newspapers:

The members of the Melbourne Cricket Club have most generously placed the gratuitous use of their ground at the disposal of Messrs. Spiers & Pond for the use of the All-England Matches, reserving to their members the pavilion and Mr McGirr's bar.

This is all the more praiseworthy, as a great deal of time and money has been expended during the past winter in enlarging and improving the ground in anticipation of the Eleven's visit. the centre turf, a space of fifty yards square, presents a beautifully level appearance, and resembles more the 'Board of Green Cloth', or a first-class bowling green. The holes and tufts that incommoded the fieldsmen round the outside portions have been carefully removed,

> and a heavy horse roller has succeeded in levelling this part of the ground. We question if there are (out of London) cricket fields at home to compete with this colonial 'Lord's'. The England men will shout for joy when they behold it, so different from what they have reason to expect. It is expected that all the booths will be erected outside the fence to give more room to the players. This will be absolutely necessary, as much inconvenience was experienced, during the last Intercolonial Match, from the crowded state of the field. If the refreshment booths are so disposed of, and a roped circle encloses the players, the public will enjoy a much better view of the game, and those engaged obtain plenty of space for batting and fielding.
>
> The painter has been at work upon the club pavilion and band stand, and the general appearance of the buildings and ground reflects great credit upon those in office.

Of the eighteen players selected to represent Victoria only two (Conway and O'Mullane) had been born in the colony: the other sixteen were migrants. The team was: George Marshall, John Sweeney, C. John Mace, John Huddlestone, Sam Cosstick, Gideon Elliott and Simon Rennie (all Richmond CC); Jerry Bryant, Richard Wardill, Charles Makinson, Tom Morres and Ben Butterworth (Melbourne CC); Tom Wray, James Stewart and George O'Mullane (East Melbourne CC); John Conway and Sam Hopkinson (South Melbourne CC), and James Thompson (Bendigo CC).

New Year's Day dawned hot with Melbourne a crowded city. People were coming from far and wide in all modes of transport to see the cricketers from England. The *Melbourne Herald* suggested next day 'that over 15,000 persons were waiting at the start of play'. At this time the population of Melbourne was 141,000 but this would have been swelled by the Western Districts families who traditionally came to Melbourne for New Year.

The organisers had issued each of the visiting players with a hat with a ribbon and also a coloured sash, each man having a different colour and these colours were printed against each player's name on the match scorecard.

The English players took the field to the playing of the national anthem. The crowd stood in silence but as the band finished they broke into a tremendous roar. This was the culmination of so many dreams.

Probably unknown to the thousands present, the ideology of the game of cricket just about to start was providing a powerful construction in cementing even further the cultural bond of the British Empire.

The Eighteen of Victoria, according to Clarence Moody, an Adelaide journalist, were 'very green, inexperienced and excessively nervous'. Had they not been too nervous to look around, however, they would have seen the Melbourne Cricket Ground at its finest. There were fruit and sweet stalls, shooting galleries, roulette wheels, young boys selling picture cards of the players, and a new grandstand some seven hundred feet long. The area underneath had been given over to publicans who boasted of having 500 cases of beer for the match.

George Marshall, publican of *The Cricketers' Arms*, was captain of the Victorian team. Born in Nottingham in 1829, Marshall had made his debut for Victoria against New South Wales some five years earlier. His career, over seven seasons, saw him score 191 first-class runs at 11.23, but little else.

Marshall won the toss, decided to bat, opened the innings himself and top-scored with 27, as his team fell for 118. George Griffith, bowling 'very swiftly' round-arm took 7/30, while George Bennett captured 7/53 'with considerable breaks which twisted both ways'.

Stephenson's team then spent nearly two days in reaching 305 with suggestions being made that his opposite number, Marshall, 'was adopting delaying tactics and that by the end of the third day he was not trying to get the Englishmen out but was playing for a draw'.

Spiers and Pond must have been rubbing their hands with glee, for by the end of the third day gate takings had covered all of their costs in promoting and launching the tour.

The *Herald* did not display the parochial views which newspapers tend to use in current times. They criticised the Victorian team saying that they 'must have been a very dry lot indeed for they were continually going out of the field to drink, and particularly at the most interesting moments of the game'. In addition: 'If they wished to delay, it was not cricket.'

Billy Caffyn made 'a very wristy' 79, and Griffith hit 61 quite rapidly including one shot when he hit the ball over the crowd between the pavilion and McGirr's refreshment rooms.

The awe in which the Victorians held their opponents, and their raw interpretation of the game, caused Stephenson to say they 'wanted in science'. As for the home fielding a local scribe was to comment:

> The Englishmen were immeasurably superior to their opponents at all points of the game except in the case of long-stopping by Butterworth. The best Victorian fielding was bungling compared to the English – and before Victoria can hope to equal their opponents they must practise to stop balls, as it leads to idleness and bad feeling to depend on nets.

John Conway took 4/60 from fifty four-ball overs but it did not prevent his side, who collapsed for 92 in their second innings (Thomas Sewell 7/20), losing by an innings and 96 runs.

The *Argus* had one criticism: 'Our attention has been called to the smoking which individuals, not knowing better, have allowed to carry on in the grandstand. Considering the large number of ladies who have been present, that practice seems not only objectionable but opposed to good manners and should be discontinued in the future.'

William Hammersley, writing for the *Herald*, also broke new ground when he coined the term 'test match' for the contest. He subsequently wrote in his *Victorian Cricketer's Guide* for the season: 'Of the thirteen [sic] matches, five only can be termed test matches; the three played at Melbourne and the two played at Sydney.'

The following day Stephenson and his team left by Cobb & Co. coach for Beechworth in the north-west of the colony. Caffyn wrote in his reminiscences of the tour: 'This conveyance was drawn by five horses – three in front and a pair behind them. A very shaky and fatiguing journey this was, and glad indeed were we all when it was over.'

The match against the country twenty-two of the Ovens Valley turned into something rather easy for the visitors. Although hospitality was unsurpassed the game took on a farcical note when all the local team fielded, for there were some heavy collisions when converging players tried to catch skied balls.

Within two days Stephenson's team had won by an innings and 191 runs. To fill in time George Griffith played eleven of the top Beechworth players on his own. Bowling his usual round-arm he dismissed the eleven for one run, which happened to be a bye. Batting himself, he scored two singles and it was all over.

The next match was back in Melbourne – due to rain only over two days – against a combined twenty-two of New South Wales and Victoria. Caffyn recalled it being 'a very different affair to the first one'. In the home side's first innings of 153, Caffyn took 7/27 but had no luck with the bat as his side fell for 111. The combined team then made 144 but time ran out with the tourists 10 without loss and the match was drawn.

The game had again been watched by a huge crowd and, when Stephenson's team travelled to Geelong, they received yet another enthusiastic welcome and scored a nine-wicket victory over the locals.

Then came a trip by sea to Sydney from Geelong's Corio Bay and an outstanding greeting by 'more than 15,000 people on the quay'. From Circular Quay the team was taken to be entertained at a 'public breakfast' and a formal dinner later that night at the Victorian Club.

The four-day match against New South Wales was won by 49 runs with the colonial Governor, Sir John Young, and his entourage present on each day. Afterwards 'a grand banquet' was put on for the team with a veritable 'Who's Who' from Sydney and the provinces present. Maybe it was this type of feasting which caused Roger Iddison to make his famous remark: 'Well o'i doan't think mooch o' their play, but they're a wonderful lot o' drinkin' men'.

The visitors then travelled to Bathurst in the Blue Mountains but a violent storm caused the game to be abandoned on the second day. Back in Sydney for another joint challenge from NSW and Victoria, England (60 and 75) lost to the combined side (101 and 35 for 8) by thirteen wickets. By now the entertainment was getting to be just a little too rich for the players: champagne breakfasts, luncheons and dinners; theatre parties; and Tattersall's Club where 'parting bumpers were drained'.

From Circular Quay the tourists boarded ship for the voyage to Tasmania. From all along Sydney Harbour to the Heads the cliff-tops were lined with people bidding farewell to these sportsmen from 'home'. Various fireworks and rockets were fired as a goodbye gesture, while Messrs Spiers and Pond could, once again, only count their good fortune.

In Hobart, William Caffyn remembered the greeting as 'another hearty reception, we being met by a deputation of gentlemen greatly interested in cricket, who, together with a band of the rifle corps, escorted us to our hotel'.

Planning for the fixture had started the previous October when advertisements for matches 'with any cricket club in Tasmania' had been placed in various newspapers. The initiative was taken by Thomas Westbrook, a trustee of the Hobart Town Cricket Ground and, reputedly, the best fielder at point in Australia.

He contacted Spiers and Pond who informed him, the following January, that any Tasmanian venture would have to pay the return steamer fares for all fourteen of the touring party and a match guarantee of £1,000.

This demand worried Westbrook who called a public meeting in Hobart to elicit help. At this meeting a Mr Gardiner, who was the manager of a circus then performing in the town, announced that he would be happy to donate a half of one night's takings to help raise the necessary money. His generosity was followed by so many further offers that Westbrook replied to Melbourne confirming the conditions.

Spiers and Pond replied with a modification of the terms which were:

> That we play a three-day match in your city, and that we bring our team to your ground at our expense and we have the privilege

> of taking all entrance fees at the gates, sub-letting sites for booths for the sale of liquors, printing etc, and every other benefit that may accrue from the ground. The committee to provide a team of twenty-two, free of any expense to us, fence in the ground, get it in proper order for play, and provide a sufficient body of police to keep the playing ground clear.

It was deals like this which helped to make the tour such a financial success.

The Tasmanian team comprised eleven from Launceston and the same number from Hobart but when the match started, on 21 February 1862, Stephenson found the pitch so bumpy that he could not even consider using his fast bowlers.

This did not really matter as the Tasmanians either gave their wickets away with loose shots or were run out by fielding of a quality they had never before encountered. The Englishmen took a comfortable first-innings lead of 67, and were only held up from their four-wicket victory by Tom Whitesides, then twenty-five.

A star batsman of the local Derwent club, Whitesides arrived at the crease with Tasmania two wickets down for 16 in their second innings. He batted for most of the second day before Stephenson stripped off his wicketkeeping gear and started to bowl fast over-arm.

Amid mounting tension, six maiden overs were sent down when, with four minutes to go until stumps, a terrific delivery from Stephenson cut back to bowl Whitesides for 50, the highest score which would be made against the tourists.

Spectators could not curb their enthusiasm and chaired their new-found hero from the pitch although it did not stop defeat early on the third day. After a scratch match to fill in time – and to compensate the three thousand spectators who had paid their 1s. 6d. admission charge – the Englishmen sailed back to Melbourne to play the only first-class match of the tour.

The idea for the fixture, styled 'Surrey versus The World', had first been put in a letter to the Melbourne *Argus* on 7 January 1862. The original game planned for this occasion was to have been the return match against Victoria but that match was postponed for three weeks.

Each side now was composed of six members of the English touring party and four leading Victorian players with James Moore of New South Wales and Fred Christy – who had played for Surrey from 1846–48 – completing the elevens.

Batting first, The World scored 211 and were dismissed exactly at the time stumps were to be drawn. George Bennett led the way with 72 and followed this up with bowling of 7/30 and 8/85 as his side won by six wickets. Both the *Argus* and, later, the *Victorian*

*Cricketer's Guide* said the contest was hard-fought and most certainly was not an exhibition match.

Then came three country fixtures in the Western Districts of Victoria. A three-day draw with Ballarat was followed by an innings victory over Bendigo, and finally by a challenge against Castlemaine. The local newspaper, *The Mount Alexander Mail* went so far overboard in their welcome that on the day the players arrived, the first ten broadsheet pages dealt with everything from the following day's proposed breakfast menu through to the colour of each person's hat.

Early colonial newspaper cricket reports tended to be lengthy, almost ball-by-ball accounts. References to the poor condition of the pitch by the visitors were written with disappointment but when, after the third day, Castlemaine had won by three wickets the *Mail* gave a whole edition to prominent citizens' views of the victory.

The success meant so much to the locals that a century later a commemorative plaque was unveiled at the Wattle Flat ground by S.C. 'Billy' Griffith (Secretary, MCC) and Colin Cowdrey, vice-captain of that year's England touring team.

The farewell match of the tour ended in controversy when the Victorian captain took his team from the field with the Englishmen only eleven runs short of victory. The argument put forward was that only three days' play had been arranged and that time was now up; but the usual procedure in those days was to regard games as timeless and to play a few extra minutes to get a result.

Stephenson and his side did not worry overmuch about this for Spiers and Pond gave half the receipts for this last match to the players. They then offered the players £1,200 to stay for another month, but they all refused because of other commitments. The team arrived home on 12 May 1862.

Charles Lawrence, however, did stay behind. He had accepted a position as coach of the Albert Club in Sydney at a salary of £300 per annum. He became a cricketer and coach of great eminence, and was later a key player strengthening and captaining the first Aboriginal team which toured England in 1868.

Lawrence, born in 1828 and a print-cutter by trade, became an all-rounder playing for Surrey and Middlesex before accepting Stephenson's invitation to tour. After taking up his Albert appointment he played at various times for New South Wales with his best bowling being 7/48 and 7/25 against Victoria at the Domain, Sydney, in February 1863.

His coaching experience had begun in 1846, when he was only seventeen. His first professional engagement had been for Perth Cricket Club in Scotland before he moved on to the Phoenix club in Dublin.

By 1854 he was back in Mitcham in Surrey, but only played for the county in two matches.

In Australia, after three years with the Alberts, Lawrence moved on to the Warwick club and, to supplement his income, he ran the Pier Hotel at Manly. Eighteen months later, in November 1866, he suffered a personal tragedy when his first wife died and his daughter, Maud, five days later, both of natural causes.

In later years Lawrence was to help sponsor the 1878 Australian team to England; to coach at the Melbourne Cricket Ground and, having settled in Newcastle, NSW, he was still fit enough to turn out, at the age of fifty-four, to play for the local twenty-two against the England touring team of 1882–83.

He re-married in 1871, and his second wife predeceased him only months before his own death in December 1916, aged eighty-eight.

Stephenson's tour had seen two of his team average over twenty runs per innings, a far cry from today's expectations. Griffith had scored 421 runs at 22.15 with Caffyn on 419 at the slightly better average of 23.27. Iddison took 103 wickets at 6.61 but no other bowler claimed so many victims. Financially the players, after various bonuses were paid and 'sponsor' money handed over, collected about £400 apiece.

Spiers and Pond made over £14,000 profit from the tour. They left Melbourne and went to live in London where they used their profits to buy properties which they then opened as refreshment rooms.

On his return home, Stephenson spoke about the predictability of Australian bowlers and how they needed more coaching. He could not know, though, how greatly Charles Lawrence's coaching and example would soon help the colonials in their quest to emulate those from 'home'. In addition, the tour had enhanced interest in the game in the whole of Australia. Although the principal aim was to make money, the visit also provided the players with an important educative role.

In the two years between Stephenson's tour and the second English tour of Australia, led by the Nottinghamshire captain George Parr, only two first-class cricket matches were played outside of England. One took place in New Zealand. The other was a clash on Sydney's Domain between New South Wales and Victoria.

The Victorian batting was weak, and for NSW Charles Lawrence was the bowling hero. For Victoria their captain, Tom Wills, took eight wickets in the match but also emerging was John Conway, now twenty-one. Despite his analyses of 5/35 and 4/31 his colony was defeated by 84 runs. The *Argus* at the time wrote of him:

> Only second to the captain of the Victorian eleven in reputation . . . Mr Conway is a powerful batsman, being able to hit and drive

with great strength. His style of batting is pretty good, but it gives one the idea of being too elaborate at times, and he has lost a great deal of that ease and freedom of wrist he once possessed. It is as a bowler, however, that he is most celebrated. He has an easy delivery, great pace, with a tendency at times to bump and break back that will try a batsman's skill to the utmost. On certain days and on certain wickets he is invincible; but he is not possessed of that equanimity of disposition that characterises [Tom] Wills, and a very little thing will at times put him off his bowling altogether. As a colonial cricketer, taken all round, he is undoubtedly the best Victoria has produced.

Another player of prominence was the Victorian all-rounder Sam Cosstick. Born in Croydon, Surrey, he had emigrated with his family to Melbourne where he became one of Richmond Cricket Club's top performers. Following Stephenson's tour, Cosstick was employed by the Melbourne Cricket Club with instructions to keep the ground in order, to play in all the club matches when required and to bowl to the members every afternoon from 2.30 pm to 7 pm. For all this his salary was £3 10s. 0d. per week.

Around this time the Melbourne Cricket Ground (MCG) was being redesigned. The arena was altered to make it a perfect oval; drainage pipes were laid underneath the ground which was then replanted. The change was remarkable. Added to all this was a revision to the Crown Lands Act which effectively gave control of the MCG to trustees of the Club.

The paperwork being in order, the Club then considered its next move. The game had been organised on a proper club basis within the colony; top-quality players were emerging, and nothing draws crowds like a series of good cricket matches.

So the decision was made to invite another team of English cricketers to tour the south-east part of Australia and the then centres of New Zealand cricket, Dunedin and Christchurch.

Amongst the players in England word had spread of the lavish hospitality and warmth of the Australian reception of Stephenson's team. It was not difficult, therefore, for George Parr, when he accepted the appointment as captain, to select a good, representative side. He only succeeded in obtaining William Caffyn from Stephenson's side as Stephenson himself, Mortlock and Griffith all declined, but the final twelve made a strong team: G. Parr (captain), A. Clarke, J. Jackson and R. C.Tinley (Nottinghamshire); R. Carpenter, T. Hayward and G. Tarrant (Cambridgeshire); J. Caesar, W. Caffyn and T. Lockyer (Surrey); G. Anderson (Yorkshire) and E. M. Grace (Gloucestershire).

The team sailed from Liverpool on S.S. *Great Britain*, arriving in Melbourne on 16 December 1863. But they arrived just after disastrous floods had hit the colony on a scale never before known. The *Argus* reported: 'There were two terrible days of storms when the city was as black as midnight and the Yarra burst its banks. . . . The city was a collection of hills rising above the lakes. Great stretches of Richmond, Abbotsford, Collingwood, Hawthorn and Toorak were all under water . . . and St Kilda Road had ceased to exist.'

Because of this chaos the England team could not go ashore at Sandridge. Instead they landed at Williamstown and went by train to Spencer Street station. Despite the floods, the usual vast gathering awaited them there, and in triumphal procession the team made their way the four hundred yards to the hotel in Swanston Street owned by the former Victorian captain, George Marshall.

They had arrived a week or so earlier than had Stephenson's side, so they had a fortnight in which to attend parties, dinners, civic receptions, banquets and picnics. On one memorable day the tourists even went on a quail shoot and bagged forty brace.

By New Year's Day the floods had largely dispersed and for the first four days of 1864 over 40,000 people would watch cricket. The first day of the contest against 'Twenty-two of Victoria' was pleasantly warm without being uncomfortably hot as 15,000 people crammed into the MCG. The Englishmen looked very fine in their uniform of white helmets and white flannel shirts with a red spot. George Parr won the toss from his opposite number, Ben Butterworth, and sent the Victorians in to bat.

The home side tried bravely but were no match for their opponents. Only the batting of the English-born Victorians – particularly a stubborn 34 from Will Greaves – took the score to 146. Parr's team scored 176 with Hayward making 61 and Carpenter 59, and after dismissing Victoria a second time for 143, they needed 114 to win. At 105 for four, with only nine runs needed and six wickets in hand, stumps were drawn, much to the annoyance of the visitors. But a draw it was, after which the party journeyed into the hinterland for four successive victories over country teams in Bendigo, Ballarat, Ararat and Maryborough. The Englishmen then left Australia to spend five weeks in New Zealand and on their return took a revenge over Castlemaine for the previous tour's defeat.

Then came their only first-class match when Parr's XI played Anderson's XI on the MCG. Once again, the teams had six Englishmen on each side – Parr's having Caesar, Caffyn, Carpenter, Tarrant and Tinley – with the balance made up by the best Australians. As a spectacle the game did not attract the numbers expected but at least it gave a chance for the locals to play with, instead of against, some of the finest cricketers of the time.

It was then time for three matches in Sydney against twenty-twos of New South Wales. It was also time to revive old friendships as NSW's principal player was Charles Lawrence. With rain causing the first match to be spread over nine days, it was Easter Saturday 1864 before the second contest started. England won the first and third fixtures, attracting crowds in excess of 20,000 on some days.

The tourists were treated as celebrities during their stay in Sydney. Crowds gathered outside their hotel in York Street hoping to catch a glimpse of them as they went in and out and even the Sydney waxworks had a figure made of E. M. Grace.

A prominent NSW cricket official of later years, Charles Beal, was very impressed by Grace – elder brother of W.G. who, at this point, was fifteen, E.M. being seven years older: 'He used to have a handkerchief stuck in the strap at the back of his trousers,' Beal wrote. 'I remember as a boy I used to imitate him, and could not think of playing without my handkerchief.'

Another Sydney boy impressed by Parr's men was Fred Spofforth who particularly admired the fast bowler George Tarrant. Spofforth wrote: 'At once my great ambition was to bowl fast like Tarrant, who, I well remember, always sent the stumps flying whenever he bowled a batsman out'.

The tourists returned to Melbourne for the final five games of the tour, the last being a return match with Victoria. Rain greatly affected the outcome and reduced the attendance. A draw was agreed which left the England team with an undefeated record.

The penultimate game had been in Ballarat where Carpenter had scored the only century of the tour. His 121 put him to the top of the batting averages, followed by Caffyn and Hayward.

After all expenses were cleared the players were left with £250 each – a goodly sum for those days. When the team sailed for home on 26 April they left two of their number behind: Grace, who was visiting friends, and Caffyn, who had accepted a coaching position with the Melbourne Cricket Club.

It was ten years before another touring team set foot in Australia. In that time the influence of both Caffyn and Lawrence was enormous both in Melbourne and Sydney. Add to this the home-grown talent of Tom Wills – a talent nurtured in England – and you have the three men most responsible for laying the foundations of Australian cricket. Without that trio there would probably have been no Giffens, Darlings, Trumpers, Spofforths, Armstrongs or Hills, let alone Woodfulls, Bradmans, Benauds, Chappells or Borders. The early development of cricket in Australia was very tenuous. A. G. Spalding's touring baseball teams, for example, were very popular. Baseball could have overhauled cricket in public enthusiasm but in retrospect it can be seen that the influence of the early English cricketers was formative.

Caffyn had accepted an offer of £300 a year to stay in Melbourne, 'as coach and general instructor of members'. Known as 'Terrible Billy', he was a fine all-rounder, a neat dapper man with bushy side whiskers. He had already let it be known that between the tours of 1861–62 and 1863–64 he had seen a notable difference in the standard of Australian play. Now he would see bigger changes still, for he was in Melbourne through the height of the over-arm controversy.

Over-arm bowling became legal in 1864 but until it did so, the rule read:

> The ball must be bowled, not thrown or jerked, or if any part of the hand be above the shoulder at time of delivery, the umpire shall call 'no ball'.

Caffyn was not impressed with 'this fancy new style of bowling'. He argued that over-the-shoulder bowling was mainly straight down the wicket or on the off-side. He loved leg-hitting and felt that this new style spoilt the game; and he had no sympathy for the Richmond bowler James Boak, said to be the fastest in the colony, who claimed he could not moderate his pace without bowling over his shoulder. Indeed James Brodie, in his *Victorian Cricketer's Guide 1860–61*, called for the law to be revised, and in conjunction with Charles Lawrence in Sydney, sent a letter to the Marylebone Cricket Club in late 1862 requesting a change.

In his later years Caffyn reflected on those days in Melbourne and the players he coached. He wrote in 1899 in *Seventy-one not out*:

> They were delightful pupils, always willing to be shown a new stroke, quick to do their best to retrieve an error, never taking offence at having their faults pointed out, never jealous of one another. When I remember all this, it is not so much a matter of surprise to me to see what Australian cricket has become today, as perhaps may be the case with some people.
>
> Their bowlers of nearly forty years ago were undoubtedly in front of the batters. Even at that time there were some of them very tricky as regards variety of pace and break, although some seemed not to have the confidence to attempt this head work when engaged in a match, at which time they were usually content to bowl straight and keep a good length. Still even at that time one was able to perceive the germs from which the present perfect Australian bowling had sprung.

Caffyn also reflected on the influence of the first two touring teams on the standard of fielding, and how his young Australians undertook hours of practice in order to improve it.

Caffyn played quite a few matches for the Melbourne club in the 1864–65 season, making his highest score in Australia of 121 against Richmond on the Punt Road ground. His influence was felt particularly in the major matches against leading clubs when his professionalism curbed some of the impetuosities of his young charges.

Melbourne easily won the Premiership for the 1864–65 season, from East Melbourne, and it must have come as a surprise to the club when Caffyn requested a cancellation of his contract in order to move to Sydney. In tandem with Lawrence, Caffyn, who by now was coaching the Warwick club, started to show results with their teaching ideals.

In 1866 Caffyn persuaded Warwick to take on Edward (Ned) Gregory of Lawrence's Albert club to assist with the day-to-day training. One of three famous brothers, and the first of a cricketing dynasty which was to last in Test cricket up to 1928, Gregory was an excellent player who, because of the times, would play in only one Test match.

The most telling story Caffyn related in his writings was when he said: 'The best bat I ever coached or saw in Australia was undoubtedly Charles Bannerman, nor do I think his superior has yet appeared in that country'. Caffyn returned reluctantly to England in 1871 due to his wife's ill-health. He had tried unsuccessfully to obtain a coaching position in Tasmania where the climate would have been cooler but the Southern Tasmanian Cricket Association secretary Thomas Sheehy replied: 'You must have been misinformed for we have not the remotest idea of employing a professional'. However, the Tasmanians did have a change of heart three months later but by then Caffyn had arranged his return home. Six years later 'Terrible Billy's' star pupil, Charles Bannerman, scored Test cricket's first century.

During the latter part of the 1860s and early 1870s various professional cricketers came to the fore such as Sam Cosstick, William Greaves, Ned Gregory, John Conway and Nathaniel Thomson. The first two, Cosstick and Greaves, had been employed by the Melbourne Cricket Club but were sacked for drunkenness. Tom Wills took Greaves' place as a paid professional and, after appeal, Cosstick was reinstated.

All played in the various intercolonial matches of the time. Grounds were becoming better tended as careful levelling and regular rolling led to better pitches which brought dramatic improvements in batting technique.

At about the time when Billy Caffyn left Melbourne in 1865 the Western Districts of Victoria were booming with cricket clubs. The tours by English teams seemed to have stimulated bush imitators and Edenhope was one settlement which formed a group of keen cricketers. William Hayman was the driving force in this team which included Aboriginals amongst its number. He noticed that the local Aboriginals were marvellous natural atheletes, so he began to teach them cricket.

They had been playing together for some time when Tom Wills arrived in the area to give coaching classes. He knew that the Victorian tribes would give no trouble, indeed he was so impressed that he organised a match on the MCG between Melbourne and the Aboriginals, which took place on Boxing Day, 1866. The *Argus* commented 'that the blackfellows had such a fearful reputation'.

The Melbourne club were worried too by the 'blackfellows', and two days before the match they elected as a playing member the noted fast bowler John James. 'It was hardly cricket,' remarked the *Argus*.

The scoreboard that Christmas season, which gave names even then, must have looked rather different to normal. It read: Tom Wills (captain), Johnny Cuzens, Billy Officer, Bullocky, Johnny Mullagh, Jellico, Tarpot, Sundown, Dick-a-Dick, Paddy and Peter. The two reserves were Lake Billy and Wattle.

Over ten thousand spectators were inside the ground at the start of play with an estimated three thousand watching from various vantage points in Yarra Park. However there was to be no fairy story, for Melbourne won easily by eight wickets. That the Melbourne club judged this match to have been important can be seen from their 1866–67 annual report which stated: 'The season was enlivened by a match between the Club and eleven aborigines of the colony, a sight which appeared to create almost as much excitement as did the first All-England Eleven matches'.

This match resulted in various fixtures being arranged around the Western Districts of Victoria before Hayman and Wills took the side to Sydney, not only for a series of cricket matches but of sporting events such as throwing the cricket ball, high jumping, and numerous track events, particularly by Tarpot who was an expert in running backwards.

In spite of fierce opposition, especially from the Central Board for Aborigines, a tour of England was arranged. After various subterfuges the team of thirteen, who had been put together by Hayman and Charles Lawrence, joined the woolship *Parramatta*. They arrived at Gravesend on 13 May 1868 with Lawrence as their captain, Hayman as manager, and a George Smith as business manager.

Three days later the *Sporting Life* announced the arrival of the team, listing the players by their native names and also the nicknames by which they would be known on tour, which were: Mullagh, Cuzens, Bullocky, Red Cap, Twopenny, King Cole, Tiger, Dick-a-Dick, Peter, Charley, Mosquito, Jim Crow and Sundown. The report also referred to the 'purity of race and origin' and added that the players were 'perfectly civilised, having been brought up in the bush to agricultural pursuits as assistants to Europeans'.

The ability of the Aboriginals to adapt their substantial skills to European ways was epitomised by their ability at cricket. Cuzens and Mullagh proved on the six-month tour to be all-rounders with remarkable ability, and the team generally played with purpose and spirit. Although they, along with Charles Lawrence, took 609 of the 714 wickets to fall and made 4212 of the 7555 runs scored, the English backers paid more attention to the assorted athletics meetings than to the cricket matches. The tourists were especially popular with their exhibitions of spear-throwing and hurling the boomerang. The tour started and finished at The Oval and consisted of 47 matches of which fourteen were won. It was a very arduous programme, during which King Cole died in June while Sundown and Jim Crow returned home in August because of ill-health.

The success of the tour in England caused considerable criticism back in Australia. While English newspapers were generally complimentary, those in Australia seemed stung by the fact that a little known group of Aborigines was holding its own in a game which was imagined to belong with the privileged white population. Worse, some of the teams challenged were not far short of first-class standard, and in the two-day match at Lord's the Marylebone Club won by only 55 runs after trailing on first innings.

The team returned home on the *Dunbar Castle*, arriving back in Sydney in February 1869. They played a match against a military team in Melbourne the following month and then split up. Twopenny moved to NSW and represented that colony against Victoria in 1870. Dick-a-Dick returned to his tribal homeland; Cuzens died of dysentery in 1871; Tarpot played local cricket, while Johnny Mullagh was appointed a professional at the Melbourne Cricket Club. In 1879 he represented Victoria against the English tourists, top-scoring in the second innings with 36.

The Central Board for Aborigines moved to protect the Aborigines and announced, in 1869, that it would be an offence to remove any Aborigine from Victoria without the approval of the Minister. This effectively prevented any further tours overseas and restricted an Aborigine from representing Victoria in another State. The reason given for this legislation was 'fear that a sharp change in climate might injure the health of the players and that they might fall into dissolute habits or be exploited commercially'.

The end of the tour marked the virtual disappearance of Aboriginals from the game. Four full or half-blooded natives would play in the first-class game in the future; but other than a blatantly politically inspired Aboriginal tour in 1988, the game had little or no appeal for Australia's indigenous population.

# 4

# The Game Develops

During the latter part of the 1860s in Australia the game of cricket appeared to be no more than drifting along. The associations had been formed in NSW (1859) and Victoria (1864), but their principal role was to organise the intercolonial fixtures which were the highpoint of the annual calendar.

Somehow the Melbourne Cricket Club had got itself into debt but it needed only one visit by an English team to put the Club back on a sound footing. That this was done was mainly due to Richard Wilson Wardill, a remarkable man who was Victoria's first great batsman, and who scored the first century in Australian first-class cricket.

Apart from his fine batting Wardill captained Victoria; was an enthusiastic member of the Melbourne Cricket Club, holding various offices; and was prominent in the first Victorian Cricket Association. He was also an active promoter in the scheme to bring to Australia the 1873–74 touring team led by Dr W. G. Grace.

Wardill had shown his mettle at the end of the 1871–72 season, and had impressed many with his organisation of the first 'Cricketer's Dinner', a highly successful social event which was held in the pavilion at the Melbourne Cricket Ground. Following this, Wardill had the ear of many influential people in the city.

He knew that the Melbourne Club had written to Grace in London in 1871 asking if he was interested in bringing out a team. Grace replied stating that his own personal fee would be £1500, exclusive of all expenses. This demand 'threw' the Melbourne Committee who had believed that, as an amateur, Grace would have taken less than any of the professionals. Another try was made in January 1872 and again the cost of Grace was too high. Yet it would have been absurd to bring out an English team without the greatest English player.

A new initiative was then taken, this time by Wardill who called a meeting on 15 May 1872 at Scott's Hotel. Thirty people attended and the Melbourne Club president, Donald McArthur, took the chair. The scheme put by Wardill was fairly straightforward particularly as £3750 had already been guaranteed: £2000 from the debt-ridden Melbourne Club itself and the balance from the South Melbourne and East

Melbourne clubs. The agreement was that the Melbourne Cricket Club would receive half the profits, although they were not going to run the tour. The guarantee was held by Thomas Hamilton, a Victorian cricketer from the 1850s and a trustee of the MCG appointed by the Victoria Colonial Governor. The only qualification agreed to that night was that Grace had to captain the team.

The scheme could not be organised for the 1872–73 season but Grace agreed to get a team up for the following season – after accepting his fee plus expenses for his wife and £170 for each of his professionals in the party.

Wardill, alas, would not see the tour. His cricket prowess suffered a grievous blow in March 1873 when, as captain of Victoria against Tasmania in Launceston, his bowling action was no-balled by the umpire William Sidebottom. Wardill, whose analysis was 1/8 at this stage, had three deliveries called for throwing. He completed his fourth over and did not bowl again.

Tasmania struggled to 124 and Victoria made 150 in reply. Wardill top-scored with 39, and added 62 for the sixth wicket with Dan Wilkie. Tasmania could make only 136 in their second innings and Victoria went on to win by seven wickets.

The Melbourne press were indignant that anyone, especially a Tasmanian, would think Wardill's action unfair. Letters appeared in *The Australasian* condemning Sidebottom's decision. Eventually the umpire decided to defend himself saying to the Launceston *Examiner* that 'he had it on good authority that Wardill's action was considered unfair by many good judges, including Tom Wills'. *The Australasian* replied with amazement saying that 'umpire Smith had passed Wardill, and as for Wills to criticise any bowler's action was akin to "Satan reproving sin"'.

Such hero-worship was not to last long. Unknown to his family and colleagues, Wardill was a gambler. During the middle of 1873 he got further and further into debt until an audit at the Victoria Sugar Company where he worked as an accountant found a discrepancy of £200. When confronted with this, Wardill confessed to embezzling £7000 – an enormous sum for those days – and asked to be allowed to see his family before the police were called in by his employers.

This act of mercy was granted: Wardill duly escaped out of the back door and committed suicide by throwing himself into the Yarra River. He was thirty-eight. The following day at the Annual General Meeting of the Melbourne Cricket Club, a statement was issued which read: 'The committee bitterly deplore the lamentable loss of Mr Wardill, our former secretary and top batsman'.

These events were a great embarrassment to Richard Wardill's younger brother Ben, who was usually referred to as Major Wardill, a rank he held in the East Melbourne Volunteer Artillery, and who was a clerk in the rival Colonial Sugar Refining Company. Ben Wardill, however, was later to become secretary of the Melbourne Cricket Club and to manage three Australian touring teams to England – in 1886, 1899 and 1902.

During the middle part of 1873, Dr Grace wrote to the Melbourne Club to say that he had succeeded in getting together a strong side which would be incapable of losing to any team put against them. But what Grace did not say was that many of the top players – both amateur and professional – had declined his invitation. These included Alfred Shaw, the leading slow bowler of the time; Yorkshire's Tom Emmett; wicketkeepers Pooley of Surrey and Pinder of Yorkshire; the Lancashire opening batsman A. N. Hornby, and others.

The team that eventually toured was W. G. Grace (captain), James Bush, Walter Gilbert, G. F. (Fred) Grace (Gloucestershire), Farrington Boult, Richard Humphrey, Henry Jupp, James Southerton (Surrey), Martin McIntyre, William Oscroft (Nottinghamshire), Andrew Greenwood (Yorkshire) and James Lillywhite (Sussex), the last six being professionals. W. G. Grace was an extraordinary performer who, in 1873, became the first cricketer to achieve the double of 2139 runs and 106 wickets. He was adaptable and fearless and combined good health with strength of character. His leadership qualities were not questioned, at least publicly.

While the English cricketers were sailing to Australia, the improvements at the Melbourne Cricket Ground were nearing completion. There was a new sloping embankment in the outer ground where, according to the *Argus* 'patrons, even though sitting, could gain an uninterrupted view over those in front'. There were seats all around the ground and the trees provided by Botanic Gardens director, Baron von Mueller, were giving excellent shade. There was a new grandstand, built by Messrs Halstead, Kerr & Co., and underneath its large sloping floors was a great public dining-room, numerous bars, oyster stalls, a fruit cart and an innovation – an electric telegraph room.

The promoters were very optimistic that their planning would bear fruit. They had even sited ten ticket boxes around the ground and built two scoreboards for spectators to see easily.

The team arrived at Fremantle, Western Australia, in mid-December and disembarked in Melbourne a few days later. In his reminiscences Grace told how he and his team were driven to Lake Oval in South Melbourne to watch a match between the home side and the Melbourne club. Some 7000 spectators were present and Grace was duly informed by an official: 'You see, we manage our crowds better than you do. Our spectators are impartial and good-tempered. We never experience any unpleasantness on our cricket grounds.'

Within fifteen minutes of being told this one of the umpires gave a decision against the batting side who needed only a few runs to win. A wrangle ensued, in the course of which a number of the crowd ran on to the playing area. In the end the players left the field and the game was abandoned.

Grace later published in his *W. G.: Cricketing Reminiscences and Personal Recollections*: 'This, I am sorry to say, was a foretaste of some experiences which subsequently fell to our lot. It was a manifestation of the spirit which still unfortunately seems to survive in Australia, though not in so malignant a form as in the 1870s.'

The tourists were eventually to play fifteen matches in a schedule which lasted until the end of March 1874. The teams they played from Victoria and New South Wales, and a joint team of the two, had sides varying from fifteen to eighteen, not the twenty-twos as ten years before.

The progress of the game in Australia had been demonstrated a year earlier in December 1872 when the side designated 'The Three Colonies' (i.e. NSW, South Australia and Tasmania) took on the powerful Victorian team in Melbourne and won by five wickets.

Although The Three Colonies had played with thirteen men, the match was seen as essentially first-class. One top cricket writer and novelist at the turn of the century, J. N. Pentelow, discussed the classification of first-class fixtures: 'The only match not absolutely eleven-a-side which I feel must be included is that played in 1872. The Colonies ought never to have accepted odds but the match was too important and the players engaged were too famous for it to be put into the same category as, say, the fifteens of Queensland versus New South Wales and the like.' The players in this match were the best available in Australia at that time and the contest was the most important fixture yet played in the country.

Captained by Ned Gregory (NSW), the Colonies team included his brother David – who was no-balled in the first innings for throwing – and other well-known players from Sydney such as Charles Bannerman, Nat Thomson and Richard Teece. In some respects the three South Australians and two Tasmanians were there to make up the numbers but the important point was that they participated.

The Victorians, although beaten, had a side of quality: Sam Cosstick, a round-arm bowler (who was to umpire in the second Test match played); Tom Wills, an all-rounder; John Conway, batsman; Tom Kelly, a batsman and outstanding fielder; Harry Boyle, over-arm bowler and future Test player; and Bransby Cooper, a batsman and former player for Middlesex, Kent, the Gentlemen, and the Marylebone Cricket Club, as well as a future Test player who in 1869 had shared a partnership with Grace of 283 for Gentlemen of the South versus Players of the South. Cooper had left England for America, but then went on to Australia where he lived for the rest of his life.

Just before the start of play the bitterness of the match the tourists had witnessed on their arrival split the Victorian eighteen. There was still such strong feeling between the players that no captain had been elected. So the match had to wait while the team held an election between two contenders, John Conway (South Melbourne) and George Robertson (Melbourne). The *Argus* said: 'The team went into committee like a solemn conclave of cardinals. One almost expected a puff of smoke to rise from the pavilion with the announcement that they had found a Pope. Eventually they elected Robertson by twelve votes to six.'

The match lasted three days and, if nothing else, was a great financial success with over 40,000 spectators each paying half-a-crown (2s. 6d.). One of the English players, James Southerton, kept a detailed diary for this tour (and the next) and he described the pitch as 'splendid and not to be surpassed in England except by having more grass on it'.

The Victorian batting line-up was impressive with Cooper top-scoring with 84 and Conway making 32. Grace took ten of the seventeen home wickets as the score reached 266. The *Argus* said the Victorians did so well that stories were afoot that 'Dr Grace was making use of the new telegraph to advise his friends in London to lay off some of their bets'.

The combination of the six-foot tall, left-handed fast bowler Frank Allan with Harry Boyle and Sam Cosstick saw the tourists dismissed for 110 and 135 so enabling the Victorians to claim success by the unbelievable margin of an innings and 21 runs. Grace scored an unbeaten 51 in the second innings which caused the *Australasian* to say: 'As a judge of a run and for speed between the wickets he is unequalled in the world. He makes safe runs where we would not dream of even stealing them. The ease and power with which the leviathan played the bowling, the shooters and bumpers, met equally coolly, not hitting the ball over the moon, but making runs simply and rapidly without apparent effort, showing, when opportunity offered, brilliant cutting and driving, defence impregnable – all this was as near perfection as it is possible to be.'

But it was to be far from a happy tour. The backers had not foreseen many of the problems which were to arise, some previously unknown in Australia, such as the apartheid between amateurs and professionals, which meant that the professionals stayed in different hotels.

There was also the colonial press which then, as now, was highly competitive and in the 1870s as vocal as any home supporter could be. But it was the accusations on the quality of the cricket which most annoyed Grace. After this initial appearance many of the newspapers accused him of bringing out a weak side, far inferior to those led by Stephenson and Parr.

Grace replied that the colonial cricket writers knew little about their task (has anything changed in 120 years?) and that his team was lacking in match practice.

*The Australian Sketcher* was so taken with the Victorian victory that it published a critique of members of the winning team, of whom the best known were:

F. ALLAN. (*South Melbourne*) – A native of Victoria, over six foot in height. A left-handed bowler, with a high delivery; varies his pace and pitch considerably, and bowls very much with his head. The most effective bowler in the colonies, and has been very successful in matches. As a batsman, has a very peculiar style of play; has improved much of late, and often scores well. A good field.

BOYLE. (*Bendigo*) – A first-class batsman; plays in excellent style. Can hit well all round. A good medium-pace bowler, requiring very careful play. Can field well anywhere.

J. CONWAY. (*South Melbourne*) – A first-class all-round player. Bats in good style, although a little too laboured in his back play. A hard hitter and quick scorer. A fast bowler and at times when on the wicket, very difficult to play. Good captain of an eleven.

B. B. COOPER. (*Melbourne*) – One of the best gentlemen players of England. Has fine defence, and plays with great patience. His back play is perfect. A middling good field, and can keep wicket.

COSSTICK. (*Melbourne*) – The professional bowler of the Melbourne Cricket Club. Fast round-arm bowler, with a low delivery, very true on the wicket, and never tires. Fast run-getter, and very hard hitter. Little too fond of slogging at times.

T. J. D. KELLY. (*Melbourne*) – Plays in capital style, and a most brilliant hitter. A very fast run-getter. At point cannot be equalled in the colonies.

MIDWINTER. (*South Melbourne*) – A very good bat, with fine

defence and good hitting powers. Good medium-pace bowler, and active field.

G. P. Robertson. (*Melbourne*) (Captain) – Native of Tasmania. Was in the Oxford University Eleven. A first-class bat, with good style. Can hit well all round, his driving being particularly good. Splendid field anywhere, especially at long leg and cover. Very quick in returning the ball.

Horan. (*East Melbourne*) – A good batsman; can hit well, and plays in good style. Medium-pace bowler; good change. A pretty good field.

By now the tourists had made their way by stagecoach into the Western Districts of the colony to play twenty-twos at Ballarat (drawn), Stawell (lost) and Warrnambool (won) before taking a boat back to Melbourne in order to catch another boat to Sydney. James Southerton noted in his diaries, before the ship had cast off, that: 'W. G. was very drunk and amused himself by shooting harmless gulls from the stern and letting them lie in the water'. Southerton did not have much respect for Grace, whom at one stage he describes as 'a damn bad captain'.

The journey to Melbourne was a storm-tossed sixteen hours of 'wretchedness' before the team transferred to the Sydney-bound ship. On arrival there the tourists visited the Albert ground on which they were to play the second major match of the tour, and which Southerton described as 'something like the ground at Eastbourne, looking very nice, being well kept all over and very green'. Their opponents were Eighteen of New South Wales, who included in their side a young fast bowler called Fred Spofforth. Spofforth, particularly, had been influenced by the on-going effect of Charles Lawrence's coaching as had many of his team-mates. Grounds were now developing and pitches becoming of far better quality.

The match took place over three days of the last weekend in January and resulted in an eight-wicket defeat for the tourists. There was tremendous jubilation both times W.G. was dismissed, all sorts of objects being joyfully thrown around as the visiting captain left the field. The *Sydney Morning Herald*, in a fit of hyperbole and in clear reference to the still-colonial status of the country, said: 'The win has proved that British blood has not yet been thinned by the heat of Australian summers'.

Following a game in the Blue Mountains against Bathurst, it was back to Sydney for the most significant fixture of the whole tour: a challenge from a combined fifteen of Victoria and New South Wales. This match, although of unequal terms, would be a severe test for the colonial players.

Batting first, the England team reached 170, mainly due to an unbeaten 55 from Martin McIntyre. Then the high expectations of the large crowd faded away as Dave Gregory, Charles Bannerman, Nat Thomson, John Conway, Sam Cosstick and Frank Allan all failed in a total of 98, James Lillywhite, the slow-medium left-arm bowler, taking 9/39. With Grace in sparkling form the visitors' second innings reached 236 which left the combined team to score the virtually unheard-of target of 309 runs to win. They fell short by 218 runs due once again to Lillywhite who returned 9/33 to claim eighteen wickets in the match.

Before the next, second, match against Victoria in Melbourne the tourists enjoyed comfortable victories in Bendigo and Castlemaine. Then they beat Victoria by seven wickets before a fortnight's visit to Tasmania where both northern and southern twenty-twos were easily vanquished.

Southerton described the Launceston ground – for the Northern Tasmania game – as 'being beautifully situated on a hill with a splendid view of the surrounding hills'. But even more interesting was his opinion that 'the bowling of the twenty-two was the best we have yet met', considering the tour was then two months old and the quality of both the NSW and Victorian bowlers had been tested.

Then it was back to Melbourne for an even draw with Victoria before a seminal visit to South Australia. A match had been arranged in the tin-mining town of Kadina, north of Adelaide, for which the local community had to pay £800 to Grace's team, and a further £900 for everything from a new grandstand to coaching lessons from Tom Wills.

In the end the visitors won in two days and spent a third playing single-wicket matches against any number of the locals. The Yorke Peninsula Cricket Association having lost £700 on the venture, then found out that the fledgling South Australian Cricketing Association had acquired the services of the England team for a mere £110.

The arrangements between Grace and SACA's Sir Edwin Smith were finalised by ship-to-shore telegraph while the England team was sailing to Adelaide. Southerton wrote: 'Adelaide did in the end get a match, thanks solely to a rather ambiguously worded contract with the promoters of the tour. The contract stipulated so many matches and W.G. held that this did not prevent them playing more. There was a fairly considerable argument with the promoters who at one stage threatened to withhold the passage money.'

In the end the South Australians lost by seven wickets, and the England team sailed from Adelaide, reaching home on 17 May. There was little doubt in their minds about the improvement in all aspects of the game in Australia.

For their visit, the professionals had received their promised £170 (£150 plus another £20 in spending money). In addition many of them had taken out cricket equipment to sell for inflated prices. They also gained from betting on the matches in which they played: for example, the six professionals put up £50 that they would defeat the combined team in Sydney. Spectators also offered side-bets. On one occasion a man approached Oscroft before he went in to bat and offered him £20 if he beat W.G.'s score.

But at the end of the tour Sam Cosstick spoke prophetic words. He said: 'Bar W.G. we're as good as they are, and some day we'll lick 'em with eleven.'

Buoyed by the success of the English team's visit, South Australia applied themselves with renewed vigour during the winter of 1874. Their first priority was to upgrade the Adelaide Oval, with importance being given to the erection of a pavilion. Then a challenge was sent to Melbourne suggesting that a Victorian eleven should play eighteen of South Australia from 7–10 November 1874. The Victorians agreed, particularly as £150 was offered to cover the team's efforts and expenses. What 'expenses' included in this context was £10 for each professional and about £15 in costs for the amateurs, a concept which remained strong in Victoria for many years.

The Victorians sent a strong side to Adelaide. Nine of their players had already appeared in first-class matches, including Horan and Boyle. The contest in itself was even up to the final day when South Australia, needing 82 to win, fell to the cunning round-arm bowling of Tom Horan and Victoria ended up victors by fourteen runs.

Eighteen months later Victoria sent an equally strong side to Adelaide and this time they were thrashed by an innings and 77 runs. The success of the South Australian Cricketing Association in such a short time was nothing short of remarkable considering the poor economic climate, the lack of good pitches, and the expense of equipment and general maintenance costs. This applied over the whole of Australia. The popularity of the game had grown in leaps and bounds. An indication of how popular the game had become is given by the percentage of column space devoted to particular sports in the main Australian newspapers of 1875. Cricket led with 37% (up from 6% in 1850), followed by horse-racing 20% (down 51%), and swimming 9% (up 8%).

In November 1875 the SACA secretary, Francis Burton, had met with John Conway, the Victorian player who was acting as agent for a prospective England touring team to be led by James Lillywhite. On his tour with Grace, James Lillywhite had shown himself to be a natural leader, particularly of the professional cricketers who were treated on that tour, at times, like second-class citizens. Lillywhite struck up a close friendship with Conway and it was Conway who suggested that Lillywhite should bring his own professional team out to tour Australia, including a visit by the team to Adelaide. By March 1876 they had agreed to play two fixtures, one in November the other in April, the first and last matches of the tour.

The SACA committee suggested offering half the gate takings for the first match. Conway disagreed, so two-thirds was then offered and accepted. Conway put two further points which the South Australians accepted, namely that the match would comprise twenty-two locals and that the ground admission charge be half-a-crown (subsequently reduced), the same as in the other colonies.

A potential rival tour was being planned at the same time, with Fred Grace liaising with elements of the Melbourne Cricket Club committee. During the English summer of 1876 both Lillywhite and Grace were discussing terms with players but the former always held the upper hand. As Lillywhite wrote to Conway: 'My team will stick to me like wax. I don't think they would come out for £500 each under Fred Grace'. The players trusted Lillywhite, trained in his youth as a tile-maker on the Goodwood estate in Sussex. By the age of twenty, in 1862, Lillywhite was in the county team, destined not to miss a match for the next nineteen years. In addition to his slow-medium left-arm bowling he was a lower-order left-hand bat.

Lillywhite had set up a complicated set of financial arrangements for the tour. He obtained backing from Arthur Hobgen, a young gentleman farmer from Chichester who put up £3000 with an agreement to take 50 per cent of the profits. Hobgen's poor health stopped him participating in the venture and he altered the arrangements for his share to a minimal amount.

Ten of the eleven players Lillywhite had chosen agreed to £200 for the trip plus shares from matches and certain profits. The person who received more, £300, was Alfred Shaw, the Nottinghamshire bowler and a man of shrewd financial sense. The team was Lillywhite (Sussex) as captain and manager; Tom Armitage, Tom Emmett, Andrew Greenwood, Allen Hill and George Ulyett (all Yorkshire); Henry Jupp, Ted Pooley and James Southerton (Surrey); Shaw and John Selby (Nottinghamshire); and Henry Charlwood (Sussex). However, without top batsmen such as Daft or Shrewsbury, the side's run-getting ability looked thin.

The three main centres in Australia where the team would play were preparing for their visitors. In Sydney, the Albert ground in the inner suburb of Redfern had been developed into a splendid venue. Facilities had been so improved that it was difficult to realise that, only a few years earlier, it had been a boggy ground. It was now a playing field with a splendid surface, fenced all round and with a sheltered grandstand. When filled to its 15,000 capacity, it held some fifteen per cent of the population of Sydney of that time.

In Melbourne the club built a new grandstand on the south side of the ground for a cost of £4,678 and had it designed in the then English traditional style. It held over two thousand people, and faced both ways so that, in summer, spectators could watch cricket on the MCG, and in winter football in Yarra Park, Richmond.

The Melbourne CC had had to make some harsh decisions. Some two months before Lillywhite's team arrived, the committee decided that champagne lunches would no longer be given during intercolonial and international matches. Instead the food would be plain but substantial and beer would replace champagne. As a compromise, at the finish of each day's play 'there would be a grand dinner for the players'. Research suggests that there was no deterioration in the standard of play as a result of the switch from champagne to beer!

The South Australian Cricketing Association had taken the risk of re-laying their pitch during the winter of 1876, and replanting with rye and clover. An unusually dry and cold winter retarded the growth and only after the tourists arrived did James Southerton explain to the curator, Thomas Dickson, how to roll a pitch.

A new pavilion had been built and temporary stands to house a three-day attendance of 21,504 who paid £1,143 at the gate. The visitors, having landed on 6 November, spent nine days in serious practice before the match. The home selectors had decided to choose twenty-six players before leaving out four after a trial match. The twenty-sixth and last name chosen was that of a seventeen-year-old youngster from the Norwood club, George Giffen. Excitement was building up. The Governor had agreed to be present, and the government gave a half-holiday for the Thursday afternoon. An offer from Mr Townsend, MP, to present prizes to the best batsman and bowler in the South Australian team was accepted. James Gooden was elected as captain, and then a major problem arose: Tom Cole had missed the practice match and when questioned, gave a weak excuse. His conduct was 'strongly disapproved' by the committee, and once again he was dropped from the team.

The day of the match arrived, and never before had the colony seen such a crowd at the Adelaide Oval. Of the 590 members, 520 turned up, so that the members' reserve overflowed before the start of play. *The Register* reported: 'There were over six thousand people inside the ground and beside these there was a very large crowd of persons who took free outside tickets for the grandstand formed by Montefiore Hill, whilst the gum trees in the parklands bore their clusters of human fruit. Taken altogether the number of spectators exceeded nine thousand.'

The estimates for the Friday were five thousand inside and three thousand outside the Oval, and for Saturday respectively seven thousand and four thousand.

The tourists won easily by an innings and 46 runs, and then moved on to Sydney – via Melbourne to sort out some confusion over fixtures – to the usual quayside welcomes given to Australia's overseas guests.

The *Sydney Mail* attributed part of the enthusiasm to the goodwill felt by people in the city for the team of professional cricketers. On Grace's tour, said the *Mail*, 'the professional element was contrasted with the amateur, not altogether to the advantage of the latter'. Grace and his fellow amateurs had been vilified in Sydney for betting on themselves and 'it had been a case of the gentlemen and professional players reversing their respective social positions'. The *Mail* concluded: 'Southerton and Lillywhite were the most gentlemanly and unassuming members of W. G. Grace's All-England XI'.

Public appproval started to wane, however, as some of the more enterprising tourists tried to make quick money. The six free days prior to the match against Fifteen of New South Wales gave time to some of the players to sell at large profits cricket equipment and photographs they had brought from home.

The New South Wales selectors had named their team. Included were the Bannerman and Gregory brothers; the fast bowler Fred Spofforth; wicketkeeper-batsman Billy Murdoch; and Edwin Evans, a medium-pace bowler and current star player.

The first day saw perfect weather as the Albert ground looked, according to a visitor, 'like an immense crowded circus. Flags fluttered from a hundred points and the green trees and the green sward were exquisitely in contrast to the dust and heat of the outside city.'

Southerton noted *before* the match: 'Everybody told us we shall have a tough job to beat the Sydney fifteen. I believe they would prefer to play with only eleven. Perhaps they will wish that they had one or two more before they have done with us.'

For Southerton it was pride before a fall, for NSW won by two wickets late on the fourth day. But the point seemingly missed by him was the progress of the game in the short time since his previous tour. The crowd exceeded 30,000, and the takings of £2,400 represented a huge profit for the tourists.

They did not, however, come away from the match as conquered heroes, even though this was the best game of the tour. The spectators more than once disagreed with umpiring decisions, which in every case were given by the English team's twelfth man. Southerton, not used to Australian style barracking, commented on 'the crowd's extreme partisanship' and recalled the Sydney spectators' attitude on his last visit. Alas, the next English tourists would face much worse.

After two country games 'on appalling wickets' the team went to Melbourne where Fifteen of Victoria won by 31 runs. It was a rain-affected match in which the bowlers dominated, and once again the difference in standards between the teams was edging closer. More country fixtures followed before successive games back in Sydney against New South Wales.

The first, against Fifteen, was easily won by NSW who then challenged the tourists to an eleven-a-side match. That Lillywhite agreed so readily is a credit to him but it was a good gamble as England had the better of a drawn game – which was the initial first-class fixture against a colonial side.

George Ulyett topped the batting with 94, followed by Pooley with 36, Selby 31 and Shaw 23 in a total of 270. For NSW, Evans took 5/96 and Tom Garrett 4/69 with Spofforth 1/79 being the other wicket-taker. Then New South Wales lost two quick wickets before play ended on the first day, which became 28 for five the next afternoon before Evans (30) saw the total to 82. Following on, NSW were 140 for six when stumps were called. For England, Shaw took 4/19 and 4/35 and Hill 4/11.

The England team next spent nearly two months in New Zealand before returning to Melbourne to play in what would be the first match in Test cricket, the organisation of which had started only on their departure over the Tasman Sea.

The success of the drawn match with NSW had made Lillywhite's team confident that they could defeat a combined Australian team on level terms. John Conway was asked to make the arrangements. He did this by contacting the leading players direct without bothering any of the cricket associations.

The NSWCA were offended by this – as associations have tended to be ever since – and just before the NSW players chosen left for Melbourne they passed a resolution:

> It has been publicly notified that a game is about to be played between the All-England Eleven and a combined eleven of New South Wales and Victoria. This association desires to place on record that the game has been arranged without any reference to the association, and cannot be regarded as a match in which chosen representatives of NSW take part.

Various other squabbles took place before the game, for example Spofforth withdrew when he discovered that Billy Murdoch would not be the wicketkeeper; Frank Allan, who was chosen to replace

Spofforth, pulled out as he preferred to go to the Warrnambool Agricultural Show; while England found themselves a man short, having to leave Ted Pooley behind in New Zealand as he had been arrested on what turned out to be a false charge.

Southerton struck a far less confident tone than previously when he wrote in his diary about 'our first match against the combined eleven of Australia'. 'I did not feel at all comfortable at this prospect,' he remarked, 'after reading our letters from home which enclosed a leader from the *Daily News* on losing our match at Sydney.'

On the morning of the great day – 15 March 1877 – the All-Australia team elected Dave Gregory (NSW) as captain, an honour he cherished all his life – especially as Victorians outnumbered New South Welshmen in the side. He captained a team of whom only five were native-born but they are now recorded as Australia's first Test cricketers, namely: Charles Bannerman, Nat Thomson, Tom Horan, Dave Gregory, Bransby Cooper, Billy Midwinter, Ned Gregory, Jack Blackham, Tom Garrett, Tom Kendall and John Hodges.

Gregory won the toss and decided to bat in front of barely a thousand spectators at the Melbourne Cricket Ground. Southerton recalled that 'when 130 was up, Bannerman had scored over 100'. At the close, after just 195 minutes of play, Australia were 166 for six with Charles Bannerman unbeaten on 126. Both sides then went out to dinner together and spent the evening at the opera. As news of Bannerman's innings had spread around Melbourne during the day the crowd had risen to four thousand. The Englishmen were impressed and said so later, particularly as he had had little support from the other players. Lillywhite even went so far as to say 'of all the English batsmen, only W. G. Grace himself could have played a finer innings'.

When Melbourne woke up to the fact that the combined Australia team had a chance of beating the cricketers from 'home' on an equal basis, 12,000 people flocked to the MCG. They hoped Bannerman would carry his bat but when he was on 165, and the score 240 for seven, a rising ball from Ulyett hit him on the hand and split a finger. After a ten-minute delay it was obvious that he could not continue and but for this injury one can only wonder what his score might eventually have been, especially as the next best score in both Australian innings was 20.

The *Argus* was so excited that it asked for a Charles Bannerman subscription even before the match was over, but better was to happen. Australia finally reached 245 with England replying with 196 which included 63 by Jupp and Billy Midwinter taking five wickets for 78. Australia's second innings, however, was a disaster as Alfred Shaw took 5/38 and Ulyett bowled the injured Bannerman for four. All out for 104 early on the final day, Australia had left the tourists just over four hours to score 154 for victory. But the left-armed Tom Kendall bowled throughout the Englishmen's innings to claim 7/55 and rout the visitors for 108. The Australians had won by 45 runs, but only three thousand were present to witness the historic occasion.

The victory had an effect as no other sporting success would, or could, have on the new country. Nationalistic fervour caught on with the *Australasian* leading from the front:

> The victory of the Australian Eleven over the English cricketers is no ordinary triumph. For the first time a team representing the cricketing prowess of England has been beaten on equal terms out of that country. The event marks the great improvement which has taken place in Australian cricket; and shows, also, that in bone as muscle, activity, athletic vigour, and success in field sports, the Englishmen born in Australia do not fall short of the Englishmen born in Surrey or Yorkshire.

Not only the newspapers evinced this new surge of confidence. The witty and cynical columnist, Marcus Clarke, issued a pamphlet later in 1877 called *The Future Australian Race*. At present, argued Clarke, Australia was reaping the benefits of 'the best bone and sinew of Cornwall, the best muscle of Yorkshire, the keenest brains of Cockneydom who had come to Bathurst, Ballarat and Bendigo during the gold rushes. The warm climate and lavish portions of meat, necessarily washed down by large quantities of fluid, would in time produce a super race that would flourish for five hundred years. No doubt need be felt,' he added, 'about the present generation of Australians. Read the accounts of the boat races, the cricket matches, and say if our youth are not manly.'

One important factor in this surge of nationalism is the reaction of the press around the colonies of Australia. Suddenly the papers give the feeling that, virtually overnight, the cricketers had shown they possessed 'the manhood and the muscles of their English sires', as wrote the leader writer of the *Australasian*. From now on the newspapers would pay diminishing respect to the theme of colonial degeneration.

The aftermath of triumph continued. The Victorian Cricketers' Association presented every player with a gold medal; Dave Gregory's, of course, slightly bigger than the others. The subscription for Bannerman raised just under £88 and another for Blackham and Kendall a little over £23, rather less because they belonged to two inner suburban working-class clubs, South Melbourne and Richmond respectively.

Meanwhile the tourists had left Melbourne to play three matches in the country cricketing centres of Bendigo, Ballarat and Ararat –

all resulting in draws.

A return match was arranged in Melbourne a fortnight later and the Australian selectors, for the first of many times, interfered with a winning team by dropping Cooper, Horan and Ned Gregory. In their places came Fred Spofforth and Billy Murdoch from New South Wales, and Tom Kelly, the Irishman from Victoria.

Since the takings for the first Test had exceeded all expectations, this match was to be for the benefit of the tourists. It must have paid well for, after the game, Southerton cabled home £156 and was most annoyed at being charged a bank fee of £1.9s.0d.

On the last day of March 1877 the second Test match started with Dave Gregory winning the toss again and choosing to bat. Over the four days the crowd would total 15,000 of whom half were present as Shaw bowled to Thomson. Australia did not do too well that first morning, being 60 for four at lunch. Midwinter's 31 held the middle order for a short while but some awkward seam bowling from Hill, with 4/27, saw Australia dismissed for 122. This caused the betting fraternity at the ground to cry 'fix, fix'. In their opinion the first Test had been rigged in order to enhance the gate for the return encounter.

It took four good individual innings for the England batsmen to get a grip on the match. Spofforth bowled extremely fast, but even so Blackham, the wicketkeeper, stood hardly any distance behind the stumps. In the third over Shaw was stumped from a fast rising delivery and at the end of the first day England were 7 for two. The morrow brought a revival: Ulyett scored 52; Hill and Greenwood both made 49 and Emmett 48. At the close England were dismissed for 261, a lead of 139.

The third day was crucial for Australia, and the MCG staff worked long and hard during the night to prepare as good a strip as possible. Southerton wrote: 'I assure you that in Australia they are not in any way behind in looking after their own interests'.

On a fine pitch Gregory and Thomson had an opening stand of 88. Then in came Charles Bannerman who started his innings by driving Lillywhite for four, and was then dropped by Emmett at point. Three successive shots then went to long-on for four from Hill's bowling and Bannerman had scored 30 in 13 minutes. Ulyett came on and took a wicket with his first delivery as Bannerman lunged forward and was caught behind by Jupp from an edge. The wickets fell regularly and at stumps Australia were 207 for seven which they saw to 259 on the last day. It looked easy for the tourists but by lunch they were only 9 for three wickets and it took an innings of 63 from Ulyett to see them to victory by four wickets. It had been a tense match and the tourists were relieved that there was now only the return fixture against South Australia to play before their departure for home.

## AUSTRALIA v ENGLAND 1877 (First Test)

At Melbourne Cricket Ground, 15, 16, 17, 19 March
Australia won toss
Result: AUSTRALIA won by 45 runs

**Australia**

| First innings | | Second innings | |
|---|---|---|---|
| C. Bannerman retired hurt | 165 | b Ulyett | 4 |
| N. Thomson b Hill | 1 | c Emmett b Shaw | 7 |
| T.P. Horan c Hill b Shaw | 12 | c Selby b Hill | 20 |
| D.W. Gregory* run out (Jupp) | 1 | (9) b Shaw | 3 |
| B.B. Cooper b Southerton | 15 | b Shaw | 3 |
| W.E. Midwinter c Ulyett b Southerton | 5 | c Southerton b Ulyett | 17 |
| E.J. Gregory c Greenwood b Lillywhite | 0 | c Emmett b Ulyett | 11 |
| J.M. Blackham† b Southerton | 17 | lbw b Shaw | 6 |
| T.W. Garrett not out | 18 | (4) c Emmett b Shaw | 0 |
| T.K. Kendall c Southerton b Shaw | 3 | not out | 17 |
| J. Hodges b Shaw | 0 | b Lillywhite | 8 |
| Extras (B 4, LB 2, W 2) | 8 | (B5, LB 3) | 8 |
| 1/2 2/40 3/41 4/118 5/142 6/143 7/197 8/243 9/245 | 245 | 1/7 2/27 3/31 4/31 5/35 6/58 7/71 8/75 9/75 | 104 |

*First Innings*—Shaw 55.3-34-51-3; Hill 23-10-42-1; Ulyett 25-12-36-0; Southerton 37-17-61-3; Armitage 3-0-15-0; Lillywhite 14-5-19-1; Emmett 12-7-13-0. *Second Innings*—Shaw 34-16-38-5; Hill 14-6-18-1; Ulyett 19-7-39-3; Lillywhite 1-0-1-1.

**England**

| First innings | | Second innings | |
|---|---|---|---|
| H. Jupp lbw b Garrett | 63 | (3) lbw b Midwinter | 4 |
| J. Selby† c Cooper b Hodges | 7 | (5) c Horan b Hodges | 38 |
| H.R.J. Charlwood c Blackham b Midwinter | 36 | (4) b Kendall | 13 |
| G. Ulyett lbw b Thomson | 10 | (6) b Kendall | 24 |
| A. Greenwood c E.J. Gregory b Midwinter | 1 | (2) c Midwinter b Kendall | 5 |
| T. Armitage c Blackham b Midwinter | 9 | (8) c Blackham b Kendall | 3 |
| A. Shaw b Midwinter | 10 | st Blackham b Kendall | 2 |
| T. Emmett b Midwinter | 8 | (9) b Kendall | 9 |
| A. Hill not out | 35 | (1) c Thomson b Kendall | 0 |
| J. Lillywhite* c & b Kendall | 10 | b Hodges | 4 |
| J. Southerton c Cooper b Garrett | 6 | not out | 1 |
| Extras (LB 1) | 1 | (B 4, LB 1) | 5 |
| 1/23 2/79 3/98 4/109 5/121 6/135 7/145 8/145 9/168 | 196 | 1/0 2/7 3/20 4/22 5/62 6/68 7/92 8/93 9/100 | 108 |

Bowling: *First Innings*—Hodges 9-0-27-1; Garrett 18.1-10-22-2; Kendall 38-16-54-1; Midwinter 54-23-78-5; Thomson 17-10-14-1. *Second Innings*—Hodges 7-5-7-2; Garrett 2-0-9-0; Kendall 33.1-12-55-7; Midwinter 19-7-23-1; D.W. Gregory 5-1-9-0.

Umpires: C.A. Reid and R.B. Terry

* *captain*
† *wicketkeeper*

Before leaving Adelaide on the evening of 19 April the tourists were given by SACA a farewell dinner at the Globe Hotel in Rundle Street. Lillywhite presented Conway with a locket 'on behalf of the eleven' and 'for all the trouble you have taken in making and carrying out the arrangements of the trip'.

Lillywhite also sowed a seed in Conway's mind by suggesting to him that he consider organising a team of Australians to tour England. If Conway needed any moral backing the press, on hearing whispers of such a venture, let their views be known in no uncertain manner. As the *Australasian* of 29 December 1877 put it:

> They wish to show John Bull that we can play cricket here as well as the old folks at home can. They are proud of their skill, as they ought to be, and wish to prove at Lord's and The Oval and other grounds in England that the colonials are worthy descendants of the good old stock from which they have come. The visit of an Australian eleven

## AUSTRALIA v ENGLAND 1877 (Second Test)

At Melbourne Cricket Ground, 31 March, 2, 3, 4 April
Australia won toss
Result: ENGLAND won by four wickets

**Australia**

| First innings | | Second innings | |
|---|---|---|---|
| N. Thomson lbw b Hill | 18 | b Lillywhite | 41 |
| C. Bannerman b Hill | 10 | (3) c Jupp b Ulyett | 30 |
| J.M. Blackham† c Lillywhite b Hill | 5 | (10) lbw b Southerton | 26 |
| T.W. Garrett b Hill | 12 | (7) c Jupp b Lillywhite | 18 |
| T.J.D. Kelly b Ulyett | 19 | (4) b Southerton | 35 |
| W.E. Midwinter c Emmett b Lillywhite | 31 | c Greenwood b Lillywhite | 12 |
| F.R. Spofforth b Ulyett | 0 | (8) b Hill | 17 |
| W.L. Murdoch run out | 3 | (5) c Shaw b Southerton | 8 |
| T.K. Kendall b Lillywhite | 7 | b Southerton | 12 |
| D.W. Gregory* not out | 1 | (2) c Ulyett b Lillywhite | 43 |
| J. Hodges run out (Lillywhite) | 2 | not out | 0 |
| Extras (B 8, LB 5, W 1) | 14 | (B 10, LB 7) | 17 |
| 1/29 2/30 3/50 4/60 5/96 6/104 7/108 8/114 9/119 | 122 | 1/88 2/112 3/135 4/164 5/169 6/196 7/203 8/221 9/259 | 259 |

Bowling: *First Innings*—Shaw 42-27-30-0; Lillywhite 29-17-36-2; Hill 27-12-27-4; Ulyett 14.1-6-15-2. *Second Innings*—Shaw 32-19-27-0; Lillywhite 41-15-70-4; Hill 21-9-43-1; Ulyett 19-9-33-1; Emmett 13-6-23-0; Southerton 28.3-13-46-4.

**England**

| First innings | | Second innings | |
|---|---|---|---|
| H. Jupp b Kendall | 0 | b Kendall | 1 |
| A. Shaw st Blackham b Spofforth | 1 | (8) not out | 0 |
| A. Greenwood b Hodges | 49 | c Murdoch b Hodges | 22 |
| H.R.J. Charlwood c Kelly b Kendall | 14 | b Kendall | 0 |
| J. Selby† b Kendall | 7 | (2) b Spofforth | 2 |
| G. Ulyett b Spofforth | 52 | (5) c Spofforth b Hodges | 63 |
| T. Emmett c Kendall b Spofforth | 48 | (6) b Midwinter | 8 |
| A. Hill run out | 49 | (7) not out | 17 |
| T. Armitage c Thomson b Midwinter | 21 | | |
| J. Lillywhite* not out | 2 | | |
| J. Southerton c Thomson b Kendall | 0 | | |
| Extras (B 5, LB 12, NB 1) | 18 | (B 8, LB 1) | 9 |
| 1/0 2/4 3/55 4/72 5/88 6/162 7/196 8/255 9/259 | 261 | 1/2 2/8 3/9 4/54 5/76 6/112 | 122 |

Bowling: *First Innings*—Kendall 52.2-21-82-4; Spofforth 29-6-67-3; Midwinter 21-8-30-1; Hodges 12-2-37-1; Garrett 5-2-10-0; Thomson 11-6-17-0. *Second Innings*—Kendall 17-7-24-2; Spofforth 15-3-44-1; Midwinter 13.1-6-25-1; Hodges 6-2-13-2; Garrett 1-0-7-0.

Umpires: S. Cosstick and R.B. Terry

will be productive of immense good, both to the colonies and the old country. Much ignorance still exists in Great Britain respecting the colonies. Australia is regarded still as an almost *terra incognita*. The Australian Eleven will dispel much of the illusion still existing as to the Australian colonies. They will travel about and visit the different counties and be brought much into contact with the class of person who would be desirous of emigrating. Eleven stalwart Australian natives will be seen at Sheffield and Manchester and Birmingham and other places, in the cricket field, and people will say that the country that can produce such fine men and good cricketers cannot be a bad one by any means. Their hitting powers will testify that the beef and mutton of the country they represent is the right sort, and their activity in the field will be the best argument that the climate is conducive to energy and muscle. People at 'home' read and hear much of Australia.

And the Britishers will, if our men are properly supported,

see an Australian eleven in the cricket field, and when they have won a few matches and beaten the British cock on his own ground, they will have rendered good service to the colonies, and enhanced the prestige of that 'Britain of the South' which they represent, and which everyone of the Eleven can claim as his native land.

# 5

# Overseas

During the southern winter of 1877 John Conway was busy. His concept of a team to England – which had to be competitive and not just based on regional representation – had received the support of Dave Gregory and the leading players, but, despite the excitement of the press, not a word of encouragement had come from the cricket associations of either New South Wales or Victoria. Conway had not approached the South Australian Cricketing Association – which was strange, for they were in constant contact with Lillywhite on various issues, not least that of obtaining a professional coach – and Dave Gregory had urged Conway to check the availability of other players who might care to be considered. For example, on 19 April 1877 Conway wrote to the Tasmanian cricketer, John Arthur:

> It is intended if possible to send an Australian team to England, taking in India en route after playing a series of matches in the Australian colonies. Would you form one of the team if sufficient inducement is held out? It is intended to make all the colonies interested in order to ensure the economical working of the team. I may state that Charles Bannerman, Spofforth, the Gregorys, Thompson, Murdoch, Garrett and Coates have already promised their cooperation, and have sanctioned my actions in this matter. Would you favour me by asking Bailey (Launceston) if he would like to join the party?

Two days after the invitation arrived at his home in Longford, near Launceston, the thirty-year-old Arthur died 'in mysterious circumstances'. But he had passed the invitation on to George Bailey, and Bailey became the only Tasmanian on the first 'white' tour to England.

Conway's financial deal to the players was that each of them had to subscribe £50 towards the expenses with all, bar one, to share equally in any profits. The exception was Alick Bannerman, brother of Charles, who, joining later, received a fixed sum for the tour: not a wise decision in retrospect as the final tour dividend was

£750. For some, like Fred Spofforth who worked at the Bank of New South Wales for £175 per annum, this dividend represented four years' wages.

It was agreed that funds for the England visit should be raised with a sixteen-match minor tour around Australia and New Zealand. The players assembled in Sydney and on 3 November 1877 left for Brisbane. John Conway, having set up the tour, was also its manager.

The team would stay together, with two changes, for the next fourteen months until they disbanded on 12 January 1879. The first change was sad. On the Australasian part of the tour the drinking problem that afflicted Tom Kendall grew worse and worse so the tour management had to make a harsh decision. After deciding to omit Kendall for the visit to England, their first choice as replacement, Nat Thomson, declined the invitation. It was then that the twenty-year-old Alick Bannerman joined the team.

The other person to join was Billy Midwinter and therein lies a story. He was born near Cirencester, in Gloucestershire, in 1851 and was taken to Australia with his family when a youngster. He first came to cricket notice in 1868 when playing for Bendigo and subsequently he turned out for the Carlton, South Melbourne, and East Melbourne clubs. He obtained a position as a professional with the Melbourne club and represented Victoria, his first-class debut being against NSW at the Albert ground on 5 March 1875.

In 1877, Midwinter returned to England and to Gloucestershire and accepted terms to play professional cricket for the county club. There was never any suggestion that it was not a long-term arrangement between both parties. Although he did not return to Australia prior to Conway choosing the touring side, Midwinter had agreed with James Lillywhite – acting on Conway's behalf – that he would join the side on its arrival in England. This selection aroused some strong comment even in the Australian press for they knew he was under contract to Gloucestershire.

Midwinter's first match for the 1878 English season was for Gloucestershire but only in an internal trial. Then he joined the tourists who had arrived at Liverpool on 13 May and played in their first match against Nottinghamshire at Trent Bridge a week later. He proved himself a powerful asset for the Australians by carrying his bat in the second innings.

He played in further matches for the tourists until the morning of 20 June 1878. Then, when practising in the nets at Lord's prior to the fixture against Middlesex, Midwinter was confronted by W. G. Grace, captain of Gloucestershire. Reminded strongly of his contractual obligations, Midwinter was 'removed to The Oval' where Gloucestershire was playing its first county match of the season, against Surrey.

Dave Gregory, John Conway and Midwinter's closest friend, Harry Boyle, hired a coach and gave chase across London. Outside The Oval a rather heated debate took place between Grace and the Australians. Grace won his point and the tourists did not see Midwinter again that season.

Interestingly, Midwinter was paid a £10 match fee by Gloucestershire – about five times the average – and even though he had been put under a lot of pressure by both sides, the Gloucestershire club promised him an end of season benefit match thought to be worth at least £500. It was actually played the next season: ruined by rain with the club throwing in a £100 ex-gratia payment, a most unusual move, to top up his coffers.

In truth the 1878 Australians were a rough side, rough in their behaviour and rough in their attitudes. They became over-fond of criticising the English umpires and, despite the forecasts of the *Australasian*, they left behind a poor impression.

But the illusions and mythologies of cricket do not always tell such stories. It is the good side which usually prevails, as it should, especially when one considers the all-important second match of that 1878 tour.

The Australian captain, Dave Gregory, was thirty-three years old. Most of his players were under twenty-five, but they were mentally tough and physically prepared for a tour which would comprise thirty-seven matches and numerous other events, including single-wicket contests and cricketing functions.

James Lillywhite had drawn up the programme and it was with a sense of irony that the Australians noted the number of matches they would play against fifteens and eighteens. It was only sixteen years since the first tour of Australia when the English had had to play mainly against twenty-twos.

Despite the efforts of Lillywhite and Conway, the Australians were denied a match against a full-strength England team, a refusal which became even more adamant after the innings defeat by Nottinghamshire in the Australians' first match.

Then came 27 May 1878, a day which Lord Hawke was later to describe as 'this marked the commencement of the modern era of cricket'. It was the fixture against the Marylebone Cricket Club at Lord's. The *Globe* newspaper stated: 'The eleven chosen [by MCC] was as good a one as could be found to represent London and England, and probably nearly as good as the Club has ever turned out'.

It was assumed, as a matter of course, that MCC would win easily. After all, the MCC attack was shouldered by the Nottinghamshire pair, Shaw and Morley, who had more than got the better of the Australian batsmen a few days earlier. Most commentators of the time believed that the English batsmen were a class above their colonial counterparts.

The weather was cold and unsettled, the pitch was very damp, and conditions seemed to favour the home team but what happened was that the Australian bowlers Spofforth (6/4 and 4/16) and Boyle (3/14 and 6/3) humbled the MCC batsmen twice in a day.

The match started at three minutes past noon with MCC batting. W. G. Grace hit Allan's first ball to the boundary and was caught from the second. Boyle bowled Booth in the next over to make the total five for two. Hornby and Ridley took the score to 25 after which Gregory made his one and only bowling change: Spofforth for Allan.

The situation altered dramatically as Spofforth took six wickets for four runs in 23 balls including a hat-trick, the first of three by him in first-class cricket. MCC were all out for 33 as the attendance started to rise. From around five hundred people at the start of play, 4742 had gone through the turnstiles by the finish – and paid receipts of £120, all of which was given to the Australians, the MCC paying expenses.

The Australians replied with 41, a first innings lead of just eight runs. Midwinter (10) was the only batsman to reach double figures as Alfred Shaw (5/10) and Fred Morley (5/31) shared the wickets.

There was an even more dramatic collapse as MCC batted a second time. W. G. Grace was dropped by Murdoch off Spofforth's very first ball, only to be bowled by the second. Webbe was bowled next delivery and in Boyle's first over he bowled Booth and Ridley: four wickets were down for just one run. Hornby was hit by Spofforth next over and forced to retire. Flowers and Wild added fifteen before the final six wickets – including Hornby who returned with Grace as his runner – fell for just three runs. All out for 19 meant MCC had left the Australians needing only 12 runs for an amazing victory. At twenty minutes past six Australia had won in a day by nine wickets.

Harry Boyle had taken six wickets for just three runs and Spofforth four, making his haul 10/20 in the match. Over in four and half hours, the estimated four hundred Australians in the ground cheered with great joy. 'The news spread like wildfire and created a sensation in London and throughout England.'

*Punch* acclaimed the victory with a poem which included a celebrated pun:

The Australians came down like a wolf on the fold,
The Mary'bone Cracks for a trifle were bowled;
Our Grace before dinner was very soon done,
And our Grace after dinner did not get a run.

The *Globe* commented: 'Seldom in the annals of modern cricket has so small a score been made as by the Marylebone Club yesterday, and never was so severe a humiliation inflicted individually and collectively upon the members of the Club. . . . Its best batsmen were bowled out one after the other as if they were novices. No pretence of luck or chance, even if it were made, could avail to explain the unprecedented event.'

And of the Australian cricketers, *Home News* said: 'Their fielding is the admiration of all who behold it; they have among them many excellent bats, but their great strength is in their bowling. Left-handed Allan is known as the 'Crouching Panther', or the 'Bowler of a Century'; Boyle is described as the 'very devil', but Mr Spofforth, as the 'Demon Bowler', carries off the palm. His delivery is quite appalling; the balls thunder in like cannon shot; yet he has the guile when seemingly about to bowl his fastest to drop in a slow which is generally fatal to the batsman.'

The Marylebone Cricket Club committee was called into urgent conclave and they quickly issued a challenge to Dave Gregory and his team. A return fixture starting the next day was what was required. The Australians turned it down saying that a couple of extra rest days would be more than welcome considering the arduous nature of their itinerary. Perhaps they felt that they should simply revel as much as possible in the victory.

The London newspapers were at a loss to explain the defeat: the Australians, claimed the *Pall Mall Gazette*, had 'no consummate an all-rounder of the stature of Grace, nor did they have such a master of the bowling craft as Shaw'.

This view, which appeared on the day following the match, still showed that the press believed that MCC had the better batting and bowling. So explanations of defeat drew on 'the element of luck', the 'strangeness' of the Australian bowling and the 'contemptible' batting of the MCC who presumably underestimated their opponents. The same newspaper was scathing of the home bats: 'men who are so nervous or so out of practice that they cannot keep half-volleys out of their wickets have no right to appear in a first-class match'. The one point that the English press was prepared to concede was that the Australians were a fine fielding side and superior to the English team. During the tour it was noted that the Australians pioneered the practice of more attacking and aggressive fielding rather than bowling to set fields: dispensing with long-leg and long-slip, popularising the silly mid-on position, which became known as 'Boyley's Mid-on' (because he became a specialist there) and returning the ball to the keeper on the full from the deep whereas the English practice had always been to return it on the first bounce. Six of the eleven, Spofforth later claimed, could throw a cricket ball over one hundred yards and the Australian throwing was more accurate than the English. The Australians also had two very fast movers: Tom Horan and Alick Bannerman. And Jack Blackham, who was an exceptional wicketkeeper of pioneering technique and who had introduced the practice of keeping without a long-stop – thereby providing an extra fieldsman in an attacking position – was the focal point of the fielding 'attack'.

The importance of the victory cannot be overestimated because it proved that the Australians could be worthy opposition to the leading English teams and, as *Sporting Life* correctly predicted on 29 May, 'the Australians are sure to draw [crowds] wherever they go'.

The victory also assured that the 1878 tour would be a profitable venture and help to establish that tours were an attractive and money-generating proposition. The victory also created the suspicion, which was proven to be a reality as the tour progressed, that while England might still have an edge in batting, the tourists' bowling, allied to their fielding, was superior to the English. Spofforth himself later reflected on the significance of this victory:

> I well remember that, when we left Lord's and returned to our hotel, we could scarcely realise our victory, and all the evening callers kept pouring in with congratulations. It is impossible to overestimate the importance of this victory in its effect on the future matches and the destiny of Australian cricket, for another defeat like that at Nottingham might have made us lose heart, besides giving the English public a far lower idea of our merits than we deserved.

But while Spofforth and Boyle were partners in the overwhelming of the MCC batsmen, it was Spofforth who took the limelight. Tom Horan (better known in later life as the cricket columnist 'Felix') recalled how, whenever their train later stopped on the way to matches, a crowd would gather round their carriage enquiring, 'Which be Spofforth?'

Back in Australia the victory seemed yet again to enhance the growing surge of nationalistic pride. This was the first time that a bunch of home-grown colonials had taken on the might of 'home' and beaten them.

As success came to the team so the tone of Australian comment during June and July 1878 illustrated the pride, mixed with some Anglo-Saxon loyalty, which went out to the players who were generating a phase of cricketing nationalism. The quotes from newspapers of the time show the depth of feeling. The *Illustrated Sydney News*, for example, had: 'We must, though, all remember that we are from the old stock, perhaps improved by grafting on Australian soil';

while *The Town and Country Journal* remarked: 'The manly qualities of the parent stock flourish as vigorously in these distant colonies as in the mother country.' *The Australasian* added: 'The win over the MCC shows that any fear which may ever had been entertained about the possible physical degeneration of the English race in the bright Australian climate is hitherto wanting in any support of evidence'.

These reactions and others were all summed up by the *Illustrated Sydney News*, at the end of the English part of the tour, on 5 October 1878:

> If it had done nothing more than to prove to the millions of our friends at home that the climate of Australia had no enervating influence on the Anglo-Saxon race that would have been a great deal.

The Australians were at once satisfied that they possessed 'the manhood and the muscle of their English sires'. However, what is of great importance is that from 27 May 1878, the Australian press contained a diminishing number of references to the theme of colonial degeneration. The Federation of the Colonies was still twenty-three years hence, but the independence of the mind had possibly just occurred.

For the rest of the four-month tour of England the Australians made their mark all over the country. In first-class fixtures they won nine and lost four of the seventeen played, while of the twenty other matches, nine were won and three lost. In the month after the MCC match, the Australians defeated Yorkshire, Surrey and Middlesex. By this time, however, it was clear that a new power had arrived in the cricketing world.

The tour was a tremendous financial success, although the rough nature of the Australians' manners ruffled a few feathers en route. The great pity was that there was no Test match on the tour nor was there to be one in 1880 on the second tour – for the Australians would undoubtedly have given a good account of themselves.

Fred Spofforth, however, did make a quite remarkable impact. In the preliminary tour of Australia he took 281 wickets, added 326 in England, 69 in North America on the way home, then another 88 during the run-down tour of Australia: a total of 764 wickets at a cost of only 6.08 runs each: an incredible performance.

Among the batsmen Charles Bannerman took the chief honours. At Montreal he scored a century, so that not only did he make the first Test hundred, he was also the first Australian tourist to score three figures in England, New Zealand and Canada.

But by the end of the tour of England, the Australian cricketers were perhaps the best known sporting celebrities in the country. Arrangements for a second visit were already under discussion. International cricket had clearly begun. England's traditional assumption of superiority over colonial cricketers was gone forever.

The 1878 tour also had other repercussions. The 'amateur' Australians emerged far better paid on their initial investment of £50 than even the most accomplished English professional. These same professionals also noticed the much better treatment accorded to the Australians who were of no higher status than themselves. Rumblings of discontent manifested themselves among the English professional cricketing class and the ultimate result was the strike by Nottinghamshire players in 1881 and, shortly thereafter, an enhancement of the standing and earning capacity of all professional players.

The tour was also the final nail in the coffin of the travelling elevens within England – like the United England Eleven and the Gentlemen of the North – who for many years had been spreading the game around the country. Now the game in England started looking for overseas competition. The success of Spofforth, Boyle, Garrett and Allan had yet another beneficial effect on English cricket: the standard of pitches. Contemporary descriptions of the Australian bowlers remark on their high actions, whereas England's champions were mainly more round-arm.* The tourists' success made imitation inevitable with the result that English pitches, always rather unpredictable, became positively dangerous with the propensity to higher, sharper, bounce induced by the new actions. Greater attention to, and rapid improvement in, groundsmanship was the obvious and necessary outcome, and it paved the way eventually to more batting artistry on reliable pitches and bowlers working on the subtleties of their arts, instead of relying on accuracy.

After the Australians left England on 18 September, they played six matches in America and Canada before steaming into Sydney on 25 November 1878. There they were met by an enormous flotilla in the harbour and a crowd of 20,000 (about ten per cent of the city's population) gathered at Circular Quay to meet the team.

They were, as Spofforth recalled, 'the heroes of the hour.' He added:

> I shall never forget the reception – an immense contrast to our cool send-off. Innumerable steamers and rowing boats came down to Port Jackson to meet us, and all the principal streets of the city were decorated with flags and flowers, while the old motto, 'Advance Australia!' seemed to span every corner. We were driven through

*Over-arm had only been legalised as recently as 1864.

> the town by Mr Want, in a four-horse coach, and at the Town Hall the Mayor met us and presented an address of congratulation. At Melbourne and Adelaide the same thing was repeated.

At Sydney Town Hall the welcoming speech to the players was made by the New South Wales Cricket Association president Richard Driver, MP. He committed his colonial government to reimbursing back-pay to the civil servants – Dave Gregory, Charles Bannerman and Tom Garrett – on the grounds that 'they had brought prestige and future benefit to the colony'. Driver persuaded thirty-two of his fellow MPs to endorse his commitment but the Colonial Secretary, Henry Parkes – a non-cricket person – rejected it out of hand.

The team had arrived home to find that Tom Wills was no longer coaching in the Western Districts but was in an outer Melbourne asylum, being kept under restraint because of his alcoholism. (Two years later he managed to elude the asylum attendants and stabbed himself to death with a pair of scissors.) Charles Lawrence was working for the railways in Newcastle, and a bit further west, Sam Cosstick, now curator at the Albion ground in Maitland, was relying on handouts for the fare to Sydney to watch the big matches.

In an intercolonial fixture on the new Association ground at Moore Park – later to be known as the Sydney Cricket Ground – New South Wales had defeated Victoria. The hero for NSW had been Ned Sheridan, one of those who had declined to go to England.

At almost the same time as the Australians returned, a team of English players disembarked in Adelaide. They had been invited to tour by the Melbourne Cricket Club who, in April 1878, had asked the leading English amateur, Isaac Walker, to organise an all-amateur team to tour. When this was found impossible, two professionals, George Ulyett and Tom Emmett, were included in the party, particularly to add depth to the bowling. On the death of one of his brothers Walker had to withdraw from the tour so Lord Harris agreed to substitute as tour captain.

The team found themselves in Adelaide just at the time when a new cricket coach arrived in the colony. At the end of the third England tour James Lillywhite had been asked by the South Australian Cricketing Association to obtain the services of a coach. On his return home, Lillywhite looked no further than his own county side and offered terms to the twenty-one-year-old Jesse Hide at the sum of £200 per annum.

*Wisden* had commented on Hide's first season for Sussex in 1876 by saying: 'Young Hide proved a fairly good change bowler. Moreover he was the only fast bowler of the county who did not bowl a wide ball for the season'. Over the next two seasons, Lillywhite and Hide became firm friends, with the England captain pushing his protégé at every opportunity.

Born in Eastbourne on 12 March 1857, Jesse Bollard Hide was a middle-order right-hand batsman, and a fast right-hand round-arm bowler. He arrived in South Australia on 14 November 1878 and the first reaction of the SACA committee members there to welcome him was one of amazement: he seemed so young to be a professional coach. Yet Hide's influence was immediate. He organised regular practice for the colony's players and had the task of selecting teams for the 12 December start of the fixture against England and, a fortnight later, against the Australian tourists.

Planning was progressing for the matches. For the Australia match, John Conway had only required 12.5 per cent of gross proceeds, so, as it turned out, SACA made a healthy profit on the fixture for very little work.

But it was the English match which took priority. On 1 December Lord Harris sent a cable from his ship requesting that, as this was the first match of the tour, he wanted to play twelve in his team. The SACA committee agreed, but in turn made their side eighteen players instead of the proposed fifteen. Then, to make matters worse for the South Australians, their planned 'grand dinner' for Lord Harris and his players had to be cancelled as none of Adelaide's leading caterers was willing, or had the necessary knowledge or staff, to organise such a function.

Adelaide, the centre of a virtual city-colony (now city-state), was a free settlement which, to this day, revels in its 'Englishness'. The thought of an actual Lord, a person of nobility, being in their midst seemed to send the committee into a frenzy of organisational activity.

Anyone who was anyone had to be seen at the match, even if they did not watch a ball being bowled (as still happens over a century later) just to be in the presence of an actual Lord. So much did the hierarchy enjoy themselves that their response from the ground caterer to a massive account for unpaid lunches was to instruct the Association's treasurer to pay it out of cricket funds. On the first day of the match *The Register* reported 'on the large number of carriages at the ground', adding, 'with at least seven hundred and fifty ladies present in the members' enclosure.'

South Australia lost by four wickets and the England side then moved to Melbourne to draw with Fifteen of Victoria over three days. At the same time the Australian tourists were making themselves unpopular in Adelaide by losing gracelessly and complaining bitterly over the umpiring. The team's behaviour under Dave Gregory's leadership had not been good in England; it was even worse in America and on their return home was giving cause for concern. Matters would come to a head, as far as Gregory was concerned, in early February.

In Adelaide *The Register* commented on the biting criticism laid against the home umpire: 'Mr Kennedy, the Australians' umpire, made three mistakes in one day – all in favour of his "own" side – and two of them so palpable as to be condemned by nine-tenths of the spectators.'

The Australians went next to Melbourne where they took part in what is now known as the third match in Test cricket. Their English opponents were mainly amateur gentlemen cricketers with public school and university backgrounds. They were used to refined and courteous behaviour and certainly had little idea or concept of the raucousness of Gregory's team.

The morning of 2 January 1879 brought an early thunderstorm which did not deter Lord Harris, who won the toss, from batting. England lost Ulyett second ball to Spofforth. At 26 for four Spofforth performed the first Test hat-trick by dismissing Royle, MacKinnon and Emmett and finished with 6/48 as the Englishmen slumped to 113 all out. Australia then secured a lead of 143 with Alick Bannerman leading the way with a slow, stubborn 73. Emmett and Ulyett bowled 121 of the 160 overs with Emmett taking 7/68: not a bad effort for the two professionals of the party!

Lord Harris batted well in England's second innings but could do little as his colleagues collapsed to the pace of Spofforth. With 7/62 the 'Demon' recorded match figures of 13/110, and the Australians won by ten wickets. Lord Harris suggested that his team's defeat was to do with the conditions, especially bad light, more than anything else.

A trip to Tasmania and a five-wicket loss to New South Wales preceded the return match in Sydney on 7 February against Dave Gregory's colonial team. Gregory himself had been dropped from the first match, held in late January, because he had failed to attend pre-match practice and had ignored the selectors' requests for an explanation. It might have been better for everyone concerned if he had been left out again, for his obstinacy was considerably responsible for what was to follow.

On Friday 7 February 1879 the English tourists began a return match against New South Wales at the Association Ground, Moore Park, in front of some four thousand spectators. Spofforth as well as Gregory were playing for NSW and so the bookmakers were offering attractive odds against the Englishmen winning. Batting first, the visitors reached 267 with half-centuries from Hornby, Ulyett and Lucas. For NSW Spofforth, 5/93, and Edwin Evans, 5/62, shared the bowling honours. At the close NSW had scored 53 for two which became 177 all out with Murdoch carrying his bat for 82 and Emmett taking 8/47.

As the follow-on rule was only 80 runs in those days, NSW had to bat again.

Murdoch returned to the crease late on the second afternoon to open the second innings but, after only twenty minutes, he was given run out by umpire George Coulthard. NSW's hopes of avoiding defeat rested heavily on Murdoch, the favourite of the ten-thousand crowd. His dismissal was given by a man who had been brought to Sydney by Lord Harris as the English team's umpire. Coulthard was actually a Victorian professional cricketer – he had been employed by the Melbourne Cricket Club for the previous two seasons as a net bowler – but so far as the Sydney crowd was concerned he was one of Lord Harris's men.

Coulthard's competence as an umpire had been called into question on the first day when he turned down a caught-behind appeal against Lord Harris. The *Sydney Morning Herald* said: 'The decision was admittedly a mistake'.

The first sign of trouble after Murdoch's dismissal came from the members' pavilion, then, as now, sited at an angle to the batting crease so the spectators there could not possibly have judged the fairness or otherwise of Coulthard's decision (said, later, to have been very close but accurate). The uproar in the pavilion soon spread around the ground with the feeling being that Coulthard should be replaced.

Before the riot began in earnest it was clear that no batsman was coming in to replace Murdoch. Noticing this, and suspecting that the NSW captain, Dave Gregory, intended to make an issue of it, Lord Harris walked to the pavilion and met Gregory at the gate. Gregory informed Harris that the NSW team were objecting to Coulthard's umpiring and competence. Harris pleaded with Gregory to drop the objection and carry on with the game, but to no avail. While he was talking to Gregory, Harris saw the ground being invaded and within a few minutes as many as two thousand spectators were milling about the playing area, jostling and abusing the English players.

Lord Harris's version of events was printed in the London *Daily Telegraph*:

> I asked Gregory on what grounds the objection was raised and he said, at first, general incompetence, but afterwards admitted that the objection was raised on account of the decision in Murdoch's case. I implored Gregory as a friend, and for the sake of the New South Wales Cricket Association, which I warned him would be the sufferer by it, not to raise the objection, but he refused to take my view of the case.
>
> Looking back, I found that the ground had been rushed by the mob and our team had been surrounded. I at once returned to the

> wickets, and in defending Coulthard from being attacked, was struck by some larrikin with a stick. Hornby immediately seized this fellow and in taking him to the pavilion was struck in the face by a would-be deliverer of the larrikin, and had his shirt nearly torn off his back. He however conveyed his prisoner to the pavilion in triumph.
>
> For some thirty minutes or more I was surrounded by a howling mob, resisting the entreaties of partisans and friends to return to the pavilion until the field was cleared, on the grounds that if our side left the field the other eleven could claim the match. I don't suppose they would have done so, but I determined to obey the laws of cricket, and may add that for an hour and a half I never left the ground, surrounded during the whole time, except for two short intervals, by some hundreds of people.
>
> At about five o'clock the crowd was cleared off somehow. I then took the opinion of the Eleven as to changing the umpire, and it was decided 'nem con' that there were no grounds for the objection, and that we should decline to change him. I informed Gregory of the decision, whereupon he said, 'Then the game is at an end'.

Lord Harris then turned for help to the other umpire, Edmund Barton (a future Australian Prime Minister), and asked whether he was entitled to claim the match on a forfeit as the two NSW batsmen, Alick Bannerman and Nat Thomson, had now left the field. Barton replied: 'I'll give it to you in two minutes if they don't return'.

Harris next requested Barton to see what Gregory intended to do. Barton returned saying that the two batsmen were going to resume their innings. Lord Harris then wrote:

> However before the batsmen could appear, the crowd had covered the ground for the second time. After twenty minutes it was cleared again for the second time also. Bannerman and Thompson then took their places at the wickets, but before a ball could be bowled the crowd broke in for the third and last time. I remained on the ground until the time for drawing the stumps, surrounded as before.

Barton and Coulthard then called off play for the day with NSW 18 for one wicket. The *Sydney Mail* estimated that an hour and a half's play had been lost. The riot took place on a Saturday afternoon and on Monday the newspapers were aghast at what had gone on. The *Sydney Morning Herald* called it 'a national humiliation'.

But cricket was seen to be more important than any other event, for that very weekend the bushranger Ned Kelly and his gang had raided the NSW town of Jerilderie: yet it was cricket that occupied the front pages.

Lord Harris had written his report on the Sunday and sent it off to London. He suggested that the disturbance began with bookmakers in the pavilion and was accelerated by the attitude of Gregory; and he criticised some of the NSWCA committee for their uncricketlike behaviour to their guests.

However, tempers had cooled by Monday and Lord Harris received a deputation from the NSWCA who apologised profusely for the riot. Harris politely told them he did not think the Association as a whole were responsible for the attack but he could not say that the events would be easily forgotten.

When Harris's letter appeared on 1 April 1879 in England, it was quickly reprinted in the Australian press.

Two months later a NSWCA meeting was convened at Tattersall's Hotel in Sydney in which a reply was sent to London to the *Daily Telegraph*. It was pointed out that the Australian press and public had been loud in their protests at the riot. It was added that betting was prohibited by the trustees of the ground and that placards to that effect were posted throughout the pavilions and enclosures. The letter went on:

> Lord Harris, by what we feel to be a most ungenerous suppression of these facts, has led the British public to suppose that in New South Wales, to quote his own words, 'a party of gentlemen travelling through these colonies for the purpose of playing a few friendly games of cricket should have been insulted and subjected to indignities', while the Press and inhabitants of Sydney neither showed surprise, indignation, nor regret.
>
> We cannot let a libel upon the people of New South Wales so unfounded as this to pass without challenge. The country upon which such a reproach could be fastened would be unworthy of a place among the civilised communities, and the imputation is especially odious to Australians, who claim to have maintained the manly, generous, and hospitable characteristics of the British race.

The NSWCA then pointed out that there had been a good deal of exaggeration in the reports. Dealing with the umpiring the letter continued:

> Previous decisions of the professional brought from Melbourne to act as umpire for the English Eleven had created real, though suppressed, dissatisfaction, and one, giving Lord Harris a second

'life', was openly admitted to be a mistake, and when Mr Murdoch, the hero of the hour, was, at the crisis of the game, given run out by what a large proportion of the spectators both in the pavilion and round the enclosure, as well as the batsman himself, whether rightly or wrongly, took to be a most unfair decision, the excitement and indignation of a section of the spectators led by the juvenile element unhappily broke through restraint.

The present demonstration was against the umpire whom Lord Harris still considers competent whilst admitting he had made mistakes. It was certainly not against our gallant visitors. The betting men to whom Lord Harris alludes, and of whom only one or two were present, were not members of this Association at all, and it is completely unjust to assign the demonstration to any such agency. Bad as it was, it sprang from no mercenary motive.

The match itself faded into insignificance. It was all over in just an hour on the Monday morning. Rain followed by a hot sun had made the pitch unplayable and the final nine NSW wickets fell for 31 runs. As a sequel to the match, the *Sydney Morning Herald* reported:

Our English readers will be glad to learn that steps have been taken to wipe out the disgrace of the discreditable attack on Lord Harris and his cricketers. Two men (named) were recently charged at the Water Police Court with having participated in the disorder arising in consequence of Murdoch being declared out by the umpire for the English team. Both men expressed deep regret for what had occurred, and pleaded guilty, and it was in consideration of this rather tardy contrition, and the good character given them by the police, that the Bench fined them 40 shillings, and to pay 21 shillings professional costs and 5 shillings costs of the court.

Mr Driver, who appeared for the prosecution, stated that the inmates of the Pavilion who had initiated the disturbance, including a well-known bookmaker of Victoria who was at the time ejected, had had their fees of membership returned to them, and they would never again be admitted to the ground. The Bench referred to the kindly hospitable treatment the Australian cricketers received in England, expressing deep regret that Lord Harris and his team should have met such a disagreeable experience.

It is obviously impossible to tell now whether or how far NSWCA officials did provoke the riot, but certainly the strange role of Dave Gregory needs to be examined.

The *Sydney Mail* carried a report from one of its journalists which said: 'I believe Gregory was coerced by certain persons in the pavilion not to send another man in when Murdoch was given out'. Interestingly enough, one of Harris's team, Charles Absolom, independently wrote the same type of detail. But knowing the background of Gregory's track record as a captain, nothing should be of a surprise in those early days of the game in Australia. And yet . . .

Dave Gregory continued playing first-class cricket for New South Wales for three more seasons. He continued to do well in his chosen civil service career and in 1897 became Paymaster of the Colonial Treasury. When Federation took place in 1901 he was offered the post of Head of the Federal Treasury and with it a knighthood. He refused both offers because the position would have entailed a move from Sydney to Melbourne.

A fit and active man he spent his retirement in and around his home in Turramurra, in what is now the north-west suburbs of Sydney. He died in 1919 at the age of seventy-four and is buried in Gore Hill cemetery beside the Pacific Highway just north of Sydney city centre. A mystery remains, however. Why is so prominent a person lying in an unmarked grave with not even a headstone to acknowledge his place of rest?

Once the NSW match was completed, Lord Harris refused to keep his team in Sydney for the scheduled return match against Australia, which would have been, historically, the fourth Test match ever played.

The English tourists, therefore, wound up their visit in Melbourne. Against Victoria they had a win and a loss; and at the farewell dinner Lord Harris made placating noises in the aftermath of the riot. On their departure the *Bulletin* revealed that the Melbourne Cricket Club had lost £6000 on the whole venture. And no wonder! The Englishmen's wine bill came to more than that.

# 6

# Ashes to Ashes

The era of Dave Gregory was over by the time the second Australian team was gathered in January 1880. After the usual tour of the country for warm-up matches and to gather finance for the venture, a team emerged but without Charles Bannerman who was unwell. Nor were Frank Allan or Tom Garrett available.

Harry Boyle, a Melbourne warehouseman, was originally given the captaincy, but he was a taciturn man, and the rest of the team felt he was not the right person for the job. So, as the SS *Garonne* sailed through the Suez Canal, the friendly, good-humoured Billy Murdoch was elected in his place.

Born in Bendigo, Victoria, in 1854, Murdoch moved to Sydney as a child with his family. A graduate of Sydney University, he had started playing cricket as a child in Balmain with his lifelong friend Fred Spofforth and later represented the famous Albert Club before appearing for NSW in 1875–76. He eventually made five tours of England with Australian teams and then, as he was domiciled in Sussex, he toured South Africa with the England team in 1891–92, one of the few men to have played Test cricket for two countries.

In later years George Giffen wrote of Murdoch that it 'was a delight to play under his captaincy', and commented: 'No matter how tight the hole we were in, Billy with a smile of assurance and a cheery word, would go in himself and often master the bowling with his splendid defence. It was an education to watch how he cut or drove the ball, seldom mistiming it one iota.'

The selection for the 1880 tour of England had been very carefully considered. The intercolonial matches saw good scores for Victoria by George Alexander, and as Alexander had been appointed manager of the tourists they knew they had available a more than adequate reserve.

The tour was backed by the cricket associations of New South Wales and Victoria. South Australia was not approached and the committee of SACA expressed their concern when, in late February 1880, their coach Jesse Hide travelled to Melbourne with the Association treasurer Alex Crooks. Hide, for one so young, already had a great influence on South Australian cricket with such players under his wing as George Giffen, 'Affie' Jarvis, John Noel and the brothers Alick and Billy Slight.

As Crooks went to discuss finances with the VCA, Hide saw Boyle and Alexander. *The Register* on 4 March 1880 rejoiced in the news 'of Affie Jarvis's selection in the team of Australians to visit England'. The committee's relief was noticeable. They were constantly worried that another colony might try to outbid them for Hide's services; and they had, in fact, written to Boyle and Alexander only days before the announcement was made:

> A very strong feeling of regret exists among the committee and the public generally that one or two of our players had not been selected to accompany the eleven and that if it were not too late such a selection would give the greatest satisfaction here.

Finance for the tour also came, in part, from two of the major clubs: East Melbourne and Melbourne. That they were able to put up money in this way was due to the extraordinary boom in Rules football during 1879. East Melbourne's profit was £708 and Melbourne's £802. The accounts for both clubs following the 1880 tour show dividends of £434 and £531 respectively with the Victorian Cricketers' Association profit on the tour being £119 (less £10 for the returning celebration luncheon!).

Just before the team sailed for England a telegram was received informing the players they would be regarded as professionals and that Lord Harris would not be prepared to meet them. Although this cable turned out to have no substance – since Harris in the event did not carry out his threat – the Australians on arrival in London on 13 May found that the main internal county fixture lists had been settled and that they had only five county matches to play, two of which were against a Yorkshire team who were not under the control of their county committee.

Several different elements needed to come together before the tour found its proper momentum: the very different outlook of Murdoch from that of his predecessor Gregory; a friendship between Murdoch and W. G. Grace; and a private meeting between them and Lord Harris. Once peace had been obtained with Harris and he had dropped his insistence that the Australians 'admit that their trip is one of pleasure and that they are only accepting expenses', moves were made to try and organise a Test match.

W. G. Grace tried unsuccessfully to arrange a Test at Lord's but, as the tourists were touring the north of England, playing mainly against local eighteens, public interest in their success was growing. Then Lord Harris was asked by Charles Alcock, Secretary of the

Surrey County Cricket Club, to choose an England team for a match at The (Kennington) Oval, Sussex CCC having agreed to postpone their fixture against the tourists at Hove in order for the match to be accommodated in early September.

Before that the first-class matches had seen Australian victories over Derbyshire, Yorkshire and Gloucestershire with the return match against Yorkshire left drawn. After the Test there were three draws, including Sussex, and a one-wicket defeat by Nottinghamshire. In a minor match at Scarborough just before the Test match Spofforth had his finger broken and he was ruled out of the big match.

It was the first defeat on the tour and Harry Boyle was very indignant about it. As he wrote to his Victorian teammate Tom Horan:

> Knowing that we were not beaten fairly, I would not have cared at the result if Spofforth had not had his finger broken by a bowler called Frank, who was put on at the latter part of our first innings at the Scarborough umpire's end. He did not no-ball Frank, and when we went in the field in the second innings Spofforth asked the Scarborough umpire if he would no-ball Spofforth for bowling like Frank. The umpire said 'Yes, you try it', and then Spofforth asked why was Frank not no-balled. The umpire answered: 'That's my business'. In the second innings our umpire, at whose end Frank now went on, cautioned him not to continue throwing, but he kept on all the same. Next morning Frank started to Alick Bannerman, who, on the delivery of the second ball, drew away from the wicket, and some of the fielders called out to bowl the wicket down, which was done amidst great cheers, but Alick not having played, was, of course, not out. Murdoch protested against the throwing of Frank, before the game started and during its progress, but it was of no use – they wouldn't remove him.

The first Test match to be played in England started on 6 September 1880 at the Kennington Oval. In front of 20,736 paying spectators and hundreds on the roofs of surrounding property, the Grace brothers, E.M. and W.G., opened for England. W.G. went on to score the first English century in Tests before being the fourth batsman out at 281 when he was bowled by Palmer. His innings of 152 contained 12 fours and was the backbone of England's 420. The second day, with 21,758 present, saw a pitch deadened by overnight rain. Australia totalled 149 and were forced to follow-on. Three wickets then fell for 14 and the task of avoiding an innings defeat looked remote. But to the rescue came Billy Murdoch, especially when he was joined by Percy McDonnell.

McDonnell went for 43 and at stumps Murdoch was on 79 and the score 170 for six. The final day saw the Australians make a terrific effort to save the game. Murdoch was supported first by the manager, George Alexander, who had been forced to play because of his team's injuries, and then by the barrister, William Moule. Alexander made 33, and Moule 34 in a last-wicket stand of 88 with Murdoch.

When the Australian second innings closed at 327, Murdoch was unbeaten on 153 with a five and 18 fours to his credit. Needing just 57 runs to win England very soon found themselves at 31 for five. However W. G. Grace and Frank Penn saw them through to a five-wicket victory.

As a sidelight the match was the first in which three brothers played – the Graces E.M., W.G. and G.F.; W.G. and Alfred Lucas shared the first century partnership in Test matches, while Murdoch became the first Test captain to score a century which was also his first in first-class cricket.

The tour had healed the wounds of the Sydney pitch invasion with Lord Harris. He was very taken by the friendliness of Murdoch and by the outspokenness of Spofforth who shared Harris's distaste for throwing and time-wasting. The team's share of the Test match receipts was £1100 which added to their handsome tour dividends. Before they left London the Australians were given a farewell banquet by the Lord Mayor of London at Mansion House. Each of the thirteen tourists was presented with a silver tankard and, in addition, Billy Murdoch received a loving-cup subscribed by a group of Australians who were living in England.

On their way home the team played ten minor matches in New Zealand and, in so doing, the Victorian and South Australian players missed playing in the initial first-class match between Victoria and South Australia. Although beaten by seven wickets, the remarkable progress of the Adelaide team since the coaching appointment of Jesse Hide was still causing admiration and amazement. The Victorians also won their traditional Christmas match against NSW before both sides combined to play the returning Australians.

In a relatively low-scoring game Spofforth (7/55 and 5/50) and the returned Midwinter (7/107 and 4/104) dominated the bowling for their respective sides. The Australians won by 178 on the MCG but, two months later in Sydney, lost the return match by 246 runs.

Billy Midwinter had rejoined the Victorian team for the southern summer of 1880–81, and then he commuted back and forth to Gloucestershire with surprising regularity given the slowness of transport at the time.

When the Nottingham professional, Alfred Shaw, arrived in Australia on 16 November 1881 with the sixth English touring team, Midwinter joined them. The tourists were all professionals and had been formed by Shaw, James Lillywhite and the brilliant and artistic Nottinghamshire batsman, Arthur Shrewsbury. The side included also previous visitors to Australia in John Selby, Tom Emmett and George Ulyett. Among the newcomers was Shrewsbury himself; the left-handed batsman from Nottinghamshire, William Scotton, of whom *Wisden* said, 'He carries caution to such extremes it was often impossible to take any pleasure from seeing him play'; Richard Pilling of Lancashire, the best wicketkeeper of his time; and Yorkshire's left-arm bowler Edmund Peate.

This tour was the first of three organised by Shaw, Shrewsbury and Lillywhite in the 1880s. They also dabbled in other sports, particularly soccer, but it was cricket in which they made their money.

Not all Australians welcomed yet another cricket tour; indeed the *Victorian Review* was quite scathing about the direction being taken by Australian society altogether. James Hogan wrote that he placed first among the main characteristics of Australians 'an inordinate love of field-sports', and asserted that the colonies gave greater numerical support to cricket and football matches than did England, despite the much smaller population. 'Of late years sports have assumed a prominence out of all proportion,' he wrote, 'and Trickett, the rower, and Murdoch, the cricketer, who achieved nothing more than what an ignorant South Sea islander could do if he wished, are to be cheered and lauded while men of brains are to be treated with cold neglect.' *Town Life in Australia* agreed with Hogan. Their writer, Robert Twopenny, said: 'In Australia, not to be interested in cricket amounts almost to a social crime.'

The England team arrived in Sydney on 16 November 1881 following a loss-making tour in America. In Australia the visitors started with five up-country fixtures against twenty-twos before taking on New South Wales at the Sydney Cricket Ground where, in front of enormous crowds, they won by 68 runs late on the fourth day and then went off to play a one-day match on 14 December at Cootamundra. This was the home town of Billy Murdoch, but it is latterly more famous as being the birthplace of Don Bradman.

What happened over the following few days soured the tour to such an extent that, on their departure from Australia the following March, the tourists split into three groups, each going home from Suez their own separate ways. As the *Australasian* put it: 'Professional cricketers who keep late hours, make bets to some amount, and are seen drinking champagne to a late hour with members of the betting ring when they ought to be in bed, must not be surprised if people put a wrong construction on their conduct. They have only themselves to blame.'

That there were tensions within the party all along is without question for, without realising it, the three organisers had chosen two men who were having a marital dispute over a third party. At Cootamundra a fight took place between those two players and, at the height of the battle, John Selby let slip a remark about a matter of bribery. He was immediately told to shut up by George Ulyett who added: 'Now, if you don't drop it, I'll take you both and "jowl" your heads together'. The other protagonist, William Scotton, had been offered (according to *The Sportsman* of 30 May 1882) £250 to be a non-trier in the forthcoming match against Victoria, in which Ulyett and Selby were each to receive £500 if Victoria won.

When that bribery attempt failed Selby and Ulyett approached Midwinter. Not only did he refuse their offer to 'throw' the game but he reported the matter to his captain, Alfred Shaw. For his trouble Midwinter was beaten up by the two conspirators.

The four-day match against Victoria on the Melbourne Cricket Ground went down to the wire with England winning late on the final day by the narrow margin of 18 runs. The match was reported in detail by *The Argus* which was also devoting space to such matters as the charges brought by the Royal Police Commission against certain police officers in connection with the extermination of the Ned Kelly gang the previous year, and the murder of the informer Aaron Sherritt.

Victoria, batting first on a good wicket, scored 247 for eight on the first day. During the night it rained quite heavily and, although play started on time, batting was much more hazardous. Victoria added only four runs to their total, after which England were dismissed for 146. Following-on, Arthur Shrewsbury was unbeaten on 80 with 'Joey' Palmer taking 7/46 as the tourists reached 198. With the Victorians needing 94 to win, the weather again intervened and, when play resumed, they had no answer to Ted Peate's bowling (6/30) and fell for 75.

In later years, when discussing the match, Peate said:

> There were circumstances connected with Victoria's second innings which I cannot fully refer to. I got two wickets in the first over – McDonnell and Horan – for nothing. Midwinter bowled an over from the other end, and sent down long-hops to leg . . . Then came in Boyle, who spooned one gently back to mid-on. He dropped it right enough . . . There was a tremendous amount of betting on the match. The bookmakers were standing up doing business as if they were in Tattersall's ring . . . The bookermakers [*sic*] were very

> badly hit by the result of the match. Certain of their schemes failed, much to the satisfaction of most of us.

Twenty years later Alfred Shaw admitted to defending his team by denying that any attempts at rigging had taken place. He confessed to being told by one of his players during the match that heavy odds – as much as 30 to 1 – were being laid against his team. He continued:

> There were certain influences at work beneath the surface which it is necessary to speak of in order to convey a true version of this remarkable match. It had been hinted to me that two members of our team, both now dead [Selby died in 1894, Ulyett in 1898, neither was named by Shaw], had received a promise of a bet of £100 to nothing on the Victorians winning. I gave no credence to it at the time I heard of it, but certain cases of misfielding compelled me to come to the conclusion that the rumours were not without foundation. Whatever the scheme actually was, it failed. A remarkably curious circumstance was that after one ridiculously easy catch had been dropped, a batsman was out by the ball going up inside the fieldsman's arm and sticking there – not, I have reason to think, with the catcher's intentional aid.

That odd things took place during the match is without question. Easy catches were dropped; certain bowlers performed at half-pace and certain batsmen tried hard to get themselves out. What went wrong for the conspirators was that the weather and two players innocent of the betting had played a large part in the England win.

After the match the team went to Adelaide to play Fifteen of South Australia over Christmas. The match was drawn with George Giffen, now twenty-two, making a splendid 95 which immediately saw him selected for the Australian team for the New Year's Test match in Melbourne.

In the first of the four Test matches of the 1881–82 season Billy Midwinter made his debut for England having previously played for Australia. Although a draw was always on the cards, over 40,000 people witnessed the four days' play. Horan scored 124 in Australia's first innings while the leg-break bowler, William Cooper, took nine wickets in his debut match.

The Englishmen then sailed on to New Zealand for five weeks as NSW and Victoria played their return match in Sydney on 10 February 1882. It was an amazing game for high scoring. Billy Murdoch won the toss and decided to bat. He came to the wicket when the first wicket fell at 21 and departed when the score was 572 for six having become the first Australian to score a triple century in a first-class match. His 321 comprised 38 fours, 9 threes, 41 twos and 60 singles off ten Victorian bowlers. His score remained the highest on the Sydney Cricket Ground until Don Bradman made 340 against Victoria nearly fifty years later.

In NSW's 775, Tom Garrett made 163 and Sam Jones 109. When Victoria replied Fred Spofforth took 6/122 as only 'Joey' Palmer, with an unbeaten 76, held the side together. Following-on Victoria reached 322 due to Tom Horan's 102 and Jack Blackham's 96. Even so, it was a crushing defeat for Victoria but it placed Billy Murdoch firmly in front of the public as Australia's current top batsman.

When the England team returned from New Zealand, three Test matches were played in four weeks with a game against Victoria and a country fixture squeezed in between. The second Test, in Sydney, was a see-sawing match with the bowlers on top for most of the time. For Australia, Palmer took 7/68 and 4/97 while the English owed their second-innings score of 232 mainly to an opening partnership of 122 between Ulyett (67) and Barlow (62).

After Australia won by five wickets, Sydney also staged the third Test, eleven days later. The home side was in charge for most of the match, aided by a record fourth-wicket partnership in their first innings of 199 between Percy McDonnell (147) and Alick Bannerman (70). Australia won by six wickets.

Three days later the fourth Test started in Melbourne but, like the first Test, it was drawn, this time owing to sailing schedules forcing a premature finish. These were the last Test draws in Australia until the 1946–47 series.

All in all the tour had been a financial success, and it showed that there was now a big public demand for international cricket. A glut of it came in the 1880s. The enthusiasm for these English visits was not shared, however, by the New South Wales Cricket Association. Although the Association did give its blessing, and on one occasion its patronage, to the tours to England, even as early as 1881, it was beginning to have misgivings that these exchanges were turning the public away from the intercolonial contests and, more particularly, the club matches in Sydney. As its annual report for 1881–82 states: 'This question of the visits of Australian teams to the mother country has arrived at a stage which calls for special attention. The refusal of members of returned teams to take part in the intercolonial contests has shorn these matches of much of their wonted interest.' The report concluded: 'The intercolonial matches were a matter of first importance and one to which all others should be subservient'.

The annual report for 1883–84 returned to the problem: 'The constant visits of Australians to England and of Englishmen to the colonies are proving disastrous to club cricket'. Two years later the 1885–86 report said: 'The visits of Australian elevens to England and of English teams to the colonies have become so frequent that they threaten to exercise a prejudicial influence on local cricket.'

Club cricket in Sydney was certainly on the wane. In the early 1880s it was common for several thousand people to attend matches between such clubs as the Alberts and the Warwicks. Now crowds rarely exceeded a few hundred. Other major centres around the country were not experiencing these problems, however. Melbourne seemed unable to stage enough sport of any kind, and the other cities of the continent had not been affected in any detrimental way. Not until 1890 did the NSWCA realise that their main problem was the manner in which their club competition was structured.

Organised cricket had now been in existence for sixty years. Intercolonial rivalries were building up; six English teams had visited the country; there was little control as yet by colonial associations and none at all on an international level. Large crowds were attending the big matches and new heroes had emerged: Dave Gregory, Fred Spofforth, Billy Murdoch and Jack Blackham.

The home season of 1881–82 had seen some outstanding events in club cricket, despite the gloom of the NSWCA. Sam Morris, a coloured cricketer whose parents were West Indian, scored 280 for Richmond against St Kilda in Melbourne. George Giffen had made 158 for Norwood in Adelaide, and in Sydney Alick Bannerman made a century in each innings, 111 and 104 not out, for Carlton against Alberts.

Two days after the fourth Test of 1881–82, the Third Australians left Melbourne. Sailing in the SS *Assam* they arrived at Plymouth on 3 May. There were five new players in the side: Tom Garrett, Sam Jones and Hugh Massie from NSW; Tom Horan of Victoria and South Australia's George Giffen. Garrett and Horan had toured in 1878 but the other three were on their initial tour. Billy Murdoch was again captain.

It took the English public only two matches to realise that the 1882 Australians were an outstanding team. In their opening match at Oxford against the University, Massie scored 206 in three-and-a-quarter hours. The next fixture at Hove saw Murdoch make an unbeaten 286 in a total 643, and he had the cheek to ask the umpire, Payne, about the legality of Blackman's bowling. Palmer took 8/48 and 6/62 which, added to Giffen's 7/78 from the opening fixture, was a very good start indeed.

Throughout the tour the weather was unusually cold and play was frequently interrupted by rain. The Australians deserved great credit therefore for winning as many as 23 out of 38 matches, with only four defeats.

As in 1880 only one Test was played, and that took place over two days on 28 and 29 August 1882. It will live as one of the mightiest battles of Test cricket history. It was the second epoch-making match with which Fred Spofforth will always be associated. Surely none of the 38,194 crowd ever forgot those two tumultuous days.

There had been heavy rain in London over the weekend of 26 and 27 August, but on the Monday morning Murdoch, on winning the toss, decided to bat as he felt that the wet pitch would not improve. But the Australians began badly and were 48 for six at lunch. Play was then delayed for an hour and a half; and twenty minutes after the resumption Australia were dismissed for 63, Barlow 5/19, Peate 4/31.

Spofforth then attacked the English batsmen, taking 7/46 in a sustained spell of fast, accurate bowling. The England total of 101 gave them a lead of 38, a handy advantage considering the conditions.

Further rain in the night delayed the resumption on the second day until 12.10 and even then conditions were hardly fit for play. The English bowlers could get neither a proper grip nor a firm foothold. This gave Hugh Massie his chance, and he scored 55 out of 66 in 54 minutes before being bowled by Steel. Murdoch made 29 but the others failed and the side was all out for 122, leaving England to make 85 runs to win.

There had, however, been an incident. Sam Jones, batting at number eight and in partnership with Murdoch, completed a run and then moved out of his ground to pat down the pitch. Lyttelton picked up the ball, threw it to W. G. Grace who whipped off the bails and appealed. Jones was given out by umpire Thoms but as the batsman was clearly not trying to score a run, the action irritated the Australians as being a little too keen. *Bell's Life* disapproved of Grace's action saying: 'It was strict cricket but it was taking advantage of a young player's thoughtlessness'.

England's chase for the runs began with Spofforth encouraging his teammates. 'It can be done,' he kept saying loudly. The innings started at 3.45 as Hornby opened with Grace. *Bell's Life* claimed later that the mixture of silence and wild cheering of runs helped to unnerve the batsmen. Spofforth then took two wickets in successive deliveries to leave England 15 for two. Grace and Ulyett took the score to 51 before they both fell in the space of two runs. There followed twelve maiden overs in a row to Lyttelton and Lucas sent down by Spofforth and Boyle.

Spofforth then whispered to Murdoch, and Bannerman deliberately misfielded a ball so as to give Spofforth the chance to bowl at Lyttelton. Four maidens later he was successful: 66 for five. At 70, Spofforth caught and bowled Steel. The batsmen were frozen and had completely lost the ability to get the ball past the fieldsmen. Horan later wrote: 'I observed the incoming batsmen. They had ashen faces and parched lips.'

Spofforth, with awesome speed, clean bowled Maurice Read. The tenseness of the struggle infected the crowd who cheered Lucas as a hero when he struck Boyle to the boundary; but Spofforth took revenge, bowling Lucas next over: 75 for eight. Boyle then captured two wickets in three balls and Australia had won a remarkable game by just seven runs.

The stunned crowd sat quietly for a moment and then let out all their tension with a huge roar. Spofforth was carried shoulder-high to the pavilion as people gathered themselves together to realise that 'the Demon' had taken 7/46 and 7/44 to claim 14/90 for the match. It was the first Australian Test victory on English soil.

Four days later the *Sporting Times* printed a mock obituary, written by Reginald Brooks, son of the editor of *Punch*:

In Affectionate Remembrance of English Cricket
Which Died at The Oval on 29 August 1882

Deeply lamented by a large circle of
sorrowing friends and acquaintances

R.I.P.

NB The body will be cremated and the ashes taken to Australia

This was the 'legend' of the Ashes created. *Bell's Life* reflected: 'Though England for the first time had to lower her colours to Australia at home, we were beaten by a magnificent eleven, before whose prowess it was no disgrace to fail.'

After the drama at The Oval the remaining eight matches paled into insignificance. Murdoch completed the tour with 1582 runs at 31.64 to head the batting averages with Spofforth leading the bowling with his 157 wickets costing 13.24 runs each.

W. G. Grace wrote in his memoirs: 'The 1882 Australians were the best team sent to the mother country. So brilliant were their achievements, and so completely did they captivate the British public, county cricket suffered complete eclipse. They were foemen worthy of our steel, plucky, resolute and resourceful, and they proved their ability to meet, and in most cases beat, the best teams we could set against them.'

Some months later the editor of *Wisden*, Sydney Pardon, stated that Grace had planned to retire to his medical practice until the success of the Australians revived his ambition to carry on in the first-class arena.

It had been a wet summer and the Australians' efforts were all that more praiseworthy. Murdoch captained the side well with Charles Beal as a most diplomatic and efficient manager.

On 28 September 1882, the day prior to the team's departure, a banquet was given in their honour at the Criterion Hotel in London. In response to the toast to 'The Australian Cricket Team', Billy Murdoch said:

> I feel my position tonight very keenly for it is one I cannot but be proud of, and I am sure it is one that will be envied by the sportsmen throughout Australia. I desire on behalf of myself and my colleagues to return you our warmest thanks for the very great honour you have done us in so kindly receiving the toast which Sir Henry Barkly proposed. It is very gratifying to us to find that our exertions in the cricket field are considered worthy of such generous recognition and such openhanded hospitality. When we quitted Australia we did so as a band of cricketers, determined to do our best to uphold the reputation of the land of our birth, to leave no stone unturned to gain the laurels so dear to every true sportsman. In this spirit we started on our daring enterprise to beard the English lion in his den. The result you know. Since landing here in May we have been constantly engaged in playing matches. On all occasions we simply did our best to play up to the true letter and spirit of the game, and we always tried our very hardest to win. I can assure you that on the few occasions we lost there were not fourteen more grieved men in the world. We knew very well that the eyes of all Australia were upon us, and that the honour of Australia had been entrusted to our hands. The laurels we have won we shall on our return place at the feet of our fellow countrymen, and hope that the verdict be that we have been tried and not found wanting. If I may be permitted to say so, I feel at present something like your very able General Wolseley must feel when he contemplated the result of the Egyptian campaign. He was sent out to do a certain thing – to crush Arabi – and he has done it. I was sent home as a captain of an Australian cricket team to beat England and I am proud of having done it. Personally I have attained the height of my ambition, having captained a team which has beaten a representative Eleven of England. Having done this, I do not wish any more to play cricket. I do not care any more to run the risk of commanding a team which may possibly sustain defeat, but if I am called upon to occupy such a position I shall only be too proud to do so, and shall do my very best to win.

> There are several gentlemen present tonight who have played cricket in Australia perhaps forty years ago. They, I trust will feel gratified at witnessing the cordial reception given tonight to those who have followed their example. English teams which have visited these colonies have taught us what we know of cricket. When the first went out there we knew little or nothing of the game, but we have since improved, as we have endeavoured to show on our present tour. If we have attained any position as cricketers, you in England have yourselves to thank for it, for you have been our instructors. We have been very ready and willing to learn, for the cricketing spirit is as strong in Australia as in England. It is the national game of the colonies, and we shall always be ready to take up the willow and do battle with any who desire to meet us in the field. . . . Before resuming my seat I desire to propose the toast, 'The English Cricketers, and success to Cricket', coupled with the names of Mr A. N. Hornby and Mr C. I. Thornton.* Both these gentlemen have always exhibited the true spirit of the game, and I thank them for the cordiality of their relations with us.

The toast to Murdoch and his team had been 'drunk with great heartiness'. At the same time, in Melbourne, Frank Grey Smith, the president of the Victorian Cricketers' Association, was addressing the Annual General Meeting.

He said: 'During the coming season a team of Gentlemen Players intend visiting these colonies, who will, we feel sure, receive a hearty welcome and although the team is a strong one, the Victorian Cricketers' Association feel confident that the cricketers of this colony will be able to hold their own with them.'

A tour of Australia in 1882–83 had been organised by the Melbourne Cricket Club who, according to their minutes, 'have made arrangements whereby the English eleven will play all their metropolitan matches on the Melbourne Cricket Ground'. What this meant in practical terms was no more going over Brunton Avenue to play on the East Melbourne Cricket Club's ground to get a better share of the gate takings.

The touring team was a mixture of amateur and professional players under the captaincy of the Hon. Ivo Bligh, the Kent batsman. The historical significance of the tour was the pledge by the captain to bring back 'The Ashes' of English cricket following the obituary notice in *The Sporting Times*.

*Hornby was captain in the 1882 Test, and Thornton, the famous hitter, and founder of the Scarborough Festival, acted as a sort of godfather figure to the early Australian teams.

The team left England in two groups, met up at Suez, sailed to Ceylon and, three days out of Colombo, their ship was involved in a collision and had to turn back for repairs. Fred Morley, the team's only fast bowler, was injured in the chest and, although he carried on gamely throughout the tour, his injury left him all but ineffective.

The team arrived in Adelaide ten days later than expected. They disembarked at Glenelg on the Friday morning of 10 November 1882, rushed to their city hotels to change, and then proceeded to the Adelaide Oval for the start of play. After two days of an even contest against Fifteen of South Australia, Bligh received his instructions from the Melbourne Cricket Club secretary, Major Ben Wardill. The team were to reboard their ship, the P & O steamer *Peshawur*, and continue to Melbourne.

The SACA committee were offended by the rush to leave Adelaide. A banquet had to be cancelled and what was worse, 'the gentlemen members of the team, who had been elected honorary members of the Adelaide Club, were unable to use the facilities'. As the *Register* also noted: 'The gentlemen stayed at the South Australian Club Hotel during their time in the city while quarters were provided for the professionals at the Prince Alfred Hotel.'

The Englishmen reached their main destination, Melbourne, on 14 November and at a celebration dinner that night, Ivo Bligh repeated that he and his eleven 'had come to beard the kangaroo in his den and try to recover those ashes'.

Bligh, later Lord Darnley, was twenty-three years of age, a Cambridge Blue and excelled at other sports including racquets, tennis and golf. His team was by no means the best England could have chosen: there was no Grace, Ulyett, Shrewsbury, Lucas, Peate or Pilling; but it included some extremely capable players in Barlow, the two Studds, Steel, W. Read, Barnes, Bates and the luckless Morley. The Third Australians, still on their way back from England, were undoubtedly a collection of great players. The matches arranged between the two sides were eagerly awaited. There were to be two Tests in Melbourne and one in Sydney, although later in the season the Australian team were to demand, and be granted, a fourth Test in Sydney.

Before all this happened, the Melbourne club was amazed at the reception given to the tourists. This caused Ben Wardill to write to SACA on 28 November, sounding them out for a Test to be played in Adelaide. He asked if SACA would accept five per cent of gross takings as their fee. The South Australians refused and said:'ten per cent or no match'.

A fortnight later the Australian team arrived in Adelaide to play South Australia with Murdoch, Bannerman, Garrett, Massie, Bonnor,

Spofforth and Jones all reluctant participants. They had wanted to play for NSW against the tourists, but had to fulfil their Adelaide commitment. Without them NSW lost by an innings and 144 runs. However, at a banquet at the Adelaide Town Hall, Murdoch told the SACA committee that arrangements had been made in London some months earlier for three Tests to take place: Melbourne, Adelaide and Sydney. The committee now knew why Wardill had written.

Bligh's team arrived back in Melbourne after Christmas for the first Test which started on 30 December. So far on tour they had defeated weakened Victorian and NSW teams, and in country matches had had a win and five draws.

Public excitement had built up in Melbourne so that, over the three days, some 54,000 people attended the match. Murdoch won the toss and Australia reached 258 for seven at stumps on the first day. George Bonnor was the star for Australia, on four occasions hitting the ball into the Ladies' Reserve. Bonnor eventually top-scored with 85 out of 291 before England collapsed for 177 on a pitch affected by overnight rain. Following-on they made 169. Palmer had figures of 7/65 and 3/61 and Australia won by nine wickets.

As the tourists went off to Tasmania for a fortnight, the South Australians were growing even more concerned about lack of communication from Wardill regarding their Test. The SACA chairman, John Colton, knew that the local Football Association secretary, John Creswell, was going to Melbourne and he asked him to open negotiations, not with Wardill, but with the players of both sides.

This was to be John Creswell's first involvement in senior cricket matters – he currently also being secretary of a minor cricket association – but by no means his last. Within a few months he became Secretary of the South Australian Cricketing Association and the instigator of much progress in Australian cricket. History has failed to appreciate his full worth.

Creswell was unsuccessful in his initial dealings with Wardill and four weeks later it was announced that an extra Test was to take place, initially in Melbourne, then in Sydney. The SACA committee tried everything to have their match confirmed, including sending telegrams to Bligh and the other associations. SACA then claimed breach of contract and, some months later, Ben Wardill admitted this was the case and paid appropriate compensation.

On their return from Tasmania the Englishmen had a fortnight of success. The second Test, in Melbourne again, saw them victorious by an innings and 27 runs as Billy Bates (7/28 and 7/74) skittled out Australia in two and a half days. Bates not only took the first English Test hat-trick – McDonnell, Giffen and Bonnor in the first innings – but became the first Test player to score a half-century and take ten wickets in a match.

Both teams then travelled to Sydney for what was originally to be the deciding Test starting on 26 January 1883. In front of 23,000 spectators on the first day England scored 247 to which the Australians had replied with 133 for one when heavy rain set in. This completely ruined Australia's efforts and only a gritty 94 by Alick Bannerman and appalling fielding by England saw the score to 218. The bowlers now took charge: Spofforth 7/44 in England's reply of 123, and Barlow 7/40 in Australia's 83, as the tourists won by 69 runs.

Bligh claimed 'the ashes' at a dinner following the match at which he accepted an embroidered 'Ashes' bag from Mrs Annie Fletcher, wife of the Paddington Cricket Club secretary. In Melbourne, a pair of bails was burned and their ashes placed in a small engraved urn which was also presented to Bligh. 'The Ashes' now existed.

The English team next went to Queensland and arrived in Brisbane after a rough, three-day journey by steamer. They found the standard of play astonishingly low compared to other parts of the mainland and won both encounters against eighteens by innings margins. But the visit had at least two good effects. The profits from the first match, £413, enabled the young Queensland Cricket Association to purchase the picturesque Albert Sports Ground on Bowen Bridge Road by the side of the bamboo fringed banks of Breakfast Creek. The other was a move by Brisbane officials to improve their standards. After some negotiation they appointed Ned Sheridan, from Sydney, to be the coach of the Stanley Club, a decision which had the same catalytic effect as Jessie Hide's appointment had in South Australia.

The fourth Test in Sydney saw, as an experiment, a different pitch used for each innings. A. G. (Allan) Steel made an unbeaten 135 for the visitors who gained a one-run lead on the first innings but could not hold on to it. Australia won on the fourth day by four wickets. Following his two earlier appearances for Australia, followed by four for England in 1881–82, Billy Midwinter represented Australia in this Test, a unique achievement.

Had Australia retained the Ashes or had England won them back? The Melbourne *Argus* on 4 January 1883 published an itinerary showing a fourth Test, plus a date for a fifth Test. Bligh stated that only three Tests were on the original schedule, so that England had won the Ashes. No-one argued with him and his ruling stood. Indeed, because Bligh was a quasi-titled Englishman, no Australian worth his salt would have dared to take such an argument further. Cricket was very important to Australian nationalism but when anyone from the ruling class of 'home' made a statement it was believed almost without question.

There was still a feeling in the country in the early 1880s that

Australians were in Australia because they were not wanted in England or because they could not make a success of life there. As cricket was only played against England, it was very important to win on an even basis to prove that Australians were near to being the equals of their rivals.

To this feeling that Australians might be cast-offs, whether by necessity or choice, was added a genuine fear of the effects of the Australian climate and what it had evidently done to the despised and decaying Aboriginal people. Prowess in manly sports – for this was also the era of muscular Christianity – especially cricket, could help to set these doubts to rest.

The heroes of cricket were around for all to see: Bonnor, Blackham, Boyle and Horan of Victoria; Spofforth, Murdoch, Bannerman and the Gregorys of New South Wales; Hide and Giffen in South Australia, with local heroes in other parts of the colonies. And what heroes were the Victorians on 24 March 1883 when they quite amazingly dismissed the pride of South Australia for 23 and then 79, to win by an innings!

Bligh's team now returned to England where his 'regaining' the Ashes was greeted with satisfaction. The captain himself, however, came back to Australia not long afterwards to marry Florence Morphy of Beechworth, whom he had met early on in the tour.

# 7

# Disagreements

The rest of 1883 saw South Australia lose Jesse Hide, who returned to Sussex, but gain a new secretary when John Creswell was appointed on 22 October. In Queensland, the Stanley Club went as missionaries to the outer reaches of the colony playing as far north as Rockhampton and Bundaberg. The island colony of Tasmania was celebrating the opening of the new cricket ground on the Domain in Hobart. It placed the southern Tasmanian cricketers on an equal footing with their cousins in the north who had had their original ground at Launceston since 1850. The only problem in Hobart was that the top-dressing cut up so badly during the opening match against the Melbourne Cricket Club that the pitch took months to repair.

The Tasmanians did, however, have the foresight to look further afield for their cricket, and early in 1884 conducted a five-week tour to New Zealand. Just a few weeks earlier, on Boxing Day 1883, Billy Murdoch had scored 158 for NSW against Victoria in Melbourne. However Tom Horan (126) and Henry Scott (114 not out) carried Victoria to a three-wicket victory.

The following day Murdoch surpassed himself by making an unbeaten 279, with seventeen fours, for the newly selected Fourth Australian team who played a Combined Team. McDonnell chipped in with 111 as the score rose to 619. The match ended in a draw but it was a most entertaining fixture for the Melbourne crowd to watch. Murdoch made only 25 and 0 in the return match against Victoria in Sydney, but when the new tourists played a second match against the Combined Team in Sydney, he scored 83.

The last first-class match of the 1883–84 season between South Australia and Victoria contained an interesting experiment. Four-ball overs had been used in all cricket in Australia but in this fixture the SACA (John Creswell) and VCA (Edward Heather) secretaries agreed to use six-ball overs because they felt that four-ball overs caused too much field-changing and cut down the actual playing time. (England still used four-ball overs, changing to five in 1889 and six in 1900.) It so happened that the match was one of the best so far played between the colonies, with Victoria winning by four wickets.

The following week South Australia played the Fourth Australians. It was to be the home team's last odds match in these fixtures, for the colony was now nearly strong enough to field even teams against all comers.

At Creswell's instigation the SACA committee wrote to John Conway on 29 February 1884 to open negotiations for Adelaide to stage its first Test match the following December. It took all Creswell's skill to obtain guarantees to cover such a venture but Conway finally agreed terms on 26 September.

The Fourth Australian team to England was again in the charge of Billy Murdoch and George Alexander as player-manager. The other changes from the 1882 tour were William Cooper, Billy Midwinter and Henry Scott replacing Garrett, Horan, Jones and Massie. The trip was a purely business venture, with none of the colonial associations involved. The players put up agreed sums to fund the tour and any losses. This time, however, three Test matches were scheduled.

The side left Melbourne on 11 March 1884 on the P & O steamer *Sutlej* and arrived at Plymouth on 29 April. They faced a most ambitious programme of fixtures, thirty-two in all, which started with a match against Lord Sheffield's XI on 12 May through to playing the South of England on 12 September.

Exactly half the programme had taken place – with ten wins and two draws – before the first Test started in a damp Manchester on 10 July. It was the first time a fixture of such importance had been staged outside of London and a drawn match due to rain started Old Trafford's 'wet' reputation.

The second Test, at Lord's, a few days later was a completely different story. Australia was dismissed for 229 with a last-wicket stand of 69 between Scott (75) and Boyle making the total look respectable. England were 135 for five in reply with the game evenly poised. Then Allan Steel took control. His 148 in just under four hours thrilled the 16,386 Tuesday crowd and proved to be a match-winning innings. Ulyett, with 7/36, puzzled the Australian batsmen in the second innings and just after lunch on the third day England had won by an innings and five runs.

Then the London newspapers found out that the Australians had been paid the entire proceeds from the Test: a princely sum of £1334. This had been agreed beforehand between Alexander and Lord Harris because the tourists depended on this money to cover their costs, but the press were extremely biased in stating their opinions. For all the other games the Australians had received only a share of the gate money, an arrangement appreciated by the county clubs as the visitors' popularity always boosted takings.

At Kennington Oval on a blazing hot August day Australia finished the first day of the third and last Test at 363 for two. This became 551 the next day, for declarations were not then allowed. But it was Billy Murdoch who stole the show, scoring the first double-century in Test cricket. His 211, with 24 fours, took just over eight hours and his stand of 207 with Henry Scott was a Test record for any wicket.

When England batted Scotton made 90 but could not stop a slide to 181 for eight with an awesome deficit looming. Then in came Walter Read to score 117 before having his stumps shattered by Harry Boyle. Read's century came in 113 minutes from only 36 scoring shots and it remains the highest Test innings by a no. 10 batsman. England's total reached 346 and, following-on, they had made 85 for two when the match was drawn.

Although the series was lost by Australia there were still matches to be played and at the end 18 games had been won with seven draws and seven defeats. With virtually an eleven-man squad, due to an injury to Cooper but with Alexander as a replacement, the team carried on manfully. Murdoch, McDonnell and Giffen passed 1,000 runs while Spofforth's 205 wickets cost him 12.50 runs apiece. He took five or more victims in a match on 22 occasions.

The tourists proved to be crowd-pleasers but there was another side to them, of which the *World* gives a hint:

> The Australians' visit has made all other matches seem tame and insipid, for it has introduced a bloodthirsty spirit.
>
> The Australians make their own terms, insist on them, not always very gracefully, and play too obviously for the money's sake. They arrogate to themselves the rank of gentlemen.

Murdoch's team had indeed met with a certain amount of hostility in England. But the *Australasian* of 11 October 1884 said:

> During the tour of the Australian cricketers they have one and all been subjected to spiteful criticism from certain portions of the English press; but it has been left to *The Illustrated Sporting and Dramatic News* to outvenom all other vituperative productions. As a specimen of narrow-minded and insulting abuse its remarks outstrip anything that has yet been levelled at the Australian cricketers.

The *Australasian* – whose cricket writer 'Felix' (Tom Horan) was no supporter of Murdoch's team – was very near to actually finding a scoop on events that were shortly to unfold. Their indignation had been sparked when they received a copy of *The Illustrated Sporting and Dramatic News* which read:

> These Australian adventurous spirits have undertaken their enterprise less for honour than for filthy lucre, demanding a sort of commission for their services: and a seemingly correct and uncontradictable report has it that each player returning to the vast colonial regions of Australia took home £900 in his pocket. Win or lose, they accept their expenses all the same. The present generation of lovers of the once noble game must have seen enough of the Australians to last them for life, and their intrusion into the mother country will be regarded henceforth as a veritable nuisance, carried out to its bitter end.

Time and again during the 1880s the criticisms of touring sides seemed to revolve around financial matters. By the time the professional team of English cricketers arrived in Australia for the 1884–85 season – James Lillywhite, Alfred Shaw and Arthur Shrewsbury arranged and managed their second speculative venture to Australia with John Conway acting as their agent – there was a distinct possibility that the issue of money could again cause problems.

On this tour James Lillywhite acted purely as an umpire, Shaw was manager and Shrewsbury captain. The party, containing no amateurs, was in Shaw's estimation the strongest team yet to represent England in Australia.

The SS *Orient* docked at Port Adelaide on the morning of 29 October 1884 and the South Australian secretary, John Creswell, boarded and told the tourists the sad news – which he had just received by cable from England – of the death of Fred Morley who never recovered from the injuries he sustained on the previous tour.

To put it mildly, Creswell was a persuasive man and, before any of the England team were allowed to disembark, he had obtained their signatures on a contract to play the first Test of the tour in Adelaide.

The tourists then went off to start the first of their eight fixtures prior to the Test. Creswell, meanwhile, was not getting caught up in fawning over the Englishmen as his committee were doing. He cabled the homecoming Australian team at Albany, Western Australia, where their ship had landed. When he got no reply he took a ship to Melbourne to start negotiations. The day after the English team arrived in Melbourne, the SS *Mirzapore* docked and with it Murdoch's Fourth Australians. Creswell bailed up Murdoch and the team manager, Alexander, at the Continental Hotel and only left them when he had the contracts signed and the arrangements confirmed.

By this time, the Melbourne Cricket Club was coming to terms with tragedy. Their new two-storey pavilion, designed by William Solway and opened in 1881, had burned to the ground during a fire on 31 August 1884. Everything had been destroyed and the only bonus the club had was that their insurance company paid up within the week. The £2900 insurance money went towards the £11,490 cost of a new stand. In order to raise some of this money the Melbourne Cricket Club backed an Australian tour to England in 1886.

But back in November 1884, trouble was brewing. *The Age* of 1 November claimed 'that the [1884–85] Englishmen are not desirous of arranging any matches in Australia against Murdoch's Eleven'. Further down the report the journalist notes: 'Alexander informs me that upon suggesting such a meeting to Conway, the Australian agent for Lillywhite's team, he was referred to Lillywhite who replied that he could make no arrangements.' The significance of this article was that it was the first hint of trouble between the teams and furthermore, while the article was being printed, the Australian team was still at sea.

Whatever the problems, it was clear by his statements to the press that Lillywhite had had a disagreement with Alexander over financial matters. He was certainly no fool, knew the side profits that were being made, and wanted his players to share in them. *The Age* of 22 November 1884 said that the Australians 'were amazed at statements being made to the effect that public opinion could and would be aroused to force them into playing on the English manager's terms'. By this time England had played and beaten Victoria for whom Alexander, Blackham, Boyle, Cooper, Midwinter, Palmer and Scott from the Fourth Australians had all refused to play.

The Victorian Cricketers' Association was furious, suspended the players concerned, initiated an enquiry and, what was worse, according to the 1884–85 annual report: 'Owing to the poor financial returns your Association returned the percentage on same, amounting to £19 6s. 9d. to Messrs Lillywhite and Co'.

The Englishmen then travelled to Sydney to play New South Wales and again members of the Fourth Australians refused to play against them. This did not seem to affect the attendance as over 30,000 people turned up to watch the match.

Not until 27 December 1884 did the reasons for the behaviour of Murdoch's players become public knowledge. The attitude Lillywhite held towards the Australians did indeed stem from a disagreement between himself and Alexander. *The Age* published correspondence between the two men in which Lillywhite offered Murdoch's team thirty per cent of the gate takings for two Tests: early January in Melbourne and late February in Sydney.

When the Australians rejected this offer, Lillywhite arranged to play against substitute teams and told Alexander: 'I have not the slightest doubt that both matches will pay us better than playing you at 30%'. Murdoch's team felt that they should get an equal amount of money, less expenses, to the Englishmen: whereas the tourists, being aware of the large profit made by the Australians in England, wanted a bigger share of the takings.

In the *Australasian* of 27 December 1884, 'Felix' (Tom Horan) said that the final offer put to Lillywhite was 'over-generous to the Englishmen'. The irony in this was that, after Alexander's final refusal to an offer of around forty per cent of the Melbourne gate, Horan was appointed captain of Australia by the Victorian Cricketers' Association which was choosing the team.

While all this was going on, a fascinating intercolonial contest was taking place on the Melbourne Cricket Ground. New South Wales had scored 403 in even time – Murdoch 97 – and Victoria replied with 482. Blackham was the backbone of the innings, making 109, and it was mid-afternoon on 30 December when NSW started their second innings.

Suddenly wickets tumbled for no apparent reason as NSW fell to 'Joey' Palmer (6/26) and were dismissed for 74. As the match had been expected to carry on into the New Year, in those days of unrestricted games, a cable was quickly sent to Benalla where Lillywhite's team was playing a local twenty-two. The message was to return to Melbourne at once so that a start could be made to the big match on New Year's Day.

Before play began, the new Australian captain, Horan, wrote in the *Australasian*: 'It would be a good thing for Australian cricket if Murdoch's men never played here again'. It was an extraordinary comment for Horan to make and after England had won the Test by ten wickets in under four days, Horan changed his mind. He then wrote: 'Everybody would like to see them playing again,' in reference to Murdoch's players.

Besides the money problems, there had been a breakdown in relations between John Conway and the Australian team. The Australians resented the fact that Conway was representing the Englishmen and pushing forward their monetary wishes. Despite denials, Harry Boyle, Jack Blackham, 'Joey' Palmer and Henry Scott wrote a lengthy account of Conway's alleged underhand dealings. This was published in the *Australasian* on 17 January 1885 and could well account for Horan's complete change of sides in his 'Cricket Chatter' column.

The arguments raged and, while they did, the tourists played a dozen matches, only one of which was first-class: a victory over NSW prior to the third Test in Sydney. In this match four of the

NSW members of Murdoch's team agreed to play, with the result that the Australians won, by six runs.

Hugh Massie took over from Horan as captain and the Australians' victory was put down to two events: a tenth-wicket partnership of 80 between Garrett and Evans on the second morning following a fierce storm the previous day; and ten wickets by Spofforth (4/54 and 6/90) including at one stage three wickets in four balls.

James Lillywhite was now expressing his concern at the Victorian Cricketers' Association's attitude, since they had now disqualified their Australian players for refusing to play in the return intercolonial in Sydney. Lillywhite wrote a letter to the VCA on 5 March 1885 in which he requested that the suspension on the players be lifted, 'as I wish to have them in a team of Australians for the Englishmen to play in Melbourne in late March'.

The motive for this letter became crystal clear as Lillywhite added: 'We wish to play them to try and recoup ourselves for the unsuccessful tour we have had financially up till now'. The VCA replied that 'when the disqualified players advise us of their willingness to play, we will reconsider the disqualifications'. Because the VCA did not consider it important enough to let their players know of this, Murdoch returned to his law practice at Cootamundra and was lost to Australian cricket for five years.

Jack Blackham returned as captain for the fourth Test in Sydney as the Victorian ban did not cover him there, and in any case the NSWCA had, on 19 January 1885, decided not to endorse the VCA's action.

The Englishmen batted first in the match to find themselves facing George Giffen as the opening bowler. His 7/117 from 52 overs kept Palmer and Spofforth fairly fresh for the third morning when they ripped through England's second innings. For Australia, George Bonnor scored the then fastest century in Test cricket, reaching his hundred in even time with four fives (hits out of the ground then scored five runs) and 14 fours. Australia won by eight wickets in under three days but would lose Blackham, Bonnor, Palmer and McDonald for the fifth Test four days later.

Again there were more squabbles, arguments and suspensions for a match which England won easily by an innings and 98 runs (Shrewsbury scoring 105 not out). But it was a sad end to an unfortunate tour which coincided with the ending of an era in Australian cricket. A successor would have to be found for Murdoch, and from London it was reported that the Marylebone Cricket Club had decided not to welcome any of the Australians who had been ungentlemanly enough to demand extra financial gain for playing the game of cricket.

The English tourists left Australia on 6 April 1885, following a drawn match against South Australia, but their departure left Victorian cricket in turmoil. Nor did the coming winter ease the situation as the VCA chairman, Mr Justice Williams, conducted a vendetta against certain members of Murdoch's Australians. His Honour tried hard to convince the players to take up amateur status and, when he realised his campaign had little or no support, the VCA lifted the bans on 10 November 1885, and in its 1885–86 annual report said: 'The removal of the disqualifications was considered the most important matter dealt with by the Association during the season'.

Nearby, the Melbourne Cricket Club had made their decision. Following a members' meeting, the club had decided to send a team to England in 1886. It was the first time the club had tried such a venture and they did so largely on the advice of Lord Harris, Albert Hornby and Ivo Bligh who all said that a team backed by the Melbourne CC would be far better received in England than a team privately promoted.

It also meant the end of his activities for John Conway who had been so involved in cricket for the past quarter of a century. Alas, the rift between himself and the Australians under Murdoch's captaincy never really healed and, when he died in 1909, only seven people turned up to his funeral: four obscure members of the family plus Frank Allan and Tom Horan of the cricketers and a man to whom Conway had given praise in a cricket publication many years earlier. Horan then wrote a fine obituary of Conway in the *Australasian* saying that, 'the fact the first Australian team did so well in England is well known and to Jack Conway, and to him alone, the credit is due him,' adding, 'and I hope that our MCC will take steps to have some permanent memorial on the pavilion walls to keep green the name and work of the dead and gone old warrior'.

Horan, under his pen-name of 'Felix', had written in the *Australasian* on 27 September 1885 about the Melbourne Cricket Club. 'It is the leading cricket club of Australia and stands alone in influence, wealth, power and position. It is supported by the best and most influential men in our community. Its members-roll numbers about 1800 and its revenue from subscriptions alone is over £3000 per annum.'

It is also important to look at how the Melbourne club could take the initiative to fund the 1886 tour when the two Test matches had, according to their annual report of September 1885, 'brought in the sum of £96 to the club'. The answer is to be found in the financial statements of the club dating back over the previous twenty years. Good housekeeping from past tours to Australia had seen profits go into an 'All-England Eleven Account' which was now showing a credit of £1229. By the time the 1886 tour was over, this figure had increased considerably with the committee protesting on one hand that 'the Club adopted this enterprise with no idea of gain' and later on in their report admitting that 'the financial results of the trip were fairly successful'. The profit was £1083.

As with many things in Australian cricket during those times, an idea or proposal from the South Australia Cricketing Association secretary, John Creswell, tended to light a beacon to which others were guided.

On 3 March 1885, Creswell had written to both the NSWCA and VCA suggesting that the three associations get together to choose the next Australian team to tour England. It was also put to the other associations that the team be responsible to a joint committee who would in turn undertake all organisational and financial matters, and that SACA 'would be prepared to undertake their equal share in accordance with the others'.

The NSWCA replied quickly saying that they had no interest in pursuing this idea further. However, the VCA did circulate the idea to their constituent clubs, whereupon Carlton and Melbourne publicly stated their support while South Melbourne was strongly against. At the VCA annual general meeting, held on 14 September 1885 at the Hawthorn Cricket Club, the clubs gave it approval but added this was provisional on the NSWCA changing its mind.

The NSWCA refused to budge. On 22 September, therefore, the VCA Secretary, Edward Heather, wrote to Creswell relating a feeling of hopelessness in taking the matter any further. This decision then enabled the Melbourne Cricket Club to act. As their annual report later said:

> *Australian Eleven* – The season 1885–86 marks an epoch in the history of the Club, an Australian Eleven for the first time having been sent to England under its exclusive control. As authorised by the special general meeting on 12 December 1885, the Committee, after being faced by many and harassing difficulties, succeeded in forming what was considered by cricketers generally as the strongest all-round team available in the colonies, consisting of – Messrs Blackham, Bruce, Bonnor, Evans, Giffen, Jones, McIlwraith, Garrett, Jarvis, Palmer, Spofforth, Scott and Trumble. The history of its formation and as yet unfinished tour in England is so familiar to the Members that it is not proposed to dilate here upon the subject; but a pamphlet, containing the scores and main incidents of the visit, will probably be published.
>
> In the early part of last year the Committee had under consideration, in connection with the projected visit of an Eleven to England, the formation of an English Eleven to visit the colonies this season, under the auspices of the MCC, and obtained the sanction of the

> Club to the undertaking at a special meeting held for the purpose in March of this year, and, as then intimated, very favourable promises of assistance had been received from the cities and inland towns of this and the other colonies. The Secretary was instructed, in accordance with the promises made to the Club, to get together the strongest team of amateurs and professionals that could be obtained, arrangements for their tour through the colonies had been made, and an attractive programme, including four matches with the Australian Eleven, was framed.
>
> Some time after Mr Wardill's arrival in England, and after he had opened negotiations with several leading cricketers to come out, he wired to the Committee that he had found Messrs Shaw, Shrewsbury and Lillywhite had determined to bring out their team, whether he brought out a team or not, and the Committee, being of opinion that the presence of two English teams in the colony was not desirable, instructed Mr Wardill to use every endeavour to arrange with Messrs Shaw and Co. to postpone their visit. These endeavours having proved fruitless, Mr Wardill was instructed to stop all further negotiations for bringing out a team, and arrangements were made here with Messrs Shaw and Co.'s agent for playing all matches in Melbourne on the Club's ground.

When the Melbourne Club was considering the selection of their team for touring England in 1886 they were aware of the threatened move to ban certain players in England. They were very careful therefore in choosing their side. Omitted were Murdoch, McDonnell and Alick Bannerman, whose absence caused immense criticism, while Horan, Boyle and Massie were unavailable. Chosen as captain was the twenty-seven-year-old Henry Scott, a doctor who had made his debut in the 1877–78 season for Victoria. A top-order batsman, Scott had toured England in 1884 under Murdoch, but it was his misfortune in a way to be following the blazing success of Murdoch's captaincy with a team which looked good on paper but was, in fact, growing jaded. Murdoch's tours of 1880, 1882 and 1884 had gone on and on, with visits also to New Zealand and the United States. The players had become too familiar with each other, despite certain newcomers on this tour, William Bruce, Edwin Evans, John Trumble and John McIlwraith.

Following the traditional Christmas match in Melbourne, where Victoria (Scott 111, McIlwraith 133) defeated NSW by an innings, a trial match was held over New Year between Victoria and An Australian XI (McIlwraith 125). This was supposed to be a guide to the forthcoming tour but as the NSW cricketers did not take part owing to 'a financial dispute', it was of little use as a guide to form.

One member of the Fifth Australian team who did cause eyebrows to be raised was George Giffen, the South Australian all-rounder. In a four-day intercolonial fixture against Victoria which started on 11 March 1886, Giffen opened the batting and scored 20 and 82. Even more remarkably he opened the bowling and took 9/91 and 8/110 in a total of 117 overs. South Australia won by 40 runs and the Adelaide *Observer* was moved to say: 'Giffen's performance stands out as one of the best ever accomplished by any man'.

The Melbourne Cricket Club wrote to Creswell on 8 January asking if SACA were interested in holding a match on the Adelaide Oval in late March between their Australian team en route to England and a Combined XV from Victoria and South Australia. The SACA Committee agreed so long as they did not have to pay the expenses of any of the players. The Melbourne CC secretary, Ben Wardill, replied on 30 January protesting at this stance but the committee remained firm. Wardill accepted this, but then wrote again on 12 February wanting the combined team to be only thirteen. The committee agreed. On being told of this change, the Australian captain, Henry Scott, insisted on the combined side reverting to fifteen and so the committee obliged Melbourne once again.

The four-day match took place on 18, 19, 20 and 22 March with the Combined XV (330 and 245) gaining a draw with the Fifth Australians (422 and 100 for six).

Seven of the tourists sailed from Adelaide on 28 March; the other six, along with the manager, Ben Wardill, left on 10 April. They all met up in Naples and arrived at Plymouth on 4 May to find that the late decision in confirming the tour had caused the county secretaries considerable difficulties in arranging a proper itinerary.

Compared with the previous tours this one was disappointing, not only for the lack of success – only nine wins from 39 games – but also for the indiscipline of certain players. Friction had developed before even one match was played and throughout the tour Scott and Wardill spent a considerable amount of time adjudicating quarrels. The cricket historian, Arthur Haygarth, noted in *Scores and Biographies*: 'The cares of leadership affected Scott's run-getting, for disputes among his players were many and he did not have the strength of character to cope with this situation'.

The tour started with the customary match at Sheffield Park against Lord Sheffield's XI and not until the fifth match did a victory come the Australians' way, when Oxford University was beaten by 25 runs in a low-scoring match. Four further victories were recorded up to the first Test at Old Trafford in early July, but disaster was following disaster. Spofforth dislocated the middle finger of his bowling hand and missed the next six games. Palmer's skill had declined and Evans, at thirty-seven, was only a shadow of his former self. Bonnor was injured in July and did not play again on the tour while Giffen took a long time to find his form.

All three Tests were lost with the defeats getting successively heavier. At Old Trafford, Jones with a first innings 87 and Spofforth with a 4/82 were the best of a poor display in a four-wicket loss. At Lord's, Spofforth took 4/73 in a defeat by an innings and 106 runs, and Spofforth again took most wickets at The Oval with 4/65 in an innings and 217 runs debacle.

The editor of *Wisden*, Sydney Pardon, summed it up well when he wrote: 'Scott led the team with the best of intentions and greatest sincerity, but he was no Murdoch. It is exceedingly doubtful whether even an ideal captain would have pulled the team through its engagements unless, indeed, he had been backed by that confidence and energy which we so seldom see in any teams'.

Despite this the tour was a financial success and wherever the team played they outdrew any attendances at county fixtures. At the tour's end Scott stayed in London to further his medical studies, eventually returning to Australia to practise at Bathurst, then at Scone where he became both mayor and chief magistrate. In later life, when he was asked if he would have liked to continue in cricket his reply was: 'I have captained Australia and hit a Test century. Many would have liked two such honours as these.'

Nice words indeed from Scott, but in those days of the mid-to-late 1880s the game of cricket was suffering. The lack of success, and the nature of this and subsequent touring teams who were all criticised for being too mercenary, tended to make this period a slack phase in the development of cricketing nationalism. Also, at home, 1886 saw a six per cent drop in wages, and nearly ten per cent unemployed. It was not a good year for Australia as a whole.

Even so, 1886 was only one bad year in a decade of optimism. Fortunes in land and buildings were made overnight, and even banks and insurance companies were becoming infected with the fever of speculation.

In Brisbane, the Queensland Cricket Association was looking at a new site for a ground at Bowen Bridge Road, which they eventually developed by importing Victoria's Merri Creek soil to make pitches. The standard of play was fairly high in Brisbane club cricket during this time, but there was a lack of any intercolonial matches. Also, in the Queensland countryside, two English sides had paid fleeting visits in 1883 and 1885. Another fixture against Lillywhite's 1887 team was the last match with a team from outside the colony until Victor Trumper's team played in Bundaberg, Gympie and Maryborough in 1906.

* * * *

The internal bickering within Victorian cricket saw Percy McDonnell and George Bonnor transfer to New South Wales for the 1886–87 season. McDonnell stayed seven years in Sydney, playing for the old Carlton club, before moving further north to play and coach in Brisbane. Billy Murdoch and Fred Spofforth had gone the other way by moving to Melbourne to live and, although Murdoch refused to play for Victoria against his former side, Spofforth had no such scruples.

McDonnell returned to Melbourne as a NSW team member and gave his old friends a hiding in their intercolonial fixture. He scored 239 in even time with three fives and 16 fours. When he was dismissed the total was 300 for three – over seventy nine per cent of the runs scored were his.

The first important game of the 1886–87 season was played in Melbourne when Victoria drew with yet another England team under the sponsorship of Messrs Lillywhite, Shaw and Shrewsbury. Discounting Shaw, the team only numbered eleven players, a situation which caused problems later in the tour. The visit was badly promoted while some of the English side's fixtures clashed with intercolonial matches. Attendances were also down and one has to wonder whether, if Conway's hand had been on the lever, everything would have been different.

The tour was Lillywhite's fifth; the fourth for Bates and Shaw; the third for Barnes, Barlow, Scotton and Shrewsbury, and the second for Briggs, Flowers and Read. The new men were William Gunn and Mordecai Sherwin, who both forsook a season of playing soccer for Notts County; and George Lohmann on the first of his three tours 'down under'.

This season Australia had two new fast bowling stars: Charles Turner and Jack Ferris, both of New South Wales. Their opening attack for their country would be unbroken for four years. Turner, known as 'the Terror', took one of the season's classic hat-tricks in the match against Victoria in Melbourne by bowling Palmer, Horan and Trumble with similar deliveries. At the other end Ferris, the twenty-year-old left-arm paceman from the Belvidere club, took four wickets on his intercolonial debut.

By the time the Tests came around – there being only two during the season – McDonnell found himself captain of a team split by dissent. The players quarrelled amongst themselves, with their local associations and, regrettably, with the England players too. McDonnell, though, was respected. George Giffen said of him: 'He was one of the best and jolliest of players. An appropriate name would have been Percy 'Greatheart' McDonnell, for it was when things were going wrong that he was seen at his best. If I live to be a hundred

I will never see more elegant, graceful and effective batting than his two innings at Adelaide in the Test of 1884.'

McDonnell has been the only Australian captain, so far, who could read Greek philosophers and playwrights in their own language. He appreciated Aristotle's logic and chuckled at *Lysistrata*. Maybe that was behind his reasoning for being the first Test captain who, on winning the toss, invited the opposition to bat – and on his initial time in charge.

The Test, in Sydney at the end of January 1887, saw Turner (6/15) and Ferris (4/27) bowl unchanged on their debuts as England fell for 45 runs in their first innings on a rain-affected pitch. Sadly, it was to be Spofforth's last Test and he picked up a consolation wicket at the end of England's second innings. In his eighteen Tests, the 'Demon' had taken 94 wickets at 18.41. He played the game for eleven more years at first-class level, both in Australia and England, before retiring with 853 victims to his name.

The Test fluctuated, with Alick Bannerman at one time failing to score for an hour. His brother Charles watched at close hand; he was making his Test debut as an umpire. In the end England won by 13 runs, Billy Barnes taking 6/28 to ensure victory for the tourists.

However, Barnes was not that lucky. He had a bitter argument after the game with McDonnell – neither side got on well and there were accusations of cheating – threw a punch, missed, and hit a brick wall, injuring his hand so badly he could not play in the second Test. Then Spofforth threw a haymaking punch at Barlow who was experienced enough in boxing to duck and weave around.

With Barnes injured, Reg Wood, a former Lancashire player now living in Melbourne, joined the party to play in his sole Test in Sydney at the end of February.

Between the Tests a row broke out in Adelaide over what was called 'loss of time payments'. Walter Giffen, George's younger brother, was complaining that he could not afford the loss of wages to play in Melbourne in an intercolonial match. Others joined him in asking for payment to play and, although the matter was resolved, it had a knock-on effect for the second Test. This saw Blackham, Bruce, George Giffen, Palmer and Trumble refuse to play while Jones had to cry off due to illness. This resulted in five new caps, namely Reg Allen, Fred Burton, John Cottam, Walter Giffen and Jack Lyons.

The Australian newspapers were saying that the English team was the finest all-round team to tour, so it was little wonder the last Test resulted in defeat for Australia by 71 runs. Rain again affected the game with the bowlers on top throughout. Ferris (5/71 and 4/69) and Turner (5/41 and 4/52) led for Australia, while Lohmann's 8/35 made him the first man to take eight wickets in a Test innings.

As with so many matches on the tour, the attendance was poor and a proposed third Test was cancelled when it was found that the NSW contingent could not play. A fascinating match was then proposed in its place: Smokers versus Non-Smokers on the East Melbourne ground over four days in mid-March 1887. The Smokers, led by Arthur Shrewsbury, and their opponents, captained by Harry Boyle, both contained English and Australian players.

At 514 for two, Shrewsbury fell for 236 having hit 40 fours in just over five hours. The innings concluded at 803 for nine which was then the highest total recorded in first-class cricket. The Smokers made 356 and were 135 for five when the match ended in a draw. William Scotton played the last ball of the match, picked it up as a souvenir and promptly became the first player in Australia to be given out 'handled ball'.

After a final match against South Australia, the tourists left Australian shores despairing of making any profit, having declined to visit New Zealand on their way home.

Domestically, the Victorian Cricketers' Association noted a sad loss to the game at this time. As the Secretary, Edward Heather, wrote:

> The construction of the new line of railway from Hawthorn to Kew has led to the demolition of the local Cricket Ground, on which a terminal railway station has been erected. This has led to the disbandment of the Kew Club. The destruction of the ground is regrettable, as it was very carefully laid out only a few years since by the Kew Recreation Association, and with the well-designed hall and grounds adjacent, formed not only an ornament to this picturesque suburb, but afforded one of the most central and convenient sites in the district for sports fixtures of all kinds.

Heather had also been busy on other fronts. He had written to the secretaries of the other colonial associations stating that the VCA was intending to hold a conference in Melbourne on 10 February 1887 to discuss the alteration of three of the Laws of Cricket. These concerned having six balls to the over; to loosen up the leg-before-wicket law, and either to widen the wicket or narrow the bat.

The only unanimous agreement amongst delegates concerned the six-ball over. Many other matters were discussed and delegates reported back on the benefit of such gatherings. The seeds for the formation of an overall Australian cricket body had been sown.

However, the Melbourne Cricket Club were still at the forefront of the game in Australia and their president, Frank Gray Smith, let his feelings be known concerning events proposed for the 1887–88 season by referring to the 'English Amateur Team' due to tour:

> As members are aware, the Secretary of the Club when in England made arrangements for the visit of an Amateur Team of Cricketers during this season, and at a special meeting of the Club, held on 29 January 1887, the scheme received formal sanction.
>
> Mr G. F. Vernon and Mr W. W. Read were entrusted with the selection of the team, and they have been assisted by Mr I. D. Walker and Dr W. G. Grace throughout their whole proceedings. The result has been the selection of a first-class team, consisting of Messrs W. W. Read, W. E. Roller, A. E. Stoddart, T. C. O'Brien, A. E. Newton, M. P. Bowden, G. F. Vernon, and the Hon. M. B. Hawke, assisted by Bates, Beaumont, Abel, Peel and Attewell, and their departure has been fixed for the middle of September by the Orient packet *Iberia*.
>
> Another team, organised by English professional cricketers, is also announced to be coming at the same time. The Committee stated their opinion last year that the presence of two English teams during the same season was not desirable, and they accordingly postponed their recorded intention of (for a third time) inviting an Amateur Eleven to Australia until the present season, in order not to clash with a professional project of the kind then in progress. On the present occasion, however, their engagements were absolutely complete before the intention of the professionals became public; and in any case they could not consent that the Club should stand aside a second time in succession for the benefit of those who make these visits purely as a monetary speculation.

It was a classic catch. The amateur tourists, supported by the most influential club in the country, competing with a professional band of cricketers intent on making money. Australia would not see such a season again for a further ninety years.

Australian cricket was undoubtedly in decline, and the financially disastrous twin tours about to take place added to the fall in popularity. No longer were Australians fawning over common-or-garden English players. The *Bulletin* went as far as to say:

> The Australians, whether amateur or professional, will never consent to be spat upon by dirty little cads whose soap-boiling or nigger-murdering grandfathers left enough money to get the cads' fathers 'ennobled' and to enable the cad himself to live without working.

Considering its powerful position in Australian cricket, the NSWCA were very quiet during the turbulent 1880s. Their main cause for concern during the 1887–88 season was the resignation of Dave Gregory from the selection panel owing to a clash of personalities with the other two selectors.

Sydney cricket itself was in the doldrums, the saddest decline being that of the great Albert club. On 30 April 1887, Charlie Turner, playing for Carlton, dismissed the whole Albert side for just ten runs.

Tasmanian cricket had set a precedent in 1884 by sending a representative team to New Zealand, but the following three years saw no visits to Tasmania by any side until the English amateur team played four matches in 1887–88.

In comparison to all the other colonies the first sixty years of cricket in Western Australia showed little progress. In 1878 the Perth Cricket Club had passed a resolution pressing for a decent ground on which to play. The club had the money but had no control over the land they wanted to improve. However on 2 October 1885 the Perth-based Metropolitan Cricket Club passed the following motion: 'The officers of the club are instructed to consider the question of forming a cricketing association and to make their report upon the subject as soon as possible to a general meeting of members.'

To effect this instruction a meeting of the committees of the various cricket clubs in Perth was convened and held at the United Services Hotel on Thursday 12 November 1885. After a full discussion it was unanimously agreed:

> That it is desirable to form a Cricketing Association of the recognized Perth cricket clubs subject to the Municipal Council letting an adequate portion of the Recreation Ground for the exclusive right of playing matches thereon by such Association.

Even though the first step had been taken to improve Western Australian cricket, the more far-sighted followers thought that two further steps were necessary. First, the game needed a 'home' of its own where a cricket ground could be developed; second, better local competition, inter-colonial games and matches against visiting international sides would have to be organised. Until 1887 there had been nine tours by English teams to Australia but none had played in Western Australia.

At a meeting in February 1887, John James, President of the Western Australian Cricketing Association, suggested they consider a tour to the eastern colonies. He recognised the high cost of such a venture but with support from the centres visited they might recoup their initial outlay. The meeting agreed that such a proposal was possible. Letters were sent to the other colonies and a subscription list opened to raise the £600 required. The tour did not go ahead.

Through correspondence between Perth and connections in Melbourne a professional cricket coach was engaged by the Metropolitan Club. The player contracted was William Duffy, a groundsman and player from the Richmond Club, and his duties were to coach youths as well as the club. He arrived in Perth at the start of the 1887–88 season.

In December 1889 a further significant move occurred. It took the form of a deputation to the Governor, Sir Frederick Broome, by the President of the Western Australian Cricketing Association, John James, and two members of the Executive, Sidney Parker and Jack Lovekin. James pointed out that, until the Association had exclusive use of an area of ground which they could develop for cricket, the game would not progress.

The deputation requested that a portion of Perth Reserve 27A be vested in the Cricketing Association. This was an area of twenty-eight acres at the eastern end of Perth. To the elation of the members of the Cricketing Association, Broome recommended that the 'Southern portion of 27A be leased to the WACA for 999 years'. In concluding the minute His Excellency stated: 'The necessary action can be taken and I am glad as almost my last act of my long administration of this Government to be able to serve so good a cause as that of cricket'.

Four years later Western Australia would play their first first-class match. However, only after the First War would interstate matches take place on a regular basis.

# 8

# Revival with Lord Sheffield

In 1887 Australian cricket was in disarray. The players were unhappy with their financial prospects and no-one wanted yet another English tour. The Melbourne Cricket Club was concerned at the behaviour of the Test players and then horrified to discover that two touring teams were to be in Australia at the same time.

The colonial cricket associations all lacked funds and the thought of them promoting any tours was beyond comprehension. So the players turned to the Melbourne club for their future survival in the game.

Melbourne had invited George Vernon of Middlesex to bring a team to Australia under the captaincy of Lord Hawke. These arrangements had been made during the tour of 1886, but not until late in 1887 did the announcement of a rival tour reveal any problem. Somewhere or somehow, the New South Wales Cricket Association had obtained funds to ask Lillywhite, Shaw and Shrewsbury to return with their professional troupe.

The professionals were to be captained by C. Aubrey Smith (later knighted, and an actor of Hollywood fame), but as expected the two tours killed off interest and the Melbourne club recorded a loss on their tour of £3583, saying afterwards: 'It was hardly anticipated that the club would escape loss in bringing out a team from England under the circumstances existing at the time, and that anticipation has been realised'.

Lord Hawke in his reminiscences wrote:

> There was never such a prominent case of folly. The fact was that it had nothing to do with us at home at all, and arose from the rivalry then existent between the Melbourne Club and their neighbours at Sydney. The Melbourne Club had endeavoured to collect a side from the mother country in the previous winter, therefore it had merely been postponed, whereas the Sydney authorities asserted that for all they knew when they wanted an English eleven to take part in the celebration in New South Wales, the Melbourne project had been abandoned.

Lord Hawke was referring to the centenary celebrations of the first settlement in Australia in 1787. Sydney celebrated with a cricket tour. Melbourne celebrated with the huge Centennial Exhibition and imported the full London Philharmonic Orchestra. Hawke was not in Australia for very long as his father died suddenly and he had to return to England; but like James Lillywhite he ran into the old amateur-professional problem. The newspapermen noticed that the amateurs and the professionals were not staying in the same hotels and, as Lord Hawke said, they threatened to take it up as a grievance. Hawke wrote:

> It is rather curious that the Australians themselves do not realise that our professionals prefer to be on their own off the field rather than to be in the same hotel as the amateurs. Indeed, I know that some of our professionals would prefer to have second-class passages on board ship rather than having to dress each night for dinner. This is not in the least diminishing the perfect accord between English amateurs and professionals.

Not for the last time in Australian cricket, officials of the NSWCA had blundered in on arrangements already made and their attitude had a lot to do with the problems which beset the game at the time.

Although the NSWCA were asked to reconsider their plans both tours went ahead. Vernon's team boarded the Orient steamer *Iberia* at Tilbury with Lillywhite's side joining at Plymouth. The first port of call was Adelaide on 25 October. The South Australians, unaware of the joint travel arrangements, had called a meeting a fortnight earlier in order to arrange for the usual greetings and a civic reception. The plan was for a formal greeting at Port Adelaide; an escort to the hotels (The South Australian for the amateurs; The Prince Alfred for the professionals); a greeting by the Mayor and the usual great rejoicings. When Lillywhite, Shaw and Shrewsbury disembarked first with their team, mild panic set in amongst the welcoming party. Although going by train to Sydney for their first match at Parramatta, the team were staying in Adelaide for two nights. Undaunted, the SACA secretary John Creswell immediately invited them to join in the partying, an action which reduced Melbourne Cricket Club's animosity towards the rival tour.

Vernon's team had two days to practise before meeting South Australia on even terms. The four-day match was a huge success with 20,443 people watching the game. The visitors (104 and 291) defeated South Australia (118 and 206) late on the last day by 71 runs, but not without an extraordinary series of incidents. From the last ball of the third day's play 'Affie' Jarvis (45) had been run out by a careless call from his partner, George Giffen. The next morning with the score on 116 for one, Giffen proceeded to run out Jack Lyons. Giffen, a first-day hero for taking a hat-trick, was now the villain of the piece for five runs later he also ran out his brother Walter. There was a dispute when the umpire, Fisher, gave George out instead of Walter and, brotherly love being what it is, and after disputing the umpire's decision, both batsmen stormed from the field. After somewhat of a delay, George returned to the crease and continued his innings as though nothing had happened.

As both touring teams now started wandering the country, attendances began to decline. Vernon's team played 26 fixtures, eight of which were first-class, while Lillywhite's side played 22, of which seven were first-class. This was too much cricket for Australians to absorb, and Lillywhite's team lost £2400.

The season saw 19 first-class matches take place, the most up till now, and a figure unbeaten until the 1894–95 season. It could be argued that a match played in Brisbane from 30 November 1887 should have been recorded as Queensland's initial first-class fixture, when Aubrey Smith's XI played L. C. Docker's XI, with twelve members of the Lillywhite team being equally divided with ten Queenslanders. However Queensland had not as yet participated on level terms in intercolonial cricket and, in the future, only two of the ten local players did so. Official first-class status therefore could not be given.

Two players, Percy McDonnell and Charles Turner, played in twelve matches each, a number unheard of previously. Yet the highest run-scorer was the NSW batsman, Harry Moses, with 815 runs from nine matches and a best score of 297 not out against Victoria in Sydney. The bowling honours went to Turner who took 106 wickets at an average of 13.59 – a domestic record.

The colonies played in ten matches against the touring sides plus three of their own intercolonial matches. Vernon's team played two important fixtures: over New Year against a Combined Australia side in Melbourne with a victory by an innings and 78 runs. The Combined side was weakened by the refusal of seven top players to take part, although a more balanced contest, also in Melbourne, in early March saw Vernon's team defeat the Sixth Australians by 87 runs.

Lillywhite's players, styled 'A. Shrewsbury's XI', played and defeated a much better representative Combined Australia in Sydney by five wickets. Their two matches against the Sixth Australians were both won with ease.

The only Test match for the season took place in Sydney from 10 February 1888. The two touring sides agreed to combine together for the fixture although the Australians were weakened by the refusal of George Giffen, Tom Horan, Billy Bruce and 'Affie' Jarvis to play because they wanted more money.

In a low-scoring encounter, England won by 126 runs on the fifth morning after two whole days had been lost to rain. Turner's match figures of 12/87 still remain the best for any Test match on the Sydney Cricket Ground.

When their tour was completed in mid-March, Vernon's team played in a one-day match for the benefit of Billy Bates who had been hit in the eye while at net practice in Melbourne and had missed most of the tour as a result. Considering this loss, and that of Lord Hawke, the team had done superbly well in trying circumstances. The professional venture also left in mid-March, but for New Zealand. It was the last speculative joint venture by Lillywhite, Shaw and Shrewsbury.

By far the most important event in Australian cricket thus far took place at the end of 1887. On 19 October 1887, Edward Heather, the secretary of the Victorian Cricketers' Association, wrote from his South Melbourne office to the secretaries of the Cricketing Associations of New South Wales, South Australia, Western Australia and Tasmania proposing that a conference be held in Melbourne just before Christmas to discuss the future of intercolonial matches.

The various associations met to discuss Heather's proposal and all of them gave it their support, although Tasmania was unable to send a delegate. The minutes of the conference read as follows:

REPORT OF CRICKET CONFERENCE

A meeting of delegates from the Cricket Associations of New South Wales, South Australia and Victoria, was held at the Oriental Hotel, Melbourne, on 21 December 1887.

The following delegates were present:
NEW SOUTH WALES – Messrs Allen, Beal and Sheridan
SOUTH AUSTRALIA – Messrs Creswell, Gunn and Leake
VICTORIA – Messrs Budd, Greig and Madden
Mr Budd was elected chairman.

Mr Sherlock, representative of the West Australian Association, applied that he might be admitted to take part in the conference.He was admitted.

The order of business and the matters to be discussed were arranged, and the meeting adjourned till next day, when there were present the whole of the delegates.

The various subjects were carefully considered, and the following resolutions were adopted and recommended for adoption by the several Associations represented.

1 – That the patronage of the Associations shall not be granted –

(a) To any English team visiting the colonies for three years after the season 1887–88;

(b) To any Australian team visiting England for four years from this date;

2 – That in all matches played under the patronage of any of the Associations, six balls be bowled to the over;

3 – That this conference is of the opinion that some alteration should be made in the laws of cricket with regard to leg before wicket, so that the bowler should get the benefit of his skill, and that the proper authorities in England be communicated with, with a view to carrying out this recommendation;

4 – That no player other than a professional shall be allowed a greater sum in compensation for loss of time than ten shillings per day;

5 – That each Association manage its own matters in connection with the luncheons;

6 – That each of the colonies of New South Wales, South Australia and Victoria meet the other two colonies in each season, one match to be played at home and one away.

NB – The New South Wales delegates did not vote on this recommendation.

The background to this conference was long and complicated, with South Australia the least affected. Victoria and NSW were suffering financial hardship due to their top players constantly touring with the privately run, self-styled 'Australian' teams. This meant that the associations could not field their best teams, and that consequently attendances – and therefore finances – were rapidly declining.

The 1888 Australian tour to England was promoted and managed by Charles Beal of Sydney, who had also managed the 1882 team. But Beal, who later became a very influential NSWCA member, failed to induce such players as Billy Bruce, George Giffen, Harry Moses, Fred Spofforth or Hugh Trumble to join his party. With Percy McDonnell as captain the new tourists were John Edwards, Jack Ferris, Jack Lyons, Harry Trott, Charlie Turner and John Worrall, with Sammy Woods replacing Sammy Jones on tour when he contracted smallpox.

A minor controversy arose in late March, before the team left Australia. Two former Test players, Billy Murdoch and Fred Spofforth, were going to live in England. However, during this period, there were stirrings in the colony of an indigenous nationalism. While a middle-class Melbourne cheered Spofforth's suggestion that he would regard it as an honour to play for England against Australia, the more radical paper, the *Bulletin*, commented sarcastically: 'Spofforth, the erstwhile demon bowler, having come in for money, leaves next month to take up residence in England.' Later the *Bulletin* added: 'If Turner keeps up his present form with bat and ball the Britishers will forget about Spofforth who at his best was only a one-part demon.'

The forty-match tour undertaken by the Sixth Australians of 1888 included three Test matches in a hectic schedule which lasted nearly five months. Having lost all three 'warm-up' matches before they sailed, the team was regarded as the weakest yet to leave home shores. However, after the Australians had won their first five games on tour, confidence in them rose so much that *Wisden* said: 'There can be no doubt that the team that sailed from Adelaide last March did not deserve a quarter of the bitter and contemptuous things said about them by newspapers of their own Colonies'.

The soft pitches prevalent during the summer were of benefit to the two main strike bowlers, Ferris and Turner, and the team achieved far better results than the 1886 side. In fact, the contrast was enhanced further by the fact that McDonnell repaired the damage caused by Scott's team and the relations with English players were most cordial both on and off the pitch.

But it was the two strike bowlers who caught the eye: Turner took a quite amazing 283 first-class wickets at 11.68 in 36 outings (in all matches 314 at 11.38) while Ferris claimed 199 wickets at 14.74 in one more game (in all 220 at 14.23).

The run-up to the first Test saw exactly half the programme completed, and with the weather poor all three Tests were completed in two days. For the Lord's Test the Australians brought in the English-based Sammy Woods, a colourful and versatile sportsman who hailed from Sydney.

Heavy overnight rain prevented the match from starting until mid-afternoon and, on winning the toss, McDonnell elected to bat. But Australia were bundled out for 116 in just on two hours. By stumps England were also struggling at 18 for three wickets which, next morning, turned into a debacle as Turner (5/27) and Ferris (3/19) shot them out for 53. Twenty-seven wickets fell that day: Australia replied with 60 after which England went only two runs better with Turner (5/36) and Ferris (5/26) devastating once again. The English papers were mortified. *Cricket* commented: 'The selection of the English eleven by the sub-committee of the Marylebone Club gave, it must be stated, anything but satisfaction'.

Then, a month later at The Oval, the England team was chosen by the home club's committee. They naturally went for five of their own Surrey players, while the Australians remained unchanged. The two days' play attracted 30,957 spectators who, from the outset, saw England on top when the local hero, George Lohmann, took two spectacular catches in the first hour to dismiss McDonnell and Bannerman. Australia never recovered, scoring 80 and 100 to lose by an innings and 137 runs. The next fortnight continued to be a nightmare for the tourists as they suffered three defeats and a draw before the final Test at Old Trafford.

Whatever the conditions – and they were poor – this was the shortest completed Test match, as in six hours and 34 minutes England claimed victory by an innings and 21 runs. Excuses could be made but the facts were there for all to see. New Australian blood was badly needed.

The Australians returned home, landing at Adelaide on 22 November. The following day they started what would turn out to be the only first-class match played by South Australia against an Australian team. With George Giffen in his usual devastating form the South Australians won by eight wickets, but the attendance over three days of just 1,971 spectators showed that the novelty of such fixtures had worn very thin. The profit was a mere 6s. 8d.

South Australia's only other fixture for the 1888–89 season was an away one against Victoria, but even George Giffen, with 135 and 19 as well as 6/82 and 7/77, could not stop his side being defeated, though only by 15 runs.

The Cricket Conference decision of December 1887 which agreed for each colony 'to meet the other . . . in each season, one match to be played at home and one away' had left the members of the Victorian Cricketers' Association in a quandary. They realised that they could not afford to stage two matches a season having, at the end of the previous financial year, assets of only £168. South Australia agreed to play only once but the New South Wales Cricket Association waited until the last possible moment before giving the VCA a reply to their request. Then, the NSWCA Secretary, Dave Gregory, wrote from Sydney refusing to delay the home and away series. As cables passed between Gregory and his Victorian counterpart, Edward Heather, the Melbourne Cricket Club just, by chance, happened to offer NSW a firm five-year contract to play matches under their own auspices each season.

Naturally, the Melbourne club said that they were approached by the NSWCA but the surviving records show this not to be the case. The Melbourne club's annual report for 1888–89 states: '. . . but before finally accepting this NSWCA proposal the MCC appealed to the Association of Victoria to reconsider their objections'. The VCA's response was to ban the Melbourne club from the Association on the grounds they were interfering in matters which had nothing to do with them.

A Victorian side then played Tasmania on the East Melbourne ground, winning by nine wickets in the final over of the match. After this the Melbourne club invited twelve players to play against NSW – against the wishes of the VCA – the following week. NSW was victorious by six wickets. The return fixture a fortnight later saw the Victorian team win by twelve runs. To rub salt into the wound the NSWCA invited some Victorian players to stay behind in Sydney to represent 'Combined New South Wales and Victoria' against 'The Sixth Australian Team'. The match was a farce from the start. Bruce and Horan could not spare the time to remain in Sydney for the game and, by the time the 'Combined' team started their second innings they had already lost Harry Donnan, Sam Morris and Syd Callaway who had to return to work. The innings closed at 38 to give the Australians victory by 214 runs.

Realising that maybe they had been goaded into doing something unwise the VCA then approached the Melbourne club with a view to lifting their ban and to take over the running of all intercolonial matches. The Melbourne CC, slightly gloating, recorded as follows:

> Shortly after the last meeting the Committee were approached by the VCA with a view to the latter resuming control of the intercolonial matches with New South Wales. The VCA volunteered to rescind the Resolution 'boycotting' this Club, and on that being done, our engagement with the NSWCA was transferred to the VCA by consent of all concerned.
>
> The Committee stipulated that the two matches played against New South Wales under the auspices of the MCC should be recognised by the Victorian Association as Intercolonial Matches, and these matches have accordingly been incorporated in the records of the Association.

The first news that an American team intended to visit Australia during the 1888–89 season came in Tom Horan's 'Cricket Chatter' column in the *Australasian* on 27 October 1888. Horan revealed that 'Mr A. G. Spalding intended the tour mainly to be an exhibition of baseball but some cricket would also be included.'

Spalding, the founder of the sports goods firm which bears his name, had been the leader of a baseball team which visited England in 1874 and also played six cricket matches. This 1888 team left San Francisco on 18 November for Auckland and during the long voyage shipboard life became tedious. Then, according to Harry Palmer's book of the tour *Athletic Sports*, 'the ship's captain had a cricket alley set up, with canvas roof and sides and a coconut matting wicket'. This enabled the party to keep fit with several hours of cricket practice a day. 'The party expected to play almost as much cricket as baseball,' Palmer added.

The Americans arrived in Sydney from New Zealand on 14 December and the following day played an exhibition baseball match on the Albert Ground with 'Chicago' playing 'All-America'. On Monday 17 December the two teams met again but this time at cricket. All-America (67) beat Chicago (33) by 34 runs, much to the disgust of George Anson, the Chicago captain. Throughout the trip Anson had been telling the baseballers what a good cricketer he was and they had listened with respect during his coaching sessions. His Chicago teammates had great expectations when Anson went in to bat, but they dissolved into laughter when he was caught first ball. Anson then retired to a far corner of the Albert Ground to practise with Clarence Duval, the tourists' negro 'mascot'.

The following morning came the big cricket match when 'An American Baseball XVII' played a combined Sydney eleven. The local team comprised four NSW players and seven top club representatives. The only two bowlers used by Sydney, Percie Charlton (an 1890 Australian tourist) and Arthur Gregory, eventually skittled the Americans for 87 with Anson scoring 15 and Fred Pfeffer 16. The Sydney side lost a quick wicket in reply and had reached 115 for six when the match ended. According to Palmer, 'the Australian fielding could not compare with that of the Americans, which elicited much applause'. He went on: 'It was said after the match that had the American bowling been half as strong as their fielding, they would have matched the Australians'.

Next day the Americans left for Melbourne and on Saturday 22 December, in front of 7000 spectators, played a baseball match on the Melbourne Cricket Ground with several local club cricketers mixed in with the Americans. The Melbourne CC report on the match said that the Americans 'gave some perfect exhibitions of the game', but concluded: 'In the opinion of the Committee, the game is one that will recommend itself to members, while in no way deteriorating [*sic*] from the excellence of the exponents of cricket'. Albert Spalding's tourists played a final exhibition baseball match on 5 January 1889 prior to their departure for Ceylon and Egypt. However, they did leave one record behind when the American, Ed Crane, beat the then Australian record of 126 yards and 3 inches for throwing the cricket ball. He threw 128 yards, 10½ inches.

During the late 1880s and early 1890s the various football codes were declining in popularity around Australia much more than was cricket. The reasons were fairly easily seen in that cricket was not only more popular but the people who played and supported it were primarily drawn from members of the public who were least affected by the economic climate; whereas among the working classes, for whom the football codes were far more popular, the depression was having a longer-lasting effect.

Melbourne, by now accepted as Australia's financial heart, was particularly badly hit by the depression. In 1889 two large companies became insolvent and several big land speculators were found guilty of fraudulent practices amounting to more than £1 million. Strikes paralysed the city and dislocated trade and commerce. A mass rally of 60,000 workers scared the government who held the military ready to deal with expected riots. Wool and wheat prices slumped, land became unsaleable and banks closed their doors. Severe unemployment hit Sydney and Melbourne in particular.

The first match of the 1889–90 season was controversial to say the least. The Victorian team, captained by Jack Blackham and managed by the former Richmond under-arm bowler Robert Greig, arrived in Adelaide on 12 December 1889 and in the evening enjoyed the hospitality of Mayor Lewis Cohen at the Town Hall. Next day they batted first against South Australia scoring 278 for seven by stumps. The second day, Saturday, having been dismissed for 320 (Reedman 5/50), Victoria captured the first home wicket with only 17 runs on the board.

The South Australian captain, George Giffen, joined Jack Lyons and, as Giffen wrote later in *With Bat and Ball*:

> The contest is one in connection with which appears a black mark against me on the records. It was the occasion on which, when I had made nine, I refused to obey the Victorian umpire's adverse decision of 'hit-wicket'. Our own umpire had declined an appeal for leg-before against me. In making the stroke I slipped down, and while in the act of rising again, was said to have knocked the wicket with my foot, and a bail fell off. The cover fieldsman appealed and Mr Flynn of Victoria gave me out. However, I knew I had not touched the wicket and moreover, had got into my head the idea that the ball was dead and that a second appeal could not be made, so I declined to leave the crease. The upshot of it was that Jack Blackham agreed to play on under protest and I scored 85 before being bowled by Hugh Trumble. Of course, afterwards I realised I had acted wrongly and I was not sorry when our last wicket fell at the end of the match with the Victorians 18 runs to the good.

Although George Giffen wrote those words some years after the event, at the time he was in no mood for reflection. The South

Australian Cricketing Association committee meeting of 7 January 1890 records that a letter dated 14 December 1889 (the second day of the match), signed by Messrs Greig and Blackham, was handed to the SACA secretary, John Creswell. It contained an official protest 'regarding the late match and one of the South Australian side who would not go out when given out by an umpire'.

The letter added that: 'a case has been stated to the Marylebone Cricket Club, London, and forwarded by us to them'. The committee were not going to be bullied and Creswell was instructed to write to Edward Heather, secretary of the VCA, asking if there was any truth in this claim, and if so, what right had a colonial captain and manager to do this without their Association's approval.

The Norwood Club delegates, Will Whitridge and George Giffen, then proposed and seconded a motion officially informing the VCA that, owing to the unsatisfactory umpiring of Mr Flynn, the SACA would suggest that in future each Association submit a list of umpires' names for approval.

Heather replied on 15 January 1890 to say that the VCA were not going to contact the Marylebone Cricket Club, and that current arrangements regarding umpires were satisfactory. The first statement was not quite correct for, although George Giffen's actions had been widely debated in the Melbourne press and at the 12 January VCA committee meeting (when his ears would have been burning at the condemnation), the Victorians had *privately* sent letters to the Marylebone Cricket Club, and to Dr W. G. Grace.

The SACA committee were beside themselves with anger. They unanimously agreed to tell the Victorians that intercolonial matches would be suspended pending an agreement on umpires, and that Creswell and Giffen would write jointly to London explaining the South Australian side of the case. Heather replied on 12 February saying: 'Your letter regarding the future appointment of umpires was read at our 9 February meeting and received'.

Nothing more was heard from the VCA until Creswell received a letter nearly eight months later from Edward Heather suggesting dates for the next match. The committee replied that the game would only take place if the umpiring issue was resolved.

The VCA committee met on 11 November at the Mechanics Institute, South Melbourne, and unanimously passed the following resolution: 'That a reply be sent to the SACA stating that whilst the VCA are anxious to play the match, they are unwilling to do so subject to the contingencies contained in the SACA secretary's letter of 15 October, and also Rule 18 of the VCA rules states that the appointment of the umpire is left to the selection committee'.

The SACA committee discussed this resolution on 18 November at considerable length, but it was agreed only to note, 'that the letter be received'.

By now George Giffen had realised that his behaviour, and loyal backing by the Association, could be the cause of a disruption in matches against Victoria. He asked his fellow Norwood delegate, Will Whitridge, to give notice of a motion which would reopen discussions with Melbourne. Whitridge duly wrote to Creswell on 24 November and the motion was presented at the next day's committee meeting – and deferred.

On 2 December the motion was brought on, and read:

> That all previous resolutions regarding the appointment of umpires in matches with Victoria be rescinded; and that this Association (while still believing that it is desirable to exchange the names of umpires prior to any intercolonial match) rather than be the cause of any stoppage to the matches, desires to withdraw its letters referring to this match; and that this Association will be prepared to send a team to Victoria as suggested by the VCA. [The motion was lost.]

Four days later a special SACA committee meeting was called, with all delegates present (for the first time in fourteen months), on a request signed by Messrs Whitridge and Giffen (Norwood); Ballans and Maddern (South Adelaide) and Gunn (Adelaide) and a petition of members which contained over eighty signatures. Whitridge proposed a slightly amended motion which was carried, and Creswell was told to send it to the VCA at once but 'without any remarks'.

The VCA was patronising, but the match went ahead without trouble. In fact, the South Australians were given a special 'smoke night'. by the VCA president, Robert Best, and George Giffen won the five guineas vice-president award for the best player of the match. It was hardly a surprising gift as Giffen had scored 237, and taken 5/89 and 7/103, as South Australia won by an innings and 62 runs. As the 1890–91 VCA Annual Report stated: 'It is evident that South Australia evokes the same amount of interest as do the contests with NSW, owing mainly to the superb batting power of players such as Giffen'.

Australian cricket was now in a void, described by Tom Horan in the *Australasian* as 'a period of decadence'. Crowds had slumped due to lack of interest, too many tours by English teams, and the prevailing economic climate; and as Victoria were defeating NSW by eight wickets, just after Christmas 1889, nearly ten per cent of the population was out of work. The slump of 1888–91 was nearly as serious economically as the Depression of the 1930s.

The beginning of 1889 had seen the start of what is now known as Tasmania's 'modern era', with a match on the East Melbourne ground which Victoria won by nine wickets. Tasmania's best performance came from Claude Rock, a Cambridge Blue who also appeared for Warwickshire in its pre-first-class days. His 102 in a second innings of 195 at least made the match respectable.

The return match, played on the Domain in Hobart starting on 8 January 1890, was an unmitigated disaster for the local team, who were crushed by an innings and 147 runs. They had only themselves to blame. Victoria scored quickly on the first day, making 338, and then had time to dispose of two Tasmanians for 30 that evening. The next morning, two Tasmanian batsmen, Charles McAllen and George Vautin, sauntered up to the ground just after midday, not expecting to have to bat until much later. This was unpardonable enough, but McAllen was also Tasmania's captain. Of course, the unthinkable had happened. With play commencing at 11.20 am (appointed hours of play in those times, in Tasmania at least, were considered a great nuisance), Tasmania by noon had subsided to 39 for seven, with William Sidebottom unable to bat because of an injury. Harry Trott, 1/6 overnight, suddenly had 5/6, then conceded a boundary, and finished the innings with an analysis of 5.4-3-10-6. With McAllen and Vautin still not present, Tasmania was forced to close its first innings at 39. History does not record what was said in the Tasmanian dressing-room that afternoon, but in the follow-on, Vautin batted at number eight (Sidebottom was still unable to bat) and McAllen, batting last, was given out lbw for 0, to complete for him and his side a most miserable match.

McAllen kept his place in the side, however, for the next game against Victoria, at Melbourne in March 1891, although he was replaced as captain. Again, the match did not go well for the Tasmanians, who had to admit defeat by nine wickets, but it did have a special significance for it marked the debut of two cricketers who were to represent the island with distinction for many years: Charles Eady and Edward Windsor.

Following their disagreement and subsequent rapprochement with Victoria, the New South Wales Cricket Association met in November 1889 to discuss whether they should now play against South Australia. It was felt to be a time to expand and the decision was made: invite South Australia to play home and away, and also send a team to New Zealand.

On 12 November the NSWCA secretary, Dave Gregory, wrote to the SACA secretary, John Creswell, asking what terms SACA would give for a NSW team to visit. Creswell replied: 'the same terms as we play Victoria'. Gregory wrote again on 3 December agreeing to the terms as long as the first match was played in Sydney. The South Australians agreed, and the date was set for 14 February 1890.

Before the visit SACA had a problem when their selector, Will Whitridge, was faced with a players' revolt over 'loss of time payments'. Wally Giffen, as ever in the forefront of such matters, pushed their case so hard that the SACA committee overruled their selector who had refused to countenance the matter. Giffen got his money and so did other members of the team but on the field of play they lost the initial encounter with NSW by nine wickets. It was not an easy match for them as they were up against the likes of Murdoch, Bannerman, Moses, Jones, Garrett, Gregory, Donnan, Ferris and Charlton. The trip was also expensive – they lost £234 while NSW made a profit of £170.

The other NSW team, under the captaincy of Coleman Davis, sailed from Sydney in mid-January to play the first of their seven matches in Auckland. The side had only one Australian representative, the fast bowler Syd Callaway who later settled in Canterbury and played for New Zealand. Another of the tourists, Alfred Clarke, would also play for Otago, Wellington and New Zealand.

Only the first match was drawn, and NSW won the final six; but an incident took place in Wellington at the Basin Reserve where the home captain, Billy McGirr, requested that the umpire supplied by the visitors be replaced after several dubious decisions had gone against his team.

Initially Davis refused to withdraw his umpire (who was his father) but changed his mind when the Wellington Cricket Association president, William Levin, explained that, if the game was abandoned, the WCA would be under no obligation to pay NSW the guaranteed gate money.

Back in Australia the press were often scornful in their treatment of both players and officials. When Billy Murdoch returned home for a visit after two years in England he was given a quite amazing roasting, with the *Bulletin* leading the way. George Bonnor escaped the critics' wrath on his return after three years' absence even though his boasting caused him to be somewhat of a figure of fun. At thirty-five, and eighteen stone in weight, Bonnor could still be a big hitter. In April 1890, playing in the Blue Mountains for Bathurst, he scored an unbeaten 297 in a club match, against Oriental, out of a total of 423.

A group of senior players had decided to tour England during 1890. They agreed that the sole selector and manager should be Harry Boyle, and he named his side in early March. George Giffen and Harry Moses declined to tour, and on 7 March, Alick Bannerman and George Bonnor withdrew.

The team needed a reserve wicketkeeper to Blackham, and the New South Wales contingent all plumped for Sidney Deane, the current NSW 'keeper who was twenty-four. The Victorians preferred Jack Harry, who was thirty-two and an occasional player for East Melbourne. Faced with an impasse Jack Blackham said he had heard of a Tasmanian called Burn who was keeping wicket very efficiently. So Ken Burn, the East Hobart batsman, was called up to join the team. On boarding the tourists' ship in Adelaide it was discovered that Burn had never kept wicket in his life. Blackham had mistaken him for James Burn, a Hobart club player.

Apart from Ken Burn, who was to play at first-class level until 1910, the other new members of the team were: John Barrett (Victoria) and Percie Charlton (NSW) who both saw the trip as a chance to further their medical studies; Syd Gregory (NSW), the son of the Sydney Cricket Ground's curator and part of the famous cricketing family; Hugh Trumble (Victoria) brother of John, the 1886 tourist; and Francis Walters (Victoria). The rest were Billy Murdoch (captain), Blackham, Ferris, Jones, Lyons, Trott and Turner.

Murdoch and his wife left Australia some weeks before the rest of the team and so avoided reading the savage newspaper criticism which greeted the 'selection' of Burn. As Australia entered the 1890s wild and intemperate reporting seemed to become the norm. At the same time the players were picking their own teams and selecting their own captains, with the tours just being money-making exercises: the 1890 tour was no exception.

Likewise, the colonial associations were going their own way. Sydney and Melbourne, in the guise of the NSWCA and VCA, were constantly bickering as were their own delegates whose committee-room infighting set trends which still exist a hundred years later. Witness the NSWCA upheavals of 1888 and those of 1988.

The 1890s brought in also the continuation of noisy, vulgar, uninhibited spectators, particularly in Sydney where more of a ruffian class seemed to frequent matches. Again, this type of action, so far from going away, was to continue in various forms up to the present time. Barracking, now part of Australian folklore, is considered by some to be a sub-cultural element of antipodean society. Little had really changed from the Lord Harris riot of 1879, although by 1979 there were more policemen available to evict troublemakers from the various grounds around the country.

The mistaken selection of Ken Burn served, oddly enough, as a catalyst for change. Questions were asked. How could such an error take place? Why were overseas tours not controlled by governing bodies? The shadows which had clouded Australian thinking in the 1870s had by now disappeared and in the 1890s a cricketing nationalism was growing that was self-confident, balanced and truly national. The colonial associations were beginning to think towards some form of Australian cricket council.

Tom Horan summed up the position of the 1890 tour in his 'Cricket Chatter' column in the *Australasian*:

> Some time back a home paper in a pleasant cricket sketch dubbed our men 'swallow cricketers' because they had a knack of turning up regularly in England with the swallows in spring. It can hardly be said that the designation is inappropriate, for ever since the first team left these shores under Gregory and Conway in 1878, our men have made a biennial flight to England, and, like the swallows in their annual flight, have invariably arrived in time to see the old land in the prime of its verdant beauty. It was thought when the last team returned that our cricketers would no longer follow the habits of the happy birds that change their sky and 'live their lives from land to land', but recent announcements show that the old biennial migration is to be maintained, and that the 1890 exodus will be under the management of the veteran 'swallow cricketer' H. F. Boyle. It will be the first time that he has winged his way home as manager and I heartily wish him success.

The team, which arrived in England on 26 April to start a 39-match tour that would finish in late September, was the first Australian side to lose more matches than they won. Of their 34 first-class fixtures, sixteen were lost and only ten won. At the outset the newcomers had little chance to settle in on unprotected batting strips, and Billy Murdoch lacked his former agility. Then came a series of injuries: Jones was a virtual passenger, and Murdoch, Ferris, Barrett and Trott were indisposed at various times. Sammy Woods – as in 1888 – was invited to join the side but this time he declined, so the assistant manager, Roly Pope, made up the number in three first-class games.

Twenty-one games passed, including a black June without a single win, before the first Test took place at Lord's in front of a packed house. Jack Lyons, opening the batting with Charlie Turner, took only thirty-six minutes to reach his fifty and set a record for fast scoring in Tests. But Australia were still dismissed for 132. However, Lyons showed his ability as a bowler too, taking 5/30 from 20 overs as England gained a first-innings lead of 41 runs.

Dr Barrett opened with Turner in the second innings and proceeded to carry his bat for 67, a remarkable feat on his Test debut. Australia fell for 176 and England easily won by seven wickets thanks to an unbeaten 75 by their captain W. G. Grace. It was also the first time that no byes were conceded in a Test.

The Australians were now finding that, as the county championship was being better organised than before, crowds were watching those fixtures rather than following the tourists. The players themselves were also accepting this trend: Andrew Stoddart preferred to play for Middlesex against Yorkshire – who in turn refused to release Peel and Ulyett – rather than take part in the second Test at The Oval.

England won this match in less than two days on a rain-affected pitch. Such a poor Australian performance was a sorry end to Murdoch's career for Australia in Test cricket, as the scheduled third Test at Old Trafford was abandoned without a ball being bowled. At the end of the tour Murdoch elected to return to England and join Sussex, subsequently confounding his critics who said he was 'over the hill'. In seven seasons for the county he played 137 matches, being captain in most of them. Ferris also went on to play county cricket with Gloucestershire, and both Australians later (1891–92) played for England in a Test match against South Africa at Cape Town.

The tour had seen Ferris (186 wickets) and Turner (179) totally dominate the bowling attack while Murdoch (1394 runs), Barrett (1226), Trott (1211) and Lyons (1029) led the batting.

Plans to tour South Africa following the tour of England fell through as did a visit to India. As it was, a match was played in Ceylon on an eleven-a-side basis. The 1884 Australians had easily defeated an Eighteen side but the progress of the game on the island was revealed by the 1890 Australians only drawing a game after gaining a 92-run lead on first innings. Harry Trott scored 52 and Syd Gregory 41 with Tom Kelaart taking 3/42 for Ceylon. The tourists arrived back home on 11 November 1890, just in time to start a new season of inter-colonial matches.

In 1890–91 five first-class matches were played, with Victoria involved in four. In the first match, in Adelaide, Jack Ferris took 8/84 and 6/108 as NSW beat South Australia by six wickets. Victoria defeated NSW and Tasmania in low-scoring games, while NSW turned the tables in Sydney by defeating Victoria by an innings. The top game of the season started on New Year's Day in Melbourne when George Giffen had yet another of his amazing performances. He scored 237 out of 407 runs scored while he was at the crease, then took 5/89 and 7/103 as South Australia won by an innings and 62 runs.

Although Jack Lyons had taken over Bonnor's mantle as the most powerful hitter in Australia, his 104 in November 1891 for South Australia against Victoria in Adelaide was dwarfed by Giffen. In what is now acclaimed as one of the finest-ever all-round performances in the game, Giffen scored 271 in seven hours then proceeded to take 9/96 and 7/70 as South Australia won by an innings and 164 runs.

W. G. Grace, who was watching, was impressed enough to say: 'In Mr Giffen, South Australia has the best man in Australia, and one of the best all-round men in the world'.

The reason for Grace being in Adelaide had originated towards the end of the Australians' 1890 tour when Henry Holroyd, the third Earl of Sheffield and president of the Sussex County Cricket Club, had discussed with Harry Boyle the possibility of taking an England team to Australia. After Boyle returned home he and Sheffield corresponded, while Boyle took soundings on the potential success of such a venture. Sheffield was assured that he would be well received, but he was urged by Boyle 'to bring W. G. Grace to ensure the success of the tour'.

Lord Sheffield then invited Grace to lead a team. The England captain was forty-three and weighed nearly eighteen stone. A tour by a man of his age and size, especially after a heavy county season, would be a major undertaking. Grace initially refused but Sheffield agreed to the financial terms put to him and an understanding was reached.

Sheffield then made contact with Ben Wardill, secretary of the Melbourne Cricket Club, who had been let in on the plans. They felt it wise initially to appoint an Australian agent, so Wardill saw Frank Illingworth, the former secretary of the East Melbourne Cricket Club who worked for Harry Boyle's firm, Boyle & Scott.

By arrangement, a story appeared in the London press on 8 February 1891, and was reprinted two days later in the Melbourne *Argus*. It read: 'A scheme has been put forward under the auspices of the Earl of Sheffield to take a team of English cricketers to Australia. The arrangements for carrying out this project are making favourable progress.'

The NSWCA and SACA responded at once to Illingworth's request for patronage, with the VCA following some time later. The Victorians, still harbouring nightmares over the 1887–88 fiasco, were not initially convinced of Lord Sheffield's financial support, but planning went ahead and, as soon as it was known that Grace was coming, the Australian newspapers became jingoistic at the thought of the great man playing once again on colonial soil.

Ever the diplomat Sheffield, in a letter published in the Melbourne *Leader*, wrote:

> I have long awaited to see your country and your cricket, and as I was compelled by my failing health to decide upon taking a long sea voyage and spending a winter away from England, it occurred to me that if it was convenient to you in Australia to see us, I could combine a voyage for health with a visit of English cricketers . . . I was very much afraid you might find that a visit of English cricketers

> would do much to dislocate local cricket, but the Australian clubs have most generously waived all objections, for which I am deeply grateful and which I warmly appreciate.

The tour, which was the subject of much talk, in a way provided a diversion from the depression which was affecting most of the continent. Collapsing financial institutions and an inability to raise funds in London saw the country in a very poor economic condition. Lord Sheffield's tour, however, certainly proved a crowd-puller, and the Test matches attracted 64,000 in Melbourne, 53,000 at Sydney and 28,000 at Adelaide.

The England team left London's Albert Dock on 2 October and arrived at Port Adelaide at noon on 9 November: the journey was becoming faster as the steamships improved. The South Australian cricket fraternity was out in force and His Lordship gave them an effective opening speech. The team then went straight to the Adelaide Oval for lunch and there they saw Giffen's great innings.

Ben Wardill arrived in Adelaide two days later to link up with the manager of the visiting Victorian team, William Ryall, another Melbourne club man. Wardill, still secretary of Melbourne CC, had taken over from Illingworth as the English team's agent and Ryall had been acting *pro tem* since the tourists' arrival in Adelaide.

On Wednesday 18 November 1891, the SACA chairman, Yorke Sparks, and secretary, John Creswell, took Lord Sheffield to lunch at the colony's most prestigious gentleman's establishment, The Adelaide Club. They raised with their guest matters concerning a return fixture between the colony and the tourists, and also details of the Test match to be played in late March.

Lord Sheffield, according to the detailed notes made by Creswell and preserved in the archives of the State Library of South Australia, spoke warmly of the standard of play in the recent intercolonial match and of how the colonies should forge closer links. He intimated that the British government would like to see the colonies federate and how, from a trading point of view, it would be easier to deal with one government than with six colonial administrations.

Sheffield went on to argue that sport and trade (politics?) were inexorably mixed, which was why it was felt that, as cricket was the seemingly national game on the new continent, then a tournament of some kind to bind them closer still would be worthy of consideration. Unknown to his hosts, Sheffield had already spoken on these lines to Major Wardill who, two days later on his return to Melbourne, sent a lengthy letter to the new NSWCA secretary, John Portus, successor to Dave Gregory.

Wardill told Portus to 'do all possible in your power to give a warm welcome to Lord Sheffield and his party', and he concluded with: 'Lord Sheffield asked me if the Associations would accept a trophy . . . for competition by the three colonies in any way agreed upon by them'. This letter leaves no doubt that Lord Sheffield gave the first notice of his intention to donate funds, for what is now the Sheffield Shield, during his initial stay in Adelaide.

Another matter of considerable importance was running parallel with the England tour. This started on 6 November 1891 when, at a meeting of the New South Wales Cricket Association, the subject was raised yet again of an Australian Cricket body. The issue had been debated for the previous thirty-five years, and had last been seriously raised two years earlier. Then, at a dinner at Clements Café in Melbourne, the visiting Tasmanian manager, George Davies, had put forward the idea of a federal cricket council. 'There was,' the *Argus* then reported, 'cordial approval of the suggestion.'

Nothing came of it, however, until Dave Gregory, in one of his last acts as NSWCA secretary, wrote on 10 November to all his colonial counterparts putting forward the following resolution:

> That it is desirable that a sub-committee of three be appointed to consider as to the propriety of an Australian Cricket Council being formed for the purpose of dealing with the matter of Australian Elevens visiting elsewhere, or of Elevens visiting the colonies.

The Victorians and South Australians agreed almost by return, but the Tasmanians felt that their cricket was too weak to join such a venture. With Queensland and Western Australia expected to join 'at a later date', it was left to the three main colonies to arrange for the creation of a new ruling body. Correspondence flowed between the three for the next sixteen months. Then, on 13 March 1891, the NSWCA sent out proposed recommendations of which the VCA reported: 'After full consideration of this proposal by a special committee, your Association unanimously decided to co-operate in the creation of such a body'. SACA concurred.

The playing season of 1891–92 started well. Following Giffen's performance against Victoria, the Englishmen found themselves up against his bowling at Adelaide when he took 7/152 from 41 overs. But Lord Sheffield's team still won their opening match by an innings and 62 runs in front of 16,349 spectators. His Lordship was handed a cheque for £272 as his share of the profits.

During the match Lord Sheffield was approached by Creswell acting as an emissary for Frederick North, secretary of the Western

Australian Cricketing Association. North was prepared to offer £150 for the tourists to play a match in Perth on their way home. Sheffield did not consider the money enough and declined.

The England team moved on to Melbourne for an innings victory over a demoralised Victorian team. Grace carried his bat for 159 which included a six and ten fours while Sharpe, Attewell and Lohmann took the wickets for the tourists. New South Wales put up slightly more resistance with Charlie Turner taking 6/45 and 5/77 as his side lost by four wickets. Six country matches then followed before the New Year Test on the Melbourne ground which had just seen a revived Victoria defeat NSW.

New Year's Day 1892 saw the introduction of six-ball overs into Test cricket and the Australian debuts of the all-rounder, Syd Callaway, and batsman Harry Donnan of NSW, and of the Victorian all-rounder Robert McLeod. W. G. Grace captained England on his Test debut in Australia and lost the toss. In a game of average scoring, no player stood out as Australia won by 54 runs in front of 61,000 spectators over the four days. Their patience was rewarded following Alick Bannerman's two stone-walling innings of 45 (in 195 minutes) and 41 (241 minutes).

As England played six further country matches, South Australia were claiming the unofficial title of intercolonial champions with an innings and 53 runs victory over NSW in Sydney. Jack Lyons scored 145 and George Giffen 120, their second-wicket stand of 234 taking just 170 minutes against a Test attack of Turner (4/132) and Callaway (6/95). As NSW collapsed, Giffen the bowler again came to the fore with 7/122 and 5/28. It was because of this match, beyond all else, that South Australia was recognised as a cricket power equal to NSW and Victoria. As this victory brought home to the NSWCA that there was life over the Great Dividing Range, the important conference shortly to be held on cricket unification would be not only equally represented but would have equally balanced voting. Two weeks later Victoria played in Sydney and won by an innings.

The second Test was one of the best yet played in the colonies. Australia fell for 145 to the brilliance of George Lohmann (8/58). England replied with 307 in which Robert Abel carried his bat for 132. His 325-minute innings contained eleven fours and was the first time ever that an English player had batted throughout an innings. The Australians' second innings was in trouble before it started with Harry Moses unable to bat. Trott then fell for a single after which Alick Bannerman and Jack Lyons set about restoring Australia's pride. Two wickets fell on the third day with Lyons scoring 134 in 165 minutes with sixteen fours. Giffen (49) assisted Bannerman who finally fell on the fourth day for 91 made in 448 minutes. So defensive was the NSW opener that, of the 204 balls delivered to him by Attewell, only five produced runs.

McLeod jumped up the batting order and, on his dismissal, rushed home to Melbourne having learned of the death of his brother. Billy Bruce (72) held the tail together as the total reached 391. The 10,000 crowd then went home in high excitement as, in the twenty minutes of play remaining, England lost three wickets for just eleven runs, including Grace who was superbly caught behind by the new Australian captain, Jack Blackham.

Only 'Drewy' Stoddart (69) held up the inevitable on the final day as George Giffen (6/72) and Charlie Turner (4/46) saw Australia to victory by 72 runs. There had been problems over a runner for Moses – which did not eventuate – and also a substitute fielder for McLeod. Eric Hutton, a young Victorian University student who was in Sydney, was lined up to field. Grace was reported to have asked Blackham, 'Is he a better field than McLeod?' Blackham replied (yes), to which Grace retorted, 'Then get someone else'. Harry Donnan became the second substitute fieldsman.

Grace's refusal to allow a substitute for Moses early in the game annoyed the crowds and he was subject to a considerable amount of heckling and barracking during the match. Some sections of the press were determined to embarrass him. This letter, purporting to come from the pen of Grace, appeared in the *Daily Telegraph*:

> I must admit that our gentleman players had a very scrubby fag end, but after all, we pulled through respectably, and I have the money, which is the only thing I wanted, for to tell you the truth, I care so little for colonial opinion that you may publish this letter if you like, it will show the cads what I think of them. A good deal was said about my stopping away from the lunch at various places. My reason was that I didn't want to fraternise with the tinkers, tailors and snobs who are the great guns of your cricket world. To take their money was a fair thing in return for work done, but to hobnob with a lot of scum was a far different thing. Fancy the chance of a greasy butcher on his travels walking up to me one day at Lord's with 'How d'ye do, Mr G.; I lunched with you in Australia'. My dear fellow, as far as I can see, colonial society is low, shockingly low. You have plenty of money, no doubt, but your gentlemen are yet unborn. I suppose, including yourself, I met about three during the whole of my trip.

This letter had been concocted, apparently as a 'joke', by Richard Egan Lee, on Grace's departure from Australia in 1874. Its author had since died, but Grace was not pleased to see it reprinted and insisted that an emphatic denial was published in the *Daily Telegraph* the day after the second Test finished on 4 February 1892. The tourists then went off for four minor fixtures, victory over NSW and a couple of matches in Tasmania before easily defeating Victoria.

Grace and his team also had to bear the consequences of some of the then current English attitudes to Australian cricket that filtered back to the colonies. A NSW official, Victor Cohen, was preparing to organise another tour of England in 1893, but was meeting with stern opposition in England, especially from Lord Hawke, who disliked the disruption to the county programme. At a meeting in London on 11 December 1891 Hawke said: 'I do not think that there is any chance of a representative team strong enough to meet the leading counties coming in 1893. The matches of the present team in Australia show that they are nothing like powerful enough to send a really good team to England. The whole thing is a money-making business from start to finish.'

These comments were made before Australia won the first two Test matches, and the editor of the *Sportsman* in London prophesied the fate of Lord Hawke's comments with unerring accuracy when he wrote, 'It is, however, a trifle early for Lord Hawke's remarks about our cricketers proving too strong for the colonials on their own soil, and if the complexion of affairs is altered before Lord Sheffield's team returns home, an unfortunate lever will be provided which may turn the laugh against us.'

To make matters worse *Blackwood's*, the well-known magazine published in Edinburgh, took a shot at Australian cricket in its January 1892 edition. It called into question the manners of the Australians on the field, their motives in touring England, the extent to which betting influenced Australian cricket, and concluded with the claim that the highest classes of Australian society had shed their connections with cricket. This was too much for Lord Sheffield, and he published a statement that neither he nor his team concurred with the views that appeared in the magazine.

As the build-up to the final Test in Adelaide took place, so did the realisation of many dreams. The meeting to form a national cricket body was set down for Friday 25 March 1892 although the idea still had its sceptics. Major Wardill, writing to the new NSWCA secretary John Portus, said: 'You see the VCA appointed five delegates – nice trip for them! – and for yours also, but I think that is all that will eventuate from the Cricket Conference.'

Wardill had actually written to Portus on another matter, namely the finances of the tour. Originally the England team's expenses were estimated at £11,000 but they finished at £16,000 with receipts failing to cover costs by some £2,700. Lord Sheffield considered this to be a fair price to pay although it did take Wardill some time to elicit from His Lordship the £150 promised for the making of a cricket trophy.

Before the third Test, W. G. Grace was up to all sorts of schemes. He boycotted an official function; he complained about the preparation of the pitch; he tried to have the long end of the ground roped off and even refused to let Jack Blackham toss with his so-called 'lucky penny'. As it was, Grace won the toss, batted first, saw Stoddart score 134 in 230 minutes with three chances going to ground, before torrential rain ended play on the second day at tea-time with England 490 for nine.

The (uncovered) pitch was so ruined that, in reply to England's 499, Australia could only score 100 and 169, with Johnny Briggs claiming 6/49 and 6/87. It was England's biggest margin of victory in a Test and meant that they finished the tour on a high note.

The effect of this tour on Australian cricket 'was dramatic', according to the *Australasian* who said 'it was like an electric current'. Tom Horan, in his article 'The International Match' published in the same paper on 9 January 1892 wrote:

> Those who were under the impression that the visit of Lord Sheffield's team would not be beneficial to Australian cricket have changed their minds, and it is now the concurrent testimony of all that the visit has caused a cricket revival which has surpassed even the most sanguine anticipations of those who viewed the tour favourably when it was first proposed.

The nationalistic idea was certainly gaining ground. Talk amongst politicians was turning to federalism and to 'one Australia'. Cricket made its first tentative steps along these lines on the evening of 21 March 1892 when the fifteen delegates to the Cricket Conference met socially at Adelaide's Prince Alfred Hotel. They were:

| | | |
|---|---|---|
| South Australia | John Creswell | (SACA Secretary) |
| | Mostyn Evan | (Lawyer and SACA Chairman) |
| | George Giffen | (Current Test cricketer) |
| | Yorke Sparks | (Stock agent and SACA Trustee) |
| | Will Whitridge | (Journalist and current Test umpire) |
| Victoria | William Bruce | (Lawyer and current Test cricketer) |
| | Harry Budd | (VCA delegate) |
| | Robert Greig | (VCA delegate) |

| | | |
|---|---|---|
| | David Maddern | (VCA Vice-President) |
| | Samuel Row | (Accountant and VCA delegate) |
| New South Wales | Victor Cohen | (NSWCA Treasurer) |
| | John Gibson | (Former NSWCA Secretary) |
| | John Portus | (NSWCA Secretary) |
| | George Reid | (NSWCA President) |
| | Richard Teece | (NSWCA Vice-President) |

The serious side of business took place at 8 pm on Friday 25 March 1892 in the Exchange Room of the Adelaide Town Hall. There the fifteen representatives thrashed out a formula by which they agreed to form *The Australasian Cricket Council.* Chaired by Yorke Sparks, the meeting looked to having Queensland and Tasmania join in due course, and by the very name of the Council was hoping to be able to include New Zealand as well.

When discussing the objects of the Council, the SACA delegates pushed hard for the inclusion of a rule dealing with the regular playing of intercolonial matches; but they were outvoted by Victoria and NSW who were no doubt mindful of their own recent dispute on such matters.

The aims finally agreed were:

(a) The regulation of visits of English or other teams.
(b) The regulation of visits of Australasian teams to England or elsewhere, in conjunction with the governing cricket bodies of the places visited.
(c) The settlement of all disputes or differences between Associations represented on the Council.
(d) The appointment of umpires for international or intercolonial matches played in Australasia.
(e) The alteration or amendment of, or the addition to, the Laws of Cricket in Australasia.

The delegates decided to take the aims of the Council back to their respective Associations (all of whom gave ready acceptance), and to meet again in Sydney in September.

During April 1892 Wardill and Portus agreed that the money donated by Lord Sheffield for his trophy should reside with the new Council for them to take the appropriate action.

The three Associations met before the next meeting to thrash out their policies towards the various motions. New South Wales and South Australia were firmly for an intercolonial trophy but

*(Above)* The old Albert ground in Sydney: one of the few photographs of a big single-wicket match in progress: 12 of New South Wales v. 7 of England, on 27 January 1874. *(Australian Cricket: A History)*

*(Below)* Twenty-two of South Australia play W.G. Grace's team at Adelaide Oval, 26 March 1874.

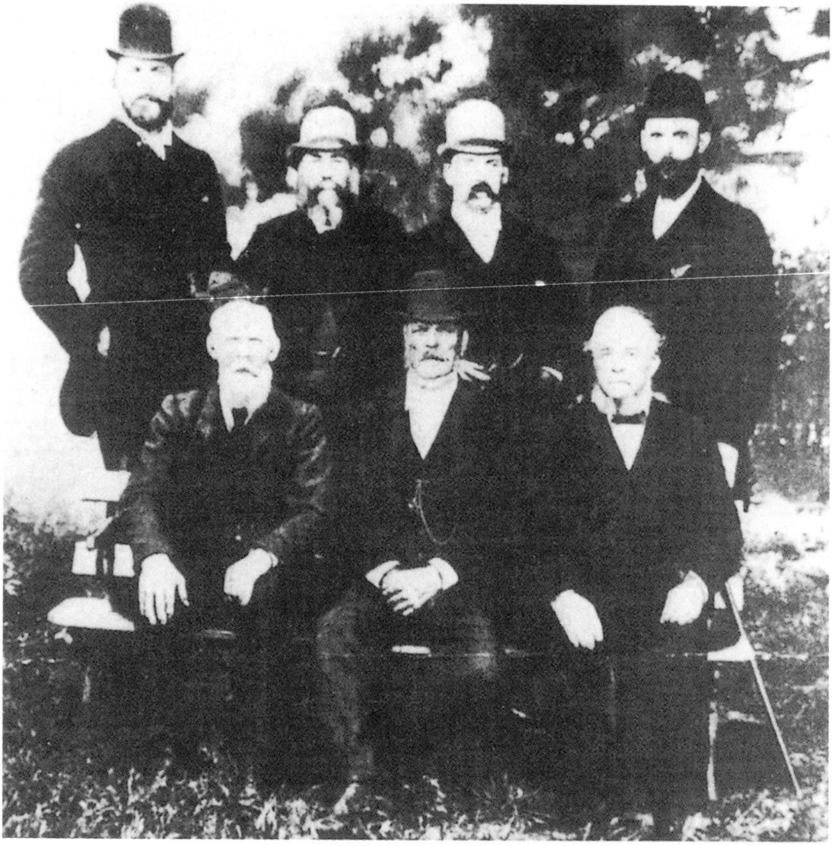

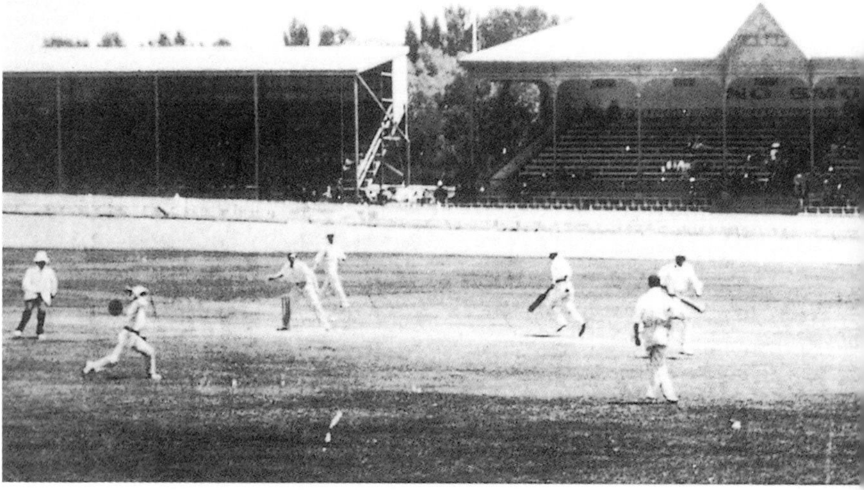

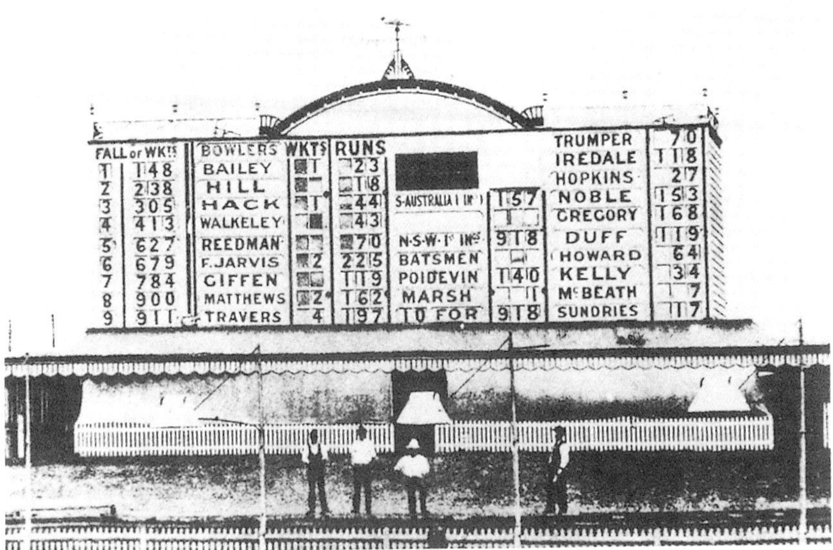


*(Left)* A photograph, taken *c.*1890, of Charles Lawrence (bottom left) with a group of old cricketers: George Bonnor, Nat Thomson, Charles Beal and Harry Boyle in the back row; Lawrence himself seated with George Moore and Henry Hilliard. Lawrence came to Australia with the 1861–62 touring team, and stayed. *(True to the Blue)*

*(Above)* Scoreboard showing NSW's defeat of South Australia by an innings and 605 runs, Sydney, 1900–01. *(Below)* Australia v. England, third Test at Adelaide, January 1902; Darling and Trumble batting.

*(Above left)* Clem Hill; *(right)* Victor Trumper; *(centre)* Montague Noble (*Hulton-Deutsch*); *(below)* 1902 team to England: (back row) Kelly, Saunders, Armstrong, Noble, Howell, Major Wardill (manager); (seated) Hill, Duff, Darling (captain), Trumper, E. Jones; (front) Hopkins, Carter, S.E. Gregory.

*(Above)* May 27, 1912: Warren Bardsley hits the ball to the boundary for Australia against South Africa in a triangular tournament (also featuring England) at Lancashire cricket ground. T.J. Matthews took a hat-trick in each innings for the men from Down Under.

*(Below)* The 1912 team to England, one of the worst-behaved Australian sides ever to tour abroad.

*(Left)* George Giffen in 1918; *(above)* Trumper in his late years – he died in 1915 at the age of thirty-seven *(True to the Blue)*; *(below)* 'Giffen's early risers'. The veteran used to coach young players well into his sixties.

*(Above Left)* Warwick Armstrong (MCC); *(above right)* Charlie McCartney (MCC); *(below)* Armstrong leads out his team, May 1921. *(Hulton-Deutsch)*

*(Above)* The 16th Australians, 1926, whose loss of the Ashes caused bitter criticism at home. *(Below)* The scoreboard as the players leave the field on 28 December 1926, when Victoria made the world record total of 1,107.

the latter was concerned about finances as debts were building up.

For that reason only one of the four South Australian delegates – Mostyn Evan – could travel to Sydney for the Cricket Conference, with Augustus Robinson, an early SACA committeeman and assistant secretary who was now resident in Sydney, being asked to take another delegate's place. Evan would also table the proxy votes for the two unable to attend.

The Australasian Cricket Council held its first meeting on Tuesday 13 September 1892 at the Oxford Hotel, Darlinghurst, an inner-Sydney suburb. Richard Teece was elected chairman and John Portus secretary. The most pressing issue concerned the 1893 tour to England including the selection of the team, and it was not until late afternoon that the Council addressed domestic problems. Then it was a matter of deciding what to do with Lord Sheffield's £150.

With hardly any debate Robert Best (Victoria) moved a motion: 'That the sum of money given by Lord Sheffield be divided equally amongst the Associations of Victoria, New South Wales and South Australia, to be devoted in a manner that each governing body may determine'. The Victorians had made their move, and what was worse, Mostyn Evan of South Australia actually seconded the motion!

To the rescue came Augustus Robinson, the ring-in South Australian delegate. He proposed an amendment: 'That the money be devoted to the purchase of a premiership shield, to be held by the premier colony for the year, and that a sub-committee of Messrs Cohen (NSW), Robinson (SA) and Kelleher (Victoria) be appointed to draft the necessary rules'.

After more discussion the amendment was put. The chairman did not vote, and it was 6–5 for creating the Sheffield Shield. It was that close.

The meeting adjourned for the day, and after dinner the sub-committee got down to work. The next day they presented their proposals which were unanimously agreed. Perhaps the most important proposal was the third:

> That the first competition for the possession of the Shield be held on the occasion of the next intercolonial match between any two of the three colonies and that the colony winning the match hold the Shield until it suffer a defeat in an intercolonial match, upon the happening of which event the shield shall pass into the possession of the colony inflicting defeat; similarly for all succeeding contests.

John Portus wrote later: 'After a couple of other items had been dealt with on the agenda, Mostyn Evan made a half-hearted attempt in moving a motion: "that in the opinion of this Council, it is desirable that the three colonies meet each other an equal number of times in every season for the Sheffield Shield". Evan would not stipulate the number of times the colonies should meet, and was reluctant to speak on it. The motion was passed, but it was toothless.' The Council went on to change the law regarding the follow-on, and it also resolved to form a panel of umpires for intercolonial matches.

It took a number of letters between Lord Sheffield and Ben Wardill before details 'of the trophy I am giving to the Australians for competition' came to fruition. Then tenders were called in the major newspapers around the country before the Australasian Cricket Council's annual general meeting of 28 December 1893 at the Vienna Café, Melbourne, awarded the contract to Philip Blashki, a jeweller of Bourke Street, Melbourne.

The Sheffield Shield was finally completed on 14 July 1894 and since that time has been the premier cricketing trophy in Australia.

Friday 16 December 1892 was an historic day in the annals of Australian cricket, for it saw the first day of play in the new Sheffield Shield competition. South Australia played New South Wales in Adelaide and, despite having to follow-on, the home team won by 57 runs. According to the rules then in force, South Australia should have won the Shield. However, the Victorians were able to change the rules mid-season so that, particularly after their home victories over NSW and South Australia, they won the trophy. It was a staggering piece of arrogance.

The season 1892–93, quite apart from seeing the launch of the Sheffield Shield competition, was an extremely full season, the more so as there was no English tour. Other than the six Sheffield Shield matches, Tasmania put up a good performance against Victoria in Launceston; Queensland, in their initial first-class match, defeated NSW by 14 runs at the Exhibition ground in Brisbane; and Western Australia played their first two first-class games, losing by ten wickets in Adelaide and by an innings in Melbourne. The Western Australians also played an exciting match against the Melbourne Cricket Club which, for some unexplained reason, has never been given first-class status even though all twenty-two players were of the required standard.

The large number of six selectors announced, on 12 January 1893, who the thirteen players would be to go on a tour of England which had been organised, and would be managed, by the NSWCA treasurer, Victor Cohen. Originally 1892 was suggested but Lord Hawke had protested that the county matches would be disturbed and 1894 was proposed by Nottinghamshire. It was later agreed that the Australians would tour in 1893 and the South Africans in 1894.

All six selectors toured: the forty-year-old Jack Blackham as captain; Alick Bannerman, George Giffen (who would not tour unless his brother Walter was selected), Jack Lyons, Harry Trott and Charlie Turner. Other former tourists to travel included Billy Bruce, Syd Gregory, Affie Jarvis and Hugh Trumble. Harry Graham and Robert McLeod were the newcomers along with Walter Giffen although the new Australasian Cricket Council (ACC) did flex its muscles and insist on the inclusion of the former Queensland all-rounder, Arthur Coningham, who was then playing for New South Wales.

The players felt that, as the ACC had no control over them and certainly no finances of which to speak, then they should not accept the dictate of the Associations. Eventually Coningham went as the fourteenth man on the tour but played in no Test matches. A volatile and over-confident man, Coningham spent his life surrounded by scandal though as a sportsman he was adept at billiards, rowing, shooting and rugby as well as cricket.

Try as it might, the ACC's aims of controlling international cricket got off to a stuttering start. The players still controlled the finances and the Test teams were run as a fiefdom. Regular tours were improving playing skills and establishing the reputations of cricketers from Australia. With Murdoch, Ferris, Woods and, previously, Midwinter playing on the English county circuit the improving standard of play from the colonies was easy to see. However, the original English visitors to Australia were not forgotten. As the Melbourne Cricket Club's annual report for 1892–93 said: 'The services of Charles Lawrence have been again secured as a coach for the junior players, his efforts during the past season having been greatly appreciated and produced good results'.

# 9

# The Australasian Cricket Council

The twenty-two years from 1893 to the beginning of the European war in 1914 was a period of high drama in the growth and development of Australian cricket.

The era was known on the cricket field as 'The Golden Age'. It was a time of superlative effort and contests with all aspects of the game providing wonderful entertainment. Sportsmanship was also of the highest standard as the newer, younger players started to make their mark; names would emerge such as Joe Darling, Frank Iredale, Ernie Jones, Albert Trott, Clem Hill, Monty Noble, Frank Laver, Victor Trumper, Warwick Armstrong, Reggie Duff, 'Tibby' Cotter. Charlie Macartney, Warren Bardsley and Charlie Kellaway.

But behaviour off the field was poor with many of the main figures in the drama of colonial, then State, committee-rooms being beyond anything a simple cricket-loving public would believe. Even now, a century later, many people do not wish to hear stories which dent or even shatter their myths and illusions about Australian cricket and cricketers of the time. It was not uncommon, however, for there to be fist-fights in committee rooms; corruption and bribery, and the fixing of matches.

The economic situation around Australia was weak and the worst-hit colony was Victoria. The public debt in early 1893 was horrendously high as development saw the expansion of Melbourne. The Victorian government approved a £44 million scheme for the railways while the first cable trams began to rattle through the city streets.

Sydney saw equally fast growth with public buildings designed to dominate their surroundings and to display the city's prestige and prosperity. The New South Wales Cricket Association was starting an important decade: they would revolutionise club cricket by making clubs form themselves from districts; they established the Country Week, and found that running the Association was no longer a hobby, and had to employ a salaried secretary.

In Adelaide the depression, and the very wet winter of 1893, spelt gloom and doom among many. Food marches by the hungry became a regular sight with the first signs of a socialist revolt coming from the Port Adelaide wharfworkers. During the year Mostyn Evan had become the Association's chairman but he was showing no sign of exerting any authority. The other colonies criticised South Australia for not spending enough money on improvements at the Adelaide Oval, nor on promoting the game.

A comparison of the financial situation of the four major cricket organisations of the time shows that in mid-1893:

> *MELBOURNE CRICKET CLUB*: Building assets valued at £17,400: Profit on year £2,500: Debt £9,475.
> *SACA*: Building assets £8,100: Profit £802: Debt £1,327.
> *VCA*: Building assets – nil: Profit £1316: Debt £1,080.
> *NSWCA*: Building assets – nil: Profit £395: Debt nil.

The 1893 tour of England was one long sad procession which had its genesis in the players' resentment of the Australasian Cricket Council because the ACC was seeking to take power away from the players and to control money matters.

The ACC secretary, John Portus, had written to Lord's giving details of the team, adding that 'the Council had approved' of the selections. This riled the players and they turned on Victor Cohen, the instigator of the tour and now team manager. Cohen had been influential in the formation of the ACC and the players regarded him as little more than an ACC spy in their midst.

Matters went from bad to worse. On his return to Australia after the tour, Cohen told a gathering of pressmen that players had assaulted him; that some of them were drunk most of the time; that he was publicly abused at Lord's during the first Test; that on the way home players had broken into his cabin and taken his account books, and that a few members of the party were totally unmanageable.

The team's captain was the highly strung and nervous Jack Blackham. For all his coolness and bravery behind the stumps he was a tense, nervous figure in the pavilion and unable to prevent his anxieties from spreading around the dressing-room. The players themselves behaved abominably: fighting regularly broke out and dissent was common. As *Sporting Life* said:

> Fines as penalties for ill-natured behaviour lost effect because they were not enforced. Manager Cohen complained of disrespectful language and said he had to defend himself from assault by 'some drunken brute'. Members of factions within the team lost

their tempers on a railway journey into Sussex. When the train reached Brighton, porters saw one of the Australians' compartments spattered with blood.

The tour had started on 8 May 1893 at Sheffield Park with an eight-wicket defeat by His Lordship's team. In fact twenty matches were played, with varying success, up to the first Test at Lord's in mid-July.

Blackham's opposite number as captain was Andrew Stoddart, who was deputising for the injured W. G. Grace. Before the match heavy rain made the pitch difficult which gives all the more credit to the four-hour innings of Arthur Shrewsbury whose 106 contained nine fours. Stanley Jackson's cavalier innings of 91 took only 105 minutes. In reply to England's 334, the Australians were 75 for five before Harry Graham, twenty-two years old, came to the rescue.

His dashing innings of 107, with a five and twelve fours, came in just 140 minutes. Graham flayed the bowling as he emulated Charles Bannerman by scoring his maiden first-class hundred in his first Test innings. Everything seemed so rosy for Graham at that point but his habitual drinking and his way of 'living life to the full' saw him die at the age of only forty. As *Wisden* put it: 'Had he ordered his life more carefully, he might have had a much longer and more successful career'.

Graham's century and further rain saw the match left as a draw, although Stoddart declared England's second innings closed at 234 for eight wickets, the first Test captain to make such a decision. A month later, however, England thrashed the Australians at The Oval winning by an innings and 43 runs. Grace was back as captain, Jackson scored 103 in exactly two hours with 13 fours, and the match was for the benefit of Maurice Read, who had just played in his last Test. The sum of £1200 was raised for him.

George Giffen took 7/128 from 54 overs as England amassed 483. Played in almost tropical heat the 13,061 second-day crowd saw seventeen wickets fall as Australia were dismissed for 91 and, following-on, they were dismissed on the third day for 349. Only Harry Trott's 92 in 125 minutes with 17 fours saved the tourists from a worse defeat.

The final Test at Old Trafford was drawn, with only Billy Bruce (68) and Alick Bannerman (60) getting past 36 for Australia in either innings. It was not only an unsatisfactory tour, but it was made worse when the team played their first match in America a month later. A full Test team was beaten by an innings and 68 runs by Philadelphia at Belmont Park. A return match a week later saw the Australians take revenge by six wickets but the damage had been done, and the recriminations went on for weeks following the team's arrival back in

Australia. Now there was no sense of nationalistic pride, just an acute public embarrassment at a national sporting team devoid of friendship, loyalty or pride.

In the domestic season of 1893–94 George Giffen scored 205 against New South Wales in Adelaide shortly after his return home. With another century in Melbourne Giffen led his South Australian team to their first of only a dozen Sheffield Shield titles.

In mid-January 1894, Coleman Davis took his second New South Wales team to New Zealand. He included in his party the twenty-year-old Monty Noble, a stylish and powerful batsman and a brisk off-break bowler, but Noble had a disappointing tour, scoring only 97 runs at 10.77 and taking four wickets at 39.50.

After defeating Auckland and Hawkes Bay, drawing with Wellington and Otago, and losing by an innings to Canterbury, the New South Wales team took on the first representative New Zealand team, although the match is not recognised as a Test match. The formation of the New Zealand Cricket Council was still ten months away, and it was the Canterbury Cricket Association which was responsible for organising the fixture. Their sole selector, A. M. Ollivier, chose the seminal national side after consultation with the selectors of the other provincial cricket associations. Even so, the *Wellington Evening Post* complained about the suitablity of Ollivier as selector and about the CCA 'running the whole show'.

New Zealand's first captain was Len Cuff, the Canterbury batsman. He lost the toss on a wet Thursday afternoon, 15 February 1894, and watched Davis's team struggle to reach 147. New Zealand then did no better themselves, going from 58 for three overnight to 116 with the New South Wales opening bowler, Sydney Austin, taking 7/63. NSW struggled on the second afternoon against some tight Kiwi bowling but eventually won by 160 runs when New Zealand collapsed for 79 in the fourth innings, Austin claiming 6/35.

The *Canterbury Times* did not hold back from attacking the local players. It deplored 'the non-existence among the New Zealand ranks of a determined, vigorous and skilful player who, instead of playing back the bowling in a feeble, half-hearted manner, would have treated a considerable number of Austin's deliveries with but scant courtesy'.

On 27 December 1894, a conference of provincial cricket association delegates met in Christchurch's City Hotel and formed the New Zealand Cricket Council. They had no wish to join in any Australasian Cricket Council and at no time did the fledgling NZCC or any of the provincial associations receive any approach from Australia for them to do so.

In Western Australia progress had been gathering pace ever since the Governor, Sir Frederick Broome, granted the WACA 'twenty eight acres at the eastern end of Perth' back in December 1889. After a great deal of work the groundsman, William Duffy, formerly from the Richmond Club in Victoria, pronounced the turf pitches at the new Cricketing Association ground as being ready for use. So, on 3 February 1894, six matches took place between local sides and visiting teams from the goldfields of Coolgardie and Kalgoorlie.

This event, coupled with the previous season's eastern tour, gave the game in the west such impetus that the WACA trustees borrowed £3000 to pay for buildings and improvements at the ground. Excitement in Perth was such that the WACA secretary, Frederick North, cabled the VCA secretary, Edward Heather, on the opening of the turf pitches: 'Great success. Association wants to arrange match with you as projected season before last'.

Heather studiously ignored this request but he did follow up a similar suggestion from the Queensland Cricketing Association. However he had to report back to his committee: 'It was suggested by the QCA that a Victorian team should visit the colony, but in consequence of the many engagements of our cricketers, it was found impracticable to comply with the request'.

But Queensland did at least get a game in Sydney where they gave NSW a fright. No-one had anticipated the Brisbane players nearly equalling the Sydneysiders on their own Moore Park ground. The visitors were put in to bat, after which rain finished play for the day with Queensland at 25 for two. This became 113 on the Monday morning with the wicket dry, but tricky, after the rest-day sun had done its work. NSW gained a 47-run lead to which Queensland replied with 246, an excellent total considering the state of the pitch and their lack of experience. After reaching 142 for two, the home side started to falter and only won by two wickets as the veteran Tom Garrett took a long blade to the raw northern attack. The moral victory boosted Queensland cricket for a while but its real lesson was that they still had a lot to learn.

The 1893–94 Australian season ended on a very sour note when Jack Blackham, the Victorian captain, criticised the Sydney umpire, Jack Tooher, for delaying the start of the fourth day's play by fifty-one minutes in the Shield match against NSW. Tooher held that the pitch was too wet to commence play but Blackham disagreed. Recriminations followed with the NSWCA insisting on an apology before matches between the colonies could continue. Blackham was forced by the VCA to issue a limited apology just before the 1894–95 season got under way. It was the beginning of the end for Blackham's career. He was to play only one further Test before retiring.

Changes were taking place in cricket all over Australia. In March 1894 the trustees of the land at Moore Park had changed the name of the arena to the Sydney Cricket Ground but without informing the NSWCA. The association delegates felt this was the thin edge of the wedge as the SCG secretary, Philip Sheridan, had formed the Sydney Cricket Club in 1888 to try, it was suggested, to equal the status of Melbourne.

In Sydney a new local competition began with clubs allocated electoral boundaries from which they could draw their players. At the same time Bulli soil, taken from a local creek, produced pitches which rolled out hard and fast but had outstanding adhesive and water-resistant properties.

The Sydney Cricket Ground curator, Ned Gregory, prepared his first Bulli soil pitch in August 1894 and its performance was so pleasing that the NSWCA decided to offer a pound-for-pound subsidy to district clubs which spent money on Bulli soil to improve their pitches.

This soil appeared to be better than the Merri Creek soil which was being exported from Melbourne. The South Australians sent their curator, Charley Checkett, to see Ned Gregory's Bulli pitches at Canterbury (NSW), Manly, North Sydney, Rushcutters Bay, Wentworth Park, Sydney University and Sydney Number Two Ovals. Checkett also visited Melbourne to look at suburban pitches of Merri Creek soil at East Melbourne, Richmond, Fitzroy, Hawthorn and Hawksburn. He was not impressed by what he saw, so the Adelaide Oval 'wicket soil' continued to be taken from sections of the Adelaide Hills.

On 24 January 1894 a special meeting of members of the Melbourne Cricket Club gave their committee the authority to open negotiations with their Sydney counterparts to bring out an English team at the end of the year. It could not have been a more important stroke of fate for both organisations. The financial boom had burst and the City of Melbourne Bank had closed its doors. The Melbourne CC was in debt by £2336 and only a £500 overdraft arranged by president Frank Grey Smith saved the club. Melbourne's half-share of the tour profit came to £3599 so that, when the day came in 1895 for the official liquidation of the Bank, the club was able to pay its debts in full.

On 21 August 1894 the Melbourne Club announced that they 'had invited Mr A. E. Stoddart to bring out an English team of cricketers during the coming season. A programme of matches has been drawn up in conjunction with the Cricket Associations of Victoria, New South Wales, South Australia, and Queensland, and with the sanction of the Cricket Council of Australasia, which will, it is believed, prove of a most interesting character. The visiting team will embrace players most of whom are entirely new to Australia, and the team is considered as representative of the best talent in England. Mr Stoddart has spared no trouble in obtaining the services of the leading amateurs and professionals; while, on this side, the promoters have received offers of the generous support of Australian cricketers. Five Test matches against Australia are to be played, two of which are arranged for the Melbourne ground.'

As Ben Wardill and Phil Sheridan were busy with tour matters so the NSWCA and VCA were starting another row. This time it was charged that weak Victorian teams were being sent to Sydney which affected the NSWCA's gate takings.

The England touring team left Tilbury on 21 September and arrived at Port Adelaide on 30 October. As preparations were being made for the match against South Australia, the Adelaide *Advertiser* said: 'The representatives of the colony can hardly hope to win this match, but we feel certain that they will do her no discredit'. It was a slight understatement as the tourists collapsed in their second innings to give South Australia their first-ever victory on equal terms against an England team. Joe Darling scored 117, and the selectors chose him for the first Test the following month.

The crowd of 25,500 gave an indication as to how popular Stoddart's team would prove to be. The next match, in Melbourne, saw Archie MacLaren score 228 against a star-studded Victorian side in such style that the England opener's innings caused the *Argus* to report: 'It is doubtful if an innings of equal length both in runs and time has been seen on the MCG marred by fewer bad strokes'. By early December, following their easy win over NSW, the Melbourne *Herald* was saying of the England team: 'They are lifting Australia out of its financial depression'.

After Queensland was overwhelmed in Brisbane, the first Test took place in Sydney in mid-December 1894. The changes in the Australian team were marked from the previous match sixteen months earlier. Out went Bannerman, Bruce, Graham, Trumble and Robert McLeod. In came Joe Darling, Frank Iredale, Ernie Jones, Charles McLeod (younger brother of Robert), and John Reedman. Changes in the series would also see the Test debuts of Arthur Coningham, Jack Harry, Albert Trott and Tom McKibbin: as a result of the changes only a few of the 'old guard' survived.

The Test provided excitement all round. Syd Gregory batted for 244 minutes and hit 28 fours in his 201, the first double-century in a Test in Australia. His stand of 154 in 73 minutes with Blackham still remains a ninth-wicket record as Australia reached 586. George Giffen with 161 and 41 became the only player to score 200 runs and take eight wickets (4/75 and 4/164) in an Ashes Test. England replied with 325 and, following-on, 437, with Australia 113 for two at the end of the fifth day needing only 64 more runs to win. When rain fell overnight, the Australian captain, Jack Blackham, knew his team was in trouble. Early morning sunshine turned the track into a classic 'sticky wicket' which Briggs (3/25) and Peel (6/67) exploited so successfully that England won by ten runs. It was the first instance in Test cricket of a team winning after following-on. It was also Blackham's thirty-fifth and final Test for Australia as injury now forced him to retire. His twenty years of first-class cricket had covered all of Australia's formative period.

The Sydney attendance of 62,113 (paying £2832) was overhauled in four days in Melbourne when 67,000 (paying £2879) saw England victorious by 94 runs after again being behind on first innings. It was Stoddart's own second innings 173 which turned the game England's way.

For the Adelaide Test Australia made four changes including bringing in Albert Trott, the twenty-one-year old younger brother of Harry. Playing in extreme heat in mid-January 1895, Albert scored 110 in two innings without being dismissed, and then bowled Australia to a 382-run victory by taking 8/43 from 27 overs. Young Trott carried on in the fourth Test at Sydney, being unbeaten on 85 and sharing a match-winning partnership with Harry Graham who scored 105 with 13 fours. With Australia winning by an innings and 147 runs the series was all-square at two wins each.

The fifth and final Test was dubbed 'the match of the century', and no wonder! It had everything a deciding contest could want. The Australian selectors made a massive blunder in dropping Charlie Turner – and in response Turner kept to his threat never to play Test cricket again. The selectors, apparently, had thought Tom McKibbin and Albert Trott could share Turner's bowling role and between them would make more runs.

The five days of the Test attracted crowds to Melbourne from all over the country. Special trains were laid on from Adelaide and Sydney, with spectators even arriving from outback Queensland. The attendance was enormous for the times: 95,023 people paid £4,004. As the *Argus* said on 4 March: 'There appears to be an idea somewhere that there is a Depression here. To the spectator on Saturday (crowd 29,123) at the MCG that word had no meaning'.

The Australian captain, George Giffen, won the toss, batted, and saw his team reach 414. England had Archie MacLaren's 120 to thank for their total of 385. It was still very even. The turning-point came early on the last morning with England needing 297 to win. The visiting batsman, John Brown of Yorkshire, should have been dismissed by the second ball he faced. Instead he went on to score his first fifty in 28 minutes which is still the fastest half-century in Test cricket. His century took 95 minutes and when he was finally out for 140, England eased themselves to a six-wicket victory and the Ashes.

The Australasian Cricket Council arranged a meeting in Adelaide to coincide with the mid-January Test. The main item on the agenda was to consider a change to the follow-on law as adopted by the Marylebone Cricket Club – which was unanimously agreed. The change was from 100 runs to 150 runs for a match of more than three days. This was difficult for Australia as all matches were played to a conclusion – be they two or five or more days.

Each colonial cricket association now had to submit a list of umpires to the ACC whom they wished to be considered to officiate in Test matches and other first-class fixtures. Each delegate had multiple votes, with the top umpires from each Test-playing colony being on the Test panel. The result of the voting announced on 10 December was:

> Maximum votes – J. T. Wallace (Queensland: not eligible for Tests because Queensland did not then host any), W. Slight (SA), S. Morris (Victoria), G. E. Downs (SA) and J. A. Tooher (NSW). These were then followed in voting order by: E. Sheridan (Queensland), E. J. Briscoe (NSW), C. Bannerman (NSW), J. Phillips (Victoria), P. Argall (SA), J. Harry (Victoria), T. A. Reeves (SA), G. H. G. Searcy (SA), T. Flynn (Victoria), I. A. Fisher (SA), A. D. McLennan (SA), J. Humphreys (NSW) and R. W. Crockett (Victoria).

However, not one of the top-rated umpires was chosen to stand in any of the Tests because of colonial jealousies. Also, of the eighteen chosen umpires seven came from South Australia.

On 10 December, Percy Bowden, now secretary of the NSWCA, sent a telegram to the other two Associations asking them to consider the claims put forward by the Queensland Cricket Association regarding their having a representative on the Test selection panel.

Both the VCA and SACA thought the request 'cheeky' and implied so in their replies. During the meeting of the ACC the South Australian delegation pushed hard for the Council to take over the arrangement and financing of all intercolonial matches, but met stiff opposition from the other delegates. Various other minor matters were decided upon but, just as the meeting was closing, the three Melbourne Cricket Club members among the four Victorian delegates announced that they were sponsoring another England tour in late 1897 with Andrew Stoddart, once again, as captain of the team. So much for combined decision-making.

Domestic matters filled the rest of the 1894–95 season although the Australian winter did see arrangements finalised for Queensland to play in Sydney, and Tasmania to visit Melbourne as additional matches to the eight Sheffield Shield fixtures. Tasmania lost by an innings while Queensland put up a good fight before losing to NSW by nine wickets. Arthur Coningham scored 151 and 51 but Queensland also had a good unbeaten 77 from Dr Robert MacDonald, a stubborn right-hand batsman who later played for Leicestershire. MacDonald held a number of important roles in cricket administration including that of being the future Board of Control's representative in London during the problems of the early 1930s.

Another ACC meeting was held on 5 October 1895 in Sydney but only minor cricketing issues were discussed. The next gathering, held in Melbourne on 27 December, was probably its most important one so far. The delegates selected the Ninth Australian team to visit England following an official invitation from the Marylebone Club. However, the ACC in reality only rubber-stamped the selection made by Percy McDonnell (of Queensland, who was 'vide' [*sic*] a NSW representative following the ACC rejection of Queensland), George Giffen (South Australia) and Harry Trott (Victoria) who would captain the team. The manager's position was between Harry Musgrove (Victoria) and Will Whitridge (South Australia). The vote was six each with the neutral chairman's deliberative vote going to Musgrove.

Despite the changes made by the ACC, the 1896 team was not free of troubles. Although the team selection was made under new rules, the players, not unanimously, decided to remove one of their companions, Jack Harry, from the team before the tour began. They were successful. They then selected a replacement and, to its discredit, the Council failed to act to preserve their original selection. Musgrove requested Jack Harry to attend a meeting with the team executive and himself and they informed Harry of the team's decision to retire him on injury grounds, despite medical opinion to the contrary. He was offered £50 as compensation. After legal assistance Harry accepted dismissal on the payment of £160 compensation.

This negligence on the part of the Council made the players more aware of their power; and this was demonstrated by the players before the year was over. Despite an agreement with the ACC in which the team was to return by a specific date to enable the players to join in the first-class matches in Australia for the 1896–97 season, the side failed to fulfil its contract. Furthermore the manager, having planned matches in North America and New Zealand which caused the delay, was a party to this. During the tour the Council lodged its protest with the team but no reply was received until a further protest was made. The team then expressed its regret at the Council's action and stated its unanimous decision to fulfil its own plans. Musgrove was reported to have said that 'the whole trouble has been caused by the wire pullers in one of the colonies represented in the Council', a strange comment for the Council's appointed manager to make.

Another case, which the Australasian Cricket Council faced at their meeting in Melbourne before the departure of Trott's team, concerned the former Test fast bowler Jack Ferris.

Ferris had played for Australia against England and for England against South Africa. He represented NSW for four seasons, and played county cricket for Gloucestershire until he burnt himself out. After arriving in South Australia in late 1895 Ferris played in three club matches for Norwood and impressed the SA selectors enough to include him in their team for the tour to Melbourne and Sydney. Telegrams were sent to the NSWCA and VCA asking if they had any objection to him playing for South Australia. Both Associations quickly gave permission, and the matter was discussed at the ACC meeting for a clear definition to be made on players changing colonies and subsequently representing their new colony in intercolonial matches. The ACC vacillated on the issue before passing it back to the individual Associations for a decision. This revealed how basically weak the ACC was becoming in matters of importance which they had been constituted to resolve.

At the same meeting the South Australian delegates made a push for John Creswell to take over as ACC secretary (which he did almost immediately).

Another New South Wales team visited New Zealand in late 1895 and over New Year played a challenge match in Christchurch. Captained by Tom Cobcroft, the NSW side defeated Canterbury, Otago and Wellington before losing to New Zealand by 142 runs. Even a superb bowling effort by Syd Callaway (7/77 and 8/98) could not stave off defeat. The *Canterbury Times* described his efforts as 'irresistible' and 'really phenomenal'.

In Melbourne Jack Worrall, the former Test player, caused quite a sensation in February 1896. Playing for Carlton against Melbourne University he scored an unbeaten 417 in a then world record total of 922. It was the first score of over 400 in Australia and made on the same day that East Melbourne reached 876 against Richmond and Melbourne's 683 versus St Kilda.

The Ninth Australians left Adelaide on 19 March 1896, following their four-day match against The Rest of Australia in Sydney. In a tight finish the tourists won by two wickets with McKibbin's ten wickets being the star turn.

On arrival in England the team practised at Mitcham in Surrey before going to Sheffield Park for the customary opening fixture against His Lordship's side. The first day, a Monday, saw 24,930 spectators present, including the Prince of Wales, as the Australians faced a near Test-strength team in a drawn match.

Of the twelve games before the first Test, seven were won and three drawn. The initial defeat came after a victory over 'An England XI' in which Fred Spofforth faced his old friends and reminded them of his ability by taking 6/49 and 5/51. Then came Thursday 11 June 1896. Against MCC at Lord's, Hugh Trumble took 6/84 as the home team reached 219. The Australians were then routed for 18 with Pougher taking five wickets in fourteen balls, finishing with a hat-trick. J. T. Hearne had an analysis of 4/4 and, as Australia crumbled again, he took 9/73. It was an ignominious defeat.

Despite this, the Australians were being cleverly captained by Harry Trott who was proving himself a fine tactician. Nine of the fifteen players were new to English conditions: Joe Darling, Clem Hill and Ernie Jones from South Australia; Charles Eady from Tasmania; Frank Iredale, Harry Donnan, Tom McKibbin and James Kelly of NSW; and the Victorian Alfred Johns.

For the first Test at Lord's, which started on 22 June, Eady, Hill and Kelly made their debuts for Australia. In front of a first-day crowd of 30,414 Australia were dismissed for 53 in just 75 minutes. It was a remarkable collapse against the Surrey bowling pair of Tom Richardson (6/39) and George Lohmann (3/13).

In reply England were 286 for eight at the close (Bobby Abel 94, W. G. Grace 66) which reached 292 next day. The tourists were 62 for three when Syd Gregory joined Harry Trott. They then added a record 221 in 161 minutes for the fourth wicket with Trott (143) scoring a century on his Test debut as captain. Gregory made 103 but the rest gave little support and England won easily by six wickets.

Six victories followed for the tourists before the second Test at Old Trafford. It was an unforgettable encounter which swayed both ways. Frank Iredale scored 108 and George Giffen 80 in Australia's 412. England replied with 231 and, following-on, 305 of which Kumar Sri Ranjitsinhji, His Highness the Jam Sahib of Nawanagar (known to his friends as 'Smith') scored an unbeaten 154 on his debut. The Australians limped to 125 for seven to win the match by three wickets.

All-square to the final Test at Kennington Oval which, unfortunately, was ruined by rain. England got home by 66 runs in a low-scoring match, with the top Australian performance being Hughie Trumble's with 6/59 and 6/30. England had retained the Ashes but the Australians had won a lot of friends. They were a popular, highly regarded and disciplined side – a far cry from the tourists of three years earlier.

This idealism was carried further. Anglo-Australian ideals played an important role in many sports both in Australia and elsewhere. There was no distinction between Australian and British competitors at the 1896 commencement of the modern Olympic Games. Athletes represented both countries without distinguishing between the two. Sport helped to dramatise that special bond which was felt to exist between the countries which made up the British Empire.

But even now, did Australia have an identity? It did in cricket, but in what else? Even with the labour troubles of the decade after 1886 there was still puzzlement at the flags waved by the proletarian masses. As P. F. Donovan wrote in his *Australia and the Great London Dock Strike: 1889*, what was 'the Australian flag' that floated above a Hyde Park rally? Was the spirit of Eureka still alive? And if so, with what section of Australian society?

Cricket, as a game, always seemed to weave its way through the maze of imponderable or unanswerable questions which dogged Australians as they came up to their national puberty with the federation of the colonies in 1901. Yet it was cricket which was the first Australian sport to form itself into a national body, although petty parochialism caused the experiment to die. Australia's sub-cultures leave stereotypes on the mind – untrue as they may be – which get passed from generation to generation. Tasmanians are considered deficient in brain-power but good at interbreeding; Victorians, so it is said, are tainted with a born-to-rule mentality which stems from being Australia's 'royalty', known better as 'the squattocracy'; Queenslanders are affected by the sun and portrayed as country cousins; Western Australians are 'sandgropers'; South Australians 'croweaters'; and people from the Northern Territory allegedly perform feats unknown to the rest of mankind.

Those from New South Wales put up with taunts from the other States knowing full well that they are superior. It is said that the ultimate contradiction in terms is 'Sydney socialite'. In cricketing terms New South Wales has always felt that it led the way especially as it produced cricketers of such consummate skill and variety.

Cricket historians in the twentieth century have usually been based in Sydney. The names roll off the tongue: Davis, Garnsey, Moyes, Fingleton, Pollard and Robinson just to name half a dozen. However, if they did have a fault, it was to put Sydney at the centre of the Australian cricketing world – and then work outwards. Little, if anything, has been written about the people who played such prominent roles in the development of the Australian game – particularly Frederick North from Perth, John Creswell in Adelaide, Maurice O'Connell in Brisbane and, all-importantly, Augustus Robinson of Adelaide, Sydney and finally, Melbourne.

The New South Wales Cricket Association in 1896 was so full of its own importance that it started the slide which led to the demise of the Australasian Cricket Council. At the January meeting of the NSWCA, the South Sydney District Cricket Club delegate, Jack Waine, said that the ACC, 'was useless and ought to be broken up'. Waine was a senior member of the Association's council and so his comments were taken seriously. The following month the NSWCA convened a special meeting to vote on a number of motions submitted by the Glebe District CC delegate, Leslie Abrams, said to be, 'one of the Association's most active men'.

His first two motions were: 'That in the opinion of this Association the Australasian Cricket Council is not required for the purpose of promoting the game of cricket in the Colonies and should be at once disbanded'. Followed by: 'That this Association do now withdraw from the Council'. The motions were not carried, so Abrams submitted them again at the end of 1897, once more without success. However, it was clear that the ACC's days were numbered.

The NSWCA had a hard core of members who had been behind the ACC's formation in order to try and exert NSW authority over the game in Australia and to take over control of the tours to and from England. National good did not come into it: it was a grab for power. Jealousy over the Melbourne Cricket Club's authority and influence, and over the Sydney Cricket Ground trustees' joint ventures, left the NSWCA out on a limb – and not for the first time.

The South Australians, led by the far-sighted John Creswell, saw what Abrams' motions would bring about. They carefully lined themselves up with Melbourne, therefore, and on 19 May 1896 asked to become joint venturers in the 1897–98 tour to be led by Andrew Stoddart. Major Wardill in Melbourne did not object to the idea but Philip Sheridan, manager of the SCG, refused to countenance the suggestion.

The ACC met in Melbourne on 29 December 1896 in the new VCA clubrooms at Messrs Young and Jackson's Hotel in the centre of the city. Two points of interest emerged from the discussions, one of which concerned the follow-on rule which, it was suggested, could be 200 runs, and the second was about time-wasting. The ACC motion on this seems all too familiar: 'That in view of the complaints which have been made by the Press and public as to the waste of time in intercolonial matches, definite instructions are to be given to umpires to report such incidents'.

On their way home from England, the Ninth Australians played five matches in New Zealand in November 1896. Huge crowds saw matches against the odds in Auckland, Wellington, Invercargill and Dunedin before the highlight of the trip: a match against New Zealand in Christchurch. Australia batted cautiously and built a total of 304 with New Zealand falling to the pace of Ernie Jones (8/64 and 5/58) for 129 and, following-on, 247. The tourists were pressed hard for victory which came by five wickets in the game's final over.

The following month Queensland played eight fixtures on a six-week tour with the important game being a clash with New Zealand at the Basin Reserve, Wellington, immediately after Christmas. Although New Zealand won by 182 runs the Queensland visit did not produce the financial windfall hoped for by the NZCC.

The 1896–97 domestic season in Australia provided one item of special interest. It was the bowling of NSW's Tom McKibbin who took 7/51 and 8/74 in Adelaide (where South Australia's first mixed race player 'Dick' Bailey made his debut); 5/47 and 3/80 in Melbourne; and in Sydney 4/62 and 4/101 in the return against South Australia, followed by 8/111 and 5/129 against Victoria. McKibbin had taken three domestic seasons to claim over 100 Sheffield Shield wickets – a remarkable feat. His final tally of 136 Shield wickets in eighteen matches was a credit to his bowling, however dubious his action.

At the end of the season a team led by George Giffen and managed by the South Australian lawyer and committeeman Mostyn Evan, toured Western Australia under the title of a 'SA Invitation Eleven'. The trip started on 13 April 1897 at Fremantle, finishing six games later on 6 May at Northam. The invitation had originally been declined by the SACA, who were furious that such a prominent person as Evan should organise the trip behind their backs. Still, that was typical of a man who entered cricket to improve his social standing, and who used to preach to the ACC exactly the opposite of what he did.

Elsewhere, cricket authorities were trying to pursue those ideals which they perceived as typifying Victorian England. They wanted to publicise the manly aspects of cricket in particular and sport in general, and so by implication prove that participation in these activities was to be considered 'moral'.

South Australia had always been an egalitarian society, particularly as it was the only colony not to be convict-based. Therefore it came as quite a shock when the SACA tried hard to push this 'muscular Christianity' ethos. They failed in 1897, but left a legacy in writing and within their committee structure, which still holds today, that only one of their own ever gets elected to the Association's main ruling body.

Andrew Stoddart's second team to visit Australia arrived off Largs Bay, near Adelaide, on 24 October 1897. There had been a problem prior to departure over whether Ranjitsinhji could tour as the NSW Government had a Bill before Parliament called 'a deterrent tax', under which all non-white people entering the colony had to pay £100. After an initial fuss the politicians agreed to waive the tax for Ranji.

In the first match of Stoddart's tour Clem Hill scored a double-century for South Australia while, in reply, Ranjitsinhji made 189. Ernie Jones took 7/189 and, in turn, was no-balled on the third day for throwing by the umpire, Jim Phillips, when he sent down 'an extra fast one'. After a draw in Adelaide, victories over Victoria and New South Wales were followed by six country fixtures prior to the first Test in Sydney.

The Sydney Cricket Ground trustees, joint sponsors of the tour, were careful to look after their investment – so much so that they took the unprecedented step of postponing the start of the Test. They did this after rain fell on the night of Friday 10 December 1897, and did so without consulting the captains. Stoddart was indisposed so Archie MacLaren captained England when play finally began on the Monday morning. England then scored freely on a pitch which had dried out over the weekend. MacLaren made 109 and Ranjitsinhji a glorious 175 in just 215 minutes as the tourists reached 551. Australia replied with 237 and, following-on, made 408 in a far better display of aggressive batting. Joe Darling scored 101, the first century by a left-handed batsman in Test cricket, while Clem Hill made 96. England easily won by nine wickets but it was to be their only success on the tour.

The Australian team was now starting to develop into a powerful side, admirably led by Harry Trott. That the defeat was an aberration was shown by the New Year Test in Melbourne a fortnight later. Monty Noble replaced Jack Lyons in the Australian line-up while Charlie McLeod moved up to join Joe Darling as opener. McLeod repayed the move by scoring 112 as his side reached 520. England replied with 315 and in the follow-on, only 150, of which Noble took 6/49 to cement his place in the team. The victory, though, did have a down side, when Jim Phillips no-balled Ernie Jones again for throwing. The general view at the time was that Tom McKibbin was the bowler who should have been called, and this feeling was acted on by the three selectors who replaced him with the NSW farmer Bill Howell.

The heat in Adelaide in mid-January was stifling. Also proper pitch preparation was made difficult for the curator, Charley Checkett, who had just one day from the finish of the intercolonial fixture against NSW to prepare a Test strip.

The local hero, Joe Darling, scored 178 on the first day, and on the second 18,000 spectators paid a record £844 to see Australia move on to 552 for nine. Finally dismissed for 573 the Australians had England where they wanted them. Their totals of 278 and 282 (203 of the runs were made by MacLaren and Ranjitsinhji) saw yet another home victory by an innings margin.

Ranjitsinhji had been barracked by the crowd who disliked the Indian's critical references to their ground in his newspaper articles. Ranji had also made some rather unnecessary comments about local players which encouraged the spectators to urge Ernie Jones to attack vigorously. After the game South Australia's power-broker Sir Edwin Smith sought out Ranji and peace was resolved over 'a glass or two of local wine'.

The curator, Checkett, received numerous compliments over his fine pitch. He had spent much time trying to persuade his cricket committee to spend £11 on 'a number of the new, revolutionary, Wedler vortex sprinklers'. The result of this purchase was a quite outstandingly lush outfield with the playing surface better than ever.

The last two Test matches were dominated by three South Australians. At the MCG Clem Hill scored an unbeaten 182 on the first day which included a seventh-wicket partnership of 165 with Hugh Trumble, still an Ashes record. Next morning Hill was dismissed for 188 made in 302 minutes but the real problem of the day was the smoke from bushfires which were raging around Melbourne. England began their innings in debilitating heat and from the stands it was occasionally impossible to follow deliveries from Ernie Jones who was by far Australia's best bowler. Australia won by eight wickets.

The Sydney encounter saw Jones again at his best with 6/82 and 3/61 as Australia won by six wickets, but it was Joe Darling's match. His 160 in the second innings took only 175 minutes and contained thirty fours with his century coming up in only 91 minutes with a record twenty boundaries. Darling became the first batsman to score three hundreds (101, 178 and 160) in the same Test rubber and was also the first to pass 500 runs in a series. The Tests also gave the captains different results. Harry Trott remains the only man who has asked England to follow-on in three successive Tests. On the other hand, the England captain Stoddart may have lost the Ashes but he consoled himself with a £1500-win in an Australian lottery.

On 19 March 1898, a fortnight after Australia's 4–1 Ashes win, the *Bulletin* said: 'This ruthless rout of English cricket will do – and has done – more to enhance the cause of Australian nationality than could ever be achieved by miles of erudite essays and impassioned appeal'. These assessments were probably correct as it had become obvious how Australian cricket teams were helping the progress towards federation: the emu and kangaroo on their caps and blazers being an emblematic advertisement for the coming 'Commonwealth of Australia'. But in England, Lord Harris also argued that cricket 'had done more to draw the mother country and the colonies together than years of beneficial legislation could have done'.

It had long been an object of imperial policy to foster a sense of

Australian nationality in such a way as to encourage the colonies to form a federation. The documents of the behind-the-scenes manoeuvring over the reasons underlying Lord Sheffield's tour have yet to be released, but it is becoming evident that Sheffield was coerced into becoming the benefactor as cricket history now portrays him.

If any English defeat against Australia seemed to enhance the cause of federation, it would have been celebrated as earnestly in the Colonial Office in London as in the *Bulletin* office in Sydney: politics, once again and quite naturally, going hand in glove with sport.

As the century came towards its close the Melbourne Cricket Club could look back at its influence on Australian cricket. The Stoddart tour had shown the Club a profit of £2388 on tour-gate receipts of £24,677. This added to the Club's efforts in the seasons when they had brought out English sides to the colonies: 1878–79, 1881–82, 1887–88 and 1891–92. Then for 1894–95 and 1897–98 they had been joint sponsors with the trustees of the Sydney Cricket Ground.

The Melbourne Club, having good reason to feel satisfied in its involvement with England teams, now intended to finance an Australian team to England and did so under the guise of: 'The Club was invited by the leading players in Australia to organise a tour to England . . . and at once accepted the proposal'.

Behind those words, written by the Assistant Secretary, George Atkinson, was a far more interesting story. Rumblings regarding the Australasian Cricket Council were coming from the Colonial Associations and being directed at Melbourne CC. At the same time the players were becoming impatient with their own Associations.

In early February the Queensland Cricket Association had written to the other Associations congratulating them on deciding to bring all intercolonial fixtures under ACC control. Then came the news that the Melbourne Club was once again going to ignore the ACC and had laid plans for an Australian team to tour England in 1899, with Ben Wardill as manager. It seemed that the players' cartel was behind this tour and the South Australian committee, on 14 March 1898, passed a motion instructing their delegates: 'To use their best endeavours to assist the Cricket Council to carry out the objects for which it was formed'.

In a last ditch effort to keep the ACC alive the NSWCA formed a sub-committee to consider pooling the takings of intercolonial matches, with the Australasian Cricket Council being responsible for distribution of profits.* They also put forward a plan for a percentage of the profits to be set aside in a fund to bring out English teams, instead of just the Melbourne CC and SCG trustees having control. The Colonial

*This was a move by NSWCA delegates which took place as soon as it was found out that Melbourne CC was backing the 1899 tour.

Associations all approved this idea and agreed to support it at the ACC meeting scheduled for 29 July, with the added suggestion that the colonies would only play each other *once* in a season when England were touring.

Then out of the blue came a bombshell. The new ACC secretary, John Creswell, received a letter dated 12 July 1898, signed by twelve leading players,* requesting that their Associations consider withdrawing from the ACC. Special meetings were arranged in all colonies and the ACC delegates were let known the players' views in no uncertain fashion. Creswell, at the ACC's Melbourne meeting, made sure that the players' views were discussed – for the NSWCA delegates were firmly opposed to the players having direct representation, and the Melbourne CC members of the Victorian delegation abstained. However Creswell, of all those present in Young and Jackson's room that day, was astute enough to know how powerful the players' lobby could be. Horse-trading went on between SACA and VCA delegates which basically came down to 'if the VCA supported the SACA push for player representation, then SACA would support the Melbourne CC right to organise an Australian team to England'.

The player representation motion was passed and, on his return to Adelaide, Creswell was instructed to call meetings of the players to let them vote in two delegates from each of the three major Associations.

The next ACC meeting was due for 2 September, also in Melbourne, but the problems were becoming urgent. The South Australian and NSW players were as one on ACC representation, but the NSWCA would not even give their players a hearing. The VCA supported their players, but their delegates to the ACC would not, as doing so conflicted with (three of the four delegates who represented) the Melbourne Cricket Club.

The meeting did result in a win for the players after a surprising backdown by the Melbourne/VCA delegates, who must have realised that they needed the top players for their next tour of England. The consequence in October was to find Hugh Trumble and John Worrall as the Victorian players' representatives along with Jack Lipscomb (St Kilda CC) and George Moir (North Melbourne CC), with not a Melbourne CC delegate in sight. The NSWCA refused to budge, their delegates – Ted Briscoe, Coleman Davis, Charles Lloyd and Richard Shute – being all dyed-in-the-wool officials. The flashpoint would come sooner rather than later.

As the 1897–98 season drew to a close a match took place on 23

*Darling, Hill, Worrall, Gregory, Noble, Trott, Trumble, Kelly, Howell, Jones, McLeod, Iredale.

and 30 April 1898 on the Waverley Ground in Sydney. It was between a 'Combined Team' and Paddington, and was a benefit match on behalf of Ned Gregory, the curator of the SCG and the designer of the first of the large Australian scoreboards. The funds raised just passed the £100 mark but what is of significance is that it was the first such benefit match played in Australia.

Attitudes in Australia were changing. Just as the triumphs over England were having their effect on national feeling the colonial associations were, as a consequence, becoming important institutions with large budgets and a growing number of clubs to control.

John Portus, having resigned as the honorary secretary of the NSWCA, the subsequent appointment of Percy Bowden was as the first full-time association official. In Perth, the WACA had followed suit and appointed Harry Brown of the Metropolitan Club as their paid secretary.

The 1898–99 season now saw Victoria win the Sheffield Shield; Western Australia play their initial first-class match on home soil; Queensland entertain South Australia for the first time; and New Zealand make a seminal tour in Australia. But the season belonged to an up-and-coming young player from New South Wales: Victor Trumper. His two double-centuries saw him top the Australian aggregates with 873 runs at 62.36, scored in just nine matches.

In December 1898 Tasmania visited Sydney and in their match against NSW were dismissed for 130 by mid-afternoon on the first day. At stumps NSW were 293 for four. Next morning, Saturday 10 December, Trumper joined Frank Iredale at the crease with the score 313 for five. They were parted 258 runs later (Iredale 196) after which Trumper continued on his merry way so that, when NSW was finally dismissed for 839, Trumper remained undefeated on 292, made in 268 minutes. At the time it was the greatest number of runs scored by a batsman in a day's play. The third day saw Tasmania dismissed for 222, NSW winning by an innings and 487 runs, again a new record.

The tour by New Zealand was approved by the NZCC at their meeting in Christchurch in February 1899. With just £134 in the bank it was an ambitious gamble but one essential to the development of the game. Factional in-fighting saw six of the original thirteen players selected changed, and resulted in the secretary of the Wellington Cricket Association urging that the tour be abandoned. It went ahead nevertheless, with the first two matches being played in Tasmania. In Hobart, the tourists fought an evenly contested draw over three days before going on to Launceston to defeat Tasmania by 150 runs. But it was very different in Melbourne and Sydney.

Batting first against Victoria, the New Zealanders ran up a score of 317 and had the home side at 129 for five. Then came two days of frustration as Peter McAlister scored a career-best 224 before being the last wicket to fall at 602. New Zealand eventually lost by an innings and 132 runs. Far worse was to follow in Sydney where the pace of the pitch quite demoralised the New Zealanders who fell easy victims to the quick spin of Bill Howell (5/22) and latterly to Tom McKibbin (7/30) to lose by an innings and 384 runs.

However, it was Victor Trumper who again took the honours. His 253 was scored in five-and-a-half hours and was an imperious exhibition of the graceful batting for which he became renowned. It was the sheer quality of Trumper's batting which made the New Zealanders realise that they were just novices on the world stage. Hugh Trumble declared 'that the standard of their cricket has declined since I was there in 1896'. He suggested that the provincial associations should look to employing coaches 'who could be procured in Australia for £2 a week'. His advice was heeded and soon the Victorian all-rounder Albert Trott was coaching in Hawkes Bay, Charles Bannerman in Christchurch, and Sam Jones in Auckland.

In March 1899 the tenth Australian team – as selected by Joe Darling (South Australia), Hugh Trumble (Victoria) and Syd Gregory (NSW) – left home for their tour of England. Even before they left the players were being hailed as the strongest team ever to leave Australia. They had originally been thirteen strong but, under pressure, also took the young Victor Trumper whose job would also be to act as assistant to the tour manager, Ben Wardill.

Joe Darling, twenty-eight years of age, was a staunch Presbyterian who had an abhorrence of both drinking and smoking. Born in the lower Adelaide hills he had attended Prince Alfred College school before going to study at Roseworthy Agricultural College in the near north of South Australia. A member of Adelaide's establishment, Darling was a natural leader in the eyes of those who wanted to push the Victorian ethos of muscular Christianity.

Darling was determined to see that any touring side under his command behaved in a proper way. There would be none of the poor conduct of some previous tours. His edicts to the players were obeyed because they trusted him even though he was the closest any Australian captain has come to being a disciplinarian.

There were five players new to England on tour: Bill Howell, Monty Noble and Victor Trumper of New South Wales, and Charles McLeod and Frank Laver from Victoria. They enjoyed an English summer of tropical weather and assisted the tourists to three victories and a defeat in the seven matches up to the first Test.

Following a two-day victory over Lancashire at Old Trafford, the

Australians spent their extra day at the local races as guests of Lord Marcus Beresford. He told them to back a horse called Portobello which won at very long odds. As most of the team had taken their host's advice – particularly Ernie Jones – any immediate financial concerns were dissipated.

The five-Test series against England was the first of such length in England, with the initial fixture at Trent Bridge, a new venue for this level of the game. England were captained by Dr W. G. Grace who was playing in his last Test at the age of fifty.

Australia batted first with Trumper making a duck on his debut. It was an unspectacular draw marred only by the outrageous behaviour of the umpire, Barlow, the former Lancashire and England Test player, who for his conduct was reported to Lord's by Joe Darling. Lord Harris agreed with the Australian captain saying that Barlow was unsuitable, 'because of misplaced loyalties to his old team'.

The second Test at Lord's in mid-June saw Archie MacLaren take over from Grace as England's captain but he could not stop Australia recording an easy victory by ten wickets. Ernie Jones took ten wickets in the match with Clem Hill and Victor Trumper both scoring 135. The tourists were now in top gear, recording victory after victory and attracting enormous crowds. Rain spoilt the final day of the drawn third Test at Headingley, with the fourth Test at Old Trafford effectively destroyed by the old follow-on law. This stated that any team 120 runs or more behind their opponents was compulsorily made to bat again. This saved Australia and infuriated England, and the law was soon changed.

The fifth Test at The Oval was also drawn, again with Australia following-on. Syd Gregory scored 117 after England had reached their highest total in a Test at home with 576, scored in little over a day's play.

The courteous behaviour of Darling's team did a lot to change the English view that Australian cricketers were a rough-mannered, ruthless lot with a very mercenary outlook. The reception the side received around the country was far more charitable than it had been towards many of the other touring teams. In particular there was widespread praise for Darling's handling of the team's discipline.

But there was one match which, amongst all others, had a profound effect on all who saw it. At Hove from 27–29 July 1899, the Australians played a drawn match against Sussex. Darling lost the toss and Sussex batted all the first day for 414. At three o'clock next day Victor Trumper walked to the crease with Australia 62 for one. At 624 for four, Darling declared, with Trumper unbeaten on a quite amazing 300. It was not only the highest score made by an Australian in England, passing Billy Murdoch's 286 not out on the same ground in 1882; it was the moment when Trumper's great ability burst upon the other Australian players and the press.

At the conclusion of the tour in early September the players decided against going on a visit to South Africa as it looked as if war was about to break out there. On the day of their farewell reception at London's Mansion House, *The Times* of 11 September carried a leading article which declared: 'Mr Darling's eleven of 1899 is the best that has ever come from the Antipodes'. It was also a benefit and a good omen for the cause of imperial cricket that the last Australian team to visit the 'old country' in the colonial era should win, so that the Ashes were in Australia when it became a Commonwealth.

On 30 November 1899, the magazine *Cricket – A Weekly Record of the Game* carried an article by Jim Phillips, the Test umpire who officiated in matches in both countries. He said that Australia's success, particularly in the series just finished, was attributable to its freedom from snobbery:

> In generalship the Australians are easily first. They play more in unison, they exchange views in the dressing-room, and their captain is thereby assisted materially in many of his plans. A varied past experience in cricket in both countries leads me to attribute much of their success to this.
>
> Off the field an Australian captain receives the benefit of the opinions of his comrades as if he were chairman of a board of directors. The average English captain is more of an autocrat. He rarely seeks advice from his men. If a consultation be held it is invariably confined to the amateurs and the batsmen, not the professionals and the bowlers. I can recall instances when I have been standing umpire when able and intelligent professional players on an England side have seen the fallacy of some plan of their captain, but nothing has been said by them, no suggestion made, to remedy the mistake.
>
> Another mistake is made in England which does not improve cricket as a science – that is, the system of isolating professionals off the field. Surely, if a man is good enough to play on the same side he is good enough to dress in the same dressing-room. It is there most useful hints and ideas are exchanged when a game is in progress, which cannot be done so well on the field.

George Bull, an Australian journalist, raised other matters, taking particular notice of the Australian grounds which were far superior to those of England especially when it came to facilities, playing surfaces and crowd control. There was also, inevitably, an authentic Australian complaint that 'one-half of the English dressing rooms don't even boast a shower-bath!'

These minor, yet significant criticisms reflected how Australian cricketing nationalism had changed over forty years. Gone was the deference of the 1860s and gone too was the feeling that lingered through the 1870s that Australia was an extension of Britain. Also blown away from the sub-conscious of the nation were the old fears of physical degeneration.

The country was now, although the Australasian Cricket Council was in its death throes, united behind its cricketers. As the *Review of Reviews* said in its edition for September 1899:

> The doings of the Elevens are treated through all Australia as events of grave historical importance. For the go 'home' and thrash the Englishmen is the summit of the schoolboy's ambition.

The article continued to say that the bond between the two countries was close but that the nature of the relationship had altered:

> The passion for cricket burns like a flame in Australian blood, and, in the case of an All-England Eleven, the passion is intensified by an unfilial yearning on the part of young Australia to triumphantly thrash the mother country!

At both ends of the Empire the word *cricket* was coming to be used, by the end of the century, as a moral metaphor at large. It had become a synonym for honourable dealing with other men off the field as well as on. From late 1899, for instance, a story is told in *Tasmanians in the Transvaal War* concerning a lack of grasp of cricket metaphors. The author, John Bufton, writing in 1905, quotes a story which had its roots following the 1899 visit of Joe Darling's Australians in England.

The story went that Paul Kruger, the Boer leader in South Africa, 'quakes with fright as the news that a contingent of Australian soldiers is on its way to the Transvaal: "And I hear that Eleven of them have just defeated all England"!'

# 10

# The Decline of Player Power

The Australasian Cricket Council died on 2 January 1900 at Scotts Hotel in Melbourne, with the sum of £28. 7s. 9d. to its name and little else. Although the excuse of player representation had been given for the demise of the ACC, in reality the reason lay in the intransigence of the New South Wales Cricket Association. They wanted control of cricket in Australia and were unhappy at the influence exerted by the Melbourne Cricket Club.

The NSWCA had met in the Association's rooms at Engdine Chambers, Elizabeth Street, Sydney, on 15 May 1899. John Gibson, who had moved for the ACC's establishment nine years earlier, said that: 'The Council has become a farce. Its history resembles a game of shuttlecock and the NSWCA has been the shuttlecock'. He continued: 'The Melbourne Cricket Club has to understand that it is not going to be allowed to govern cricket in Australia'.

The motion to withdraw from the Council was carried unanimously. In a letter to the Marylebone Cricket Club in London, Billy McElhone, an influential NSWCA executive member, said 'the sole cause of the Association's withdrawal from the ACC was over the matter of the players' representation'. This claim, apart from being very doubtful, only serves to prove further the NSWCA's paranoia over the Melbourne Club.

Much as the VCA and SACA tried to keep the Council alive, it was impossible to do so without New South Wales. Following discussions with Ben Wardill and commitments given by the Melbourne Cricket Club, it was agreed to hold a final meeting during the match when South Australia were playing in Melbourne.

Four of the seven delegates present at the end were Test cricketers – Joe Darling, Clem Hill, Jack Worrall and Hughie Trumble – and the Australian captain seconded the motion which read:

> That the Australian [*sic*] Cricket Council be dissolved; that Mr Creswell and Mr Whitridge be appointed as a committee to liquidate the affairs of the Council; that out of the balance, after payment of all debts, a donation of £10. 10s. be paid to the Hon. secretary Mr

> Creswell for his services in connection with the Council's business and liquidation of the affairs; that any balance remaining be equally divided between the Victorian Cricket Association and the South Australian Cricket Association, being the existing members of the body.

Next day the Melbourne *Argus* reported:

> At the conclusion of the meeting, Mr Joe Darling proposed the health of Mr George Moir, the chairman. Mr Moir had been very prominent in the work of the Council, and had shown great ability for the work, and it was not his fault that the results had not been better.
>
> Mr Moir in replying, regretted that circumstances had compelled the Council to end its existence, but he felt sure that ere long a body would be found capable of thoroughly managing Australian cricket. In all the doings of the Council, he had been satisfied, with Mr Darling, that playing members should have a voice in the control of affairs. The men who were playing the game were in touch with what was going on, and he was satisfied that they should be represented on the governing body. He hoped soon to see some arrangements to come whereby the cricket of Australia might be satisfactorily managed.

Ironically enough George Moir's words would be echoed in 1987 by a later Australian captain (Greg Chappell) when he made a plea to Australian cricket administrators using virtually the same phrases. Nearly two years later, in November 1901, the NSWCA – by now clearly envious of the Melbourne club's position – passed a motion urging the formation of a national cricket board but the proposal fell flat when the players made it clear that they would oppose any such move.

The turn of the century saw New South Wales take the Sheffield Shield from Victoria; Joe Darling move to Tasmania to take up farming; and a gangling batsman called Warwick Armstrong score 270 for South Melbourne in a VCA club game against Melbourne. Matches were being played to raise money for the Imperial Patriotic Fund which, along with Smoke Concerts and Sports meetings, raised the sum of £340 to assist the Australian forces fighting in the Boer War.

The Melbourne Cricket Club sent their first team to New Zealand in mid-February 1900 to play in seven fixtures. Six were called 'first-class' and saw three-day successes over Auckland, Wanganui (now known as

Central Districts), Wellington, Canterbury and New Zealand, with the Otago match left drawn. Harry Graham scored 169 against Canterbury; Hugh Trumble 135 and David Mailer 105 versus Auckland; Mailer, again, made 88 in Wellington and the top scorer against New Zealand was Alan Russell with 98. Trumble achieved the best bowling analyses on the tour with 7/35 against Canterbury and 6/25 in a second-class fixture with Southland.

By 1900, the popularity of cricket had dropped even though large crowds still turned up to watch the stars play in club matches. Sports pages remained popular but the popularity of different sports fluctuated: at this time 47% of all sports news was devoted to horse-racing, whereas only 11% was being devoted to cricket.

Unemployment had dropped to 7%, a far cry from the 11% of 1896. Sydney had now overtaken Melbourne in population, while gold fever saw thousands of men migrate to Western Australia, mainly from Victoria.

For most of the 1890s the colonies of Australia had held intercolonial conferences with a view to becoming a federation but not until early 1900 was that agreement reached. Federation, it was announced, would take place on the stroke of midnight on 1 January 1901, and the capital city would be Melbourne (until 1927, when it was moved to the new city of Canberra). Victoria had been in the vanguard of the movement for Federation and the choice of Melbourne saw scenes almost as jubilant as when Victoria had separated from New South Wales nearly fifty years earlier.

The official proclamation of the Commonwealth of Australia was read out in Sydney. No longer were there colonies: there were States. Happiness ruled Australia. Adulthood had arrived. Then came a shock when, on 23 January, Queen Victoria died. The newspapers ran black borders for ten days and some even had black borders around every single column. From a cricket point of view the match in Launceston between Tasmania and Victoria was delayed by a day to allow for the national shock to pass.

The Melbourne Cricket Club had originally wanted an England team to tour in the 1900–01 season but with all the other events taking place around the country this proved impossible to arrange. They had asked the Marylebone Cricket Club to make the necessary arrangements in England and select the team. However, the powers-that-be at Lord's were having difficulties: on 13 May 1901 they announced that it was impossible to recruit a representative English team and subsequently withdrew from the venture.

Archie MacLaren, the Lancashire captain, was then persuaded to attempt the task. It did cost the Melbourne club some money: 'the advance on account of the England Eleven amounts to £333. 2s. 10d.

which, it is expected, will be recouped from their account this coming season', read the Club minute.

The Melbourne Club also announced: 'Mr MacLaren has succeeded in getting a very powerful side, which, with the exception of himself and Hayward, is composed of new men on Australian wickets'. They added: 'Mr John McLaughin, one of our vice-presidents, is now in England and in personal communication with Mr MacLaren, so members may be assured that the best team available will represent England'.

It needed to be 'the best' England team for batsmen in Australia were seemingly running wild. When NSW visited Adelaide in December 1900, Clem Hill had scored an unbeaten 365 for South Australia. In the return match three weeks later NSW made 918 – Syd Gregory 168, Monty Noble 153, Leslie Poidevin 140 not out, Reggie Duff 119, Frank Iredale 118 and Victor Trumper 70. This was a new world record total which saw the bowlers suffer: Joe Travers took 4/197 and Fred Jarvis 2/225! At the same time Warwick Armstrong was scoring centuries for Victoria while Victor Trumper had previously made 230 against Victoria in Sydney.

MacLaren's team arrived in Adelaide on 4 November 1901 and for their first three days were fêted by local cricket officials. Then came the crunch as, over four days, South Australia won by 233 runs, Clem Hill scoring 107 and 80, and the veteran George Giffen taking 7/46 and 6/47. The tide turned in Melbourne when MacLaren's side won by 118 runs, but it was defeat again in Sydney when NSW won by 53 runs.

The first Test took place in Sydney in mid-December when Australia was thrashed by an innings and 124 runs. After the English openers, MacLaren (116) and Hayward (69), put on 154 for the first wicket the tourists reached 464. Joe Darling gave no excuse for his side's totals of 168 and 172, and for the second Test he brought in Warwick Armstrong and Reg Duff for their debuts and dropped Charles McLeod and Frank Laver.

The Melbourne Test on New Year's Day 1902 saw wickets tumble on a rain-affected pitch. Australia were dismissed for 112 and, in reply, Noble claimed 7/17 as England fell for 61 in just 68 minutes. Joe Darling then changed his batting order and although Australia were 48 for five at stumps it was their tail-end batsmen who had been dismissed. Twenty-five wickets had fallen in the day – a record in Australia.

Next morning the pitch rolled out well and the batting stars who had been held back all performed as expected. Reggie Duff became the third Australian to score a century on his Test debut and he remains the only Australian to score a century against England as the penultimate batsman visiting the crease, at no. 10! He and Armstrong, who had also been held back, responded with the first hundred partnership for the tenth wicket in Test cricket. Clem Hill scored 99, the first man to be out for that score in Tests. As Australia reached 353 it was records all the way. Sidney Barnes took 6/42 and 7/121 for England which Monty Noble answered with his second innings 6/60 as England had the worst of the weather. When Hugh Trumble finished the match with a hat-trick Australia had won by 229 runs.

Then came the third Test in Adelaide, that most English of outposts. As the Adelaide *Register* reported: 'The weather was gloriously fine for the opening day, and the Oval was brilliant with flags and banners. Long lines of streamers hung from the roofs of the pavilions, and over the smokers reserve floated the Commonwealth flag and a large green-and-gold ensign with "Australia" emblazoned in gold letters. The front of the Governor's enclosure was decorated with the Union Jack and a display of cricketing colours: the green and gold of Australia; red and white check and blue background of England; red, yellow and black of South Australia; dark blue of Victoria and light blue of New South Wales.' The 'innocence' of the Edwardian golden age was complete: Statehood; Independence: Nationalism and The Empire. And South Australia's home-grown hero, Clem Hill, scored 98 and 97, to help Australia win by four wickets on the sixth day.

Local officials had their dreams realised when 48,105 people attended the match, paying £2258. This meant that, at the end of the financial year, SACA's debt was reduced by forty-five per cent.

Joe Darling, having retained the Ashes, handed over the captaincy to Hugh Trumble and returned to his farm in Tasmania. The final two Tests, in Sydney and Melbourne, were both won by Australia with some ease. Whereas the Australians' fielding, catching and Kelly's wicketkeeping were top-class, the tourists persistently fumbled balls, dropped easy chances and generally became demoralised. Australia had won the series 4–1 and Clem Hill was the first player to score 500 runs in a series without making a century.

As the England team departed, the controversies grew. The NSWCA, jealous at the financial success of MacLaren's tour, particularly when they heard that the Melbourne Club had given over £1000 to local clubs as 'donations', demanded a percentage cut of the profits. Percy Bowden wrote to Major Wardill saying: 'It is to be regretted that you . . . have not adjusted the claim of this Association . . . this charge has always been acknowledged as a just one and paid . . . for previous tours.' Wardill sent a cheque for ten guineas.

John Creswell, on the other hand, was offered twenty per cent of the tour profits for the SACA – and demanded one-third which, surprisingly, he got with little fuss. Wardill knew that, much as he disliked Creswell's hard businessman's approach, he would need his support in the near future.

In early August 1902 Edward Heather sent a letter to both Creswell and Bowden. In it he put the Victorian Cricket Association's proposal concerning the disposal of the Sheffield Shield:

> (i) That the shield becomes the property of the Association who won the first ten series of matches from the beginning of the competition;
> (ii) That the Shield should be placed in a leading pavilion of one of the clubs of the states for exhibition, and insured jointly at the expense of the states against burglary and fire;
> (iii) If approved of, Lord Sheffield be communicated with to obtain his sanction.

The South Australians debated the issue in committee and resolved: 'That this Association is in favour of continuing the present arrangement during the life of Lord Sheffield.' The 'present arrangement' still stands in the 1990s: the winner of the round-robin competition wins the Shield, but with the addition that the two top teams of the round-robin competition play off in a Final.

Then followed another letter from the VCA in which Heather wrote: 'The NSWCA agree with our suggestion that the Sheffield Shield become the property of one of the states. However, they suggest it be for whoever wins three series of matches commencing from the 1902–03 season.'

Three weeks later the VCA president, James Aitken, said at their Annual General Meeting in South Melbourne: 'Your Association, after consideration, suggested to the NSWCA and SACA that to secure finality in connection with the Sheffield Shield, it would be desirable for the state winning the first ten matches to become absolute holders. No decision has yet been definitely arrived at.'

With the South Australians now being firmly for the retention of the Shield they soon persuaded the other two Associations to leave matters as they were and the whole idea was forgotten fairly quickly.

At the end of the 1901–02 season two diverse pieces of cricket history were recorded. In Brisbane, New South Wales played Queensland in a tight match which started on 29 March. A draw was a fair result but what was of unusual interest was that this is the only time when two aboriginal players have faced each other in Australian first-class cricket. For NSW, Jack Marsh took 2/64 and 3/67 while Albert Henry, also a fast-bowler, took 1/59 and 1/38.

Also at the end of March and the beginning of April, in a match spread over four Saturdays, Charles Eady, a tall, bulky Hobart solicitor, made a world record score of 566 for his club Break o' Day.

The match, against Wellington, saw him score his runs in 473 minutes in a total of 911. His seventh-wicket stand with Walter Abbott realised 429 of which Abbott made 143.

In the newly federated country, however, matches between New South Wales and Victoria were akin to Test matches as the young States competed with each other. The game was being played more cleanly, for gambling was being stamped out at the grounds, particularly in Sydney where a more artisan type of spectator tended to dominate. The number of half-days, usually Wednesdays and Saturdays, plus a growing number of public holidays, particularly during the summer, helped sport to grow. Cricket grew among tradesmen and warehousemen in a similar way as it had in the eastern parts of America in the 1850s, but cricket continued to grow in Australia whereas in the United States baseball supplanted cricket.

District, or Electorate, cricket grew in the cities and created local interest and loyalty. As country towns grew larger so did their local associations. The cricket club became the nub of the community, with the Western Australian Cricketing Association finding themselves solvent purely due to profits from bar takings.

Major Ben Wardill, Secretary of the Melbourne Cricket Club, organised, arranged and managed the eleventh Australian team to visit England in 1902. Captained again by Joe Darling, who was taking a respite from his farm in Tasmania, and with Victor Trumper as his deputy, the side was finally selected in early March 1902. New to England would be four players who had made their debuts against MacLaren's tourists: Warwick Armstrong, Reggie Duff, Bert Hopkins and John ('Jack') Saunders. Hanson Carter went as reserve wicketkeeper but he was going to have to wait over five years before making his Test debut.

The Australians had also arranged to tour South Africa after their English trip, a move intended to restore friendly relations following the 1899 tour postponement and Australia's involvement in the Boer War.

The 1902 Australians may well have been the strongest team ever to visit England. Warwick Armstrong always thought so and he captained the great side of 1921. The other comparable teams of 1948 and 1989 also played against weakened sides – by war, and by politics – but the 1902 tourists played a full-strength, unravaged England team.

Both Darling's men and MacLaren's tourists sailed for England in March 1902 on the mailboat *Omrah*. They arrived in late April to a London in the second year of Edward VII's reign. Gone were the dowdy years of late Victorian England. It was now the days of 'make-hay-while-the-sun-shines', or in modern parlance 'The Empire

Rules. OK'. It was an England of jingoism; of a country which gloated over *their* victory in the Boer War, without knowing the full truth; which talked of *their* Empire; of how the natives wanted to be led by *their* English masters. It was an England where white racial superiority was taken for granted – although it was in order for Ranjitsinhji to play cricket for England because he was a prince who became the heir to the throne of Nawanagar. But it was also an England where no woman had the vote, as women already did in Australia.

The tour was dominated by Victor Trumper. His batting was supreme in what was a fairly wet summer. He scored 2570 runs in 36 matches at an average of 48.49. He made eleven centuries with a highest of only 128 and that against Cambridge University.

There was a mystique about Trumper. His batting was stylish and he had ability seldom before seen in a batsman. But however great a player he was, legends of him grew without a basis of fact. He was the illegitimate son of a housemaid, born in Auckland, New Zealand, and he only arrived in Australia when one of his mother's cousins agreed for him to become a member of her family. Had this not happened, would the world of cricket now be praising the Kiwi batsman Victor Coghlan?

The Trumper 'industry' went off the rails years ago and fact is now blurred with fiction. In his time, Trumper's contemporaries were full of praise for his cricketing ability. Albert Knight in *The Complete Cricketer* wrote in 1906: 'Trumper with the bat does all things perfectly. There is the simplicity and depth of a full melody,' and then went on to describe Trumper as 'Australia's Crown Prince of Cricket'. During his short but eventful lifetime he was described by cricket's sternest critics as 'the wizard of the willow', 'the incomparable', 'a genius beyond compare', 'the dazzling cavalier' . . .

In an article for the *Strand Magazine* of September 1912, Jack Hobbs, the great Surrey run-scoring machine, when commenting on the soundness of Australian pitches, wrote:

> The same prevalence of ideal batting conditions has given us Victor Trumper, the 'Champagne of Cricket'.
>
> He is the most perfect batsman in his scoring methods I have ever seen. He makes every orthodox stroke quite after the best models, and in addition he has several strokes of his own which it is quite hopeless for other batsmen to attempt.
>
> The way in which he hits a good-length ball round to the leg boundary where there are no fieldsmen is enough to break the heart of any bowler, and this is only one of his characteristic shots. He is a past-master of every method of scoring four off a ball most batsmen would be content to play with care, and has more strokes

of this type at his command than any other cricketer.

The former England captain, Charles Fry, said in a broadcast on Sydney radio station 2FC in late 1932:

> Trumper captured the hearts of English cricket lovers. No matter how many runs Bradman makes, Vic Trumper's name comes up time and again, and his great deeds are discussed. He took a hold on the hearts and minds of people in England as no other batsman has done. It was not only the runs he made but how he made them. He did everything so easily and with such infinite grace. We were not in the least annoyed when he flogged our bowling, he did it so nicely. He will always live in English cricket as something unique, as perhaps the greatest of all!

But there was another side to Trumper which concerned his off-field activities. Business ventures failing; bankruptcies, and a final indignity of being sacked as Treasurer of the NSW Rugby League. *The Bulletin* of 18 March 1908 says Trumper was dismissed for 'not being able to account for certain funds'. The *Sydney Morning Herald* on 13 March 1909 reported that Trumper 'mismanaged the League's affairs'. On 22 April 1909 the *SMH* added that Trumper had 'made illegal deposits', and on the story went. The legends of Victor Trumper's prowess and modesty allow little room for stories such as these.

The first seven matches of the 1902 tour saw four wins for the Australians and three draws before the first Test at the end of May. The venue was Edgbaston, Birmingham, a new ground for the staging of Tests. The English selectors, led by Lord Hawke, chose a team, captained by Archie MacLaren, which is usually considered to be the strongest England batting side ever to come together. All of them had scored centuries in first-class cricket and represented the nucleus of the game's 'Golden Age': MacLaren, Fry, Ranjitsinhji, Jackson, (J.T.) Tyldesley, Lilley, Hirst, Jessop, Braund, Lockwood, Rhodes.

MacLaren won the toss and batted on the first of the three days, England scoring 351 for nine by the close. Rain next morning saw England declare at 376, with the Australians unable to cope with the drying pitch when they batted. In just 85 minutes the tourists had been dismissed for 36 runs, half of them scored by Trumper. Rain the next day restricted play to 75 minutes and Australia escaped with a draw.

They did not escape the next match, at Headingley against Yorkshire, when the influenza wracked team – it was a virulent strain which affected the majority of the party and lingered – fell to the bowling of the Test players, George Hirst and Stanley Jackson, for 23 runs. As the tourists approached the Lord's Test they were at their lowest ebb, but fate would play its hand as only 105 minutes' play was possible for the whole Test.

Moving on to another new Test venue, Bramall Lane, Sheffield (the only time a Test was played there) the Australians were recovering well enough from their illnesses to endure the appalling smog created by the city's smokestacks. The visibility was so poor that the players on the field could see the gas lamps burning in the pavilion at lunchtime.

Darling won the toss for the first time on the tour, and would have been pleased with the 49-run credit after each side had completed their first innings. Then Trumper and Hill both played memorable innings: Trumper making 62 out of 80 in 50 minutes, and Hill 119. Noble then assisted Australia to victory with bowling of 5/51 and 6/52.

The final Test matches, at Old Trafford and The Oval, were two of the finest ever played. At Manchester from 24–26 July the advantage seemed to swing from one team to the other all the time. Australia batted first with Trumper in devastating form. He was 103 not out at lunch when the score was 173 for one, all scored in 105 minutes. The century opening stand with Reggie Duff (54) took only 57 minutes, with Trumper eventually out just after the first break for 104. Clem Hill (65) and Joe Darling (51) assisted the total to 299, following which Saunders and Trumble saw England to 70 for five at the close.

Stanley Jackson (128) and Len Braund (65) played England out of this seemingly hopeless situation and took the total to 262. With a first-innings lead of 37 all looked well for Australia until they were 10 for three in their second innings. Aided by fielding lapses Gregory and Darling then carried the score to 64 before a final rot set in. Dismissed for 86, the Australians had left England needing just 124 for victory.

Trumble (6/53) and Saunders (4/52) were in devastating form after lunch on the final day as England slumped after being 44 without loss. In the tightest of all possible finishes Australia won by three runs and at the end the Australian players ran from the field like dervishes in a display of emotion previously unknown to the more staid English supporters. In the dressing-room Joe Darling fell into a chair as the momentous events suddenly sank home.

A week later the tourists found themselves on the south coast playing against Sussex at Hove. Monty Noble must have enjoyed the sea air for his 284 out of 580 for six turned out to be the Australians' only double-century of the tour. Six weeks later against the South of England at Bournemouth, Hugh Trumble gained the best bowling figures with 9/39 and 6/29. Trumble with 137 wickets and Saunders with 123 easily led the wicket-takers over the five-month tour.

The final Test, from 11–13 August 1902, was every bit as dramatic as the previous one. Australia had the Ashes, so only pride was at stake for the Englishmen. The selectors dropped Ranjitsinhji – he had now played his last Test – and brought back Gilbert Jessop who had missed the Manchester drama.

Australia batted first for 324 of which Hugh Trumble made an unbeaten 64. He then bowled unchanged taking 8/65 as England fell for 183, which could have been worse had Clem Hill not dropped an outfield catch which would have caused the home side to follow-on. Patchy batting second time around by Australia saw England left to make 263 to win on a worn pitch.

This far from easy task looked impossible when the score became 48 for five. But then came Jessop. He flayed the Australian attack scoring his fifty in just 43 minutes and then went on to record what was then Test cricket's fastest century in just 75 minutes. Even though Trumble was again bowling unchanged it was Warwick Armstrong who ultimately dismissed Jessop for 104. As *The Times* said the following day: 'As long as cricket lasts Mr Jessop's great performance will be remembered'.

Stanley Jackson, who had held up one end, continued on to 49 before being seventh man out at 187. George Hirst was now the mainstay of the English batting with his calmness essential as the score neared the winning target. Lockwood and Lilley departed, and when Rhodes, the last man, came to the crease to join Hirst 15 runs were needed.

The pair picked off the runs slowly although they were fortunate that Armstrong dropped a slip catch as he overbalanced. It was one of cricket's historic last-wicket partnerships and gave England's season more respectability than perhaps it deserved.

Ten more fixtures had to be completed before the Australian team could board the SS *Dunvegan Castle* on 20 September to sail to South Africa. Eighteen days at sea would give the players a well deserved rest. They could also reflect on a tour which saw Test cricket completely dominate the competition for the county championship. It was the first time this had happened and it pleased neither Lord Hawke nor Lord Harris to whom the county structure was the essential basis of the game.

The batting of Victor Trumper had caught the public's imagination: they had seen nothing like it before, but on the field and off Joe Darling's captaincy had been second to none. Not only had he led the side well; he had kept the party keen through an arduous summer and, of more importance, had kept any factions or cliques from forming.

After landing in Cape Town the cricketers took the train across the Karoo to the highveld and Johannesburg, a city just over twenty years old. The day after their arrival, the Australians started their initial Test match on South African soil on a matting pitch and at an altitude of seven thousand feet.

The noted South African cricket administrator Maurice Luckin wrote in his *History of South African Cricket*: 'That South Africa should be able to hold its own against the choice of the Australian cricketers fresh from a triumphant season in Great Britain was in some circles unthinkable'. The Old Wanderers ground in the heart of Johannesburg (now the site of the main railway station) had seen nothing like it before as the crowds flocked in to see the men they had previously only heard about. But it was not that easy for the visitors: South Africa made 428 for seven at the end of the first day and took the total to 454 when play resumed the following Monday morning.

The matting pitch played havoc with the Australian bowling as Louis Tancred (97), Charles Llewellyn (90), Dave Nourse (72) and Ernest Halliwell (57) took to the six-man bowling attack. In reply only an unbeaten 82 from Reggie Duff, Clem Hill's 76 and Victor Trumper's 63 saw the score to 296. The Springbok captain, Henry Taberer, enforced the follow-on which saw two wickets fall before Hill and Warwick Armstrong (59) pulled the match round. Hill, 22 overnight went on to 138 at lunch on the last day: his 116 made in one session being a then Australian individual record. Darling declared at 372 for seven but the game by that time was destined to be a draw.

The day following the Test, the Australians started a fixture at Berea Park in Pretoria against 'Fifteen of Transvaal'. In a drawn match 1213 runs were scored with Victor Trumper carrying his bat for 218.

Without a break it was back to the (Old) Wanderers ground for the second Test and after a day and a half the Australians had a first-innings deficit of 65 runs. Then came a splendid knock from Warwick Armstrong when he opened the second innings. He remained unbeaten on 159 out of 309, over half of the runs on a difficult matting track.

South Africa never looked capable of scoring the 245 needed to win and fell to the vicious left-arm medium-paced spin of Jack Saunders who took 7/34. Australia won by 159 runs late on the third day, a Tuesday. They then changed, packed, thanked their hosts and walked over the road to the old railway station. There they took the night train over the Drakensburg range and arrived the following lunchtime in hot, steamy Durban.

At Old Lord's they played 'Fifteen of Natal' whose team included many names soon to become famous in Springbok cricket: Nourse, Dalton, Deane, Vogler and Bissett. The match was drawn with the stretched coconut matting causing Natal wicketkeeper Deane no end of trouble: his 28 byes in Australia's first innings being a virtually unheard-of figure. If a matting pitch is not laid absolutely flat, nor pulled taut enough, a spin bowler can be unplayable and a fast bowler decidedly dangerous.

Then came a delicate cruise along the southern coast with ports of call at East London and Port Elizabeth until Cape Town was reached at the beginning of November. There the Australians played an evens contest with Western Province on the spectacularly beautiful Newlands ground with Bill Howell enjoying a match to remember. He made 20 and 57 not out in a low-scoring match, and took 8/31 and 9/23, bowling unchanged. After a day's break it was straight into the third Test. Darling won the toss and watched Clem Hill make an unbeaten 91 and Victor Trumper 70 in a score of 252.

The Springboks fell to Howell (4/18) and Saunders (4/37) for 85, and looked doomed following-on in front of a record crowd for a cricket match in South Africa. Then, the 11,000 spectators had their special holiday Monday transformed as Jimmy Sinclair scored South Africa's fastest Test century. His 104 took just 80 minutes and included six sixes and ten fours, all in a total of 225. Australia won by ten wickets and took the series, but it had not been as easy as that suggests. Darling's team had made many friends and their influence would be felt around the country, particularly as they were the first fully representative national team to tour the land.

Three days later the Australians sailed from Cape Town, reaching home a fortnight before Christmas 1902. But the South Australian and New South Wales players had little time to spend with their families for the first Sheffield Shield match of the new season started in Adelaide on 19 December. Five weeks later NSW were celebrating their fourth successive victory and the Shield title.

Victor Trumper, who had been rewarded for his efforts on tour by the public of New South Wales subscribing one hundred guineas through a special fund, was able to play only five times for his club, Paddington, due to first-class commitments. In one of these matches against Redfern at the Redfern Oval, he made 335 in two hours and forty minutes in an innings comprising 22 sixes and 39 fours – the highest score in Sydney cricket at the time.

Towards the end of the 1902–03 season, NSW cricket saw the resignation of their vice-president John Gibson. He had served for over thirty years, being honorary secretary from 1875–82 and then honorary treasurer, and had done much to stabilise the Association in its period of expansion.

A team of English cricketers, put together by Lord Hawke and captained by Pelham Warner, toured New Zealand during 1902–03. At the end of their sojourn in March they played three matches in Australia on their way home, losing to Victoria in Melbourne and drawing in Sydney against NSW. In South Australia, due to a prior booking of the Adelaide Oval by the 'League of Wheelmen', the fixture took place on the suburban Unley Oval; the only first-class fixture in the State ever to have been played away from Adelaide. The locals took advantage of the rough pitch to defeat the visitors by 97 runs.

The need for a more relaxed style of cricket, with less competition, saw the formation in June 1903 in Sydney of the City and Suburban Cricket Association. To other Australians, particularly Victorians, the thought of not playing a game to win but just for its social value was anathema. The original twelve CSCA clubs were Callon Park, Cammeray, CBC Bank, Double Bay, Glenwood, I Zingari, Leichhardt, Nondescripts, Sydney District, Wayfarers and Willoughby. A month later eighteen more clubs joined and, from that day to this, City and Suburban matches have provided recreation for thousands of cricketers who just enjoy participating in a match.

On 27 June 1903 Major Ben Wardill sent a cable to the NSWCA, VCA and SACA regarding a tour by an England team for the following 1903–04 season. It read:

> Negotiations were entered into by the Melbourne Cricket Club committee with Mr A. C. MacLaren to bring out another team, under the auspices and management of this Club, during the coming season. Mr MacLaren, however, was unable to bring a team at the desired time, and the committee then cabled to the Marylebone Club, asking that body to revive the schemes of 1900 (which it will be remembered fell through owing to the war in South Africa) and of 1901, when the Marylebone CC was again asked to bring out a team, but were unable to do so. On this occasion the head authority of cricket in England has accepted the invitation from the committee and has undertaken to bring out a representative team. The Melbourne Cricket Club has no responsibility at all with regard to the visit, and is only pecuniarily interested in the matches played upon the Melbourne Ground, but the committee have, at the request of the Marylebone CC, prepared the programme of matches in Australia, and will welcome with great pleasure the advent of a team under the management and prestige of the highest cricketing institution in the world, and having for its captain Mr P. F. Warner.

Although the stranglehold the Melbourne Cricket Club had on Australian cricket was weakening (and the South Australian secretary, John Creswell, was strongly agitating behind the scenes for an Australian

Cricket Board of Control), they were still performing all the tour negotiations. The reason for Wardill's cable was to pass on the conditions for touring as sent by the Marylebone Cricket Club secretary, Francis Lacey. These were:

(i) Invitations must come from all three principal cricket associations;
(ii) All matches must be played to our laws;
(iii) We take half gross gate in Test matches with usual guarantees in others;
(iv) Fixtures to be made subject to our approval on our arrival;
(v) Three days' rest before each Test;
(vi) Only members to be admitted to grounds without payment;
(vii) Phillips to accompany team as umpire.

Archie MacLaren had asked Wardill to postpone the tour until the 1904–05 season as the top players, Barnes and Lockwood, were not available. Wardill had refused and turned to Lacey for help. This resulted in Pelham Warner being appointed captain in late June with his touring side being selected a month later. They left England for a five-week voyage to Australia, landing at Port Adelaide on 2 November 1903, right into the middle of a fascinating row between John Creswell of SACA and the senior cricketer, George Giffen. As the State associations became more organised, the power of the players was gradually slipping away, with players' demands no longer gaining the response of earlier times.

The South Australian team to play England starting on 7 November 1903 was announced on Wednesday 28 October. Two days later Creswell sent the following letter to the players:

> 30 October. Dear Sir, I have to inform you that you have been selected to play in the match against England. Kindly let me know at once if you are able to play, and the amount of your loss of time, if any. J. Creswell, secretary.

Creswell received the following, by messenger, early on Monday morning:

> 2 November. Dear Sir, I beg to claim £10 for match England v South Australia, 7 November and following days. Yours truly, George Giffen.

Creswell sent a reply next morning:

> 3 November. Dear Sir, Your application for the sum of £10 for

> loss of time in connection with the forthcoming English match was considered last night by the Ground & Finance committee, and in reply thereto I beg to state that they regret they cannot accede to your request, but will be pleased to allow you the sum of £5 for loss of time. Please let me know as soon as possible whether this is acceptable, and oblige, John Creswell, secretary.

To which Giffen replied:

> 3 November. Dear Sir, Yours of today to hand. My application was for expenses, not for loss of time altogether. If your committee cannot see their way clear to accede to my request I am sorry to say I will not take part in the forthcoming match against England. Yours, George Giffen.

Next day Giffen received from Creswell:

> 4 November. Dear Sir, Replying to yours of the 3rd instant, I am instructed to inform you that the committee cannot see their way clear to grant you more than £5 for expenses and for loss of time in connection with the forthcoming match. Please, therefore, let me know as soon as possible whether you intend to play or not, and oblige. John Creswell, secretary.

The following morning Creswell obtained Giffen's response which said:

> 5 November. Dear Creswell, Re my declining to play in the forthcoming match. After due consideration and on the advice of friends, I hereby withdraw my previous intention of not playing, on the condition that my expenses are handed to the secretary of the Children's Hospital. Yours, George Giffen.

An immediate reply was sent the few yards from Creswell's Waymouth Street office to Giffen at the General Post Office:

> 5 November. Dear Sir, Replying to your letter of even date, I am instructed by my committee to inform you that they positively decline to hand over any moneys payable to you to any person or body other than yourself. Should you play in the match the amount you will receive will be £5 already offered you, and the committee require to know by four o'clock today whether you propose to play on the terms offered. J. Creswell, secretary.

Giffen's letter which concluded the correspondence read:

5 November. Sir, Yours of even date to hand. As stated in my letter of this morning, I have decided to play in the match merely out of courtesy to the English team. As your committee refuse to hand any moneys payable to me for my services to the Childrens Hospital, I will undertake to do so myself and will forward you the secretary's acknowledgement in due course. Yours, George Giffen.

A row between Creswell and Giffen was akin to an irresistible force meeting an immovable object. Player power was on the decline, but not yet dead, and Giffen's stance meant little in reality as the match would be his penultimate first-class appearance at forty-four years of age.

'Of the fourteen players in Warner's England team, seven were entire strangers to Australia', stated *Wisden* when commenting on the tour. Strangers they may have been but the team settled down well, winning three and drawing one of their four first-class matches which led up to the first Test in Sydney.

There they met an Australian team captained by Montague Alfred Noble who, in his prime years as an all-rounder (1899–1905), would have been worth his place in the Australian side either as a batsman or a bowler. A disciplinarian, like Darling, Noble could not abide slackness or slovenliness in any shape or form and, as his teammate Hugh Trumble said: 'With Noble, woe betide the inattentive or carelessly dressed fieldsman'.

On the art of captaincy, Noble wrote in his book *The Game's the Thing*: 'Many qualifications are necessary adequately to equip the man selected as captain and he may learn just as much as his mentality will allow. The great leader is the embodiment of all the hopes, virtue, courage, and ability possessed by the ten men under his command. If he is not, he is but the shadow and lacks the substance of captaincy. He will not last.'

Noble won his first toss from Warner and he proceeded to score his maiden Test century on his debut as captain. It was his twenty-third Test and his 133 was the backbone of Australia's 285. The Saturday, second-day, crowd of 35,499 – the second highest yet recorded in Australia – paid a record £1772 to watch England pass Australia's total, and then gain a healthy lead. By the third afternoon R. E. (Reginald) Foster, on his debut, had made the highest score by an Englishman in Australia, and it would remain the best in Test cricket for a quarter of a century.

His 287 runs came in 419 minutes, with his final 214 runs all coming on the third day. He shared in three century partnerships, and his tenth-wicket stand of 130 in 66 minutes with Wilfred Rhodes remains an Ashes record. In answer to England's 577, the Australian batsmen tried valiantly to overcome the deficit. Victor Trumper scored an unbeaten 185, reaching his century in 94 minutes, but even so England won by five wickets. The total attendance of 96,339, paying £4274, were both new Australian records.

Then it was virtually straight on to Melbourne for the New Year Test when England scored 221 for two on the first day. They were precious runs, for rain seriously curtailed the second day's play and also ruined the fourth day. The Australians had no answer to Wilfred Rhodes' guile as he claimed 7/56 and 8/68 to give the tourists a 185-run victory and a two–nil lead in the series. The captains agreed after the match that, in future, the pitch should be rolled each night if it had rained during the day in order to give the strip a chance to recover. They also agreed that the outfield could be cut each morning before play: both innovations are still in current use.

Adelaide in mid-January saw Trumper score yet another century (113); Clem Hill become the first batsman to score 2000 Test runs; and Syd Gregory's 112 enabled him to equal Trumper's record of four Test centuries against England. All this in Australia's 216-run victory.

Between Tests the tourists played Tasmania twice, New South Wales and Victoria. The latter match caused eyebrows to be raised for, on a wet wicket at the MCG, Victoria were dismissed in their second innings for just 15, a figure which still remains the lowest first-class score in Australia. The innings lasted for 45 minutes, Rhodes taking 5/6 from 37 balls and Arnold 4/8 from 36 balls, with Saunders being 'absent hurt'. The *Argus* had a field day referring to 'missed catches' and, stating the obvious: 'This was the worst score ever by an Australian team against English bowling'.

The fourth and fifth Tests in Sydney and Melbourne were played back to back. The Australians brought in a twenty-year-old, Albert 'Tibby' Cotter, the NSW fast bowler, in place of Bill Howell, and the Victorian batsman Peter McAlister for Warwick Armstrong but Monty Noble was the only Australian to shine, being not out in both innings – the latter the only home half-century – and taking 7/100 in the first innings. England won by 157 runs.

With England having regained the Ashes, Australia surprisingly made only one change for the final Test: the South Australian batsman, Algy Gehrs, coming in for Syd Gregory who was injured. Australia won a low-scoring match by 218 runs, and Hugh Trumble took a hat-trick in his last appearance for his country. The Australian public was fascinated by the series with 314,284 attending the five Tests and paying gate receipts of £12,441. Even so the Marylebone Cricket Club lost £1500 on the venture.

During Test match time in Melbourne in those days before radio broadcasts, one of the greatest problems was for cricket followers to find out the score. Newspaper information quickly became dated so the *Argus* started a news-agency system. As a public service the newspaper posted telegrams relating the latest score outside all the leading suburban news agencies. This enabled the public to keep up to date with events. It also gave the *Argus* a huge boost in popularity.

A small incident took place, following the end of the fifth Test, which proved to be the catalyst that led to the formation of a national cricket body in Australia. It also saw the beginning of the end of the major influence of the Melbourne Cricket Club. The move had more to do, however, with NSWCA jealousy, their urge to control the game, and naked cricket-political ambition than with the good of the game itself.

In March 1904 Syd Gregory was the innocent victim of an administrative muddle between the Victorian Cricket Association and the Melbourne Cricket Club. Both he and Warwick Armstrong had been named as Australia's twelfth man for the final Test. When this was realised, Gregory was sent a letter and a cheque from Ben Wardill, secretary of the Melbourne Cricket Club, with a note apologising to him for the confusion and money to cover his costs.

Gregory returned the £8. 18s. 6d. cheque and explained that as he was one of the players chosen for the match – which had been confirmed to him by two of the selectors – he was entitled to the full £25 match fee. Gregory was paid that money by return.

This caused the Melbourne Club and the Victorian Cricket Association to review their relationship for, although the Melbourne club backed the tour financially, it had been the Marylebone club's insistence that the State associations choose the Australian teams. The incident also galvanised the VCA president, James Aitken, and the secretary, Edward Heather, to consider, most carefully, the structure of the game in Australia. Their first move came following representation from the cricketers themselves, who had formed their own Trade Union, the League of Victorian Cricketers. A conference was arranged for 29 July 1904 to reorganise the game in Melbourne. This resulted in general agreement on a new structure, known as District Cricket, in a report dated 23 August 1904, which was passed at a meeting of all clubs on 25 September 1904.

One of the Sydney District Cricket Club delegates to the NSWCA was William McElhone, a solicitor with a rare debating skill. He first became a delegate in 1896, then for the East Sydney Club, and for Sydney itself from 1900. He was to attain high office in the NSWCA but, more important, and over and above the groundwork laid by other State associations, he was the influence behind his Association's formation of what became the Cricket Board of Control.

Meanwhile, in Sydney there had twice been conflict between the NSWCA and the trustees of the Sydney Cricket Ground, as the NSWCA Annual Report of 25 July 1904 details:

> The Colts' Match was played upon the University Oval this year, owing to the Trustees of the Sydney Cricket Ground having given permission for a professional sports meeting to be held on the ground on the King's Birthday, the day set apart for the Colts' Match. The Association, thinking that the Trustees had exceeded their powers, decided to ask for an injunction, restraining them from proceeding with the proposed sports meeting.
>
> The time, however, was too short to proceed in the matter, and the suit was turned into one of decree, which has since been decided in favour of the Association, the Court holding that during the cricket season the Association has the first right to the use of the ground for cricket purposes, thus setting at rest the long series of troubles which have arisen, owing to the fact that the Trustees would not recognise the Association's standing under the Deed of Grant.

The second point of conflict concerned the proceeds from the matches against England:

> Considerable ill-feeling was occasioned by the action of the Trustees in refusing to recognise the Association in the distribution of the proceeds of the English matches, and accounting to the Marylebone Club representatives direct for their share of the proceeds, the Association contending that as all arrangements for the tour in this State had been made by them with the Marylebone Cricket Club, including the engagement of the ground, the Trustees should have accounted for the whole of the proceeds to the Association direct, instead of dividing the proceeds, which they had no right to do, with the Marylebone Club. By thus doing, the Trustees would have avoided casting an unnecessary slight upon the Association.

In mid-November 1904, the South Australian Cricket Association became aware of clandestine discussions taking place between Edward Heather and Percy Bowden regarding a national body. The SACA secretary, John Creswell, also found out that Billy McElhone had promised the Queensland Cricket Association executive member, Joseph Allen, a Test match for Brisbane if, and only if, the QCA would back NSW on the controlling body issue.

The wheeling and dealing was now in full swing, with McElhone strongly against the players having any say in the matter. He was mindful of such derogatory remarks which Joe Darling, Clem Hill and George Giffen had made about the NSWCA and particularly 'the freeloaders that appear at New South Wales matches'. He was prepared for a fight. When it came, it would fester on until 1913.

The story of the formation of the Australian Board of Control for International Cricket, and its junior committee, the Interstate Conference, is almost lengthy enough to fill a book in its own right. Suffice it to say that on 6 January 1905, in Sydney, a constitution was drafted which empowered the new Board to take control of all tours by Australian teams, to appoint umpires, and to draft any changes in the laws of cricket.

McElhone virtually railroaded the whole issue, brushing aside what had been planned as a Melbourne-based body. Promises made to the Queensland and Tasmanian Associations – which were not kept – saw New South Wales present what was basically a *fait accompli* to the rest of the country. McElhone's zeal had been accelerated when the 1899 Australian team arrived back in Australia and Joe Darling called the Melbourne Cricket Club, 'the Marylebone of Australia' – which indeed it was. Darling later accused McElhone of 'rigging the Board minutes', followed by 'making unauthorised decisions' and 'making a grab for power'.

The first formal meeting was held at Wesley College, Melbourne, on 6 May 1905. South Australia attended but only as observers, not joining as full members until 13 July 1906. The original member associations, therefore, were New South Wales and Victoria, with Queensland joining on 22 September 1905, then South Australia, next Tasmania on 9 August 1907, and finally Western Australia on 15 October 1914.

The 1903–04 domestic season had seen some particularly high scoring in Sheffield Shield matches. In Sydney Reggie Duff scored 271 and Monty Noble 230 against South Australia in a NSW total of 681. In the return match a fortnight later in Adelaide, NSW reached 624, on their way to their third successive title. The following season NSW, dominating cricket for the summer, won all four matches.

The team for the 1905 tour of New Zealand and England was finalised on 9 January 1905, and it was to be the last time the players had any say in the appointment of their captain. Joe Darling got the job after Monty Noble had led the side in New Zealand. There were fifteen in the party with the new tourists being 'Tibby' Cotter (NSW) and two surprise choices in Algy Gehrs and the reserve wicketkeeper, Phil Newland, both from South Australia.

Newland's selection had little to do with cricket. His parents were part of the Adelaide establishment; he had gone to the right school, and his was the first of many Australian selections strongly influenced by Freemasonry. Hanson Carter's omission this time was a regrettable error. But at least one good thing came from the tour and that was the advent of a scorer cum baggageman in the shape of William Ferguson for whom this would be the first of thirty-nine Test tours.

The Twelfth Australians left Sydney on 1 February 1905 bound for Auckland where they defeated a local fifteen by an innings. Rain saved Fifteen of Wellington from defeat with both Canterbury and Otago easily beaten. Then came two matches on even terms with a New Zealand team which included Harry Graham and Syd Callaway, the Australian Test players who were, by then, living in the country.

The first match, at Lancaster Park, Christchurch, saw the Australians give the locals a lesson in batting. Trumper (84) and Hill (118) scored 132 runs in 90 minutes in the first session of play which was followed by an unbeaten 126 from Warwick Armstrong in a total of 533. Then Armstrong took the ball and claimed 5/27 and 5/25 as New Zealand, following-on, held out for a draw in front of 10,000 spectators, an enormous crowd for New Zealand, let alone Christchurch.

A two-day boat trip to Wellington saw a second match played on the Basin Reserve starting on 16 March. Umpiring again at the New Zealand Cricket Council's invitation was Charles Bannerman who happened to be coaching in New Zealand at the time.

Drizzle delayed the start of play and, on winning the toss, Monty Noble put New Zealand in to bat and saw them dismissed in under two hours for just 94. Conditions improved so much on the second day that 3,000 people paid to enter the ground on a Friday afternoon to see Trumper and Hill (129) amass 269 runs in 117 minutes. At one stage they added a century in just 37 minutes.

After Hill was stumped, Trumper's innings ended when he had scored 172. The Wellington *Evening Post* said of Trumper: 'This was a batting exhibition the likes of which people in Wellington had never before witnessed and probably never would again'. Noble declared at 593 for nine; Armstrong took 6/51 and Australia won by an innings and 358 runs.

The team then sailed across the Pacific, playing a match in Suva against Eighteen of Fiji before going overland through Canada and America, arriving in Liverpool on 26 April 1905. The tourists' first match, just over a week later, was played at Crystal Palace against a Gentlemen of England side captained by W. G. Grace, now fifty-seven.

Seven matches were played up to the first Test and the visitors remained undefeated. Warwick Armstrong recorded an unbeaten 248 in the second meeting with the Gentlemen of England while Frank Laver took 8/75 and 4/36 in the match with Oxford University.

Australia went into the first Test at Nottingham worried about their main strike bowler, 'Tibby' Cotter, who had lost his form. The gamble of playing him did not work, but worse was to follow as Trumper had to retire hurt early in his first innings with a back strain. It was then downhill all the way for Australia as Joe Darling's negative tactics, designed to regain the Ashes, and his counterpart, Stanley Jackson's luck in winning all five tosses, saw England keep them.

Frank Laver provided a modicum of joy at Trent Bridge with 7/64 as England won by 213 runs. At Lord's, rain ensured a drawn match which was the same result as at Headingley. Darling's instructions to Armstrong to bowl down the leg-side and for McLeod to bowl off-theory resulted in extremely boring cricket. Still, the Leeds crowd enjoyed Jackson's best Test score of 144 and Johnny Tyldesley's second-innings century.

Cotter missed the second and third Tests, and in between time caused the Sydney *Referee*'s correspondent to write: 'I hope we shall see no more of the monstrous style of bowling adopted by Cotter. Deliberately to pitch halfway down the wicket, with no other object than to frighten the batsmen by making the ball go over their heads, is emphatically not cricket.'

After the third Test the tourists passed 600 in two of their following three games: 620 against Hampshire, and 609 for four declared versus Somerset at Bath in which Warwick Armstrong made 303 not out, the highest score of his career. A fortnight later Noble scored 267 out of 556 against Sussex.

The fourth Test at Old Trafford finally saw the Ashes slip away from Australia's hopes. Jackson scored another century for England who won by an innings and 80 runs by lunch on the third day. The final Test at The Oval always seemed as though it was going to be drawn. With only three days allocated for Tests in England, the perfect pitch and excellent weather was unlikely to produce any other result. Reggie Duff, in his final Test, became the first player to score a century in both his first and last appearances for his country. When Duff returned to Australia he lost all his form, however. Within two years he was lost to first-class cricket, and fell on hard times. He died in 1911 and is buried in Sydney's Gore Hill cemetery only yards from the unmarked grave of Australia's first Test captain, Dave Gregory.

The end of the 1905 tour saw the curtain come down on a number of other Test careers, including those of Darling, Kelly and McLeod, for by the time Australia played another match at the top level over two years would have elapsed.

The Australian season of 1905–06 was overshadowed by the formation of the Board of Control and the Melbourne Cricket Club's attempted poaching of players from New South Wales to play in a non-Board Australian team.

One match dominated a Shield season won yet again by NSW. In Melbourne over Christmas 1905, NSW reached 805, with Monty Noble making 281 and Jim Mackay 194 in a second-wicket stand worth 267 runs. The NSWCA did, however, show a kinder side to its tough dealings when, on hearing of Joe Kelly's decision to retire from the game due to injury, they granted him a benefit match. Played between NSW and the Twelfth Australians – who won by 79 runs – the Association could report: '. . . with the result that £1400. 12s. 7d. was handed to Mr Kelly'.

The Marylebone Cricket Club was becoming more and more the influence to bind Australian cricket together. They declined an invitation from the new Board of Control to send out a touring team for the 1906–07 season, 'until the Board was truly representative of Australian cricket'. While this was going on the Melbourne Cricket Club sent a team to New Zealand under the captaincy of Warwick Armstrong.

Ten matches were played around the country including one against New Zealand. The representative match, played at Christchurch from 23–27 March 1906 was dogged by bad weather. It was a low-scoring encounter with play possible on only three days. New Zealand made 77 and 167 in reply to 228 and so just avoided defeat. Armstrong scored 83 and took 4/23 and 4/72 in a good all-round display.

Also at the end of the 1905–06 season, Victor Trumper led a strong New South Wales team on a tour around Queensland. In his side were his fellow Australian tourists, Bert Hopkins and 'Tibby' Cotter. With the assistance of the theatrical entrepreneur J. C. Williamson, Trumper's side made all their arrangements without consulting either the Queensland or New South Wales Cricket Associations, a decision which incensed officials of both bodies. The QCA secretary, George Colledge, wrote an irate letter to Percy Bowden which was leaked to the press. The resulting newspaper comments blasted the QCA, with *The Courier* accusing: 'Mr Colledge is trying to stir up trouble, if not to block the tour altogether'.

Queensland country associations at this time were also in dispute with the QCA. They felt the treatment they were receiving was very poor, even contemptuous. Their support of the tour saw it start in late April 1906 with a game against Eighteen of Charters Towers. Then followed fixtures in Townsville, Rockhampton, Charters Towers again, Mount Morgan, Bundaberg, Maryborough, Gympie, and with two concluding matches against Brisbane select elevens.

During the game in Maryborough the local cricket authorities entertained the visitors with typical Queensland country hospitality. When the time came for speech-making the local cricket association president, Charles Gorry, caused controversy by attacking the QCA. He claimed the Association was not representative of Queensland cricket, and that it ignored country areas, and overlooked star country players when picking representative teams. These comments were given considerable publicity followed by a groundswell of agreement within the State, a situation the QCA studiously ignored until they themselves had the opportunity to reply.

This happened at a farewell dinner given by the QCA to Trumper's team at the Grand Hotel in Brisbane at the end of the tour. The Association president, Colonel Foxton, let rip at Gorry who happened to have been chosen that night to propose the toast to 'Cricket'. The ensuing embarrassment saw Trumper propose a toast to the QCA and then leave quickly with his team.

A cynic might suggest that Foxton's and Gorry's successors are continuing the debate to this very day!

Apart from squabbling administrators, the tour was a great success and resulted in a cricket boom in the country areas. Games between various country centres increased and up until the outbreak of the European war quite a number of unofficial sides went on end-of-season tours around the State.

Considering the activity surrounding the early years of the Board of Control, the 1906–07 season was relatively quiet. Right up until September 1906, an England tour was expected but after the Marylebone Cricket Club insisted that the Australians put their administrative house in order first, this was put back a year.

New South Wales won the Sheffield Shield for the sixth consecutive time with Austin Diamond's unbeaten 210 against Victoria being the competition's only double-century. However, in a match which started in Brisbane on 10 November 1906, Charles William Gregory, younger brother of Syd, scored 383 for New South Wales against Queensland. On the second day of the match he scored 318 runs, progressing from an overnight 48 to 366. When he was finally out on the last morning, his innings had taken 345 minutes and he had hit 55 fours.

A sickly child, it had always been hoped that Charles would regain his health and take his place alongside other members of the famous Gregory clan. Alas, four years after this major feat, at the age of thirty-two, he was dead.

In the *Sydney Morning Herald* of 24 January 1907 it was noted that ' . . . it is apparent the game of cricket is fast degenerating into a business rather than a sport'. *The Bulletin*, exactly six months later, referred to 'veiled professionalism in Australian cricket being rampant'. This was of particular significance when viewed with the amateur beliefs of the era.

One man who was to dominate Victorian cricket administration was Ernest Edward Bean. He, and his counterpart in NSW, Billy McElhone, were the two strong men of the new Board of Control. Both were dedicated to preventing the players having any influence on how the game was run. Bean was a cunning man who worked for the Victorian Government Printing Office and who became the Board's second chairman – after McElhone – in 1906–07. He had been born in North Melbourne in 1866, and played for the club of his area, making his first-class debut in the 1887–88 season. Between then and 1905 Bean made eight appearances for Victoria but he built up a large number of enemies of whom he openly expressed his contempt, none more so than Warwick Armstrong with whom he conducted a vendetta for over thirty years. Armstrong, inevitably perhaps, was triumphant in such issues. He was nothing if not abrasive himself.

Warwick Armstrong was an important employee at the Melbourne Cricket Ground for a number of years before he moved to Sydney. As pavilion clerk, he had a staff of twenty-four men whom he organised to provide practice for, and equipment to, members of the club.

Despite his constant activity, Armstrong's weight soared but it appeared to have little effect on his playing ability. Besides his 438 against University, he also scored an unbeaten 200 against Williamstown in 1905, then his 335 in New Zealand against Southland and 251 against Essendon scored in three hours on the first January Saturday afternoon of 1907. What was so remarkable about this innings was that Armstrong twice hit the Essendon leg-spinner, Harry Forsythe, right out of the Melbourne Cricket Ground, a feat performed by only George Bonnor (on three occasions) in 1881 and Bill Howell in 1901.

Armstrong was paid £19 a month in his position although during the cricket season he would spend most of his time either bowling in the nets or playing for various Melbourne CC teams. He was also a remarkably generous man. When Syd Gregory was declared bankrupt in 1903 – due to the embezzlement of a so-called trusted employee at his sports shop – Armstrong went out of his way to help get Gregory started again. Gregory was discharged from bankruptcy two years later and in February 1907, a benefit match for him raised the sum of £641.

The Board of Control – which amounted really to Bean and McElhone – was now organising Australian cricket in its own way. McElhone sent letters to the South Australian, Queensland, Victorian and New South Wales Cricket Associations on 5 April 1907 asking if they would all underwrite the Marylebone Cricket Club's £10,000 guarantee for an England team to tour in the 1907–08 season.

A meeting was arranged for 19 and 20 April 1907 in the VCA rooms at Young & Jackson's pub in central Melbourne. When the South Australian and Queensland delegations arrived, they found that the two other States had already sent a cable to London agreeing to all the conditions; but at least the meeting was able to approve the applications of the Tasmanian and Western Australian associations for full and observer status respectively.

By the next Board meeting, on 9 August in Sydney, the delegates were able to approve the setting up of a panel of Test umpires; a Test Fund for the proceeds of matches before an end-of-tour distribution; and the final arrangement of the dates of Sheffield Shield fixtures for the coming season. If nothing else, McElhone's enthusiasm was bringing some semblance of order into cricket's organisation.

The season of 1907–08 would, in fact, see two touring teams in Australia: the England team for a full tour, and also a party of cricketers from Fiji. The 9 August Board meeting had originally rejected the Fiji tour 'due to the strong objections of Mr E. E. Bean (Victoria) and Mr W. McElhone (NSW) who both stated that it would be in breach of the government's White Australia policy'. That is what the minutes said, yet on 20 August, McElhone wrote to all Associations saying that the Board had now granted patronage to the Fiji tour. All secretaries wrote back asking for explanations but none were forthcoming.

What in fact had happened after the Board meeting was that the Melbourne Cricket Club delegate Edward Mitchell, KC, had been so incensed by the racialist attitudes put forward that he contacted the Fijian tour manager, G. V. Allen of Sydney, and told him to get the team organised and that, if needed, the Melbourne Cricket Club would give them the patronage to tour.

Mitchell then told McElhone what he had done. The ensuing row between the Melbourne silk and the Sydney solicitor eventually saw Mitchell withdraw from Board administration. The idea met with wide public approval, however, and when the Board next met, the South Australian delegate, Joe Darling, asked for the previous meeting's minutes to be read. It was found that these sanctioned a Fijian tour. As Joe Darling noted in his papers:

> At the next meeting of the Board, I moved that the minutes of the previous meeting be read. McElhone, who was responsible for the minutes, strongly objected, saying it was not the annual meeting. I was not going to be 'bluffed' and when my motion was put, it was carried by a small majority. As soon as the minutes were read, I challenged them as being 'faked' and not a true record of the business

> of the last meeting. The minutes as actually recorded showed that the Board had agreed to send an invitation to the Fijian team to visit Australia. The minutes were faked as the Board had definitely turned down the application. McElhone, the secretary, had voiced his opinion against a team of black fellows visiting White Australia, and yet contrary to the Board's decision, he recorded the Board's approval in its minutes.

The Fijian team was led by Lieutenant Eric Marsden, captain of the Victorian Army team and cricket coach on the island of Bau from where most of the team came. The Army connection enabled him to gain the ear of Major Ben Wardill who arranged a full and proper itinerary.

The Fijians arrived in Australia in November 1907 and were, in reality, captained by Ratu Penaia Kadavulevu. They played twenty-six matches, losing only five and winning the same number. Against the States all matches ended in honourable draws although the Australian teams were on top in most cases, except in Tasmania where not only was a first-innings lead obtained but bad weather stopped a probable shock win.

The South Australians paid the Fijians a great compliment by persuading forty-nine-year-old George Giffen out of retirement to lead the team. When the SACA secretary John Creswell received a letter from the private secretary to the South Australian Governor, Sir George Ruthven le Hunte, stating that not only did he intend to watch the whole match but also wished to host a reception for the team, the SACA committee were surprised but immediately started making serious plans for the match.

The Fijian team attended Government House dressed in their usual lap-laps (much to the amazement of the committee wives). They were astonished when le Hunte gave the welcoming speech in fluent Fijian and only later found out he had been the first administrative officer of the Lau Islands in Fiji back in 1875.

Le Hunte did as he had promised and stayed for all two days along with a gaggle of local dignitaries who could not quite grasp the Governor's keenness. Giffen put Fiji in to bat and took 6/58 as they made 147. At stumps on the first day South Australia were 147 for eight, but next morning Giffen remained unbeaten on 32 when the innings closed at 198.

The large Saturday crowd gave great support to the 'fuzzy-wuzzies', who in their second innings were 48 for three when Sokidi joined Meleti at the wicket. In the next 70 minutes they added 172 runs with graceful hitting, and at tea were 226 for four. Giffen, who at one time had 2/7, by then had bowling figures of 2/73. He was certainly not used to being treated in such a manner, so during the tea interval he changed and stormed off back to work at the General Post Office. He never played on the Adelaide Oval again.

The England team, led by Arthur Jones of Nottinghamshire, sailed from Tilbury on 20 September 1907 and, for the first time, played a match against Western Australia in Perth as the initial fixture of their tour. During the following five weeks, as they moved through Adelaide, Melbourne, Sydney and Brisbane they remained undefeated.

In Brisbane, Jones contracted pneumonia and had to stay in hospital. This meant the English team needed to call on the Nottinghamshire batsman, George Gunn, who was in Australia on a private visit. When the time came for the first Test in Sydney in mid-December the visitors' captaincy passed to Frederick Fane.

The Australians were to blood six new players during the series, four of them from the start. Hanson Carter finally earned his reward as wicketkeeper on Kelly's retirement. With Darling having retired, and Duff, Hopkins and McLeod not selected, the other newcomers were Gervys Rignold Hazlitt, who bowled right-arm off-breaks at medium pace; the New South Wales batsman Charlie Macartney, later to be dubbed the 'Governor-General' due to his authoritative manner; and Vernon Ransford, a left-handed batsman from Victoria. Later in the series Jack O'Connor, a fast bowler from South Australia, and Roger Hartigan, a stalwart of Queensland cricket, were brought in. On his retirement from the game, Hartigan served on the Board of Control for thirty-five years.

Fane won the toss and batted; he opened the innings and was dismissed after scoring just two runs. In came George Gunn, having arrived at the ground with literally minutes to spare in answer to the team's plea for assistance. Having not lifted a bat for three months, Gunn surprised everyone by making a century in his first innings for his country. His 119 out of 273 was what was needed as 'Tibby' Cotter (6/101) had cleared through the top order batsmen. Gunn also top-scored with 74 in England's second innings but could not stop Australia gaining victory by two wickets.

On to Melbourne for the second Test over the New Year's holiday and one of the most dramatic of matches. England gave a debut to Jack Hobbs and, with Jones still unwell, Fane continued as captain and saw his team take a 116-run first-innings lead. The sides were so well balanced that the spectators – who paid one shilling to enter the ground or half-a-crown for the stands – would not know the result until the last moment.

Australia made 397 in their second innings, and it took the final England pair of Barnes and Fielder to score the 39 precious runs for victory. The game should have ended in a tie but for a panic-stricken throw by Gerry Hazlitt when the scores were level. The game was watched by 91,386 spectators who paid £4071 for the privilege, an excellent start to the presidency of Mr Justice Cussen who had taken the reins at the Melbourne Cricket Club, and would remain in charge for the next twenty-six years.

Melbourne itself was changing. Still the capital of Australia, the city was emerging well from the land-bust and banking traumas of a decade earlier. But it was still the Melbourne of a rowdy Bourke Street on a Friday night; of street orators and musicians; of street pedlars and lively music-halls. Then, as now, the city was the base for about half of Australia's business, a fact which constantly irritated those based in Sydney.

While the Test match was taking place the Brisbane *Courier* reported: 'At Laidley, Queensland, on New Year's Day 1908, a bowler named James Higgins of the Milton Cricket Club, bowled a bail 51 yards off the wicket. The distance was measured by four of the players.'

The Test teams travelled together by train to Adelaide and arrived to find that John Creswell, the SACA secretary, had just been fined two guineas by the local magistrates court. As the Adelaide *Register* said: ' . . . he allowed his sheep to graze on the pitch next door to the Adelaide Oval'.

Hartigan and O'Connor now came into the Australian side for Hazlitt and the injured Cotter. The game was played in intense heat with England gaining a first-innings lead of 78. They then let the match slip as Hartigan scored 116, and Clem Hill, batting at number nine as he was suffering from influenza, scored a courageous 160 in 319 minutes. At the end of the fourth day, with the score on 397 for seven, Roger Hartigan, unbeaten on 105, sent a telegram back to Brisbane. He worked for a local auctioneer who had given him leave for only four days and the cable requested an extension, 'as I am still batting'. The reply came back: 'Stay as long as you are making runs'.

England failed to make any headway as they chased 429 for victory and lost by 245 runs. Even with the heat, it was surprising that the attendance was Adelaide's lowest for thirteen years. Nor did Melbourne's fans exactly flock to the next Test three weeks later, when England put up a very weak display to lose by 308 runs and so let Australia retain the Ashes. The series was marred by slow, over-cautious batting by both sides.

Warwick Armstrong, on his home ground, was by far and away the highest scorer with a second-innings unbeaten 133. Arthur Jones had recovered enough to captain the tourists but the talking point was Victor Trumper's inability to get off the mark in both innings. Much newspaper space was devoted to this national calamity with the Melbourne *Argus* stating: 'Before the contest nobody would have dreamed of such a remote contingency as the great Victor Trumper making two duck eggs in a Test match. Any man who had cared to gamble on such a thing would have received fantastic odds.'

The fifth match in Sydney was the one hundredth Test played and the 81st between the two countries. It was attended by Sydney's lowest average daily crowd since the debacle tours of 1888. More people should have attended, for not only did Australia win by 49 runs to clinch the series 4–1 but Victor Trumper made up for his double failure in Melbourne. In front of his home crowd Trumper scored 166, 'which rates among the finest innings ever played in Australia', wrote J. C. Davis in the *Referee*. 'It was in every way a great innings, played at a critical time uphill, and it fully merited the zestful applause that greeted him as he retired.'

After games in Adelaide and Perth, the tourists departed leaving the new Board of Control with a deficit of £2600 which the three major States had to make good. No Board money reached Tasmania, Queensland or Western Australia, however, although it could have done if Billy McElhone and Ernie Bean had wished. They dismissed Joe Darling's plea that moneys should be distributed to all Board member States. Darling added that it was scandalous that Tasmania, which had already produced three Test cricketers (Bailey, Burn and Eady), received no financial assistance to improve their standards.

The Sheffield Shield season had been truncated by the England tour and only four matches were played. In the first match Warwick Armstrong made 231 as Victoria thrashed South Australia, and in the last, Frank Tarrant's 206 saw Victoria defeat NSW to claim their first Shield premiership since 1901.

On 6 March 1908, the Queensland Cricket Association secretary, George Colledge, in one of his last acts before retirement, wrote to all other associations pleading for home and away Shield matches each season. Then on 29 May, at the Board meeting in Sydney, a motion to elect Queensland to the Sheffield Shield competition was lost by seven votes to five. The replies to his letter drifted back to Colledge – all negative: no-one wanted to make such a commitment.

After the Fijians returned home there was some public speculation as to whether or not their matches should be counted as first-class. A lead was needed from a position of authority but, surprisingly, the Board of Control refused to give a ruling. The Victorian Cricket Association decided to take the matter on.

At a meeting held in the Mechanics' Institute, South Melbourne, on 22 June 1908, the executive recommended that the following be ranked as first-class:

(a) International matches;
(b) All matches between English or other representative visiting teams, and interstate teams;
(c) All interstate matches, and matches against New Zealand;
(d) All matches of a representative character played on even terms and comprising first-class players, including Australia, the Rest of Australia, North versus South of Tasmania, and the First versus Next Eleven of the States competing for the Sheffield Shield.

Although this ruling made no specific mention of Fiji, for many years the Associations against whom they played considered the matches to be of first-class status.

The ruling of the VCA was then passed on to the NSWCA and SACA, 'for their consideration'. In supporting the definition at the VCA meeting, Ernie Bean remarked that no pronouncement had ever before been made as to what constituted a first-class match. 'Representatives of the press included some games, and excluded others. Tasmania and Queensland had been left out of the first-class; but surely it would improve cricket in these States if they were included. The three associations could and should settle the matter.'

The NSWCA met on 20 July 1908 to consider the question, and agreed to the Victorians' definition, but excluding the North-South game in Tasmania, and internal games of other States. The SACA followed suit at a meeting in late August 1908. This legislation remained in force until May 1947, when the Imperial Cricket Conference not only reached an agreement in defining a first-class match, but also agreed that, in future, the status of teams would be determined by the governing body in each country.

Australians were making names for themselves world-wide in 1908. Norman Brookes was the world's top tennis player; in swimming Frank Beaurepaire was beating all comers; and boxing fans had the long-awaited Tommy Burns—Jack Johnson bout for the heavyweight championship of the world.

It was also the time when Joe Darling finally retired. He sold his sports shop in Adelaide, and his various franchises, to go and concentrate on the family's farming business in Tasmania. On 28 September 1908 the SACA gave him a farewell party. The speeches showed in how much esteem Darling was held, particularly in his fight for players' rights. In reply Darling went straight on to the attack by criticising the Board of Control for their manipulations and lack of care for the players' well-being. He added: 'During my cricket experience here in South Australia this Association has shown more consideration for their players than any other Association in Australia. It has been a pleasure to play for SACA and to be treated with respect, as players should be. We often asked for reasonable things and they had been granted. If the other Associations had treated their players so well we would not be seeing the problems that are now existing in NSW.' The NSWCA had, in fact, suspended a number of players who had criticised them. Billy McElhone would only accept subservient players, and certainly not the outspoken Monty Noble.

The 1908–09 Sheffield Shield season saw New South Wales regain the trophy with some tremendous scoring. In Adelaide NSW reached 713 (Bert Hopkins 218, Monty Noble 213) as South Australia were thrashed by an innings and 527 runs. It was higher against Victoria as NSW made 815 (Noble 213, Bardsley 192). But the scoring did not stop there. In one of the two Test trials, Bardsley scored 264 for Australia in a total of 648 against The Rest of Australia in a match played in Melbourne.

The high scoring even affected schools cricket. The final of the Great Public Schools competition, played at North Sydney Oval from 19 March 1909, saw Sydney Grammar School pile up 916 against Shore Grammar. For Shore, Claude Tozer, nephew of Percie Charlton and a future NSW batsman, scored 140 out of 301. However, it was Sydney's Eric Barbour and Frank Farrer who stole the show. Barbour, one of eight players in the match who went on to play first-class cricket, opened the innings and scored 356 out of 606 for five while he was at the crease. He batted for 370 minutes and hit 65 fours. Farrer made 229 in 210 minutes as Sydney won by an innings and 519 runs.

Curiously enough, Sydney's 916 beat the Australian Public Schools record which had been established only the previous Saturday. Then, in Melbourne, Wesley College had reached 710 against Geelong College with Jimmy Proust scoring 459. But Sydney's 916 remained a world school record for only six years – until Melbourne Grammar, aided by James Sharp's unbeaten 506, scored 961, also against Geelong.

Although by 1909 Australia was eight years into its nominal independence from Britain, the more influential members of society still responded with exaggerated respect to royalty or their representatives. In late February the president of the South Australian Cricket Association, Sir Edwin Smith, received a letter from an aide-de-camp to the Governor-General of Australia, Lord Dudley, which said that Lord Dudley was shortly to be in Adelaide for a few days and had expressed a desire to play a match against the committee. Smith called together a full executive meeting plus delegates of clubs, senior and junior, as well as many cricket personalities. Sub-committees were formed with Smith putting himself in charge of the 'Catering and Entertainment Sub-Committee'. His first words at the initial meeting were: 'We shall have champagne'.

Cricket clubs around Adelaide and its country areas were then informed, 'that all matches and net practice were cancelled for the week prior to the match'. Adelaide Oval gatemen were told they would be needed for duty on the two days of the contest which had been set down for 10 and 11 March. The Oval caterer, Mr Schroeder, prepared a feast and a local wine distributor handled the bulk order of champagne.

Unfortunately the general public did not share Sir Edwin Smith's enthusiasm. Only forty people paid at the turnstiles to watch the match and to observe an excellent turnout in the members' area mixing with the vice-regal party. By the time the accounts had been tallied and Mr Schroeder had purchased cheaply the large residual amount of champagne, the cost to the Association was horrific.

A fortnight later, however, on Wednesday 24 March 1909, the SACA secretary, John Creswell, collapsed and died. He was only fifty years of age. The reaction to the news was one of genuine grief in South Australia. *The Observer* said in a lengthy tribute:

> Genial John Creswell, the bluff, the homely, the hearty, is dead! . . . He was the busiest man in Adelaide. The Australian counterpart of the American hustler . . . and Jack was one of the best fellows in the world: a splendid friend, and those who knew him loved him as few men are loved.

Other tributes to Creswell poured in from far and wide. Sir Edwin Smith was devastated and so were many of the Australian cricketers, for Creswell had been their staunchest ally. Now there would be no effective opposition to the machinations of McElhone and Bean. The power in Australian cricket had transferred to Sydney.

*The Bulletin* on 17 September 1908, summed up the furore that was being created by the Board's stand against the players:

> 'The Players', those indefinite wraiths that have haunted Australian cricket like a nightmare for the past two years, are making their last effort to keep Australian tours on a boodle [money and pleasure] basis. Hitherto the Australian XI has gone to England practically on its own, and whatever money was made was divided among the players according to their own sweet will. That the men did not share equally is well known, and that they shared according to the value of their play is doubtful. Weird stories are told of young players (Trumper reportedly was one of them) going 'on terms', which meant they were squeezed, and only got a show on the team on the understanding that they took a sum below what was due them on a fair and equal division of profits. Certain individuals who

considered themselves the salt of the expedition demanded special rates, and got them . . .

Cash hunting is obnoxious. The Board was created to control international campaigns . . . the Board of Control *must* take charge of the coming expeditions . . . the players are all allegedly amateurs.

For the 1909 visit to England, the Board assumed control for the first time, but not without battles before, during, and after the tour.

The English magazine *Cricket* published a long letter on 28 January 1909 from someone using the pseudonym 'An Australian in England'. The letter attempted to explain the causes of the differences between the leading Australian players and the Board, saying that the main problem was money and 'the division of the surplus of profits on English tours'. The letter continued that the Board held an idealistic view which was diametrically opposed to the practical attitude of the players. The anonymous writer went on to advocate the resolving of these differences in the interest of selecting 'the best Australian eleven'.

The Board was in no mood to be conciliatory, and so McElhone first tackled the issue of profits and expenses. Of the leading players Victor Trumper had been at odds with cricket administrators for four years over excess claims, likewise Warwick Armstrong and 'Tibby' Cotter. Early in 1908, therefore, the Board had laid down conditions for the distribution of profits from the 1909 tour:

*For the Board*: 6% of the first £6000, plus 12½% of the remainder of the tour receipts;

*For the Players*: Equal shares of the surplus remaining after deducting the tour expenses and the Board's proportion of the tour receipts. No players to be allowed 'special terms'.

The leading players were bitterly opposed to these conditions but, if they wanted to fight, they knew it would have to be to the end as Billy McElhone was the opponent. McElhone was determined to ensure that the 1909 finances were strictly controlled. In his view the players should not expect to preserve their amateur status while drawing professionals' rewards. This was a complete reversal from previous tours where the players had been professionals in all but name, and it marked a policy change in Australian cricket which would last for nearly seventy years.

To try and forestall opposition from the players, McElhone shrewdly invited Monty Noble, Clem Hill and Frank Laver to make representations of their case to the Board's tour sub-committee. Noble and Hill had previously indicated their unwillingness to tour because of their dissatisfaction with the Board's terms. But, given the opportunity to prove their points, the players failed to produce documentary proof from financial records of previous tours to show that the Board's offer was anything but fair. They failed, therefore, to convince the officials that there should be changes. The days of rich pickings were nearly at an end: at least for seventy years. The only concession the players obtained was the right to choose their own tour manager.

Having established, at least to its own satisfaction, its authority in financial matters, the Board turned its attention next to controlling team selection. For the 1907–08 Test series, they had appointed a selection committee consisting of Frank Iredale (New South Wales), Joe Darling (South Australia) and Peter McAlister (Victoria). This had not been a happy combination for McAlister was generally believed to have talked his fellow selectors into picking him as a batsman for four of the five Tests (8 innings, 166 runs). Most of the players felt also that he was reporting back to Bean and McElhone on dressing-room talk.

In December 1908 the Board reappointed Iredale and McAlister. Since Joe Darling had moved to Tasmania, Clem Hill was his natural successor from South Australia. But the retention of McAlister was curious. Both Monty Noble and Hugh Trumble had offered themselves for consideration and their credentials were far superior. This meant that McAlister was immediately marked down as a 'Board's Man', a derogatory title that is still given to one or two players in the 1980s and 1990s who were considered to be in a similar position.

The seeds of future dissension were now firmly sown, but the players still had one or two aces to play. On 5 February 1909, the *Sydney Morning Herald* said: 'The certainties for England have had a meeting and appointed Mr Frank Laver manager of the team'.

This move by the players – who were in Sydney for a four-day fixture, 'The Australian Eleven' versus 'Rest of Australia', the first of two tour trial matches – was an interesting one. Laver had managed the 1905 team to everyone's satisfaction, but had not been included in any of the trial teams. This was seen to bear the hand of Bean and McAlister.

The Board may have had good reason to be apprehensive at filling both the manager's and the captain's positions with men openly antagonistic to them; but they certainly would not have foreseen the players choosing their manager before the team had been announced. It was a *fait accompli*, and much as McElhone disliked it, he had no alternative but to endorse Laver's appointment if a strong side was to be sent to England.

It was in this climate of distrust and suspicion that the touring team was selected, but McElhone was an experienced political fighter. With the support of most of the NSW and Victorian Board delegates they, as expected, confirmed Monty Noble as captain but they appointed Peter McAlister as his deputy. The players later retaliated by not appointing McAlister as one of the two tour selectors to assist Noble.

McAlister had held a grudge at not being selected for the 1905 tour and persuaded the Board – in his position as a selector – that to go as vice-captain would give him a great deal of say and control over the players. He also had himself appointed as Treasurer on the grounds he could then oversee the manager. McAlister's mediocre Test record hardly justified his place as a player and all three issues caused a split in the Board with voting on each occasion being 6–5.

The votes themselves showed certain interesting movements. Tasmania's delegate, William Campbell, voted against because his Association wanted more representatives in the Test trials than just the wicketkeeper, Norman Dodds (who played brilliantly; scored an unbeaten 80 in his only innings, and then went home to cricket obscurity). South Australia's delegates were split as usual: Harry Blinman and Clem Hill, both players, voted against whilst Mostyn Evan, who eventually became chairman of the Board of Control, voted for McAlister. Queensland (Foxton and Allen) also voted against while Victoria had one abstention (Aitken) with Bean and Rush plus NSW's McElhone, Green and Gibson voting in favour.

This type of 'block voting' became firmer as the years wore on. It was usual for NSW and Victoria (six votes) to oppose South Australia and Tasmania (four votes) with Queensland (two votes) being offered the metaphorical bribes. In fact, McElhone's promise in 1905 to Queensland that they would shortly be granted a Test match was not honoured until November 1928.

When the team to tour was finally announced on 15 February 1909, sixteen had been chosen with the newcomers being Warren Bardsley, William Carkeek, Roger Hartigan, Charlie Macartney, Peter McAlister, Jack O'Connor, Vernon Ransford and Bill Whitty. Carkeek got the reserve wicketkeeper's job in front of Woodford (South Australia) and Gorry (NSW), it was said, by being a close friend of McAlister! However, what raised eyebrows was the omission of Dodds.

In January 1909 the former Australian captain, Harry Trott, toured Tasmania with his Bendigo club and encountered Dodds in a number of matches. In an interview with Tasmania's *Daily Post*, Trott said: 'I consider Dodds the best wicketkeeper in Australia. The selection committee should give him a chance of winning his way into the side.' After Dodds' Test trial and rejection, the Launceston *Daily Telegraph* suggested that Dodds was branded ineligible because of a 'peccadillo'. The offence was said to have happened a year earlier when Arthur Jones' England team spent a fortnight on the island. Then Dodds 'incapacitated himself for a day through a little indiscretion in his choice of a boon companion from amongst that [England] team'. Nice words and flowery prose, but the question left unanswered was: 'Who was Dodds' homosexual companion?'

The implication of prejudice against Dodds was on the part of the national selectors, as Tasmania's selectors noted: 'Dodds has never since that time repeated the occurrence, but, on the other hand, he has kept wicket in all the important matches with consistent brilliancy'. Even the Speaker of the Tasmanian parliament, Sir George Davies, who saw the Test trial, said that 'the selectors have been unfair to Dodds, Tasmania and Australia'. Dodds, known as 'Joker' to his close friends, was not accepted for military service, and died in 1916 aged forty.

Despite these disputes the Board of Control gave Monty Noble the second Test trial as a benefit match. The return was in excess of £2000, something of a fortune in 1909. Noble, now thirty-six, was making his fourth visit to England. A sidelight on his character is that he possessed a splendid baritone voice and he was often heard as a soloist at concerts given by the Sydney Choral Society, and also when he was in the choir at St Mark's, Darling Point, where, in his youth, he had been a bell-ringer.

Noble had obtained thirteen of his own choices from the Board for the tour of England, but the tour was taking place a year later than planned. Originally the Australians had been invited as part of a Triangular Tournament, but the Board refused to countenance such an idea. The Marylebone Cricket Club pressed the concept but withdrew it in July 1908 after receiving a letter from McElhone. Another plan, put forward by the players, was to have a short tour of South Africa before arriving in England. Again, this was turned down.

The players were unaware of the communications behind the scenes between the Board and the South African Cricket Association. The Springboks wanted to tour Australia during the 1908–09 season but McElhone refused, saying: 'It would interfere with planning for Australia's (1909) tour of England'. As the following season was inconvenient to the South Africans, it was agreed that they should tour Australia during the 1910–11 season – but this was kept from the players.

When the Thirteenth Australians arrived in London in April 1909, Monty Noble insisted that the team hold an election for captain. McAlister argued that the Board of Control had already appointed a captain but Noble was not satisfied. He wanted the players to agree to his leadership, not the Board. The players elected Noble by a large but not unanimous vote and in the process pointedly omitted McAlister from being allowed to deputise for Noble as vice-captain.

Noble had to be a firm captain for so many promises and commitments, made in good faith for and on behalf of the team, had been broken or changed by Billy McElhone and the Board. It was ineptitude on the part of the Board – who lacked any experience in organising tours – to agree to play six days a week for the whole tour; to place players together as room-mates on an arbitrary basis; to refuse cash advances to selected players to cover pre-tour expenses; to insist that McAlister be the tour treasurer; to renege on promises not to interfere with the players' financial terms; and finally to forget to check players' contracts or see that they were in order and correctly signed.

The tour started slowly, with Warren Bardsley scoring 219 against Essex at Leyton, the first of his two double-centuries. Then a couple of defeats in six matches before the Tests caused the English public to underrate a fine squad of tourists. Interest polarised around the five Tests but twenty of the other thirty-four fixtures ended in a draw.

The weather was largely to blame for the lack of results although England easily won the first Test at Edgbaston. Rain created havoc with the pitch as Australia collapsed to Blythe (6/44 and 5/58) and Hirst (4/28 and 5/58) to lose by ten wickets. The only Australian to emerge with credit was Warwick Armstrong who took 5/27 and top-scored in the visitors' first innings.

From then on the Australians' superiority showed through. As Sydney Pardon confirmed in *Wisden*: 'I cannot help thinking that the selection committee, like the general public, were inclined to underrate the Australians'. After the selectors had called on twenty-five players for the series Pardon added: 'It is evident that we shall want practically a new England eleven'. Pardon had not grasped, however, how much Australia owed their success to Noble. As the tourists were being written off so the Australian captain revived his players. The second Test at Lord's showed the come-back. Cotter, Noble and Laver bowled England out for 269; Vernon Ransford hit an unbeaten 143 to gain his side an 81-run first-innings lead; Warwick Armstrong claimed 6/35, turning his leg-breaks a long way and getting a high bounce, which then left McAlister – of all people – to score the winning run.

The Australians did not lose again for three months. The Headingley Test, on the first three days of July 1909, saw Charlie Macartney claim both his best innings and match analysis. After Australia had fallen for 188 on a decidedly awkward pitch, Noble made one of his inspired bowling changes. He handed the ball to Macartney and told him: 'You go on and get them out and I'll bowl at the other end to keep the runs down'.

Macartney proved unplayable. His left arm seemed to be like a huge steel spring as he took 7/58, and Noble kept his promise with 13–5–22–0. Macartney followed with 4/27 in the second innings.

Australia won by 126 runs and in the course of the match Syd Gregory completed his 2000th Test run.

In between Tests in July, Peter McAlister absented himself from the touring team to attend a meeting at Lord's. He was joined by Dr Leslie Poidevin, the former NSW player, and jointly they became the official Australian delegation to a meeting entitled the *British Colonial Cricket Conference*. This title was quickly discarded as discussions took place with the representatives of the Marylebone Cricket Club and South African Cricket Association. The *Imperial Cricket Conference* emerged and one of their initial decisions concerned – as McAlister's report back to Melbourne stated – 'The desirability of holding triangular contests was agreed to'.

McAlister also stated that he would inform the Board at their next meeting 'on other matters dealt with'. In reply, Ernie Bean thanked McAlister for his efforts and added ' . . . how you were subjected to so many unsportsmanlike attacks from sections of the Melbourne press,' and followed with 'your judgment has been subsequently vindicated by success'.

Monty Noble was very unhappy with McAlister's influence at Board level, and disliked intensely his reporting on tour affairs. He himself was being hounded by McElhone in NSW and finally his resilience snapped. Not long after his return from tour Noble gave up playing the first-class game he loved and quit the argumentative scene (except for one appearance in 1918–19). In his letter to the Board of Control dated 13 January 1910, he said:

> The exigencies of my business demand that close personal attention be given it. It is with the greatest regret, therefore, that I am compelled to retire from first-class cricket and sever connections with a game in which I have been so keenly interested.

Noble, in short, had been driven from the game by the Board, and thereafter only took part in club administration on an honorary basis. First Joe Darling: now Noble: soon Clem Hill. The sorry tale of Australian cricket politics would claim many fine men right up until the present day.

# 11

# Triangular Troubles

The last two Tests of the 1909 tour had both ended as draws. At Old Trafford Frank Laver took 8/31 to record the best analysis by any visiting bowler in Tests in England. Then, in mid-August, at The Oval, Warren Bardsley scored centuries (136 and 130) in each innings to become the first batsman to achieve such a feat in a Test match.

With the Ashes won the tour carried on for another two months, which included a fortnight's holiday in the Scottish Highlands. The tourists departed on 13 October knowing that the visit had grossed £13,228, of which the Board would retain £1003, while the sum of £7359 would be divided between the sixteen players.

On the way home the party split into two groups, the first arriving in Ceylon in late October. In Colombo, Noble led a team which played a strong island eleven at the Galle Face ground. His opposite number, D. B. Gunasekera, gained honour for Ceylon by obtaining a first-innings lead. Warwick Armstrong scored 59 not out in the Australians' second innings after claiming 5/51. 'Tibby' Cotter thrilled the locals with a quickfire 61 while for Ceylon, A. T. Pollocks scored 38 with R. E. S. Mendis claiming 5/19 in an entertaining draw.

A week later Peter McAlister led a team in which Warren Bardsley's second innings unbeaten 31 was top score. Tom Kelaart had bowling figures of 6/31 and 3/42 as Ceylon won easily. Unfortunately McAlister – along with Bardsley, Ransford, Carter, Whitty and Carkeek – were the subject of a letter of complaint sent by the Ceylon Board to their Australian counterparts who ignored the allegations. No-one knows precisely what these were, although usually such complaints related to unpaid bills, treating local people discourteously or taking goods without payment.

During 1909 the England team had been weakened by the apparent resolve of the selectors not to pick the all-rounder Jack Crawford who was in dispute with his Surrey county committee over money and the captaincy. In August Crawford talked to Victor Trumper about the possibility of emigrating to Australia and playing for a State team. Knowing how weak South Australia was, Trumper wrote privately to Clem Hill who was given approval by SACA to send Crawford an offer. A position was obtained for Crawford as a resident master at Adelaide's St Peter's College at a salary of £160 per annum. In addition the SACA committee offered Crawford £50 to arrive before the second Sheffield Shield match of the season. The NSWCA, however, objected to Crawford playing on residential grounds – there being an unofficial three months' qualification rule between the major associations in operation since 1890; but as the VCA raised no objection, and perhaps too because he had toured in Australia in 1907–08, the NSWCA complaint was disregarded.

The season resulted in South Australia's second Sheffield Shield win, and Crawford scored the winning boundary in Sydney to clinch the victory. Crawford was to stay in Adelaide for four and a half years, living in idle luxury in the South Australian Hotel for a large period of that time as a 'guest' of the management. He taught for only a short time, then did some farming, and from 1911–14 was, at least nominally, the South Australian coach. However, his demands and whims eventually made him a liability to the association and when he left for New Zealand in May 1914 – leaving behind a heartbroken young wife, numerous debts, and much bad feeling – the SACA committee resolved to be far more careful in future about importing players.

A high spot during the 1909–10 Australian season came during a grade match in New South Wales when the experienced North Sydney wicketkeeper, Ted Long, stumped seven batsmen and caught another in a single innings against Burwood. These eight dismissals equalled the then world record but only gained Long one representative call for his State. He did, however, distinguish himself later in the Australian Imperial Forces team.

The NSWCA during January 1910 granted a benefit match to Charlie Turner, but it raised him the sum of only £331 after expenses. They also concluded an agreement with the Trustees of the Sydney Cricket Ground. The death of Philip Sheridan, who had been SCG manager for many years, removed a stumbling block in obtaining permanent and priority use of the ground for cricket. The agreement, signed on 14 January 1910, basically carried on until it was contested in the courts in late 1977.

By coincidence the VCA were then concluding their agreement with 'the Trustees of the Metropolitan Cricket Ground and the Committee of the Melbourne Cricket Club'. Their seven-year contract was for all top matches to be played on the MCG, 'for the sum of £925 per annum rising to £1000 by 1915–16 if four international teams play on the ground during that period'. This contract carried on in various forms up to the present day.

Also in January 1910 the Board of Control decided to send a representative team to New Zealand the following March. Warwick

Armstrong was invited to captain the team on a nine-match tour to include two unofficial Tests.

The first match saw Wellington defeated by six wickets. Auckland were next, losing by an innings before Canterbury gave the tourists a major fright at Lancaster Park, Christchurch. The home side had the Australians grasping for a draw having outplayed them for the whole match.

After a long, hot summer in New Zealand the weather broke a week before the first unofficial Test, so softening the Christchurch pitch. Armstrong seized the advantage by winning the toss and asking Dan Reese, his opposite number, to bat first. Bill Whitty took 6/53 and as the pitch dried out, Australia replied with a first-innings lead of 151. New Zealand were 201 for four at the close of the second day but overnight rain saw the next day washed out and with it all New Zealand's hopes: Australia won an easy nine-wicket victory.

The second unofficial Test, in Wellington, saw local frustrations at the Kiwi selectors' choices. Four top players had been dropped and the burden again fell on Reese, who top-scored in his side's first innings with an unbeaten 69. David Smith made 102 for Australia who owed their 162-run victory to the pace bowling of Whitty (2/71 and 6/28) and a new Tasmanian bowler, Ashley Facey, whose first-innings 7/71 caused Reese to say that his country 'desperately required a fast bowler of the Facey type'.

Cricket in Australia was losing its popularity at this time, if anything, to horse-racing but it was due also to a steady rise in unemployment. In the year 1909 to 1910, unemployment rose by 52%, and by 1911 another 71%, and in 1911–12 by a staggering 392%. In numerical terms, those out of work in 1909 totalled 1223 for the whole country which, by 1912, had become 12,441. Therefore the 'entertainment pennies' were not around to be spent, and by 1914 crowd attendances had slumped alarmingly.

Squabbles were still affecting the game in Australia. On his return from England Peter McAlister's enmity with Frank Laver had reached such a pitch that, when the players returned and the Board asked McAlister for his financial records as tour treasurer, he announced that he had not kept any but had left it to Laver with whom he was not speaking.

Since the Board had hoped to gain knowledge of the cricketers' financial killings of which they had heard rumours for so many years, McAlister's news came as a shock. So the Board approached Laver for his records. Laver replied that this had been McAlister's job although he had been willing to assist at any time if asked. In the same letter he told the Board that he had been unable to get some of the players to sign the Board's contract. In further correspondence Laver maintained that McElhone had told him that his duties would virtually be the same as on the England visit in 1905, when he was tour manager.

Laver added that he had bought books to keep for the Board but when his tour contract arrived he found that the accounting had been taken out of his hands and assigned to McAlister. As a result he had used the books, which the players paid for, to put down personal mementoes of the tour, together with a record of all transactions, private and otherwise, and at the end of the tour he had presented each member of the team with a book as a souvenir.

In recent years, some of these books, along with Laver's personally inscribed photograph album given to each player, have come up for sale at auction. The latest – the one inscribed to Hanson Carter – fetched £720 at Christie's saleroom in Melbourne in 1990. However, Colin Sinclair, who had replaced McElhone as Board Secretary (McElhone becoming chairman of the Board a year later) accepted Laver's view that his books contained many personal and private entries and agreed, officially, 'that it would be improper for them to be disclosed'.

McAlister, after refusing his album of photographs from Laver, then wrote and had printed a series of defamatory notes, mainly about his former friend and teammate. The issue continued to bubble beneath the surface, since the Board continued to back McAlister although the players believed he was lying.

In Tasmania the debts were mounting as the game there too was declining. The Northern and Southern Associations could not even agree to accept an offer from the NSWCA to tour during 1910.

The subject of obtaining a cricket coach was discussed by the TCA but still no agreement could be reached. The Secretary, Philip Facy, said at the Annual General Meeting: 'Clubs were asked to donate £10 each towards obtaining a coach for the association. Most declined the responsibility. Schools were then asked to contribute in the knowledge they would receive professional benefit for their efforts: again, most declined. Your committee then made inquiries in the various cricket centres in Australia for suitable men, but has not heard of a first-class coach being available.' Facy probably forgot to add that no-one in any prominent cricket position would have dreamt of dropping down the ladder to coach on the island.

On the other hand, by 1910, Western Australia had played a number of first-class matches against South Australia, Victoria and New South Wales, and they had enticed two interstate cricketers to move west: Ernie Jones, the former Test fast bowler from Adelaide, and Arthur Christian, the Victorian all-rounder. Having also played two matches against Arthur Jones' English tourists in 1907, the WACA felt they now had a chance of meeting more teams. Alas, only one 1912 interstate tour was to be their reward, plus a seat on the Board of Control in 1913.

WACA's finances were so poor in 1910, that the club survived going in to debt only by profits from the bar at the ground. Membership had dropped to 212 which brought in £184 out of an annual income of £945.

Comparative figures at this time were:

| | *Members* | *Membership income* £ | *Annual income* £ |
|---|---|---|---|
| South Australia | 1007 | 2037 | 10,819 |
| Queensland | 285 | 49 | 900 |
| Tasmania | 436 | 335 | 1551 |
| NSW | N/A | N/A | 9063 |
| Victoria | N/A | N/A | 7709 |
| Melbourne CC | 5495 | 10,707 | 12,958 |

NB. As neither the NSWCA nor VCA owned grounds they did not have memberships.

Between 1908 and 1911 Queensland built up a strong team led by John Hutcheon who, in years to come, would be responsible for Queensland's entry into the Sheffield Shield competition. When Hutcheon went to England to further his law studies at the end of the 1910–11 season there was a considerable downturn in Queensland's cricketing fortunes which had prospered under his captaincy.

Meanwhile, communication between the Australian Board of Control and the South African Cricket Association continued. A tour by South Africa for the 1910–11 season had been agreed upon but, even so, the arrangements did not go through smoothly. Six months before the tour was planned to start the South Africans sent a cable to the Board: 'We cannot possibly send a team unless we are assured of half the gross gate takings with a minimum guarantee of five thousand pounds.' This threw the Australian Board into a minor panic. Meetings were convened of all the State associations who reported back to the Board secretary, Colin Sinclair. After discussion with the chairman, Mostyn Evan, Sinclair replied to Johannesburg: 'Agreement to guarantee of five thousand pounds, provided your team is approved by us, and you approve of our programme for your tour. We decline to concede half gross gate takings but offer instead half gross ground takings.' Gate takings included the stands while ground were only for entry – a large difference financially.

After more to-ing and fro-ing, the financial aspects of the tour were agreed which was just as well since the Springbok captain, Percy Sherwell, and his team had already set sail from Durban.

The first South African team arrived at Port Adelaide late on the afternoon of 31 October 1910, to be greeted by some four hundred cheering well-wishers. After speeches, Sherwell and his team were taken to the Adelaide Oval where South Australia was in the process of defeating Victoria. The Shield season of 1910–11 took second place to the Springboks' tour, but regrettably, because of the tour, NSW and South Australia cancelled their match which would have been the championship decider.

It was also a time of change in that the St George Cricket Association in Sydney had tried out eight-ball overs in the 1909–10 season for a couple of matches and for 1910–11 were playing all their matches this way.

The Springboks' tour of England in 1907 had created a 'googly craze' and many people in the game were wondering whether top batsmen would ever master this type of bowling. But they failed to realise that Australian pitches were far, far different from those in England or South Africa, so that the tourists' decision not to include a genuine fast bowler in their party was a bad error of judgment.

Reggie Fitzgerald, the team manager – he was also vice-chairman of the Transvaal Cricket Union – said in his tour report: 'We hope this tour will help to bring the people of the great dominions of the Empire into closer touch'. He added that meetings between the two countries, 'should be opened up with a series of intercolonial visits'. Maybe his reasoning was due to the breaking of the British umbilical cord when South Africa was granted independence in 1910.

In the first match South Australia were easily beaten with Dave Nourse scoring an unbeaten 201 and Reggie Schwarz, one of the googly bowlers, taking 6/66 and 5/64. Then came defeats by Victoria and New South Wales, followed by victories over Queensland and Toowoomba. A fixture in Brisbane against an Australian XI saw the Springboks escape with a draw from a side which was a virtual second-string national team.

For the first Test Clem Hill took over the Australian captaincy in succession to Monty Noble with Charlie Kelleway, the young NSW batsman, making his debut. Hill won the toss and batted on a rock-hard Sydney pitch. Trumper was run out early, but then Bardsley (132) and Hill (191) added 224, after which Gehrs (67) and Armstrong (48) kept up the scoring-rate. At stumps Australia were 494 for six, which is the highest total for the first day of any Test match. This became 528 next day and, after rain had taken all but a few minutes of two days' play, the Springboks collapsed on the drying uncovered pitch to lose by an innings and 114 runs.

Three minor matches followed before the second Test in Melbourne. Here it was a different story as all eight bowlers in the South African team sent down an even number of overs as Australia reached 348. At stumps on the second day the visitors had a first innings lead which eventually stretched to 158. Aubrey Faulkner scored 204 in 315 minutes for the South Africans which remained a national record for twenty-seven years.

Victor Trumper's 159 saved the Australians from ignominy but even so the Springboks were left to make only 170 to win. Trumper's score, reached in 168 minutes, was a wonderful example of how to play spin bowling. He kept producing late cuts as googlies turned in from the off, hitting them through gully to the boundary. Then came disaster for the tourists as South Australia's left-arm paceman, Bill Whitty, aided by a strong cross-wind, achieved a career-best 6/17 as South Africa collapsed for 80.

In Adelaide South Africa gained revenge when they won the third Test by 38 runs in a match which saw forty wickets fall for 1646 runs, then the highest aggregate in Tests. Victor Trumper's unbeaten 214 was a new Test record for Australia and his four-hour innings contained 26 boundaries. When Dave Nourse was bowling and swinging the ball prodigiously, Trumper leg-glanced him to the boundary under his upraised left leg. This was a stroke originally played by Billy Murdoch and copied by Ranjitsinhji. Percy Sherwell, the South African wicketkeeper as well as captain, remarked that 'Trumper did not offer a chance, nor did he play a single false stroke'.

The fourth Test in Melbourne in mid-February was a sad affair. Australia was dismissed early on the second day for 328 and, in discussions during the interval, Billy Murdoch, the former Australian captain, made a forecast that five South African wickets would fall before the lunch break.

His judgment proved to be correct and, while having lunch with the committee he said: 'I'll never make another prophecy again. I've brought bad luck on those boys.' He then said, quite suddenly, that he felt ill and just as abruptly nosed forward on to the table. A committeeman, Dr Ramsay Mailer, saw he was suffering a stroke and arranged for him to be taken to hospital; but Murdoch did not recover consciousness and died two hours later.

All the flags around the MCG were lowered to half-mast. The Melbourne *Argus* said: 'News of his death under any circumstances would have created profound regret, but on such an occasion, in such surroundings, the event was infused with a note of tragedy and pathos that made a very deep impression.'

It was also the end of an era for the Melbourne Cricket Club as its secretary, Major Ben Wardill, was retiring because of ill-health. The

1911 Annual Report said: 'Having regard to his long and faithful service, extending over thirty-one years, the committee decided to grant him six months leave of absence on full pay, with a pension of £400 per annum at the expiry of that period.'

The report then added: 'Applications were invited throughout the Commonwealth for the position of secretary and after full consideration Mr S. M. Tindall was appointed to the position.' Sidney Tindall, formerly of Lancashire and London County, lasted only a few months in the post before departing under a cloud; and his death in Sydney eleven years later, when he fell from a tram, was covered in suspicion and mystery. The club then elected Hugh Trumble as Secretary, and he remained until 1938, but even nowadays, when listing its secretaries, the Melbourne Club tries to forget Tindall's name.

In the fourth Test match the South Africans had been beaten by 530 runs after the Australians scored 578 in their second innings, the first time such a large margin of victory had been achieved by Australia. In Sydney two weeks later Australia clinched the series 4–1 with a seven-wicket win. The new hero for Australia was Dr Herbert Hordern, the googly bowler who had just returned home after a long stay in America. He had come up through the ranks of the North Sydney Club at the turn of the century before his studies took him abroad. Once, in Jamaica, he had taken 8/55 and 8/31 and awoke the following morning to find five little black boys carefully examining his bowling hand. His figures in the last two Tests were 3/39 and 5/66, followed by 4/73 and 2/117: not flattering returns but enough to quell the batsmen's lust for runs.

Of the twenty-two matches the Springboks had played on tour they had won twelve and lost seven, including four of the Tests. The Tests had attracted 213,603 spectators who paid £8891 which was nowhere near enough to cover the tour's costs. A subsequent levy on the State associations to make up the shortfall saw a reluctance to issue another invitation. Not until 1931 would Australians see another South African team.

In club cricket in February 1910, two feats of remarkably quick scoring were recorded. For Trinity against Mercantile, in Cairns on 10 February, Laurie Quinlan reached an unbeaten century in a recorded time of eighteen minutes with seven sixes and eight fours. Meanwhile in Maitland, Laurie Hawkins, playing for Millfield against Aberdare, made 92 not out in twenty-five minutes with ten sixes and four fours.

Another touring team during the season had the nomenclature of 'New Zealand Teachers', but it was in fact a team of top cricketers who all happened to be in the profession. Captained by Harold Lusk (Canterbury), the players included Grant (Hawke's Bay), Donohue

(South Canterbury), Olson (Poverty Bay), Holland (Wanganui and Manawatu) and Trevena (Manawatu).

The eight-match tour culminated with a fixture on the Sydney Cricket Ground against their NSW counterparts which ended in a draw. Lusk was the star of the visit, scoring the only century (114 against NSW Country), making 409 runs at 58.43, and claiming 23 wickets at 19.96; a good captain's performance.

When, in the Australian winter of 1911 Sydney Smith was elected as secretary of the Board of Control, and McElhone as chairman, their first task was to write to Frank Laver demanding that he hand over the books on the 1909 tour finances. Laver repeated his arguments and offered to attend a Board meeting to answer any queries about receipts and expenditure. This was refused, and both men set about trying to destroy Laver's reputation.

For the previous two years McElhone had been trying to do the same to Monty Noble. He was aware that Noble was esteemed throughout Australia as embodying the highest standards of sportsmanship, but McElhone was prepared to smear a national hero in order to give the Board of Control true authority. There are, unfortunately, many present-day Australian cricketers who would argue that nothing has changed.

The players of those early years had controlled the game. They were not only sickened by the antics of McElhone and Ernie Bean, they bitterly opposed handing over administration of the game to men who had never played top-class cricket. In the forthcoming clashes lifelong friendships were to be broken and only the intervening European war calmed matters down.

On a lighter side, the South Australian Cricket Association committee met on 25 September 1911. When the agenda reached membership matters, the chairman, Mostyn Evan, said: 'Gentlemen, today we reach two milestones with regard to membership. The first is that we have before us our first application from a lady for election as a member, and secondly the Association reaches one thousand members for the first time in its existence'. South Australia, the first colony to give women the vote, now became the first cricket association to elect a female member. The Melbourne Cricket Club, forced by law in 1985 to accept women on to their thirty-year waiting list, will probably end up one hundred years behind South Australia in electing women to full membership.

Four days later Clem Hill joined Algy Gehrs, George Giffen and nineteen others at the SACA annual general meeting. Hill, essentially a calm man, was a steward with the Adelaide Racing Club and, later, after his wife had died, he took up the post of Chief Steward in Melbourne. His family were well-off and he had been educated at one of Adelaide's top public schools. All six brothers played first-class cricket as well, and his father John had hit the first century on the Adelaide Oval.

How little Hill would realise that the quiet gentlemanliness of an Adelaide cricket meeting would become, in a few months, a cricket meeting brawl in Sydney.

The Board of Control's election, for selectors to choose the Australian teams for the forthcoming five Tests against England, was blatantly rigged by Bean, McElhone and an uneasy Syd Smith. Hugh Trumble allegedly got no votes in the election (having picked up a majority the previous year); Victor Trumper got four out of eleven but inexplicably did not get elected, while the Board's friend Peter McAlister apeared to be elected by acclaim without bothering with votes. Frank Iredale and Clem Hill joined the panel for a season of unbridled acrimony. Hill and McAlister taunted each other from the very first selection meeting.

The crunch came on 2 February 1912 when the selectors met to choose the team for the fourth Test. Hill had had enough of McAlister's snide remarks, obnoxious telegrams and downright lies. They came to blows and fought a wrestling match for nearly twenty minutes. Hill, having been harassed beyond endurance, subsequently resigned as a selector.

The press splashed the story over their front pages, and the *Australasian* even gave a blow-by-blow account – but worse was to follow. Another important question at issue was whether Australian touring sides would retain the right to choose their own managers. The players had chosen Frank Laver as their manager for the England tours of 1905 and 1909 and it was well known that they wanted to choose him also for the 1912 tour. The players trusted Laver to do the job, and no-one else.

On New Year's Eve 1911, a meeting of Board delegates quietly changed their constitution, so breaking the last of their promises made to the players. From now on the Board would choose the team manager. When the time came for a manager to be appointed, McAlister thought he had the offer of the job in the bag, but in a twist of all twists, McElhone switched his allegiance and nominated the NSW candidate, Ernest Hume. Ernie Bean, furious, transferred the Victorian votes to the Queensland nominee, George Crouch.

The upshot of this was that the six players who insisted on their right to choose a manager – Warwick Armstrong, Hanson Carter, Albert Cotter, Clem Hill, Vernon Ransford and Victor Trumper – all refused to be selected for the team to England.

A special meeting of the NSWCA on 13 March 1912 was called to censure NSW's three Board members, McElhone, Smith and H. G. Howlett. McElhone fought like a caged lion and won the day by accusing the Melbourne Cricket Club of stirring up all the trouble.

Victor Trumper, a delegate at the meeting, rose to deny McElhone's comments but as Trumper had been involved in stranger matters of late concerning the sport of rugby league, his views did not carry the weight they would have done in earlier years.

The players made it plain that they considered McElhone their chief oppressor. In March 1912 Clem Hill wrote in a letter to the *Sydney Morning Herald*: 'If it is considered desirable that the control of Australian cricket should be placed in the hands of one man, by all means do it openly, but don't pretend to invest the Board with this control when you know an individual controls the Board'. In a speech at about the same time, Monty Noble described the Board as a 'democratic body being ruled and governed by a despot'. In both cases the man complained of was, of course, McElhone. The Board's supporters, too, recognised that McElhone was largely responsible for subduing the players and openly held a special dinner for him at the Sydney Town Hall in August 1912.

McElhone left the Board in 1914. He became President of the NSWCA from 1921–31, and Lord Mayor of Sydney in 1922. When he died in 1932 the *Sydney Morning Herald* described him as 'inflexible and unchangeable'.

What nearly became forgotten in all the cricket politics was that an England touring team was in Australia for the 1911–12 season. They won the series 4–1 which caused the touring captain, Pelham Warner, to say: 'At the present time Australian cricket is honeycombed with an amount of personal feeling and bitterness that is incredible and this must, to some extent, have militated against our opponents showing their true form'. On arrival in Adelaide, Warner had requested the SACA secretary, Joe Riley, to contact the Board to ask why they had failed to confirm the team's itinerary or to answer a cable from the Marylebone Cricket Club president, Lord Desborough. Apparently the Board had simply ignored the cable.

After defeating South Australia by an innings, the tourists took the train to Melbourne. On the journey Warner collapsed with a ruptured duodenal ulcer and took no further part in the tour, the captaincy passing to Johnny Douglas. The tourists remained undefeated up to the first Test in Sydney in mid-December although they admitted to being bemused by the fact that most of the cricket publicity concerned the feuding between the Australian players and officials.

The Test was a triumph for Herbert Hordern whose googlies claimed twelve of the Englishmen's wickets. Australia batted well enough on the first day to attract 35,526 spectators for the Saturday when they reached 447, with Trumper making 113 and the debutant, Roy Minnett, 90. Trumper was the second player to pass 3000 Test runs, behind only Clem Hill.

Although the match just went into a sixth day, Australia were victorious by 146 runs and moved on confidently to Melbourne. However, they did so having heard that, two days before the Sydney Test, their old colleague Reggie Duff had died a youthful and sad end. A whip-round in the dressing-room paid for the funeral and later on the NSWCA paid for a headstone.

The second Test made a sensational start. England's opening bowler, Sidney Barnes, took 5/6 as Australia fell to 38 for six. There was no recovery even though Warwick Armstrong hit a second-innings 90, and England were triumphant thanks to Jack Hobbs who scored the first of his twelve centuries against Australia.

The Australian spectator, who had always been vocal, seemed to enjoy this series more than others as a number of the Englishmen lost their cool at various jibes. Johnny Douglas was different: his smile or a wave in the right direction would delight his barrackers whereas the touchy players continued to be so. This sparked a debate about spectators in the Melbourne *Argus*. It deplored what it called 'such American behaviour' and declared that the purchase of a ticket did not confer the right to make a nuisance of oneself. Clem Hill felt that the crowds were as well behaved as at any time, adding 'that the objectionable comments would soon end with the removal of one or two louts from the stands'.

The five Tests attracted 342,275 spectators, the largest number in Australia's history who paid the then almost incredible sum of £16,297 at the gate. The smallest crowds were at the third Test in Adelaide when only 36,350 saw England bowl out Australia for a ponderously slow 133 made from 60 overs. The pitch was difficult early in the game and the curator, Charley Checkett, blamed the lack of preparation on the just completed Sheffield Shield match against NSW. England replied with 501, Jack Hobbs making a superb 187, but Douglas caused a controversy when he asked his opposite number, Clem Hill, to discipline Kelleway and Hordern for using resin to improve their control of the ball. Hill refused to acknowledge that an Australian would do such a thing.

England made their seven-wicket victory and departed for Tasmania. After an easy win in Launceston came a fixture in Hobart. There the locals watched in awe as Frank Woolley hit two sixes and 43 fours in an innings of quite amazing hitting. His unbeaten 305 stood as the highest score by an Englishman in Australia for just over fifty years.

While Australian cricket supporters were still discussing *the* fight, Clem Hill lost the toss in Sydney; Douglas put Australia in to bat and yet again the brittle batting let them down. Scores of 191 and 173 hardly exceeded being combined and put against England's first-wicket pair. Hobbs (178) and Rhodes (179) set an Ashes record opening partnership of 323 which lasted until beaten in 1989. Gunn and Frank Foster piled on the agony and the visitors won by an innings and 225 runs.

The political quarrels showed up yet again during the final Test as Clem Hill bowed out of the international game. England won by 70 runs which would have been greater had Hordern not claimed ten wickets in the match.

The decision of the leading six players not to go to England for the Triangular Test series of 1912 forced the hand of Pelham Warner. He made strenuous attempts to prevent what he realised would be a financial disaster for the tournament. He sought the aid of the Prime Minister, State Governors and assorted politicians. He persuaded the Board of Control on three occasions not to announce the touring team and met all six defectors more than once to try and persuade them to change their minds.

On 29 February 1912, three weeks before the Fourteenth Australians left for England, the *Sydney Morning Herald* published a letter from Monty Noble which read:

> I say that the Board of Control has acted unjustly and dishonestly and has violated its own constitution. I am a strong supporter of the Board as a Board, and I believe in the principle of Board control, but I am strongly against its present personnel. They have had six years now to bring everybody into line, and to legislate for Australian cricket, and they have absolutely failed. In these six years they have not been credited with one single act of conciliation or forbearance. They have held the pistol of coercion at the heads of the players the whole time, and gradually taken from them all their privileges. Where a happy issue and solution of the present crisis might easily have resulted, we now have the spectacle of a non-representative team going to England.

The legacy of the 1911–12 showdown has been a continual mistrust between Australian players and administrators which lasts even to today. Although the players and Board managed to close the gap before the 1914 war, there were still grudges which were taken even to the grave.

Ernie Bean, for example, continued his feud with Warwick Armstrong. He stayed on the Board until 1929 and was also secretary of the Victorian Cricket Association from 1916–25, an extraordinary double-act. He died in 1939 aged seventy-two.

Peter McAlister rather faded from the cricket scene although he was seen quite often at the MCG. He played no more cricket after 1910, and died in Melbourne in 1938 aged sixty-eight. In 1914 Frank Laver took a team to New Zealand, much against the Board's wishes. He was a most popular and likeable man whose obituary in *Wisden* outstrips many others in quality and substance. He died young, aged forty-nine, in 1919.

The Australian team which went to England in 1912 was one of the weakest and worst-behaved ever assembled. Captained by the forty-two-year-old Syd Gregory, the players set all 'records' for alcoholic consumption, disorderly conduct and 'fraternising with the locals'.

Gregory would not discipline the players, and the manager, George Crouch, was completely out of his depth in the handling of affairs. The team had no idea of social graces and long before the tour's end had been socially ostracised by their hosts. It must have hurt Victor Trumper, who was in England as a journalist, to witness what was happening, and, sensibly, he declined various offers to appear in the Tests.

The tour started with a defeat at Trent Bridge against Nottinghamshire, although in the third match versus Essex, Charlie Macartney hit the tour's only double-century, 208, as his side won by an innings. The first of the six Tests was against South Africa at Old Trafford. William 'Barlow' Carkeek, Sid Emery and Claude Jennings made their debuts but it was the leg-spinner, Jimmy Matthews, who caused the sensations. He took a hat-trick in each of the South Africans' innings as Australia won the match in under two days.

England then easily accounted for South Africa at Lord's, and a fortnight later rain spoilt one of the key matches of the tournament when Australia were the opponents, also at Lord's. In three and a half hours on the first day England made 211 for four, and added another 30 runs in twenty minutes next day. The inevitable draw contained a slightly sad touch as Charlie Macartney became one of the few batsmen dismissed on 99 in a Test. The next clash saw England defeat South Africa again before Australia took on the Springboks once more. In the first meeting Kelleway (114) and Bardsley (121) scored centuries, now they did it again scoring 102 and 164 respectively as Australia won by ten wickets at Lord's. The sixth match of the series, between England and Australia at Old Trafford, was left drawn after only five hours' play was possible all told, and the same happened at Trent Bridge when the two visiting teams met.

England then thrashed South Africa at The Oval to set up a perfect tournament climax at the same South London ground in late August 1912. But the Australians disgraced themselves. Other than Hazlitt's 7/25, and the usually consistent batting of Charlie Kelleway and Warren Bardsley, the rest of the team failed utterly as England won by 244 runs, and took the title by virtue of having the most victories.

Stories of the Australians' behaviour on tour abounded. On a trip to Ireland, stewards refused to serve brawling Australians on the ship. Drunken cricketers collapsed on the decks and teammates had difficulty reviving them when the ship reached dock.

As alcohol clouded the players' judgment news of their behaviour reached the Board of Control. On 1 August, Crouch received a cable from McElhone in Sydney who stated that he felt it was not advisable to continue with the tournament. Other Board delegates resented McElhone's interference but in any case Crouch did not know how to act in such a situation and let the instruction rest.

The England part of the tour finished in mid-September after which the Australians sailed for America and matches in Philadelphia, New York, Winnipeg and British Columbia. The majority arrived back in Melbourne on 25 November, in disgrace and with a loss on the tour of £1286.

Behaviour had worsened on the American leg of the tour and, on receipt of Crouch's scathing report, the Board of Control set up a committee to investigate matters. Matthews, Carkeek and Smith were called to give their side of the story – although Smith did not attend, saying he was ill. None of the three played for Australia again and others were lucky not to have had disciplinary action taken against them. However, the Board secretary, Syd Smith, made the suggestion, which was agreed, that in future the Board must have the power to say whether, for reasons other than skill at cricket, a player was a fit and proper person to represent his country. This would result in a court case in future years.

The 1912 tour was a catalyst for the Board. With the 'big six' dropping out, the Board now had total control and 'player power' would hibernate for some sixty-five years before the challenges would again go out against cricket's ruling body in Australia.

New South Wales comprehensively won the Sheffield Shield in 1911–12 but, in a fairly mediocre season, it was the turn of South Australia in 1912–13. Victor Trumper scored 201 against South Australia in Sydney but his health was starting to fail – he contracted Bright's Disease which affects the kidneys. Emerging from Victoria was the Collingwood all-rounder, Jack Ryder, who scored 521 runs and took 35 wickets in his seven matches.

In February 1913, the NSWCA granted a testimonial match to Victor Trumper in which NSW played the Rest of Australia. As the

NSWCA annual report says: 'A record for such a benefit in Australia was established'. The match plus a public subscription raised £2950, a figure which was only beaten three times in ensuing years.

Charles Bannerman was by now the NSWCA coach. He would have gained great satisfaction when one of his protégés, Herbert Collins, an opening batsman, scored a career-best 282 against Tasmania at the end of the season. However what must be called into question is the granting of first-class status to a number of the matches in which Tasmania participated.

In an average season, a State with Test players might call on around twenty cricketers but, in the 1912–13 season, Victoria called up 33 players from the ranks of their district clubs. In fact 25 of these played in the space of three weeks in January 1913. For several their first-class careers were brief: two played in only one game and a dozen in less than ten.

The problem arose when three Victorian sides were playing at the same time. The Sheffield Shield side was in Sydney: the second eleven was on the East Melbourne ground playing their New South Wales counterparts; while another 'first' team was on the main Melbourne ground in a fixture against Tasmania.

The Tasmanian match was granted first-class status even though the VCA said at the time: 'The executive committee decided to send out a team composed of players not eligible to appear [for the second eleven] and not qualified on merit to participate in Sheffield Shield matches. Several of the original selection could not be spared from business and the side that took the field proved somewhat weak in bowling.' In the match, Victoria totalled 725 runs in two innings – and still lost!

Naturally the Tasmanians loved it. The TCA secretary Philip Facy said: 'After a tremendous uphill struggle, we gained victory by 54 runs,' and he then eulogised each player's achievements, 'on the billiard table wicket [*sic*]', and referred to Tasmania's players, 'reaching a high standard'. One can only wonder what his reaction would have been had they beaten Victoria's second, then first elevens.

Times were changing as progress was enveloping the country. By 1913, Australians were becoming more sophisticated particularly with the inventions of the era. The dashing influence of the motor car, which was reasonably priced considering it had to be imported, made Australians amongst the most motor-minded people of the world, an attitude still prevalent in today's society.

Men were examining the newspapers for the new vehicles: the Lanchester; the Hurtu; the Waverley; the Bianchi and the Siddeley-Deasey. Women, on the other hand, had let the new fashions take over: they were almost showing their ankles! Their beachwear was even more daring. Bathing suits were above the knee and, on some secluded beaches, one could even see men bare to the waist.

Costs seemed to rise each year although unemployment was lower in 1913, at 5.3%, than it would be again until 1941. A lady's skirt cost eighteen shillings; straw boaters seven shillings and sixpence; a two-passenger Hupmobile £230; a sports Buick £285, while cigarettes were one shilling for a packet of twenty. But the bonus there was a free cigarette card with the possibility of a picture of Victor Trumper or Clem Hill or Warwick Armstrong. There was even one of Peter McAlister: as a contemporary wrote, 'The face glaring out at you was that of a fanatic'.

A gentleman's suit could be purchased for under four pounds and the Melbourne Cricket Club had to inform members that, reluctantly, club blazers would have to be put up from twenty-two shillings and sixpence to twenty-five shillings.

The Empire was stable, mighty, and possibly becoming arrogant. Lord Hawke, in the Introduction to a massively over-sized book entitled *Imperial Cricket*, which was published in 1912, wrote the following:

> On the cricket grounds of the Empire is fostered the spirit of never knowing when you are beaten; of playing for your side and not for yourself. This is as invaluable in Imperial matters as in cricket.

# 12

# War and the AIF

In early 1913 the Melbourne club committee had to make a hard decision. This was to cut down the finest trees on the ground: the eleven lovely old elms planted by Stephenson's eleven back in 1862. Not only did the trees take up too much room, their removal would allow an extra five thousand spectators into the ground.

Edgar Mayne, the South Australian batsman who had played the occasional Test, had struck up a friendship, when in North America with Gregory's side, with Richard Benjamin, the promoter. Now Mayne, acting as an agent, started approaching various cricketers asking whether they would be interested in going on a five-month tour around America and Canada.

A team was got together and Mayne approached the Board of Control for their patronage, which was refused by the chairman, Ernie Bean, who had taken over from McElhone in 1912. So the players went unofficially.

On the voyage to the USA the players held their usual election for captain and chose Austin Diamond, the English-born NSW batsman. Later Diamond was to say: 'The Board should remember that it was through private tours such as this that international cricket began. Private tours were the genesis of Australian cricket. The Board should encourage cricket in Canada, where there are thousands of Englishmen, because of the strong chance of developing cricket there as it has been in South Africa.'

The team played 53 matches of which five were first-class. Charlie Macartney topped both batting and bowling averages. He scored 2390 runs at 45.92 and took 189 wickets at 3.81. The only defeat was by the strong Germantown club in Manheim, USA, who won by three wickets.

The 1913–14 Sheffield Shield was won in an unspectacular domestic season by New South Wales. However there were three tours to which the Board gave permission to proceed.

The first was when a New South Wales team toured Ceylon under the captaincy of Ernest Waddy. The idea for the visit had been put to Waddy by S. P. Foenander, a writer and influential cricket administrator on the island. Waddy had made soundings in Sydney, obtained the support of the NSWCA, and embarked on the tour in December 1913. They played nine matches, losing only once which was the return match against the full Ceylon side. Waddy scored the only century of the tour, 127 against Up-Country. It was more of a flag-showing exercise than anything else and the impression left was one of good humour and bonhomie.

With improved communications it was surprising that more teams from New Zealand did not visit, nor entertain more Australian teams. Harry Trott had taken his South Melbourne team across the Tasman in early 1913, and the following December a full-strength New Zealand side played nine matches on their second tour of Australia.

Captained by Dan Reese, the tourists won four and drew one of their minor fixtures, and also played four State games. Queensland was defeated by twelve runs at the Exhibition ground in Brisbane after which came the match against NSW which started on Boxing Day 1913. Facing such a strong team presented an impossible task for the Kiwis. Charlie Kelleway first took 7/53 with his fast swing bowling. Then came Charlie Macartney (142), Herbie Collins (104) and Jack Scott (84) as the visitors crumbled to defeat by an innings and 247 runs. The hard and fast conditions in Sydney confounded and confused the New Zealanders who then travelled on to Melbourne not knowing what to expect.

What they found was a Victorian side led by the reinstated captain Warwick Armstrong, and another defeat by an innings. The game was over in under two days with the sparse crowd paying only £156 at the gate. It was not quite as poor in Adelaide for the final match when 5144 paid £202 to watch three days of cricket.

But what was of far more importance was the impression the team made on the ladies of Adelaide. The social column of *The Register* reported: 'The gentlemanly conduct of the players, their refined social graces, and most pleasant demeanour made them the focal point for attention by Adelaide's young beauties at His Excellency's garden party'.

What effect such attentions had on the team might be judged by their excellent performance against a South Australian side led by Clem Hill. Dan Reese scored 96 and 130 not out, and his second-innings declaration only just failed to produce a result.

Returning home aboard the SS *Victoria*, the New Zealanders were joined by an Australian team which was to make a sixteen-match tour of the country. The side had been organised by Arthur Sims, a former New Zealand captain who then took over as leader of the Australians. Sims had suggested to Monty Noble and Frank Laver that they select a team of top Australian players to tour New Zealand and that he would meet all expenses. More importantly, Sims said that all profits were to be shared amongst the players. This immediately caused the Board of Control secretary, Syd Smith, to refuse to give approval to the venture.

The players went anyway and their calibre showed how much notice they took of the Board. Laver was named as manager of a team which included Warwick Armstrong, Jack Crawford, Herbie Collins, Arthur Mailey, Monty Noble, Vernon Ransford and Victor Trumper.

As Tom Reese, a nephew of Dan Reese, recorded in 1927 in his *History of New Zealand Cricket*: 'The Australians veritably smashed their way through the Dominion'. The tourists' scoring included eighteen individual centuries and innings totals of 658 against Auckland; 653 versus Canterbury; and 922 against South Canterbury. This latter figure is still the highest recorded in the country and Jack Crawford's 354 was a record.

In fifteen innings Trumper amassed 1246 runs and joined with Sims to create a world eighth-wicket record partnership of 433 against Canterbury. Armstrong had a batting average of 56, and 89 wickets at 14 runs each.

The Australians won both of the representative matches at Dunedin and Auckland. In the first match Armstrong took 5/80 and Arthur Mailey a second innings 7/65 as the visitors won by seven wickets on a damp pitch. At Eden Park in Auckland the Australians virtually smashed their way to 610 for six before Sims declared. Edgar Waddy led the way with 140 followed by the South Australian, Charles Dolling, 104, Jack Crawford 134 and Warwick Armstrong's unbeaten 110 which followed his 6/47. The 8000 crowd loved the match, applauding everything. They needed to, as the sunny glories over Eden Park soon faded with the call to arms for a war half a world away.

In October 1913 the former Board chairman, Mostyn Evan, wrote to James Gardiner, president of the Western Australian Cricketing Association, asking if he would allow a move to gain a representative for his State on the Board of Control. Gardiner immediately gave a positive reply and Evan successfully moved such a resolution at the Board's annual general meeting in Melbourne on 14 November 1913.

The Board, however, immediately put the Western Australians at a distinct disadvantage. Not only were they just granted one delegate (instead of three) but, 'such delegate or proxy must be a bona fide resident of Western Australia'.

The South Australian Cricket Association met on 5 December in Adelaide and passed a motion which read: 'In the opinion of this Association, Western Australia should be on the same footing as far as proxies are concerned, as the other Associations'. This imbalance, although corrected and somewhat adjusted, still penalises the WACA through to the present day. Instead of one-third of a vote they now have two-thirds of a vote!

It was at this meeting also that the Board finally laid down hard and fast rules which their constituent Associations had to obey. First, however, they had to be approved.

The first major resolution concerned profits:

> That in future the whole of the net profits earned in Test Matches played in Australia be taken by the Board of Control and distributed to the various Cricket Associations represented on the Board, on an equitable basis, and that the Constitution be altered accordingly.

Then came the move on selection:

> That in Section Two of the Constitution the following words be added after the word 'Board' – 'The names of the players so selected shall be submitted to the Board for approval, and in the event of the Board not approving of the name or names of any players so submitted for the reasons other than of cricketing ability only, then the Board shall direct the Selection Committee to submit the name or names of other players in his or their stead.'

And finally, to circumvent the players appointing their own man, it was proposed,

> That Section Nine of the Constitution be repealed, and the following substituted in lieu thereof: 'There shall be a Manager and Treasurer of every Australian Team visiting England or elsewhere, and he or they shall be appointed by the Board'.

These resolutions were put to the State bodies for ratification and, apart from a few minor protests, their approval was given.

Another matter which occupied the minds of the delegates was an invitation from the German authorities to send a cricket team to compete in the 1916 Olympic Games which were scheduled to be held in Berlin. The delegates were in somewhat of a quandary over this. They had scheduled an Australian visit to the West Indies in early 1916, after which the team would carry on to England for a tour of the usual duration. After a discussion in which certain delegates spoke of their 'German brethren' and 'our Aryan kith and kin', a vote was taken on whether to participate in the Olympics and narrowly lost. One of those sympathetic to the Germans was, within the year, organising young cricketers to 'fight the Empire's menace'.

Following Jack Crawford's abrupt departure as the South Australian coach, the SACA approached Charlie Macartney who proved ready and willing to leave Sydney and move to Adelaide. A five-year contract was signed with Macartney who was to start in September 1914. When the war in Europe intervened, SACA informed Macartney their offer had to be withdrawn. On the surface the SACA offer looked innocent enough. However, the South Australians would continue to buy players throughout the 1920s and 1930s in blatant contravention of guidelines agreed between the States. It was a policy that Queensland would continue from the 1960s onwards.

During the latter part of 1913 and the first half of 1914, peace moves were going on behind the scenes of Australian cricket. Billy McElhone had announced his intention to retire from the Board; Ernie Bean suffered from an illness, while Syd Smith, consolidating himself as the secretary, had a weak chairman in James Allen of Queensland because Allen's time was mainly taken up as mayor of South Brisbane.

Richard Benjamin, the American promoter of the 1913 tour, was engaged during the northern winter of 1913–14 to organise a further tour of North America for 1914. Interestingly – and amazingly – he was unable to make any headway with the top players who told him to put his ideas to the Board of Control.

Who? What? Why? When? How? These questions are unanswerable as no records survive – if there ever were any at all – of what went on behind the scenes. A lot of the bitterness disappeared when McElhone left the scene: McAlister was relegated to the VCA executive committee as well as being a Victorian selector; and the Melbourne Cricket Club, under Hugh Trumble's watchful eye, was content to accept that it was no longer going to be the 'Marylebone' of the south.

From the few surviving letters and reports it would appear that Syd Smith in Sydney, and Warwick Armstrong in Melbourne, had much to do with the healing process. Armstrong's employers, the Melbourne club, gave up to the VCA its own direct representation on the Board, a move which they were under no pressure to make.

Then came the choice of national selectors: Clem Hill (South Australia), Ernie Bean (Victoria) and Leslie Poidevin (New South Wales). Had there been no rapprochement these three men could not possibly have worked together. As it was, they met on 20 June 1914 in Melbourne to choose the team scheduled to tour South Africa in the 1914–15 season.

Some players were genuinely unable to tour for one reason or another. These included Hill, who had made himself unavailable, Minnett, Trumper, Hordern and Ransford. The selectors had a difficult choice, for tour allowances were low and the previous season had not brought forth any startling new talent. In the end they chose the South Australian lawyer, Gordon Campbell, as player-manager with Warwick Armstrong as captain plus twelve well tried and true players.

With war looming the tour was put back for a year, then cancelled altogether. This meant there was a fairly full turnout for the 1914–15 Sheffield Shield competition: the last of 'The Golden Age'. Victoria won through the batting of Warwick Armstrong and Dr Roy Park, and the bowling of Bert Ironmonger who, formerly a Queenslander, was persuaded to move to Melbourne by Hugh Trumble when he spotted him while on tour.

By a quirk of fate Syd Smith received a letter dated 27 May 1914 from John Shuter, the acting secretary of the Marylebone Cricket Club, which detailed in an appendix all the financial arrangements of the Australian tours to England in 1899, 1902, 1905, 1909, and 1912. The figures so wanted by McElhone were now at hand: too late for any action but interesting in themselves.

The Australian team's profits were (according to Lord's):

| | | |
|---|---|---|
| 1899 | – | £ 8,000 |
| 1902 | – | £ 5,000 |
| 1905 | – | £10,000 |
| 1909 | – | £ 8,080 |

and under Board control, 1912 – loss £2,739.

Shuter's letter, in the absence of secretary Francis Lacey who was seriously ill, showed how much the Marylebone Cricket Club now accepted the Board of Control as the only Australian body with whom to discuss matters. Maybe they were happy to be dealing with only one authority? Maybe, too, it was fortunate that Ben Wardill had retired and no longer knew the intimacies of cricket's workings.

Shuter wrote:

> In endeavouring to arrive at a scheme to govern the financial arrangements of future overseas visits of Australian and British teams respectively, my Committee assume that the MCC will be an acceptable authority in the former, and the Australian Board of Control in the latter case – acceptable, that is, not only to the Clubs which supply the players, but also to each other.
>
> It seems to my committee that the first point needing agreement is the maximum number of players to compose a visiting team, and we have based our calculations on the supposition that it will consist of fifteen players and a manager, which we suggest to you as an adequate number.
>
> The next point is what would be acceptable to the members of the visiting team as 'compensation' for loss of time, interruption

to and risk of loss of business by absence from home, and I am to suggest to you that for 16 persons a sum of £5,600 should suffice.

The third point would seem to be to agree what items should be included in the 'reasonable expenses' of the team.

These would probably be covered by the items:

1. Steamboat passages, railway fares, and such cab fares to boats, railways, hotels and grounds as are authorised by the manager.
2. Board and lodging (exclusive of drinks).
3. Tips.
4. Washing.
5. The remuneration of a scorer, and a baggage man together with their board, lodging and travelling expenses. But these men to be engaged in the country visited, and only for the period that the team is in that country.
6. The payment of a sum of not more than £50 (Fifty pounds) for the purpose of entertaining guests, or for giving the team wine or cigars to mark an excellent performance on some special occasions.
7. Cost of arranging fixtures, together with all postages and telegrams.
8. The cost of colours for the team.

These respective amounts, that is, 'compensation' and 'reasonable expenses' to be secured by the visiting authority taking half the gross gate money, or in the case of up-country or outside matches such sum as may be arranged. But should the auditors find that these takings do not suffice to cover the above expenditure, as agreed, then the visiting authority shall be entitled to claim and receive out of the stand money at Test matches such an amount as will cover the deficiency, provided that such an amount shall not exceed one half of the amount taken at the stands in Test matches. Any such claim on stand money to be presented together with an audited balance sheet within six months of the date of the last match of the tour.

With regard to auditors I would suggest that you should have the power to nominate an auditor in England to whom the accounts of the English tours in Australia could be submitted, and we should have the power to nominate in Australia an auditor to whom the accounts of your tours in England could be submitted.

To sum up. The visiting authority shall, under any circumstances, take half the gross gate, or where necessary such sum as may be arranged for up-country and outside matches, but should the sum acruing therefrom be found by the auditor to be insufficient to cover the cost of 'reasonable expenses' and also provide a sum of £5,600 for the purpose of 'compensation' then the visiting authority shall be entitled to claim from the stand receipts in Test matches such sum – but not exceeding a moiety of such stand receipts – as will make up the difference.

My Committee hope that this scheme may be acceptable to you.

We shall have also to address you on the subject of the regulations for the conduct of the game, but it is proposed to do that in a letter which will shortly follow.

On 3 July 1914 Syd Smith circulated the letter to all the State Associations. However time ran out, and by the time the ideas were revived in 1919 both parties were looking for a different formula. But even without the war the players would have found life ever more different, in a cricketing sense, from those days when they had ruled themselves.

Once war was raging in Europe the word 'patriotic' needed to be associated with all types of sporting endeavour. Cricketers played 'for exercise only' and woe betide anyone who was found to be enjoying himself. Extremes of jingoism were inevitable in this climate although the VCA chairman, Ernie Bean, went much too far in the 1915 VCA annual report when he wrote about 'draft-dodging cricketers'.

The *Australasian* on 10 July 1915 reported 'that the Sheffield Shield season has been abandoned'. The following month, at the annual general meeting of the Melbourne Cricket Club, the president, Mr Justice Cussen, said that 'cricket and sport generally had been thrown into comparative insignificance owing to the crisis'.

The war was taking its toll but not only on the battlefront. On 28 June 1915 the cricket world was shocked to hear of the death of Victor Trumper. He was thirty-seven and had died of chronic inflammation of the kidneys. He was buried three days later in Waverley cemetery having been borne there on a horse-drawn hearse with a funeral cortège over three miles long. His pallbearers were Warwick Armstrong, Warren Bardsley, Hanson Carter, 'Tibby' Cotter, Syd Gregory and Monty Noble. The hero of the Golden Age had gone.

Then Gerry Hazlitt died, aged only twenty-seven. He had a weak heart and always knew he was living on borrowed time. Dr W. G. Grace died in England, as did Albert Trott, who committed suicide. Harry Trott, Tom Horan and old Charles Lawrence died also. 'Tibby' Cotter was killed in Palestine; Ben Wardill died at home, but the VCA were also able to report: 'That Captain R. Grieve of the Brighton Club had won the Victoria Cross'.

All the cricket Associations around the country went into limbo. Frank Iredale had replaced Percy Bowden as the NSWCA secretary in 1914, but at the end of hostilities the Association's bank balance was only £9. 11s. 0d. The other cricket bodies were nearly as badly off: Tasmania could not afford to print an annual report; Western Australia had £319. 3s. 1d. but only because they stood down their secretary John Rushton who, however, resumed duties when the war was over; Victoria had £2141; South Australia £3176; Queensland had a few pence; while the Melbourne Cricket Club was in debt to the tune of £2985.

Times were difficult, but the public wanted to see cricket again. Various patriotic matches had been arranged during the war years with the self-imposed ban on top matches being hastily lifted almost as soon as the armistice was announced.

The South Australian Cricket Association had its share of war profiteers, none more so than the Cricket Committee chairman, Norrie Claxton. The Federal Taxation Department won a case against him for a substantial sum of money and Claxton resigned. His eventual successor, Harry Hodgetts (around whom a far greater scandal would occur in 1945), was at the time secretary of the Adelaide Stock Exchange.

The Victorian Cricket Association held a lengthy meeting on the evening of 17 November 1918 and the following day Ernie Bean, now its secretary, sent telegrams to all Associations which read: 'Victorian Association meeting last night agreed to the resumption of interstate matches as from the New Year. Would like to learn of your wishes.'

The South Australians replied by return and suggested New Year's Day in Melbourne for the first meeting between the sides for four years. Cricket was still alive in Australia although, having been bitten by the behaviour of Jack Crawford, the SACA turned down the offer of England batsman Jack Hobbs who wanted to emigrate. 'He was,' said SACA, 'too old to be considered.'

The Australian Board of Control met at the NSWCA offices in Bulls' Chambers, Moore Street, Sydney on 6 December 1918. There they basically split the Board's committee into two parts: one to deal with international matters; the other, called the Interstate Conference, to cover domestic matters.

International matters were put on one side while the delegates considered reforming the game. For some reason the Board secretary, Syd Smith, took the chair as the 'nine wise men' made decisions. The Victorians wanted to scrap the Sheffield Shield competition and replace it with interstate matches 'played for the joy of competing'. Ernie Bean fought for this concept which was, and still is, alien to the Australian psyche.

What was immediately agreed was that the Shield competition would start at once while its long-term future was discussed by the three main Associations. However, within days, an influenza epidemic swept the country and travel between States was severely restricted by government order.

Bean's idea was that the Shield would go to the team with the best record over three seasons, then matches would become just 'friendlies'. He took this concept to the Victorian Cricket Association meeting held on Monday 13 January 1919, and the club representatives duly endorsed his view.

'The other states are tired of it,' he claimed, 'and when it is dropped some other trophy "might" be played for.' Why this confusing attitude should have prevailed is a mystery as, at the Interstate Conference on 17 October 1919, the Victorian delegation voted with the South Australians to retain the Shield. On 10 November 1919 the VCA adopted this recommendation. What prompted the change of heart is not clear nor, probably, ever will be.

Back at the original Interstate Conference other important decisions made were:

(i) Times of matches to be from 11.00 am to 6.00 pm in line with the Marylebone Cricket Club ruling.
(ii) Overs to consist of eight balls (which lasted until 1979).
(iii) Umpires' payments to be regularised.
(iv) Definition of a Colt. (Under-25.)
(v) Batsmen outgoing to cross with those incoming, on the field of play.

The first first-class match after the war was played on the Melbourne Cricket Ground, starting on 26 December 1918. At the age of forty-six Monty Noble came out of retirement to lead the New South Wales team. The Victorians won by 216 runs. Financially the game was a resounding success with takings being the highest of the century so far.

A few days later Clem Hill led South Australia in a match dominated by Warwick Armstrong and Jack Ryder, both of whom had lost none of their all-round skills. Then, on the Sydney Cricket Ground, in front of a three-day crowd of 25,000 who paid £1405, New South Wales beat Victoria and the NSW secretary, Frank Iredale, wrote: 'Whatever doubts may have lingered in the minds of the followers of the game in this State as to the attraction of the match were speedily dispersed.'

With the cessation of hostilities in Europe, the Australian Corps Headquarters in London had to provide entertainment for thousands of troops waiting to be sent home. Before the signing of the armistice, three games had been played in London between England and the Dominions, and these included Charlie Kelleway, Roy Park, Charlie Macartney, Johnny Taylor, 'Johnnie' Moyes, Cyril Docker, Clarence Pellew and Allie Lampard. There followed, on 31 January 1919, an Australian Imperial Forces Order, No. 1539, issued to all ranks:

> AIF Sports Control Board. The following proposals for the formation of an AIF Board of Control to encourage sport in all units and supervise organisation and selection of representative teams. The Board to consist of a president, two representatives from units in France, one from AIF depots in the United Kingdom, one from London, and one representative of the Australian Comforts Fund.

The AIF Sports Board had the support of the Australian Board of Control who appointed Major Gordon Campbell, the former South Australian wicketkeeper, as its representative in meetings at Lord's, to discuss a proposed AIF team and subsequent tour.

The Cricket Board stressed that it should retain control of the AIF team and it gave first-class status to their matches. Much of the organisation was undertaken by the Surrey County Cricket Club and, with the Board's agreement, they appointed Howard Lacy as manager of the team.

The AIF Board started trials in February 1919 to ensure selection of the best available players and, as the news spread, so applications poured in from many former first-class cricketers. After some initial matches, the captaincy was given to Herbie Collins of New South Wales following a decision by the Army authorities to relieve Charlie Kelleway of the post because of poor behaviour. The team then ignored all considerations of rank, so that Lance-Corporal Collins was giving orders to a side which contained seven commissioned officers without anyone questioning his authority.

The AIF team showed fine form, especially considering that some of them were carrying war injuries. In 28 first-class matches around Britain, there were 21 individual centuries, the highest being Clarence 'Nip' Pellew's unbeaten 195 against Worcestershire. There were also 27 occasions when five or more wickets were taken in an innings, with Allie Lampard's 9/42 against Lancashire being the best of his career.

The AIF were not defeated until their twelfth match when they played a virtually Test-strength Gentlemen team at Lord's. The AIF eleven only lost on three more occasions and were generally a very sound side. Herbie Collins was the best of the batsmen although he averaged only 38.45 from his 1615 runs made in 27 matches. Jack Gregory's 131 wickets at 18.19 marked him out as a future Test fast bowler and he took five or more wickets in an innings on ten occasions.

The crowds that watched the AIF on tour were far above expectations. After years of war new names were being spoken of by a public desperate for sport. Australians of whom they would now hear much more included Collins, Pellew, Oldfield, Taylor and Gregory.

An AIF second eleven also toured and played against public schools, county colts and the top clubs. In all they played 55 matches losing only eleven. Very few of them, however, played more than first-grade club cricket on their return home.

The prestige of the principal fourteen AIF players was such that the Sports Control Board received a telegram from the South African government in Pretoria asking if it was possible for the team to visit on their way back to Australia. The players, anxious to get home, were unanimous in refusing such a request, but the army thought otherwise and the Minister of Defence, Senator Pearce, issued the necessary edict to the cricketers who, being serving officers and men, had to accept.

The vice-president of the South African Cricket Association, Sir Abe Bailey, a millionaire, was able to give a guarantee against any financial loss. The South African public had been following the AIF in England, so that by now those initially unknown players were virtually household names. The team arrived in Cape Town on 13 October 1919, on the same day, as it happened, that the Associations back in Australia started squabbling over who would host AIF matches on their return home.

The South African Cricket Association gave the tourists four whole days for practice at the Newlands Cricket Ground before their first match against Western Province. A two-wicket win was followed by a draw against Transvaal in Johannesburg, and victories over Natal in matches at Pietermaritzburg and Durban. A return to Johannesburg and an innings win over a strong Transvaal team preceded the first of two fixtures against the full South African side.

The *Cape Argus*, in an appraisal of the AIF team, said:

> Their youth and keenness are splendid assets when it is remembered that youth, in their case, is allied to valuable experience. As a fielding side and in the art of placing a field they have little to learn from the average international eleven and if, from the batting, stars of the first magnitude are absent, there is compensating evenness of skill that makes them all the more formidable.

A heavy downpour two days before the match started at the Old Wanderers ground in the heart of Johannesburg did not deter Billy Zulch from batting when he won the toss. In between the showers South Africa had no idea how to play the bowling of Jack Gregory (5/72) and Herbie Collins (5/52) who bowled unchanged. In reply to 127, Collins and Gregory – a right-handed bowler but a left-handed bat – then opened the AIF innings with a stand of 70, when Gregory departed for 32. Collins then just went on and on and was only dismissed when the score had reached 428 for five wickets. His 235 occupied 315 minutes and it was only through tiredness that

Jimmy Blanckenberg claimed Collins' wicket. A minor collapse saw the total finish at 441 after which Zulch entertained with a lively 135, but the result was never in doubt. The AIF won by eight wickets in four days.

Zulch had justified his status as the best South African batsman, scoring his runs in 195 minutes against the pace of Gregory and guile of Collins. His opposite number had, however, captured more headlines as Collins' double-century was the highest by an Australian against South Africa, surpassing Victor Trumper's 214 in Adelaide in 1911.

The second unofficial Test four days later on the same ground started with a Springbok collapse on a good wicket. Only Zulch (42) and the wicketkeeper, Tom Ward (29), with an opening partnership of 76 really bothered the bowlers. Ten wickets fell for 41 again to the pair of Gregory (6/46) and Collins (4/28) after which the AIF amassed 456 with good all-round batting.

The innings and 129 runs AIF victory saw the *Cape Times* comment: 'The South African team was well beaten and while one believes the South African side has not reflected its true worth, the superiority of its opponents has been emphatically demonstrated. The tour has served its purpose: the Australian team has given us good, honest, clean cricket and has revealed our weaknesses. The AIF team was hard to beat due to their skill, their keenness, their combination and their batting.'

After a draw with Western Province at Newlands the team prepared for their return home. Before they did, the South African Cricket Association held a farewell dinner for them at Cape Town's Royal Hotel. In his speech Herbie Collins said: 'The strength of the South African team was not revealed in the two representative games. Some of the players failed to do themselves justice, perhaps because of the importance of the occasion.'

While the AIF team were sailing home, the row in Australia about who, and where, the 'soldier cricketers' would play, had become public. Against the wishes of the South Australians, Tasmanians and Western Australians the AIF was scheduled to play only the other three States.

The first match, against Victoria, was easily won. *The Referee* reported: 'The Victorians were taken aback with the bowling of Gregory who made a sensational debut into Australian first-class cricket by taking 7/22 in the Victorian innings of 116.' The Queensland fixture a week later was ruined by rain, but only after Bert Oldfield had demonstrated his wicketkeeping ability with some quality catches.

Against New South Wales, Jack Gregory turned in a brilliant all-round performance. In the AIF first innings he scored 122 out of 265: he then took 5/65 as NSW gained a 14-run lead: next he scored 102 in the second innings; and ended with 3/65 as the AIF won by 203 runs. The NSWCA annual report of July 1920 suggested that, 'many of these players will be seen in our big matches next season'.

Alas, that was not to be the case. Over half of them returned to their pre-war occupations in banking and farming. It was a disappointment, for their sparkling play was precisely what was needed after years of fruitless devastation and the elimination of so much of the nation's youth.

# 13

# Armstrong and 1921

During the war the Australian government established its primacy with numerous laws which overrode the previously sacrosanct legislation passed by the State parliaments. One such Federal law was to place a tax on all forms of entertainment which was passed on to the States to administer and collect. This Amusement Tax made for some farcical situations: one being that entrance tickets had to be purchased at one ticket office after which customers had to go to another ticket office to pay the tax and have their tickets stamped accordingly. Only then could admittance be gained to cinema, dog-track, or whatever.

Cricket and football associations warned their State governments early in 1919 that, with the huge upsurge of interest in sport, the vast crowds attending venues and the odd amounts of money taken at ticket boxes meant that it was very difficult to handle quickly the crowds who turned up near to the advertised starting times. Incidents inevitably took place: in Brisbane, Sydney and Melbourne, but the worst was in Adelaide on 5 July 1919 when a football crowd got out of hand at the Adelaide Oval. The South Australian Cricket Association had been fearful of such a drama which happened before the Norwood versus Port Adelaide match. The large waiting crowd lost patience and stormed the entrance gates with an estimated 15,000 gaining free admittance. Anticipating the forthcoming summer all the entrance gates at Adelaide were rebuilt. In Melbourne and Sydney more turnstiles were provided, but the crowd problems were to continue for some years to come.

In all, the 1919–20 season was to see nine first-class matches other than the three with the AIF. Six were in the Sheffield Shield – won by NSW – and three others were against Queensland. Tasmania, regrettably, did not figure highly. As Frank Iredale wrote in his NSWCA report: 'A team of cricketers from Tasmania came over to Sydney and played a series of matches in the city and suburbs. Opportunity was given them to meet a NSW second team. Your players, however, were too strong for the visitors, who were beaten easily.'

Many of the old – and not so old – players now passed from

the scene. Dave Gregory died on 4 August 1919: Frank Laver on 24 September, aged just forty-nine; and another Trumper died when Victor's legal father Charles died in July 1920. The war years and immediately after saw the passing of Francis Allan, Jack Barrett, George Bonnor, Bransby Cooper, Jack Harry, and Charles McLeod.

During 1919 Jack Gregory had impressed everyone and he remains the only Australian bowler to have taken a hundred wickets in his debut season. This was all the more remarkable as, before the war, his North Sydney club had not considered him to have shown much promise. Then, in January 1920, when the AIF played Victoria, Gregory first came across the former Tasmanian player, Ted McDonald. Within a short time they would become a pair of devastating opening bowlers for Australia.

The Board of Control had originally invited the Marylebone Cricket Club to send a touring team to Australia for the 1919–20 season. This invitation was declined on the grounds of 'unseemly haste' following the war, but a second invitation was found impossible to refuse and, despite certain misgivings, the powers at Lord's selected their strongest available team. The captaincy was given to Johnny Douglas of Essex with the Yorkshire secretary, Frederick Toone, as manager. In the team was Wilfred Rhodes, now forty-three, who first played Test cricket in 1899.

The tourists arrived in Fremantle on 22 October for a week's quarantine due to a passenger having contracted typhus. This meant that the journey to Adelaide would have to be completed by train – a four-day trek judging by the number of official receptions en route. Speeches at Cook, Tarcoola, Quorn, Peterborough, Port Augusta and Port Pirie were shared by Johnny Douglas and Rockley Wilson before they arrived in Adelaide.

There to meet the tourists were Clem Hill, George Giffen, Mostyn Evan, both the South Australian and Victorian teams who had just completed a Shield match, the Board of Control delegates, and the Lord Mayor, Frank Moulden. After a night's rest at the Grand Central Hotel, there was a 9.30 am official welcome at the Town Hall at which Rockley Wilson commented: 'Australians seem to have two great national sports – cricket and speech-making'.

The four-day match that followed, which England won by an innings and 55 runs, was an enjoyable affair. Entertainments were arranged for the players and officials, which included the visiting captain's father, J. H. Douglas, acting as referee during the Saturday evening's State Boxing Championships.

The team moved on to Melbourne to defeat Victoria, also by an innings, but against NSW they suffered a six-wicket defeat.

Meanwhile trouble was brewing. The Victorian selectors for the

1920–21 season were Ernie Bean, Peter McAlister and Matthew Ellis. Bean was honorary secretary of the VCA and a delegate for North Melbourne (even though he lived at Brighton beach, a technical infringement of the rules): McAlister represented East Melbourne and was working at the Metropolitan Board of Works in Spencer Street; and Matt Ellis, a former Victorian leg-break bowler, was a Fitzroy man through and through.

Ellis had no quarrels with anyone but the other two selectors were trying to persuade the Victorian team that Warwick Armstrong, at forty-one, was too old for the State captaincy. When that failed they leaked to the Melbourne press their view that he was past his prime as a player.

Armstrong replied as only he could some ten days after the England match. Against South Australia in Melbourne he scored an unbeaten 157 out of 310, and in the second innings he made 245 in a score of 724. His match tally of 402 runs was then the highest aggregate for two centuries in the same match.

In Sydney NSW scored 802 against South Australia, Warren Bardsley 235, in the Sheffield Shield's first drawn match. Bardsley then scored another 235 as NSW made a record 770 in their second innings in the return fixture in Adelaide. Victoria were then due to play NSW in Sydney in the last match of the season although NSW had already won the trophy.

By this time three Tests had been played, and Australia had won them all. In the first at Sydney twelve players had made their debuts, seven being Australians: Herbie Collins, Jack Gregory, Arthur Mailey, Bert Oldfield, Clarence 'Nip' Pellew, Jack Ryder and Johnny Taylor. The four survivors from pre-war were Warwick Armstrong, Warren Bardsley, Charlie Kelleway and Charlie Macartney.

In their 377-run victory Collins scored 104 on his debut; Armstrong made 158 in his first match as Australian captain – an appointment fought by Bean in Board of Control meetings; and Australia scored 581 in their second innings which was a record.

Australia's second Test victory in Melbourne by an innings and 91 runs had Pellew (116) and Gregory (100) scoring their maiden Test hundreds with Gregory chipping in with 7/69 and 1/32. Only Jack Hobbs with 122 made England's outplayed team look more than average.

Adelaide in mid-January saw the debut of Ted McDonald linking up with Jack Gregory for the first time. However, it was a batsman's match – allowing for Arthur Mailey's 5/160 and 5/142 – with the six centuries scored being a record that would stand until 1938. For England, Russell was unbeaten on 135 and Hobbs made 123. For the Australians, Collins scored 162, Kelleway 147, Pellew 104 and Armstrong 121 and they won by 119 runs.

During his innings Armstrong's leg was badly bruised by the English fast bowler, Henry Howell, but he still travelled to Sydney with his Victorian team a few days later. It was the one hundredth meeting between Australia's two great cricketing rivals and a feast was expected. But Armstrong was ruled unfit to play by a doctor whom Bean believed was lying; and the Victorian selectors, including Bean, did not believe Armstrong either and removed him from the State captaincy. A public meeting was called to protest against the selectors' action and the VCA was forced to back down in a humiliating volte-face.

A few days later, on 11 February 1921, Armstrong was given a prolonged standing ovation by the large Melbourne crowd as he led the Australian side on to the field for the fourth Test. On the second day Armstrong had a recurrence of his malaria, and he decided not to bat unless it was absolutely necessary. He drank a few whiskies thinking that he would not be needed until after the following day's rest day. Alas, a slump occurred and Armstrong was forced to bat. 'As he walked to the crease,' wrote the journalist Ray Robinson in *Between Wickets* 'he saw among the sea of faces the countenance of Bean, wearing, besides his waxed-end moustache, an expression that seemed to say, "I've got him now!" The sight of the teetotal Bean, gloating, sobered Armstrong to such an effect that he made 123 not out. When Armstrong came off the field, with Australia leading, by 105 runs, Bean was drunk.'

Arthur Mailey had match figures of 4/115 and 9/121 and Australia won by eight wickets. The fifth Test, which Macartney top-scored with 170 on the Sydney Cricket Ground, was won by nine wickets which gave Australia the series five–nil.

The Tests had attracted huge crowds, with many thousands more milling outside newspaper offices where scores were posted on special boards. Adelaide's attendance of 109,704, paying £7007, was a new record, with the whole series attracting 478,020 people who paid £40,731: figures quite startling at the time but which within two decades would be doubled.

In the season before the war, the six Sheffield Shield matches saw 74,442 spectators attend who paid £2217 to watch. The first Shield season after the war saw the comparable figures rise to 148,959 and £6813 respectively.

During the war the New Zealand Cricket Council virtually lapsed. On its revival its debts were wiped out and the Council was left with £16. The Council made many attempts to attract touring sides, but England, the AIF, and two other Australian sides all declined.

Finally, in February 1921, the Australian Board of Control relented and sent a team of promising players, all of whom were on the verge of Test selection. Captained by Vernon Ransford it included future Test stars in Percy Hornibrook, Bert Ironmonger, Alan Kippax and Vic Richardson.

The Australians drew big crowds all around New Zealand with the two unofficial Tests alone returning a profit of £600; and they won eleven of their fourteen matches, with the other three drawn. Arthur Liddicut headed the batting averages with 727 runs at 60.50 followed by Ransford, 550 runs, including three centuries, at 61.10. Hornibrook claimed 81 wickets at 8.90 runs each and Ironmonger took 59 at 10.90.

The first of the fixtures against New Zealand, in Wellington in late March, saw the international debuts of Roger Blunt and Ces Dacre who would both have notable careers for their country. Rain affected the whole game which ended in an honourable draw with Liddicut top-scoring with 83 for Australia and Alfred Brice taking 7/80 for the Kiwis.

In Auckland on April Fools' Day the tourists won the toss and batted in front of a large crowd. The weather was perfect and the pitch excellent. Despite losing their last three wickets for one run the Australians amassed 663 runs in just 430 minutes with centuries from Lampard (132), Ransford (128) and Richardson (112). Their superiority showed as of the New Zealand bowlers' 108 overs, only four were maidens. The result, indeed, was never in doubt as Ironmonger (4/93 and 5/34) and Lampard (3/63 and 4/47) broke the back of the New Zealand batting. This tour was the start of many across the Tasman Sea by Australian second elevens or by various Shield teams. A Test match between the countries was a long way in the future.

The impressive performance by Ransford's team was largely lost on the Australian public, however, for their interest lay in the forthcoming tour of England. The choice of captain should never have been in doubt for Warwick Armstrong was in every sense the colossus of the Australian game. But Armstrong had enemies, and none more virulent than Ernie Bean. The Board's decision boiled down to a vote of confidence in Armstrong and, although Syd Smith's minutes were doctored to show no sign of dispute, the decision went Armstrong's way by only one vote.

Life since the end of the war was becoming rather expensive for the Victorian public. Fares on the cable trams had gone up by fifty per cent. Instead of paying one penny a section to reach the Melbourne

Cricket Ground it now cost three halfpence a section. But if the tram was too expensive, there were other forms of transport: 25,000 cars, no less, were on the roads of Victoria. This caused the Melbourne Cricket Club to approach the City Council's Parks and Gardens Committee. The suggestion was that, now there was a parking problem in the city of Melbourne, could a small area of land be put aside for use as a car park when matches were in progress? Approval was given to the idea – which allows cars to be parked on the parklands around the MCG – and it is still in use today.

The team selected for the 1921 England tour, with Armstrong as captain, had the Board of Control secretary, Syd Smith, as its manager. It was such an experienced side that eleven of Armstrong's players had captained their State or club teams.

After a couple of matches in Western Australia the team sailed from Fremantle on 18 March 1921. As their ship was behind schedule a planned fixture in Ceylon had to be cancelled but the players did find time to visit Nice and Monte Carlo. As the rest travelled to London by boat-train, Hanson Carter and Syd Smith daringly flew from Paris to Cricklewood – the first Australian cricketers to arrive in England by air.

The Board of Control had prepared a hopelessly inefficient schedule for the team and at a meeting on board ship the team had decided to break their Board contracts and change the tour itinerary. The original schedule, arranged by the Programme Committee, had the team finishing a match against a strong county in the early evening; travelling overnight to far corners of the country; and possibly fielding the next day if they lost the toss. Nor was there any provision for a rest day before the Tests. Syd Smith tried his best to obtain them by writing to the counties concerned, but only two agreed to assist.

Armstrong pointed out to his team that they had signed contracts 'for a deplorably organised programme'. Tommy Andrews replied: 'I'd have signed anything to get away on this trip'. And Andrews was right, for the tour by the all-conquering Australians has gone down as one of the finest there has been.

The figures speak for themselves. Four players took one hundred wickets: McDonald (138), Mailey (134), Gregory (116) and Armstrong (100). Thirty-three times a bowler took five or more wickets in an innings, starting with Ted McDonald's 8/41 on the very first day of the tour and Arthur Mailey 10/66 – hence the title of his autobiography – against Gloucestershire at Cheltenham towards the end of August.

The all-round batting ability of the team saw eleven of the fifteen score thirty-two centuries between them with Macartney and Bardsley making eight each. Six tourists scored in excess of a thousand runs: Macartney (2317), Bardsley (2005), Armstrong (1213), Andrews (1212), Gregory (1135) and Taylor (1019). Bardsley made 209 out of 708 for seven declared against Hampshire at Southampton but the finest innings of the tour was played by Macartney.

He was one of the most dazzling and brilliant attacking batsmen the game has seen and, although he played many great innings, the one which saw his genius at its peak was played against Nottinghamshire at Trent Bridge on Saturday 25 June 1921. That day he set the record for the highest number of runs scored by one player in a single day's play in a first-class match.

Bardsley was out to the first ball of the second over of the day which brought Charlie Macartney to the crease. The day was hot: the ground was packed: the pitch perfect. At lunch, after just an hour and twenty minutes, the Australians were 151 for two: Macartney on 77.

There was no relief for the Nottinghamshire bowlers in the two hours between lunch and tea when a phenomenal 333 runs were scored. At one time 200 runs came in 68 minutes. Macartney's individual 200 came in 145 minutes: his 300 in 205 minutes. At tea the score was 484 for three, Macartney on 308 having passed the previous highest score by an Australian in England, Warwick Armstrong's unbeaten 303 against Somerset at Bath in 1905.

His fourth-wicket stand of 291 with Pellew (100) came up in just 105 minutes and shortly afterwards Macartney was leg-before-wicket to Joe Hardstaff (senior) for 345, made in 235 minutes out of 540 runs. His innings comprised 212 runs in boundaries: four sixes and 47 fours.

The Australians at the close were 608 for seven and went on to total 675 on the Monday morning. Nottinghamshire in reply made only 58 and 100, so that the Australians won by the huge margin of an innings and 517 runs in two days.

The great strength of the Australians on tour lay in the fast bowling partnership of Gregory and McDonald. The English batsmen in the Tests were demoralised by them: McDonald claimed 27 victims and Gregory 19.

The first Test at Trent Bridge, the hundredth match in the series, was over in a day and a half with Australia victors by ten wickets. Gregory's 6/58 helped rout England for 112; then McDonald took 5/32 as the home team fell for 147. It was all too easy.

Lord's in mid-June witnessed crowd problems as an immense gathering caused a crush so great that the Marylebone Cricket Club had to issue an apology! This was greeted by dissent from many but nothing was done. Australia won by eight wickets in two and a half days as the England selectors chopped and changed their team.

This was England's seventh successive Test defeat since the war and it raised unprecedented criticisms in the London press. The selectors took a severe battering. Clearly the old easy-going approach to Test cricket was a thing of the past.

For the third Test at Headingley, Lionel Tennyson took over the captaincy from Johnny Douglas; but he could not stop the rot as Australia won their eighth Test in a row, this time by 219 runs in just under three days' play. Macartney (115) scored the Australians' only Test century of the series, which happened to be his fourth in consecutive first-class innings.

The first day of the Old Trafford Test in late July was wholly lost due to rain. On the second day of the three scheduled for the match Tennyson won the toss for England and batted. England reached 341 for four at ten minutes to six when Tennyson declared the innings closed.

Hanson Carter told Armstrong that the declaration was against the rules which applied to two-day games. Armstrong told his players to stay on the field while he went to discuss matters with the England captain. The rules said no closure was allowable in two-day games unless one hundred minutes' batting time was available to the fielding side. Tennyson argued but Armstrong won, so that twenty-five minutes' play was lost before England resumed batting. In the confusion Warwick Armstrong took the ball and bowled what was his second consecutive over: a rare blunder indeed. Heavy rain overnight ruined the match which was left drawn.

Between the Tests, Armstrong attended an Imperial Cricket Conference meeting at Lord's and proposed that Test umpires should not be appointed until the morning of a match. In discussion with Lord Hawke it became clear that Armstrong was justifiably concerned about the amount of betting going on and felt that this change of rule 'would remove them from temptation'.

The final Test at The Oval was also drawn after both teams scored large first-innings totals. The English selectors had made things somewhat easier for the Australians by choosing thirty players during the series. However, throughout Australia's unbeaten run, Archie MacLaren, the former England captain, had told anyone who cared to listen that he could pick a team to beat the tourists. He was given his chance in late August 1921 when asked to choose an 'England Eleven' for the Australians' thirty-fourth match of the tour.

The venue was the Saffrons ground at Eastbourne in Sussex and the match was a see-sawing game. Even though his side was dismissed in its first innings for 43, MacLaren's team eventually won by 28 runs. MacLaren had made his point. One further defeat, by C. I. Thornton's XI at Scarborough, meant that the 1921 Australians had matched the achievement of their 1902 cousins by incurring only two losses on a full England tour.

The profit at the conclusion of this part of their venture saw the Australians to the good by in excess of £9000. However, there was still a short visit to come to South Africa and this reduced the final profit to £5250. The Board paid a bonus to each player of £300 for even they recognised that this was one of Australia's finest teams.

The support in Melbourne for Warwick Armstrong was nothing short of hero-worship, so that the public's disappointment was felt when Armstrong handed over the captaincy for the South African tour to Herbie Collins. A mixture of continuing malaria attacks and persistent injuries to his left leg forced Armstrong to spend time in a Durban hospital. He decided then to retire from cricket and shortly after his return took up a position with a distillery company in Sydney.

Armstrong's first-class record, which stretched from 1898 to 1921, contained 45 centuries among his 16,158 runs. His bowling showed an equally fine return with 832 wickets at under twenty runs each. He played in fifty Test matches and in his latter years of playing was known as the 'Big Ship' due to his ever-expanding girth. His fame – and his good investments, his benefit match and his whiskey dealings – brought forth fortune so that when he died in 1947 he was a wealthy man.

The team left England on 30 September for the three-week voyage to Cape Town. A two-day train journey to Johannesburg followed where they scored an easy win over Transvaal. Against Natal four days later, Jack Gregory showed his worth with eleven wickets, form which carried on into a dull drawn first Test in Durban. Gregory's half-century plus eight wickets could not, however, force an Australian win even though, batting at the end for South Africa, hanging on for a draw, was a one-eyed Norwegian called Eiulf Nupen who was making his Test debut.

An overnight train to Johannesburg and another four-day drawn Test. On the first day Australia scored 450 with Herbie Collins making 203 which remains Australia's only double-century in a Test in South Africa. But the star, again, was Jack Gregory who scored his 50 in 35 minutes and exactly double that time for his century. It is still the fastest hundred in time (not balls faced) in Test cricket. When the Springboks batted Gregory took seven wickets but once more time ran out on the tourists.

After an easy victory over Western Province in Cape Town in which Arthur Mailey claimed eleven wickets, the final Test was all over in three days. Jack Ryder scored 142 as South Africa fell to the total dominance of the Australian bowlers by ten wickets.

There was little time for more than just one farewell banquet in Cape Town before the team boarded the *Ascanius* on 1 December for the three-week trip back to Australia, having been away for nine months. More celebrations followed and, after his team had dispersed, Armstrong was asked how the 1921 side compared with Joe Darling's 1902 team of which he was a member.

Knowing that in 1902 both sides were at full strength whereas in 1921 English cricket had not recovered from the war – and had selectorial inadequacies – Armstrong, ever the realist, said: 'The 1902 side could play twenty-two of my chaps and give them a beating'.

# 14

# Sport and Politics

The 1921 tourists arrived home too late for the start of the 1921–22 Shield season, but after the Test players rejoined their States it was Victoria all the way. Jack Ryder notched up 242 against South Australia and Ted McDonald took 8/84 as NSW were defeated in Sydney.

Match receipts for the Victoria and NSW clashes were phenomenal for the times: £2859 in Melbourne; £2256 in Sydney with the crowds being 62,369 and 36,458 respectively. (Melbourne charged lower prices and had more 'outer', or unsheltered, accommodation, while Sydney had more seats.) All this at a time when a good-sized house in a quality Sydney suburb could be purchased for £400.

Victoria went on tour to both Tasmania and Western Australia after the completion of their Shield matches. Their Colts, and then Second Elevens, were so strong that they could have held their own against the first teams of other states. Emerging players had a fruitful season: Bill Ponsford scored 162 against Tasmania in Launceston while his young partner, Bill Woodfull, took 153 off Western Australia in Perth. This followed Ponsford's 186 not out against South Australia Colts and 227 not out versus the New South Wales second eleven. It was remarkable progress even for such a talented player.

Cricket in Perth was starting to regain momentum after the war. The Western Australian Cricketing Association made a profit in 1921 of £1224 (a good percentage of which was still coming from the bar) and began on a number of fundamental ground improvements. Two thousand extra seats were installed by the end of March 1922 and work started on a splendid new grandstand which, when completed, was a credit to both the architect and the foresight of the WACA committee of management.

Some three thousand feet of new drains were laid under the playing area which enabled surface water to drain away rapidly. Even a new press box was built which, according to the chairman, Keane Bolton, 'enables the reporters to do their work under more favourable conditions'. A certain type of local soil was found to be perfect for pitch preparation and the land where it was found was sold to the WACA by the State government for a nominal sum.

District cricket was reorganised with the top six teams now playing each other home and away. Claremont won the premiership from Subiaco-Leederville with East Perth's Leo Bott scoring an unbeaten 208 to record the first double-hundred of the century in district matches. At the same time country cricket was also expanding. Kalgoorlie was still a strong area, as were Northam, Katanning, Moora, Merredin and the far north of the State known as Nor' West.

In Tasmania, unfortunately, the standard of the game was at best marking-time and, towards the end of the 1920s, probably declining. Queensland cricket, however, was improving, as was shown by a good victory recorded over NSW at Brisbane in December 1921.

On 31 May 1921 South Australia celebrated their Jubilee with a gentlemen-only celebration dinner at Adelaide's South Australian Hotel. The evening was full of nostalgia and, after the formalities had been dispensed with it was time for the 'old brigade' to tell a few stories. Normally George Giffen would have captivated the audience, but for once he was overshadowed. 'Affie' Jarvis, rough and ready as ever, gave a speech fondly recorded as 'downright humour of the most pronounced type'. The stories and reminiscences 'kept the audience in roars of laughter' for some considerable time.

In the SACA committee rooms, however, a challenge had been made to the accepted order. The late John Creswell had conceived a committee system which entrenched the local cricket establishment. Although they could never be outvoted, the Adelaide committeemen were aghast when a person of working-class origins, Harry McKay, was not only nominated by a sub-committee but, incredibly, was elected. Wheels worked within wheels. Pressure was put on McKay to resign and on the cricket sub-committee to withdraw the nomination. Then came the crunch. It was found that McKay had once been fined a nominal few shillings for an arithmetical error perpetrated by his accountant when submitting McKay's taxation forms. A proven criminal on the committee and a working-class one at that! McKay was removed and the person who forced him off was Harry Hodgetts, an Ernie Bean/Billy McElhone clone if ever there could be said to be one.

During this season the Victorian Cricket Association held a conference in order to bring their country cricket clubs and associations into some kind of order. As the game was expanding so rapidly, the VCA felt it ought to be involved in the administration and organisation in the country. The senior districts showed the depth of the game. Grade associations had been formed in Ballarat, Bendigo, Hamilton, Geelong, Benalla, Swan Hill, Maryborough, Warracknabeal, Healesville, Tallangatta, Sale, Bacchus Marsh, Echuca, Euroa, Ararat, Panmure, Bairnsdale, Colac, Mildura and Wonthaggi. Add to this the enormously popular city competitions of first-grade and sub-districts' premierships, and the VCA boast of 'one thousand teams under our auspices playing each Saturday' was not an exaggeration.

By now the Melbourne Cricket Club had a waiting list of some 1300 people who were advised that 'their wait for election could be as long as five years'. During the early part of April 1922, the Club decided to revive their annual match against the Combined Public Schools. This was very much a social occasion with the 'CPS' being the equivalent of a combined Eton/Harrow side in England. To boost their team the Club included the former Test captains, Monty Noble and Warwick Armstrong. The attendance was large for both days with the Schools winning by 121 runs.

The New South Wales Cricket Association now introduced a system of sixteen first-grade clubs, a number unaltered until the mid-1980s. Waverley won the first expanded premiership with the new teams of Marrickville and Mosman second and third respectively. In the Gordon versus Central Cumberland match at Chatswood on 25 March 1922, 'Johnnie' Moyes, now twenty-nine, scored 218 for Gordon in 83 minutes. His rate of scoring was 50 in 20 minutes; 100 in 40 minutes; 150 in 62 minutes and 200 in 72 minutes. In his score he hit seven sixes and 36 fours and the total at the fall of the first wicket, when he was dismissed, was 263. As NSWCA secretary Frank Iredale said: 'There is nothing in the records to compare with this rapid rate of scoring'.

The NSWCA made two other important moves during early 1922. The first was to purchase all of the property between 252a and 256 George Street, Sydney, for the sum of £22,165 of which £14,666 was in the form of a mortgage. It was a brilliant investment as rents wiped out any debts in a relatively quick time whilst the property valuation grew strongly. The other move concerned country cricket. Like other states the NSWCA realised the importance of organising country clubs and associations. A 'city versus country' match was originated and good quality cricketers emerged from Bathurst, Orange, Young, Forbes, Newcastle, Wagga, Tamworth, Goulburn and Marulan. The revitalisation of country cricket was growing apace.

The 1922–23 season saw a much changed England side tour South Africa while Archie MacLaren captained another England team on a tour to Ceylon, Australia and New Zealand. After a drawn match in Perth against Western Australia, the team recorded three successive defeats in Adelaide, Melbourne and Sydney. MacLaren gave much time to conducting press interviews and ceaselessly criticised the eight-ball over. On his team's return in March 1923 to play four drawn matches, MacLaren, stirred up by Lord Harris, kept repeating his opposition to the Australian law change until the newspapers gave up reporting his views.

The last match of the tour took place in Adelaide over three days in mid-March. The South Australian opening batsman, the bespectacled Arthur Richardson, scored 280 out of 495 with two sixes and 35 fours. In a way it was an innings of reward for the South Australian Cricket Association because, two months earlier, they had agreed that Arthur Richardson become their first professional cricketer. As there was an unofficial ban on professionalism in Australian cricket, the SACA found a way around the problem. It was a method they would continue to use for many years.

In January 1923 Richardson received a lucrative offer to transfer to and live in Melbourne which would then make him eligible to play for Victoria. On hearing this the acting SACA president, Bernard Scrymgour, called a special committee meeting and within two days Richardson had a job with an Insurance company as an 'inspector', as well as being appointed Association coach. Financially the SACA paid 'insurance premiums' to the Federal Mutual Fire Insurance Company who paid the same amount in salary and expenses to their new employee. The same scheme would work for another seventeen years until the NSWCA finally called the SACA bluff.

The Sheffield Shield season saw NSW claim the title on scoring difference from Victoria, but it was a non-Shield match which made the headlines. Victoria entertained Tasmania in a four-day match which started on 2 February 1923 at the Melbourne Cricket Ground. They expected, according to the secretary, Ernie Bean, 'a close contest after the warmly commended play of the Tasmanians in Launceston during the preceding season'.

Instead, the four-day crowd of 16,400 saw an extraordinary match. Curator Bert Luttrell had prepared a wicket, described as 'granite hard and glass smooth', which gave the batsmen complete mastery. The Victorian team consisted mainly of fringe players who were just about, or just had, fought their way into the Sheffield Shield team. One of these young hopefuls was the twenty-two-year-old St Kilda player, Bill Ponsford.

Tasmania batted first, being dismissed for 217, and at stumps Victoria had already reached 116 for one. The third wicket fell the next day with the score at 200 and Ponsford walked out to bat. While he was at the crease 801 runs were scored in 477 minutes in quite the most amazing sequence of run-getting in Australian cricket history. At the end of the second day Victoria were 672 for five with Ponsford unbeaten on 234. In the day 556 runs had been scored with the Melbourne *Herald* reporting that, 'Ponsford passed records like a fast car shooting past milestones'.

The Tasmanians were now toiling as Ponsford passed Armstrong's individual Victorian record of 250, and five minutes later the Victorian record total of 724 was broken. Next to go was Trumper's Australian record against Tasmania of 292, then Frank Woolley's English record against Tasmania of 305. Later, Charles Gregory's all-Australian record of 383 was shattered. After lunch on that fateful third day, Bill Ponsford passed Archie MacLaren's world record innings of 424 – which MacLaren, who was in Australia at the time, did not take very graciously.

'The next objective', the *Herald* wrote, 'was one thousand runs for his side and here his partner, Leonard Mullett, did a most sporting thing. He was facing the bowling at 999 and could have scored easily, but wishing to give Ponsford the distinction he blocked the over, and then Ponsford with a pat to mid-on got the thousandth run and more cheers. Then realising there were no more worlds to conquer he hit out and was caught.' Ponsford had made 429 runs in three minutes under eight hours, hitting 42 fours. Victoria's total reached a previously unheard-of 1059, and they won the match by an innings and 666 runs.

In Sydney at the beginning of the season, the NSW trial match had been designated as a benefit for Charles Bannerman. The game, H. L. Collins' XI versus C. G. Macartney's XI, raised £490 for the old international.

Joe Riley, the South Australian secretary, now received a letter dated 25 November 1922 from Joe Darling in Tasmania. In it Darling suggested that the SACA should organise a Testimonial Fund for the benefit of George Giffen. He added: 'I would be prepared to contribute towards such a fund, and I also would propose that two benefit matches should be played; one in Melbourne and one in Sydney. My reason for doing this is that I am firmly convinced that few people realise how much George jeopardised his prospects in life by playing so much big cricket, and I thought that now he was reaching the age of retirement from the Post and Telegraph Department, then something should be done in the matter.'

Darling related how Giffen had virtually forced Victoria and NSW to play home and away matches each season, adding: 'If George had not brought about this change then I am of the opinion that Jones, Hill, Lyons and myself would never have been heard of. Clem Hill had George to thank for his first trip to England in 1896, as the three selectors had not chosen him, and it was through Giffen that a meeting of the team had been called, and Hill included. George Giffen has always gone out of his way to encourage junior players, and I consider he has done far more for the game in South Australia than has any other player.'

Darling's letter united the SACA in a way not previously seen. Everyone wanted 'to do their bit for George'. The Committee immediately decided to donate the proceeds of the February match against Victoria to the newly formed 'George Giffen Testimonial Fund'.

At the suggestion of the SACA president, Joe Darling wrote to the NSWCA and VCA with his proposals. In his letters of 8 December 1922, he put forward the idea of playing the Sheffield Shield winners against the Rest of Australia. Both bodies declined the match, but the NSWCA forwarded a donation of £50 and the VCA agreed to open a subscription list through their clubs as well as approving the decision on takings in the forthcoming match.

The Testimonial Fund committee then started ordering and circulating souvenirs: five thousand buttons were made with Giffen's portrait on them; a booklet of his cricketing career was printed, as were ten thousand match programmes. The result was totally unexpected, but very welcome: the largest Sheffield Shield attendance (26,161) yet recorded at the Adelaide Oval.

Helped by hefty donations from the VCA and Melbourne CC, the fund finally closed at £2020. But then came a problem. The fund trustees felt that they could not give George the money (although he was advanced £30 at one time) as it would, in their opinion, soon find its way to his favourite haunt – Adelaide's suburban Morphettville Racecourse. They considered an annuity for him but found that commission and government licence fees would claim too large an amount, so they decided to set up their own Trust. A public meeting of subscribers was called on 17 April 1923 and of the £1964 left after all expenses had been paid, £1700 was invested, with Giffen getting the balance as well as a pension of £150 per annum.

At this period the popularity of cricket was growing all the time. From a virtual complete lack of interest in the game before the European war, the general public seemed now unable to get enough of it. Attendances were rising, and they continued to do so through the Depression years. Radio was a new means of communication and the station 3AR opened in Melbourne in 1923. In Sydney sport was regularly broadcast on the airwaves and between the two cities a huge new audience was being addressed.

Suddenly the sporting heroes of the day came alive in the living-rooms of ordinary people. They could hear Monty Noble giving his cricket lectures or a young Bill Ponsford cackling down the wires saying how many blisters he had on his hands and feet following his mammoth innings. This popularity was carried on into print. Newspapers were employing cricketers to give their opinions on current fixtures or to speculate on series. Space given to horse-racing declined so that the acres of newsprint on cricket seemed to grow and spread.

The mid-1920s was a period of lull before storm. A low 7.1% of the population was out of work: wages were reasonable for the times: the returned war veterans were building the Great Ocean Road around the coastline of Victoria: land grants saw trench warriors become farmers; and yet winter sports were declining in popularity. Was it only the great Australian sun which kept cricket booming?

The 1923–24 season was quiet. There were no touring teams to disrupt a Sheffield Shield season dominated by Victoria. A new batsman was emerging in Sydney, twenty-five-year-old Alan Kippax of the Waverley Club. It was not just his skill and style but his complete confidence in himself. His Shield ventures were good: 170 in Adelaide, 197 against Victoria in Sydney, and 248, also in Sydney, against South Australia. This earned him a trip to New Zealand in February 1924 with the NSW side captained by Charlie Macartney. The team contained six Test players and of their twelve matches, eight were won with the other four left drawn. Seven of the eight victories were by an innings and the scores included 752 for eight against Otago and 599 for eight versus Canterbury. At the end of the tour Gilbert Cochrane, the NSW manager, remarked that, with NSW being such a strong side, maybe they should in future play only representative or combined teams.

Two matches were played against New Zealand. The first, at Christchurch, saw NSW win by eight wickets, a margin which would have been larger had not a series of catches gone to ground. Hunter Hendry scored 110 and opened the bowling in this match, but he did better in Wellington, taking 8/33 to dismiss New Zealand in their first innings for 89. The match finished in under two days with NSW victors by an innings and 126 runs.

Young players were emerging from both city and country. In addition to Ponsford in Victoria, South Australia had the unrelated Richardsons, Arthur and Victor. Clarrie Grimmett, the Kiwi turned Aussie, moved from Melbourne to Adelaide and his future Test partner Bill O'Reilly was making an impact on the game in the bush where he and the young Don Bradman competed. Archie Jackson and Bill Woodfull were soon to be Test openers and Leslie O'Brien Fleetwood-Smith, from the Wimmera region of Victoria's Western Districts, was a schoolboy left-arm spinner of growing fame.

These were happy years for Australian cricket. The sun seemed always to shine and big scores were the order of the day. Interstate matches took the players on long leisurely trips invariably broken by a couple of days to play local sides in places like Ballarat, Newcastle, Goulburn, Broken Hill, Toowoomba and, latterly, Kalgoorlie.

Players used to look forward to the train journeys; to the comfortable rooms provided by basic hotels; to the comradeship and the sing-song around the piano at night. It was not all innocence but the players accepted their lot with few murmurings. However, one trade-union style of cricketer emerging in Adelaide was Victor York Richardson, a supreme athlete in many sports. In April 1924 he led a delegation of players to meet SACA officials over payments for 'loss of time money'. He won his case, but his card was marked for the future.

Changes were taking place in the committee rooms. Player power was dead and buried, but cricket associations were now attracting successful businessmen with social ambitions. They had to start as one of two delegates from clubs to state associations, who then, in turn, elected members to the Board of Control. This gave power to men who had their favourite players irrespective of ability, which caused parochialism around the national selection table. One player to suffer badly because of interstate rivalries was Alan Kippax who, for most of his prime, 1921–26, was disgracefully ignored at a time when the Victorians were pushing for the inclusion of comparatively ordinary players such as Hendry and Hartkopf.

A delegate's first priority was to convince his club that he was doing all in his power to promote their players within the state association or the Board of Control. He would have to attend hundreds of meetings during his career and, to give a later example, Sir Donald Bradman attended 1713 major South Australian committee meetings during his term of office. Add to this club executive meetings through to the Imperial Cricket Conference, and Bradman's estimated attendances between 1935 and 1986 would number around 3200 meetings.

Bradman, admittedly, was a rare exception in that he was a player cum brilliant administrator. The bulk of cricket committeemen tended to wallow in their own self-importance. They too would attend meetings; give views, unhelpful in many cases; criticise the players; then have a good lunch or prop up the Association's bar – all at the expense of cricket. So many, unfortunately, lived up to this image that the rift between administrators and players gradually grew wider and wider. However much today's administrators say that matters have changed, the players often tell a different story.

And so it was in 1924, only some twelve years after the great rift. Player domination had ceased in general terms, yet there would always be troublesome individuals to whom the Board would defer because their loss to the game, and to its finances, could have caused even more problems.

The Twentieth England team to tour Australia arrived in Fremantle, Western Australia, on 14 October 1924. Captained by Arthur Gilligan, the Sussex opening bowler, now thirty, and managed, again, by the

Yorkshire secretary, Frederick Toone, the side was as representative as any team had been. After four matches in the west the tourists travelled by train to Adelaide where Arthur Richardson cemented his Test place by scoring an unbeaten double-century as England won by nine wickets.

Six further matches followed which included an excellent three-wicket victory over New South Wales before the first Test started in Sydney on 19 December 1924. New into the Australian team by sheer weight of their State performances came Bill Ponsford and Vic Richardson as well as Arthur Richardson. Gone from the last Test side were Ted McDonald, who was now living in England, Charlie Macartney, who had suffered a nervous breakdown, Jack Ryder (soon to return), and Warwick Armstrong.

Herbie Collins won the toss for Australia and batted on what looked like a placid Sydney pitch. But it was totally the opposite in character, and it was only by the sheer skill of Collins (114) and Ponsford (110) that the Australians lost just three wickets on that first day. For England, Maurice Tate bowled fast and so accurately that the former Australian captain, Clem Hill, said in the dressing-room later that evening: 'That's the toughest bowling I have ever seen on the first day. If Tate had had any luck, your whole team could have been out twice before lunch.'

Australia went on to score 450, and although he was carrying a leg injury Jack Gregory's 5/111 saw the home side to a 152-run first-innings lead. Johnny Taylor (108) dominated the second innings which included a remarkable last-wicket stand of 127 with Arthur Mailey (46*). The match, which saw both the introduction of the eight-ball over and the start of the famous Hobbs and Sutcliffe opening partnership for England, was eventually won on the seventh day by Australia by 193 runs. (All Tests in Australia from 1881–82 to 1946–47 were played to a finish.)

The teams travelled together to Melbourne, for the New Year game, where Australia brought in the leg-spinner, Bert Hartkopf, for Hunter Hendry. Bob Crockett returned to umpire the match with a career behind him of 28 Tests and thirty-eight years of first-class experience. He was able to keep going for only two more seasons before his failing eyesight caused him to retire. By then he had umpired in 32 Tests, and he was awarded a Testimonial worth £1043.

The interest in this Test was tremendous. The attendance in Sydney, 165,706, was thought good: now the spectators numbered 236,258, with gate takings of £22,600. Also there was the radio station 3AR paying £75 for broadcasting rights for the season in Victoria. As the new morning newspaper the *Sun-News Pictorial* reported on 1 January 1925:

> Wireless operators [i.e. listeners] will obtain a first-hand description of every incident in the Second Test match which begins today . . . The 3AR broadcasting station has secured the services of the Victorian Eleven captain, E. R. Mayne, and will describe the progress of the game. A special land line has been run from the studio in Elizabeth Street to the MCG, where a special observer from 3AR will transmit over the telephone to the broadcasting studio a complete description of the match.
>
> The enterprise of 3AR marks a new era in the use of radio. The wireless operator in the remotest part of Australia will be able to learn the many turns which the game may take within a few seconds of the time at which the spectators on the ground become aware of them. 3LO, the other broadcasting station, will also broadcast the scores every half hour.

Herbie Collins won the toss in front of a record crowd of 48,321 and then saw Australia bat for two days. The total reached 600, the then highest score in Test cricket, with Ponsford (128) scoring his second century in as many Tests and Vic Richardson (138) making his initial hundred. England fought back well to 479, with Hobbs (154) and Sutcliffe (176) putting on 283 for the first wicket. Sutcliffe (127) reached three figures again in the second innings but this could not stop Australia winning by 81 runs.

Before the third Test in Adelaide a week later, the Governor-General of Australia, Lord Forster, unveiled a specially commissioned oil painting of George Giffen which had been financed by the Adelaide Post and Telegraph Cricket Club. The painting may have been of one individual, but it represented much more. The old warrior was now sixty-five, and his friends were beginning to pass on: Alick Bannerman had died three months earlier and shortly so would Billy Bruce (by suicide), Frank Iredale, Fred Spofforth, Jack Saunders and a close friend of Giffen's, Jack Lyons.

Yet again Herbie Collins won the toss and Jack Ryder celebrated his recall with an unbeaten 201 out of a total of 489 and then 88 in the second innings (out of 250). Jack Hobbs scored 119 in England's first innings of 365 but on the seventh day Australia won a very close contest by 11 runs to reclaim the Ashes.

Relations between the teams were excellent, and this sportsmanship conveyed itself to the crowds. England turned the tables by winning the fourth Test in Melbourne by an innings – after Gilligan had won the toss for the only time in the series. The last Test in Sydney, however, was over in four and a half days, Australia victorious by 307 runs. Clarrie Grimmett and Alan Kippax made their debuts with Grimmett, aged thirty-three, taking 5/45 and 6/37.

After two more matches to finish the tour, Toone went into conclave with the Board Treasurer, Aubrey Oxlade, and startling figures emerged. The gross gate receipts had totalled £95,171 which, after the paying of amusement tax of £8479, saw the Marylebone Cricket Club take back to London the sum of £35,120. The number of spectators who watched the tourists topped the one million mark for the first time – 1,052,820.

No wonder Syd Smith, in his annual report to the Board of Control, wrote: 'The interest displayed in the game during the past season was phenomenal'. Smith went on to praise Arthur Gilligan 'who possessed a charming personality and a most tactful manner'.

But underneath the pleasant surface, had the English visit been more than a cricket tour? Under the 'Fifty-Year Rule', documents from the Australian Archives, previously labelled 'Top Secret', have now been made available to historians and researchers. Item Number N4673 shows, for example, that the Australian secret services had been informed by their counterparts in London that both Arthur Gilligan and Frederick Toone 'were members of an organisation known as the British Fascists'.

The academic journal, *Sporting Traditions*, states: "During the years 1920–40, Australian political life was influenced by various ideologies imported from Europe. Bolshevism added clarity and rigour to Australian radicalism; and class-conscious Australian, workers found much to celebrate in the successful revolution which brought about the Soviet Union. At the other end of the political spectrum many members of the 'governing' classes were inspired by Benito Mussolini and subsequent fascist movements in Europe. Fascism came to be widely perceived as the antidote to the Communist Revolution. Conservative journals even canvassed the prospects of an antipodean Mussolini emerging to teach sections of the militant Australian working class lessons in industrial relations.

"But was there the genesis of fascist sentiment and organisation to be exploited in Australia? And how soon after Mussolini's march on Rome in October 1922 did Australians come to be interested in fascism? What precisely did Monty Noble mean when he wrote, in his book *Gilligan's Men,* that these were 'days of national unsettlement and disruptive influences generally'?

"By late 1924, when the keenly anticipated England tour started, the 'White Australia' policy was well in place. But some people saw the cricket tour in a wider cultural and political context. Specifically it was hoped that the tour might ameliorate some of the social tensions that had become all too apparent in post-war Australia.

"Indeed almost everything in Australian society seemed on the verge of being turned upside down. The certainties of the Victorian and Edwardian eras had vanished. Cubism, jazz and the 'Black Bottom' seemed to be affronts to the Australian ruling class's cultural hegemony, while in political terms 'the rising tide of Labor' – militants within the newly-formed Communist Party of Australia and radicals committed to the socialisation objectives of the Australian Labor Party – all seemed hell-bent on following in the footsteps of Lenin's Bolsheviks. Just twelve months before the English cricket team arrived in Australia unprecedented scenes of rioting and looting had taken place in the streets of Melbourne in the wake of a police strike. The reverberations of this 'Bolshevik Orgy' were still being felt. Like the royal tour by the Prince of Wales in 1920, which sought to counter 'pernicious influences in the far reaches of the Empire, a cricket tour exemplifying 'the Englishman at his best, dignified, cautious, charming and optimistic in face of all kinds of difficulties', as the journal *Labour History* put it in 1980, might perform a stabilising function. In the minds of some it could provide some cement for an apparently faltering social fabric. At least it could serve as a temporary diversion for the militants within the working class.

"England may have lost the series 4–1 but in social terms, the tour was far more productive. At glittering receptions such as at Melbourne's Windsor Hotel the cricketers were fêted visitors as Australia's self-proclaimed gentry lined up to be introduced. Especially popular was the touring captain, Arthur Gilligan.

"Indeed much of the propaganda surrounding the tour focussed on Gilligan's personal characteristics. A competent fast bowler prior to suffering a serious injury in the 1924 season, what he now lacked in cricketing ability ('except for his brilliant fielding and inspiring captaincy he was a passenger,' said *Wisden)* Gilligan apparently compensated for in sportsmanlike behaviour. A product of Dulwich College and Cambridge University, and a gentleman of independent means, Gilligan had served with the Lancashire Fuseliers during the European war. *Cricket* recorded that he possessed 'one of the most jovial personalities imaginable'. Monty Noble enthused that Gilligan was 'the type of man who, in the most unostentatious way, can do more than all the politicians and statesmen to cement the relations between the Homeland and the Dominions'. He was the epitome of the English gentleman, a good sport of 'debonair countenance' and a fine 'Empire builder'.

"However, the information received from London by the Australian secret services (controlled by the Federal Police until 1947) was that both Gilligan and Frederick Toone (whom *Cricket* described as a 'hard-headed business-like son of good old Yorkshire') were members of the British Fascists. Presenting themselves as empire loyalists prepared to save civilisation from Bolshevism, the movement briefly enjoyed great popularity, though the membership statistics available to the Australian secret service were greatly exaggerated.

"The question which remains unanswered is: To what extent did Gilligan and Toone push their beliefs on tour? On his return from the tour Gilligan wrote an article for *The Bulletin of the British Fascists.* Entitled 'The Spirit of Fascism and Cricket Tours' he argued that: 'In cricket tours it is essential to work solely on the lines of Fascism, that is, the team must be good friends and out for one thing, and one thing only, namely the good of the side and not for any self-glory.'

"There is little reason to believe that this type of rhetoric struck a responsive chord among its target audience – the Australian working class. By the end of 1925 there was industrial turmoil in the maritime industry. On the other hand it seems likely that some members of the Australian bourgeoisie not only shared Gilligan's view that cricket enhanced the 'crimson ties of friendship . . . and the crimson bonds of kinship', but that they also followed the England captain's lead in terms of hitching their own wagon to fascism. Some of them were perhaps among the 'heaps of good friends' Gilligan's team claimed to have made in Australia.

"Shortly after the departure of the English cricketers, officers of the Commonwealth Investigation Branch became aware that an Australian legion of the British Fascists had been established in several of the capital cities. In Sydney, for instance, enrolment forms, internal memoranda and propaganda were uncovered.

"It may be coincidental that the Australian chapter of the British Fascists was established so soon after the England tour, but, on balance, it seems likely that Arthur Gilligan simply followed the advice issued by the Fascists' Recruiting and Propaganda Department. This was to: 'Talk about the movement to everyone you meet' and 'Always carry at least one enrolment form and one of each of the other pamphlets with you wherever you go'. The literature of the fascists probably arrived in the luggage that Gilligan and Toone brought to Australia in 1924."

The records of the Australian Board of Control for International Cricket show absolutely no dealings – officially – with any outside body concerning the tour manager or captain. In fact, most of their season seemed to be spent answering letters to Lord's, for the Marylebone Cricket Club put the Board under enormous pressure to withdraw first-class status from the Victoria versus Tasmania match of the previous season. It was not Victoria's enormous total of 1059 that caused concern, so much as Ponsford's 429 which rankled, as it beat Archie MacLaren's English record of 424.

The Board meeting held in Melbourne on New Year's Eve 1924 rejected any move to downgrade the fixture; and the motion was passed in front of three guests: Messrs Toone, Gilligan and Johnny

Douglas who were present to hand over a letter to the Board from Lord Harris. His Lordship, as Chairman of the Cricket Committee of MCC, demanded an immediate end to the eight-ball over in Australia, a proposal which the Australian Board would not even consider.

After Victoria won the Sheffield Shield for the 1924–25 season, and as a reward, their players were taken on a twelve-match tour of New Zealand. Originally Tasmania had been due to go, but the TCA was still too broke even to print an annual report. So, captained by Edgar Mayne, the Victorians found the standard of cricket in the country had improved. Seven games were drawn, while Wellington won their match by 19 runs. Canterbury, Auckland and Hawke's Bay all exceeded 400 runs in an innings and the tour brought in a welcome profit of £358 for the NZCC.

Bill Woodfull scored four unbeaten centuries, including 212 against Canterbury. His 110 against the full New Zealand side in Wellington was the basis for Victoria's six-wicket win although Vernon Ransford's 6/38 was by far and away the best bowling return of his career.

The two teams sailed from Wellington to Christchurch, and started their second and final representative match on 27 March 1925. New Zealand batted and made 237 with Victoria just having begun their innings when the rain came. Most of the Saturday's play was lost although by Monday, the final day, the pitch had dried out. Victoria went to 349 for four before Mayne declared. Woodfull by now was on 150 and Ransford 100, their fifth-wicket partnership having raised 235 runs. The match was drawn, but as New Zealand's captain, Billy Patrick, had earned high praise for his leadership, he was appointed to lead the team on a two-month tour of Australia which started in Brisbane on 4 December 1925. Having never batted in such heat before, the Kiwis lost their match with Queensland by an innings and 92 runs. Two country matches followed before Victoria were the opponents in Melbourne. The hospitality shown to the tourists could have been the reason for the New Zealanders' turn in fortune.

Their drawn matches against Victoria (in which Hunter Hendry scored an unbeaten 325), South Australia, and New South Wales caused the Sydney *Daily Telegraph* to devote generous praise to the New Zealanders. 'Since the tour opened in Brisbane the team has shown wonderful improvement. It possesses some enterprising batsmen, and [William] Cunningham is a bowler of outstanding ability.' The report concluded with the apt comment: 'The standard of cricket in the Dominion is improving. Australia should do everything possible to assist New Zealanders in putting the game on a sound basis.'

Sadly, the Board of Control's almost immediate reaction to this suggestion was to cancel any plans for the 1926 team to England to visit New Zealand en route. Instead it was agreed: 'That all members of the Australian team should visit Tasmania'.

In 1925 the New South Wales Cricket Association's secretary, Frank Iredale, became so seriously ill that he was granted sick leave on full pay, and the executive knew they would have to search for a successor. It was said of Iredale, although not in a critical spirit, that 'he was too keen a player to be an efficient administrator', and 'that he preferred to mix with the players at the practice nets than deal with paperwork at his desk in the city'. He died on 15 April 1926, aged fifty-nine.

Coincidentally, all three major Associations changed their secretaries around this time. The remnants of the old guard were gone: memories of the 1912 row and Board fights were now becoming old men's stories. The new breed were hard, tough men and the toughest of them was William Henry Jeanes, who took over as South Australian secretary in September 1926 and as Board of Control secretary shortly afterwards. His background was in local government, having become a Town Clerk at thirty years of age, in 1913. His proven administrative ability, especially his record during the war years as chairman of the Sports Executive for the South Australian Allied Forces Welfare Committee, showed the SACA executive that they had a forceful character to succeed the retiring Joe Riley.

In Victoria, the underestimated Harry Brereton took over from Ernie Bean on 31 August 1925 and occupied the post until the end of 1950. Meanwhile, in Sydney, the NSWCA appointed Harold Heydon as secretary on 27 April 1926 at an annual salary of £520.

Haydon had previously been secretary of the Sydney University Sports Union and admired for his efficiency and capacity for hard work; but he was not popular with the players and tended to be autocratic towards them.

The advent of Heydon and Jeanes, and, to a lesser extent, Brereton – whose diplomacy and ability were not recognised by outsiders and who was looked down upon by the NSWCA as a 'football type' rather than a 'cricket person' – soon created a 'them and us' scenario between players and administrators; and by the end of the repercussions which followed the 1926 tour of England, a virtual clean sweep would have occurred through the corridors of Australian cricket.

# 15

# The Changing of the Guard

At a meeting in Melbourne on 30 and 31 December 1925, Queensland's Board of Control delegates, John Hutcheon and Roger Hartigan, put forward their Association's claims for entry to the Sheffield Shield competition. It was the Queensland Association's Jubilee Year but they had to wait until the Interstate Conference meeting in Adelaide, on 7 May 1926, to know whether their application had been successful.

After a lot of hard bargaining over lunch, the resumption of the full Conference saw the Queensland delegates still having to wait for another hour while the question of playing days was discussed. They were reduced to four-and-a-half from being timeless since the competition began. Then came the motion, moved by the South Australian Bernard Scrymgour, and seconded by Ramsay Mailer from Victoria, that Queensland be admitted, and it was passed unanimously.

The Queensland Cricket Association then determined on a membership drive, not only to improve the finances of the Association but also to persuade the Brisbane public to support their team now that Sheffield Shield status, and shortly Test recognition for Brisbane, had come about.

To assist the membership drive, the secretary, Richard Stephens, wrote on 30 July 1926 to the Sheffield Shield holders, the NSWCA, asking permission to display the Shield in a shop-window. On 3 August Harold Heydon replied from Sydney that, as NSW was only the custodian of the Shield, the other states would have to agree. This duly occurred and on 10 September the Shield arrived in Brisbane where it was shown on display for three weeks. It is the only time the Sheffield Shield has been to Queensland.

New South Wales had made the 1925–26 season seem like a run-spree with totals of 708, 705, 642, 593 and 554 with Alan Kippax scoring an unbeaten 271 against Victoria. To help the selectors pick the Sixteenth Australians a match between Australia and The Rest was held in Sydney in December 1925. When The Rest won by 156 runs the selectors – Herbie Collins (NSW), Jack Ryder (Victoria) and Clem Hill (SA) – virtually ignored the result and chose to send nine of the losing side to England.

At their meeting on 30 December 1925 the Board delegates fought for their favourite players to be selected. Collins got the nod as captain but it was a narrow vote before Bardsley was chosen as vice-captain rather than Ryder. Twelve names were announced next day as touring players, with the rest in dribs and drabs. These included Arthur Richardson (SA) who was thirty-seven and whose selection over Alan Kippax was described by Monty Noble as 'a crime against the cricketing youth of Australia'.

Six of the players were new to England: Grimmett and Richardson of South Australia; Ellis, Ponsford and Woodfull of Victoria, and Everett from New South Wales. After matches had been played in Tasmania the team arrived in Ceylon to take on a good representative side on 23 March. Played at the Colombo CC ground the Australians won by 37 runs due to the bowling of Macartney (recovered from his nervous breakdown) and Everett.

The gods seemed to be against Collins and his team from the outset, for a strange imbalance showed when they succeeded in winning only two and drawing eleven of their first thirteen first-class matches up to the first Test. Other problems facing them were an unusually wet summer, the General Strike in May and industrial unrest generally, a considerable number of illnesses through the team, and a lengthy injury list. In the final accounting, only four batsmen passed 1000 runs, the 'pace' attack was non-existent, and only Mailey and Grimmett were effective wicket-takers. It was a case of too many mediocre all-rounders and too few top specialists.

The initial six weeks of the tour made it clear that only the leg-spinners, Mailey and Grimmett, were capable of dismissing opponents in three days. It was Mailey who recorded the best bowling on tour, 9/86 against Lancashire and 8/83 at Nottingham. In all, Arthur Mailey took 126 wickets, while Clarrie Grimmett captured 105. The rest trailed way behind.

Of the batsmen four players reached four-figure aggregates with Bill Woodfull's 201 against Essex the only double-century. He scored 1672 runs followed by Macartney on 1561, Bardsley 1424 and Andrews 1234. However, the aggression which usually characterises Australian sides in England was missing from this tour. It was also the first time a visiting team had blatantly used county games simply as warm-up matches for the Tests.

In the first Test at Trent Bridge Woodfull made his debut without batting. Fifty minutes' play was possible on the first day, when England made 32 without loss, after which heavy rain ruined the rest of the contest. Lord's, a fortnight later, saw three blazing June days as Bardsley carried his bat for 193; Macartney scored an unbeaten second innings of 133, and another match was drawn. It was this game which brought home to the Australians that Jack Gregory had lost his pace; a fact confirmed by his going wicketless for the first four Tests whilst conceding over 200 runs.

Bardsley captained Australia for the next two Tests at Headingley and Old Trafford as Herbie Collins had neuritis. At Leeds, Bardsley, as Australia's oldest captain, was dismissed with the first ball of the match after having won the toss from the England captain, Arthur Carr. Macartney, dropped from the fifth ball of the first over, then made an unbeaten 112 in the two hours before lunch.

Macartney (151) along with Woodfull (141) put on 235 for the second wicket after which Richardson (100) flogged the tired English attack. After 366 for three overnight became 494, England looked beaten at 182 for eight. A ninth-wicket stand of 108 saw the total to 294 and, following-on, England were able to hang on for a draw.

The authorities at Lord's, concerned that England had now drawn five successive Tests at home, began to make moves to increase the three playing days to four. Their worries were compounded when, in the fourth Test at Old Trafford, only one innings was completed. For Australia Woodfull (117) and Macartney (109) scored centuries in a score of 335 to which England replied with 305 for five and that was all.

However, the tour agreement was that the final Test would be timeless if the sides were still level on results. Interest in the match was intense and became even more so when the England selectors dropped their captain, Carr, and replaced him with the twenty-five-year-old Percy Chapman. They also, in a shrewd move, recalled Wilfred Rhodes, now forty-eight.

Chapman won the toss, batted and saw his team fall for 280, Mailey claiming 6/138. Australia gained a 22-run lead on the first innings but it was England who were worried as heavy rain fell on the second, Monday, night.

Herbie Collins then made a grave error in starting the third day with Arthur Richardson bowling off-breaks while England's openers played him with false caution. This enabled the pitch to dry out and prevented Jack Gregory being used on a spiteful wicket. Altogether it was superb batting by Jack Hobbs (100) and Herbert Sutcliffe (161) that produced 172 runs for the first-wicket partnership and turned the game around.

England were finally dismissed on the fourth morning for 436 which left Australia needing 415 to win at their leisure; but further rain put an end to any hopes the tourists had of victory, especially after Rhodes had claimed four important wickets during the afternoon – those of Bardsley, Ponsford, Collins and Richardson.

Once the team returned home, retribution was swift. Collins found himself relieved of his positions as captain of his club, Waverley, and of New South Wales. He was also vilified in the newspapers for the tour selections and for the final Test defeat. Collins retired, citing 'ill health' as his reason. He had been one of the most respected men in Australian cricket, yet only five years after this he was in such financial distress that he was applying to the New South Wales Cricketers' Fund for help. Assistance to Collins had been recommended by the NSWCA treasurer, E. A. Tyler, who wrote as follows:

> I have to report that I interviewed Mr H. L. Collins in regard to his present financial position. He informs me that he has been right up against it for a considerable time, has tried in every possible way to get employment or means of earning his livelihood, but has failed almost completely. He has an invalid mother who has no hope of recovering. So short has he been of money that on occasions he has not been able to buy the necessary medicine, and more infrequently they have been short of food.

It was a distressful situation. A former Australian captain so poor at the age of forty-three that he sometimes went without food. It provided proof, if proof were needed, that all the honours the game could bestow did not help to pay the bills. Collins may then have been just another victim of the Depression, which in 1931 was at its worst, but he was known to be an enthusiastic gambler, and this probably contributed to his difficulties. In any case, he continued to be dependent on the NSWCA for years afterwards. The Cricketers' Fund was providing him with money as late as 1938.

Clem Hill had taken his sickly wife to England to watch the team he had helped select. After The Oval defeat he found himself removed not only as a selector but from the Board as well. While Hill was on his way home, Harry Hodgetts wormed his way on to the Board of Control at Clem Hill's expense, but such huge indignation swept Adelaide cricket circles that, on Hill's return, Hodgetts resigned his position and stood for re-election. Judicious calling in of old-school-tie favours saw Hodgetts re-elected by the narrowest of margins. The following day he travelled to a Board meeting in Sydney to start an unbroken twenty-year run as a South Australian delegate. Only a lengthy prison sentence then stopped his attendance.

The loss of the Ashes also brought a halt to the ambitions of the touring manager, Syd Smith. His grade club, Gordon, still incensed at the omission of Charlie Kelleway from the Australian side, dropped Smith as their delegate to the NSWCA. This automatically stripped him of his positions within the Association and cost him his post as secretary of the Board of Control. In fact, though Smith did not realise it at the time, the Board had already dismissed him before the Gordon club's decision and appointed Bill Jeanes in his stead.

Smith retaliated by holding on to the Board's letters and as the Board minutes of 25 March 1927 record, declined to accept a parting gift: 'Mr Sydney Smith, Junior, intimated that in view of the fact that the Board had afforded him no explanation as to why his services were no longer required, after apparently giving entire satisfaction for fifteen years, he had no alternative but to decline to accept the memento'.

Queensland began their quest for the Sheffield Shield on 26 November 1926 in Brisbane. Although NSW won by eight runs it was for Queensland a glorious defeat that was watched by 23,000 spectators at the old Exhibition Ground. Run-scoring was also prolific in the Victoria match which followed. Victoria's second innings 518 in Brisbane ended still 235 runs short of its victory target. But the game of all games took place in Melbourne over Christmas 1926.

Bill Ponsford, in a remarkable season, in successive matches played innings of 214, 151, 352, 108 and 116. And he finished off with 131 for Australia versus The Rest in Charlie Macartney's benefit match in Sydney to give him a total of 1229 runs at an average of 122.90.

In Melbourne NSW won the toss and were dismissed by 5pm for 221, but when Victoria batted it was a different story. In 322 minutes they scored 594 runs for the loss of only one wicket. Woodfull and Ponsford broke Trumper and Duff's 1902–03 Sheffield Shield first-wicket record of 298 by scoring 375 in 223 minutes, before Woodfull was out for 133. Hunter Hendry then scored 100 to add 219 for the second wicket in 113 minutes. In came Jack Ryder, and he proceeded to hit 295 out of 449 in 245 minutes including six sixes and 33 fours.

Ponsford was out for 352, just 13 short of Clem Hill's record 365 scored in 1900. After playing a ball from Morgan on to his wicket, Ponsford, on reaching the dressing-room, commented, 'Cripes, I'm stiff'. After three quick wickets had fallen, Hartkopf joined Ryder with the score at 657 for five. Ryder commented to his new partner, 'Don't take any notice of me, I've gone mad'. Together they added 177 in 94 minutes. With Jack Ellis in, the score passed 918, the previous Shield record held by NSW.

The 1000-run mark arrived after 574 minutes when wicketkeeper Ellis pushed a three, and ran down the wicket yelling, 'Three to me and 1000 up. Long live Victoria'. Ryder was out trying to hit Andrews for six to bring up his 300. Ellis and Blackie continued on to pass the previous world record score of 1059 made by Victoria against Tasmania four years earlier. Finally Ellis was run out when the total stood at 1107, scored in 630 minutes.

In the NSW bowling analyses Arthur Mailey bowled 64 overs to take 4/362 and, along with the other bowlers, had stuck gamely to his task. Afterwards Mailey made several now legendary comments such as, 'It was rather a pity that Ellis got run out at 1107 as I was just striking a length' and 'Very few chances were given but I think the chap in the tweed coat dropped Ryder in the shilling stand'. After Ryder had struck him for his third six, Tommy Andrews remarked to Mailey, 'That's his weak spot. We'd better put a man there'.

Not surprisingly, NSW was demoralised and succumbed for 230. Archie Jackson confirmed his promise with 59 not out, and Hartkopf took 6/98. Victoria won by an innings and 656 runs. In a contemporary cartoon a NSW fieldsman is depicted saying, 'Wait till we get you in Sydney'. It had an ironic outcome. A month later Victoria, caught on a sticky wicket in Sydney, was dismissed for 35!

At long last it was to be South Australia's season, their first Shield since 1912–13. It was the bowlers more than the batsmen who excelled: Harry Whitfield topped the averages with 13 wickets at 13.54 but the deciding factors were Norm Williams with 35 and Clarrie Grimmett with 30 victims.

In February 1927 the Melbourne Cricket Club sent a strong team to New Zealand. Managed by Hugh Trumble, who had toured in 1900, the side was captained by Warwick Armstrong and included Vernon Ransford, Hunter Hendry and Hans Ebeling. Out of the thirteen matches scheduled, two matches were played against New Zealand. Basil Onyons topped the batting averages with 842 runs at 56.13; followed by Armstrong, 323 at 53.83; Hendry 424 at 53.00; and Ransford 499 at 41.58. As expected, the State players figured in the bowling with Ebeling claiming 58 wickets at 17.63 followed by Armstrong's 39 at 23.05.

The two 'Tests' – as the Melbourne Cricket Club's 1926–27 annual report decided to call them – against New Zealand were both drawn, with the home team having the upper hand in both. The club, very modestly, said:

> The New Zealand tour of 1927 will always rank as one of the most pleasant and successful undertakings the club has ever enjoyed. The welcome the team received throughout New Zealand was exceptional. . . There is no doubt that the visit of the club team did an immense amount of good to New Zealand cricket, and it was a distinct pleasure to help in any way we could the advancement of the game, and particularly any encouragement we could give to the New Zealand players about to leave on their first visit to England . . .

> Many of the leading sportsmen in New Zealand treated the team in a royal manner – luncheons, picnics, beautiful drives, when time permitted – and it is pleasant to know that the representatives of the club at all times behaved themselves as gentlemen, and made themselves very popular throughout both islands. The financial result of the tour to the New Zealand Cricket Council, after paying all expenses, showed a clear profit of just on £1000, and this in some measure must be attributed to the glorious weather experienced during the two Test matches.

When the Board of Control met in Melbourne on 25 March 1927 for a short meeting, the item which took most of their time was a discussion of the gift from the Canadian city of Calgary of a buffalo's head. The NSWCA had hold of the item, 'but declined to accept any responsibility for its preservation' as there was 'the risk of the head being destroyed by moths and silverfish'. Then, after debate, 'Mr Bull (NSW) proposed and Dr Robertson (Victoria) seconded that the head be presented to the Sydney Museum'. Other than various agenda matters concerning delegates' free passes to grounds, giving presents to each other, and the quality of the lunch, the subject of a possible Indian tour to Australia in 1927–28 was put on one side.

Just after the meeting finished the Board chairman, Harry Gregory of Western Australia, who was a novice at cricket politics, was approached by the Test wicketkeeper Bert Oldfield for permission to take a team to Singapore and Malaya for a private tour. Gregory immediately agreed, and the tour was a huge success. But at the next Board meeting in September 1927 the delegates revised their constitution so that no future chairman could authorise such a visit.

Oldfield's team played nine fixtures: three in Singapore, the rest in Malaya. It contained seven Test players, but in Kuala Lumpur in June, it was beaten over three days by Malaya by 39 runs: Harold Hennessey was the Malayans' match winner, his pace bowling claiming 7/42 and 3/30 in sapping humidity. *The Straits Times* positively chortled: 'Our friends from down under, good sportsmen as they are, will forgive the people of the country a little justifiable jubilation on such an historic and unlooked-for occasion'. Singapore's sports-mad Governor, Sir Hugh Clifford, sent congratulatory cables to the Malayan team and the event went down as the happening of the times in the annals of local cricket history.

Three weeks later, on the Padang in Singapore, it was a different matter. Billy Woodfull (157) and Tommy Andrews (145) added 268 for the Australians' third wicket in just under even time. It was slow going in the shimmering haze with Macartney (16), Mayne (5), Everett (9), Oldfield (7) and Bardsley (0) not exactly exciting the spectators;

but Macartney, with 4/19 and 4/16, assisted most in the dismissal of Malaya for 69 and 136 to give the tourists a quick revenge. Charlie Macartney, who had the role of speech-maker, pleased his hosts at the formal dinner afterwards at the Grand Hotel de l'Europe by saying that: 'Cricket in Malaya is ever so much better than we had been led to believe or had expected'. After all this, Warren Bardsley demonstrated his skill as a pianist while Sam Everett gave the press the impression that he was so taken with Singapore, he might settle and do business there. 'What an acquisition for the Singapore Cricket Club he would be!' daydreamed the *Straits Times*.

Around this time in New South Wales cricket circles an undermining cancer was starting to show itself: sectarianism in the shape of Catholics against Freemasons was the type of discord unwanted in sport but, alas, its reverberations in New South Wales cricket can be felt even into the present day. The friction did not really start to be seen publicly until the early 1920s. There had certainly been a strong Masonic influence in the NSWCA long before then. Richard Driver, in those formative years, was a Mason, as was the former secretary John Portus. Against that, Billy McElhone, who had been such a prominent character before the first war, and was the Association president throughout the 1920s, was a Catholic.

In the late 1920s and early 1930s – and in fact onwards through Syd Smith's lengthy presidency (1936–66) – a high proportion of the men prominent in the NSWCA were Masons. They included Aubrey Oxlade, Sydney Webb and Harold Heydon. Catholics complained amongst themselves that they were kept out of senior positions because Masons had formed a ruling clique. Although the Catholic and Mason differences were well enough known in the cricket world they were rarely brought out into the open. Even sportswriters who tried to publicise such matters were firmly slapped down by their editors. Like so much in cricket, myth and illusion ruled supreme – and that is how it continued to be in the inter-war years.

Late in the evening of Monday 29 November 1927, the great George Giffen died at the age of sixty-eight. He had been regarded as the best cricketer Australia had produced, the 'W.G.' of Australian cricket. He had played in thirty-one Tests and toured England five times. Yet even to the end he was coaching youngsters in the art of the game. His home was near to the parklands of Adelaide, and a group of boys known as 'Giffen's Early Risers' met before breakfast on summer mornings to be coached by the old champion. It would have pleased him to know that two of them would play for Australia.

A bachelor, George Giffen was buried with his parents and sister in Adelaide's West Terrace cemetery. Giffen's name was so revered that the Australian Cricket Society, in late 1991, refurbished his vandalised grave, rebuilding the headstone, and arranged a ceremony of dedication to a wonderful cricketing career.

In April 1927, just months before Giffen's death, a picnic was held in the Belair National Park in the Adelaide Hills, organised by the Postal Workers Club, of which Giffen was a pensioner member. A bet was laid by some of his old colleagues. They had argued amongst themselves as to how many times old George could hit a single stump bowling from twenty-two yards away. It was agreed to let him bowl 24 deliveries and bets were taken. To the amazement of all, Giffen, who had not bowled for some time, hit the single wicket 21 times while the three deliveries that failed to hit were extremely near misses. The old champion still possessed his skill.

The 1927–28 season did not see an Indian team tour Australia, nor was one allowed to tour New South Wales as had been the original idea. The Board refused the proposal on the grounds that, as there was no controlling body for cricket in India, how could a national team be selected? The two main organisations in India, the Calcutta Cricket Club and the Bombay Quadrangular Committee, replied that this was nonsense and that they could put an All-India team together of a very high standard.

Board members Oxlade and Bull then started to prepare an itinerary which had the Indians touring from early January to April 1928 and they presented this to the Board meeting held on 15 September 1927. After lengthy discussion, in which the 'White Australia' policy again reared its ugly head, the vote to invite All-India to tour was lost by the seven votes of Victoria (3), Queensland (2), Western Australia (1) and Tasmania (1) to the six votes of New South Wales (3) and South Australia (3).

The Secretary, Bill Jeanes, wrote in pencil on the margin of his Agenda paper, 'a bad error of judgment' and intimated in a file note that the Victorian delegation had voted against the Indians because they wished an invitation to tour New Zealand to be accepted instead.

As the two-day Board meeting was being held in Sydney, the NSW delegates were able to get approval quickly from their executive to push, the following day, for NSW to be allowed to invite, and sponsor, an Indian side to tour. The next day Aubrey Oxlade proposed: 'That the NSWCA be, and is, authorised if it so desires to invite a team from India to play in NSW or any other states if required. The NSWCA to accept all responsibilities.' Billy Bull seconded the motion, but as Bill Jeanes noted, 'After discussion it was withdrawn by consent'. This avoided the NSWCA suffering another 7–6 vote defeat.

However, the NSWCA did get permission to play the New Zealand team who were calling at Sydney on their way home from a tour of England. As the visitors had received high praise in England the NSW selectors chose their strongest team to play against cricketers who, shipbound for nearly five weeks, were eager to return home after an absence of seven months.

The three-day game, which started on 28 October 1927, attracted just 813 spectators. Those who did attend saw NSW bat first with Jack Gregory (152) and Tommy Andrews (134) putting on 262 runs for the second wicket after which Alan Kippax (119) and Archie Jackson (104) added 176 for the fourth. The Kiwis had the enthusiasm knocked out of them by the NSW power batting, and at one stage the score stood at 505 for three. An eventual ten-wicket loss came almost as a relief.

While the Board of Control worried about the revelation that the sum of three farthings had been lost on some tickets sold for the first Test at Nottingham in June 1926, a sub-committee chose the team to tour New Zealand during February and March 1928. They appointed the South Australian, Vic Richardson, as captain and included Test players such as Grimmett (who was born in New Zealand), Kippax, Oldfield, Ponsford and Woodfull. Also chosen were players who were on the verge of international honours such as the pace bowler Harry Alexander; Don Blackie; the eighteen-year-old Archie Jackson, and Queensland all-rounder Ron Oxenham. The team played thirteen matches and half of their eighteen innings exceeded 400 runs. It was a run harvest unseen in New Zealand for many years: 472 v. Nelson; 375 v. Wellington; 448 v. North Otago; 454 v. Otago; 597 v. Southland; 404 v. Canterbury; 431 v. Auckland; 427. v. Taranaki; 428 v. Wanganui; and then, in the first unofficial Test, 573 for five declared.

This match, played at Eden Park, Auckland, was ruined by rain. Even so, the gate takings of over £1000 established a new record for New Zealand. Batting first, Australia had Ponsford (86) and Woodfull scoring 184 for the first wicket in 140 minutes. Kippax (16) failed, but after that Woodfull had a partnership of 218 with Karl Schneider (68) before being the fourth batsman out with the score at 490. Woodfull had scored 284 in just over six hours. New Zealand struggled after Richardson's declaration but the weather saved them from an innings defeat.

Four days later at Carisbrook, Dunedin, the damp conditions caused problems for the Australian bowlers as New Zealand batted slowly to reach 162. In his element, Grimmett took 6/47, and later on shared a match-winning partnership of 69 for the Australians' eighth wicket with Oxenham. The tourists won by seven wickets as heavy rain started to fall.

* * * *

In Victoria the membership of the Melbourne CC was continually rising. In just over a year, it had gone from under 4000 (waiting list 4040) to 5200 (waiting list 2740). In turn the annual subscription rose to £3 which saw a 1927 membership income of £11,254 turn into £19,532 by August 1928. But as the club grew, so something had to give. In October 1927 it was announced that the club would build a new members' pavilion at a cost of £80,000. In moved the wreckers and the old pavilion, built in 1881 at a cost of £5170, crumbled under the hammers.

With the old pavilion had gone its history and there were regrets. But the new edifice would provide accommodation for 3000 (compared to 1800 in the old one), a buffet room, a large members' bar, dining-rooms, a long-room and much more. In recent times cosmetic changes and certain additions have been made and without doubt it ranks as the premier cricket pavilion.

While the building work was going on, Victoria played their three home Sheffield Shield matches between 16 December and 3 January. Within those nineteen days, Bill Ponsford scored 1013 runs in just four innings. He had already scored 133 in Adelaide but now he broke the world record with 437 against Queensland, then 202 and 38 off the New South Wales attack, followed by 336 from the South Australian bowlers. The *Sun News-Pictorial* commented:

> A young batsman made history last Saturday. Now we wonder if there is anywhere a bowler who can also make history – bowling history. He would be very welcome. The season is now well advanced and we still wait in vain the appearance of the super bowler who can deal with the super batsmen. England, apparently, also waits. Opportunity is beckoning to the brilliant bowler, and he is badly needed in both countries.

Victoria walked away with the Shield, due mainly to Ponsford's 1217 runs at an average of 152.12. Even Woodfull's 645 at 129.00 paled in comparison. But the tables were turned in club cricket. Carlton's Woodfull topped with an average of 133.00 whilst St Kilda's Ponsford could record only 121.00!

The only other player to make a large score during the season was Alan Kippax. His unbeaten 315 for NSW against Queensland in Sydney was made in 328 minutes with 41 fours and was the highest score of his career.

Tallish, rather slim, with his shirt-sleeves rolled down, Kippax was a charming, cultured, right-handed batsman, orthodox in his stroke-play but never dull or boring. He was very quick-footed and could get to the pitch of the ball when facing the spinner or walk inside the line of flight when the short one came along. Despite not always being well treated by the Test selectors, he remained a brilliant and prolific batsman, captaining his State for several years.

The 1928–29 Shield was won by New South Wales and this had a lot to do with a young player who had scored 118 on his debut for NSW in Adelaide in December 1927. He was Donald George Bradman.

Back in February 1921 a carpenter called George Bradman had taken his twelve-year-old son to Sydney to see England beaten by Australia. Young Donald was enchanted by Charlie Macartney's innings of 170 and told his father he would never be content until he batted like his hero, and on the same ground.

As the 1922–23 season approached, the young Bradman became the scorer for his uncle's team in Bowral, and when the side was short of a player he was allowed to play albeit with a cut-down bat as Don was on the small size for his age. His fascination with the game saw him practise as much as possible even down to catching a ball returning at all angles from the base of the backyard water tank.

It has long been the boast of cricket people in Australia that players of promise are noticed early and advanced rapidly. If there was ever an example of this it was the rise of Don Bradman from his local Bowral team to Test selection in just under two years. In 1925–26, Bradman had scores of 300 against Moss Vale and 234 against Wingello. He also took 51 wickets with his leg-breaks at 7.80 and held 26 catches.

A NSWCA coaching scheme saw the Association secretary, Harold Heydon, write to Bradman on 5 October 1926: 'The selectors have had under consideration your record in cricket in the past season, and in view of such record they particularly desire to see you in action.' Bradman was asked to attend on a Monday night at the Sydney Cricket Ground where young players were coached and showed their skill in front of the NSW team selectors.

The rest of Bradman's rise to fame has been chronicled many times. Least to say, when he made his debut against South Australia in Adelaide he became the sixteenth Australian cricketer to make a century on his first-class debut. Although Bill Ponsford's high scoring overshadowed everything else during that 1927–28 season, the emergence of the two young NSW batsmen, Bradman and Archie Jackson, showed the rich potential in NSW cricket. Another to attain top status was Bill O'Reilly who often bowled to Bradman when both were playing country cricket.

Of all of Bradman's contemporaries, O'Reilly was the one who could be his highest acclaimer as well as his fiercest critic. Each respected the other's play and toured regularly, yet O'Reilly was a Catholic and Bradman became a Mason. The behind-the-scenes jousting did, occasionally, become public.

A player who earned the wrath of the Board of Control was Arthur Richardson. The former Test player had walked out on the South Australian Cricket Association in September 1927, when he signed a three-year contract as coach to the Western Australian Cricket Association. To their credit SACA did not follow up Richardson's breach of contract and it was a great irony when the South Australians urged the Board of Control not to take action against him when he wrote an article in the *Sporting Globe* on 21 March 1928 criticising the financial assistance given by the Board to the WACA. Richardson commented that 'a paltry amount had been allotted to West Australia out of the profits of the last Australian tour of England'. To cover themselves, the WACA replied in the *Sporting Globe* of 11 April 1928 contradicting Richardson and saying that they 'had participated equally with all other states'. The Board agreed to drop the matter as 'the WACA had subsequently made a public correction of Richardson's statement' and 'that no further action be taken'.

What action the Board could have taken is open to speculation but Richardson was certainly badly informed for the Western Australian Cricket Association's share of the 1926 tour profit was, in fact, overgenerous. A glance at the WACA's annual report of 31 August 1927 showed the Board's contribution as £2324 plus £114 interest. The major associations of NSW, SA and Victoria actually received less.

The net result was that Arthur Richardson's untimely comments started a chain of events in which the future distribution of tour profits became divided on an unequal basis for many years, a situation only rectified in the late 1980s.

The September 1928 Board meeting also made some long-term decisions on policy. They wiped out any appeals from India for a tour even after receiving a letter from Colonel M. G. Rolandson who stated 'that a provisional Board of Control has now been formed in India and the office has been transferred from Bombay to the Roshanara Club in Delhi'.

The members then refused even to discuss a letter from Algy Frames, Secretary of the South African Cricket Association, which pleaded for an Australian visit in the 1930–31 season. Instead, the NSW delegates proposed sending a cable to Frames in Johannesburg 'asking if it is prepared to send a team to Australia in season 1931–32 if satisfactory terms can be arranged'. Although the visit did take place 'satisfactory terms' were not finalised until the tour was a month old and even then the South Africans returned a financial loss.

The delegates, in setting out the Australian playing schedules for future years, were taken aback when a cable was read from 'The

West Indian Cricket Association' stating that they were unable to tour Australia in 1929–30 as an England team was scheduled to visit them, but 'we would appreciate an invitation for later'. A tour in 1930–31 was subsequently agreed.

But what really upset the Board was a series of complaints emanating from Lord's over the forthcoming 1928–29 England tour of Australia. The Board's refusal to let the tourists visit New Zealand for two matches elicited a series of letters from both the Marylebone Cricket Club and the New Zealand Cricket Council. However, the letters from Lord's which particularly annoyed the delegates came from the Marylebone secretary, William Findlay, who wrote 'that regret is expressed that your Board should have seen fit to decide to play one of the Test matches at Brisbane during the tour instead of two at Sydney as previously'.

The Board had promised Queensland a Test ever since its formation in 1905 and now Lord's was objecting. Most of Queensland's important matches had been played at the Woolloongabba ground in South Brisbane but from 1923 interstate matches were played on rotation between there and the Exhibition Ground in Bowen Hills. The facilities for spectators were far better at Bowen Hills and so the Board, early in 1924, set up a sub-committee of Clem Hill, Harry Rush and Syd Smith. They reported that they could find no fault with the amenities but felt 'that the pitch would not last for four or five days' continuous play'.

This report cost Queensland a Test that year but after a QCA committee had overcome the problems, a Test match was duly allocated. With a new pitch laid with Merri Creek soil by the Melbourne Cricket Ground curator, Bert Luttrell, all was in order. This information was passed to Findlay at Lord's who replied in July 1928: 'It is assumed that your Board when making its decision has thoroughly considered the matter and in the circumstances the Marylebone Cricket Club committee do not feel justified in making any objection'.

The demands from the Marylebone Cricket Club regarding the England tour of Australia, which started in Perth on 18 October 1928, took up many hours in Board of Control meetings. The insistence from Lord's that the visit be organised in a military fashion eventually cost the Board – and, thereby, the state associations – a considerable amount of money.

Percy Chapman of Kent, who had captained England in the Oval win of 1926, was selected to captain the touring team with Frederick Toone, the Yorkshire secretary, once again manager for his third trip to Australia. Toone was a master of detail, and his managerial skill left the Australian Board floundering in his wake. Bill Jeanes, when administering his first England visit, acknowledged that he learned a lot from observing Toone's work. As subsequent tours would show, Toone's death in 1930, not long after returning from Australia, robbed the cricket world of a fine administrator.

There were six matches up to the first Test, during which Chapman continually sought the advice of his professionals. For an amateur player to do such a thing was previously unknown and it contributed to the tourists' high cricketing skills which they demonstrated to the Australian public.

The first four matches were drawn as England scored plenty of runs: 406 against Western Australia; 528 versus South Australia (who replied with 524, Vic Richardson 231); 486 against Victoria; 734 for seven against New South Wales (Wally Hammond 225), after which there were victories against an Australian XI in Sydney and Queensland in Brisbane.

The public were flocking to see the tourists. Successive Saturdays in Sydney saw 42,757 and 27,020 spectators – and that was only at the start of the visit. Queensland's first Test began on 30 November 1928 with the Australians giving caps to Don Bradman and to Bert Ironmonger, the slow-medium left-arm spin bowler then aged forty-five. From the eleven who had played in Australia's previous Test the missing faces were Herbie Collins, Warren Bardsley (now a selector), Charlie Macartney, Tommy Andrews, Arthur Richardson and Arthur Mailey.

The Australian Board members were so unsure of themselves that they consulted Counsel, Mr Maughan, K.C., of Sydney, to ask if they could appoint a chairman of selectors. Legal opinion said they could not under their present constitution. However, what they were able to do was to decline a player's selection on the grounds of 'matters other than cricket'.

The four selectors then picked a team which relied, not on current form, but on the statistics contained in Ernie Bean's writing books. This bizarre state of affairs saw some interesting choices during the series as well as factional fighting which resulted in gross ineptitude. As the Board became more trapped in its own mire so the English tourists grew in stature.

The choice as Australian captain was the Victorian, Jack Ryder. The Board then spent an enormous amount of time arguing over whether Vic Richardson or Billy Woodfull should be vice-captain until it was realised that Richardson had not been chosen by the selectors. Then came the farcical situation – which happened all season – of players not being notified of their selection but still being expected to turn up on time for the Tests or trial games. Then, to cap matters, the Board met for the whole day prior to the third Test discussing what their official reaction should be to the news of King George V's ill-health.

Of the four selectors only Warren Bardsley (NSW) – whose grovelling to the NSWCA delegates for the job was something else – had played the game at the highest level. Ernie Bean (Victoria) and Jack Hutcheon (Queensland) were iron-fisted administrators who had little time or thought for the players, while Charles Dolling (SA) was a man of the Adelaide establishment whose wife gave dinner parties and 'entertainments' to visiting cricketers.

The selectors gambled on a first Test side that had the thirty-three-year-old Jack Gregory as its youngest bowler and it showed. England won the toss and batted for most of the first two days, scoring 521. It was the end for Jack Gregory, and for his family dynasty, as cartilage problems had caused him to break down. He knew it was the end and, with tears streaming down his face, announced: 'Boys. I'm finished'.

Gregory's opening bowling partner, Charlie Kelleway, then went down with food poisoning and it became a question not just of an Australian defeat looming, but by how much. Australia fell behind by 399 runs on first innings with Chapman deciding to bat on and set Australia a target. Late on the fourth afternoon the first declaration in Test cricket in Australia took place as Australia were set 742 to win.

Ponsford was dismissed early, bad light finished play for the day and heavy overnight rain ruined the pitch. Bill Woodfull carried his bat for 30 as the Australian total finished on 66. England won by the record margin of 675 runs.

Don Bradman, whose scoring for New South Wales had forced him into the Test team, was made twelfth man for the second Test in Sydney a fortnight later. The selectors brought in Otto Nothling and Don Blackie, who was forty-six. Warren Bardsley said he opposed Bradman's omission but was outvoted three to one. It was a ghastly error, judged by his performance in the third Test.

Australia batted first in front of 40,723 spectators who saw the pace of Harold Larwood shatter a bone in Ponsford's left hand and sideline him for the rest of the series. Woodfull, with 68, top-scored as Australia made 253. A record Sydney crowd of 58,446 acclaimed Jack Hobbs on the second day, the eve of his forty-sixth birthday, as he was presented with a cheque from a fund organised by the *Sydney Sun* newspaper. Hobbs only made 40, but Wally Hammond, setting about the Australian bowlers, scored 251 in 461 minutes, hitting 30 fours in an England total of 636. The Australian batsmen fought hard in their second innings as Woodfull (111) and Hendry (112) put on 215 for the second wicket. Ryder hit a quick-fire 79 but in the end England romped home by eight wickets. The *Sydney Morning Herald* could not believe that 170,109 people had seen a Test match. Could it ever be beaten?

Nine days later, in Melbourne, it was not only beaten but pushed to one side. The first day saw 63,247 in attendance, the second 62,259. In all, 262,467 watched the third Test, paying out £22,562. Not bad for a State in which 11.1 per cent of the workforce was unemployed.

Jack Ryder knew that to lose the match meant that England retained the Ashes. The local boy, Ted a'Beckett, came into the side along with Queenslander Ron Oxenham in order to boost the pace attack. They took only one wicket each in the match, but this time England did not find it so easy. It was a see-sawing match with Alan Kippax (100) and Jack Ryder (112) scoring centuries in Australia's 397 to which England gained a first-innings lead of just 20 runs, due mainly to Wally Hammond's second successive double-century. Woodfull (107) opened the second innings with a century but the most talked about performance was that of Bradman. He had scored a polished 79 in the first innings and with his 112 in the second he was the youngest cricketer to score a century in a Test – a record which lasted for exactly one month.

The press described his crisp stroke-making, his perfect defence and his almost brash confidence. The *Argus* said:

> Soon after lunch the lad found himself left to play almost a lone fighting hand. The bowling was definitely mastered and Bradman hit it unmercifully. The bowlers and fieldsmen, overcome by the heat of one of Melbourne's muggiest days, must have prayed for relief from the torture of Bradman. He refused to relax, and when at last he had piled up his first 100 in a Test – he has played in only two [Test] matches – the crowd went wild with joy. It was another one of those great demonstrations for which the M.C.G. is famous. For minutes thousands cheered, clapped and stamped, and the tired Englishmen were glad to sit on the grass until it was all over.

England won by three wickets, scoring 332 for seven (Sutcliffe 135).

Between the Tests the tourists usually played country matches but in January 1929 they played two matches in Tasmania, winning them both as Douglas Jardine scored 214 in Launceston. After a four-day draw against South Australia the fourth Test started in Adelaide on 1 February.

This was one of cricket's most finely balanced Tests, as the totals of 334, 369, 383 and 336 show. But the selectors had allowed themselves to take a chance with their second prodigy after Bradman. When Archie Jackson, nineteen years and 152 days old, was given the nod, Arthur Mailey, the Balmain Club's only previous Test player, rushed down from his office at the *Sydney Sun* to Alan Kippax's sports store in Martin Place, where Jackson worked, to bring him the news.

In the days following Jackson's selection, Jack Ryder sought the advice of Kippax about the youngster opening the batting. Kippax's reported reply was: 'I am sure he expects to open'. And open he did, with Billy Woodfull, after England had made 334 in intense heat. Jackson was the sixth Australian to be dismissed, when the score was on 287. He had scored not only a debut century, 164, but had played an innings which those who played and watched that day still remember vividly. It was one of the game's immortal innings, and now Jackson was the youngest player to score a century in a Test match. It dominated a match which England won by 12 runs on the seventh day, even though Hammond scored a century, 119 not out and 177, in each innings.

The Test created a new record attendance for Adelaide of 137,447 who paid £12,435 for the privilege. But this made it very obvious that the SACA would have to provide extra seating accommodation. A fortuitous bequest as well as profit from the Test saw Adelaide Oval seating limits rise to 11,125 within the year.

Just before the final Test the tourists played Victoria in Melbourne and found themselves for once on the receiving end of a big score. As the Victorian total moved up to 572 for nine, Bill Woodfull was unbeaten on 275. Jack Ryder declared at that point only because England's pace bowler, Harold Larwood, was bowling short-pitched deliveries at Bert Ironmonger, whose batting was woeful to say the least. The match ended in a draw.

The selectors finally gave Ryder the fast bowler he wanted for the fifth Test. Thomas Wall, always known as 'Tim', had proved to be a prolific wicket-taker for his club, Prospect, and for South Australia. Also included in the team was Percy Hornibrook who could bowl both left-arm orthodox and medium-pace, and Alan Fairfax, a top-order batsman and right-arm medium-pace bowler. Hendry, Blackie and a'Beckett were dropped. At last, Ponsford excepted because of his injury, the selectors had got the team right.

The match was 'timeless' and ended on its eighth day. On the first, Jack Hobbs became the *oldest* batsman to score a century in Test cricket. His 142, along with Maurice Leyland's 137 and Hendren's 95, saw England to 519. The Australian reply fell just 28 runs short with Bradman making 123 and Woodfull 102. The scoring was desperately slow but the spectators did not seem to mind. With only fourteen wickets falling in the first four days the match was a nightmare for the bowlers.

The game turned on Tim Wall's second innings effort of 5/66 which left Australia needing 286 runs to win. That they did win, by five wickets, was also a turning-point after the low ebb of the series and the 1926 debacle, and Jack Ryder was carried shoulder-high from the field. He deserved the tribute, for Australia's fortunes were now looking up after their defeat of one of the finest teams England had ever assembled.

There had been, however, an unpleasant situation on the fourth day of the fourth Test in Adelaide which did not augur well for the future. During the England second innings Clarrie Grimmett had been infuriated by an incident when Walter Hammond was in the seventies (he went on to score 177), and Douglas Jardine was at the bowler's end. Hammond spooned what looked like an easy catch straight back to Grimmett but slightly on the leg side. As Grimmett moved to take the catch he ran into Jardine's elbow and the ball dropped down by the batsman's feet.

Grimmett swung around and called to the umpire, George Hele: 'He did that on purpose'. The umpire took no action and at the end of the over Grimmett renewed his protest. When the players came off the field at the end of the day's play, pressmen surrounded Grimmett as he came through the gate and in the dressing-room he was asked: 'Did you appeal for that interference by Jardine?' Grimmett said: 'No, but it was deliberate'. He was soon put in his place and told he should have appealed in the correct way. When asked about the incident, umpire Hele replied: 'There was no appeal'.

The pressbox at the time was convinced that an appeal for 'obstructing the field' would have been upheld. As it was, the hundred or so runs which Hammond scored after the incident swung the game to England.

When, after a final match in Perth against an Australian XI, the tourists sailed for home, Bill Jeanes started to tot up all the figures. The total number of people who had attended the England matches was a quite staggering 1,290,420 who paid a total sum of £107,947. The Marylebone Cricket Club, as the backers of the tour, grossed £40,427. After deducting minimal Board expenses the shareout to the States was on a percentage basis. The big three – NSW, Victoria and South Australia – got the lion's share, with Queensland, Western Australia, and Tasmania receiving lesser amounts.

It had all been very successful.

The domestic season of 1928–29 also saw an inordinate number of runs scored and in the overall aggregates for the season Don Bradman (1690), Alan Kippax (1079) and Jack Ryder (1045) all passed four figures. In Shield matches Bill Ponsford had scored an unbeaten 275 against South Australia in Melbourne but there were two other innings which caught the eye.

In the Christmas fixture between New South Wales and Victoria at Melbourne, Victoria batted first, scoring 376 with centuries from Jack Ryder (175) and Ted a'Beckett. NSW's reply was dismal as they slumped to 113 for nine. Late on the Monday afternoon Alan Kippax, then 20 not out, was joined by Hal Hooker and it was not until just after noon on Wednesday that they were parted. Their world record tenth-wicket partnership of 307 took 304 minutes with Hooker contributing 62 and Kippax left unbeaten on 260. The match ended in a draw but the record stands unbeaten to this day.

Over the Australia Day holiday weekend in late January 1929, the hapless Victorians travelled to Sydney to play a NSW side already declared champions. The home side batted first with Bradman already showing what a run-machine he had become. He passed Billy Murdoch's record of 321 for the highest individual innings at the Sydney Cricket Ground by scoring a chanceless, unbeaten, 340 in just eight hours. Alan Fairfax scored 104 as NSW declared at 713 for six, but in the end they could only draw the match.

Bowlers occasionally missed out on the plaudits which tend to go the way of batsmen. However Clarrie Grimmett more than once took pride of place this season with his 71 wickets in 13 matches, and in the 1929–30 season he would do even better and take 82 wickets from 11 games.

In early 1929, the NSWCA had received a letter from Warren Bardsley in which he asked for the support of the Association at the Board of Control. His proposal was to take a team of cricketers to Malaya in May 1929. The Board approved the tour subject to a condition which would cause trouble in later years. It read: 'That on completion of the tour the Board be supplied with a full financial statement'.

Ernie Bean was against such a venture and had a motion passed which instructed Bardsley, through the NSWCA, to show all correspondence to the Victorian delegates of the Board. Bean was horrified with some of the names who had accepted invitations to tour and promptly warned off the Victorian players. Bardsley reported to the next Board meeting on 12 September 1929: 'That I am unable to finalise arrangements to take a team of Australian players to the Malay States'.

The winter months of 1929 saw the state associations utilise their financial windfall from the recent England tour. Grounds were improved, coaches appointed, extra office staff employed. But just around the corner was perhaps the worst economic depression of modern times.

# 16

# The Bradman Factor

As Jack Ryder's men were winning the fifth Test in Melbourne in March 1929, so Lord Mayor Luxton, while the match was still in progress, had called a meeting of twenty-two municipalities in and around Melbourne to discuss ways of providing work for the unemployed. Even *The Age* and the *Argus* published leading articles on the matter giving the Depression, as it came to be called, more emphasis than the cricket.

It was like the 1890s all over again. Thousands left the cities around Australia and took to country areas hoping to find menial work. But country poverty had always been endemic in Australia and the Depression was far worse in the bush. The urban poor went to Toorak in Melbourne; Hunters Hill in Sydney; Dalkeith in Perth; Beaumont in Adelaide; anywhere in Brisbane and Hobart just to beg at the doors of those who lived in the wealthier suburbs.

To put the figures in their context – 11.1% of the workforce was unemployed in 1929. This rose to 19.3% in 1930; 27.4% in 1931; and, at its top, 29% in 1932. The peak of unemployed in the States was 27.4% in Tasmania in 1931, and in 1932 Queensland 18.8%, Victoria 26.5%, Western Australia 29.5%, NSW 32.5% and, worst of all, South Australia with 34%.

Attendances were obviously affected at all sporting events although the Melbourne Cricket Club which, naturally, attracted a wealthier type of member than most ordinary cricket clubs, survived the crisis remarkably well. General receipts dropped from £40,516 in 1928–29 to £30,165 in 1931–32; yet the club paid off a debt of £11,000 and even declared a small profit.

The year 1929 finally saw the departure of Ernie Bean not only from the Board of Control but from active participation in Victorian cricket. Likewise, in Sydney, Billy McElhone was too ill to carry out his role as President of the NSWCA; and the Board itself was going through a change, but more of personnel than of attitudes.

During the England tour there had been a number of complaints lodged against umpires, and those for the final match in Perth were reported for 'certain incidents . . . which were regarded by the

Western Australian Cricket Association as unsatisfactory'. A copy of the letter was sent to Lord's with the reply, tabled on 12 September 1929, from the Marylebone Cricket Club stating 'it was evident that some misunderstanding had arisen in the cases referred to in the correspondence which were regretted'. A further report from the WACA which 'dealt with other incidents in the same match' were read at the Board meeting 'and subsequently withdrawn'.

Whatever the problems were they seemed to have been solved by the time another England team played in Perth in late October 1929. This time it was Harold Gilligan's team who stopped off for five matches on their way to a three-month tour of New Zealand to mark the first official series of Test matches between England and New Zealand. They defeated Western Australia and South Australia quite easily and drew with New South Wales in a high-scoring encounter. Victoria defeated the visitors by seven wickets following Don Blackie's 5/82 and 7/25, and then Queensland had a totally unexpected victory by five wickets.

The bonus for Australia from the last full England visit was the emergence of both Don Bradman and Archie Jackson. They certainly increased the attendances of the previous year, 1927–28, but even they could not stop the slump in crowd figures as the problems of the Depression hit home. The two young cricketers became the idols of schoolchildren around the country. The radio was becoming more popular and their performances were broadcast to a wide audience. Newspapers fed hero-worshipping readers with stories of each coming and going: suddenly it was the era of mass adulation.

Illness would kill Archie Jackson – tuberculosis finally took him in February 1933 – so the mantle shifted to Bradman. But not before both had played major parts in Australian cricket in the early 1930s. In a Test trial match in Sydney in December 1929, Bradman overshadowed everyone by scoring 124 and 225. In the same match Jackson made 182, Kippax 170, and Ponsford 131, while Clarrie Grimmett took the bowling honours with ten wickets. However, it was the Sheffield Shield match between New South Wales and Queensland, played in Sydney starting on 3 January 1930, which effectively raised Bradman on to a pedestal of cricketing immortality.

New South Wales batted first and made 235 with Bradman caught behind for just three runs. Queensland fell short on first innings by eight runs and Bradman walked out to bat again with the NSW score on 22 for one. Displaying a wider range of strokes than had ever been seen before, Bradman was 205 not out by the end of the second day's play. Resuming on the Monday morning, Bradman admitted later that he had his sights on Bill Ponsford's record of 437, which had been scored against Queensland two seasons earlier. When Bradman went from 434 to 438 with a ferocious hook off a short pitched delivery from Hugh Thurlow the crowd erupted to acclaim the new record. Leo O'Connor, the Queensland captain, called for three cheers and when Kippax declared at 761 for eight, four Queensland players chaired an embarrassed Bradman from the field. It was the highest individual score in first-class cricket, 452 not out, and it was scored in 406 minutes and included 49 fours.

Needing 770 to win, Queensland collapsed to 84 all out, with Sam Everett claiming 6/23 from 8.5 overs.

Among those watching that day was Charles Bannerman, scorer of the very first Test century. Later that afternoon Bradman and Bannerman were photographed together – a unique opportunity for the 79-year-old veteran died eight months later.

Bradman dominated the season yet again, scoring 1586 runs at an average of 113.29. Second highest scorer, from the same number of innings with 844 at 56.27 was the promising young batsman, Stan McCabe, a NSW teammate of Bradman's. On the bowling side, a feat not given as much prominence was Clarrie Grimmett's superb return of 82 wickets from eleven matches. His nearest rival was Queensland's medium-pace bowler, Alec Hurwood, who claimed 46 victims in nine matches.

Encouraged by Queensland's admission to the Sheffield Shield in 1926, Western Australia now embarked on a programme of development designed to elevate it eventually to the same status. One of its ideas for placing before the other States the talent that otherwise lay unnoticed in Perth, was the institution of a Second Eleven competition, rather ostentatiously named the All-States Competition.

The manager of the Western Australian team that toured the eastern states in 1929–30 was Alf Randell, an old State player and a tireless worker for cricket in the west. He was given the brief to lobby the other states to support the scheme, and he received favourable audiences in both Melbourne and Hobart. He revealed that the competition would be between Western Australia, Tasmania, and the second elevens of the other states; the intention was to have the two junior states lift the standard of their play, and ultimately for them to join the Sheffield Shield as full members. He conceded at the time that there was a huge gap between the two states and the Sheffield Shield partners, and that it would have been counter-productive for both the Sheffield Shield competition, and Western Australia and Tasmania, if the latter states were to enter it immediately.

The Western Australian proposal was formally put to the Interstate Conference on 11 September 1931, and the details released to the public for the first time. The States would be divided into two groups, Western Australia, South Australia and Victoria playing a round-robin in Melbourne, and Queensland, New South Wales and Tasmania doing likewise in Sydney. The winner of each group would then play off in a final in Melbourne. Tasmania and Western Australia, of course, could field their strongest sides, but the other states were restricted to players who had appeared in a maximum of two Sheffield Shield matches. The competition would be held every other season, with Western Australia and Tasmania making their usual unilateral tours to the other centres in the off season.

The Interstate Conference decided nothing definite, and the idea lapsed until the next Conference, held on 23 September 1932; but the Western Australians' persistence forced the formation of a sub-committee to frame recommendations for consideration by the constituent Associations. The VCA strongly supported Western Australia in these early stages, and even offered a Shield for the competition, to be known as the Donald Mackinnon Shield after a long-serving and recently deceased president.

The recommendation by this sub-committee that effectively killed the scheme was that all expenses be shared equally by the competing states. The whole idea had roused considerable interest in Tasmania, but because the cricket authorities in that State lacked the resources, they rejected the idea in its proposed format. It was calculated that the cost to Tasmania for sending a team alone would have been £220, about £70 more than the annual visit to Victoria. Cost-cutting measures such as abandoning the traditional Tasmanian North versus South matches, and providing allowances to married players only, were talked of so that, in the end, the Tasmania conditions of entry were laid down as follows:

(i) Tasmania to play in Melbourne. (It was thought at the time that Western Australia might be prepared to swap zones and travel to Sydney.)
(ii) Tasmania to pay its expenses only, and not to be asked to share in the heavier expenses of the other states.
(iii) The matter of player allowances to be left to each state.
(iv) The VCA to accept any Tasmanian invitation to send a team to play in Tasmania. (Tasmania relied on these games to raise money to send their teams to the mainland.)

It was a measure of Tasmania's poverty that the cost of installation of a sewerage service at the TCA ground in Hobart was seen as an effective barrier to participation in the scheme. Equally, a more forward-looking approach might have realised the long-term benefits for Tasmanian cricket that participation in the competition would have provided.

Western Australia shortly afterwards made clear that they were not prepared to travel to Sydney. In the event, South Australia joined Tasmania in opposing the scheme and at the Interstate Conference of 24 September 1933, the same sub-committee was instructed to consider the alternatives put forward by the two dissenting states. No agreement could be reached, however, and a resolution was passed at the Conference of 21 September 1934 'that the Western Australian Cricket Association be advised that owing to many difficulties, the All-States Competition cannot be proceeded with'.

The Western Australians did not give up, however. During the 1935–36 season, Alf Randell visited the various states to present a modified proposal, with the request for a special conference to consider it. Apathy from the other Associations delayed any action until the late 1930s, and when it looked as though Western Australia might succeed in getting a competition started in the 1939–40 season, war had broken out and ruined the preparations. After the war, the impetus for a Second Eleven competition was removed because Western Australia was admitted to the Sheffield Shield competition itself. Much energy had thus been spent on a competition that never really got beyond the agenda notices.

But back in the last week of January 1930 the Australian selectors – now Charles Dolling, Dick Jones and Jack Ryder – were preparing to announce the team to tour England that year. Ryder was outvoted by his fellow selectors and knew then that his Test career was over. When the team was finally announced it included only four who had toured before: Bill Woodfull, who was appointed captain, Bill Ponsford, Clarrie Grimmett and Bert Oldfield.

Every state seemed to complain about someone or other who had been left out and there was genuine fury at Ryder's omission, for he was the working-class hero of Melbourne and had lived in Collingwood all his life. Vic Richardson was appointed vice-captain, and the party comprised fifteen players. The Board of Control discussed whether to send a sixteenth man, with the NSW and Victorian delegates agreeing but losing out in a vote to the bloc opposition of the other states. The man in view was Ryder himself. From the day the team was announced Ryder never spoke another word to the NSW representative, Dick Jones, nor attended any function organised by Jones – who for many years was chairman of the Sydney Cricket Ground trustees.

Bill Woodfull had to be persuaded to accept the captaincy vacated by Ryder's non-selection. It was quite a job for the tour manager, William Kelly, a Melbourne auctioneer and Board delegate, to get Woodfull to allow his name to go forward for ratification. But it eventually did and was passed unanimously by the Board which was more than could be said for Vic Richardson's election as vice-captain which only came on the chairman's deliberative vote.

Richardson's off-field interests in South Australia were already becoming of concern to SACA officials and their qualms were passed on to other Board delegates. However, it was not felt that the Board had sufficient reason 'for matters other than cricket' to deny the multi-talented Richardson an English tour.

The team attended numerous receptions and dinners while they were together, and before leaving Australia played matches in Tasmania and Western Australia. At Launceston, Stan McCabe made 103 and Alan Fairfax took eight wickets as the tourists won by ten wickets. In Hobart, Bill Woodfull scored an unbeaten 166 and Don Bradman 139 in a match which petered out into a draw. Kippax made 114 in an innings victory in Perth but the eye was caught by Grimmett's accurate bowling in the two games in which he played. In 62 overs, he claimed a dozen wickets at 14.82 each on pitches that were unresponsive to his leg-spin and top-spin.

The team left Fremantle for Ceylon and a match at the Colombo Cricket Club ground which was spoilt by rain. The Australians suffered a minor collapse, going from 154 for four to 233 all out, due solely to the swing bowling of Edward Kelaart who took 6/65. Ponsford scored 62 in an hour, with two sixes and five fours, and Woodfull 54. Ceylon were 52 for one when the rain arrived.

The Australians arrived in England on Wednesday 23 April 1930, and the first match started at Worcester on 30 April. Don Bradman entertained the full house there with 236 as the Australians reached 492 before declaring. Other large totals on tour were 406 for two (Ponsford 220 not out) against Oxford University; 504 for eight (Woodfull 216) versus Cambridge University; 427 against Lancashire; 405 for eight at Northampton and 432 at Folkestone against An England Eleven. Other notable individual efforts were Bradman's other double-centuries, an unbeaten 252 against Surrey and 205 not out at Canterbury versus Kent.

Clarrie Grimmett's 10–37 at Sheffield in the Yorkshire match was the best analysis of his career (which would stretch for another twelve years). In all Grimmett would claim 1424 wickets in his 31-year first-class involvement in the game, taking five wickets or more in an innings 127 times and ten or more in a match on 33 occasions. He was quite a remarkable bowler who hardly ever sent down a ball without wearing his cap and who was rumoured only ever to have bowled one wide and never a no-ball. He was wizened, small and prematurely bald. His action was short, jerky and almost round-arm. His stock ball was the leg-break, but he probably took most wickets with his top-spinner.

In the twelve matches up to the first Test, the Seventeenth

Australians gained a considerable amount of attention as their run-scoring feats continued. Yet the tour management was not happy and in mid-May sent a cable to the Board which read: 'In the view of the [manager, treasurer, captain, vice-captain and third selector] undersigned it is imperative in Australia's interest that another bowler of the type of Ironmonger or Chilvers should be chosen for the England tour'. They were looking for a strong partner for Grimmett. Bill Jeanes canvassed the Board delegates, 'and a majority had replied against the request'. William Kelly was cabled the decision along with details as to how to vote at the forthcoming Imperial Cricket Conference.

Bradman had become the first Australian to score 1,000 runs in England by the end of May and the crowds were now flocking in to see him. He was short, but looked every inch a cricketer, had small feet, magical wrist-work and his footwork was lightning fast.

In the first Test at Nottingham the English first-innings stuttered as the batsmen showed a distinct dislike for Grimmett's bowling. His clever mixture of leg-spin, top-spin and googlies caused more problems than any of the pacemen. Grimmett's 5/107 shone out as England made 270, with Australia, batting on an uncovered pitch which had absorbed heavy overnight rain following the first day, having only Alan Kippax's half-century to show in a total of 144.

Grimmett (5/94) again was the tourists' spearhead as England's second innings reached 302, and all was in train for an interesting finish with Australia set to make 428. At the end of the third day Australia were 60 for one with Ponsford and Bradman looking safe. The last morning saw the score move on to 198 for three at the first interval. Stan McCabe, on his debut, was partnering Bradman and they were pushing the score along rapidly when there occurred an incident which has entered cricket's lore.

England's second substitute fielder (for Larwood) was a Nottinghamshire ground staff man called Syd Copley – who was to play in only one first-class match. At 229 for three McCabe hit a delivery from Maurice Tate. Copley, at mid-on, sprinted towards the ball and dived forward to take a spectacular catch. He rolled over and over but did not let go of the ball. That catch swung the Test.

Not long afterwards, Bradman's innings came to an end. He had made 131 in 260 minutes, slow scoring for him but essential in the situation. After that the tail fell away and England notched up a 93-run win; England's ninth victory in successive matches under Percy Chapman's captaincy.

England recalled the Indian player Prince Kumar Duleepsinhji, nephew of Ranjitsinhji, for the second Test at Lord's and also gave a debut to the Australian-born fast bowler George Allen, known as 'Gubby'. Duleepsinhji had played one previous Test, against South

Africa a year earlier, but was subsequently left out of the England team because, it was suggested, the Springboks objected to playing against him.

Chapman batted on winning the toss and could only have marvelled at Duleepsinhji's batting. He held the top and middle order together, making 173 in 235 minutes as England reached 425, early on the second morning. Then came batting of a quality and brilliance that gave the Saturday full-house a day not to be forgotten.

Ponsford (81) lost his wicket with the score on 162 immediately after the teams had been presented to King George V. Then came a batting blitzkrieg as Billy Woodfull (155) and Bradman added 231 in two and a half hours. Their shots ranged around Lord's, causing the spectators to give prolonged applause as boundary after boundary was signalled by umpires Chester and Oates.

Woodfull was stumped just before the close, but Bradman had the rest day to contemplate his unbeaten 155. He carried on to 254 when play resumed on the Monday before Chapman took a marvellous low catch at extra-cover. In recalling his innings – even sixty years later – Bradman still insisted that this was his most perfect innings which was ended by a catch as brilliant as any he ever saw.

The score at the time was 585, with Bradman's 254 being then the highest score made in a Test in England, beating Billy Murdoch's 211 at The Oval in 1884. And to think the 'young Don' was still two months short of his twenty-second birthday! The Australian innings continued on to 729 for six before Woodfull declared 304 runs ahead.

A fighting 121 by Percy Chapman – who was dismissed just after swallowing a bluebottle – could not stop England falling to a seven-wicket defeat. Grimmett took 6/167 in 53 overs as, yet again, the majority of England's batsmen could not fathom his spin.

The reaction back in Depression-riddled Australia was nothing short of remarkable. Suddenly a weight seemed to have been lifted from the young nation's shoulders. In Sydney, where news of the victory arrived before dawn, thousands of people waited outside the offices of the *Sydney Morning Herald* for the scores to be posted on a board. With so many out of work a new young hero was just what they wanted.

After two county fixtures the Australians moved on to Headingley for the third Test. Ponsford was unfit and replaced by Archie Jackson who, although not knowing it at the time, was starting to show the symptoms of the tuberculosis which would prematurely end his life. Jackson made a single as Woodfull won the toss for the first time, and decided to bat.

Then came a Bradman onslaught of proportions previously unknown in Test cricket: 50 runs in 49 minutes; a century in 99; at lunch unbeaten on 105 becoming the third Australian behind Trumper and Macartney to score a hundred in this time; at 138 reaching one thousand Test runs in only his seventh match; 200 in 214 minutes; at tea 220 not out having scored 115 in the two-hour session of play; at twenty-five minutes past five reaching, then passing, Reggie Foster's record Test score of 287 made in Sydney in 1903; and at the close of play remaining unbeaten on 309 out of 458 for three.

The next morning *The Times* said: 'To mention the strokes from which he scored most of his runs is to go through the whole range of strokes known to modern batsmen. It was, in fact, an innings so glorious that it might well be classed as incomparable – and how the Yorkshiremen loved it'. The *Daily Express* commented: 'When Bradman exceeded Foster's record, the enthusiasm was so terrific that play had to be stopped until the noise diminished'.

Next morning Bradman took his score to 334 before he was caught behind. He had hit 46 fours in 383 minutes but it was his audacious footwork and hard hitting all around the wicket which had captivated the capacity crowd. Alan Kippax made 77, the rest very few and Australia's total reached 566.

England's reply reached 212 for five at the close and, as forecast, rain on the Monday following the rest day saw only a few minutes' play. For the home side Wally Hammond scored a delightful 113 but it all became rather academic and the match was left drawn.

Behind the scenes the tourists' manager (Kelly) and treasurer (Howard) were 'terribly gung-ho cricketing chaps' but with little knowledge on how to keep up correspondence or look after the ledger books. Spending was high and only after their return to Australia was the true condition of the accounts really found. For the Headingley Test, passes – which had to be paid for – were freely handed out and even elementary records were incorrectly recorded: one example being children's admission charges improperly recorded, which deprived the Australian Board of Control of £290. Another was Treasurer Howard's £156. 17s. 2d. 'entertaining' in the week following the final match of the tour.

The fourth Test at Old Trafford was badly affected by rain and left drawn. Australia made 345, Ponsford 83, to which England replied with 251 for eight, Stan McCabe surprising everyone by taking 4/41 from seventeen very precise overs.

Three rainy weeks later came a shock. Before the fifth and final Test the England selectors decided to change their captain, Percy Chapman, and replace him with Bob Wyatt. By agreement the match was to be played to a finish, so that England's openers, Jack Hobbs and Herbert Sutcliffe, played with the utmost caution from the start. This did not stop Sutcliffe making 161 as England reached 405, Clarrie Grimmett bowling 66 overs for 4/135.

The Australian innings started after lunch on the second day with Woodfull (54) and Ponsford putting on 159 for the first wicket. Ponsford (110) added only 31 with Bradman before he was bowled by Ian Peebles. At close of play on the second day the Australian score was 215 for two, which became 403 for three at the end of the third day with Kippax (28) the only wicket to fall and Bradman going from 27 to 130. It was tedious play.

Rain produced a lively pitch for the fourth day as Bradman struggled against the pace of Harold Larwood. Archie Jackson (73) aided Bradman to a fourth-wicket record of 243, and not too long afterwards Bradman's 438-minute effort came to an end. Caught behind for 232, the third time he had passed 200 in the series, Bradman finished with an aggregate of 974 Test runs at an average of 139.14, a monumental effort and one highly unlikely to be beaten.

McCabe (54) and Fairfax (53) continued Australia's domination of England's bowlers and the innings closed at 695 with the leg-spinner, Ian Peebles, taking 6/204 in 71 overs. Jack Hobbs, in his last Test, fell early and England were 24 for one wicket overnight. Rain ruined the fifth day and when play resumed on the sixth, Percy Hornibrook's left-arm spin (7/92) for once outshone Grimmett as England fell for 251 giving Australia the series 2–1 and the Ashes.

The newspapers made some interesting and amusing observations. *The Times* commented favourably on Bill Woodfull's captaincy and how he encouraged his young players. 'No praise is too high for Woodfull. He showed all the qualities of a great captain.' The *News Chronicle* suggested that: 'As long as Australia has Bradman she will be invincible' and added: 'In order to keep alive the competitive spirit, the authorities might take a hint from billiards. It is almost time to request a legal limit on the number of runs Bradman should be allowed to make.'

When the team returned home huge crowds greeted them in Perth, Adelaide, Melbourne and Sydney. There was a virtual hysteria around the country to see the cricketers. When Bradman returned to work at Mick Simmons' sports store in central Sydney some two thousand people stood outside just to get a glimpse of him. Yet his fame and growing fortune were earning him enemies: Vic Richardson, who had played a minor part in the first four Tests but was dropped for the fifth, commented on radio four days after the team arrived home: 'We could have played any team without Bradman, but we could not have played the blind school without Clarrie Grimmett'.

In one sense Richardson was right. The bowling honours for the tour went to Clarrie Grimmett with 144 wickets, and only Percy Hornibrook (96) came near him. Bradman headed the batting averages with 2960 first-class runs, followed by Kippax (1451), Woodfull (1425),

Jackson (1097) and McCabe (1012). What these figures indicated was that, while the batting was very strong, it was not balanced by equally powerful bowling.

The Board of Control's ban on players writing for newspapers was ignored by Don Bradman on tour. He sold a series of articles to the London *Star* which appeared from 4–15 August 1930. The manager, William Kelly, did not give permission for them and considered that Bradman had breached his tour contact. On his return home Bradman was fined £50 by the Board.

While the Australian team was in England, a number of associations were looking at the possibility of night coaching. They had received letters from Robert Herford, secretary of the Western Suburbs Cricket Club in Sydney, who detailed the particulars of night coaching sessions promoted successfully by his club. 'Amongst other things which we have found most satisfactory', he wrote, 'is the use of specially constructed white cricket balls. If your Association decides to coach at night we will have pleasure in donating a white ball for your examination and use.' Alas, it was not to be. Only forty-seven years later did the white ball come seriously into use.

During the tour the Board had met in Melbourne and agreed 'to make enquiries in respect to the standard and conditions generally respecting Indian cricket'. The Queensland delegates were very keen on a visit to the sub-continent and got the other delegates to agree to contact the Indian Board to send an invitation. They stated that Australia could tour in either the 1933–34 or 1934–35 seasons.

Meanwhile the final details for the 1930–31 visit by the West Indies were in hand. A cable from Barbados from the Secretary of the West Indies Board of Control included the information 'that including managers, the party would comprise seven whites and eleven natives' and went on to stress 'that all should reside at the same hotels'.

Around the country the State Associations were meeting to discuss the West Indian team's social activities without fully realising that there could be a 'culture clash' on their arrival. Then the Board informed the Associations that they had to make themselves completely aware of the 'White Australia' policy being pursued by the various state and federal governments.

Bill Jeanes – in his role as secretary to the Board of Control – discovered that it would be necessary to obtain permission from the Department of Home Affairs for the eleven black players to land in Australia. He duly made the necessary application which was granted only on the condition that the Board would give a written undertaking to be responsible for the departure of the eleven blacks from Australia within a period of six months.

The West Indies team arrived in Sydney on 18 November and the seven whites (five players and two officials) were put into a separate hotel from the rest of the team. The tourists' hierarchy immediately complained and from then on all stayed together.

As they travelled around on tour the keenness of individuals and Associations to arrange social activities ran into problems when they found that the majority of the tourists were Roman Catholics who refused to play golf or to go touring on Sundays. Both the captain, G. C. 'Jack' Grant, and the assistant manager, Joe Scheult, were lay missionaries who took their charges to early matins or mass – depending on their religion – virtually every day. This played havoc with Association schedules: they just had not come across a team like this before. The West Indians conducted themselves in such a correct and friendly way that the Anglican Archbishop was moved to write positively about them in a diocesan journal. They attended Mayoral functions at virtually every venue; enjoyed other sporting events and even an Orpheus Society recital. But when they attended official cricket dinners held by the Board and the Associations the West Indians became offended at the 'gentlemen only' nights and the ribald speeches which followed.

The tour was a financial disaster, but then it was never expected to make money. Of their fourteen first-class matches the West Indies won four and lost eight. George Headley scored 1066 runs at 44.41 to top the batting averages while Learie Constantine's 47 wickets at 20.23 led the bowling. Defeats against the three major states led up to the first Test in Adelaide.

Against Victoria the tourists were completely at sea facing the bowling of Bert Ironmonger who took 5/87 and 8/31. Bill Ponsford scored 187 but it was the innings of Keith Rigg (126), a right-handed middle-order batsman from the Hawthorn-East Melbourne club, that particularly caught the eye. Although he was to play in eight Tests, Rigg did not show his full ability at the top level.

The (now five) Australian selectors gave Alec Hurwood his chance in the first Test and he repaid their faith by taking seven wickets. He then took four wickets in the second Test and was discarded: a familiar story for many. Jack Grant won the toss and elected to bat in the first-ever match between the two sides. Bartlett made 84, Roach 56 and Grant himself an unbeaten 53 as Clarrie Grimmett had a field day on his home pitch taking 7/87. In reply to 296, Australia fairly raced to 376 with Alan Kippax scoring 146 and Stan McCabe 90.

The West Indian team had not been chosen for the harder and bouncier Australian pitches and their morale slipped as Grimmett

(4/96) and Hurwood (4/86) teased out their inexperienced batsmen. The Australians' ten-wicket victory came with an unbeaten first wicket stand in their second innings by Ponsford (92) and Jackson (70).

After a visit to Tasmania, the West Indians had luck against them in the second Test at Sydney. Rain completely altered the character of a perfect batting pitch after Australia had won the toss, batted and made 323 for four on the first day. Even Ponsford, 174 overnight, was out for 183 after a struggle when play resumed. The Australians' 369 was a winning total as the Caribbean cricketers fell for 107 and 90.

Then followed a fixture against Queensland in which the West Indians faced the pace of the aboriginal fast-bowler Eddie Gilbert. The Queensland government's treatment of aboriginals was appalling, and Gilbert had to have a permit even to be in the city of Brisbane at all. The QCA had to guarantee his boarding and they were also responsible for his behaviour. However Gilbert took 5/65 and 2/26 in an impressive performance although the tourists won easily.

The third Test in mid-January at the Exhibition Ground in Brisbane was another nightmare for the West Indians. Here they faced a second-wicket deluge of runs as Ponsford (109) and Bradman (223) put on 229 runs together. Then Kippax (84) joined his NSW partner and 193 runs came in just two hours. Bradman's innings, which concluded early on the second day, was scored in just five hours. In reply to 558 only George Headley, a remarkably fine batsman, could stop the rot, but his unbeaten 102 out of 193 could not save the follow-on. Clarrie Grimmett took nine wickets in a match which Australia won by an innings and 217 runs.

The fourth Test in Melbourne followed a now predictable pattern. The West Indies fell to Ironmonger, 7/23 and 4/56, while Bradman scored 152 and the match was over in two days. Luck, however, finally fell upon Grant's shoulders in Sydney for the final Test. He declared his team's two innings closed at just the right time so that his bowlers could gain maximum assistance from a 'sticky' pitch. Frank Martin (123) and George Headley (105) got some revenge against their tormentors, and Australia's only resistance came from Alan Fairfax who scored a half-century in each innings. The West Indies thus finished their tour with a totally unexpected Test victory.

Don Bradman, as expected, dominated the 1930–31 season scoring 1422 runs and yet, down the other end of the statistics, the bowlers had a comparable year, particularly Grimmett with 74 wickets and Ironmonger 68.

The domestic season had begun with a 'thank-you' to Jack Ryder who had not only lost the Australian captaincy but was also voted out as a selector. The Victorian Cricket Association arranged a Ryder's XI versus a Woodfull's XI (which was, in fact, a full-strength Test side) which, after expenses, brought in just about £3000 for the testimonial.

Victoria won a narrowly fought Sheffield Shield contest which saw Bradman score two double-centuries (258 versus South Australia and 220 versus Victoria) and one other century, with the highest innings coming from Queensland's Cecil Thompson who scored an unbeaten 275 in Brisbane against NSW, as his state made 687, their then highest Shield total. Yet wherever one turned, there was Bradman. He was the greatest crowd-drawer of the 1920s and 1930s. No-one before or since has matched his appeal and for the West Indies series it was his face and name which was used prominently in match advertisements. But the Bradman legend continued to be a product of the Depression, just as Australians continued to need sporting heroes.

Radio was now regularly providing a service for people to listen to the exploits of their cricketers. By the early 1930s cricket dominated the sporting airwaves. In addition to an expanded press coverage a much larger audience was created as a wireless set became an essential part of a home. In 1924, when Test cricket was first covered only 1400 people held a radio licence; but by the early 1930s this number had increased to 370,000.

As with television in later years, the cricket authorities were wary of radio, fearing that it would reduce attendances at matches. The Interstate Conference, which comprised state administrators, was worried by dropping Shield attendances and considered that radio, at least in part, was to blame. Attendances for the five seasons from 1930 were about fifty per cent down on the five seasons before 1930.

The drop in crowds, however, had little to do with the introduction of radio. It was caused mainly by the Depression. It is more likely that radio helped to expand cricket's audience, a point which journalists sensed rather more quickly than officials. In Melbourne, for example, the *Argus* pointed out as early as 4 January 1929 that 'if the Victorian Cricket Association loses anything by having Test matches broadcast, it gains also because thousands rush to the ground when news goes forth that interesting events are imminent. This was especially noticeable when Bradman was nearing his century.'

The *Sydney Morning Herald* suggested that cricket's audience was further swelled since in 'thousands of homes, the housewife who never went to a match is being educated while the radio is turned on in the points and personalities of cricket'. (In later years, 1977, a whole marketing strategy would evolve around cricket and women under the guise of 'the lowest common denominator'.) Overall, the expanding coverage was good for the game and whetted the appetites of many people who now, suddenly, wanted more.

During the height of the economic Depression, 1930–34, South Australia had the highest rate of unemployment in the country. From

1927 to 1935 more people were out of work (on a percentage basis) in Adelaide than in any other city. The SACA, aware of the problems associated with unemployment, came up with a number of novel ways to look after their members. Some asked to pay off their subscription by doing labouring work at the Oval: others asked for time to pay or a suspension for a year or two: some asked to pay half, that being for either the cricket or football seasons but not both. Remarkably, membership figures dropped from a 1930 peak of 3135 to a 1932 low of 2758 (down 12%); but it rose in 1933 to 3251.

The SACA was also aware of the general plight of the community. A donation of cricket materials was made to the Kuitpo Unemployment Colony, and men from the Exhibition Unemployment Camp were allowed free access to district matches.

The Association had to cut costs, and the first to be affected were the casual staff. Gatemen and stilekeepers were reduced in number, their work increased and their pay halved. There were no complaints.

It was the same in the other States. The Depression years in Sydney produced an exodus of New South Wales cricketers to Queensland. Players who were frustrated at their failure to find employment, or a place in the star-studded NSW team, went north hoping for better things. Unemployment was half in Brisbane compared to that in Sydney although it was still heavy. However, Queensland cricket was to benefit with such new players as Gordon Amos, Roy Levy, Charles Andrews, Ernie Laidler and, from Bradman's St George club, Frank Ward, a talented leg-spinner.

When Charles Bannerman died in 1930, he left his widow Mary so short of funds that the NSWCA made her a grant of £50 within a few months of his death. With times so tough, other players started to be dependent on the Association and Harold Heydon, at his own request, had his salary reduced by ten per cent.

The share market crashed and thousands of people went from a comfortable life to one of poverty. There were soup kitchens; shelters for families in inner city areas; and suicides. Alongside city rivers, particularly Brisbane and Adelaide, long lines of hessian shacks housed the homeless. It was ugly, brutal, depressing.

In April 1931, a meeting was held in London between government representatives and three senior members of the Marylebone Cricket Club. Notes of this meeting, which are housed in the archives at Lord's, have never been revealed. It has long been privately suggested by one prominent person connected with the issue at hand, and who had intimate knowledge of certain planning, that the British government had realised what a political animal the game of cricket was becoming and how it felt it might be used for its benefit.

Five years earlier the Imperial Conference of 1926 had defined the 'position and mutual relation of the group of self-governing communities composed of Great Britain and the Dominions'. It declared its members to be 'autonomous communities within the British Empire, equal in status, in no way subordinate one to another in any aspect of their domestic or foreign affairs, though united by a common allegiance to the Crown, and freely associated as members of the British Commonwealth of Nations'.

Not long after this Whitehall meeting had taken place, and in order to remove all doubts as to the autonomy of the Dominions as recognised in the 1926 declaration, the British Parliament enacted the 1931 Statute of Westminster. It laid down that no future Act passed by Britain should apply to any Dominion unless that Dominion requested it; nor could any law passed by a Dominion be declared invalid by Britain. The Crown now appeared to be the sole legal force unifying the Commonwealth. So, it could be argued, some thirty years after the event, Australia's independence had been officially approved by their former colonial mentors.

There appeared, in the eyes of the British government, to be a need for some type of sporting achievement to take place which would boost the morale of the unemployed and in some way take their minds off the more urgent matters at hand. To that end it was, therefore, important that cricket, as a recognised international game, should be the chosen sport in which Britain could be shown as reigning supreme.

It was also necessary to make the oldest sporting 'enemy' insist on a challenge and equally important to win, under whatever circumstances could be found. So, completely out of the blue, Bill Jeanes in Adelaide received a cable on 20 May 1931 from the secretary of the Marylebone Cricket Club asking if Australia wanted an England tour for the 1932–33 season or should it be scrapped? Jeanes replied at once: 'Tour on'.

Two days later came another cable from Lord's: 'If English tour in Australia 1932 considered feasible, please send suggested programme. Findlay.' To which Jeanes answered: 'Your tour 1932 essential. Arrival and departure dates required urgently assist preparation programme.'

The Board of Control held a special meeting in Melbourne on 11 June 1931 to discuss the unusual moves coming from London. As unswerving loyalists to the Marylebone Cricket Club, no delegate would question the existence of an ulterior motive. British values included an ethic of fair play and, according to many, they were superior values to those in Australia. But one New South Wales delegate raised his suspicions at the meeting. Frank Cush 'was not sure of the Marylebone motives' and their 'calling for the programme at such an early date' was strange enough for the matter to be adjourned until a later date. As for the 'urgent' request from Lord's – they did not reply to Jeanes' cable of 22 May 1931 until 11 September 1931.

The domestic season of 1931–32 was anything but exciting. New South Wales won the Sheffield Shield as attendances fell all around the country, with the season's most talked about match being the very first, when NSW played Queensland in Brisbane on 6 October 1931. Just before play began, Archie Jackson started coughing blood and he was rushed to hospital. Within a week he was diagnosed as suffering from tuberculosis.

When the match began, Eddie Gilbert produced an opening spell described by Don Bradman later as the fastest spell of bowling he had ever encountered. Gilbert took the wicket of Wendell Bill with his first ball and then gave Bradman a horrific few moments until defeating him with his sixth delivery. At 21 for three Alan Kippax retired hurt and it took an ultra-courageous effort from Stan McCabe to tame Gilbert. McCabe's unbeaten 229 saw NSW to an innings victory in a strange match in which nine batsmen failed to score.

Don Bradman has always been the subject of rumours and, prior to this season, his name was linked with a number of Lancashire League clubs. The South African tourists arrived for their second visit to Australia while these stories were at their height. Moral splutterings came from many different places, even from England where the *Observer* of 6 September stated:

> No sporting interest would be served by bringing Bradman to Lancashire. He is an ornament to his own country and in that capacity will always be welcome here, but as a salaried run-getter for an English club he would be only a reminder of how money deranged the order of things.

On 3 November, Bradman went to the Blue Mountains town of Blackheath to play in a match to celebrate the opening of the club's new ground. A huge crowd saw an amazing few minutes when, in partnership with Wendell Bill, Bradman scored 100 out of 102 in three eight-ball overs. Bill's two singles during Bradman's pillage won him more applause than any of his six first-class centuries.

The South African tour had been the subject of much discussion between their Cricket Association and the Board of Control. On 17 April 1931 they had cabled Bill Jeanes:

> Association perturbed financial position Australia – particularly

> Government embargo against money leaving Australia and adverse exchange. Essential you secure Government undertaking that all our funds will be permitted to be transferred to South Africa at conclusion of tour. We are most anxious that no circumstances will arise to prevent our visit and trust you hold similar views notwithstanding financial Depression.

Jeanes was able to confirm that the South Africans could take their money home but would not guarantee making up any shortfall due to the exchange rate. All went quiet for two months until on 11 June the South Africans sent another cable: 'In view general Depression and your Board's inability to meet exchange position, which we fully appreciate, our Association suggests cancellation of our visit on terms originally agreed.'

What was being put forward, which the Board had to consider, was that the South Africans just took '15% of net profits', or 'alternatively are you prepared to consider a visit to South Africa'? or 'alternatively would you prefer no visit at all made by either party?' The Board cabled back: 'Accept 15% net profits'.

After a number of further cables the tour party was selected. The captain was Horace Brakenridge 'Jock' Cameron, a wicketkeeper-batsman from Eastern Province, with Denys Morkel of Western Province as his vice-captain. The tourists arrived in Fremantle and within three days were playing a drawn match against Western Australia. Then followed a win in Adelaide where Clarrie Grimmett took eight wickets and his South African counterpart, Quintin McMillan, claimed eleven, including a second innings 9/53.

In Melbourne, Victoria won by 87 runs, Bill Woodfull 121, Bert Ironmonger 5/87 and 5/21, and in Sydney, Don Bradman said 'hallo' with 135 and the new opener, Jack Fingleton, chipped in with 117 in a close draw. Moving on to Brisbane, the South Africans drew with Queensland at the Woolloongabba and then prepared themselves for the first of the five timeless Tests they would play over the next eleven weeks.

Bill Woodfull won the toss on the morning of 27 November 1931 as the 'Gabba became Test cricket's twenty-fourth venue. Bradman came in on the fall of Ponsford's wicket at 32 for one, and was dropped on 11 and 15. The Springboks then paid for their errors as the young Australian proceeded to score exactly 200 by stumps. The following day, Saturday, saw Bradman reach 226 when he was leg-before-wicket to the left-arm spin of Cyril Vincent. The score reached 450 which South Africa pulled back by 126 for three by the close. Then came the rain. For three solid days the heavens opened but then the whole ground dried out quickly. Play resumed late on the fifth day and the

South Africans – who were much more at home playing on matting than on a turf pitch – fell apart. Ironmonger claimed nine of the wickets to fall as Australia won by an innings and 163 runs.

Bradman followed the tourists and, two days later in Sydney, scored 219 as NSW reached 500. Then came more rain and the game was left drawn.

The Bradman nightmare for the Springboks started again in the Sydney Test as his 112, alongside Keith Rigg's 127, saw yet another innings victory, this time just after tea on the third day. Then it was Melbourne on New Year's Eve and Jock Cameron must have thought that luck was with him at last. His medium-paced opening attack of Sandy Bell and Neville Quinn saw the back of the Australians for 198 with only three batsmen reaching double figures. The Springboks took the lead on the second afternoon and continued building on their advantage for another day. Ken Viljoen (111) scored his side's only Test century in the series in a score of 358.

The match was then transformed as Woodfull (161) and Bradman (167) added 274 for the second wicket in front of the series' largest daily crowd of 31,786. It was Bradman the crowd wanted to see and for the first time Melbourne had an example of the extraordinary effect this cricketer had on them. As soon as people knew he was batting they just poured through the turnstiles. As the *Argus* said: 'Bradman was a magnet and there were thousands who could not attend business. Suddenly they discovered they had a most pressing appointment at the Melbourne Cricket Ground'. Another aspect was revealed by the Deputy Director of Postal Services who said 'that the volume of mails was abnormally low' and he could put it down only to the cricket. This was the 'Bradman factor' in action.

Recent studies of all of Bradman's innings in Australia and the crowd attendances with and without him show that overall he added 91% to the gates of the time. In the years of the Depression this was manna from heaven to the various State Associations.

As the Australian score climbed past 500 it became obvious to all watching that the visitors would have no chance in their second innings. Grimmett (6/92) and Ironmonger (4/54) saw to that. With the series now won the Australian selectors continued with their policy of blooding young players. Most of them played in only one or two Tests but two, Bill O'Reilly and Jack Fingleton, were to enjoy long periods at the top.

In Adelaide for the fourth Test the Springboks made 308 after Cameron had won the toss and decided to bat on one of curator Alby Wright's perfect pitches. Alas, Clarrie Grimmett was on his home turf and returns of 7/116 and 7/83 were unanswerable. Between the South African innings the Australians had made 513 with Bradman once again dominant. Coming in when the first wicket fell at nine, he remained unbeaten on 299 having run out his last partner going for that one extra run. Dropped twice at 14 and once at 20, on two occasions by Bruce Mitchell in the slips, Bradman's innings remained the highest for Australia in a home series for thirty-five years. With a ten-wicket win under their belt the Australians went to Melbourne for the final Test.

The fifth Test lasted exactly five hours and fifty-three minutes, the shortest on record. It had a match aggregate of 234 runs for the 29 wickets to fall. Most of the play took place under conditions that are provided only by Australian 'sticky' wickets, caused by hot sun following heavy rain. Both teams were ill-equipped but since the Australians had more experience of such conditions they fared better.

South Africa's first innings lasted 89 minutes for 36 runs of which eight were extras. Their second innings took 105 minutes, which brought forth 45 runs. Bert Ironmonger claimed 5/6 and 6/18 and Clarrie Grimmett, who had taken 33 wickets in the first four Tests, was not even invited to bowl. It was the Springboks' third defeat by an innings and the series was lost by five matches to nil.

But yet again it was a Bradman year. In his total domination of the game he scored 1190 runs against the South Africans, 806 of them in five Test innings. In all matches he scored 1403 at 116.92 and even in Sydney grade cricket he made 785 runs at 112.14 in a limited number of appearances.

Ever since 1927 the Board of Control had operated a strict rule that no team comprising players who were under the jurisdiction of any of the six State Associations could make an overseas tour – or play overseas – without Board approval. The Board deliberated long and hard over allowing cricketers to play in England, with Alan Fairfax, in particular, having to plead for his authority to play in the Lancashire League.

Arthur Mailey received permission to take a side to tour the United States and Canada in 1932, a venture he organised with a number of commercial outlets. The Board agreed provided they confirmed the team chosen; that full accounts were presented on return; and that no player receive more than £100. Only the first condition was kept.

The team selected included Vic Richardson as captain with Test players Don Bradman, Hanson Carter – now fifty-four – Alan Kippax, Stan McCabe and Mailey himself as player-manager. They left Australia in May 1932 to play 51 matches in one hundred days. None of the matches was first-class and half were against odds. The pitches on which they batted, and often the outfields, were certainly not of the standard expected, but the players all enjoyed the tour.

The statistics are extraordinary: the Australians scored over 10,000 runs of which Bradman made 3779 with 18 centuries. His 260 against Western Ontario is still the highest individual score made in Canada. The unexpected success of the tour was Leslie O'Brien 'Chuck' Fleetwood-Smith. His left-arm spinners claimed 249 victims at just nine runs each. Arthur Mailey took 240 wickets at 6.50.

One of the fixtures that was particularly remembered was against the actor, and ex-England captain, Aubrey Smith's Hollywood team. Smith, then sixty-nine, opened the batting: Boris Karloff fielded in the slips; Douglas Fairbanks, jr, spent part of the game explaining the rules to Jean Harlow, while Joan Crawford admired the physique of Vic Richardson with whom she had become particularly friendly. The social aspect of the tour was remembered above all else.

In some ways it was an age of innocence. Cricket was played as a game to be enjoyed. It was fun. But soon it was to lose its virginity.

# 17

# Bodyline: Causes and Effects, 1932–34

When pressed, the main victim of England's 1932–33 tour of Australia, Don Bradman says: 'I have always given the Marylebone Cricket Club the benefit of very considerable doubt that they did not know what was planned to happen on that tour'.

There is no doubt whatever that during the year or more before the England touring team left home shores on 17 September 1932 that planning had begun on two fronts: one, to regain the Ashes; and two, to combat Bradman within the then existing rules of the game. To this end the Marylebone Cricket Club committee decided to elect a three-man selection committee to act for two years rather than the customary one.

Pelham Warner was on this committee, in fact he would be announced as joint tour manager along with Richard Palairet. He was also on a programme committee, a most unusual move as at all times the host nation provided a programme for the visitors' consideration. Quite cleverly the powers at Lord's had put Warner as chairman together with the former England captain, Percy Chapman, and the permanent Australian representative on the Imperial Cricket Conference, Richard Mallett.

They sent a cable to Bill Jeanes on 22 October 1931 detailing their wishes for the itinerary which said in part: 'Owing to climate play first Test Brisbane or not at all', and went on seemingly to give considerable prominence to the New Zealand leg of the tour by stating: 'This shows our wish to visit New Zealand as we cannot well refuse request of New Zealand government. Invite your co-operation and help.'

When the Australian Board read this they were united in their views. There would be no changes to the Australians' proposed itinerary, and if the England team wanted to visit New Zealand they could do so after their Australian commitments were over. Anticipating that the Australians would bow to Lord's wishes, Warner had instructed New Zealand Cricket Council secretary William Winsor to go to Melbourne to negotiate with the Board. On the day of the scheduled meeting Winsor was kept waiting in an ante-room of the Victorian Cricket Association until just after nine in the evening before being called in to receive the Board's view.

The Board minutes then read: 'Mr Winsor expressed regret at the decision. His Council would not let the matter rest at this stage but would make further representations to the Marylebone Cricket Club and hoped to have success in that direction. He added that he would have great difficulty in convincing his Council that the Australian Board had not been most unreasonable and had committed a most unfriendly act. He expressed the opinion that the present action will terminate friendly relations for some years to come between Australia and New Zealand.' Eventually the England team did visit New Zealand but not until late March 1933 which saw both Test matches ruined by seasonal rain.

As well as affecting their domestic economies, and thus their workforces, the Depression had also strained trade and diplomatic relations between England and Australia. World trade dropped by twenty-five per cent which for Britain was a devastating blow. British exports fell by thirty-two per cent in volume terms, and by half in value terms, in the three years to the end of 1932. On the world market the prices of raw materials and foodstuffs declined dramatically. Australia, as a major exporter of primary products – wool, wheat, butter, lamb – found its export earnings plummeting and its debts mounting.

In March 1930 the Australian government had asked Britain to allow it to defer an interest payment on a huge war loan. This worried the financial gurus in London, and on 16 June 1930 the British Trade Commissioner in Sydney wrote to the Department of Overseas Trade in London:

> I think we should be doing something to lead Australia to come to us for help, and having achieved that we should expect 'sanctions' in return. I need not elaborate that idea, but I am afraid that unless something of the kind happens, not only may Australia be in imminent danger for a long time of being unable to meet her overseas commitments but we may lose a very valuable opportunity for bringing her back into the fold not only chastened but more appreciative of the value of the imperial tie.

Two months later the Commissioner sent another report:

> The Westminster Bank alone could make Australia default immediately . . . the country is in an appalling mess, worse, much worse, than a few months ago, but not so bad as it will be . . . the country is now absolutely bankrupt . . . but for the imperial idea there would be no nation, there is no justification for equality and they cannot possibly meet their commitments. So why, I ask you, should we take all this lying down?

In December he cabled, 'You cannot possibly over-estimate in your own mind the serious present situation so that you should be prepared to accept anything'. On 24 August the London *Observer* commented: 'There seems to have been a decision by the British money market, to put it bluntly, that Australia must be taught a lesson'.

And so the strategy was to exploit the difficult economic circumstances in order to exert pressure on Australia, thereby reinforcing its economic reliance and dependence on Britain. The Commissioner hoped to impede the desire for greater autonomy which had become more manifest during the 1920s. Australia, Canada and South Africa had pressed at the 1926 Imperial Conference for the status of the Dominions to be redefined as 'autonomous communities within the British Empire, equal in status' although 'united by a common allegiance to the Crown'.

Matters became worse for Britain in 1931 when the Scullin government in Australia imposed a series of high protectionist tariffs on imported goods *and made no exception for British items*. There was a special customs surcharge of fifty per cent imposed on a large range of imports, and non-essentials were prohibited. In British eyes worse was to follow when a further ten per cent duty was levied on all imported goods.

Then came another row as Australia insisted on a home-born successor to the retiring Governor-General, Lord Stonehaven. The traditional procedure, until then, had been for the Dominions Office in London, in collaboration with the King, to present the Australian government with a short list from which to make a choice. The Australians dispensed with this and proposed the seventy-five-year-old Chief Justice, Sir Isaac Isaacs. 'A Jew was one thing but an Australian . . .' The British government was horrified.

The Australian Prime Minister, Jimmy Scullin, refused to give way and raised the matter at the 1930 Imperial Conference where, with the support of Canada and South Africa, he got what he wanted: an Australian-born Governor-General. However, the Scullin government fell in November 1931, to be replaced by the United Australia Party led by Joseph Lyons. Then the NSW State government was dismissed for its second default on a loan payment to Britain and subsequently an economic austerity programme was imposed over the country.

The resolution of Australia's immediate problems took place at the Imperial Economic Conference, held in Ottawa from 21 July to 20 August 1932, where Australia's delegation was led by Stanley Bruce, a former Prime Minister who thereafter became the resident Minister in London. The final compromise reached gave Dominion foodstuffs an imperial preference on the British market in exchange for British exports receiving favourable treatment in the Dominions. The latter was achieved by the tariffs on all non-British imports being increased. Both Britain and Australia had highly protected economies and the Imperial trade war led to many bitter exchanges in the press and letters of complaint to the Dominions Office from disgruntled British manufacturers who claimed they had been unfairly treated in Australia. This did nothing to improve Anglo-Australian relations, already strained by the insistence of the Australian government on showing that independence meant what it said.

Many politicians and diplomats hoped that the 1932–33 cricket tour to Australia would help re-establish harmony and mutual understanding. Others saw the Test series as an opportunity to find a new national pride amidst world chaos. For some in Australia, cricket was an important aspect in the formation of the emergent nation's identity and self-consciousness. Matches against the 'mother country' were a yardstick in measuring that growth. For others in London, to quote their Sydney man's comment, the tour offered Britain an opportunity to bring the troublesome Dominion 'back into the fold not only chastened but more appreciative of . . . the imperial tie'. And that is why the tough, uncompromising Douglas Jardine was chosen to lead the side.

During the second war, Pelham Warner was the so-called 'Deputy Secretary' at the Marylebone Cricket Club. It has been widely assumed that, in this period, he culled the Club's records of many papers, particularly those critical of himself and, more importantly, those relating to the planning and execution of the 1932–33 tour.

A widespread belief also exists that there were a number of meetings in early to mid-1932 between J. H. Thomas, the Secretary of State for the Dominions, and certain influential members of the Marylebone Cricket Club, particularly Lord Hawke who had been added to the selection committee as chairman. Decisions were made which would cause cricket-loving people around the world to discuss the tour from then until the present day.

Numerous publications over the past sixty years have tried to give one view or another about the series. It was, in many ways, a clash of cultures which was particularly prevalent in the composition of the two governing cricket bodies: the Marylebone Cricket Club ruled by tradition and the aristocracy; the Australian Board of Control for International Cricket run by men who shared a common social heritage, an average education, and a commercial-professional background.

The Board men found great delight in hobnobbing with people of higher social status. As an example, the minutes of the Board meeting held on 22 September 1932 record the Board's desire 'to entertain the English team at a dinner in Melbourne during the second Test match', but added that, 'the Australian team not be included'. As matters turned out the dinner was organised by the Victorian Cricket Association president, Canon E. S. Hughes, who not only invited the Australian team but any State players and officials who could attend.

Prior to the series the members had a problem with Don Bradman who had written to the Board, 'for permission to write comments upon and descriptions of first-class cricket matches for the press during the season as well as participate in the game as a player'. The then chairman, Dr Allen Robertson, replied to Bradman that the Board's resolutions on player-writers must be adhered to unless 'you can advise me that you are employed solely as a journalist and support such statement with a letter from your press employers'.

Some fuss was raised as Bradman was contracted to the Frank Packer newspaper and radio empire but after common sense prevailed – following Bradman's threat not to play in the Test series – he replied to Robertson, as given in the Board minutes, 'saying that he could not state that he was solely employed as a journalist', and added that, 'he accepted the conditions as laid down by the Board and considered that his application had been rejected and that the matter was closed'.

The Board minutes then immediately recorded: 'The General Secretary of the Australian Journalists Association conveyed the thanks of the Association to the Board of Control for its decision that only cricketers who are employed solely as journalists should be allowed to write for newspapers on Test cricket matches'.

But however hard the Board tried to impose its rules, Bradman was looked upon publicly as the man who had become a success in the midst of the Depression. He was a symbol of hope for all who were struggling under the black cloud of unemployment, of numbing debts and the pain of hunger. As it happened, the England captain Douglas Jardine came to be considered the exemplar of all that the working-class Australians loathed: he was the haughty representative of a privileged class who cared little for the hardships they were suffering.

The England team opened their visit with a match against Western Australia which started on 21 October 1932 and, within a day, a complaint about Douglas Jardine had been laid by the WACA to the Board of Control. Sent by the president, His Honour Mr Justice

T. P. Draper, the WACA executive was furious at Jardine's refusal to attend the ground, 'until 12.33 pm, on Saturday 22 October, to inspect the wicket which had been damaged by rain, although the captain of the Western Australian team and the umpires were on the ground at the official time fixed for the resumption of play at noon'. Not knowing how to handle such a matter the Board ignored it.

When the tourists arrived in Adelaide in early November they were feted in the usual way: civic receptions; government lunches; social rounds of golf; sightseeing, dances, cinemas, theatres. Away from all this Douglas Jardine and Pelham Warner were invited to meet with Allen Robertson, the local Board delegate Bernard Scrymgour, and Bill Jeanes at the SACA offices in Pirie Street, Adelaide to discuss matters of common interest. The tourists wanted, particularly, to vary the playing conditions of the tour and after a lengthy discussion Jardine got his way.

Up until the match against An Australian XI in Melbourne the English batsmen were in excellent form. They then fell for just 60 runs in their second innings with the medium-paced Lisle Nagel claiming 8/32. Jardine was not playing and had gone fishing, with his deputy, Bob Wyatt, taking over as captain. He set a leg-side field for Bradman and on both occasions fast bowler Harold Larwood claimed the Australian's wicket.

Bradman failed again the following week when playing for NSW against the tourists and subsequently withdrew from the team for the first Test. Although Board officials were satisfied with the various medical reports which said he was 'seriously rundown', Jardine believed that Bradman had had a nervous breakdown.

But Bradman, as astute and aware as he always was, had already communicated to the NSW delegates to the Board the nature of the English team's tactics. He later wrote: 'Its purport was obvious to me. I promptly confided to responsible officials my predictions regarding the future, but found little sympathy for my views'. Jack Fingleton supports Bradman in this for he also raised the issue and was left feeling that the Board could not believe that any English team would bowl at a batsman deliberately to hurt him.

This all took place in Melbourne, and now the teams faced each other in Sydney in the first of five controversial Tests. Woodfull won the toss and batted, and watched as Stan McCabe scored a splendid unbeaten 187 against Larwood (5/96 and 5/28) and his partner Bill Voce. He scored 25 fours in his 242-minute innings by hitting with a boldness which endeared him to the large, and vocal, Sydney crowd. In reply to 360, the Englishmen took the attack to the four main Australian bowlers: Wall and Nagel, the pacemen; Grimmett and O'Reilly, flight and spin.

At 423 for two – Sutcliffe 194, Hammond 112, Nawab of Pataudi, on his debut, 102 – the England side had looked set for a huge score. In the end they made 524 to which Australia's miserable reply of 164 on a good pitch was only enough to see them draw level with the tourists.

The ten-wicket victory was not won with universal acclaim. The leg-theory bowling had been picked up for what it was by the old players who were now reporting from the pressbox. Eric Barbour and Tom Garrett condemned it with Garrett, who had played in the first Test in 1877, saying in a letter to the *Sydney Morning Herald*: 'I can unhesitatingly say that this is the first occasion that I have ever seen bowlers deliberately bowling at the batsman'. Joe Darling called it 'Bradman theory' while John Worrall in the *Australasian* wrote of an attack 'in line with the body'. Hugh Buggy in the *Melbourne Herald* used the term 'Bodyline' for the first time and it was picked up by all and sundry as an appropriate way to describe the England tactics.

The crowd for four days had been an enormous 158,193, and there was at least one NSWCA official who seemed to realise the implications of Jardine's tactics particularly on such a large crowd who had been extremely vocal. The NSWCA secretary, Harold Heydon, immediately wrote to the Board (and SACA) secretary, Bill Jeanes, warning of the danger of crowd disturbances at Adelaide and elsewhere.

What is of importance to note is that the records of the major cricket associations, mainly from a period of mid-December 1932 to March 1933, have been tampered with. Usually reliable documentation is not in place, and yet there is no question of these moves being officially sanctioned. Even the discovery in 1983 of a large trunkload of relevant papers in the Victorian coastal town of Barwon Heads proved of premature joy to researchers as their quick subsequent disappearance stymied any background revelations.

Following a country game in Wagga and two fixtures in Tasmania the second Test saw Australia recall Ironmonger for Nagel and the English leave out Verity. These moves were decisive as O'Reilly and Ironmonger won the game for Australia on the fourth afternoon. Australia and England played probably the best match of the series in Melbourne with a third-day record crowd of 68,238 and the total reaching 200,635.

Larwood and Bowes both bowled fast with Woodfull, on one occasion, being hit in the chest. Radio helped to keep the public informed with the Postmaster General's department organising the most extensive interstate hook-up it had ever undertaken. There was now virtually a wireless in every home and the whole country was keeping abreast of events as they happened.

Australia scored 228 to which England replied with 169 (O'Reilly

5/63). The match was superbly balanced and the holiday Monday crowd had their reward when Bradman, who had been out first ball two days earlier, now proceeded to score an unbeaten 103 out of an Australian total of 191. On the final day the pitch took spin awkwardly. O'Reilly earned 5/66 and Ironmonger 4/26 as Australia won by 111 runs. The series was level but now came the trouble.

Two days before the Melbourne Test, Jack Blackham had died aged seventy-eight. He was a tough man and in his day fought fire with fire. Now Australia was led by a gentleman in Bill Woodfull who refused to allow his team to retaliate in kind. He was battered from head to toe by the English bowlers and suffered so much from their attentions that his wife was to claim in later years that his death was due to the injuries received in this series.

The England team arrived in Adelaide on 10 January 1933. With unemployment in the area at thirty per cent there were a lot of people keen to watch the visitors at practice in the Adelaide Oval nets. Five thousand turned up to see them the next day which angered Jardine so much that he summoned Bill Jeanes to the ground and told him to close the gates and to exclude the public. This was the only time, before or after, that this has happened in Adelaide.

Jeanes already had enough on his plate regarding the England captain. A lengthy and detailed complaint concerning Douglas Jardine had been received from the Tasmanian president, the former Test player Charles Eady, who was now a member of the State's Legislative Assembly. The Tasmanians had been incensed by Jardine's whole attitude during the tourists' short visit to the island with further complaints being lodged by Colonel L. M. Mullen, chairman of the TCA; Douglas Green, the Tasmanian vice-captain, and the secretary R. J. Shield. The Board decided that their only action in this and other matters should be to pass copies on to the Marylebone Cricket Club.

The third Test started on 13 January and lasted for six days. The NSWCA annual report summed it up perfectly when it read: 'This match aroused greater feeling than probably any other Test match ever played. The injuries to Woodfull and Oldfield, the cable of protest by the Board of Control to the Marylebone Cricket Club, and various other incidents so worked on the feelings of the crowd that play throughout was marked by extraordinary scenes.'

England batted until the second morning, scoring 341 after being at one stage 30 for four. 'Tim' Wall claimed 5/72 and walked off in awe as Adelaide's record crowd of 50,962 looked on. The scenario that followed is well known. The Adelaide crowd's anger was provoked initially by Jardine's decision to move his men into the (legside) bodyline trap after Woodfull had been hit a stunning blow in the chest by Larwood. The Australian captain then later rebuked the England team manager, Pelham Warner, when he went into the dressing-room to express his sympathy, and Woodfull also complained at length to the Board members at the ground.

For a man like Woodfull to complain was significant. The Board members present consulted their colleagues and, on a majority, sent a cable to Lord's protesting about the 'bodyline' tactics. They did, however, make a fundamental error in their draft by including the word 'unsportsmanlike'. It severely exacerbated the situation. You can call an Englishman pretty well anything, but to question his sporting attitude is the worst offence imaginable. Lord's picked on the word and cables flew between the MCC and the Board.

Diplomats and politicians became involved in the fuss even to the extent of a serious rift in relations between the two countries. Australia, as a nation, was too much in debt – in all senses – to Britain to call a number of bluffs and in the end had to back down. It was the old colonial story once again – 'We can rape, loot and pillage you, but don't call us unsporting in the process.'

The match went on. Bert Oldfield retired hurt with a fractured skull, Ponsford top-scored with 85 runs and the most bruises, and Australia reached 222. Right to the end of the innings, with the crowd baying for his blood, Jardine kept the bodyline field. England's second innings of 412 was an excellent display of batting considering that the pitch was deteriorating all the time. In the end Australia needed 532 to win, an impossible task. Woodfull carried his bat for 73 as England won by 338 runs.

Behind the scenes activity intensified between the Tests with Jardine saying that the fourth Test would not be played unless the Board of Control made a complete retraction of their claims. How a touring captain could get away with Jardine's attitudes and threats does not say much for his senior management colleague, Pelham Warner.

After further government intervention, the Board withdrew the offending word. This satisfied Jardine but did nothing to lessen the animosity among the players. The England captain was loathed by the Australians and even sixty years later mention of the name can bring a look of utter disdain to the face of Don Bradman.

In Brisbane in the fourth Test Woodfull won the toss and batted in intense heat with Australia looking to be in a good position at the end of play with the score on 251 for three. On a lifeless pitch in front of a total crowd of 93,143 – a figure never again reached – the score finished on 340. Run-making was slow and laborious with England scoring 35 runs an hour. The tourists gained a 16-run first-innings lead and after Australia's second innings of 175, the total needed to win the game and the Ashes was just 160.

Eddie Paynter won the match for England with a six on the

same day as Archie Jackson died in nearby Ingarfield Hospital, aged twenty-three. The train which took both teams south for the final Test in Sydney also carried Jackson's body. He was given one of Sydney's biggest funerals with a mile-long cortege. The pall-bearers were Woodfull, Richardson, Bradman, Kippax, Oldfield and Ponsford.

Woodfull won the toss for the fourth time in the series on 23 February 1933. Even though the rubber had been won, Jardine persisted with a bodyline attack, but yet again it was the overall batting which decided the match, not the intimidatory bowling. Australia scored 435 to which England replied with 454, Wally Hammond 101 and Harold Larwood, as a night-watchman, a Test-best 98 in what was to be his final appearance for his country. Other than a stand of 115 for the second wicket between Woodfull (67) and Bradman (71), the Australians' 182 was another poor batting display. England hit off the necessary runs to win by eight wickets and the series by four matches to one.

There were, however, certain unsavoury off-shoots from the series. In Adelaide the University team adopted bodyline for a District match against Glenelg with SACA banning the practice at their Cricket Committee meeting on 15 February. In Sydney, junior cricketers, particularly those who played in the Centennial Park leagues, saw an alarming rise in head injuries. The VCA took quick action, while the Board acted with quite amazing haste.

During 1933 Aubrey Oxlade, the Board's vice-chairman who had relinquished the chairmanship in 1930 and regained it in 1933, came to play an increasingly prominent role in the Board's dealings with the Marylebone Cricket Club over bodyline. At the NSWCA's meeting in April he said that unless the 'canker' of bodyline was removed no Australian team would visit England in 1934. Oxlade was speaking during the discussion of a resolution, later carried, which said: 'That this Association considers bodyline bowling is against the best interests of the game and urges all affiliated and recognised associations and clubs to discourage it'.

On 20 June Oxlade wrote to Board chairman Allen Robertson: 'I am fully of the opinion that under no consideration should the tour of our team in England be abandoned', and went on to suggest the bluff and bluster needed to try and get bodyline outlawed. The real reason appeared to come from the former Board secretary, and now NSWCA executive member, Syd Smith. At the annual meeting of the St George Cricket Club he was asked if a team would go to England the following year. 'It has to go,' he replied. 'We cannot afford, from an Empire point of view, to allow the Tests to be abandoned. They mean more than cricket. They mean friendships between England, Australia, South Africa, New Zealand and the West Indies.'

That was the crunch. The concern about the Empire. When Oxlade took over the chairmanship from Robertson in September 1933 the 1934 tour still lay in question. Cables went back and forth from England to Australia until the break came. Australia confirmed the tour on 14 December following which Lord's hinted that bodyline would not be used again. Under no circumstance would the English admit wrong-doing. They never did. And most certainly not to colonial cousins.

The States acted more quickly. At the Interstate Conference of 23 September 1933, South Australia introduced the following motion, intended to apply to Sheffield Shield matches:

> Any ball delivered which, in the opinion of the umpire at the bowler's end, is bowled at the batsman with intent to intimidate or injure him, shall be considered unfair, and 'no-ball' shall be called and the bowler notified of the reason. If the offence be repeated by the same bowler in the same innings, he shall be immediately instructed by the umpire to cease bowling, and the over shall be regarded as completed. Such bowler shall not again be permitted to bowl during the course of the innings then in progress.

The law had a wider application than the Sheffield Shield. Western Australia, Victoria and Tasmania had already indicated their support for it, and Queensland did so on the day, but New South Wales were implacably opposed. They had not applied it to Grade cricket, and New South Wales officials, supported by prominent umpires, regarded it as a 'mind-reader's' law, being impractical and perhaps leading to regrettable incidents. But because theirs was a lone voice of dissent, the motion was carried.

Whatever one's thoughts on the 1932–33 England tour it certainly provided a financial windfall for the State associations. The tourists had been watched by 1,278,056 spectators who paid £100,682 in admission charges and goodness knows what else on refreshments and souvenirs at the grounds.

What with all the fuss over the tour, the Sheffield Shield competition took second place. New South Wales won yet again but the star performance came on 3 February 1933 in Sydney when South Australia's 'Tim' Wall took the bowling honours. NSW had batted first and at lunch were 87 for two. As *Wisden* reported: 'After lunch Wall's fast bowling was almost unplayable. Fingleton, McCabe, Rowe and Cummins were sent back in one over without a run being scored, and Wall took all ten wickets for 36 runs – eight for five runs after the interval and six clean-bowled. The pitch gave him little assistance, but a stiff breeze helped him swing the ball.' Wall's analysis was 12.4 overs, 2 maidens,

36 runs, 10 wickets. He was the first player to take ten wickets in a Shield innings, a feat which, until that time had been accomplished on only one other occasion in Australian first-class cricket, by George Giffen for Australia against The Rest in Sydney in 1884. Wall was a schoolmaster by profession, principally at St Peter's College, one of South Australia's top public schools. As a fast bowler he had a long flowing approach and a vigorous kicking action as he neared the crease. Altogether he played eighteen times for Australia, and toured England in 1930 and 1934. He retired from first-class cricket in 1936. He suffered much from depression and died by his own hand, his third attempt, at the age of seventy-seven in 1981.

The Australian winter of 1933 offered a chance for the game of cricket to recover after the traumas of the previous season. Testimonial matches were being arranged for the benefit of six cricketers: Herbie Collins, Charlie Kelleway and Tommy Andrews of New South Wales; Don Blackie and Bert Ironmonger, Victoria; and Ernest Jones, the South Australian fast bowler.

Jones' case was a particularly sad one. In late 1932 Clem Hill, who was the link between the old cricketers and SACA, had informed the committee that all was not well with Ernie Jones' financial situation. Hill took a great interest in the old players' welfare and made sure that as many as possible knew of invitations for various Association functions.

At Christmas 1932 Jones was retired from his employment and granted a pension of 32 shillings a week. With his rent at 11s. and a sick wife to look after, life was very hard for him. On 27 February the SACA agreed 'to approve of immediate assistance' and 'to agree to help meet the expenses of his wife's illness and to supplement Jones' pension by £1 per week'.

On 2 March, in his small artisan dwelling in the south-west corner of Adelaide, Jones was visited by SACA officials. He discussed with them his financial situation which had been totally depleted by medical expenses for his wife. Jones was then told that SACA was going to award him a testimonial the following season and that, in the meantime, the Association would meet all of his wife's medical expenses, which would be considered as an advance payment on any monies raised for him. Various fund-raising activities and the gate from the match against NSW saw the total raised just exceed £1000. Ernie Jones' outstanding debts of £80 were paid off and some shrewd investments saw Jones paid an amount of £7 per month for the rest of his life.

The 1933–34 domestic season saw Don Bradman head the batting once again with 1192 runs at 132.44, but it was Victoria who won their first Shield for three years. A tour of New Zealand had been in the planning stages for some time and the party was due to leave in early February 1934 for an eight-week visit. The original captain chosen was Vic Richardson, with Keith Rigg as vice-captain, but when the Board of Control announced that pay for the tour was fifteen shillings a day, players started to drop out.

The New Zealand Cricket Council had assumed all was well following the visit which their president, Arthur Donnelly, made to Melbourne to attend the Board meeting held on 29 December 1932. Donnelly requested, and was granted, the Board's approval for Australian tours to his country 'in 1933–34 and subsequent seasons', and 'that Australian teams touring New Zealand should be international teams but his Council would like each team to contain a few first-class players and would greatly appreciate the arrangement of such a tour in the 1933–34 season'.

What the NZCC did not want was a team of 'has-beens' along with club cricketers who would never make the grade. Following ten days of alterations, Donnelly stated that the NZCC, frustrated by 'daily cablegrams regarding changes in the team' and fearing a heavy financial loss, had cancelled the tour. The Sydney *Daily Telegraph* claimed: 'The whole affair has been a sorry one due in no small measure to the policy of the Australian Board of Control'. The *Labour Daily* thundered: 'The Board has shown a deplorable lack of vision, a total disregard of its duties to the game in the sister dominion, and rank parsimony in its attitude to the players'.

The New Zealand press had a field day: 'New Zealand Council Tells Australians Not To Come', said a headline in the *Auckland Star*. In the story Donnelly spoke of a 'budgeted loss of about £500 on the tour' and 'complaints from affiliated associations about the amounts of guarantees asked of them'. Finally, with the Australian defections, the estimated loss doubled.

Within two years of making his debut for New South Wales, Don Bradman was receiving star treatment from both press and public. The 'Bradman Factor' saw gate receipts nearly double for matches in which he played. He was worth thousands of pounds to the Association each year, yet in the 1933–34 season he was earning just ten shillings for each Sheffield Shield match in Sydney plus a few extra shillings to compensate for loss of salary.

Since 1931 Bradman had made it clear that he was prepared to leave NSW in order to better himself. He considered many offers but realised that, for the time being, he should stay in Sydney. He was under contract to the Sydney *Sun* newspaper; radio station 2UE, and the gentlemen's outfitters F. J. Palmer & Co. However, all of these contracts ended on 1 February 1934, and with nothing substantial in prospect he decided to look elsewhere.

Recently discovered documents, held in Adelaide under lock and key for nearly sixty years, reveal what made Bradman change States and go to live in South Australia. The cause was Vic Richardson and from not long afterwards until his death in 1969, there was an almost paranoid hatred of Bradman by Richardson and, through him, by his extended family.

During the period 1926 to 1933, the South Australian Cricket Association had become more and more anxious at the off-field activities of Vic Richardson. A group of players, whose ringleaders were the Test cricketers, Phillip Lee and 'Jack' Nitschke, plus a bodyline series twelfth man, Bert Tobin, were like acolytes in a number of nefarious activities which sent Adelaide's rumour-mill humming.

The catalyst was the third bodyline Test in January 1933 when the SACA finally realised that they had lost control of their players and that drastic action had to be taken. The question was: who is tougher than Richardson? The name which came to their minds was Don Bradman.

Discussions were held in private and two important decisions were made. First of all, the Association would adopt a policy of virtually buying players from other States and let them play on a quasi-professional basis. Naturally the SACA would not pay them. Goodness, no. They would, instead, give money to the players' new employers so that it could be honestly denied that the new recruits were being paid for playing cricket. Secondly, the tough uncompromising Harry Hodgetts – a long-standing Board member – would quietly seek out Bradman to discover his reaction to a move south.

Bradman was receptive to Hodgett's overtures and a meeting was arranged for when the NSW team arrived in Adelaide on 14 December 1933 to play their Sheffield Shield match against South Australia. In the greatest secrecy Bradman met the four heavyweights of the SACA: Bernard Scrymgour, Roy Middleton, Harry Blinman and Harry Hodgetts, with Bill Jeanes in attendance. He was told what the situation was of the game and the players in South Australia and could he clean it up?

After receiving Bradman's assurance the Committee formally convened and passed a resolution which read: 'That this Association would be justified in endeavouring to secure Bradman's services, and to achieve that objective to substantially subsidise any remuneration he could otherwise obtain'. Scrymgour suggested the figure should be up to £500 per annum but the former Test cricketer and current junior coach, Joe Travers, disagreed. He no doubt foresaw the cricketing benefit of bringing Bradman to South Australia. Cricket had been falling off in popularity amongst youth as tennis became the new popular sport. With Bradman in the State, surely cricket would regain its rightful place? Travers moved 'to subsidise his salary for a term of five years at the rate of up to £750 per annum'. Carried unanimously.

Scrymgour also announced at the meeting 'that it was understood that C. L. Badcock, a Tasmanian player, was desirous of coming over to the mainland to improve his cricket . . . and had a preference for South Australia'.

The arrangements for Bradman and Badcock then went hand-in-hand, with Harry Hodgetts involved in both cases. He left Adelaide on New Year's Eve and arrived in Launceston on 2 January 1934 (following Badcock's superb 274 for Tasmania against Victoria the previous day) to meet Badcock and his lawyer Harold Bushby (who was the Tasmanian delegate on the Board of Control). 'Jack' Badcock, as he was always known, agreed to give South Australia a first refusal, but he was holding off on any decision until after the proposed Australian tour of New Zealand. When that was called off Badcock entered into a formal agreement with SACA.

By this time Harry Hodgetts had offered Don Bradman a position in his stockbroking firm. In addition Bernard Scrymgour, who was a stickler for keeping matters 'correct', wrote to Aubrey Oxlade, chairman of the NSWCA, advising him of the negotiations taking place to secure Bradman for South Australia. Oxlade replied thanking SACA 'for their candour'.

Don Bradman nominally started his employment with H. W. Hodgetts & Co., sharebrokers of Grenfell Street, Adelaide, on 14 March 1934, but in reality it was intended he would start at the conclusion of the 1934 tour of England. Bradman met with the SACA Finance Committee on 15 March to finalise his agreement. His salary would be £700 per annum (£500 when out of Australia).

When the planning started for the 1934 Australian tour of England, the Australian Board resolved to ask the Marylebone Cricket Club if 'Kennington Oval could be removed from the list of Test match grounds'. The Board had received continually bad reports on the state of the ground from the tour managers of 1921, 1926 and 1930 and now felt it time to make their views known. The reply from Lord's, as expected, was negative.

The selectors who met to choose the touring team were Charles Dolling (SA), Bill Woodfull (Victoria), and 'Chappie' Dwyer (NSW). They announced their side on 31 January 1934 to the Board meeting in Sydney. Woodfull was unanimously confirmed as captain. For the deputy's position, Bradman won the job by a majority of the three over Kippax who, however, became the third selector.

The chosen team showed that the selectors were looking for new talent with Len Darling, Bromley, Barnett, Brown, Chipperfield, Ebeling and Fleetwood-Smith having played only three Tests between them. The others were Grimmett, McCabe, Oldfield, O'Reilly, Ponsford and Wall.

Before their departure the tourists played three warm-up matches. In Launceston they could not have failed to be impressed by Jack Badcock's century against them, while Woodfull, for the Australians, scored 126 in Launceston and 124 in Hobart. A draw in Perth, in a rain-affected match, saw Woodfull's total reach 295 runs in three innings. It was an encouraging sign.

The team left Fremantle on the SS *Orford* and enjoyed a relaxing and sociable voyage to England broken only by the usual match in Ceylon. In fact the time was spent so socially in one instance that it had cricketing repercussions eighteen months hence.

The fixture in Colombo was, as always, eagerly awaited by the local Association who were far from disappointed by the play. Ernie Bromley scored 80, an innings which saw the *Islander* remark: 'It was compared to that of Frank Woolley at his best'. The bowler who impressed most was the fast-medium Hans Ebeling who took 3/24 in ten overs in a drawn game.

When the players arrived in England they were forbidden to discuss anything with the press, let alone bodyline. Bert Oldfield even refused to tell newsmen whether he had been seasick in the Bay of Biscay.

Pre-tour practice took place at an indoor cricket school run by their former colleague, Alan Fairfax, now domiciled in England. But much had been going on in the previous months. Douglas Jardine had announced from India, where he was leading England's team on a successful tour, that he was retiring and would report on the 1934 tour from the pressbox for the London *Evening Standard*. Harold Larwood had been made the scapegoat for the bodyline policy by the powers-that-be at Lord's and refused to make himself available for Test cricket. He continued to play until 1938 when the injuries he suffered on the bodyline tour became too great for him to bear. Ironically, in 1949, he was to emigrate to Australia.

At various pre-tour functions, especially those held in the closeted clubs of London, Woodfull was given assurances that bodyline would not be used against them. The County Cricket Advisory Committee had made the decision six months earlier but only now were the Australians being informed.

In a number of interviews before the first match at Worcester

Woodfull said that his star bowlers were Grimmett and O'Reilly. As it turned out both Grimmett and O'Reilly each took 109 wickets but a pleasant surprise was 'Chuck' Fleetwood-Smith who claimed 106 victims with his left-arm googlies and 'chinamen'. The Australian captain also made reference to the strength of his batting line-up and how correct he was, for six players passed the thousand-run mark. McCabe made 2078 runs, with eight of the 33 hundreds scored by the Australians in first-class matches, with a highest score of 240 against Surrey. Bradman was next with seven centuries in his 2020 runs with a county best of 206 at Worcester. Ponsford made 1784 runs, Bill Brown 1308, Woodfull 1268 and Len Darling 1022.

There were ten matches around the country (five wins, five draws) before the first Test at Trent Bridge, Nottingham, starting on 8 June 1934. The Australians introduced two new batsmen to Test cricket, Bill Brown and Arthur Chipperfield. It was the latter who would get the attention, and sympathy, as he was dismissed for 99 directly after a nervous lunch break on the second day. In spite of that Australia reached 374 and then 273 for eight declared against England's 268 (Grimmett 5/81, O'Reilly 4/75) and 141 (Grimmett 3/39, O'Reilly 7/54). Interestingly enough, this was to prove to be Australia's only victory against England in the period 1928–38 which was gained without Bradman getting a century – he made just 29 and 25 in the match.

Woodfull's fears about the fielding ability of his side proved unnecessary as, from the first time they played, Brown, Chipperfield, Bromley and Darling were superb with Bromley's throwing a particular delight. A win and a draw took the tourists to the second Test at Lord's a fortnight later.

This game became known as 'Verity's match' as the Yorkshireman's bowling triumph on the last day gave England their only victory against Australia at Lord's in this century. All seemed straightforward for the Friday and Saturday. The England captain, Bob Wyatt, won the toss, chose to bat, and saw the wicketkeeper Leslie Ames (120) and Maurice Leyland (109) both score centuries in a total of 440. The Australians in reply were 192 for two, Bill Brown 103 not out, at the close of the second day.

Then came weekend rain and by Monday morning the uncovered pitch was ready for the deadly slow left-arm bowling of Hedley Verity. He proceeded to take 14 wickets for 80 runs in the day including the last seven in an hour. Australia had no answer to the conditions, falling for 284 (Verity 7/61) and 118 (Verity 8/43). A sidelight on this performance was that it led to the British Broadcasting Corporation allowing its radio commentator, Howard Marshall, a scorer/assistant at all further Tests.

England's victory by an innings and 38 runs did not seem to affect the tourists who, after two further provincial wins, played out a draw in the third Test in Manchester. As *Wisden* records: 'From first to last the sun blazed down, the heat being at times almost unbearable'. England made 627 for nine declared (O'Reilly 7/189) to which Australia replied with 491 (McCabe 137). The sides then just played out time.

Victory over Derbyshire and a draw with Yorkshire took the Australians to Headingley for the fourth Test. England batted first but could make only 200 on a pitch which appeared to be acceptable. Then came trouble as Australia fell to 39 for three at stumps with Ponsford still there on 22. Next day, Saturday, was a joy for lovers of good batting as 455 runs were scored for the loss of just one wicket.

Ponsford and Bradman added 388 for the fourth wicket until, near the close, Ponsford, on 181, struck his own wicket trying to cut Verity. Bradman remained on 271 at the weekend with a huge Monday crowd turning up to see if he could beat his own world record there of 334 in 1930. Bill Bowes, on his home ground, thought otherwise and bowled Bradman for 304. He had hit two sixes and 43 fours in a stay of 430 minutes.

The visitors' total moved on to 584 on the third day to which England replied with 188 for four. Heavy rain that night upset all predictions and after two more wickets fell on the final morning another storm ended the match. There followed five first-class draws and a couple of minor matches before the climax of the series at The Oval started on 18 August.

A week earlier, however, had seen the first real unpleasantness of the tour. Bradman was in a nursing home, recovering from a torn thigh muscle sustained in the fourth Test, while the rest of the side went to play Nottinghamshire. The Trent Bridge crowd were vocal from the start believing that the Australians had been responsible for the criticism of their hero Larwood – who diplomatically did not play in the match – and for complaining about bodyline.

The noise grew stronger when Bill Voce bowled numerous short-pitched balls, with five men on the leg side, four of them in the leg-trap where they could pick up deflections. Woodfull made 81 and Voce took 8/66, all of them caught. At the end of play Bill Woodfull told the Nottinghamshire secretary, Dr Gould, that the agreement under which Australia were touring England had been broken. Woodfull is reputed to have said that the county committee must make a decision, but if Voce took the field when Australia batted a second time the tourists would return to London without finishing the match.

Voce suddenly developed shin-soreness and took no further part in the match which was drawn. The local committee then apologised to

Lord's for Voce's bowling, but suffered their own traumas during the winter when a packed members' meeting condemned their action.

The Oval Test was scheduled to be played to a conclusion but it lasted only four days. The pitch was lifeless but Woodfull's winning of the toss and the Australians' batting display saw victory in sight very early on. Bill Brown (10) departed when the score was 21, after which Ponsford and Bradman scored at the rate of around 80 runs an hour. Wyatt's confusing field placings did not assist his bowlers as the Australian pair made 451 in 316 minutes before Bradman was caught behind for 244, which included a six and 32 fours.

Ponsford was finally out on the second day having been at the crease while 574 runs were scored. His 266, made in 460 minutes with 28 boundaries, was a fitting finale in his final Test. The innings reached 701 to which England really had no reply. Woodfull did not enforce the follow-on and finally left England needing 707 runs to win. With Grimmett taking 5/64 the Australians won by the huge margin of 562 runs and for the second time in four years regained the Ashes on their captain's birthday.

The tour concluded with four top matches. Against Sussex at Hove Alan Kippax scored 250 in a brilliant, stylish display. The tour finished with a minor match against the North of Scotland in mid-September. The Eighteenth Australians had lost only one match – a Test – throughout the whole tour and had overcome constant setbacks through illness and accident. Ernie Bromley had developed appendicitis on the eve of the final Test but worse was to follow. Bradman collapsed with a gangrenous appendix and, following an emergency operation, lay near death for several days. The cricket world held its breath as the game's greatest living hero fought for survival. As the post-operative period grew longer so the threat of peritonitis receded. Bradman, now joined by his wife, convalesced in the south of France and, on his return to Australia, went to his father-in-law's farm at Mittagong so missing all of the 1934–35 cricket season. However, his recovery was remarkable and by mid-1935 he was ready again for action.

The rest of the team had left Tilbury on the SS *Orontes* on 29 September 1934, arriving back in Australia just in time for their new season. But the opening pair of Bill Woodfull and Bill Ponsford had announced their retirement from first-class cricket. The Victorian Cricket Association arranged a Testimonial match for them and in the 1935 annual report stated that 'it was very well patronised and was a fitting send-off to two great cricketers for Australia and Victoria'.

In his last match, played between 16–20 November 1934, Bill Woodfull scored 111 and even took a wicket. That weekend he had been informed from Government House that 'His Majesty, the King, has conferred the honour of a knighthood on William Maldon Woodfull for services to the game of cricket'. The citation recorded his 35 Tests, 25 as captain, and hinted at his superb handling of matters during the bodyline crisis.

Woodfull's immediate reaction was to decline the honour. Following Dave Gregory, Woodfull was the second Australian cricket captain to refuse a title. In later years he revealed: 'Had I been awarded it for being an educationalist, then I would have accepted it. But under no circumstances would I accept it for playing cricket.'

# 18

# A Feast of runs and crowds

Suddenly everything in Australian cricket seemed quiet. Woodfull and Ponsford had retired: Bradman was recovering from illness. The 1934–35 season was virtually anonymous. Fleetwood-Smith (63) and Grimmett (58) took far more wickets than anyone else while on New Year's Day Queensland's Charles Andrews (253) scored the Shield's only double-century. Victoria easily claimed the domestic trophy by winning five of their six Shield encounters.

The State of Victoria had celebrated its centenary in 1934 when the Duke of Gloucester paid an official visit to the main events which were held at the Melbourne Cricket Ground. More than 80,000 people crammed into the stands and outer ground which forced the committee to consider expanding the facilities. In late 1935 it announced a plan for rebuilding the outer areas which would increase the accommodation to over 100,000 people. The new stand was to be 1250 feet in length with changing rooms for footballers and cricketers, refreshment booths, casualty rooms and seating space for 35,000. The cost was anticipated as £100,000. Although the club was still paying off the new members' pavilion, it planned to raise the extra funds by increasing membership from 5200 to 6200. The stand was finished in January 1937 and lasted until 1990 when it was demolished to make way for an even grander edifice.

At the beginning of the 1935–36 season an England team en route to New Zealand played six matches on their way from west to east around the country. Led by the Surrey captain, Errol Holmes, the visitors drew against Western Australia and Victoria, defeated South Australia, Queensland and an Australian XI, and suffered a ten-wicket defeat at the hands of a virtual New South Wales second eleven.

For many years the South African Cricket Association had been trying to persuade the Australian Board to make a full tour of their country. There had previously been only three brief visits by Australian teams, all on their way home from England, in 1902, 1919 and 1921. Eventually the Board relented and negotiations started to take place.

The South Africans held a meeting at the Wanderers Club in

Johannesburg on 3 January 1935 to discuss the finances of the impending Australian visit and were quite happy with anticipated receipts, 'so long as Bradman is in the team'. Their joy was confirmed on 29 April when the side was announced with Bradman as captain. Communications between the Board and their star player confirmed Bradman's fitness and willingness to tour. Harold Rowe of Western Australia was to manage the side which included Sievers, of Victoria, who was a replacement for Hans Ebeling who had withdrawn for business reasons.

Suddenly, on 8 August 1935, came the news that Bradman had withdrawn. The Board were upset by this because, originally, Bradman had been omitted by the selectors and then reinstated. However, in the way of Australian cricket politics another South Australian, Vic Richardson, was appointed captain in his stead, but Bradman's withdrawal had nothing to do with his health, nor with the game of cricket. It was forced upon him by an outside authority and was the aftermath from a situation which occurred on the 1934 tour of England.

However, Bradman was fit and willing to lead South Australia in domestic matches and in this capacity he replaced Vic Richardson, but those who appointed Bradman had no intention that the captaincy should be removed from him on Richardson's return, not the least of these being Bradman's new employer, Harry Hodgetts. Dick Whitington, the journalist-cricketer, has related how, at a farewell function in Adelaide to Richardson and Grimmett just before they left for South Africa in 1935, Hodgetts declared what a fitting tribute it was that Richardson be appointed captain of Australia, 'at the end of his career'. At this Clem Hill, bristling with anger and indignation, exclaimed: 'End of his career! Bunkum!'

By then Richardson had already been told the score by certain members of the SACA committee, so that the new Australian captain knew it was the end of the line for him as far as South Australia was concerned, because he would never accept to play State cricket under Bradman's captaincy. Richardson went to South Africa spawning hatred of Bradman, and found a number of like minds among his touring colleagues.

Little did the other South Australian tourist, Clarrie Grimmett, realise that his 92 victims in all matches would also be his last for Australia. On his return, and although he remained playing first-class cricket up until 1941, he was 'dumped'. Bradman held the view that he was no longer good enough for Test cricket and he preferred the over-rated Frank Ward who toured England in 1938. Grimmett's spin partner in South Africa, Bill O'Reilly, claimed 95 wickets in what he described as 'the happiest tour I ever went on'.

And what a tour it was. Of the sixteen first-class matches, 13 were won – ten of them by an innings – and the remaining three were drawn. At the start, Natal, Western Province and Transvaal were easily dismissed before the first Test took place in Durban. In four days South Africa were beaten by nine wickets as Arthur Chipperfield (109) scored his only Test century; Stan McCabe made 149 and the spin trio of Grimmett, Fleetwood-Smith and O'Reilly took eighteen of the Springboks' wickets.

Both teams moved straight to the Old Wanderers Ground in Johannesburg where rain caused a draw as Australia was making a startling bid for victory. On the newly laid turf pitch, South Africa made a slow, grafting, 157 to which Australia replied with 250. Then the Springboks attacked with Dudley Nourse hammering the tourists' bowling to all parts of the ground for 231, then South Africa's highest individual score in Test cricket. His innings included 36 fours and came in eleven minutes short of five hours.

All out for 491, South Africa had left Australia to score 399 for victory. At the end of the third day the score was 85 for one with Stan McCabe on 59, made in just 43 minutes. By lunch the next day he had moved on to 138 having lost Jack Fingleton (40) when the score was 194. With typical highvelt stormclouds brewing the Australians hit out after the break. In the end the light grew so bad that the umpires called the players off for their own safety. By then McCabe was on 189 and Australia was still 125 runs short of what would have been a quality victory. Ten minutes later a thunderstorm ended the match.

The itinerary had not been planned with the players' needs in mind for straightaway they had to take the train to Cape Town. Rain ruined New Year's Day for the 5000 spectators inside the Newlands ground but play did start on time next day after Richardson had won the toss from his opposite number, Herbie Wade. It took Bill Brown (121) and Jack Fingleton (112) only three hours to run up 233 for the first wicket, which proved to be the decisive partnership of the match.

Richardson declared overnight at 362 for eight as torrential rain cascaded down on the third morning. Wade did not want to resume play but the umpires insisted on a start forty minutes before tea. The inevitable happened, and South Africa were all out for 102 (Grimmett 5/32) and were forced to follow-on. Although the pitch was rolled between innings it only saved South Africa for a short while from defeat. Grimmett (5/56) claimed ten wickets in the match to pass S. F. Barnes of England and become Test cricket's leading wicket-taker.

The social life of the tour was exceptional with the players fêted at every opportunity. They now had six weeks of easy cricket around South Africa and Rhodesia: in East London against Border, Bill O'Reilly took 8/73 and 5/32; at the Ramblers Club in Bloemfontein against Orange Free State, O'Reilly (4/38 and 5/34) and Grimmett (5/35 and 5/67) totally confused the locals. Four days later, in Johannesburg, O'Reilly took 7/54 as yet another innings victory loomed. Keeping up the good work at the DeBeers stadium in Kimberley, the Griqualand West batsmen could not fathom O'Reilly who took 7/88 and 6/54 and in the return against Western Province he took 6/35 and 6/64.

Grimmett and O'Reilly provided a fascinating contrast. Whereas Grimmett had a short, jerky run with an almost round-arm action and bowled his leg-breaks slowly, O'Reilly's run-up and action formed an ungraceful whirl of arms and legs – he was as tall as Grimmett was short – and bowled at a far greater pace and with abnormal bounce. Their partnership was a cause of great jealousy back in Australia as news came through of their success. Why this should be so was initially a puzzle to both men, although in later years they would claim that, had they been less successful, their careers would in all probability have been extended.

The fourth Test in Johannesburg lasted for only two days with 13 wickets falling on the first day and 17 on the second as Australia won by an innings and 184 runs. The South Africans were simply outplayed as their scores of 157 and 98 attest. Bill O'Reilly had 5/20 from 21 overs in the Springboks' first innings but the bowling honours went to Clarrie Grimmett: 3/70, then 7/40, saw him become the first bowler to take over 200 Test wickets.

While Jack Fingleton was scoring his third Test century in a row (112, 108 and 118) in Durban, the fifth Test was a fitting finale for the skills of Grimmett. He was claiming ten or more wickets in a match for the third successive time, with his 7/100 and 6/73 taking his series tally to 44 wickets at an average of 14.59. Grimmett's final Test career figures of 216 wickets at 24.21 was a record until Alec Bedser overtook it in 1953. The match itself was another innings victory to Australia who took the series four–nil.

When the South African press stated that the Australian team was the finest group of cricketers yet to have toured the country there was no disagreement. Vic Richardson's leadership had a flair which would not be seen again until the advent of Richie Benaud a quarter of a century later. The spirit Richardson aroused was responsible for each player's raised standards. For all his faults the captain's air of larrikinism* pulled a diverse group in the same direction.

*A larrikin, in Australian terminology, is basically a non-conformist; not a law-breaker but someone who could, at times, be distinctly naughty. Origin, *c.* 1890.

While the South African tour was in progress, the Board of Control had reluctantly agreed that a team be allowed to play in India and Ceylon. The Board had been asked a number of times by various Indian authorities to allow a tour to go ahead. Heavy pressure in 1934 saw a strong note sent to India by Board members completely ignorant of the standard or type of play on the sub-continent. Then a request by the Rajputana Cricket Club to tour in 1935–36 to play club matches received a 'it is regretted that the application cannot be entertained' brush-off.

The Board now looked askance at a letter dated 2 January from Frank Tarrant, an itinerant Australian cricket professional and businessman who wrote from the Guest House, Patiala, Punjab, Northern India. The Board members knew about Ranjitsinhji, Duleepsinhji and the Nawab of Pataudi and were fascinated by the struggle between the Maharajadhiraj of Patiala and the Maharajkumar of Vizianagram for the control of Indian cricket. Ironically, Bill Jeanes received Tarrant's letter on 26 January, the day Indians were forced to celebrate 147 years of European settlement. However the signs were not good for Tarrant, an outstanding all-rounder for Victoria and latterly Middlesex, who had served as cricket aide to both the Maharaja of Cooch-Behar and the Maharaja of Patiala and had made occasional appearances in Bombay's Quadrangular competition since 1915. He had also umpired in India's first two home Test matches against England in 1933–34.

Tarrant's letter, received by Bill Jeanes on 26 January, was felt by the Board to have breached protocol because it did not come directly from the Board of Control for Cricket in India (BCCI). It read:

> I should like to inform you that the Indian Cricket Board of Control has requested His Highness the Maharaja of Patiala to send me to Australia to select and bring a team of Australian cricketers to India for a three-month tour. Only about 16 matches are to be played.
>
> The entire financial responsibility will lie with me as the representative of His Highness, Maharaja of Patiala, who is financing the tour. I am herewith asking your permission to get together a side from the different states. I shall certainly not interfere in any way with your selection of the players for South Africa. There will be ample talent among the players who are left behind. It is planned that the team should arrive in Bombay on November 23 and leave again for home on February 23, 1936. As this tour will be a private concern there can be no chance of financial profit to the Board of Control. Remuneration to the different players will be settled personally by myself.

Please put this matter before your Board at your earliest convenience and send me a reply to my Australian address.

The Board delegates suggested that the letter was presumptuous and audacious and rejected it. Tarrant arrived at Port Adelaide on 2 March 1935 to find Bill Jeanes waiting for him with the news that the Board 'would not countenance his venture'. There was a chink in the Board's armour, however. Tarrant had persuaded Aubrey Oxlade of the benefits of the venture. Oxlade, a solicitor, was able to get his colleagues to give the venture their support subject to a number of harsh conditions. It took Tarrant five months before he could complete arrangements and even then the Victorian delegates vetoed suggested team members for whom they did not have to give any explanation. Such players, even retired ones, as Woodfull, Ponsford, Mailey (at forty-nine!), Gregory, Hornibrook and Kippax were all prevented from touring.

After months of in-fighting the Board was adamant that the word 'Australia' should not be used. On 6 September 1935 they ruled: 'The team must at all times be known as "The Maharajah of Patiala's Team of Australian Cricketers" ' and added: 'Under no circumstances must any Test match or any match designated a Test match or any match against All-India be played'.

The team was captained by Jack Ryder (aged 45) with Charlie Macartney (49) as vice-captain. Also included were Bert Ironmonger (52), Jack Ellis (45), Hunter Hendry (40), 'Hammy' Love (39), Ron Oxenham (44), Arthur Allsopp (27), Tom Leather (25), Ron Morrisby (20), Harry Alexander (30), Lisle Nagel (30), Frank Bryant (27), Wendell Bill (25) and Fred Mair (34). At the Board's insistence Tarrant could only select 'players who have retired and those not required for the Sheffield Shield competition'. After gathering in Melbourne, the players boarded the SS *Mongolia* on 8 October for an historic visit to the sub-continent during which 23 matches would be played of which 17 were first-class. The tourists – by now generally styled 'Australians' – won eleven, drew nine and lost three of their fixtures. Jack Ryder went out of the top level of the game with 1121 runs at an average of 48.74 while Queensland's Ron Oxenham took 101 wickets at 8.19 runs apiece.

The only match in Ceylon took place in Colombo over three days starting on 25 October 1935 when Oxenham claimed his career-best figures of 9/18 in the Ceylon first innings and Wendell Bill made the game's only century. After an innings victory the Australians sailed to Bombay where they were met formally and with speeches of greeting.

From that moment on, the Australians were feted wherever they travelled along the 13,000 miles of the remarkable Indian railways system. At Bombay they were each allocated one of a host of Hindu and Muslim bearers who would materialise whenever summoned and carry out all the duties their temporary masters desired. However there was one matter above all which won the hearts of the Indians, particularly the princes who lavished hospitality on their guests. As the Karachi correspondent of the *Associated Special Service* reported: 'The Australians have made it known that they will not take advantage of any club facilities offered by a social institution which does not accord to Indians the same status as to themselves'. This attitude, puzzling as it was to the Australian Board who were firmly for the 'White Australia' policy, resulted in the princes opening their homes and their hearts to the visitors.

Tarrant and the Australians were the outstanding success of the social season as indeed, at the same time, across the Indian Ocean, were Vic Richardson and his team in South Africa. Pity the keen amateurs and quasi-professionals going through the domestic season in Australia for 'ten bob' a day!

The early games of the tour at Rajkot, Jamnagar, Ahmedabad, Ajmer, Karachi, Poona and Bombay saw Ron Oxenham take five wickets or more in an innings on seven occasions including 7/31 and 7/13 against Central India. Ryder (139* and 101*), Bryant (155), Bill (107) and Macartney (106*) all hit centuries up to the first unofficial 'Test' played in Bombay over four days starting on 5 December 1935.

By giving names to the teams for the 'Tests', the Indians hoped to circumvent the Australian Board's ruling. The first match was officially His Highness The Maharaja of Patiala's Team of Australian Cricketers versus His Highness The Maharaja of Patiala's XI of All-India. To the newspapers it was All-India versus Australia and when such a title appeared in the Australian press letters were fired off to India by the Board secretary, Bill Jeanes, and the chairman Aubrey Oxlade.

Further letters followed to the Indian Board secretary, Anthony de Mello, 'calling attention to the reports and asking if the names of the matches in question had been correctly reported'. De Mello did not reply: maybe he wondered if all the Australian Board had to worry about was the nomenclature of cricket matches?

India were outplayed but nonetheless put in a brave performance on the coir matting pitch. Lala Amarnath top-scored with a second innings 41 as India reached 163 in both innings. Ryder made 104 in 205 minutes with ten fours as the Australians reached 268, and a nine-wicket victory came on the final day.

In the matches up to the second 'Test' in Calcutta (staged on one of the days an official Test was being played in Cape Town by Vic Richardson's team) only Ron Morrisby's 119 at Nagpur stood out as members of the team went down with the various illnesses and ailments that often afflict visitors to the sub-continent. The 'Test' itself was a two-day affair ruined by rain and cricket politics, particularly when one of India's best cricketers, the quick bowler Amar Singh, watched the match from the stands. The Indians scored 48 and 127 to the Australians' 99 and 80 for two.

In Amritsar against Southern Punjab, between 'Tests', Ryder scored 115 and Oxenham's medium-pace claimed 3/40 and 7/14 as another innings victory was recorded. Then came the third 'Test' at Lahore against a new opposing captain in Wazir Ali, who had made his Test debut at Lord's in 1932. He was a good all-round cricketer, an attractive right-handed batsman and a medium-pace change bowler.

Wazir handled his team superbly and top-scored in both innings with 77 and 92. The crowds, which became larger with each passing day, gave encouragement to the splendid bowling of Baqa Jilani and Mahomed Nissar, and the superb boundary fielding of Bhaya. Ron Oxenham's leg injury reduced his effectiveness as India scored 149, and with no Oxenham in the second innings, India's 301 was a winning total. The Australians made 166 first time around but could not match the Indians' keenness and fell to defeat by 68 runs. As *The Hindu* reported: 'The atmosphere vibrated with triumphant joy'.

In Patiala two days later Wazir Ali scored 132 in a drawn provincial match in which Ron Morrisby scored 145, 'with his wonted nonchalance', and Wendell Bill 118. Then came a draw in Delhi in a match abandoned due to the death of the British Monarch. After this it was on to Secunderabad for an important fixture against the influential Moin-ud-Dowlah's selection.

It was, at last, a team of genuine Test strength to face the Australians and the Indians did not let their supporters down. Lala Amarnath claimed his century in ten minutes over two hours, being particularly hard on the bowling of the grade cricketers, Leather and Mair. He eventually went for 144 which contained 24 fours and left Hussain (73) and Palia (61*) to take the score to 413 for five before Vizianagram declared. There was little answer to the bowling of Amar Singh who took 4/51 and 6/36 as the Australians lost by an innings and 115 runs.

The low point of the tour came when Madras dismissed the tourists for just 47, who then surprised probably even themselves to win by one wicket following an unbeaten last-wicket stand of 70 between Leather and Oxenham. The pitch at Madras for the fourth and final 'Test' two days later was euphemistically described in *The Hindu* as one 'which did not favour the batsmen'. India started with 189, but were able to gain a first-innings lead of 27 thanks to Nissar's 5/61 and Amar Singh's 5/54. Charlie Macartney had 6/41 as India fell for 113 second time around, leaving the Australians

*(Above)* A gathering of old cricketers at a 1929 reunion: Vernon Ransford, Clem Hill, Monty Noble, Hugh Trumble, J.M. Gregory, Joe Darling, John Worrall, Warwick Armstrong, Peter McAlister; *(below)* The Australian team of 1930 arrives at Dover: standing from left, Kelly (manager), Woodfull (captain), Fairfax, McCabe, Hornibrook. *(Hulton-Deutsch)*

*(Above)* Adelaide Oval, third Test, 1932–33, of the 'Bodyline' series. The police comment on the day was that, if one spectator had jumped over the fence, a riot would have followed.

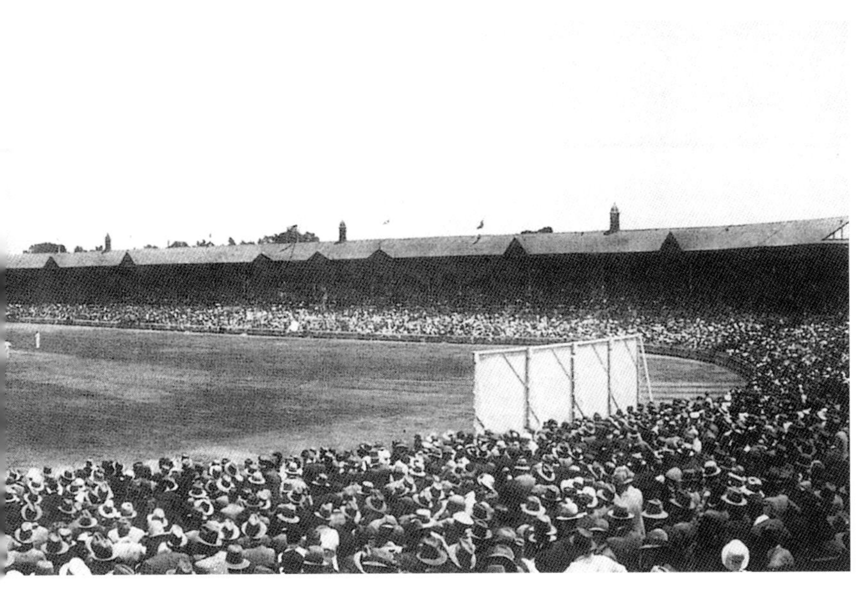

*(Below)*: *(left)* Woodfull struck a blow to the body; *(right)* Oldfield hit on the head.

*(Above left)* Australia's openers, Woodfull and Ponsford, here seen at Nottingham in 1930 *(Hulton-Deutsch)*. *(Above right)* Bradman 1930 *(Ken Kelly)*. *(Below)* Victor Richardson *(left)*; and Clarrie Grimmett, Australia's most-feared bowler at this time.

*(Above)* The Australian and England teams being photographed during the Lord's Test, 1938; *(below)* relaxation from cricket – Ted White, Don Bradman, Ernie McCormick and manager Bill Jeanes at golf, also in 1938 *(Hulton-Deutsch)*.

*(Above)* Bradman was in great form in England throughout the 1948 tour *(Sport and General)*; *(below)* Syd Webb, Syd Smith and Aubrey Oxlade, Sydney, 1952.

*(Above)* A typically swashbuckling stroke from Keith Miller.
*(Below)* As usual the 1953 team played their first match at Worcester: (back row) Hill, Hole, Benaud, G.A. Davies (manager), Miller, Ron Archer, Langley, McDonald; (seated) Craig, Morris, Hassett, Lindwall, De Courcy.

*(Above)* The Australian team for the fourth Test against West Indies, 1960–61; *(below)* the dramatic climax to that match was the stand between Mackay and Kline who resisted the West Indies in a last-wicket stand for 102 minutes to force a draw.

the apparently easy task of scoring 141 runs for victory and the series.

Jack Ryder held the top order together with an 80-minute innings of 41 but on his departure Nissar cleaned up the tail with 6/36. The Indians won by 33 runs so that the series finished all-square. After the match Ryder told *The Hindu*: 'We ourselves have been sadly handicapped due to illness and injuries but we have tried to do our best and we could not have done better'.

In his last column in *The Hindu*, Charlie Macartney wrote:

> It has been a hard tour but most enjoyable and our only regret is that we have not had our full complement from whom to choose our elevens. However, we have done our best to please and if we have succeeded in that we are happy. And maybe our work has been of some little instruction to some and if so then that will give us added pleasure.
>
> Goodbye, good friends in India, and thank you very much for all you have done to make our stay among you enjoyable.

In his final press conference Ryder fearlessly predicted that India would one day become a powerful and influential force in world cricket. At the same time he earnestly appealed to the Indian Board to make a commitment to eradicate matting pitches.

Tarrant, understandably relieved and delighted at the impressive beginnings to India-Australia cricket, remained in India. From the Motibagh Palace on 18 April 1936 he submitted the statement requested by the Australian Board who, on receipt, pulled it apart and demanded much irrelevant detailed information. Tarrant ignored the churlish letters they sent to him and it was not until January 1937 – and only then on the 'advice' of Marylebone Cricket Club president, Lord Somers – that the Board decided to: 'Remove Tarrant's line from the Agenda'.

Tarrant's reaction has never been recorded. He died in Melbourne in January 1951 some five years before Ian Johnson led the first official Australian team to India.

Domestically the 1935–36 season was dominated by Don Bradman who, forcibly kept in Australia, proved his worth for his new State, South Australia. He scored 1173 runs as his team claimed the Sheffield Shield for the first time in ten years. At Christmas, against Queensland in Adelaide, he scored 233 and, a week later in Melbourne, took the Victorian attack apart in making 357. One of South Australia's other imports, Jack Badcock, scored 325 in the return match against Victoria but it was an end-of-season fixture which produced the records.

Tasmania, trying hard but fairly unsuccessfully to raise their standards, won two home matches by overgenerous declarations against Victoria before venturing on to the mainland. Victoria scored 531 to win by an innings but in Adelaide the Tasmanians were hit for 688. Bradman and Ron Hamence (121 on his debut) put on 356 in only 181 minutes for the third wicket. Bradman went on to get 369 in 253 minutes with four sixes and 46 fours, and in the process he passed Clem Hill's record of 365 not out made for South Australia against New South Wales in 1900. Hill sent a telegram: 'Congratulations you little devil for breaking my record'.

At the Board of Control meeting held in Sydney on 23 April 1936, 'the Victorian Cricket Association forwarded for consideration a suggestion made by Monty Noble in connection with the New South Wales sesquicentenary celebrations'. Noble was one of a group who wanted an 'Imperial Team' – comprising players from England, South Africa, New Zealand and the West Indies – to visit the country and play a series of matches against Australia The Board would have none of it and told the VCA and Noble in no uncertain way. This resulted in a letter to Jeanes dated 20 May 1936 from the NSW minister in charge of the celebrations, Hon. John Dunningham, MLA. The minister urged the Board 'to earnestly consider a proposal to arrange an "Empire Cricket Match"', along the lines suggested by Noble. Dunningham received an equally sharp response.

The pressure was stepped up. On 17 June Hon. Michael Bruxner, the Deputy Premier of NSW, wrote to Aubrey Oxlade 'asking for reconsideration and reversal of its former decision'. Oxlade replied that the letter would be considered by the September Board meeting. Bruxner demanded an immediate answer which Oxlade refused.

On 10 September the Board sent a formal refusal which caused the NSW government to accuse it of not acting in the best interests of the game, nor that of Australia. The Federal government then became involved and on 29 October a formal letter was sent to Oxlade virtually demanding a positive decision. All expenses and organisation would be met by the NSW State government who 'were prepared to assume the whole financial responsibility of the undertaking'. Pressure was also put on the Board's NSW delegates who, at the meeting on 31 December, pleaded for a change of heart by their colleagues. It was of no use. The Victorians were certainly not going to assist NSW in any way and Harry Hodgetts and Roy Middleton said South Australia was not interested although their other delegate, Clem Hill, was. In retrospect it seems a disgraceful attitude for the Board to have taken, particularly in defying a State government in the way they did. Their autocratic ways put them, yet again, offside with people whose help and assistance were needed in a number of ways.

Australian cricket had survived the Depression in a far better way than might have been expected. Unemployment was falling rapidly and by the time the 1936–37 English tourists sailed on 12 September 1936, just under ten per cent of the Australian workforce was looking for a job. Newspapers, now fatter, offered page upon page of cricket, and it was a poor newspaper that did not employ at least three former Test players. For the England visit, and particularly following the paucity of correspondents covering the Jardine tour four years earlier, a phalanx of all-star cricket writers travelled with the tourists, including Bruce Harris, Neville Cardus, C. B. Fry, Gilbert Mant, William Pollock, Jack Hobbs, and Ross Slater.

The England team was captained by George 'Gubby' Allen, Australian-born but very much part of the British establishment. His leadership and fair play was to heal many of the wounds caused by the previous tour. Allen had also found a 'soul-mate' in the Australian captain and between them Allen and Bradman spent much time, energy and thought in the following decades eradicating many of the evils which crept into the game.

Even before Allen's team landed in Fremantle on 13 October 1936, advance bookings had broken all previous records, and the summer's cricket proved to be outstanding. Altogether 953,096 spectators watched the five Tests and 1,336,951 people saw the tourists in action. Financially, both the Board and the Marylebone Cricket Club made larger than expected profits which came from Test match takings of £89,956 and an overall tour figure of £115,544. These returns were highly acceptable to the business-oriented Board members who debated long and hard such matters as whether they should allow medical claims for doctor's fees on Leslie Fleetwood-Smith's injured hand.

The Board had little hesitation in appointing Don Bradman not only as captain but also as a selector. He had proved his worth and his fitness when South Australia had won the Sheffield Shield the previous season. Attendances in Adelaide had rocketed with Bradman in the side, whereas in Sydney his loss to the NSWCA was a financial disaster.

A virtual Test trial was played in Sydney from 9–13 October when Vic Richardson's South Africa side played a Don Bradman team for the benefits of Warren Bardsley and Jack Gregory. Bradman's team won by six wickets, the captain himself scoring 212. The selectors also noticed a century from Bill Brown and that Frank Ward's leg-spin claimed a dozen victims.

Ward's display set up an intense struggle for spin bowling places in the Australian team. Ward had arrived in Adelaide some eighteen months earlier as an itinerant cricketer. He did not cut a fine figure: his clothes were dishevelled, there were holes in his shoes and his hair was matted. However he was so successfully taken in hand by Cecil Starr, the occasional South Australian player, that Ward made his Test debut in December 1936.

The English team began their tour in Perth with an easy victory over Western Australia and a high-scoring draw against a Combined team in which Jack Badcock made a splendid 167, particularly with his hooking of short deliveries from the pace attack of Copson, Allen and Voce. After a country match en route, the England team arrived in Adelaide expecting to play against Bradman. However, the night before the match the Bradmans' first child had died in an Adelaide hospital, so naturally he stood down. Frank Ward took ten wickets and Grimmett only two. The writing was on the wall for the veteran whose dislike of Bradman was an open secret.

England won in Adelaide, drew against Victoria in Melbourne and suffered defeat against a mediocre New South Wales combination. An Australian XI in Sydney thrashed the tourists in all but the result for they were saved by an unbeaten 118 from Maurice Leyland. Badcock scored 182 and, out of the blue, Arthur Chipperfield had taken his best figures of 8/66 and ten wickets in a match for the only time in his career.

The visitors then hit their stride in Brisbane against Queensland, failing by only one wicket to record a massive victory. Charlie Barnett scored 259 for England and shared an opening stand of 295 with Arthur Fagg (112). Then came the first Test over five days with a diplomatic gaffe on the first morning when Queensland's dictatorial chairman, Jack Hutcheon, barred Charles Fry, the former Test player and distinguished figure at Lord's, from the Woolloongabba pavilion because he was commenting on the match for a London newspaper. In Brisbane journalists were forced to remain behind a barbed wire fence separating them from the players.

Bradman had four new players in his side: Jack Badcock, Frank Ward, Morris Sievers and Rayford Robinson, but between them they were only ever to play fifteen Tests. Allen won the toss and batted with the England players finding some difficulty against the home bowlers, particularly McCormick who dismissed Worthington, Fagg and Hammond by the time the total was 20. Once the attack had been neutralised, Maurice Leyland (126) scored England's first Test century at the ground as they totalled 358 and Australia moved to 151 for two at the end of the second day. Under the conditions of play for the tour, only the ends of the pitch could be covered overnight, and rain helped Bill Voce (6/41) obtain alarming lift with the ball next morning.

Jack Fingleton was able to claim his fourth century in successive Test innings but Australia were all out for 234. With injuries depleting the home attack the tourists' second innings 256 was decisive. More rain turned the fifth day into a farce as a typical Brisbane 'sticky' – so loved by Bill O'Reilly – saw Australia slump to Allen and Voce for 58, their lowest total at home in this century.

England played Queensland Country at Ipswich between Tests before moving on to Sydney for another rain-affected encounter. In hindsight the Australian selectors erred in playing Badcock (ill), McCormick (lumbago) and Ward (broken nose which inhibited his breathing) and could only watch as England took two days to score 426 for six. Wally Hammond's unbeaten 231 was his third double-century against Australia.

Heavy rain on the rest day and a thunderstorm on Monday morning persuaded Allen to declare immediately. Bradman went first ball to Voce who took 4/10 as Australia made only 80. Following-on, with the pitch drying out, Australia did somewhat better, scoring 324 but still lost by an innings and 22 runs. This prompted quite a considerable debate in the newspapers and on the wireless as to why Australia was two down in the series, and on the tour conditions, while England went to Newcastle to play the locals and the Australian selectors plotted for the New Year's Day Test in Melbourne.

Like with so many organisations in the old Empire, the thought of having any titled person in one's presence was enough to raise one's own social standing. The Board of Control therefore wrote with some trepidation to Lord's in June 1936 asking if the Marylebone Cricket Club president, Lord Cobham, 'would pay them the honour of allowing the Board to entertain him should he visit Australia during the forthcoming Test series'. They appeared to be unaware that the MCC presidency changed each September, but were delighted when, on 10 September, Lord Somers replied 'as the new president of MCC'. He felt 'that it would be a good plan if one or two of us could come over in an unofficial capacity on a friendly visit during the forthcoming Tests'.

Plans were put in train to entertain Lord Somers with no expense spared. When the official notice of the impending visit arrived from Lord's it re-emphasised the 'unofficial nature of the president's presence'. Harold Rowe, the Western Australian delegate, was deputed to receive his Lordship at Fremantle in late December and to look after his needs which, naturally, included a banquet organised by the WACA. After this Lord Somers travelled on to Melbourne where he was met by Allen Robertson and Bill Jeanes at Spencer Street Station and escorted to his hotel. That night, the second day of the third Test, the Board held a glittering gala dinner at the Windsor Hotel for his Lordship and the touring team.

The large crowds were causing the health authorities concern in each of the four Test centres. In Adelaide the city council pointed out that 'there was a marked lack of lavatory accommodation for women', and added: 'It is obvious from the increase of women attending cricket matches in recent times that the original proportion of accommodation for females is altogether out of ratio and that steps must be taken in the near future to provide increased facilities'.

Catering was another problem, particularly in Melbourne where there were daily attendances of 87,798 (4 January); 79,630 (1 January); 77,181 (27 February); 65,235 (2 January); 64,826 (5 January) and 63,340 (1 March). First-aid post facilities were stretched to breaking point; there were not enough police or attendants on duty and, in one instance, members of the Melbourne Cricket Club committee helped to man the turnstiles.

The turning-point in the series for Australia came on New Year's Day, 1937. The selectors had made four changes, two of them at the last minute when Sievers and Rigg came in for McCormick and O'Brien. Not being aware of Rigg's late inclusion the *Sun News-Pictorial* said: 'It is one of the mysteries of the game why he has escaped selection. He has done everything a batsman could do to deserve it.' The paper had a point. In his previous two matches on the Melbourne Cricket Ground, Rigg had scored 97 and 105 against South Australia and 100 and 167 not out versus New South Wales.

But Australia had a problem. For the first time since 1928 they had to go into a Test match without a genuine fast bowler to open. In those days there was no quick air travel as today and Victoria had no-one to whom the selectors could turn. So the opening attack was to be Morris Sievers and the occasional medium-pace of Stan McCabe.

Luckily Bradman won the toss. He decided to bat, and the tension was so great that, when Bill Voce bowled the first ball of the match, a roar went up from the spectators. It was, though, a poor day's cricket in which Australia reached only 181 for six by the close. Then came the rain and play on the Saturday was delayed. As Neville Cardus reported for the *Manchester Guardian*:

> The patience of the crowd was exemplary. The women talked profusely and the bars were well supported. So the morning dragged on while the police guarded the pitch as though it were the Crown jewels. There were repeated visits by the captains to the wicket and the crowd counted them out. But there was no need for the reading of the Riot Act. Cricket crowds are well broken in. If they can stand Test matches they can stand anything.
>
> Apparently the captains could not agree, for when they left the scene the umpires had a look and walked around the pitch

> warily, as though half expecting it to get up and shake itself and wet everybody. Profound consultation went forward. It did not require to elaborate the doctrine of relativity. The problem of establishing objective wetness or dryness of a cricket pitch is as deep and mysterious as all your metaphysics from Descartes to Professor Whitehead. It is a serious business and no mistake; let us be grateful for the cheering quality of Melbourne ale.

When play finally started the pitch was a 'gluepot' and, after only a short while, Bradman declared at 200 for nine. The sun then found a way through the clouds, the temperature rose and Sievers claimed a Test best 5/21 before Allen closed England's innings at 76 for nine. Bradman was no fool, however. He chose to open his second innings with the tail-enders, O'Reilly and Fleetwood-Smith, and by close of play had only lost the former. Sunday came and went: more drizzle but nothing too disturbing. After a delayed start on Monday the Australian score rose to 97 for five when Bradman walked to the wicket to join Jack Fingleton. They batted for the rest of the day and for all except a few minutes on the Tuesday. Their sixth-wicket partnership of 346 is still a Test record and Fingleton reached 136.

Bradman carried on into Wednesday morning until he was caught by his opposite number, Allen. In all Bradman had batted 458 minutes for his 270 runs and had scampered 110 singles. The Australian total reached 564 which was too much for the tourists who lost by 365 runs.

The match had virtually brought Melbourne to a standstill. The *Sun News-Pictorial* commented: 'There will be no rise in bread prices while the Test cricket is on. A meeting of the Master Bakers' Council that was to take place yesterday to consider an increase has been postponed until Thursday afternoon, as the Council were unanimous that watching Bradman yesterday was more entertaining than risking the wrath of housewives by raising prices.'

Before the fourth Test the tourists played three matches. Tasmania were easily beaten in Launceston and rain ruined the games in Hobart and Adelaide. Before the Test started in Adelaide, however, the Board of Control had a lengthy meeting with Lord Somers, 'to discuss matters affecting the Marylebone Cricket Club and this Board, and cricket affairs generally'. Nothing came out of this, however. The war intervened before any ideas could be enacted!

During this match a little piece of history was made when Alan Kippax sat in a corner of the telegraph box situated by the press area in the Adelaide Oval and, for the last ten minutes of each day's play, spoke by radio-telephone directly to BBC listeners in Britain. He would have told his listeners of a very even first three days, with

England gaining a 42-run lead on first innings. The last three days belonged to Australia, particularly to Don Bradman and Leslie Fleetwood-Smith.

With England's fieldsmen set to prevent boundaries, Bradman played a quite incredibly disciplined innings. He had stands of 109 with Stan McCabe (55) and 135 with Ross Gregory (50) making his debut. Bradman's second successive double-century, 212, which helped Australia's score to 433, took him over seven hours.

Then Fleetwood-Smith took over. Following 4/129 from 42 overs in England's first innings, he took 6/110 from 30 overs in their second. His bowling of Wally Hammond immediately at the start of the last day's play swung the match which Australia went on to win by 148 runs.

All square at two Tests each set up an interesting finale for Melbourne, but before that England played two country fixtures in Geelong and Canberra before losing to New South Wales and scraping a draw with Victoria.

Then came five scintillating days of the fifth and final Test in a series played with a sportsmanship so pure that old-timers seem to remember it like a first love. In fact, the match was watched by the seventy-eight-year-old Tom Garrett, now the last survivor of the first Test played sixty years earlier. Australia batted first and immediately set about amassing a huge score by completely overcoming the English attack. Bradman made 169, Badcock 118, McCabe 112 and Gregory 80 in a total of 604, against which Kenneth Farnes earned an impressive analysis, 28.5-5-96-6.

Not everyone was watching cricket, however. Thieves broke into the house of Harry Brereton, the Victorian Cricket Association's secretary, in the then outer suburb of Glenferrie and ransacked the place. Naturally he and his family were at the match.

The critics particularly enjoyed Ross Gregory's 80. Neville Cardus commented: 'Heaven bless us, we have again witnessed strokes in a Test match, gay and handsome and cultured strokes'. Sadly, it was to be Gregory's last Test for he was not available (although some say the selectors passed him over) for the 1938 tour, and he was killed in 1942 serving with the Royal Australian Air Force, aged twenty-six.

Having to face Australia's highest-ever score against them at home, the tourists failed to avoid the follow-on. England made 239 and then seemed to lose heart. Defeat by an innings and 200 runs was the final result in a series which Australia had clawed back after being two matches down.

With all the interruptions of the England tour, the Sheffield Shield season was pushed into the background. Some teams, hit by Test selections, were weak but that did not stop Victoria easily taking the title. Fleetwood-Smith captured 53 wickets altogether including 7/17 and 8/79 against Queensland in Melbourne.

As summer turned to winter, Bill Jeanes received another lengthy letter written on Tasmanian parliamentary notepaper. Joe Darling had again been thinking about the players: 'I am submitting some proposals for the establishment of a Trust Fund for the benefit of International Cricketers and I would like the Board to give them some consideration'. The consideration was immediate because Harry Hodgetts refused even to discuss Darling's letter. So much for the players.

As the 1937–38 season got under way the New Zealanders who had toured England in 1937 arrived in Adelaide on 30 October to play three matches in Australia on their way home. It was a relaxing time for the Kiwis especially with the hospitality laid on by SACA. When the match took place New Zealand made 151 with South Australia 64 for two at the close, Don Bradman unbeaten on 11. Next morning as spectators were still queuing at the gates, Bradman in his only innings against New Zealand was caught behind without adding to his score. Many of the crowd outside the ground, on hearing this news, turned and walked away. The NZCC later admitted that his early dismissal cost them hundreds of pounds worth of gate takings.

Jack Badcock made 114 and Frank Ward had figures of 4/59 and 7/62 as South Australia won by ten wickets. Victoria then beat New Zealand by five wickets with a young Lindsay Hassett, a very talented player from Geelong College, scoring an unbeaten 127. Then in Sydney an eight-wicket win to New South Wales saw the emergence of another young batsman, Sidney Barnes. A virtual street urchin in his youth, Barnes was a tough kid whose cocky attitude would always be getting him into trouble. Against the Kiwis he scored 97 and impressed all who watched him.

A testimonial match in Adelaide for Vic Richardson and Clarrie Grimmett saw each player receive £1028, which would have been much more had rain not washed out the final two days' play. Then came the 1937–38 Shield season in which NSW were clear winners but again it was Bradman – with the season's only double-century, 246 against Queensland in Adelaide – and Fleetwood-Smith (who took 9/135 against South Australia in Melbourne) who shone most.

On the voyage to England in April 1938, the Australians stopped off in Naples. There Don Bradman, the captain of the side, counted 36 destroyers, 72 submarines and 8 cruisers in the harbour. He wrote home: 'I guess they were not built to rust. It's obvious that Europe is contemplating a grim future.' Indeed. This was also the year of the annexation of Austria by Nazi Germany, but to Australians this was not going to affect the tour.

At the Board of Control meeting in Melbourne on 27 January 1938 approval was given to the selectors' choices. Stan McCabe was elected vice-captain and, as one of their better moves, the Board of Control voted Bill Jeanes as tour manager although he was also given the extra, onerous, task of being its treasurer. Autocratic and gruff, Jeanes was nonetheless an excellent administrator who deserved the OBE he was awarded in the June Honours List. He made sure, for example, that a proposal to play in Cairo en route was rejected as were four matches tentatively planned for Jamaica on the way home.

As usual there were two matches in Tasmania and one in Western Australia as a gentle warm-up for the team. In Launceston the Australians defeated Tasmania by 386 runs and in Hobart by 485 runs, then in Perth the victory was by an innings and 126 runs. The SS *Orontes* left Fremantle on 21 March and arrived at Southampton a month later. They stopped off in Ceylon for a match on 30 March and in front of 11,000 people scored 367 (Badcock 116, Hassett 116) to Ceylon's 114 for seven. An honourable draw.

The tour in England started in sensational fashion. At Worcester the Australians scored 541 (Bradman 258 and Fleetwood-Smith 8/98); against Oxford University 679 for seven; at Leicester 590 for five; versus Cambridge University 708 for five (Hassett 220); against the MCC at Lord's 502 (Bradman 278); at Northampton 406 for six, and against Surrey 528, when O'Reilly also took 8/104. But in between all this, on the last day of the Leicestershire fixture, came news from Australia of the death of Peter McAlister, aged 69. Considering the way he had backed the Board in its early days their brief minute acknowledging his passing left a sour taste.

During the early stages of the tour Bill Jeanes was finding out what life was like for the touring party and the individual players. Virtually all the requests he sent back to the Board in Australia were rejected, some of them vehemently so. He asked: 'In view of the international situation should the Board consider a War Risks Insurance for the manager and players?' Unanimous refusal. Then, when Sid Barnes was injured, Jeanes cabled on 23 April asking for an additional batsman 'in view of the strenuous programme and limited reserves'. Refused again. Then followed a request which was sent to Jeanes from the Australian High Commissioner in London asking if the team could be photographed helping Australia's fruit exports. Allen Robertson, as Board chairman, refused the request out of hand.

Next, the Australian Broadcasting Commission wrote asking if Jeanes and Bradman could link up from London to their Sydney studios for a ten-minute discussion on the eve of the first Test. This time, shocked refusal.

The subject of players' wives arose and, after a month of cables to and fro, the Board caved in to pressure to allow wives to meet their returning husbands in Colombo on the way home to Australia. However, the Board did show one piece of belated generosity when they received a letter from Mrs Chipperfield complaining that she had only found out about her husband's appendicitis operation, and in which hospital it took place, from an enquiring journalist. It was agreed: 'That the Board refund to Mrs Chipperfield the cost of her telephone call to Dundee'.

The first Test at Nottingham was played on a pitch representing a batsman's paradise. The England captain, Wally Hammond, won the toss and by the close of play his side had reached 422 for four. Charlie Barnett (126) and Len Hutton (100) had already scored centuries with two more to come next day as Denis Compton (102) and Eddie Paynter (216 not out) took the score to 658 for eight when Hammond declared. It was the first time four batsmen had scored centuries in the same Test innings and Compton, at 20 years and 19 days, was the youngest Englishman to score a hundred against Australia.

The third day began with Australia on 138 for three with Stan McCabe unbeaten on 19. As wickets fell around him McCabe unleashed a memorable display of aggressive strokes. So fine was McCabe's performance that day that Bradman called his players out on to the balcony of the dressing-room to watch it. Of the 300 runs scored while he was at the crease, 232 came from McCabe's bat. Neville Cardus called it one of the greatest innings ever seen anywhere in any period of the game's history. Bradman has always said it was the greatest innings he ever saw or hoped to see. McCabe made his runs in even time with a six and 34 fours, and he scored 72 of the last 77 runs.

But it did not prevent Hammond enforcing the follow-on. Bill Brown (133) and Don Bradman (144 not out) then realised they had to play for a draw as victory was impossible. Their slow play annoyed the last-day crowd who became extremely vocal. They had been spoilt by the McCabe innings and wanted more.

Ten days later came the second Test at Lord's which saw the biggest crowd of the tour, 117,173, pay £26,422 to watch two quality double-centuries in another drawn match. Hammond won the toss, batted, and found himself 210 not out at the end of the first day. Lord's was in a perfect condition with the Saturday attendance of 33,800 seeing the fifth-wicket partnership of 186, with Ames, finish at 457 when Hammond (240) was bowled by McCormick. The England captain had batted for 367 minutes and hit 32 fours in his chanceless innings. The fourth-wicket partnership of 222 in 182 minutes with Eddie Paynter (99) is still England's highest against Australia.

Then came Bill Brown to open the innings for Australia and also to be there at the end, unbeaten on 206 made in two minutes longer than Hammond. It was Australia's one-hundredth century against England and the total of 422 remains the highest throughout which anyone has carried his bat in a Test. After rain on the third night McCormick made the ball lift alarmingly on the final morning. Three quick wickets saw England slump to 76 for five, but the recovery came, then a declaration, and time for Bradman to score an easy century before the close.

Bill Brown scored an unbeaten 265 two days later against Derbyshire at Chesterfield. A week after that the third Test at Old Trafford was abandoned without a ball being bowled. The rain gave the Australians a much-needed week off in order to relax and recover from two-and-a-half successive months of touring.

Resuming after their rest, the tourists thrashed Warwickshire and Nottinghamshire before tackling England again in the fourth Test at Leeds. The Australians brought in the playboy of the tour, Merv Waite, for Chipperfield, but he took just one wicket in the only two Tests in which he played. ('Bradman got the runs,' he said to me in an interview shortly before he died in 1985. 'I got the roots.') His pace was just not needed at Leeds as, after weeks of bowling on over-prepared pitches, O'Reilly and Fleetwood-Smith were given a soft track which took spin and made batting far from easy.

Hammond batted on winning the toss and his 76 was the backbone of England's 223, in which O'Reilly took 5/66. Bradman (103) scored his third hundred in successive Test innings at Leeds as Australia took a 19-run lead. On what turned out to be the third and last day, England found themselves at 73 for one. O'Reilly had six men around the bat and became angry when no-balled bowling to Joe Hardstaff. The next delivery was a fast leg-break which removed the batsman's bails. Hammond then went first ball caught at short-leg, and next over Fleetwood-Smith had Bill Edrich stumped. In five deliveries the match had been turned and Australia were on their way to keeping the Ashes.

England were all out for 123 with O'Reilly taking 5/56 to claim 10/122 for the match. Fleetwood-Smith's total figures were 7/107. With dark clouds looming Bradman told his batsmen to force the pace. It took 32.3 overs, one rain delay, and lots of tension before Australia won by five wickets. The players left the field and within minutes it was swamped by a cloudburst. Another 50 runs or so could well have seen the match go England's way. It was that close.

Three days later, at Taunton, Bradman scored his third double-century of the tour as Somerset were easily beaten. Four first-class and four-non-first-class matches were played up to the final Test at The Oval which started on 20 August 1938 and was due to be played to the finish however long that took. England stacked their team with batsmen while Sid Barnes made his Test debut in place of Ernie McCormick even though this meant that Australia's opening attack would be Waite and McCabe.

Hammond won his fourth successive toss and batted with Edrich partnering Hutton. Edrich (12) was leg-before to O'Reilly with the score on 29, after which Leyland and Hutton batted for the rest of the day. At the close, England were 347 for one, Hutton on 160 and Leyland 156. The perfect pitch was a joy for the England batsmen and the second wicket did not go down until the score was 411, when Leyland was run out for 187. Their 382–run partnership was the highest made by England against Australia.

All this time Len Hutton was grinding on and on. The Australian bowlers could not penetrate his defence and his cautious play frustrated them. Three quick wickets fell near the close of the second day which saw England still batting at 634 for five, Hutton on 300 and Hardstaff 40.

Over 30,000 people turned up on Tuesday morning to see if Hutton could beat Bradman's Ashes record Test score of 334. Hutton was made to fight for every run as he neared the magic figure. Finally a boundary off Fleetwood-Smith and the record was his, albeit in double the time it took Bradman. On 364 Hutton was well caught by Hassett in the covers off O'Reilly and so ended the then longest innings in first-class cricket: 797 minutes, which contained 35 fours, 15 threes, 18 twos and 143 singles. Hardstaff was on 169 when Hammond finally declared at 903 for seven.

Among the records that fell, Leslie Flee twood-Smith's 1/298 was the most runs any bowler would concede in Test history in a single innings. His 87 overs were only two more than O'Reilly's 85 which, with 26 maidens, gave him figures of 3/178. With Bradman breaking a bone in his ankle while bowling and Fingleton unable to bat with knee injury, the nine-man Australian team had little hope of survival. Bill Brown (69) was first in and last out in the tourists' 201. Then only a stand of 74 between Ben Barnett (46) and Sid Barnes (33) delayed England's thrust for victory. The final margin of an innings and 579 runs was a crude reminder of the fallibilities of any great team.

Six more matches saw the tour to its close. The Australians had won 20 of their 36 matches and only suffered two defeats – against England and at a Scarborough Festival jaunt. The Board of Control received £36,841 as their share of the tour receipts, down from the 1934 figure of £40,505.

In August 1938 the Board lost the services of Clem Hill as a South Australian delegate. Hill's wife had died and he had decided to leave Adelaide for Melbourne and a new position as a handicapper to the Victorian Amateur Turf Club. SACA put on a sparkling farewell dinner for him in late September, the invitation list to which was a sporting 'Who's Who?'

Hugh Trumble, secretary of the Melbourne Cricket Club, died on 14 August 1938. Harry Hodgetts and Clem Hill represented the SACA at the funeral a few days later. Don Bradman was still in England at this stage but, on his return, it was suggested to him that, should he wish to apply for the position as Trumble's successor, the job was his for the asking. Bradman – and one hundred and fifty other people – applied and, to the never-ending gratitude of all South Australians, he missed out on the position by the casting vote of the chairman. The post went to the former Victorian and Australian representative, Vernon Ransford.

But 1938 was also the centenary year for the Melbourne Cricket Club which had been formed only three years after the founding of Melbourne itself. On Saturday night, 10 December, the club celebrated the one-hundredth anniversary of Melbourne's first cricket match when the club played a military side. Four days later the club held its Centenary Ball with guests, all in period dress, in the Members' Pavilion. It was historic in many ways, but especially as it was the first occasion when ladies had been admitted to the lounge and dining-room areas.

A four-day centenary match was held between the Australian team and a combination under Keith Rigg's captaincy. Bradman showed that he had recovered from his injury at The Oval by scoring 118, the first of a record equalling six successive first-class hundreds. Stan McCabe made 105 with Bill O'Reilly and Leslie Fleetwood-Smith dominating the bowling in a drawn match.

At their meeting held at the Australian Jockey Club on 22 September 1938, the Board finally agreed to the pesterings of the New Zealand Cricket Council to send a team on tour there for the 1939–40 season. It was only ever to be an Australian second team and the Board laid down strict conditions on the team's title.

There were plans afoot also for a side to tour North America in 1939 under the managership of Edgar Waddy but war, declared on 3 September 1939, put paid to both tours.

Three full seasons of cricket were played in 1938–39, 1939–40 and 1940–41 although only the first two counted for the Sheffield Shield. South Australia and New South Wales were the winners and in the unofficial season NSW were again top. The dominating performances were by players already well known to the cricketing public: Bradman, Brown, Hassett and, latterly, Barnes with the bat; Fleetwood-Smith, initially, Grimmett and O'Reilly with the ball.

Before the Shield season of 1938–39, Clarrie Grimmett had been coaching in India for the Rajah of Jath. The break must have done him good as he topped the Shield averages for the season with 27 victims at 20.85. Fleetwood-Smith took 30 wickets, but expensively at 39.73, and it marked the start of his decline. But it was the batsmen who prospered, centuries and double-centuries coming with apparent ease. Badcock's unbeaten 271 for South Australia against NSW was the highest of the season, followed by Percy Beames' 226 not out for Victoria and Don Bradman's 225.

South Australia had won the Sheffield Shield but in doing so they caused something of a controversy. The NSWCA secretary, Harold Heydon, wrote to SACA in mid-January 1939:

> This Association has been giving consideration to the question of 'professionalism in Australian cricket', especially with regard to players participating in Sheffield Shield matches. Many reports affecting South Australian players in relation to the above matter have reached our committee and we would care to be informed if certain of your players are in receipt, directly or indirectly, of any monetary consideration from SACA for playing cricket.

The SACA committee resolved that the correspondence be minuted as 'received'. Bill Jeanes sent a reply in early February which was a classic 'no answer' letter, to which Harold Heydon replied on 6 March: 'My Association express regret at the nature of your reply and can only assume that the players named in our original letter are in receipt of subsidies from you and are therefore professional cricketers'. Jeanes acknowledged the letter saying: 'It will be placed before the committee at its next meeting'.

On 27 March, Heydon wrote again asking: 'Has any further action been taken on this subject?' to which Jeanes replied: 'No'.

There was no further correspondence on the issue, and no record of any official discussion can be found in the records of the NSWCA. Nor did the subject reach Board level. Maybe NSW were annoyed for, as their 1938–39 Annual Report says: 'This state experienced its worst season in Sheffield Shield cricket since the war . . . South Australia was fortunate in having all its players available throughout the season . . . the absence of [our] leading players from the team for matches in Sydney was reflected in the public patronage, and the financial result was the worst for very many years.' Heydon was, of course, quite correct in what he assumed. Bradman, Badcock, Ward and Grimmett were professionals in all but name and in breach of Australia's unwritten rules of the time.

On 7 September, four days after war had been declared in Europe, at the SACA annual general meeting, the president, Harry Blinman, said:

I refer to the calamitous war in which we have been plunged in order that an adventurer and bandit should endeavour to achieve his ambition of world domination. However, at the moment there is no reason to expect that interstate and District cricket will do other than follow their usual course. The morale of the community is much more likely to be benefited by the holding of manly sports and the continuation of our activities will be accepted as in keeping with the Prime Minister's counsel to the people of Australia to carry on in the normal way.

Blinman was repeating the news given to the Board of Control by the Prime Minister, Robert Menzies. It was agreed to hold the Sheffield Shield competition 'for the morale of the people'.

The 1939–40 season saw Bradman play two unbeaten innings of 251 and 90 against Queensland in Adelaide; in the next match Badcock scored 236 against Queensland as South Australia reached their highest ever score of 821 for seven.

At the New Year, Bill O'Reilly took 8/23 and 6/22 as NSW thrashed Queensland in Sydney and at the same time Bradman made 267 against Victoria in Melbourne; Bradman then scored an unbeaten 209 in Perth against Western Australia, and to finish off the season in style NSW beat 'The Rest of Australia' in Sydney in early March 1940 to record their total supremacy. Their recovery since 1938–39 had been largely due to promising youngsters coming through the ranks. Bradman had scored 1475 runs in nine matches at an average of 122.92 with only Hassett (897 at 74.75) and Brown (857 at 61.21) anywhere near him. Clarrie Grimmett captured an amazing 73 wickets in nine games followed by Bill O'Reilly with 55 in seven matches. Also emerging was a wicketkeeper of great quality in Queensland's Don Tallon. The previous season he claimed 34 dismissals – including twelve in one match, equalling the world record which still stands – and was now consolidating his position as a batsman too.

Two years earlier the Sydney Cricket Ground Trust had named their new stand at the ground the 'M. A. Noble Stand'. It was a fine edifice and a deserved honour for a supreme cricketer, so therefore it came as a shock to everyone when Noble died at his home in Randwick on 22 June 1940, aged sixty-seven. Three weeks later Bill Howell also died, aged seventy, and it was the start of five years of extended obituary notices exaggerated by the war. Those years would see the passing of former great players such as Tom Garrett, Ernie Jones, Tommy Matthews, Charlie Turner, Johnny Taylor, Joe Darling, Charlie Kelleway and Charles Eady.

The years between the wars had seen Australian cricket at its peak. In many ways it was an antipodean 'Golden Age': runs, wickets, high-quality fielding, crowds, glory and honour were part of the cricketing way of life. The Board of Control and the autocratic State administrators were perhaps, in retrospect at least regarding the latter, good for the developing game. No other sport had been built up in this way with most of the money it attracted going back into the game, in many cases the redevelopment of grounds. The crowd records set in the period culminated in the English tour of 1936–37 with even greater crowds expected had the planned 1940–41 tour gone ahead.

# 19

# 'No-one remembers us now'

The 1940–41 season saw Sid Barnes dominate domestic cricket. His 1050 runs from eight matches placed him 400 runs in front of the next highest scorer, Jack Badcock. Bill O'Reilly still topped the bowling, his eight games netting him 55 victims. Of the eleven matches played during the season two stand out. The first was played just after Christmas 1940 when Arthur Morris, a young left-handed batsman from the St George Club, scored 148 and 111 on his debut for New South Wales against Queensland, a feat not previously accomplished.

The other outstanding fixture started in Melbourne on 1 January 1941 and was titled 'D. G. Bradman's XI versus S. J. McCabe's XI' and was played 'for patriotic funds'. The first-day crowd of 8690 saw McCabe's team reach 449 for nine with 137 from Barnes and 105 from Badcock. Bradman's side managed only 205 and 141 with the Australian captain performing poorly. Wise heads started saying he was finished!

The only match of the 1941–42 season took place in Brisbane in late November 1941 when Queensland defeated NSW by 29 runs. The Interstate Conference held in Sydney on 25 September 1941 had agreed on ten three-day games for the season, a policy scheduled to carry on until the war in Europe was over. But all this went by the board on 7 December, with the Japanese raid on Pearl Harbor, which was followed on 19 February 1942 by the devastating air-raid on Darwin.

Australia was now really at war and not simply involved in someone else's conflict. The government brought in the black-out: digging squads tore up parks and gardens for air-raid shelters; and all the major cricket grounds were taken over for military use. There was no more top cricket in Australia for nearly four years.

The new Labor Prime Minister, John Curtin, unlike his predecessor, was not sports-minded. However, when he said: 'In view of the seriousness of the national situation . . . the continuance of sport in this time of crisis . . . should be discontinued', everyone obeyed.

What would have been the 1942–43 season did not happen in Australia

– it was the darkest part of the war – although in faraway Egypt and Palestine Lindsay Hassett was organising matches in the desert between Australians and other combinations. Some states resumed club matches in 1943–44 although – as in the previous war – games 'had to be for exercise only and not for competition'. Then on 25 February 1944 the NSWCA circulated a letter which stated that 'due to the dire shortage of cricket material there was a risk that an almost entire cessation of the game would be caused'. Apparently none of the Associations had previously given much thought to the matter.

Letters were sent to sporting retailers throughout Australia in order to ascertain their stocks, with the replies causing so much concern that Associations immediately put embargoes on their donations of equipment to military camps and for patriotic purposes. The NSWCA were galvanised into action as it was necessary, clearly, to obtain bats from England and matting from India.

On 12 July 1944 the VCA wrote a circular enclosing correspondence between themselves, NSWCA, QCA, the Department of War Organisation of Industry, the Department of Supply and Shipping, and the Division of Import Procurement. The VCA had taken control of the situation, but having made little progress with the public servants, turned to their trump card, the VCA Patron, Robert Menzies.

A week later, on 19 July, the VCA circulated a copy of a letter from the Director of Import Procurement to Menzies which said: 'We have authorised the importation of ten thousand cricket bats for Slazengers Pty Ltd . . . as regards to coir matting from India, the stocks are so small and demand so extensive that disposal is being restricted to hospitals and ships exclusively'. The Director was slightly incorrect in his figures for eventually twelve thousand bats arrived.

With Hassett's team being such a success in Egypt, the Royal Australian Air Force formed teams which played in England when on leave from their service duties. It is said that Pelham Warner, while watching Flight-Sergeant Keith Miller and Squadron-Leader Keith Carmody bat for the RAAF against a British Services XI at Lord's in 1943, determined that arrangements should start for a RAAF/AIF team to play immediately the war was over.

On 1 August 1944, Harold Heydon advised the Board of Control that the NSWCA had been approached by the RAAF to allow Jack Chegwyn, a Randwick and NSW player, to organise and conduct a cricket tour of Northern Australia and New Guinea. The RAAF said that 'the tour would be by a civilian team comprising players from all states and that they would be playing only service teams'. Also, the RAAF stressed, 'there would be no remuneration to players but transport and accommodation would be supplied by us'.

The RAAF added that they were officially asking the Board 'for permission for the New Guinea portion of the tour'. The necessary authority was granted but, as it turned out, only the Australian part of the tour took place. It was, however, a successful and popular venture and became the first of many private tours which Chegwyn would organise over the next twenty years.

The success of Lindsay Hassett's team in the Middle East had been noted at the highest level of the Australian army. The powers at Lord's then took a hand in late 1944 when the Australian Prime Minister, John Curtin, and the Forces commander, Field-Marshal Thomas Blamey were both in London. Invited to watch a RAAF versus British Services fixture at headquarters the idea was put to them of the benefit of an Australian Services team. Both took the bait and, within a short time, soldier-cricketers were finding themselves transferred to a unit called the 'AIF Reception Group'.

The idea behind this Group was to help welcome home the thousands of prisoners-of-war and organise victory celebrations. But the cricketers had a different role. When they arrived at the Cumberland Hotel in Eastbourne, Sussex, the motive for their being there was made apparent: they were to be the 1945 Australian Services team who would play a twenty-match tour of England, including five unofficial Tests, from 19 May to 15 September before going on to India, Ceylon and a tour back home.

After VE-Day, 8 May 1945, the two Australian teams – AIF and RAAF – amalgamated under the management of Flight-Lieutenant Keith Johnson who had flown in from Australia. He was the Board of Control's choice to look after the team and organise their schedule. The AIF had played in one-day matches at Eastbourne (twice) and Dulwich, while the RAAF had easily beaten the British Empire XI at Lord's.

In the first of the 'Victory Tests' played at Lord's from 19–22 May 1945, *Wisden* described the clash between England and Australia as 'giving intense pleasure', and the finale as 'dynamic'. England had batted first 'after heavy rain overnight' and 'on a green pitch'. In front of a first-day crowd of 18,000, Squadron Leader Les Ames top-scored with 53 for England in a total of 267. Australia moved to 82 for two at the close and on the following Whit Monday, with over 30,000 people present, took their score to 455 with Keith Miller, the young Victorian all-rounder, scoring 105 in 210 minutes with only six boundaries. *Wisden* said: 'He was always getting runs with the soundness characteristic of most Australians'.

Rain fell as the Australian innings finished with England batting again on the third morning 'on turf drying in sunshine'. The leg-breaks of the NSW bowler, Cec Pepper, took 4/80 as England moved to 294. Needing 107 to win in just seventy minutes, the England captain, Wally

Hammond, did not waste time and moved his field quickly. As time ticked down, so did the runs required with Pepper, unbeaten on 54, making 'the winning hit off the fourth ball of the last possible over'. Australian Services won by six wickets, having been watched by 67,660 people over three days.

The team, whose bond of friendship would last them all their lives, was: Jim Workman (a South Australian whose only first-class cricket was for this team); Dick Whitington (SA), Lindsay Hassett (Victoria), Stan Sismey (NSW), Keith Miller (Victoria, and later NSW), Ross Stanford (SA), Cec Pepper (NSW), Albert Cheetham (NSW), Graham Williams (SA), Charles Price (of NSW but who only played for Services) and Reg Ellis (SA). The other four members of the team were Keith Carmody (NSW, and later Western Australia), Bob Cristofani (NSW), Jack Pettiford (NSW, and later county cricket for Kent), and A. W. 'Mick' Roper (NSW).

Then followed various matches all around England until the second Victory Test at Bramall Lane, Sheffield. The bomb-scarred ground held 50,000 people over three days who paid £7311 to watch, as *Wisden* reported, 'the finest match of the season'. Carmody replaced Stanford from the Lord's side, and top-scored with 42 as the Australians could reach only 147 in reply to England's 286. With Miller bowling ferociously England's second innings only reached 190. On a cold final day, needing 330 to win, the Australians opened with a partnership of 108 between Whitington (61) and Workman (63) but could not sustain the momentum, going down to defeat by 41 runs.

At Eastbourne in late June the Services defeated their New Zealand counterparts by ten wickets – Price scoring an unbeaten 139 and Hassett taking 5/31, and in mid-July a promising match with Yorkshire ended in a draw, being spoilt by rain. The third 'Test' against England took place at Lord's. Cristofani replaced Price and proceeded to take 4/43 and 5/49 to swing the match Australia's way. The London crowds were increasing: this time 84,000 watched a game in which Len Hutton made 104 and 69, the top scorer in each of England's innings.

The build-up to the match had been somewhat different. An eclipse of the sun followed by storms of wind and rain led to only a slight delay on the first day and, as luck would have it, the rain held off during the playing hours. England had a 60-run first-innings lead which was extended to 224. The initial Australian reply was slow but in the end they won by four wickets with time to spare.

The scoring started to increase in fixtures played between 'Tests'. Keith Miller scored 111 against Yorkshire at Sheffield followed by an amazing 189 by Lindsay Hassett at Portsmouth against a strong Royal Navy team.

Lord's was the venue for the fourth of the five 'Tests' and now over 93,000 turned up over three mid-week days in early August 1945. Pettiford and Stanford replaced Cheetham and Carmody in the Australian side, who batted first and scored 388 with Keith Miller's 118 taking 198 minutes and containing ten fours. The new British Prime Minister, Clement Attlee, watched the second day's play and saw England move past the visitors' score with only four wickets down. Cyril Washbrook made 112 as Hammond finally declared at 468 for seven to allow Australia to wipe off the deficit. The perfect pitch was always going to see a draw with only 21 wickets falling to some rather varied bowling.

The final 'Test' took place at Old Trafford from 20 August. As at Sheffield the match was staged by the Inter-Services Sports Committee who paid German prisoners-of-war three-farthings an hour for painting the outside of the buildings and for repairing certain sections of the ground. The decision to repair and make safe proved correct as 72,463 spectators paid £11,627 to watch a truly magnificent sporting spectacle.

Keith Carmody was chosen for Australia in place of Jim Workman but the gamble failed, as Carmody fell cheaply in both innings. Miller's unbeaten 77 saved Australia who still only reached 173 to which England replied with 243 on the second day. It would have been more but Bob Cristofani's quick leg-breaks had the English batsmen in all sorts of trouble as he claimed 5/55 from his 22 overs.

'After nearly six years of transport restrictions the sight of dozens of special omnibuses labelled "Cricket Ground" was something remarkable,' wrote *Wisden*. The crowds brought in by the buses even endured pouring rain but their enthusiasm was particularly evident when the Australians were reduced to 87 for seven in their second innings. Then Bob Cristofani played the innings of his career. For NSW he had once managed to score 31 but now he square-cut, hooked and off-drove in a manner not seen from him before. His century (101) came from 126 runs and when Australia were finally dismissed for 200, Cristofani remained unbeaten on 110, the only century of his career.

There was no heavy roller to use between the innings – it had been requisitioned and was somewhere in the Middle East having been used to lay out airfields. This did not bother the English batsmen who needed to score only 141 in plenty of time for victory, which came for the loss of four wickets.

There were still matches to play, particularly against Nottinghamshire (won), Surrey (lost), Sussex (won) and Combined Counties (won). But the last big match was at Scarborough for the revived festival week. The Australians had a ball: Cec Pepper's 168 was the only first-class century he would score, Dick Whitington made 79,

Stan Sismey 78 and Keith Miller 71 in a total of 506. The reply, by H. D. G. Leveson-Gower's XI (a virtual Test team in disguise) was 258 and, following-on, 140 with Reg Ellis taking 5/43 and 5/24. It was a fitting finale to a series of matches played in a most pleasing spirit and watched by large crowds everywhere.

Yet back in Australia the series counted for virtually nothing. Interstate matches were due to start again on 23 November 1945 and all the Australian public appeared to be concerned about was whether Bradman would play or not. The reason for this lay partly in Bradman's having been invalided out of the army in 1941, partly because he had since been suffering severe muscular pains and spasms. He himself did not really want to go on playing cricket, but considerable political pressure was put on him to do so.

The Services players who performed so creditably in that wonderful northern summer of 1945 have now all been forgotten bar those, such as Hassett and Miller and Whitington, whose exploits or performance took them to greater fame. Some, like Cristofani, Pepper and Pettiford returned to England. Others such as Ellis, Workman, Stanford, Price, Williams, Roper and Cheetham returned to public obscurity. But just when they were looking forward to returning home to Australia after the end of their programme in England, news came through that they had first to tour India and Ceylon. They were understandably reluctant after so long away, but as Service personnel they had to obey the instructions of their military superiors.

It was to be a ten-match tour of two months' duration and to be exactly the opposite of the happy-go-lucky attitude of Hammond's England team. In India the Services were crushed by a lack of adventure, defensive captaincy and appallingly biased umpiring. This latter problem turned the players into such a moody group that Bob Cristofani, at one point, stormed from the field in disgust.

Five drawn matches was not a good start to a tour which included three unofficial Tests. Following matches in Lahore, Delhi and Bombay, the first 'Test' started on 10 November in the Brabourne Stadium, Bombay. Hassett batted on winning the toss and saw Carmody (113) and Pettiford (124) score centuries before he chipped in himself with 53. Cec Pepper (95) and Jim Workman (76) saw the score to 531 halfway through the second day after which the Indians batted slowly and surely to reach 339 and 304, so drawing the match.

Defeat in Calcutta by two wickets against East Zone was the prelude to the second 'Test' in the same city at Eden Gardens. This time India took strike first and as the *Calcutta Illustrated News* reported: 'Indian batting on the first day lacked brilliance', which was quite an understatement. It was in fact a tortuous day's play. The second morning saw India dismissed for 386 after which the Australian

Services team stepped up the tempo, scoring at nearly double the rate of their opponents.

Whitington made 155 with 15 fours and Pettiford 101. After them came Keith Miller who, according to the *Illustrated News*, 'gave an exhibition prior to the close of his innings which will long be remembered. With effortless grace he hit Vinoo Mankad four times over the ropes. He put the crowd in a good mood and the fans gurgled in joy.' The lead was 86 which the Indians passed easily on their way to 350 for four declared, Vijay Merchant unbeaten on 155. Left to score 265 to win in exactly an hour Hassett declined the opportunity and a draw resulted.

What the Australians had not expected was opposition of such a high standard; but has any Indian team since been represented at the same time by such class players as Vijay Merchant, Lala Amarnath, Vinoo Mankad, Rusi Modi, Gul Mahomed, Vijay Hazare and Mushtaq Ali?

The only victory of the tour followed the Calcutta match when South Zone was defeated in Madras by six wickets, after which came the third and final 'Test' against India. In front of a total crowd estimated 'in excess of 200,000' who paid 'a record Rs 1,420,000' the four-day match started on 7 December 1945. Batting 'in a gloomy atmosphere' the Australians had Hassett (143) and Pepper (87) as their main scorers in a total of 339.

The Indian reply of 525 had the local journalists digging deeply into their thesauruses for words to describe such a score. When Lala Amarnath made 113 in two-and-a-quarter hours he 'struck the spark of battle, ruffled the dignity of the bowlers and scattered the field by driving, cutting and pulling with power and grace'. Rusi Modi went even better than his colleague by scoring 203, the first double-century by an Indian in a match at this level. Dropped at 20 and 162, Modi's runs came in 319 minutes with 24 fours as Hassett tried out ten bowlers in the innings.

Facing a daunting task the Australians batted slowly but surely, ending the third day at 148 for one. On the final morning Carmody was given out leg-before wicket to 'Montu' Banerjee for 92, made in 200 minutes with nine fours. It was the first of four highly suspect decisions of this nature which saw the tourists slump to 275 all out. Amidst great excitement the Indians crept towards their winning target, nervously losing four wickets along the way.

The main purpose of the tour had been to revive India's international cricket which was soon shown when the Indian Board asked the Australian Board for assistance in various administrative matters in preparation for proposed overseas tours. Agreement was soon reached for India to tour Australia in 1947–48 although the Indian

High Commissioner in Canberra had to exert considerable political pressure before it was officially accepted.

The Australian Services team then met a full-strength island team in Ceylon. Keith Miller scored a quickfire 132 and Hassett 57 as the Australians raced to 306. Ceylon were no match and it took all of Hassett's juggling with the bowling to extend the game to the end of the second day.

While the team was heading to Perth the Australian Board fixed up matches against all the States and even debated the NSW idea of having a final game against a Rest of Australia side. The South Australians, including Bradman, were opposed to any such fixture and their view finally won the day.

The five-week tour of Australia started on Christmas Eve in Perth with a drawn game against Western Australia. The team had arrived at Guildford airport and spent three days being wined and dined at the Palace Hotel so it was no wonder they had some difficulty in concentrating on a match they should have easily won. In Adelaide they came up against Reg Craig (141) and a now fully fit Don Bradman (112), and played out another draw. Victoria was a different matter with the Services going down to defeat by an innings and 156 runs. Against New South Wales, the home batsmen plundered the Services bowling attack with Bill Alley (119), Sid Barnes (102) and Ken Grieves (102*) leading the way. By now it was an obviously tired side who lost by an innings although Keith Miller did liven things up with an unbeaten 105.

On to Brisbane for another draw in mid-January as illness and defections weakened the Services team. Then came their final contest as a unit, against Tasmania in Hobart over the January holiday weekend. Ross Stanford scored a first-day 153 in splendid fashion with 13 fours in his four-hour innings. Cec Pepper took nine wickets in the match and amid 'great excitement' the last Tasmanian pair held out for the final five minutes. Then it was all over, and the players dispersed.

History has virtually forgotten them, but in 1990 Ross Stanford summed up their existence and experience: 'No-one remembers us now or what we did. But we have our cherished memories and that is all that counts.'

# 20

# Resumption

The first formal Board of Control meeting since the end of the war started in Sydney on 11 October 1945. It was extremely lengthy and started with part of Bradman's captain's report from the 1938 tour of England. Two main points were decided: firstly, to tour New Zealand at the end of the current season in lieu of the cancelled 1939–40 visit; and, secondly, to issue a formal invitation to Lord's for England to tour in 1946–47. Bradman was very much against the New Zealand tour and, as it turned out, passed the captaincy over to Bill Brown.

Bradman, at the time, had considerable business worries. The first the South Australian Cricket Association were aware of any problem was on 19 June 1945 when the SACA vice-president and Board of Control delegate Harry Hodgetts wrote to Bill Jeanes saying: 'With regret I desire to notify you that I wish to withdraw from my position as a trustee of your Association and from membership of all committees'. It was the only thing Hodgetts could do as government investigators had found fraud on a massive scale within his business.

It became fairly clear that Hodgetts had been cooking the books for some time and there was little doubt that others knew of this. Hodgetts was, in reality, no loss to the Board of Control having shown little rapport with the players or understanding of their needs. His voting record showed a man using the game for ulterior purposes. When his stockbroking firm collapsed and criminal proceedings were issued against him his deficiencies were shown to be £82,854 with 238 unsecured creditors named and debts totalling £102,926.

Bradman, as an 'employee', was stated as being owed £762, which represented a year or more's salary. Adelaide's rumour-mill worked overtime, so much so that stories are still told to the present day. However, Bradman left H. W. Hodgetts & Co. and, with a seat on the Adelaide Stock Exchange, set himself up as Don Bradman & Co. of Grenfell Street, Adelaide.

As the old order were passing on so the aftermath of war would bring new recruits to the game. Charlie Turner and Charles Kelleway had died during 1944 and, in Melbourne, Clem Hill had fallen from a tram and sustained serious injuries. He died on 5 September 1945 and in his passing a link with many old cricketers was broken. Then four months later came the news that Joe Darling had died in Hobart at the age of seventy-six.

The 1945–46 domestic season was not competitive although, had it been so, Victoria would have won the Shield from NSW. The best displays were 200 from Sid Barnes, who was captain of NSW when they played Queensland in Brisbane, and from George Tribe of Victoria, a left-arm spin and googly bowler who took 9/45, also in Brisbane. Both men topped their respective tables: Barnes in batting with 794 runs at 88.22; Tribe in bowling with 40 wickets at 19.03.

The Australian selectors who chose the team for New Zealand were Edmund 'Chappie' Dwyer (NSW), Jack Ryder (Victoria) and Don Bradman (South Australia). They had a long hard look at all available players and, with one exception, chose the best cricketers on show. The odd one out was the volatile Cec Pepper who, after a number of verbal and written complaints about his language on the field of play, was never really considered a suitable tourist. Pepper went off to play league cricket in England and to enjoy a successful umpiring career.

After Bill Brown had been chosen as captain of the New Zealand party, Bill O'Reilly was elected as his deputy with Lindsay Hassett as the third touring selector. The team arrived in Auckland in late February 1946 and played their first match at Eden Park almost at once. Large crowds turned out to watch the Australians and they were not disappointed. Against Auckland the Australians scored 579 (Miller 139, Hassett 121, Barnes 107); versus Canterbury 415 (Brown 137); against Otago 420 (Brown 106), and in Wellington 415 (Hassett 114). This led neatly to the first-ever Test match (although not confirmed by the Imperial Cricket Conference until March 1948) between the neighbouring countries.

The contest lasted for eight hours and thirty-eight minutes spread over two damp days and watched by in excess of 40,000 people. The New Zealand captain, Walter Hadlee, gambled by batting on winning the toss. The soft pitch caused such serious problems that the Kiwis went from 37 for two to 42 all out – eight wickets falling for five runs in a few minutes either side of the lunch break. Australia were 149 for three at the close, Brown having made 67 and Barnes 54.

Next morning the tourists added 50 more runs before Brown declared at 199 for eight. It was a shrewd move, for within two hours New Zealand had been dismissed for 54 – a humiliating defeat by an innings and 103 runs. But such was the public's interest in cricket after the war years that the NZCC's gate-takings were a record, in excess of £3000.

The thirteen Australians who made the tour received £1 per day from the Board of Control, the same as had they been playing in Shield games. With such a profit the NZCC asked the Board if the allowance could be increased. The refusal was blunt. Four of the team were still in uniform and most were concerned about whether they could find jobs on their return home. All were out of pocket after the tour with only a blazer to show for their efforts. And the Board wondered why the players despised them.

While the latter stages of the Pacific war were still in progress the Western Australian Cricket Association was preparing its case for admittance into the Sheffield Shield competition. Alf Randell, who attended an Interstate Conference in Sydney on 12 October 1945, was told to make a full and definite proposal which the WACA spent hours in drafting. They originally wanted to enter for the 1946–47 season but this was rejected by the other states.

Randell therefore had to go to Melbourne on 16 March 1946 to put the WACA case and, according to his notes, 'encountered a searching examination'. The Interstate Conference then agreed to admit Western Australia but only on a conditional basis and, at the next meeting in Sydney on 12 September, put down some grossly unfair financial constraints which were to last up to 1954. Randell had to undergo yet another interrogation in Melbourne on 3 January 1947 after which he was given the news that his bid had been successful.

Preparations were, by now, in train for the forthcoming tour of Australia by an England team to be captained by Wally Hammond. Matters of moment flowed backwards and forwards between both cricket authorities including a letter from the Marylebone Cricket Club which asked 'if it was thought desirable that players should take dress clothes with them'. The note continued: 'It must be pointed out that such clothes are, at the present time, very expensive here in Britain and purchase of them would involve the surrender of a number of clothing coupons'.

The Board of Control, with little understanding of conditions in war-torn Britain, could scarcely contain their indignation. Jeanes replied: 'I have brought the matter to the attention of my Board and the chairman has expressed the view that there might be occasions upon which the visiting team would feel uncomfortable if they were not able to "dress". We feel that it is most necessary that the players be required to include dress clothes in their kit.'

At their subsequent meeting on 12 September 1946 the Board went ahead and arranged a series of formal dinners throughout the country with the most formal of all scheduled for the Hotel Windsor in Melbourne on 4 January 1947, 'in which dinner jackets will be worn'. In deferring the important cricket items on their agenda for the following day, the Board members had a lengthy discussion as to the menu, number of speeches, quotations for food, type and style of music and the invitation list.

Life in Australia just after the war was free and easy compared to that in Britain. Food parcels sent 'back home' was as natural a thing to do for Australians as being able to laze on a beach or buy virtually any consumer durable required. Mass migration to 'the land of milk and honey' was not yet fully under way but it had started. Far from work being hard to obtain, the situation was now reversed, where people were lured from one job to another on the promise of higher pay. Skilled workmen were a precious commodity and in some States unemployment was down to a level where it was only the unemployable who were left as representing the official statistics.

The first post-war England team left Southampton on 31 August and reached Australia only 24 days later, much to the surprise of the Australian Board who had not allowed for such a swift passage. For the English cricketers it was to be the start of a long, six-month tour, the final three weeks of which would be spent in New Zealand.

The appeal of the tour sent the memberships of State Associations or equivalents to all-time highs. In Perth, membership increased by 1186 resulting in a 260 per cent increase in the subscription income. This saw additional seating for one thousand people erected at the WACA ground and, according to the WACA's annual report: 'The executive embarked upon a bold plan for the general improvement of the ground which will involve a heavy outlay'. In Adelaide the membership rose to 3837 and, for the first time in their history, the SACA had to create a waiting list. Income rose to unprecedented heights and the SACA profit for the season was a staggering £6662.

In Melbourne the VCA recorded a profit of £9502, of which £5000 was distributed direct to the clubs. The Melbourne Cricket Club recorded a profit on cricket matches of £17,992 while their waiting list for membership grew to 7085 and the comment that: 'There does not appear, at present, much prospect of an early ballot for new full members'. It was the same story in Sydney where the trustees of the Sydney Cricket Ground found that their newly created waiting list quickly had over 5000 applicants waiting for membership. Meanwhile the NSWCA continued to buy property with their surplus monies and recorded assets of £79,800.

The Queensland Cricket Association recorded a profit for the year of £1433 after liaising with the Brisbane Cricket Ground Trust in spending a large amount of money to provide new and improved facilities for spectators. Even cricket's poor relations in Hobart had the TCA annual report mentioning an unexpected £1408 profit of which '£1300 was spent on much needed ground improvements'. It then added an interesting sideline that 'a large amount of maintenance work has accumulated at the ground but cannot be done due to the difficulty of obtaining labour'.

As the England cricketers were warming up in Western Australia in early October so the other States were in negotiation with the Australian Federation of Commercial Broadcasting Stations over the granting of broadcasting and filming rights for the season. The filming rights were easily arranged. Twentieth-Century Fox paid each State Association a fee of £40 to cover all matches while Paramount, Movietone and British Empire Films paid £25 for each Test.

The New South Wales Cricket Association came to an agreement fairly easily with the radio representatives, gaining a fee of £1200, but it was less easy around the rest of the country. In the end the WACA and TCA gained £150 each with the SACA, VCA and QCA benefiting by £800.

But for all the publicity and massive press coverage in Australia, the view of the English media that their team was too old proved to be valid even before the first Test had taken place. The tour, coming so soon after the end of the war, was mainly one of goodwill and that was exactly what it became.

The first serious match, against Western Australia, saw Hammond (208) score his team's only double-century of the tour. The match was drawn as were fixtures against a Western Australian Combined Team, South Australia, An Australian Eleven, New South Wales and Queensland with only a win over Victoria to show before the Tests began.

It had been ten years since 'Gubby' Allen's team had signed off and now an England side would again play Tests on Australian soil. Don Bradman had been appointed Australian captain and the Brisbane Test saw the debuts of the talented left-handed batsman from Sydney, Arthur Morris, along with the Victorian bowler George Tribe. Batting first, the home team were 46 for two when Bradman was joined at the crease by Lindsay Hassett. The pair then proceeded to add 276 for the third wicket, a record yet to be passed in Ashes matches. The partnership was not without its controversy as Bradman was given not out by umpire George Borwick when a bump ball was taken at second slip. Hassett (128) has always said the umpire was correct and Bradman, then on 28, went on to score 187 which was a match-winning score. During the lunch interval following the incident the English players were extremely agitated over the affair and ensuing years have seen the story become one of the most discussed in Test cricket.

That, along with two fortuitous thunderstorms, saw Australia on top for the whole game. Their total of 645 was just too much for

England who struggled on a typical Brisbane 'sticky' to 141 (Miller 7/60) and, following-on, 172 (Toshack 6/82), to lose by an innings and 332 runs.

Then came a country match for the tourists before the second Test in Sydney. Australia had a problem, albeit a pleasant one. Ray Lindwall had contracted chicken-pox in Brisbane and the selectors were faced with a surfeit of outstanding bowlers who could replace him. There have been a number of times in Australian cricket history when a second 'Test' team could easily have been chosen and this time was one of them. Any one of ten top bowlers could be selected and in the end the choice went to the big Victorian paceman, Fred Freer, who was to play in his sole Test.

Hammond decided to bat on winning the toss and saw only two of his batsmen – Edrich (71) and Ikin (60) – prepared to use their feet against the off-spin of Ian Johnson and the leg-spin of Colin McCool. A total of 255 did not look too bad when Australia were 159 for four, but then Bradman, who batted down the order because of a leg injury, joined Sid Barnes and in the next 393 minutes they scored 405 runs for the fifth wicket to create a current long-standing Test record. Barnes took 642 minutes to score his 234. Remarkably Bradman also made 234, with both batsmen being out within four balls of each other. The Australian score reached 659 for eight before Bradman declared on the penultimate morning. England fought back well, being 247 for three at stumps with Bill Edrich carrying on to an excellent 119. But on his dismissal the tourists' innings folded and defeat by an innings in successive matches had not happened to an England side since January 1898.

Before the third Test started in Melbourne on New Year's Day 1947, half the Sheffield Shield programme had been completed. Victoria were by far the strongest side and easily took the first title since the end of the war. Their strength in reserves was crucial and with Test and representative selections they called on thirty players during the season. By the New Year, Victoria had won three matches out of three with scores of 548, 543, and 560 for eight declared. Afterwards their scores were 466, 356, and 450 for three declared.

In retrospect, and with the benefit of modern methods, it now seems rather bizarre that Don Bradman was not only a delegate on the Australian Board of Control but also had to attend meetings while play was in progress during the third Test. The Board meeting started at noon on 30 December 1946 and carried on for five days in the VCA offices in Flinders Street.

After worrying about the forthcoming Saturday night 'Dinner jackets must be worn' dinner, the Board discussed various matters: a protest from Australian National Airways over the decision 'prohibiting cricketers from travelling by air in numbers in excess of three at any one time'; the Federal Government's 'disproportionate Entertainments Tax levy'; and a fight between the NSW and Victorian delegates as to which State was going to supply wood to Lord's for their new memorial gallery. Late on the second day the meeting got down to discussing the game of cricket.

Don Bradman then spoke, and discussed at some length the players' views on a number of issues. He had consulted Wally Hammond on the best ball to use for Tests and both had agreed on A. G. Thompson's 'Turf' ball. Hotels used, and their facilities, were reported upon with Bradman adamant that the players should have single rooms at all times. His obvious care for the cricketers was as refreshing as it was vital. It had been nearly forty years since a Board man had spoken so passionately about the players' needs and wishes, and not surprisingly, all Bradman's requests were met.

Bradman left the meeting on New Year's morning to play in the Test just as his fellow delegates were discussing the following season's tour by India. By the time Australia had reached 253 for six at the close of the first day the Board's agenda had reached the item marked: 'Bradman's Tour Report, 1938'. Amazingly, this excellent report was not finally fully discussed for another nine months and even then not in detail before the writer was thanked for his efforts and the matter dropped from the agenda paper.

The Australian innings was saved on the second day by Colin McCool's only Test century. His three-hour innings saw the score to 365 to which England replied with 351 by late afternoon on only the second day. Yet the six-day game was going to end in the first drawn Test in Australia since March 1882. Three Australians were responsible for this turn of events: Arthur Morris with 155 and then, after an Australian collapse, a tail-end partnership of 154 runs in only 88 minutes between Don Tallon (92) and Ray Lindwall (100). Left to score 551 in seven hours, England survived a barrage of bouncers from Lindwall and Miller to see the final score to 310 for seven.

The match had been watched by the largest crowd of the series, 343,675, with 72,022 on the fourth day and 70,863 on the third. Takings of £49,390 reflected the change in the value of money from the previous tour ten years earlier when a slightly larger crowd paid nearly half the amount for the same number of days' cricket.

After two draws in Tasmania and one in South Australia, the tourists prepared themselves for the fourth Test in Adelaide. As in the previous match there was little to choose between the two sides after each had completed an innings. England scored 460 to Australia's 487, all made in temperatures of a century plus. What did mark the game out for special attention was that Denis Compton and Arthur Morris both scored hundreds in each innings which is the only occasion that a batsman on each side has achieved this in the same Test. As the match headed towards a draw, the English wicketkeeper, Godfrey Evans, created a record which is referred to frequently: it took him 97 minutes 'to get off the mark' in his second innings.

Two more draws, in Melbourne and Sydney against Victoria and NSW respectively, led up to the tourists' final Test in Sydney which started on the last day of February 1947. With Australia having retained the Ashes, the small crowd and poor weather did not augur for a spectacular clash. The damp, overcast conditions and rain on the second day saw the bowlers in control for the first time in the series. Once again the first innings was close: England 280 (Lindwall 7/63) to Australia's 253 (Wright 7/105). With Len Hutton ill, the top England batting looked brittle the second time around. Three stumpings by Tallon off McCool helped reduce the tourists' score to 186 after England had seemed like taking a clear advantage. Needing 214 to win, the Australians looked surprisingly shaky. The pitch was deteriorating all the time as Wright and Bedser bowled superbly. The struggle finally ended in a five-wicket victory for Bradman's side in the last over of the penultimate day's play.

Australia had won the series three-nil and brought back big cricket to a nation in need of sporting success. Financially the tour was a great success with the Board recording a profit of £39,722, but post-war Australia gave cricket a number of new situations to face. The NSWCA, in a decision of considerable merit, arranged for a report to be prepared listing the most pressing problems facing the game. It had been noted that there had been a marked rise in attendances at club fixtures during the war but these figures were obviously exceptional.

The report, compiled by the State selectors, could nearly as easily apply today, forty-five years later. Of the five identified problems the first was 'the increasing counter-attraction of other outdoor summer games and pastimes, particularly golf, and also tennis, surfing and motoring'. Next came, 'the growing popularity of racing and other kinds of gambling'. The third was the most relevant in the society of the day: 'The increased competition for jobs among young people – who were therefore concentrating less on cricket – combined with a reluctance of employers to give cricketers time off to play or practise'; the fourth was 'a loss of interest in cricket at schools, in part because boys were turning to swimming, tennis and softball'; and fifth was 'the rapid disappearance of open spaces in Sydney where boys could play the game'.

The chief concern of the five selectors, headed by 'Chappie' Dwyer, and comprising Selby Burt, Alex Marks, Arthur Vincent and Billy Wells, was that standards were likely to fall. Their report was relevant around the country, so much so that the associations in South Australia and Western Australia, influenced by the NSWCA findings, commissioned their own reports and came up with near enough the same answers. Nowadays, the pull of television sport would be relevant although back in post-war Australia it was felt that radio was having a similar effect.

There was also another leak from the cricketing ship and that concerned the number of Australian first-class or top Grade players who moved to England to play in League, or County, cricket. NSW lost Bill Alley, Cec Pepper, Jack Pettiford, Ken Grieves, and Jock Livingston, while from other States Fred Freer, Bruce Dooland, Jack Manning, George Tribe and Ben Barnett (who went to the Leagues) added to the exodus.

The demand for Australia to tour various countries was discussed at length during the September meeting of the Board in Sydney. New Zealand wanted a tour in early 1948; the West Indies Board had asked the Imperial Cricket Conference to pressurise Australia to agree to tour the Caribbean from January to April 1949; South Africa wanted to tour Australia, then changed their minds and wanted Australia to visit them, while India wanted a return tour as quickly as possible to the forthcoming visit which they were making to Australia.

The Indians, however, were not making life easy for the Board secretary, Bill Jeanes. No reply had been received regarding their approval of the playing and financial conditions laid down and after a number of unanswered cables the Board recorded: 'That on not having heard from India on these questions it is assumed that such conditions are accepted'.

Jeanes did get a telegram from the Indian Board which said: 'Arrangements have been made for the team to travel to Australia by the Orient liner *Orion*, arriving at Fremantle on 6 October'. On checking with various agencies Jeanes subsequently found that the Indians would arrive in Australia by plane. Then came a later telegram which read: 'Our party will comprise 17 players, manager, baggage supervisor and masseur'. The missive gave the names of the three officials but failed to list those of the players.

Captained by Lala Amarnath and managed by the Indian Board secretary, Pankaj Gupta, the team finally arrived at Guildford airport, Perth, in time to play in a drawn four-day match against Western Australia. Two more draws followed – against South Australia and Victoria, in which Amarnath scored an impressive unbeaten 228. NSW defeated the visitors by an innings but the big surprise came when

India defeated An Australian Eleven in Sydney with Vinoo Mankad taking 2/93 and 8/84 with his slow left-arm bowling.

It was during this match that Don Bradman (172) scored his one-hundredth first-class century. As the entire crowd rose to greet the single which took him to three figures the reality was that it was his 295th innings compared to the next fastest to score a hundred centuries, Wally Hammond, who needed 679 innings. Denis Compton later did it in 552 innings but, even so, the genius of Bradman always seemed to make record-making easy.

While this was happening in Sydney, across the continent in Perth the Western Australians were playing South Australia in their initial Sheffield Shield fixture before a less than expected overall crowd of 10,188. Having lured Keith Carmody from NSW, the newly appointed captain-coach scored 198 as Western Australia scored 444 and went on to win by an innings and 124 runs.

The Indians moved on to Brisbane and defeat by Queensland by just 24 runs after Mankad had claimed nine more wickets. This led on to the first Test which saw Australia get the benefit of a good pitch before rain allowed only two hours' play over three of the scheduled six days. Before the deluge Australia had made 273 for three on the first day with Bradman declaring at 382 for eight. The captain's 185, in his first Test against India, was the backbone of the innings.

Ernie Toshack, with his left-arm slow-medium bowling, then took the final five Indian wickets for just two runs in nineteen deliveries as the tourists fell for a miserly 58. Following-on they did slightly better with 98, Toshack 6/29, but still lost by an innings and 226 runs.

The second Test, in Sydney, was completely ruined by rain with only ten hours play possible during which Mankad created Test history by running out the non-striker, Bill Brown, for backing-up. India scored 188 and 61 for seven, Australia 107 and the match was drawn. The Indians then played two leisurely country matches whilst the Test men went back to their States to play in Shield fixtures.

A trend was now beginning to evidence itself in Australian newspapers which has, unfortunately, grown worse as time progresses. For the previous season's England tour, the Sydney journalist Clif Cary had launched attack after attack on various players which culminated in a particularly outspoken book entitled *Cricket Controversy*.

For the Indian tour the former South Australian batsman, Dick Whitington, now a cricket writer for *The Sun* newspaper in Sydney, was carrying on a long feud with Don Bradman in the columns of his publication and those others who took his syndicated articles. So incorrect were his charges that the South Australian Cricket Association described them as 'unfair criticism and not based on fact'.

A discussion with Whitington got nowhere as his articles started to become more vitriolic and adopted a tabloid style familiar today. His editor said: 'Whitington is employed by us because of his special qualifications as a cricket writer and he is quite competent to express any views he deems necessary in the interests of the game'. The Australian Journalists' Association had by now become involved, saying that: 'The articles by R. S. Whitington are under consideration by the Federal Executive'.

For once, activities in the press box were becoming as interesting as those on the field of play. The sniping went on and reached the stage where the Board of Control seriously considered making representations in each State to the newspaper proprietors. Unfortunately the trend had started which saw player/journalist relationships deteriorate, never to recover.

The third Test in Melbourne, which started on New Year's Day 1948, lasted only four days and was yet again affected by rain. The Indian captain must have regretted his pre-tour decision not to accept the Australian offer to cover Test pitches for yet again rain on an uncovered pitch cost India dearly.

Australia reached 355 for eight on the first day, Bradman 132, in front of a holiday crowd of 45,327 people. This became 394 on the second morning to which India replied with 291 for nine declared. Amarnath gambled slightly with his third-day declaration as heavy overnight rain had changed the character of the pitch. Bradman countered by putting his tail-end batsmen in first. The ploy worked for, at 32 for four, Bradman joined Morris (100*) for an unbroken fifth wicket partnership of 223. Bradman's unbeaten 127 made him the first player to score a century in each innings of a Test against India.

Declaring overnight, Bradman set India 359 to win on a pitch again devastated by further rain. India fell for 125 and Australia won by 233 runs. India then went to play two fixtures against Tasmania, winning by an innings and 139 runs in Hobart and having the worst of a draw in Launceston.

The Indians arrived in Adelaide for the fourth Test as the SACA committee had just made a momentous decision. Bill Jeanes had received a number of complaints during the season from Association members stating that women were drinking in the members' bar at the Adelaide Oval. The committee were shocked to hear that this was going on and immediately instructed their secretary to put up a sign saying 'that the bar was for the use of men only'. They were no doubt incensed by the recent Health Department warning which stated: 'The Ladies Conveniences have been declared to be in an insanitary condition' and instructed SACA 'to take steps to amend this condition' prior to the Test match.

Neil Harvey, a left-handed Victorian batsman, made his debut in the Test which saw Australia's total reach 674, the highest score reached in a home Test. Don Bradman made 201, the last of his twelve double-hundreds; Lindsay Hassett remained unbeaten on 198 and Sid Barnes scored 112. For India Vijay Hazare became the first batsman from his country to score a century in each innings – 116 out of 381, then 145 out of 277 as Ray Lindwall claimed his Test-best figures of 7/38 in Australia's victory by an innings and 16 runs.

The fifth Test in Melbourne was equally as one-sided, with the winning margin being an innings and 177 runs. The highlight of the match was the innings of Neil Harvey (153). At 19 years and 121 days he became the youngest player to score a century for Australia.

The Indians lost to Western Australia on their way home but could excuse themselves by saying that they were beaten by the newly crowned Sheffield Shield champions. For in a domestic season of shocks the newcomers had grabbed the trophy at their first attempt.

There was now to be a turning-point in Australian cricket. The Twentieth Australians would soon depart for England and the tour would bring Don Bradman's Test career to its conclusion. Australian cricket was in fine fettle although the inept Board of Control was still a battleground for the strife and jealousy that brought about its formation. In sitting in judgment on the players it controlled, Board members had difficulty in recognising the members of the Australian team. Cricketers with intimate knowledge of the game were unwelcome on the Board, with Bradman being the only exception. But, as the tour of 1948 would show, Bradman was quite exceptional.

## 21

# Bradman and after, 1948–51

Before the selection and departure of the 1948 Australian team to England, the Board of Control received a number of requests for the side to visit different countries on their return home. The Australian High Commissioner in Malaya requested that two matches be played, one in Kuala Lumpur, the other in Singapore. Then the Fiji Cricket Association wanted a match in Suva if the team were travelling via North America. Soon afterwards came a suggestion to play matches in Canada while going from east to west by train. Last came a communication from the Indian Board of Control who wanted a game in Bombay as sailing hours would permit such a fixture. All these requests were refused even before the selectors – Messrs Bradman, Dwyer and Ryder – made their choice on 11 February 1948. Bill Jeanes was asked to take the manager's position but he turned it down, and the job went to NSW Board delegate Keith Johnson, who had managed the Australian Services in 1945. Bradman was confirmed as captain. It was a risk for him to undertake such a tour, particularly bearing in mind that during part of the war he had been afflicted with muscle spasms, while a rib injury suffered in the final Test against India caused him some discomfort for a time.

At the age of thirty-nine Bradman could have toured as manager but one can only speculate about the pressures he was put under to play. He was unique in that he had become a symbol: a prime example of success from humble origins. He was 'Australia' to many people in the cricket community and had represented hope to those who needed a hero during the Depression years.

His touring team, like everything done by him, was chosen with great care. The batting was immensely strong, with the bowling mainly reliant on pace. In the two warm-up matches against Tasmania in early March, Barnes (111), Harvey (104) and Hassett (100) scored centuries in Hobart with Brown, Morris and Loxton doing well in the return at Launceston. In Perth a few days later Bradman (115) and Morris (each 115) stood out as another large Australian score was made.

Just after the SS *Strathaird* had sailed from Fremantle on 19 March, Bill Jeanes received a request from the Ceylon Cricket Association asking if the team could now play two matches instead of one when they reached Colombo. The suggestion was that the team could then fly direct to Bombay to rejoin their ship. The Board chairman, Aubrey Oxlade, refused even to consider the argument so the single match took place on 27 March at the Colombo Oval. *The Islander* newspaper had the headline 'Bradman will definitely play' which guaranteed a crowd in excess of 20,000.

The result was a predictable draw as rain spoiled the latter stages. The Australians had found the going slightly difficult in the morning and only after Ian Johnson had the pitch measured during the lunch interval was it found to be only twenty yards in length. From then on the bowlers delivered the ball from two yards behind the crease. As Ceylon Board official Eddie Melder wrote: 'Such readjustments added a little spice to the game'.

The Australians arrived at Tilbury on 16 April to a resounding welcome and an immediate presentation by Bradman to the British people of 17,000 food parcels brought over from the State of Victoria. Throughout the voyage Bradman had worked on the various speeches he would have to give to numerous receptions, but with the bulk of his side having undergone military discipline there was never any need to lay down the law. They were all at ease in dinner suits and totally unconcerned when functions demanded full dress.

The tour opened at Worcester with Bradman (107) scoring his expected hundred and Hassett making 138. With forty photographers following him to the crease, and a young radio commentator named John Arlott giving descriptions of the match from the boundary, Bradman had new pressures to contend with for the next five months.

During the tour in non-Test matches the Australians' scoring was prodigious. Their highest was 774 for seven against Gloucestershire, Arthur Morris 290; then 721 in a day against Essex; 632 versus Surrey; 610 for five against the Gentlemen at Lord's, Lindsay Hassett 200; 560 for five against Somerset; 552 at Lord's against MCC; 549 for five against Sussex and 522 for seven at Hastings versus the South of England. The team scored 47 centuries in first-class matches, more than ever before on an England tour, yet the best bowling performance was Ian Johnson's 7/42 against Leicester in the second match.

With ten victories and two draws behind them the Australians went into the first Test at Nottingham in confident mood. Norman Yardley, who had been Hammond's vice-captain in 1946–47, now won the toss for England, batted, and then watched as his team fell to 74 for eight by the tea interval. Bill Johnston caused the most trouble with his fast left-arm deliveries that swung, dipped and varied in pace. A revival to 165 was nowhere near good enough as Bradman (138) scored his twenty-eighth Test century in 288 minutes while Hassett (137) took 354 minutes over his. After dismissing Australia for 509 England faced a 344-run deficit which they reached for the loss of six wickets. Denis Compton held the innings together with 184, scored in ten minutes under seven hours, but even this could not stop Australia eventually running out victors by eight wickets.

Two matches against counties followed the Test and Bradman's pulling power was obvious in the fact that against Yorkshire at Bramall Lane 51,824 saw the three days of cricket in cold weather. Six weeks earlier, against Yorkshire at Bradford, only 12,128 had attended a match in which Bradman did not play.

Then came five glorious days in late June at Lord's when Australia showed their prowess in front of a total attendance of 132,000 who paid a then record £43,000. With thousands locked out each day the atmosphere was electric as Arthur Morris (105) got the Australian score ticking over nicely. A total of 350 was good enough as Lindwall, 5/70, reduced England to 215 early on the third morning. The Saturday crowd then sat back and watched Barnes (141), Bradman (89), Miller (74) and Morris (62) slaughter the home attack of Bedser, Coxon, Wright, Laker, Yardley, Edrich and Compton. A declaration at lunch on Monday at 460 for seven gave England five sessions in which to hold out. On a rain-affected pitch Toshack found conditions ideal for him and his 5/40 saw Australia home by 409 runs.

The margin of Australia's two Test victories had the newspaper writers of the day questioning the structure of the game in Britain. They did not seem to realise that Australian cricket had recovered much more swiftly from the war and that the cycle of the game had given the tourists world-class players which England scarcely possessed.

Relief came for England in Manchester when the third Test was ruined by rain. Compton had scored a courageous unbeaten 145 for the home side following a retirement with a nasty head blow. England gained a first-innings lead but the weather meant that a draw was inevitable.

The itinerary then sent the tourists south to Lord's for an easy victory over Middlesex and then back north for the fourth Test at Leeds. This match became a contest remembered by most followers of the game for its quite amazing fourth innings.

At one time England were 423 for two with Washbrook (143), Edrich (111), Hutton (81) and Bedser, sent in as night-watchman, going strongly; but the pressure from the Australian bowlers saw a mini-collapse to 496 all out which was a huge challenge for the tourists. After losing three early wickets for 68, Neil Harvey went to the crease for his first Test innings in England, and proceeded to score 112 in partnerships with Keith Miller (58) and Sam Loxton (93). Later Lindwall made 77 as the Australian score fell just 38 runs short of England's.

Going in to bat again only a quarter of an hour into the fourth day the English batsmen consolidated their lead, reaching 362 for eight at the close, a lead of exactly 400. Yardley surprised the pundits by batting for five minutes on the last morning before declaring and leaving Australia to score 404 runs in 345 minutes to win the Test and the series. No team then had ever scored 400 for victory in the fourth innings of a Test and when Hassett (17) was caught and bowled by Compton with the score on 57 the odds against them lengthened.

But then Bradman joined Morris and they were not parted until six minutes past five that afternoon. The stand was worth 301 runs made in 217 minutes: no wonder the Yorkshire crowd stood to applaud Morris back to the pavilion following his 182 scored in 291 minutes with 33 fours. Keith Miller (12) fell quickly, going for the runs and, with a quarter of an hour to go, Neil Harvey scored the winning runs. Bradman remained not out on 173, made in 255 minutes with 29 fours, the last of his 29 Test centuries.

The celebrations lasted long into the evening. The owner of the hotel where the Australians stayed overnight possibly unwisely gave Lindsay Hassett the keys to the bar. Next morning the tourists were fortunate to bat first against Derbyshire – using openers who had not played in the Test – but they still managed to score 456 and win by an innings.

The final Test at The Oval started on 14 August and by the end of the first day Australia had the game virtually won. England had collapsed for 52 to the pace of Ray Lindwall who took 6/20, and only Len Hutton (30) – first in, last out – saved the score from being much worse. The humidity was perfect for the visiting bowlers but it was not exploited by the home attack. At 117, Sid Barnes (61) fell to Eric Hollies and then rushed off the field to film Bradman's last Test innings.

In one of the game's most emotional moments Don Bradman walked to the crease, the crowd standing and the ground echoing to applause. He needed just four runs to get a Test aggregate of 7000 and a Test career average of 100. Norman Yardley led the players in three hearty cheers for the Australian captain as he took guard against Hollies. The first ball was a leg-break which was played with a correct dead bat. The second, a googly of perfect length, went through the defence and bowled Australia's greatest cricketer. On his return to the dressing-room Sid Barnes told Bradman he had filmed his entire innings.

Arthur Morris took the batting honours with 196 out of Australia's 389 and even though Len Hutton (64) held the England top order together again an Australian win was never in doubt. By winning the series four-nil the tourists had entertained the vast crowds who watched them and, more importantly in certain eyes, had recorded a profit of £79,608.

The tour concluded with five more first-class matches and two minor fixtures in Scotland. The final record, with the team playing in 38 matches, four of which were minor, and not recording a single defeat, was superb. The tourists sailed home from England on 23 September as arrangements were in hand in Australia for Bradman's testimonial match to be played in Melbourne from 3–7 December 1948; but the Interstate Conference did not obtain unanimity on the Bradman match from NSW until they were granted permission to hold a testimonial for Alan Kippax and Bert Oldfield which had been postponed from the 1939–40 season.

To add to the congestion in the fixture list, Albert Moir, MP, moved a motion at the South Australian Cricket Association's annual meeting which did not have the support of the committee. Moir's motion required that 'they grant a testimonial cricket match for the benefit of Mr Arthur Richardson during the forthcoming season'. The motion was carried easily and eventually the South Australian home fixture against Victoria in March 1949 was chosen for the event. Sympathy ran high in Adelaide for Richardson, who had been badly advised by a cricketing friend to invest his life savings in Harry Hodgett's firm only weeks before it collapsed. In the end Arthur Richardson collected £2130 from the testimonial.

The Kippax-Oldfield testimonial match had been played between Hassett's XI and Morris's XI in Sydney in late February. In a casual encounter the NSW opening batsman, Jack Moroney, scored 217 as Morris's team won by eight wickets, and £6030 was split evenly between the two recipients.

The Bradman match in Melbourne was a far greater affair. Every innings was a delight as Hassett's XI 406 (Lindwall 104) and 430 (Hassett 102) tied with Bradman's XI 434 (Bradman 123, Meuleman 100) and 402 (Tallon 146*, Morris 108). After expenses Bradman received £9342, the highest figure ever reached in such matches.

Behind the scenes the Western Australian Cricket Association had been basking in their success. In March 1948 an invitation arrived from the Ceylon Cricket Association which asked 'that if in the event of satisfactory terms being arranged, would Western Australia tour Ceylon?' The Board raised their usual disruptive points but the WACA committee continued processing the idea. Dates were arranged for a tour in April and May 1949, an itinerary raised and players asked about their availability. The project collapsed in August 1948 when the Board refused to sanction the financial arrangements. It would take another forty-two years before Western Australia would finally play on the sub-continent.

At the Board meeting held in September 1948 a matter was first raised which, in later years, brought about a catastrophic split in Australian cricket. The subject was television and it was raised by Eric Yeomans, the Victorian delegate, who proposed that the Board examine how this new means of mass communication would affect them. Yeomans suggested 'that the secretary write to the Marylebone Cricket Club asking for their experiences on the televising of cricket matches, and particularly as to the efficiency of television as applied to such matches and the fees received for such rights'.

The arrogance of the Board over radio broadcasting defied belief. At the Interstate Conference (the Board by another name where domestic matters were discussed) held in Sydney on 16 September 1948, the NSW Sports Broadcasting Association (SBA) – which represented all radio stations – proposed that in exchange for broadcasting Shield and club matches the SBA would 'give the fullest publicity to all matches and to the Associations' cricket activities; the commercial stations to give three free advertisements each day prior to matches, and that cricket interviews, stories and features would become part of the overall sporting presentations'. The Conference, totally unimpressed, replied by asking how much the stations would pay for broadcasting.

In January 1950, Eric Yeomans again referred to the subject by suggesting that the cricket and radio authorities should work together as they complemented each other. The criticisms thrown back at him showed a bigoted attitude towards the radio stations. The view was that it was the stations who should chase the Board to beg for broadcasting rights. As time would show, Yeomans had the right idea.

New South Wales won the Sheffield Shield in 1948–49 and in the following season. They were far superior to all the States except Victoria who chased them hard in both years. In the former season, Lindsay Hassett's 205 against Queensland was the only Shield double-century with Ian Johnson's 43 wickets showing how things had changed since before the war. In 1949–50, Bob McLean's incredibly slow 213 for South Australia was also the sole Shield double-hundred although Jack Iverson's 46 wickets topped the bill, three more than Johnson's haul.

The Australian selectors – Bradman, Dwyer and Ryder – now looked hard and long at the talent available to them before choosing the team to tour South Africa in 1949–50. Bradman, who had been knighted in the previous New Year's Honours list, fully expected his successor as captain to be Lindsay Hassett, yet when the votes were counted he only won the position by seven votes to six over Arthur Morris who had no experience of captaincy. Writer Ray Robinson said at the time that the near decision had 'prevented a disgusting act of ingratitude' and that 'once again Hassett's notable achievements with the Services team had been devalued'.

Three Test players were unavailable for the tour: Sid Barnes, who said that the money offered by the Board was a pittance which would cost him too much; Don Tallon; and Bill Brown. The team was the seemingly usual five each from Victoria and NSW, with two each from South Australia and Queensland; but there were howls of dismay when the team was announced and Keith Miller's name was missing. A feud with Bradman – resolved in later years – had seen the vote go against him but as Miller was contemplating his future, Bill Johnston was injured in a car crash soon after arriving in South Africa, and Miller flew out to join the team.

The four newcomers to the party were the NSW fast left-arm bowler Alan Walker, who was also an international rugby player; the right-hand opening batsman, Jack Moroney, from Sydney; Queensland's batsman Ken Archer; and South Australia's Geff Noblet, a medium-pace bowler with a suspect action.

Hassett's captaincy impressed from the start. His warmth of personality and sense of fun contrasted with Bradman's efficient but cold methods. It was a happy tour with the players remembering particularly the hospitality offered to them.

After defeating Zululand in the opening match the team recorded five first-class wins and three draws up to the first Test in Johannesburg on Christmas Eve. The venue was a rugby stadium, Ellis Park, as the Old Wanderers ground in the centre of town had been demolished and the new facilities in the (then) outer suburb of Kent Park had not yet been completed.

Hassett won the toss, batted, and saw both opening batsmen back in the pavilion without scoring. In typical captain's style Hassett scored 112 and Sam Loxton 101 as the total reached 413 by the middle of the second day. Keith Miller, making only his second appearance on tour, then took 5/40 in a devastating spell which reduced the Springboks to 137. Following-on they did little better, reaching 191 with Bill Johnston, now recovered, being the destroyer this time with 6/44.

The second Test on New Year's Eve in Cape Town saw a more even display from the Australians. The first-day score of 312 for four saw Moroney with 87, Miller 58 and Hassett 57. Then came Harvey, after the New Year's celebrations, with 178, an innings which had the knowledgeable Newlands crowd applauding with delight. Hassett declared at 526 for seven and then patiently worked his bowlers in even spells as South Africa made 278, McCool 5/41. Hassett enforced the follow-on and, even though South Africa's captain, Dudley Nourse, scored 114, the Australian tactics of patience – and 5/32 from Ray Lindwall – saw them winners by eight wickets.

Innings victories against Eastern Province and Border led up to the third Test in Durban where Nourse won his only toss of the series and was well satisfied with his team's 240 for two at the close. An inch of rain fell overnight and made the pitch difficult. Eric Rowan scored 143 and Nourse 66 but the tail fell away and the Springboks were all out for 311. *The Natal Mercury* suggested that the pitch 'may remain on the tough side' and how correct this proved as the 17,000 spectators whooped with joy as Hugh Tayfield's 7/23 saw the Australians dismissed for 75!

The second day had seen eighteen wickets fall for 146 runs and it left Nourse the weekend to decide whether or not to enforce the follow-on. *The Natal Mercury* said on Monday: 'The question will need some careful study of the wicket [*sic*] this morning before the South African captain makes his pronouncement'. Nourse decided to bat again and on a drying, but still awkward, pitch his side fell for 99. Hassett's captaincy came in for great praise as he allowed the South Africans to bat while the pitch dried out. He cut down the runs by fielding men on the boundary and allowing only singles. It was shrewd and it worked.

Needing to score 336 in 435 minutes Australia were 80 for three at the end of the penultimate day. Only two wickets fell on the final day as Neil Harvey – batting completely out of character – took five and a half hours to score a match-winning and unbeaten 151. The *Mercury* said: 'Renowned for their fighting qualities as cricketers, the occasion brought the best out of the Australians. They fought a rearguard action of no mean proportion in the final innings. That indomitable spirit to win through, no matter what the circumstances may be, was in most marked evidence.'

Two more victories – against Transvaal and North Eastern Transvaal – led up to the fourth Test at Ellis Park. Morris (111) and Moroney (118) opened for Australia with a stand of 214 on a pitch perfect for batting. Miller chipped in with 84, and Hassett (53) and Harvey (56*) scored half-centuries before the declaration at 465 for eight. Lindwall and Miller then reduced South Africa to 148 for six after which the home team staged a good recovery. At 275 for seven overnight, the score reached 352 by lunch on the final day. With a draw inevitable Moroney (101*) and Harvey (100) enjoyed themselves with centuries, Moroney's making him the only player to score a hundred in each innings in matches between the two sides.

The depth and power of Australia's batting made up for a slight weakness in the bowling attack but for all that Hassett's team was far better balanced than Nourse's. The fifth Test at St George's Park, Port Elizabeth, was a prime example. The Springbok bowlers failed to utilise the strong sea-breeze as Australia made their highest total in South Africa, 549 for seven declared. Hassett led the way with 167, Morris followed with 157 and Harvey with 116. The Springboks were always up against it, falling for 158 and 132, and so allowing Australia to take the series four-nil. Harvey's 660 runs at 132.00 remains the record aggregate for these contests.

In all first-class matches the Australian batsmen scored thirty centuries with Harvey's aggregate 1526 runs followed by Morris on 1411 and Moroney 1331. The bowling was very evenly distributed with Johnson taking 77 wickets, Johnston 56, McCool 51 and Lindwall 50 being the top four. But the Australian team sailed home during April 1950 knowing that age was beginning to catch up with many of them and that competition from younger players would be fierce.

A number of times during 1948 and 1949 pressure from the New Zealand Cricket Council on various issues forced the Australian Board on to the back foot. The Test match of 1946 had belatedly been given Test status but not the two matches of March 1905. The NZCC were adamant that the 1905 matches were Tests but this was rejected by the Australians on the grounds that 'We don't want to change our records by retrospectivity'. What New Zealand did win, however, was a tour by a strong Australian side, again captained by Bill Brown.

The tour comprised a mixture of first-class and two-day minor matches. All told there were ten centuries with Bill Brown's 184 against Otago being the highest. Against Wairarapa at Masterton on 29 March 1950, the NSW left-arm paceman, Alan Davidson, took 10/29 from thirteen overs. He then scored an unbeaten 157.

Australia won ten and drew four of their fourteen matches with the main fixture being against a full New Zealand side starting on 17 March in Dunedin. Walter Hadlee won the toss and decided to bat and although the Kiwis finished at 231 they had a great deal of trouble reading the spin of Jack Iverson, whose middle finger flicked the ball with either off-spin or leg-spin motion. But it was leg-spinner Doug Ring, with 7/88, who achieved considerable turn and subsequent success.

Rain delayed the start of play on the second day, but Australia were soon 42 for four. From an overnight 120 for five the pitch had dried out enough for Don Tallon to score 116, with seven sixes, and the total to reach 299. New Zealand then collapsed to 67 for nine, still one run behind Australia, before Hadlee stone-walled and played out the last tense 22 minutes for a draw. On his return to Australia, Bill Brown made an interesting observation: 'The New Zealand fielding was much better than the Australians'. High praise indeed.

At the turn of the decade changes took place within some Associations although people such as Bill Jeanes, Aubrey Oxlade, Syd Smith and Jack Hutcheon – all of whom had been cricket's decision-makers for a quarter of a century or so – were still in place with their fixed ideals. At one time, Jeanes had had an assistant: he lasted just three months. The only person who seemed capable of working with him was the former South Australian batsman, Roy Lonergan, who was twice enticed from Sydney to be second-in-command.

Pressure was the accepted thing at the time because, so often, one man was doing a job which should have been done by many. Lonergan died mysteriously in 1956 but prior to that, in January 1950, pressure had forced the NSWCA secretary, Harold Heydon, to resign. He went to Killara Golf Club as secretary – a sinecure in many ways. At the end of the year Harry Brereton, the long-standing VCA secretary, handed over to Jack Ledward. In Perth the energetic Les Truman was putting the WACA on its way to becoming the pride of Australian cricket.

In NSW, Heydon's successor was his assistant Alan Barnes. Here was a less forceful man and one much more personable, who brought a new management style to the Association. Like his predecessor, Barnes was totally committed to the job and available at all times. He managed affairs with great efficiency and was just the man for the Board to turn to when Bill Jeanes finally retired and his successor, Jack Ledward, found the going too tough.

During the southern winter of 1950 it was announced from Lord's that the forty-year-old Northamptonshire captain, Freddie Brown, would lead the England touring team a few months later. He was the third choice behind Norman Yardley and George Mann who both declined the trip for business reasons. Brown then insisted on a team of mainly young players to tackle the rampant Australians.

Arriving at Fremantle on 9 October, the team had two country matches prior to meeting Western Australia. A draw plus victory against South Australia took the tourists to Melbourne for another draw, this time with Victoria. Then came NSW in Sydney as a total crowd of 53,643 watched four days of superb cricket. NSW declared at 509 for three, following 168 from captain Arthur Morris and 214 in cavalier style by Keith Miller. Rain ruined a splendid match on the final day as England chased runs following a generous declaration.

Defeat by NSW Country in Newcastle was not taken seriously although a rain-ruined match against Queensland did curtail batting practice before the first Test. And what an amazing Test it turned out to be. Australia batted first on a good 'Gabba' pitch and made only 228 in what was an excellent day for England. The opening medium-pacers, Trevor Bailey and Alec Bedser, took the bulk of the wickets, while Neil Harvey's 74 stood way above his colleagues.

Then came the rain. An overnight storm washed out Saturday's play and the pitch was not good enough to use again until just before lunch on the scheduled third day, Monday. Even so, 12,000 spectators turned up to watch twenty wickets fall for just 102 runs. Openers Reg Simpson and Cyril Washbrook batted with all their skill as Johnston (5/35) and Miller attacked with guile. It became very obvious that England's goal was to avoid the follow-on and as soon as this had been achieved, Brown declared at 68 for seven.

When Australia had to bat again on a treacherous pitch Jack Moroney was out to his first ball for the second time in the match. Morris and Loxton followed and suddenly Australia were three wickets down for no runs. This became 19 for five and then 32 for seven when Hassett declared.

Freddie Brown was nonplussed at this shrewd move of Hassett's which was underlined when Simpson's stumps were scattered first ball by Lindwall. By the close England had slumped to 30 for six which became 46 for eight early on the last day. It was then that Len Hutton (62*), batting down the order, took control and had it not been for two unnecessary errors by his partners, Australia's 70-run victory might not have been.

Before the second Test England played against An Australian XI (a Test side, and match, in all but name) in Sydney. The Australians scored 526 (Jim Burke 128, Arthur Morris 100) and had England following-on yet again before time ran out. Ken Archer came in to partner Morris for the second Test in Melbourne which lasted for four days – two either side of Christmas. The even contest saw Australia dismissed on the first day for 194 and England on the second replying with 197. After a two-day break the virtual one-innings challenge got under way with Australia reaching 181. The heavy atmosphere was making for a gripping contest and at the close England were 28 for two.

In theory there were two days for England to score another 151 runs to win with eight second-innings wickets still to fall. The tactics Brown decided to use were based on stone-walling and scoring off the very poor deliveries. Only Len Hutton played any strokes and his 40 took 160 minutes before he mis-hit Bill Johnston to mid-wicket. The game was slowly slipping from England's grasp as wickets fell due to this over-cautiousness of the batsmen. When Johnston had Doug Wright leg-before, Australia had won by 28 runs in a match which, for the first time in fifty-four years, failed to see either side reach 200.

The tourists moved on to Sydney to take comfort from getting the better of a strong New South Wales side. Len Hutton hit 150 and Reg Simpson's 259, scored in nine hours, was the highest by an Englishman against NSW.

Meanwhile the Board of Control were meeting in the NSWCA offices in George Street along with their New Zealand counterparts with whom they were failing to curry favour. As the Board were changing direction and trying to arrange tours over the Tasman Sea each season, so the NZCC were in the position of holding such overtures in abeyance until they had arranged their own, growing, international programme.

As the federation of Australia had taken place on 1 January 1901, the Australian Jubilee Celebration Committee now felt the need to call the third Test, starting in Sydney on 5 January 1951, 'The Jubilee Test'. It proved a popular name as a number of subsequent Tests have been so called. The AJCC, in their wisdom, also decided to present a Jubilee Trophy to the winners of the match. The Board approved of the gesture but were not impressed by the design of the trophy.

England started well on a perfect pitch and by the end of the first day were 211 for five, a good score considering the stifling heat in which the match was played. The following day, Saturday, the largest Sydney crowd for nineteen years – 51,796 – saw England lose two front-line bowlers in Bailey (fractured thumb) and Wright (torn leg tendon) and with them, effectively, the match.

The tourists totalled 290 with Keith Miller taking 4/37. He then went out and played a typical swashbuckling innings of 145 and remained unbeaten as Australia's 426 gave them a comfortable lead. With the pitch wearing Hassett brought on Jack Iverson and his 6/27 saw Australia win the match and the series.

The tourists recorded three first-class victories prior to the fourth Test in Adelaide in early February. It followed the same pattern as the others with Australia winning by 274 runs. Arthur Morris scored 206 and Jim Burke an unbeaten 101 on his debut. For England, Len Hutton carried his bat for 156 out of his team's 272 in the first innings and Freddie Brown missed the final day having wrapped his borrowed car around a lamp post the previous night on his return from a convivial dinner at Government House.

A draw with Victoria preceded the final Test in Melbourne in which England at last ended Australia's run of 25 consecutive Tests without defeat. An unbeaten 156 by Reg Simpson, and a double bowling display by Alec Bedser with 5/46 and 5/59, saw Australia lose by eight wickets in front of Melbourne's lowest crowd for twenty-one years. The glamour had gone from the tour, which not only had lasted too long, but for which Australia lacked a player of the calibre or pulling-power of Don Bradman. Ray Lindwall was slowing in pace, though not in guile, and even the young players in the side would, in most cases, be short-lived replacements. The two newcomers in the early Tests were Jack Iverson and Jim Burke. Could those pressures have been too much for them is a rhetorical question for in later years both would commit suicide.

Both Lindsay Hassett and Freddie Brown said that the series was the friendliest they could remember; but the sad fact was that it had seen a mediocre five Tests which had been reflected in the attendances. For the whole tour 967,001 people had watched the tourists and paid £140,725 for the privilege. Yet the England share of the tour profit was only £3842 whilst the Australian slice was £6655.

There had also been a slump in the number of spectators at Sheffield Shield matches with overall attendances down by twenty-five per cent. Although Victoria just won the Shield from NSW, only four batsmen reached four figures for the season – Hassett, Miller, Morris and Harvey – and, yet again, no bowler since the war ended had taken 50 wickets. The bubble was not bursting, just deflating, as subsequent tours by the West Indies and South Africa would show.

# 22

# Board Matters

During the southern winter of 1951 various restrictions on building and development were lifted by the Federal government although many draconian edicts remained in place. This enabled all of the major cricket venues around the country to carry out much more repair and maintenance than they had been able to do for many years. With labour at a premium it was very difficult for the various curators to keep good men at the grounds. In Melbourne, Bill Vanthoff found himself ringing around suburban ovals asking colleagues if they had staff to spare who could work at the MCG.

As cricket was declining in popularity, so the various football codes around Australia were gaining strength. Australian Rules matches in Melbourne, Adelaide and Perth showed attendances up by 27 per cent and revenue by 26 per cent. Rugby League in Sydney and Rugby Union in Brisbane had similar gains. For Tasmania a comparative figure would be inaccurate due to the regionalisation of their sports, but the trend seems to have been similar.

Cricket administrators were becoming more aware of the need to reform the game and to increase its popularity, yet they had no idea how to go about doing so. Their wooden thinking saw the work of a number of progressively minded committees go to waste. Clubs were noticing a drop in playing members and no longer were talented young boys walking in off the streets asking for a game. Society was changing, but the Board of Control did not have any ideas on such matters. Within the year a celebrated court case would show the Board for what it really was.

The success of the West Indies team in England in 1950, when they won a four-match series 3-1, spurred the Australian Board of Control into offering the WIBC a tour in 1951–52. In exchanges of letters the West Indies made clear that they wanted a New Zealand component in whatever schedule was drawn up. This would mean that the Australian planned visit across the Tasman Sea would be postponed.

The arrogance of the Board showed through in their dealings with the Caribbean when chairman Allen Robertson wrote virtually telling the West Indies that certain players had to tour. He asked: 'Will you indicate if Goddard will captain the team and if it will also include the nucleus of the side in England last summer, that is: Weekes, Walcott, Rae, Ramadhin, Valentine, Christiani, Gomez, Marshall and Stollmeyer. We will not be able to progress on our financial negotiations until you can guarantee us a sufficiently representative side.'

The West Indian reply concentrated more on the financial arrangements and the international situation. The Australian guarantee of £6000 'will see us with a deficit of at least £4000' wrote the WIBC. 'In the light of our heavy expenditure could this guarantee be increased to £10,000 Australian currency?' The Board, at their meeting in Melbourne in March 1951, reluctantly raised their offer to £8000.

Then came another key issue which arose out of the crisis in Korea. The WIBC wrote: 'The possibility of an international situation cannot be ignored. Suppose war unfortunately starts while the team is in Australia and they cannot obtain passages, can you help us with a suggestion as to the source from which the maintenance of the team in Australia could be met?' The Australian reply was nearly beyond belief in its tone: 'The Board considers that, in such an event, there would be ample suitable occupation available in Australia to members of the team,' and added as a finale: 'Why do you not consider taking out insurance against war occurring during the period of the tour?'

The West Indies Board of Control took this advice and found that the premium cost them seven per cent of their tour guarantee. With their overall expenses seeming to accelerate, the financial loss looming was a potential disaster. At least the WIBC had the satisfaction of the June 1951 Imperial Cricket Conference ruling that the Australian Board had to let the West Indies tour of New Zealand go ahead.

For reasons that are not discernible the Board of Control decided to change the West Indian itinerary; but they could not have made more of a hash of matters. One first-class match prior to the first Test – in which Queensland won by ten wickets on a pitch totally alien to the tourists – added to lengthy travel between venues with no time for rest and practice even had the Australian captain, Lindsay Hassett, saying at a public function: 'The West Indies have suffered from sheer stupidity in the organisation of their tour of Australia'. From a diplomat such as Hassett this comment was a stinging rebuke to the Board.

At the same time the Board had arranged the usual social rounds, albeit reduced from that imposed on previous touring teams, with the white-tie formal dinner arranged for the time between the third and fourth Tests after Christmas. For the first time the Board minute for this function reads: 'Ordinary dress'. Either standards were declining or a realisation had taken place that the West Indians did not possess such imperialistic attire.

The West Indian team assembled in Sydney in dribs and drabs during the middle of October 1951. The manager, Cyril Merry, and captain, John Goddard, went into conclave with Aubrey Oxlade and Bill Jeanes on arrival with 'certain matters' discussed and agreements on these points circulated to Board members. Although the Board minutes do not reveal what these 'certain matters' were, it is clear from subsequent correspondence that racial intolerance was high on the agenda. These matters came to a head in Melbourne prior to the fourth Test when the manager of the Hotel Federal allocated the tourists the worst rooms possible. Only following a personal visit by Board chairman Oxlade were the visitors given rooms of a slightly higher standard although it was made quite obvious to him that the management 'didn't want blacks' staying at their establishment.

To start their tour the West Indies arranged a match at the North Sydney Oval as a benefit for the noted scorer/baggageman Bill Ferguson. This kind gesture raised £600 in a match which the Board sanctioned with reluctance. However, no such inhibitions existed when the Prime Minister, Bob Menzies, asked if a match could be played in Canberra two days later against the Prime Minister's XI.

The five-Test series, which Australia won 4-1, attracted only 395,798 people to twenty days of top cricket. There was no shortage of entertainment although the third day of the third Test, played on Christmas Day, caused Adelaide's crowd total to fall to its lowest since the previous West Indies Test back in December 1930.

The economy was booming, work was plentiful, and unemployment was recorded nationally at 0.7 per cent. The beginning of the patriarchal Menzies years would last for a decade and a half. Australia was a country to which millions wanted to emigrate. It offered everything one could want: a job, food, shelter and security yet the era also saw a downward slide in cricket's popularity until it was reversed by two players who first faced each other in this series: Frank Worrell and Richie Benaud.

The Australian selectors had only one Sheffield Shield match to watch prior to the first Test. It told them nothing new as Arthur Morris scored 253, Ken Archer 104 with Ray Lindwall taking 7/45 as NSW drew with Queensland in Brisbane. Then came the West Indies match with Queensland and, after that, the first Test. Three fixtures for the whole continent and all in the space of three weeks at the same venue. The four-day Test created little of note excepting the large percentage of bowling (86%) performed by the West Indian spin pair of Sonny

Ramadhin and Alf Valentine. Doug Ring claimed 6/80 in the West Indies second innings as Australia won by three wickets with over a day to spare.

Two Shield matches in Perth and one in Adelaide gave no help to the Australian selectors before the second Test in Sydney in late November. In reply to the West Indies' 362, Australia were 106 for three when Keith Miller joined Lindsay Hassett. The pair added 235 in two sessions of play with Hassett making 132 and Miller 129. It was enough to subdue the visiting bowlers and on an easy pitch tail-enders Lindwall (48) and Ring (65) saw the score to 517. With Stollmeyer and Weekes both suffering pulled leg muscles the West Indies were always up against the big Australian lead and their ferocious fast bowling. The expected victory – by seven wickets – arrived on the fifth day.

Two poor displays of batting and fielding saw the West Indies beaten in matches against South Australia and Western Australia. But the bowling was effective with Valentine taking 5/112 and 7/52 in Adelaide and the right-arm paceman, John Trim, claiming 7/80 and 3/32 in Perth. Then it was to Adelaide for the third Test and a classic Board of Control 'stuff-up'. Lindsay Hassett pulled a muscle at net practice and the selectors named local batsman Phil Ridings as his replacement. But because all the thirteen Board delegates could not be contacted in time to approve this change, Hassett had to become twelfth man with South Australia's suspect fast bowler Geff Noblet taking his place.

This unbalanced the Australian side as the stand-in captain, Arthur Morris, soon found out. Twenty-two wickets fell on the initial day. First, Australia collapsed for 82 with Worrell's seamers claiming 6/38. Then the West Indies scored 105 with Bill Johnston taking 6/62. A reshuffled batting order had Australia 20 for two overnight. The damp pitch dried enough for Australia to get 255, Valentine 6/102, but not enough to stop the West Indies claiming victory by six wickets just after lunch on Christmas Day.

The fourth Test in Melbourne followed at once, and the tourists had only themselves to blame for not levelling the series at two each. In front of a first-day New Year's Eve crowd of 54,810, the highest daily gate of the series, the West Indies batted manfully to reach 272 at stumps. Frank Worrell (108) batted in considerable pain after being struck on the right hand by a ball from Keith Miller and struggled to his century. Australia replied with 216 next day which would have been a rout had Neil Harvey (83) not regained form in time to hold the innings together.

The match was turning into a thrilling contest with the *Sun News-Pictorial* calling it 'The Test match of the century' which was rather an exaggeration. With the iron-fist of a Bradman or a Jardine behind them the West Indies would have won. Their second innings 203 left Australia to score 260 for victory in plenty of time. Valentine and Ramadhin soon got to work on that final day and, even though Hassett scored 102, the wickets kept falling. It was 222 for nine when Bill Johnston joined Doug Ring at the crease: two batting rabbits to try and save the match.

Both batsmen were Victorians who played on the Richmond ground adjacent to the Melbourne Cricket Ground. Richmond, known as the Tigers, would have been proud of their players as with the vocal Melbourne crowd chanting 'Tigers, Tigers', much to the puzzlement of the West Indians, Johnston and Ring hit and ran single after single. The tension rose as the winning total drew nearer and a single by Johnston off Worrell brought Test cricket's fifth recorded victory by one wicket.

By now the Australian selectors had a chance to view a number of Shield matches and what they saw impressed them enough to choose three players for their debuts in the fifth Test. In came twenty-one-year-old Richie Benaud, a right-hand batsman and leg-break bowler from New South Wales whose influence on the game of cricket at the top level would continue up to the present day. Also selected was Victorian opening batsman Colin McDonald – in later years to become the supremo of Australian tennis – and George Thoms, also an opener from Victoria, for his sole Test.

The match was a bizarre one. The Sydney pitch was perfect, the temperature hovered around 40°C for the whole game, and yet nineteen wickets fell on the first day with the West Indies scoring 64 for nine in reply to Australia's 116. Gerry Gomez took 7/55 for the tourists and Keith Miller 5/26 for Australia as the West Indies reached 78 early on the second day. Then the contest took a predictable turn as the Australians ran up 377 and the West Indies, Stollmeyer (104) apart, had no answer to the attack of Lindwall and Miller to lose by 202 runs.

Although the West Indies lost the series – and their ground fielding had been truly atrocious – they had left a lasting impression of their potential which would be more than borne out on their next visit.

Cricket is played at all levels in Australia from Test matches to pub challenges. Each season all Associations organise a Country Carnival in which representative teams from country areas are selected to play a series of matches in a round-robin competition held during the holiday season in the capital cities of the various States.

In South Australia the Country Carnival for the 1951–52 season was in its third day on Wednesday 13 February. The match was Murray Districts against Upper North on Adelaide's north-west parklands at the Railways Oval when a deranged man walked on to the field of play and fatally shot one player and wounded another. The cricket community was shocked and although the killer was found to be insane, it needed a national appeal to defray the injured man's medical expenses and to provide a small fund for the widow.

Although New South Wales had won the Sheffield Shield with ease their success came second to a major scandal which had erupted over NSW batsman Sid Barnes. For the third Test at Adelaide the three selectors – Bradman, Dwyer and Ryder – had selected Barnes in the light of his batting form. For the first time the Board referred the team back to the selectors as nine of the twelve voting delegates had objected to Barnes' inclusion. Barnes was subsequently replaced, with newspapers around the country having a field day with the story.

Board chairman Aubrey Oxlade, one of the three to vote for Barnes, apologised to him in Stan McCabe's sports store in Sydney where he worked 'for the scandalous thing that has occurred'. For weeks afterwards the press speculated in the way in which only they knew how. The Board remained silent while others openly supported Barnes. In the end Barnes decided to seek guidance and was put in touch with a barrister, Jack Shand, KC. This resulted in Barnes issuing a statement to try and clear the air and to give the Board a chance of replying.

With no comment forthcoming the silent men of Australian cricket seemed to have won the day until a stroke of fortune occurred. A letter to the Sydney *Daily Mirror* from a Jacob Raith, which supported the Board, was just what Barnes needed and he immediately sued Raith for libel.

The trial in the District Court at Sydney before His Honour Judge Lloyd and a jury took place on 21–22 August 1952. The transcript has to be read to be believed. Raith, who had never met Barnes, initially defended the case on the grounds of truth and public benefit but, following the testimonies and cross-examinations of members of the Board, Raith's counsel admitted: 'That seldom in the history of libel actions had such a plea failed so completely and utterly. The Board had presented an awful image of the chaos and bigotry under which Australian cricket was administered.'

Bill Jeanes had admitted that minutes were doctored (a claim Joe Darling had made over forty years earlier); Keith Johnson, the 1948 tour manager, had been made to look a fool under cross-examination; and as an outcome of his evidence Aubrey Oxlade lost his position as chairman of the Board.

What Sidney Barnes had said in his statement was intended to dispel the rumours which surrounded him. They ranged from his behaviour on the 1948 tour to a car theft; from stealing from the players in the changing-rooms to drunkenness – and so it went on. Barnes challenged the Board to deny the rumours and to say why he had really been left out of the team. What was alleged as Barnes' worst sin was that he had lampooned the Board in his commentary for his home-movies made on the 1948 tour. Another charge against him was that at one ground in England he had gained admittance by jumping over a turnstile because he had forgotten his player's pass. It was all trivia and gossip, and the Board was flayed in court for believing it.

Any scholar of Australian cricket should read the full details of this case and the 1977 judgment to gain some idea as to how the game has been governed in Australia and to understand the closed shop which exists on the Board to this day.

Barnes never again played for Australia, and soon retired from first-class cricket. His moral victory in court told against him and he moved into the pressbox to make his views known. The conspiracy which got him, and others who did not toe the 'party line', saw him become a very bitter man. He took his own life in 1973.

Prior to the 1952–53 season cricket administrators around the country were concerned as to why the number of men playing cricket had dropped sharply. The figures were indeed bad. They ranged around one-third of players registered (1951–54) in South Australia and Western Australia to a quarter in NSW, and a fifth in Victoria. The appeal of the game seemed to have gone, fielding was admitted to be poor, batting was defensive, the game was being strangled by its own rope. At a seminar in Adelaide in August 1952, Vic Richardson advocated 'limited-overs matches being introduced to encourage faster scoring'. His proposal went to the State delegates of the Interstate Conference who rejected the idea without consideration.

Around the country the problems were clear. The Board had suggested to State Associations that matches start earlier. Most people still worked on Saturday mornings and with club matches starting at 1.30 pm it was, in most cases, very difficult to have to leave work and get to a ground all in half-an-hour. This had not previously been the case. Matches used to start at 2 pm or 2.30 pm at a time when Australian Labor laws saw shops shut on Saturdays at 11.30 am prompt, with other businesses, such as petrol stations which were allowed to stay open no later than 2 pm. Practice nights were also affected now by the fact that most players did not leave their businesses until 6 pm and then, after finding public transport to their respective grounds, they had little time to master their sport until the light drew in.

Another problem was that National Service requirements did not allow players in camp to leave before 1 pm on Saturdays even if most were just hanging around doing very little. Commanding Officers were, generally, not inclined to allow players to leave early and were not giving encouragement to their servicemen to play sport. Only when Bill Jeanes approached the Minister of Defence, Philip McBride, was an instruction issued that 'participation in sport was a desirable adjunct of military training'.

The Board of Control for Cricket in India (BCCI) was still pressing the Australian Board to visit their country for a tour. In late 1951 a formal invitation was issued asking 'if it would be possible for an Australian team to tour India next winter'. The BCCI stated that they knew the seasons clashed and asked, in those circumstances, 'if it would be difficult for Australia to send a very good side?' The Board dismissed the idea out of hand and did not even stop to consider what benefits such a tour would provide for the game of cricket on the sub-continent.

For three years the Australian Board of Control had been negotiating and organising a South African tour of Australia. Many pundits were suggesting that the team would be too weak even to compete at first-class level let alone be able to hold Australia in Tests. As the time grew near for the tour to start, the Board was getting very nervous about the whole project. Bill Jeanes was instructed to write to his opposite number in Johannesburg, Algy Frames, expressing the Board's fears of low public response and a potentially heavy financial loss.

The South African Cricket Association replied by accepting Jeanes' point of view and stating that they were prepared to bear losses of up to £10,000 on the tour which they regarded as an educational venture for their younger players. In the outcome the South African share of the proceeds was £28,754 which represented a profit of around £3000.

The South Africans, captained by Jack Cheetham and managed by Ken Viljoen, sailed to Australia on the *Dominion Monarch* to be greeted at Fremantle by the pilot's launch containing the journalist Dick Whitington. At least he got the captain's first public comment for his syndicated column!

After a country game at Northam, the tourists drew their initial first-class match which was against Western Australia. The Springbok opener, Jackie McGlew, started well with 182 which proved to be his side's highest individual score on tour. Then followed drawn games against South Australia and Victoria (in which Hugh Tayfield, the visiting off-spinner, took a hat-trick), a loss to New South Wales, and a draw with Queensland in which Russell Endean scored an unbeaten 181.

The tourists paid special attention to their fielding, particularly after hearing of the West Indies' poor standard in the previous season. There would be time spent each day on improving fielding techniques which quite amazed an Australian public used only to seeing their players practise in the nets.

The first Test in Brisbane which started on 5 December 1952 was a splendid contest, evenly fought until the final day. On the first morning Neil Harvey came to the wicket after an hour and proceeded to score a chanceless 109 in 143 minutes. The paceman Michael Melle took 6/71 as Australia reached 280, but it was Australia's leg-break bowler, Doug Ring, with 6/72 who turned the tourists' total of 221 into a deficit of 59. In heatwave conditions the Australian lead was stretched by 277 to 336 and by the end of the fourth day South Africa had scored 150 for two and looked to be on their way to an 'impossible' win. But luck failed the Springboks while fortune smiled on the Australians. Even with Keith Miller out through injury the pace attack led by a slower, but more crafty, Ray Lindwall (5/60) took the home side through to a 96-run victory. In the stifling atmosphere the Springbok batsmen fell, mainly it could be said, to their own lack of experience.

Life was equally interesting behind the scenes. The Board of Control were worried about the finances of the series and the drop in attendances. Some delegates from the Associations were advocating a purely domestic season in order to improve the standard of the Shield competition while others were equally pessimistic. 'Johnnie' Moyes wrote that: 'Attendances had fallen away chiefly because the cricket served up lacked the touch of life and adventure so essential if turnstiles are to click'. In other words, there was no Bradman.

The South African visit also synchronised with a period of blood-letting by the Board which caused feelings of great bitterness. The selectors for the season were Jack Ryder (Victoria), Bill Brown (Queensland) and Phil Ridings (South Australia). Sir Donald Bradman had declined nomination for reasons of family illness while 'Chappie' Dwyer of NSW, a selector for some years and an enthusiastic worker for the game of cricket, had been surprisingly defeated in the ballot.

When the twelve players for the Brisbane Test were named and only four NSW men were selected 'the critics in northern states at once seized their typewriters and began an attack on the selectors', wrote Moyes. He added: 'At once the New South Wales Cricket Association delegates were moved to wrath and they said many bitter things'. With reference to Dwyer's defeat, Moyes said: 'there were suggestions of secession from the Board which, some indicated, must be smashed at all costs'. Even though the NSWCA had the right idea, their methods were not correct and the festering row continued all season much to the embarrassment of the South Africans who were model tourists.

In between Tests was a fairly meaningless match in Sydney with An Australian XI getting slightly the better of a draw against the Springboks. Then came the second Test at Melbourne, played over Christmas. Cheetham won the toss in front of the lowest first-day Melbourne crowd since the corresponding match back in February 1932, just 12,675 spectators, and within the first hour his team were 27 for three. The recovery to 227 did not really seem enough.

Following the break for Christmas Day, the Australians then faced the excellent off-spin of Tayfield (6/84) and the superb catching and fielding of a truly athletic side. The Australians' 16-run first innings lead meant little once Russell Endean batted. The Transvaal batsman stayed at the crease for seven and a half hours for his unbeaten 162 which turned the game South Africa's way.

Keith Miller reached the double of 1000 runs and 100 wickets in Tests when he had Waite caught by Hole but it was Hugh Tayfield who clinched the victory, by 82 runs, with his 7/81, for a match analysis of 13/165 which remains the best for the Springboks in all Tests. It was South Africa's first win over Australia for forty-two years.

Two days later the tourists were hit by the seventeen-year-old Ian Craig. The NSW batsman became the youngest Australian to score a double-century against a touring team, being unbeaten on 213 when his captain, Keith Miller, finally declared. A draw was salvaged but it was not a good omen for the third Test, played a week later on the same ground. In a one-sided Test, Neil Harvey made 190 as victory for Australia came in under four days by an innings and 38 runs.

Two embarrassingly easy victories against Tasmania preceded a drawn fourth Test in Adelaide on a pitch described by curator Stan Williams as 'perfect'. Not perfect enough, however, for he took to heart criticisms of his lifeless track, handing in his resignation within the month. An Australian second-wicket partnership of 275 by Colin McDonald (154) and Lindsay Hassett (163) saw the first innings to 530. South Africa's last-wicket pair saved the follow-on and from then on a draw was the only possible result in five days of play.

The Australian selectors now produced a bombshell. They dropped their opening fast bowlers, Miller and Lindwall, brought back South Australian paceman Geff Noblet, and gave debuts to the lumbering Queensland medium-fast bowler Ron Archer and to Ian Craig who, at 17 years and 239 days, became the youngest Australian to appear in Test cricket. Melbourne provided a contrast. On the first day a lower than previous crowd of 10,837 saw Australia score 243 for two. Expecting, and getting, a deluge of runs on the second day a season's highest gate of 47,039 saw Neil Harvey to 205 as the Australian total ended at 520. It took South Africa until tea on the fourth day to register their reply of 435.

Eddie Fuller's 5/66 kept the Australian second innings in check as Hassett's team reached 209, Craig top-scoring with 47 to give him exactly 100 runs for the match. The South Africans started slowly in response but gained momentum as Roy McLean brought the match to a rousing conclusion by scoring 76 out of 106 in eighty minutes. A six-wicket victory was a just reward for the tourists, for it was their sheer strength of character that put together their greatest cricket triumph.

Domestically the season had been a triumph for South Australia who had one of their rare Sheffield Shield victories. Sid Barnes topped the batting averages but when he realised he was not going to be selected for Australia again he retired. On the administrative side the Board had a worrying time at the end of the South African tour when it became apparent that, following their rejection of an Indian tour, an unofficial visit was being planned.

This came as a shock to the delegates who had become used to bullying cricketers into conforming to a set of unwritten edicts if they valued continuing playing the game at its top level. It was revealed in early 1953 that Andrew Barlow, the former Test umpire, acting in an official capacity for the Board of Control for Cricket in India, was in the process of putting together a team of Australian cricketers to tour the sub-continent. Bill Jeanes made contact with Barlow and found out what the conditions were for the proposed visit.

At its meeting in Melbourne on 10 February 1953 the Board took a surprisingly light view of a 'rebel tour'. It was agreed to ask Barlow for a formal application to tour, the proposed personnel of the party, and that the Board must be in a position to agree or otherwise for the tour to proceed. A proposal by Western Australia and Queensland to ban current Sheffield Shield players from selection was surprisingly outvoted.

On 15 June, Barlow wrote to Jeanes naming sixteen players who had signed up. They were: Loxton, Thoms, Iverson, Howard and deLacy from Victoria; Burke, Walker, Flockton, Trueman and Moroney of NSW; McCool and Grout, Queensland; Langdon and Meuleman, Western Australia; and exiles Tribe and Vic Jackson who were playing county cricket in England.

Barlow also stated that the tour would leave Australia 'in the last week of September 1953 and return early in March 1954'. He added: 'That the Indian Board of Control would guarantee the players and manager £750 (Australian) as well as meeting all personal expenses'. Next day a cable arrived at Jeanes' office in Pirie Street, Adelaide, from the BCCI saying that 'they would be grateful for the approval of the Australian Board to be given to the proposed unofficial tour under the management of Mr Barlow'.

Jeanes then contacted the new Board chairman, Roy Middleton, and it was decided to send a circular to all Board delegates asking for their thoughts on the matter. The response was predictable, and the BCCI and Barlow were informed 'that the Australian Board was not prepared to give its approval to the proposed tour'.

Barlow came back on 8 July with various other points and a slightly revised team, but again he was rejected. The Indian Board then wrote to Middleton asking 'to receive a visit from Australia as soon as possible'. The reply was abrupt: 'We cannot fit you into our schedule before 1960 at the earliest'. All went quiet on the issue until a letter arrived from England. Dated 28 August 1953, one of the Board's two Imperial Cricket Conference delegates, Ben Barnett, the former Test wicketkeeper said he had been invited by the BCCI to captain a Commonwealth team to visit India during the 1953–54 season and asked for permission to approach two Australian players, Sam Loxton and Ken Meuleman. Permission was given with reluctance and only one other player, Jack Iverson, was also granted authority. All other applications were refused.

The Board's lack of missionary zeal in promoting the game in India leaves a poor taste in the mouth, especially as, at the same time, when Prime Minister Robert Menzies asked the Board to consider touring the West Indies adding that 'it could coincide with a Royal visit', action could not have been speedier, nor the revision of planned tours. The Australian government presented the Board with an itinerary in February 1953 saying: 'It is the desire of the government that an Australian cricket team should play the following series of matches in the West Indies as a highlight of the celebrations in 1955 of Jamaica being a British territory for 300 years.'

The Australian government also stated that they 'would be willing to indemnify the Board against financial loss' and that the tour should take place between early April and late June 1955. The Board's discussion lasted only minutes before full approval was given.

While the Australian team was in England during the northern summer of 1953, the members of the Interstate Conference were huffing and puffing over the rights of various radio stations to broadcast matches. They were still convinced that cricket on the wireless was stopping thousands from attending matches.

Western Australia boasted that they had squeezed £420 'from the local broadcasting authorities to cover the four seasons from 1952–53 to 1955–56 inclusive'. Tasmania had 'turned down £80 for the season as it was considered too low an offer'. So instead Tasmanian radio listeners had ball-by-ball accounts of all of Victoria's matches. Queensland announced that they had made an agreement with the

Australian Broadcasting Commission and that 'the three commercial stations broadcast from separate boxes and each paid a fee of £20 with the sanction of the ABC'. In Adelaide tenders were sought with one commercial station suggesting they should be paid to publicise the game. But the big three – South Australia, Victoria and New South Wales – got the largest slice of the ABC cake, carving up £1200 equally.

The problem of broadcasting, and subsequently television, rights would continue to bother the Board from now on. Their negative attitude of 1953 would persist and prove to be their downfall in later years.

The team chosen for the tour of England had been announced on 12 February 1953, the last day of the final South African Test. Captained by Lindsay Hassett and managed by George Davies – a Victorian delegate to the Board – the team played the usual three warm-up matches before leaving Australia. In Hobart, Tasmania were beaten by an innings: in Launceston it was by ten wickets; and the Western Australia match in Perth was drawn.

With the players being away from home for eight months it was always going to be a difficult tour. Matters were made worse by the complete lack of discipline exerted by George Davies which left Lindsay Hassett with an additional burden. Hassett had let it be known that he intended to retire at the conclusion of the visit, a fact which accelerated Australia's decline in world cricket.

In the pressbox following the tour was Don Bradman who was representing London's *Daily Mail* and Sid Barnes for Sydney's *Daily Mirror*. Barnes' inclusion as a player would have vastly improved the side but as it turned out he became so fierce a critic in his despatches home that he ruined any chance he may have had of a recall.

In the early matches Keith Miller scored an unbeaten 220 out of 542 for seven against Worcestershire and in the next match Neil Harvey made 202 not out at Leicester. The tour's best bowling, 7/20, came from Ray Lindwall in the ninth fixture which was against the Minor Counties, and then it was three-and-a-half months later that the other two double-centuries were scored – Miller 262 not out and Jim de Courcy 204 – in a total of 592 for four against the Combined Services.

Miller finished with 2040 runs at 65.80 and Lindwall topped the bowling with 85 wickets at 16.40. The team amused themselves by making sure that tail-ender Bill Johnston remained top of the batting averages with 102 runs from once out in 17 innings.

The run-up to the first Test saw seven wins and five draws as the tour selectors were impressed enough to drop McDonald and Ring to bring in left-arm paceman Alan Davidson, and leg-break bowler John Hill, for their Test debuts. Hassett's opposite number was Len Hutton – the first professional to captain England in a home Test against Australia and the first to do so in either country since Arthur Shrewsbury in March 1887.

The Trent Bridge Test was a stop-start affair with one day completely lost to rain; even so a record overall attendance of 86,000 paid £29,261 to watch a drawn match. Hassett won the toss and top-scored with 115 as his team reached 237 for three. Then came an amazing collapse as Alec Bedser (7/55) and Trevor Bailey took the final seven wickets for twelve runs with the new ball. Ray Lindwall (5/57) countered this with a masterly display of swing bowling which led to England making only 144. Bedser struck even more savagely in Australia's second innings with 7/44 in a score of 123 (Morris 60). However, rain and bad light saw England's victory attempt thwarted at the death.

It was Australia's turn to be frustrated in the second Test as the English middle-order held firm when all seemed lost. Both captains had made centuries, Hassett 104 and Hutton 145. Second time around Keith Miller made 109 as Australia's overall lead became 342. At 20 for three at the end of the fourth day, England's task looked hopeless. The Australians celebrated prematurely that night and found the world a tough place the following morning. After Compton went at 73 for four Willie Watson (109 in 346 minutes) and Trevor Bailey (71 in 257 minutes) saved the day for England.

Jim de Courcy replaced Richie Benaud for the third Test at Old Trafford which saw only 13 hours and 50 minutes play due to rain. This was the ninth successive Test between the teams in Manchester to be drawn or abandoned. Australia's innings finished on the third afternoon with Neil Harvey making 122. England batted until late on the last day and in the final hour Australia collapsed to 35 for eight against a turning ball.

The fourth successive draw took place at Headingley in late July as Hassett put England into bat, the first time an Australian captain had done such a thing since 1909. Rain affected most days with the only item of note being Alec Bedser passing Clarrie Grimmett's record of 216 Test wickets when Gil Langley gave Hutton a catch at first slip to end Australia's first innings. In the pressbox a humorist had seated Don Bradman and Douglas Jardine next to each other.

This evenly matched series for the Ashes had made the tour a huge financial success with the eventual profit being £66,000. From the English point of view, once defeat had been staved off at Lord's, the possibility of regaining the Ashes after nineteen years seemed promising.

Rain enlivened the pitch at The Oval during lunch on the first day of the final Test as Australia made 275. England led by 31 runs early on the third day after which the Surrey pair of Tony Lock and

Jim Laker, playing on their home turf, took control. Dismissed for 162 the Australians had no hope of saving the match or the series as England won by eight wickets. The Tests had been watched by 549,650 people, the largest on record, and by the time the tour had been completed 1,494,979 spectators had watched the Australians. Hassett's leadership throughout had been sparkling even though his last Test ended in defeat.

It had been Coronation year and the time when Hillary and Tensing conquered Everest. The Empire was changing to Commonwealth. The power base of cricket was changing but not enough yet to have that much influence on the game. In Australia unemployment was non-existent; consumerism was rearing its head as families could now buy what they wanted without restriction; the Menzies government was paternalistic. It was boom time 'down under'.

# 23

# The 1950s – Cricket in the doldrums

The arrogance of the Australian Board of Control for International Cricket was causing distress around the cricket world. Not only had the Indian issue created bad feeling but further sores were opened up in late 1953 when South Africa were informed 'we cannot consider touring your country until the 1963–64 season at the earliest'. Pleas, by letter and cablegram, had no effect on the Board who refused to review the matter. New Zealand, equally, were dismissed and, on appeal, offered 'a second team around 1959–60'.

Sir Donald Bradman returned to the Board on the death of the South Australian treasurer Hugh Bridgman but try as he might – and he made a strong effort – he could not convince his colleagues of the leadership qualities of Keith Miller. With Lindsay Hassett's retirement Australian cricket needed a leader who could motivate a team and who could also put a spring into their step. Miller had these qualities and was the successor to Bradman as the crowd's popular entertainer. But the Board would not accept the popularity suggestions, indeed, during the 1953–54 season in which there was no full tour, they aired their distaste for the flamboyancy of the man by spreading rumours about him. Characteristically, Miller gave them a generous demonstration of his ability by scoring 100 and 101 in Hassett's testimonial match in Melbourne in January 1954. It was the big match of the season, with 49,454 watching during the four days, between Hassett's XI and Morris' XI. Hassett went out of first-class cricket with 126 and a cheque for £5503.

But cricket in Australia was stagnating. The Sheffield Shield competition was becoming a financial drain on the State Associations, so much so that in 1952–53 the average daily attendance was 3669 which was boosted only by the large crowds who watched Victoria in Melbourne. In the non-tour season of 1953–54 the daily gate rose to 4553, however, not counting the Melbourne matches, this fell by over one thousand to 3532. By a long way the top daily crowd was the

21,169 who watched the second day of Victoria against New South Wales in Melbourne on 28 December 1953. The increased popularity of other games was taking the eye of the sporting public. The hugely successful Australian Davis Cup team saw tennis receive a boost with State competitions attracting full houses.

The decade also saw the Australian economy boom. With unemployment non-existent, leisure-time was becoming an all-important part of the new society's way of life. Virtually no funds were being distributed by State Associations to the top clubs, and local administrators were always trying to find ways to keep the game alive: the expression 'chook-raffle' was coined when a donated chicken usually could be raffled on a Saturday night to put a few extra pounds into the club kitty.

The feeling of the era was summed up by the Sydney sports journalist, Jack Pollard:

> The Australian Board of Control's need for tight financial housekeeping offered little opportunity to assist junior or schools cricket and made it an administration preoccupied with overseas tours. Social cricketers such as those who played on Sydney's Centennial Park or Moore Park, the churches' cricket association in Melbourne or the Brisbane business houses competition, had little contact with state associations and none at all with the Board. The Board's contact with the vast majority of cricketers in action around Australia was so remote the players naturally believed the Board was unconcerned with the overall strength of the game. For thousands of social players with no prospect of playing state or Test cricket their control came from the local council or the curators who pegged down their matting. After fifty years of administering Australian cricket, the men who sat on the Board of Control were virtually unknown figures, with Bradman the notable exception.

Pick up any book from this era and Pollard's view is confirmed loud and clear. Club histories of the time are fearful for the future. The economics of club cricket showed financial deficits all round.

The 1953–54 season was also the start of a remarkable run by New South Wales, who would win the Sheffield Shield for nine consecutive seasons and completely dominate Australian cricket. Their position was challenged in six of those seasons by Victoria and three times by Queensland. Of the other States South Australia finished last for seven successive years during which time their committee spent some of their meetings trying to remove a newly appointed progressive secretary. NSW won in this season from Victoria when no batsman reached four figures and the top bowler was Ian Johnson (Victoria) with 45 wickets at 22.76. Johnson's end-of-season form was spurred on when it was whispered into his ear that he was likely to be Hassett's successor.

On their way home from South Africa, the New Zealand team led by Bert Sutcliffe – in charge due to an injury to the touring captain, Geoff Rabone – played in Perth, Adelaide and Melbourne over a three-week period in March 1954. In Perth's scorching heat Sutcliffe's batting was a joy to watch with his 142 coming in just 165 minutes on the first day. The Kiwis won by 184 runs and carried on to Adelaide to record an eight-wicket victory. Sutcliffe with 149 led from the front again although victory was only gained with ten minutes to spare. Sutcliffe's third successive century (117) against Victoria, however, could not spur his team to a clean sweep and a draw spoilt their record.

Bill Jeanes' grip on Board and South Australian affairs began to wane in the early part of 1954. A Royal visit, with state and national implications, had taken its toll and he finally gave notice of his intention to resign as Board secretary. For a man in his seventy-second year Jeanes had done a sterling job for cricket since 1926. His successor was the VCA secretary, Jack Ledward, a former first-class player who had taken over the VCA position in early 1951.

An announcement from Lord's on 27 July 1954 gave details of the twenty-sixth England team to tour Australia. Len Hutton had been retained as captain with Peter May as his deputy. Geoffrey Howard, named as manager, proved a good choice as his diplomacy and charm solved many minor problems. In the team was a young fast bowler from Northamptonshire, Frank Tyson, whose reputation for speed preceded his arrival.

Within days, planning for the social side of the tour started in earnest. The usual receptions were arranged with mayors and State governors, with the Board deciding 'that they had to be hospitable to all the journalists covering the tour'. What they did not bargain for was twenty-three scribes from Fleet Street plus around forty locals for each State match, a figure which doubled for the Tests. The South Australian Cricket Association could not believe that 120 pressmen would cover the fourth Test in Adelaide but, when they checked around the country, they found this figure was the lowest.

Television and filming arrangements were organised with little problem and at each ground a special telephone line was installed 'so as Mr John Arlott can send his reports back to the BBC in London'. Sponsored cars were provided for the use of the touring players and the usual flood of speaking invitations was received by all the State Associations.

The tourists arrived in Perth on 7 October. Following a report by their manager the Marylebone Cricket Club took the unusual step of writing to the Australian Board 'expressing gratitude for the excellent practice facilities provided' and 'requested that the thanks of the Club be conveyed to those responsible'.

The tourists won their first three matches with ease before coming up against An Australian XI in Melbourne. Although ruined by rain the match gave an indicator for the immediate future when Ian Johnson's off-spin gave him 6/66 in England's only innings. During the match the death occurred of Dr Allen Robertson, one of the two top men of the Board for the previous thirty years. As fate would have it, his NSW counterpart, Aubrey Oxlade, died less than a year later. Thus a vacuum had been created which only one man could fill: Don Bradman.

Time saved the tourists from defeat in Sydney against the powerful NSW side. Colin Cowdrey, on his first tour, with a century in each innings, and Len Hutton (102 and 87) were the only batsmen competent to thwart a team quite capable of being renamed Australia. Nine of the eleven would win Test caps and five captained Australia at one time or another.

The first Test in Brisbane in late November 1954 saw the pitch fully covered for the first time in Australia with the subsequent risk of a 'Brisbane sticky' fading into the memory. Len Hutton won the toss and surprised everyone by putting Australia into bat. The response was a match-winning total of 601 for eight declared, with Neil Harvey (162) and Arthur Morris (153) adding 202 for the third wicket in 249 minutes.

The new Australian captain, Ian Johnson, had a dream start as leader as his six-pronged bowling attack gave him victory by an innings and 154 runs. His appointment, however, had not been met with acclaim around the country but it did give pride to the South Melbourne Cricket Club as Johnson became their sixth Australian captain following on from Jack Blackham, Harry Trott, Warwick Armstrong, Bill Woodfull and Lindsay Hassett. Only the Sturt Cricket Club in Adelaide can match this record.

After a draw with Victoria in Melbourne, in which Tyson cut down his run-up by about six paces and took 6/68, the England team moved to Sydney for the second Test. Johnson and Miller were injured so Arthur Morris took over the captaincy. It was a trying Test for Morris as Len Hutton started a tactic he was to use for the remaining Tests, and which has been perfected by the West Indies in more recent times, which was to slow down the bowling rate as much as possible. England's rate of 84 balls an hour (the equivalent of 14 six-ball overs) frustrated the Australian batsmen but proved a most effective weapon.

England fell on the first day for 154, and in front of Sydney's biggest crowd of the season, 44,879, Australia scored just 210 runs from fifty eight-ball overs on the second to take a lead of 74 runs. The two young English amateurs May (104) and Cowdrey (54) then added 116 which steered the tourists to 296, a lead of only 222. Australia, with over two days in which to win, then came up against Frank Tyson, who had taken 4/45 in their first innings. With strong winds blowing in from Botany Bay behind him, Tyson's astonishing pace saw him claim 6/85 as only Neil Harvey, with an unbeaten 92, held out. England won by 38 runs to level the series.

The Melbourne Test which followed was a seeming repeat of Sydney's, except that Cowdrey (102) made his runs in the first innings, while May (91) rescued England in the second following Australia's first-innings lead of 40. Australia then collapsed against Tyson, whose 7/27 came in 12.3 overs. It was grim cricket, with slow batting, slow tempo bowling and high temperatures. England won by 128 runs so it could be argued that the end justified the means.

Three weeks in Tasmania and South Australia now kept the tourists busy until the fourth Test in Adelaide. Bushfires were causing problems in Victoria and South Australia at this time with 'century heat' dominating the whole five days of the Test. Hutton used his bowlers in short bursts but it still took them nearly two days to see off Australia for 323. For once, England gained a first-innings lead, albeit only 18 runs, but they then ripped through Australia again, this time for 111. Curator Arthur Lance's pitch was certainly not to blame for the Australian debacle and, on the fifth afternoon, Godfrey Evans scored the runs which won England the match and the retention of the Ashes. The celebrations carried on long into the night at the Pier Hotel in suburban, coastal Glenelg with many Australian officials on hand to join in.

It marked the end of an era, for as journalist Bruce Harris wrote:

> I always hate leaving Adelaide and this time had additional reason for regret because Mr W. H. Jeanes, secretary to the South Australian Cricket Association, and until recently secretary also to the Board of Control, was about to retire. Bill Jeanes has always been a good friend to me ever since I first visited Adelaide in the stormy days of 1932.

Harris did not know that Jeanes had 'cracked' under his workload and been absent from his office for most of the season. He left officially on 31 March 1955 and had only a short retirement before his death just six weeks before the start of the next England tour.

With the series decided the Australian selectors brought in Queensland batsman Peter Burge for the final Test. February 1955 had seen a shocking loss of life in flooding in New South Wales and the fifth Test lost its first three days to the wet conditions in Sydney. Even then there were so many delays that the fixture became fairly meaningless and a draw was inevitable. Within a week the Australians were saying goodbye to the England tourists who had suffered only two defeats on tour – by Australia and in the return against NSW – and left for the initial Australian tour of the West Indies.

The domestic season had been curtailed in order to save money but all it did was to make the selectors' choice for the Caribbean tour more difficult as they had little to guide them in the way of form.

The Board had met, as usual, at the end of December. Their attitude to a number of important cricket issues had been so negative that, on the second day, they gave permission for the South African Cricket Association's president, Arthur Coy, to be present, and on the third day Ronnie Aird, secretary of the Marylebone Cricket Club.

Coy had flown over from Cape Town especially to see the Board and one can wonder at the chairman, Roy Middleton, who said that 'he appreciated the long journey Mr Coy had undertaken just to attend this meeting'. Had the Board been more flexible Coy would never have had to travel halfway around the southern hemisphere.

Arthur Coy was a true diplomat. He buttered up the Board delegates saying 'what a privilege it was' for 'being permitted to address such a gathering'. He described the workings of the South African Cricket Association, its Board of Control, and touched on some of the difficulties administrators found in his country. He stressed the need for overseas tours and put Australia on a par with England. 'If the mother of cricket could tour every four years,' he argued, 'so could a great cricketing nation such as Australia.'

Coy then came to the crunch and issued a formal invitation for Australia to tour in 1957–58. He then left the room while the delegates, who had virtually unanimously rejected this suggestion such a short time earlier, now rescinded their earlier motion and passed it by thirteen votes to nil: 'That Australia visit South Africa during 1957–58 season providing suitable financial arrangements could be made'.

Recalled to the meeting, Coy was told of the decision and later worked with a Board sub-committee to thrash out the financial necessities. Coy had got his tour, but what about India, the other Test-playing nation treated with such disdain by the Board? Their tour would come earlier than anyone would guess.

The final day of the meeting saw the secretary of the Marylebone

Cricket Club politely, but firmly, tell the Australian Board to get its house in order and to stop squabbling over trivial matters. Mr Aird flattered the delegates by saying 'how pleased he was to be present on such an historic occasion' and 'that his visit was one of goodwill and the desire to gain knowledge'. He then said that 'MCC was anxious for Australia to make some proposals regarding the financial conditions for future tours' and then went on to give the Board a lesson in accounting.

In a wide-ranging (one-sided) discussion the Board were told 'how worried MCC were by the negative cricket played in their domestic competition'; 'that Australia must standardise its laws of the game to conform to MCC laws'; that the dictating of tour fixtures in England 'must be left for the MCC to do and not arranged from Australia' and that 'Australian touring teams must curb the number of free tickets given out for each and every day's play, particularly for Test matches'. Mr Aird then went on to discuss Imperial Cricket Conference matters telling the Australians 'that they might care to join MCC in the direction of taking responsibility of being cricket missionaries to the less popular Test countries'.

The Board members were overwhelmed by all this and questioned Aird at some length. The meeting concluded with the usual platitudes and, immediately on the MCC secretary's departure, the agenda went back to its usual trivia and nit-picking. On the fourth day of the meeting, the Board formed itself into the Interstate Conference and discussed two important matters within a few minutes. They rejected an excellent offer from the Federation of Commercial Broadcasting Stations for the future broadcasting of Sheffield Shield matches, preferring 'silent airwaves to accepting such a derisory offer'. They then dismissed with scorn a plea by NSW delegate Frank Cush who said that 'the NSW players feel that they are getting a raw deal by not having a match in Sydney during the Christmas holiday break' and requesting the Conference 'to arrange the Shield programme so that NSW could be given a home match in this time'.

Another NSW delegate, Ewart Macmillan, in supporting Cush, said that 'the NSW players were becoming very disgruntled at their continued absence from home over the Christmas period'. The pleas were ignored but Cush insisted that the minutes recorded his displeasure: 'That on behalf of the NSW delegates we have to accept the vote against our players' wishes and we have to accept the Sheffield Shield programme, but we are not happy with it'.

The Australian team to tour the West Indies was chosen by the selection panel of Sir Donald Bradman (South Australia), Jack Ryder

(Victoria) and Dudley Seddon (NSW). These three would, in time, be looked upon as the finest selection trio Australian cricket could have. For a dozen or so years their policy was stable and the players were more aware of their strengths and failings than at any previous time in the modern game.

There were briefings for the players from the Department of Foreign Affairs as the Australian government was seriously concerned that no diplomatic incidents should take place. A tour twelve months earlier by Len Hutton's England team had seen spectator riots and over-reaction by players to adverse umpiring decisions.

In Ian Johnson the Australians had the perfect diplomat as captain, and his team spurned fraternisation with the wealthy whites in the islands for socialising with the black cricketers in their local bars. Johnson met his challenges head-on particularly by taking the local journalists into his confidence from the moment the tourists arrived in Jamaica for the start of the visit. Johnson later recollected:

> As we reached the airport reception centre we were besieged by a crowd of English reporters who had flown out to witness what they thought would be a holocaust. They were plying us with questions when I spotted a group of West Indian pressmen about a cricket pitch away.
>
> I grabbed Keith Miller and whispered that the West Indians were more important to us than the Poms, who were just after sensation. The West Indian reporters conveyed our friendliness to their readers and told them to forget the White Australia policy. We were off to a wonderful start.
>
> The crowds were extremely volatile. They'd laugh their heads off one minute and next be crying for your blood. The important thing was when they abused you not to show resentment. You had to laugh with them, not at them. By doing so you could change their hot temper to genuine friendship. The tour was the most successful ever undertaken by an Australian team and it was certainly the most enjoyable any of us were ever on.

In all, the Australians played twelve matches on tour of which nine were first-class. They remained undefeated and in Tests had nine century partnerships and twelve individual three-figure innings.

The warm-up match against Jamaica saw Arthur Morris hit 157 in an evenly contested draw. Then came the first Test in Kingston starting on 26 March 1955. Harvey (133) and Miller (147) dominated the first two days as Australia reached 515 for nine. Miller led Australia for the final three days after Johnson was injured and he took the visitors to a nine-wicket victory despite being held up by a century (104) on debut by the exciting West Indian batsman Collie Smith.

A flight to Port-of-Spain, Trinidad, for a match against the island team, was the start of the Australians' island hopping. After a draw against the locals, in which Ray Lindwall took 6/41, there was a four-day break to the second Test. Lindwall then took 6/95 in a high-scoring draw as Harvey (133), Morris (111) and McDonald (110) enjoyed the run-feast.

An easy victory against British Guiana in Georgetown by an innings and 134 runs saw the Australians' first match on the South American mainland. John Hill took ten wickets (5/50 and 5/15) and Peter Burge made 177 with some fearsome batting. The third Test in late April on the Bourda ground was a low-scoring affair by local standards and was won for Australia by Ian Johnson's off-breaks. His second innings 7/44 from 22 overs gave him the match and the first series in the Caribbean.

After a three-wicket win in Bridgetown against Barbados, Ian Johnson found himself in trouble with the Board back in Australia. On a flight between the islands Johnson, an experienced pilot, had persuaded the crew to let him take the controls of the British West Indian Airways plane. When news of this reached Australia, chairman Roy Middleton instructed secretary Jack Ledward to fire off an urgent cable to manager Jack Burge (Peter Burge's father) 'with instructions to prevent team members from piloting aircraft in the future'. The Board were worried about their insurance policy in case of any accident.

The fourth Test in Bridgetown was a superb game of cricket. Johnson won the toss and Australia moved on to 243 for five by the end of the first day with Miller and Archer having come together a few minutes earlier. The pair added a record 206 for the sixth wicket next day, after which Miller (137) was joined by his opening bowling partner Ray Lindwall who then hit his second Test century (118). Australia reached 668 and, at the close of the third day, the West Indies were 187 for six with Denis Atkinson on 19 and Clairmonte Depeiza 22.

The fourth day was a delight for the watching Barbadians for Atkinson reached 215 and Depeiza 122 as they batted together for the whole day. Their partnership, which was broken immediately next morning, was worth 347 runs, a new world record for the seventh wicket. It was to be Depeiza's only century in first-class cricket. Atkinson reached 219 and the total 510, but the die had been cast for the result as too little time was left. Johnson eventually set the West Indies a target of 408 in 230 minutes with a draw the end-result.

The final Test took place back in Kingston in the middle of June and, luckily for the Australians, the rainy season – which had seen the tour's penultimate match abandoned – held off, so the six-day game was played to its conclusion. The West Indies had first knock on the rock-hard pitch, reaching 357 with Keith Miller claiming 6/107. Then came a reply from Australia unique to Test cricket: five centuries in a total of 758 for eight declared, then the highest Test score by a country other than England. Harvey (204) and McDonald (127) put on 295 for the third wicket and, with the relatively mild West Indian attack flagging in the high humidity, Archer (128), Benaud (121) and Miller (109) had a field day. Benaud was particularly harsh on the bowling, his fifty arriving in 38 minutes and his century in 78, with two sixes and fifteen fours. With Bill Johnston unable to bowl in his final Test due to a leg injury sustained on the first morning, the Australians were a bowler short. But this had little effect on the eventual outcome as victory arrived early on the sixth morning by an innings and 82 runs.

So ended Australia's seminal tour of the Caribbean. In spite of press criticism by Australian and English journalists, the West Indian scribes had taken Ian Johnson to their hearts. He had not only led an unbeaten team but he, and his players, had gone out of their way to meet local people and to attend as many functions as possible. It had been like a breath of fresh air but, as expected, it was completely ignored in Australia.

In fact not until three months after the team had arrived home did letters start to arrive at the Board's office praising the team. The Prime Minister, Sir Robert Menzies, sent a copy of a letter written to him by Sir Hugh Foot, Governor of Jamaica, in which Sir Hugh referred in eulogistic terms to the Australian team. After referring to their skill as players and praising their sportsmanship and popularity, he added: 'The good which they have done is beyond praise or calculation'.

The Board of Control met in Sydney over three days in mid-September 1955. Aubrey Oxlade had died the previous night so a half-hour adjournment took place 'in his memory'. Oxlade had been due to take up the chairmanship once again so this short break saw the delegates horse-trade over who should take the chair. It was finally resolved to let the progressive Frank Cush take over but 'following the usual custom Mr Middleton presided over this meeting'.

Roy Middleton, the staunchly conservative Methodist from South Australia, belonged to the school of thought which did not like the players expressing a point of view. When under 'deferred correspondence' Lindsay Hassett's lengthy 'Captain's Report' from the 1953 tour of England was tabled, every single item from meal allowances to fixtures was diplomatically noted as: 'Resolved no action be taken'.

When it came to matters from the Marylebone Cricket Club the Board took a different stance. Ronnie Aird had written from London and 'expressed his appreciation on behalf of his committee for the kind way he had been received in Australia. The experience he had gained would prove most valuable to his committee in the future, and they felt that if the Board Secretary or some other representative could visit England in the near future it would be a great pleasure for MCC to welcome him, and would prove helpful to the Board as well.'

If ever displeasure was couched in diplomatic terms, this was it. Behind the scenes 'Gubby' Allen had been in Australia for a time during the Hutton tour and had spoken privately, and at length, with Sir Donald Bradman about problems the MCC saw with the Board. By the end of the Board meeting Jack Ledward 'submitted an application for leave to enable him to visit England', and added 'that the objects of the visit were to acquire first-hand knowledge of English conditions and to meet English officials'.

One subject which Ledward had to tackle was television and filming rights. Lord's were furious with the Board over the treatment meted out to the BBC and the refusal to allow filming to take place for television-showing in England. Bradman spoke at the meeting on matters raised with him by Allen with the delegates not knowing how to tackle this new problem. Their fears were compounded when a letter was tabled from Sir William Becher of the Associated-Rediffusion commercial television company in England. Becher's organisation wanted to buy the complete television and filming rights for the forthcoming 1958–59 England tour of Australia. He added that 'if this was granted they would require all facilities to the main cricket grounds in Australia and also facilities for camera positions and interviews with the players'.

As they would, to their cost, do again in the future, the Board put their collective heads in the sand on this issue resolving to tell Becher that 'nothing could be done at the present time'. Later, when Lord's wrote asking if there was any objection to the 1956 Australians being televised at net practice on their arrival in London, Roy Middleton led the diehard opposition to such a move on the grounds that it would stop people attending matches.

The Marylebone Cricket Club's secretary's visit to Australia bore fruit at the Imperial Cricket Conference held at Lord's on 14 July 1955. There it was gently suggested to the Pakistan and Indian representatives that they might care to write yet again to the Australian Board inviting them to send a touring team.

Within days both Pakistan and India had sent cables to Jack Ledward followed by lengthy, flowery, letters 'requesting the Board to permit the 1956 Australian team to make a short tour on their return from England'. Having been fully briefed by Gubby Allen on this issue and after very short discussion, Bradman tabled the dates and places for suggested Tests; arrangements for the freight of players' luggage; the need for giving the players three weeks' holiday after the

England tour; all air travel arrangements, and financial implications. The delegates could do little but raise their hands meekly in approval of these seminal tours.

The 1955–56 season in Australia was purely domestic with very little to be seen to change the selectors' thinking for the forthcoming tour to England. Richie Benaud took most wickets, 44 at 21.61, and Jim Burke made most runs, 979 at 61.19, with the official Test trial doubling up as a testimonial match for Arthur Mailey and Johnny Taylor.

Held in Sydney in mid-January 1956, Ian Johnson's team lost to Ray Lindwall's team by two wickets. The large crowd were regally entertained with centuries from Jim Burke (192), Queenslander Ken Mackay (143), Richie Benaud (101) and John Rutherford (113) with Neil Harvey (96) just failing to match the others. Rutherford made the journey from Perth immediately following a motoring accident with his consequent cuts and bruises being treated en route. His century staked his claim to be the first Western Australian to be chosen for an Australian touring team. The testimonial was a financial success for the two former Test players who shared £7182 between them.

Changes were afoot in Australian cricket in the mid-1950s. Sid Webb, QC, was appointed to the Board to represent New South Wales, in place of Aubrey Oxlade. His presence was of considerable embarrassment to another delegate as the two had clashed over a matrimonial matter some twenty years earlier which had had a direct bearing on Australian cricket at the time.

The Board, in September 1955, gave a gift of £200 to the veteran scorer-baggageman Bill Ferguson in thanks for his services to Australian touring teams since 1905. Ferguson had accompanied the team for fifty years and had only been given the 1953 tour to England by the canvassing of Don Bradman. The gift was meant as a farewell gesture but Ferguson did not grasp this, so his bitterness at being overlooked for the 1956 tour was understandable.

A change was now in the air regarding tours. In February 1956 the Board approved a second team tour of New Zealand from February 1957, confirmed the visit to South Africa for 1957–58 and a return to Australia in 1963–64, and a tour by the West Indies for 1960–61 – all of which had been worked out before the meeting by Sir Donald Bradman. His progressive thought and vision was starting to have a marked effect on the direction of the Australian game.

The 1956 touring team for England was announced at the Board meeting and it included Rutherford from Western Australia. The manager was Bill Dowling and his assistant Leo Rush, both of Victoria.

The usual pre-departure matches might well have been ominous signs of things to come. Miller (106) and Benaud (103*) scored centuries against Tasmania in Hobart with the rest of the batting there, and in Launceston and Perth, looking quite ordinary. The bowling gave nothing away with Benaud's 5/71 in Hobart the best performance by far.

With no stopover match in Ceylon because of the island's general election, the next first-class match was ten days after arrival in England when Benaud (160) dominated a drawn game at Worcester. Things looked better three days later when Miller scored an unbeaten 281 at Leicester following which Colin McDonald (195) flayed the Leicestershire attack and Neil Harvey (225) recorded the tour's only other double-century in the match against the Marylebone Cricket Club at Lord's. The ten fixtures leading up to the first Test saw two victories, seven draws and a defeat by Surrey, the first county to achieve such a success for forty-four years. Even more remarkable was Surrey off-spinner Jim Laker's return of 10/88.

England had a new captain for the Ashes series in Peter May, who had taken over from Len Hutton a year earlier. May elected to bat in the first Test under damp, grey, Nottingham skies. With twelve hours of play lost to rain and two declarations by England no result ever looked remotely possible. The Australians' problems started on the first morning when the left-arm fast bowler, Alan Davidson, slipped during his run-up and chipped a bone in his ankle.

For the second Test at Lord's, Davidson's replacement, Pat Crawford, a fellow NSW paceman, made his debut and lasted for just 29 deliveries before he limped off the field with a pulled thigh muscle. Crawford was highly regarded in Australian circles as the logical successor to Ray Lindwall but throughout his short career of only four Tests was subject to muscular injuries which caused his eventual early retirement.

An opening partnership of 137 by Colin McDonald and Jim Burke followed by bowling spells of 5/72 and 5/80 by Keith Miller saw the Australians claim their first Test victory in England since 1948. The eventual margin of 185 runs was not a true reflection of the standards of the teams. In between Tests the tourists scored their first victory against a county side when Gloucestershire were defeated by an innings and 48 runs with South Australia's orthodox left-arm spinner, John Wilson, taking the tour's best figures of 7/11 for a match analysis of 12/61.

Four days prior to the third Test at Headingley the Leeds pitch was covered in water, a legacy of the wet summer being experienced. The tourists were hit by injuries for the match: Miller could not bowl due to a knee injury; Lindwall came back into the team although his fitness was suspect; wicketkeeper Gil Langley had a back problem and was replaced by Len Maddocks, and three of the batsmen were carrying various ailments. The England team contained one major surprise, the return of the forty-one-year-old Lancashire batsman, Cyril Washbrook, who was a selector and therefore part of his own recall process.

The press criticism was loud and long. Then, on the first morning, with England 17 for three in the first hour, Washbrook joined his captain Peter May. Their partnership of 187 in 287 minutes not only kept the press quiet, it proved also to be a match-winning partnership for England (May 101, Washbrook 98). The total reached 325 on the second afternoon as the pitch started to deteriorate rapidly. The Australians were 81 for six at the close, and after Saturday's washout, their innings closed at 143 on the fourth afternoon, Laker taking 5/58. May enforced the follow-on which saw Laker (6/55) skittle the tourists for 140 and defeat by an innings and 42 runs.

Old Trafford, nine days later, saw a Test match which was to become revered in the annals of cricket history. The Australians had shown their vulnerability to spin during the tour and were having a hard time against both Jim Laker and Tony Lock. This was a low period for Australian cricket as the techniques which were so successful on the hard-baked pitches back home failed miserably on the green, damp tracks offered in England during this wet summer. When the pitches were not green-tops they were dust-bowls and from the start the Australians never had a chance in this Test.

It became known as 'Laker's Match' for the Surrey off-spinner broke several major bowling records with his match analysis of 19/90, all taken from Old Trafford's Stretford End. He claimed the most wickets in any first-class game; the only instance of ten wickets in a Test innings; the first time anyone had taken ten wickets twice in one season; and 39 wickets in a series, equalling Alec Bedser's record, with one match still to play (Laker would eventually claim 46 victims to set a new Ashes record).

England batted on winning the toss and reached 307 for three by the end of the first day. This stretched to 459 on the Friday with Australia 53 for one and unprepared for what was to come. Rain interruptions then took place at regular intervals over the succeeding three days as Australia made 84 (Laker 9/37) and 205 (Laker 10/53) to give England a remarkable win. Not since 1905 had England beaten Australia twice in a home series and to complete a Test in Manchester was a feat in itself.

As Australia had failed to regain the Ashes it would have been appropriate to blood one or two of the younger players in the final Test at The Oval in late August. However that was not to be, and the match represented the end of an era for Australian cricket. Many of the players would not be seen in Test cricket in England again: Ian Johnson (who would retire on his return home), Keith Miller, Ron Archer, Jim

Burke, Ian Craig, Pat Crawford, Gil Langley, Ray Lindwall and Len Maddocks.

The final Test lost exactly the same time due to rain as the opening Test, with a draw always being the probable result. Ron Archer said farewell to England with 5/53, his best Test return, and the always exciting Keith Miller top-scored for Australia with 61. The tourists then played in three festival matches and made a tour of Scotland before enjoying their Board of Control paid holiday.

The tour had made a profit of £52,792, which was less than in 1953, but the rain had caused thirteen totally blank days. When the financial forecasts fell below expectations all the Board of Control did was to reduce the cash distributions to the State Associations. Australia had enjoyed a wonderful run from 1933 for twenty years or so but the game and society were changing rapidly and the Board was not. They fined Miller £100 and Lindwall £50 for minor breaches of their 'non-publication policy' and ignored the wonderful service given to the game by the two players. They also ignored the fact that, in 1956, they could have called on the valuable services in England of Bruce Dooland, Colin McCool, Jack Manning, Jock Livingston, Jack Walsh, Bill Alley and George Tribe when it became obvious there were serious weaknesses in the touring side.

The Board were complacent, even with the new blood starting to trickle in. They just did not care and did nothing about the fact that the Test team did not contain Australia's best cricketers. The Board set up sub-committees to look at 'brighter cricket' but the effort was self-defeating as the members of these committees were the very people who were stifling the game. Radio broadcasters, fed up with the Board's attitude to them, made tennis and golf the top summer games with blanket coverage around the nation. In Brisbane, the Queensland administration still barred photographers and feature writer journalists from their ground. In Adelaide, SACA secretary Allan Lyon was severely reprimanded for speaking to cricket clubs on coaching matters in his spare time. His late 1956 holiday spent visiting country cricket officials saw him warned about his future conduct. As Sydney journalist Jack Pollard wrote of this period:

> Fifty years after its formation, the Board had no national junior development programme, no plans to ensure coaches were qualified and no plans to develop its own grounds. Coaching in schools was left to masters seconded to the job by their headmasters, and in district clubs the fathers of small boys were often recruited to coach and organise travel for their sons' teams. Capital city ground improvements were left to State associations.

Australians took to the car as their main means of transport to

> Test match grounds in the 1950s, discarding trams and buses, but parking facilities at the grounds remained primitive. Most had to park in the back streets of nearby suburbs and walk to the ground. The marvel of it all was that so many continued to play the game despite such supine administration.

Pollard, of course, was completely right. The arrogance of the Board had to be seen to be believed and, had Don Bradman decided to devote himself full-time to stockbroking and to ignore cricket administration, one just could not imagine into what state Australian cricket would have fallen. There is little doubt that its armageddon of 1977 would have happened much earlier had it not been for Australia's finest cricketer.

To give examples of the Board in action would all too frequently appear 'Pythonesque'. Their sense of their own importance becomes comical yet the meeting which was held over three days from 19 September 1956 contained a member still present in 1992 and others who oversaw the great rebellion of 1977.

After greeting themselves formally and electing everybody to various committees, the Board's first main item was to spend three hours debating why Lord's had refused one of their number permission to be an 'observer' at the 20 July Imperial Cricket Conference. Bruised pride causes lengthy debate. Then came a disgraceful decision when a reciprocal visit by a team of Ceylon schoolboy cricketers was refused 'as it would clash with the start of the rugby league season in Sydney and Brisbane'.

Australian captain Ian Johnson was not spared when it was agreed 'to refer his 1954–55 allowances to the Deputy Commissioner of Taxation, Victoria'. Johnson, in Scotland at the time, did not find out about this action for another year. Then came the revelation, in tour manager Bill Dowling's first report, that Pat Crawford had been told his tour contract would be cancelled if he made contact with his seriously ill and pregnant wife who happened to have booked, by chance, on the same ship to England as the Australian team. Mrs Crawford was forced to spend a week, by herself, in a Perth hotel before being able to board a ship for the voyage to England. Dowling had unloaded her in Western Australia, following discovery of her embarkation in Melbourne. The Board were furnished with copies of the whole unsavoury incident 'and unanimously endorsed the action taken'.

The Board of Control for Cricket in India was not spared either. It had approved a souvenir booklet being prepared by *The Indian Sporting Times* whose editor wrote to the Australian Board asking for photographs and profiles of the Australian players. The reply sent back to both parties said: 'It is suggested you contact some of the

English newspapers for the detail you require'. Then the President of the BCCI wrote about the air fares for the team saying: 'I am advised by BOAC/Qantas that the fare from London to Sydney with a break of journey in India and Pakistan is £299 per person and we propose arranging this forthwith'. The Board became very indignant when told by one, Sydney-based, delegate that he 'could get the tickets for £239'. The Indians were sent a cable in which they were virtually told that they were cheats and that 'the tour manager will arrange all flight arrangements'. The following month Bill Dowling wrote in one of his interim reports: 'The cheapest air fare I could get was £329 a player'. Not, one might say, a way to make friends and influence people.

The whole of the third day of the meeting was taken up with a debate on the televising of cricket in Australia. In the morning a delegation met the Board from Channel Nine, the Sydney-based television station, and various Melbourne stations. The Channel Nine team, Messrs Finlay and Sheil, were the obvious leaders in a push to try and get the Board to allow the televising of Sheffield Shield cricket in order to gain maximum exposure for the game and to allow their station to be readily connected with the sport. Finlay gave a lengthy presentation to the Board explaining the technical necessities, how many cameras would be needed and the cost. With each outside broadcast van 'costing £60,000 each', Finlay stated 'that his organisation were willing to purchase a number of such vehicles for the televising of cricket if the Board gave their approval'.

Finlay went on to describe the fee structure arranged with the Australian Lawn Tennis Association for Channel Nine's blanket coverage of the Davis Cup and that 'the positioning of cameras high up in the stands might mean the loss of a few seats but would be of no inconvenience to the general public'. The delegation was then thanked by chairman Frank Cush and left the meeting. The Board then decided not only to have nothing to do with the television stations but agreed to lobby the Postmaster-General to have a new clause written into the new Broadcasting and Television Bill, 1956.

The Board then drafted the proposed clause which, with minor amendments, was accepted by the government as a new clause in the Act. It read:

> The Australian Broadcasting Commission or the holder of a licence for a commercial television station shall not televise, either directly, or by means of any recording, film or other material or device or otherwise, the whole or a part of a sporting event or other entertainment held in Australia, after the commencement of this section, in a place to which a charge is made for admission, if the

> images of the sporting event or other entertainment originate from the use of equipment outside that place.

The clause gave the Board total power over the televising, or not, of cricket in Australia. Their incompetence and misuse of this Act twenty years hence would prove catastrophic.

# 24

# Cricket in controversy

While Ian Johnson and his team were on the Indian sub-continent, playing Tests against Pakistan and India, in Australia preparations had nearly been finalised for the Olympic Games to be held in Melbourne from 21 November 1956 for some sixteen days. A large section of the Melbourne Cricket Ground had been rebuilt, and Sheffield Shield matches transferred to St Kilda's Junction Oval. The Games did not affect cricket around the nation, which carried on as though nothing else was happening. With radio and the new television stations broadcasting the Olympics, however, cricket attendances plummeted.

In that same southern spring of 1956 there were disastrous floods on the River Murray. Huge rainfall in the catchment areas of central Queensland gave the communities along the feeder rivers notice of floods to come. But there had never been a flood of this magnitude and the result, as far as cricket was concerned, was that the game suffered badly in the country areas of four states, grounds were ruined, and players had to devote their time to more pressing matters and concerns.

On 8 October the Australian cricketers gathered at Rome's Ciampano airport for their tour of Pakistan and India. Arriving in Karachi next day the tourists were amazed to find a matting pitch laid out for their Test at the National Stadium. Their spiked boots were a serious hindrance when practising or playing on the mat. The Board had known about this, but had not passed on any detail to the manager or players.

The first day of play was historic in more than one way. It was the initial Test between the sides and it produced the slowest day of Test cricket yet recorded. Only 95 runs were scored for the loss of twelve wickets. The Australians were completely at sea when batting and all out for 80 runs. Pakistan's right-arm medium-fast swing bowler, Fazal Mahmood, took 6/34 and bowled unchanged with Khan Mohammad (4/34), the last instance of one pair of bowlers completing such a feat in a full Test innings. Pakistan were in equal trouble on the second day before a sixth-wicket stand of 104 between their captain, Abdul Hafeez Kardar (69), and Wazir Mohammad (67) all but won the game for their side.

Australia battled for a day and a half to reach 187 the second time around but again found Fazal (7/80) and Khan (3/69) too much to handle. The expected home victory, by nine wickets, came during the second over of the final day's play. It also represented the end of the brilliant Test career of Keith Miller as his troublesome knee injury – which dated back to when he was playing football for St Kilda ten years before – finally became too much for him to bear.

The team flew to Madras and, after only one day's break, started the first of three successive Tests against India. Returning to a turf pitch, but minus Archer and Davidson as well as the injured Miller, the tourists did well to restrict India to 161 with Richie Benaud claiming his Test-best figures of 7/72. The large crowd in the sweltering Corporation Stadium watched as their heroes had Australia at 200 for eight before Ian Johnson played a true captain's role by making 73 as the score moved on to 319. Ray Lindwall, who had retired with a stomach complaint after bowling only nine overs in the first innings, came back with a vengeance to take 7/43 and see Australia victorious by an innings and five runs.

The itinerary set by the Board for their players then saw a much delayed flight to Bombay for the second Test at the Brabourne Stadium with only one day in which to travel. With Ian Johnson now ill, Ray Lindwall took over the captaincy and had to use eight bowlers in each of India's innings. Illness and injury compounded Lindwall's only Test as captain although Australia did have the better of a drawn game. The century hoodoo was broken as Jim Burke (161) and Neil Harvey (140) took Australia's total to 523 for seven declared in reply to India's 251 of which Gul Ramchand (109) recorded his team's first home century against Australia. On the final day a six-hour innings of 78 by Polly Umrigar, the Indian captain, saved his side from defeat.

Immediately the game was finished both parties rushed to the airport for the flight to Calcutta. Arriving in the early hours of the morning and to be expected to greet swarms of local officials, make a speech, deal with reporters, sign autographs and ensure that the team was all together, was part and parcel of Ian Johnson's task as captain.

He led Australia for the last time at Eden Gardens in the third Test which started on 2 November 1956. It was his forty-fifth Test of which he had been captain in seventeen matches. Put into bat Australia made 177 on a pitch which took spin from the outset. Ghulam Ahmed claimed 7/49, with Richie Benaud taking 6/52 as India's reply fell 41 runs short. A slow 69 by Neil Harvey let Johnson declare and set India 231 runs to win in over two days. The gamble paid off as Benaud's 5/53 saw Australia home by 94 runs with a day and a half to spare.

Within five months of Ian Johnson returning to Australia, the Melbourne Cricket Club secretary, Vernon Ransford, retired. Applications were called for and from forty-five received, Johnson was chosen for the job. The committee had been impressed with his diplomatic skills and his ability to mix with all sections of the community. He had a strong personality and was an excellent all-round sportsman. He held the position until his retirement in 1983, and even then kept up strong connections with the game.

The Sheffield Shield season of 1956–57 was already under way when the Australians returned home. Western Australia, having been elected a full participating member, now played eight matches a season instead of four. This expansion of the competition to eight fixtures each stayed for the next twenty-one years.

Almost immediately the Test players started making good performances. Jim Burke scored 220 for NSW against South Australia; Peter Burge 210 for Queensland against Victoria; Neil Harvey 209 for Victoria versus NSW and several single hundreds. Alas, the bowling during the season was not of much consequence.

A testimonial match was held in Sydney for Bill O'Reilly and Stan McCabe in January 1957 and it acted as a trial for the non-Test tour of New Zealand which began the following month. The pair shared £7500, a sum which could then have bought four decent-sized homes in the ever-growing suburbs of Sydney. The game saw Harvey's XI defeat Lindwall's XI by seven wickets but the star of the match was the left-arm fast bowler from the South Melbourne club, Ian Meckiff, who took 6/75.

The fourteeen-man party for New Zealand, which was announced on 27 January, saw the twenty-one-year-old Ian Craig as captain with NSW Cricketers' Club president, Jack Norton, as manager. The Board were very concerned by the medical report received from England on the physical fitness of Johnson's team and issued a strict instruction to Craig and Norton to make sure 'that the team should undertake physical training on a regular basis'. The report, from Dr Lade in London, had stressed how easily certain players put on weight with constant socialising, and how he had been quite shocked at the total lack of physical exercise carried out by most of the players. His recommendation to the Board 'stressed the need for intense physical training for international cricket in the same way as for every other form of athletic endeavour'. The Board agreed and circulated his report to all associations.

When the Australian team was announced there was general relief in New Zealand. The country had been offended by the Australian Board's refusal to allow Test status to be given to the three international fixtures, so they had to be content with the calibre of the chosen players. Although the team was comparatively young it included six men with Test experience: Benaud, Burge, Craig, Favell, Harvey and Watson. Most of the others were seasoned Shield players with Norman O'Neill and Bobby Simpson having established reputations as exciting batsmen, and with a pace armoury of Ian Meckiff, John Drennan and Ron Gaunt. Barry Jarman, who was to serve a long apprenticeship as second-string to Wally Grout, was wicketkeeper and Lindsay Kline and Johnny Martin were the two left-arm spinners.

In the Sydney *Sunday Telegraph*, Sid Barnes in his cricket column decried the New Zealand Cricket Council's offer of £2 a day to the team as 'lousy'. He added:

> As far as the players are concerned, cricket tours of New Zealand are a racket, which our Board of Control falls for with the simple faith of a country yokel confronted with the thimble and pea for the first time.
>
> Our boys are going over there knowing they will draw huge crowds of New Zealanders who have not seen an Australian team for several years, and that the profits will be considerable.
>
> If New Zealand can afford to tour England and South Africa, it can afford to pay our boys better than the chicken-feed grub steak they will get on this trip. If not, then the initials on this team's blazer should be XYZ-Finish!

In the seven first-class matches on tour (the Australians won five, the other two ended in draws) Harvey had the best aggregate of 448 runs at an average of 49.77, O'Neill's 218 runs were obtained at the best average of 72.66, followed by Benaud, 323 runs at 53.83. Benaud proved himself an excellent all-rounder by taking 32 wickets at 19.31, while Meckiff (20 wickets at 10.85) was the pick of the fast bowlers.

In the first representative match, played at Christchurch's Lancaster Park from 1 March 1957, the Australians made 216 to New Zealand's 268. Then Ian Craig made an unbeaten 123 although at one time he scored only two runs in an hour while Neil Harvey (84) made 51. Craig's declaration at 284 for three gave New Zealand no time to chase the required runs and they finished on 112 for two.

The second match at the Basin Reserve, Wellington, went the same way as the first. Benaud took 6/79 and Simpson scored 67 but rain ruined any chance of a result. The end of March saw Eden Park in Auckland as the venue for the third and deciding international.

New Zealand elected to bat first on a green-top which saw Meckiff (4/28) and Drennan give the batsmen a torrid time. In reply to 198 the Australians declared at 350 for eight after a delightful innings of 102 not out from Norman O'Neill. The 17,000 second-day crowd showed great enthusiasm for O'Neill's powerful shots, giving him a standing ovation when his thirteenth boundary brought up his century. When New Zealand replied, Meckiff claimed two wickets in successive balls after which Johnny Martin (6/46) ran through the rest. The Australians won by ten wickets to take the mini-series.

At a farewell dinner, Ian Craig told his hosts that 'New Zealand cricket was handicapped by an inferiority complex'. He went on to suggest that 'pitches be made of firmer surfaces to encourage batsmen to play proper strokes' and 'the present varying quality of pitches tended to favour bowlers unduly'. Not bad for a twenty-one-year-old!

The Australian team hardly seemed to have returned home when the selectors announced the side to tour South Africa starting in early October 1957. Ian Craig and Neil Harvey, both from NSW, were elected captain and vice-captain respectively.

During the southern winter of 1957, Bill Ferguson, former scorer and baggage-master, died just after being awarded the British Empire Medal for his services to the game. Queensland's autocratic leader Jack Hutcheon, QC, also died. He had been on the Board for thirty-eight years and his loss was a blow to the influence of his State on international cricket. But whoever appeared on the Board, usually in 'dead men's shoes', there appeared to be no change in attitude.

Having said that, it was quite a change for the Board to stand up to the Marylebone Cricket Club in the way they did in September 1957. Lord's wished the forthcoming England tour of 1958–59 to be shorter than before with the States only having one match each against the touring side. The Board rejected such a suggestion out-of-hand, replying with their idea of a proper itinerary and the fact that 'we expect your visit here to be of no less than five months duration'. With Lord's having promised the New Zealand Cricket Council that they could have at least two Tests following an Australian visit the tour took on a look of endurance rather than pleasure.

One point which MCC did win was over the pressure put on the Board to tour India and Pakistan in 1959–60. Hints had been dropped at the 1956 Imperial Cricket Conference and followed up by correspondence in January 1957. The Board's discussion on this matter revolved not around the benefit to the game of such a tour – and Ian Johnson was very outspoken in favour of this – but would any tour income become subject to taxation, and how could any profit be taken out of the countries?

By June 1957 the Board of Control for Cricket in India had given the Board an assurance 'that the Australian team would be completely exempt from taxation' and added 'that better accommodation would be arranged' if the tour went ahead. Then on 1 July 1957 the Department of External Affairs in Canberra wrote to Ledward saying 'that we have been advised that President Iskander Mirza had given his assurance' vis à vis a Pakistan tour 'that no income tax would be levied on the Australian team and there would be no difficulty in remitting moneys to the Board in Australia'.

Faced with this, a strongly worded letter from the Minister of External Affairs and a telephone message from Prime Minister Menzies, the Board agreed to go ahead with the tour. But the politicians became embroiled again in cricket matters when Board delegates tried to limit the duration of the tour and the number of Tests to be played. By November 1957 they had been virtually instructed to play eight Tests between November 1959 and February 1960: three in Pakistan and five in India.

With the fitness of cricketers coming more and more under scrutiny, the Board had asked Jack Norton, as manager of the side in New Zealand, to get the players to carry out a series of exercises each day. On his return Norton reported that 'apart from trotting at least twice around the ground prior to practices, the players did not carry out the physical training programme set down by the Board'. He added: 'Some players were continuing exercises which they had been doing throughout the season and did not wish to change them'.

The Board then decided to issue an edict to the players chosen for the South Africa tour. It read:

> You must undertake the following set of exercises as far as practicable during the tour:
>
> a) Before breakfast a short run, perhaps 440 yards, then ten minutes of simple sitting up exercises without apparatus, and in addition skipping, which will promote balance and muscle tone.
>
> b) Warming up, which is recognised by all athletes as important. New bowlers should turn their arms over and limber up generally as practised by Ray Lindwall, before bowling their first ball. (This can be done whilst the field is being placed.)
>
> c) Warming down. After the game, or during intervals, it is better to jog a little, or walk, rather than relax immediately. No amount of massage or rub-down will take the place of mild exercise to empty the muscles of waste products.
>
> d) Shower and brisk rub with the towel and a short walk rather than an immediate seat in a car.

e) Avoid getting cold, keep out of draughts, wear a sweater if it feels necessary.

f) Keep away from wrestlers, weightlifters and violent exercise fanatics.

The general setting up exercises referred to are deep breathing, knee bending, touching the toes, doubling on the spot, press-ups, etc, which are known to practically everybody.

Just before the team was due to leave for South Africa the tour manager, Jack Jantke – a South Australian committee apparatchik – had a heart attack. Jack Norton took his place and enhanced his reputation with calm and efficient management.

The team was met in Johannesburg by the captain, Ian Craig, who had spent the previous few months in London on business and playing cricket for the Marylebone Cricket Club. Mature far beyond his twenty-two years, Craig blossomed under the pressure of speechmaking, press interviews and as acting-manager until Norton arrived from Australia a fortnight after the players.

Following training and acclimatisation in Johannesburg the team flew to Northern Rhodesia (now Zambia) for a warm-up fixture in Kitwe. The Northerners tried hard but Richie Benaud's 9/16 in ten overs found them wanting. Then it was to Salisbury (now Harare) for the first of two games against Rhodesia. It was appropriate that Craig (113) should score the first hundred of the tour followed quickly by Benaud (117*) and Davidson (100*) as Australia won by an innings. Three days later in Bulawayo, Craig (100) and Burke (106) top-scored in a ten-wicket victory.

Then came seven fixtures prior to the first Test. In Johannesburg, Transvaal lost by nine wickets as Simpson (103) and Davidson (100) made hundreds. Against a strong South African XI at Berea Park, Pretoria, Harvey (173) and Burge (111*) saw Australia to an innings triumph; against Natal in Durban, Burke scored 122 but Benaud won the game by taking 7/46 and 6/88; next Border were defeated by an innings in East London, then it was along the coast again to Port Elizabeth as the Australians (Burke 133, Mackay 113) recorded yet another innings win over Eastern Province (Benaud 5/45 and 5/44).

Victory over Western Province and a draw at Benoni against North Eastern Transvaal led up to the start of the Test series. Four Australians made their debuts: wicketkeeper Wally Grout of Queensland; left-arm off-break and googly bowler Lindsay Kline; the left-arm paceman Ian Meckiff; and all-rounder Bobby Simpson batsman, leg-spinner and a fine slip fieldsman.

Ian Craig now became Australia's youngest ever Test captain with his opposite number, Jackie McGlew, taking over at the last minute when Clive van Ryneveld withdrew with a hand injury. McGlew won the toss and batted for nearly two days on the lush turf of the New Wanderers ground in the northern suburbs of Johannesburg. In reply to 470, a record third-day crowd of 36,057 saw Richie Benaud on his way to 122. With a draw looming the tourists had Wally Grout claim a then world record of six catches in a Test innings with Alan Davidson taking 6/34. With Australia needing to score 304 in 268 minutes on the final day the match petered out to an indecisive conclusion.

Both teams then travelled on South African Railways' famous Blue Train to Cape Town for a New Year's Eve start to their second encounter. Craig won the toss and chose to bat on a perfect Newlands pitch. A light southerly breeze over the pavilion was of little help to the spinners although Hugh Tayfield did claim 5/120 out of Australia's 449. It was an opening stand of 190 between Colin McDonald (99) and Jim Burke (189) – who batted 578 minutes for his highest Test score – which paved the way for Australia. With the pitch breaking up, South Africa's 209 saw them forced to follow-on and, although Trevor Goddard carried his bat for 56, Lindsay Kline ended the match soon after lunch on the fourth day when he did the hat-trick, dismissing Fuller, Tayfield and Adcock for Australia to win by an innings and 141 runs.

Another win against Transvaal was followed by a high-scoring draw in Pietermaritzburg versus Natal. Benaud scorched his way to a career-best 187 and enjoyed a partnership of 246 with Alan Davidson (121) which took just over a session of play. Benaud then took 5/71 as Natal followed-on but a dogged century from Trevor Goddard (131*) kept the tourists at bay on the final day. Over five days at Kingsmead slow batting by South Africa made a draw inevitable in the third Test. The Springboks failed to capitalise on bowling Australia out for 163, taking an unnecessarily long thirteen hours to reach 384 on a lifeless pitch.

The fourth Test in Johannesburg was completely different. Benaud, promoted in the batting order, proceeded to hit the fastest century of the series. Ken Mackay (83*) and Alan Davidson (62) extended the tail with the Australians reaching 401. Benaud the bowler then set about the South Africans, taking 4/70 and 5/84 in what became an easy ten-wicket victory.

With the series won, the tourists might have given Test places to the stoic players who did not get a look-in during the first four Tests. But Ian Craig's side rammed home their superiority in the three-and-a-half days of the fifth Test in Port Elizabeth. With the sea breeze being of more benefit to the bowlers a low-scoring Test saw Australia victors by eight wickets to take the series three-nil.

Richie Benaud was the player of the tour. His fielding was excellent;

in eighteen first-class matches he scored 817 runs at 51.06 and took 106 wickets at 19.41. Added to that he was, without question, leadership material, although it seemed probable he would spend many years in the shadow of Ian Craig.

Just before the fourth Test in Johannesburg, the Board of Control had met over three days in Melbourne. After the usual preliminaries, standing orders were suspended to allow for a discussion on future Test tours. Both India and Pakistan had asked for more matches in 1959–60 than the itinerary drawn up by the Board allowed. The reaction of the Board was one of anger and Jack Ledward was instructed to send both countries 'an immediate reply by letter giving them 30 days in which to confirm their acceptance', of the itinerary otherwise 'if a reply is not received within 30 days of the letter being sent, a follow-up cable will cancel the tour'.

This high-handed attitude was no doubt behind the next item discussed. It concerned a lengthy letter sent by the Marylebone Cricket Club about the Australians' reluctance to tour all but England and, occasionally, South Africa. It set out, in detail, MCC's thinking on overseas tours from 1964 to 1986 – which in February 1958 was forward planning in the extreme. In diplomatic terms it was suggested that the Board 'could assist MCC by planning for the future' and gave 'an idea to help' which put forward 'a four-year cycle for England tours home and away, with eight years for South Africa'. Then, said MCC, 'Australia would have greater ease in fitting in regular tours to and from the West Indies and New Zealand'.

By never wishing to go against the wishes of MCC (and perhaps lose the chance of the OBEs or MBEs awarded to long-serving Board members which seemed to be recommended from Lord's), the Board immediately formed a sub-committee which worked late into the night before handing down a report next day. Not surprisingly they 'fully agreed with MCC's recommendations' and went somewhat further by scheduling tours to India and Pakistan as well. Three minor switches were made but otherwise the schedule agreed that day held up to 1971–72 when South Africa were prevented from touring Australia.

With the Test team away the Sheffield Shield season did not change tack. New South Wales walked away with the title again in 1957–58 but not as emphatically as in 1958–59 when they brushed aside most opposition with impunity.

Norman O'Neill had scored 1005 runs in 1957–58 at 83.75; and in the next year 874 at 51.41 as he made his debut against Peter May's England side. His talent was obvious to the tourists when he scored 104 against them in Perth on their second match in the country. O'Neill was a right-hand batsman, a back-foot player of the highest class, a powerful driver, and very quick on his feet to spin bowling.

Before the drawn match against a Combined XI, the England side had drawn with Western Australia, and they went on to defeat South Australia and Victoria. Then they came up against the all-conquering New South Wales side.

Neil Harvey (149), who had moved to Sydney, and Jim Burke (104) put on 246 for the second wicket; O'Neill made 84, and, once Benaud (5/48) had made the tourists follow-on, it was a matter of survival. The eventual draw showed up weakness in the tourists' order which became worse when batsman Raman Subba Row fractured his wrist just before the first Test.

The Australian selectors were in a quandary over their team for the first Test in Brisbane starting on 5 December 1958. Should they include in the team a player who, on his return from South Africa, had been apprehended by the Australian Customs service and subsequently charged with attempting to bring goods into the country and trying to avoid a sizeable amount of duty? (Subsequent tour agreements between the Board and players carried a clause which required complete compliance with Australian Customs regulations.) And whom should they choose to captain the side in place of Ian Craig who was troubled yet again with hepatitis?

In the first case they chose the player concerned who continued in Test cricket for some time although his off-field activities were a poor influence on the younger players. For their other choice they by-passed the obvious candidate in Neil Harvey and went for his NSW colleague Richie Benaud. It was a shock appointment particularly as Harvey had done an outstanding job in South Africa as the team's senior player. But in retrospect – and with no criticism of Harvey who gave splendid support to his new leader – the selection of Benaud, a Bradman protégé, was as farsighted as it was wise. Benaud's influence on the game, not only in Australia but worldwide, is felt right up to the present. Born in Penrith, a town west of Sydney, on 6 October 1930, Benaud played his grade cricket for Central Cumberland before making his NSW debut in 1948–49. In a twenty-year first-class career he scored 23 centuries in his 11,719 runs and took 945 wickets, claiming five or more in an innings 56 times. Added to that he took 255 catches.

A journalist by profession, he started his career on the now defunct *Sydney Sun* newspaper, in the accounts department. Then, under the wing of former player 'Johnnie' Moyes, he graduated to the rough and tumble of the police rounds where his crime stories earned him respectful attention. When made Australian captain he already understood the cricket journalists' needs with his grasp of deadlines and quickly had their confidence. The response to him was larger and more varied coverage of the game which brought cricket back to its media peak in Australia. Another of his innovations was the eve of Test match dinner, which was restricted to the players only, at which tactics and other relevant matters could be thrashed out in private.

The 1958–59 Test at the Gabba, from an historical point of view, was the first to be televised. The Board of Control had eventually reached agreement with the Australian Broadcasting Commission (ABC) for a payment of £5000 for the televising of the final two-and-a-half hours of each day's play in all Tests, with the added provision that 'only five extra people to be allowed into the ground as technicians'.

Peter May won the toss and batted first in what was one of the dreariest Tests of all time. No wonder the Brisbane attendance became less and less as each day wore on. England were dismissed for 134 to which Australia replied with 186 by lunch on the third day. By the close England were 92 for two which became 198 all out at the end of the fourth day: 106 runs in a whole day's play being the fewest scored in a day in Australia. England's all-rounder Trevor Bailey batted 357 minutes before reaching his half-century – then a record for the slowest in the history of the first-class game. His innings of 68 endured for 458 minutes at an average run-rate of slightly less than nine runs an hour.

Needing 147 to win in a day the Australians made a meal of their task, taking four hours and ten minutes to reach the figure, Jim Burke batting for the whole time for just 28 runs. Even so, victory by eight wickets was a fine start for Benaud's leadership.

The tourists then played three drawn matches, two in Tasmania and one in South Australia before the second Test in Melbourne. Following the team was a large contingent of English journalists who were plainly at a loss how to make excuses for the dismal, boring play of their team. So, in order to create a few headlines 'back home', stories started to appear in Fleet Street newspapers branding virtually every Australian bowler over medium-pace as a 'chucker'. The tabloid style debate – one newspaper correspondent referred to Gordon Rorke as 'a honey of a chucker' – from then on ruined any serious analysis of the series, a situation which also was to occur in 1974–75. Then, as in this series, two fast bowlers dominated the Tests to an extent which precluded the touring team's journalists from appreciating the skill of the opposition and the failings of their own players. To sum it up in the words of Jack Pollard, who spent the tour in the pressbox, 'the English journalists were growing in agitation each day over what they saw as chucking by Australian bowlers . . . [they] conducted a witchhunt against those they perceived to be jerkers and throwers'.

The Victorian left-arm pace bowler Ian Meckiff was one of those two bowlers. His five wickets in Brisbane was followed by 3/69 and a match-winning 6/38 in Melbourne. Peter May had won the toss on New Year's Eve and spent the night eleven runs short of his century. His celebration came next morning as 58,865 spectators saw him reach 113, the first England captain since Archie MacLaren in 1901 to score a Test century in Australia. In reply to England's 259, Australia next day reached 308 with Neil Harvey, in front of the season's best crowd of 71,295 scoring 167, the first Australian century against England since November 1954, eleven Tests ago.

It was now that the English press got going telling all sorts of fables to their readers back home as England's dismal batting saw them all out for just 87 runs. Meckiff dominated, and in later years umpire Mel McInnes (when interviewed for this book) said quite categorically that 'Meckiff was not a chucker and I had no hesitation in passing his action'. McInnes also related stories on how the visiting press tried to badger him into making controversial comments with trick questions. To the end of his long career he remained mute – as an umpire should.

England's total was their lowest in Australia since their 61 in Melbourne in March 1904. It left Benaud's men needing just 39 runs for victory, which came by eight wickets early on the fifth morning. The humiliations of the 1956 tour by Australia were gradually being exorcised.

Next it was straight on to Sydney to commence battle once more. May again won the toss and batted on a good pitch with his team struggling to 190 for six on the first day. Rain then took a hand in proceedings and the spinners took over. Benaud claimed 5/83 in England's 219 while Tony Lock (4/130) and Jim Laker (5/107) bowled 90 of the 129 overs in Australia's 357. England were then content to bat out for a draw as the pitch improved, with Colin Cowdrey taking over six hours to reach his hundred.

The lack of thought given to the England itinerary showed up when the team had to leave Sydney, travel the long distance to Melbourne to play Victoria (and gain a rare victory) only to return to Sydney to play New South Wales and then go back on themselves again and on to Adelaide for the next Test. For the fourth time in a row Peter May won the toss but on this occasion asked Australia to bat on one of Arthur Lance's perfect pitches.

The England captain's logic was that he had a pace attack more than a spinning one because Jim Laker had had to withdraw just before the start of play with a 'sore spinning finger'. Alas for the tourists the gamble failed. Australia took until lunch on the third day to reach 476. Colin McDonald (170) and Jim Burke (66) put on 171 for the first wicket with runs mounting slowly but surely after that. Benaud bowled beautifully when England came to occupy the crease with his 5/91 and 4/82 dominating as the visitors made 240 and 270.

Australia's ten-wicket victory came on the sixth day with the Ashes being regained after a period of five years and 170 days.

Benaud's cricketing skills and his consummate captaincy were largely ignored by the touring journalists, in contrast, for example, to Johnnie Moyes and Ray Robinson. The British press were more interested in the new Australian fast bowler Rorke who had made his Test debut in the match taking 3/23 and 2/78. Rorke's action and the way his back foot 'dragged' over the bowling crease, added to the ball being delivered from an unusual height (Rorke was 6 ft 4 in tall) made good copy. By today's standards, as laid down by the West Indies, Rorke was almost a medium-paced plodder but in 1959 he, and Ian Meckiff, were the excuse to the readers back home for the team's over-defensive performance. To them England's defeats were caused by the colonials' ability to run cricket's laws to their limits. That aside, Rorke's display in the intense heat of Adelaide was little short of a near-perfect debut.

Another excuse, leaked to the Engish newspapermen, was that the touring management, having had no response from the Australian Board, had cabled Lord's asking them to intervene in the continued appointment of umpire Mel McInnes! Peter May was particularly disappointed in McInnes' performance in the first four Tests and wanted him replaced for the final Test in Melbourne. The Board met during the Adelaide Test, rejected Lord's overtures saying 'that in their opinion the objections raised were neither tangible nor reasonable', and then sought out McInnes and suggested he might consider retiring from Test cricket.

During the Board meeting England manager Freddie Brown and his assistant Desmond Eagar were invited to attend and state any views they might have. What is of considerable interest is the exchange between Brown and Sir Donald Bradman. Chairman Bill Dowling raised the matter of 'bowlers with suspicious actions' and asked Brown for his views especially in the light of newspaper comments.

Freddie Brown said: 'I would like to make it perfectly clear, Mr Chairman, both to you and the delegates of the Australian Board of Control for International Cricket, that I am most definitely not raising any objection regarding the action of any Australian bowler. Both Mr Eagar and I, along with our captain, want to make this point to clarify any misunderstandings.' Brown then added: 'However I must make a point to you. I have visited fifteen schools so far on this tour and at practically every one there were around four or five boys of the first or second elevens who had suspicious actions.' He concluded: 'In minor matches around the country the English players have been concerned at the number of bowlers with doubtful actions'.

Sir Donald Bradman put forward a brief résumé of the problem, then said: 'Mr Brown, there are two points that should be raised. First: Whether the umpires are interpreting the law correctly; and secondly: Whether the law should be altered. In my opinion it must be one or the other.'

Brown replied: 'You are quite right. My own view is that the law is difficult to interpret, and I believe that a change in the law would be of benefit and would make it easier for the umpires to interpret. Naturally the law, if amended, would come before the Imperial Cricket Conference.'

Bradman: 'There is some doubt as to whether the Imperial Cricket Conference has any power.'

Brown: 'The Conference has no power, but is the place where opinions can be ventilated.'

Bradman: 'The present law contains the words "absolute fairness", and surely this is clear enough?'

Brown: 'I have no wish to further discuss the matter.'

The Board meeting then went on to discuss with Brown the reports received from various Australian umpires on the suspect bowling action of Jim Laker and listing various complaints – all of which the English tour management dismissed. Brown then requested more complimentary tickets for the final Test 'for the players' friends', and then changed the subject by giving the Board a lecture, via Lord's, 'for not doing more for New Zealand cricket'.

Sir Donald Bradman then asked why MCC had not raised this matter earlier and the meeting then fell into a lengthy discussion as to who should do what for which country in order to improve the game. The spat went on for some time and after the touring management left the meeting Roy Middleton proposed and Don Bradman seconded: 'That when the Board writes to MCC on this meeting disappointment be expressed that the England captain Peter May did not attend as arranged'.

Bradman then took it on himself to try and get clarity on Law 26 in the 1947 Code which then read:

> For a delivery to be fair the ball must be bowled, not thrown or jerked; if either umpire be not entirely satisfied of the absolute fairness of a delivery in this respect, he shall call and signal 'no ball' instantly upon delivery.

For months he held meetings in his own State of South Australia to get a resolution. Then the results were passed on to other States for their opinions and action, following which the Board submitted proposals to the Imperial Cricket Conference. Bradman flew to London to team up with his close friend and former rival Gubby Allen and together they pursued the problem.

Australia won the final Test of the series in Melbourne by nine wickets to wrap up a four-nil victory. Colin McDonald (133) scored his second consecutive century while Ray Lindwall broke Clarrie Grimmett's Australian record of 216 Test wickets. It had been an argumentative series with time-wasting and gamesmanship at an all-time high. Slow batting had seen only 150 runs being scored in a day become a common occurrence but even so 1,131,408 people had paid £247,267 to watch. The Board made a profit of £44,984. Their players received just £85 per Test.

As a sidelight to all this money in the game the Board were using the State Associations in order to siphon off money from radio and television concerns in a way which would remain unknown to all bar themselves. The Victorian representative, Bob Parish, whose long-term involvement with cricket and television started with this series, had managed to squeeze £1333 out of Melbourne station GTV9 for televising the Sydney Test to Victoria. The ABC paid £4000 to the NSWCA for the whole series while their radio arm saw £1125 divided between the five Sheffield Shield playing States for broadcasting.

They need not have bothered for the Shield season was overshadowed by the England tour. NSW won easily with the only individual efforts of note being Richie Benaud's 7/65 for NSW against Western Australia; South Australia's paceman Peter Tretheway taking 7/69 against Victoria; and Gavin Stevens scoring an unbeaten 259 versus NSW in Sydney. It was all, so to speak, a bit of a drag.

Later on in 1959 the Australian team would leave these pressures behind to face other pressures: Pakistan and India. The touring side was announced eight months prior to departure and, for the first time, included a specialist doctor in tropical diseases: Dr Ian McDonald, brother of Colin. Benaud was again captain, Harvey vice-captain, and Sam Loxton was tour manager of what would prove to be a test of endurance. Illness would hit many of the players, with Gordon Rorke and Gavin Stevens being so badly affected that they did not resume playing, and retired.

Before arriving in Pakistan on 9 November 1959, the Australian tourists took part in three matches. The first was the 'Queensland Centenary Match', which was supposed to represent one hundred years of the game in the State although the organisers of the fixture were incorrect in their assumption by some thirteen years, for the first game played in Queensland was in 1846. The four-day knockabout –

which was granted first-class status – saw 'Benaud's XI' 207 and 278 for two declared (McDonald 128) lose to 'Lindwall's XI' 260 and 228 for three (Harvey 112) by seven wickets.

The team then flew to Singapore to play two one-day games, beating a President's XI and a Combined Malayan team with some ease. Then came a flight to Dacca in East Pakistan and a four-day acclimatisation before the first Test. In between net practice and regular inspection of the matting pitch being prepared for the match, the tourists had to give considerable time to Radio Pakistan who had persuaded the Board 'to allow them to make recorded interviews with all the players'. It was arranged through the High Commissioner, who told the Board that it was a diplomatic necessity.

Considerable rain before the start of the Test had not drained away at all well, and as the area was in a low-level region of East Pakistan (now Bangladesh), the outfield had a distinctly unusual look, according to Qamaruddin Butt's tour book, 'green instead of its usual yellow'. The conditions did not affect the crowd of 25,000 on the first day who, 'included a fair number from across the border'. Benaud won the toss from Fazal Mahmood and put Pakistan in to bat.

The home team gave a debut to the twenty-two-year-old Quetta batsman, Duncan Sharpe, who, eighteen months later, would emigrate to South Australia. He played five seasons of Sheffield Shield cricket before settling in Melbourne and becoming a groundsman at various public schools. Sharpe (56) and Hanif Mohammad (66) were the only Pakistanis to pass the half-century mark in a game won by Australia by eight wickets. In a quite remarkable bowling partnership during the Pakistan second innings Ken Mackay (45-27-42-6) and Richie Benaud (39.3-26-42-4) caused Butt to write in the *Pakistan Observer*: 'They were dreadfully accurate and penetrating. Mackay had so hypnotised the batsmen that it was almost sacrilegious to handle him roughly. Benaud with his slow assorted deliveries halted Pakistan's progress with runs'.

The teams then travelled to West Pakistan to play the second Test at a new venue, the Lahore Stadium. Previous Tests in the city had been staged at the Bagh-i-Jinnah ground – formerly Lawrence Gardens. The flight, on a Pakistan International Airways Super Constellation, had seen Australia's Neil Harvey and Pakistan captain Fazal Mahmood dressing up as air-hostesses and serving not only their respective teams but also bemused passengers. Maybe it was the food, but Fazal suddenly became 'unfit' for the Test and the wicketkeeper, Imtiaz Ahmed, took over leadership of the team.

In front of a packed house Pakistan slowly managed to reach 146 to which Australia replied with 27 for one. The placid pitch was fully exploited by the tourists on the second day as Norman O'Neill scored

134, and Australia went on to 391 for nine when Benaud declared. Prior to play on the third morning the teams were introduced to Pakistan's leader, Field Marshal Mohammad Ayub Khan, whose military presence had seemed to scare the crowd away. The stands were sparsely filled as Pakistan plodded on to 138 for two by the close of a less than exciting day's play.

Just 150 runs in 385 minutes comprised the fourth day with only one wicket falling. The final morning saw Saeed Ahmed stumped for 166, after which Pakistan collapsed and the tourists chalked up victory by seven wickets. However the Pakistanis, in a situation that today might seem ironic, were the victims of poor decisions by their own umpires. The Australian players all believed that, had correct decisions been made, the game would have ended in a draw.

Then followed a light-hearted match in Rawalpindi in which the Australians defeated a President's XI by three wickets, after which came a dreary drawn third Test in Karachi. The game started slowly and proceeded to become an endurance test for all concerned. During the morning session on the fourth day, American President Dwight Eisenhower watched the game as Pakistan scored just 27 runs in 130 minutes. Even the support of a crowd in excess of 53,000 could not spur the batsmen along. The fifth day followed a predictable course but, even then, some 27,000 turned out to see master-batsman Hanif Mohammad reach an unbeaten 101.

Pakistan is a nation of cricket fanatics and a crowd estimated to exceed 10,000 bid the Australians farewell at Karachi airport next day as the team took off for neighbouring India. Before landing in Delhi the players would have been unconcerned by the goings-on behind the scenes which, at one time, had jeopardised the visit.

The Australian Board of Control had been very firm with the Indians over advance payments and it was only twenty-four hours before the team's departure from Pakistan that the Board received confirmation that £8343 had been paid for all eighteen first-class return air fares from Sydney, and that £3500 had been placed in the Board's Melbourne account to cover the preliminary expenses of the tour. For the next two months the BCCI bombarded the Board secretary, Jack Ledward, with promises of bank guarantees for the Australians' share of tour profits but it was not until September 1960 that a sum of £3255 was eventually received.

India, who had just returned from being comprehensively beaten in England, recalled Gulabrai Ramchand as captain for the series. The Bombay all-rounder, a veteran of twenty-eight previous Tests, won the toss at the Feroz Shah Kotla Stadium in Delhi on 12 December 1959 and elected to bat on a strangely discoloured pitch. Benaud used seven bowlers in short bursts to dismiss India for 135 and gain a first-innings lead early on the second day. As the Indian spectators became increasingly frustrated by their team's display Neil Harvey reached 114 out of a total of 468. With India never likely to win, the crowd hurled bottles on to the playing field as Benaud (5/76) and Kline (4/42) spearheaded victory in just three and a half days.

Meanwhile the Indian Board had been in emergency contact with their Australian equivalents. Kanpur, venue of the second Test, had experienced heavy rain in the three months preceding the match and to make the contest 'more fair and even' the BCCI had requested 'that the Test be played on matting'. The Australian Board's reaction was predictable and the BCCI were informed that 'we insist on sticking strictly to the agreement that all Test matches in India are to be played on turf wickets [*sic*] and that if a first-class turf wicket [*sic*] cannot be prepared at Kanpur then the Test should be transferred to another centre'. The conclusion to this belligerent reply was that India beat Australia for the first time in thirteen Tests.

The Green Park pitch at Kanpur produced differing reactions from the bowlers. Australia's paceman Alan Davidson returned 5/31 and 7/93 while, for India, the Gujerat off-spinner Jasubhai Patel took 9/69 and 5/55. The excitement for the Indian spectators grew with each day, particularly the fifth, which Australia started at 59 for two. Eight wickets fell for just 46 runs in a session of play which Australia were supposed to dominate on their way to victory. Instead it was the Indians' turn for great joy as Christmas Eve 1959 brought them a famous victory.

Just after Christmas the Australians took on a President's XI at Ahmedabad in a fixture dominated by Norman O'Neill's batting. He scored 284 of the 500 runs made while he was at the crease. His innings lasted 383 minutes against a Test-class attack and enabled Benaud to declare at 554 for six as the game petered out to a draw. The tourists then moved south to Bombay and the third Test at the Brabourne Stadium which turned into a dull, lifeless draw as players on both sides became affected by various illnesses. O'Neill (163) carried on his high-scoring spree aided by Neil Harvey with 102.

By this time the health of Gordon Rorke was giving serious cause for concern, so much so that manager Sam Loxton decided to send him back to Sydney. The Board's rather patronising minutes record that 'it was the manager's duty to get the boy home where he could receive proper treatment'. Lindsay Kline returned to Melbourne not long afterwards while Gavin Stevens was confined to a hospital in Madras where he was treated for hepatitis.

The depleted Australians then played Indian Universities in Bangalore (Burge 157, Grout 101) for the inevitable draw before travelling on to Madras and the fourth Test. The humidity and stench of the city added to the woes of the players, but it did not stop Les Favell (101) and Ken Mackay (89) posting their highest Test scores in a total of 342. Benaud's good fortune on winning the toss continued as his 5/43 and 3/43 were the best bowling returns in each innings as India collapsed for 149 and 138.

At Eden Gardens, Calcutta, in late January the Australians declined the opportunity of an easy run chase to gain their third victory. After Norman O'Neill's first innings 113, the Indians found themselves unable to cope with Davidson and Benaud's bowling. Left to score 203 in 150 minutes against an ordinary attack on a placid track, Benaud shut up shop and played for a draw. Australia won the series 2-1, and Ray Lindwall, in his final Test, took his wicket haul to a then Australian record of 228.

The players flew back to Sydney to find a crucial Sheffield Shield match about to start; Fiji touring the eastern States; and a second-eleven side in New Zealand. Although New South Wales yet again won the Shield it was the all-round performances of Bobby Simpson which caught the eye. Passed over for the tour of the sub-continent and transferred in his work to Perth, Simpson's achievements for Western Australia were quite remarkable. He scored 902 runs at an average of 300.66 with a highest score of 236 not out – and 5/45 – against NSW in Perth. He followed this with innings of 230* and 161*, but the season's highest was made by NSW's Ray Flockton, yet even his unbeaten 264 could not guarantee him a regular place in a team full of star players.

The highlight of the sixteen-match Fijian tour – the first since 1907–08 – was the fixture in mid-February against NSW on the Sydney Cricket Ground. Batting first, Fiji opening batsman Walter Apted carried his bat for 70 in a total of 163. Then came the surprise as Valentine (4/54) and the captain, Uluiviti (5/28), spun NSW out for 137. A generous second-innings declaration by Fiji resulted in NSW struggling to save themselves from outright defeat at 52 for seven when time ran out.

The team to tour New Zealand was announced three weeks before its mid-February departure. Ian Craig was appointed captain with Len Maddocks as his deputy, and of the fourteen players ten were, or would become, Test players. The New Zealand press were scathing on the lack of Test status to be given to the four representative matches. *The Auckland Star* said: 'The Australian Board of Control is yet again treating us as second-class citizens'.

Of the nine matches played, the Australians won four and drew the rest. Predictably, the tour was dominated by Bobby Simpson who scored 518 runs at 74.00, with Ian Quick, a left-arm spinner from Victoria, claiming 28 wickets of which 7/20 and 5/78 came in the first match against Auckland at Eden Park. The initial unofficial 'Test' in Wellington was affected by rain and ended in a draw as did the second 'Test' match at Christchurch.

Victory in the third 'Test' at Dunedin was due to a splendid unbeaten 129 by Simpson which included nineteen fours and came in 177 minutes. It saw Australia win by eight wickets at the end of the fourth day of a match in which the Kiwis were debilitated by injuries. No less than six of their players needed hospital treatment over the course of the game which resulted in a number of changes for the final 'Test' in Auckland at the end of March.

Australia made 381 in their first innings with Len Maddocks unbeaten on 122. New Zealand replied with 203 and then, to much local criticism, Ian Craig declined to enforce the follow-on, telling the *New Zealand Herald*: 'I have more confidence in the ability of the New Zealand batsmen than many people'. True or not, it killed the game which dragged out into a draw.

The Australians were split as to the quality of the local cricket. Simpson was outspoken in saying that 'the standard of the game in New Zealand is not improving' whereas Phil Tressider wrote in the *Sydney Morning Herald*: 'The New Zealand team has surprised the touring Australians by its high standard. It is sad that such fine players have not appeared on the Sydney Cricket Ground. A New Zealand visit should be a must for Australian cricket legislators.'

Two months after the tour, at the end of May 1960, the New Zealand Cricket Council sent the Board a cheque for £603 and a letter of profuse thanks adding: 'We are very pleased with the results of the tour which had been most successful in every way'. At their meeting on 13 September the Board were not at all happy at this amount and asked the tour manager, Clyde Smith, 'to approach the NZCC to obtain a statement of the finances of the tour'.

At the following Board meeting on 7 February 1961, Smith presented NZCC figures for the tour which showed that out of all proceeds, which came to £20,775, expenses left a profit of only £130. This resulted in Bob Parish, a Victorian delegate, introducing a motion which, inter alia, deeply questioned the figures presented. He proposed that a letter be sent to the NZCC which said that 'the receipt of further information would assist the Board's considerations of future tours'. This implied threat caused a lengthy and angry response from Christchurch, with the new Australian Board secretary, Alan Barnes, acting as a peacemaker during the winter months of 1961. The Board meeting of 13 September 1961 saw the chairman, Sir Donald Bradman, note that 'the NZCC correspondence be received'.

The furore over bowlers who were said to 'throw' blew up again during mid-1960. The South Africans were touring England and their fast bowler Geoff Griffin was no-balled during matches against the counties and in the second Test at Lord's.

Behind the scenes in Australia, Sir Donald Bradman was doing cricket marvellous service with his efforts to clarify, then to eliminate, bowling problems throughout Australian cricket. His discussions and explanations were greatly appreciated, especially his *coup de grâce* at a meeting of the South Australian Cricket Umpires' Association in May 1960. He asked the umpires present – who included five former or current Test custodians as well as six others with first-class experience – if they would view some film and give a decision on the bowler's action. The umpires saw a film of a left-hand bowler in action. They viewed it a number of times and were unanimous that the man threw the ball. Sir Donald then rearranged the film and ran it properly to show a right-armed bowler in action. The umpires gasped, for they had just branded the action of England's Harold Larwood.

Sir Donald, and the then Board chairman Bill Dowling, flew to London for the all-important Imperial Cricket Conference meeting at Lord's in July 1960. This meeting was of such a delicate nature that it needed the best minds of cricket's top men to sort it out. On his return to Australia, Bradman said:

> It is the most complex question in cricket history because it is not a matter of fact, but of opinion and interpretation. It is so involved that two men of equal goodwill and sincerity can take opposite views. I plead that a calm, patient attitude be exercised while we pursue and resolve the problem.

The next Board meeting received Bradman's reports from around Australia of his discussions with all State Associations. They then approved all of the ICC rule changes after hearing the results of the meetings and viewing Sir Donald's films – including the trick one of Harold Larwood.

In late September 1960, Algy Frames, secretary of the South African Cricket Association, wrote to Sir Donald saying: 'Cricket seems to be in the doldrums all over the world, particularly as far as gate receipts are concerned' and went on to wish Australian cricket 'a successful visit from the West Indies with greatly improved gate receipts'.

The game was in a state of torpor around Australia: Shield matches were dull and lifeless with South Australia winning three matches in eight years; Tasmanian cricket was at rock bottom with a standard so low that none of the touring teams wanted to play there; club cricketers' interests were declining in favour of other pastimes and activities; while the attitude of local and national administrators neither appreciated nor understood the changing moods and cycle of a dawning society whose members would question their elders in a way not previously known.

Australia was a patriarchal society just starting to decline. The mass migration of Anglo-Saxons outnumbering all other new immigrants would soon be reversed. The 1960s migrants from Latin and Eastern Europe would result in a new cultural awareness which would result in their children – with names such as Durtanovich, Dimattina, Sacristani, Wiener, Zesers, Frei, Jelich, Tazelaar, Duperouzel, Milosz, Veletta, Yagmich, Zoehrer, Majewski, Stobo, Polzin, Gladigau, Scuderi and Kasprowicz, to list just a few – bringing new attitudes and endeavour to a game which needed reviving.

And the 1960s revival was just about to happen.

# 25

# The Benaud Years

In September 1960 the Board of Control, in its guise as the Interstate Conference, came to an agreement with the Australian Broadcasting Commission over television rights for the 1960–61 season. For £7500 the ABC could have 139 days of Test and first-class cricket to televise around the nation. No commercial station showed any interest in the game except for the right to take two minutes of each day's highlights for their news bulletins.

Likewise, radio agreements were with the ABC except in New South Wales where commercial stations 2UE and 2UW paid a total of £780 for broadcasting in Sydney. The Board's attitude towards the media appeared to be one of having to deal with a matter of considerable nuisance value. They had no appreciation of the growing mass popularity of black and white television or of portable transistor radios.

Times were lean for cricket in 1960, with ratings modest, so that the ABC carried on while the commercial stations jumped ship. Their expert panel of commentators were articulate and highly placed personalities with the Commission. The tradition established in past years was maintained by broadcasters such as Michael Charlton who spiced his commentaries with quotations from the Bible and Shakespeare.

The game itself was still losing popularity, with officials having no real solution to combat the decline. Then came the 1960–61 West Indies tour and their player-led revival which owed so much to their flamboyant play and the exciting captaincy of both Richie Benaud and Frank Worrell. The Barbadian Worrell, the first black man to be appointed captain of the West Indies, brought to his role a remarkable perception of each of his players' potential contribution to the team effort.

The tourists arrived in dribs and drabs in Sydney and Perth between 11 and 17 October 1960, finally grouping together and playing their first match in Bunbury against Western Australian Country with only 2450 spectators present over two days, an enormous drop on the crowd who had watched England there in 1958–59.

The initial first-class match in Perth saw Bobby Simpson top-score in both Western Australian innings with 87 out of 140 and an unbeaten 221 in 444 as the tourists lost by 94 runs. Matches were then drawn against An Australian XI in Perth, and South Australia in Adelaide, before Victoria were decisively beaten by an innings and 171 runs in Melbourne when Rohan Kanhai scored 252. Then came a crushing defeat by an innings and 119 runs in Sydney as NSW had Neil Harvey (109) and Norman O'Neill (156*) in top form; and Ken Mackay scored 173 as Queensland drew with the tourists in Brisbane just before the first Test.

The 498th Test match (not 500th as is commonly believed) started at the Woolloongabba ground in South Brisbane on 9 December 1960 with Worrell winning the toss and electing to bat in front of a Friday crowd of 10,678. The West Indies scored at a rapid rate with Garfield Sobers reaching 132 in 174 minutes with twenty-one fours. Worrell (65), Solomon (65), Alexander (60) and Hall (50) saw the total to 453 as Alan Davidson claimed 5/135 for Australia. The reply of 505 had Norman O'Neill scoring 181 aided by Bobby Simpson (92) and Colin McDonald (57). There appeared nothing out of the ordinary as the West Indies second innings reached 284, Worrell with 65 again, and Davidson 6/87, in the first session of the final day.

With just 4100 people in the ground (a figure seemingly multiplied many times if you believed everyone who said they were present that day), the Australians were set to score 233 runs to win in 310 minutes. At 92 for six spectators began to leave in droves, many for the long trip south to Sydney by road to beat the rush-hour traffic, others – including officials and commentators – to go north to Gympie for the fixture against Queensland Country.

There followed a quite remarkable partnership of 134 between Benaud (52) and Davidson which took the Australians to within seven runs of victory before Davidson was run out for 80. As the last over began, Australia needed six runs to win with three wickets in hand. Wes Hall bowled six of the eight permissible deliveries as five runs were scored and two of the three wickets fell to run-outs: then off the seventh, one run needed, Joe Solomon's throw from square-leg hit the only stump he could see to run out Ian Meckiff. The match was tied, the first time such a result had occurred in Test cricket. It would take another 554 Test matches for it to happen again, when Australia would also be involved.

The impact of the match around Australia was tremendous. Many people had watched the closing minutes on television, crowding pavements in town centres as shops displayed their sets for sale with the game as a drawcard. History was made with the public watching. Regrettably the Queensland Cricket Association did not fully appreciate the historical value of their records, for a few years later the scorebooks of this famous match were thrown away.

Nonetheless a new era was dawning. Suddenly there was excitement in a Test series. Another defeat by the all-conquering NSW side led into the second Test in Melbourne. What spectators saw was a grossly unbalanced West Indies batting display where two batsmen made 86% and 81% of the runs scored in each innings, respectively Nurse and Kanhai, and Hunte and Alexander. Defeat by seven wickets was not what the apparently easy-going West Indies needed, but two victories in Tasmania put them in the right frame for Sydney's mid-January Test.

The usual partisanship of an Ashes series became lost on this tour as spectators began to enjoy, and applaud, the quality of the West Indians' play. In the first innings Sobers reached 168 with a withering assault on Australia's pacemen when they took the second new ball. In reply to 339, Australia could only reach 202 as the spinners, Lance Gibbs and Alf Valentine, took control. Three West Indies second-innings wickets fell for 22 after which Cammie Smith and Frank Worrell added 101 in only 67 minutes. Then Gerry Alexander (108) scored the only century of his career in a way which greatly entertained the crowd. Needing 464 to win, Australia lost five wickets for 18 runs in a middle order slump and the series was level at one match each, and one tied.

This inspired a large demand for tickets for the Adelaide Test to be played over the Australia Day long weekend. Those who saw the match, particularly the final day, saw a classic game which produced one of the most exciting rearguard actions in Australian cricket. West Indies stuttered to 91 for three, then Kanhai and Worrell (71) added 107 in an hour with Kanhai's 117 taking just 126 minutes and including two sixes and eleven fours. The run mountain grew to 393 with Australia replying with 281 for five when the off-spinner Lance Gibbs, with a hat-trick, took the wickets of Mackay, Grout and Misson before Benaud (77) and Hoare (35) took the total to 366.

Rohan Kanhai, the diminutive right-handed Guyanan batsman, then showed his class. A player highly significant in the development of the West Indies into a world force, his second century of the match, 115 in 150 minutes, helped his team's score to 432 for six when Worrell declared.

Set to score 460 runs to win in 390 minutes, Australia never looked like getting the runs. Six wickets went down for 144, then it was 207 for nine. Exactly one hundred minutes' play was left for Ken Mackay and tail-ender Lindsay Kline to hold out. Kline had been practising; he arrived at the crease directly from the nets where seven times in the last eleven deliveries he faced, he had been bowled.

The pair defended grimly against a five-pronged world-class attack of Wes Hall, Frank Worrell, Gary Sobers, Lance Gibbs and Alf Valentine: against the fastest of fast bowlers and the wiliest of spinners.

The batsmen stood firm. The 13,691 crowd varied from being deathly quiet to uproariously noisy. The tension was unbearable. The 66 runs scored came through a grim determination to hold on, and Mackay survived Hall's final delivery by taking a sickening blow on the chest. Australia had survived to draw the match, and the series was still level.

The cavalier approach which the West Indies brought to their game coupled with the enterprising tactics of Richie Benaud, produced a frenzied rush for tickets for the final Test in Melbourne. The Board decided to add a sixth day, if needed, to get a result and the Melbourne Cricket Club secretary, Ian Johnson, said that interest in the match was greater than for any of the football finals played at the ground.

On the morning of Friday 10 February 1961 Benaud dared the fates. After winning the toss he sent the West Indies in to bat and could not have been displeased to see them score 252 for eight by the close. The next day was one to remember, for the then greatest crowd in cricket history gathered to watch the match: 90,800 people paying an unheard-of sum of £18,089. Where was the club going to hide all that cash over the weekend? Hidden in sacks between the stacks of files outside the assistant secretary's office!

It was an amazing day. There was no crowd trouble and no difficulty in getting refreshments because whenever a seat was vacated someone else filled it. The West Indies made 292 and Australia 236 for three. The crowd loved it although one farmer, who apparently had babysitting problems, left his grey utility truck outside the ground with a large ram tethered in the rear. The ram was baa-ing dolefully throughout Bobby Simpson's (75) innings.

Australia made 356, and the tourists' second innings reached 321. Set 258 to win in two days and a bit, the Australians had reached 57 for one by the end of the fourth day. There was going to be a result. But which way? Richie Benaud said: 'I am happy with the situation. If we can't score 201 more runs we don't deserve to win.'

Melbourne seemed gripped by cricket fever. One department of the Commonwealth Bank put its staff on a three-hourly roster system: the Supreme Court press-room had to send scores around to their learned gentlemen who were taking note of proceedings at another place. Barristers, jury panels, court officials and judges wanted to know the latest events as they happened. Office workers had their ears to transistor radios and D24, the police radio station, kept police car crews up-to-date with the scores all day.

Behind the scenes South Australian representatives were talking to Gary Sobers: Western Australians to Rohan Kanhai; Queenslanders to Wes Hall. Would they be interested in playing Sheffield Shield cricket next season?

Simpson made 92, O'Neill 48, Burge 53, until finally there were only three wickets to fall and four runs to make. Then drama. A bail was dislodged as Grout played a stroke. Umpire Colin Egar did not see it: not out. The West Indians were distraught. Then Grout, hitting out, was caught in the covers.

Those last minutes were unbearable. The bars were empty, the tension taut. John Martin scored a single and then, with Ken Mackay facing Alf Valentine, two byes. It was an Australian victory by two wickets.

The crowd poured on to the pitch, presentations were made, and the new Frank Worrell Trophy – a perpetual trophy which had been announced as a surprise by Sir Donald Bradman a week earlier – was handed to Richie Benaud by Worrell himself. Two days later came a 'ticker tape' farewell through the streets of Melbourne in honour of the West Indies team. They were to be a boon to cricket the world over. Attitudes changed and so did the game. Within eighteen months the amateur and professional distinctions had been abolished; one-day limited-overs cricket came into being in England, and Australia in Richie Benaud had a captain who could be guaranteed to provide brighter cricket.

The 1960–61 tour brought in £213,531 from 956,018 spectators while the West Indies took home an amazing, unexpected windfall of £84,548. Suddenly everyone seemed to be talking cricket.

The Sheffield Shield competition had been virtually overshadowed by the excitement created by the tourists. With a tour of England imminent, new players had to be sought to replace tired, out-of-form or retiring cricketers. The Shield produced one outstanding young bowler in Western Australia's Graham McKenzie, one of the most talented, yet modest, men the game has bred. New South Wales continued their dominance of the domestic season with the Test players controlling matches when they were free from international duty.

The advent of Sir Donald Bradman as chairman of the Board of Control coincided with this change in the image of the game. He brought to the Board a leadership of great vision during his terms from 1960–63 and 1969–72 and the loss to international cricket by his involuntary departure in 1980 has been felt ever since.

Bradman, who took over from the Victorian, Bill Dowling, after the September 1960 meeting, began at once to stamp his imprimatur on the Board's proceedings. He sent delegates (circular No. 132 of 25 January 1961) a strict note in which he expressed 'his concern at the rising cost of Board expenditure'. The real meaning was for them to cut down on lengthy stays in various cities when Tests were being played and to rein in on general expenses. Bradman then made sure that the players were properly looked after, his friendship with Richie Benaud growing apace. The advancement of Australian cricket at this time owed a lot to the discussions between these two on various golf courses around Australia.

Bradman was the only Board man even to consider rewarding the men who had taken part in the historic Tied Test with special mementoes. He had taken it upon himself to get agreement informally for a presentation to be made by the Board. He had commissioned the former Test bowler, Ernie McCormick, a Melbourne jeweller, to manufacture silver tie tacks which represented both the Australian and West Indian emblems. Thirty-four were made and presented at the official farewell dinner following the final Test.

Bradman was also aware that the name 'Board of Control' had 'always held an unpopular meaning amongst Australian players' and asked delegates if they would consider changing the name. He felt 'Australian Cricket Council' would be correct, but ultimately could not carry the vote.

In early February 1961 the secretary of the Marylebone Cricket Club, Ronnie Aird, in his capacity as secretary of the Imperial Cricket Conference, sent a cable which read: 'Reports reaching London indicate the fifth Test is rescheduled for 36 playing hours. The ICC meeting in July 1959 agreed the maximum duration would be 30 playing hours'.

Bradman and the Board secretary Alan Barnes put their heads together to see if they could overcome what Bradman admitted 'had been an oversight' in agreeing an extra day with the West Indies manager, Gerry Gomez. Their solution was to apologise for the 'apparent overlooking of the ICC decision' but pointing out that 'negotiations for the tour had been commenced prior to the 1959 meeting'.

Those hectic first few months also saw Bradman push through changes to five of the Laws of Cricket which dealt mainly with the 'chucking' problem or with matters aimed at livening up the game.

In his capacity as chairman of selectors Bradman, along with Jack Ryder and Dudley Seddon, chose the team to tour England in 1961. Syd Webb (a poor choice) was elected as manager with a Victorian Cricket Association member, Ray Steele, as treasurer. On 16 February 1961 it was announced that Richie Benaud would captain the team with Neil Harvey as his deputy. The rest of the team would be Brian Booth, Alan Davidson, Frank Misson, Norman O'Neill and Bobby Simpson (making seven in all) from New South Wales; Ron Gaunt, Lindsay Kline, Bill Lawry, Colin McDonald and Ian Quick (Victoria); Peter Burge, Wally Grout and Ken Mackay (Queensland); Graham McKenzie (Western Australia) and Barry Jarman (South Australia).

As usual the team, who were the last touring side to sail to and from England, played three matches in Australia before their departure from Fremantle on the *Himalaya*. The form batsmen were Brian Booth with 65, 40, 128 and 112 in his four innings followed by Norman O'Neill who scored 112, 43 and 123, and Bobby Simpson 71, 108 and 78. The bowling, however, had not been impressive although the conditions were only helpful to the batsmen.

In Colombo, on 4 April 1961, the Australians played their usual one-day match against Ceylon. At the Colombo Cricket Club ground in front of more than 20,000 people they batted first and reached 289 for eight, O'Neill 70, Gunesekera taking 3/39. In reply Ceylon made 187 for eight, Quick, slow left arm, 4/31, with the crowd highly appreciative of the Australians' fielding in light rain for the last part of the game.

The team arrived at Tilbury on 21 April and the British press were immediately won over by Richie Benaud. He understood things such as quotes and deadlines, being a journalist himself. He was always available to the press, with his candour being treated in a proper way. He and his team were intent on playing entertaining cricket, were ready to challenge the clock, not wanting to play for a draw, and in moments of adversity they took the bold way out.

After spending a day in London on sponsorship and advertising duty – the players' reward being two Jaeger pullovers each – the next few days saw continual practice in the nets at Lord's. In the first match, the traditional opener against Worcestershire, Benaud suffered a shoulder injury which restricted him for the rest of the tour. In eleven fixtures prior to the first Test the tourists won four and drew the rest, most of which were affected by the rain.

The opening Test, at Edgbaston, was Australia's first at the ground since 1909 and they enjoyed the initial skirmishes, dismissing England for 195 early on the second day. Then came a barrage of runs as the visitors clocked up 516 for nine before Benaud declared. Neil Harvey's 114 was his twentieth Test century; Norman O'Neill made 82 despite a bad knee injury and Ken Mackay scored a solid 64. Rain then took six hours from the playing time added to which a strong England fight back by Subba Row (112) and Dexter (180) saw the match to a draw.

Benaud's injury ruled him out of the second Test at Lord's which gave Neil Harvey his only taste of Test captaincy. England won their twelfth consecutive toss and their acting captain, Colin Cowdrey, batted first on a Lord's pitch which had a markedly unpredictable bounce at the Nursery End, nicknamed the 'ridge' by elements of the press. The newspapers already had a good story before the match when the Australian manager, Syd Webb, persuaded the Board to 'gag'

*(Above)* Benaud bowling against Middlesex at Lord's in 1961 *(Sport and General)*; *(below)* Alan Davidson bowling against MCC on the same tour *(Sport and General)*.

*(Above)* South Australia won the Sheffield Shield in 1963–64. With the captain, Les Favell, are Rex Sellers, Neil Hawke, Barry Jarman and Sir Donald Bradman; *(below)* Bobby Simpson was captain of the 1964 tour to England. Here he is batting in the opening first-class match.

*(Left)* Bobby Simpson and Bill Lawry, successive captains of Australia, open the innings in the first Test at Sabina Park, Kingston, Jamaica, March 1965 *(Sport and General)*; *(below)* The Board of Control meeting at Adelaide, 1969: from left, Phil Ridings, Bob Parish, Ray Steele, Tim Caldwell, and Sir Donald Bradman.

*(Right)* Ian Chappell, a dominant leader on the field, not always in harmony with the Board *(Patrick Eager)*; *(below)* Ian Chappell's team in England in 1975 (Edgbaston): Marsh, Walters, Ian Chappell, Edwards, Turner, McCosker, Mallett, Walker, Greg Chappell, Lillee. Not in picture – Thomson *(Patrick Eagar)*.

*(Above)* Dennis Lillee's delivery stride and *(below)* his partner Jeff Thomson's slinging action, 1975. 'If Lillee don't get yer, Thommo must.' *(Patrick Eagar)*

*(Left)* Greg Chappell batting in England, 1977 *(Patrick Eagar)*; *(below)* The Australian team for the Centenary Test tour of England, 1980, under the captaincy of Greg Chappell.

*(Above)* Part of the WACA ground at Perth, November 1986, the John Inverarity stand; *(below)* the unveiling in 1988 of the Clarrie Grimmett Stone, just inside the North Gate, Adelaide Oval: from left, Len Darling, Bill O'Reilly, Sir Donald Bradman.

*(Above)* Sir Donald Bradman, who has opened the new Bradman stand at Adelaide, January 1990; *(above right)* Allan Border, captain of the 1989 side which brought home the Ashes *(Patrick Eagar)*; *(below)* 301 for no wicket: Taylor and Marsh have batted all day against England at Trent Bridge in the fifth Test *(Patrick Eagar)*.

Benaud. Webb, who had little knowledge of the game, had felt ignored as manager and was intensely jealous of his captain capturing the headlines.

Unfortunately the Board chairman was unable to override the gag put on Benaud by the tour manager, and press reports of a rift between captain and manager dominated Australian newspapers. Bradman's only comment was to say that the Board could not be held responsible for a newspaper's views. Back in England the touring players took to playing a series of practical jokes on Webb; and the press tried hard not to quote him which was easy during an exciting Lord's Test.

England made 206, and there then followed a titanic battle between the opening bowlers, Fred Trueman and Brian Statham, and the top-order Australian batsmen. Bill Lawry scored 130 in only his second Test innings as the tourists gained a 134-run lead. The English reply was in tatters at the end of Saturday's play at 178 for six following some sparkling quick bowling by Graham McKenzie (5/37) on his Test debut. Australia's five-wicket victory came with a day and a half to spare and put them one up in the series.

The Australians suffered their first defeat at Headingley in early July when England bounced back to win the third Test by eight wickets. The Australians, batting first, lost their last eight wickets for 50 runs in a collapse which saw England gain a first-innings lead of 62. Then a devastating spell of fast bowling from Trueman (6/30), who took five wickets for no runs in 24 balls, turned the match.

After three fixtures against county sides the tourists arrived at Old Trafford for what was to be a remarkable fourth Test. Dismissed for 190, the Australians were 'on the rack' as England totalled 367 in reply. The weekend break, however, seemed to encourage Lawry (102), Simpson (51) and O'Neill (67) and the score crept up to 334 for nine. Then came inspiration as Davidson, unbeaten on 77, and the young McKenzie (32) added 98 for the final wicket which left England to score 256 to win in 230 minutes.

The challenge was taken up by Ted Dexter who scored a glorious 76 in just 84 minutes. At 150 for one England looked the winners. Then came some superb captaincy from Benaud who brought himself on to bowl round the wicket and into the footmarks left by Trueman. In the next two hours to the minute nine wickets went down for 51 runs with Benaud capturing 6/70. Australia won by 54 runs with much praise being accorded to Benaud for his willingness to go for victory even though the early England batsmen had been dominant. The Ashes were retained twenty minutes before the close on the final day.

A win and three more draws against the counties led up to the final Test at The Oval which drifted into a draw. Peter Burge scored 181 in 411 minutes with twenty-two fours while Norman O'Neill made 117. England batted for over two days in their second innings to save a game which saw the end of Peter May's Test career. He wrote, 'I had never really played as well since my illness and somehow I was not enjoying it so much. There were business and domestic considerations too . . . I had also always promised myself that I would give up at the top.' He was only thirty-one.

The Australians arrived home just as the New Zealand team was playing in Perth en route to tour Rhodesia and South Africa. Western Australia sported their new signing, the West Indian Rohan Kanhai, but it was the Kiwi fast-medium bowler Frank Cameron who took the honours with 7/27 as the home team fell for 113. The match was eventually drawn with the New Zealanders having more than a fright the next day. A bad oil leak developed on their Qantas flight across the Indian Ocean and a tense, dramatic landing took place at Johannesburg airport. Five months later, on their return flight, the aircraft's brakes failed on touchdown in Perth and the plane slewed off the runway on to the grass.

Two further matches were then played in Australia. Cameron, with 5/56, bowled South Australia out for 260 after the Test batsman Les Favell had made 109. South Australia's eventual six-wicket victory was due more to the tiredness of the visitors than to anything else. Then the all-conquering New South Wales team, bristling with ten Test players – wicketkeeper Doug Ford being the odd man out – beat New Zealand by 59 runs (Benaud 5/30 and 3/52).

The success of the 1960–61 West Indies tour of Australia was considered long and hard by the Board of Control. Under Bradman's guidance the administration of the game was starting to catch up with the times. Alan Barnes, in Sydney, as Board secretary was kept busy by a constant stream of telephone calls and letters from his chairman in Adelaide. For years Bradman told Barnes to destroy all messages, notes and letters. Barnes kept them all and the seven large trunks of papers reveal the sharpness of Bradman's mind.

Less brilliant was the pettiness of cricket officialdom elsewhere. The Queensland Cricket Association, for example, complained that, following the Tied Test, 'some players stayed in the dressing-rooms until 7.30 pm'. They wanted the Board 'to ensure that players leave dressing-rooms within a few minutes of the conclusion of play'. The delegates approved the measure with Bradman outvoted. Alas for common sense!

The return to Australia of the West Indian star players Hall,

Kanhai and Sobers to play in the Sheffield Shield saw attendances more than double to the best since 1927–28 and the third best on record. The Shield was still a viable competition in the 1960s as four of the ten summers had no visits by international teams. Cricket mythology talks of the wonderful influence the West Indians had on the domestic seasons, yet in truth State Associations had to spend time soothing ruffled feathers, placating sponsors, sending search parties to find individuals who had last been seen in so-and-so's public house and, in more than one instance, sobering up a player before he went out to bat. But in retrospect the same cricket officials remember the era as being 'lots of fun' and 'breathing new life into the Shield'.

There was, unfortunately, some resentment towards the imported players, described as being 'because of the colour question'. Yet their impact was enormous. In South Australia, Gary Sobers had, through sheer ability, caused an 89 per cent increase in attendances and gate takings to rise by two-and-a-half times. The latter figure is important for it showed that the general public (non-members) was returning to watch the game of cricket. The statistics for the three stand out. Wes Hall's 43 wickets for Queensland more than doubled anyone else's efforts. Rohan Kanhai's 533 runs for Western Australia came second only to his captain Barry Shepherd, while Gary Sobers topped both batting and bowling for South Australia. His remarkable 251, followed by 3/51 and 6/72, saw New South Wales to a rare defeat in Adelaide in February 1962. It did not, however, stop NSW from claiming their ninth successive Shield title.

On 27 June 1961 Alan Barnes, as secretary of the NSWCA, wrote to himself as the secretary of the Board of Control to suggest that 'the Board suitably recognise the centenary of the first match played by an English team in Australia in Melbourne in January 1862'. Barnes reported that the NSWCA would like the form of commemoration to be 'the designation of one of the Tests' of the 1962–63 England tour as a Centenary Match. The Melbourne Cricket Club, on 16 August 1961, wrote 'seeking approval' for an Australia versus A Rest of the World game in January 1962.

The Board, on 13 September, gave weak support to the NSWCA idea and told Melbourne to go ahead with their proposal if they so wished. Behind the scenes Bradman told the Melbourne club that he did not really want anything to distract from the forthcoming England tour. The original ideas grew smaller and smaller until, in the end, all that took place was a mock game in period costume.

In December 1961 Alan Barnes received a letter from the Canadian Cricket Association who wondered if the next Australian team to tour England could be allowed to visit Canada en route. The CCA said that 'a short visit to us and the USA would be easy to finance'. Surprisingly the Board, at its February 1962 meeting, agreed to consider the proposal and asked the programme sub-committee to report back.

At the next meeting, in September 1962, the sub-committee reported that a team of fourteen players and a manager was practicable for such a tour which would be of its own volition, and not tagged on to an England tour. Costings were presented and agreement reached for a tour in 1964 which would not, obviously, contain any players chosen for the main tour. State Associations were to be contacted to see how many players would be available, if selected.

The Canadians, kept informed of these moves, expressed their pleasure. The following month the former Test umpire Colin Hoy was appointed manager. Then came amazing news from the State Associations: only five first-class players were willing to tour. The Board meeting of December 1962 noted that 'delegates expressed doubt as to whether all players had been approached on the matter', and resolved: 'That state associations be asked to resubmit the matter and reply by 31 March 1963'.

When the Canadians heard of this response they offered to pay all expenses as well as giving the players 'a weekly allowance'. They then wrote again to suggest that '1965 would be a more suitable year to tour than 1964'. This proposal produced twenty-five players (but none who had played in Tests) who expressed their interest. The Canadians, having hoped to attract 'at least two players with Test experience' in order to publicise the game in their country, lost heart and in January 1964 it was agreed to let the matter rest.

The Board then agreed to make a tour of India and Pakistan in October 1964, following the tour to England. The Board of Control for Cricket in India pushed hard for a five-Test tour 'exclusively', which meant no Pakistan Tests. So hard indeed did they negotiate for this that, in late August 1962, the Maharajah of Baroda made a special visit to Adelaide to confer with Sir Donald Bradman.

The next quarter of a century would see numerous Indian cricket officials try to persuade Sir Donald in one form or another to do what they wanted. All of their visits to Adelaide would end in failure as did Baroda's.

It was explained to him why Australia could only make a short visit to India and why it was important to visit Pakistan as well. It was also the case, Bradman said, that their seasons clashed; that the Australians did not wish to field a second-rate team for a long tour; and that Australia had to give priority to other countries with whom they had been playing for years. When Baroda returned to India, his Board's response was to offer an immediate £50,000 on top of all other profits for a five-Test series. The cash bribe had no effect on Bradman or the Board who stuck rigidly to their decisions.

The high point of Bradman's first chairmanship of the Board was the England tour of Australia during the 1962–63 season. Planning had started as long ago as 1958, and when it was announced from Lord's that the Duke of Norfolk would manage the team the social invitations became so numerous that a standard Board letter had to be sent out in reply. Around the country, State Associations were inundated with requests for the Duke's presence. For those few invitations which were accepted the Board felt it necessary to prepare guidelines advising the States on protocol.

The England side was captained by Ted Dexter with Colin Cowdrey as vice-captain and Alec Bedser as assistant manager. They arrived in Fremantle in mid-October and beat Western Australia by ten wickets in their first serious match. Then followed a series of first-class and country games which included the team scoring 633 for seven against an Australian XI in Melbourne (Ken Barrington 219*) and then losing by an innings and 80 runs to the all-powerful NSW team.

The first Test in Brisbane ended in a draw with Brian Booth scoring 112 in Australia's first innings and Richie Benaud taking 6/115. Set 378 to win in even time England refused to take up Benaud's challenge and finished 100 runs short when time ran out. Then followed four country games, victory over Victoria, and a record-breaking game against South Australia. Played over Christmas the match started in heatwave conditions and, after being interrupted by rain, finished in the cold. On the first day, a Saturday, England scored 474 for four and on the Monday resumption Colin Cowdrey took his individual score to 307, the most runs scored in a single innings by an Englishman in Australia.

This Christmas boost helped England to a surprise win in the second Test in Melbourne. Australia's first innings was bettered by just 15 runs as England reached 331, Cowdrey's 113 being the highest of his five centuries in Ashes fixtures, whilst Alan Davidson took 6/75. Brian Booth scored 103 second time around but England, left needing 234 to win, took up the challenge. The Rev. David Sheppard made 113 in 301 minutes, being run out going for the winning single. It was the visitors' first win in Australia since February 1955.

Life in Australia in the early 1960s was prospering. Work was plentiful, money abundant, and the cost of living within reasonable bounds. New towns and suburbs were springing up around the capital cities. Adelaide had Panorama, Hope Valley, Elizabeth, Marion, and Happy Valley; Melbourne saw the growth of the Mornington Peninsula as well as suburbs such as Sunshine, Plenty, Rosebud and St Albans. Sydney's growth included Doubleview, Rooty Hill, Asquith, Whale Beach and on to the Barenjoey Peninsula. Hobart had its Cascades and New Town, while Brisbane grew through Malaga, Fig Tree Pocket, Sunnybank and Bald Hills.

On farming land in outlying areas new universities sprang up on campuses of great acreage then thought to be in the wilds of nowhere but now, thirty years later, they are surrounded by suburbs. These include the Flinders University of South Australia; La Trobe and Monash in Melbourne; Macquarie in Sydney; Curtin and Murdoch in Perth and Griffith in Brisbane. These are all in addition to the old universities established in the last century.

Television was playing its part in shaping Australian life. The Board allowed cricket to be televised live during the final session of each day's play in the city in which a Test was played. The rest of the country could, and did wherever possible, receive the whole of the match, with continuous commentary.

It was now that Bradman brought not only the Board but the State Associations to the realisation of modern-day needs. In a series of circulars, recommendations, proposals, submissions and, in many cases, detailed dissertations he broached such matters as sponsorship, the need for brighter cricket, making the game more professional, the impact of overseas players on the domestic competition, the provision of spectator comfort, and the need to plan and provide stadiums for the future. His vision and advocacy, even by today's standards, were impressive and greatly to the benefit of the game. He made a special study of the eight-ball over and showed that it speeded up the game; he also spoke of how desirable it was to limit the tours to England to 100 days, or 105 days at the most.

The first sponsorship of cricket in Australia came from Bradman's direct negotiations with the British Tobacco Company and the petroleum giant Shell. Later, the Rothmans Foundation and other organisations concerned themselves with providing country and junior coaching. Money was given to pay also for intra state tours. No player benefited personally.

The Melbourne Test of 1962–63, from 29 December to 3 January, could also be known as the first beer-can match. The cans had only just come on to the Australian market and for the first time a now familiar sound was heard at the MCG: the sound of a can gently cascading from concrete step down to concrete step in the Southern Stand. Furthermore, vocal cricket spectators in the outer areas discovered a new method of expressing their displeasure at a quiet session of play: the slow clap done with a beer can in each hand.

For the Sydney Test in mid-January 1962, the selectors dropped Peter Burge and Ken Mackay and replaced them with the Western Australian Barry Shepherd, a left-handed batsman of rare talent who, unfortunately, would play in only nine Tests, and Colin Guest, a Victorian paceman making his solitary Test appearance. But it was Bobby Simpson's leg-spinners which saw England off for 279, his 5/57 being his best Test figures. Australia's reply saw them lead by only 40 runs although no-one was prepared for what happened next. Swinging the ball both ways Alan Davidson, at a brisk medium pace, left England 86 for six at the close. Davidson ended with 5/25 as victory came by eight wickets the following day. The sides were level with two Tests to play.

In the fourth Test in Adelaide Neil Harvey scored 154 and Norman O'Neill 100 in a match always destined for a draw. Alan Davidson broke down with a torn hamstring but recovered in time to play in the fifth Test in Sydney. It was his, as well as Harvey's, farewell to Test cricket. They both ended in style: Davidson took a wicket with his final delivery to record 186 wickets and 1328 runs in his 44 Tests; Harvey, with 79 appearances, 6149 runs including 21 centuries, and 64 catches – six in this Test. Harvey's skill did not desert him even in later times for, at the age of sixty in a charity match on the Adelaide Oval, his brilliant footwork and batting skill brought forth standing ovations not only from the crowd but from the jaded journalists in the pressbox.

Alas, this final Test was not a success; indeed, it proved to be one of the most boring Tests imaginable. A draw seemed likely from day one, and although the recalled Peter Burge made 103 spread over three days the captains played slowly and surely for the whole game. When Australia was set 241 to win in 240 minutes, Lawry batted the whole time for 45 runs with the series ending amid jeers and catcalls from the crowd on the Sydney Hill.

Benaud made two points to explain this seeming change of attitude: first, that Australia held the Ashes at the time; second, that with the series one-all after four Tests he could not risk a cavalier act in the fifth. Had England held the Ashes, however, he would have gone for broke. Sadly, though, the whole five Test series had made a nonsense of the hopes for bright and innovative cricket. It had turned viewers on the ABC from cricket to tennis, particularly the Davis Cup, which was shown on the three commercial stations. Bradman, on 10 May 1963, wrote to the associations:

> In my position as chairman of the Australian Board of Control it has naturally been of great concern to me that cricket should remain a healthy game, attractive to the spectator and providing the maximum enjoyment for those who play. Last season I spent countless hours discussing these aspects with leading players and officials. There was almost complete unanimity between us that the encouragement of an aggressive, positive approach was essential.

Sir Donald then went on to list numerous suggested changes he wanted to see in club cricket and ended his letter with:

> The whole purpose of my proposals is to make it profitable for clubs to adopt aggressive measures and not to profit from negative defensive, time-wasting tactics.

More interesting than the Test series had been the breaking up of New South Wales' domination of the Sheffield Shield. Victoria, competently led by Bill Lawry, had produced new star players: the left-handed opener Bob Cowper headed the Shield averages with 813 runs at 101.62; South Melbourne's Ian Redpath scored 637 runs and Fitzroy's Jack Potter – a larrikin with a brilliant mind – made 708. The bowling went three ways with Guest (39 wickets at 18.28), Meckiff (47 at 19.61) and the right-arm fast-medium Alan Connolly (36 at 27.72). Redpath's 261 against Queensland saw Victoria to 633 for four, their highest Shield score since the days of Bill Ponsford in 1927–28.

However, the Victorian Cricket Association seemed far more proud to report that 'during the Queensland match we were honoured by an unofficial and unexpected visit by HRH Prince Philip, Duke of Edinburgh, when he found a spare hour from his numerous duties connected with the Royal Tour'. Later on, when realising the significance of Victoria's triumph, the VCA 'presented each of the players with a set of cuff-links suitably inscribed'.

Kind and thoughtful though this gesture was, it did not help to pay the players' mortgages, nor school fees or the weekly groceries. But into the controversies of Australian first-class cricket had emerged, on 15 February 1962, in the match between South Australia and Tasmania, the man who would come to lead the players' attack against the establishment for more money, a pension fund, and better security: Ian Michael Chappell.

Born in Unley, South Australia on 26 September 1943, Ian Chappell's father, Martin, was a club cricketer and baseball player of the 'toughest' variety while his mother Jeanne was the daughter of Victor Richardson. Subsequently he would gain two brothers, Gregory Stephen, and Trevor Martin, both of whom would join Ian in playing for Australia.

Ian, a rebel in his youth, was a superb leader of men in his prime and a deep thinker and writer on the game with the mellowing of middle age. His family's feud with Bradman has lasted to this day with the clash of iron wills and personalities not yet documented in any material way. Yet it was this fusion which would cause the eruptions of later years.

The 1960s had begun to see a new element appear in western society:

children who were growing up having had little or no experience of war. They were ready to question their parents and buck the accepted order of things. The Australian government was stagnant after years of progress and would soon help the United States by supplying conscripts for an alien war in far-off Vietnam. Youth would rebel at what they saw as a pusillanimous policy and many facets of society would change. And change they did, especially with the advent of a popular music culture which was nothing like anything previously known. Long-haired musicians strutted their rebellious causes and found thousands, if not millions, responding to their messages around the world. 'Of course we'll play cricket,' said the young people, 'but what's the fee?'

Behind the closed doors of cricket association committee rooms around Australia no-one heard the call. They did at Lord's, creating what the public wanted in the instant cricket of the Gillette Cup: a game to be played out and finished in a day. It proved hugely popular. In Australia the associations, such as Victoria, could only gloat that, at their dinners, distinguished people such as 'His Excellency Major-General Sir Rohan Delacombe, KBE, CB, DSO attended at very short notice along with Sir Robert Menzies, KT, CH, QC, who very ably proposed the toast'. This dinner, incidentally, was supposed to be for Victorian club cricketers but of 750 invitations issued only 28 were sent to the players (and certainly not to their wives). The rift was really starting to show.

In September 1963 the Board of Control, at Bradman's last meeting as chairman for six years, decided to increase Test players' incidental expenses to £15 a match. This would cover all meals, taxi fares, laundry and drinks, although the Board would pay for hotel accommodation. There was also a match fee of £14 a day which, naturally, would not be paid if a game finished early or was disturbed by bad weather. To travel to Tests, players 'may travel when out of their home state by railway, using sleepers and parlour cars' and were to 'arrive twenty-four hours before a Test match is timed to commence, and must depart not later than the day after the match finishes'. Board members, incidentally, received half the players' allowances, plus accommodation, for just watching the Tests.

Preconceived attitudes also played an important part in the Board's behaviour. For example when, on his retirement, Neil Harvey started to write a weekly column which was syndicated around a newspaper group, he gently wondered in one article if the Duke of Norfolk, as manager of the England team, had really been a wise choice, particularly bearing in mind the changing image of the game.

Board members were affronted by this and then outraged when the Duke raised the matter with Alan Barnes when passing through Sydney two months after the tour. The Duke stated to Barnes that he himself was not offended but 'the England team expressed concern over the nature and content of Mr Harvey's article'. The next Board meeting saw the Victorian delegate, Bob Parish, move a motion: 'That the Marylebone Cricket Club be advised that this Board deplores articles written by Mr Harvey and that it wishes to entirely disassociate itself from their publication.'

Parish also took this opportunity to let Lord's know that the Australian Board did not like Test captains talking to the press after each day's play and that 'these [matters] can best be dealt with through personal talks with the captains by their respective administrators'. So now it was spelt out loud and clear: Australian administrators were better suited to inform the press than were the players. This would eliminate in the future any further Benaud/Webb or suchlike fiascoes.

Conspiracy in cricket is nothing new. The malodorous drift of it has existed in the game since the beginning. The biggest single delusion suffered by any member of the cricket-loving public is that the game is overflowing with wonderful, charming, trustworthy people. It certainly is not although, thank goodness, the unsavoury elements are in a minority.

Rumours have abounded in Australia for nearly thirty years on why Ian Meckiff was suddenly recalled to the Australian first Test team to play South Africa in Brisbane in December 1963, and why, without any benefit of consideration, he was no-balled out of the game for throwing by the umpire, Colin Egar.

Before this match Meckiff's previous Test had been against the West Indies in 1961. His Test record was rather ordinary: 45 wickets at 31.62 runs each in eighteen appearances. The start of the 1963–64 season saw him take 5/69 for Victoria against Western Australia and eleven wickets in all Shield fixtures.

A hint of what was to come arose at the Interstate Conference held in Sydney on 12 September 1963. There, the Queensland delegate, Alderman Clem Jones, raised the subject of the then Law 26 – suspect bowling actions – by moving a motion which said that infringements of the Law had taken place and that it was essential for the problem to be stamped out now, once and for all. Then, at the following meeting, Jones actually named Ian Meckiff and 'objected to the possible selection of Mr I. Meckiff on the grounds that he did not consider that Mr Meckiff played in accordance with the rules of the game in view of his bowling action'.

Jones wanted Meckiff officially barred from Test cricket and under no circumstances to be considered for selection for the 1964 tour to England. The Board demurred even in the face of a legal opinion by Syd Webb, QC, both a member of the Board and its legal adviser, which said they could ban Meckiff. Various issues arose including giving the selectors a strong hint of a certain direction to be followed.

Much conjecture surrounds the question of whether umpire Egar was given instructions to 'call' Meckiff on that fateful Brisbane afternoon of 7 December. Certain people, particularly the majority of the South African team, say that he was, whilst surviving Board members from the time generally refuse to discuss the issue. However, there seems to be little doubt Meckiff was sacrificed to end the long-running controversy and by the end of his one and only over, which comprised twelve deliveries, his Test career was over. Four calls from square-leg by Egar for throwing his second, third, fifth and ninth balls was enough. Meckiff retired to become a radio executive; Egar went on to become chairman of the Board.

The fourth South African side to visit Australia had arrived in Perth on 16 October 1963. Captained by Trevor Goddard, the team contained at least six players – Goddard, Eddie Barlow, Graeme Pollock, Peter Pollock, John Waite and Colin Bland – who would have walked into any Test selection in the cricketing world. Their initial six matches leading up to the first Test brought them three victories, a draw and two defeats.

Other than the Meckiff incident, the Brisbane Test saw Richie Benaud captain Australia for the final time before handing over to Bobby Simpson. He had a shoulder injury, and he had already told Bradman that he would not be touring England in 1964. During the game Benaud became the only Australian to pass 2000 Test runs and 200 wickets, and he continued to play in the series.

Australia batted for a day and a half to reach 435, of which Brian Booth made 169, and the Springbok fast bowler Peter Pollock took 6/95. South Africa replied with Barlow scoring 114 out of 346, but rain took over for a day and a half of play and the match was drawn.

Simpson called correctly in his first Test as captain in Melbourne on New Year's Day. Ian Redpath made his debut in place of the injured Brian Booth but had to wait until the final three overs of the first day to get a chance to bat. Simpson put South Africa in and even though Barlow scored 109, they were dismissed for 274.

Bill Lawry (157) and Redpath (97) then put on 219 for Australia's first wicket. Simpson got a duck and Shepherd 96 as the score reached 447. South Africa replied with an entertaining 306, which left Australia plenty of time to win. Simpson made the winning hit early on the fifth day in front of very few spectators, all of whom had been let in free on the Monday morning. The four-day crowd of 104,314 was far better than Brisbane's 22,561, and it turned out to be the highest of the series. This was disappointing as the Springboks were an entertaining side, well led, and full of talent.

Four days later the teams met again in Sydney. South Africa gained a first-innings lead of 42, due to 122 from the nineteen-year-old left-handed batsman Graeme Pollock. The Australians' second innings saw a good all-round display with Benaud (90), Lawry (89), O'Neill (88) and McKenzie (76) seeing the total to 450 before Simpson declared. Set 409 to win in 430 minutes, the Springboks made a valiant effort, falling short with five wickets to spare as time ran out.

The Australia Day holiday weekend tradition saw a Test in Adelaide, and this one remained for long in the memories of cricket lovers. Australia won the toss and batted with Burge (91), Simpson (78) and Shepherd (70) seeing the total to 345. The South Africans lost two wickets at 70 before Graeme Pollock joined Eddie Barlow. In the next 283 minutes they entertained the crowd with such superb strokeplay that many of the Adelaide crowd that day recalled the partnership as the finest they could remember. Their stand of 341 remains South Africa's highest for any wicket in Test cricket. Pollock was first out, his 175 containing three sixes and 18 fours. Barlow followed not long afterwards, his 201 in 392 minutes with 27 fours making him the third South African after Aubrey Faulkner and Dudley Nourse to score a double-century against Australia.

Back in South Africa the joy was there to see. Mac Pollock, Peter and Graeme's father, and editor of Port Elizabeth's *Eastern Province Herald*, spent his son's nervous nineties in the Cape Town office of A. C. Parker, sports editor of the *Cape Argus* so that at least one paper had an exclusive story the following morning.

The Springbok score reached 595. Australia's reply of 331 left the tourists needing only 82 runs to win which came before lunch on the fifth day. The fact the temperature was over the fahrenheit century mark mattered little to the 8730 spectators. They had seen a crushing ten-wicket victory.

In the *Cape Argus* the veteran journalist Louis Duffus wrote: 'It was a wonderful win, not only in its record scores and its magnitude, but in the greatness which it thrust upon Goddard, Barlow and Graeme Pollock. There has never been anything in South African cricket to equal it.'

The expectations in South Africa were nearly realised in the final Test when victory was lost by time running out. An extra hour would have seen the visitors home in an absorbing series. As it was, Brian Booth had a splendid match scoring an unbeaten 102 and 87, with Colin Bland hitting 126 for the Springboks. Richie Benaud finished his Test career with 2201 runs and an Australian record of 248 victims in 63 matches.

This last South African tour to Australia for many years was watched by 500,889 people who paid £102,962 in gate takings. The Springboks' share of £44,728, even after costs were deducted, represented a healthy profit. However, the planning and itinerary for the tour left much to be desired. The Board sent the South Africans on a magical mystery tour around the outback of Australia. In fifteen weeks, between first-class games scattered around capital cities the tourists visited – in order – Cunderdin (WA), Whyalla (SA), Ipswich (Q), Southport (Q), Toowoomba (Q), Lismore (NSW), Benalla (V), Launceston (Tas), Devonport (Tas), Geelong (V), Parkes (NSW), Warrnambool (V), Newcastle (NSW) and Cooma (NSW). They played mainly two-day matches watched by crowds averaging 750 keen country enthusiasts. Change was still some years ahead.

The 1963–64 Sheffield Shield was one of the best contests for many years, with South Australia clinching the title when defeating the holders, Victoria, in the penultimate game of the season. An interesting point about that South Australian side is that, amateurs all except for Gary Sobers, the majority have since not only succeeded in their chosen careers but are also considered to be 'prominent in the community'. It was a close-knit side which is still reflected today in the bond between them.

The first match of the season was amazing in itself. Queensland reached 613 in Brisbane – Peter Burge scoring 283, the highest innings ever for his State – and in reply New South Wales made 661 with Bobby Simpson, now returned from working in Perth, scoring 359 with 33 fours. Runs flowed during the season: Simpson (again) 247 not out versus Western Australia; Burge (again) 205 not out against Western Australia; Sam Trimble 252 not out for Queensland against NSW; Ian Chappell 205 not out for South Australia versus Queensland. The top four scorers for the season were Sobers with 973 runs at 74.84, Trimble 950 at 86.36, Ray Reynolds of Queensland 794 at 61.07, and Simpson 784 at 112.00. The bowling honours went solely to two South Australians: Sobers with 47 wickets at 28.27 and the Indian-born leg-spinner Rex Sellers with 46 at 26.63.

# 26

# Educating the Board

Always willing to come up with new concepts,the Board of Control at its September 1963 meeting thought that the idea of a Triangular Test series should be revived. Appreciating that the 1912 experiment had been a disaster they felt the 1965–66 season was an ideal time for another attempt. The feeling this time was that the three participants should be Australia, England and the West Indies. A detailed submission was prepared and sent to Lord's for consideration. The main points were:

(i) A triangular contest between the three countries would create tremendous interest in cricket throughout Australia;
(ii) It would allow the earlier return of the West Indies to Australia than under the existing arrangements;
(iii) From the financial point of view each side should benefit as, under a suggested programme, each team would participate in six Test matches. It was suggested that for Test matches between England and West Indies the nett ground receipts, less a small percentage to the local State Association, be divided equally between the two countries.

At no time was the West Indies Board of Control apprised of the Australians' idea and they only heard of it after the Marylebone Cricket Club had met to discuss the proposal. Lord's was against the plan largely because of the 1912 disaster, and their letter of 20 December 1963 to Alan Barnes made this plain. In addition the letter stated that should the proposal be brought before the Imperial Cricket Conference then it would be opposed 'with all our might'. With such a firm reply the Australian Board 'received the correspondence'.

As the final Test against South Africa was drawing to a close in Sydney, on 12 February 1964, the Australian selectors released the names of the players chosen for the tour of England, India and Pakistan. Now that Benaud, Davidson, Harvey and Mackay had retired, the team had a new look to it. The New South Welshmen, Bobby Simpson and Brian Booth were named captain and vice-captain respectively, along with Grahame Corling, Johnny Martin and Norman O'Neill, also from NSW; Alan Connolly, Bob Cowper, Bill Lawry, Jack Potter and Ian Redpath from Victoria; Peter Burge, Wally Grout and Tom Veivers from Queensland; Neil Hawke, Barry Jarman and Rex Sellers from South Australia; and Graham McKenzie from Western Australia.

The team made the usual run around Tasmania and Western Australia prior to sailing from Fremantle. In Hobart, Bobby Simpson made 143 and in Launceston Bill Lawry 99 with Jack Potter's fine pair of 83 and 62 not out, both against Tasmania. In Perth, Western Australia were defeated by eight wickets as Ian Redpath scored 202 and Norman O'Neill 135. The voyage by ship to Colombo was the last to be made by an Australian team. Following their rain-interrupted draw there with Ceylon the players took a flight on to London.

Rain ruined the pre-season net practices but the sun shone for the build-up to the first Test. The tourists had won four matches and drawn the rest and went confidently into the match at Trent Bridge, except perhaps for the vice-captain Brian Booth who arguably should have given way to the in-form Jack Potter. As Booth scored 38 runs in six innings in the first three Tests, the talents of Potter lay wasted.

The first week in June was so wet that fifteen hours' play was lost from the Test and a draw made inevitable. However Graham McKenzie took 5/53 in England's second innings and the wicket-keeper, Wally Grout, made a decision that is still spoken of in cricket circles. England's improvised opening batsman Fred Titmus, who was called in at the last minute due to an injury to John Edrich, collided with the bowler, Hawke, in responding to a call for a quick single from his fellow opener, Geoffrey Boycott. The ball was immediately thrown to Grout, over the stumps, who declined to break the wicket. It was an act of sportsmanship keenly appreciated around the cricketing world.

The second Test at Lord's was also ruined by rain since a start was not possible until late on the third day. The weather improved for the four days of the third Test at Headingley, when Ted Dexter won the toss for the third successive time but made a fatal error on the second afternoon. After bowling England out for 268, Australia were 187 for seven and in deep trouble against the off-spin of Fred Titmus and the left-arm spin of Norman Gifford. Dexter decided to take the new-ball and Peter Burge, on 38, gleefully took his score to 160 and the Australian total to 389. England never recovered from this change of fortune, sliding to 229 in their second innings and losing by seven wickets.

In the four games against the counties prior to the fourth Test,

Australia tried out the strength of the team's batting. Irritating though it may have been to the spectators – particularly those at Leicester who were very vocal – the policy paid off. Simpson won the toss and chose to bat on a perfect Old Trafford pitch. It proved to be an absorbing game for the statisticians as it was the only instance in Test cricket of both sides scoring over 600 runs each in their first innings. Bill Lawry (106) and Simpson put on a then record first-wicket partnership of 201, and by the close of play Australia were 253 for two with Simpson having reached his maiden Test century.

Two wickets fell the next day as Simpson went on to 265 at the close – Australia 570 for four. No declaration came overnight which caused great indignation among the England supporting media. The fact that Simpson was batting to retain the Ashes seemed to cross no-one's mind. He eventually fell to a catch by the wicketkeeper, Jim Parks, from the bowling of the paceman John Price for 311. It was then the third longest innings in first-class cricket, having taken 762 minutes with a six and twenty-three fours. Brian Booth made 98 and the declaration came at 656 for eight from 256 overs.

Australia's bowlers then spent the same time in the field as had England, bowling 293 overs – of which off-spinner Tom Veivers sent down 95 – without conceding a no-ball or a wide. How times change! England's batsmen defended well initially and then set themselves the follow-on target of 457. Once that had been reached the game was a certain draw. Ken Barrington made 256 and Ted Dexter 174, while Graham McKenzie had the tour's best figures of 7/153 from 60 overs.

Then came successive defeats by Glamorgan and Warwickshire (and, later on, Essex) prior to the final Test at The Oval. Although rain washed out the last day's play the match was heading for a draw. England had struggled to 182 to which Australia replied with 379, Lawry 94. A rearguard century by Geoffrey Boycott saved his side from defeat, though Australia took the series one-nil.

During the tour a number of matters arose which, in years past, would have been referred to the tour manager, Ray Steele, for a decision. With easier access to telephone communications Steele was having to confer with Australia, sometimes waiting quite a while as the Board's Emergency Committee debated a difficult point.

After wasting time over quotations for the team's laundry – Steele wanted to use the facilities offered through the Institute of British Launderers, while the Board preferred a cheaper but inefficient firm – he had to discuss the prior arrangements for 'the use of motor transport' organised by a Board member through 'a good contact' which proved to be virtually non-existent. So Steele had to negotiate through the Ford Motor Company 'to make available drive-yourself cars'. Then Steele received a cable from Board chairman, Ewart Macmillan – who must have made life difficult for the secretary Alan Barnes – asking him to negotiate a fee with the BBC for the televising 'of film not exceeding a period of three minutes' of the Australians practising in the nets at Lord's. Steele was ordered 'to obtain a fee of £20'. After this came a major exercise when the Glamorgan County Cricket Club asked the Marylebone Cricket Club 'for permission to allow the BBC to televise twenty minutes of the Cardiff match before lunch on Saturday 16 May'. Lord's asked Steele, mainly out of politeness, if he minded them granting the request to which Steele informed them he had no power to agree and had to refer the matter to Australia. After much agonising in Sydney, Glamorgan were given the necessary permission on the understanding that 'it not be taken as a precedent'.

In late April the Melbourne *Sun* and Brisbane *Courier-Mail* newspapers had printed a series of articles written by Bobby Simpson 'which referred to the prospects of the team in England'. When these articles came to the attention of the Board, Simpson, instead of playing in the match against Nottinghamshire, had to write an explanation of the articles. They had been rehashed from the London *Daily Express* of the previous February and reprinted without Simpson's knowledge or permission. This explanation did not satisfy the Board chairman and so Ray Steele had to obtain letters of denial from the paper's sports editor and the commissioning agent, Ron Roberts. Only then were the powers-in-Sydney placated.

The Board's restriction on players writing or commenting on tour had caused considerable embarrassment before they left Australia when they had to give 'no comments' to the media men seeing them off. Then came news of Norman O'Neill's book *Ins and Outs* which was published during the tour. Since it had been written eighteen months earlier, O'Neill had all but forgotten about its release and was nearly sent home for his forgetfulness. His grovelling apology 'for his oversight' was accepted with reluctance and before the Board became aware of a more appalling sin allowed by O'Neill: his wife was going to be in England in September for a fortnight. Worse was to follow: the wife of the scorer and baggageman, Dave Sherwood, arrived for a month, and the Board, to their horror, discovered that neither the team masseur nor the scorer had signed a contract with them which would not allow such goings-on.

And so it went on. Ray Steele's reports showed a man who kept things moving on an even keel whilst being bombarded with some ludicrous cables, letters and telephone calls from Australia. Far from moving with the times, the men who were running Australian cricket in the mid-1960s – with one obvious exception – were making themselves the laughing stock of the Australian game.

After a fortnight's holiday in Europe, the Australians flew from Rome to Delhi on 30 September by Air India. The food on board caused the first of numerous internal problems for the party. Jack Potter had returned to Australia having received a fractured skull during a one-day match in Holland and shortly afterwards Norman O'Neill followed suit. His illness was viral and weakened him for many months afterwards.

After just one day's acclimatisation, the team went into the first Test in Madras at the Corporation Stadium. In hot, humid conditions, the Australians did well to reach 211 with Bill Lawry making 62, after which a splendid effort by Graham McKenzie, with 6/58 from 32.3 overs, restricted India's lead to 65. The Indian captain, the young Nawab of Pataudi, scored an unbeaten 128, thus emulating his father by scoring a hundred in his first Test against Australia, his father having made 102 for England in Sydney in 1932.

The Australian victory was due in many ways to Tom Veivers' second innings 74. He shared in two record partnerships – which added 64 (with Martin, 39) for the seventh wicket and 73 (with McKenzie, 27) for the eighth. India, left to score 333 to win, collapsed for 193 despite an excellent rearguard 94 by Hanumant Singh.

Both teams flew to Bombay on 8 October 1964 to start the second Test at the Brabourne Stadium two days later. It proved to be an excellent encounter. Burge (80), Jarman (78) and Veivers (67) top-scored in the first innings while Cowper (81), Booth (74) and Lawry (68) did so in the second. Even though Tom Veivers bowled 92 overs in the match, taking 4/68 and 2/82, India hung on to win by two wickets in front of an enraptured last-day crowd of 42,000.

The third Test at Eden Gardens, Calcutta, was ruined by rain after India had taken a first-innings lead of 61 runs. This gave the players some breathing space before they flew back across the top of India to Karachi for the solitary Test against Pakistan. By now Ray Steele had had enough of Indian umpiring. He sent a lengthy report back to the Board in Australia (Manager's Report No. 7: Board Circular No. 203) in which he stated 'that the apparent incompetence of umpires in India is very disturbing'. On his return to Australia, Steele spent most of 14 January 1965 in front of the Board answering this and other 'touchy' points from his reports.

For the Test at the National Stadium, Karachi, the Pakistan selectors brought in six players for their Test debuts. Three of them – Asif Iqbal, Khalid Ibadulla and Majid Khan – would become very well known in later years. Hanif Mohammad won the toss and sat back as his opening pair Ibadulla (166) and wicketkeeper Abdul Kadir (95) put on a record opening stand of 249. In a total of 414, Graham McKenzie again bowled with consummate skill, taking 6/69 in 30 overs. By tea on the third day Australia's reply of 352 – Simpson 153 in five hours – saw them trailing Pakistan by 62 runs. Then came a strange move as Hanif instructed his batsmen to play cautiously, which saw Pakistan score only 220 runs on the fourth day. A last-morning declaration left Australia to score 342 for victory in 290 minutes. They did not bother to chase such a score but in the time available Simpson (115) became the first visiting batsman to score a hundred in each innings of a Test in Pakistan.

Within a month Pakistan were in Australia to play three States and a Test match while en route to New Zealand. They drew all their fixtures playing tough, dour cricket and making every effort not to lose a game. In the four-day Test in Melbourne, which attracted only 33,067 people, Australia gave a debut to Ian Chappell of South Australia. In the match Hanif scored 104 and 93 as Pakistan, 287 and 326, drew with Australia, 448 and 88 for two, in a highly forgettable match.

Two months earlier, the Interstate Conference, meeting in Sydney, had in front of it an application, dated 16 June, from the newly formed Tasmanian Cricket Council seeking admission to the Sheffield Shield competition. To say the proposal came as a surprise would be correct, for in 1964 the game in Tasmania was in considerable danger. While club cricket flourished in centres such as Hobart, Launceston and Devonport, links with the mainland State Associations had been virtually severed. The one consistent thread which ran through Tasmania's cricket for over a century, matches with Victorian teams, had been cut by the cost-conscious Victorian Cricket Association. South Australia had declined to repay two recent visits to Adelaide by Tasmanian teams, and New South Wales had ignored competition since 1930. Western Australia and Queensland were too far away to consider regular meetings, and the final indignity for Tasmania came when the Australian Board downgraded the first-class status of the fixtures with the England touring team. The sad fact about this state of affairs was that it was quite deserved. If you do not play top cricket your standard falls and your players move elsewhere. In this case most good Tasmanian players went to Melbourne.

The application was surprising because Tasmania had actually applied for Sheffield Shield status in 1963: that application had been refused on technical grounds and another submitted in its place. What the island needed was regular competition. The Interstate Conference, although rejecting Tasmania's application, stated that the move was premature and gave guidelines which were to be followed before another application could be considered.

The different States agreed to help Tasmanian cricket by playing, between Shield games, fixtures in Melbourne and Sydney as long as the Tasmanian Cricket Council upgraded their playing strength, built up stronger public support, and created a more secure financial base. That Tasmania did all these things over the next thirteen years was a credit to them.

The Australian domestic season of 1964–65 saw a minor change take place in the scheduling of matches which was to have vast social overtones. Sunday sport had been considered an evil by many people and cricket associations had resisted pressure by progressives who wanted to enjoy the game all through the weekend. However, in August 1964 the Queensland Cricket Association sent out a circular which stated that they intended to move a motion at the next Interstate Conference to allow for Sunday play in the Sheffield Shield.

When it was presented, the motion was passed after heated debate and protests from the Methodist members of the committee. The discussion was a prime example of what was wrong with Australian cricket administration: personal bigotry dictating an issue over the greater need of the sport itself. The only complaint ever received on the decision came from the Tasmanian Protestant Federation. Immediately on hearing the decision, Western Australia and Queensland arranged to play their matches in Perth and Brisbane on Sundays. Since the attendances at both matches improved over the previous season, by 92% and 339% respectively; it was a clear indication of what the public wanted.

New South Wales regained the Shield in a season when new names came to the fore. In Adelaide in early February 1965, NSW had a record-breaking second-wicket stand of 378 runs in 307 minutes by the left-handed batsman Lynn Marks (185) and Doug Walters, who made 253 in six hours and 42 minutes to become the youngest Australian to make a double-century.

Behind the stumps that day was an angry Barry Jarman. As proprietor of an Adelaide sports shop (Rowe & Jarman) he had personally allowed the recent Pakistan tourists to buy thousands of pounds worth of goods, clothing and equipment on an alleged credit note from the Pakistan Cricket Board. Jarman had submitted accounts for payment which had been ignored. He then asked Sir Donald Bradman to bring the matter to the attention of the Board in September 1965 only to find he had opened up a hornet's nest: there were many others in Australia who were owed money. In the end nobody got paid – and the Board washed their hands of the matter.

The team to tour the West Indies from February May 1965 was announced on 14 January. Peter Burge and Tom Veivers had both asked not to be considered for selection as neither could afford to lose money at that current time of their careers. Bob Simpson was appointed captain, with Brian Booth again as his deputy, and Bob Parish of Victoria as manager. Before the team left they now had to go through medical checks and make statutory declarations regarding many different matters, from their health to 'no wives on tour', and through to not writing or commenting to the press until their return home in June.

Just before their 13 February departure from Sydney's Mascot airport each member of the side was presented with a protective helmet by the Australian Cricket Society of Sydney. The Society advised the Board in a subsequent letter 'that owing to the expectations of the West Indian fast bowling attack these special helmets are made to protect the head and face of players against fast, short-pitched balls'. Parish, in one of his tour reports, told Alan Barnes 'that these helmets were not used by the Australian team' and 'had been discarded'.

At that very time in Melbourne, Jack Potter was still recovering from his injuries received in Holland the previous August. He sustaining a fractured skull and other adverse symptoms when hit on the head by a short-pitched delivery. Luckily Potter's academic career had given him a life outside cricket. Had he been able to wear a helmet at the time of his accident the damage would have been far less than it actually was.

The team flew to San Francisco, then on to New York where they had an eight-hour delay before finally arriving in Kingston, Jamaica, on 15 February 1965. The West Indies had never won a series against Australia but this time their team would include Charlie Griffith, a fast bowler with an action more suspect than any yet known. In March 1962 in Barbados he had knocked the Indian captain, Nari Contractor, senseless, fracturing his skull so badly that Contractor hovered near death for several days and never played Test cricket again.

The West Indies tour of England in 1963 had caused a number of umpires to report Griffith's action to Lord's. However, due to the delicate race issue, umpires were instructed not to no-ball him for throwing. West Indian umpire Cortez Jordan had called Griffith two years earlier and the Australians knew that this giant of a man could cast a pall over the series.

Following two warm-up matches in Kingston, the Sabina Park Test started on 3 March. Mayne, Philpott and Thomas made their debuts for Australia as Gary Sobers took over the West Indies captaincy from Frank Worrell. In a low-scoring encounter, in which Wes Hall took 5/60 and 4/45, the West Indies won by 179 runs. The interest was in the bowling of Griffith and one of the Australian touring party filmed his action from square-leg with his cine-camera. The resultant film was a clear indictment of Griffith's action which no official seemed willing or able to do anything about.

Three further island fixtures led up to the second Test in Port-of-Spain, Trinidad. The pitch at the Queen's Park Oval suggested to Bobby Simpson that it was worth putting the opposition in to bat. He became only the second captain to do this in the Caribbean following Bob Wyatt's two decisions in 1935. In the end Simpson had to use eight bowlers as the batsmen ran up a total of 429. In reply Bob Cowper (143) and Brian Booth (117) added 225 for the third wicket after Norman O'Neill had retired hurt having been struck on the left arm while protecting his head from a Griffith bouncer. The Australian innings carried on into the fifth day, reaching 516. The West Indies made 386 in reply as time ran out which was lucky for Australia as O'Neill, Booth and Philpott would have been unable to bat in a second innings. Then it was on to three matches at the Bourda ground in Georgetown, British Guiana (now Guyana).

Before the third Test a row developed behind the scenes over the choice of umpires for the match. The British Guiana Umpires Association objected to the appointment of Cortez Jordan of Barbados. They made their local man, Cecil Kippins, withdraw on the eve of the game which resulted in Gerry Gomez, the former West Indian all-rounder and a current Test selector, taking over the role. Gomez held an umpiring certificate although he had not previously officiated in a first-class match.

Gomez showed his mettle by ordering the ground staff to re-mark the creases prior to play on the first day. Sobers won the toss and saw his side take charge from the beginning. Their 355 was countered by only 179 from the tourists who fell more under the spell of Lance Gibbs' off-spin bowling than that of Hall, Griffith or Sobers. Left to score 357 the Australians collapsed to Gibbs, 6/29, to lose by 212 runs.

The tourists warmed up for the fourth Test by having Simpson (117), Thomas (110*) and O'Neill (101) score centuries against Barbados, so gaining a good look at the Kensington Oval pitch. The Test could not have got off to a better start for Australia as Lawry (102*) and Simpson (137*) batted all of the first day for 263. They were not parted until the second afternoon when Simpson (201) was bowled by Wes Hall when the total was 382. The next wicket fell at 522 when Bill Lawry (210) was caught by Sobers to give Joey Solomon one of his rare Test wickets. Bob Cowper made 102 and Simpson declared at 650 for six.

The West Indies were not overawed by this score. First Rohan Kanhai (129), then Seymour Nurse (201), set about pushing the score to 573 and an inevitable draw. With the Frank Worrell Trophy now in Caribbean hands the fifth Test which followed straightaway in Trinidad was a lacklustre affair. Australia won by ten wickets in under three days with Graham McKenzie ending the West Indies second innings by taking three wickets in four balls.

The top order batsmen in the tourists' line-up had been hard to prise apart over the three-and-a-half month tour. Five batsmen averaged over sixty: O'Neill 617 runs at 68.55, Lawry 791 at 65.91, Trimble 262 at 65.50, Cowper 854 at 61.00 and Simpson 784 at 60.30. The bowling was less impressive on the hard tracks of the Caribbean, only Peter Philpott's 49 wickets at 24.96 being of note.

Off the field the former Australian Test captain, Richie Benaud, was withering in his attacks on Griffith's bowling action. Now a full-time journalist, Benaud had gained a reputation for fairness and objectivity. What Benaud wrote was read as being of authority and it upset the West Indies Cricket Board of Control. Further recriminations followed as, on the return home, Norman O'Neill also let fire in the press with his opinions on Griffith's action. The Board of Control was embarrassed by O'Neill's articles but there was little protest they could make as O'Neill's contract with them had expired.

Before the 1965–66 season began, the former Australian captain Bill Woodfull collapsed and died on a golf course at Tweeds Heads in northern New South Wales. He was just short of his sixty-eighth birthday. A man who commanded respect, he had for many years been headmaster at Melbourne Boys High School. In recent times his widow, Gwen, has been outspoken regarding her husband's fatal heart attack, blaming the injuries he received at the hands of Harold Larwood during the Bodyline series. Whatever the truth of this, it was always to be regretted that the knighthood which Woodfull refused was never offered to him again.

In early September 1965 the Board met for three days to discuss mainly routine matters. There were still mutterings, however, over the Benaud and O'Neill articles, and late on the final day the Board asked Syd Webb, QC, 'to consider the drafting of a Standing Order to restrict the scope of players' publications in Australia as distinct from tour and post-tour restrictions'.

That the majority of Board members was out of touch with reality became clear a few minutes later when the Victoria delegate Bob Parish, in the 130th and final agenda item, gently put it to the meeting 'that the Victorian Cricket Association shares the concern of other Associations that the best "image" is given for cricket to the public'. Being a 'young pup' by Board standards, Parish then stated a great heresy: he said that the VCA 'had suggested that greater latitude be allowed to players and selectors in writing and commenting for newspapers, radio and television whilst the desirability of engaging a firm of public relations experts had also been discussed'.

Parish must have felt like the boy who 'asked for more'. He was told in no uncertain terms by the diehards that the last thing the Board required 'was those sort of people'. The result of Parish's attempt was a minute saying: 'It was agreed that public relations was a matter primarily for the individual state associations'.

For many years the Western Australian Cricket Association had been aware of the need for the Board to spruce up its image and it had obtained support behind the scenes from other States' cricket officials – particularly those in Victoria. However, the majority of the Board delegates and State administrations were poles apart in their thinking. In Adelaide, when the subject of play on a Sunday was discussed, the secretary, Hugh Millard, was castigated by his committee when he suggested that a vote on the subject by members 'would result in a large majority in favour'. Sensing public feeling, Don Bradman pushed for a vote, which showed seventy-five per cent of people wanting Sunday play. The result was the departure of Roy Middleton from the Board of Control and his retirement as president of SACA.

Middleton had seen the writing on the wall and retired with good grace. Others did not and were seemingly prepared to fight any move which they felt 'would cause the start of the breakdown in family life'. This was a common call from Australia's ultra-conservatives during the 1960s.

The concept of 'family life' played an important role in the propaganda aimed at potential migrants to Australia. The publicity posters, sponsored by the government and sent around the world projected an image of sun, sea, surf and sand plus father cleaning his new car in the driveway leading to a four-bedroomed house; perfectly cut lawns; a swimming pool; mother content in the kitchen or helping at the local church; children playing happily in the back yard. This was the image the world was told about Australia and, like with many such images, the affluent Board members believed this to be what was wanted. To play cricket on a Sunday or to change the status quo would be to assist in undermining the fabric of society – and that would let in the communists and radicals.

Prime Minister Menzies had almost made 'communists' a political art form during the 1950s and 1960s. Having failed to ban the Communist Party of Australia in 1952, when legislation was declared illegal by the High Court, he won the 1954 General Election on the defection of two alleged Soviet communist spies by playing on the public's fears. The undercurrents that this generated in Australian society made any progressive views an easy target for being labelled as subversive. The era of McCarthyism in the United States of America in the early 1950s lived on in Australia some years later.

Not wishing to be branded, those involved in the game of cricket, and who saw that change was urgently needed, kept quiet following the Board's rebuff to Parish. But, as always, there was one man eating away at the old guard's philosophy, one man who knew how to handle them and yet keep the new breed in check while old fortresses slowly crumbled. What Australian cricket owes to Don Bradman is inestimable.

The twenty-ninth England team landed at Perth airport on 23 October 1965 having become the first side to fly all the way to Australia by jet, albeit with a stopover for two matches in Ceylon.

The tourists were captained by the Warwickshire batsman Mike Smith with Colin Cowdrey as his deputy. The manager's job had been given to S. C. 'Billy' Griffith who was also the secretary of the Marylebone Cricket Club. The choice of Griffith was a deliberate ploy by Lord's who gave him a brief quite unlike that handed to any other manager.

The initial press conference was held at the offices of the Western Australian Cricket Association in East Perth on the afternoon of the team's arrival. At once Griffith laid down the law to waiting journalists when he said that the captain, Mike Smith, 'would not be involved in interviews during a match' though he, Griffith, 'would always be available'. This threw the local journalists, who were used to obtaining end-of-day quotes for their stories, into some perturbation.

As the days and weeks wore on, however, it became all too clear – in retrospect – that Griffith had come to educate the Board of Control; to change the internal workings of tours to and from Australia, and to cultivate Sir Donald Bradman further into the way of thinking at cricket's headquarters in London.

A win, two draws and a narrow defeat to Victoria in Melbourne took the team to Sydney for a match against New South Wales in late November. The evening before the match Griffith, assistant manager Jack Ikin, and chairman of selectors Doug Insole, dined with Sir Donald Bradman at the team's hotel in Sydney. The tourists had a problem at the time over whom to call from England as an extra pace bowler due to various injuries and ailments amongst their number. However it was the Australian Board who suffered that night – mainly due to embarrassment – as the Australian Broadcasting Commission's television current affairs programme *Four Corners* exposed the workings and failings of the Board as no other had done before. A touring journalist likened it 'to Ed Morrow and the programme he did to reveal Senator McCarthy'.

The initial part of the programme saw the English cricket writer, 'Jim' Swanton, interviewed by two journalists, John O'Grady and Frank Browne, who then turned their attention to the Board. Telephones ran hot the next day which resulted in the Board chairman, Ewart Macmillan, and the secretary, Alan Barnes, composing a lengthy letter of complaint to Talbot Duckmanton, the General Manager of ABC.

The touring journalists saw the programme as manna from heaven, so that a number of them filed rather exaggerated stories. Duckmanton's reply to Macmillan was to the effect that the programme 'was not intended to be indicative of the Commission's attitude to cricket or cricket administrators', and left it at that. Macmillan reported this to the next Board meeting which decided to let the matter rest.

The tourists then defeated NSW and drew with Queensland on their way to the first Test in Brisbane. The Australian selectors, as was their wont, had the names of a number of players under contention circulated to Board members for approval. One name was that of Duncan Sharpe, the former Quetta and Pakistan right-handed batsman who had made three Test appearances against Australia in 1959. Sharpe, having emigrated to South Australia the following year, was now under consideration to play for Australia. An objection was raised against him which saw his Australian representative career finish before it had ever started.

Three days prior to the Test, Billy Griffith telephoned Alan Barnes to ask if it was possible to vary one of the tour playing conditions. Griffith wanted the minimum follow-on deficit to be increased to 200 runs from the current 150, and added 'that this is what the Marylebone Club are requesting'. Barnes told Griffith that there was no way the Board could consider this request in the time available before the Test. The match went ahead, and Australia's acting captain, Brian Booth, correctly enforced the follow-on when England's first innings fell 163 runs behind Australia's 443 for six declared.

In Australia's only innings of a match badly affected by rain, Bill Lawry scored 166 and Doug Walters, on his debut, 155. Walters became the fifth Australian to score a hundred in the first innings of his first Test and, at 19 years and 357 days, the third youngest Australian after Archie Jackson and Neil Harvey to score a Test century. Peter Philpott took 5/90 in England's first innings of a dull, drawn match.

The second Test in Melbourne over the New Year was watched by a five-day crowd of 170,014, the largest of the five Tests, in a series which saw the lowest overall attendances for an England tour since 1921. After three-and-a-half days England (558) had a lead of 200 runs over Australia, whose second innings then lasted until just before the end of the contest. In this innings Doug Walters scored 115 to become the second batsman after Bill Ponsford to score hundreds in each of his first two Tests. The match was drawn and both teams then flew to Sydney to carry on the battle.

Mike Smith won the toss and sat back to watch Geoff Boycott

(84) and Bob Barber (185) put on an opening partnership of 234 in just four hours on a lifeless pitch. Following a mid-order slump, John Edrich (103) saw the total to 488 which would be more than enough for England to claim victory. Australia fell for 221 and 174 to lose by an innings and 93 runs.

After the England team had made the traditional journey to Tasmania, the fourth Test in Adelaide proved to be the exact opposite of the third. England took first guard on a placid pitch and found themselves dismissed for 241 with Graham McKenzie claiming 6/48. Then it was the home batsmen's turn as Bobby Simpson (225) and Bill Lawry (119) put on 244 in 255 minutes, a new record which stood until 1989. Simpson's innings took 545 minutes and contained a six and 18 fours. Some indifferent batting down the order saw the total to 516 but it was enough. Although Ken Barrington scored 102, his colleagues did not hold out too long against the Australian bowlers, whose team went on to victory by an innings and nine runs.

Ten days later the final Test started in Melbourne with the public showing what they thought of the whole series. Admittedly 68,476 people turned up for the Saturday, the second day's play, but other than that the matches lacked much entertainment. England scored 485 for nine declared, and, by the start of the final day, Australia's reply was 333 for three, Lawry having made 108. The match does, however, live in the memory for the innings of Bob Cowper. His century took 310 minutes, his double-century 535 minutes, and his triple-century came in 716 minutes. In scoring the only triple-century in Tests in Australia, Cowper had set his sights on the world Test record of 365 set by Gary Sobers. At tea on that final afternoon he was on 303 with the Englishmen knowing of his quest. An extra special bowling effort after the break by Barry Knight saw Cowper depart with 307 to his name, having been bowled after 727 minutes at the crease.

The drawn match left the series level. It was the end of the Test match road for Norman O'Neill, Peter Philpott, Peter Burge and the wicketkeeper Wally Grout who, alas, died of a heart attack only three years later at the age of forty-one.

New South Wales won the Sheffield Shield yet again in 1965–66, despite needing to use eighteen players due to Test-match calls. The top cricketer in the side was the Bankstown batsman Graeme Thomas, who scored 837 runs at 64.38 including the season's highest of 229 against Victoria in Melbourne. The star turn was Queensland's right-arm paceman, Peter Allan, who took 10/61 against Victoria in Melbourne in January 1966. Surprisingly it is the only instance of a bowler taking all ten wickets yet recorded on the Melbourne Cricket Ground.

Three days before the final Test, which started on 11 February

1966, the Board of Control met in Melbourne. Change was in the air especially in Sydney where Syd Smith had announced his forthcoming retirement – at the age of eighty-six – from the presidency of the NSWCA, a position he had held since 1935: and the Victor Trumper Trust, which was set up in 1915, finally wound itself up. More was to follow as, at last, the Victorian Cricket Association delegates persuaded their colleagues to set up a sub-committee to look into the easing of restrictions put upon Test and touring players.

Syd Webb, QC, gave a number of legal opinions on various matters concerning players' contracts and then surprised many by suggesting that the VCA concept of letting cricketers write for newspapers and magazines could 'benefit the game with its publicity'. Rather cunningly, two known forward-thinkers on the Board formed the basis of the publications sub-committee, which comprised Clem Jones (Queensland), Ray Steele (Victoria) and Webb (NSW).

From February to September the three men wrote to each other at length putting forward various ideas. Victoria were progressive; NSW moderate and Queensland completely against giving cricketers freedom within the press. At the September Board meeting Webb said that 'following extensive correspondence between the sub-committee members it had been found impractical to reach a mutually agreeable conclusion'.

Webb then proposed – to everyone's surprise – that the Board's standing orders be suspended for the 1966–67 season to allow players a certain freedom with publicity. Some delegates did not approve of the move and said so plainly. They found it yet another ploy to undermine family life in Australia just as the State of Victoria had done the previous February, when the law was changed to allow hotels and public houses to stay open until 10 pm – four hours later than had been the case since 1916.

Society was changing: life was changing. The delicate yet firm words of Billy Griffith still rankled. He had spoken at length, by invitation, to the February Board meeting and in a subtle, gentlemanly way had torn to shreds many of the Board's practices which had lain unchanged for years.

He had told them that the methods of financing tours to England should alter, and asked the Board to 'refer to the MCC's suggestion as detailed in our letter of last August'. He said England's tour itinerary of Australia must also alter – 'the value of some matches might come under your consideration'; he told them that the Board under no circumstances were to interfere in BBC Television's rights as negotiated with them by MCC; that 'your idea of awarding points for Test matches in each series would be rather difficult to apply'; and so on through a detailed and well-prepared dossier which Griffith had taken to the meeting. The Board were taken aback by Griffith's strong views – but there was no way they would not ingratiate themselves with him, so his suggestions were followed up.

The touring party to South Africa for the 1966–67 season was announced on 20 February 1966 and almost immediately Doug Walters had to withdraw when called up for National Service. The team captain was Bob Simpson, Bill Lawry was vice-captain, and the manager Bill Jacobs, a radio broadcaster from Melbourne and a delegate to the Victorian Cricket Association from the Fitzroy Club.

Although the itinerary had been finalised some time before the team left Australia, the South African Cricket Association cabled in August asking if certain variations could be made. Two changes of date and one of venue met Board approval but they did not fully understand when the South Africans put the question: 'We have had a number of requests from provinces for the Australian team to play under floodlights at night. What would be your reaction to this?' The Board asked for clarification. When this came, Alan Barnes circulated the details to the relevant delegates. But the reply was: 'The Board will not agree to the team or any of its players taking part in such matches'. It was to be another twelve years before day-night fixtures came into vogue.

Bob Parish was elected as chairman of the Board on 7 September 1966 and almost immediately he started to modernise the administration. Within a day such office equipment as a wet copier, a dictaphone, a modern Olympic typewriter and other accepted essentials were purchased; but most of the delegates did not understand the need for such extravagances.

Born in 1916, Parish played grade cricket for the Prahran club in Melbourne from 1935 to 1949 and was noted for his accurate medium-paced bowling. He was elected to the Prahran committee in 1936 and was chosen as the club's delegate to the Victorian Cricket Association in 1950. He became the club's president in 1954, a position he still holds.

One of Parish's first major initiatives was to approve a one-day 50-overs match requested by the South African Cricket Association. This fixture was scheduled for 4 March 1967 in Johannesburg and would be played between the South African and Australian Test teams which competed in the fifth Test at Port Elizabeth the previous week.

The tour of Southern Africa lasted twenty weeks and meant that the sixteen players missed the whole of the Sheffield Shield season which itself was compacted due to an Australian second eleven visiting New Zealand. Victoria won in a season in which only two double-centuries were scored (Paul Sheahan, Victoria, and Keith Ziebell, Queensland) while the English Test bowler Tony Lock took 51 wickets for Western Australia.

Simpson's team spent some days in Johannesburg practising and acclimatising at the New Wanderers ground in Kent Park. The first match was a draw against Matabeleland in Bulawayo followed by a victory over Rhodesia in Salisbury. The third match contained a shock: defeat by Transvaal by 76 runs, albeit with only eight minutes of the game left. It was the first time the Australians had lost in South Africa since tours began in 1902. Their reply was to score 504 against Western Province in Cape Town and win by an innings and 108 runs. Another win, over Eastern Province, came before a second reversal; by 190 runs against a South African XI in East London. An easy win in Natal led up to the first Test in Johannesburg.

In a five-day match, watched by 112,401 people who paid R62,493, South Africa were 41 for five after only ninety minutes' play. That they recovered to 199 at tea was due to the wicketkeeper, Denis Lindsay, making 69. Graham McKenzie claimed 5/46. Lindsay's success carried on as he took six catches in the tourists' reply of 325, and then, in the Springboks' second innings, his 182 took 274 minutes with five sixes as his side made 620, then their highest score in Test cricket. The fight had seemingly gone from the tourists as South Africa won by 233 runs, their first home victory over Australia in twenty-two attempts.

Three days later in Cape Town Bobby Simpson (153) scored his fiftieth century in first-class cricket, and along with Keith Stackpole (134), batting at seven, saw the Australian score to 542. The third day belonged to South Africa's Graeme Pollock who made 209 in just under six hours with 30 fours and left to a standing ovation from the large Newlands crowd. Watching that innings on video shows a master batsman at work and even though South Africa failed to avoid the follow-on, the basis of a quality team can be seen. Graeme's brother Peter – principally a right-handed fast bowler – saved the second innings from disintegration with a tail-end unbeaten 75. Australia eventually won by six wickets with only 24 minutes to spare in yet another absorbing match well received by the 74,165 who watched.

The Australian batsmen and bowlers appeared in good form particularly in the provincial matches. Bob Cowper scored an unbeaten 201 against Orange Free State and Basutoland while Ian Chappell made 164 and Johnny Martin took 7/69 against Border.

The third Test in Durban was fairly slow going over five days as 72,034 saw Denis Lindsay, with 137 and six catches, enjoy another good match which saw Australia follow-on and lose by eight wickets. Yet again the team bounced back in the provincial fixtures as Simpson (243) and Cowper (171) added 374 for the second wicket against Northern Transvaal in under four hours.

Only a rainstorm just after tea on the final day of the fourth Test in Johannesburg saved Australia from an innings defeat. It had been a fairly insipid display. They wilted against the Springboks' onslaught: firstly of their pacemen, then of their batsmen. Denis Lindsay scored his third hundred of the series in 107 minutes to break the record for the most runs by a wicketkeeper in a Test rubber (previously 525 by Kunderan for India against England in 1964). The attendance was 88,498.

Journalists back in Australia were by now receiving fairly detailed stories on player behaviour, having previously only heard rumours. Although these were denied at the time, a newspaper exposé referring to 'ill-feeling within the touring team' and to a Test player 'walking into a club gathering wearing only an athletic support' were subsequently confirmed as correct by some of the players. Such reports had come to the attention of the Board but were only the tip of the iceberg. It marked the start of gradually deteriorating behaviour from touring Australian cricketers.

Johnny Martin, for example, found himself in hot water with the Board on his return to Australia. On arrival at Sydney airport on 7 March he had had an altercation with a customs official over a transistor radio. What was then unforgivable in the Board's eyes was Martin's immediate reaction in talking on the subject, and the tour, to waiting journalists, so breaching the Board's tour agreement. Martin did not represent Australia again.

It took the Springboks only three and a half days in Port Elizabeth in late February 1967 to wrap up the series by three Tests to one. The South African victory in front of 59,323 at St George's Park showed that, while they were approaching world dominance, the Australian team was in need of re-building. Only Cowper passed the half-century mark with 60 and 54, while Graham McKenzie took 5/65 as Australia slumped to a seven-wicket defeat.

The teams then moved back to The Wanderers ground in Johannesburg to play the first fifty-overs match against each other. The Australians batted first and reached 323 for eight (Lawry 91, Thomas 70, Stackpole 47) only to find Graeme Pollock in devastating form. His 132 came in just 98 balls and saw his side to 327 for seven: victory by three wickets with just eight deliveries to spare in front of 11,383 wildly cheering spectators.

The team returned home to find the season over and the 'second eleven' in New Zealand. The selectors – still Bradman, Ryder and Seddon – had chosen Les Favell as captain along with his fellow South Australians Ken Cunningham, Eric Freeman, Alan Frost and Barry Jarman, plus Brian Booth, Geoff Davies, Johnny Gleeson, Norman O'Neill and Peter Philpott of NSW; Bob Bitmead, Alan Connolly and

Paul Sheahan of Victoria; and the Queenslander Peter Burge.

This team – the antithesis of their colleagues in South Africa and led by a cricketer of the 'old school' in Les Favell – played ten matches, winning two, losing two and drawing the rest, but at all times their cricket was attractive and aggressive. The Australians began by defeating Otago in Dunedin, then surprisingly lost to Canterbury in Christchurch which gave the home side the honour of being the first New Zealand team to defeat an Australian eleven since Wellington beat Victoria in 1925. Two drawn matches and a ten-wicket victory over Auckland led up to the first unofficial 'Test'. This was originally scheduled for the Basin Reserve, Wellington, but because of a substandard pitch the game was transferred to Pukekura Park in New Plymouth. It was the first international match played outside one of New Zealand's four main centres.

The first of four matches between the sides saw New Zealand victorious by 159 runs. Favell, quoted in the *New Zealand Herald*, said: 'We were out-batted, out-bowled and out-fielded,' and that is how the series remained. Three drawn games in Dunedin, Christchurch and Auckland saw the Kiwis clinch their first-ever series win. The Australians fell, in the main, to the spin of Pollard and Yuile who between them captured 38 of the 49 wickets taken by the bowlers.

For Australia Booth (179), Sheahan (135) and Burge (102) scored centuries while Connolly's 16 wickets at 22.25 included the only five-wicket haul (5/61) in an innings. It was not a good result for Australian cricket but it enabled the Kiwis to look forward to more success in their four-match tour of Australia later in 1967.

This tour, in November and December, saw South Australia win by 24 runs, New South Wales by 131 runs, and the games with Victoria and Queensland were drawn. Although good experience for the New Zealanders it did little to give them hope of a full Test series in the foreseeable future. Australian Board officials were against such a move and, when questioned, said so openly.

The records of the Australian Board of Control for International Cricket are awash with trivia yet what comes through most strongly is the remarkable mind of Sir Donald Bradman. For instance, seven years after the debate on Law 26 (Throwing) started, he was the only man on the Board sharp enough to pick up faults in the drafting of revised laws or amendments to existing guidelines.

The December 1966 issue of *Playfair Cricket Monthly* magazine caught his eye when 'Billy' Griffith, in an interview, made reference to Law 26 and how, in Australia, 'a player called by two umpires was automatically put out of cricket'. Bradman's views resulted in the Board seeking clarification on this interpretation from the MCC secretary.

This small error – which was never admitted – paled into insignificance when Bradman discovered errors in the Revised Laws of Cricket. These Laws were used throughout the game from umpiring through to player contracts and inter-Board tour agreements. Bradman's attention to the most minor detail saw the majority of the members of the (now) International Cricket Conference having to amend their various documentation.

But what was sad from an Australian point of view was that Bradman was the only Board member who bothered to go through all his paperwork with due care and attention. In the later years of the Board, post-Bradman, such sloppy and careless attitudes were to cost Australian cricket dearly, such as over the 'rebel' tours of 1985–87.

In 1967–68 the Sheffield Shield season centred on Western Australia who won the trophy under the captaincy of Tony Lock. The England spinner took 42 wickets at 17.19 with his star batsman being the dour John Inverarity who scored 726 runs at 55.84. A special highlight of the season was the home match against Victoria when the journalist-cricketer, Ian Brayshaw, took 10/44 from 17.6 overs in the visitors' first innings.

In Sydney, in November, Bobby Simpson scored a classic 277 against Queensland and then told surprised NSW officials that he intended to retire from first-class cricket three months later to devote himself to family and business matters. However he remained Australia's captain for the first two Tests against India.

The party of sixteen Indian players arrived in Perth in mid-November 1967 for a twelve-week tour. Captained by the Nawab of Pataudi, the visitors were only the second Indian team to tour Australia; but they suffered a serious setback early in the tour when Pataudi incurred a leg injury while fielding against Western Australia and he remained out of action until the New Year.

Western Australia won that match by an innings and 20 runs, Gordon Becker scoring 195 out of his side's 480 for five declared. Then South Australia won by an innings (Ken Cunningham 145) before the tourists stemmed the tide with draws against Victoria (Ian Redpath 117) and Tasmania (twice).

The Australian selectors gave debuts in the first Test at Adelaide over Christmas to Victoria's stylish batsman Paul Sheahan and NSW's off-spinner Johnny Gleeson. Chandra Borde took over the captaincy for the first Test but could do little to stop the Australian Test machine running over India to win by 146 runs. Bob Cowper made 92 and

108, and Simpson 55 and 103, a mood he carried to the next Test in Melbourne two days later when he scored 109 and shared a 191-run first-wicket partnership with Bill Lawry who reached exactly 100. Ian Chappell scored an eye-catching 151 as Australia reached 529. Graham McKenzie took ten wickets in the match, including a first-innings 7/66 as Australia won by an innings and four runs.

At the Board of Control meeting held in Sydney in September 1967, Dudley Seddon retired as an Australian selector. Two challengers fought for his position, Neil Harvey being nominated by the NSWCA, and Ray Lindwall by Queensland. Harvey won the vote and then discovered that the schedule he was expected to follow was a demanding one. Don Bradman, as chairman, wanted every player to be seen as often as could be, because of the need to select a party to tour England in 1968. As expected of them, the selectors attended all Test matches until, that is, the third Test in Brisbane which started on Friday 19 January 1967, when Bill Lawry took over as captain of Australia.

Lawry won the toss and opened the batting. Overnight Australia were 312 for seven and on Saturday morning took their total to 379. Then came the discovery that only two selectors were at the ground. Neil Harvey had excused himself and gone off to a luncheon at a nearby race-meeting. The Board chairman, Bob Parish, was informed and wrote a letter to Harvey asking for an explanation. To Queensland, who were pushing hard for a national selector to represent their interests, this error by Harvey was heaven-sent. The QCA chairman – and Board delegate – Norman McMahon fired off an official letter of protest and, although Harvey offered a logical explanation, he found himself challenged by a Queensland nominee every year from then on at the election for selectors.

Australia won the third Test by 39 runs in front of a miserable five-day attendance of only 18,895; this was Brisbane's lowest-ever Test figure and the smallest five-day crowd since 1888. The fourth and final Test, in Sydney, saw Australia wrap up a one-sided series four-nil with a 144-run victory in which Bob Cowper's 165 was the highest Test score of the season.

As the New Year Test was being played in Melbourne the redevelopment at the ground was taking shape. Following the Southern Stand, completed in 1956 for the Olympic Games, now came the new Western Stand. When it was opened in 1968 it increased the ground capacity by 19,000 to 123,000. At the same time club membership was allowed to rise to 12,800. The most remarkable feat, however, was the re-siting of the scoreboard at a height of 155 feet – or ten storeys – above street level. A self-contained unit, it had its own showers and lavatories for the scoreboard workers. In the stand the architect, Stan Evans, had to allow eighteen inches for each seat, instead of fifteen inches as in the old stand. As Melbourne *Sun-Herald* journalist Keith Dunstan wrote: 'The affluent Melbourne behind had become more ample'.

At the conclusion of the series against India the Australian selectors announced the Twenty-fifth Australians to tour England. The Queensland Cricket Association's reaction to the news that not one of their players had been chosen was predictable, with the opening batsman, Sam Trimble, particularly unfortunate not to get a place. A loyal player who had represented his State in 133 matches, Trimble scored 9465 runs for Queensland, including 24 centuries, in a career spanning sixteen seasons from 1959–75.

The team under Bill Lawry had Barry Jarman as its vice-captain. Bob Parish was the manager; the Western Australian Cricket Association secretary, Les Truman, took the treasurer's position and NSW's Dave Sherwood was scorer and general factotum.

The tour got off to a slow start. Rain washed out the opening first-class match at Worcester and caused the next three games to be drawn. So concerned was Bob Parish at the lack of play that he made a number of requests for the Board to overturn their rules on allowing Sunday play. By a small margin permission was given so that, for the first time, the Australians played against Sussex, Glamorgan and Kent on Sundays.

Sussex wanted to allow Southern Television to show parts of the match during the Saturday and Monday afternoons in order to boost interest locally; but the Board instructed Lord's to make sure no televising took place.

Somerset, meanwhile, had contacted Lord's who then passed on the county's suggestion 'that in view of the large proportion of members making up our spectator attendance we would be prepared to pay the Australians a guarantee rather than a share of the gate takings'. In 1961 the Australians had received £1116 from the match, and £864 in 1964. The Somerset guarantee of £1150 was readily agreed by the Board who were aware by early in the tour that earnings would not exceed those of 1964. The final tour attendances of 628,847 showed a marked drop from the 940,408 of four years earlier.

The first Test in Manchester in early June saw Australia on top from the start. At the end of the first day the tourists had made 319 for four and, although they lost their final six wickets for just 31 runs, England struggled to avoid the follow-on. The Australian lead of 192 was extended to leave England the mammoth task of scoring 413 to win in 552 minutes, Doug Walters with 81 and 86 recording what would turn out to be his best Test batting return in England. Eventually the Australians won by 159 runs.

The day following the Test the tourists played Warwickshire at

Edgbaston. It turned out to be a splendid day for Ian Chappell whose unbeaten 202 was the highest score of the tour. In the Essex match both Dave Renneberg (8/72) and Bob Cowper (7/42) recorded the best bowling returns of the visit as well as their own career-best figures.

The 200th Test match between the two countries at Lord's in late June was spoilt by rain. Over half the allocated playing time was lost. England, captained by Colin Cowdrey, batted on the first three days before declaring at 351 for seven. On a damp pitch Australia fell for 78 but held out for a draw at 127 for four when following-on.

Rain also affected the third Test at Edgbaston where England were once more on top for the whole match. Set 262 to make in 270 minutes to win, Australia were saved from any anxiety when the weather intervened on the last day.

With both the appointed captains injured, Tom Graveney and Barry Jarman led their respective teams for the only time in the fourth Test at Headingley, which was the Test least affected by the summer's rain. Both sides played with the utmost caution. Australia's first-innings lead of 13 runs was extended by another 312 in their second innings. With England left to score 326 runs in just under even time Graveney settled for a draw even though that meant Australia retaining the Ashes.

The fifth Test at The Oval was an altogether different affair, and featured a superb display of left-arm spin bowling by Derek Underwood at his usually varied pace of slow-medium to slow. Before that, Basil D'Oliveira, brought back from the county circuit, was badly missed on a stumping chance by Barry Jarman. Riding his luck D'Oliveira scored 158 and, along with John Edrich (164), the pair helped England's score to 494. Australia replied with 324, Bill Lawry 135, and then England reached 181. Set 352 runs to win in better than even time the visitors were 86 for five and in danger of quick defeat when a freak storm at lunchtime seemed to have saved them. The playing area was completely flooded but the reappearance of the sun combined with the efforts of groundstaff and helpful spectators, enabled play to resume with seventy-five minutes of scheduled time remaining.

Derek Underwood, taking four of the five remaining wickets to fall, had the opener, John Inverarity (56), leg-before-wicket to the final delivery so that England won a remarkable game by 226 runs with just five minutes to spare.

In retrospect, the match proved to be a catalyst for many changes. First, D'Oliveira's fortunate century, and his eventual selection as a replacement for England's proposed tour of South Africa, caused a severe rift to appear between the two nations when the government of Prime Minister John Vorster banned the Cape Coloured D'Oliveira from touring. That left only Australia to play South Africa, and after their tour of the veldt two years later South African cricket went into isolation, or limbo, for twenty-one years.

Then, during the Sunday of the Oval Test, the manager Bob Parish telephoned Alan Barnes in Sydney, who gave him the sad news of the accidental death of Stan McCabe at the age of fifty-eight. Parish then told Barnes the reason for his call. It appeared that the majority of the team wanted to terminate their tour after the final match on 3 September and not return to Australia on the scheduled flight four days later. Some wanted to play in a special Scarborough Festival match which was being organised by the Bagenal Harvey public relations company, while the majority had accepted invitations to play in some specially arranged games in South Africa during the rest of September. Added to this, Graham McKenzie and Alan Connolly had signed to play county cricket, with Leicestershire and Middlesex respectively.

What the players were doing appeared obvious to all but the Australian Board: they were trying to cash in on all offers in order to increase the miserly amounts paid to them for playing Test cricket for their country. The extent of this for the cricketers who played for the Rest of the World at Scarborough was dramatic – the money being paid to them was the equivalent of a twenty per cent tour bonus and rather better than the Board's $200 (£100 pre-decimalisation) bonus paid as an extra for the tour.

The next meeting of the Board, a fortnight after Parish's requests, saw Sir Donald Bradman, surprisingly perhaps, ask the question 'If the players wanted shorter official tours of England, then why are they prepared to extend their time away from home by playing in sponsored games?' It was agreed to wait until the January 1969 Board meeting to discuss the issue further.

By then Bob Parish had returned from England and taken up the matter of sponsors and promoters. He had sent back to Barnes numerous press cuttings on the subject and asked that they be circulated to the delegates. In his letters Parish expressed concern '*on the growth of private cricket promoters and their contractual arrangements with first-class cricketers*'. He said that the powers-that-be at Lord's 'were encountering great embarrassment in the matter' and '*it was apparent that private promotions would shortly become more evident in Australia than at present*'. This letter was dated 25 August 1968.

The New Year Board meeting, held at the Adelaide Oval, heard Parish give a lengthy résumé of the subject. The Board then agreed 'that immediate steps should be taken to amend the Constitution to adequately control the subject activities in respect of Australian players'. Syd Webb, QC, gave various legal opinions, one of which was that all the State Associations would have to amend their rules accordingly. By 24 June 1969 this had been done. The Board breathed more easily: this would curb the players' demands.

With the West Indies due to tour Australia for the 1968–69 season, the more progressive elements of the Board – mainly the members from Victoria – suggested that 'endeavours should be made to obtain a sponsor of prizes for the series mainly in relation to obtaining match results, including bonuses to players'. Although this was the proposal of Ray Steele, the job was given to the NSWCA.

This resulted, in November 1968, in W. D. & H. O. Wills (Australia) Ltd offering to put up $20,000 in prize money. For this they required two advertising signs to be erected on the inside boundary fences at all Test venues. The ground authorities at Melbourne and Sydney immediately refused, and the company withdrew its offer.

Times were changing nonetheless, and somewhat too rapidly for many. Youth was rebelling. Long hair was now the fashion. Clothes became visual colour hues; T-shirts and jeans came in for jackets and ties. Unrest over the war in Vietnam underlay the new attitudes. With the social order changing, with it went the self-discipline required to play sport. A most noticeable feature of the 1968–69 season was that umpires made far more reports to their various associations alleging ill-discipline amongst cricketers. Sadly, too, players were being suspended by their cricket committees.

The West Indies team arrived in Perth in mid-October, captained by Gary Sobers. It was their first visit for eight years and much was expected of them, although the matches leading to the first Test in Brisbane gave little away. Western Australia was defeated by six wickets; a Combined team won after a generous declaration and a swashbuckling unbeaten 188 from Ian Chappell; South Australia won by ten wickets after Chappell hit 123; the Victorian and Queensland matches were drawn, while NSW lost by nine wickets.

The first Test lasted for four days with the small attendance of 40,185 people getting full value for their $36,883. West Indies started with 296 after which only a second-wicket stand of 217 between Bill Lawry (105) and Ian Chappell (117) saw Australia make 284. The visitors' second innings of 353 owed much to Clive Lloyd (129); then, through the spin of Lance Gibbs (3/82) and Gary Sobers (6/73) the tourists gained their first victory at Brisbane by 125 runs.

Ian Chappell with 180 dominated the return drawn match with South Australia prior to the second Test in Melbourne. Put into bat by Lawry, West Indies made 200 on a damp pitch as Graham McKenzie took 8/71. Then came another large second-wicket partnership – this time 298 – as Ian Chappell (165) scored the one thousandth century in

Test cricket and Bill Lawry (205) took 440 minutes to score his runs. Writing in the Melbourne *Sun News-Pictorial* the former Australian captain Bobby Simpson commented on Lawry's discipline and strength against the tourists: 'It was one of the finest Test innings I have seen Lawry play'. Alas, the newspaper recorded also a new fashion among the young: running out to the centre of the ground to congratulate the players every time a milestone was reached, and the taking of stumps and bails. Sixteen minutes' play was lost on the Friday alone with these incursions.

Australia eventually won, on the fourth day, by an innings and 30 runs but what was of concern to observers was the fairly small crowd of 113,376. For, entertaining though the tourists were, there seemed no way in which the public could be attracted back to the game in the numbers of earlier years. The series total of 428,940, paying $277,668, was way below the figures expected of 755,000 and $488,000. The game was now losing money.

Not that this affected the Australian players who were now on top of the West Indians. In Sydney, three Australians made career-best scores in a total of 547, with Doug Walters top-scoring with 118. Only Basil Butcher's 101 saved West Indies from an innings defeat although it did not stop Australia eventually winning by ten wickets.

The fourth Test provided the most exciting finish of the series, and the perfect Adelaide Oval pitch produced the highest-scoring Test match in Australia. West Indies batted first, scoring 276 with Gary Sobers making 110 and the local medium-fast bowler, Eric Freeman, cleaning up the tail. Another Doug Walters century (110) was the backbone of Australia's 533 which was scored at a rapid pace.

In five sessions of play the West Indians scored at better than even time. Butcher (118) added to his previous century as the score climbed to 616 which included a ninth-wicket record partnership of 122 between David Holford (80) and wicketkeeper Jackie Hendriks (37*). Set to make 360 for victory in 345 minutes, the Australians went about their task with gusto. All looked to be going well at 215 for two, until Ian Redpath, backing up too far, was run out at the bowler's end, without warning, by Charlie Griffith. Ian Chappell (96) at the other end, let his opinion of this be known and it spurred him and Walters (50) on to 304 for three until panic set in after the umpire, Colin Egar, had somewhat controversially given both batsmen out in the space of eleven runs. In the end it was the tenth-wicket pair of Sheahan and Connolly who survived the final 26 balls for a draw. Only 20 runs and one wicket separated the sides.

This still failed, however, to bring about a large attendance to the final Test in Sydney where Australia gained their then biggest margin of victory by runs as Doug Walters scored 242 and 103, Bill Lawry 151, and Ian Redpath 132, in a 382-run win. The truth, however, was not that Australia were world-beaters but that the great West Indian team of the 1960s was well past its best. The fast-bowling attack of Wes Hall and Charlie Griffith had not bothered the Australian batsmen, although the all-round play of Gary Sobers saw him top both the batting and bowling averages for the tour.

The Sheffield Shield season had been dominated by the rotund figure of English opening batsman Colin Milburn. His 811 runs at 73.72 for Western Australia included an innings of 243 in Brisbane against Queensland in an opening partnership of 328 with Derek Chadwick (91). However, the success of Milburn and his fellow Englishman Tony Lock (46 wickets at 22.93) could not stop South Australia having one of their rare Shield titles. In recognition of this the SACA held a reception 'at which the two sponsors of the team handed cheques to the players as a mark of their success'. Not vast sums, as thought, but $11 each!

During 1965 and 1966 the Board of Control had tried to get an indication both from their members and from the State Associations on the future financial structure of the Sheffield Shield. Excuse followed excuse from the Board's sub-committee, and it was only when Ray Steele was elected as a Victorian delegate, to replace Bill Dowling, that progress began to be made.

When the Board formed itself into the Interstate Conference on Thursday 7 September 1967, Bob Parish and Ray Steele inserted a suggestion into a sub-committee report on Sheffield Shield finances. They asked whether 'a sponsored interstate knock-out competition could be considered'. Three months later, at the next meeting, Parish stated that 'discussions with a possible sponsor company' had taken place.

Don Bradman had a couple of companies in mind, particularly Shell, but Parish had written from England in 1968 to advise the Board that he had obtained agreement with the insurance company, Vehicle & General, for a $100,000 three-year sponsorship for a limited-overs one-day competition. This would include also Tasmania and New Zealand.

Parish and Steele were given carte blanche to get the competition organised, and in a press release dated 7 January 1969 they informed the Australian public that their initial one-day domestic competition would start early the following season, 1969–70. Not unnaturally the major semi-final and the final were scheduled for Melbourne. In an interesting move the Board appointed Richie Benaud's public relations company 'to undertake the promotional work associated with the competition'.

At times the logic of Board decisions is difficult to explain. They were slowly coming to terms with the cricketers who wished to play cricket on a year-round basis and they were granting approval to quite a number who wished to play for county or league clubs in England. Then suddenly, when Ian Chappell applied to play in England in 1969, permission was refused.

Chappell was (and still is) mystified by the decision, even more so when it is considered that Graham McKenzie (Leicestershire), Alan Connolly (Middlesex), Dave Renneberg (Rawtenstall) and Neil Hawke (Nelson), all current Test players like Chappell, were granted permission without question. Chappell and Doug Walters went instead on a coaching tour of New Zealand which caused the *Dominion* newspaper in Wellington 'to express appreciation to Ian Chappell for the coaching undertaken in the North Island'. A further application by Chappell for the 1970 English season was likewise refused by the Board.

# 27

# Sponsorship and the World XI

The Pakistan Board of Control decided, on 27 November 1968, to cancel the proposed tour of their country by Australia which was scheduled for January to March 1970. The reasons given were bound up with the government of Pakistan's refusal to allow money to leave the country. The first part of the Australians' tour, to Ceylon and India, was still viable, however, particularly after the Indian Board lodged their $103,500 tour guarantee in a Melbourne bank.

Almost immediately, the South African Cricket Association offered to step into the breach with a four-Test tour and more than adequate financial assurances. This was accepted by the Board who, without much thought, were committing their players to touring two separate continents and playing nine Test matches in thirteen weeks along with various provincial and representative matches.

The touring party was selected in early March 1969 after a plea to the Board by the selectors. Realising the strenuous nature of inter-continental tours, subsequent permission was given – albeit reluctantly – for the party to comprise fifteen players instead of the originally proposed fourteen. The former Balmain wicketkeeper, Fred Bennett, was appointed manager, a job he was to accomplish in a particularly efficient way. As a personnel officer with the Australian Broadcasting Commission, Bennett was well practised in diplomacy.

The team captain was Bill Lawry and the vice-captain Ian Chappell, and yet again Queensland's prolific opening batsman Sam Trimble was overlooked; instead he was appointed captain of the Australian second team which was to tour New Zealand in March and April 1970.

The party was the last touring selection of the chairman, Sir Donald Bradman. He had been on the selection panel for the tours of 1938, 1946, 1948, 1949–50, 1955, 1956, 1957–58, 1959–60, 1961, 1964, 1964–65, 1966–67, 1968 and now 1969–70. His decisions had made many careers and thwarted others, but whatever one's opinion, it was many years of excellent, dedicated service. He did not formally retire as a selector until 9 September 1971.

The team flew from Sydney on 15 October 1969, arriving at Colombo's Katunayake airport the next day, to play four fixtures in Ceylon. Three minor matches preceded the only first-class game which proved to be an even draw with Ceylon in Colombo.

Two days into their tour of India, Ian Chappell was told of the death, in Adelaide, of his grandfather Vic Richardson. A noted sporting radio commentator in his latter years, Richardson's main piece of advice to his eldest grandson had been given after his selection for the South African tour four years earlier. Chappell recalled: 'He took me into the kitchen at home and reminded me of his tour to South Africa in 1935–36. He looked me straight in the eye and said: "Be careful of the women over there. Some of them could be your cousins".'

Following a draw with West Zone in Poona, the Australians left the cool climate of the hills to return to the plains and the first Test in Bombay, where an extraordinary situation had arisen. Before the Test the Indian selectors decided to omit Srinivasaraghavan Venkataraghavan, the Madras off-spinner, but such was the public outcry that Subroto Guha, the Bengal fast-medium swing-bowler, agreed to stand down from the selected team to allow Venkataraghavan to come in as a replacement.

On the fourth day of the Test, with India sliding to defeat at 114 for seven in their second innings, the crowd rioted when Venkataraghavan was given out by the umpire Shambu Pan. Play continued through the uproar although Johnny Gleeson was hit on the head by a flying bottle and, as the players left the field, a wicker chair tossed from the pavilion balcony fell upon Bill Lawry. A century from Keith Stackpole (103) and 5/69 by Graham McKenzie had set up the eight-wicket victory.

Ashley Mallett took ten wickets at Jaipur as Central Zone were beaten by an innings, but he was unable to carry such success over to the second Test in Kanpur even after bowling 88 overs. The drawn match at the Green Park ground saw Paul Sheahan (114) top-score for Australia and Gundappa Viswanath (137) become the sixth Indian to score a hundred on his Test debut.

Then came the start of a run of good scores for Ian Chappell. He started with 164 in Jullundur in the drawn match with North Zone and carried on into the following two Tests with 138 and 99. The third Test was played on the Feroz Shah Kotla ground in Delhi with a pitch specially prepared for spin bowling. Even though Ashley Mallett took 6/64 in India's first innings, the spin trio of Bedi, Prasanna and Venkataraghavan ensured victory going India's way by seven wickets.

In the second innings Bill Lawry carried his bat, becoming the sixth Australian to accomplish the feat in Tests; but the pressures of the tour were starting to affect him, particularly the excitable Indian media. Incident followed incident, both on and off the field, which culminated in the fourth Test at Eden Gardens drawing from the *Calcutta Statesman* allegations of the Australian captain pushing away, with his bat, a photographer who just wandered out to the centre of the playing area while Lawry was batting with Keith Stackpole.

After the third day's play crowds queued all night for seats for the following day. The crowd rioted, the Calcutta police were pelted with stones, six people died and the Australians' hotel was invaded by a mob. A fund was set up for the victims and on his own initiative Fred Bennett, on behalf of the Board, made a substantial donation.

The fourth Test had been won by Australia in less than four days by ten wickets. The fifth and final Test followed over the Christmas of 1969. Having endured another riot in Bangalore in the match against South Zone there had been calls for the Australians to abandon the rest of the tour. Fred Bennett was given an assurance that all would be well in Madras – and it was. Crowds of enthusiasts lined the route from the hotel to the Chepauk Stadium. Doug Walters made 102 but what was more important was 5/91 and 5/53 from Ashley Mallett as victory came for Australia by 77 runs on the fourth day.

Although Australia had won the series by three matches to one, the problems encountered in India were by no means over. After his contract had expired, Lawry wrote a series of scathing articles about Indian cricket administration and the behaviour of officials to him and his team. The Indian Board complained to their Australian counterparts and received in return a letter of diplomatic niceties which 'expressed appreciation at the high level of hospitality and interest exhibited by Indian cricket authorities and the public'.

Lawry's formal captain's report to the Board so worried them that they formed a special sub-committee to consider the points he raised. A man naturally sympathetic to the players' needs, Lawry queried the Board's insurances in view of what had happened in India – even the team coach had been attacked at times and the players had had to lie on the floor for cover as the vehicle sped past stone-throwing mobs. He also queried the security of their accommodation and continued all the way through his report to question the need for touring the sub-continent at all. The riots appear to have been politically motivated – and the Board had been so warned. They took place only in certain parts of India, the precise cause remaining obscure.

After the match in Madras the Australians had to endure a difficult series of connecting flights before they finally landed at Jan Smuts airport, Johannesburg, on 2 January 1970. After India, South Africa should have offered them relief but tensions had started to build within the team. The first period of the visit was successful. There were some good individual displays in the warm-up fixtures against Northern Transvaal. Ian Chappell scored 104 and Johnny Gleeson took 3/25 and 5/49. Gleeson again did well with 6/46 and 4/59 against Griqualand West when Lawry made an unbeaten 157; and Keith Stackpole reached 123 versus Eastern Province.

During the second match in Kimberley, Fred Bennett was approached on behalf of the South African Cricket Association by Jack Cheetham and asked if he would be prepared to play a fifth Test in addition to the four already arranged. After discussion Bennett agreed provided the Australian Board gave its approval. A letter was sent to Alan Barnes in Sydney and the proposal was raised as a matter of urgency at the Board's meeting on 29 January. Delegates agreed to an extra Test but on the condition 'that all fifteen players make themselves available to play' and 'the players receive an additional allowance of $200'.

The team, by now in Johannesburg, were called to a special meeting on Sunday 1 February in the hotel lounge to hear of the proposal. The financial terms were considered derisory and Fred Bennett asked the Board for $500 each which was refused. The players then rejected the extra Test. As the South African leg of the tour made a profit in excess of $250,000 the Board's attitude appeared parsimonious, to say the least. Maybe the Board later realised this for in their final comment on the tour in September 1970 they referred to 'having regard to the relations between the Board and the players'. This was the first acknowledgement of such an issue since before the first war, and the first occasion since 1912–13 when the players overrode the Board's wishes. The Board's wording was an attempt not to be seen to be giving in to the players. But, from the players' point of view, it was a case of 'money or no play'. Had other Board members rather than Fred Bennett been in charge, a big problem could have arisen.

The four-Test series against South Africa saw the Australians totally overwhelmed. Not one tourist scored a century, with 83 from Lawry being the highest innings. Alan Connolly took 6/47 in Port Elizabeth while Mallett, Gleeson and Connolly, again, took five wickets in one innings.

The South Africans won by 170 runs in Cape Town having lost all six previous encounters on the ground which dated back to 1902. Then came Durban and South Africa's highest score in Test cricket, 622 for nine declared. Graeme Pollock made 274, Barry Richards 140, and their victory was by an innings and 129 runs. Next came a drubbing in Johannesburg for the Australians by a margin of 307 runs with worse to follow. South Africa's last official Test for twenty-two years saw them annihilate the tourists by 323 runs. No wonder the Australians did not want a fifth Test.

With the top cricketers on tour the Sheffield Shield competition for 1969–70 had been one of the most even for years. Victoria pulled off an unexpected success with a new discovery, paceman Alan Thomson, taking 49 wickets in the season. Early in the summer New Zealand had made a short four-week tour in order to play in the initial one-day Vehicle & General competition, which they won, and to fulfil three fixtures against Tasmania, Victoria and New South Wales, all of which were drawn. The Australian party, who were to return the visit and play a series of provincial and representative matches in New Zealand, was announced in February 1970. Managed by Frank Bryant, the former Western Australian batsman, the team was Geoff Davies, Kerry O'Keefe, Dave Renneberg, Tony Steele and Alan Turner, New South Wales; John Inverarity, Derek Chadwick and Dennis Lillee, Western Australia; Sam Trimble (captain) and John Maclean, Queensland; Greg Chappell and Terry Jenner, South Australia; Alan Thomson and Graeme Watson, Victoria.

Before the first of the unofficial 'Tests', the tourists drew with Canterbury, defeated Otago by an innings and fifty runs, and saw off a challenge by a New Zealand under-23 side by an innings and 20 runs as the youngsters collapsed on the first morning against the pace of Dennis Lillee (6/40). The 'Tests' in Auckland, Christchurch and Wellington were all drawn, the last two due to rain. Sam Trimble's 213 in the final encounter held the Australians together in the face of New Zealand's 410 but the weather had the last word.

During this tour, on 10 March 1970, the always perceptive Bill O'Reilly wrote in the *Sydney Morning Herald*, after the stunning four-nil defeat in South Africa and 'the humiliating absence of bite in the Australian performance', that 'the selectors should pay particular attention to the players now touring New Zealand if they are to shore up Australia's sagging reputation'. In fact, within a few months only six of the South African tourists would remain in Test cricket. At the same time, and after many years, Jack Ryder retired from selecting and Sam Loxton took his place as the Victorian representative.

The problems of the India/South Africa tour kept bubbling away during the southern winter of 1970. After a meeting of the Marylebone Cricket Club committee in June 1970, a letter had been sent to the Board by the secretary, 'Billy' Griffith, in which he asked 'if you would be kind enough to give us advice, in the strictest confidence, on the experiences of your team which recently toured India bearing in mind our proposed tour of India and Pakistan in 1971–72'. Griffith concluded: 'There are considerable doubts amongst my committee as to whether the tour should proceed.'

Alan Barnes sent the letter on to his chairman, Sir Donald Bradman (who had now taken over from Bob Parish) and Bradman's reply to Griffith detailed some of the major problems experienced by Bill Lawry and his team. Fred Bennett as tour manager added his views which together would not have made very pleasant reading for the Board of Control for Cricket in India. The TCCB cancelled their 1971–72 tour, but it went ahead a year later.

There was still the problem of Lawry, however. His actions on tour had, by now, come to the attention of the relevant cricket power-brokers who were also dithering about what to do with their captain's tour report. They could not just dismiss him because, as a cricketer, he was, without doubt, one of their finest opening batsmen; yet if he played his authority was such that the captaincy should be his.

The England tour of 1970–71 saw Lawry average over 40, which included carrying his bat in one innings. Before the final Test the Board decided to acknowledge Lawry's report of ten months earlier. After quite a battle among Board members it was agreed by seven votes to six to send Lawry a reply which neither addressed the major points he had raised nor came to any conclusion.

The South Australian Board contingent of Bradman, Jack Dunning (a former New Zealand Test player) and Mel McInnes (the former Test umpire) wanted to ignore Lawry's report. Clearly with Bradman as chairman of selectors Lawry had lost the support of his backers. He received the Board's letter just two days before hearing on his car radio that he had been sacked as Australia's captain.

Awards, sponsorships, trophies and minor entrepreneurial ideas were now becoming part and parcel of cricket life. As with any new avenue of venture, it was seemingly uncoordinated and prizes were offered in bits and pieces, often as one-off presentations. Gillette (Aust) Pty Ltd were sponsoring knock-out competitions for the district clubs in the major cities, but were soon threatening to withdraw their sponsorships 'unless the local newspapers gave the competitions more publicity'.

In Perth the television station TVW6 announced that they were going 'to grant the sum of $500 for the fastest century scored in first-class cricket in the 1970–71 season'. In Brisbane there was to be a 'throwing the ball contest' during the lunch break of Sheffield Shield matches, and in Adelaide the four South Australian sponsors for the season were Nestlé, Cadbury, Colgate and Luv Pet Foods. These moves caused the Board of Control to make a fundamental shift in its policy. A suggestion by Bob Parish (Victoria), strongly supported by Frank Bryant (WA), Clem Jones (Queensland), Ray Steele (Victoria), Max Jillett (Tasmania) and Fred Bennett (NSW) saw a resolution passed at the September 1970 meeting which said: 'That this Board is favourably inclined to suitable sponsorships for matches under its control and should actively seek such sponsorships'.

By January of 1971 the secretary, Alan Barnes, was reporting on the money coming into the game. The Australian Broadcasting Commission had paid its advance of $30,000 for the year's cricket and Vehicle & General had handed over $80,000 'for their total seasonal fee'. Other payments came from Regal Reprographics ($250) for being allowed to use the Board's name in its NSW advertising; Honey Pool ($400) for the 'Man of the Match' award in Perth; Rothmans of Pall Mall (Australia) Ltd ($5500) for 'the international knock-out match' in Melbourne; Radio Station 3XY, Melbourne ($500) for the 'Man of the Test Series'.

In retrospect the sums seem small but the Board nonetheless was very pleased. Their view was that the players were doing well financially and pointed out that the 1969–70 tourists' allowance of $2820 for 23 weeks away from Australia represented $123 per week. With average weekly earnings for adult males in the private sector in Australia being $74 per week this meant the players were getting 66 per cent more payment than the average worker. So, asked the Board delegates, why were they complaining?

For the 1970–71 Test series against England the Australian players were paid $180 for each Test, a figure which some Board delegates thought to be over-generous. To put this sum into some kind of perspective, player income represented exactly 2.95% of the gate receipts which, after expenses and payment to Lord's, saw the Board's share represent 38.12%. The payment to Lord's was MCC's share of the tour receipts plus their guarantee over and above this.

In 1970–71 a regular player in the Sheffield Shield competition would have earned around $1120 for playing in every match of the season. With absences from work and associated travel (and a number of players were refused leave of absence by their employers) many cricketers were losing money by being involved with the game. Two early retirements, by players who today would be considered national treasures, were Bob Cowper and Paul Sheahan: two men who have now reached the peak of their chosen professions. Cowper now lives in Monaco, having made a fortune in finance; Sheahan is Principal of Geelong College, one of Australia's top private schools.

With the attitudes of Board delegates apparently changing, the New Zealand Cricket Council chanced their arm and wrote to Barnes in August 1970. They proposed that 'a New Zealand team make a short tour of Australia in the 1973–74 season and that an Australian team visit New Zealand in the same year, the two tours to embrace a series of Test matches in each country'. Bob Parish immediately took up the Kiwis' call and recommended to the Board that six Test matches be played, three in each country. He not only won his case but also made sure that a letter was sent to the Board of Control for Cricket in Pakistan stating: 'We are not prepared to arrange for a visit by

Pakistan to Australia in 1973–74 as you have suggested'.

At long last New Zealand was getting what it wanted and as a result used the next five seasons' short visits to Australia for the limited-overs competition as a blooding experience for its young players. Eventually New Zealand withdrew from a competition which, even today, has never captured the public's attention.

With so many changes coming into the game at all levels each tour to, and by, Australia appeared to be a catalyst for one reason or another. The England tour to Australia in 1970–71 was no exception.

The tour started in Adelaide with the team, led by Ray Illingworth and managed by David Clark, arriving on 20 October 1970. After a country match, the first principal fixture was against South Australia at the Adelaide Oval with the tourists running straight into the South African, Barry Richards, who was spending a few months with the local side. Richards scored 224 in South Australia's 649 for nine declared and the tourists batted out their second innings to draw the game. Then came a shock defeat in Melbourne by six wickets against Victoria when the new paceman, Alan Thomson, took 6/80 in England's first innings to clinch his spot in the team for the first Test.

Doug Walters scored an unbeaten 201 as NSW declared at 410 for five in Sydney. Once again the English batsmen held out in their second innings for a draw with Brian Luckhurst (135) and Geoffrey Boycott (129*) putting on 228 for the first wicket. A repeat performance came in Brisbane where Sam Trimble made 177 out of 360 in a one-innings draw which saw the Australians totally confident for the Test which started at the 'Gabba on 27 November 1970.

A shocking umpiring error in the first hour of the Test let Australia off the hook as Keith Stackpole (207), who was clearly run out when 18, and Doug Walters (112) added 207 for the third wicket. That the last seven wickets then fell for 15 runs was an ominous sign, but in reply to 433 the tourists made 464 and a draw was then on the cards. England's batting and over rates were slow, a factor which was to frustrate the Australians later on in the series.

The team then flew across the continent to play a draw with Western Australia and to participate in Perth's first Test match. Months of effort by the Western Australian Cricket Association was rewarded with a crowd of 84,142 – double that of Brisbane – and unexpectedly high gate receipts of $110,337.

In the first Test the selectors had given a surprise debut to Western Australia's rather rotund and clumsy-looking wicketkeeper Rodney Marsh. Now they gave a first selection to South Australia's Greg Chappell, the younger brother of Ian Chappell, who rewarded them with an innings of 108. Although Ian Redpath scored 171 in a match which was finally drawn, the imbalance of the scoring and wicket-taking left the selectors in little doubt as to the need to rebuild the side. By the time of the final Test in Sydney half the Australian team had been replaced.

Before and just after Christmas the tourists came up against South Australia again, as Barry Richards (146) and Greg Chappell (102) showed their worth in yet another draw. Victory over Tasmania by nine wickets and an abandoned fixture in Launceston due to incessant rain led up to the planned third Test in Melbourne on New Year's Eve.

On the first morning England won the toss and put Australia in to bat but, before the players could take the field, down came the rain. It continued until the end of the third day by which time the Test had been abandoned. A conference then took place between Sir Donald Bradman and Bob Parish representing Australia; and the manager of the touring team, David Clark, the MCC president Sir Cyril Hawker and treasurer 'Gubby' Allen. They agreed to re-schedule the Test for three weeks later and, in place of the current match, a one-day limited-overs international should take place on what would have been the fifth and final day.

This very first one-day international took place on Tuesday 5 January 1971, with an attendance which surprised the Board delegates who were present: a crowd of 46,006 who paid $33,894 passed through the turnstiles. England scored 190 in 39.4 eight-ball overs (Edrich 82, Mallett 4/34) and lost to Australia 191 for five in 34.6 overs (I. Chappell 60), by five wickets.

Although nothing was reported at the time, the conference of the five cricketing elder statesmen also discussed one other major issue and made a suggestion for another. Considering that the one-day game had already proved extremely popular in England, as well as bringing much needed finance into cricket, a private discussion between Bradman and Allen was aired for the benefit of the three other men present. The suggestion – to remain completely confidential – was for there to be a World Cup in cricket which would comprise all the Test-playing nations competing on a round-robin basis in limited-overs matches. The idea was to hold the tournament in England because, with the benefit of daylight lasting well into the evenings, matches could be completed in one day.

Parish, Hawker and Clark were taken with the idea and it was agreed that Allen would go back to London and put the suggestions on paper to be circulated as a memorandum to all relevant bodies.

The second matter discussed at this meeting arose from conversations between Sir Donald Bradman and David Clark earlier in the tour. Bradman felt that something needed to be done to enliven the

Sheffield Shield competition and Clark put to him the concept used in the County Championship of having bonus points for batting and bowling sides reaching required targets. The current Shield system had been in place since 1957–58 and was clearly in need of revision. Bradman prepared a memorandum which was passed by the Interstate Conference and his recommendations came into force for the 1971–72 season. The points system stayed in place until 1981–82 when a move inspired by Kim Hughes brought about another change.

In the fourth Test in Sydney, which started on 9 January 1971, England played their replacement fast bowler, Bob Willis, for the first time. For Australia this match would mark Graham McKenzie's sixtieth and final Test, in which he took his 246th wicket to place him two behind Richie Benaud's Australian record.

Illingworth won the toss and batted on a difficult pitch with an uneven bounce. Only the spinners, Gleeson and Mallett, caused much concern as England totalled 332. Redpath and Walters scored half-centuries in Australia's reply of 236 but then it was England's Geoffrey Boycott who wore down the home bowling attack. When the declaration came at 319 for five, Boycott remained with 142 scored in 410 minutes of dull, dreary cricket. He did, however, carry out his captain's instructions which left Australia nine hours to score the runs needed for a remarkable victory. It was not to happen despite Lawry's resistance, for John Snow took 7/40 in 17.5 overs and England won by 299 runs, their largest margin of victory in Australia by runs since 1936.

A week later came the additional Test, played in Melbourne, which developed into a bouncer war from the very first over in which Snow bowled four at Stackpole. The crowd were stirred up and over two thousand of them took great delight in dashing to the wickets to congratulate Ian Chappell (111) when he reached his century late on the first day. The fielding side was roundly abused by the rather emotional spectators. Ian Johnson, the secretary of the Melbourne Cricket Club, said to the Melbourne *Herald*: 'It was a disgraceful performance. The adults were either sheer exhibitionists or drunken louts.'

Two days later, before 65,860 people, four mounted troopers moved to the players' gates: no-one rushed the field as England's Brian Luckhurst (109) completed his century. England made 392 in reply to Australia's 493 and a draw was appearing to be the result. One cricket writer called it the 'Ho-Hum' Test; another said the match was 'the corpse which needed the kiss of life'.

The now seemingly endless Test cavalcade moved on to Adelaide with the England team gaining the sharp end of the popular newspaper writers' ire. That England settled for a draw in Melbourne was met by a crowd reaction of a constant barrage of abuse and the banging of beer cans for a good part of the final day. In Adelaide for the sixth Test the crowd were far better behaved although they did vent their feelings at England's opening batsman Geoffrey Boycott. During the first afternoon Boycott was facing Australia's new fast bowler, Dennis Lillee, and on taking a quick single was given run out by umpire Max O'Connell. The player's reaction was one of disbelief and he disputed the decision only to be told by Ian Chappell to 'get on your bike'. Boycott walked off to loud derision from the 22,307 crowd who slow-handclapped him to the pavilion. In the stands Boycott's constant companion turned to the woman sitting next to her and said: 'Listen to the crowd's reaction. They know Geoffrey was in and the umpire was wrong.' Mrs O'Connell did not reply.

Lillee took 5/84, the first of 23 hauls of five or more wickets in a Test innings, as England reached 470. Australia managed exactly half in reply but Illingworth did not enforce the follow-on, preferring to let Boycott (119*) bat on to extend the lead to 468 before declaring. Bill Lawry's 21, which proved to be his last Test innings, was followed by a second-wicket partnership of 202 between Keith Stackpole (136) and Ian Chappell (104) but it was to no avail and the game petered out into another draw.

The final Test in Sydney started on 12 February with Ian Chappell, the newly appointed captain, winning the toss and putting England into bat. His instructions to the Australian bowlers were to try and intimidate the English batsmen. As a result balls hit the tourists almost from head to toe. The crowd were fired up by this display as England fell for 184.

The second day saw the roles reversed and, at 195 for seven, fast bowler John Snow hit Australian tail-end batsman Terry Jenner on the side of the head. The batsman collapsed on to the turf. The obvious happened as the noisy crowd became aggravated at the sight of Jenner leaving the field, blood streaming down his shirt. Beer cans flew over the fence and Snow was officially warned by umpire Lou Rowan for intimidatory bowling. More cans followed as Illingworth led his players from the field.

After discussions with the Board secretary, Alan Barnes, and once the groundstaff had cleared the litter, the England team resumed the match and ended up by winning by 62 runs on the penultimate day, so claiming the series and the Ashes. The upshot of the disturbance was that Sir Donald Bradman called for an official umpire's report and statements from all concerned. These papers were then sent to the Test and County Cricket Board at Lord's. After their consideration of the matter and the interviewing of players a formal apology was sent to the Australian Board in July 1971.

The domestic season of 1970–71 was dominated by Barry Richards. His 1538 runs at an average of 109.85 broke a number of Don Bradman's South Australian records on the way. It saw South Australia claim one of their rare Sheffield Shield triumphs but it also brought home to officials the world of cricket professionalism.

The previous season Adelaide had seen the West Indian bowler Lance Gibbs playing for South Australia. His main value had been through his employment with Coca-Cola Bottlers, where he had led their sponsored cricket coaching scheme. At the end of the season Gibbs wrote a delightful note to the South Australian Cricket Association giving profuse thanks for the faith put in him and hoping that his coaching work had been of benefit.

The ease of dealing with Gibbs, where so much of the arranging had been conducted in gentlemanly manner, was in sharp contrast to the legal necessities entered into to gain the services of Barry Richards. The usual agreement had been sent to him for signature and what came back in reply was totally unexpected: a legal document from a firm of solicitors in Durban. Many clauses were altered, and the monetary benefit increased. Professionalism hit Australian cricket with a thud especially as the Association's solicitors now became involved. Many weeks of legal papers going to and fro saw a final document agreed only days before Richards was due to arrive.

With Ian Chappell at the helm in South Australia – as well as of Australia – the SACA annual report for 1971 said: 'Ian proved himself a worthy captain and we look forward to him leading many more victorious teams. A feature of the season's success was the happy relationship and enthusiasm among the players.' Those words were to cause considerable embarrassment to the South Australians through the decade as Chappell's relationship with them deteriorated. Also his international team became known as 'The Ugly Australians' for their behaviour both on and off the field of play.

A social problem that has previously been swept under the carpet concerns the private lives of cricketers, particularly those who have played in Test matches. They were normally not revealed. In April 1969 Leslie Fleetwood-Smith had been charged with vagrancy in Melbourne City Court and by March 1971, when he died, he was a derelict again, living rough as he had done for many years. In the 1970s Jack Iverson, Sid Barnes and Jim Burke would join cricket's list of suicides, while in the 1980s two former players were sent to prison. In the late 1980s two other players were convicted for drug trafficking but their penalties were hushed up so as not to interfere with their Test careers. Other former Test players would find themselves used by glib-talking businessmen in order to put their names to shady deals while another found himself married to a woman who was a convicted terrorist. The seamier aspect of the game could, sadly, take numerous pages to relate.

During the Australian winter of 1971 Sir Donald Bradman and Bob Parish investigated the situation regarding the proposed South African tour due to start in mid-October. While Bradman made enquiries 'of various government authorities, diplomatic and police channels' as well as 'other sporting administrators, ground authorities and other avenues', Parish was secretly putting together an alternative tour which would include the largest sponsorship to date for the game.

Realising what was going on, the Indian Board contacted every known concern to plead for a chance either to tour Australia or have Australia tour India. In August the Indians suggested twin tours: the first half of the season in India, the second in Australia. These were rejected by the Australian Board on the grounds that 'it would interfere with the selection arrangements for the 1972 Australian tour of England'.

The Board meeting in Sydney on 8 September 1971 rubber-stamped Bradman's recommendations and issued the following statement:

> The Australian Board of Control for International Cricket to-day reviewed all aspects of the proposed South African tour of Australia in 1971–72.
>
> Whilst there was substantial evidence that very many Australians felt the tour should go on the Board was equally made aware of the widespread disapproval of the South African Government's racial policy with restricted selection of South Africa's team.
>
> The Board faced the unenviable situation that whatever decision it made would meet with the displeasure of a large percentage of the people but it could not let that factor influence it in coming to a decision.
>
> It weighed carefully the views expressed by responsible Australian authorities including political leaders, union officials, church dignitaries, police commissioners, ground authorities, administrative officials and others.
>
> There could be no doubt the tour would set up internal bitterness between rival groups and demonstrations on a large scale would be inevitable.
>
> The police would be called upon to provide massive and prolonged protection at matches and elsewhere.
>
> The Board has complete confidence in the ability and willingness of the police forces to maintain law and order but had to question whether it was reasonable in the circumstances to ask these men to

undergo the severe ordeal which would be demanded of them to enable cricket to be played in peace and at the same time other members of the public being deprived of their services. Also was it reasonable to expect international cricketers to perform under the trying circumstances which would prevail?

Having deeply considered all these matters the Board felt it was in the best interests of Australia, of the game of cricket and all those associated with it that the tour should not take place.

Accordingly with great regret the Board decided to advise the South African Cricket Association that in the present atmosphere the invitation to tour in 1971–72 must be withdrawn.

The Board wishes to commend the South African Cricket Association and its players for their courageous stand against their Government's apartheid policy in cricket.

It earnestly hopes that the South African Government will in the near future so relax its laws that the cricketers of South Africa may once again take their place as full participants in the international field and the Board will give its utmost support to the South African Cricket Association to try and bring about this end.

The Board, having reached their decision, then turned to Bob Parish and his alternative proposal, of which the delegates had been forewarned the previous week. It was to have a 'World XI' tour along similar lines to the one in England in 1970 when their visit by the South Africans was cancelled. The crunch of Parish's announcement was a $70,000 sponsorship from the Melbourne *Herald* newspaper group with the contract noting, 'such to embrace payment of fees for television rights of $20,000 in respect of the televising of matches in Melbourne and Sydney'. Later on Parish negotiated 'commercial television rights for the States of Queensland, South Australia and Western Australia for a minimum of $6000 each and in the case of Tasmania, $1200'.

Parish's scheme was an excellent piece of work for he was more than aware of the commercial needs of the time. His *fait accompli* was accepted by the Board delegates who tried to put their own various imprimaturs on the deal but were politely baulked with 'the matter will be given earnest consideration', none of which ever took place. It was fascinating to watch as each State delegation tried to put a good face on the negotiations of the cancellation of the Springbok visit and the now approved alternative. The Queensland delegate Clem Jones, who was a Labor politician, could not separate cricket from politics and this is reflected in his motions. Others wanted to fight on.

The World XI tour was arranged with great speed. Bill Jacobs of Victoria was appointed the tour manager with Gary Sobers as captain and a cast of the best players that the cricket world had available.* The players got together in Melbourne in early November 1971 but their first two matches against Victoria and New South Wales were spoilt by rain. The game against Queensland, however, began to show that the visitors were not just a scratch side but a team of demanding professionals who would provide brilliant, if not sometimes bruising, cricket.

The World XI defeated Queensland by 38 runs in a game in which fortunes fluctuated from the start, after which came the first unofficial 'Test' against Australia. In an amazing match – which was drawn due to rain – only fifteen wickets fell in four innings with five centuries scored. Ian Chappell made 145 and 106, Keith Stackpole 132, while the South African Hylton Ackerman scored 112, and West Indian Rohan Kanhai 101.

A win by 72 runs over Western Australia preceded the second 'Test' in Perth which Australia won due to a devastating spell of bowling by Dennis Lillee. His 8/29 from 7.1 overs was as brilliant a spell of the fast-bowler's art as anyone could wish to see. He took twelve wickets in the game in which victory came by an innings and eleven runs.

South Australia won easily in Adelaide; Tasmania was beaten in Launceston, and a Combined XI drew in Hobart. This led up to the New Year's Day third 'Test' in Melbourne which still lives in the minds of many who watched it. Said to be the best five-day game in Australia since the Tied Test of 1960–61 it started in favour of Lillee who took 5/48 in a total of 184. The Australians weathered the barrage of bouncers from Sobers, England's Tony Greig – who with his height had the ability on the hard Australian pitches to bounce the ball usefully although his action was not fast – and South African Peter Pollock to reach 285, with Greg Chappell unbeaten on 115.

Then came Sobers the batsman, who played one of the most magnificent innings seen on the Melbourne Cricket Ground. He scored 254 runs in 376 minutes with two sixes and 33 fours in a superb display of forceful cricket. The World XI ended up with a 413-run lead with Sobers' stand with Peter Pollock (54) adding 186

*Gary Sobers (WI), captain; Intikhab Alam (Pak), vice-captain; Hylton Ackerman (SA); Graeme Pollock (SA); Peter Pollock (SA); Asif Masood (Pak); Zaheer Abbas (Pak); Bishan Bedi (Ind); Farokh Engineer (Ind); Sunil Gavaskar (Ind); Bob Cunis (NZ); Norman Gifford (Eng); Tony Greig (Eng); Richard Hutton (Eng); Bob Taylor (Eng); Clive Lloyd (WI); Rohan Kanhai (WI).

in three hours for the eighth wicket. Pollock said later: 'It was my greatest cricket experience. There can be no greater cricketer'. In reply Doug Walters made 127 but the visitors won by 97 runs.

The fourth unofficial 'Test' took place in Sydney two days later with Australia firmly in the box seat until rain washed out the final day. Keith Stackpole made 104 out of 312 after which Perth medium-fast seam-bowler Bob Massie took 7/76 – a sign of things to come. With a 35-run lead Stackpole (95), Ian Chappell (119) and Greg Chappell (197*) scored at over 50 runs per hour to reach 546 in front of grateful fans who, a year earlier, were demonstrating with beer-cans and abuse. The World XI went from 155 without loss to 164 for five just before the close on the fourth day but Sydney's fickle summer weather then came to the rescue of the visitors.

Adelaide staged the final unofficial 'Test' over the Australia Day holiday weekend at the end of January. John Benaud (99) and Greg Chappell (85) fought off the bowling attack of Tony Greig (6/30) for Australia to reach 311. South African Graeme Pollock (136) and Pakistani Zaheer Abbas (73) top-scored in the World's 367 which made the game look fairly even. However only an unbeaten 111 from Ian Chappell out of 201 stopped the game ending in three days as the spin of India's Bishan Bedi and Pakistan's Intikhab Alam saw the World XI to a nine-wicket victory early on the fourth.

The tourists were watched by altogether 399,853 spectators who paid $301,804 in gate money, a pair of figures comparable to those expected from a South African visit.

In domestic matters, the Sheffield Shield was won for the third time by Western Australia in a season in which all of Australia's leading players were available and keen to prove their worth to the selectors. The new panel of Neil Harvey, Sam Loxton and Phil Ridings – who had captained South Australia for some ten years – travelled widely to watch Shield matches and could not help being impressed by what had happened in Western Australia. The win represented a triumph for the coaches and their policies – Ken Meuleman, Peter Loader, Hugh Bevan, Wally Langdon, Laurie Mayne and, finally, Tony Lock who changed the balance of power in Australian cricket with his positive actions that turned Western Australia into a formidable Shield-winning team. Crowds at the WACA in 1971–72 were the highest in the country with 25,636 watching the Shield decider against second-placed South Australia in late February.

Between late July and mid-August 1971, Sir Donald Bradman received three letters at his home in Kensington Park, South Australia. All were marked confidential and no copies were sent for reference to Alan

Barnes for Board information, nor were they in the future.

The writers were the treasurer 'Gubby' Allen; the secretary 'Billy' Griffith; and Australia's permanent representative to the International Cricket Conference, Ben Barnett.

The official letter from Griffith said in part, 'May we suggest that a closer understanding between the Marylebone Club and the Australian Board of Control on matters arising at International Cricket Conference meetings and of mutual interest might be achieved if representatives of MCC, possibly one or more of Messrs Allen, Griffith and Insole [a MCC committee member], visited Australia for talks during the 1971–72 season'.

At the Board meeting in Sydney on 8 September Bradman, according to the minutes, 'read portions of letters received by him'. He did not say much to the delegates who, realising that something was amiss, gave Bradman the go-ahead to arrange a meeting. Bob Parish, Syd Webb and Ray Steele agreed to attend with Bradman as did the Board secretary Alan Barnes.

After further correspondence it was agreed to hold the meeting over two days on 26 and 27 January 1972 at the Victorian Cricket Association offices in Exhibition Street, Melbourne.

Even in early 1972, to travel halfway around the world for a meeting must have meant that matters of considerable importance needed to be aired. The party of three from Lord's arrived in Melbourne on Monday 24 January and booked into the Hotel Windsor a short walk from the VCA offices. Bradman met Allen privately the next afternoon before dining with all three in the evening.

Barnes was told to keep notes only, and that under no circumstances were minutes to be kept of the gathering. In speaking about the meeting when the Board next met, Sir Donald said that 'the English cricket authorities requested that they personally discuss with Board representatives items deemed in need of verbal discussion and clarification as between England and Australia'. It was interesting to note that minutes of the meeting 'would be circulated when the MCC response to the draft minutes, which had been submitted for endorsement, had been received'. As Barnes took no minutes this comment was a sop to the delegates.

The importance of this meeting has been confirmed by three of those present but none (most are now deceased) gave any hint or information as to what was said or why three MCC men found it necessary to circle the globe for a chat. As it was they all returned to England without even watching any cricket.

When the tour sub-committee of the Australian Board of Control started to study the itinerary for the 1972 visit to England, some three years prior to departure, the last thing on their mind was money. Times and attitudes moved quickly in the early 1970s and only months prior to the team's departure changes were being made to the tour schedule. Out went any thought of playing a match in The Hague as requested by the Netherlands Cricket Association, and the proposed visit to Ireland, which had always taken place in the past, was cancelled. The reason was an offer by the organisers of the Scarborough Festival of £2000 for the Australians to play a three-day match at the end of the tour.

Then came an offer from the Test and County Cricket Board for the Australians to play three one-day internationals at the end of August at Old Trafford, Lord's and Edgbaston. The bait was an extra £2000 a match, a figure initially rejected. When raised to £2500, the games were promptly slotted into the itinerary.

The Board made yet another internal appointment when Ray Steele was 'unanimously elected' as manager for the 1972 tour in late December 1971. This caused quite a stir among the cricket fraternity, so much so that one Western Australian Cricket Association committeeman was moved to write to Alan Barnes suggesting that such appointments should be open to all administrators. Barnes' non-committal reply brought forth a detailed submission to which the Board in September 1972 resolved 'that the correspondence be received and that further communication between the Board and the gentleman concerned be terminated'.

One person who did incur the Board's wrath, albeit in 1926, and who never returned as a delegate, was Sydney Smith. His death in April 1972 at the age of ninety-two was mourned throughout New South Wales. From being a delegate to the NSWCA from the Petersham Cricket Club in 1906, Smith had gone on to become NSWCA president from 1935–66 and had been a life-member since 1937. His obituary by the NSWCA recorded Smith as: 'One of the outstanding personalities of the game' and as 'an able and distinguished administrator whose contribution to cricket is without parallel in the history of the NSWCA'.

The success of Western Australia in the 1971–72 Sheffield Shield competition was reflected in the selectors' choice for the England tour, for in the side were six of the team – Ross Edwards, John Inverarity, Dennis Lillee, Rodney Marsh, Bob Massie and Graeme Watson.

The players began the tour in a most unfortunate way when thirty-two items of luggage were lost in San Francisco en route to England. Their arrival in London on 19 April heralded a tour in which one-day limited-overs matches first began to play a significant role. Ten such fixtures took place of which three were internationals against England and another three versus county sides.

Of the ten first-class fixtures leading up to the first Test at Old Trafford, the tourists won three and drew the rest with Bob Massie's 6/31 against Worcestershire being passed over without comment by the touring scribes. The twenty-five-year-old bank clerk from Perth had made his first- class debut six years earlier and had been chosen for the tour because of his impressive displays of medium-fast bowling for Western Australia. With an ability to swing and cut the ball in either direction, Massie was devastating in humid conditions.

The Old Trafford Test saw England captain, Ray Illingworth, win the toss on his fortieth birthday and watch as Tony Greig top-scored in both innings of his Test debut. The conditions were alien to the Australians, of whom only Keith Stackpole, with two half-centuries, appeared to master the situation. England's first-innings lead of 107 was increased by a second innings of 234 although Dennis Lillee did claim 6/66, including three wickets in four balls in his final over. Set 342 runs for victory in plenty of time the Australians were 147 for eight when Gleeson joined Marsh at the wicket. Their 104-run partnership in 82 minutes showed what could be done if the bowling was attacked. Marsh scored 91 in two hours but after his dismissal England claimed victory by 89 runs, recording their first victory in the first Test of a home series against Australia since 1930.

The following match at Oxford saw the only double-century of the tour when the opening batsman, Bruce Francis, scored 210 at The Parks. Francis, a complex, emotional character, played in the first three Tests before being dropped. In later years he would come to the forefront again in cricket but for vastly different reasons.

The second Test at Lord's lasted for three-and-a-half days and became known as 'Massie's Match'. With conditions suited to his style of bowling, Massie returned figures of 8/84 and 8/53 in his first Test to become one of only five bowlers who have taken eight wickets in an innings on their Test debut.*

Illingworth had won the toss and watched his side struggle to 272. A century from Greg Chappell (131) – one he himself always rated as his best from a technical point of view – saw Australia finish on 308 just before tea on the Saturday. Then came England's total collapse in the face of Massie's second onslaught with victory going Australia's way by eight wickets early on the fourth day. The gate for three days – no charge on the last – saw 96,538 people pay £82,915 which more

*The others are A. E. Trott, 8/43 for Australia v. England, 1894–95; A. L. Valentine, 8/104 for West Indies v. England, 1950; N. D. Hirwani, 8/61 and 8/75 for India v. West Indies, 1987–88; and L. Klusener, 8/64 for South Africa v. India, 1996–97.

than proved the financial benefit brought by a Test played at Lord's.

Massie's ten wickets against Leicestershire prior to the third Test at Nottingham raised Australia's hopes again. However, although he bowled well at Nottingham, he took only two wickets in the last two Tests that followed; and six months later his Test career was over and he returned to his job in the Commonwealth Bank's city office in Perth.

How did Massie 'lose it'? He has said that the conditions at Lord's for that famous match were absolutely perfect for his bowling – very akin to Perth's 'Fremantle Doctor', a late-afternoon wind that brings with it overcast conditions and high humidity. 'Different weather,' he said, 'and it could have been 0/100 and 0/100.' He failed in the West Indies a few months later and faded out of first-class cricket in 1974–75. He only ever played 52 first-class games in ten seasons – and 28 of them were for Western Australia.

Put in to bat at Trent Bridge on a green pitch Keith Stackpole (114) led the Australian charge to 315. The England reply of 189 saw both Lillee (4/35) and Massie (4/43) in full control after which Ross Edwards, playing in only his second Test, scored a sound unbeaten 170 which enabled Ian Chappell to declare at 324 for four. Set 451 to win in nine-and-a-half hours the England side made no attempt to score the runs. Opener Brian Luckhurst (96) made England's highest individual score of the series, batting for 325 minutes in front of a bored and ever-decreasing crowd.

Having not officially received their captain to hear his views since the days of Richie Benaud eleven years earlier, the Board now received such a request from Ian Chappell. In Steele's fifth report as manager, after the third Test, he indicated that Chappell wished to meet with the Board to discuss matters 'raised by the captain and the players whilst on tour'.

The fourth Test at Headingley was a farce. Over in under three days the grossly underprepared pitch was grassless and had obviously been tampered with. Ray Steele allowed play to go ahead even after protestations from his captain and the team. The pitch took spin from the outset with Chappell's gamble on batting first in order to get the best from the track backfiring as Australia fell for 146. England's reply of 263 owed much to an eighth-wicket partnership of 104 between Illingworth (57) and Snow (48) who both took a long handle to spinners Mallett (5/114) and Inverarity (3/26). Derek Underwood (6/45) found life a joy as Australia's second innings collapsed for 136 on the Saturday afternoon. England ran out winners by nine wickets and thereby retained the Ashes.

Between Tests, Derbyshire County Cricket Club approached Australian pace bowler Dennis Lillee to enquire if he would be interested in playing county cricket for them during the 1973 season. Lillee indicated his willingness knowing that current Australian players Ross Hunter, Terry Jenner, Tony Mann, Graham McKenzie, John Maclean, Paul Nicholls, Ian Redpath, Marshall Rosen and Leslie Varis were all playing in England and so sent off to the Board a formal application for approval.

The refusal arrived just over six weeks later and came, like Ian Chappell's request in 1969, as a total surprise. The Board had told the Western Australian delegate, Frank Bryant, 'to discuss the matter with Lillee on his return to Australia' and if he did not co-operate 'and was desirous of proceeding with the Derby negotiations and the Board being required to approve the necessary application, such would be declined by the Board'. As events unfolded it would have made no difference. Lillee went to the West Indies a few months later and broke down with stress fractures in the back following which he spent many months fighting to regain his fitness. But for all that, it was an example of extraordinarily autocratic behaviour by the Board, who were worried that Lillee's 'flamboyant style' might cause offence to English cricket officials.

The final Test, at The Oval over six days, was an excellent game of cricket played without the tension of having the Ashes at stake. England scored 284 in their first innings with Lillee taking 5/58 including three wickets in four balls for the second time in the series. Australia's reply of 399 provided the first instance in Test cricket of brothers scoring centuries in the same innings: Ian Chappell making 118 and Greg 113. Lillee again (5/123) showed his mettle – and pace – as England's second innings totalled 356 which left Australia over a day and a half to score the 242 runs needed for victory and to square the series.

The five-wicket win saw the end of the Tests which had been watched by 383,345 people who paid £261,283. Lillee had taken a record 31 wickets and Massie 23, but now came an innovation: three limited-overs Internationals.

Played for the Prudential Trophy, the fixtures at Old Trafford, Lord's and Edgbaston were acted out in front of packed houses as England won the first match by six wickets; Australia the next by five wickets with the decider going to England by two wickets in a breathtaking finale.

The English public were very impressed with Ian Chappell and his team. He had proved to be an adventurous captain quite different from his predecessor, Bill Lawry. His public relations had been good with no interference from his manager. In view of later events it was perhaps ironic that the next Board of Control meeting saw a motion passed unanimously which: 'Expressed the Board's appreciation to Mr

Chappell for his leadership of the 1972 Australian touring team' and 'requested him to submit a report' on any matters he would care to raise with them.

If ever that was a Pandora's-box . . .

# 28

# Disciplinary Problems

In January 1973 the Board of Control found it necessary to issue a letter to all State cricket associations concerning 'the behaviour of players on the field'. The reason lay in numerous reports by umpires from the start of the 1972–73 season which culminated in incidents during the South Australia versus Western Australia match in Adelaide in mid-December 1972. From that game the Test umpire Max O'Connell wrote in his report: 'During the current season I have noticed an increase in foul language and bad sportsmanship on the field during first-class matches with this current match being the worst of them all.'

By standing up to the players in this way, O'Connell's umpiring career would suffer in later years. One State captain used to write in his reports: 'This man should never again umpire a first-class match'. Those umpires who ignored poor on-field behaviour tended to be looked upon by certain senior players as 'one of us'. Those who complained were undermined. The Board tried to exert authority over growing player power but all they did was to frustrate or hurt well-meaning projects. Two prime examples happened during this season.

The first concerned the Spastic Centre of New South Wales who, in order to raise much needed funds, asked John Benaud if he would captain a team against another comprising Test players. The match was scheduled for Drummoyne Oval in Sydney on a Sunday in early October 1972. It had taken the Centre's public relations officer, the former Services player Charles Price, a number of months to put together two teams, mainly of cricketers but also with a few television personalities, and to publicise the match throughout New South Wales. He had even sold television rights to a local commercial station and had obtained sponsorship for the printing of programmes and the provision of supplies for players and guests.

Benaud, a journalist like his brother Richie, had also given the event publicity through various newspaper articles, one of which was spotted by a Board delegate during their mid-September meeting. When he raised the matter formally Alan Barnes was instructed to find out what was going on and why the Board had not been approached for permission to hold such a function.

Delegates, hot under the collar at such a 'flagrant' disregard of their authority, talked about 'refusing to let this matter proceed'. Then came a hand-delivered letter from the Spastic Centre, with a grovelling apology: 'We were completely unaware of the correct procedures involved in seeking the participation of players from affiliated organisations in matches not arranged or approved by the Board of Control or state cricket associations concerned. With this apology we apply for permission to stage our charity match and hope you will forgive our oversight and grant the necessary authority.' Suitably placated the Board resolved: 'To raise no objection to the match and to the participation of players invited by the Spastic Centre'.

The second instance came about when the Wallsend Cricket Club in Newcastle, northern New South Wales, decided it was time to organise a testimonial match for the all-rounder and former Test player, Johnny Martin.

Martin was a country boy from Burrell Creek near Taree where each year the Martin family gathered to play a Burrell Creek XI. After his retirement from first-class cricket in 1968, Martin became postmaster at Burrell Creek and coached the Wallsend club. When he had a heart attack in November 1971, his cricketing friends opened a fund for him and agreed to raise money with a special match.

The local committee decided to approach as many cricketing bodies as they could in search of funds, donations of cricketing items which could be auctioned, and general support. The Wallsend club could not do enough for Martin as, in his time with them, he had restored the club to prominence. The titles they gained in 1969, 1970 and 1972 were the club's first since 1937, while Martin's infectious cheerfulness was a timely reminder to local people of the enjoyment they could get from the game.

Letters were sent off to all state associations, the top clubs around Australia as well as to governing bodies in countries in which Martin had played. The letter sent to the Marylebone Cricket Club was referred to Ray Steele on tour who passed it back to Alan Barnes.

Wheels were then put into motion. An official complaint, approved by Board delegates, was sent to the New South Wales Cricket Association pointing out that not only did the Wallsend club have no right to contact Lord's direct, they should have gone through the Newcastle District Cricket Association who would then have passed any letter to the NSWCA who would then have passed it to the Board who would have refused permission for it to be sent.

The Board were so furious that they insisted the 'indiscretion' be punished by the Newcastle Association. NDCA chairman Tom Locker wrote to Barnes in October 1972 saying: 'The Wallsend club have been appropriately admonished'.

The testimonial for Martin went ahead and was a great success.

The 1972–73 season was going to be busy for the Australian team. A three-Test home series against Pakistan was to be followed by five Tests in the West Indies. Before that, however, the Board had made an interesting move. Negotiations for radio and television rights had moved to the Board's control from the Interstate Conference (a body acknowledged by many to have served its purpose) and although the Board officially acknowledged the work carried out on the subject by the NSWCA and VCA, in reality Bob Parish had done the hard graft during many weeks of committee meetings and with a plethora of suggestions. Parish achieved a sum of $32,900 for television rights from the Australian Broadcasting Commission, with another $8000 for radio. At no time did any commercial television concern show any interest in the season as the tourists were 'not a high profile team'.

The era of 'them' and 'us' had now dawned. With the itinerary arranged by the Board, top players were now going to play non-stop from late October 1972 through to the end of April 1973 for a minimal financial reward. The players had two main complaints: that they were not able to survive on Board payments and, secondly, that the administrators took no account of their needs and interests when making decisions.

Fast bowler Dennis Lillee and batsman Ross Edwards had both been sacked by their respective employers in Perth because cricket had kept them away from their jobs for most of the previous year. Many other players were being forced into premature retirement because they could not make an adequate living from the game.

At 4 pm on Friday 5 January 1973, Ian Chappell sat down to face the Board during their meeting at the NSWCA offices in Sydney. 'Cricket House' at 254 George Street was a splendid building, owned in full by the Association through careful housekeeping over many years. The NSWCA also owned playing fields and blocks of flats, all of which supplemented their income.

The meeting with Chappell was the start of the parting of the ways which, within five years, would see legal costs reduce the NSWCA's assets to those encompassed in rented office space in nearby Clarence Street.

Things had been going well for Chappell. He had taken career-best bowling figures of 5/29 to see South Australia to victory over New South Wales in Adelaide in early November 1972, and he had scored four half-centuries in as many Shield matches. Against Pakistan in the first Test in Adelaide over Christmas, Chappell scored 196 and had led his team to victory by an innings. In Melbourne the following week he scored 66 and 9 in a 92-run win. Not only was he one of his country's top batsmen but he was also fully in charge of his team.

Chappell knew that Bill Lawry's criticisms of the 1969–70 tours to Ceylon, India and South Africa had much assisted his downfall. Nothing had been done from Lawry's report. Now the players were complaining openly about inadequate travelling arrangements, too few rest days – particularly after a gruelling Test match – sub-standard hotel accommodation, and poor-quality food on overseas tours.

The Board felt they were being magnanimous in giving Chappell 'permission' to address them, but they had no idea how much they were either ignoring or misjudging the mood of the players. As one delegate stated, when giving an interview for the research for this book: 'We honestly thought we were doing our best for cricket at the time'. In response to that Ian Chappell said: 'They just did not understand what I was saying'.

The record of the meeting noted that Chappell showed deference to the delegates, stating at the outset that 'he felt the relationships between the players and the Board were quite good but could possibly be improved'. He then listed a number of issues to which the Board delegates listened to in, mainly, an awkward silence:

(i) The tours of England were far too long and should conclude at the end of the final Test. One-day internationals, which were extremely popular, should be played early in the tour in order to capture the public's interest of the players and the forthcoming Tests.
(ii) Chappell suggested that the Board might advantageously talk with representatives of the players from time to time and that a player liaison person be appointed as an intermediary as soon as possible.
(iii) He suggested that further encouragements should be given to the players by incentive payments for wins and/or for crowds on a percentage basis. Provident funds would generally encourage players to stay in the game.
(iv) Chappell felt that although the standard of umpiring in Australia was better than in all other countries, save England, he thought that each captain should report fully on the umpiring of each match.

Ian Chappell also raised a number of other points which ranged from 'limited-overs games in England are developing defensive fielding', and suggesting law changes to make such contests more exciting for the spectators through to the 'penalising of slow over-rates in Sheffield Shield cricket'.

Chappell recalled afterwards that his representations were not well received by the Board.

The programme thrown together by the Board for the 1972–73 season saw New Zealand play one first-class match in Adelaide (in which Ian Chappell scored an unbeaten century) and two one-day fixtures; Pakistan play (and lose) three Tests as well as partaking in a short tour, and then the Australian team packing their bags in mid-season to go off to the West Indies. The Pakistan team, captained by Intikhab Alam, defeated Queensland and Tasmania but lost badly to Western Australia (where Rodney Marsh scored 236, the highest score of his career) and Victoria (with Keith Stackpole 136 and Paul Sheahan 143 not out, tearing the attack apart). The Tests followed a regular pattern and were all compressed within a period of twenty-one days. No wonder Chappell complained.

The first Test in Adelaide was a triumph for local players as Ian Chappell scored 196 and the off-spinner, Ashley Mallett, took 8/59. Rodney Marsh chipped in with six catches and 118 runs, so becoming the first Australian wicketkeeper to score a Test hundred. Victory came early on the last day by an innings and 114 runs.

The Melbourne Test, two days later, saw another Australian success, this time by 92 runs as John Benaud (142), Ian Redpath (135), Paul Sheahan (127) and Greg Chappell (116*) all made centuries. The match also saw the debut of two bowlers who would play a large part in Australia's future teams: fast bowler Jeff Thomson and medium-pacer Max Walker. It was Walker, with 6/15 in Sydney, who saw Australia to an unexpected win by just 52 runs after the Pakistan bowlers had reduced Australia's second innings to 184.

With Paul Sheahan and Ashley Mallett unavailable, the selectors announced the party to tour the West Indies on 4 January 1973. Ian Chappell was named as captain. Jack Pollard summed up what happened next:

> In the three weeks between the announcement of the team and their departure, the players were peppered with letters from the Board of Control advising them on luggage arrangements, match fees and payments, when they would be required to wear dinner suits, what they could and could not say to the media, and the ban on wives accompanying them until after the last tour match. Their tour contracts stipulated that they could not pilot aircraft in which the team travelled and that they had to get the Board's approval of

any manuscripts they might have with a publisher. There was also the customary stern warning that they had to pay for all their own alcohol.

The team arrived in Kingston, Jamaica, on 28 January 1973 to be greeted by hundreds of fans and a reggae band which followed them around the island. After three wins in the country to start the tour, the Australians took on the West Indies at Sabina Park. Both sides scored 428 in their first innings which virtually guaranteed the game would end in a draw. Keith Stackpole made 142 second time around with Chappell's late declaration allowing his bowlers more match practice.

Then came a draw with the Leeward Islands followed by victory over Barbados in which Ian Chappell (209) and his brother Greg (142) added exactly 300 for the third wicket. The second Test at the Kensington Oval five days later on an adjoining pitch saw both Chappells score 106 and Doug Walters 102 as the match became the fifteenth draw in the previous seventeen Tests played in the Caribbean.

More island-hopping followed. In Trinidad a frustrating match against the locals ended when the final pair of Inshan Ali and Raphick Jumadeen held out for over an hour to deny Australia victory. The Test match three days afterwards was a different story even though Ian Chappell should not have played. He had sprained his right ankle playing tennis between fixtures, and he dropped himself down the batting order. Batting first, the Australians scored 308 for six on the first day with Doug Walters (112) collecting 100 of the 130 runs made between lunch and tea. In reply to 332 the West Indies made 280, and then Ian Chappell showed his courage. His 97 pain-wracked runs scored on a turning pitch helped his team to 281. Left to score 334 the West Indies were 268 for four at lunch on the final day with victory in their grasp.

Chappell then spoke to his team in a way a seafarer might describe as 'salty'. His words had their effect with a wicket coming from the first delivery after the break. Just 21 runs later the Australians were celebrating a most unexpected success by 44 runs. O'Keeffe (4/57) and Walker (3/43) had run through the tail to put Australia one up in the series.

Victory over Guyana went before the fourth Test. After three days' play the contest was even: the West Indies had Clive Lloyd's 178 to thank for their 366 while Australia relied mainly on Ian Chappell's 109 for their 341. The Sunday rest-day and a deluge of tropical rain changed the game. Jeff Hammond (4/38) and Max Walker (4/45) went through the West Indies for 109, their second lowest total in a home match, and Australia won by ten wickets twenty minutes into the final day.

The incident-free tour ended with a final Test ruined by rain in Port-of-Spain, Trinidad. The Australians were never in any danger of defeat after a 100-run first innings lead. At the end of the tour it was obvious that Ian Chappell had cemented his place as captain. His leadership had shone out, with his opposite number Rohan Kanhai completely outmanoeuvred.

Dennis Lillee was at the peak of his powers at the beginning of the tour but he broke down with stress fractures in the back. The injury was serious and it would not be until November 1974 until Lillee returned to the Test arena. Yet without him, Marsh, Edwards and Massie the Western Australian team had taken the Sheffield Shield in a remarkable fashion. Three outright wins in Perth over Victoria, Queensland and South Australia in just four weeks saw the Shield go west.

In August 1973 the Queensland Cricket Association offered Greg Chappell the chance to move to Brisbane from Adelaide. The opportunity put to Chappell both in cricket and business terms saw him accept the Queensland proposal. Qualification for the State was by residence only. It would also give him the chance to develop his experience of captaincy so that he would be prepared to take over from his brother in due course as leader of the national team. Late as ever, the South Australian Cricket Association came up with various incentives but by then the horse had bolted.

In September 1973, Sir Donald Bradman and Bob Parish finally got their way. The Board's Constitution Review Committee had laid down new guidelines. The Interstate Conference was abolished and the Board renamed itself the Australian Cricket Board. As well as taking full control over all cricket matters the Board gave the WACA an extra delegate and, therefore, another share of the dividend handed out by the treasurer (i.e. it rose from a $\frac{1}{13}$ share to $\frac{2}{14}$ share.) As a NSWCA delegate, Tim Caldwell, pointed out to his executive prior to them rubber-stamping the change: 'The new Board will now have complete authority in respect of all television, radio and sponsorship negotiations involving cricket in Australia'.

In December 1972 a mini-revolution had hit Australia with the election of a Labor government led by Gough Whitlam. It would remain in office for just under three years but for now, after twenty-three years of ultra-conservative rule, new government departments were created from the ashes of former ministries. As a new bureaucracy blossomed in Canberra for the Federal government so the States followed suit. Thousands of new public servants were employed. Departments of Tourism, Recreation and Sport sprang up and cricket, as an Australian majority sport, soon had these new government officials bombarding administrators with lengthy surveys to complete and requests for detailed information.

The Board was not exempt from such tentacles, to the extent that Alan Barnes, in August 1973, became exasperated by the upsurge in paperwork from government: 'a considerable amount of correspondence has come from them and responses have been very time-consuming'. Then came an intrusive request wanting 'detailed information on the financial arrangements of the Board' which Barnes took to the next meeting.

Victorian delegate Len Maddocks stated that his Association had spent some time looking at all these demands for information and offers of assistance, and had come to the conclusion that government funding, especially for coaching, should be accepted. The Board then appointed Maddocks chairman of a similar committee and, following his meeting with the Federal Minister in Sydney the following December, the Board soon came round to the view of the benefit of grant aid.

Being a former Test cricketer, Len Maddocks was taking a risk by throwing his ideas around at his first Board meeting. Late on the second day he raised (under Agenda Item 73 out of 114) the question of 'the possible provision of benefits or retirement allowances for Australian players'. In his opinion 'this matter should be further examined with the Board conducting in depth research possibly by way of a sub-committee'. Maddocks got his committee, his second, and the job of chairing it. He would find the task a hard slog before finally getting the Board to establish a proper Players' Benefit Fund.

The 130th and final meeting of the Australian Board of Control for International Cricket took place in Sydney over the days of 5, 6 and 7 September 1973. Two items of note stand out. The first concerned the 1974–75 tour by the England team and the itinerary drawn up by the Board. Lord's was pushing for four one-day internationals in the schedule, whereas the Board said they would reluctantly grant one. After a lot of paperwork, and the Board not budging, just one such match was arranged for Melbourne on New Year's Day.

Once more the Indian Board were asking for tours on a much more regular basis but the Australians were not at all keen to go deeper into the friendship. Knowing the Board were meeting, the persistent Maharajah of Baroda made a special trip from India to discuss the possibility 'of arranging a cycle of future tours between our two countries'. He arrived at Mascot airport on the second day of the meeting and within two hours was being received as an official guest.

His Highness would have needed all his internal strength to compose himself as the best he was offered over the next four years was a short tour to India by an Australian second eleven team. As Pakistan had recently refused such an offer, considering it 'insulting', His Highness likewise declined but with the good grace of a man raised at an English public school. The Board then tried to spell out many of cricket's facts of life as they saw them, particularly the Australian team's commitments for future years. Then the Board produced their *coup de grâce*, 'the problem of the exchange control' which His Highness simply dismissed by saying: 'there is no real problem there which could not be adequately resolved'.

This threw the delegates, as it had always been their prime excuse for avoiding the sub-continent. So in a typically British way the minutes record: 'After an exchange of pleasantries the meeting went into recess and the Maharajah was entertained to a cup of tea'.

With His Highness out of the way, the Board's tour sub-committee held forth. As their guest was still trying to persuade them 'to tour India instead of having a replacement tour for the South Africans in 1975–76', the tour sub-committee agreed on a date. Soon afterwards the Maharajah was offered, and accepted, a full five-Test tour of Australia in the 1976–77 season. Honour was satisfied all round.

The Australian neglect of New Zealand finished when the party led by Bevan Congdon arrived in Melbourne in late November 1973. Their first match was against a Victorian team, captained by Keith Stackpole, who were on their way to a Sheffield Shield title. With eight current or future Test players the Victorians made the Kiwis fight all the way in order to finish with a draw. NSW (with eight more current or future Test players) then beat the tourists by seven wickets, and Queensland (with seven such players) won by an innings in just two days. Then South Australia (with five such players) won by five wickets just before the first Test in Melbourne.

The Melbourne Cricket Ground has been used for many events over the years, most of which were sporting. But before the New Zealanders set foot on the famous turf there had been an International Eucharistic Congress. The members' pavilion then had been a mass of black and white – not the famous Collingwood Football Club's fans but priests all in black on one side and nuns all in white on the other.

Now, with the New Zealanders present, the newly renovated MCG was showing faint signs of the commercialism that was to come. The Club had accepted fence advertising for the first time so that an Ian Chappell drive would not 'rattle the pickets' but twang against a Benson & Hedges sign – or Toyota's, or Foster's or the State Bank or even against Melbourne's famous Four 'n' Twenty Pie's sign.

As the late December Test took place, members of the Melbourne Cricket Club could stroll the pavilion corridors and see hundreds upon hundreds of pictures and paintings adorning the walls. The collection of cricket, football and other sporting lithographs had been put together over the previous two years by Hans Ebeling, a club vice-president who had played one Test match in 1934. He found these treasures in an old attic where they had lain since being stored, and subsequently forgotten, in 1926. The collection was restored and put on show, a superb contribution to the history of Australian sport. At exactly the same time, however, similar wonderful collections in Adelaide and Brisbane were carted off to the local rubbish-tips.

The Board's Umpires Appointment Committee comprised Bob Parish (Victoria), chairman; Frank Bryant (WA); Clem Jones (Queensland); Ray Little (NSW); and the former Test umpire Mel McInnes (SA). When the committee met to determine the umpires for the first Test they had before them a detailed report from NSW umpire Tom Brooks and a confirmation note from Reg Ledwidge, both of whom took charge of the New Zealanders' match against New South Wales in early December. They were also aware of an oral communication to Mel McInnes from South Australian umpires, Robin Bailhache and Max O'Connell. All four umpires considered that the Kiwi left-arm spinner, David O'Sullivan, threw the ball and they wanted guidance from the Board under the constraints of the then Law 26.

Brooks had raised the issue orally with Alan Barnes because he wanted to know if his Test career would be threatened if he applied the Law. Realising the diplomatic repercussions Barnes told Brooks to hold fire until the Board met in January. Bearing this in mind the Appointment Committee gave Brooks only the first Test to officiate – and O'Connell the second – prior to the Board meeting before the third Test.

After discussing the various reports the full Board sent instructions to all State secretaries that they were not to discuss 'any application of the Laws with umpires during a match' and to tell umpires making such enquiries 'that the decisions were his responsibility'. When Ian Chappell raised the issue with the Board, saying 'In my opinion there are occasions when New Zealand player David O'Sullivan's bowling action is illegal, and why has no Australian umpire called him?' there was a general gnashing of teeth from Board delegates. Chappell was told it was a privilege for him to be allowed to address the Board and he should not abuse this honour.

Ian Chappell won the toss in Melbourne and decided to bat on a pitch described by the NZBC commentator, Alan Richards, as 'sub-standard'. This did not affect the Australian batsmen as Stackpole (122), Walters (79) and Greg Chappell (60) scored almost at will before the second afternoon declaration came at 462 for eight. It was enough as the Australian spinners got going and the wickets kept falling. Victory by an innings and 25 runs on the fourth day saw the Melbourne *Truth* comment that the visitors 'were inadequate' and adding: 'The opposition is so feeble it provides no experience for our up-and-coming young players'.

The writer, the former Australian representative wicketkeeper Ray Jordon, nearly ate his words three days later when the second Test started in Sydney. Put into bat by Ian Chappell the Kiwis enjoyed their first day of Test cricket in Sydney. John Parker (108) became the first New Zealander to score a century against Australia and in the second innings John Morrison (117) followed suit. In between the tourists had scored 312 and 305 to Australia's 162. At 30 for two overnight on the penultimate day the Australians looked a beaten side and were only saved by the third and then the last day's play being washed out. Suddenly the New Zealanders were looked upon with a greater respect.

Then, for no apparent reason, came their collapse in the third Test at Adelaide. The weather played a factor but by then the damage had been done. The New Zealanders were not holding their catches and dropped a dozen as Australia made 477 in perfect weather. Rodney Marsh clubbed 132 and Doug Walters stroked 94. The Kiwis fell for 218 and 202, their last innings in very poor weather conditions, to lose by an innings and 57 runs. Twenty minutes after the final delivery heavy, continuous, rain flooded the playing area.

Nothing, however, was done about O'Sullivan.

The renamed Australian Cricket Board had met in the boardroom of the Adelaide Oval two days before the third Test. Much of their early discussion was routine. Then came a bombshell – the revelation of the negotiations conducted by Bob Parish in obtaining sponsorship from the tobacco company W. D. & H. O. Wills (Australia) Ltd. Parish had given some details away in circulars to delegates on 25 October and 10 December 1973, but until everything was spelt out no-one had much idea of the success of Parish's hard work. He had obtained $50,000 for the New Zealand series and Sheffield Shield matches, followed by $100,000 for the 1974–75 visit by England.

Naturally Sir Donald Bradman was fully involved with this progressive move and his clear head saw through the excitement to the correct and proper distribution of the monies. For four of the six State associations, this money was their largest 'cricket' income of the season.

The 1970s was a trying, not to say traumatic decade for Australian cricket; a decade which wrought fundamental changes to its structure, organisation and operation. Cricket was transformed from a semi-amateur sport where Test and leading players were paid relatively small amounts of money, to a fully-fledged professional operation with leading players employed on well remunerated contracts. However, the decade was punctuated by a series of clashes between players and administrators as players asserted their rights regarding remuneration, playing conditions, and for their views on the organisation and administration of cricket to be taken into account.

Ian Chappell was at the centre of, or associated with, most of the disputes which occurred during this period. One of the leading batsmen of his era, Ian Chappell was an outstanding, if not brilliant, captain, who, between 1971 and 1975 transformed Australia from a mediocre team to acknowledged world champions. Often described as a 'players' man' Ian Chappell not only led players on the field, but also, and more importantly, fought for their rights off the field. Richie Benaud has described him, in his book *On Reflections*, as someone who 'was never averse to speaking his mind, particularly if it was to do with some bungle made by an administrator, or if his players were being harshly treated by the Australian Cricket Board'. Phil Tresidder, editor of *Australian Cricket*, described Chappell as 'a crusader for players . . . a modern-day sporting shop steward seeking better conditions, pay and sponsorship for his colleagues'.

Chappell had addressed the Board once. Now he was to do it again but in a far more demanding way. On entering the meeting Chappell presented the delegates with copies of a summary of items which had arisen from his meetings with State captains around the country. The men present had no idea of these discussions, and blanched visibly.

Having done his homework, Chappell then launched into his prepared text. He started by questioning details on the Sheffield Shield competition, then moved on to suggested tours of non-Test nations by Australian second elevens; rotation of umpires; the need for national junior cricket development; liaison between State associations and players; a player draft system; expansion of the domestic one-day competition; the suggested introduction of light meters, and rest days in Test matches.

By this time the Board had had enough. Chappell was asked if he could attend the following day, and on his departure fury was vented against him. The delegates insisted that the chairman, Tim Caldwell, 'inform Mr Chappell of his position' and that 'Mr Chappell's attendance at a Board meeting was a privilege granted him'.

When talks resumed next day Ian Chappell faced a line of cold faces; but he carried on by discussing ground administration costs; income tax deductions from Test players' match payments; the need for a players' provident fund, and – the real crunch – an increase in payments to players for all types of senior cricket. Chappell recalled later that his representations concerning the last two items 'were not well received by the Board'.

Ian Chappell was now in the gunsights of certain Board delegates who sought to make life difficult for him until a suitable replacement captain could be found. The first such opportunity came earlier than expected. Following the Australians' tour game in Dunedin against Otago in mid-March 1974, umpire Eric Dempster lodged a formal complaint with the tour manager, Frank Bryant, concerning Ian Chappell's 'foul and abusive language on the field of play during the match'. When this complaint came to Sir Donald Bradman's ears he raised the matter at the subsequent Board meeting. Conveniently forgetting a number of points – the propriety of an umpire writing a letter direct to a tour manager; a New Zealand Council member telling Bryant 'to forget the matter', and the New Zealand Cricket Council deciding to take no action – the Australian Board decided that chairman Tim Caldwell should 'verbally [*sic*] warn Mr Chappell as to his future conduct'.

This return tour to New Zealand was not a happy one with star Kiwi batsman Glenn Turner receiving more than his fair share of on-field comment. Turner's wife, an Indian, came in for particular attention with crude racial comments being used to weaken his strong batting concentration. Although team spirit was high in the Australian camp, their turn-out and behaviour left a great deal to be desired.

The six-and-a-half-week tour was badly affected by rain but even so showed a profit of just over $6000. Of the four first-class games against the provinces the Canterbury, Auckland and Otago fixtures were drawn, while Northern Districts were beaten by an innings and 236 runs in Hamilton following centuries from Ian Chappell and Doug Walters.

The first Test in Wellington was a statistician's dream. On a pitch which was lifeless a run aggregate of 1455 was the highest recorded in New Zealand but it was the Chappell brothers who took the honours. Greg Chappell set the then record for the most runs scored in a Test with a career-best 247 not out, followed by 133. His brother Ian made 145 and 121 which provided only the second instance in all first-class cricket of brothers each scoring a hundred in both innings of a match. Australia scored 511 for six declared to which New Zealand replied with 484, captain Bevan Congdon 132 and Brian Hastings 101. Australia batted out time to 460 for eight with Ian Chappell having no thought of declaring.

Two days later in Christchurch came one of the most exciting Tests staged in New Zealand. Australia scored 223 on a pitch made damp by light drizzle to which the Kiwis made 255 with Glenn Turner getting 101. The Australians came up against Richard Hadlee (4/71) and Dayle Hadlee (4/75) in their second innings which reached 259. At stumps on the penultimate day New Zealand were 177 for four.

On the final morning Glenn Turner hit a no-ball from Geoff Dymock backward of cover for four to raise three figures and to become the first New Zealander to score a century in each innings of a Test. Thirty-four minutes later, Ken Wadsworth hit the winning boundary. Success had been achieved over Australia for the first time. It was also New Zealand's eighth Test win in 113 matches.

The sporting press in New Zealand rejoiced while the Australians went off to play their infamous game against Otago which caused the umpire's protest at the 'foul and abusive language'. The three-day match at Carisbrook was played in freezing conditions with the tourists' behaviour not endearing them to the crowd. Even though Marsh played, Ian Chappell kept wicket and, when batting, threw his bat at every ball. In Australia's second innings Marsh and then Greg Chappell adopted a go-slow attitude and steadfastly and pointedly refused to take runs when they were available. The match was drawn but in terms of tact, diplomacy and public relations, the tourists lost heavily.

The third Test lasted for just three days. The Eden Park pitch had been unresponsive to bowlers during the season so the groundsman decided to transplant grass to inject some life into it. The toss should have been crucial but it was not. An unbeaten 104 from Doug Walters, after Australia had been put in to bat, saw the score to 221. New Zealand's reply was only 112, with worse to follow when their bowlers got no life from the pitch as Australia raced away. On the Saturday, the third morning, in front of 35,000 – a record crowd for Auckland in Tests – Ian Redpath carried his bat for 159, scored in 348 minutes with twenty fours, and the total reached 346. Set 456 to win in plenty of time the New Zealanders collapsed for 158 to let Australia win by 297 runs.

Australia had drawn the mini-series and then went on to win the two one-day internationals. According to media reports of the time 'attitude was one of the main differences between the two sides'. NZBC commentator Alan Richards summed up with: 'When an Australian innings was threatened with disaster, their batsmen usually answered the challenge with bold attacking strokes in an effort to regain an ascendancy. Too often in similar circumstances New Zealand's batsmen surrendered the initiative as they became engrossed in subdued defence'.

During the Australian winter of 1974 a number of cricketers accepted various appointments or took up invitations to play in different parts of the world. The poor behaviour within the game in Australia at the time spread overseas with these individuals. In an old colonial country two Test players, apart from appalling on-field behaviour, decided to demonstrate potty training on the bar of one of cricket's best known clubs.

Although they were on a 'private' tour, these players were reported to the Australian Cricket Board by the president of the Board of the country in which the incident occurred. This complaint joined a list of others received in Australia from Boards of Control, Associations, Clubs and various individuals.

Private correspondence to Sir Donald Bradman made him aware that some action needed to be taken. With an England visit imminent he arranged for two senior officials, Gubby Allen and Doug Insole, to be in Australia to meet with chairman Tim Caldwell, Bob Parish and himself in Adelaide before the fifth Test in January 1975.

Although their discussions did little more than make all sides aware of the ever-growing problem, it would not be for another nine years that the disease of lack of discipline could be said to have been fully eradicated.

The Federal government of Prime Minister Gough Whitlam was the most radical of Australia's short history. The conservative parties, so used to considering themselves to have a divine right to rule the country were, in late 1974, starting the process which would cause Whitlam's government to be unconstitutionally removed from office. The government had put more money into sport than had ever previously occurred. But Board delegates, conservative by nature, could not understand why the government was not giving them big handouts and complained bitterly to the Minister of Tourism and Recreation. There was a further 'letter of concern' sent not long afterwards when the new fourteen-member Australian Sports Council was formed and no Board delegate was appointed to it.

On being apprised by Alan Barnes of the government's view of the Board – which was that it was an unrepresentative body which cared only for first-class cricket, and that it was incompetent – it was agreed to send a deputation, comprising the three New South Wales delegates, to meet the Minister for a general discussion.

The facts were – although this was unpalatable – that money was being pumped into cricket but through activities unconnected with the Board. Youth coaching and the game at levels which did not come under the all-encompassing control of State associations, were receiving funds for all sorts of projects.

This resulted in a far-reaching decision. The Board realised that the time had come for them to employ a public relations company in Canberra to look after their interests at government level. Having had for so many years the ear of Prime Minister Menzies, the need for a lobbyist in the corridors of power was a strange new experience. Arrangements were made, a company appointed, and the fee agreed was $1800 per annum.

# 29

# Test Match Pay

The 1974–75 England team captained by Mike Denness of Kent, and with Alec Bedser as manager, arrived in South Australia in late October for a four-and-a-half month tour of Australasia which would take in eight Tests, two of which would be in New Zealand. After drawn games with South Australia and Victoria, the tourists defeated New South Wales and Queensland although Greg Chappell did take 122 and 51 from the English bowling attack. All this gave the England players little warning of the barrage that would face them in the Tests.

Eight days before the start of the Brisbane Test, on 29 November 1974, Lord Mayor Clem Jones, acting in his capacity as a member of the Brisbane Cricket Ground Trust, dismissed the curator and took over the job himself. Although a well-meaning man and generous to a fault, Jones had interfered in cricket matters before in Brisbane to the detriment of the game. Now he sat atop the heavy roller and prepared a strip which had uneven bounce at one end where England lost sixteen of their twenty wickets.

Ian Chappell (90) batted on winning the toss and saw his side to 309. Brisbane's best attendance for sixteen years then saw the unpredictable Jeff Thomson – who had moved north from Sydney to live and play locally – take 3/59, then 6/46 as Australia won the match by 166 runs. The pace of Lillee and Thomson kept the touring team's masseur, Bernard Thomas, very busy as he dealt with bruises and minor fractures.

Suddenly Australia were on top of the cricketing world. Ian Chappell had got them there by treating with disdain the accepted principles of gentlemanliness and by not letting the game's administrators get the better of him. A chant, like those of the football codes, echoed around Australian, and subsequently English, cricket grounds:

Ashes to Ashes
Dust to Dust

If Lillee don't get yer
Thommo must

In the raucous atmosphere of the Melbourne Cricket Ground this chant, with an accompaniment of tin cans struck together, a descant from the inebriated, and a seemingly chorale style Gregorian plainchant from those sitting in the heavens, made a frightening sound for the old enemy.

But before Melbourne came the second Test in Perth. There Lillee took four wickets and Thomson seven. England made 208 with Colin Cowdrey, a reinforcement to the party at the age of forty-two, making his first Test appearance since June 1971 and Fred Titmus his first since February 1968. Australia then scored at a rapid rate with Doug Walters (103) getting a century between tea and stumps on the second day, finishing from the last ball of the day with a six over square-leg off Bob Willis. Ross Edwards (115) stayed while the total went to 481 after which England put up little resistance and lost by nine wickets.

Having lost to Western Australia prior to the Perth Test, the tourists were unlucky not to beat South Australia before Christmas when they finished six runs short with five wickets in hand. The third Test in Melbourne was a close-run affair. England's 242 saw Australia reply with 241, then the tourists made 244 (Amiss 90) and, for some inexplicable reason, Australia did not chase the runs and finished with two wickets left still standing and eight runs short of their target. The crowd, even so, exceeded a quarter of a million people which brought forth record Australian gate takings of $251,771.

Two tours later, in 1982, a slightly smaller crowd would pay $933,152. Two further tours later in 1991, a crowd of half the size (129,530) would hand over $876,480.

Then came only the second one-day international Australia had played. Just 18,977 people wandered into the MCG on New Year's Day 1975 to see England win by three wickets with 23 balls remaining.

The selectors brought in the NSW opening batsman, Rick McCosker, for his Test debut as his weight of Sheffield Shield runs meant he could not be ignored. His previous five innings were 138, 136*, 164, 125 and 2. McCosker scored 80 on his home turf in Sydney as the fourth Test moved Australia's way from the start. Adding on to their 110-run first-innings lead Ian Chappell's side could do little wrong as their score mounted second time around. A 220-run second-wicket stand between Ian Redpath (105) and Greg Chappell (144) enabled the declaration to come at 289 for four. When Ashley Mallett (4/21) had Geoff Arnold caught at short-leg, Australia had not only won by 171 runs and regained the Ashes but it was also Mallett's one hundredth Test wicket.

The beaten tourists then went to Tasmania to draw in Hobart and win by an innings in Launceston. Then came a splendid win, by 187 runs, over NSW in Sydney before going to Adelaide for the fifth Test over the Australia Day weekend.

Mike Denness put Australia into bat after the first day had been lost due to water seeping under the covers following overnight rain. His gamble nearly paid off when the score was 84 for five. It took the recalled Terry Jenner (74) and the tail-end batsmen to get the total to 304. Lillee and Thomson fired England out for 172 and then the Australians suffered a blow. During the rest day, spent at the local vineyard of former Western Australian wicketkeeper Wyndham Hill-Smith, Thomson tore fibres in his right shoulder while playing tennis and did not bowl again in the series. His 33 wickets was the third highest against England in a rubber behind Arthur Mailey's 36 in 1920–21 and George Giffen's 34 in 1894–95.

Ian Chappell declared midway through the fourth day at 272 for five and had England on the rack at 94 for five at the close. The tail-end kept going until late afternoon on the fifth day before Australia gained their fourth victory, this time by 163 runs.

Rain in Melbourne before the sixth Test not only kept the crowd figures down but gave England their solitary success in the series. Ian Chappell's gamble of batting first backfired as Australia fell for 152. At 18 for two England were starting to wilt but then Dennis Lillee limped off with a leg injury and the English batsmen grew in stature. With no Lillee and no Thomson they played as though out of the bunker. Denness (188) and Fletcher (146) took the score to 529 with Max Walker claiming his Test-best figures of 8/143. Greg Chappell (102), Ian Redpath (83), Rick McCosker (76) and Ian Chappell (50) gave Australia the start they needed in reply but with the series won, the wickets fell easily and the loss was by an innings and four runs.

There was little doubt that the Australians were far fitter than the tourists and this counted a lot towards their success. Along with Ian Chappell's leadership there was a magical enthusiasm among the players that even today – now that all have retired – still comes out in their conversations on the era.

There were many pundits who put money on Queensland winning that elusive Sheffield Shield in 1974–75. They had good victories over South Australia (twice), New South Wales and Victoria but lost the title to Western Australia because of a lack of batting bonus points. Times were changing: the highest score of the season had been McCosker's 164 with South Australia just scraping a solitary century from Ian Chappell (100). It made the selectors' choice for the World

Cup and 1975 tour of England somewhat hazardous. In the end they chose a balanced team which was managed by Fred Bennett. Of the sixteen selected Jim Higgs, Alan Hurst, Bruce Laird and Richie Robinson did not appear in any of the World Cup matches.

The day before the start of the sixth Test, Ian Chappell again attended a Board meeting. This in itself was recognition of Chappell's hold over the players for no captain had ever before faced his administrators on three occasions. He again spelt out a number of issues. The Board delegates found these pushy, but by now there were some who were feeling slight twinges of rapport with what Chappell was saying.

Later, Richie Benaud would write: 'Chappell himself would disclaim any suggestion of militant shop-steward style thinking but he has certainly livened things up in the four years of his captaincy, in a game where the top players have always been ridiculously underpaid'.

Ian Chappell himself was also jotting down a few notes. His life story, *Chappelli*, published early in 1976 noted:

> The Board has a responsibility to see that the leading Australian cricketers are satisfactorily rewarded . . . I think it's time that the Board carefully considered the principle of binding the leading Australian players to full-time contracts in much the same way as other sportsmen, businessmen and celebrities are contracted.

For the 1974–75 series the players received a fee of $200, up from the $180 of 1970–71. Following Chappell's agitation the Australian Cricket Board paid a further $200 'bonus' per player per Test as well as a sponsor's bonus of $157. In actual payment a Test player's income per match had increased from $180 to $557 from one England tour to the next.

With the assistance of Len Maddocks, Chappell's push for a provident fund saw such a scheme introduced for this series with the players credited with $100 a Test for the first twenty Tests and $200 a Test thereafter. Monies so accrued would be paid to players 'at the discretion of the Board', two years after their retirement from first-class cricket. State associations had smaller funds for their representative players. For the 1974–75 series the gate receipts and sponsors' income came to $891,442. Of this the players were paid $40,104; a player's share of 4.5% which at least was better than the 2.95% of 1970–71.

To put the players' argument into another context, the Melbourne Test after Christmas paid, as previously noted, $251,771 of which $2400 went to the chosen twelve. At the same time, just down the South-Eastern Freeway at Kooyong, John Newcombe received $10,000 for eleven hours' work playing tennis in the Australian Open. All wicketkeeper Rodney Marsh had to do was to talk to his brother

Graham to discover how well golfers were rewarded in comparison with cricketers (one hundred and thirteen times better in 1974).

At the end of the Sydney Test, Dennis Lillee told a journalist that he believed players should be contracted to the Board and receive annual salaries ranging from $25,000 to $30,000 per annum. Alan Barnes reacted to these comments in a way which summed up the Board's whole philosophy when he said: 'The players are not professional. They are all invited to play and if they don't like the conditions there are 500,000 other cricketers in Australia who would love to take their place.'

This attitude hardened the players' resolve and sent Ian Chappell off to meet with Bob Hawke, then the president of the Australian Council of Trade Unions. Chappell raised with Hawke the possibility of players organising themselves into a union or association. There were also suggestions at the time that many players both at Test and Shield levels would contemplate striking in an effort to have their pay increased. It had got to that stage and would, in time, get far worse.

The tremendous pride Ian Chappell engendered into his players saw them progress much further in the first World Cup than had been considered possible. The pundits had not seen it that way before the tournament for, on their way to England, the Australians had spent a week in late May 1975 playing five one-day matches in Canada. They won two, drew two and, in a historic encounter, lost to Eastern Canada in Toronto by five wickets.

An unbeaten 80 from Ross Edwards and 5/34 in his twelve overs from Dennis Lillee saw Australia defeat Pakistan by 73 runs at Headingley in their first match of the three preliminary round fixtures. A century from Alan Turner (101) saw Sri Lanka out of the way in round two, before a loss to the West Indies by seven wickets at The Oval. However, this did not stop Australia qualifying for the semi-finals in which Gary Gilmour (6/14) bowled splendidly to enable England to be beaten by four wickets.

The final at Lord's on 21 June 1975 against the West Indies was a game which reflected all that was good about the limited-overs style of cricket. Ian Chappell sent the West Indies into bat and kept them subdued until Clive Lloyd arrived in the middle with the score at 50 for three. Rohan Kanhai (55) became the anchorman as Lloyd hit 102 from 82 balls with two sixes and twelve fours as his team reached 291 for eight in their sixty overs. The Australians batted defiantly but five run-outs, mainly due to the splendid fielding of Vivian Richards, saw their score to 274 leaving the West Indies as World Cup winners by just 17 runs.

The pre-Test county matches started with a stunning defeat by Kent by four wickets. Ian Chappell misjudged the pitch and declined to enforce the follow-on when 213 runs ahead on first innings. There were no such errors against Hampshire, MCC and Glamorgan all of whom were beaten. This led up to the first of the four-Test series which was played over four days at Edgbaston.

The England selectors gave a debut to Essex batsman Graham Gooch but it proved to be captain Mike Denness's last Test. His head had been on the chopping block since the last tour of Australia and his misjudgment in sending the tourists into bat backfired badly. An even display from Chappell's team saw them reach 359 midway through the second day. In the next twelve hours Lillee (5/15 and 2/45), Walker (5/48 and 2/47) and Thomson (0/21 and 5/38) took Australia to victory by an innings and 85 runs.

At Lord's on the last day of July England's new captain, South African born Tony Greig, led from the front scoring 96 of England's 315. Only two Australians seemed to contest the reply: Ross Edwards with 99 and Dennis Lillee whose unbeaten 73 was the highest score of his first-class career. The English tactics in their second innings were just to avoid defeat, even with a lead of 47 runs. John Edrich made 175 in nine hours before Greig's declaration meant that only a draw was probable. The fourth day also saw the first of a series of exhibitionist acts brought on by alcohol and bravado: a male streaker.

The third Test at Headingley ended prematurely in a draw following the vandalisation of the pitch by a group campaigning for the release of a convicted criminal. In the end it mattered little as constant rain would have brought the same result. Gary Gilmour took 6/85 and 3/72 and Rick McCosker was unbeaten on 95 when the vandals struck.

The final Test at The Oval produced England's longest first-class match. The actual playing time amounted to 32 hours and 17 minutes and still the game ended in a draw. The Australians had a second-wicket stand of 277 in 343 minutes between McCosker (127) and Ian Chappell (192) as the score mounted to 532 for nine declared. Lillee, Thomson, Walker and Walters bowled England out twice but there was not quite enough time to go for that second victory.

The short tour had been hugely successful with McCosker scoring 1078 runs at 59.89, Ian Chappell 1022 at 53.79 and Doug Walters 784 at 60.31. All the bowlers did well with Lillee's 41 wickets costing 22.12, Walker's 36 at 30.81 and Thomson's 34 at 34.50.

On the evening of 31 August, team manager Fred Bennett and Board chairman Tim Caldwell held a meeting with the Australian players in the team-room of their London hotel. Bennett was able to reveal a profit to the Board of $78,000 to which the players pointed out that they were actually out-of-pocket after receiving $2734, the equivalent of $182 a week for the 105-day tour. They complained that this was poor pay from such a successful tour, after which Bennett said: 'The players feel $500 for each Test against the West Indies in 1975–76 would be reasonable and that is the figure we will bring up at the next Australian Cricket Board meeting.'

What the players were not told was that the popular British entertainer, Tommy Steele, had obtained the support of Lord's in proposing a sponsored one-day match between England and Australia following the final Test. Steele was willing to put up a substantial sum of money – most of it to go to the players – for the fixture to take place. From Sydney, Steele was informed 'that the Board is not interested in your proposal'.

Ten days after the hotel-room discussions Caldwell chaired the fifth meeting of the newly constituted ACB in Sydney. The delegates discussed the proposals put to them by Fred Bennett and agreed to allow the players' match fee to rise to $400. They did little else, finding the whole subject rather distasteful and passed the buck to the State associations.

According to Dennis Lillee both Bennett and Caldwell had indicated that they would look into the players' various complaints and seek to initiate action. Lillee said:

> We heard no more about it. That was the annoying and frustrating thing. We just never seemed to be getting anywhere in our effort to get a better deal with the Board. At times we felt we were making some headway, then all of a sudden a brick wall would appear at the end of the passage. Always that brick wall was there and it seemed a waste of time talking to them about anything.

There is little doubt the Board was in some confusion at this meeting. Bradman, Maddocks and Parish led the discussions with at least half of the delegates and the Board secretary hopelessly out of their depth in the face of the players making demands previously unknown, and putting pressure on the Board to act quickly.

The Board members were much happier making decisions such as refusing a plea from the United States to play a one-off international in Sydney between Australia and America, sponsorship to be provided by the Peter Stuyvesant Trust. They liked the 'thank-you' letter from the Middlesex and former England wicketkeeper, John Murray, who wrote conveying his appreciation to the Board for approving the Australians' match against Middlesex in aid of his benefit. They debated at length a request submitted through the Queensland Cricket Association by the Paraplegic and Quadriplegic Association, 'that two paraplegics be allowed to take out drinks with the twelfth men on the first day of the first Test in Brisbane against the West Indies'.

What they could not stomach was the request by West Indies' wicketkeeper Deryck Murray – who wrote on behalf of the West Indies Players' Association – for details of the Board's Players' Retirement Benefit Plan. Murray's request had been returned to the WICBC with a patronising note. By return the WICBC wrote officially asking for the same information as had Murray, and the details required were sent 'on the understanding that the matter be regarded as confidential'.

Players of all countries were united in pushing for better remuneration, insurance, conditions and retirement benefits to which cricket administrators had never given much consideration. On the third morning of the Board meeting a shocked Alan Barnes read out a cable just received from the WICBC in Trinidad:

> Deeply regret due increase demands sought by our players must request additional $A45,000 added to tour guarantee of $A205,000 otherwise tour may have to be cancelled. Regards Burnett, WICBC.

It was left to Bob Parish to telephone Trinidad to explain that the sponsorship packages he had arranged would bring the West Indies players a minimum of $9000 and much more if they were successful. This calmed matters down until the third Test in Melbourne at Christmas when three senior West Indian officials (Messrs Burnett, Murray and Walcott) had met three Board members (Messrs Maddocks, Parish and Steele) not 'to ask for extra money' but to see 'if the Australian Board would care to resolve to pay a bonus to the West Indian Board'. Request refused.

Next day Ray Steele faced a deputation from touring players Clive Lloyd, Deryck Murray and Lance Gibbs. They enquired of Steele, in his capacity as Board treasurer, as to 'what the Board intended to do in regard to the payment of a bonus to the West Indies players?' Steele refused to countenance such an idea. Instead he pushed through a scheme to reward the Australian players with a bonus (based on playing in all six Tests and one limited-overs international) of $4770 each from the Board and sponsors combined.

Although this sum may seem good in its context it must be set against what the England captain, Tony Greig, obtained in the 1975–76 season when playing for Waverley in the Sydney district competition. His playing fee for club cricket was $20,000, while other fees for guest appearances, endorsements and other activities pushed that figure past $60,000 for just five months' work. The following season Waverley employed English opening batsman Geoff Boycott and his fees exceeded $70,000. At the same time, Sheffield Shield cricketers, who played for the whole season, were paid $480 from which, with various sponsorships, they could reasonably expect to earn between

$1000 and $2500 a season depending on individual and team performances.

The situation was getting so bad for Australian cricketers – and the inflation rate from 1972–75 was 115% – that Gary Sobers wrote from Barbados offering to present the Test team 'with cricket clothing'. Alan Barnes replied curtly, but politely, 'advising Mr Sobers of the Board's requirements in this direction'.

Then Richie Benaud's organisation, D. E. Benaud & Associates 'advised of their unavailability to continue promotions' on behalf of the Board. Bobby Simpson's company offered to manage the players and, when they accepted, the Board made sure 'that Bob Simpson & Associates were to be advised that the Board is not yet ready to accept this type of promotion'. The Canberra public relations company had met a stone wall in trying to put the Board's point of view to central government, but, instead of giving them more room and scope to expand, the Board seriously considered dumping them 'as a waste of time and money' – although they expressed it officially in much more pleasant terms.

The cauldron was boiling up and the players knew it, so they pressed onwards with the benefit of a lucky break. Terry Jenner had been somewhat critical of the selectors following his omission from the team to tour England and had subsequently breached the Board's Player/Writer Rule. Alan Barnes had written to Jenner, care of the South Australian Cricket Association, who had then forwarded the letters to South Africa where he was playing and coaching.

Jenner ignored these letters and, on his return to Adelaide, sought a meeting with Sir Donald Bradman. There Jenner admitted 'that the statements attributed to him were correct and that they had been made on the spur of the moment in circumstances of great disappointment'. The crunch of Jenner's point to Sir Donald, however, was why was he being picked on when fellow South Australian spin bowler Ashley Mallett 'had also made certain strong statements regarding selection and had not been similarly written to by the Board'.

No answer was forthcoming, so Jenner was kept in the dark. What had happened was that the Australian Journalists' Association had written to Sir Donald on 16 May 1975 'expressing concern' that two of its members, namely A. A. Mallett and I. M. Chappell, were bound by an agreement which prohibited them from talking to or writing for the media. The AJA had met to discuss this and resolved to seek clarification from the Board of its policy on communication by players with the media during the Australians' tour of Canada and England. This letter galvanised Sir Donald into action and he made a number of private enquiries of AJA members whom he knew. The implications described to him made him very concerned as to what might happen if the Board were challenged on a point of law alleging that the Board was stopping cricketers earning a living through their normal professions.

Aware of the pending AJA letter, Ian Chappell had left a note at the SACA offices in Adelaide before departure, informing Sir Donald that he intended writing certain articles while away on tour. To get around the rules, Chappell's articles read: 'As told to . . .'; but even after a letter from Sir Donald and constant counselling from Fred Bennett, Chappell's articles still appeared and there was nothing the Board could do about it. Jeff Thomson and Rodney Marsh also challenged the Board in this way and found that opposition crumbled before them. The first stirrings of real rebellion had begun.

It became very obvious in late 1975 that Alan Barnes could not cope with being both NSWCA and Board secretary. Something had to give, and it was decided that Barnes would relinquish the NSWCA position to his assistant Bob Radford and take over the Board full-time with the offices relocated within Sydney.

Although the Board was unable, or unwilling, to see the wood for the trees at least the various State Association secretaries were more aware of what was happening. New blood had been attracted to the Victorian Cricket Association when, in January 1972, David Richards had become assistant secretary. He was promoted to secretary on 1 July 1973 on Jack Ledward's sudden retirement and went on to become Board secretary in 1980.

Seeing at close hand what was going on, Richards was able to persuade Ansett Airlines and Melbourne's Hilton Hotel to sponsor a seminal meeting of State secretaries which was held on 28 August 1975 at the VCA's new premises in Jolimont Street opposite the Melbourne Cricket Ground. Besides Richards, those attending were Bob Radford (NSWCA), Darby Munn (SACA), Brian Bellon (WACA), Tom Veivers (QCA) and Peter Hadlow (TCC).

Officially they 'discussed matters of mutual interest' but this encompassed a great deal. They were aware of the growing militancy amongst the players (which blew up into a short-lived strike by South Australian players in late February 1976); they knew that the Board had lost its grip at grass-roots level; provident funds were growing in the States but not at Board level which was causing resentment; the Board had little concept of the commercial side of the game; the players wanted to go out into the business community to find sponsors, and marketing by the Board was non-existent. Added to all that was a total lack of understanding at Board level of public relations or the needs of the media.

After the State secretaries had met, David Richards produced a report for the Board in which he, ever so gently and very politely, suggested they might care to give due consideration to the possibility of the VCA producing 'a national souvenir programme for the forthcoming West Indian tour'. It was a simple request as a need had been identified. The Board threw the idea around for two days at their meeting with delegates seeming to think it was all right. Richards was given the go-ahead. In fact the Board were so taken with Richards' diplomacy and ability to please them that they appointed him as a pro-tem assistant secretary to the Board while the organisation took place for a special one-off Test match in March 1977 against England to celebrate the one hundred years of Test cricket. Richards would prove his worth in a most admirable way.

As the September 1975 Board meeting broke up, Tim Caldwell passed the reins of power over to Bob Parish mouthing the usual thanks, but concluding with: 'I extend my very best wishes to Mr Parish, whose services the Board are most fortunate to have, for a happy and fruitful term as chairman'. If only Caldwell had known what he was saying.

Before the 1975–76 series against the West Indies began, Ian Chappell seemed to sense a move against him by the faceless men who ran Australian cricket. At just thirty-two years of age he stepped down from the captaincy which was then taken on by his brother Greg. Ian's Test record as leader had seen fifteen wins out of thirty games with ten drawn. Particularly at the present time (1993) it is possible to assess Ian Chappell's contribution to the game with some awe. The mellowing of middle age has brought forth the true, deep thinker he really is behind that brash Aussie-male-macho image.

Just six weeks after the Australians arrived home from England, the West Indies started their fifth tour of Australia. With Clive Lloyd as captain, the tourists had played two matches in Papua New Guinea prior to arriving in Adelaide. Once in Australia the West Indies would have exactly one hundred days with very little success.

Draws against South Australia (Gary Cosier 130) and Victoria (Ian Redpath 105, Alan Hurst 7/57) preceded a narrow 52-run win over NSW (Alan Turner 106*) and an impressive innings and 90-run victory against Queensland. The ground in Brisbane was a disgrace yet again as Lord Mayor Clem Jones took on the curator's job. His lack of preparation left the pitch in a precarious state and two electrical storms on days leading up to the first Test did not help.

The Australian team lacked Ross Edwards, one of the best fieldsmen of the time who had now retired, and Doug Walters, who had been injured during a Shield match in Adelaide and was out for the season. Not surprisingly both teams included two spinners: Jenner and Mallett for Australia, and Gibbs and Inshan Ali for the tourists.

On winning the toss the West Indies batted as if there was no tomorrow. They were 125 for six by lunchtime and all out before tea for 214. Australia's reply was equally as quick, 366, with Greg Chappell on his debut as captain scoring 123. The suicidal tendencies of the visitors carried on and, with Greg Chappell reaching 109 not out second time around, Australia won by eight wickets in under four days' play.

The West Indies were then beaten by Western Australia by 115 runs in a game which had virtually everything: 39 wickets falling for 1507 runs; five centuries; six half-centuries; and a bowling display from spinner Bob Paulsen which saw his first-innings 1/153 turn to 8/71 in the second. Kim Hughes (102) and Ian Brayshaw (100*) top-scored for WA whose 291 for nine declared, and 520, defeated the West Indies' 479 (Vivian Richards 175, Roy Fredericks 108, Clive Lloyd 105) and 217.

The scoring mood carried on into the second Test. Australia reached 329 of which Ian Chappell (still playing in the side under his brother's captaincy) made 156 after which came a West Indian onslaught. In a superb attacking innings Roy Fredericks scored 169 in 212 minutes from 145 balls with a six and 27 fours. He reached 50 in 45 minutes off 33 balls and 100 in 116 minutes off 71 balls. The Australian attack was torn apart on a perfect batting pitch. Clive Lloyd scored 149 as the scoring raced on to 585. In another three-and-a-half-day Test, Australia lost by an innings and 87 runs. The crowds of 64,383 in Brisbane and now 66,062 in Perth appreciated what they had seen. The next Test was in Melbourne, with the promise of a specially large attendance.

Before that the teams played a one-day international in Adelaide which Australia won by five wickets in a game which lacked any real atmosphere. Then came a desperately dull draw against South Australia. Boxing Day morning 1975 dawned light and bright as 85,661 spectators streamed into the Melbourne Cricket Ground. There was lots of talk of a new world-record crowd but as Ian Johnson said in the *Sun News-Pictorial*: 'The weather cost us up to 15,000 people. It was just a little too hot for comfort, especially for those who waited to see what it was like before deciding where to go'.

Yet again the Test lasted under four days. Lillee (4/56) and Thomson (5/62) kept the crowd on their toes with a bowling display which dismissed the West Indies for 224. In addition to three streakers the West Indies' concentration was broken by blood-curdling cries of 'Thomm - oooooh . . . Thomm - oooooh . . .' and also 'Lill - eeeee . . . Lill - eeeee . . . Lill - eeeee . . .', the war-chant which represented a generation. Free from conflict for the first time in many years, the halcyon days of the Whitlam government were now over. Jobs a-plenty were a thing of the past. The new regime, led by the tall, austere Malcolm Fraser, son of a farmer-politician, would see Australia governed by Melbourne's establishment for the next eight years. The squattocracy* would divide and rule: the Test match was an outlet for the dark economic unknown to come.

The Fraser government's deep involvement in cricket started slowly. The Department of Tourism, Recreation and Sport had been incorporated into the larger Department of Community Development under Senator Ivor Greenwood. Not only did the Senator spend much of the match at the ground with the Club's committee but he also made sure he appeared in the players' changing-room usually, coincidentally, with a photographer.

Ian Redpath (102) and Gary Cosier (109 on Test debut) scored centuries as Australia scored 485. Only Clive Lloyd (102) with a captain's innings saved the defeat from being worse than by eight wickets. In Sydney there was a repeat performance where Australia won by seven wickets with 182 not out from Greg Chappell and a stunning 6/50 from Jeff Thomson.

The fifth Test in Adelaide saw centuries in each innings by opening batsmen: Ian Redpath (103), then Alan Turner (136). Gilmour, Thomson and Lillee shared the bowling honours in a 190-run Australian victory. It was same again for the sixth Test in Melbourne: 101 from Redpath and 109 not out from McCosker in a 165-run win and the series by five matches to one. Such one-sided results actually saw crowd figures decline instead of rise. For the Tests 746,311 people paid $1,110,685: the first one million dollar series.

On the West Indies' side, the effect of losing the series so heavily resulted in a re-think of their tactics and mental attitudes under Clive Lloyd's guidance – and this saw them bounce back to the top of world cricket.

And the Australian players? Ian Redpath announced his retirement from the game at the peak of his career. He could not afford to be away for so long from his antique shop in Geelong for such little financial reward. The same had happened to Paul Sheahan, a schoolmaster, and to Keith Stackpole and Bob Cowper, both business executives. Then came the real shock: Ian Chappell announced *his* retirement. The *Sun News-Pictorial* in Melbourne thundered: 'It is monstrous that the man of the match in the sixth Test, the ballast, the anchor of the Australian Test side, should be allowed to walk out ahead of time'.

When the news was made public that Ian Chappell was moving to Melbourne for the 1976–77 season to coach and play District

*The squattocracy were farming people (mainly Victorians) who had settled on free land in years past. Succeeding generations became the blue-blooded farmers, collectively regarded as rich and influential, who ruled the conservative political parties.

cricket for North Melbourne because the pay was better than for Test cricket, all but those ostriches with their heads in the sand knew that a breaking-point was coming.

Behind the scenes Sir Donald Bradman had been very annoyed by a number of events over the series, particularly the very slow over-rates bowled by the West Indies. In a formal discussion with manager Esmond Kentish and his assistant, Keith Walcott, Bradman pointed out that as few as eighty balls an hour had been bowled compared to the English minimum of 111. Kentish replied that the West Indies considered ninety balls an hour to be acceptable and said further that the slow over-rate could be allied to the bowling of eight-ball overs rather than six-ball overs.

Bradman was far too polite to point out that his research, for personal use only, had found that eight-ball overs actually quickened the game. He then turned to the front-foot aspect of the no-ball law and expressed his dissatisfaction with it. Kentish waffled a reply knowing that Bradman was right and that the West Indies bowlers had been exploiting a weakness in umpire interpretation.

During the Australian winter of 1976, Board chairman Bob Parish became aware of moves by the Gillette company – who sponsored the domestic one-day competition – to try and organise a series of limited-overs matches between the winners of Gillette trophies in Australia, England, South Africa and the West Indies (once established). To that end, Gillette had requested D. E. Benaud & Associates to prepare a feasibility study on the project. Richie Benaud became active in the matter when the Board gave in-principle support subject to a favourable report. Nothing came of the idea, but what it did do was to make Benaud even more aware of the poor standing of international cricketers.

Players were now being looked upon by the business community as usable commodities. Two Queensland players were the target of large offers: Greg Chappell was presented with a package deal by a group of Adelaide businessmen worth $8000 a year for five years to play cricket plus an annual salary of $25,000 for employment. Jeff Thomson signed a contract worth $63,000 annually with the Brisbane radio station 4IP to work for the station and to play cricket.

With cricketers retiring from the game owing to their inability to continue playing on the terms offered by the Board, Ian Chappell spoke his mind yet again. He argued that 'an annual salary for Test cricketers approaching $30,000 plus increases each year to cope with inflation' should be paid by the Board. Chappell had received only $470 from his Sheffield Shield matches in 1975–76, a season in which his leadership qualities led South Australia to one of their rare domestic trophy triumphs. At the same time Dennis Lillee calculated he made around $150 a Test after taxation and deductions for expenses, which meant $30 a day for five-day games.

In February 1976 the players had reached such an impasse with cricket's authorities that they held a dinner in Melbourne's Hilton Hotel. Present were Greg Chappell, Rodney Marsh, Rick McCosker, Ian Chappell, former Test batsman Bob Cowper, and the then president of the Australian Council of Trade Unions and future Prime Minister, Bob Hawke. Basically the players were seeking advice from Hawke on how to proceed to improve their economic lot. Hawke, a cricketing enthusiast and an accomplished player, suggested that they should avoid using the terms 'union' and 'strike' in discussions with the Board. He also proposed the concept of a 'players' liaison officer' who would act as a conciliator or intermediary between players and administrators. Bob Cowper was given this role and a fairly lengthy brief. He was to arrange match payments and annual salaries for Test players followed by a plethora of other matters which the cricketers felt the Board should know. These would include the players' views on playing conditions, tour programmes, sponsorships and promotion. Sponsorships had got out of hand with cricketers signing individually to endorse products in opposition to those supported by the Board. Cowper's role was to meet twice a year with the five Sheffield Shield captains and, after receiving their views, pass them on to the Board for action.

To prepare the way for this a letter was sent to Alan Barnes who put it on the agenda for the September 1976 Board meeting in Brisbane, held in the Queensland Cricketers Club in the aptly named Vulture Street. The delegates, who had received copies of Cowper's proposal to digest before the meeting, were vehemently against the idea. In voting against it, cricketing politics came to the fore with the three major associations (nine votes) bullying the three minor associations (five votes) into a unanimous decision. In particular, there was no way Tasmania would rock the boat: they were just on the verge of acceptance into the Sheffield Shield competition and nothing was going to affect their ambitions.

Five men dealt with this move by the players: the three Victorians, Bob Parish (chairman), Ray Steele (treasurer) and Len Maddocks along with former chairman Tim Caldwell (NSW) and Sir Donald Bradman (SA). They would not be dictated to by the players but would set up a 'Cricket sub-committee' comprising three Board representatives and each Sheffield Shield team captain. The terms of reference were:

To consider and report to the Board on any matters referred to it by the Board and on any matters raised by the players or that it considers are pertinent to the welfare of the game.

The sub-committee was instructed to 'meet at least once a year and more often if approved by the Board'. It was a classic Civil Service tactic: form a committee to keep the workers quiet and all problems will be lost in a talking-shop. As a future Australian captain, Kim Hughes, said: 'It was all a waste of time. The Board set the agenda and items for discussion became more and more trivial as the years wore on. It did nothing and solved nothing. If the Board tell you it was successful then they are only doing so to protect their entrenched viewpoint.'

Looking back on those times, David Richards, now chief executive of the Board, said the players 'wanted a players' association and the Board set up a Cricket Committee'.

Freed of his responsibilities as Australia's captain, Ian Chappell gave considerable thought to the future of Australian cricket, and even more so when he was contacted by Bob Cowper. Cowper had had long discussions with a former Perth journalist, John Cornell, who was now managing the actor Paul Hogan and producing quality television programmes. Cornell, deeply interested in the players' grievances, felt something should be done. He was contracted to the television station, Channel Nine, which was owned by Australia's richest man, Kerry Packer.

In February 1976, Packer had asked to meet the Board's representatives so that he could make an offer to them for exclusive rights to televise Test and Sheffield Shield cricket. Bob Parish and Ray Steele kept Packer waiting for four months during which time they negotiated with the Australian Broadcasting Commission a television deal worth $69,000 for each of the following three years. When Packer was finally granted an audience with Parish and his sub-committee in Melbourne in June 1976, he offered $500,000 a season for the next five years. Parish told him the ABC contract was signed and sealed.

Whereas the Board had a guarantee of $207,000, they had also just turned down $2,500,000. Packer went away convinced that something should be done as sport was not only becoming a television medium per se, it was also opening up a highly lucrative advertising market. The potential was there, but how to harness it? The answer came later in the year when John Cornell told Packer of the players' plight. Ian Chappell had provided considerable information but Cornell had also been made aware, through a high-level leak at the Queensland Cricket Association, of certain items which had been discussed at the September 1976 Board meeting.

Cornell knew that, of the $800,000 the Benson & Hedges company were planning to put into the game for the following three seasons, over seventy per cent would go straight to the Board or to State administrations. Not only was the players' reward minimal, in percentage terms their share of gate and sponsorship for the 1976–77 season would actually decrease from 7.54% the previous season to 5.55% (and, worse, to 4.44% for 1977–78).

Cornell suggested to Packer 'a series of one-day and Test matches organised privately and played as an adjunct to, but not necessarily in opposition to, the traditional game'. Packer's reply was: 'Why not do the thing properly? Let's get the world's best to play Australia's best.'

Kerry Packer, soon afterwards, formed the company which became known as World Series Cricket with 98 shares at $1 each. The major shareholder was Publishing and Broadcasting Ltd, a subsidiary of Packer's main company, Consolidated Press.

Another person involved was the former Western Australian footballer, Austin Robertson, a Perth journalist and friend of Cornell's, and also manager to a number of sportsmen, including Dennis Lillee. Ian Chappell went to South Africa in mid-1976 but on his return to Australia he and Cowper instructed Robertson to contact the players. Over a period of some months the required cricketers all signed and were paid their initial fees. Not only in Australia but all over the cricketing world players were giving their nod of approval, in great secrecy, to Packer's plan. Richie Benaud and his promotion company were hired as consultants, particularly to advise Packer how to handle the Board once the existence of WSC became known.

All was quiet. It took just one drunk player in 1977 (and, amazingly, the same person again in 1984 for another unauthorised venture) to blurt out the whole story to an astounded group of journalists at a cricket function.

A hastily arranged tour by Pakistan filled in the first part of a heavy 1976–77 season in which Australia played six Test matches in a period of under twelve weeks. The tourists agreed to an extraordinary itinerary, just five matches, three of them Tests. However, as the tour did not start until mid-December the Australian selectors had an unusually long time to assess the form of players in the Sheffield Shield. Exactly half the twenty matches were over by the end of November and the in-form players then were among batsmen, Richie Robinson (Victoria), Bruce Laird (WA), Jeff Moss (Victoria) and David Ogilvie (Queensland), none of whom would be selected now but would win future Test caps. Of the bowlers Jeff Thomson (Queensland), Dennis Lillee (WA) and the spinner Kerry O'Keeffe (NSW) were regularly taking wickets.

The Pakistan team was easily defeated on a fast Western Australian pitch in the first match, with home batsman Kim Hughes scoring an unbeaten 137 to set up a six-wicket win. Then came the first Test in Adelaide which started on Christmas Eve. Mushtaq Mohammad won the toss and batted, saw his side lose two quick wickets and watched as his batting partner Zaheer Abbas was dropped from a skyer when Jeff Thomson and Alan Turner collided in attempting the catch. Both were knocked out, and Thomson dislocated his shoulder, an injury which kept him out of Test cricket for six months.

Pakistan scored 272 and, after Christmas, Ian Davis (105) and Doug Walters (107) saw Australia to a score of 454 and a good lead. Pakistan then owed their survival to a last-wicket partnership of 87 between Asif Iqbal (152*) and Iqbal Qasim which held up the Australian quest for success. In the end the home batsmen did not try to run-chase and the game was left drawn.

New Year's Day in Melbourne saw Australia win the toss and start on their way to scoring 517 for eight declared with Greg Chappell making 121 and the red-haired, overweight Gary Cosier a career-best 168 from just 206 deliveries. In reply Pakistan were 270 for two before collapsing to 333 all out. Dennis Lillee took 6/82 but in the process earned warnings for excessive use of the bouncer and then for taking too long to complete an over. Dennis was provoked. In typical Lillee fashion, he said later: 'At the end of it all I had a fairly interesting exchange with some of the "gentlemen" sitting on their fat backsides in front of the Members' Stand.' He took 4/53 in the second innings as Australia won by 348 runs. He was named Man of the Match. Frank Tyson wrote: 'Seldom have I witnessed a fast bowling performance of such impressive proportions on a wicket [*sic*] which was so exasperatingly slow'.

Then followed a drawn match in Brisbane against Queensland in which a local batsman, Martin Kent, came to the attention of the travelling media with an unbeaten 122 in a sizzling partnership of 210 for the second-innings fifth wicket. Along with Phil Carlson (99) their stand took just over two hours.

Over four days in mid-January 1977, however, serious flaws started to appear in the Australian team. On a reasonable Sydney pitch the Pakistan pace-bowler Imran Khan took 6/102 and 6/63 as Australia fell for 211 and 180. Asif Iqbal made 120 in Pakistan's 360 as they went on to win by eight wickets.

The Australian selectors did not spend long over their choice for the short tour of New Zealand which started ten days after the Sydney Test. With an official chairman now appointed (before this he had been called quaintly 'the pilot member' of the selection committee) in Phil Ridings, he, along with Neil Harvey and Sam Loxton, gave the captaincy to Greg Chappell and the vice-captaincy to Rodney Marsh. Whether it was a mistake to appoint Marsh is open to conjecture as in future years his non-appointment as captain meant a hard time for Chappell's sucessor.

The New South Wales member of parliament, Roger Wootton, was made manager of the team. In retrospect, Wootton was treated with a lack of courtesy by the players during their five-week absence from Australia. He had no inkling of the WSC arrangements going on behind his back, and looked extremely foolish when the story eventually broke.

The team flew to Christchurch on 28 January and before the end of the month had lost two limited-overs fixtures to New Zealand. Then came four successive victories over provincial sides: Northern Districts by 113 runs (O'Keeffe 5/70 and 5/55); Wellington by 50 runs (O'Keeffe 4/39 and 6/74); Central Districts by 65 runs, and Otago by 48 runs (O'Keeffe 6/50 and 2/66).

The first Test in Christchurch was a triumph for Doug Walters and a slap in the face for his adversaries. Captain Greg Chappell had introduced early morning fitness runs on tour and, on the first morning, Walters was last out, wearing a singlet advertising his favourite brand of cigarettes. On the second morning he wore a T-shirt which stated: 'Jogging Can Kill'. On neither run was he sighted until the last two hundred yards. In the match he scored 250 of Australia's 552 at Lancaster Park sharing a record seventh-wicket stand of 217 in 187 minutes with Gary Gilmour (101). Walters' score is the highest in Test cricket by a number six batsman.

New Zealand replied with 357, Kerry O'Keeffe continuing his success on the local pitches by taking 5/101 – his 35 wickets in five matches costing 16.48 apiece – and late on the fourth day, following an Australian declaration, the Kiwis were set 350 runs for victory in 390 minutes. When the final hour began New Zealand were 260 for eight. Against all the odds and some ferocious Australian pace bowling Bevan Congdon (107*) and Dayle Hadlee held out for a draw.

Luck did not hold for the Kiwis two days later in the second Test at Eden Park, Auckland. Australia won with almost two days to spare by ten wickets after Dennis Lillee returned figures of 5/51 and 6/72.

How some of the players concentrated on the match could be questioned for, all the while, John Cornell and Austin Robertson were getting players' signatures on paper. Greg Chappell 'after a lot of thought and heartache' signed on for a fee of around $12,000, a salary of $35,000 for five years, and a $5000 per annum consultants' and commentators' fee. Likewise Lillee got his wish: payment at last, $35,000 for three years. The contracts varied: Ian Redpath, coming out of retirement, got $16,500 for one year, with Western Australian swing bowler Mick Malone getting $19,000 a year for three years. The revolution had started.

Back in Australia the Sheffield Shield competition continued on its way. With six outright wins Western Australia walked away with the title but it was events in Adelaide which caught the eye. A young fresh-faced left-hander, David Hookes from the West Torrens club, had made his first-class debut the previous season against the West Indies. Now, in a purple patch he scored five centuries in six innings, the last four in succession: 163 and 9 against Victoria; 185 and 105 in the tied match versus Queensland, and 135 and 156 against New South Wales. Having been dropped earlier in the season for poor form, Hookes had certainly come back with a bang.

His displays saw the selectors gamble with him – successfully – for the special one-off Test against England in Melbourne in mid-March. Alas, Hookes' great natural talent went to waste through his inability to accept the disciplines needed at the highest level of the game. Instead he stayed playing for South Australia until 1992, breaking most State and Shield batting records along the way.

The idea of a Test match to celebrate the centenary of Test cricket between England and Australia had come out of a discussion early in 1963 between John Trumble, of the famous Victorian cricketing family, and the then Prime Minister, Sir Robert Menzies. The minutes of the Board dated 11 September 1963 record that Trumble and Menzies suggested: 'That the centenary of English/Australia Tests in 1977 be fittingly celebrated and that a visit to Australia by an English team be arranged for that year'.

The Board agreed to note the idea and to keep the matter open on file. Their principal aim from then on, until receiving a detailed submission from the Melbourne Cricket Club ten years later, was to try and persuade successive Postmasters-General to strike a special commemorative postage stamp to mark the occasion.

When the Trumble family raised the matter again with Menzies, he contacted Melbourne Club committeeman Hans Ebeling, who was able to get approval from his committee to make an approach to the Victorian Cricket Association. When the VCA took the project on board, both parties wrote officially to Alan Barnes in order to get the matter discussed at a subsequent Board meeting.

On 5 September 1973, Board delegate and VCA president Ray Steele put the Trumble/Ebeling proposal to his fellow Board members. While a postage stamp still held priority in most minds the concept of 'a suitable commemorative match on the Melbourne Cricket Ground in March 1977' was not rejected. However, no delegate was going to vote for such an event 'until further enquiries on the idea had been made with the Marylebone Cricket Club'.

Twelve months later in September 1974, Board delegates were very pleased to hear that 'the Postmaster-General Senator Reg Bishop had advised that he had approved the inclusion of the proposed commemorative 1977 cricket stamp in his Department's tentative stamp issue programme for that year'. This caused much urgent discussion and, after a while, it was resolved 'that the matter of the design of the stamp be appropriately discussed with the relevant section of the Department'. Ray Steele was delegated to inform the Melbourne Cricket Club of the excellent progress the Board had made in this regard.

It seemed that most of the men who made up the Board were more excited at the prospect of a postage stamp than in staging any special match. It needed the firm hand of Bob Parish to relate his correspondence and telephone conversations with Donald Carr, secretary of the Test and County Cricket Board.

Carr was not too sure as to whether the England team's itinerary would allow a special Test, but he gave Parish a promise that every effort would be made to schedule such a contest. With the help of Len Maddocks, Parish pushed through a proposal 'to stage a commemorative Test match'.

Parish was finding it difficult to get some of his fellow delegates to take the matter seriously and also for them to dismiss the idea of a Victorian 'plot' against the other States. Even to the present day 'States Rights' is a daily issue in Australian life, it being enshrined in Section 92 of the Commonwealth (Federal) Constitution. New South Wales was the senior State of Australia, claimed their cricket administrators, so why can't the match be played in Sydney?

Bob Parish was astute enough to ignore the quasi-political whinings of his colleagues although it took him until the last day of the September 1975 Board meeting in Sydney to get his way. He spelt out to the Board 'how important this proposed fixture is to Australian cricket'. He talked about the history of the game, the first Test in 1877 and how he wanted the dates to be as near as possible in March. He then hit the jackpot and a unanimous vote when he said: 'It is proposed to extend an invitation to His Royal Highness, The Duke of Edinburgh'. With that Parish won hands down.

From then on, the postage stamp was virtually forgotten as Parish proposed 'that a sub-committee be set up comprising the three Victorian Board representatives, representatives of the Melbourne Cricket Club, and Sir John Holland of the Victorian Historical Committee; that all arrangements be left in the hands of the sub-committee; that Mr David Richards, secretary of the Victorian Cricket Association, be appointed as assistant secretary of the Board for this purpose; and that copies of all relevant correspondence be forwarded to the Board secretary for information'.

The vote was carried, although not unanimously. Parish had got his way and watched as the Great Man just shrugged his shoulders. He was not against the idea, although he was not happy with some of the arrangements. However, word of the match became known, as Lord's gave it their blessing, and various ideas flowed in from cricket aficionados around the country. The majority were treated with contempt and when one did hit the Board's agenda paper (Mr J. Dixon of Frankston, Victoria, who suggested that there should be both an English and an Australian umpire for the Centenary Test) it resulted in a motion saying: 'That no English umpires' representative, as such, be invited'.

David Richards organised the whole event splendidly, and detailed news of it was released at a specially convened press conference in Melbourne on 15 September 1976. The cricket world was told of the greatest gathering of former Test stars: 244 would accept and 26 decline due to age or infirmity. It became the greatest reunion in cricket history.

And the postage stamp? It took the Board half-a-minute to approve the design six months before its appearance. After that it was never mentioned again.

# 30

# WSC v. The Board

As the members of the Australian Cricket Board went about their business they remained totally unaware of the great storm about to erupt. The fact that not one player, nor any State official who was in the know, passed on any hint or information showed the disdain in which cricketers held the Board.

As a try-on, Eric Beecher, the then editor of the Australian *Cricketer* magazine, wrote to Alan Barnes requesting information about the Board's finances, annual reports and constitution. Under current New South Wales State legislation, the Board was not compelled to furnish these to the Companies Office, hence the secrecy which surrounded their workings. The reply to Beecher was waffled nonsense which the next meeting of the Board endorsed at their gathering in Sydney on 12 January 1977. They gave far more attention to a report received from the Watsonian Cricket Club in Scotland which, 'praised the cricketing ability and general behaviour and deportment of Mr K. J. Hughes of Western Australia who had received Board approval to play in Scotland during the Australian winter of 1976.'

At this meeting Bob Parish informed delegates of the details of correspondence and discussions he had had with Talbot Duckmanton, general manager of the Australian Broadcasting Commission, concerning payments for television relays to Australia from the 1977 tour to England. Duckmanton had been told by the Test and County Cricket Board: 'That we are prepared to offer exclusive live rights in Australia for a sum of $120,000'. The ABC felt that this sum was unreasonably high considering that they were only going to charge $35,000 for the six 1978–79 Tests to be beamed back to England.

Duckmanton asked for the Board's help and Parish agreed to discuss the matter with TCCB representatives at a special meeting planned for Melbourne in March.

While this was going on, the television magnate, Kerry Packer, offered the TCCB $118,000 for exclusive rights to the five Tests being played between June and August. When Lord's referred the offer back to Australia Parish informed the March meeting that the ABC interests must be preserved. On hearing this Packer was outraged and doubled his original offer to $236,000 which won him the rights he sought.

This action caused the Board to move quickly. Further talks were held with Talbot Duckmanton, with Parish and Barnes signing a long-term contract which gave radio and television rights to the ABC until 1979. It was all arranged in undue haste, for a paltry sum of money and without consideration to other parties. A possible sale of some television rights to the former Test player, Ron Archer, manager of Brisbane's 0/10 Network, fell through when Archer found out the conditions to be imposed, which included only 30-second 'bites' for television news bulletins.

Too late the Board realised that they had not acted quickly enough to quell the past grievances of players. The inaugural meeting of the Cricket sub-committee in Adelaide on 22 December 1976 had the Board delegate, Ray Steele, saying 'it was an unqualified success' and he felt that 'it had materially assisted in overcoming communication problems which had existed with the players'. In a way Steele was right for it formed the vehicle through which player payments were increased for the various domestic and overseas tours which occurred in the following two years.

But this did not stop the top players signing with Kerry Packer. He was providing them with alternative employment and to a man they deserted the Board. As the writer Jack Pollard observed: 'The fact that so many signed at a point when match fees were rising and no organisation existed to stage WSC games, demonstrated how unanimous was the players' discontent and how badly ACB officials misjudged the players' mood'.

All these manoeuvrings were put to one side, however, for the Centenary Test at Melbourne. Like a dream being fulfilled, the match lasted until the final hour of the last day with an astonishing result. England, captained by Tony Greig, put Australia into bat and almost immediately there was drama as Rick McCosker had his jaw broken from a rising delivery bowled by Bob Willis. Then came a collapse as only Greg Chappell, who made 40, held his ground while Australia fell for 138. Dennis Lillee (6/26) and Max Walker (4/54) now struck back, dismissing England for 95 on the second day. The weather was balmy, the pitch in superb condition: the only possible explanation for two batting collapses was that the occasion had been too overwhelming for the players. It all came right, however, in the respective second innings. Rodney Marsh became the first Australian wicketkeeper to score a century against England with his unbeaten 110. Ian Davis (68), Doug Walters (66) and David Hookes (56) all hit out until Chappell declared at 419 for nine. Even McCosker, his face encircled by bandages, added runs with Marsh in a situation which Dennis Lillee described as 'one of the most courageous acts I ever saw'.

Tony Greig had to ponder his task. To make 463 runs to win in 590 minutes was an awesome task but his players stuck to it. Dennis Amiss (64), Mike Brearley (43), Alan Knott (42) and Greig (41) himself all tried valiantly but they were overshadowed by Derek Randall.

A permanently fidgety character, Randall talked to anyone and everyone. He was not disturbed by Melbourne's gregarious Bay 13 crowd chanting 'Lilleeeeeee Lilleeeeeee' and howling for blood. When his innings finally came to an end he had scored 174 off 353 balls in 446 minutes with 21 fours.

Dennis Lillee (5/139) finished off the tail and the great occasion was over. The Australians had won, by 45 runs, the very same margin of victory as in 1877. Enjoyed by 248,260 spectators who paid $418,019 in gate money, the five days had epitomised all that was good in the game of cricket.

In retrospect it seems quite strange that a gathering of the cricketing clans in Melbourne did not produce any leaks or discussions on the proposed breakaway movement. As early as September 1976, the Melbourne Cricket Club secretary, Ian Johnson, had a sense that something strange was happening when the Club received a letter from the general manager of the local television station, GTV9, making an application for the use of the ground for a series of cricket matches from December 1977 to February 1978. After consulting with his committee Johnson wrote back asking whether the proposed matches had been approved by the VCA or the Board. He had no reply from the Packer group nor was there ever any application to play on the MCG.

The day after the Centenary Test, Ross Edwards joined WSC and took his $8333 signing-on fee for a contract of $25,000 a year for two years. This signing completed the list of twenty-eight players from Australia drawn up by Ian Chappell. Now it was time to sign up eighteen West Indians, and twenty-two others for a Rest of the World team.

From all around the cricketing world players were signing up, many to secure their futures, others as a final fling before retirement. Some who were not approached by WSC, were to say that they had been, but had refused in order to stay with the establishment.*

*Players under contract to WSC and PBL Marketing were:
AUSTRALIA: Ray Bright, Greg Chappell, Ian Chappell, Trevor Chappell, Ian Davis, Ross Edwards, Gary Gilmour, David Hookes, Martin Kent, Bruce Laird, Robbie Langer, Dennis Lillee, Rick McCosker, Graham McKenzie, Ashley Mallett, Mick Malone, Rodney Marsh, Kerry O'Keeffe, Len Pascoe, Wayne Prior, Ian Redpath, Richie Robinson, Jeff Thomson, Max Walker, Doug Walters, Graeme Watson, Kepler Wessels, Dennis Yagmich. *(see overleaf)*

The signings went on until a few days before the twenty-eighth Australian team flew to London, on 21 April 1977. The official team was chosen by the regular selection panel of Phil Ridings, Neil Harvey and Sam Loxton. Dennis Lillee was unavailable to tour because of vertebrae fractures, a return of his old injury. In the circumstances the chosen management team of Len Maddocks (Victoria) and his treasurer Norman McMahon (Queensland) could not have been more inappropriate. Their almost total lack of control over the tourists, along with some unfortunate behaviour by certain members of the side, no doubt brought on following the Packer revelations, has left the 1977 tourists as being one of the less admired in Australia's cricket history.

For the nineteen-week tour the players' pay had risen dramatically. Even allowing for a 115 per cent rise in the Consumer Price Index since the last full tour in 1972, their $10,890 fee represented a figure 83 per cent higher than the adult male average weekly earnings. In 1972 it had been just 40 per cent higher.

The party arrived in London to find the weather affecting all matches. They did not complete a game until mid-May and by then the revelations of Kerry Packer's plans had been made. The subsequent newspaper coverage affected the team badly and the players split into camps, the most ostracised being the four non-Packer players, Cosier, Dymock, Hughes and Serjeant.

The Board too took the whole issue so badly that, when Bob Parish flew to London to attend the International Cricket Conference, he refused to discuss anything with the Australian captain, Greg Chappell. Tony Greig was sacked as England's captain and Richie Benaud found himself shunned by players he had known for years. Morale in the team was low, under the constant threat that they would be sent home.

Greg Chappell had continually to air his displeasure with his team's performance particularly after their second successive one-day international defeat. Only his determined 125 not out in the rain at The Oval saw Chappell pull back a victory in the three-match series.

The tour was past the halfway mark before the first Test began. Unusually, this was at Lord's and was staged as a Jubilee Test to

---

WEST INDIES: Jim Allen, Richard Austin, Colin Croft, Wayne Daniel, Roy Fredericks, Joel Garner, Gordon Greenidge, Desmond Haynes, David Holford, Michael Holding, Bernard Julien, Collis King, Clive Lloyd, Deryck Murray, Albert Padmore, Vivian Richards, Andy Roberts, Lawrence Rowe.

WORLD TEAM: Dennis Amiss, Asif Iqbal, Eddie Barlow, Bob Cunis, Tony Greig, Haroon Rashid, Denys Hobson, Imran Khan, Javed Miandad, Alan Knott, Garth Le Roux, Majid Khan, Mushtaq Mohammad, Graeme Pollock, Mike Procter, Clive Rice, Barry Richards, Sarfraz Nawaz, John Snow, Derek Underwood, Bob Woolmer, Zaheer Abbas.

celebrate the twenty-five year reign of the monarch. It produced gate receipts of £220,384 and an attendance of 101,050.

A new reign in cricket started with the appointment as England's captain of Mike Brearley. A cultured, educated man, Brearley had an ability to bring out the best from even the most average player. As one Australian Test cricketer said of him two years later: 'Mike Brearley has a degree in People'. Clear thinking, calmness under pressure, and decisiveness were his major qualities: the three Australian captains who faced him over the next four years were no match for him.

The first day of the Test saw England dismissed for 216, as Pascoe, Robinson and Serjeant became three of Australia's six new Test caps for the series. A debut 81 from Craig Serjeant, the Perth pharmacist, saw Australia to 296 as Willis took 7/78. Rain then lost nearly a day's play and the match fizzled out into a draw.

At this time, while the players were trying harder to please the large English crowds, events in Australia were moving quickly. The Board was tut-tutting and the New South Wales Cricket Association was spending its assets on legal fees. Much went on behind the scenes, particularly in Sydney, and only the effluxion of time will see the whole story eventually surface. State and Federal politicians became involved, as did businessmen. Not only were the Board outflanked, they acted in the way people expected.

The classic story concerns the Sydney Cricket Ground and the Trust which ran the complex. On 17 May 1977, WSC applied for the use of the SCG on thirteen days during 1977–78 and offered $260,000 for the privilege. On 25 July the Trust declined the application. Next day the Trust was sacked by the NSW government of Premier Neville Wran, a man generally known by his nickname of 'Nifty'. The Trust was immediately reconstituted – which caused the NSWCA to institute an action in the NSW Equity Court challenging the Trust's right to let WSC use the ground on dates that were needed for Sheffield Shield and Test cricket.

The NSWCA case rested on the Sydney Cricket Ground and Sports Ground Amalgamation Act, 1951, which gave the Association priority use over the ground during the cricket season. The same such right applied to the NSW Rugby League during winter. In court Mr Justice Helsham decided in favour of the Association. It was a very short-lived triumph for the government immediately rushed through a Bill stripping the NSWCA of its traditional right over the SCG. However, the legislative process did stall WSC for a season and they had to make do with the neighbouring Sydney Showground arena.

Back in England relations were getting worse between team and management, and clashes bordering on violence were reported. The second Test, at Old Trafford, saw Greg Chappell score 112 and Doug

Walters 88 but morale was so poor that defeat by nine wickets scarcely worried the team. The third Test at Trent Bridge had a similar pattern. Rick McCosker scored 51 and 107 in Australia's seven-wicket loss, although this was made worse by the news during the match that the Packer cricketers were to be banned from playing Test cricket.

The players were now just going through the motions in non-Test fixtures. A good win over Lancashire prior to the fourth Test was soured by the boiling over of tension against the four non-Packer players who were constantly joking amongst themselves as to who would be Australia's next Test captain. The Test, at Headingley, is remembered for Geoffrey Boycott (191) scoring his one hundredth first-class century, so becoming the first man to accomplish such a feat during a Test. Australia's display was woeful. They were dismissed for 103 and 248 to lose by an innings and 85 runs.

The end of one of Australia's least happy tours came with a draw in the fifth Test at The Oval. Mick Malone, in his solitary Test, took 5/63 and scored a career-best 46, as did Max Walker with his unbeaten 78. Rain caused nearly two days' play to be lost but at least the Post Office scores service could claim success: 22,556,000 calls throughout the series.

By now Kerry Packer had launched his action against the International Cricket Conference for banning his players from all matches under their jurisdiction. The High Court in London, after a case which lasted for thirty-one days, gave its ruling fairly and squarely in favour of Packer. They ruled that no one body had a monopoly of the game of cricket: the Australian Cricket Board was stunned.

Prior to this judgment Bob Parish had released a lengthy statement, a response which came four months after the Board's initial reaction to the formation of WSC. In retrospect one can see a Board completely confused and hurt as to why its senior players had chosen to sign with a private promoter. Parish tried, in nine detailed pages, to argue Board policy. In one instance he said: 'the Board reaffirms that it will pay to the players the maximum it can afford after taking into consideration its responsibility to Australian cricket at all levels'.

Parish argued the point that the selfish few would jeopardise cricket down to 'school, junior and country grades', without realising that the opposite was the case. Any sport with mass television coverage, presented in a way to capture an audience, will bring new participants to the game. A prime recent example has been the boom in rugby at junior and local levels following the successful television coverage of the 1991 World Cup held in Britain and France.

Far from being the pariah the cricket establishment made him out to be – and in certain cases still does – it can be seriously argued that Kerry Packer was the saviour of the game. For there was an immediate response in England where the Cornhill Insurance Company attached their name and sponsorship to Test cricket. The harmonious relationship lasted for many years.

The crude facts were that the majority of the men running Australian cricket in 1977 were inadequate for the job. Pleasant men though they may have been, they were lost in the sea of change that was enveloping the sporting world. As one delegate of the time has said: 'When I first started to play we were paid £1 a day for first-class matches. The players then [referring to 1977] were just downright greedy. If it was good enough for us why not them?' Another said: 'What we did at the time we thought was the best for Australian cricket. We just had no idea of the depth of feeling of the players.'

The Board's attitude to the WSC fixtures was succinctly summed up by the treasurer, Ray Steele, who said that he hoped nobody would watch their matches. To try and stop people from watching the sport you enjoy because a part of it was being organised by a person you disliked encapsulated the overall problems in Australian cricket at that time. It was like the story of the little boy who, on being bowled, picked up his bat and went home.

In his first season of World Series Cricket in 1977–78, Packer produced numerous innovations to the game. He made it exciting for a completely new audience, both at the grounds and on television. He built up a large and enthusiastic following for matches which were keenly competitive and not just the exhibition games the purists claimed they would be.

There were six 'Supertests' and numerous one-day matches for both 'The International Cup' and in rural areas for 'The Country Cup Championship'. Proper cricket in the bush, instead of the occasional, patronisingly given one-day match against a touring team, created a huge growth in cricket support. So much so that, within a short time of this WSC venture, the Board announced that some Sheffield Shield matches might well be allocated to country centres. The financial success of New South Wales' one game a season in Newcastle has constantly proved this policy to be correct.

The first Supertest, held at VFL Park,* Waverley – a south-eastern suburb of Melbourne – saw WSC Australia make 256 and 192 and lose to the West Indies, 214 and 247 for seven, by three wickets. A fortnight later in mid-December at the Sydney Showground WSC Australia, 251 and 182, again lost to the West Indies, 336 and 101 for one, by nine wickets.

The tables were turned in the third match, held at West Lakes, Adelaide, when WSC Australia 388 (Ian Chappell 141) and 267 for

*VFL stands for 'Victorian Football League'.

eight declared (Laird 106) defeated West Indies 145 (Greg Chappell, 5/20) and 290 (Vivian Richards, 123) by 220 runs.

Then followed three Supertests against Tony Greig's World XI. Back in Sydney in mid-January, WSC Australia 304 (Laird 106) and 128 (Roberts 6/69) lost to World XI 290 (Vivian Richards 119, Walker 7/88) and 145 for six by four wickets.

Gloucester Park in Perth witnessed a quite splendid match at the end of January 1978 when the World XI scored a staggering 433 for one from 74 overs at the end of the first day's play. Eventually the World XI made 625 (Barry Richards 207, Vivian Richards 177, Greenidge 140, Bright 5/149) and defeated WSC Australia, 393 (Greg Chappell 174) and 159, by an innings and 73 runs.

The final five-day match took place back in Melbourne in early February, with spectators enjoying a run glut, including a partnership of 219 between Rick McCosker and Greg Chappell. In the end WSC Australia, 538 for six declared (Greg Chappell 246 not out, McCosker 129) and 167 (Garner 5/52), defeated World XI 434 (Vivian Richards 170) and 230 (Walker 5/62, Lillee 5/82) by 41 runs.

With the Indians due to tour for the 1977–78 official season, the Board searched for a successor as captain to Greg Chappell. The players left did not fit the bill so they turned to Bobby Simpson who was still playing grade cricket in Sydney for Western Suburbs. At forty-one Simpson had not played first-class cricket for ten years but he accepted the challenge offered to him.

Although Simpson succeeded on the field he became somewhat of a thorn in the side of the Board with his continued ideas for improving the players' lot. This was the last sort of advice the Board needed at this juncture. Before the season began they could not even agree their own financial report, despite their own self-auditing. They fiddled while Rome burned: a sum of $23,436 was transferred from 'the team sponsorship account', i.e. players' money, into 'the account to be used to defray the Board's anticipated administration costs'; then the 1976–77 player payments for bonus and sponsorship were fixed which added a good line to the Board's press release that denied the players' complaint of poor payment for the season. In fact the Board tried every move they knew to put themselves in a good light. The disguise fell apart when the Queensland Cricket Association was told that payments to players in matches under their control 'were excessive'.

Requests, which in past years had either been ignored or rejected, were now looked upon solemnly. A letter from the secretary of the Department of Environment, Housing and Community Development 'requesting the name of a suitable coach who would be willing to coach for a period of three months in India', had received a nil response from the State Associations. Normally the answer would have been 'no interest', now it was felt: 'That the Board had an obligation to do all in its power to submit the name of a suitable person, because it would be disastrous from a public relations point of view if the matter was successfully dealt with by a private promoter'.

Muddle upon muddle took place regarding promotional activities, and main sponsors, Benson & Hedges, became quite irate at some of the Board's plans. Even legal action taken against Messrs Caldwell, Parish and Barnes by World Series Cricket (as an aftermath of the London case, Packer took action in the Australian courts to stop the Board interfering with WSC activities) could have been resolved by an immediate round-table conference instead of costing tens of thousands of dollars in legal fees before a settlement was agreed.

Yet again it fell to the Great Man to spell out some facts of life to his colleagues. Bradman twice, on successive days in September 1977, warned his fellow delegates on the Packer troubles and the issue of television rights. On 8 September he said in a Board meeting 'that we should remain with the Australian Broadcasting Commission for only the next year but the time has now come for discussion on the question of exclusive rights'. The next day he repeated his warning in response to a bid from Ron Archer who sought exclusive television rights for the 0/10 Network 'at the conclusion of the existing contract with the ABC'. Even before WSC cricket started Bradman could see the dead-end road up which his colleagues were travelling.

Probably the most amazing statement made to that very difficult Board meeting came from Ray Steele when he reported 'that the Television Sub-Committee had not been able to sell commercial television rights for 1977–78'. However he did add 'that the 0/10 Network had purchased the rights to the domestic limited-overs competition for 1977–78 for $10,000 as compared to $9000 in 1976–77'. Great joy was expressed at this news. The fact that Kerry Packer's Channel Nine – through its various companies – paid around $25,000,000 in setting up and televising World Series Cricket showed that the protagonists were living in completely different worlds.

At the conclusion of the Board meeting the chairman, Bob Parish, said that he hoped it would be a good cricket season and that the final arbiters would be the public and people of Australia. He concluded: 'Let us hope our friends stop with us'.

The Board was fortunate that the official Test series with India was so evenly balanced with Australia finally winning by three matches to two. Crowds for the twenty-five days of play came to 256,594, just a few more than those who watched the five days of the Centenary Test. It could have been a lot worse as fourteen of those Test days had attendances of only four figures.

The Indian tourists played their first serious match against South Australia in early November 1977, winning easily by six wickets. Then came the same result against Victoria and New South Wales, and an improvement to a margin of an innings and 123 runs over Queensland.

The first Test in Brisbane was a thrilling affair. Six Australians made their debut: Wayne Clark, Paul Hibbert, Tony Mann, David Ogilvie, Steve Rixon and Peter Toohey. The new curator at the 'Gabba overwatered the pitch which gave the Indian spinners an ideal surface. The new Australians fell to the spin of Bishan Bedi (5/55) for 166 but the Indians then surprised everyone by only scoring 153 on a pitch which had rolled-out into a perfect track. Then came the revival with Bobby Simpson scoring 89, and a valuable last-wicket stand of 50 between Alan Hurst and Jeff Thomson, who had been prevented from joining WSC by his commitment as a Public Relations executive to a Queensland radio network. Left to score 341 in over two days the Indians fell short by sixteen runs even after a splendid 113 from Sunil Gavaskar.

The Indians flew west and were badly beaten by the Western Australian cricket machine. The strength of the game in Perth could afford to lose players such as Lillee, Marsh, Laird, Malone and Langer and still demonstrate its great ability. The second Test was another splendid contest with the result coming with just two wickets and twenty-two deliveries remaining. The free scoring of both sides was reflected in the aggregate of 1468 runs made in the match. For India, Sunil Gavaskar (127) and Mohinder Amarnath (100) scored centuries with Bishan Bedi claiming 5/89 and 5/105. The Australians had 176 from Simpson – the oldest Australian to score a century in a home Test – and a quite amazing 105 from night-watchman Tony Mann. The Australian fourth-innings score of 342 for eight was the highest ever to win a Test at home.

Two narrow defeats sent the downhearted Indians to Tasmania, who celebrated their initial season in the Sheffield Shield by beating the tourists by 84 runs in Hobart and by three wickets in Launceston. All the more credit to Bedi who made three tactical changes in his team for the third Test in Melbourne where he took 2/71 and 4/58 and his spinning partner Bhagwat Chandrasekhar 6/52 and 6/52, as Australia were routed by 222 runs.

Two days later in Sydney the fourth Test saw Bedi (3/49 and 2/62), Chandrasekhar (4/30 and 2/85) and their fellow spinner Erapally Prasanna (1/14 and 4/51) rout Australia by an innings and two runs. This brought forth changes from the Australian selectors for the final Test in Adelaide: four new boys in Ian Callen, Rick Darling, Graeme Wood and Bruce Yardley with a recall for Graham Yallop. The gamble paid off as Yallop (121) and Simpson (100) led the charge to 505. India reached 269 in reply but the follow-on was not enforced. Darling's second half-century then took Australia to 256 which left India plenty of time to score 493. The fact that they reached 445, and the second highest fourth-innings total in Test cricket, was an immense credit to their discipline. Australia's 47-run win and the three-two series victory came on their captain's forty-second birthday.

It was an unfortunate season for Tasmania to be blooded into Sheffield Shield cricket, and no-one was surprised that the surfeit of first-class cricket saw attendances fall all around the country. Western Australia retained the trophy, winning seven of their nine matches outright. Queensland produced the season's highest run-getter in the red-bearded David Ogilvie who became the fifth batsman to pass one thousand Shield runs in a season. His 1060 runs, including six centuries, came at an average of 58.89.

The Australian team to tour the West Indies from February to May 1978 was announced before the final Test against India. The side chosen was, at best, no better than a good club combination with one or two star players. The chosen fifteen were: Wayne Clark, Kim Hughes, Craig Serjeant, Graeme Wood and Bruce Yardley (WA); Ian Callen, Jim Higgs, Trevor Laughlin and Graham Yallop (Victoria); Steve Rixon, Bobby Simpson and Peter Toohey (NSW); Gary Cosier and Jeff Thomson (Queensland) and Rick Darling (SA). The selection caused a storm in Queensland with both their delegates to the Board being reprimanded for their adverse comments. They really had no case for there were far better cricketers left behind, particularly in Western Australia; it was a typical case of wanting pro-rata State selections instead of choosing by ability.

A number of matters concerning the tour worried the Board delegates as they convened their meeting in Adelaide prior to the fifth Test. They were made aware of a drugs problem in Australian sport which had never before been considered by them, particularly not in regard to cricket, and they were equally concerned that the more excitable press might pick up the fact that one player enjoyed the company of other men. As it was no stories on either made the back pages of any newspaper.

Then came a submission to the Board from the Australian captain. Never before had such an issue been debated as Bob Parish read, 'a letter to me from R. B. Simpson Promotions Pty Ltd proposing that they be appointed to perform public relations work for the Board during the Australian team's tour of the West Indies'. Parish went on to explain that Simpson had put to him the fact that 'he would suffer financially by reason of his inclusion in the team, and the appointment of his company to perform the Board's public relations functions would assist this aspect'.

Clearly the Board wanted to assist Simpson in any way they could, but under no circumstances could it be seen that the captaincy had a condition of employment attached to it. As always Sir Donald Bradman produced the solution which saw the sponsorship sub-committee utilise Simpson's company 'in ways beneficial to the promotion of official cricket'.

When Simpson attended the Board meeting on the morning of the fifth Test against India – prior to going on to the field and making a century – he proved to be a quite different type of visitor from the two Chappell brothers who had preceded him.

Simpson had prepared his brief, not to antagonise, but to get his way by playing to the unwritten rules acceptable to the men surrounding him. The austere boardroom, with a solitary kitsch picture of the Queen staring down at him, would have made him realise these were worried men, for the thick files of paper in front of each contained details which a number found difficult to grasp. To their visitor it made a black-comedy impression. There was no doubting these Board delegates were well-meaning people, but whatever the rights and wrongs, the professionalism of Packer's backroom staff with their commercial expertise made the Board's men look dull, slow, and lacking in enterprise.

In replying to a profuse welcome of grateful thanks Simpson said that the main purpose of attending 'was to engender a good relationship between players and administrators, and to ensure that cricketers remain playing under the Board's auspices'. In referring to 'the recent cricket series conducted by a private promoter', Simpson felt 'the situation should be accepted'. He pushed the Board to consider a number of possibilities: a regular newsletter to first-class cricketers (which, when it did appear, read like a Parliamentary report and was ignored by most players); a player representative on any disciplinary committee; better promotion of the game by the Board; a suggestion that State Associations meet player-representatives from each grade or district club on a regular basis for an exchange of views and, importantly, a general wish from the players for the immediate introduction of six-ball overs (a request granted a year later).

In an unusual move, as Simpson rose to leave the meeting, all fourteen delegates stood to applaud him. That had not happened to Ian Chappell.

Simpson's words could not have come more sweetly to the ears of David Richards. The young VCA secretary had been trying to drum into the Board the need for far better cricket promotions and, along with Tom Worrell of Sportsplan Marketing, had presented a number of options for consideration.

What Richards and Worrell knew from their market research was that the Sydney and Melbourne media were moving away from blindly supporting the Board and were taking a much softer line towards WSC. Public opinion was accepting 'the move towards this Americanisation of cricket' for Packer's 1978–79 plans were creating considerable interest. The innovations of coloured clothing and cricket under floodlights had great public appeal and Richards, in an excellent report, made a number of fairly radical suggestions. The Board had to act and, by giving Richards a virtual *carte-blanche*, served unwritten notice to Alan Barnes that his style of administration was nearing its conclusion.

When the history of the Australian Cricket Board comes to be written, one hopes that some of their more esoteric debates are recorded. A proposal that was discussed seriously in 1978 was for 'an international competition' to be held in Australia during December 1979 and January 1980. The idea was that 'this could provide active and attractive play in a period free of other international competition'. The *Pacific Cup* would enable Australia to play a series of one-day matches against India, New Zealand and Sri Lanka plus the other cricketing nations of Fiji, Bangladesh, the United States, Malaysia and Papua New Guinea. This form of thinking had obviously taken into consideration the likely spectator support for, say, Bangladesh against Malaysia at the Melbourne Cricket Ground or the United States versus Papua New Guinea in Sydney.

Even though the Packer organisation had their 'mole' in Australian cricket administration, no word of this plan ever reached their headquarters in Park Street, Sydney. The Board's proposal was discussed many times by the Programme sub-committee and was only shelved when both sides agreed to a peace.

The touring team flew from Sydney on 12 February with Bobby Simpson as captain and Fred Bennett as manager. The vice-captaincy position had revealed a typical Board farce as, in the five days from the announcement of the team, three different players had been named as vice-captain. First the position was given to Graham Yallop; then to Craig Serjeant and finally to Jeff Thomson – all because of internal squabblings on the inevitable 'State's rights'.

The Board circumvented any legal problems by only selecting players 'who had made themselves available for Australian Cricket Board-controlled matches in the 1978–79 season'. Although this effectively ruled out the WSC players, it did not stop Jeff Thomson from defecting some months later.

The first match, at Warner Park, St Kitts, saw the tourists get off to a good start. Wood (122) and Simpson (113) scored centuries while Higgs (6/91 and 6/71) bamboozled the locals with his leg-spin.

A horrific 132-run loss in a one-day international at St John's, Antigua, was effectively forgotten when Trinidad were beaten by six wickets at Queen's Park, Rick Darling scoring 105 and Bruce Yardley taking nine wickets in the match with his fast off-spin.

The first Test in Trinidad was a debacle. The West Indies, with all their WSC players available, just walked over the young Australians by an innings and 106 runs in two-and-a-half days. A respite in Barbados for Serjeant (114) and Simpson (102) to make hundreds against the islanders preceded the second Test in Bridgetown. Again it was a hopeless task as the West Indies won by nine wickets in half the allotted time. Graham Yallop made a minor piece of cricketing history by wearing a helmet, a first in Test matches.

As the tourists were in Georgetown playing Guyana at the Bourda ground – with unbeaten centuries from Yallop (118) and Cosier (114) plus 123 from Darling – the West Indies Cricket Board of Control found themselves at crisis point with their players. Before the first Test the players had demanded more money and from then on relations had worsened. More of the West Indian cricketers signed up with WSC and, after various selection changes for the third Test in Georgetown, the Packer players withdrew from the team. A new side was selected with the captaincy passing from Clive Lloyd to Alvin Kallicharran.

The West Indies Board chairman, Jeffrey Stollmeyer, tried hard to patch up differences but, with the WSC players refusing to say if they were available for the forthcoming tour to India, a new team had to be blooded. Kerry Packer flew to Barbados, met his cricketers, and also appeared on television to say how poorly the Caribbean associations paid their players. This gave him widespread support throughout the islands, a situation he exploited the following year.

Without their menacing pacemen the West Indies were now at the Australians' level for the last three Tests. Jeff Thomson and Wayne Clark shared eight wickets on the first day in Georgetown as the West Indies reached 205. Simpson (67), Rixon (54) and Wood (50) made half-centuries as Australia gained a first-innings lead of 81. The West Indies hit back to make 439 and the question was, could Simpson's young Australians score Test cricket's third-highest winning total to pull the series back to two-one? The fact that they did was, in part, due to a courageous fourth-wicket partnership of 251 between Wood (126) and Serjeant (124).

The balance turned for a fortnight following that three-wicket victory. Four days later Wayne Clark took 7/26 and 5/45 as the Windward Islands were beaten by 52 runs, after which the West Indies lost a one-day international, at Victoria Park, St Lucia, by just one run. Back in Port-of-Spain the fourth Test was a most even contest for the first three days. The West Indies scored 292: Australia 290. Second time around West Indies reached 290 and all looked set for another thrilling finish. But it was not to be. Off-spinner Derek Parry took five wickets for six runs in 24 balls as Australia collapsed for 94.

Victory over Jamaica by two wickets was followed by the fifth and most controversial Test of an unsatisfactory series. In the Jamaica match the umpire, Douglas Sang Hue, twice called Bruce Yardley for throwing. When Sang Hue was appointed to umpire the final Test the Australians objected. A replacement umpire, Wesley Malcolm, was chosen along with the experienced Ralph Gosein.

The Australians held the upper hand throughout. Peter Toohey (122) scored his solitary Test century out of 343, after which Trevor Laughlin's medium-pace claimed 5/101 as the West Indies reached 280. Batting with aggression Toohey (97) and Wood (90) enabled Simpson to declare at 305 for three, giving the West Indies the whole of the fifth day to survive. At 88 for five it looked all over but Kallicharran played a captain's innings of 126. At 258 for eight, Vanburn Holder was given out by umpire Malcolm which left the last pair 38 balls in which to hold out. The crowd rioted at Holder's dismissal and hurled stones and debris on to the field. All attempts to complete the match that day were fruitless and an attempt to finish the game next morning failed when umpire Gosein refused to officiate.

The tour was a financial disaster for the West Indies Board. They lost over £106,000, money they could ill afford. In trying to field their strongest team, then being in dispute with their players, cost the WICBC in many ways whereas the West Indian WSC players benefited as they had won an extra $78,735 in prize money from Packer's first season of cricket.

On his return from the West Indies, Bobby Simpson expressed his intense dislike of WSC and all it stood for. His speech to the National Press Club in Canberra made enemies of some former friends. But the Board recorded: 'Mr Simpson's address had been very well received and had contained a substantial amount of factual information which assisted in the promotion of official cricket'. Delegates resolved: 'That the tape of Mr Simpson's speech should be obtained and circulated to all state associations'.

As much as they fawned over Simpson, the Board had to draw the line somewhere. Simpson asked Parish for a guarantee that he would be picked for the Tests against England in the 1978–79 season should he stay in first-class cricket. The Board refused any such promise and so Simpson retired again, with ten comeback Tests behind him. It would be eight further years before the Board again pleaded with Simpson to help them out of trouble once more.

When Simpson addressed the Board in Adelaide in January 1978, the

Victorian delegate, Len Maddocks, asked him if he knew, apart from Western Australia, if there was any pressure to form a players' association. Simpson did not know of any, adding that the young players were still too new to do anything that would not encourage them to feel that they were part of the game. Yet a Professional Cricketers' Association (PCA) of Australia had been formed, four months earlier, in September 1977. Its life of just under five years fell into two parts, the first from its beginning through to its registration under the New South Wales Companies Act in January 1979, roughly the period in which WSC operated.

The advent of WSC had encouraged the players to put into effect their previous desire to form a players' association. The inaugural executive comprised Ian Chappell as president, Greg Chappell vice-president, Ross Edwards secretary, Rod Marsh treasurer, with Mick Malone and David Hookes as committee members.

The PCA did not want to confine its membership to Packer players, so it sought to enrol Board cricketers and to develop relationships with overseas Associations in order to form an international body. The Association of Tennis Professionals (ATP), formed in 1972, was their model, and in November 1977 the Australian tennis player John Newcombe addressed a PCA meeting with his subject being the workings of the ATP.

Membership fees were set realistically at $50 for Packer players and $10 for those under the Board. The official players formed their first Branch in Western Australia with moves made in Queensland and South Australia. The international aspect never got going, mainly due to the opposition to WSC of the English Cricketers' Association. However, the West Indies Association co-operated fully with Australia, and during 1977–78 Sunil Gavaskar had discussions with Ian Chappell prior to the formation of an Indian offshoot.

Other major functions performed by all Cricketers' Associations during the Packer period (1977–79) were to provide members with taxation, superannuation and other financial advice, and the establishment of a code of discipline to govern player behaviour on the field. Not only did players earn higher incomes from playing for WSC compared with what they had previously received from the Board, but they also experienced a closer and more cordial relationship with their management and employers.

When, in June 1978, the Australian Cricket Board called a special meeting in Sydney the delegates met to find out how much the first season of the 'split' had cost official cricket. The finances of all State Associations had been badly hit. Victoria was worst off with a drop of $260,953 and a financial year loss of $111,605. New South Wales' loss of $70,696 in 1976–77 had now blown out to $184,912, making a two-year loss of in excess of a quarter of a million dollars. The Queensland loss for 1977–78 was $108,135, with somewhat less disastrous figures in South Australia, Western Australia and Tasmania.

The Board discussed the latest matters 'regarding private promoters' and their strategy at the forthcoming International Cricket Conference meeting at Lord's in July 1978. They were becoming so desperate at the losses being reported, including their share of legal costs due to the High Court in London ruling for Kerry Packer, that application for grant aid was made to the Australian government. As Prime Minister Malcolm Fraser was actively helping Kerry Packer, this avenue of help was never going to be forthcoming.

The Packer issue was having a profound effect on cricket and the game's administrators all around the world. No-one could see a way out of the impasse: traditional cricket felt trapped, and trapped in a way superbly summed up by Ray Steele some months earlier in the High Court. When asked by counsel for the plaintiffs whether he thought the Packer contracts with his players were legal and enforceable, Steele replied: 'I do not doubt it. There is a saying in Australia that the only way out of a Packer contract is by becoming pregnant. I do not suppose that applies to many of our cricketers.' But Steele misjudged Packer, as did many within the establishment. The WSC players were not only more than fairly treated by their boss but with personal thoughtfulness and kindness as well.

What happened behind the scenes in Australian cricket over the next twelve months has never been fully chronicled – nor will it be while most of those involved are still alive, as with Bodyline. What can be said is that a small group of diligent cricket historians have pieced together a sensational train of events which culminated in two intimate dinners and the announcement of a rapprochement. It was not until 1987 that leaked documentation came to light which detailed a chain of events running parallel to the officially given story from the time. Unfortunately it is still not possible to publish the details.

The Churchillian mood of the Australian Cricket Board during the 1977–78 season was not so strong when they gathered in Sydney again in September 1978. Unknown to the Board suspicions were already being felt within the ICC secretariat at Lord's that something was going on behind the scenes on which the game's world governing body was not being informed. The then ICC (and MCC) secretary, Jack Bailey, recorded at the time his thoughts on this and wrote in *Conflicts in Cricket* how 'I brushed them aside as being the result of an over-suspicious nature. Yet they kept on returning like a still, small voice. They insisted that the Australian Board had already had some form of dialogue with Packer.' Bailey knew that the ACB had given their word not to do such a thing and so he allowed his suspicions to rest.

The Board's first act that September was to change their constitution to allow Bob Parish an extra year – subsequently extended to two – as chairman in order to keep continuity. The work being generated by the Board, the continual stream of overseas visitors, and the urgent late night meetings were taking their toll on the secretary, Alan Barnes.

A senior WSC man, who was friendly with both sides, remembers: 'The conditions under which Alan Barnes worked were an utter disgrace. I used to visit him in his cramped office with one, solitary, secretary stuck away in a corner of Cricket House. His health was failing fast and he became stooped and hunched up like a man twenty years his elder. The paranoia shown by Board delegates towards Packer all came through Barnes. He worked all hours possible in an atmosphere which became more schizophrenic as he became aware of what was really going on. The pressures built up so much one just wondered when we would be told of his sudden death. When it was all over with the split and Barnes retired he took three years to recover and by 1983 was his old self again. His very private stories of Board activities were an eye-opener.'

Barnes was aware that during the southern winter of 1978, Walter Hadlee, chairman of the New Zealand Cricket Council, was putting considerable pressure on the Australian Board 'to come to some compromise with World Series Cricket'. Hadlee, who had been quite vocal at the ICC meeting, told Bob Parish what the long-term effects on the game would be unless someone did something soon.

Board delegates, and the new assistant secretary Alan Walsh, had attended various seminars and conferences during July and August which dealt with Packer's activities. The Australian Institute of Management had held a marketing seminar on: 'The activities of private promotion in cricket', the conclusion of which would not have been pleasant for the Board to hear. Likewise the Department of Economics at Melbourne University presented a detailed paper at a conference held at Sydney's Macquarie University, the results of which did not make happy reading for the establishment.

The delegates discussed these and other activities. The New South Wales trio admitted that rural areas in their State were actively supporting 'this type of cricket' and admitted that the reason could be 'perhaps because some country areas had been neglected by our Association'. They also spoke of Packer's right-hand man, Richie Benaud, 'organising coaching and giving help to local bodies and police boys' clubs at no cost to local associations'.

The Board were coming near to admitting that their years of

neglect were now catching up on them. But it did not stop them spending a lengthy period of time discussing whether they could oppose Bill Lawry being elected as a Life Member of the Marylebone Cricket Club; whether to allow the seventeen-year-old 'Master Tau Ao of Papua New Guinea to play club cricket in Queensland'; or to reprimand the Western Australian Cricket Association for having the temerity to ask for prior warning of their players gaining Test selection 'so proper media details could be prepared for issue to the local press'.

Seen in retrospect, trivia still dominated a lot of the Board's time and, when the delegates did knuckle down to items of substance, they appeared lost and confused. Packer's professionalism left them high and dry for the 1978–79 season which was why, sooner rather than later, Bob Parish had to act.

The Board's marketing plans for the season were so amateurish that, on looking back, an element of surprise would be in order that such jumbled proposals were ever given the green light. Their own consultants, Sportsplan Marketing Pty Ltd, had recognised the constraints that their clients had imposed on them and tried, to little avail, to push a 'new image' during July 1978 on visits around Australia.

The Board's own public opinion survey at this time told them that both the public and media strongly believed:

(i) That Board cricketers were seriously underpaid compared to WSC cricketers, and
(ii) That Kerry Packer had brought about the new upward match payments for ACB controlled cricket.

The Board's strategy to counteract this public conception was:

(i) To issue a set of seventy-two playing cards which had photographs of Shield players on them. This would encourage recognition;
(ii) To allow Brandella, a division of Dunlop, to advertise their products as 'endorsed by the Australian Cricket Board', in return for a 5% royalty. A specially prepared sales brochure sent to all cricket clubs produced a negative response;
(iii) The organising of 'World Cup package tours to England, 1979'. Response was very limited from the thousands of leaflets printed, particularly as major travel agents could offer better and cheaper packages.

And so it all went on.

The Sportsplan organisation wrote in a confidential report to the Board dated 7 September 1978: 'At this stage, whilst we are not as advanced in some areas as we would like, we are confident that we will be able to present an effective promotional campaign this season'.

And that, unfortunately, summed it all up in one word: hope. For the 1978–79 season would prove to be a total disaster for official Australian cricket.

The amount of money being dealt with by the Australian Cricket Board had risen beyond Alan Barnes' control. For the financial year ending on 31 July 1978 income had come to $940,020 with expenditure at $898,545. Realising this, assistant secretary Alan Walsh took over financial control with his first task being to look into a system of contracting players, and what sort of financial guarantee should be offered. Bob Parish argued that 'the Board should recognise that it had a competitor which would need to continually replenish its supply of players'. He hoped that by providing contracts this would, in due course, eliminate Packer's source of cricketers. What he did not know was that Kerry Packer, World Series Cricket, and Publishing and Broadcasting Ltd had foreseen this and had taken the appropriate action. All the Board was doing was to copy Packer and play by his rules.

With hindsight it is now clear that WSC won the hearts of Australians for the 1978–79 season although English writers and supporters would say otherwise. In its second season, with Andrew Caro as a cost-cutting managing director, WSC was able to attract increased support from sponsors and the public plus the introduction of a song 'C'mon, Aussie, C'mon', which is still popularly recognised today as Australia's cricket anthem.

WSC started with a fifteen-day tour of New Zealand in which their Australians played a World XI in one three-day and eight limited-overs matches. In the main match, played at Auckland's Mount Smart Stadium the Australians 184 (Greg Chappell 74) and 196 (Greg Chappell 89) defeated the World XI 128 (Lillee 7/59) and 85 (Lillee 5/30) by 167 runs. The World team had their revenge winning five of the one-day games.

The players then flew to Perth for a round-robin series of one-day matches, which now included the West Indies. With Packer's winner-take-all motive, the players competed for $10,000 and for the long-forgotten Swan–Channel Nine Cup. The West Indies eventually won the series defeating the Australians in the final by one wicket on a damp Gloucester Park pitch.

With so many players under contract, WSC decided to form the Cavaliers and scheduled them to play twenty-four one-day and two-day games against the three major WSC teams in country towns around Australia. With these fixtures and the coaching of thousands of schoolchildren by international stars, the Packer organisation won the hearts of many. What must have hurt the Australian Cricket Board were the attendance figures in the country: figures far higher than those for the occasional visit of official touring teams.

The official England touring party, captained by Mike Brearley and with Doug Insole as manager, arrived in South Australia in late October 1978. After a warm-up match in the citrus region of Renmark the visitors played South Australia in Adelaide and lost by 32 runs. This was the first time they had come up against fast bowler Rodney Hogg, a deep-thinking player with a diffident air. Hogg's speed brought him six wickets and a Test debut four weeks later. The England team then drew in Melbourne against Victoria, defeated NSW in Sydney by ten wickets, and beat Queensland in Brisbane by six wickets. This match finished on 27 November and the first Test started on 1 December.

Like most of metropolitan Australia, the tourists tuned into Channel Nine the following day to witness the first WSC match to be played under the newly constructed Sydney Cricket Ground floodlights. What they and others witnessed was the acceptance of day/night cricket by the Australian public. Over 50,000 people attended with the gatemen instructed to let everyone in on that memorable night. A festival atmosphere was felt around the ground and nowhere was the fuddy-duddy feeling of Board cricket present. Every journalist in the pressbox had a telephone; television monitors were available to provide instant replays; the dressing-room doors were open to all pressmen – even those the players and management disliked; the cricketers wrote what they liked about the game in newspapers; spoke readily on radio and gave television interviews by the side of the playing-field on their dismissal. Even the players' wives were allowed to join them and to stay at the same hotels.

That very day the Board's sub-committee met to strengthen further their Player/Writer rule by imposing financial sanctions on any cricketer who dared to speak to the press within three months of the end of a tour or during the Australian season. The contrasts could not have been greater.

Packer's one-day matches, twenty-one in all around Australia, ended with four finals games taking place in Melbourne between WSC Australians and WSC West Indians. Nearly 79,000 spectators watched as the West Indies won by three matches to one and collected $35,000 in prize money.

The four Board one-day internationals attracted 43,448 fans in which Australia defeated England by two matches to one with the other abandoned. Not once did the official attendances come near to those of WSC, and worse was to happen in the Test series.

It is worth comparing the spectator interest in both WSC and Board international matches for the season. WSC attracted 585,240 people to their fixtures whereas the Board had both England and Pakistan touring for a figure of 551,007 for exactly the same number of days of cricket. PBL Marketing were very forthcoming with information for this book and their archival records clearly show a five-year plan to take over the game in Australia. Not only had they drawn up an itinerary for a third season, and pre-booked grounds in advance, they were actively looking at making a tour of England during 1980.

The five WSC Supertests for 1978–79 took place between 8 December and 4 February. All were day/night matches scheduled over four days. The first, at Waverley, Melbourne, saw the World XI score 175 and 257 to defeat WSC Australians 150 (Le Roux 5/39) and 180 by 102 runs. A fortnight later at the Sydney Cricket Ground the World XI 471 (Asif Iqbal 107) defeated WSC West Indies 217 and 210 by an innings and 44 runs. The third Supertest in Melbourne was drawn when the West Indies refused the challenge of scoring 252 runs in 206 minutes for the $11,000 prize money. The scores were WSC Australians 366 (Wessels 126, Hookes 116) and 304 for nine declared; West Indies 419 (Rowe 175) and 126 for two.

Having used the first three matches as a minor round, the fourth became a Qualifying Final. At Sydney from 21 January, the West Indies 163 (Bright 6/52) and 89 (Lillee 7/23) lost to WSC Australians, 185 (Croft 5/65) and 68 for none, by ten wickets. A fortnight later in the Grand Final, WSC Australians, 172 (Le Roux 5/57) and 219, lost to the World XI, 168 (Lillee 5/51) and 226 for five (Barry Richards 101 not out), by five wickets leaving Tony Greig to claim the $61,000 first prize for his World team. Twelve days later two of Packer's teams would be off to the Caribbean for a most interesting two-month tour.

England captain Mike Brearley, having watched the first Sydney floodlight match on television was asked for his comments. He said he did not really want to pre-judge the innovation but 'would certainly like to attend one when we are next in Sydney'. The invitation from Ian Chappell was handed to Brearley within the day.

With Jeff Thomson refusing to play for the Board and retiring temporarily until being allowed to switch to WSC, the Australian selectors brought in Rodney Hogg from South Australia and a new wicketkeeper in Queensland's John Maclean, for the first Test in Brisbane which started on 1 December. The first morning was a disaster for Australia after the newly appointed captain, Victorian Graham Yallop, decided to bat first. At 26 for six the statisticians went to the record books but the tail hit out to see the total to 116. Hogg took 6/74 as England gained a 170-run lead and it was only due to centuries by Kim Hughes (129) and Yallop (102) that England's seven-wicket win did not come before the fifth afternoon.

The tourists then flew to Perth to inflict a crushing two-day defeat on Western Australia prior to the second Test. For the first time since 1936, England won the first two Tests of a series in Australia when they completed an unexpectedly easy victory on the last day. Yallop had put England into bat and only had one penetrative bowler, Hogg (5/65), in his side as they scored 309. Peter Toohey's unbeaten 81 saved Australia from a complete collapse and England built on their 119-run first-innings lead by scoring 208 second time around, Rodney Hogg's 5/57 giving him ten wickets for the match. The inexperienced Australian batsmen gave the England bowlers little trouble as the tourists won by 166 runs.

Behind the scenes Board delegates seemed to be in continual contact with each other, holding sub-committee meetings or writing reports. Sir Donald Bradman was trying to persuade his colleagues not to get embroiled in South African matters as his extremely reliable network had told him Pakistan, India and the West Indies were very much against any ICC fact-finding mission to the republic.

The Prime Minister, Malcolm Fraser, and the Department of Foreign Affairs were by now dictating to the Board on a number of issues. Correspondence was flowing back and forth to Canberra as the government tried to tell the Board where it could, and could not, tour. This pressure eased the following year as the politicians turned their attention to the Olympic Games, banning Australians from competing on hazy political grounds.

There was still the matter of television rights to sort out. The 0/10 Network wanted exclusive rights to the domestic one-day competition, which they got, and also opened negotiations with the Board to take over Test coverage when the Australian Broadcasting Commission's contract ran out in March 1979. It was also fairly obvious by this time that Board delegates were weakening in their resolve against Kerry Packer and Channel Nine. With television rights soon available, one or two were suggesting that the professionalism and innovations introduced by Channel Nine were appealing to the public more and more while the ABC coverage was stodgy, vague and insipid. Progress had happened so rapidly that the Board had received a considerable number of letters arguing against the patronising tones of the ABC, their stilted voices and historical anecdotes compared to the brash, loud but modern commentary from Channel Nine.

England tour manager Doug Insole told the Board at their January 1979 meeting in Adelaide he felt that WSC, through its extensive television promotions of the game, 'was gaining in popularity while from reports he had heard . . . there were rumblings of discontent among WSC players'. He added that 'the money involved was substantial and the players were interested in that. However, the England WSC players were not happy with the type of cricket in which they were engaged.'

The third Test took place in Melbourne over the New Year holiday with the Australian selectors choosing a new middle-order batsman, the left-handed NSW player Allan Border. Border's initial contribution was 29, but he was at the crease as Graeme Wood scored his second Test century, his 100 coming in 392 minutes. In reply to Australia's 258 the England batsmen made 143 in very slow time, Hogg taking 5/30 in 17 fiery overs. In what turned out to be a low-scoring game the Australians' 167 proved to be good enough second time around. Hogg took 5/36 as England's batsmen struggled in the conditions and eventually the home team gained their only win of the series by 103 runs.

The day after the Test a meeting took place in the VCA boardroom between Bob Parish, Ray Steele and Sir Donald Bradman along with various ICC representatives. The visitors had been to India and Pakistan before arriving in Australia and their main concern was the forthcoming World Cup in England in mid-1979. There was indication that England players in particular would not play against any team which contained WSC players – and at least three countries were planning to include such players in their squads. The result of the meeting was nebulous and it was only a few days later that a secret, hitherto unreported, meeting took place in the northern suburbs of Sydney in order to resolve this problem.

Meanwhile, the fourth Test was taking place just twenty miles south at the Sydney Cricket Ground where the smallest Test match crowd to watch England there in a quarter of a century saw Australia lose a game they should have won. The 93-run defeat allowed Brearley successfully to defend the Ashes he had won eighteen months earlier.

By now the majority of delegates to the Board were in a state of controlled panic. Their marketing strategy for the season had collapsed and a report by Tom Worrell of Sportsplan Marketing made their gloom even deeper. Their meeting in Adelaide prior to the fifth Test was a litany of problems.

Four main matters needed discussing. The first concerned the Fraser government's involvement in trying to find a resolution to the impasse with WSC. The Prime Minister had already indicated his wish on cricket matters which did not concern WSC, but now on his direction the Minister of Home Affairs, Bob Ellicott, QC, had requested that 'the Board chairman and other representatives' meet him to discuss the problem. Before meeting Ellicott, the Board wanted to straighten out existing legal problems which included accepting a $45,000 pay-off from WSC to release Jeff Thomson from his contract; of paying $9000 of the $18,362 legal bill incurred by the WACA in their court case with Dennis Lillee on the announcement of 'commercial cricket' in May 1977, and to drawing up correct legal contracts for all Board players to sign. Incidentally, the Board's legal expenses for the last four months of 1978 alone came to $68,292!

The third issue was a full, frank assessment of the Sheffield Shield competition. Attendances in 1978–79 were the lowest that had ever been the case since the competition started in the 1892–93 season. On forty of the ninety-two days of Shield cricket the crowds were in three figures with an overall average daily gate of 1458: even Packer's troupe in the bush were getting many more.

Everyone put forward their own suggestions, some of them quite radical, until as always the wise voice of Sir Donald Bradman came through. He pointed out that any alterations to playing days would see a drop in memberships of Asssociations, and that would see income fall steeply. In the end the only real decision taken was to adopt six deliveries an over instead of eight in all future first-class games.

Then came probably the most remarkable discussion on the current official Australian team. Sir Donald Bradman led the revolt against a proposal to have a team manager yet there was almost unanimous support that the team needed a coach. A man who had the respect of the players was needed and one who was also a fine tactician in the game. Only one name was ever discussed and surprisingly he was an Englishman, the Lancashire player, Jack Simmons, who was currently coaching and playing in Tasmania. Simmons had just led Tasmania to success in the Gillette Cup one-day competition and had also advised the Board on matters ranging from the national Colts Competition through to the need for captains to liaise on Umpires' Reports. No decision was taken and the subject lapsed in view of pending events.

The final two Tests of the season saw England win by 205 runs in Adelaide and then by nine wickets in Sydney before an aggregate crowd of just 22,617. The only highlights for Australia were Graham Yallop's 121 out of 198 in Sydney, the fifth highest individual contribution (61.11%) in a team total in Test history, and Rodney Hogg's final figure of 41 wickets in a series, a record by an Australian in a home rubber against England.

Then came Pakistan to play in two Tests. Their first, in Melbourne starting on 10 March, coincided with the Moomba festival which kept attendance figures down. It was an acrimonious short series which saw gamesmanship reach very low levels. At 4.30 pm on the final afternoon of a very ordinary first Test, Australia needed 77 runs to win with seven wickets in hand. Allan Border (105) had made his first Test century before becoming one of Sarfraz Nawaz's victims. The Pakistani pace bowler took all of those seven wickets for one run in just 33 balls, and finished with 9/86, as the visitors gained an unexpected win by 71 runs.

Western Australian Kim Hughes was appointed as Australia's captain for the second Test in Perth which started in the middle of autumn, on 24 March. Australia won by seven wickets but by then no-one was really interested. It had been far too long a season with saturation point having been reached long before Allan Border hit Australia's winning runs on 29 March. The Board had lost $445,000 when they should, in normal circumstances, have returned a huge profit from playing eight home Tests in four months.

To make matters worse, the WSC Australians were on tour in the West Indies. They played five Supertests and ten one-day matches between 20 February and 15 April 1979. The one-day fixtures were split: the West Indies winning initially by three games to two, then whitewashing the Australians five-nil at the end of the tour. In the first Supertest played at Sabina Park, Kingston, Jamaica, the West Indies 188 and 481 (Lloyd 197) defeated WSC Australians, 106 and 194, by 369 runs.

Crowd riots saw the second Supertest at Kensington Oval, Barbados, abandoned as a draw after WSC Australians had scored 311 and 294 to the West Indies 239 and 133 for four. Further crowd trouble at the Queens Park Oval, Port-of-Spain, Trinidad, did not stop the visitors winning the third Supertest as WSC Australia 246 (Laird 122, Holding 5/48) and 282 (Greg Chappell 150, Padmore 6/81) defeated the West Indies 230 (Thomson 5/78) and 274 by 24 runs.

Crowd violence reached its peak during the fourth Supertest at the Bourda in Georgetown, Guyana. The match saw WSC Australia, 341 (Greg Chappell 113) and 117 for three, draw with the West Indies 476 (King 110). Heavy rain had flooded the outfield and play was impossible after three days yet ground announcements said play would take place. When this did not happen mobs wrecked the pavilion, burnt club records and forced the players to seek refuge in the dressing-rooms. It was all very ugly and for the rest of the tour the players just went through the motions. The final Supertest on the delightful Recreation Ground in St Johns, Antigua, saw WSC Australians 234 (Greg Chappell 104) and 415 for six (Marsh 102*) draw with the West Indies, 438 for nine declared (Rowe 135, Lillee 6/125).

The venture helped to rescue the financially stricken West Indies Board. Packer made sure they received good ground rental fees plus a proportion of the gate monies. He also gave the Board an ex-gratia payment to compensate them for any loss of interest in their Shell Shield inter-island competition.

Prior to joining his players in the Caribbean, Kerry Packer had had a meeting with two senior ICC officials. He knew that members of Brearley's official England team were angered that their rates of pay were well below those of the rebels and some, in spite, wanted to ban Packer players from English county cricket. He told the meeting that if this ban became fact he would take his troupe to England, and nobody disbelieved him.

The cricket world was, and in the main, standing four-square behind the official game. Had they known what was going on behind the scenes between two Australian officials and WSC men then there would have been grave disappointment. In his book *Conflicts In Cricket* the former ICC and MCC secretary, Jack Bailey, spells out in detail the shock when he heard that a compromise had been reached. As has been stated earlier, the exact details of the negotiations and payments are inappropriate to discuss here. However, at its meeting in Sydney on 23 and 24 April 1979, the Board agreed to a deal with Channel Nine. It spelt the end of the old order of cricket administration in Australia with the long-term price a heavy burden to bear.

Within a year the full effect of the rapprochement came to fruition when the greatest of them all was forced into not renominating. The sell-out had been that high.

# 31

# The Rapprochement

At noon on Wednesday 30 May 1979 Bob Parish made a public statement on behalf of the Australian Cricket Board:

> I am pleased to announce that the agreement between the Australian Cricket Board and PBL Sports [Public and Broadcasting Limited, henceforth known as PBL Marketing] has been signed and will be lodged with the Trade Practices Commissioner. Under the agreement the Board has granted PBL Sports the exclusive right, for a term of ten years, to promote the programme of cricket organised by the Board and to arrange the television and merchandising in respect of that programme. For the first three years of the agreement the Board has agreed that PBL Sports may arrange a contract for the televising of the programme with the Channel Nine Network.
>
> World Series Cricket will cease to promote cricket matches in Australia or elsewhere during the term of the agreement. However, under the programme the World Series logo will continue to be worn in international one-day matches by Australian players. The Australian Cricket Board will have the exclusive responsibility for the selection of Australian teams and has agreed that no player will be excluded from selection by reason only of that player having participated prior to the commencement of the 1979–80 cricket season in any match not authorised by the Board. There will be no change in Board policy that Australian teams will be selected only from those players who participate in Sheffield Shield cricket.
>
> It is envisaged that the programme each season will comprise five or six Test matches and an international one-day series, to be known as the Benson and Hedges World Series Cup, of fifteen matches plus a final which will be the best of five matches. These international matches will involve two overseas teams and the Australian team. The programme will also include the Sheffield Shield Competition and a one-day series of nine matches between the States. Playing conditions of all matches will be under the control of the Board

> and the Board has agreed to consider favourably the introduction of the thirty-yard circles in limited overs matches, day/night matches and, on an experimental basis, the use of coloured clothing in Benson and Hedges World Series one-day limited overs international matches.
>
> The programme for the 1979–80 season will not be finally determined for some weeks. England and India have accepted invitations to come to Australia in 1979–80. The Board has agreed to ask the Indian Board to defer their visit until next season 1980–81 and will invite the West Indian Board to send an official team to participate in the 1979–80 programme.
>
> The Board is unanimously of the opinion that its decision to accept the proposal from PBL is in the best interests of Australian and International cricket.

The financial arrangements sounded excellent when first announced: 'A total of $265,000 prize money will be provided,' said Parish. What he did not tell the world was that Packer had won hands-down with a financial deal which must have made him very content.

Four of the fourteen Board delegates during those fateful times all expressed the view that they thought they were doing their best for Australian cricket. The deal gave the Board $1,150,000 annually for ten years, *non-indexed*. By 1986 inflation had ravaged this figure to such a small percentage of cricket income that the Board's pleading for a revised figure to be agreed was accepted by PBL.

In those early days of peace, as Bob Parish flew around the world making excuses – particularly to Lord's who were, and still are, furious at the turn of events – the PBL executives started their takeover. Board meetings were hijacked by Packer's executives; State Associations received more paperwork than they knew how to deal with; players were suddenly handed new contracts which told them for whom they could and could not do promotional work, and a publicity campaign started which carried quotes such as this from the Victorian Cricket Association:

> Australian cricket once again has rosy prospects. The events of the past two years must be left there – in the past! The Association is fully committed to playing its part in making this agreement work and calls on players, officials and the public to rally behind a reunited Australian team.

The Australian side to make a short tour to England for the 1979 World Cup was managed by David Richards and was: Alan Hurst, Trevor Laughlin, Jeff Moss, Davnell Whatmore and Graham Yallop

(Victoria); Kim Hughes (captain), Graham Porter and Kevin Wright (WA); Andrew Hilditch and Allan Border (NSW); Gary Cosier and Geoff Dymock (Queensland); Rick Darling and Rodney Hogg (SA).

All matches were limited-overs affairs with an initial warm-up match against Middlesex at Southgate rained off. New Zealand (52) were then beaten at Arundel by 153 runs in early June as the team started to show promise. This fell apart four days later as Kent (281) won a high-scoring match over Australia (208) by 73 runs. The next day's fixture at Southampton against Hampshire was abandoned after an hour with the outfield waterlogged.

The Australians' three World Cup matches were not quite the results looked for by the twelve hundred supporters who had flown over for the tournament. At Lord's on 9 June, Australia (159) lost to England by six wickets; at Trent Bridge, Pakistan (286) won by 89 runs while at Edgbaston, Canada (105) lost to the Australians by seven wickets. In the final the West Indies won their second successive title by defeating England by 92 runs.

On their arrival home the Australians found out who the selectors had axed for the forthcoming tour of India. Out went Cosier, Laughlin and Moss, in came Jim Higgs (Victoria), Peter Sleep (SA), Graeme Wood (WA) and Bruce Yardley (WA). A mid-tour reinforcement pace bowler was Geoff Lawson (NSW).

Ten days before the team's departure, a special Board meeting was held in Sydney to sort out the beginnings of the new era in Australian cricket.

PBL executives, led by Packer's right-hand man Lynton Taylor, were present and virtually dominated proceedings. Board delegates were both confused and angry by their visitors' dictatorial stance but there was little, if anything, they could do about it. Bob Parish reported on how copies of the agreement had been distributed to all representatives at the June 1979 ICC meeting at Lords: 'With the financial clauses deleted,' Parish hastened to tell the Board.

Then came the crunch. PBL wanted a top first season and the Board were told to confirm that the visit by India had been put on hold. England and the West Indies were wanted for three Tests each plus a series of one-day internationals. PBL wanted the Frank Worrell Trophy to be part of the West Indies deal but Lord's flatly refused to do the same with the Ashes.

PBL also took over the negotiations from the Board on the financial arrangements for both touring teams. Lord's wanted $600,000 for England to which PBL, in their letter of instructions to Parish dated 3 August 1979, said $500,000 was quite sufficient – and that would also go for the West Indies to whom the Board had offered $485,000.

Now came the publicity and promotional side of things. The Board were told that coloured clothing was to be worn for one-day internationals; gross gate receipts and the supply of auditors was PBL's responsibility (and they caught one State Association almost at once taking a quarter of gate monies as a matter of course); the rules of one-day cricket would be rewritten; white balls would be used in these matches, and the individual awards would be under the titles of Classic Catches, Strike Rates, Player of the Match, Player of the Series, and International Cricketer of the Year.

For years the Board had refused to countenance suggestions of having a reduced rate of entry fee for old-age pensioners. Now they had to give concessions for the elderly, unemployed and social security cardholders such as unmarried mothers and the disabled. There were also to be black sightscreens for matches in which the white ball was used; revised hours of televising all types of cricket; on-ground entertainment such as sky-divers, performing dogs, exhibitions of American football, but (as one delegate gleefully asked before being put down) definitely no brass bands.

The list went on. PBL would produce official programmes and tour brochures; there would be Cheer Leaders during the day/night games; PBL would have a final say in perimeter advertising; public address systems would announce new batsmen and bowlers; the McDonald fast food company would sponsor the domestic one-day competition which would be revised; an electric drinks buggy would be used for interval refreshments; where possible corporate hospitality tents would be erected – and so the innovations went on and on.

The one thing the Board did recognise was that it would be impossible for Alan Barnes to oversee the new order. Ray Steele told the meeting that: 'There is a vast amount of detailed work to be undertaken which is most important to the successful conduct of cricket in the 1979–80 season. In these circumstances I suggest that Mr David Richards, secretary of the Victorian Cricket Association, be seconded from that Association to work for the Australian Cricket Board.' Richards, the perfect man for the job, was initially given the title of 'Marketing Manager' and it was he who smoothed the path as both sides walked back down the aisle.

As part of the conciliation process the Professional Cricketers' Association (PCA) of Australia had elected Ian Redpath as their president with Ian Chappell as his deputy and Richie Robinson as secretary. They wanted to establish a good relationship with the Board and, to this end, Redpath spoke to Ray Steele. He suggested a meeting between representatives of both parties, an idea Steele derided when reporting to the August 1979 Board meeting. Steele told the delegates that the Cricket sub-committee was the way for players to air any possible grievances they might have.

When the WSC players realised that decisions taken at the Cricket sub-committee meeting were passed over at the Board meeting in September 1978, they wrote to all Shield and State practice squad players on 9 February 1979 seeking to enrol them as members. The WSC dominated group said in their letter that the PCA's aim was, 'to represent *all* professional cricketers' and that it should 'not be regarded as a militant breakaway group'. It continued saying that the PCA's 'objectives can be broadly summarised as being for the promotion of professional cricket and the protection and support of individual players'. It ended: 'The purpose of our Association is to represent professional cricketers as a body at discussions at state, national and international levels for the betterment of players and the game'.

The PCA also contacted all other cricketing countries suggesting that their Associations send a representative to form an International Cricketers' Association, but it was the hostile response from England which stopped this concept dead in its tracks.

Following Ray Steele's stand, the PCA used September and October 1979 to have a series of meetings around Australia where their executive sought to convince non-Packer cricketers of the wisdom of becoming members, especially as the annual subscription was now only $25. Notwithstanding the reluctance of some Board players to line up with Packer's men the PCA succeeded in signing up over 75 per cent of all Test and Sheffield Shield players, reaching a peak membership of 67 members in June 1982.

That the PCA failed in its aims and objectives was due to the Board using the age-old tactic of just ignoring them. There was no Board confrontation with the PCA, only the comment that delegates felt: 'That there is no real role they can perform given the existence of the cricket sub-committee which provides a regular forum for players and the Board to exchange viewpoints'.

With its inability to develop a bargaining relationship with the Board the PCA, in the words of Dennis Lillee, 'gradually disintegrated'. It quickly became a spent force and, although Ian Chappell tried hard to interest other players in taking a leading role and rejuvenating the Association, it was to no avail. The PCA had little money and, when it finally fell apart in 1988 the balance in the account of $252 was given over to the cricketing charity, the Primary Club of Australia.

The Australian team, managed by Victorian Cricket Association committeeman Bob Merriman, left Australia on 21 August 1979 for India. The tour was being made unusually early in the Indian season in order to enable the team to return home to fight for representative places with WSC players. This meant that play was frequently interrupted by the monsoon which was only part of the reason not one first-class match was won. As ten of the fifteen tourists had never represented their country abroad before it was no disgrace to lose the six-Test series by only two-nil.

The first few days were a learning curve for the new boys. Their Air-India jumbo-jet lost power in an engine en route which meant a return to Singapore and an emergency landing. Then, on arrival at Meenam Bakkam airport in Madras, they were met by armed police, and on a further flight to Srinagar for the first match the welcoming party was the military security forces. This was because of threats to Kim Hughes and his players from the Jammu and Kashmir Liberation Front based just over the border in Pakistan.

Following draws with North Zone at Srinagar and South Zone in Hyderabad (Allan Border 113) the first Test started in the Chepauk Stadium, Madras, on 11 September just half-an-hour after the Board had started their sixth annual meeting in Perth.

In Madras, Hughes (100) batted first and enjoyed a 222-run third-wicket stand with Border (162). In reply to 390, India scored 425 (Jim Higgs 7/143) with bad light and heavy rain seeing the game to an expected draw. Three days later in Bangalore the south-west monsoon ruined the second Test which also ended without a result.

The tourists then went inland to Delhi for yet another drawn match, this time with Central Zone before taking on India in the third Test in Kanpur. The match swung either way with Geoff Dymock's left-arm pace claiming 5/99 and 7/67 as Australia were left 312 minutes on the final day to score 279 for victory. They collapsed ignominiously against the fast-medium swing of Kapil Dev and the off-spin of Shivlal Yadav and lost by 153 runs.

Hughes scored 126 against West Zone in Ahmedabad in yet another inconclusive fixture after which it was back to Delhi for another drawn Test at the Feroz Shah Kotla ground. The old warhorse, Ramesh Saxena, steered his East Zone side to a four-wicket victory in Cuttack as Hughes, not taking the game seriously, bowled his batsmen rather than his bowlers. This trait of the Australian captain was unbecoming and, regrettably, continued through to his retirement from the game ten years later.

The fifth Test at Eden Gardens, Calcutta, started on 26 October. Sheffield Shield matches had commenced back in Australia and Hughes would have felt the pressure knowing that Greg Chappell had marked his return from WSC by taking 185 off the Victorian attack in Brisbane. Hughes made 92 and Yallop 167 in 520 minutes as Australia reached 442. India scored 347 and Hughes then declared his second innings to give India a chance of making 247 runs in even time. Bad light stopped play with India 47 runs short in the most pulsating game of the series.

The black clouds hovering over Australia's Test players would have caused deepening gloom as news filtered back from home. The opening Shield games had also seen ex-Packer men doing well: Thomson 7/58, Trevor Chappell 150, Bruce Laird 117, Mick Malone 5/83, Dennis Lillee 6/94, Thomson, again, 6/51, and on it went. The Australians' morale was low as they took the field for the sixth and final Test at the Wankhede Stadium, Bombay, and, indeed, only three would play in Australia's next Test three weeks later. The match lasted for just three-and-a-half days as India won by an innings and 100 runs to win their first series against Australia.

The Packer rift had cost the Australian Cricket Board $810,000 in lost income, money they had to make up. On the other side Kerry Packer was presented with a bat signed by all the WSC players to thank him for turning the game into a professionally run business, and to extend their own careers. According to John Benaud, Packer would often pat the bat affectionately and call it: 'My six million dollar bat'. In reality the financial gains were far more than that.

Even though the players were going to gain more money, feelers were put out in August 1979 to see what reaction there would be if some cricketers had an offer put to them to join a proposed 'International Team' to tour South Africa. No takers came forward even though the West Indies Board were convinced that some players had given in-principle agreements. Nothing more would be heard on this for three years.

Socially, the September 1979 Board meeting in Perth had been a most enjoyable affair. The State was celebrating its 150th anniversary and delegates had a lengthy luncheon at Parliament House with the Premier, Sir Charles Court. The Western Australian Cricket Association also arranged a lunch with other breaks described by Bob Parish as 'having outstanding catering arrangements'.

Less outstanding was the dictatorial attitude of PBL Marketing. David Richards had worked hard prior to the meeting to sort out the season's innovations which were presented to delegates at a special function at the studios of Perth radio station 6PM in Subiaco. Disliked as many of these were, the new styles of clothing and equipment were a *fait accompli*. All the delegates could do was to ask a few questions concerning marketing arrangements before returning to the WACA ground in East Perth to resume their meeting.

It must have been heartbreaking for many of those fourteen Board men as the responsibility for running Australian cricket was taken from them. A letter from the International Cricket Conference to the Board concerning the release of WSC players from their Packer contracts was read prior to the meeting by PBL who had already drafted a reply to Lord's for the delegates to approve. No change to this reply would be allowed and the rubber-stamping took place amid much muttering.

Probably the least liked state of affairs was PBL's taking over of negotiations regarding the forthcoming visit by Mike Brearley's England team. Lynton Taylor had said that, if Lord's did not accept PBL's generous offer, 'then we would have no objection to accepting a tour of Australia by New Zealand in lieu of England'. On hearing this, Parish immediately contacted George Mann, chairman of the Test and County Cricket Board, and it took the old-boy network to resolve gently an issue which the hard-bitten businessmen had created.

From now on any Australian cricketer chosen to represent his country not only had to sign a contract with the Board, it was compulsory for him to sign a commercial agreement with PBL Marketing. Like it or not, if the player was told to attend a certain place at a certain time he had to obey. The sight in the early 1980s of professional cricketers bouncing on trampolines in shopping malls or selling cheap television sets in a bulk-store promotional activity was demeaning to put it mildly. Totally immune to criticism, PBL Marketing carried on in such a way that within five years players were rebelling against them as much as their predecessors had against the Board in 1977.

The one item of the rapprochement the Board has always kept hidden away is their financial agreement with Kerry Packer. This book has revealed that figure for the first time but, back in late 1979, the Australian Trade Practices Commission had indicated that they would make this figure public. Bob Parish immediately slapped an injunction on them and it took all his powers of persuasion, along with those of Ray Steele, for the Commission to agree to keep all matters confidential.

As the Board's power and influence started to wane, so their authority, as it drained away, was passed to other people. The idea of a permanent team manager and travelling physiotherapist was suggested and the appointment of such people was approved in September 1979 subject to the agreement of PBL. However, circumstances dictated that such a role did not fully evolve for some time.

The 1979–80 season was always going to be awkward and even more so for the disgraceful behaviour of some of the returning senior players. No longer was cricket a gentleman's game in Australia: it was a tough uncompromising battle, with no quarter given in any direction.

On 4 November 1979, during the second day of South Australia's match against Tasmania in Devonport, the visitors' captain, Ian Chappell, was reported by the umpires for his behaviour. Chappell was subsequently suspended by the Board for three weeks, a punishment confirmed by the Cricket committee of the South Australian Cricket

Association on 12 November. The day following the end of Chappell's enforced lay-off he captained South Australia in a match against the touring England team, and this time he was reported by an umpire who was officiating in his one and only first-class match. Chappell was given a suspended six-weeks sentence after which he was reported again in the NSW match in late February and announced his retirement from the game prior to the SACA taking the drastic action they intended.

By 1982 Chappell had been forgiven enough for his portrait to rejoin those of other South Australian captains on the wall in the Association's dining-room. From the day in 1977 when WSC had been announced it had been taken from the appropriate wall and hung for two years behind a toilet door until placed in proper storage.

The marketing men who had taken over Australian cricket in 1979 were always very wary of the Great Man. He was the only one who could see through their bluff and bluster with his pithy comments and acute dissection which resulted in their crash-through policies being reined back. Very early on the policy had been somehow to get him to resign and Ian Chappell's second offence provided just the opportunity needed.

It was decided by the Board's Emergency committee, which comprised Bob Parish (Victoria), Tim Caldwell (NSW) and Phil Ridings (SA), to ask Sir Donald Bradman to convene a disciplinary committee comprising himself and two other Board members. This was to take place in Adelaide a week after Chappell's offence with all parties agreeing to be present.

As Sir Donald Bradman said later: 'It was a set-up. The two other Board members cried off with feeble excuses and I had to sit alone in judgment. I heard the case; found Chappell guilty as charged, and suspended him forthwith for a period of six weeks. I sent my report to the Board who did not back me up. Chappell's sentence was suspended. I had no other course of action than to see the season through and not re-nominate again.'

That was not quite the end of the matter. On 18 December 1979, Newcastle solicitors Turnbull & Hill sent two letters to Bob Parish. One, marked 'without prejudice' contained a proposal that the suspended sentence on Ian Chappell be lifted, the other lodged objection to the whole disciplinary proceedings. At a specially called Board meeting in Melbourne on 28 December – which Sir Donald Bradman did not attend, nor did he give an apology for absence – the delegates present went through the motions of rejecting Turnbull & Hill's letter and getting their solicitors, Stephen Jaques & Stephen, to reply accordingly.

Following the meeting the second Test against the West Indies took place. Shortly afterwards, following an absence of four years, Ian

Chappell was recalled to the Australian Test side, a position he held until his final retirement from the game at the end of March 1980.

In attempting to exert their authority over the game, PBL Marketing went completely overboard in the 1979–80 season. Not only did both England and West Indies tour, but fourteen highly forgettable one-day internationals took place as well as the Sheffield Shield and a revamped domestic McDonald's Cup limited-overs challenge. What was even more galling for the Board was the fine which PBL imposed on them for not playing the full twenty contracted one-day internationals.

The England tour started with a draw against Queensland in Brisbane, victory over Tasmania in Hobart, various minor matches and the Chappell-incident drawn game in Adelaide. The first Test in Perth saw England captain Mike Brearley put Australia into bat and at 219 for seven Dennis Lillee walked to the crease carrying an aluminium bat. It was a ploy to obtain publicity for the bat with the Channel Nine television commentary team being aware in advance of Lillee's proposed action. After receiving four balls from which Lillee scored three runs, Brearley complained to umpire Max O'Connell that the unusual bat was damaging the ball. Lillee's behaviour for the next eleven minutes before the bat was changed was a disgrace. Had the Board had control over their own house they would have suspended Lillee. As it was their letter to him of 28 December could only say: 'Your behaviour was reprehensible. As a senior player it is your responsibility to set an example and not to denigrate the game.' Lillee was 'severely reprimanded' and laughed the matter off. Two years later he would commit a far worse offence at the same ground.

Ian Botham took 6/78 as Australia reached 244 (Hughes 99) with England failing to match that figure by 16 runs. Allan Border scored 115 in Australia's second innings 337 which was all too much for the visitors. Left-armed paceman Geoff Dymock claimed 6/34 as England fell for 215, opening batsman Geoff Boycott being left stranded on 99.

A return match against Queensland and victory by 138 runs led up to the second Test in Sydney. By now it was common knowledge that Australian captain Greg Chappell had made a detailed report to the Board concerning one of the Perth Test umpires, Don Weser. Chappell had been so disturbed by certain matters that he said in a letter to the Board's Tim Caldwell 'that he was prepared to elaborate further on his captain's report on umpires to members of the Umpires' Appointment Committee, if required'.

This was player-power unknown since the turn of the century and, following the Sydney Test, Chappell and his deputy Kim Hughes wrote an extraordinary letter to Alan Barnes. They started by complaining about the state of the pitch saying: 'It had been allowed to be saturated two days prior to the start of the Test match', and went on to criticise the ground authorities 'for allowing members of the public to be admitted to the ground prior to any decision being made on the fitness of the ground for play'. Far from being offended by this letter the Board actually investigated the complaints and supported the players. A letter of apology from the Sydney Cricket Ground Trust said: 'The particular events which led to the saturation of the wicket [*sic*] will not occur again.' What happened was that the ground staff watered the pitch too much, and then left the covers off overnight when it rained heavily. The pitch did dry out but was far too green in places. This assisted the fast bowlers, making them dangerous.

Greg Chappell's fortune on winning the toss and putting England into bat on the still damp pitch paid off as Lillee (4/40) and Dymock (4/42) bowled England out for 123. Australia gained a lead of 22 runs in the poor conditions with only an unbeaten 98 by David Gower saving the visitors from a humiliating defeat. With Greg Chappell also remaining unbeaten on 98, Australia won by six wickets in just three days' actual playing time.

England then won in Canberra against NSW by eight wickets prior to their third Test in Melbourne. The itinerary split between one-, four- and five-day games, plus the West Indians having their share of the same, was unsettling for Brearley's team. He had to endure a considerable amount of personal abuse for looking after the best interests of his team with an inflammatory television commentary not helping to quell the tide of feeling against him. Australia won the third Test by eight wickets in early February as Lillee took 6/60 and 5/78, and Greg Chappell scored 114.

The one-day series had not gone the way the promoters had imagined. England were clearly on top in the eleven (with one abandoned) minor-round matches, winning five of their seven games. However, in the finals the West Indies won by two runs in Melbourne and a decisive eight wickets in Sydney to claim the Benson & Hedges Cup. Nor did the thirteen matches attract as many spectators as anticipated. The lowest crowd was 6120 for a day/night match in Sydney between the two tourists with Australia against the West Indies in a day-game in Melbourne attracting a high of 39,833. In all 257,333 people paid $830,421 to watch the initial series of official one-day matches.

Attendances were also poor for the West Indies sojourn around the country, other than Tests. Their highest daily crowd was 4199 for the middle day of their match against South Australia in Adelaide, a match they won by nine wickets following some splendid bowling by Rodney Hogg (6/95). This was followed by a 260-run win in Devonport against a Combined Team after which the first Test was played in Brisbane.

The match became the first drawn Test in Australia for three years, ending a sequence of sixteen games which had produced definite results. It was also the first five-day Test without a rest day since South Africa played England at Cape Town over New Year 1957.

Bruce Laird made his debut for Australia as an opening batsman, scoring 92 and 75 which created a record for the highest number of runs without a century by any batsman in his first Test. Australia made 268 to which the West Indies replied with 441. Sensing that his team were not going to win, Greg Chappell (124) and Kim Hughes (130*) saw the match to safety before a cursory declaration gave the visitors a few minutes at the crease.

The second Test in Melbourne over the New Year saw 1979 depart with the Australians struggling to save the match. The first day of January 1980 saw a decisive West Indies victory by ten wickets in front of a very poor aggregate attendance of 89,045.

Adelaide hosted the third Test at the end of January with the Australians thrashed by the sixth-largest victory by a margin of runs in Test cricket. Their 408-run drubbing saw a West Indian team gaining ample revenge for the humiliations of the 1975–76 series. The tourists then departed for New Zealand and one of the worst-behaved Test series yet known.

The Sheffield Shield season ended with Victoria defeating South Australia in Adelaide to snatch the trophy from their host's certain grasp. For all his faults, Ian Chappell had led South Australia superbly, pulling them up from near to bottom to their final runners-up position. Victoria also claimed the McDonald's Cup by defeating NSW in the final.

When the playing season was finally over, Ian Johnson, secretary of the Melbourne Cricket Club, made a prediction. He said that by the turn of the century, 'you will find that Test matches, as we know them, will not be played. In their place we will have a Test series which will comprise five matches with each match like an American baseball series. That is, a match will consist of five one-day games.' Johnson still thinks that this will happen.

Behind the scenes the Australian Cricket Board seemed to have all the troubles of the world heaped upon them. On 21 December 1979 the Australian Broadcasting Commission lodged an injunction against them, PBL Marketing, World Series Cricket and other Packer-owned companies claiming breaches of Section 45 of the Trade Practices Act and seeking relief. The said Act, introduced by the Whitlam government in 1974, was a far-reaching piece of legislation which in itself was innovative and has been copied by many legislators around the world. Section 45 dealt, *inter alia*, with monopolies and price-fixing arrangements. It was heard in the Federal Court in Sydney by Mr Justice St John with PBL Marketing magnanimously agreeing to pay all costs (which actually came out of cricket revenue not passed on to the Board).

The ABC action also went on to concern the merchandising and marketing of cricket as well as the main point of television rights. Bob Parish discussed the problems with John Norgard, chairman of the ABC, but could reach no satisfactory conclusion. In the end the ABC won their case in court by gaining television rights for areas of Australia not covered by Channel Nine. The irony of the outcome was that the ABC had to pay Channel Nine $600,000 per annum, indexed annually, for permission to televise whereas, in the settlement between the Board and WSC, the non-indexed television component was only $420,000. So ironically, His Honour's judgment actually benefited PBL Marketing by $180,000 a year with the Board gaining nothing and indirectly paying all costs.

Another major problem the Board had to overcome was the hostility engendered towards it by the press who went as far as sending a letter of complaint to Bob Parish. It was quickly recognised by David Richards, 'that, as expected, some members of the media were not in favour of the Board's settlement with World Series Cricket and this was causing an unsettling effect'. Officially the journalists were complaining about the lack of television monitors in the Sydney pressbox; television cables blocking their line of sight in Melbourne; the unavailability of luncheon facilities at most grounds; the lack of detailed information on sponsors, prize money and the rules for one-day games; the lack of proper press releases and numerous other minor grievances.

Without meaning to, the journalists had conceived in certain minds the realisation that a happy and contented media were a compliant media. Moves were put in train within a short time which saw in five years the emergence of a travelling 'media mafia'. Those who supported the Board and wrote to their wishes were subliminally rewarded. Those who questioned were left out in the cold. By the end of the 1980s this media manipulation had become so blatant that even members of the public were aware enough to buy certain newspapers for their cricket comment against buying others which just reprinted *in toto* the plethora of Board press releases. Thc net effect of this policy was for the game in Australia to lose a number of quality writers who gave up reporting cricket in disgust.

PBL Marketing's report for their initial year of running Australian cricket makes interesting reading. Their main television *modus operandi* was to target advertising towards 'the lowest common denominator', i.e. women and children, before firing on all cylinders at men watching from their armchairs at evenings and weekends.

Surveys showed a tremendous shift in the age and socio-economic fabric of those who actually attended games in this first season of rampant commercialism. The vast majority who passed through the turnstiles were under forty years of age, with women attending in much larger numbers than before. PBL's aim for 1980–81 was to target the children's market, which they did very successfully.

In his report to the Board meeting held in Melbourne in early February 1980, Lynton Taylor said there were several matters which were of concern to him, the most serious being 'the urgent need to streamline the organisation for cricket administration'. Alan Barnes took the hint and gave notice of his intention to retire at the end of the meeting. This precipitated moves at virtually all six Cricket Associations with changes in Perth, Adelaide, Melbourne, Sydney and Brisbane. New administrators took over for the new era which left one wondering how Bill Jeanes, Harold Heydon, Harry Brereton or even the redoubtable Ernie Bean would have coped.

On 18 December 1979 Brian Hawkins, head of the South-West Asia desk at the Department of Foreign Affairs in Canberra, wrote to Bob Parish to advise him that the forthcoming Australian tour of Pakistan could go ahead. Hawkins stated that the political situation in Pakistan 'would continue to be monitored but there was no current reason why the Board should not carry on with its planning for the visit'.

Two weeks later Fred Bennett was appointed as team manager with a brief to visit Pakistan almost at once to check on accommodation and all aspects of security arrangements. While Bennett was in Pakistan the ongoing problem of tour finances was coming to a head. After estimating all their costings the Australian Board asked their Pakistan counterparts for a tour guarantee of $A250,000 which included a profit of $A30,000. When the Pakistan Board refused, the programme was cut from eight matches to five with $A150,000 as a guarantee.

The tour party was announced on 30 January 1980, but the initial politicking came, amazingly, not from the Pakistanis but from the Australian Board. At their meeting in Melbourne on 8 February, there was the first vote for ages as to who would be Australia's captain. The traditionalists wanted Kim Hughes, the realists went for Greg Chappell, despite his original defection to WSC. The vote was as close as could be possible with Chappell getting the nod.

The team flew from Sydney on 16 February and arrived in Bombay the next day in time to watch the second day of the Jubilee Test between India and England at the Wankhede Stadium. Then it was on to Karachi that evening and three days of acclimatisation before playing a drawn match against the President's XI in Rawalpindi. Ray Bright used his flight and changes of pace effectively to take 5/93 and 6/29 to start a pleasant tour. His 29 wickets at 19.44 each had him head and shoulders above any other Australian bowler.

Australia's first Test in Pakistan for fifteen years was dominated by slow bowlers who accounted for 28 of the 33 wickets to fall. The National Stadium in Karachi saw both orthodox left-arm spinners in Iqbal Qasim (7/49) and Ray Bright (7/87) recording the best innings and match analyses of their Test careers. Bright's 10/111 remains a record in matches in this series.

It took Pakistan just over three days to record a victory by seven wickets on a very helpful pitch. This pleased the locals who were living in a country ravaged by corruption, and drugs, and religious and military power struggles. Having won one Test the Pakistanis were now content to draw the remaining two. The second started virtually straight after the first, this time at the Iqbal Stadium, Faisalabad. No result was ever going to be possible – so lifeless was the pitch – that Greg Chappell just let the Australian innings carry on into the fourth day. He scored 235 before being given out leg-before-wicket when dancing down the pitch, and Graham Yallop made 172 in a total of 617. Pakistan reached 382 for two in reply as all eleven Australians bowled, the first time this had happened since 1884.

Allan Border then had a dream run. He scored 178 in the draw against a Governor's XI in Multan followed by 150 not out and 153 in the third Test at Lahore's Gaddafi Stadium. With the Test drawn Pakistan claimed their first series win against Australia as Greg Chappell in his sixtieth Test passed the 5000-run mark.

Chappell was a relieved man, for prior to the tour he had discussed with Brian Hawkins of the Department of Foreign Affairs the procedures needed to be put into place and the evacuation plans for the team should the internal situation deteriorate. The Australian ambassador to Pakistan, John Petherbridge, had his embassy staff on stand-by to assist, but in the end the Pakistan Prime Minister's personal assurances that there would be no trouble held good.

Following the February 1980 Board meeting the Emergency Committee had a good hard look at the whole organisation and administration of Australian cricket. They quickly came to the conclusion to relocate the Board from Sydney to Melbourne – which took place in March 1981. The three men involved, Messrs Parish, Caldwell and Ridings, then made the decisions which had a fundamental effect on the structure of the Board. They decided to advertise for an Executive Director to replace the retiring Alan Barnes with David Richards being the only serious candidate. He commenced his duties on 1 October 1980 having been with the VCA for the previous nine years. Richards' successor at the VCA was assistant secretary Ken Jacobs, a personable man and highly efficient administrator.

What had now been created was an executive never available to Alan Barnes. Within a short time Richards had founded an administration which slowly but surely took power away from the fourteen delegates. The appointment of staff, as money flowed in from PBL, saw the work performed by delegates become more and more trivial although they still said they were the decision-making body. As the 1980s wore on so more sub-committees were formed to occupy delegates' time and to avoid their becoming involved in the matters their predecessors had loved to debate endlessly. From now on the relevance of the newly scheduled quarterly Board meetings had far less impact on the Australian game than in the past. The honest truth was that, by the beginning of the 1990s, just ten years after reorganisation, the Board could run itself without the input from any of the delegates – who were now quaintly called 'directors'. The changes had been that significant.

At the end of the Cricket sub-committee meeting in Melbourne on 4 February 1980, Greg Chappell again raised the issue of the Professional Cricketers' Association. He was fobbed off by Bob Parish with the suggestion of putting 'a formal submission to the Board'. While Chappell was in Pakistan the Board decided to appoint Bob Merriman as 'Coordinator of the Cricket sub-committee'. It was a shrewd move as he was a man respected by both sides. The attraction of Merriman for the Board was that he was both an industrial relations specialist and a cricket administrator. Prior to being appointed as a Commissioner to the Australian Conciliation and Arbitration Commission in May 1980, Merriman had been an industrial relations practitioner in the vehicle industry.

Merriman also had a number of years' experience in cricket administration in Geelong and had impressed everyone with his skills as manager of the Australian team to India in 1979. In retrospect David Richards maintains that Bob Merriman played a vitally important role from 1980, in building bridges between the players and the administration (not the delegates) in the period following the rapprochement. Dennis Lillee in his book *My Life* praised Merriman whom he saw as being 'very keen to do the right thing by both parties'.

The advent of Merriman signalled the beginning of the end for the PCA who not only were undermined but had no bargaining power with the Board. The major reason for the PCA demise could be argued as being the logistical and financial problems associated with maintaining an organisation with a small membership distributed across six States. But, as it was, Merriman's counselling and guidance saw rifts healed, misunderstandings corrected and the start of an improvement in player behaviour. With the top cricketers now on Board contracts, misbehaviour could be expensive – as one or two would soon find out.

Times were changing. The Cricket sub-committee was now deeply involved in players' income-tax matters with suggestions made that, when a team toured overseas and that country's taxation rates were lower than Australia's, then could the tourists be employed by that country's Board for this purpose? Only Lord's considered the matter worthwhile with the Test and County Cricket Board making investigations and putting suggestions to the Australian Board. Nothing came of it but it showed the shift in the top players' thinking.

Soon after the players returned from Pakistan, the selectors announced the team for the short tour to England to celebrate their centenary of Test cricket. Out went Beard, Hookes, Lawson, Malone and Wiener and in came John Dyson (NSW), Ashley Mallett (SA), Len Pascoe (NSW), Jeff Thomson (Queensland) and Graeme Wood (WA).

The first match in early August at Southampton saw Allan Border (95), Greg Chappell (86) and Bruce Laird (85) get into their stride as Hampshire were defeated by ten wickets. From then on it was draws or defeats with Surrey winning by 59 runs at The Oval and Nottinghamshire victorious by an innings and 76 runs at Trent Bridge. England won both one-day internationals on the run-up to the only Test.

Following the style of the remarkably successful Melbourne Centenary Test three years earlier, the organisers invited all the surviving English and Australian players to attend even though the match was played at Lord's instead of The Oval. Lord's was chosen not only because of its accepted place as the headquarters of the game, but also because it was far better equipped to handle the crowds expected. This proved a correct move as receipts for the Test amounted to £360,850 from an attendance of 84,938.

The week before the Test was one of nostalgia as these events prove to be. Alas the game did not provide the memories of its Melbourne equivalent, more the opposite. Fifty minutes was lost to rain on the first day and nearly five hours on the second. On the third morning rain left the ground sodden in patches on the Tavern side and after the fifth inspection umpires Bird and Constant were involved in a scuffle with angry Marylebone Cricket Club members. It soured the whole match which fell away into an embarrassing draw.

Greg Chappell had earlier won the toss and watched as Graeme Wood (112) scored a century by the close of the first day. Then Kim Hughes became the third batsman after Jaisimha (India) and Boycott to bat on all five days of a Test match. His match double of 117 and 84 were made in a style and manner which bespoke a batsman at the peak of his career. In all, Hughes struck five sixes and 25 fours, faced 308 balls and scored his 201 runs in 346 minutes. His six into the top tier of the pavilion was a shot to be savoured and remembered.

Chappell declared his first innings at 385 for five late on the third day. England then struggled to 205 (Lillee 4/43, Pascoe 5/59), and Chappell declared again at 189 for four, setting England a target of 370 runs in even time but the challenge was not taken up by the England captain, Ian Botham.

After the Test Phil Ridings, the tour manager and Board chairman-elect, and Alan Barnes both attended a later than usual International Cricket Conference at Lord's. On their return home Ridings took over from Parish and in November Barnes, then aged sixty-four, suffered a stroke in his office. The toll on his health had been taken.

Soon after the players returned home Greg Chappell met with the Cricket sub-committee and related the problems caused at the Centenary Test. It was resolved that, should weather interfere in Australian Tests in future, then umpires should publicly involve captains, groundstaff and administrators. Revolutionary stuff from a man who was 'unwelcome' only two years earlier. In fact the whole attitude of the players had changed. Now they were being given some responsibility they were acting with far more conservatism than before. At their meeting in Adelaide on 1 October 1980 they were openly critical of PBL Marketing, 'being unanimous that PBL's question of prize money distribution and their proposal for change was not in the best interests of the game and clearly indicated that PBL did not understand the game nor the players'.

Greg Chappell then presented a well-thought-out and deeply researched paper on future Australian tours to England. His two main proposals were 'that after the 1981 tour, future tours should involve four-day matches against County teams. Five matches should be played against the top five counties of the previous year with six fixtures against combined teams representing the remaining twelve counties'. His second proposal was, 'that the Test and County Cricket Board should accept that Test matches are for thirty hours with lost time being made up on rest days'.

The Board took no action on Chappell's proposals but what was showing was the thinking now going on in a Test cricketer's mind. A Woodfull or a Hassett would never have dreamt of bringing forth such ideas.

In the summer of 1980–81 both India and New Zealand toured, each playing three Tests. New Zealand began by losing their first Test in Brisbane in just three days. Captained by Geoff Howarth, the Kiwis made 225 to which Australia replied with 305, Graeme Wood 111.

Then Dennis Lilliee struck, taking 6/53 as New Zealand crumbled for 142. Victory was Australia's by ten wickets.

In mid-December in Perth it was a repeat performance. Lillee took 5/63 as New Zealand scored 196 and 121 to Australia's 265 and 55 for two. Then followed a Melbourne Test after Christmas in which the New Zealanders could rightly argue that a poor interpretation of the Laws by umpire Robin Bailhache cost them a more than reasonable chance of victory. On a sub-standard pitch, in which it was later found that couch grass had incorrectly been sown, Australia were put into bat and had reached 279 for nine when the last batsman, Jim Higgs, was caught by wicketkeeper Warren Lees from the medium-paced bowling of Lance Cairns. Umpire Bailhache called a very late no-ball saying the delivery was intimidatory. This decision allowed Doug Walters to go from 77 to 107 and complete the last of his fifteen Test centuries. The last-wicket record partnership of 60 proved decisive on the last day as Australia struggled to survive for a draw.

India started the first of their three Tests in Sydney on 2 January 1981. The Test lasted only three days, much to the annoyance of PBL Marketing who by now had lost six lucrative days of Test cricket television advertising which at peak times was worth $8000 for a 30-second slot. For the limited-overs day/night games this fee rose to $50,000. India made 201 in both innings to Australia's 406, Greg Chappell's 204 taking 408 minutes and coming from 296 balls with 27 boundaries.

Crowds fell badly this season, averaging only 47,555 for each Test. Adelaide met this average for the second Test as Kim Hughes scored a career-best 213 in 383 minutes from 303 balls. Graeme Wood made 125 as the Australian score mounted to 528. India replied with 419 and a Greg Chappell declaration set up an exciting finish. Needing to score 331 runs in 265 minutes, India reached 135 for eight with the tail-enders ducking and weaving against the fire of Lillee, Hogg and Pascoe.

In Melbourne on 12 February India, put into bat, made 237; then Allan Border (124) led the way in his team's reply of 419 and what looked like a comfortable situation. India, crippled by injuries, fought back to 324 second time around which left Australia needing only 143 runs to win in over a day. They then collapsed to be all out for 83, giving India victory by 59 runs, which could all have been so different. At 165 in their second innings, captain Sunil Gavaskar (70) was given out leg-before-wicket by umpire Rex Whitehead. Television replays clearly showed the ball hitting Gavaskar's bat and his protests came to nothing. He stalked off the pitch with his batting partner Chetan Chauhan and only the calming affect of manager S. K. Durrani saw Chauhan resume his innings with his new partner Dilip Vengsarkar. The match could so easily have been forfeited by India, yet had reference to television been allowed the umpire could have had a chance to reconsider his decision.

PBL Marketing were now fully in charge of Australian cricket and pulling the strings. Melbourne was to have a new electronic scoreboard – the old one eventually finding a new home at Canberra's Manuka Oval – and Sydney would follow suit, their fine scoreboard having a grossly ugly concrete stand built in front of it in the mid-1980s.

On 28 November 1980 Lynton Taylor wrote to the South Australian Cricket Association telling them, 'they were lagging behind the rest of the cricketing world by not having an electronic scoreboard'. A representative from a Japanese electronic company visited the Adelaide Oval for discussions, at the behest of PBL, but nothing was ever done to spoil the beauty of one of cricket's loveliest grounds.

The one-day series went through its usual ritual with India being eliminated. Of the finals matches New Zealand won the first, in Sydney, by 78 runs and Australia the second, in Melbourne, by seven wickets. Then came the most controversial one-day international yet played. Sunday 1 February, a hot steamy Melbourne day, with 52,990 present saw Australia bat first. Greg Chappell had just passed his half-century when he hit a ball from Lance Cairns to Martin Snedden who took a spectacular catch in the outfield. Chappell waited for the umpires to give a decision, claiming he had not seen the catch taken. Neither had the umpires, although yet again television would have confirmed it for them. It incensed the New Zealanders, who had to obey the two inexperienced umpires' decision, as Chappell went on to score 90 out of his team's 235 for four.

Worse was to follow. New Zealand reached 229 for eight with one ball remaining when Greg Chappell instructed his younger brother Trevor, who was bowling, to send down the final delivery under-arm. For all their huff and puff when approving the rules of the tournament as prepared by the Board, PBL had not given this situation any thought. Nor should they, for it was completely outside the spirit of the game although within the Laws. Trevor Chappell bowled as instructed and then all hell broke loose. New Zealand Prime Minister Robert Muldoon called it 'an act of cowardice' and said 'it was appropriate that the Australians were dressed in yellow'. Malcolm Fraser, the Australian Prime Minister immediately telephoned Board chairman Phil Ridings to voice his disapproval, while politicians in both countries joined the majority in condemning Greg Chappell's action.

The match had finished late on the Sunday afternoon. In Adelaide, Sir Donald Bradman went straight to his study, examined the rules pertaining to the game and by early Monday morning his detailed draft of suggested changes was with every Board delegate. Within three weeks all State Associations had passed them into law with the Board confirming likewise.

Under considerable pressure, Greg Chappell issued a statement apologising for 'a decision made under pressure and in the heat of the moment'. Two days later he made a brilliant 87 as Australia won the fourth match to take the finals series. The following morning Chappell announced his unavailability for the forthcoming tour of England.

The country was being saturated with cricket. The incessant barrage of the television game was causing people to move away from watching with at least two products advertised between each over being boycotted by shoppers.

The Shield season saw a big decline in attendances. The days of five-figure daily crowds were long gone. Three times in Perth and once in Sydney did a four-day aggregate exceed 10,000 with the season's average daily numbering just 1944 spectators. Some matches just scraped to three figures: the goose that laid the golden egg was suffocating the rest. Western Australia did not mind; they won the title yet again with a side of eight Test players and a South African, Ken McEwan, who played in unofficial Test sides. At least one record was set when, on 9 January 1981 in Brisbane, Queensland and Tasmania took part in the 1000th Sheffield Shield game.

At their January 1981 meeting, the Board decided to take only sixteen players to England rather than seventeen, the traditional number. The reasoning was 'owing to all the one-day matches needed to be played'. The obvious happened during the tour and the young NSW left-armed paceman, Mike Whitney, was called up to join the party.

Western Australians Kim Hughes and Rodney Marsh were named captain and vice-captain respectively. The manager was Fred Bennett of NSW, with Peter Philpott as coach.

The team left Sydney on 28 April 1981 and arrived at Colombo's Katunayeke airport the next day to play in an unofficial Test and three one-day internationals. Then it was on to London for the start of a three-and-a-half month tour.

The Thirtieth Australians played in only seventeen first-class matches, far fewer than their predecessors. As a result only seven centuries were scored – Dirk Wellham's unbeaten 135 at Northampton being the highest – and only thirteen lots of five or more wickets in an innings were taken by the bowlers, Geoff Lawson's 7/81 in the second Test topping the list. No batsman exceeded Allan Border's 807-run aggregate, while Terry Alderman topped the wicket-taking list with 51 at 20.86.

Rain badly affected the tour up to the three one-day internationals in early June, which Australia won by two matches to one. Then came the first Test at Trent Bridge, Nottingham, and debuts for Trevor Chappell, the last of the three brothers, and swing bowler Terry Alderman, one of the most civilised of men to play the modern game.

Kim Hughes put England into bat in a match which would see Sunday play for the first time in a Test in England. In a low-scoring game England, with six past and future Test captains in their line-up, fell to Alderman (4/68 and 5/62) and Lillee (3/34 and 5/46) for 185 and 125. Trevor Chappell scored the winning runs on the Sunday afternoon as Australia won by four wickets.

The second Test at Lord's saw Hughes again put England into bat. The gamble paid off as Lawson's 7/81 saw the home team dismissed for 311 to which Australia replied with 345. A draw was always on the cards but it produced a turning-point in the series when, after the game, England captain Ian Botham handed in his resignation. The subsequent decision of the local selectors was to recall Mike Brearley as leader and hand him the task of turning the tide for his side who by now had gone twelve Tests without a win.

The third Test, which took place at Headingley, Leeds, over five days from 16 July, has gone down in the annals of cricket history as one of the finest Tests ever played. For this series the Australian Broadcasting Commission had won the rights to televise the Tests back to Australia. Unlike their commercial rivals, staff at the ABC were quasi-civil servants and they took their salary grievances out on the watching public by 'pulling the plug' just before the start of play each day on this and subsequent Tests. From then on Channel Nine could do no wrong in televising cricket to their domestic market.

Hughes won the toss and batted first: Dyson (102) scored the first of his two Test centuries with Hughes making 89. The declaration came at 401 for nine with Botham claiming 6/95. Lillee, Alderman and Lawson skittled England for 174 and, following-on, they reached 135 for seven when Graham Dilley (56) joined Botham at the crease. Relieved of the pressures of captaincy, Botham proceeded to hit his way to an unbeaten 149 and Australia, set 130 to win, lost by 18 runs as fast bowler Bob Willis claimed career-best figures of 8/43. It was a crushing, devastating blow for the Australians from which they never recovered. It also left Kim Hughes in the public perception as a man who could snatch defeat from the jaws of victory.

Following this loss the tourists had the first of their only two victories against county teams when an inspired Allan Border (115 and 70*) saw the Australians to a seven-wicket success over Worcestershire. At Edgbaston three days later, Mike Brearley's superb captaincy saw England again win by a narrow margin, this time 29 runs. Hughes was completely out-manoeuvred as Brearley pressured every batsman, made precise field changes and never allowed England to lose the initiative, even after they were 69 runs behind on the first innings.

The embattled Hughes was, by now, losing the support of his own team and at Old Trafford in mid-August another Botham batting blitz stopped the Australians in their tracks. Terry Alderman took 4/88 and 5/109 while Graham Yallop (114) and Allan Border (123*) scored centuries but they could not stop England winning by 103 runs and retaining the Ashes.

The sixth Test at The Oval saw Australia have the better of a drawn game. Dirk Wellham (103) scored a century on his debut – the first by an Australian in England since Harry Graham's in 1893 – while Allan Border's unbeaten 106 showed him to be a player of quality. Dennis Lillee took eleven wickets in the match (7/89 and 4/70) with Terry Alderman finishing with 42 wickets, the most by any Australian bowler in this series.

As the Australians flew home it was clear that Kim Hughes would not retain the captaincy for the home series against Pakistan and the West Indies. However, the Board were having doubts over Greg Chappell. They had felt badly let down by his displays earlier in 1981 and later in that year did not give him the wholehearted support a captain should have.

David Richards, exerting his new power and authority, obtained from Greg Chappell a further apology for the New Zealand incidents in the precise words he believed were needed. It was all a little far-fetched, for Greg Chappell was a man who brooded on and felt for the game. He would have realised his error of judgment and had little need for an administrator to run around getting an assumed correct wording on a piece of paper just to smooth the perceived sensibilities of Board delegates.

With the Board's former decision-making process now passing to the administration, the meetings prior to the start of the 1981–82 season took on the role more of serving a large business concern than a sport. The role of the game in Australia was becoming the end-point of a concentrated commercial build-up to a climax of on-field activity.

The players were still in England when the State Secretaries Pre-Season Conference was held in Sydney. At the American business inspired hour of 7.30 am on their first day the dazed State officials met their Board counterparts at a breakfast meeting at which PBL Marketing performed. The Board's commercial arm – as they were now described – presented their marketing and promotional activities for the season aided by four pretty girls and two cliché-speaking executives. The secretaries were told of the ticket agency that would now be used for all cricket bookings (an agency which would collapse amid allegations of fraud and missing money with its well-known chairman eventually serving a prison sentence), and of the merchandising to be sold for the season, of which none of the profits would find their way into the States' coffers.

After PBL's departure came the new era of Board instructions. No longer did State associations do their own thing: now they were locked into form-filling; standardised reports; computerisation; group travel bookings with named companies, hotels and airlines; fixed allowances for player payments, umpires' fees, scorers' expenses and food costs; statistical match returns; an administration handbook 'which must be followed'; payroll tax forms; the compulsory purchases of Telex machines; marketing logos; advertising on cricket equipment; fees for endorsements; approved suppliers of goods; a new national coaching plan to follow; no refunds on pre-sold tickets as a policy; all dealings with the ACB's Parliament House lobbyist to be conducted through the Board; experimental laws; cricket scholarships; tours by non-Test countries. And so it went on.

It was all quite exhausting.

The team arrived home from England on Saturday 5 September and by the following Wednesday Kim Hughes had flown across the continent for a meeting of the (now) Cricket committee in Melbourne. Hughes raised all the points Greg Chappell had brought up two years earlier concerning the England tour, none of which have ever been acted upon.

In general discussions the players were seen to get their ways on minor issues. They came up with ideas on payments particularly for the twenty 'key players' the Board had put under contract. They felt they needed a 'cricket manager' for the domestic season; came up with a new concept – of a chairman, a captain, and a manager – for the selection committee (which the English took up and the Australians rejected); and suggested a panel of six recommended umpires for Tests – which the Board accepted for the following two seasons.

As the meeting drew to its lunchtime conclusion David Richards gave an explanation as to why he had recently sent out a letter to all players warning them of the consequences of going to play or coach in South Africa. The Fraser government was clamping down on the sports where individuals had South African contacts, particularly in view of the recent violent Springbok rugby tour of New Zealand. Richards gave the players' representatives a report on the latest ICC meeting and its refusal to accept the recommendations of a fact-finding mission.

Within five months the first group of rebel cricketers, from England, would tour South Africa. Australian players too were already being considered.

# 32

# Politicking

Pakistan were the first tourists to Australia for the new season, arriving in Perth on 13 October 1981. After drawn matches against Western Australia, Queensland and Victoria the first Test started on the WACA ground on 13 November. Visiting captain Javed Miandad put Australia into bat and would have been satisfied at the end of the day to see them at 159 for seven.

Fifteen wickets fell on the second day as Pakistan collapsed to 62 (Lillee 5/18, Alderman 4/36) in reply to Australia's 180. There was no reason for their inept batting display and at 26 for eight the record books were out. Only 26 from Sarfraz Nawaz saved the blushes. Kim Hughes (106) led the Australian counter-attack with Greg Chappell declaring at 424 for eight.

On the fourth afternoon Pakistan were 96 for three when Dennis Lillee was responsible for one of the ugliest scenes yet observed on a cricket field. Miandad, facing Lillee, turned a ball to the legside for a single and trotted up the pitch. Lillee deliberately obstructed Miandad who pushed him out of the way. Lillee then proceeded to kick Miandad on the shins and as umpire Tony Crafter came between them so Miandad raised his bat to ward off the Australian fast bowler. Lillee raised his fists as if wanting to fight before the umpire calmed matters down.

Whatever disciplinary action was going to be taken, the Board were virtually impotent to give Lillee the suspension his behaviour warranted. They knew that PBL Marketing had, in Lillee, a considerable commercial asset and under no circumstances was his absence from the television screen going to be tolerated. The players' disciplinary meeting fined Lillee $200 and asked Miandad for an apology for provoking Lillee in the first place. Umpires Crafter and Mel Johnson, who had a close-up view of the incident, objected to the penalty on the grounds it was manifestly inadequate. The Board took over from the players' self-disciplinary committee and handed Lillee a suspension from two one-day internationals.

The Test finished early on the fifth morning in victory for Australia by 286 runs. Lillee then sat out the limited-overs games in Melbourne and Sydney before returning for the second Test in Brisbane. He took 5/81 and 4/51, including Miandad twice, and also became the third bowler in Test cricket to take 300 wickets. Greg Chappell with 201 on his home pitch in 411 minutes from 296 balls and with 22 fours steered Australia to victory by ten wickets. The great disappointment was that ten days of good Test cricket had seen 50,664 spectators go through the turnstiles whereas the three one-day internationals between the Tests had attracted 53,894.

The Melbourne Cricket Ground pitch continued to be a disgrace and the Club knew it. They were going to dig up the whole wicket area but had to wait until the international season was over in late January 1982. When Miandad won the toss on 11 December he knew that by batting first he would be in pole position. He declared Pakistan's innings closed at 500 for eight – much to the annoyance of the television commentators who sat through two days' fairly tedious cricket – and then dismissed Australia for 293 (Wood 100) and 125 to gain Pakistan their first victory by an innings against Australia. Imran Khan had captured Pakistan's leading wicket-taking record during the match and the vast outfield had seen Majid Khan score an all-run seven when Lillee had been driven to the long-off boundary.

The West Indies team had arrived in Sydney on 9 November for their three-month tour and, before their first Test, they beat South Australia by 226 runs, NSW by nine wickets, Queensland by an innings and 92 runs, and drew with Tasmania.

The four-day crowd of 134,801 was the highest aggregate of another saturated cricket season, and they saw Kim Hughes fight his way to an unbeaten century as Australia made just 198 on Boxing Day. Then came a sensation as, in the few minutes before stumps were drawn, the West Indies lost four wickets for just ten runs, Lillee claiming three of them. The atmosphere was gladiatorial with the whole ground enveloped in an atmosphere of expectation. Even the cynics in the pressbox were enthusiastic.

The following morning all was calm as the West Indies resumed their innings until at 2.55 pm the crowd went wild again. It was then that the left-handed Larry Gomes snicked a Lillee delivery to Greg Chappell at first slip. The Australian captain took the catch and Lillee had broken the world Test record previously held by Lance Gibbs with 309 wickets. Music blared over the loudspeakers as the crowd stood and roared their approval. For the companies advertising on Channel Nine at that time, their message was getting to nearly one-third of Australia's population.

Lillee's 7/83 was a Test-best as the Australians fell behind by only three runs on first innings. Laird (64), Wood (46) and Border (66) gave Australia a surprisingly good start in their second innings as all the other batsmen failed on the treacherous pitch. The West Indian batsmen could not cope either and fell to defeat by 58 runs.

Two days later in Sydney the sides met again for a draw. Yardley's bowling claimed him ten wickets for the match including a Test-best 7/98 while John Dyson's unbeaten 127, his Test highest, took him over six hours as Australia batted out time. Then followed a glut of easily forgettable one-day matches and a final series in which the West Indies defeated Australia by three matches to one.

The third and final Test in Adelaide was a splendid match played in the right spirit and at the end had the right result. Put into bat Australia lost four wickets in the first half an hour before pulling back to 238. The West Indies scored quickly to reach 389 after which Border (126), Hughes (84) and Laird (78) dominated in Australia's 386. Needing 236 to win the West Indies reached their target early on the final evening as their captain Clive Lloyd hit the winning boundary. His team then ran on to the ground and, lifting their captain high, carried him in triumph to the dressing-room. Memories of the 1975–76 debacle were gradually being erased.

The domestic season of 1981–82 had seen the surprise of South Australia taking the Sheffield Shield in quite dramatic fashion on the final day of the season. This rare success was due solely to the influence on the team of John Inverarity. Holder of the then record for the most number of Shield runs, Inverarity had moved to Adelaide to take up a senior teaching post and had offered his services to the SACA. He was immediately drafted into the side with his tactical acumen and common sense prevailing. It was said by many in Australia that the choice of Inverarity instead of Simpson during the WSC interregnum would have seen the emergence of one of Australia's greatest captains.

Prior to the start of the one-day finals, the Cricket Committee had met in Melbourne to thrash out a number of issues. Other than three Board delegates, the executive director and coordinator, the players present were Greg Chappell (Queensland), Jim Higgs (Victoria), David Hookes (SA), Kim Hughes (WA), Geoff Lawson (NSW) and Roger Woolley (Tasmania).

Chairman Phil Ridings started by giving the players the news they wanted to hear: of course the captain could attend Board meetings. So could Bob Merriman, the cricket coordinator, and, added Ridings: 'They may discuss any matter they choose to bring before the Board'. Having won such a major victory the players have hardly since used the prerogative granted to them. Whether it was hot air or not, only Greg Chappell utilised this form of contact and even then he became quickly disillusioned.

The players discussed at considerable length the Board's Code of Behaviour. Surprisingly, they did not unite behind Dennis Lillee and were openly critical of his incident with Javed Miandad. It was agreed to amend this disciplinary code for the following season and to ask Channel Nine not to show replay after replay of any problem until it had been dealt with at the close of each day's play. The players also realised that the Sheffield Shield was a most important competition and, to add spice to it, suggested a final between the teams finishing on top of the table. This was adopted by the Board and came into being for the 1982–83 season.

With a short tour of New Zealand soon to take place the Board appointed Greg Chappell as captain before choosing the team. This was done specifically to allow Chappell to join the selectors in making their decisions as it was realised that, following the under-arm incident in Melbourne, the Australians would be given a hostile reception. In deciding to take only thirteen players – Australia's smallest number of tourists – it was also agreed that all would be seasoned professionals.

There were three one-day internationals – of which Australia won two – two drawn first-class matches and three provincial one-day games. The first of the three Tests was a rain restricted match at the Basin Reserve, Wellington, in which under ten hours' play was possible. A fortnight later at Auckland's Eden Park ground, the Australians were comprehensively outplayed by New Zealand, being defeated by five wickets. Graeme Wood scored a century in Australia's second innings but it was to no avail as his colleagues gave him little assistance.

Greg Chappell was a model of decorum during the tour with player behaviour reaching new levels for the modern game. The crowds ranged from boisterous at the Tests to unruly during the limited-overs fixtures. Attendance records were broken everywhere and the New Zealand Cricket Council reported a profit on the series of over $NZ58,000.

Chappell went to Lancaster Park in Christchurch for the final Test in the right frame of mind. He scored a first-innings 176 in 266 minutes and then hit the winning runs as Australia won by eight wickets. By his own efforts Chappell had done a considerable amount of repair work to an incident now put behind him.

The whirl of cricket tours continued as, three days after the team returned home from New Zealand, the side to tour Pakistan was announced. Chappell declined selection due to business matters, Lillee was injured again and Pascoe did not want to go. The selectors decided to revert to Kim Hughes as captain with Allan Border as his deputy. The new players were Ian Callen (Victoria), Geoff Lawson (NSW), Wayne Phillips (SA), Greg Ritchie (Queensland), and Peter Sleep

(SA). The choice of manager in Colin Egar, the former Test umpire, proved to be a poor decision as his belligerent and disciplinarian attitude had a negative effect on the players.

Before the team flew to Rawalpindi on 9 September the, by now, very influential Cricket Committee met in Melbourne. The players were putting forward proposals and ideas, the Board approving or suggesting changes, with the players having virtually the final say. In this situation Greg Chappell was the ideal man at the helm of the playing side of the game. His maturity and understanding compared more than favourably to that of Kim Hughes who was prone to tantrums and regular ego-trips.

At the meeting, the Board's growing number of apparatchiks – some of whom David Richards found difficulty keeping in check – reported to the players on numerous issues ranging from the new Melbourne Cricket Ground electronic scoreboard not showing any controversial replays, through to the political unrest in Pakistan, particularly Hyderabad. In return the players requested the removal of Robin Bailhache from the list of Test umpires; a detailed submission from the Board on options for the tours of Sri Lanka and to England for the World Cup in 1983; increases in player payments and contributions to the Retirement Benefits Payment Scheme; television video replays for the players to study; Test cricketers to be unavailable for designated domestic matches during the season; Test match venues only for Shield matches with exceptions by discretion only; future tour contracts to contain clauses which prohibited players gambling on matches in which they played; the Board chairman to investigate specified incidents which happened during the season; and so on went the list. It was player power, but not power being in any sense misused: with Greg Chappell at the helm, that would not happen in any case.

The six-week tour of Pakistan was a shambles from beginning to end. Because of its clash with the Commonwealth Games in Brisbane only two reporters went with the team and their copy barely made Australian newspapers due to the apathy engendered towards it. Australia lost all three Tests, two of the three one-day internationals with the other abandoned due to rioting, while the three other first-class matches were drawn.

After games against the Patron's XI, the Board XI, and Pakistan in a limited-overs fixture, the first Test started in Karachi on 22 September. Hughes batted on winning the toss and saw his side reach 218 for five at the close. His players' concentration was sorely tested by unruly spectators setting light to a marquee by the side of the playing area and by various missiles being thrown at the fielders.

After being dismissed for 284, the Australian fielders then had to try and concentrate through a series of umpiring decisions which caused them to become quite agitated. Their concern filtered through to batsman Moshin Khan who, when on 58, played defensively to a delivery from Jeff Thomson and then instinctively knocked the ball away when it rebounded towards his stumps and was given out 'handled the ball'. He was only the third batsman in Test cricket to have been given out in that way after Russell Endean and Andrew Hilditch. Captain Imran Khan declared the Pakistan innings closed at 419 for nine after Kim Hughes had twice taken his players from the field. They had been pelted with rocks, vegetables and other projectiles and this caused the Australian captain to warn the Pakistan authorities of his determination to leave the country should any of his players be hurt.

With their concentration gone, the Australians put up only token resistance for the rest of the game, eventually losing by nine wickets early on the fifth day. Two days later in Faisalabad the tourists went out to field for six long sessions of play as Pakistan set about reaching 501 for six as the declaration came before play began on the third day. Australia replied with 168 and 330 – Greg Ritchie 106 not out in only his second Test – to lose by an innings and three runs.

With considerable tension between captain and manager not helping team morale, a crushing nine-wicket defeat in Lahore did not come as any surprise. Graeme Wood (85) top-scored in Australia's 316 to which Pakistan replied with 467 for seven declared and went on to record three Test wins in a series for the first time. The final limited-overs match two days later was abandoned after Lawson, Callen and Ritchie were struck by missiles while fielding. The Australian team were just able to return to their hotel, to pack and flee to the airport to await their flight out of the country, and safety.

With all the political unrest in Pakistan, the tour should never have taken place. However, if PBL Marketing wanted two overseas teams a season to visit Australia then reciprocal tours had to be made.

The Australians arrived home the day before the England touring team arrived. The visitors, lacking the cream of their players who had been suspended from Test cricket for three years following a rebel tour to South Africa, were captained by pace-bowler Bob Willis and had Doug Insole as manager.

A month earlier the Board had met in Melbourne to discuss a number of issues, not least their concern over the amount of money PBL was taking from the game. The accounts for 1981–82 had now been audited and made for some fairly horrific reading. Bearing in mind that there was more money in the coffers than ever before, the amount of profit going to Kerry Packer's companies showed what an excellent businessman he was. Of the season's $3,492,864 gate takings, exactly $90,005 was left to be distributed to the six State Associations with nothing left to add to the Players' Retirement Benefit Scheme. Had every available player suddenly demanded their payment the total at 30 June 1982 had already reached the nominal figure of $330,200 which twelve months later had become $451,850.

The money flowing into cricket would grow and grow. Even the disastrous tour of Pakistan saw the return of a $54,266 profit. But it was the 1982–83 season which would see the big take-off in crowd figures and income. For the first time attendances topped the magical seven-figure mark for Test and international games: 1,189,934 and $5,271,390 respectively. However, and this was the figure which caused considerable media comment, the amount of money distributed to the States was only $65,000, with another $22,365 going into the Retirement Benefit scheme.

From 1985 onwards, these figures were not available to State Associations and only to senior members of the Board's administration. The secrecy had started during the 1981–82 season when, at the request of Consolidated Press, the Fraser Government had agreed to amendments to various sections of company legislation. The result was that for future tours to Australia the actual guarantee paid to overseas cricket Boards would not be made public. When a Board official let slip in 1984 that the West Indies had demanded, and received, a guarantee in excess of $2,000,000 there was considerable embarrassment.

The England tour started in late October 1982 when Queensland defeated the tourists by 171 runs with Greg Chappell (126) and Kepler Wessels (103) recording centuries. It was only Queensland's second success against an England team, the first being in 1928. Then came a draw with South Australia and victory by one wicket over Western Australia on a very poor Perth pitch.

On 4 November the Australian Cricket Board had announced the team for the first Test in Perth with Greg Chappell winning the captaincy back from Kim Hughes. The choice was a close run thing when put to the vote, but Chappell won because he had the backing of Board chairman and chairman of selectors, Phil Ridings.

In my book *Fight for the Ashes, 1982–83* I wrote:

> It had been common gossip amongst the cricketing fraternity that some kind of arrangement had been made between Ridings and Chappell. These rumours were around wherever England had played; Brisbane, Adelaide and now Perth. Scurrilous though they might seem they were all of the same consistency. It was said that Chappell would regain the captaincy in return for speaking out at regular intervals against South African cricket. The ACB were quietly worried that the tempting financial tentacles of South

African promoters would snare some of Australia's best cricketers, and the consequences of that move were all too well known.

The Test in Perth will be remembered as the first in which a player was injured on the field of play by a spectator. On a well-prepared pitch, next to the offending one used a week earlier, England, who had been put into bat, had reached 402 for eight by the second afternoon when a number of spectators jumped the boundary fence and headed towards Terry Alderman. Waving Union Jacks, these young men, the children of emigrants, with their closely cropped haircuts and climbing boots wished to inform Alderman that the English batsmen were on top of the Australian bowlers. As he was hit, Alderman grabbed his assailant and in doing so dislocated his shoulder which also caused considerable nerve damage. Carried from the field on a stretcher, Alderman would not be able to appear in Test cricket again until March 1984. It took over seven years for his insurance claim for loss of earnings to be met.

Greg Chappell took his team from the field while the dozen police on duty made 26 arrests. Within a few minutes of the resumption England had been dismissed for 411 to which Australia replied with 424 for nine declared, Greg Chappell 117. England batted out their second innings and the match was left drawn.

England defeated New South Wales by 27 runs on their way to Brisbane for the second Test. The Australian selectors brought in two Queensland players for their debuts: fast bowler Carl Rackemann, a farmer from Wondai, and the South African Kepler Wessels.

For the next three years Wessels would be a controversial figure both on and off the field of play. There is little doubt he used his recently gained Australian citizenship as a flag of convenience but, at the time of his Australian Test debut and subsequent maiden century, only a few of the travelling journalists knew what was really going on.

Between the Tests, Western Australia had played New South Wales in Sydney in a domestic one-day fixture. After the match, Kim Hughes had been approached by former Test batsman Bruce Francis who discussed with him the possibility of his interest in playing in South Africa. Hughes immediately notified the Board who were also aware of the presence in Australia of former South African bowler Hugh Tayfield who was supposedly writing on the England tour for the Johannesburg *Star* newspaper. Armed with a cheque book and backed by one of the Republic's cricketing sponsors, Tayfield was authorised to pay any Test player up to $100,000 for a five-week South Africa tour.

The Board told PBL Marketing to get their solicitors to write to Francis warning him that the Board had Australia's top twenty-five players under contract and to leave them alone. Three players had already signed and with the Board issuing a public warning these agreements were cancelled. The matter lay dormant for just over a year.

Greg Chappell won the toss at the 'Gabba and put England into bat. Geoff Lawson in a splendid match took eleven wickets, with 6/47 as England fell for 219. Wessels, first in and last out, scored 162 in Australia's 341 and the advantage was with the home team for the rest of the match. Lawson (5/87) and Thomson (5/73) saw off the England fightback and eventually Kim Hughes hit the winning boundary to see Australia winners by seven wickets.

On their way to Adelaide, the tourists drew with Victoria, a match which saw the first use of the giant electronic scoreboard and the dangers of its distraction upon the players. On a number of occasions, English fielders instead of chasing the ball were looking up at the big screen to see what had just happened.

The Adelaide Oval is a beautiful ground, all the more so in mid-December before the summer heat discolours the playing surface and surrounding embankments. Maybe Bob Willis was distracted for, on winning the toss, he put Australia in to bat. On the two previous occasions an England captain had done such a thing (Peter May in 1959 and Mike Denness in 1975) Australia had won easily.

Greg Chappell (115) scored an elegant century on the first day as Australia took complete charge and totalled 438. Geoff Lawson again became the main wicket-taker with 4/56 and 5/66 as England reached 216, and following-on, 304. Australia won by eight wickets on the fifth morning to go two games up in the series.

England then travelled to Hobart for a six-wicket win over Tasmania prior to going on to Melbourne for what was one of the most exciting Test matches ever played. There was absolutely nothing between the two teams on each of the five days and victory came by what was then the narrowest runs margin in Test cricket.

On the first day England, put into bat, made 284; Australia scored 287 on the second; England 294 on the third – the only instance in Test history of sides being all out at the end of each scheduled day's play. On the fourth day Australia's ninth wicket fell at 218 still 74 runs short of victory. Then the drama started as Allan Border and last batsman Jeff Thomson battled to save the match. At the close they were still there with the score on 255. Next morning, Thursday, dawned dull and overcast. Rain overnight had caused a few problems for the groundstaff but by the start of play the ground was perfect.

Inside were over 18,000 spectators, let in free of charge as, quite obviously, the game could have been over after just one delivery. The tension was quite unbearable as the victory target got closer and closer. Then, after 128 minutes together for 70 runs, Thomson edged a ball from Botham to Tavaré at second slip. He fumbled the ball, knocking it upwards for Geoff Miller to run behind him to complete a remarkable catch. England had won by just three runs in the 250th Test between the old enemies.

In a way the fifth Test was an anticlimax. In the first over of the Sydney Test, local batsman John Dyson (79) was palpably run out but given the benefit of the doubt by umpire Mel Johnson. A call for a television replay judgment would have saved many claims of umpires' bias by the visiting press. As this was Kim Hughes (137) scored his only century in Sydney as the match ground out to a draw. Australia had regained the Ashes lost in 1977 and gave Greg Chappell the high point of his long and distinguished career. At his post-match press conference he announced his decision to step down as Australia's captain for the forthcoming one-day series in which New Zealand would make up the numbers.

After fifteen minor-round matches played around Australia, England were eliminated from the final series. It then took Australia just two more matches to win the World Series Cup and to conclude a most successful season.

On Friday 11 March 1983, when the players met the Board in Melbourne, it was unanimously agreed that the format for the season had been perfect. After three years of experimenting the right formula had been found. To cap the season off, New South Wales had beaten Western Australia over five days in Perth in the first Sheffield Shield Final in front of a crowd of 16,443. The Board were happy, particularly with the 84,153 spectators who turned up at Melbourne for a one-day match. All was sweetness and light.

During the 1982–83 season a full Sri Lankan team had made a short tour of Australia playing first-class matches against New South Wales, Tasmania and Victoria. Then, in April, Australia made an equally short tour of the island to play in four one-day internationals and the inaugural Test between the sides. Played at the Asgiriya Stadium in Kandy, Australia gave debuts to left-arm spinner Tom Hogan and wicketkeeper Roger Woolley. There was rejoicing in Tasmania as Woolley became his State's first Test representative this century – not counting, of course, those who were born on the island and gained honours elsewhere.

Greg Chappell captained Australia for the final time as Kepler Wessels (141), Graham Yallop (98) and David Hookes (143*) slaughtered the Sri Lankan bowling. In just four sessions of play the score had reached 514 for four before Chappell did the humane thing and declared. In two days Sri Lanka fell for 271 (Yardley 5/88) and 205 (Hogan 5/66) to give Australia victory by an innings and 38 runs.

The team flew home at the end of April for a short break before proceeding to England for the third World Cup competition. Greg Chappell withdrew from selection and the captaincy reverted to Hughes for the eighth time. The tour was a disaster, however. Australia started by losing to Zimbabwe, of all teams, by 13 runs and followed this with a loss by 101 runs to the West Indies. Then came victories over India by 162 runs, and by 32 runs against Zimbabwe in the return fixture. Two losses finished the tour: by seven wickets against the West Indies and by 118 runs against India.

Prior to the World Cup a Young Australian team had made an eight-match tour of Zimbabwe under the captaincy of NSW batsman Dirk Wellham. Of the fourteen players chosen only two of the Tasmanians, Phil Blizzard and Stuart Saunders, failed to gain representative honours in one form or another. It was one of the best behaved teams to have left Australian shores for many years with players from the team even now talking about the comradeship that existed between them.

On the other hand, the majority of the team in England were in the game for what they could get out of it. If one looks at any main reason for their abject failure it could be put at the door of the South African cricket authorities who continually disrupted the Australian team preparation by waving lucrative contracts under their noses.

The Australian rebel tour of South Africa was conceived by Graham Yallop and Kepler Wessels over dinner one night in Leeds with Dr Ali Bacher, managing director of the South African Cricket Union. All was going well until a Test cricketer, while drinking with journalists, told the whole story: the same player who had divulged the Packer story in 1977! When the story broke, the tour was put on hold for a short time to allow matters to cool down.

The Australian Cricket Board were always, contrary to their constant denials in the media, fully aware of what was going on regarding South Africa. On Thursday 28 July 1983 they summoned all State Association secretaries to Melbourne to discuss specifically the South African problem and the performance of the Australian team.

As the Board staff expanded, with fresh senior appointments being made, the old story of more office space being needed became a fact. In four years the Board numbers had grown from Alan Barnes, an occasional assistant and a part-time typist to some twenty people, many of whom were supplied with company cars and travelled the country on a regular basis. Because of the change in government legislation, and as this was not a public company, the final fully publicised financial statement for the year ending 30 June 1983 showed a Board income of $506,651 and administration expenses of $423,691. Four years earlier both figures had been $40,000!

What was even more galling to those who studied financial statements was the 'official' total income from cricket in 1982–83 which was given as $2,087,309 whereas the 'Confidential: Eyes Only' PBL Marketing accounts showed the true figure of $8,705,717, and even then this did not include television advertising revenue, radio fees or other associated income.

As this figure 'grow'd like Topsy' with the expansion of the game and the ravages of inflation, so the percentage of money actually finding its way back into cricket grew less and less. Kim Hughes said: 'When I was captain I was given quite an insight into the way PBL Marketing had the Board over a financial barrel. By the time of the West Indies visit in 1983–84, from a gate of $490,010 (22 January) in Melbourne just $27,832 found its way to the Board. It was disgraceful.'

By now the internal workings of Australian cricket were starting to fragment in a way which would see four years of disgraceful antics both on and off the field of play. The 1983–87 era was a very dark time for the game with committeemen as much, if not more, to blame as the players themselves.

Kim Hughes cut a very sorry figure at this time. His loyalty to official cricket in the days of Packer had seen him treated as a pariah by the cricketers who returned to the fold in 1979. Senior players talked of him with open contempt, and in doing so told journalists, who in turn formulated public opinion against Hughes.

The administration once again lost any semblance of respect the players might have had for them by forcing the Test men to sign draconian contracts and by not giving loyalty to the team when it was most needed.

In September 1983, at the Board's annual meeting, Fred Bennett took over as chairman from Phil Ridings. Bennett immediately saw the need for change, but push as he might he could not get his way with other Board delegates. He was also aware of the demands sent to 'Key Players' by the Board insisting 'that you confirm your current contract to us by 2 September 1983 and your agreement for us to extend it to the end of the 1984–85 season'.

The players, at the Cricket Committee meeting held on 26 August, were furious at the Board's demands. David Richards attempted to calm matters down but rebellion was once again in the air. Ray Steele tried to tell the players the contracts were not really water-tight but 'the Board was in a position where it had established its forward tours programme for several years ahead and so it was now able to make a longer term commitment to its international standard players'.

The reality was the perceived idea that, to get the top players to sign for $12,000 a year, would stop them signing for rebel South African tours at $100,000 a year.

Cricket politics now dominated, but the game had to go on. Pakistan were the tourists for the 1983–84 season with the West Indians arriving for the World Series Cup. Captained by Imran Khan, the Pakistanis opened their tour with a match against Queensland in Brisbane only to find Greg Ritchie (196) and Kepler Wessels (127) in strong form. Escaping with a draw, Pakistan then won well against South Australia and were beaten by Western Australia on the lead up to the first Test in Perth.

With Imran Khan injured, Zaheer Abbas captained Pakistan for the first three Tests. He put Australia into bat at the WACA ground and spent nearly two long days in the field as the score went to 436 for nine before Hughes declared. South Australian opening batsman Wayne Phillips made his debut and proceeded to share a second-wicket stand with Yallop (141) of 259. Phillips scored 159 from 246 balls in a fraction over five hours to give an exciting start to a Test career which would become erratic to say the least. With paceman Carl Rackemann in fine form with 5/32 and 6/86, Pakistan fell for 129 and 298 to lose by an innings and nine runs.

Then came a draw with NSW in Sydney before the second Test in Brisbane. Lawson took 5/49 to skittle Pakistan for 156 after which Greg Chappell (150*) and Allan Border (118) had a run feast against a weak visiting attack. Hughes declared at 509 for seven but torrential rain saved Pakistan from certain defeat. The tourists then defeated Victoria before playing out a drawn Test in the heat of Adelaide.

The Australian batsmen started well in the third Test with Wessels (179) and Border (117*) scoring centuries in a total of 465, but Pakistan passed this on their way to 624. Kim Hughes made 106 as Australia batted out time on one of Les Burdett's perfect Adelaide pitches.

The Australian selectors gave Melbourne debuts to Queensland medium-pace bowler John Maguire and the eccentric New South Wales off-spinner Greg Matthews in the fourth Test which started on Boxing Day. In another drawn encounter the game belonged to the much maligned Graham Yallop who scored a career-best 268. His innings was the seventh longest in all first-class cricket, taking 716 minutes in which he received 517 deliveries and scored 29 boundaries. It was a purple season for Yallop who, three weeks earlier, had taken 220 off the Pakistan attack when representing Victoria.

The fifth Test in Sydney was the end of an era for Greg Chappell, Dennis Lillee and Rodney Marsh who all finished their international careers at the same time. If ever a Test was stage-managed it was this one. Knowing it was to be his final match Greg Chappell invited his parents over from Adelaide and brought his wife and children down from Brisbane, aware that he always performed best when under great pressure.

Chappell did not disappoint his legion of admirers by taking 182 off the Pakistan attack. His innings of 530 minutes from 400 deliveries with 17 fours, first took him past Bradman's Australian record of 6996 Test runs, then to the 7000 mark making him the sixth Test player to reach such a figure. He ended a splendid career with 7110 runs at 53.86; 24 centuries; 122 catches – also a record; and 47 wickets at 40.70.

Meanwhile the ever-controversial Dennis Lillee took a wicket with his last ball in Test cricket to finish with 355 wickets at 23.92 which contained 23 occasions of five wickets or more in an innings and seven achievements of ten or more wickets in a match. Rodney Marsh also stepped down having taken 355 dismissals in 96 appearances.

The departure from the cricket scene of three made-for-television heroes – with victory over Pakistan by ten wickets – saw the end of a fourteen-year partnership. All three had been deeply involved in the Packer schism and in varying ways had fallen foul of the Australian Cricket Board. They had angered traditionalists with their various escapades and shared a mutual dislike of Kim Hughes, giving him little help and making his position as captain ever more difficult.

The West Indians arrived yet again for the World Series Cup. This time they had come direct from a full tour of India and, after a shock defeat by Queensland in a warm-up match, proceeded to dominate the one-day tournament totally. In the finals the West Indies won two games and tied another against Australia with their match in Melbourne on 22 January attracting a record one-day crowd of 86,133.

Late in February the Australian team embarked on their fifth tour of the West Indies having previously visited the Caribbean in 1955, 1965, 1973 and 1978. The choice of Colin Egar as manager was debated long and hard by the Board's Emergency Committee but, as his application was the only one received, he was given the position.

Even with the three old stagers now missing the disruptive elements within the touring party gained the upper hand. At least five players were seriously reprimanded for their poor behaviour with one, at times, having to be physically restrained from causing further damage or injuring a disliked colleague. Nor did the captain, Kim Hughes, add to the gracefulness of the visit, being fined by the tour management for a disgraceful display of churlishness at Pointe-à-Pierre in the game against Trinidad and Tobago. In the first Test in Georgetown, Guyana, the Australian tail-end pair of Tom Hogan (42*) and Rodney Hogg (52) ignored their captain's instruction to 'hit out or get out' and instead batted for two-and-a-half hours to add a record 97 runs for the tenth wicket.

The unpopular tour continued with Lawson being fined $300 for disputing umpire David Narine's rejection of a leg-before-wicket appeal, and a travelling newspaper photographer, Ray Titus, captured dramatic photographs of Rodney Hogg being physically restrained from hitting Kim Hughes on the field of play.

The first Test was eventually drawn, with Vivian Richards captaining the West Indies for the second Test in Trinidad. There, Australia were saved from defeat by Allan Border who remained unbeaten on 98 and, again, on 100 while salvaging his side from what appeared to be a certain innings defeat.

While the Australians were playing in the controversial match against Trinidad and Tobago, the Cricket Committee were meeting in Melbourne with problems to be ironed out. Hughes, Border and Hookes, who were elected members, asked to be kept in touch with the decisions as, prior to their departure, there had been an unfortunate occurrence at Sydney airport.

Only Tom Hogan had signed and returned his tour contract before the team assembled, with some others reluctantly doing so under pressure at an airport hotel in front of the Board's chairman and executive director. One player was stopped in the airport lounge and told if he did not sign his contract which bound him, and his colleagues, to the Board without a guarantee of payment for two years, then he could not board his flight. It was all very unseemly and resulted in David Richards getting a signature but alienating the players far more than he ever realised.

With nothing to lose, Greg Chappell led from the front at the Cricket Committee meeting on 23 March 1984. Backed up by NSW captain Dirk Wellham, Chappell quite tore into the Board for forcing unwanted contracts on the players. To try and calm matters down David Richards stated that, 'a complete review of contractual arrangements would now be taking place'. Richards went on to 'note that concern had also been expressed by the players regarding certain aspects of the Key Player agreements'. The legal costs for what was, in reality, an exercise for the Board to try and lay down the law to the players was given to the meeting by Fred Bennett as 'being $8756'.

Bennett continued in his role of trying to pacify by, 'strongly emphasising my, and the Board's desire that in future such problems can be ironed out via the Cricket Committee so that this forum's effectiveness will be maintained'. He added: 'I am looking forward to jointly discussing and reviewing the matter of contracts in the future'. Even though he tried hard to placate the committee and, through them, the players, the die had been cast for Australian cricket's second major upset.

While this was going on, David Richards was fighting on behalf of the Board for more independence from the decisions being made by

PBL Marketing. Following the February 1984 Board meeting, Richards advised Lynton Taylor that not only did the Board want to keep separate the Test and one-day series for the 1984–85 season, they would also not brook the PBL idea of taking Perth off the schedule for major matches.

The reaction from PBL, in a telex to the Board dated 18 April 1984, is as amazing a piece of paper as any in this new era. The frenzied attack started with Lynton Taylor saying that the agreement between PBL and the Board 'was that World Series Cup matches would be scheduled in the major markets'. He added 'that the principle of playing the best matches at the best venues was behind our Clause Four'. Further: 'Your actions will not only reduce the financial returns but more importantly it will degrade the competition nationally as matches of little interest will be televised live in Prime Time throughout the country'. And so it went on and on. Taylor concluded: 'I am adamant that I will not accept a further reduction in major matches for Sydney and Melbourne. I place the Board on notice that if they continue to press this course I will insist on my right under our agreement that Test matches be conducted during the months of December and January only; one-day matches during November and February with a best of five finals'. Taylor went on to criticise the fact that Adelaide and Brisbane as well as Perth wanted major one-day matches. 'No sensible, logical argument can be made to justify the stance that is being taken. This action indicates an unprofessional approach to business practice and a continuing attempt to recile [*sic*] from the basic tenets of our understanding.'

David Richards immediately prepared a summary for the Board delegates setting out the options as discussed by the Emergency Committee of Fred Bennett (NSW), Norman McMahon (Queensland) and Lawrie Sawle (WA). There was to be a four-week rest while Taylor was away overseas for the Board to decide whether this was to be the Armageddon so many had predicted would eventually come.

In late May the Board backed down but the damage of Taylor's telex had been done. From then on there was an open whispering campaign against PBL, and Taylor in particular, with occasional savage articles appearing in the Australian press written by those journalists who were part of the Board's Masonic 'media mafia'.

Back in the West Indies things were going from bad to worse with the tour. The last three Tests were lost and the West Indies won the one-day series 3-1, with one match abandoned. In the third Test in Barbados, Wayne Phillips scored 120 of which 80 out of 99 came in stands for the last two wickets. The West Indies gained a first-innings lead of 80 runs and then skittled Australia for 97, eventually to win by ten wickets.

The fourth Test in Antigua saw Allan Border score 98 as Australia were beaten by an innings in under four days. Then followed another ten-wicket loss in the final Test in Jamaica to end one of the worst displays from an Australian team in many years. Some players spoke out openly on their return home about the lack of team spirit with David Hookes and Roger Woolley being prominent in stating their views.

Jack Pollard, in his summary of the tour, added another dimension when he wrote: 'Greg Matthews caused alarm among the team management when he was discovered smoking "funny cigarettes". No action was taken and this was treated as a minor indiscretion.'

During the tour, the Sheffield Shield season reached its conclusion back in Australia. Tasmania had shocked the pundits by finishing third on the table but, as it turned out, the second final was between Western Australia and Queensland in Perth. Yet again there was to be no Shield seen in Brisbane as Western Australia won by four wickets late on the fifth day.

More changes were taking place in Australian cricket as the mid-1980s approached. The Melbourne Cricket Club were reluctantly forced by the Victorian State government to allow women access to the long-room and members' area of the MCG. For the first time in 145 years females entered the hallowed portals. In the *Age*, Jane Sullivan wrote: 'We waited for the portraits of past Melbourne Cricket Club secretaries to grow pale; for eighteenth-century cricket bats to rattle in their mountings, or for a sacrilegious female to be struck down by the ghost of W. G. Grace. But nothing happened. The invasion of one of the last male strongholds in Melbourne was one of the quietest on record.'

The southern winter of 1984 saw the first move by the Australian Cricket Board to escape the clutches of PBL Marketing. A State secretaries conference was held in early August at the Queensland Cricketers Club at which former federal Senator, Ron McAuliffe, chairman of the Queensland Rugby League, spoke at length. He informed those present on how the QRL had become ensnared in the tentacles of the NSWRL, and how Queensland finally broke away. The parallel with cricket was staggering and McAuliffe gave his audience a detailed and informative lecture on how to go their own way particularly regarding finances and forward planning. The secretaries were impressed, and one, in presenting his report to his committee, wrote: 'I personally found Mr McAuliffe's address stimulating and it was interesting to note the foresight and the eventual rewards that are now being reaped by the Queensland Rugby League through the initiative that was taken by members of their administration in putting their house in order.'

With the State Associations' administration having received the hint, all of them moved out into their wider communities to garner sponsorships, business involvements and sporting promotions as they had never done before. Not only did this see the States become much more financially independent but also, by a series of good fortune, PBL Marketing's dominance had, by 1987, been reduced to a supporting role.

During the winter Graham Yallop spent some time in Wales where his wife's family lived. On his way back to Australia he stopped over in Johannesburg and spent a number of fruitful hours with the South African Cricket Union's managing director, Ali Bacher. They agreed that an unauthorised, or rebel, tour to South Africa by a team of Australian cricketers was needed and made arrangements for players to be approached.

With the Australian Cricket Board fully aware as to what was going on, but issuing public denials of any knowledge of events, 72 first-class players were approached of whom 41 said they were definitely interested. This apparent lack of loyalty was based on two issues: one was the way the Board had forced contracts on to the senior players but, more importantly, the players loathed PBL Marketing, what it was doing to (not for) the game, and the individuals connected with the company.

Just before the start of the 1984–85 season, the Board sent a team to India for a series of one-day internationals staged to celebrate the Golden Jubilee of the Ranji Trophy. Australia won three of the five matches with the other two abandoned. The team left India to return home, arriving in Singapore on 10 October. There the majority of the team met Ali Bacher along with some players who had flown in direct from Australia. Contracts were signed and cheques written out: a rebel team was formed.

The West Indies toured Australia in 1984–85 for the fourth time in six seasons. Arriving in mid-October they started their first-class matches with draws against Queensland and South Australia followed by a nine-wicket victory over Western Australia. Then came the first Test in Perth against an Australian team of whom ten of the selected twelve would be playing in South Africa within the year.

The West Indies were put into bat by Kim Hughes and then proceeded to run riot. By tea on the second day they had reached 416 with only Alderman (6/128) and Hogg (4/101) the successful bowlers. The Australians collapsed for 76 and, following-on, rallied to 228 to lose by an innings and 112 runs. The Caribbean machine then suffered a severe backfire the following week when New South Wales defeated them by 71 runs in Sydney. The Australian selectors noted that fifteen wickets fell to the NSW spin pair of Bob Holland

and Murray Bennett, both of whom would make their Test debuts during the season.

The second Test in Brisbane was another shattering defeat for Australia, this time by eight wickets, yet the drama came after the end of the match. Bowing to the pressure from his critics Kim Hughes announced his decision to resign the captaincy of the Australian team. He was a broken man after enduring much from his former colleagues who had never forgiven him for sticking by the establishment during the Packer interregnum. Hughes, as a player, was now a shadow of his former self and his decline over the following five years was very sad to watch.

Holding the strings behind the scenes was Greg Chappell. He had tried to talk to Hughes. He had even gone as far as addressing a team meeting in very blunt tones. Nothing had worked, so he had quietly told Hughes it was time to go. Chappell was a very worried man at this time and, as a Test selector, used his knowledge and wisdom in the best way he could. Allan Border was the heir-apparent, although he appeared to be the last person to know. Border had no ambitions to become captain; the job was just thrust upon him.

Journalist Peter McFarline summed up the situation in the *Age* on 28 November 1984 when he wrote:

> The Australian Cricket Board loves to bombard the public with news of the new professionalism that has come to Australian cricket. The death of Kim Hughes's captaincy is no such thing. It is Tammany Hall stuff. Those responsible for it should be the ones taking a long look in the mirror.

Should anyone fail to grasp the politicking in Australian cricket, particularly at that time, it became known later that, since early 1983, Kim Hughes had tape-recorded all of his home telephone conversations with Australian cricket officials. The reading of those transcripts defies belief.

# 33

# Official and Unofficial

The fall of Kim Hughes had its reverberations. Former Test captain Bill Lawry, in Adelaide for the third Test, said at a Rotary Club luncheon: 'What happened to Kim Hughes in Brisbane was like being dragged down like a dingo in the pack and devoured by your own from within and without'. He then added, 'And it is going to be a long time before Australian cricket recovers from that moment in Brisbane'.

At a dinner, held in Adelaide's Hilton Hotel during the Test, the South Australian Cricket Association celebrated their one hundred years of Test cricket on the Adelaide Oval. Twenty-two captains of teams that played in that time were present with Kim Hughes gaining a standing ovation from most in the 800-strong gathering.

Most: for earlier in the day the Board had met in the SACA offices to receive a report on Hughes' resignation from the newly appointed Australian team manager Bob Merriman. After a quick discussion they brushed the issue away to deal with other matters considered more important. In all honesty they were pleased to be rid of Hughes and welcomed his successor, Allan Border, with open arms.

The whole style and tenor of Board meetings had now changed. No longer the detailed eye of a Bradman to look over every piece of paper, or of an Alan Barnes to look after each and every whim and fancy. Now it was rule by executive: all the delegates really had to do was – after a lot of hot air – rubber-stamp the proposals put in front of them. They were now the victims of their own creations. In fact so little notice did they take of the 'late correspondence' put before them that they virtually ignored a letter from former Test opening batsman Bruce Francis warning them of an impending rebel tour should they not change their stance towards South Africa.

Francis, a highly intelligent man, was the brains behind the organisation of the rebel tour. His insistence on playing the game by the unwritten rules saw his letters to the Board dismissed as the work of a crank. But Francis would have the last laugh.

On 4 December 1984, Allan Robert Border, aged twenty-nine, formerly of Sydney now of Brisbane, held his first press conference as Australia's captain. In the Ansett lounge at Melbourne's Tullamarine Airport and, according to *The Age*, 'flanked by the now ubiquitous officials of the Australian Cricket Board', Border showed he was going to be his own man right from the start. Admitting he was taking over the captaincy reluctantly Border added: 'I have been a little bit disappointed with the circumstances surrounding my appointment'.

Border was to be similarly disappointed with his first match in charge of the Australian team. A loss by 191 runs was a hard start even though Geoff Lawson (8/112 and 3/69) had bowled superbly. There was better news for his second match in charge – the fourth Test in Melbourne. Recalled opener Andrew Hilditch scored 70 and then a match-saving 113 as the game finished in a draw. Then came the climax to his first twenty-nine days as captain when, on 2 January 1985, Australia defeated the West Indies in Sydney by an innings and 55 runs.

Batting first, Australia had declared at 471 for nine, an hour into the third day. Then in four hours they dismissed the West Indies for 163, Bob Holland's leg-spin claiming 6/54. Following-on the tourists did little better with Holland taking 4/90 to claim ten wickets for the match.

While this was going on, Sri Lanka were in Australia for their second tour and to play in the World Series Cup. They had a splendid start to their visit by defeating Western Australia in a first-class game but losing in a one-day match. Then came two wins over Queensland before the three-way international competition.

The general public's lack of interest in the World Series Cup was their answer to the overkill of the West Indies in Australia. This did not worry the West Indies Board who had obtained their $2,000,000 tour guarantee plus a share of profits and winnings. In fact the series was so one-sided it became boring. The West Indies won all ten preliminary round games and then beat Australia in the best of three finals matches.

As the Sheffield Shield slipped further into obscurity, yet another one-day competition followed WSC. Called the 'World Championship of Cricket', it contained all the then seven major cricketing nations for a tournament which lasted from 17 February to 10 March 1985. Staged by the Victorian Cricket Association as part of the State of Victoria's 150th Anniversary celebrations, the spectacular opening took place under the new Melbourne floodlights. The obvious opening match, Australia versus England, drew 82,494 spectators to see Australia win easily by seven wickets.

Attendances fell as Australia lost to Pakistan and India leaving those two countries to fight out the final and for India to win by eight wickets. As the Australians trooped wearily back home to rest – all except those from New South Wales and Queensland who contested a thrilling Sheffield Shield final in Sydney which NSW won by one wicket – it was off again on yet another mad-cap venture. This time the Board had agreed for their cricketers to play in a tournament in Sharjah at the invitation of the United Arab Emirates. In their two matches, Australia defeated England then lost to India. It was during this ten days in the desert that Kim Hughes was approached to become captain of the rebel team.

On 20 March the Australian selectors, Lawrie Sawle (WA), Greg Chappell (Queensland) and Rick McCosker (NSW) announced the seventeen-man team to tour England. They chose Murray Bennett, Bob Holland, Geoff Lawson, Greg Matthews, Steve Rixon and Dirk Wellham (NSW); Allan Border, Craig McDermott, Greg Ritchie and Kepler Wessels (Queensland); Andrew Hilditch, Rod McCurdy and Wayne Phillips (SA); Terry Alderman and Graeme Wood (WA) plus David Boon (Tasmania) and Simon O'Donnell (Victoria). They left out Kim Hughes.

The Board delegates and executive had, however, promised Hughes selection. With this in mind he had arranged to rent a house in England for his family and had provisionally employed a nanny for his three young children. When David Richards phoned him at home with the news Hughes was stunned. But the South Africans were delighted.

When the rebel tour story finally broke it was revealed that ten of the intended tourists had South African connections. Wood, Wellham and Phillips were then told by Kerry Packer to renege on their contracts and he would make up their loss of earnings. Bennett, Hilditch and Matthews pulled out; Wessels denied any involvement until found out later; and Alderman, McCurdy and Rixon withdrew from the England tour.

They were then replaced by Carl Rackemann, John Maguire and Ray Phillips, the Queensland wicketkeeper, only to find that Rackemann and Maguire had signed with Bruce Francis. With confusion reigning, the Board then chose Jeff Thomson and fellow paceman Dave Gilbert (NSW) in their stead.

The Australian Cricket Board huffed and puffed. They then decided to take the rebel cricketers to court for breach of contract but, as always, the Board had neither done their homework nor listened to advice.

On 23 January 1979 in the aftermath of Jeff Thomson's court case against the Board, Sir Donald Bradman had warned: 'That the Board should obtain legal advice regarding the effect the Thomson case would have on the validity of the Board's future contracts.' Nothing was done. Then, on 8 February 1980, at his final Board meeting, Bradman virtually pleaded with the delegates to tighten up the Board's contracts with the players, warning them that another venture such as Packer's World Series Cricket could happen again and the Board must be properly prepared.

Bradman was ignored and now, on 24 April 1985, Board chairman Fred Bennett faced the media in the dining-room of the New South Wales Cricketers Club. He criticised the South Africans for pinching Australian players; was pleased that the Minister for Foreign Affairs, Bill Hayden, had supported the Board in Parliament and denied many of the facts which had been accurately reported in Australian newspapers.

The Board was shown up in April and May 1985 for what it had really become: totally toothless and unable even to provide its players with binding contracts. The irony of the situation was that, of the fourteen Board delegates at the time, three were actively involved in business in South Africa (one of whom was selling cricket equipment to the Western Province Cricket Union in Cape Town) whilst over the next two seasons four would watch part of the unofficial Test series.

With players being signed by all sorts of organisations – approved or otherwise – Fred Bennett was a lonely man. A well-meaning, pleasant individual, he was drowning in a sea of litigation. One Sunday morning in late May 1985 he went to see the man who controlled everything. He was greeted, and farewelled, with two words.

Eventually a compromise was reached with the South Africans who, by now, had claimed the big name they needed to captain the side in place of original choice Dirk Wellham; and that was Kim Hughes. Along with Hughes were fellow Western Australians, Terry Alderman, Tom Hogan and Greg Shipperd; Victorians, Graham Yallop, Rodney Hogg and Michael Taylor; New South Welshmen, John Dyson, Steve Rixon and Steve Smith; Queenslanders, Trevor Hohns, John Maguire and Carl Rackemann; South Australians, Mike Haysman and Rod McCurdy, and Peter Faulkner from Tasmania.

The Thirty-first Australians arrived in England at the beginning of May 1985 for a four-month tour in which thirty fixtures would be played. Of these, twenty were first-class of which the Australians won only four.

Lacking the services of the four rebel fast bowlers the Australian attack looked, and was, threadbare. Only Craig McDermott was effective in the Tests, except for the match-winning effort at Lord's by leg-spinner Bob Holland.

Captain Allan Border had a magnificent summer. He scored eight centuries in his 1355 runs at an average of 71.31. His only fault was not to appreciate his own ability as a left-arm spinner. Had he done so at least one Test result might have been different.

The three one-day internationals were all won by the team batting second. Australia won by three wickets at Old Trafford and four wickets at Edgbaston while England were victorious by eight wickets at Lord's.

The first-class matches started with a victory over Somerset by 233 runs, then six drawn games leading up to the first Test at Headingley. There Border batted first on winning the toss with his vice-captain Andrew Hilditch scoring 119 in a total of 331. England's lead was eventually 202 with the Australian bowling figures looking quite horrific. Hilditch (80) again and Wayne Phillips with a tail-end 91 saw Australia to 324 but it was not enough. England won by five wickets in the final hour of play.

Eleven days later it was on to Lord's for Australia to claim their only Test win of the tour. Having dismissed England for 290 (McDermott 6/70) early on the second morning Australia were 101 for four when Ritchie (94) joined Border at the crease. They added 216 runs for the fifth wicket and on Ritchie's dismissal Border went on to reach 196. His 450-minute innings from 318 deliveries and containing 22 fours was the highest score by an Australian captain at Lord's since Woodfull's 155 in 1930.

Australia made 425 and then it was the turn of Bob Holland to reach the peak of his eleven Test match career. His 5/68 from 32 overs turned the game Australia's way and victory came on the final morning by four wickets.

The third Test at Nottingham was a high-scoring draw. England captain David Gower made 166 out of 456 to which the Australians had Graeme Wood (172) and Greg Ritchie (146) top-scoring in 539. England then batted out time in an unsatisfactory match.

The following Saturday, 20 July, the Australians played Glamorgan at Neath and this time their bowling attack was exposed for what it was. The Pakistani pair of Javed Miandad (200*) and Younis Ahmed (118*) put on an unbeaten 306 for the fourth wicket, a record not only for the county but for any wicket against a touring side.

David Boon scored an unbeaten 206 against Northamptonshire, form which took him into the fourth Test five days later to top-score with 61 in Australia's 257. England replied with 482 for nine declared, and left Australia just over five sessions to bat out for yet another draw. Two pleasing aspects of the match had been Craig McDermott's 8/141 and Allan Border's fourteenth Test century – an unbeaten 146 scored from 334 balls in five-and-three-quarter hours.

The brittle bowling and some inept batting let the tourists down in the final two Tests. England won by an innings and 118 runs in

Birmingham and then by an innings and 94 runs at The Oval. It was the start of a very poor run for Australian cricket although financially the tour had been a great success: 373,000 spectators paying £2,467,030.

The day after the final Test the Australian Cricket Board met in Melbourne for its twelfth Annual General Meeting. Although the South African question dominated proceedings two other issues had to be carefully considered. The first was the constant barrage of bad publicity the Board was getting regarding their sponsorship by Benson & Hedges for Test cricket. Media manager Ian McDonald, a former Melbourne tabloid newspaper writer, said afterwards: 'It is of concern to the Board that so much time has yet again been devoted to defending the right of sport to accept tobacco company sponsorship against attacks by minority groups with no broad community support for their attitudes'.

If McDonald was speaking for the Board he was very wide of the mark. Cigarette smoking was becoming socially unacceptable in Australia at this time. Two State governments had banned tobacco advertising and the rest swiftly followed suit. This was one of many gaffes McDonald would make during his tenure of office while speaking on behalf of his employers.

The other matter concerned the former West Indian captain Clive Lloyd. Towards the end of the previous season the West Indies had played a Prime Minister's XI in Canberra. The night before the match, on 22 January, Prime Minister Bob Hawke had entertained Lloyd at his official residence, The Lodge.

Hawke, rather rashly, offered Lloyd the position of team coach to the Australians, and wrote to Fred Bennett the following day to tell him what he had done. After consultation with the Emergency Committee Bennett replied that: 'We are not prepared to be involved in any scheme involving Lloyd as national team coach'. Bennett also had to placate the West Indies Board who felt that the Australian Board were up to some form of mischief.

On receipt of Bennett's letter the Prime Minister consulted his very high-profile Minister of Sport, John Brown, and they came up with the concept of adding cricket to the sports being introduced into the Australian Institute of Sport. They argued that Lloyd could then take over as director of the proposed Australian Cricket Academy, a coaching school of excellence for promising young cricketers. The Board replied to this idea: 'If Lloyd is resident in Australia at the time the Academy is in operation, the Board will give consideration to using his services in some way'.

The Board meeting also saw a distinct shift in the balance of power when Treasurer Ray Steele ceased to be a delegate and Bob Parish stepped down from the executive. Parish was replaced by another Victorian delegate, Malcolm Gray, Ray Steele's son-in-law.

In mid-September a team of Australian 'B' cricketers made a short tour of Zimbabwe. They played five one-day internationals without success but did win one of the two unofficial Tests. The side was the cream of Australia's up-and-coming young players but they were, in the main, promising yet not good enough. Eight of the fourteen were to play Test cricket of whom only Dean Jones and Steve Waugh became established in the side.

New Zealand were the first of the two touring teams for the 1985–86 season. After playing two minor matches in Queensland they drew with South Australia for whom Glenn Bishop (202) and Peter Sleep (133*) put on 297 for the fourth wicket. In reply, Martin Crowe scored a spectacular 242 not out. Crowe missed the draw over Queensland but carried on his good form into the first Test in Brisbane in early November 1985. He scored 188 out of 553 for seven declared but the real Kiwi hero was fast bowler Richard Hadlee. He took the fourth best bowling analysis in the history of Test cricket with 9/52 and 6/71 as Australia crumpled to defeat. The New Zealand win by an innings and 41 runs would have been far worse had not Allan Border (152*) and Greg Matthews (115) put on 197 for the sixth wicket.

Matthews (111) scored another century against New Zealand three days later as New South Wales drew their match in Sydney but it was his colleague, Bob Holland, who took the honours during the second Test in Sydney. Australia won by four wickets with just 23 balls to spare but it was Holland's leg-spin which claimed 6/106 and 4/68 on his home pitch that swayed the match.

The Australian Cricket Board was very concerned at the low attendance figures for the season and the fact that many of the major cricket writers were following the Australians in South Africa. Whispering campaigns were mounted against some of the scribes and in future years they would become aware of a deep-seated resentment against them for reporting the unauthorised tour.

The day before the third Test in Perth, Jeff Thomson became the first Queensland bowler to take 300 Sheffield Shield wickets when he had Graeme Wood caught in the slips in the match against Western Australia in Brisbane. On the same day India started their first-class matches by playing South Australia, eventually running out winners by four wickets.

The third Test in Perth was played on a WACA pitch which had been relaid only two months earlier and its uneven bounce caused numerous problems to the batsmen. Allan Border (83) and David Boon (50) were the only Australians to pass the half-century mark as Hadlee (5/65 and 6/90) tore the heart out of a poor batting line-up. New Zealand won by six wickets to claim their first series win in Australia and to become the inaugural holders of the Trans-Tasman Trophy.

Hard as they tried to make the Tests appealing to the public the Board remained worried about the drop in spectators. David Richards tried to get around this when the season was over by comparing the figures of 1985–86 to those of 1980–81 'when New Zealand and India last toured together'. In reality the Indians had never been a crowd-pulling side and their three drawn Tests in the space of 25 days was programming at its most ludicrous. It was little wonder numbers were down.

Five players were given debuts during the season with the talented opening batsman Robbie Kerr of Queensland dropped after two Tests. In Adelaide for the first Test, Merv Hughes, Geoff Marsh and Bruce Reid made little impact as Australia 381 (Ritchie 128, Boon 123) drew with India 520 (Gavaskar 166*). The attendance over five days of 30,315 was the fourth lowest at Adelaide in ninety years.

The on-running show then moved to Melbourne for the now traditional Boxing Day start. Put into bat, Australia reached 262 due mainly to an unbeaten century from Greg Matthews. India gained a lead of 183 and looked winners when Australia were 205 for eight on the fourth day. However a tail-end rally led by Allan Border with 163 and a final day thunderstorm saved the game for the home side.

Australia were humiliated but not beaten by India in Sydney at New Year. Kapil Dev declared his team's innings closed at 600 for four, and then led his bowlers on the attack. David Boon made 131 out of 396 and Australia's follow-on saw them finish at 119 for six as India tried to press home that final advantage.

Australian cricket was now at its lowest ebb for many years. Kepler Wessels had refused to sign a Board contract which considerably reduced his salary, and attendances at the six Tests had only been 283,109. Luckily for the Board the one-day series did not let them down when 499,253 watched the seventeen matches, with Australia defeating India in the finals.

In South Africa the Australians played fourteen matches – five of which were first-class – prior to the first unofficial 'Test' in Durban which started on Boxing Day 1985. South Africa's innings was dominated by a quite startling exhibition of batting by the left-handed Graeme Pollock, now forty-one, who scored 108 out of 393. Australian pacemen Rodney Hogg (5/88) and Carl Rackemann (5/115) shared the wickets, with the Australians' reply of 359 led by Victorian batsman Michael Taylor who scored 109. The match was drawn as both sides tried to find out each other's strengths and weaknesses.

The delightful Newlands ground in Cape Town was the setting for the second 'Test' on New Year's Day. On a perfect pitch no result was ever going to be possible in the scheduled four days. John Dyson (95) and Kim Hughes (97*) top-scored for the Australians and Rackemann took eight more wickets.

After two days of the third and final 'Test' at the Wanderers ground in Johannesburg, the Australians were on their way to victory. Rackemann had bowled splendidly by taking 8/84 as South Africa fell for 211. Opener Steve Smith, with 116 from 163 balls including 17 fours, led the batting, but suddenly it all went wrong. Rodney Hogg pulled a hamstring which blunted the attack and a final day thunderstorm changed the pitch dramatically. Needing 250 runs to win in plenty of time, the Australians were undone by humid conditions which none of the players had previously encountered. For South Africa their captain Clive Rice and paceman Garth Le Roux both took hat-tricks as the tourists fell for 61 and defeat by 188 runs.

The six one-day internationals saw the Australians go two up by winning in Johannesburg and Durban, then lose four in a row in Port Elizabeth, Cape Town, Johannesburg (again) and Pretoria. Kim Hughes had enjoyed a tour away from the back-biting and politicking of his days as official captain. However, he would spend most of the Australian winter of 1986 in court fighting the cricket authorities' ban on him playing club cricket. His eventual victory cost the WACA – who passed the legal costs to the Board to pay – the sum of $397,000, money which could have been far better spent on the game itself.

On 15 February 1986, the official Australian team started a short tour of New Zealand. The (now) four selectors of Lawrie Sawle (WA) chairman, Greg Chappell (Queensland), Dick Guy (NSW) and Jim Higgs (Victoria) chose the best team available. Three wins and a draw took them up to the first Test of the three-match series. Played at the Basin Reserve, Wellington, the game was badly interrupted by rain. Australia, put into bat, made 435 in which Greg Ritchie (92) and Greg Matthews (130) added a record 213 in 275 minutes for the fifth wicket. New Zealand had scored 379 for six before the rain.

Three days later, at a cold Lancaster Park in Christchurch, Australia put into bat, achieved a first-innings lead for the first time in ten Tests. Allan Border was the star of the show. He scored 140 and then an unbeaten 114 to become the second Australian after Greg Chappell to score hundreds in both innings of Tests on two occasions. The match ended in a draw after autumn rains once again interrupted proceedings.

A win and a draw against provincial sides led up to the third Test in Auckland. Initially all seemed to be going well for Australia. Geoff Marsh scored 118 in a total of 314 with New Zealand's reply being 258. At the end of the third day Australia were 32 for two and looking fairly comfortable. They then lost the series in the first forty minutes next morning when five wickets fell for 12 runs with the final total of 103 being Australia's lowest against New Zealand. The Kiwis went on to win by eight wickets and retain the Trans-Tasman Trophy.

In mid-March New South Wales drew with Queensland in the Sheffield Shield final to retain the trophy they had won the previous season. Then it was off for a three-week tour of Zimbabwe to play in eight matches two of which were against the national team. The first match at the Harare Sports Club was drawn with the second won by 70 runs due to a fine performance from Mark O'Neill (Norman's son) who scored 132 and 55 not out, and took 2/19 from eleven overs of leg-spin.

On 1 April 1986 Phil Ridings, as president of the South Australian Cricket Association, read a letter to his committee which he had just received. It indicated Sir Donald Bradman's intention to retire from his last cricket position and said:

> I would be happy to retire forthwith if the committee so wished, but otherwise I thought it sensible for me to see out the financial year and make my retirement operative from early July.

Sir Donald continued by thanking all his colleagues for their kindnesses on behalf of his wife and himself.

On 30 June 1986, Sir Donald Bradman attended his 1713th and last official SACA meeting. It had been a career without parallel in the annals of cricket in Australia. Trying to calculate Bradman's other cricket involvement is a near impossible task but it is fairly clear that, at the peak of his influence, in his first spell as the Board chairman in 1960-63, he attended 546 official cricket meetings in Australia and overseas. It is a phenomenal record by anybody's standards considering, particularly, that he would have been fully prepared for each and every one. His influence had not been lost to the game for in mid-1985 his skill and ability had been called on by the Board to resolve the problems caused by the South African defections. If the Board had used his skill from the beginning they could have saved themselves around $245,000 in cumulative legal fees.

At the Board's April 1986 meeting in Canberra former Australian captain Bobby Simpson was appointed as full-time cricket manager along with physiotherapist Errol Alcott. Both men worked together during the winter on the players' level of fitness and skill particularly in preparation for the tour of India which was due to start in late August.

In June, Simpson flew around Australia for meetings with the national players and to give talks to various State training squads.

Much to his regret, and that of others, Bob Merriman's position was downgraded so that the team operations and administration were left to a clerk from the Board's office. Merriman took the hint and resigned from his position as Cricket Committee coordinator and returned full-time to his judicial post. He was a great loss to Australian cricket, had done an enormous amount to heal rifts after the WSC rapprochement, and was still in harness when Packer, in 1986, sold most of his companies and departed from involvement in the game of cricket.

At the Board Annual General Meeting in Sydney on 12 September the Victorian delegate, Malcolm Gray, was elected as chairman for a period of three years. His first priority was to look at the relationship between the Board and PBL Marketing for, after many years of frustration, the time had come to make a firm stand against the dictatorial attitude of the so-called 'marketing arm'.

Board treasurer Des Rundle had given away quite a bit at the SACA annual meeting in Adelaide the previous night when he said: 'From a Board point of view we are reviewing our involvement with PBL Marketing, the main reason being to ensure more money goes to the grass roots of the game'. Rundle had prepared a confidential report for the Board based on his first ten months in office as Treasurer since succeeding Ray Steele. Rundle had seen figures which he did not like and his report on these matters shook delegates to the core. Consternation followed, as well as the shredding of much, but not all, of the offending documentation.

The team selected for the six-week tour of India in September and October 1986 was now announced. When it reached India Geoff Marsh made 139 in Bangalore against the Indian Board President's XI, Greg Ritchie 124 against Bombay in Gwalior followed by 95 in Chandigarh versus an Indian Under-25 team. None of the bowlers had taken more than four wickets in an innings which worried the tour management as they went into the first Test in Madras. In front of 30,000 chanting spectators on the first day, and in extreme heat, David Boon scored 122 from 258 balls in five-and-a-half hours.

Resuming at 211 for two on the second morning, Dean Jones, playing in only his third Test and his first for two-and-a-half years, endured 45°C heat, 60% humidity, severe stomach and leg cramps, vomiting attacks and heat exhaustion to score a double-century. His 210 came in 503 minutes from 330 balls and contained 27 fours and two sixes. On his dismissal he was taken straight to hospital and put on a saline drip. Following his departure Allan Border made 106 from 178 balls and the Australians were 556 for six at the end of the day.

Border made the decision to bat for just under an hour on the third day, to the annoyance of the huge crowd in the Chidambaram Stadium in the suburb of Chepauk. When declaring at 574 for seven little could

Border guess how this, the 1052nd Test match, would turn out. Greg Matthews took 5/103 as India made 397; Kapil Dev with a captain's innings of 119 leading the way. Tensions ran wild on the fourth day with verbal abuse between the players being a regular occurrence. At the end of play Border made his decision to declare at 170 for five which left India the whole of the last day to score 348 for victory.

India started off well, losing only the local player Kris Srikkanth before lunch. By mid-afternoon the score was 158 for one before Mohinder Amarnath fell, then Sunil Gavaskar (90) went with the score on 204. India needed 144 from 25.3 overs but lost two quick wickets. Pandit (39) and Shastri together reached 291, and then Sharma (23) added 40 with Shastri before he was out at 331 for seven. There were now three-and-a-half overs left to score 17 runs.

At 334 Moré (0) was leg-before to Bright and ten runs later Bright (5/94) bowled Yadav (8). Umpire Dara Dotiwalla incurred the wrath of Allan Border by suggesting the over-rate could be hurried along a little as the last pair of Ravi Shastri (48*) and Maninder Singh came together. Four runs were needed with one over left.

Greg Matthews (5/146) took the ball. Shastri blocked his first delivery, took two runs to mid-wicket from the second and a single, also to mid-wicket, off the third. Maninder missed the fourth delivery which hit him on the pads, with the fifth spinning in sharply and hitting him on the front pad. Umpire Vikramraju agreed with the Australian's triumphant appeal and Test cricket had its second tied match.

Manager Bob Simpson ran on to the field to congratulate his team and to tell them that as play had exceeded the official playing schedule by an hour-and-a-quarter they had just forty minutes to change and rush to the airport for their next flight around the sub-continent.

Four days later unseasonal rains delayed the second Test in Delhi until late on the fourth afternoon. Both teams had some batting practice on the final day as the game was left drawn. At Baroda on 10 October the final provincial game was played with Delhi the opponents. With the Australians using the game as a warm-up for the final Test both Greg Dyer (106) and Dave Gilbert (117) made the only centuries of their careers.

The final Test at the Wankhede Stadium in Bombay saw 1078 runs scored at 63.41 per wicket as only 17 wickets fell in five days, with none falling on the fourth as Vengsarkar (164*) and Shastri (121*) shared an unbroken sixth-wicket partnership of 298 in 388 minutes. The game ended in a draw, as did the series, but even in a dull series history had been created.

Between the Tests six limited-overs internationals had been squeezed into the itinerary. India was successful by three games to two, with one abandoned.

On 8 October, in Melbourne, the Australian Cricket Board laid on a garish launch to publicise the forthcoming visit by an England team captained by Mike Gatting. Titled 'The Clashes for the Ashes', the cynical press wrote of the series 'as the battle for cricket's wooden spoon' as it was generally agreed at this time that both countries were far from being at their strongest compared to the rest of the cricketing world.

The refreshing change was the new Board chairman, Malcolm Gray. In the months prior to his election – it being Victoria's turn to sit in the hot seat – a number of clandestine meetings had taken place, some originating from the Board's staff, to see if Phil Ridings would nominate out of turn. Eventually Ridings declined, and Gray's tenure of office saw the power in Australian cricket swing back more to the delegates and away from the paid employees.

The England team arrived in Australia on 12 October and on their way to the first Test in Brisbane lost to Queensland by five wickets, defeated South Australia by the same margin, and drew with Western Australia.

The Australians had been home only three-and-a-half weeks prior to the first Test, and even in that time most players took part in three Sheffield Shield matches. The never-ending rush started on 14 November when Border won the toss and put England into bat. It was the start of a dismal series for Australia as England reached 456, with Ian Botham (138) registering the highest Test score by an Englishman on the ground. Australia struggled to 248 and, following-on, only had Geoff Marsh (110) to boost the total to 282. Late on the fifth afternoon England had won by seven wickets but at least Australia had created some type of record: at 6ft 8in. Bruce Reid had become the tallest player to appear in an Ashes Test, surpassing Tony Greig (6ft 7½in.), George Bonnor and Lisle Nagel (both 6ft 6in.).

On their way to Perth for the second Test, England were badly defeated by eight wickets by a New South Wales side who then went to New Zealand to beat Wellington by 105 runs and Auckland on a superior scoring rate to win a short-lived tournament sponsored by a New Zealand computer company.

Meanwhile the England team were dominating the second Test. Chris Broad (162), David Gower (136) and Jack Richards (133) saw their side to 592 for eight wickets declared, England's second highest total in Australia – exceeded only by their 636 at Sydney in December 1928. Australia's 401 included 125 from Allan Border and after that the match petered out into a draw.

Meanwhile, in South Africa, Kim Hughes' team, bolstered by the recruitment of Kepler Wessels, played nine matches, three of them first-class, prior to their first of two series of unofficial one-day internationals. The four fixtures against South Africa were played under lights in Verwoerdburg (Pretoria), Johannesburg, Cape Town and Durban in front of capacity crowds. The Springboks won by two matches to one, with one abandoned.

The enthusiasm of the rebel team was in contrast to the official Australians, who changed their wicketkeeper for the third Test in Adelaide. Greg Dyer of NSW replaced Tim Zoehrer (WA) who, from then on, would always be the bridesmaid as second choice 'keeper. A benign pitch saw a draw inevitable from the first day. David Boon (103) top-scored in Australia's 514 for five declared and Allan Border made an unbeaten century in the second innings. Afterwards he called the contest 'a wasted match'.

Boxing Day saw two Australian teams, a continent apart, on their respective ways to being beaten by superior teams. In Melbourne, England retained the Ashes through their first three-day victory in Australia since 1901. Australia's pathetic scores of 141 and 194 to England's 349 caused Robin Marlar to write in *The Australian*: 'Kerry Packer's chicken has finally come home to roost, as some of us in England have long predicted. It may have taken almost ten years, but the evil done when a commercial interest aided and abetted by a generation of senior players took over the game in Australia, may now be shown for what it really is.'

In Johannesburg, Kim Hughes' team were making much more of a fight of their game against South Africa. The unofficial Australian pace attack had blunted the usually rampant South African batsmen as Rod McCurdy (6/67) and then John Maguire (6/61) kept the Springboks down to 254 and 182. Needing to score 295 for victory, Hughes (54*) tried hard to force the win but, with his lengthy tail collapsing around him, had to suffer defeat by 49 runs.

In Australia the hounds of the press were baying at the door of the Australian Cricket Board, who all retreated to Perth for a series of one-day matches to celebrate the America's Cup yachting race being held in nearby Fremantle. Pakistan and the West Indies joined the fun with England defeating Pakistan in the final by five wickets.

While the one-day frolics were taking place in Perth westwards over the Indian Ocean the second unofficial Test was starting in Cape Town. Put into bat the South Africans took ten-and-a-half hours to score 493 with former captain, Peter Kirsten, making 173 on his home ground. The Australians were 170 for four until John Dyson (198) and Michael Haysman (153) added 225 for the fifth wicket in 349 minutes and eventually saw their side to a three-run first-innings lead. Springbok captain Clive Rice then allowed Kirsten (105*) to complete his second century as the match became a tame draw.

The muddle which had become Australian cricket sadly came to public note yet again prior to the fifth Test against England in Sydney which started on 10 January 1987. The Australian selectors were widely reported as having had a communication breakdown when picking the side, with the Board's media manager announcing the chosen twelve and in doing so naming incorrectly a player who had the same surname as the one intended to be chosen.

The laughing echoed around the cricketing world. Richie Benaud in the Sydney *Sun* called it 'bewildering'; Alan Shiell in the Adelaide *Advertiser* said, 'Explanations must be given for their latest aberrations'; Michael Owen-Smith in the Cape *Argus* in South Africa wondered 'if all the stories one has heard about the Australian Cricket Board, and not believed because, surely, no one body could be that stupid, are in fact all true.' In London the *Daily Telegraph* said the Board 'bewildered and bemused Australia's cricket followers', with Sandeep Nakai of *The Hindu* in India commenting: 'Surely these are not the same people who only a few months ago actually privately criticised the Indian Board?' And so it went on.

Then, at the Board meeting held in Perth on 6 January, and after 'receiving a report from the selectors', the delegates refused to endorse the selectors' choice for vice-captain. With David Boon omitted from the side, Dirk Wellham was named as Allan Border's deputy. By a large margin the Board voted against Wellham and chose Western Australian farmer Geoff Marsh in his place. In reality, Wellham was obviously in charge on the field during that final Test, his tactics and placings being the most superior seen by an Australian that summer. Wellham, in all but name, guided the team to their first Test win in fourteen games. He never played for Australia again.

By now there was a crisis in Australian cricket. With favourable reports coming back from South Africa on the emerging talents of young Australians such as Steve Smith, Michael Haysman, Rod McCurdy, Peter Faulkner and Greg Shipperd, the Board tried to get various newspaper sports editors to tone down their coverage of the rebel tour.

Then the 'Fleet Street' newspapers, all of whom had one or more journalists in Australia, went on to the attack, particularly over the selection problems. In *The Times*, John Woodcock said he thought 'there was a real probability the selectors had made a mistake'; the *Daily Mail* report spoke of 'blundering selectors'; the *Guardian*'s Matthew Engel said it 'was a lovely one'; the *Daily Telegraph* described the selectors as 'Australia's four great fonts of wisdom'; and the *Star* headlined 'What a XXXX-up!'

Even though Australia won the final Test by 55 runs from the last ball of the penultimate available over to lose the series by three matches to one, the knives were out for the Board. The normally compliant Australian cricket media let years of frustrated, pent-up feeling run wild. Throughout the one-day World Series Cup fixtures, which England won easily, the criticism went on and on. If ever the press was the cause of a scheduled tour being cancelled it was this barrage which saw David Richards organise for the Board to by-pass the planned 1988 tour to the West Indies. He told the WICBC that the tour would be a financial flop as the series would be one-sided. It would have been a massacre and have done no good whatever to Australia's young players.

Back in South Africa, Kim Hughes' team failed by a whisker to defeat the South Africans in the third unofficial 'Test' in Durban. Steve Smith (137), Michael Haysman (115) and John Dyson (101) led the batting with leg-spinner Trevor Hohns (6/98 and 3/27) showing his class during a bowling spell which had the purists smiling.

In the final 'Test' in Port Elizabeth the tourists again came up against the legendary Graeme Pollock, forty-three years of age and still one of the finest of post-war batsmen. In his last big match Pollock scored 144 in 263 minutes in a manner which caused even the 'rebels' to acknowledge his consummate skill. The match petered out into a draw with the second series of one-day games seeing South Africa winners by three matches to one.

Of the 'rebel' players four would return to Test cricket: Alderman, Hohns and Rackemann with Wessels becoming South Africa's first Test captain following their readmittance to the fold. Kim Hughes stayed in South Africa to play provincial cricket for Natal but even that ended in acrimonious circumstances and he returned to Perth to resume employment with his brother-in-law's building concern.

In Australia, a below-par Sheffield Shield season had ended with Western Australia taking their tenth success by drawing with Victoria in the final. Western Australian opening batsman Michael Veletta recorded the highest individual score for his State with his 262 runs coming in 766 minutes from 550 balls.

However, the record-breaking match of the season took place on the Adelaide Oval in early March when Tasmania were the visitors. The second and third days' play saw a quite remarkable unbroken fourth-wicket stand of 462 between David Hookes (306*) and Wayne Phillips (213*) as South Australia's score reached 643 for three declared, and an eventual innings victory.

In early April, Australia made up the numbers in a four-way one-day tournament in Sharjah. The team enjoyed a well-deserved break, even though they lost all of their matches by fairly wide margins.

Time flies when you're having fun, or so it would seem, for on 9 May 1987 the realisation dawned that it was ten years, to the day, that news first broke of Kerry Packer's involvement in cricket. Many of his players had now retired with most leaving the game. One person still deeply involved was former England captain Tony Greig, now domiciled in Sydney.

On reflection Greig said that the war which was going to free cricketers from financial hardship and liberate them from the chains of colonial attitudes had, instead, 'created an unworkable situation in international cricket'. He added: 'Modern cricket cannot afford the wage-and-workload spiral that stems directly from the Packer revolution'.

In a wide-ranging interview in *The Australian* Greig put the crunch point when addressing the Australian Cricket Board: 'The administrators now have to ask themselves: "Do we want this to be a full-time profession or not?" Once they decide it is not going to be a profession everything else falls into place.'

This was a radical reaction from a man who once went to the barricades to champion the revolutionary theory that cricketers were professionals with a right to be paid as such. What impression this might have had on Board chairman Malcolm Gray is unknown, yet it was around this time that a change started to come over the whole game in Australia. By his helpful, pleasant attitude and ability to listen Gray gained many an ear during his time in office. The nadir of Australian cricket had now been passed.

# 34

# The Crowds decline

The southern winter of 1987 saw the Board change the timing, then cancel, another planned tour, this one to Sri Lanka. During these months Bobby Simpson worked closely with Allan Border and the selectors prior to the squad being named for the fourth World Cup to be held in India and Pakistan later in the year.

The newly formed Australian Cricket Academy in Adelaide saw the appointment of former Australian representative, Jack Potter, as head coach with Board cricket co-ordinator Peter Spence as his deputy. Once the Academy was opened the first two annual intakes proved the worth of such a concern. It was to be regretted that constant interference by the Board in matters which did not concern them saw both Potter and Spence resign before the third annual intake of fifteen boys had completed their course.

The team for the World Cup was not expected to do more than provide opposition for the suggested stronger teams. The selectors made some fundamental changes to a side they regarded as experimental. The team was Geoff Marsh, Tom Moody, Bruce Reid and Mike Veletta (WA); Greg Dyer, Peter Taylor and Steve Waugh (NSW); Allan Border and Craig McDermott (Queensland); Tim May and Andrew Zesers (SA); Dean Jones and Simon O'Donnell (Victoria) and David Boon (Tasmania).

Before the tournament, when politicians in India were regularly making provocative comments, Malcolm Gray took the initiative in laying down firm guidelines for Australia's participation. Gone was the prevarication of years past and in its place came a completely new style of management. Gray flew to Hong Kong in mid-May for talks with International Cricket Conference chairman Colin Cowdrey, which then saw England take as strong a stance as Australia.

In early June, Sir Donald Bradman took the opportunity of 'exchanging views' with a delegation of Indian World Cup organisers who met him at the Adelaide Oval. Led by the chairman of the organising committee, N. K. P. Salve, the Indians had rushed to Melbourne to clarify matters with Malcolm Gray and then 'sought

Sir Donald's views and advice on the political problems threatening the staging of the World Cup'.

At a Board meeting on 12 June, Gray's mild-mannered ways could not hide the fact that he was in full command of Australian cricket. The Indians had been very impressed with him, so much so that he confidently said, 'India gave assurances there would be no problems with the tournament'. And he was proved correct.

Australia won their first match, in the heat of Madras, by defeating joint-hosts India by one run on 9 October. Then followed victories over Zimbabwe, also in Madras, by 96 runs, and New Zealand at Indore by three runs. India won the return in Delhi by 56 runs after which Australia were back on their winning ways, defeating New Zealand by seventeen runs in Chandigarh and Zimbabwe by 70 runs in Cuttack. Having qualified for the semi-finals the team moved to the countryside for three days of relaxation in Bhubaneswar before flying to Pakistan.

In Lahore, Australia turned the tables on Pakistan, inflicting an eighteen-run defeat on the other joint hosts who had been expected to win. Pakistan captain Imran Khan vowed to gain revenge at the tournament four years later in Australia.

The lead-up to the final at Eden Gardens, Calcutta, on 8 November 1987 saw, ironically, the pitch prepared by Les Burdett, curator of the Adelaide Oval. His expertise had been called for by the Bengal Cricket Association who wanted to prepare a fair pitch instead of one that was traditionally slow. Burdett succeeded in his task and, in front of 90,000 spectators, Australia won the World Cup by defeating England by just seven runs.

The reward for the players returning home was a summer of five Tests against three different countries, and a new contract system offered to them by the Australian Cricket Board. Prior to flying to Calcutta for the World Cup final, Malcolm Gray had led the pre-season press conference at the North Sydney Oval. He stated that all player contracts, except Allan Border's, would be for two years and would be worth a minimum $12,000 for each cricketer. Border was on a five-year contract worth $50,000 per annum.

Gray also announced a change in the eligibility for provident fund monies, reducing the threshold to twenty credits (one credit equalling one Test or three one-day internationals or a combination of both). The result of this move was, for the first time in many years, a fully contented squad of players who were now being paid a fair amount of money with guaranteed minimums. Why it took so long for the Board to organise themselves in this way is the great unanswerable question.

˛alcolm Gray innovation was gently to clear the decks personnel who had become time-servers or were the 'right ɔr a position. He persuaded the Board to approve of the ˌppointment of a new representative in London to look after Australia's interests, particularly at ICC meetings. The position went to Bob Cowper who, many years earlier, had been the players' choice to look after their concerns. It was an appointment which gained Gray much favour in a number of quarters.

Not long afterwards it became clear that Gray had been consulting Allan Border, senior players, State administrators and sponsors over all innovations which concerned them. The result was startling. For the first time in memory a warmth was creeping into the game. It was all a far cry from the military regimentation of years ago or the lack of understanding shown by Alan Barnes' infamous comment on hearing of player discontent when he said: 'There are 50,000 other cricketers willing to play for Australia'.

Where there was gloom there was now light. Attendances at Sheffield Shield matches started to rise albeit at times with some gimmicks from the State Associations. South Australia signed a $500,000 three-year deal with the local brewery as did the NSWCA with theirs. Tasmania obtained a $40,000 annual agreement with a computer company while in Western Australia the Rural and Industries Bank signed a long-term contract with the Cricket Association worth $2.1 million. Also in Perth, the redevelopment of the WACA ground carried on apace with the $8 million southern stand nearly complete.

Suddenly grounds were changing. The Sydney Cricket Ground, Melbourne Cricket Ground and Adelaide Oval all were building or preparing to build large new stands. In Hobart a Test match would shortly be played on the new Bellerive Oval and, as always, when something was successful, the Federal government wanted to get in on the act.

At the behest of an anonymous civil servant an 'Aboriginal Cricket Association' was formed for the sole reason of providing a political front for a group of aboriginal-descended men who could play cricket to tour England in 1988 at government expense. The shameful story of how a group of men were used as purely political pawns was another blot on Australia's use of their indigenous peoples for self-gratifying motives. The standard of play on the tour was of a lower club level with opposing sides often quietly requested to put out weak opposition to let the tourists be seen to put up a good showing.

Flanked by Australian High Commission officials and other flunkies the team toured England for seven weeks in the northern spring of 1988. They returned to Australia amidst plenty of propaganda and after dispersal were never again heard of in a cricketing context.

The 1987–88 season had started with New Zealand, captained by former South Australian player Jeff Crowe, defeating Western Australia by an innings and 96 runs, and then losing to South Australia by three wickets. After that came three Test matches in three weeks during December.

In Brisbane, Allan Border put the Kiwis into bat which paid off handsomely. Australia were able to bowl first on a surface which had had its preparation hampered by torrential rain and which would have been ideal for Richard Hadlee's bowling. It was New Zealand who collapsed, and with David Boon scoring 143 on the second day, Australia's victory was never in doubt. It came on the fourth afternoon by nine wickets and gave Australia their first pair of successive Test wins for four years.

The second Test in Adelaide was played in stifling heat on a bland pitch ideally suited for a timeless Test. Andrew Jones (150) and Martin Crowe (137) scored centuries for New Zealand in their 485 for nine declared with Allan Border (205) making a double-century in Australia's 496. In a drawn match, Border's twenty-second century saw him complete 7000 Test runs and pass Greg Chappell's Australian record aggregate of 7110.

In Melbourne, after Christmas, one of the decade's most exciting Tests took place amid controversy, recrimination and a finish as tense as any for years. New Zealand had attracted crowds of only 28,153 in Brisbane and 30,083 in Adelaide but on the first day in Melbourne 51,087 (out of a final total of 127,184) turned up to see New Zealand get away to a fine start by reaching 242 for five. Alas, there had been a major controversy when New Zealand were on 119 for one.

Andrew Jones (40) had shared a second-wicket partnership of 87 with John Wright, when he edged a ball from paceman Craig McDermott. Australian wicketkeeper Greg Dyer claimed the catch after rolling over and holding the ball up. Umpire Tony Crafter, sensing something was not right, initially declined to give Jones out. His colleague at square-leg Dick French indicated the ball had carried, as it had, and Crafter raised his finger. As Jones walked off television replays showed the ball bouncing out of Dyer's gloves and on to the ground where it was scooped back into his gloves before, in a sitting position, he appealed for the catch.

The tension between the two teams rose appreciably, and the next morning's newspapers contained no apology from Dyer but, on the other hand, threats from the Board's media manager to sue those who made criticisms. In events so extraordinary to outside journalists but, alas, now common in these circles, the Board's apparatchick said: 'We are looking at taking action against the New Zealand press'.

Those Australian journalists who wrote the story as they saw it, and were critical of Dyer, had it let known to them that any further escalation or criticism could well see them excluded from briefings or receiving media releases. Those who wrote approved stories were duly rewarded. The New Zealand journalists were so disgusted at this treatment that they occasionally let their copy run away with them.

Dyer at this stage had seemed to have earned a permanent place as Australia's wicketkeeper but following this dispute his confidence clearly dropped. Another incident in Adelaide the following season, far more unsportsmanlike than this, saw him removed from the captaincy of New South Wales. He retired from first-class cricket at the end of that season.

New Zealand went on to make 317, to which Australia replied with 357 (Peter Sleep 90). The debutant Victorian all-rounder, Tony Dodemaide, added 6/58 to his first innings half-century as New Zealand were dismissed three deliveries into the final day for 286. With Australia needing to score 247 from 92 overs the tension rose as the score mounted with wickets falling. At 209 for five all looked on course for victory. At 227 for nine defeat was staring Australia in the face. Richard Hadlee bowled unchanged from 5.17 until the finish at 6.49 pm as Craig McDermott (10*) and Michael Whitney (2*) survived the final 29 balls to draw the match, secure the Trans-Tasman Trophy and provide Allan Border with his first series victory in eight attempts. It had been a splendid finish.

In 1988 Australia celebrated two hundred years of white rule, and the government dubbed the time as the Bicentenary. All sorts of functions took place around the country including a one-off Test match against England at the Sydney Cricket Ground which started on 29 January.

The Ashes, although not at stake, were on exhibition in the main hall of the State Bank of NSW in Martin Place, Sydney. Cricketers from the past arrived in Sydney for the Test and celebration dinners with the commercial hype being quite considerable. The match, regrettably, proved more a contest of attrition than the anticipated festival match and became a tiresome, boring draw. The Board budgeted for the five-day match to attract over 200,000 spectators: in fact only 103,831 attended.

One of the biggest losses was suffered by the New South Wales Cricket Association, one of whose events was a celebration banquet in a marquee on North Sydney Oval. An Association committeeman put their losses alone at $179,000 instead of an anticipated profit.

In the match England took nearly two days to score 425, during which time opening batsman Chris Broad (139) was fined $1200 for

*(Above)* That ball! With his first delivery in an Ashes Test, Shane Warne dismisses Mike Gatting at Old Trafford on 3 June 1993. For the remainder of the series only Gooch handled Warne with any assurance. *(Adrian Murrell/Getty Images)*

*(Below)* Master of the sledge, scourge of all Poms and all-round fine figure of a man, Merv 'the Swerve' Hughes plays up to the camera in 1993. He was nicknamed 'Sumo' by the English fans and 'Fruitfly.' by his countrymen after the great Australian pest. *(Ben Radford/Getty Images)*

*(Above)* Captain Hook: Alan Border lashes out during the First Test against South Africa, Johannesburg, 4–8 March, 1994. He retired at the end of the series with an exceptional record: 156 Tests, 11,174 runs, average 50.56. *(Mike Hewitt/Getty Images)*

*(Below)* Michael Clarke who made a dashing 151 against India in his Test debut at Bangalore on 6-7 October, 2004, has made six centuries in 33 Tests, and is vice-captain of his country. *(Hamish Blair/ Getty Images)*

*(Above)* Runs on the board: Mark Taylor shoulders arms after his record innings of 334 in the second Test against Pakistan in Peshawar, 17 October, 1998. *(Ben Radford/Allsport/Getty Images)*

*(Below)* Late declaration: Mark Waugh and Shane Warne own up to accepting money from an Indian bookmaker four years previously, 9 December 1988. *(Laurence Griffiths/Allsport/Getty Images)*

*(Above)* Upping sticks: Mark Waugh and Darren Lehmann race for the pavilion after securing victory in the World Cup Final against Pakistan at Lord's, 20 June 1999 *(Grahan Chadwick/Allsport/Getty Images)*

*(Below)* Shane Warne traps English opener Marcus Trescothick lbw for 33 in the second innings of the fifth Test at The Oval, September 2005. England were in trouble on 109 for four, with a lead of only 115, only for Kevin Pietersen to score 158 to force a draw. Warne captured 40 wickets in the series. *(Jon Buckle/Empics Sport/PA Photos)*

*(Left)* Left-hand batsman Michael Hussey debuted as an opening batsman in 2005-06 against the West Indies and has proved the epitome of reliability in the middle order with eight centuries from just 23 Test matches. *(Jon Buckle/ Empics Sport/PA Photos)*

*(Below)* Eyes on the prize: Glenn McGrath dives to take a freakishly brilliant catch to dismiss Michael Vaughanof England during the second Test at Adelaide Oval, 24 November, 2002. *(Nick Wilson/Getty Images)*

*(Right)* The best wicket-keeper batsman in the history of the game, Adam Gilchrist blasted 33 international centuries (17 Test, 16 ODI) besides making 888 dismissals. *(Gareth Copley/PA Photos)*

*(Below)* Top of the world: The Australian squad celebrate their 125-run victory over India. Back row: Bevan, McGrath, Gilchrist, Ponting, Martyn, Lee, Hayden, Harvey, John Burchanan (coach); front row: Hogg, Bichel, Hauritz, Maher. Missing from picture: Lehmann and Symonds. *(Hamish Blair/Getty Images)*

*(Above)* Stuart Clark, lean and mean in the McGrath mould, captured 26 wickets at 17.03 in the 2006-07 Ashes series and has gathered 76 wickets at 20.77 in 16 Tests since 2006. *(Tom Shaw/Getty Images)*

*(Below)* Three Australian Test heroes, left to right, Justin Langer, Glenn McGrath and Shane Warne celebrate their last Test match (and 5-0 Ashes victory) with their children at the Sydney Cricket Ground, January 2007. *(Torsten Blackwood/AFP/Getty Images)*

*(Above)* Opening batsman Matthew Hayden made a strong comeback in both forms of the game in the 2000s. From 94 Tests he has scored 8242 runs, average 53.51 and was top run scorer in the 2007 World Cup with 659 runs and three centuries. *(Aman Sharma/AP/PA Photos)*

*(Below)* Glenn McGrath went out on top as the leading bowler at the 2007 World Cup with 26 wickets at 13.73 to take his career tally to 381 wickets from 250 one day international matches. *(Hamish Blair/Getty Images)*

knocking over his stumps on dismissal. Australia fell for 214 and then played out time for nearly two days in scoring 328 for two, David Boon remaining unbeaten on 184. The highlight of the final day was a pressbox presentation to Bill O'Reilly who, at the age of eighty-two, was ending his Test match reporting career with the *Sydney Morning Herald*.

A Sri Lankan team had been playing various country and State one-day matches during January and, at the beginning of February, warmed up for their solitary Test by playing in a draw with Victoria in Melbourne.

Having been pressurised by the ICC to grant a Test to Sri Lanka, the Board eventually gave way and scheduled the match for Perth in mid-February. The public gave their thoughts on such a match with only 10,587 turning up to watch four days of cricket.

Unable to host tours because of continued civil unrest and without a domestic first-class competition, Sri Lanka were desperately short of four- and five-day cricket. The Australian Cricket Board did not help by scheduling only one first-class game before the Test so, quite naturally, the Sri Lankans were more than rusty.

Australia batted first with Dean Jones (102) and Allan Border (88) leading the way to 455. It was more than enough, with Sri Lanka managing only 194 and 153 in reply.

The World Series Cup between Australia, New Zealand and Sri Lanka saw a ridiculously one-sided contest although Sri Lanka did manage one win, in defeating New Zealand in Hobart by four wickets. Australia defeated New Zealand in the finals to add to their trophy list for the season. Domestically, Western Australia retained the Sheffield Shield by defeating Queensland in the final by five wickets.

During February and March 1988 the SACA and VCA were joint hosts for a Youth World Cup. The cream of cricket's young players took part in an eight-team competition with Australia, England, Pakistan and the West Indies making it through to the semi-finals which were played on the Adelaide Oval. Pakistan defeated West Indies by two wickets, and Australia overcame England by seven wickets. The final was an excellent game of cricket played at a high standard with Australia winning by five wickets to claim the Bicentennial Youth World Cup.

With another proposed tour of Sri Lanka cancelled because of continuous political problems on the island, the Australian Cricket Board considered quite seriously a tour of Zimbabwe. Allan Border let it be known to the Board executive meeting held in Adelaide on 22 March that he was not interested in touring on the proposed dates of 7 to 21 April. Subsequently the whole idea was dropped and the selectors went ahead in choosing the side to tour Pakistan in September and October.

During April a series of three matches were played for charity between the England and Australian teams of 1977 vintage. In Perth, under lights, in front of 19,500 spectators England 215 (D. Randall 69) lost to Australia 216 for seven (G. Chappell 59*) by three wickets. Three days later in Adelaide, watched by 7363 on a working-day Wednesday, Australia 212 (G. Cosier 72*, P. Lever 3/34) defeated England 185 (D. Amiss 73, D. Walters 3/12) by 27 runs. Finally, with 8435 watching in Brisbane, England 136 (D. Walters 3/14, K. O'Keeffe 3/37) lost to Australia 137 for three (D. Hookes 94) by seven wickets.

The appeal – not necessarily of these types of matches but of the players involved – saw a Perth crowd outstrip that of the whole four days of the recent Test, with the Adelaide and Sydney attendances higher than any Shield match.

On 22 April 1988 the Australian Cricket Board announced that NSWCA delegate and Sydney solicitor Alan Crompton had been appointed manager of the team to tour Pakistan in September. Crompton was destined not to go as he would have other more important matters at hand for, on 18 July, the first of a number of arranged 'coups' took place in Australian cricket. That night, at the annual general meeting of the New South Wales Cricket Association, the majority of the 'old guard' were swept from office. A self-styled 'Sydney reform group', who for some time had been disenchanted with the direction in which their Association was moving, succeeded in electing a majority of their supporters on to the NSWCA executive. Fred Bennett and Dick Guy lost their Board positions and the interstate movements to claim more Board delegates' places and reduce the number of 'yes-men' started to gain momentum.

However, success was not at hand. Tasmania, under the guidance of Brian Davison, had overturned their old guard a couple of years earlier while Queensland's reform group made slow but steady progress. South Australia was a lost cause because its committee system, set up in 1897, was so watertight that no 'unapproved' person could ever get elected.

The real setback to the reform groups – who had been meeting informally around Australia for some time – came when Greg Chappell resigned in total frustration from all his numerous positions from Test selector to chairing Board coaching committees. Chappell had become only the third Australian captain, behind Joe Darling and Sir Donald Bradman, to be elected to the Board, and for ten months he had sat and fumed at what he found was going on. He then called a press conference in Melbourne, after informing David Richards of his intentions, and spoke with aplomb and diplomacy. As Michael Horan wrote in the Melbourne *Sun-Herald*: 'Greg Chappell tipped a monumental bucket on Australian cricket administration'. Horan added: 'Chappell said he simply realised he was beating his head against a brick wall'.

In his remarks Chappell called cricket administration in Australia 'archaic', adding: 'It makes it difficult for one or a number of people to effectively change things. Once I came to the realisation that I wasn't getting any satisfaction from doing it, then I was better off doing something else'. He concluded: 'I believed I could no longer achieve or offer very much. It's a whole multitude of things. I just think the system is wrong. It is very difficult for the right people to get involved,' and here Chappell put what so many people knew: 'The wrong sort of people are getting to make decisions that are very important, but of which they have no understanding'.

And with that Greg Chappell walked out of Australian cricket. When asked his views Allan Border expressed sadness saying: 'It's really sad that a person of that calibre should resign for those reasons. It seems to be an indictment of the current administration.'

Colin Egar was appointed manager of the touring team to Pakistan in early August. The tour started in Lahore with a drawn game against the Patron's XI, Geoff Marsh scoring 136, after which came another draw, this time in Quetta against the Baluchistan Governor's team.

Then came the first, and most controversial, Test of the short tour, marred by unacceptable umpiring and played on a bald pitch. Pakistan scored 469 for nine declared with Australia in reply making 165 and 116 to lose by an innings and 188 runs. Manager Egar had protested 'from the word go' to the Pakistan authorities about the pitch and umpires, and it took strong words by telephone from Australia to stop Border and his team returning home immediately.

As Border said: 'I can write down the scenario now. The next two Tests will be played on bland pitches and will be drawn. It's the same old story in Pakistan.' And so it came to pass. The second Test in Faisalabad saw Border score an unbeaten 113, with Australia way on top in the third Test in Lahore as time ran out.

A three-day match in Peshawar gave Geoff Marsh (106) the opportunity to score a century in a high-scoring draw. The only one-day international, played before 25,000 spectators in Lahore, saw the scores finish level but Pakistan given the match on the basis of losing fewer wickets.

The team then flew to Hong Kong for a one-day match scoring 398 in 46.1 overs (Dean Jones 131, Mike Veletta 88) to defeat Hong Kong, 219 for eight in 50 overs, by 179 runs.

On their return home the Western Australian players had to play against the Ranji Trophy holders, Tamil Nadu, in the first ever first-class match by an overseas province in Australia. Put into bat in Perth the Western Australian openers, Geoff Marsh (209) and Mike Veletta

(166*), scored 374 for the first wicket in just 363 minutes. Tamil Nadu were in complete disarray and Graeme Wood declared after 101 overs, just after the start on the second day, at 438 for two. WA went on to win in less than three days by an innings and 51 runs. However, a few months later the same Tamil Nadu team scored 912 for six in a Ranji Trophy match against Goa. If nothing else this gave an explanation as to the high standard of WA cricket. A week after their opening display, Marsh (223) and Veletta (157) put on 310 for the first wicket against Tasmania at Bellerive Oval in Hobart. It was a good start to the season.

To celebrate their 150th anniversary, the Melbourne Cricket Club held three weeks of exhibitions and dinners between late October and mid-November 1988. In keeping with their role in Australian cricket the club opened its ground to the public and put on tasteful displays of its history at the newly completed Australian Gallery of Sport. The whole ground was a wonderful museum of past sporting events. The big occasion was held on the actual birthday, 15 November 1988, when 2200 members sat down to dinner in an enormous marquee erected on the ground. It was a splendid affair and with it came the news of planned ground developments which would increase its capacity to 115,000.

The Australian Cricket Board held its fifteenth annual general meeting at its offices in Jolimont Street, opposite the Melbourne Cricket Ground, on 8 September. There were a number of issues of concern, particularly the problems besetting the tour of Pakistan (and, later, an official complaint from the Pakistan Board regarding the Australian manager) and the invitations sent to some forty cricket officials around the country to attend the centenary of Test cricket in South Africa.

The Board, with a number of new delegates, agreed that Malcolm Gray should continue as chairman and proceeded to involve themselves with the forthcoming season rather than anything else. The South African invitations were considered matters for personal judgment with the Board, correctly, not wishing to intervene.

What happened over the following three months was a campaign by the federal and state governments to prevent any cricket officials going to Johannesburg. In South Australia, Phil Ridings was told that the State government would cancel the lease to the Adelaide Oval and refuse to lend money for the redevelopment of the ground's new grandstand; in Victoria, Ray Steele was threatened with removal as a trustee of the MCG, which the Victorian Cricket Association needed so as to be able to play on the ground; and the federal government indicated their intention to withdraw funding from various cricket projects.

So much for the innocent who try to argue that sport and politics do not mix.

The official Board launch of the 1988–89 season took place at the Victorian Arts Centre on 25 October. Other than to introduce the touring West Indian team and to announce that twenty-six players were now under contract, the Board also let it be known that it and its New Zealand counterpart 'had launched a joint venture to stage the 1992 World Cup cricket tournament'. David Richards told the gathering of media representatives that the application 'would be put to the January meeting of the International Cricket Conference'.

The West Indies team arrived in Perth on 24 October from Sharjah, but they were unable to train prior to their first match as their luggage had been mislaid en route from the United Arab Emirates. This showed in their initial first-class match when they were beaten by Western Australia by seven wickets in front of 12,858 spectators. The visitors' attractiveness continued into their next fixture, an innings-and-twenty-run win over South Australia when 19,467 people turned up, the highest for a four-day match in Adelaide since 1969. In Sydney, for a draw with NSW, 17,819 spectators watched West Indies' captain, Vivian Richards, register his one hundredth first-class century, the first Caribbean player to record such a feat.

It was during this match that an announcement was made that the West Indies team had signed a ten-year promotional agreement with the International Management Group. From now on IMG would handle all tour contracts, sponsorships, marketing and promotional activities and television rights. The immediate result was that newspaper photographers were asked $250 for each photograph and an Australian Cricket Society function was cancelled when the tour manager, Clive Lloyd, suddenly demanded a $3000 appearance fee. Ian Chappell was also caught out when, having flown from Sydney to Adelaide to film a segment for his Channel Nine sports programme, the West Indians, who had previously agreed, now refused to be filmed. In the Adelaide *News* the question was asked: 'Has the monster, which Ian Chappell helped to create by the formation of World Series Cricket, now turned and threatened to engulf the cricket world?'

The West Indies showed their superiority in the first Test in Brisbane when defeating Australia by nine wickets in just three-and-a-half days. Only Stephen Waugh, with a second-innings 90, made any impression against a rampant West Indian attack in which Courtney Walsh claimed a hat-trick and Vivian Richards his one hundredth Test catch.

After a draw against Victoria the tourists moved to Perth for the second Test. It took them until eleven minutes from the end of the final day's play to win by 169 runs in a match which saw Australian pace-bowler Merv Hughes (5/130 and 8/87) claim a hat-trick and

Vivian Richards (146) score his twenty-third Test century.

During the match umpire Robin Bailhache had warned West Indian fast-bowler Patrick Patterson for intimidatory bowling. This brought forth the revelation on Channel Nine's television commentary that Allan Border had been so concerned over the bowling action of another West Indian during the Brisbane Test that he had asked to view film of the bowler. Studied in slow motion, and from a number of angles, it resulted in a report being sent by the Australian captain to the Board.

Following yet another draw, this time with Tasmania, the third Test in Melbourne started, unusually, before Christmas which was reflected in the overall attendance figure of 108,408. It was yet another case of Australia being overwhelmed by the West Indian juggernaut, this time by 285 runs. No Australian batsman scored more than 42 (Stephen Waugh) in innings of 242 and 114.

It was now time for the selectors to change the team. In came former 'rebel' leg-spinner Trevor Hohns; a new opening batsman in Mark Taylor and a new lease of life for another 'rebel' in swing bowler Terry Alderman. The effect, short- and long-term, was to be dramatic.

But not so dramatic were the attendance figures. After a good start the popular attraction of the West Indies had become less and less until Melbourne Cricket Club secretary John Lill had, surprisingly, gone into print with criticism of the Board's scheduling of the tour. He put forward the case that, had the usual Boxing Day start taken place, attendances for the third Test would have doubled. This sent the statisticians to their books with the Sydney *Sun-Herald* on 1 January 1989 devoting three pages to showing graphically the decline of interest in Test cricket in Australia with average daily attendances falling from 36,481 (England 1936–37) to 30,621 (West Indies 1960–61), 26,805 (England 1974–75), 22,264 (England 1982–83), 14,523 (West Indies 1984–85), 12,963 (West Indies 1988–89). The Board's reaction, according to the newspaper was: 'It is not correct that crowds are down', while the rest of those interviewed, ranging from former players to journalists to 'the-man-in-the-street', all focussed on the prohibitive cost of attending Test matches in Australia. The doomwatchers had a field day until the fourth Test started in Sydney on 26 January.

It was Australia Day, a national holiday, and led from the front by the captain, the team chased away those years of despondency. The first day started with the West Indies batting in their usual manner to reach 156 for two just before tea. Then Border brought himself on to bowl his left-arm spinners and the West Indian batsmen collapsed. Border took a career-best 7/46 as the visitors reached 224. In a disciplined innings, the Australian batsmen scored slowly but surely: Boon made 149 in a day-and-a-half; Border 75 in six-and-a-half hours, and Stephen Waugh an unbeaten 55 in three hours as the score mounted to 401. Border (4/50) again ensured that the West Indies had to fight for their runs and success came his way just after lunch on the fifth day by seven wickets. Border became the first Australian captain to take ten wickets in a match with his 11/96 being the fourth-best ever by a Test captain.

The mood was buoyant for the fifth Test in Adelaide. Australia batted for most of the first two days with Dean Jones (216) recording his side's seventh double-century against the West Indies, and then having a record partnership for the ninth wicket with Merv Hughes (72*). In reply to Australia's 515 the tourists came up against the recalled left-arm pace-bowler Michael Whitney who achieved his career-best figures of 7/89. After a much quicker second innings, Border declared overnight on the fourth day but the West Indians declined the challenge and batted out for a draw.

Pakistan also toured during the season in order to act as the third team for the World Series Cup. They played one first-class match – a draw against New South Wales – and one-day games at extremities of the country. They then won only two WSC fixtures and left the country as anonymously as they had arrived. West Indies defeated Australia 2-1 in the finals and all that was left of a rushed season was for Western Australia to claim once again the Sheffield Shield when they drew with South Australia in the final in Perth.

After the official season was over, New Zealand lost to Western Australia in Perth in a match arranged to commemorate the launch of Air New Zealand's first direct flight from Christchurch to Perth. Then a proposed first-class match between Worcestershire and Queensland was cancelled due to torrential rain and replaced with two one-day matches, both won by Queensland.

The season's finances were looked at long and hard after the Board reported a drop in profits from $345,894 to $41,157. The usual receipt figures from major games were not given out for the season although intelligent guesswork would suggest takings during the Tests of $2,128,230 from 323,759 spectators and $4,064,765 from 479,581 who attended the one-day internationals. The other tour games were watched by 98,766 people who paid $395,064 for the privilege. Which begs the question of costs when a profit to distribute is only $41,157 against an income from home tours of $6,588,059!

With the growth of cricket administration in Australia the Board felt it necessary to explain, in late 1988, its role and functions to an increasingly bewildered public. The fourteen directors (who used to be called delegates and whose functions had not changed) were the Board and under them came the Executive Committee. Stemming from the Executive Committee came the specialist committees covering Playing Conditions, Cricket, Selection, International, Financial Review, Programme, Coaching, Umpires, Youth Council, Kanga (or Kwick) Cricket and Cricket Academy.

The directors and committees were serviced by an administration comprising a Chief Executive, General Manager, Administration Manager, Accountant, Media Manager, Director of Coaching and Australian Coach who in turn had access to the administration and secretarial staff of nine. Also employed by the Board were Kanga (junior) Coordinators in each State as well as consultants ranging from PBL Marketing to the quaintly named Government Affairs adviser who was based in Canberra.

When the former secretary Alan Barnes died in Sydney on 14 March 1989 the entire Executive Committee attended his funeral to pay their respects to a man who for twenty-one years carried on his shoulders the work now done by so many.

# 35

# 'The Nervous Nineties'

When the International Cricket Conference met at Lord's in late January 1989, Malcolm Gray, David Richards and Bob Cowper represented Australia. Their main success was when the ICC representatives voted by 20-12 to award the 1992 World Cup jointly to Australia and New Zealand. This resulted in a World Cup Organising Committee being formed with the first of many meetings held on 31 March in Melbourne with Malcolm Gray and Des Rundle representing Australia, and Barry Paterson and Graham Dowling, New Zealand.

The Board also had another matter on its collective mind. In keeping with the apparent policy of threatening to sue anyone who criticised them the administration had taken umbrage in mid-February when the Alice Springs magistrate, Denis Barritt, made reference to the Australian team. In the process of sentencing a man on an indecency charge, the magistrate drew an analogy between the case and the public antics of the Australian team which included 'kissing and hugging on the field of play'.

David Richards said later that the Board had referred the matter to its solicitors to determine if the team had any legal redress. 'The extraordinary comments would seem to be totally unrelated to the matter before him,' Richards said. 'Accordingly the Board cannot understand why these comments were made. However they are regarded as being clearly defamatory and on this basis have been referred to our solicitors.'

Most people with a basic knowledge of Australian law, state and federal, would have known that Mr Barritt's comments – correct or otherwise – were covered by privilege. Nothing further was heard of the matter except, maybe, the peals of laughter around Australia as every news bulletin on radio and television, and the following day's newspapers, carried the story in prominent positions.

The Board's financial statement for 1988–89 fails to indicate the cost of fees for legal advice for the year.

At their meeting held in Melbourne, which started on 27 April, Board directors were given details of Allan Border's new three-year contract. Said to be worth $300,000 the concept behind the offer was to stop the Australian captain giving any consideration to retiring from the game. Also on the agenda was a most difficult rearrangement of the following season's itinerary following David Richards' return from Karachi with the news that the Pakistan Board had double-booked tours for 1989–90. This resulted in an Australian season which would defy belief.

The northern summer of 1989 proved to be the best for Australia since Bradman's all-conquering side of 1948. Success seemed to breed success from the tourists who were managed by Lawrie Sawle and coached by Bobby Simpson. In twenty first-class matches on tour the Australians only lost one, against Worcestershire in their initial fixture. The pitch was sub-standard and Simpson refused the offer of an additional one-day game on the scheduled third day saying: 'We could not be guaranteed a pitch good enough to produce an even game'. Then followed a draw with Somerset and victory over Middlesex (Marsh 100*) before the three one-day internationals.

At Old Trafford England won by 95 runs; there was a tie at Trent Bridge, and Australia won at Lord's by six wickets. The three matches were watched by 52,871 spectators who paid the enormous sum of £854,246 – and that did not include the members who were admitted without charge.

The next two matches were versus county sides prior to the first Test. Against Warwickshire, Dean Jones scored 248 in 331 minutes from 284 balls with twelve sixes and nineteen fours. His sixes were a record for any Australian batsman in first-class cricket, with his third-wicket stand of 349 in 225 minutes with Tom Moody (144*) establishing another milestone. The match was drawn. Three days later Derbyshire were beaten by eleven runs.

Then came the start of a six-Test series which would be watched by 339,602 spectators who would pay £4,244,321 at the turnstiles or booking offices. The excitable section of the volatile English press had all but ignored the deliberate Australian build-up to the Test. They had virtually disregarded the form of Mark Taylor, the devastating swing bowling of Terry Alderman, the growing confidence of Stephen Waugh, and the quality of Allan Border's captaincy. They told silly stories, as was their wont, and the masses fell for it.

On 8 June at Headingley, England captain David Gower won the toss and put Australia into bat. Taylor (136) and Waugh (177*) then scored their first Test centuries; Waugh and Hughes (71) added 147 for the seventh wicket, Australia's highest in a Test in England; and Border's third-morning declaration at 601 for seven was the second highest score at Headingley behind Somerset's 630 in 1901. England replied with 430 (Allan Lamb 125, Terry Alderman 5/107) after which the Australians took the long handle to the home attack. After scoring at more than a run a minute the declaration came at 230 for three which left England to score 402 to win in five hours. With only Gooch (68) holding out, Alderman took 5/44. England fell for 191 in four hours to give Australia victory by 210 runs.

Morale in the tourists' camp was sky-high as they next defeated Lancashire by nine wickets and Northamptonshire by 272 runs (Border 135) before going to Lord's for the second Test. Trevor Hohns came into the side for Greg Campbell and from then on the team remained unchanged in the Tests. Gower (57) batted on winning the toss but England were dismissed for 286 before the close. Hughes took 4/71 with his pace, periodic bouncers and occasional leg-breaks unsettling the batsmen.

Australia's 528 was a model of solid team batting which was obvious to a capacity crowd who paid £1,249,472 to see Stephen Waugh score an unbeaten 152, David Boon 94, while Geoff Lawson, who put on 130 in 107 minutes for the ninth wicket with Waugh, made 74. Only an England fifth-wicket stand of 139 between Gower (106) and Smith (96) saved England from a worse defeat. Alderman took 6/128 as England made 359, and at five o'clock on the fifth afternoon Waugh hit the winning boundary for Australia to record victory by six wickets to go two up in the series.

By now the English press had turned on David Gower. He was so shocked at their questions and probing into his personal life (for which there was no reason) that he stormed out of the mid-match press conference, so breaking that tenuous umbilical cord that exists twixt captain and the fourth estate.

The visiting Australian press were bemused by all this. In *The Australian* on 26 June, Terry Brindle wrote: 'David Gower is unloved by an English public which sees his apparent acceptance of failure as a luxury, unappreciated by professionals who see his as an amateur philosophy on the game and – perhaps most importantly – offside with an English media which creates kings and coffins with equal facility.'

The die was now cast and the Australians knew it. After a draw with Glamorgan (Veletta 134*) the third Test at Edgbaston was ruined by rain: Dean Jones scored 157 out of 424 with England's reply of 242 just avoiding the follow-on on the last morning. Then came a draw with Hampshire (Waugh 112, Boon 103) and victory by an innings and 146 runs against Gloucestershire (Jones 167*, Taylor 141, Lawson 6/30) in two days.

Old Trafford, Manchester, hosted the fourth Test which started on 27 July with England batting until just before lunch on the second morning for 260 of which Robin Smith made 143 and Geoff Lawson claimed 6/72. Stephen Waugh (92) led the way in Australia's 447 after which Terry Alderman's 5/66 broke the back of England's innings. 'Jack' Russell (128*) and John Emburey (64) held up the Australian victory roll by adding 142 for the seventh wicket but the Ashes were to be Australia's at 5.41 pm on the fifth day when David Boon swept a ball to the square-leg boundary to give Australia their one hundredth Test win against England.

It was the first time since 1934 that Australia had regained the Ashes in England and, by coincidence, both Australian captains, Bill Woodfull (22 August) and Allan Border (27 July) celebrated their birthdays during the matches in question.

The day after the Australians' success the Board met in Melbourne for their mid-winter meeting. The most controversial item on the agenda – and one which would have international repercussions during the 1992 World Cup – was the acceptance of Richie Benaud's new draft rules for international one-day games played in Australia. The main recommendation was that the best solution for interrupted matches was to calculate the target score using the equivalent number of highest scoring overs, instead of using the average run-rate. The Board argued that this would enliven games 'by meaning the side batting second, when the overs were reduced, would be facing a higher target score'.

Meanwhile the English press were hardly bothering to report on Australia's success although the former Test player, Mike Selvey, did write in the *Guardian*: 'When the winning hit was made Border, sitting padded up on the team balcony, was swamped by teammates. He and Bobby Simpson have schemed and plotted this moment all summer. And before that England have been outplayed, outwitted and outgunned by an Australian side blessed with skill, spirit, self-belief and good luck.'

As the sun slanted across the misty hills and valleys of central Victoria the day after the Ashes victory, an old man in a nursing home in the town of Kyneton had the news read to him. His failing eyesight meant that eighty-eight-year-old Bill Ponsford, a member of that 1934 team, could only listen to what had happened. No doubt the thoughts came flooding back in memory of his hugely successful final Test of all those years ago.

By now the tour was a breeze. Nottinghamshire were defeated by 196 runs (Boon 102*) and Leicestershire by nine wickets. Then came the fifth Test at Trent Bridge where the records flew thick and fast as Australia set about beating England in the most comprehensive fashion imaginable. Their victory, achieved inside four days, was the biggest by an innings margin in Ashes Tests since 1946.

Batting first, the Australian openers, Geoff Marsh and Mark Taylor, became the ninth pair to bat throughout an uninterrupted day of Test cricket and the first to do so in England. At the close the score was 301 without loss with Marsh falling first on the second morning: his 138 taking 432 minutes from 382 balls with fifteen fours in a stand of 329. At 430, Taylor fell for 219 scored from 461 deliveries in 554 minutes with 23 fours. At 602 for six Border declared and then let his bowlers at the England batsmen. Of 255, Robin Smith scored 101, Terry Alderman taking 5/69, and following-on England reached just 167 to lose by an innings and 180 runs.

Now the English press were in a stupor. As Rob Batsford reported for Reuter's: 'English cricket writers have exploded nearly all their wrath and, with expletives deleted, they tend to treat Australia's triumphant progress – and England's demise – with black humour.'

The last two county fixtures saw a draw with Kent (Jones 128) and a 150-run win over Essex. Although David Boon scored a first-innings 151, most attention was paid to the fact that NSW batsman Mark Waugh scored an unbeaten century for Essex while his twin brother Stephen did the same in Australia's second innings. This was the first instance in any first-class match of twins scoring centuries for opposing teams.

The sixth Test at The Oval was spoilt by rain and petered out into a frustrating draw. The Australians were on top throughout and bad light on the final afternoon probably cost them their fifth victory of the series. Dean Jones scored 122 and Alderman took 5/66 to finish off a highly satisfying series from the Australians' point of view.

In all first-class matches the tourists had scored twenty centuries with four players – Taylor (1669), Jones (1510), Boon (1306) and Waugh (1030) – passing one thousand runs. Alderman (70), Lawson (69) and Hughes (47) were the top wicket-takers.

The whole tour had been a success on and off the field. Memories of the previous three visits were erased as Border and his men pushed forward relentlessly. Attendances were good with 528,000 spectators watching the 32 matches and in the process paying £5,363,380 for the honour.

The Australian team then concluded their tour with four one-day matches, defeating Holland by 57 runs and four wickets on successive days in The Hague, and Denmark by 45 runs at Copenhagen's Brondby Stadium followed by a 54-run victory at the Slagelse Stadium.

The team returned home to wide adulation. It was a time, in Australia, when the economy was starting to slide and the future for many beginning to look grim. Unemployment had taken a sharp turn upwards with banking scandals rocking Australia's financial community. But whatever the problems, the cricketers received a ticker-tape parade through the streets of Sydney following a celebratory dinner held under Prime Ministerial patronage in Melbourne.

Western Australia toured southern India for a fortnight during mid-September 1989 to play their return fixture with Tamil Nadu and three one-day games. The first-class fixture at the Chidambaram Stadium in Madras was spoilt by rain after Tamil Nadu had scored 503 and Western Australia replied with 271 for eight. In the one-day fixtures WA lost to Tamil Nadu by ten runs in Coimbatore but won by 29 runs in Madras. Against Karnataka in the Chinnaswamy Stadium, Bangalore, WA lost by seven wickets. The tour was impracticably scheduled for the hottest and most humid time of the year. The sponsors did not get much benefit from either series and it was unappreciated by both players and the few spectators who watched the contests. A few months later the idea was scrapped.

In late September the Board's sixteenth annual general meeting took place in the new Victorian Cricket Association offices in Melbourne. Malcolm Gray stepped down as chairman after three very successful years and by the Board's unwritten regulations, the chairmanship had to go to a South Australian. Phil Ridings and (now Finance Director) Des Rundle declined to put their names forward so former Test umpire Colin Egar rose through the ranks to take Australian cricket's top position. The democracy of the Board showed through as a Dry Cleaner replaced one of Australia's top financial experts. However, before the election of the chairman, a number of rumblings were heard with various suggestions being made, particularly that of WA's Lawrie Sawle having his name put forward or for Gray to carry on. The appropriate deals were struck among Board directors when they enjoyed dinner together the night before the meeting.

The second week of October saw the naming of two well-known cricket landmarks. In the Adelaide suburb of Glenelg a new stand at the local Oval was named after the founder of the Adelaide Oval, Yorke Sparks, while in the NSW highlands town of Bowral a far more important event took place. In the town where Sir Donald Bradman spent much of his early life, a Bradman Museum had been built next to the Bradman Oval to honour the great man.

On 13 October a dinner was held in Sydney to mark the occasion and the following day Bradman, then eighty-one, along with his wife Jessie, returned to Bowral to open the $700,000 building. The concept of a Sydney barrister, the museum was an excellent idea to honour one of Australia's favourite sons. Along with Melbourne's Gallery of Sport in which cricket dominates, Australia's culture in this area is far ahead of many in the concept of having 'living' museums in which younger generations can watch and experience the game and heroes of yesteryear.

After a short break at home, and playing in the first two club matches of the new season, Australia's cricketers flew to India in mid-October. They were to participate in the Nehru Cup – another one-day competition dreamt up by the Indian Board – in order to celebrate the centenary of the birth of Jawaharlal Nehru.

Six nations took part with the competition having started by the time the Australians arrived. After defeating Hyderabad in Secunderabad by 162 runs, the Australians lost to England, Pakistan and India; defeated the West Indies and Sri Lanka, but failed to qualify for the finals, which Pakistan won, and returned to Australia at the beginning of November.

The Board launched their season on 11 October with details of the three touring teams to Australia and of the three late season tours being made to New Zealand, Sharjah and the United States of America. They also announced the purchase of a property at 90 Jolimont Street in Melbourne for the Board's new headquarters. The palatial two-storey building was secured with a mortgage of $1,100,000 from the Commonwealth Bank with the balance of $600,000 coming from regular funds.

New Zealand arrived for their short tour in early November 1989. After defeating Western Australia by seven wickets in a one-day game, and drawing a first-class encounter the Kiwis drew against South Australia in Adelaide before returning to Perth for the one-off Test.

Australia showed how they felt about New Zealand captain John Wright's decision to put them in to bat by taking nearly two days to score 521 for nine declared. David Boon made exactly 200 in 451 minutes from 326 deliveries with 28 fours, and Dean Jones fell leg-before-wicket one run short of his century. New Zealand's response of 231 saw Border enforce the follow-on. It took the then slowest century in Australian cricket (462 minutes) by Mark Greatbatch to steady the Kiwi ship. When stumps were finally drawn the left-handed batsman remained unbeaten on 146 scored in just under eleven hours to deny Australia victory.

The Sri Lankan team toured Australia from mid-November to mid-February, visiting all parts of the continent. The itinerary was described by David Richards as 'far from ideal', yet no effort was made to spare the visitors from some humiliating fixtures. Where first-class opposition could have been slotted into the schedule with outgrounds used, such as happended with NSW (Canberra) and Victoria (Sale), the Board had filled in with one-day games against country combinations. This unsatisfactory state of affairs – and the Board's refusal to allow Sri Lanka to visit New Zealand during their 39 days of useless wandering around the Australian bush between the second Test and the start of the one-day series – saw them chalk up 19,375 miles in twenty-two separate journeys.

In fixtures against the States Sri Lanka drew against New South Wales, South Australia and Tasmania, and lost to Victoria at Sale (a new first-class venue) by an innings and three runs. However, the Sri Lankans confounded the pundits by putting up an excellent performance in the first Test in Brisbane. The Woolloongabba ground became the first venue in Australia to have hosted a Test involving each of the eight Test-playing teams when Sri Lanka took the field after having put Australia in to bat. Tom Moody (106), on his second appearance, scored a century as Australia reached 367. Then came the surprise as visiting batsman Aravinda de Silva scored a splendid 167 to give his side a 51-run first-innings lead. The Australian response was to bat through to the end of the match at 375 for six. Mark Taylor made 164, and when 76 he reached 1000 Test runs, becoming the first batsman to attain such a mark in his debut calendar year of Test cricket.

Exactly 1132 Test matches had taken place before the island of Tasmania was honoured with their first fixture at the game's highest level. The best week in the State's cricket history started with a banquet for 500 people in Hobart followed by a full meeting of the Australian Cricket Board and then the match at Bellerive Oval in the suburb of Clarence.

Captain Arjuna Ranatunga put Australia into bat on a hard and fast pitch. Tasmanian David Boon faced the first ball while local umpire Steve Randell officiated at the bowler's end with the Tasmania member of the ABC radio commentary team, Neville Oliver, describing the start over the airwaves. Medium-pace outswinger bowler Rumesh Ratnayake took his Test-best figures of 6/66 as Australia were dismissed for 224. Rohan Mahanama (85) and Aravinda de Silva (75) put on 128 in three-and-a-quarter hours for the fourth wicket as Sri Lanka failed by six runs to equal Australia.

Then came an Australian onslaught as Taylor (108) Jones (118*) and Waugh (134*) set about the tiring Sri Lankan attack. The unbeaten sixth-wicket partnership of 260 came in under four hours, much to the delight of the excellent Hobart crowd. Set 522 for victory in five sessions the tourists tried hard but lost wickets regularly in the process. Their eventual defeat by 173 runs did not fully reflect their prowess and ability.

The Sri Lankans then started their aimless wander around Australia in between World Series Cup matches. They won just one match – against Pakistan in Perth – before leaving Australia two months after the end of their last Test. Australia and Pakistan fought out the World

Series Cup; Australia winning with ease against a Pakistan team who had had an exhausting season both home and away.

Prior to the WSC finals, Pakistan had lost to Western Australia by an innings and 78 runs and scrambled a draw with Queensland. The captain, Imran Khan, put Australia into bat in the first Test at Melbourne on Boxing Day 1989. On a firm pitch Australia struggled against the pace of Wasim Akram (6/62) and were dismissed for 223. Not to be outdone, the Australian pace trio of Alderman, Rackemann and Hughes skittled the tourists for 107. Mark Taylor (101) and Allan Border (62*), who was captaining Australia for a record forty-ninth time, top-scored as the total moved on to 312 for eight before the declaration was made. Pakistan fought valiantly to save the match with Ijaz Ahmed taking exactly seven-and-a-half hours over his 121 but defeat came by 92 runs with half-an-hour left to play.

The second Test in Adelaide was drawn, but with some outstanding individual performances. Dean Jones scored 116 and 121 not out to become the tenth Australian to complete a century in each innings of a Test. Pakistan all-rounder Wasim Akram scored 52 and 123 while also taking 5/100 and 1/29. Imran Khan made 136 and took 2/61 in Adelaide's fifth successive Test without a result.

Before the match the South Australian Cricket Association had formally opened their new $11 million grandstand at the southern end of the Adelaide Oval. Previously the site of the Creswell stand, named after arguably Australia's second-best cricket administrator, the new complex was named after Sir Donald Bradman who performed the opening ceremony.

When Pakistan moved on to Melbourne for a match against Victoria, the side became embroiled in a disgraceful display of questioning the umpire's authority. Robin Bailhache had officially warned leg-spinner Mushtaq Ahmed three times for following through on the pitch and subsequently banned him from bowling any more during the innings. The Pakistanis disagreed and walked off the field. After half-an-hour a compromise was reached with the umpire's authority undermined – the VCA secretary, Ken Jacobs, persuaded the umpires and Intikhab Alam, the Pakistan team manager, to agree that one of the official warnings to Mushtaq was not correctly given, thereby reducing his transgressions by one – but that did not stop Victoria winning the match by 59 runs.

Before the third Test in Sydney the Cricket Ground Trust unveiled a new $1 million surveillance system. Hooliganism at cricket matches in Sydney had been rife for nearly fifteen years and ninety-five electronic cameras were positioned strategically around the ground to catch the troublemakers.

They had no need to worry, for only 13,864 spectators braved the three days on which play took place. A cyclone had poured seventeen inches of rain on Sydney and no cricket was possible until the third afternoon. Even extending play to a sixth day did not help as Pakistan 199 (Alderman 5/65) drew with Australia 176 for two (Mark Taylor 101*).

During the season the Australian Cricket Board had been in the news, usually for the wrong reasons. In December it announced the possibility of moving the third Test against Pakistan from Sydney to Brisbane 'if the pitch at the Sydney Cricket Ground was not up to Test standard'. This annoyed the Trust who had recently spent $300,000 on upgrading the area.

Then came an incident during the WSC match in Perth between Australia and Sri Lanka when Channel Nine held up play for eight minutes during which time a television microphone was replaced in one of the stumps. The replacement stump then stood taller than the rest and had to be adjusted before play could proceed. The official WACA complaint to the Board was treated with contempt which caused broad headlines in Australia's newspapers. *The Australian* titled their story: 'Board's silence sure sign of guilt' and said: 'For too long have television dollars dictated how, where and when sports events are to be played'.

The leader writer commented: 'The Australian Cricket Board's stonewall silence over Channel Nine holding up the WSC match was an announcement of guilt and embarrassment', adding: 'Could you imagine Ian Chappell remaining silent during his playing days while a technician ran out on to the field to replace a microphone in the closing overs of a one-day match when the outcome hung in the balance?'

To cap off a poor season of public relations the Board had to read a detailed account of their budgeting and 'financial embarrassment' in the Melbourne *Age*. The Melbourne Test had attracted only 66,865 spectators in five days which saw the Board talk about 'the unusual nature of the season's fixtures'. David Richards added: 'We have framed our budget to suit the needs of the season'. The financial statements later in the year showed how fortunate the Board had been to have had a successful playing and financial tour of England a few months earlier.

The other touring team to Australia in a very busy season was English county side Lancashire. They played eight one- and two-day games in Tasmania and Western Australia, winning three and losing five.

New South Wales won the Sheffield Shield by defeating Queensland by 345 runs in the final at Sydney. The season had seen the emergence of two young batsmen with vast potential: Mark Waugh of NSW, and

South Australia's Darren Lehmann. Waugh scored 967 runs at 80.58 and Lehmann 953 at 52.94. It was not necessarily how many runs they scored but the way they did it. Waugh was rewarded with a WSC match, while Lehmann was twelfth man for the third Pakistan Test.

But it was the Western Australia versus South Australia match in Perth in mid-December 1989 which caught the eye. Australian vice-captain Geoff Marsh, recovering from a broken toe, opened the WA innings with Michael Veletta (150) and scored a career-best 355 not out in ten-and-a-half hours. It was not until two minutes past two o'clock on the second day that the pair were parted with the score on 431. Marsh made the first triple-century by a Western Australian and his score the tenth highest in Australian first-class cricket history.

The Australian team had little time to relax after the international season had ended for they were soon off to New Zealand to play in a three-way one-day series which also included India. The team won all five of its matches, including the final against New Zealand in Auckland by eight wickets.

As agreed with the New Zealand Cricket Council a solitary Test was played in Wellington as a reciprocal fixture for the one in Perth at the beginning of the season. The timing was unwise as the city had started its rainy season and the match took place in quite inappropriate conditions.

Australia batted first and struggled to 110 on a pitch New Zealand captain John Wright described as 'the slowest I have ever played a Test on'. When New Zealand batted night-watchman Martin Snedden claimed a new world record when he remained stationary on 6 for an officially timed 94 minutes. New Zealand reached 202 and in reply Australia's night-watchman Peter Taylor (87) and Allan Border (78*) were the only two scorers of note in a total of 269. Needing 178 to win New Zealand won easily by nine wickets, so breaking Australia's run of fourteen successive Tests without defeat.

The next port of call for Australia's cricket wayfarers was Sharjah in the United Arab Emirates. Six countries took part in the oddly named *Australasia Cup* tournament which saw Australia win their first three matches before losing in the final to Pakistan by 36 runs in front of over 20,000 spectators. This match finished on 4 May 1990 and eight days later a team, captained by David Boon, played Pakistan in two one-day matches in America. These contests, for the *North America Cup*, were arranged by the United States Cricket Control Board who wanted to play a four-match series.

David Richards flew to America in early May to finalise arrangements and immediately rejected plans for a fixture at the Houston Astrodome. He demanded, and got, an appearance fee of $US100,000 for the services of the Australian cricketers, and for only two matches.

Board chairman Colin Egar became team manager for the two games played at the Downing Stadium, New York – which Australia won by five runs – and at the Los Angeles Colosseum – which Pakistan won by four wickets.

The Australian Cricket Academy was well into its third year in July 1990 when the head coach, Jack Potter, followed the decision of his deputy Peter Spence, and handed in his resignation to the Board. Strong efforts were made by representatives of the Australian Institute of Sport to have both men reconsider their positions but to no avail. They had had enough of the politicking of the Board's administration and had openly approached the AIS for help in getting the 'empire-builders' off their backs.

Potter's individuality had gone against him. He was always aware that he had been second choice for the job. Originally it had been earmarked for John Inverarity, but he had withdrawn his application at the last minute when he became aware to whom he would be responsible. In two-and-a-half years of solid, intense work Potter had produced the cream of Australia's top players of the mid-1990s and beyond. His treatment by the Board, in many issues best left unaired, was nothing short of shameful. Potter, previously an academic, left the game to concentrate on his highly successful business. The eventual new appointee, Rodney Marsh, was little short of a figurehead.

The shift in the balance of power in Australian cricket was all but completed following the Board's seventeenth annual general meeting held on 14 September 1990. In their palatial new offices (valued at $2,416,668) the Board said farewell to Bob Parish after his thirty-three years representing Victoria. He was honoured with a special retirement dinner at the Hilton Hotel in Melbourne the night before the meeting, when the Board flew a number of former cricket administrators to Australia to mark the occasion.

Parish had served a total of eight years as chairman of both the old Board of Control and the current Board. When he joined cricket's ruling body in 1957, aged forty-one, he became the youngest member to be so elected. Along with Don Bradman, Parish had moved Australian cricket in the right direction with his firm control and foresight. Now he was gone and only South Australia's Phil Ridings and Queensland's Alan Pettigrew had been present prior to 1980.

The Board directors were now being farmed off to various sub-committees and only meeting together on four occasions each year. The seven executive members were meeting monthly to agree on administration matters and to sign the cheques. The real power had passed to the top three administrators whose public edicts were gratefully used by a cricket media happy to have press releases sent to them on a virtual daily basis.

Before the forty-second English team to visit Australia arrived in Perth in mid-October 1990, coach Bobby Simpson predicted defeat for the tourists in all facets of their visit. Having been coach for the northern summer at Leicestershire, Simpson said in an interview in *The Times* on 7 September: 'I have not seen anything over here that makes me think Australia will not win'. The team, captained by Graham Gooch, played three one-day warm-up matches before meeting Western Australia. England narrowly avoided defeat when their last pair held out for the final thirty minutes of the game. There was no such luck against South Australia who won by six wickets in a one-sided contest.

Instead of having a sixth Test the powers at Lord's had agreed to a match at Hobart's Bellerive Oval against An Australian XI. Poor weather spoilt the game as a contest but England's acting-captain Allan Lamb (154 and 105) scored a century in each innings, a feat not quite matched by opposing captain David Boon (67 and 108).

The first Test, which started at the Woolloongabba ground in Brisbane on 23 November, lasted for under three days. Allan Border put England in to bat and saw them dismissed for 194 on the first day. England repaid the compliment by bowling out Australia for 152 on a pitch which both captains agreed was perfect for Test cricket. The bizarre Test continued with Terry Alderman (6/47) bowling England out second time around for just 114. Needing 157 to win Geoff Marsh (72*) and Mark Taylor (67*) scored at ease to bring Australia a surprisingly early victory by ten wickets.

The tourists then played four one-day matches, two of which were in Adelaide against the Australian Cricket Academy, and one each against the Prime Minister's XI in Canberra and a Bradman XI in Bowral. The Bowral match was to benefit the Bradman Trust and Museum with all $40,000 proceeds being donated to the governing body.

Ballarat's Eastern Oval became Australian cricket's thirty-fourth first-class venue when Victoria were the hosts for England to play for the Sir Robert Menzies Memorial Trophy. At 301 for one it seemed as though Victoria would cause England some trouble but, with calculated declarations, the game ran through to an exciting finish and an eventual draw.

The second Test started in Melbourne on Boxing Day 1990 in an arena lacking the whole of its vast Southern Stand. Built in 1936, paid for in 1989 and demolished in 1990, the enormous stand had made way for an eventual new edifice capable of increasing the ground capacity to 115,000. With restricted viewing only 49,763 turned up on the first day to see England bat well enough to score 239 for four. Next morning David Gower reached his century and England 352 (Bruce Reid 6/97) with Australia failing by 46 runs to match the visitors' score. At 103 for one in their second innings by mid-afternoon on the fourth day, England looked safe and a draw certain. At 147 for four at tea no-one would have guessed that England would lose six wickets for three runs in 54 minutes as the gangling Reid claimed 7/51 to make his haul thirteen wickets for the match. Australia lost opener Mark Taylor and night-watchman Ian Healy with the score at 10 but Geoff Marsh (79*) and David Boon (94*) then easily took their time to record an eight-wicket win for Australia.

Australia were full of confidence going straight into the third Test at the Sydney Cricket Ground. The forty-eight touring English journalists and commentators were giving their team a frightful hammering back home with every little nuance, expression or indication by any player blown up into stories of dissent or poor relations with the umpires.

What was perhaps even worse was that no-one had informed the four hundred or so Marylebone Cricket Club members, who were touring Australia, that the reciprocal arrangements between the two bodies had expired four days earlier and not been renewed. As Marylebone members were being turned away from the ground so the ticket touts did a roaring trade. 'I had to keep rather rowdy company in the public stand,' said one English gentleman for whom the SCG outer had come as something of a culture shock!

Australia batted until just after tea on the second day, amassing 518 with Greg Matthews (128) scoring his fourth Test century and David Boon (97) just missing out on his. England replied with hundreds from Michael Atherton (105) and David Gower (123) with Gooch declaring at 469 for eight. Although Australia scored 205 in their second innings there was no chance of a result and the game was called off early with England 113 for four.

England then suffered a humiliating defeat by six wickets against a New South Wales side lacking its top players. A win over Queensland by ten wickets at the new venue of Carrara Oval on the Gold Coast led up to the fourth Test in Adelaide.

While the teams were preparing for the match, played over the Australia Day weekend, a somewhat sad event was taking place on virtually the same latitude across the Indian Ocean. Former Australian captain Kim Hughes, who had been playing for Natal in South Africa's Currie Cup competition, had been considered not good enough even for the province's second team. His acrimonious departure from Durban and immediate return to Australia was a sombre end to a career which started in glory and ended in acute embarrassment.

The first day of the Adelaide Test was a triumph for Mark Waugh on his debut. Having replaced his twin brother Stephen, Mark walked to the crease with Australia on 104 for four. Mike Selvey in the

*Guardian* wrote: 'Just occasionally there occurs an individual performance so perfectly sublime it transcends the contest itself. Mark Waugh in his first Test innings for Australia made a century of such stunning, rounded perfection that, for a while in the afternoon sunshine, batting was elevated above the level of the purely functional modern mode and transported back to the Golden Age.'

Mark Waugh's century had come with fifteen boundaries in four minutes under three hours. He had steadied an Australian innings which was rocking but finished at 386 (Waugh 138). England replied with 229 (McDermott 5/97) which then saw Allan Border give serious consideration to a sporting declaration. In the end after Boon (121) had made a century the innings closed at 314 for six, which left England to score 472 runs to win the game – an impossible task, so the match petered out into a draw.

Watching the game, Sir Donald Bradman was moved to remark that there was a definite similarity between Mark Waugh and Archie Jackson. Bradman said that although Jackson, a contemporary of his, was slightly taller and a wristier player, the adjectives stylish, quick-footed and attractive applied equally to both men.

The final Test in Perth was the last match of a tour by a now dispirited England team. It took them just 87 minutes into the fourth day to lose the match by nine wickets and the series three-nil. Yet all had started so well after Graham Gooch had won the toss and seen his team to 212 for three at the tea interval on the first day. Then came the collapse with seven wickets falling for 32 runs in just over an hour. Craig McDermott took his career-best figures of 8/97.

There was no overt reason for the England collapse. Admittedly the day before the Test had been the hottest on record in Perth, 45.8°C, but the temperature had cooled down by the time play began on a typically hard and fast WACA pitch.

Allan Border, playing in his 117th consecutive Test, was content to let the poor England team give more away to his players than they deserved. Catch after catch went down which caused Gooch to say: 'This England side is the worst fielding side I have ever seen'. The *Sunday Times* in London was more blunt: 'The team is tired and beaten. Batting collapses signal culpable selection as well as a lack of fighting spirit.' Australia made 307, and England's second innings 182 was a weak effort. Marsh and Boon quickly scored the runs needed to win and a one-sided series was over. How right Bobby Simpson had been.

The season's World Series Cup was played over a period from the end of November 1990 until mid-January 1991 so as to enable the Australian team to fly to the West Indies for a five-Test series.

Australia won nine of their ten WSC games, losing by one run to New Zealand in their only defeat before easily defeating the Kiwis in the finals.

It was an inexperienced New Zealand side who toured, variously from late November onwards. Lacking their former captain Jeff Crowe who refused to endure the hostile Australian cricket press after years of vilification, the Kiwis endured a bizarre itinerary. They played their eight WSC qualifying matches in a three-week period to mid-December then had to return a month later for the finals.

Old-style visits between Australian state teams and New Zealand provincial sides were starting to be revived in the late 1980s with New South Wales visiting Wellington and South Australia playing six matches against Central Districts. In November 1990, Wellington became the first New Zealand provincial team in Australia for sixty-six years. They played three non-first-class fixtures at Canberra (twice) and Gosford before meeting NSW at North Sydney Oval in a four-day match.

As Wellington had won the Shell Shield in 1989–90 and New South Wales the Sheffield Shield, the match was an international championship fixture. It was their sixth first-class meeting, with NSW 375 (Small 115) and 258 for five declared (Small 126, to become the first NSW batsman since Charlie Macartney in 1911 to score a century in each innings against a touring side) defeating Wellington, 218 and 255, by 160 runs.

The final visiting team of the season was Lancashire again, who toured Western Australia in March and April 1991. They played seven matches, all of which were of the one-day variety, against the top clubs, finishing with a defeat against Western Australia by 33 runs at the WACA.

The Sheffield Shield season saw the emergence of two fine young players. Batsman Stuart Law of Queensland (a Cricket Academy product) topped the batting with 1087 Shield runs at 77.64, while Victorian pace-bowler Paul Reiffel took 49 wickets at 21.48.

Victoria defeated NSW in the Shield final in Melbourne by eight wickets but the game of the season was played in Perth from 20–23 December 1990. The match, between Western Australia and New South Wales, was originally intended to be the first first-class match in the cricketing world to be played under floodlights. However, after originally agreeing for this, and the return fixture in Sydney, to happen the Australian Cricket Board changed their minds and refused to sanction the concept.

WA captain Geoff Marsh won the toss and put NSW into bat on a perfect pitch in ideal conditions. NSW were 137 for four when Stephen Waugh joined his brother Mark at the crease at 2.15 on a Friday afternoon. By three o'clock the next day when NSW captain

Geoff Lawson declared, the score had risen to 601 for four. Mark Waugh was unbeaten on 229 and Stephen on 216. They had added a world fifth-wicket record partnership of 464 in just 407 minutes. It was a remarkable partnership in many ways, not least that neither batsman played a false shot. WA scored 314 and then followed-on with their own record eighth-wicket stand of 242. It was Western Australia's highest ever second-innings total (475 for seven) in their 449 first-class fixtures to date. In all, it was an astonishing match.

The Australian Cricket Academy played a dozen matches during the season mainly against second eleven teams. However, it was decided to send a party of thirteen to tour Sri Lanka during January and February 1991 to play four four-day and two one-day matches. The Sri Lankan Board, after long deliberation, ruled the matches non-first-class although it is suggested this decision might not be final. Both of the limited-overs matches were won with the other games being evenly split.

The Australian tour to the West Indies had been labelled by sections of the media as 'the unofficial championship of the world'. All the pressure seemed to cause was a tour dogged by bad sportsmanship, no little controversy and umpires who did not appear to know some of the basic rules of the game.

The tour lasted for three months, starting in mid-February 1991, at Warner Park, Basseterre, on the island of St Kitts. This was the introduction for nine of the Australians to the game in the West Indies. The match against a West Indian Board XI, with a number of unpleasant situations, was drawn but only after another incident which was unbecoming of first-class cricketers. In the Australians' second innings, West Indies Board fast bowler Tony Gray had a caught-behind appeal against Geoff Marsh turned down by umpire Phil White. *The Australian* reported: 'Gray ran the length of the pitch and turned on a tantrum which would have thrown Australia's code of behaviour commissioners into all-night session. It was a virtuoso vulgar performance by any standards.'

Then followed victory over Jamaica by an innings and 137 runs, and a surprise win over the West Indies by 35 runs in the first one-day international at Sabina Park, Kingston. The first Test started on 1 March with Australia in a strong position before rain wiped out the fourth and part of the fifth days' play. West Indies made 264 (McDermott 5/80) with Australia 371 in reply, David Boon unbeaten on 109. The West Indies started their fight-back well, but the weather intervened and a draw became inevitable.

The four remaining one-day internationals followed with Australia winning three to inflict upon the West Indies not only their first one-day series loss at home but in the fourth match at Kensington Oval in Bridgetown the first West Indian defeat in any type of international fixture played there since January 1935!

The second Test in Guyana was watched by some 30,000 spectators who saw the West Indies win on the final afternoon by ten wickets. But it will be a Test remembered by many as one in which umpires Cumberbatch and Duncan showed their ignorance of the laws of the game.

The worst of a number of errors – all recorded for posterity by the cameras of Australia's Channel Nine network – was the dismissal of Dean Jones on the fourth day. Up to that point the West Indies had been on top scoring 569 (Border 5/68) in reply to Australia's 348. Second time around the Australians were 73 for three and in poor shape when Jones was incorrectly ruled 'run out'. He had been bowled by a Walsh no-ball and had headed off towards the pavilion under the misapprehension that he had been dismissed. His batting partner, Allan Border, shouted for him to get back into his crease. West Indian Carl Hooper then threw down the wicket and the whole team jubilantly appealed to umpire Cumberbatch at square-leg, who complied by upholding the appeal.

The Laws of Cricket (1980; 27:5) which state that, 'a batsman cannot be given run out if a no-ball has been called unless he attempts to run' were pointed out to the umpires forty-five minutes later at the tea interval. They refused to reconsider their decision and it was generally felt that the West Indian players were guilty of malpractice. Relations between the two sides then deteriorated rapidly.

The tourists flew to St Vincent for a four-day draw against the West Indies Under-23 team before facing the third Test at the Queen's Park Oval in Port-of-Spain. Torrential rain fell over the first two days and what play was possible saw Australia take until the fourth morning to reach 294. Although a draw was certain, both teams used up the remaining time for batting practice in Test conditions.

A draw with yet another West Indies Board combination in Barbados preceded the fourth Test which started on 19 April. Poor batting, which affected both sides, saw the two first innings completed by mid-afternoon on the second day with the West Indies gaining a 15-run lead. Then came the onslaught as the Caribbean cricketers pulled the Australian attack apart. Gordon Greenidge made his highest Test score of 226 as his team went on to 536 for nine before Vivian Richards declared. Defeat stared Australia in the face after Taylor (76) and Boon (57) were parted, with the final six wickets falling in three-quarters-of-an-hour for 18 runs. The West Indies won by a massive 343 runs to retain the Frank Worrell Trophy, having been watched by 45,000 spectators over the five days who paid altogether $US620,000.

The Australians adopted a noticeably more aggressive stance for the final Test at the St John's Recreation Ground in Antigua. Batting first they scored 403, Mark Waugh unbeaten on 139, before seeing the West Indies just avoid the follow-on with 214. Mark Taylor (144) led the way in the second-innings 265 which gave Australia an unassailable lead of 454 runs. Victory came by 157 runs as an apparently uninterested West Indian team put together 297.

The series, shown on television in a number of countries, will be remembered for its acrimony and bad feelings. Opposing players repeatedly abused each other on the field and all the umpires had to do was to look at the television replays after each day's play to know that their standards were not of the highest quality. Oh my Woodfull and my Ponsford long ago!

The Australians then had a gentle wind-down to their Caribbean adventures with a short tour of Bermuda. They won all three matches, defeating the island's top club, St George's, by 18 runs at Wellington Oval, then the President's XI by 34 runs at Lord's Oval in St Davids, before playing and winning by 93 runs against the full Bermuda side at Somerset Field.

# 36

# The Fifth World Cup

Politics and the Australian Cricket Board are regular bedfellows, so it was no surprise when an invitation was extended to Mr Krish Mackerdhuj to attend the Sydney Board meeting on 11 February 1991.

Mr Mackerdhuj, the radical left-wing president of the Durban-based South African Cricket Board – which mainly represented the interests of South Africa's large Indian community – was in Australia to brief government officials on the latest developments in the Republic. His pronouncements, in the nine years he had held office, were a little short on the game and heavy on Marxism. Now he was to meet the fourteen directors of the Board, conservative to their bootstraps.

The two-hour presentation made by Mackerdhuj and his clear and concise answers to the directors' questions showed how much pragmatism had replaced rhetoric. With readmission to cricket's family staring them in the face no-one in South African cricket was going to stand out. The Board supported the request made to them to back the Springboks at the mid-year International Cricket Council meeting, which duly saw the success Mackerdhuj wanted.

When the Board gathered in Adelaide for their eighteenth annual general meeting on 12 September 1991 they could reflect on a year in which the Australian game had risen against most of the other Test playing countries. In his report, David Richards stressed the need 'to face the challenges which threaten the future of Test cricket'. He listed three factors: independent umpires, slow over-rates and intimidatory bowling, and tore into the West Indies administrators for not controlling their players in the recent Test series. The Board meeting before the AGM had looked closely at implementing ICC rules regarding bouncers and intimidatory bowling for the Sheffield Shield competition, but had rejected the guidelines on the grounds it would affect the development of Australia's young fast bowlers.

In between these meetings there was an important gathering in Melbourne in mid-August when delegates from all World Cup participating countries discussed the *modus operandi* of the tournament and were introduced to the marketing side of things. The gaudy players' uniforms were not received with overwhelming joy, Marylebone Cricket Club secretary John Stephenson calling them 'pyjamas' and biting his lip hard when asked for his views.

At least the news was good on the home front. The Victorian Cricket Association announced a profit of $581,579 on a turnover of $2.06 million while the Tasmanian Cricket Association finally sorted out their administration after years of intra-island wranglings.

Allan Border's anointed successor, Mark Taylor, was named, by the Australian selectors, as captain of the party to tour Zimbabwe for three weeks in September. The squad included a number of outstanding young players who would, no doubt, form the backbone of the Test team in future years. The team was Michael Bevan, Wayne Holdsworth, Mark Taylor and Stephen Waugh (NSW); Peter McIntyre, Paul Reiffel and Shane Warne (Victoria); Jamie Cox and Rod Tucker (Tasmania); Denis Hickey and Tim Nielson (SA); Stuart Law (Queensland) and Tom Moody (WA).

The visit fulfilled three motives. Firstly it gained international experience for the younger players and, secondly, it gave Zimbabwe some warm-up matches before the World Cup. But, most importantly, it gave the Australian selectors an ideal opportunity to see how Taylor coped with the job of captaincy.

The three one-day matches saw Zimbabwe win by two games to one with the Australians defeating Zimbabwe B in a three-day fixture in Mutare by six wickets. The first of the two four-day games was played in Bulawayo against the full Zimbabwe team. Experience told as the Test players Tom Moody (141) and Steve Waugh (119) scored centuries as Australia, 483 and 20 for no wicket, defeated Zimbabwe 193 and 309 (Reiffel 5/43) by ten wickets.

Not used to the African heat the team found playing in 34°C rather tiring but pulled themselves together for the final match at the Harare Sports Club. Zimbabwe batted first in front of a sizeable crowd with their captain Duncan Houghton scoring an unbeaten 105 out of 239 (Hickey 5/72). The Australians replied with 383 (Law 94, Moody 85, Tucker 62), after which the young leg-spinner, Shane Warne, gave a superb display of his craft taking 7/49, his best analysis so far in first-class cricket, as Zimbabwe reached 179. The Australians made 36 for one to win by nine wickets and conclude a short, friendly, successful tour. It was as though the West Indies tour of five months earlier had been conducted on another planet so different was the attitude in which the game was played.

As somewhat of an experiment the Board had agreed for the Sheffield Shield winners to travel to England to play the County Champions in both one-day and four-day contests during September.

The Victorian team prepared for their matches with Essex by playing newly-elevated Durham in one-day (lost) and three-day (drawn) fixtures.

The limited-overs match at Chelmsford, in front of a full house, saw Victoria 274 for three (Dean Jones 86*) defeat Essex 215 (Merv Hughes 5/41) by 59 runs. Then came the last match of the longest first-class season in English cricket history when the weather and the Essex players' knowledge of their home pitch so nearly brought off an inaugural victory. Essex scored 343 for nine declared to which Victoria replied with 168 (Merv Hughes 60*) and 56 for eight, and the match was drawn.

The Board's Cricket Committee met for their usual discussions in Melbourne in late September with one item high on the agenda of both Board and players. The Sri Lankan cricketers had complained bitterly about racist comments during their tour of two seasons ago and former West Indian captain Vivian Richards had echoed this point of view in his report on the series a few months earlier. It was agreed that Allan Border should warn his players on such a sensitive matter 'and get on with the job if conflict develops'. The other issues were routine – a far cry from the militant days of not so long ago – and covered the season's itinerary, ground facilities, travel and accommodation, over-rates, players' awards and the code of behaviour.

The New Zealand World Cup squad played a number of pre-season one-day matches in South Australia early in October 1991 before returning home for further training. With the World Cup the dominating factor for the season, the domestic one-day trophy, now called the FAI Cup, was cleared and out of the way within the first month of 1991–92. New South Wales won the Cup, defeating Western Australia in Perth, little suspecting that five months later the same teams would fight out the Sheffield Shield final on the same ground. On that occasion Western Australia would be victorious and claim yet another Shield triumph.

Prior to their tour of Australia, which started in mid-November 1991, the Indian team had played three one-day internationals against the redeemed South Africans who would now participate in the World Cup later in the season. Following three one-day matches after their arrival in Australia the Indians played their only first-class match before the first Test when losing by an innings and eight runs to New South Wales in the country town of Lismore. The *Sydney Morning Herald*'s cricket correspondent now wrote: 'The elite of Indian cricket is in disarray in the run-up to the first Test match with Australia,' and added: 'The Board of Control for Cricket in India must now rue their decision to turn down the Australian Cricket Board's original offer of four first-class matches before the opening Test in the first five-Test series between the two countries in Australia since 1977–78.'

This match, at Brisbane, was a milestone in the history of the game in that it was the first to be played under the supervision of a referee – in this case the former England captain Mike Smith. In implementing the new ICC code, Smith had to look for player dissent; to ensure the stipulated over-rate of fifteen per hour was fulfilled, and to give opinions as and when necessary.

In leading his team out on to the field on the morning of 29 November, Allan Border set a record for Test match appearances. His 126th Test was now one ahead of former Indian captain Sunil Gavaskar who was watching from the pressbox. Australia had early success, at one time seeing India 83 for six but a rearguard action took them to 239. Australia replied with 340 but India fell apart again, reaching only 156, as victory came to Border's side by ten wickets with over a day to spare.

By now the West Indian team had also arrived in Australia, to make up the numbers for the World Series Cup with seven of the twelve matches taking place prior to the second Test in Melbourne on Boxing Day. With the Great New Southern Stand officially opened, the Melbourne Cricket Ground was a spectacular place to be as Australia completed their third successive Test victory inside four days.

India had batted first for 263 with pace-bowler Bruce Reid claiming 6/66 on the well-grassed pitch. Solid batting throughout saw Australia to 349 before Reid again (6/60) scuttled India for 213. Allan Border scored the single needed as Australia won by eight wickets. The Indian manager, Abbas Ali Baig, made a well-deserved complaint to the Australian Cricket Board regarding the standard of umpiring, which fell on deaf ears, but he did not go as far as contacting the match referee.

For the third Test in Sydney, which started on 2 January 1992, the Australian selectors called up the twenty-two-year-old leg-spinner Shane Warne who had played in exactly seven first-class games. He took only one wicket on his debut but retained his place for the following Test.

This was the only Test of the five which India deserved to win, being on top for the whole match. Rain destroyed their victory chances after Australia had scored 313 (Boon 129*) and 173 for eight in reply to 483. Ravi Shastri made 206 in 572 minutes, spread over three days, and Sachin Tendulkar (148*) became, at 18 years and 256 days, the youngest century-maker in a Test match in Australia. It took Allan Border (53*) 158 minutes with a succession of tail-enders to hold out for a draw.

Between Tests, the WSC competition finished its qualifying rounds which saw the West Indies surprisingly eliminated, and Australia easily defeat India in the two finals matches.

The fourth Test started in Adelaide on 25 January with the wish of curator Les Burdett for a result after a sequence of six drawn Tests on the perfectly prepared pitch. The Indian captain, Mohammad Azharuddin, put Australia in to bat with his gamble paying off splendidly. The home side fell for 145 with India scoring 225 in reply. The Australians' second innings was a different matter as first Taylor (100), then Boon (135), made centuries, with captain Allan Border left stranded on 91 as the score reached 451. Set 372 to win from 103 overs the Indians made a tremendous effort, failing by just 38 runs to stop Australia going three up in the series. Azharuddin reached 106 and Prabhakar 64 but to no avail as McDermott took 5/92 to lead the victory charge.

With the final Test fairly meaningless the Australian selectors, realising the time for wholesale change was nearing, brought in Victorian batsman Wayne Phillips, and his teammate fast bowler Paul Reiffel, for the Perth match. Allan Border protested vigorously against the changes to his side, which had an undermining effect on the two new players. Phillips scored 8 and 14, whilst Reiffel took 0/46 and 2/34: not exactly memorable debuts.

The Perth match saw umpire Tony Crafter officiate in his thirty-third Test, one more than Bob Crockett who stood from 1901–25. Crafter first stood in 1978 and, in an interview in the *West Australian* newspaper, said: 'The pressure has got stronger year by year, and the appealing noticeably more aggressive'. It was also the Test in which the Indian fast bowler Kapil Dev claimed his 400th Test wicket.

The match started in scorching heat on the first day of February – Perth's tenth day of the year when the temperature passed the old hundred mark – with David Boon (107) hitting his third century of the series. In reply to Australia's 346, the Indians scored 272 with Sachin Tendulkar's 114 being described as 'a stunning century'. Ian Chappell, commentating on Channel Nine, added: 'I wish there was a way of making this boy an Australian'.

Then came the Australian rush as Dean Jones (150*) and the recalled Tom Moody (101) put on 173 in even time for the fourth wicket, with the declaration coming at 367 for six. Set 442 to win on a lively pitch India stumbled from 82 without loss to 141 all out as left-arm pace-bowler Michael Whitney took 7/27 from twelve overs to see Australia winners by 300 runs.

This was the first Test match in history – of which this was number 1186 – in which a positive result had been achieved without a single batsman being bowled out. With the Test series over it was now back to the one-day game for the fifth World Cup.

Since the Australia/New Zealand bid to stage the 1992 World Cup had been successful, a joint committee had gathered at regular intervals. Meetings had taken place in Auckland, London, Melbourne and Sydney on, virtually, a monthly cycle to consider and evaluate the enormous logistics for such a tournament. Planning was so meticulous that, when South Africa came into the reckoning, it took little effort to reschedule the programme.

The reason for such quality decision-making had been the choice of joint-chairmen. On the Australian side Malcolm Gray stood head and shoulders above the others on his Board while New Zealand had the same type of man in Auckland's Peter McDermott. It is interesting to note that the sub-committees, on which these two men did not serve, were the ones whose decision-making caused wails of anguish as the tournament wore on. Sponsorship, obtained from the Benson & Hedges Company, totalled $A250,000.

As the teams made their way to Australia from around the world, many played in warm-up matches either against each other or the various States. Over 17,000 people attended the Western Australia versus South Africa game in Perth on the same day when Victoria played India, Tasmania took on Pakistan, and Zimbabwe lost to Queensland.

Just prior to the official opening dinner for the competing teams the Australian Cricket Board announced their decision not to appeal against a Victorian Supreme Court ruling which *inter alia* had found that their rules governing interstate cricket were completely invalid. Not for the first time had the pronouncement of the Board's directors been found wanting by Australia's legal system.

But nothing was going to spoil the party. The 'Welcome Dinner' saw Malcolm Gray deliver a quote which will no doubt find itself well used, when he told his Sydney audience: 'This dinner represents the most extraordinary collection of cricket talent and knowledge, with the possible exception of when Sir Donald Bradman dines alone'. The teams scattered the following day with Australia flying to Auckland to play New Zealand.

Allan Border's team were exhausted following a season of far too much cricket. Although favourites for the tournament they never showed any inclination or determination to retain the World Cup. They lost to New Zealand by 37 runs and then returned to do a circuit of their own country. Australia's progress saw a defeat by South Africa in Sydney by nine wickets; victory by one run in Brisbane over India; a loss in Sydney against England by eight wickets; Sri Lanka defeated in Adelaide by seven wickets; a defeat by 48 runs against Pakistan in Perth followed by two successes, against Zimbabwe in Hobart by 128 runs and the West Indies in Melbourne by 57 runs.

Fifth place saw Australia eliminated which worried the organisers who feared for the attendance at the final. In the semi-finals Pakistan defeated New Zealand in Auckland, and England controversially were declared winners over South Africa in Sydney. The competition rule for deciding rain-affected matches came into force in Sydney with unfortunate consequences for South Africa, and a hammering for the responsible sub-committee by the world's media. In true Australian Cricket Board fashion, the office administrator was sent to face the press with his outrageous views fuelling the criticism instead of dampening it down.

A controversial 'World Cup Final Banquet' grotesquely scheduled for the evening prior to the Final – with 'compulsory attendance by all players and officials' written into participating teams' tour contracts – saw the Australian liking for poor-taste comedians result in a walk-out by two senior England players and yet another thrashing for the Australian Cricket Board in the world's media.

But it was not all bad. A report by business consultants Coopers and Lybrand predicted that the Australian economy would benefit by some $A30 million from the World Cup, mainly through present and future tourism. It suggested that many of the worldwide television audience of one billion people in twenty-nine countries would decide to visit Australia because of what they would have seen of the tournament.

On 25 March 1992, in front of 87,182 spectators at the Melbourne Cricket Ground, Pakistan defeated England by 22 runs to claim the World Cup for the first time. It was a success few would have resented for Pakistan's captain Imran Khan. Not many people would have been thinking, as Imran Khan lifted the trophy above his head, of the beginnings of the game in Australia. It had been just a century since the early Melbourne Cricket Ground pavilion had been burnt to the ground. Now an edifice worth $150,000,000 had risen in its place.

The game had developed in a way no-one could ever have envisaged, yet some things had not really changed. The players' clothing was as gaudy today as it had been garish long ago; administrators seemed to be of the same quality while committeemen were still full of their own self-importance.

Who knows what would have happened had Joe Darling controlled the destiny of the Board; or George Giffen carried out some of his threats; or Warwick Armstrong been put in charge of team matters; or Bradman had not existed; or Greg Chappell had not resigned from the Board in despair. Or if . . . Or if . . .

# 37

# The Story So Far

Time was passing; players were coming and going; administrators were pontificating and the media kept an eye on the game. Australian cricket was evolving to such an extent that John Woodcock wrote in *The Australian*: 'It was said of the first Australians to play Test cricket in Adelaide in 1884 that "they did not trouble to practise". Anything less applicable to their side today would be hard to imagine. It exhausts me just to watch Allan Border and his players at work. Their three-hour training sessions see them hardly letting up for a moment. The captain is as fit as any of them, though he is thirty-seven.'

As the Australian cricketers drove themselves to peaks of fitness, Woodcock reflected on past tour captains to Australia and how they would have coped. 'Most Test captains that I have known would have found today's pace more than they could cope with. Freddie Brown had his fortieth birthday on the 1950–51 tour and I fancied the doctor would have advised him against such a violent exercise as the Australian side takes today.' As Woodcock wrote, the annual report of the Leicestershire County Cricket Club was released. They had previously appointed Australian coach Bobby Simpson as their cricket manager to try to change their fortunes.

The report commented: 'There are differences of opinion about what he did or did not achieve during his time with the club. However, as tangible evidence of any success is difficult to recognise, it is likely that cricket historians in the future will judge his appointment as a mistake.' Former Leicester and England player Jack Birkenshaw was appointed in Simpson's stead, and his county finished the 1992 season in eighth position from next to bottom the previous year.

As the 1991–92 season drew to a close the agency Australian Associated Press reported a story from the Australian Cricket Board. It came after a call by Victorian Sports Minister Neil Trezise for umpiring standards to be improved. Board chairman Colin Egar was quoted as saying: 'Behind the scenes there have been discussions taking place. I'm doing certain things. I can't say when or exactly how I will act because it's all in its infancy. What I will say is that anything that is available to help in such a professional sport should be used and it should be made more use of than it is now.' Egar added: 'Neil Trezise is certainly on the right track when he says that something has to be done.' A fortnight later the Board met in Sydney with the Trezise suggestion quietly put to one side.

On 3 February 1992, a small paragraph appeared in the gossip column of a London newspaper which stated that 'the cricketing collection of the late Sir George (Gubby) Allen will be auctioned in Newbury next month'. It was only on examination of the photographs, diaries and assorted paperwork that twenty-four letters came to light. These were written to his parents during the 1932–33 tour of Australia by Douglas Jardine's team and turned around many previously perceived ideas on the Bodyline series. Allen wrote of Jardine being 'loathed', of 'changing his mind every five minutes' and being 'difficult and whines away if he doesn't have everything as he wants'. In a letter sent in January 1933, Allen commented: 'The leg-theory brawl seems to be blowing over slightly. I thought the MCC reply was magnificent, so dignified after their [Australia's] common outburst. The whole thing has given Douglas a great fright and seems to have done him good. He is less bumptious and seems to look on the leg-theory in a more gentlemanly light.' The letters were purchased at auction by the library of the University of New South Wales.

The ACB met in Sydney during the second week of May 1992 and took time to consider the financial aspects of the World Cup. The New Zealand profit was around £5 million and although the ACB do not publish anything like full accounts, information sent to the ICC secretariat at Lord's suggests that a sum nearly double that of the Kiwis' was tucked away in investments for future use.

A month later, on 12 June, the Board's executive met at the WACA ground in Perth. There they discussed the format for the domestic one-day series and decided to up-grade the competition from a lacklustre two group-two game each affair to a round-robin tournament. The planned extension would give more scope for television coverage and a subsequent boost to the required sponsorship figure.

This sudden new demand took the sponsors, FAI Insurance Group, by surprise and resulted in a termination of their involvement. In severing it, FAI chief executive Rodney Adler delivered a stinging attack on the ACB. 'The Board has put its fees up significantly,' he said. 'It amounts to a threefold increase and we believe that is outrageous in the middle of a recession. We believe in moving our sponsorships around but we would have continued on in this case particularly given that the competition is to have such a new look. We love cricket and it's been good for us but we did not consider negotiations were being carried on sensibly.'

Away from the politicking, the players selected for the tour of Sri Lanka held a five-day training camp in Darwin, Northern Territory, in order to acclimatise for their crowded schedule. They then flew to Colombo for a three-Test series as well as three one-day internationals.

After a drawn match against a President's XI in Kandy, the Australians lost the first one-day match in Colombo by four wickets. Then came a remarkable Test at the Sinhalese Sports Club ground which Sri Lanka had all but won on the final day before a dramatic collapse gave Australia victory by 16 runs. In reply to the visitors' 256, Sri Lanka passed 500 for the first time since they entered the Test arena in 1982. They reached 547 for eight declared with Asanka Gurusinha (137), Romesh Kaluwitharana (132*) and Arjuna Ranatunga (127) all getting to three figures. The Australians battled in the high humidity to reach 471 in their second innings but all looked lost as Sri Lanka needed only to score 181 from a minimum of 58 overs.

Just after the tea interval the score was 127 for two. The crowd of over 10,000 people were singing, chanting and exploding firecrackers. At last, so it seemed, the seasoned batsmen were taking their responsibilities carefully and leading their team away from the troubles besetting the island. The spirits of the population needed lifting as they were jaded by the interminable ethnic conflict in the north of the country. But the Sri Lankans failed the challenge. They panicked and turned victory into an inglorious defeat. Young leg-spinner Shane Warne, coached and coaxed by Terry Jenner in the off-season, reacted positively. Unafraid to give the ball air he took the last three wickets for no runs in eleven balls. The win ended a dismal run for Australia on the sub-continent. They had not won a Test in Pakistan since 1959, nor in India since 1969, and could only report their victory over Sri Lanka in Kandy in 1983.

Sri Lanka were demoralised. The second Test at Colombo's Khettarama Stadium ended in a draw as did the third at the Tyronne Fernando Stadium in Moratuwa – both being venues new to Test cricket.

The June 1992 meeting of the Directors of the Australian Cricket Board had before them an internal report, part of which dwelt on the Australians' failure to progress past the qualifying rounds of the recent World Cup. Although various excuses were presented by the administration the Board accepted a recommendation put forward by the four selectors who referred to the team's 'poor preparation'. The selectors 'admitted that in hindsight members of the national team should have been rested from two arduous Sheffield Shield matches between the end of the five-Test series against India and the beginning of the World Cup.' They concluded with a message to the State

Associations noting that in a similar circumstance 'the team as a whole will be rested to make it as fair as possible on all States and remove the burden from individual players who may be pressured into playing by local officials'.

The following month, on 17 September in Melbourne, NSW director Alan Crompton was elected as chairman of the Board. A Sydney solicitor, Crompton had managed a number of Australian teams on tour with his highlight being the visit to India for the successful World Cup of 1987.

The effect of Crompton's leadership was noticeable almost at once. Within a week came the announcement that for the 1992–93 season, three umpires would officiate in all State matches, each one controlling two sessions per day instead of three. The reasoning behind the move was simple: the main one being to reduce the stress and fatigue of umpiring during the heat of the Australian summer and also to reduce the problems of being subjected to constant television replays which were having a disheartening effect on certain umpires.

A week later, at the end of September, Crompton was able to announce the continuation of Australian cricket's major sponsorship. The Benson & Hedges deal was due to continue until the end of March 1996 but the sponsorship of sporting events by tobacco and alcohol companies had recently come under intense scrutiny by the Federal Government. With some State governments going so far as to impose a ban on tobacco advertising the Board had been concerned enough to seek clarification from Canberra. Crompton said that the Board had obtained an assurance that the sponsorship could continue 'until the end of the 1995–96 season'. This was certainly good news for they relied upon such income to meet numerous commitments.

What was not revealed until a few days later was that the June meeting of the Board had decided to discipline all-rounder Greg Matthews for publicly stating his opposition to smoking. The May edition of *Woman's Day* had run an article entitled 'Greg Hits Smokes For Six!' in which Matthews claimed he had given up smoking with an accompanying photograph of him crushing a cigarette packet.

The Board decided to withhold twenty-five per cent of Matthews' contract fee and refused to pay him for the months of July, August and September. Crompton, in a statement, said that Matthews had 'shown disrespect for Test cricket's chief sponsor'. The fine amounted to several thousand dollars with Crompton adding that 'it is not normal policy to comment on matters of internal discipline. However, the Board wishes to set the record straight. The players' contract and code of conduct have always contained a requirement that a player shall not denigrate the sponsorship and shall not otherwise do anything which is detrimental to the game or its sponsors.'

As expected, there was uproar from all sections of Australian society. The Board had struck yet again. The Minister of Health, Peter Staples, said it 'exposed the sheer hypocrisy of tobacco sponsorship of sport', while Minister of Sport, Ros Kelly, and Justice Minister, Senator Michael Tate, gave their opinions of the Australian Cricket Board. The Australian Medical Association and the Australian Doctors' Fund applauded Matthews' declaration and sent in donations to help pay the cricketer's fine. The furore may have quietened down but not the public's respect for those running the game. What was interesting was a comment made by the Australian Rugby League Players' Association president, barrister Kevin Ryan, whose sport also has a major cigarette sponsor. He said 'Matthews' contract would be declared "harsh and unconscionable" if challenged in court', a point raised yet again by a legal expert whenever the ACB contract system came under scrutiny.

As the 1992–93 season was about to get underway, Bill O'Reilly died in Sydney on 5 October, aged eighty-six. After his retirement from Test cricket in 1946, O'Reilly spent the next forty-two years covering the game he loved from the pressbox for the *Sydney Morning Herald*. His knowledge of the game was awesome and his memory of detail quite exceptional. The hours he gave me in reciting past events for this work provided much of the new material for the period of his playing career.

A week later in Perth's Supreme Court another unfortunate legal case was taking place when Test umpires Peter McConnell and Terry Prue sued the Sydney newspaper, the *Sunday Telegraph Mirror*. The paper had accused them of bias in an article headlined 'Aussie Cheats'. The story referred to the views of former Indian Test captain Sunil Gavaskar and had been published the previous January. It was alleged in the article that they had made biased decisions in favour of Australian batsmen during the series against India.

After a two-week trial, the jury found for the umpires and awarded them $25,000 each. Both men had risked financial ruin because of the high legal costs, with McConnell announcing during the trial his retirement from umpiring 'because of the distress caused by the report'.

The tenth West Indian Test touring team, captained by Richie Richardson, arrived in Perth at the end of October 1992. Within four days they were embroiled in controversy with allegations of gamesmanship being made against them. Australian fast bowler Craig McDermott, in a provocative chapter in his book *McDermott: Strike Bowler*, said that the 1991 series in the West Indies was the 'most unpleasant' in which he had ever played. 'I have never before or since encountered so much personal hostility on the field as I did then,' he wrote. 'The sledging I was subjected to was unlike anything I had known. I would go as far as to say that it was the most savage and persistent sledging I have ever heard anywhere, at any level of cricket.'

After the usual denials of McDermott's claims, the tourists played in two warm-up matches before defeating Western Australia by 236 runs at the WACA. Then came a drawn game in Hobart against An Australian XI captained by wicketkeeper Ian Healy. Stephen Waugh returned to form with 95 and an unbeaten 100 and the signs for the future of Australian cricket were good.

Damien Martyn, a twenty-one-year-old middle-order batsman from Perth, scored 39 and 44; Darren Lehmann, the precociously talented Victorian left-handed batsman, 16 and 54 not out; and opening batsman Matthew Hayden of Brisbane made 46 and 53, all against a four-pronged West Indian pace attack of Test standard.

A week before the first Test, New South Wales took the tourists apart in Sydney. Mark Waugh scored an unbeaten 200 and Mark Taylor 101, in a score of 473 for six declared. The West Indies fell for 183 but followed-on in a more confident mood, letting the match drift to a draw.

The Australian selectors dropped Dean Jones and replaced him with Damien Martyn for the Brisbane Test, a move greeted with some scepticism in the press, particularly in Jones' home town of Melbourne. Other changes from the previous Test side which played in Moratuwa were Stephen Waugh, Merv Hughes and Bruce Reid coming in for Tom Moody, Shane Warne and Tony Dodemaide.

Behind the scenes, player discontent was simmering. Most had been reluctant to sign the new contracts offered to them and waited until the Board executive had had their November 1992 meeting in Hobart. From the Board came the news the players wanted to hear: they had won the pay-rise sought and their match fees would be increased to just under $4000 a Test per man. Their previous pay had been $3750 a Test and $1250 for each limited-overs international.

Although spectator involvement in the Australian game tended to be at the highest level, the source of players was still through the ranks of grade or district cricket. These players were usually watched by a handful of spectators – a far cry from the five-figure attendances who used to watch Bill O'Reilly playing for St George at Hurstville Oval before the war.

It was such a loyal following who saw a remarkable grade innings in mid-November when sixteen-year-old Brian Clemow played for Manly against Bankstown. The High School student scored an unbeaten 287, the third highest innings in the history of Sydney grade cricket. His 310-minute innings contained a six and 36 fours and was compulsorily completed at 440 for four in the statutory 85 overs. Only Victor Trumper with 335 in 1902–03 and Harry Donnan, 308 in 1896–97, had scored higher totals, and both of them were established Test cricketers at the time.

The Test series started in Brisbane with the West Indies scrambling to obtain a draw. Over the five days Australia were on top, even though the tourists obtained a first-innings lead, due in the main to Keith Arthurton's unbeaten 157. Needing 231 runs to win in 270 minutes, the West Indies hung on to be 133 for eight at the close.

The new International Cricket Council's code of conduct came into action when umpire Steve Randell reported Australia's Allan Border and Merv Hughes to match referee Raman Subba Row, accusing them of showing dissent. Hughes attended the disciplinary hearing and apologised saying 'it was a spur of the moment comment' and hoped umpire Randell 'would have no hard feelings'. Hughes was fined $400. Border, on the other hand, refused to acknowledge the disciplinary tribunal, did not attend, nor offer any comment. His fine was $2000, the heaviest imposed on any international player since the code was implemented. Subba Row, furious at Border's non-appearance, made the decision to impose a two-match Test ban on the Australian captain. Before handing down his sentence, Subba Row decided to inform ICC chairman, Sir Colin Cowdrey. The sanction sought was vetoed and in its place a fine was decided upon.

The contrasts between the old and the new that first day of December 1992 could not have been more pronounced. As Border was being fined so Sir Donald Bradman, aged eighty-four, made a rare and popular public appearance. The Mortlock Library of South Australia held the opening ceremony of an exhibition of Bradman's cricketing memorabilia which, during its run, attracted more paying customers than any other held previously. Hundreds of photographs, trophies, newspaper banners, caps, blazers and assorted ephemera were on display. The Bradman factor was still potent.

Pakistan were the third team to visit Australia during the 1992–93 season in order to make up the numbers for the World Series Cup. Their World Cup winning form of the previous season deserted them as they could win only one of the minor round of eight matches. The West Indies easily defeated Australia in the finals to take the trophy for the sixth time in fourteen seasons.

Attendances varied at the one-day matches. In Melbourne on 15 December, 74,450 spectators saw Australia defeat the West Indies by four runs in a thrilling encounter whereas only 6254 watched an equally exciting game in Adelaide three days earlier in which the West Indies defeated Pakistan by the same margin.

Then came the revelation that the Victorian Cricket Association were formulating a proposal in conjunction with the New South Wales Cricket Association arguing strongly for Melbourne and Sydney to be given a larger share of international matches – much along the lines proposed by Lynton Taylor a decade and a half earlier. The attendance for five Test-days' cricket in Brisbane had been 31,689, a figure easily bettered on just the first day of the second Test in Melbourne when 49,414 were present.

Over the years, Brisbane and Perth had regularly been the weak links in the Test chain although limited-overs internationals always attracted near capacity crowds. The VCA proposal, which was submitted to the ACB early in 1993, was to reschedule Test matches to the more popular venues. Politically the issue was dynamite although financially it made common sense.

The second Test, which started on Boxing Day, attracted 138,604 spectators who saw Australia win by 139 runs. Allan Border (110) recorded his twenty-fifth Test century and shared a fifth-wicket partnership of 204 with Mark Waugh (112), the second-highest stand for this wicket in Tests between the countries. Australia's first innings 395 eventually gave them a 162-run lead, which extended to 358 near the end of the fourth day. The West Indies looked good at 143 for one, but finally fell for 219, leg-spinner Shane Warne claiming 7/52. The last time an Australian leg-spinner had taken five wickets in a Test innings in Melbourne had been Bill O'Reilly with 5/51 against England in 1936–37.

Prior to the third Test, which started in Sydney on 2 January 1993, the Australian Cricket Board released details of the planned itinerary for matches against South Africa in 1993–94. After three Tests in Melbourne, Sydney and Adelaide in December and January, three further Tests would be played against the Springboks in Cape Town, Johannesburg and Durban during March. The wheel had turned a full circle.

The 83,320 spectators who watched the five days of Test cricket in Sydney experienced a game of joy for the statisticians. Both teams passed 500 with the West Indian batsman Brian Lara scoring 277 in just under eight hours at the crease.

Australia batted first scoring 503 for nine declared, Stephen Waugh's century being his first in Tests for over three years. Allan Border, in his 136th Test, made his 10,000th Test run when he reached 21, thereby joining Sunil Gavaskar as being the only players to achieve such a feat. The West Indies made 606 and a draw was inevitable.

The result in Adelaide also had the statisticians rummaging through their records. Richie Richardson won the toss for the first time in the series and saw his side fall for 252. Australia replied with 213 following which the recalled Australian off-spinner, Tim May, took 5/9 in seven overs as the West Indies crumbled for 146. With two full days to score

186 to win, Australia had the chance to go two up with one to play in the series.

But wickets started falling on the final morning with debutant Justin Langer (54) holding up one end as others fell to the West Indies pace quartet. When Langer was out the score was 144 for nine but Tim May (42*) and Craig McDermott (18) added 40 runs in 88 minutes before McDermott was controversially given out two minutes before the close of the fourth day. He had attempted to sway out of the path of a rising delivery from West Indian paceman Courtney Walsh. The ball struck the peak of his helmet and, according to the umpire, deflected from his glove to be caught behind by wicketkeeper, Junior Murray. The 15,000 crowd were stunned into silence as the West Indies had won by the smallest possible margin.

The whole of Australia seemed to be struck with cricket fever that Tuesday – which also happened to be Australia Day. Some departmental stores in the Eastern States stayed open until the final delivery, they being half-an-hour ahead of Adelaide time. At the Australian Tennis Championships at Melbourne's Flinders Park, tennis correspondents from all parts of the world watched the climax on television monitors in the vast media centre. Some knew little to nothing about the game but were caught up in the tension. At the end a *Los Angeles Times* reporter said: 'McDermott was ripped off. He didn't hit that ball. No way.' The one-run victory saw the West Indian players let off steam in their Adelaide Oval dressing-room. So much so that the damage bill payable to the SACA ran into four-figures. David Holford, the manager of the touring team, said, 'The damage was the result of an outpouring of emotion after a magnificent victory', and that 'it was nothing malicious'.

Allan Border's dream of defeating the West Indies in a series was fading away. The following week in Perth it totally collapsed as Australia were beaten by an innings and 25 runs before lunch on the third day, the quickest completed Test match since Australia defeated New Zealand in 1945–46. A month later the WACA dismissed curator Scott Hamilton.

It was not a happy match for Border: a pair for the first time in his seventeen-year career and a warning from match referee Donald Carr following yet another umpires' report. It was Border's 138th Test, with three more to come as the Australians were off to New Zealand to play in Christchurch, Wellington and Auckland, plus five one-day internationals prior to touring England in mid-1993. Also in the Perth team was twenty-four-year-old Western Australian fast bowler Jo Angel, who became the 355th cricketer to play in Test matches for Australia.

As the Australian players started their tour of New Zealand in late February 1993, the ACB announced details of a new sponsorship arrangement with the brewing company Lion Nathan, producers of the XXXX brand of beer. The package depended upon on-field success in New Zealand and, latterly, England, with guaranteed individual fees of $19,500 and $25,000 respectively.

At the same time, in Perth, former Test players Ian Botham and Vivian Richards were starting a series of theatre speaking engagements. On their first night, in answering a question from the audience, Richards suggested that Allan Border had possibly 'shirked his responsibilities' by batting too low in the order in recent Test matches. Sensitive as always, the Board let it be known that they felt 'cricket fans should boycott the show' and that 'a legal opinion is being sought as to whether Richards' remarks are defamatory'. Media manager Ian McDonald said: 'We are putting the matter in the hands of our legal advisers'.

The first Test in Christchurch saw Australia put in to bat on a Lancaster Park pitch which the groundsman, Russell Wylie, felt was under-prepared due to heavy autumn rains. The gamble failed as Australia scored 217 for three by the end of the first day.

Next morning Allan Border went in to bat in front of 3100 spectators. As his score rose so did the applause until, on hitting a boundary to bring up his fifty, he received a standing ovation as he had simultaneously passed Sunil Gavaskar's record of 10,122 runs in Test matches.

Sir Donald Bradman led the praise, saying: 'Not only does this recognise his skill as a batsman, it is also a tribute to his physical fitness and tough character because it has taken many years of toil to reach such a milestone'.

Border went on to make 88, and Australia won the Test by an innings and 60 runs. New Zealand, expecting to have held the trump cards, scored only 182 and 243 in reply to 485; and Australian leg-spinner Shane Warne had match figures of 7/86 from 48 overs.

Warne went on to be the star of the series, revealing amazing accuracy as well as penetration, as he went on to take 17 wickets at 15.05 at 1.6 runs per over, although the Kiwis gained a draw at Wellington and levelled the series with a five-wicket win at Auckland. The weakness for the Australians was their batting, highlighted by the fact that Merv Hughes finished third in the averages. Mark Waugh was dropped for the final Test but Justin Langer, who made a pair in that game, fared worse by missing selection for the English tour party, and went into the cricketing wilderness. The drawn series meant that Allan Border's side was unable to dent the New Zealanders' 16-year unbeaten record at home.

The domestic season had run its usual course. Wayne Phillips had made 205 for Victoria against NSW in Sydney and Jamie Siddons 189 not out for South Australia in Perth against Western Australia. On 11 December, Dirk Wellham became the first player to have captained three State teams when he led Queensland in Sydney against NSW.

# 38

# That Ball – the End of the Border Years

It was delivered by Shane Warne in the first Test of 1993 at Old Trafford. It swerved into Mike Gatting, pitched a good foot outside the leg stump, spun hard out of the rough and took the off stump, leaving the batsman completely nonplussed. As Patrick Murphy later observed in *Wisden*: 'Gatting looked understandably bewildered as he dragged himself off the field. Thereafter only Gooch played Warne with conviction: never perhaps has one delivery cast so long a shadow over a game, or a series.' The ball quickly became 'That Ball', 'The Ball from Hell' or 'The Ball of the Century'. By reviving what had begun to seem an antique craft in the game he, more than any player, changed the complexion of cricket in the 1990s.

Allan Border was equalling Joe Darling's record of leading three Australian sides to England in 1993 but his single-minded pursuit of victory revived the 'Captain Grumpy' tag when not all things went his way. Entering the first Test at Old Trafford in June, however, the Australian team was rolling along smoothly. From 12 first-class and limited-overs matches Australia had won 10, drawn one, and the only defeat was a technical one-day loss to Northamptonshire on scoring rate. In the three-match Texaco Trophy limited-overs series the Australians beat England 3–0.

The opening Test was enthralling, with Wagga Wagga pair Mark Taylor (124) and Michael Slater combining with an initial Test partnership of 128 on a pitch which favoured spin early. Australia, 289, led England, 210, after Warne began, with 'that ball', to assert his dominance, and a second innings of 432 for five declared in which Ian Healy (102 not out) reached his maiden first-class century left England a day and a half to survive. They struggled, though Graham Gooch batted superbly until given out handled ball for 133, punching it away after a defensive shot to a short ball from the irrepressible Merv Hughes. While the Victorian combination of Warne (8/137) and Hughes (8/151) won the match, the fact that Warne's figures were the best by an Australian leg-spinner in England since Bill O'Reilly's 10/122 at Headingley in 1938 spelt the greater long-term significance. An immediate worry for the Australians was the operation on Craig

McDermott for a twisted bowel which ended his tour and saw him replaced by Paul Reiffel.

Few Tests have been as one-sided as the match at Lord's in which Australia lost four wickets to England's 20. Michael Slater (152) and Mark Taylor (111) posted 260 in five hours on the first day, with Taylor appearing anonymous by comparison with his partner. Slater's immaculate driving, and his delightful jig on reaching his century accompanied by kissing the Australian badge on his helmet, warmed the hearts of the crowd and the wider television audience. David Boon (164) then weighed in with his first Test century on English soil, so that only Phil Tufnell's bowling Mark Waugh for 99 spoilt the Australian party of 632 for four declared. On a plumb batting pitch England should have been able to draw the match but, with the exception of Michael Atherton, who batted 495 minutes for scores of 80 and 99, the spin pair of Warne and Tim May, along with Hughes, proved too difficult to counter.

Nottingham represented England's opportunity to get back into the six-Test series. David Boon's second century saw Australia pass England's first innings but hundreds by Gooch and debutant Graham Thorpe allowed England to declare, setting Australia 371 to win in 77 overs. When Andy Caddick swung the ball alarmingly in the second session Australia was in trouble at 115 for six until the cool heads of Steve Waugh and newcomer Brendon Julian saw the game safely to a draw.

An Ashes revival was snuffed out at Leeds where another awesome Australian total of 653 for four declared matched the Lord's result as England could only score 200 and 305 in reply. After Boon (107) brought up his third Test century in successive matches, Border (200) and Steve Waugh (157) batted for the record books in an unbeaten fifth-wicket partnership of 321. Paul Reiffel's Test-best figures of 5/65 in the first innings combined with those of Hughes, who became the seventh Australian bowler to reach 200 Test wickets, and May to secure the series.

Australia won convincingly (if more modestly) by eight wickets at Edgbaston. Reiffel (6/71) went one better than his Headingley performance, and after a cultured 137 from Mark Waugh in Australia's 408 Warne and May shared all ten England second innings wickets.

At The Oval England salvaged a modicum of dignity from a summer of despair. After a solid first innings batting performance on a quick wicket Devon Malcolm and Angus Fraser hit the pitch hard, and Steve Watkin moved the ball off the seam to gain a surprising victory by 161 runs.

It is easy to be wise with the benefit of hindsight but a clear-eyed observer then was former Australian leg-spinner and coach Peter

Philpott who, in an article in the July 1993 edition of *The Cricketer* after the first Test at Manchester, made a number of remarks about players both inside and outside the Australian team which are worth recalling at length nearly ten years later.

Summing up the batting Philpott noted 'some magnificent stroke-players' in Mark and Steve Waugh, and picked out Damien Martyn as 'likely to enjoy the flat English pitches and underwhelming English attack' with Mark Taylor, David Boon and Allan Border providing the 'solid core'. Taylor was also seen as the heir apparent to the captaincy but possessing technical flaws, being 'vulnerable outside the off-stump, off both the back and front foot'; Matthew Hayden as able to 'batter English bowling off the front foot'; and Michael Slater as 'a busy player with sound defence and a strong array of shots'.

Allan Border was regarded as 'a great Test player and still a useful one'; Dean Jones as 'dangerous'; Jamie Siddons as 'probably better' than Jones; Darren Lehmann as 'a powerfully built stroke-player who has the ability to destroy any attack in the world'; and Michael Bevan as possessing 'a touch of genius' comparable with Neil Harvey and Gary Sobers. He also described three youngsters in the wings: Justin Langer as 'correct and determined, a Test player'; Greg Blewett as 'oozing ability'; and Tasmanian teenager Ricky Ponting as having 'a touch of class and maturity far beyond his years'. He summarised that it was doubtful if any cricketing nation had as great a depth of batting available to it as Australia in the 1990s.

How prescient was this? Philpott was not so confident about the bowling although he viewed Craig McDermott as 'a word-class swing bowler of real pace'; Merv Hughes as 'a far more skilful bowler than he is given credit for'; and Paul Reiffel as 'a bowler who is always at you and seldom bowls a bad ball'. Among the emerging breed of pace men he thought New South Wales speedster Wayne Holdsworth the most likely successor to McDermott and Hughes, but saw Julian as possessing technical deficiencies. Michael Kasprowicz and Joe Angel were seen as Test possibles. In the spin department he regarded Shane Warne as 'a youngster of great potential who spins the ball hard, has the control and variations, and is a very good all round cricketer' but doubted whether he was as good as the hype surrounding him, and had a feeling that by the end of the tour Tim May might supplant him as the number one spinner.

In his discussion of wicket-keepers Ian Healy and Tim Zoehrer, Philpott felt both were more than competent but one gains the feeling that, while he agreed with the view of some followers that Zoehrer was the better batsman and keeper, as well as leg-spinner, he believed Healy would maintain his place.

It must be said that Philpott was a superb judge and perhaps the time can now be seen as a turning point in Australian cricket. Of course, no-one gets everything right. Maybe Lehmann and Bevan have disappointed him but surely that would be for lack of opportunity in the Test arena rather than their lack of ability. Of all the batsmen only Siddons never received a Test chance and he should have. Among the bowlers Holdsworth sank without trace, May would seem like the world's best off-spinner one season and then go missing the next, but the comments on Angel, Kasprowicz and Julian are spot on. Perhaps the big surprise was that Warne has more than lived up to his hype. There is only one absentee. The missing man had then just one first-class season behind him and was yet to lift his head above the horizon. Glenn McGrath.

At the time, for all the positives about the tour, there were still complaints about negative leadership at Lord's and Headingley where the Australians took their first innings into the third day on both occasions. And in his 1993 report on the Ashes series in *Wisden,* John Thicknesse noted that Border would be 'remembered with respect rather than affection' for condoning and even participating in the sledging of opponents and umpires. Nevertheless, Border represented stability and from 1984 he had been Australia's only captain whereas England had eight in the same period. It was not possible to argue about the recent Ashes numbers – 11 wins, 5 draws, 1 loss – in his last three series but there was an argument that it was time to move beyond mere stability.

An increase in the amount of cricket per day in the Sheffield Shield competition in the 1993–94 season attracted criticism from the players. The ACB increased the minimum number of overs to be bowled per day from 96 to 100 with a penalty of 0.1 points subtracted for each over short; a factor which ended up denying Western Australia a place in the Shield final. From 576 balls to 600 balls did not seem a big requirement and was a long way short of the 915 balls bowled by the West Indies on the last day of the fourth Test at Adelaide in 1961.

Martin Crowe brought a New Zealand side to Australia in October-December 1993 for a three-Test tour but the Kiwis never recovered after the loss of their captain in the first Test in Perth with a knee injury, and appalling catching which broke the spirit of their main strike bowler Danny Morrison. Australia lost Merv Hughes, who was recovering from restorative surgery after his bone-grinding tour of England, but regained Craig McDermott.

Glenn McGrath made his debut in the first match in which Ian Healy's undefeated 113 was the chief contribution to Australia's dawdling 398 and to which New Zealand replied with 419 for nine before declaring early on the fourth day. Mark Taylor muddled through the early part of his second innings but eventually raised 142 and shared an opening partnership of 198 with Michael Slater who fell for 99. A negative declaration by Allan Border just before lunch on the final day, when his side led by well over 300, saw the game peter out to a draw when it had been possible to force a win. The result certainly raised the ire of Geoff Lawson who expressed the view that Border had 'never shown willingness to take risks during his reign' and was now not making the best use of the talent at his disposal.

The next two matches were never in doubt and Australia won by an innings in each. At Hobart the home side had three century-makers – Slater (168), David Boon (106, his first Test century in Tasmania) and Mark Waugh (111) – before Border declared at 544 for six and Shane Warne and Tim May mopped up with 16 wickets between them. In Brisbane it was Border's 150th Test match and, batting second, the captain made his 27th and last Test century (105). Steve Waugh's unbeaten 147 saw Australia to 607 for six declared. Warne was again the destructive bowling force with eight wickets as the Australians reclaimed the Trans-Tasman Trophy.

A poor attendance of only 61,385 for the entire New Zealand series raised the question about the low quality of some Test match contests. Mark Waugh, for one, pointed out that a century he scored for New South Wales against Victoria in December was more difficult than the one he had made at Hobart in November.

South Africa's first Test tour of Australia for thirty years got under way in December with a new format which meant each country would host three Tests back to back. In two first-class and four limited-over matches before the Boxing Day Test in Melbourne the Proteas' form was poor with just one win. The first Test was ruined by rain to such an extent that only four hours play was possible on the first three days. Then Australia and Mark Taylor (170) batted well into the fourth day until Taylor declared at 342 for seven whereupon the South Africans batted out time. An interesting sideline to the match was that the South African captain Kepler Wessels became the first player since Billy Midwinter in 1881–82 to play both for and against Australia.

The visitors' surprise victory by five runs in Sydney shocked the Australians and was described by the United Cricket Board of South Africa managing director Ali Bacher as 'our finest achievement ever'. It reminded local followers of the collapse against England at Headingley in 1981. Shane Warne continued his devastation with an outstanding match analysis of 12/128 (7/56, 5/72) as South Africa fell for 169 and 239. Set only 117 to win, Australia appeared to be travelling easily at 51 for one until fast-medium Farnie de Villiers smashed through the middle-order by taking three wickets in five balls, and then finished off the tail to grab his own sparkling match figures of 10/123.

While Allan Border was straightforward in his appraisal of the result – 'we are letting ourselves down in the tight ones' – the player who suffered most was Damien Martyn, a replacement for the injured Steve Waugh, who lingered 106 minutes in the second innings for six runs before lashing out to be caught at cover with just seven runs required. He went out of the side for the next six years.

Australia squared the series at Adelaide mainly through Steve Waugh whose 164 and fifth-wicket partnership of 208 with Border set Australia on the road to 469, and whose four first-innings wickets smashed through the South African middle-order. Leading by 320, Australia's second innings declaration gave them seven and a half hours to dismiss the tourists and this they achieved despite stout defensive resistance. Warne took his 100th Test wicket in his 23rd Test and Ian Healy made his 200th dismissal. Warne was the star of the series with 18 wickets at 17.05 with McDermott close behind with 14 wickets at 17.57.

The Benson & Hedges World Series involving South Africa and New Zealand in December-January was won by Australia after first falling behind in the finals. After finishing on top in the qualifying matches Australia lost the first final to South Africa before winning the remaining two games. Worth mentioning in this comeback was the restoration of Dean Jones to the one-day side. When Jones made 98 and won the Man of the Match award in the World Series Cup match against South Africa in Brisbane on 9 January, it raised his prospects of touring that country later in the summer. As Mark Ray has reported, Jones dictated comments to him for a *Sunday Age* column in which he stated that he was more relaxed batting in the absence from duty of coach Bob Simpson. Simpson might have been affronted but his threat of legal action against Jones, also revealed in Jones's book, *Deano, My Call*, was surely excessive.

In the short-term it is obvious that Simpson was the winner and Jones the loser as, the same month, Simpson was re-engaged as Australia's coach for a further two-year term with his contract to expire on 30 June 1996. Jones made his final tour in Australian colours to South Africa. He was unable to regain his Test spot and, after playing seven of the eight one-day games, was omitted from the tour of Sharjah which followed.

New South Wales won both the Sheffield Shield and Mercantile Mutual Cup competitions from Tasmania and Western Australia respectively and comprehensively, while Matthew Hayden won the Player of the Year award for his stellar season in which he scored seven hundreds in six matches. Hayden had scored 1136 runs at an average of 126.22 in a high-scoring season in which Michael Bevan, Justin Langer, Darren Lehmann and Dene Hills also topped 1000 runs.

Hayden was unable to break into the Test side in the series at home but made his Test debut as a later replacement for Mark Taylor at Johannesburg, where a ball from 'White Lightning' Allan Donald broke a bone in his hand. Hayden thus became the sixth of the most recent players – Glenn McGrath, Damien Martyn, Justin Langer, Joe Angel and Michael Slater were the others – chosen for Australia who had attended the Australian Cricket Academy, which seemed to indicate there was but one way to the top. Certainly it appeared significant that Darren Lehmann, who had declined an Academy invitation in 1989, continued to be ignored.

Some of Allan Border's team to South Africa in February-April 1994 were not even born when Bill Lawry had led Australia to a 4–0 defeat 24 years before but on this occasion they divided both the Test series 1–1 and the limited-overs matches with four wins apiece. After defeating Northern Transvaal in the opening first-class match, the side then lost three of four one-day internationals in the first half of that competition, before defeating Orange Free State, for whom Hansie Cronje made a career-best score of 251.

South Africa's 197-run win in the opening Test at the refurbished Wanderers Ground at Johannesburg was a sign that the home team was a force to be reckoned with. The match was evenly balanced after the first innings but Cronje's continued dominance with a second innings hundred allowed Kepler Wessels to declare with a lead of 454, a target well beyond the Australians.

Steve Waugh's all-round abilities were mainly responsible for the Australians hitting back at Cape Town, where some observers thought they hit below the belt. Merv Hughes, in a frustrating final series, was reported by referee Donald Carr for verbally abusing batsmen, although Shane Warne's uncouth send-off to Andrew Hudson when he bowled him in his first over was much worse. Warne ran down the pitch to continue his tirade and had to be restrained by wicket-keeper Ian Healy from carrying the abuse further as the batsman was half-way off the arena. Carr fined Hughes and Warne 1,000 rand ($450) each for their actions but a surprising outcome was Bob Simpson's announcement that no further action would be taken by management. Back home there was mounting criticism of the behaviour of the Australian team, particularly their excessive disputing of umpire's decisions, and the failure of the coach and captain to stem it.

Even Border himself had been reported twice for dissent by leading umpire Steve Randell. With the press keeping pressure on the ACB, the Board chairman Alan Crompton and chief executive Graham Halbish flew to South Africa and increased the fines on the two errant cricketers to $4,000 each.

After the Proteas crawled to 361 in nine and a half hours on a slow,

low Newlands pitch, Australia's reply of 435, in which David Boon (96) and Steve Waugh (86) led the scoring, took two hours longer. This seemed to leave little prospect of a result and at 69 for one the South Africans were travelling comfortably in their second innings until Steve Waugh engineered a middle-order breakthrough after tea on the fourth day and went on to finish with 5/28 from 22.3 overs, the best figures of his Test career. In the end Australia gained an easy win by nine wickets.

Defensive batting cost the home side victory in the last match at Kingsmead, Durban after Wessels' enterprising action of putting the Australians into bat saw them prised out for 269 on the second day. In a display reminiscent of batting by Jackie McGlew and John Waite at the same ground in January 1958, the South Africans took 14 hours to reach 422 at the rate of 2.05 runs per over, leaving little time to force a result. Mark Waugh unfolded a pretty match-saving innings of 113 on a tedious last day while Allan Border was more than happy to accompany him.

For the final three hours of spiritless cricket Allan Border was aware that the innings might be his last. The question of 'might' was a curious one. While Australia was successful in three of the four remaining one-day international matches in Border's last stint as Australian captain, the home season had been regarded as a Test farewell and he had even enjoyed a tribute celebrity match played at the Gabba. The trouble was that he had made no formal retirement announcement.

The situation was awkward. In his last nine months as captain, including the 1993 Ashes tour, Border had led Australia in 15 Tests for 8 wins, 3 losses and 4 draws while, in 23 limited-overs international matches in the same period, Australia had won 15 and lost 8. The wonder that was Shane Warne had taken 85 wickets in those games and 102 wickets in 18 Tests between February 1993 and March 1994, exciting pundits' projections of 600 Test career wickets. If there was a push for a change at the helm it was not because a now high-quality side was performing poorly: merely below its potential. But the push of the legend with 156 Test caps, 11,174 Test runs, and who had led his country 93 times, had not become shove.

Unfortunately by early May there were some complicating factors connected with the issue. Four senior players – Mark Taylor, David Boon, Ian Healy and Steve Waugh – were interviewed by the Board and the outside perception was that these interviews were related to the captaincy. Furthermore, the ACB wanted to announce the team to tour Pakistan in August. As Gideon Haigh wrote in *The Border Years*: 'When matters crystallised suddenly, with a 9–10 May ACB convention of possible captains for a touring side for Pakistan, Border felt exiled.' While there was no criticism of Border from the Board, a possible misinterpretation of journalists' reports of the ACB meeting led to him gruffly announcing his retirement on 11 May 'with a heavy heart' and stating: 'It's like a part of me has died.'

Retirement for any top sportsman is a sort of premature death and while the public invariably like their heroes to go out on top with a grand exit, the personal feelings of the player often demands giving something back to the game they love. The young Allan Border in Sydney grade cricket would have been aware of Bob Simpson maintaining a high level of performance in that competition nearly a decade after the first stage of his Test career had ended.

In his second season of first-class cricket (1977–78) for New South Wales, Border played under Simpson's captaincy and witnessed his successful return to Test cricket the same summer. By contrast, when Rod Marsh retired in early 1984, Border believed that he quit the game too early when he still had a couple of good years to give. Thus Border himself played two more years in the quieter pastures of the Sheffield Shield as the next chapter reveals. The final departure from international cricket might have been anguished but playing on for Queensland meant that a powerful connection with the game was not severed completely. While professional pride demanded high performance, Border could leave the playing side of cricket in a gentler manner.

# 39

# The Taylor Era

If Allan Border's departure was messy, the handover to his successor was smooth. Mark Taylor impressed before the ACB at the May meetings and was given increased powers as captain with Bob Simpson taking a reduced role in the operation of the team. Nevertheless, Taylor's Test captaincy got off to a bad start in September-October 1994. Not only did the Australians pluck defeat from the jaws of victory on the last day of the match at the National Stadium at Karachi, where Pakistan had never lost in 30 previous encounters, but he also had the personal ignominy of completing a pair.

The Karachi match is one of the most famous Test clashes, although it would subsequently attract negative attention associated with bribery allegations. Middle-order batsman Michael Bevan top-scored on his debut in Australia's 337 to lead Pakistan's 256. David Boon (114 not out) then provided almost half his team's second innings of 232 which left the home side 314 to win. When the Pakistanis lost their ninth wicket for 258, the task seemed beyond them. Shane Warne (5/89) maintained pressure until the end but a difficult missed stumping chance by Ian Healy with two runs remaining allowed four leg byes and a one-wicket win to Pakistan.

At Rawalpindi in the second Test Australia dominated the first innings exchanges. Following on, however, Salim Malik's long innings of 237 saw his side to safety before Victorian fast-medium Damien Fleming became the first Australian bowler to take a hat-trick in his debut Test.

The first triangular series in Pakistan for the Wills Cup now intervened. Australia won five of six matches against South Africa and Pakistan including the final at Gaddafi Stadium, Lahore. The same ground was used for the final Test two days later. The game was drawn, with the bat generally on top. Salim Malik's second innings hundred gave him over 500 runs for the series, while Shane Warne's 18 wickets put him well ahead of the bowlers on either side.

Michael Atherton's English party arrived at the end of October before the Australians returned. They played seven matches before the Ashes series began but their form was mediocre. Michael Slater (176) put Australia and himself on the front foot in the first Test in Brisbane in late November with a dashing knock and brilliant partnership with Mark Waugh (140) whose innings was his fiftieth first-class century. England were left chasing 507. A strong position of 211 for two at stumps on the fourth day left hopes of a draw until Shane Warne got into his stride with career-best figures of 8/71 as Australia won by 184 runs.

In the second Test at Melbourne on Christmas Eve, David Boon's 131 set up a winning opportunity and Warne and McDermott again did the damage with 17 wickets between them. Warne's hat-trick on the final morning capped an easy win.

Australia retained the Ashes at Sydney, perhaps the result of a hard-hearted declaration by Michael Atherton. Leading by 448 midway through the fourth afternoon, Atherton declared with Graeme Hick 98 not out, a controversial decision which may possibly have undermined team morale. Michael Slater (103) and Mark Taylor (113) slammed on an opening partnership of 208 and the tail fought off defeat in fading light.

Australia lost the fourth Test at Adelaide but the series was won 3–1 following the fifth Test at Perth in which Greg Blewett (115) equalled Bill Ponsford's record of making centuries in his first two Tests. Michael Slater was the leading run-getter for the series with 623 runs and Craig McDermott and Shane Warne led the attack with 32 and 27 wickets respectively. Part of the fascination with watching Warne was increased for the armchair viewer, at least, by the introduction of 'Spin Vision', a fascinating example of close-up camera technology which enabled the watcher to follow the bowler's flipper or big-spinning leg-break with equal wonder. Importantly, however, the Ashes Test series also attracted 478,000 spectators to the games. An obvious benefit was the ACB finally taking charge of the marketing of the game for the first time since its contractual linkage with Channel Nine in 1979.

Zimbabwe did well on their first major tour of Australia but odd scheduling made their task of competing in the limited-overs international matches difficult. Australia won the World Series from an Australia A side which played alongside England and Zimbabwe but whose records did not count for official purposes. Australia A was popular with local supporters as it showcased emerging talent but not the Australian team who found their own support and identity undermined.

Mark Taylor continued his winning run in February 1995 in the Centenary Cup in New Zealand. There Australia won a round-robin limited-overs tournament involving the host nation South Africa and India before departing on the biggest challenge of all, a series in the West Indies to determine the championship of world cricket.

Taylor wasted little time stamping his imprint on the team by demanding unity in the dressing room and involvement with action in the middle. This was important when strike bowler Craig McDermott tore ligaments in his left ankle jumping off a wall on a Georgetown beach prior to the Test series. The Australians had just lost the one-day series 1–4 and their Test hopes appeared doomed. With Brian Lara in thrashing form, Shane Warne faced the prospect of being belted by the West Indian batsmen as Pakistani leg-spinner Abdul Qadir had been by the Australians in 1983–84.

Instead, new heroes emerged. Glenn McGrath captured 5/68 in Australia's ten wicket win in the first Test at Bridgetown and 6/47 in the first innings of a nine-wicket loss at Port-of-Spain in the third Test. The Australians were unlucky to be deprived of a win due to rain in the second Test at Antigua but the West Indies regained confidence on Joey Carew's underdone pitch at Trinidad where Curtley Ambrose took nine of his 13 wickets for the series. With the score one match apiece, the Australians must have recalled their one-run loss to the West Indies at Adelaide in January 1993 and their subsequent destruction in the Perth Test which followed. Could Ambrose and Courtney Walsh lift their team one more time in the deciding Test on the glass-like surface at Sabina Park?

The West Indies were travelling well at 103 for one but being dismissed for 265 near the end of the first day was not what captain Richie Richardson had in mind. The second day saw the Australians in trouble early before Mark and Steve Waugh gave gritty performances against a barrage of short-pitched bowling to add 231 runs for the fourth wicket. After Mark left, Steve batted on for a monumental 200 in 555 minutes, stopping to mop his perspiring brow with the red handkerchief in an innings described by Robert Craddock as one in which 'his concentration never wavered, his tenacity never buckled, his courage never faltered'.

When the West Indies, trailing by 266 runs, collapsed for 213 their great era had ended. Steve Waugh's heroic innings at Kingston, and 429 runs at 107.25 for the series, laid the foundation for the return of the Frank Worrell Trophy to Australia for the first time since 1976. Well might West Indian skipper Richardson rue his graceless remark that this was the weakest Australian side he had played against, for it underlined his opposite number's aptitude for team building.

If abroad Australia had once again reached the top of the cricketing heights, at home Queensland succeeded in a longer quest for their own Holy Grail. The northern state had been the butt of Australian sporting humour over the failure to capture the Sheffield Shield in 62 years of trying but finally put the issue beyond doubt when, after dismissing South Australia for 214 on the first day, they amassed a huge score of 664 and went on to win by an innings and 101 runs. In a year which saw a triumph of the aged, 33-year-old Dean Jones won the Sheffield Shield Player of the Year following his 1,216 runs at 76.00 and career-highest score of 324 not out, and 34-year-old Carl Rackemann was the leading wicket-taker with 48 wickets.

While Rackemann was the only player to experience the double glory of celebrating his state's Shield win and then enjoy the Australians' West Indies' celebrations as a replacement for his state team-mate Craig McDermott, Allan Border's season was nearly as perfect. To the surprise of many, Border was one of the keenest participants in pre-season fitness trials, an inspiration to team-mates throughout the season, and particularly when carrying the injury of a broken bone in his forearm in the last two games. He was also as exhilarated as anyone when singing Queensland's victory songs at season's end.

The year saw a number of innovations. Day-night, first-class cricket was introduced for the first time with three matches played under lights; quarters cricket – playing 50-over matches in 25-over sessions – was trialled in a game between England and Western Australia; a half-time spectator pitch inspection was offered during the Mercantile Mutual Cup final at the MCG; and money prizes of up to $1,000 were also awarded to spectators catching sixes hit into the crowd during limited-overs games. Only the prizes for catching sixes remains, and this is a dubious practice considering that a patron injured as a result of such an attempt might have a strong legal claim against the ACB and state associations for failure to exercise duty of care.

The 1995–96 season has been described as the most turbulent in Australian cricket since the Packer era. It began with serious concerns that the claims of corruption could cause a cancellation of the Test series against Pakistan but the problem seemed to be alleviated when Salim Malik, after being omitted from a home Test series against Sri Lanka, appeared unlikely to tour. However, when Pakistan supreme court judge Fakhruddin Ibrahim found that allegations against Malik seemed to have been concocted, he returned to the side.

But the tour got off to a bad start with accusations of ball-tampering by Pakistan. The ACB impounded the ball used by the Pakistanis in their opening tour match against Western Australia after umpires Terry Prue and Ross Emerson revealed concern about the scarring to one side of the ball. However, despite the destabilising effect of the incident, the series passed without conflict.

In the first Test in Brisbane the brilliant leg-spinning of Shane Warne, backed by superb fielding, put the game firmly within Australia's grasp. Warne's 7/23 saw Pakistan routed for 97 in under three hours in the first innings and the tourists were then tumbled out for 240 in the second after being forced to follow on, giving Australia victory by an innings with a day and two sessions to spare. Warne's figures of 11/77 for the match were the best analysis by any Australian bowler in a Test against Pakistan but a match attendance of 16,099 was a poor level of support for the home side.

Hobart provided better crowds for the second Test staged just four days later, when Australia earned a comfortable win by 155 runs. After a third consecutive loss with a day to spare – to Victoria – it was not expected that Pakistan would turn around the result in the Sydney Test. As it turned out, although Warne returned match figures of 8/121, he was trumped by Mushtaq Ahmed's second successive nine-wicket haul. The Australians again found a modest fourth-innings victory target beyond them as they lost seven wickets for 51 on the final morning.

Despite pre-match speculation, controversy in the first Test against Sri Lanka in Perth centred on allegations of ball-tampering by the visitors rather than off-spinner Mutthiah Muralitharan's action. After Sri Lanka were dismissed in the last over of the first day for 251, Australian openers Michael Slater and Mark Taylor got away to a blazing start before the Sri Lankans were warned for altering the condition of the ball in the 17th over. Continuing with the same ball Michael Slater, in a Test-best 219, Mark Taylor (96), Mark Waugh (111) and debutants Ricky Ponting (96) and Stuart Law (54 not out) thrashed the Sri Lankan attack to amass 617 for five declared to set up an easy win. At this point, no-one would have predicted that this would be Law's only Test appearance. Slater set a record Test score for Perth and the five-hundredth Test century for Australia. Muralitharan bowled 54 overs without complaint from umpires Khizer Hayat and Peter Parker in taking 2/224, the only bowling double century registered in Tests in Australia.

The largest crowd (55,239 on Boxing Day) to attend Test cricket in Australia for ten years witnessed a major controversy when umpire Darrell Hair called Muralitharan seven times for throwing in the second Test at the Melbourne Cricket Ground. This incident, which caused Sri Lankan skipper Arjuna Ranatunga to remove his bowler from the attack and leave the field to consult match referee Graham Dowling, overshadowed the rest of the match that Australia won by ten wickets. The calls were made against Muralitharan in his fourth, fifth and sixth overs but he returned to complete 38 overs for the innings.

David Boon announced his retirement before the third Test at the Adelaide Oval and his side allowed him to sing the victory song one more time although the margin of 148 was the closest of the series. Boon's 107-Test, 7,422-run career ended with a couple of modest scores but Steve Waugh produced a flawless seven-hour 170 which saw Australia to a third consecutive first innings score of 500 and thereafter there was only one possible winner. At the end of the match, Waugh won two Toyota cars valued at $60,000 as International Cricketer of the Year and few would dispute his right to the title. In the two Sri Lankan Tests he averaged 362 to boost his Test career average above 50 for the first time.

The World Series involving Sri Lanka and the West Indies as well as Australia was marked by another throwing controversy regarding Muralitharan. Umpire Ross Emerson repeated umpire Hair's action from the Melbourne Test by no-balling Muralitharan seven times for throwing from the bowler's end. Australia defeated Sri Lanka in both finals in a competition marked by the brilliant batting of Michael Bevan who scored 389 runs at an average of 194.50.

The sixth World Cup staged in India, Pakistan and Sri Lanka in February-March 1996 was an expanded competition with new countries Kenya, United Arab Emirates and Holland included for the first time but the increase in quantity produced a loss of quality with many one-sided games. Security worries in Sri Lanka following Tamil Tiger bombings in Colombo also caused Australia and the West Indies to forfeit matches there.

Australia was one of the favoured teams and reached the semi-final at Muhali, where they twice recovered from impending defeat against the West Indies. Australia lost four wickets for 15 before recovering to a competitive 207 for eight, then saw the West Indies lose eight for 37 from 50 balls after being in a comfortable position at 165 for two wickets, to lose eventually by five runs. As captain Taylor admitted: 'I thought the West Indies were home and dry – it was the most unbelievable win I have played in.'

The final in Gaddafi Stadium, Lahore on 17 March saw Sri Lanka run out well-deserved winners by seven wickets with Aravinda de Silva and Arjuna Ranatunga in control. When the game ended, players, administrators and security guards protecting Pakistani prime minister, Benazir Bhutto, looked awkward on a small dais where the official presentations were made. And Channel Nine commentator, Ian Chappell, made the security staff look edgy as he marshalled the prime minister into place with a guiding arm. While Mark Waugh was the top run-getter in the competition with 484 runs at 80.66 and three centuries, it was the explosive starts by the Sri Lankan openers that changed the paradigm for limited-overs cricket.

At home the Sheffield Shield continued with the Australian players available for the last games. Not surprisingly South Australia and Western Australia contested the final at Adelaide Oval in April since, with the exception of Jason Gillespie, neither side had a representative in the World Cup team. The match was as fine a climax to the season as had been experienced in the competition's history. Adam Gilchrist's smashing 189 from 187 balls was one of the most brilliant batting displays seen on the ground and brought this wonderful player to public attention. The nail-gnawing 15 runs in the final session and 59-ball resistance by Shane George and Peter McIntyre, which enabled South Australia to win its 13th Shield before a closing crowd of 13,000, showed that run scoring is not everything and was as intense as cricket can get.

In May 1996, 60-year-old Bob Simpson, Australian coach for ten years and a major contributor to Australia's rise to the top of world cricket, was replaced by Geoff Marsh, a change endorsed by Mark Taylor, Marsh's former opening partner, and the previous Test captain, Allan Border.

Taylor himself was experiencing a loss of form which saw him play 21 innings without a half-century from Boxing Day 1995 to June 1997. His position in the side was not under threat although, as Ian Healy revealed in his autobiography, there was considerable unrest at Pretoria in 1997 when batsman Michael Bevan was played as a specialist spinner to keep Taylor in the side. According to Healy: 'More than one team-mate would insinuate that the tour selectors weren't choosing our strongest side for the sake of the captain while one or two players complained some players' careers were being jeopardised by our selection strategies.'

Australia made its first tour under Geoff Marsh as coach on a two-week tour of Sri Lanka during August–September 1996 for a four-nation limited-overs competition, the Singer Cup. Ian Healy led the Australians in Mark Taylor's absence following back surgery, and the team was minus Shane Warne whose spinning finger remained stiff. Australia defeated both India and Zimbabwe but lost to Sri Lanka on the way to the final when the Sri Lankans again triumphed.

A month later the Australians were back in India for a four-week tour which included a one-off Test match and the Titan Cup, a triangular limited-over series with South Africa. Taylor resumed his leadership but India won the Test by seven wickets. The Australians also lost all five limited-over matches in what was a less than ideal preparation for the West Indies series to follow.

Courtney Walsh's West Indian side arrived in Australia in November with the ambition to regain the Frank Worrell Trophy but in a topsy-turvy season Australia maintained its ascendancy in the Test series while missing out on the finals of the limited-overs international matches. The Tests were played in a fine sporting spirit until the last match in Perth.

The first Test opened in Brisbane to a crowd of 17,116 – the biggest in fifty years – and it was fitting that local hero Ian Healy (161) should stamp an indelible impression on the game by becoming the first Queensland-born player to make a century at the Gabba. Respect for the baggy green cap was also highlighted on the first morning when players formed a guard of honour and Mark Taylor presented caps to Test debutants, Matthew Elliott and Michael Kasprowicz. Australia's 479 in the first innings met with a weak reply and only Sherwin Campbell's dogged second innings century enabled the West Indies to survive into the final session of the match before finally succumbing by 123 runs.

The margin in the second Test at Sydney, which began just three days later, was one run more. Jason Gillespie debuted for Australia and Matthew Elliott was moving smoothly in his second innings 78 when a spectacular mid-pitch collision with Mark Waugh led to him tearing a cartilage in his right knee and retiring from the match and the series. The home team's advantage was won by its spinners, Shane Warne and left-arm wrist spinner Michael Bevan, who took control of the end game.

For the third Test in Melbourne, Australia recast the batting line-up with Matthew Hayden and Justin Langer coming in for the injured Elliott and Ricky Ponting. The opening day crowd of 72,891 was stunned when Australia lost 27 for four and the ball remained on top thereafter. A victory target of 87 was not achieved by the West Indies until four batsmen had departed. McGrath's removal of Sherwin Campbell and Robert Samuels took him to 100 wickets in 23 Tests.

After the limited-overs international matches were completed, the Test series resumed in Adelaide. Curtley Ambrose's withdrawal on the morning of the match gave the Australians a huge boost and they went on to record a win by an innings and 183 runs, the largest margin between the countries since their first series in 1930–31. The game was virtually over by the end of the first day when the West Indian's paltry 130 had been passed by the Australians for the loss of just two wickets. The revelation in the match was Michael Bevan, who was restored to the side from twelfth man duties in the previous Test. Not only did Bevan's grim five-and-a-half hour undefeated 85 make a major contribution to Australia's impregnable position but his career-best figures of 10/113 snatched the limelight away from Shane Warne and ensured a series win for his country.

Between the fourth and final Tests came the sad announcement of Craig McDermott's retirement from cricket. An injury to his left knee while playing a grade match in Brisbane in September gave him continued trouble and he was forced to acknowledge that he would have to close his distinguished career in second place behind Dennis Lillee with 291 wickets from 71 Test matches.

Bevan continued his good batting form on a cracked and scarred Perth pitch which saw the West Indies turn the tables inside three days and narrow the series margin to 3–2. Curtley Ambrose proved the danger man in the first innings with 5/43 and then Brian Lara (132) finally unveiled his scintillating strokeplay in a stand of 208 with Robert Samuels; during this partnership, confrontation ensued between the players which led to the umpires warning both teams as to their conduct. The West Indies' ten-wicket win was overshadowed on the final afternoon of the game by Ambrose's last over in which he overstepped the crease nine times in completing the longest over in Test history.

The West Indies were not the only tourists during the summer. An England A side came and went with little notice, and tour manager David Graveney complained that the Australians had little regard for English cricket. This was reflected in the programming of the seven-week tour which saw only three of the six four-day games given first-class status.

Pakistan toured during December and January and won the World Series Cup for the first time. The Australians failed to make the finals for the first time since the inaugural season in 1979–80 and brought to an end a sequence of six wins in the past seven seasons.

The non-stop nature of cricket saw the Australians make a busy two-month tour of South Africa in February-April 1997. Seventeen matches were played, including three Tests and seven limited-overs international games, but the main feature of the tour was that, for the first time, Australia named separate squads for the Tests and one-day matches. The new situation would produce pluses and minuses. A gain would be a sharing of the workload: lost was the sense of team identity for those players categorised as either Test or one-day specialists.

Australia went into a so-called world championship battle at The Wanderers, Johannesburg following five successive wins and exited easy victors of the first Test by an innings and 196 runs. Steve Waugh (160) and Greg Blewett (214) shared a fifth-wicket partnership of 385.

After an innings win over Border, the Australians entered the second Test at Port Elizabeth full of confidence only to get the fright of their lives. On an uneven green pitch only an amazing turn around on the third morning put the visitors back in the match. Australia's unlikely two-wicket victory added insult to injury when Ian Healy brought up the win with a six over square leg off South African captain Hansie Cronje.

Australia maintained an unchanged team for the final match at Centurion but were humbled by eight wickets. The Australians could claim that they received the worst of some poor umpiring in the match but Ian Healy's action of disputing his second-innings dismissal and then throwing his bat towards the dressing room as he left the field brought him a two-match suspension.

The 2–1 margin in the Test series could easily have been reversed and, in any event, represented a great fightback by South Africa. Australia sent home opening batsmen Matthew Hayden and Matthew Elliott, middle-order Justin Langer and Glenn McGrath (to rest an injury) from the Test party and replaced them with Michael Di Venuto as an opener, all-rounder Brendon Julian, swing bowler Adam Dale, and wicket-keeper batsman Adam Gilchrist to cover for Ian Healy's suspension. Australia won the limited-overs series 4–3, with perhaps the decisive moment coming in the third match when Mark Taylor stood down from the competition, after which Healy took over the captaincy in four games and Steve Waugh in one.

Back on home ground, Western Australia defeated Queensland to win the Mercantile Mutual Cup at the WACA Ground in March. However, Queensland turned the tables on the same opponents at the same ground a month later. Led by Stuart Law, the Queenslanders won the Sheffield Shield for the second time in three years. Queensland's victory margin was a comfortable 160 runs. Justin Langer topped the Shield averages easily with 712 runs at 142.40 while Andy Bichel won the Shield Player of the Year award after taking 25 wickets at 16.56 in just three games.

Mark Taylor's Australian side was on the road again in 1997 when England gained the early initiative by winning all three Texaco Trophy internationals before the first Test at Birmingham.

A diabolical performance on the first morning, when the Australian scorecard read 54 for eight at one point before recovering to 118, cost the side dearly. Nasser Hussain (a career-best 207) and Graham Thorpe rammed home the advantage with an attacking fourth wicket stand of 288 out of 478 for nine declared. Mark Taylor (129) saved his career with his second-innings century and Greg Blewett became the only batsman to score centuries in his first three Ashes Tests, but England hit 119 runs in under an hour and a half to win by nine wickets with a day to spare.

In a rain-ruined second Test at Lord's Glenn McGrath gave the Australians a victory chance by returning career-best figures of 8/38 in removing England for a minuscule 77 by lunch on the third day but England easily saved the match.

Twin centuries by Steve Waugh and a return to bowling form by Shane Warne saw Australia equal the series with a comfortable 268-run win at Old Trafford.

There was a light-hearted intermission with limited-overs matches against the Minor Counties, Scotland and John Paul Getty's XI during which time Shane Warne was given ten days' leave to return to

Australia to see his wife Simone and newborn daughter Brooke, a far cry from the old days.

Rain interrupted play on the first day of the fourth Test at Headingley, but then Jason Gillespie ran through the English batting on the second morning to finish with a career-best 7/37 out of 172. Australia started appallingly to be 50 for four and, if Matthew Elliott had been held at slip by Graham Thorpe on 29 from debutant Mike Smith, they might have trailed England's score. Instead Elliott (199) and Ricky Ponting (127), added 268 runs for the fifth wicket and Australia recorded a win by an innings and 61 runs.

Australia sealed the fate of the Ashes with an easy 264-run victory at Trent Bridge. Ian Healy brought up his 300th catch in England's first innings but the most interesting sideline to the game came when the brothers Waugh were batting and faced the brothers Hollioake at the bowling crease.

A loss at The Oval in the sixth Test made the series result 3–2 to Australia. Needing only 124 for victory Australia succumbed for 104, 19 runs short of their target. But 3–2 flattered England as the tourists had seven century-makers to England's three and captured their wickets at a cost of 24.84 runs compared with England's 32.19.

Money hung over negotiations between the Australian Cricketers' Association (ACA), the player representative body headed by Tim May, and the ACB during the 1997–98 season. Talk of a strike arose in November 1997 after the ACA sought to share power with the Board and perhaps greedily claim 40 per cent of ACB revenue for its members. At this time the Board's financial figures showed income of $54 million in 1996–97, of which $9.5 million (18 per cent) went to the players, a relatively low amount when the Board and state associations were holding reserves of more than $20 million. As the season unfolded and a new seven-year television deal was struck with Channel Nine for $175 million (an increase of $10 million per year), and increased player payments (20-25 per cent) were pegged to this, dissatisfaction withered.

Stephen Fleming's young New Zealand side arrived amid the turmoil but its search for Test respect showed little sign of being realised following innings losses to Queensland and New South Wales. Given this lack of form, Australia's win in the first Test in Brisbane by 186 runs was relatively modest. The Kiwis slipped into an even lower gear while scoring 82 and 173 against Victoria, so it was not surprising that Australia should dominate the second Perth Test with an innings win on a cracking pitch. Yet a dull game saw history made. On the first day, when the floodlights were turned on during the final session, it was a first in Test cricket. And then on the second day, when

Mark Waugh drove spinner Daniel Vettori high on to the roof of the Lillee-Marsh Stand, it had historians searching their memories for a bigger hit.

Australia had retained the Trans-Tasman trophy and the third game in Hobart was to be revived with enterprising declarations after rain interruptions. Fleming's declaration at 251 for six, with his side 149 behind, prompted Taylor's second-innings closure at 138 for two, setting the New Zealanders 288 to win on the last afternoon. A juggled batting order and a breezy start saw 72 runs on the board in 40 minutes, but after Shane Warne (5/88) had bitten through the middle order, the New Zealand last pair put up shutters in the last half hour to stave off defeat.

Hansie Cronje's South African team arrived in November and proved tough opponents. In nine games, they had five wins, three draws and only a single loss to New Zealand in a one-day international match before the Tests began. More importantly, they beat Australia in two limited-overs matches.

Scoring was tedious but the cricket intense in the first Test at Melbourne which attracted an attendance of 160,182. The Proteas had to survive eight hours in the fourth innings to save the game. This seemed unlikely but Jacques Kallis's six-hour century, in his first game against Australia, saved his side.

Shane Warne put Australia ahead in the Sydney Test with match-winning figures of 11/109 (5/75, 6/34) as he spun the tourists out for 287 and 113 in reply to Australia's 421, in which Mark Waugh's even 100 topped the score. Warne's tally springboarded him to his 300th wicket in his 63rd Test, while Steve Waugh became the third Australian to play 100 Test matches.

Warne's success prompted the interesting selection of Stuart MacGill for Adelaide where two leg-spinners were paired for the first time since Warne's once-only partnership with Peter McIntyre three years previously. An even batting performance, including a hard-hitting half-century from number eleven Pat Symcox, guided the Proteas to a commanding 517, to which Australia replied with 350. Mark Taylor, who carried his bat through the innings for eight and a three quarter hours for 169, was the Australian hero, while Shaun Pollock produced the best South African bowling figures against Australia with 7/87 from 41 overs. The South Africans' second innings declaration left Australia chasing 361 in seven hours but the challenge was never attempted.

The game ended controversially when an appeal for hit-wicket against century-maker Mark Waugh was turned down with 50 balls remaining. It led to a post-match tantrum by Hansie Cronje who slammed a stump into the umpire's dressing room door. However, it was really poor catching that robbed the visitors of any chance of levelling the series.

Australia took a while to get going in the Carlton & United Series. The axing of Test captain Mark Taylor and wicket-keeper Ian Healy – who were replaced by Steve Waugh as skipper and Adam Gilchrist as gloveman and opening bat – was unpopular at first, and particularly with Taylor as he wrote later in his autobiography, *Time to Declare*. 'Suddenly at a certain time in the cricket season, I became a disappearing man . . . It was demeaning. I was supposed to be a senior player, a senior figure in Australian cricket, yet I was not rated good enough to play one form of the game.' In his book Taylor went on to say he was ready to resign the Test captaincy and had to be talked out of it by friends. Steve Waugh definitely felt the pressure as his first six innings yielded just 12 runs and Gilchrist only won acceptance after his century in the second final in Sydney. The Australians won only three of their eight qualifying matches and lost five times in succession to the South Africans before being defeated in the last two finals.

Soon afterwards the Australians were on their way to New Zealand for a 10-day stopover tour in which they played four one-day international matches before going on to India and Sharjah. Honours were shared with the host nation. In India they played a six-week tour in February-April. It was a Test Series with strange turnarounds in the first and third matches.

The expected man-to-man duel between Shane Warne and Sachin Tendulkar was won convincingly by the Indian master after Warne dismissed him cheaply in their first encounter. Tendulkar scored 446 runs at 111.50 whereas Warne, bowling an unaccustomed off-theory, took 10 wickets at 54.00 apiece. After Australia's 328 led India's 257 on the first innings in the first Test at Chennai, Tendulkar's second-innings hundred enabled Mohammad Azharuddin to set a victory target of 347, enough for his spin attack to wheedle the Australians out.

Australia's run of nine Test series wins in a row under Mark Taylor ended at Eden Gardens in unmistakeable fashion. Dismissed at the end of the first day for 233, their bowlers were then pummelled to the tune of 633 for five declared in even time. The Australians occupied the crease for six hours in their second innings but could muster only 181 against an accurate probing attack. The figures of opposing leg-spinners Warne, with 0/147 from 42 overs compared to Anil Kumble's 8/106 from 59 overs, remains a matter of wonder for statisticians.

Australia gained their first Test win in India since 1969 in the final match at Bangalore despite six players suffering bacterial attacks and after Tendulkar and India had looked in control on the first day. Mark Waugh's undefeated 153 was the dominant innings as Australia's 400 just trailed India's 424 at tea on day three before Michael Kasprowicz (5/28) used reverse swing to wreck India's second innings for 169. Needing 194 to win, Mark Taylor's 102 not out set his team on an easy road to an eight-wicket win.

Not one but two limited-overs series remained and the Steve Waugh-led side finished on a high note. Australia defeated India in the final of both the home triangular Pepsi Cup series, which also involved Zimbabwe, and then played brilliantly to win all four preliminary games before going down to India and the blade of Sachin Tendulkar in the Coca-Cola Cup final in Sharjah immediately afterwards. If there were any doubts about Tendulkar's class before this tour they were swiftly dismissed as he recorded 1,130 runs at 113.00 in all matches against the Australians.

On the domestic front, Western Australia made up for its losses in the two previous Sheffield Shield finals by defeating Tasmania to win its 14th title. Tasmania's consolation prizes were that opening batsman Dene Hills won the Player of the Year with 1,132 runs and his 33-year-old team-mate Colin Miller, reinventing himself as an off-spinner to support his medium-pace, broke 'Chuck' Fleetwood-Smith's 63-year-old record in taking 67 wickets for the season.

Cricket's first (and maybe last) appearance in the Commonwealth Games in Kuala Lumpur in September 1998 saw Australia send a full-strength team for games which were not given the status of official one-day international matches. Steve Waugh's side defeated Canada, Antigua, India and New Zealand and took a silver medal after losing to South Africa in the final.

Mark Taylor's Test side embarked on its tour of Pakistan in September-November and in the first Test match in Rawalpindi not only won, for the first time in forty years, but did so by an innings. The statistical highlight was Ian Healy's catch of Wasim Akram on the last afternoon which gave him his 356th dismissal in Test matches, taking him past Rod Marsh as the world's most successful Test wicket-keeper.

Bat dominated ball in the second Test in Peshawar where only 18 wickets fell for 1468 runs. Mark Taylor achieved an incredible milestone over the first two days of the match, equalling Don Bradman's record Test score for Australia before declaring with his own score on 334 not out and the team's total at 599 for four. Much debate raged over Taylor's decision and his modest comment was: 'I am proud that I have equalled Bradman's record, and that is more than satisfying for me.' Pakistan batted for nearly two days in compiling 580. Taylor's 92 in the second innings enabled him to join Graham Gooch as the only batsman to score 400 runs in a Test as the Australians batted out time.

Pakistan remained undefeated in the National Stadium, Karachi in the third Test but the drawn game gave Australia its first win in Pakistan for 39 years.

Alec Stewart's English side arrived in Australia in late October 1998. The series starter in Brisbane was drawn in Australia's favour with England struggling against the wiles of Stuart MacGill when a thunderstorm ended play.

A fast bouncy wicket for the match at Perth, which began four days later, produced an administrator's nightmare – a three-day Test. England had no answers to McGrath, Damien Fleming and Jason Gillespie, with swing bowler Fleming capturing the star figures of 5/36 out of 112. Gillespie (5/88) then mopped up the second innings with 4/1 in six balls as Australia went on to a seven-wicket win.

Match-fixing and bribery investigations were big news on the eve of the Adelaide Test following an ACB press conference at which it appeared there had been an official cover-up by the Board regarding the connection of Mark Waugh and Shane Warne with corruption in cricket.

Bad as Waugh's and Warne's admissions of being 'naïve and stupid' for accepting amounts of $6,000 and $5,000 for passing on pitch and weather reports to an illegal bookmaker in Pakistan in 1994 were, a worse disclosure was that the ACB had kept secret their investigation, which led them to fine the respective players $10,000 and $8,000 in 1995. It produced outrage among Australians at all levels. Mark Wallace in the *Canberra Times* wrote emotionally but hit a bathetic note by stating that Waugh and Warne had 'tainted the great game of cricket, tainted the baggy green cap and broken the hearts of a million kids'. A lot of kids probably got over it but Prime Minister John Howard spoke for a large constituency of social conservatives when he said that 'knocking cricket off its pedestal is something that's going to deeply disturb Australians'.

It was hard for the cricket itself to compete with the off-field scandals as news, even when local hero Jason Gillespie was made twelfth man after his seven wickets in the previous Test. Justin Langer secured his number three position with an eight-hour 179 and England could never muster enough batsmen in either innings to withstand Australia's penetrative and versatile attack as the home side retained the Ashes in convincing style.

Greg Blewett cashed in for an Australian XI against England in Hobart by making 382 runs in two innings without being dismissed before the next Melbourne Test, which saw over 60,000 people attend on a bitterly cold Boxing Day, that was completely washed out. Batting first, England left Australia 175 to win in the fourth innings. At 103 for two a home victory seemed a formality but an inspired spell of bowling by Dean Headley of 4/4 started the crumble and

Australia's loss of their last three wickets for one run saw England claim an incredible win by 12 runs at 7.33 pm.

Australia brought back Shane Warne after his shoulder injury as part of a three-man spin attack for Sydney with Colin Miller and Stuart MacGill but, on a sharp-turning pitch, it was MacGill who took the heaviest toll. After Darren Gough's hat-trick and Michael Slater's masterful second-innings 123 out of his team's total of 184, England had 287 to chase in the fourth innings but had no answer to MacGill's tricks as he finished with 7/50 and the outstanding match analysis of 12/107. The final series margin to Australia was 3–1.

To stay on top was the biggest challenge, as Allan Miller noted, and Mark Taylor's Australians had done that and were a far more accomplished outfit than England for the sixth time in a row. In all, Taylor had led Australia to 11 wins from 14 series, and 26 wins against 13 losses and 11 draws from 50 matches. Since claiming the world title from the West Indies in 1995 he had won nine out of 11 series, the only two losses coming in a single Test in India in 1996 and a three-Test series on the sub-continent in 1998.

There is never an easy time to retire but for Taylor, a chirpy yet dignified leader, the time on 2 February 1999 was right. Just over a week before he had been named Australian of the Year, following in the footsteps of his predecessor Allan Border as a winner of the award. He had also recently received the Sir Donald Bradman Medal of Honour for his contribution to Australian sport and was the subject of an hour-long special edition of the television programme, *This Is Your Life*. As it came to a close, Taylor's career had a neat symmetry about it. His first Test match had been at the Sydney Cricket Ground in January 1989 and his international career, after 104 Tests, 7525 runs and 113 limited-over matches, was ending on the same ground in the same month, ten years later. Australian cricket was strong when he took over its leadership and stronger when he left it, and he had made a significant individual contribution to that success.

# 40

# Waugh Time

Due to Steve Waugh's hamstring injury, the Australian limited-overs team captaincy was divided during the summer of 1998–99 between Waugh and Shane Warne. In the Carlton & United Series conducted during January and early February, Australia won seven of ten preliminary games and two finals against England, although Sri Lanka provided much of the controversy and excitement. The no-balling of Mutthiah Muralitharan for throwing against England at Adelaide Oval on 23 January sparked a protest, then a walk-off and finally a remarkable victory by the Sri Lankans. Warne's enterprising leadership briefly raised media speculation about Mark Taylor's Test successor on the tour of the West Indies in February-April 1999.

Appropriately Waugh was given the job when the Test series began in Trinidad. The cricket was slow until Australia set West Indies 364 in the fourth innings to win. No-one could have predicted the scale of the West Indian demise for just 51 off 19.1 overs, with Glenn McGrath snaring 10/78 (5/50, 5/28), the first ten-wicket haul of his career.

The West Indians bounced back at Sabina Park where Steve Waugh's even 100 led the scoring in Australia's 256 and the home team wobbled to 37 for 4 at stumps on the first day. A remarkable second day's play saw Brian Lara (213) and Jimmy Adams (94) add 340 runs on the way to a winning position. Glenn McGrath took 5/93 out of 431 but no Australian batsman topped 30 in a weak second innings which allowed West Indies a ten-wicket win.

A brilliant Test match at Barbados saw Australia gain an early ascendancy on the back of a 281 fifth-wicket partnership between Steve Waugh (199) and Ricky Ponting (104) out of 490 and a West Indian fight back from 98 for six to 329. Veteran fast bowler Walsh blasted out the Australians for 146, leaving the home side 308 to win. Again a superb innings by Lara (153) overcame the consistent wicket-taking of McGrath (5/92), so that when he cover-drove Jason Gillespie for four to snatch a one-wicket win pandemonium broke loose.

Australia's attempt to retain the Frank Worrell Trophy required a win in the last Test in St. John's, Antigua and for that reason Steve Waugh and coach Geoff Marsh were forced to drop third selector

Shane Warne whose 2/268 in the first three Tests demanded his replacment by off-spinner Colin Miller. Australia batted a long time in each innings for 302 and 306, enough runs to force a win. Although Brian Lara made a magical 100 from 84 balls in the first innings, his dismissal for 7 in the second set Australia on the victory path and allowed them to tie the series two wins apiece. Both sides had outstanding players but in some respects the series could be seen as a play-off between Steve Waugh and McGrath and Lara, Walsh and Ambrose.

After such enthralling contests the limited-overs international matches to follow might have been anti-climactic except that they provided their own perils. After each side had won two matches the fifth game in Georgetown, Guyana ended in a tie when Steve Waugh took three runs from the final ball as 2000 spectators invaded the ground and the players on both sides were fortunate to escape injury. As Waugh noted: 'It only takes one guy who's had plenty to drink to run out there with a knife, à la Monica Seles, and it's over for you.'

Four days later the final match in Bridgetown, Barbados was interrupted in an even more dangerous manner when glass bottles were thrown on to the field after local player Sherwin Campbell was controversially run out following a collision with Brendon Julian as the West Indies sought victory. Thinking of their lives rather than the result of the game, the Australians agreed to reinstate Campbell and a revised run target due to the ten overs lost because of the hold-up. The three-all result in the series was immaterial. Waugh's comment this time was: 'It's better to let the crowd have their way than getting killed on the way home.'

Speaking of home, a State Player Contract system was introduced following an agreement between the ACB and the Australian Cricketers' Association (ACA) under which the ACB gave each state $240,000 to make 20 selected squad-members payments ranging from $5,000 to $40,000. In a much gentler atmosphere than the West Indies tour, Western Australia, playing in its fourth consecutive final, won back-to-back Sheffield Shields by upsetting Queensland in Brisbane by an innings and 31 runs. Australian limited-overs stars Darren Lehmann and Michael Bevan had phenomenal seasons, averaging 134.75 and 106.00 respectively, while David Saker headed the bowling aggregates with 45 wickets.

The finale to the long season was the seventh World Cup where Australia opened with a win against Scotland at Worcester on 16 May, but when the next two matches, against New Zealand and Pakistan, were lost, they were in danger of not progressing beyond the preliminary rounds and needed to win seven games in a row to claim the greatest prize in the abbreviated form of the game. They did so when Darren Lehmann cut Saqlain Mushtaq to the boundary at Lord's on

20 June. The side's strength of character was most evident in a spine-tingling, tied semi-final against South Africa at Edgbaston. Overall the notable performances came from big guns such as the Waugh brothers, Ricky Ponting, Michael Bevan, Glenn McGrath and Shane Warne who stood up to be counted when they were needed most.

International cricketers no longer rest and Geoff Marsh became a casualty of the hectic life on the circuit when announcing his resignation just a month after being reappointed for a further two years. Marsh's replacement, John Buchanan, did not have the first-class playing credentials of his predecessors but was noted for his abilities as a technical analyst as well as his success in bringing Queensland their first Sheffield Shield win and a second title during his five-year term.

The Sri Lankan Tests of 1999–2000 represented Australia's last series loss before their long period of dominance. At Kandy a terrible accident befell Steve Waugh and fast bowler Jason Gillespie. In attempting to catch a ball which landed between them at short fine leg, Waugh and Gillespie crashed, a collision which sidelined the Australian captain for the rest of the match with a broken nose and Gillespie (broken leg and wrist) for the summer. Thereafter Shane Warne, winning the political game of re-selection, recaptured his Test place (from Stuart MacGill) and form in taking 5/52 out of Sri Lanka's 234. With Australia routed for 188 and 140, Sri Lanka ran out winners by six wickets.

Rain ruined each of the remaining Tests. Australia's 0–1 result was disappointing for the new captain Waugh, whose hopes of a comeback after Kandy were swamped by monsoons.

While these games were going on, an Australia A side led by Adam Gilchrist played five limited-overs matches against India A on a week-long tour of the United States. All matches were staged at Woodley Field, Los Angeles, starting at the inhospitable hour of 8am and were watched by nobody.

Australia's first visit to Zimbabwe with a full Test side lasted just over a fortnight. The Australians were too strong for the home side in the only Test, and the three one-day internationals were also won easily by the visitors.

Although they did not know it, the Harare Test marked the beginning of the Australians' long chain of victories yet for Ian Healy it represented the end of the road. Healy wanted to play one more Test on his home ground and make five more dismissals, to give him 400, but even this great gloveman, whose brilliance in taking sharply spun Warne leg-breaks out of the leg-side rough made him the prince of modern wicket-keepers, had to face the reality that his time had come.

A typically fractious Pakistani side, chock-full of talent, started its tour of Australia in late October and experienced three defeats before the first Test in Brisbane, which coincided with the referendum for an Australian republic. Pakistan scored solidly to mount 367 just before lunch on the second day but the Australian openers, Michael Slater and Greg Blewett, reached 233 without loss by stumps and Australia rocketed to 575. Swing bowler Damien Fleming's 5/59 in the second innings (and match analysis of 9/124) was chiefly responsible for removing the visitors for 281 the second time around as the Australians won by ten wickets.

The Test series might have been under way but on 17 November came the biggest news of the Australian summer with the commercialisation of the major domestic competition following its four-year sponsorship by National Foods Limited for an undisclosed financial underwriting. In return the sponsor was to receive media exposure valued at $22 million, exclusive signage rights on the players and grounds, and the renaming of the competition as the Pura Milk Cup in place of the Sheffield Shield. Diehard traditionalists were shocked that a competition which had been losing around $6 million a year for some time should be sold out when the ACB was reporting annual revenue of $70 million. Coming just 11 days after the referendum which had extended the life of the Australian constitutional monarchy, it was perhaps a reflection of the fact that Australia was more revolutionary when it came to sport than politics. The 'tradition' which gave an English earl 108-year naming rights after donating £150 for the manufacture of a trophy for an intercolonial (state) cricket competition had now ended.

After achieving its only first-class win of the tour against South Australia, Pakistan was in the box seat to grab another victory in Hobart after making 222 to Australia's 246 and following with 392 in the second innings. This total set the home side the improbable task of scoring 368 to win. Australia crumbled to 126 for five but an incredible 238-run, sixth-wicket partnership between left-handed Western Australian pair Justin Langer (127) and Adam Gilchrist (149 not out) took Australia to a miraculous four-wicket win.

Remarkable as the Hobart game was, it has also passed into legend as the place where the 'can't bowl, can't throw' jibe occurred. Those words, picked up by a television microphone, were alleged to have been uttered by Shane Warne about Scott Muller and sent the media into a frenzy with the *Australian* newspaper heading one story: 'How a teammate sledged a rookie'. The admission four days later by Channel Nine cameraman Joe Privetera that the voice was his convinced few people and kept the saga running for weeks, with 'Joe' becoming the most likely suspect regarding various forms of malpractice and misdemeanours around the country.

The third match in Perth continued the pattern of three-day Tests in that city. The Australian pace attack combined to dismiss Pakistan on a bouncy wicket for 155 on the first day and, although Australia were shaky at 54 for four, another huge partnership of 227 for the fifth wicket by Langer (144) and Ricky Ponting (197) – ending a sequence for the latter of three consecutive Test ducks – saw Australia to 451. Pakistan never looked likely to force Australia to bat again as the home side maintained its ascendancy.

India began their Australian tour in November and enjoyed a good first Test morning at Adelaide Oval to have the Australians reeling at 52 for four before yet another mountainous fifth-wicket partnership of 239 between Steve Waugh (150) and Ricky Ponting (125) plus a late innings blast by Shane Warne (86 in 100 balls) took the home side to 441. India subsided in the fourth innings after Sachin Tendulkar was controversially given out lbw ducking a short ball from Glenn McGrath which did not rise. If Warne had held a standard first slip's catch, Damien Fleming would have had a second Test hat-trick as well as the best bowling figures of 5/30.

Consistent batting by the Australians in the second Test in Melbourne saw them win again, overcoming what was a largely one-man resistance from Tendulkar.

If these results were bad enough for the visitors, the Sydney defeat must have been devastating. Glenn McGrath (5/48) and Brett Lee destroyed the Indians for 150, after which Australia remorselessly compiled 552 for five with Justin Langer (223) and Ricky Ponting (141 not out) leading the way. McGrath was again in annihilation mode as he claimed 5/55 in the second innings and 10/103 for the match. The only consolation for the tourists was V.V.S. Laxman's extraordinary innings of 167 on the last afternoon, a taste of batting immortality to come.

Australia continued to maintain their hold on the Carlton & United Series by winning nine games in succession, including hitting their highest-ever score in Australia of 337 for seven in the deciding final in Sydney.

A six-week tour of New Zealand began in mid-February with early problems for the Australians. Shane Warne was accused of harassing a boy who photographed him smoking prior to the first limited-overs international, and an ugly crowd disturbance during the third match at Dunedin saw the tyres of the visitors' team bus slashed. Australia still took the series.

After a six-year absence, Damien Martyn returned to the Test arena at Auckland where Australia had to fight hard against the wiles of 21-year-old, left-arm orthodox spinner Daniel Vettori, whose outstanding match analysis of 12/149 took him past the 100-wicket milestone. Nevertheless, the home side failed in the difficult task of scoring 281 in the fourth innings, with Colin Miller (5/55) making the early breakthroughs. In the end, Australia won fairly comfortably by 62 runs.

The second Test at Wellington resulted in the Australians' ninth successive Test victory, breaking Warwick Armstrong's team's national record set in 1921. Yet the match could easily have gone the other way. On a seaming first-day wicket New Zealand recovered from 66 for five to reach 298, thanks to an aggressive century from Chris Cairns. Then the Australians were in trouble at 51 for four before Michael Slater (143) and Steve Waugh (151 not out) shared a fifth-wicket stand of 199 on the way to 419. New Zealand's 294 in their second visit to the crease set Australia 174 to win, a target they might have found difficult had Daniel Vettori not been off the field for most of the innings with a back injury. The third Test in Hamilton again gave the Australians a six-wicket margin but the New Zealanders were far more competitive than the 3–0 scoreline indicated. However, a rejuvenated Justin Langer's brilliant 122, at a run a ball, put the issue beyond doubt. Adam Gilchrist additionally celebrated his side's tenth consecutive win by becoming the first Australian wicket-keeper to complete ten dismissals in a Test.

Back home, Queensland won the first Pura Milk Cup final at Allan Border Field, Brisbane when they played a painstaking draw against Victoria in the final. Each side scored at the rate of about one run every two minutes and Queensland's 285 and 343 occupied the bulk of the match after Victoria were out for 182. Victorian captain and former Test pace man Paul Reiffel enjoyed a great personal triumph, taking 9/130 to give him 59 wickets and make him leading wicket-taker for the season, although Queensland's Michael Kasprowicz achieved an astonishing 42 wickets at 11.64 in six matches. Matthew Elliott was the only batsman to reach four figures with 1,128 runs.

In May the ACB disclosed how it ranked the top 25 contracted players according to usage, fitness, team spirit, attitude and team balance. The base retainer for players ranged from a minimum of $80,000 for a newly contracted player to $315,000 (up from $220,000 the previous year) for captain Steve Waugh.

Nothing succeeds like excess should have been the motto for the scheduling of three home and three away limited-overs international matches by the cricket boards of Australia and South Africa in April and August, building on the epic 1999 tied World Cup semi-final between the two nations. Only one game echoed that performance. The second of three matches, played indoors in Melbourne's Colonial Stadium on a drop-in wicket grown in a glasshouse in central Victoria, produced a tie, although the intrusion of cricket into the Australian Rules football season left most people in the host state underwhelmed. As commentator Neville Turner noted, playing indoors with musical accompaniment gave the games the flavour of cricket in a disco.

Moving from entertainment to the sober side of cricket, measures were taken to stamp out any whiff of corruption. Before their matches in the 2000–01 season, the Australian players signed a declaration that none of their on-field actions resulted from deals with bookmakers. The declarations resulted from the lingering taint of corruption in international cricket and the view of ICC anti-corruption chief Sir Paul Condon that deals were still being made.

Australia's first visit to Kenya in September 2000 was brief. Because the ICC Trophy was a knock-out format, Australia's loss in its limited-overs match against India in Nairobi meant the end of their tour.

Jimmy Adams' West Indian team arrived in Australia in November with its usual quantity (if not quality) of fast bowlers and a batting line-up that would depend too heavily on Brian Lara. Australia's dominance was quickly established in the first Test in Brisbane before the biggest opening day crowd (19,541) since the Bodyline series. Glenn McGrath (6/17) dismissed Brian Lara for a duck and then mowed down the rest of the West Indian batting order before tea for 82, so that when Michael Slater and Matthew Hayden opened with a century partnership the game was as good as over. It lasted until just after lunch on the third day.

Australia's world-record twelfth successive Test win in Perth was achieved in truly remarkable fashion since they already had a stranglehold on the game after the first three-quarters of an hour. Again it was McGrath who did the damage, his stellar career hitting fairytale heights as he dismissed Sherwin Campbell, Lara (his 300th Test wicket) and Jimmy Adams with consecutive balls for a sensational hat-trick. At 22 for five, it was feared that the West Indies would be blown away before lunch. However, the match reached a third day before Australia recorded an innings victory.

A brilliant innings of 231 by Brian Lara against Australia A in Hobart gave West Indies hope for the third Test in Adelaide where McGrath was finally subdued. Lara scored 182 and the West Indies' 391 was a solid total against an attack where home-town fast bowler Jason Gillespie (5/89) and Colin Miller (5/81) divided the wickets. Australia edged ahead with 403 and Colin Miller's second innings dismissal of Lara for 39 proved the turning point in the match. Miller's 10/113 was a match-winning effort and, despite losing five wickets, Australia still reached 130 to claim the Frank Worrell Trophy. An extra 40 runs to chase and an adequate finger-spinner in the visitors' attack might have seen the result reversed.

Australia gained an easy win in Melbourne. Steve Waugh's hard-nosed 121 assisted his team to 364 after which a paralysed West Indies saw no runs registered until the seventh over. Andy Bichel (5/60) captured the best figures of his Test career as the visitors were removed for 165, and Jason Gillespie (6/40) smashed through the top order the second time around. Only the cultured batting of 19-year-old Marlon Samuels, who reminded long-time observers of Frank Worrell as he top-scored in each innings, providing any solace for the losers.

For only the third time in Australia a series ended with a 5–0 result although the West Indians' Sydney performance was probably their best of the summer. An opening stand of 147 was incredible given the pattern of previous games and the visitors would have been disappointed when Stuart MacGill (7/104) ran through the rest of the innings for 272. At the start of the second day Colin Miller provided the most colourful moment (and one of the funniest) in Test cricket history when he lifted his baggy green cap at the bowling crease to reveal bright blue hair. Australia needed 173 in the fourth innings to win, and got there for the loss of four wickets.

The renamed Carlton Series in January-February 2001 revealed Australia as equally adept at either form of the game. For the first time in the competition's 22-year history a side went through a series undefeated. To give an idea of Australia's batting dominance, three players – Darren Lehmann (197.00), Damien Martyn (149.00) and Mark Waugh (108.40) – had three-figure batting averages. More than any other year, the other two teams, namely the West Indies and Zimbabwe, merely made up the numbers.

Eight days after the WSC final, the Australians opened their most difficult campaign, their object being not so much to retain the Border–Gavaskar Trophy as to win their first series in India since Bill Lawry's team in 1969–70. They started well and claimed their sixteenth consecutive Test victory with an emphatic ten-wicket win at Mumbai. For Steve Waugh, putting the Indians in to bat on a grassy wicket reaped dividends as they fell for 176. But the Australians were soon in trouble themselves at 99 for five until a brilliant record sixth-wicket partnership against India of 197 by Matthew Hayden (119) and Adam Gilchrist (122 off 112 balls) led them to 349. With only Sachin Tendulkar passing fifty in both innings, a second innings of 219 left the Australians with an easy win and confidence sky-high. What followed were two remarkable matches, showing Test cricket at its best.

At Eden Gardens, Kolkata, Australia reached 193 for one at tea on the opening day before a great comeback by the Indians who captured seven wickets for 98 runs in the final session, including a hat-trick by 20-year-old Sikh off-spinner Harbhajan Singh. He despatched Ricky Ponting, Adam Gilchrist and Shane Warne to the dressing room with successive balls. If the pendulum was even, it swung decisively Australia's way on day two as Steve Waugh (110) and Jason Gillespie staged a long partnership which helped Australia to 445. India's response was a feeble 171 and they were forced to follow on. Early on the third day, the match seemed over with Tendulkar out for 10 at 115 for three. A century stand by V.V.S. Laxman and captain Sourav Ganguly put respectability into the second innings but at the end of the third day the Indians trailed by 20 runs with only six wickets left. Then came the magical play of Laxman and Rahul Dravid on the fourth day which saw them add 335 runs, batting all day. When Laxman (281) and Dravid (180) were finally parted, they had added a record fifth-wicket partnership of 376 and India's declaration at 657 for seven set Australia an improbable target of 384 runs from 75 overs. After a brilliant start, the Australians lost their way and fell for 212 against Harbhajan, whose match analysis of 13/196 (7/123, 6/73) made him one of three Indian superheroes for the match.

With the series tied the Australians needed to win the last Test at Chennai. A mammoth 203 by Matthew Hayden, who ended the contests with an Australian record of 549 runs at 109.80 for a three-Test series, was the guiding hand in his side's 391, although Steve Waugh's freak handled ball dismissal at 340 for four was immediately followed by Harbhajan Singh (7/133) spinning out the last six in rapid succession. India's first innings was more solid as five of their first six batsmen passed fifty, including a century from Sachin Tendulkar who again maintained his mastery over Shane Warne on the way to 501. Harbhajan's incredible success continued as Australia were out for 264. His second innings figures of 8/84 gave him 15/217 for the match and a superb 32 wickets at 17.03 in the three-Test series. The Indians finally needed only 155 to win and were cruising at 101 for two but the great fighting spirit of the Australians came to the fore as they got within two wickets of success.

There was little rest. The day after the Test, an unofficial Australian XI captained by Darren Lehmann, and including former Test all-rounder Greg Matthews and ex-Queensland wicket-keeper Ray Phillips, played and lost a fundraising match against India for victims of the January Gujarat earthquake before a crowd of 35,000. And three days later a five-match, limited-overs international series began in Bangalore which the Australians went on to win 3–2.

A few weeks earlier, as the Indian Test series was about to begin, a long shadow was cast over Australian cricket with the death of Sir Donald Bradman on 25 February. He was a great man who enjoyed a wonderful marriage partnership and led a life full of accomplishments. Yet when his innings ended (at 92), the expression of national grief – much of it media-led – went on so long and was so disproportionate as to seem positively unhinged. Throughout a month-long passing parade, Bradman's son John emerged as a dignified figure in calling for people to remember his father as a man rather than as a god.

At home, the second Pura Cup attracted only 95,000 spectators, a paltry one-third the total of fifteen years before. In a tight final, the Cup was won by Queensland who defeated Victoria for the second successive year. Martin Love topped the batting averages but it continued to be the pace attack of Joe Dawes, Andy Bichel and Adam Dale who put their side in winning positions. The trio became the only men to take 40 wickets apiece in the competition as they bowled themselves to the top three places in the averages. In the limited-overs Mercantile Mutual Cup, New South Wales won their sixth title but ironically the side they defeated in the final (Western Australia) won the inaugural round-robin Champions Cup in Perth after defeating teams from Central Districts (New Zealand), Bombay (India) and Kwa-Zulu (South Africa) in a further one-day competition.

Steve Waugh's Australian tour of England started much later than usual. The first game at Worcester did not begin until 1 June, after which Australia won the NatWest triangular series of international limited-overs matches.

England's hopes of regaining the Ashes were quickly snuffed out. In the first Test at Edgbaston, an amazing first day's play saw England recover to 294 after Alec Stewart and Andy Caddick added 103 runs in under an hour for the last wicket but then suffered the audacity of Michael Slater plundering four boundaries from Darren Gough's opening over. Australia reached 133 for one at stumps. Steve Waugh and Damien Martyn (his first Test century) each then scored 105 before Adam Gilchrist tore the bowling apart with 152 off 143 balls. Australia's 576 was completed in just 545 minutes and England had no answers in their second innings in which nine players recorded single-figure scores.

At Lord's the Australian supremacy continued. Glenn McGrath (5/54) and Jason Gillespie provided incessant pressure to dismiss England for 187 and Mark Waugh's (108) bolstered the middle order as Australia raised 401 at roughly four runs per over. Gillespie (5/53) led the attack in the second innings and after England were out for 227, their only solace was picking up two cheap wickets in Australia's small run-chase.

The ball dominated the third Test at Trent Bridge, particularly on the first day when 17 wickets fell. Again the probing accuracy of Glenn McGrath (5/49) was too good for the home side but England struck back to have Australia 105 for seven at stumps. However, Adam Gilchrist and Gillespie put the game back on even terms on the second morning before Shane Warne (6/33) gained a second-innings ascendancy. Finally, the Australian batsmen took charge in the fourth innings to win by seven wickets.

England's win at Headingley shouldn't have happened. That it occurred was for the best of reasons. After frequent rain stoppages, stand-in captain Adam Gilchrist declared at the fourth-day, tea-time score of 182 for four, with his side leading by 314 runs and with the aim of making a clean sweep of the series. History was on Gilchrist's side. The only previous team to score more than 220 to win in a fourth innings at Leeds had been Don Bradman's 'Invincibles' in 1948. By a nice statistical quirk, Mark Butcher played the innings of his life to equal The Don's 173 not out to see his side home by six wickets.

Australia's batsmen gave England little time for glory when, three days later, they put the home side's attack to the sword. Matthew Hayden, Justin Langer, Mark and Steve Waugh clobbered the bowling to reach 641 for four in just 624 minutes.

England's sustained defence, led by a patient century from Mark Ramprakash, managed 432, but the second time around the twin skills of Glenn McGrath (5/43) and Shane Warne saw them fall for 184 early on the fifth day. It was a great match and a great series for Australia's key strike bowlers, with Warne claiming 11/229 (7/165, 4/64) for the match and 31 wickets for the series as well as becoming the first Australian bowler to pass 400 Test wickets.

McGrath ended the series with the striking figures of 32 wickets at 16.93 and overtook Dennis Lillee as Australia's second-highest wicket-taker. In the Test batting averages, Steve Waugh finished with 107.00, while Damien Martyn's average of 104.66 from 942 runs meant that he was only the third Australian after Don Bradman and Bill Johnston to top three figures on an English tour.

In looking at Australia's Test performances from November 2000 to August 2001, the team played 13 matches winning ten and losing three. They played a superb brand of attacking cricket and their losses were brought about only by some herculean individual performances from their opponents.

The fight for the Trans-Tasman Trophy in the 2001–02 season proved keen and, after an eight-year failure to win a Test match against Australia, the New Zealanders came close to snatching the series.

Rain washed out a third of the first Test at Brisbane, in which declarations were made in three innings. Steve Waugh's rapid second-innings declaration at 84 for two left the visitors an attainable target of 284 in 57 overs. In a bold attempt they almost got there, falling just 10 runs short on a day in which 459 runs were scored and 11 wickets lost.

Rain truly destroyed the Hobart Test after a destructive batting display by the Australians, in which Justin Langer and Matthew Hayden produced their second, successive double-century stand and Ponting (157 not out) surpassed his three previous home-state scores of 4, 0 and 0 by a wide margin. Australia compiled 558 for eight declared with the New Zealanders unable to complete their first innings.

Australia were under the cosh in the Perth Test where New Zealand reached 534 for nine. There were two large partnerships of 199 for the second wicket between Lou Vincent (104) and Stephen Fleming (105), and 253 for the eighth wicket between Nathan Astle (156 not out) and Adam Parore (110). Australia reached 351. With a strong lead, the New Zealanders set Australia a run chase of 440 from a minimum of 107 overs. On the last afternoon, the home side struggled to reach 381 for seven when they were satisfied to settle for a third draw.

South Africa's supposed tilt at the world's Test crown came to nothing. The first Test in Adelaide proved a one-sided affair after a keen first innings struggle, Australia's 439 being answered by the Proteas' 374. Eventually, the Australians set a victory target of 375. The South Africans were never in the race following Shane Warne's magic in removing Gary Kirsten with the last ball of the fourth day.

Steve Waugh's team easily retained the Mandela Trophy after the second Test in Melbourne. Rain interrupted the first day but rigid batting left the Proteas all out for 277 on the second. Australia's 487 was almost enough for an innings victory since Jacques Kallis (99) stood alone for the second match in a row, before being run out trying to keep the strike.

Justin Langer (126) and Matthew Hayden (105) compiled their fourth 200-run partnership of the summer in Sydney as Australia reached 554. The most excitement in the game, however, was the rare pairing of leg-spinners Shane Warne and Stuart MacGill who finished with 13 wickets between them. After a limp 154 in their first innings, South Africa reached 452 in their second, going down by ten wickets.

With the Test series behind them the Australians made a slow start to the triangular limited-overs international matches known for the first time as the VB series. Same sponsor, different name.

In the most exciting of these contests, South Africa, New Zealand and Australia each won four games but the Australians were eliminated from the finals owing to some controversial manipulations of incentive points.

The Australian tour of South Africa was due to begin just nine days later but first the selectors signalled the partial end of an era by controversially axing Steve Waugh from the captaincy of the one-day international team and replacing him with Ricky Ponting within two days. In the first Test at Johannesburg the Australian Dominators really lived up to their name by recording their largest-ever Test win by an innings and 360 runs.

The Australian batting was positive on the first day in reaching 331 for five, with Matthew Hayden (122) leading the way. However, they were nothing short of brutal on the second, with Damien Martyn (133) and Adam Gilchrist (204) combining in a sixth-wicket stand of

317 at 5.5 runs an over, so that Australia were able to declare at 652 for seven in just over five sessions. The South Africans were shell-shocked and capitulated for 159 and 133 before the end of the third day.

With South Africa in seeming disarray, Australia had to work much harder than expected in the second Test in Newlands, Cape Town, especially after the Proteas lost six wickets for 92 before reaching 239. Magic man Adam Gilchrist was again the inspiration of his team as his blazing stroke play (138 in 108 balls) pushed the total to 382. In the second innings, consistent scoring by all the South African top order against the persevering leg-spin of Shane warne (7/161 off 70 overs) saw them reach 473, setting Australia 331 to win. It was a big task but Ricky Ponting eventually sealed the match and raised his century with a six off left-arm unorthox spinner Paul Adams into the Railway Stand.

South Africa made a superb comeback at Durban to take the third Test with a stirring fourth-innings run-chase after the Australians looked in control. Overall, the outstanding player of the series was Adam Gilchrist, who smashed 473 runs off 474 balls at an average of 157.67 in addition to his 14 dismissals behind the stumps, while Warne and McGrath maintained their illustrious standards. Mark Waugh then joined Steve Waugh as a one-day casualty when he was omitted from the side which went on to thrash the South Africans in the seven limited-overs international matches.

In Australia, Queensland won its third successive Pura Cup and New South Wales its second title in a row in the ING Cup. The Queenslanders had the leading performers in all departments of the first-class game with Martin Love and Jimmy Maher alone topping 1,000 runs, Michael Kasprowicz finishing the leading wicket-taker with 49 wickets, and Wade Seccombe ending as the top wicket-keeper with 49 dismissals.

April put the cricketers into winter hibernation except for those plying their trade on the county circuit and the interruption brought by Pakistan's brief tour in June to play three limited-overs matches. Australia lost the deciding match in Brisbane by 91 runs when Shoaib Akhtar (5/25) provided an irresistible display of fast bowling.

The ACB dithered over renewing its battle with Pakistan in a three-Test series in October 2002 because of political instability related to the war in next-door neighbour Afghanistan and instead agreed to matches in neutral venues in Sri Lanka and Sharjah. The neutral venues did not appeal to Australian captain Steve Waugh, who stated after his side's narrow 41-run victory at the Sarvanamuttu Stadium, Colombo that such games were only good for television watchers. 'From a player's point of view you want some atmosphere at the ground.'

The first Test against an undermanned Pakistan gave the Australians a fright after early dominance. The great Pakistani fight-back began when Shoaib Akhtar and Saqlain Mushtaq smashed through the Australian second innings and resolute batting gave them chance of victory. However, the slimline Warne had other ideas and he proved the match-winner with 11/188 (7/94, 4/94), the sixth ten-wicket haul of his career.

In Sharjah, in blazing temperatures which reached 51 degrees in the stadium, the Pakistanis melted in the second Test. Matthew Hayden's courageous seven-hour century (119) was more than Pakistan could muster in both innings combined; their totals of 53 and 59 being the fourth-lowest match total in Test history. In the third Test at the same venue, Australia's 444 was again far too good for their opponents who went down by an innings margin and gave the Australians a clean sweep of the series.

Nasser Hussain's English side arrived in Australia in mid-October and were quickly dubbed 'walking wounded' as Darren Gough and Andrew Flintoff struggled to recover from injury and surgery. Australia entered the first Test in Brisbane in early November with two notable changes. When elegant 37-year-old, 128-Test, 8,029-run veteran Mark Waugh was replaced by Darren Lehmann in the middle-order there was an inevitable Sydney lament, but Andy Bichel's retention of his place on his home ground at the expense of Brett Lee was received with less complaint. A power-packed first day saw Matthew Hayden (197) and Ricky Ponting add 272 for the second wicket to put Australia in charge, a position they maintained. After a solid English reply, Hayden's second century of the match (103) gave the home side a lead of 463 but England's supine surrender in just two hours knocked the lights out of the series from the outset.

The visitors fought hard for a day at Adelaide Oval, but after Michael Vaughan's dismissal in the last over for a brilliant 177, it was again Australia all the way. England slipped from 295 for three to be all out for 342 and, in reply, Australia batted with arrogant ease to compile 552. Ricky Ponting's fourth century (154) in five Tests and his third-wicket partnership of 242 with Damien Martyn were the highlights of the innings. When Vaughan was caught from a spectacular freak diving outfield catch by Glenn McGrath in the second innings, the heart went out of the English batting and poor shot-making ended the game in double quick time.

'Same Old England' was one Australian newspaper headline when it might have been 'Same Old Australia' following another innings victory at Perth. After England were out for 185 on the first day, only Glenn McGrath failed to reach double figures (and he was 8 not out) in Australia's total of 456. Then, for the second time round, insufficient batsmen fired for England. With the Ashes remaining safely in Australia's keeping, the main question was whether Australia could inflict a 5–0 Ashes series whitewash for the first time since Warwick Armstrong's side in 1920–21.

The break in the Tests for the triangular VB series during December probably broke the Australia's momentum, especially following the loss of Shane Warne for several weeks with a dislocated shoulder. The Boxing Day Melbourne Test began with an act of Australian murder and ended with an English sting in the tail.

Matthew Hayden and Justin Langer were totally in control as they belted 100 runs in an hour after lunch on the first day, before Hayden (102) was dismissed for his third century of the series. From then on, the Australians maintained their savage pace to reach 551 for six with Langer's 250 in 578 minutes from 407 balls the biggest of his 13 Test centuries. England wilted to 118 for six, raising fears of another three-day match but recovered to 270 before Steve Waugh enforced the follow-on. A superb, fighting 145 by Michael Vaughan helped England to 387, setting Australia a victory target of 107. Remarkably the game went into a fifth day and the Australians were left running scared as they revived memories of small-chase failures of the last twenty years and lost five wickets to a dangerous pace attack of Andy Caddick and Steve Harmison. Although the Australians led 4–0 in the series, there had finally been a contest.

Steve Waugh equalled Allan Border's international record of 156 Test appearances in Sydney and wanted to win again but Australia *sans* Warne, *sans* McGrath (side-strain), and with a tired Gillespie, went down by 225 runs. Michael Vaughan (183) slammed his third century of the series to win the Man of the Match award, Andy Caddick took 10 wickets in a Test for the first time in his career and Adam Gilchrist crashed 133 from 121 balls in the first innings, but the most glorious moment was seized by Waugh in front of his home crowd. Coming after an appalling second innings in Melbourne, he needed 69 runs to become only the third batsman to reach 10,000 runs in Test history when he arrived at the crease on the second afternoon and not many people would have backed him to achieve it. Instead Waugh raised a brilliant century in the most gripping manner, as he cover-drove the last ball of the day with Bradman-like vigour for four.

# Chapter 41

## Eighth World Cup and Waugh's End

Ricky Ponting returned to lead Australia to success in the rest of the VB Series in January 2003 but the competition was less newsworthy than two other comebacks.

Darren Lehmann bounced back into the one-day side against Sri Lanka at the Brisbane Cricket Ground on 15 January after a frustrating season in which he failed to capitalise on his restoration to the Test team. Opening the batting in the limited-over international match against Sri Lanka in Perth on 22 December, he scored a brilliant century, at a run a ball, only to contract a mystery infection in his right leg which hospitalized him for several days and caused him to miss the final two Ashes Tests. Lehmann vented his frustration by unleashing an insult that was both racist and sexist within earshot of the Gabba dressing rooms, bringing him suspension for five matches on the first-ever charge of racial vilification in international cricket, which not only blighted his own impeccable playing record, but also led to additional charges of misogyny from leading Australian feminists.

Shane Warne was crashed for 26 runs in an over by Justin Langer in his return from injury in an ING Cup match for Victoria against Western Australia at the MCG on 10 January. Afterwards he expressed his keenness to play in the VB Series finals before dropping the bombshell of the year on 23 January by announcing his retirement from limited-over cricket as soon as the World Cup was over. Warne's decision meant that he became the first Australian player to plump for partial retirement. In making his announcement, Warne stated that he did not want to be dumped from the one-day side as the Waugh brothers had been. "A year or so down the track I don't particularly want to get the tap on the shoulder." The good news was the likely extension of his Test career; the bad that the great (but ageing) Australian team was beginning to break up.

The Australian side for the World Cup was led by Ricky Ponting (Tasmania) and comprised Michael Bevan, Brett Lee and Glenn McGrath from New South Wales; Queenslanders Andy Bichel, Matthew Hayden, Jimmy Maher and Andrew Symonds; South Australians Jason Gillespie and Darren Lehmann; Victorians Ian

Harvey and Shane Warne; and Western Australians Adam Gilchrist, Brad Hogg and Damien Martyn. It was a team which boasted a brilliant batting line-up and potent bowling attack. The major shadow over the event was the political instablility in Zimbabwe and Kenya which saw England forfeit their opening match against Zimbabwe in Harare and New Zealand their fourth game against Kenya in Nairobi. The Australians' match against Zimbabwe in Bulawayo would eventually pass without incident.

On the eve of Australia's first cup match against Pakistan on 10 February, however, came a major shock with Shane Warne's admission to his team-mates that he had tested positive for two diuretics, hydrochlorothiazide and amiloride, in a urine sample taken by the Australian Sports Drug Agency (ASDA) in Sydney on 22 January. The result required him to be sent home to await the results of a second test before a hearing. Over the next few days Warne again put forward the 'naïvety' defence he had used back in 1998, regarding his admission of furnishing information to bookmakers, only this time he combined it with 'vanity' – he had taken his mother Brigitte's Moduretic 'fluid tablet' to improve his appearance on television.

At the eight-hour hearing in Melbourne on 21 February before a three-member ACB anti-doping tribunal – Queensland Court of Appeal Justice Glen Williams, sports medicine expert Susan White and former Test player and selector Peter Taylor – evidence was taken from Warne, his mother, ACB medical adviser Dr Peter Harcourt, ASDA officers, ACB doctor Trefor James and physician Greg Hoy who presided over Warne's recovery from his recent shoulder injury.

Although the panel could have banned Warne for two years his sentence was reduced to twelve months because there was no evidence of anabolic steroids in Warne's sample. Amid the instant reaction from Warne that he was a victim of 'anti-doping hysteria', and opposing views which argued he had been treated either too harshly or too leniently, the tribunal published its findings on 26 February. These criticised him for 'extreme vagueness' and inconsistency. Although his team-mates in South Africa, and Steve Waugh at home, gave messages of support it had to be recognised that Warne had let his team, as well as himself, down.

While Steve Waugh's thrilling Sydney Test century would have been a fairytale ending to his career, he kept Australian cricket followers and the ACB in suspense about his future until mid-March. Returning to New South Wales colours, he enjoyed outstanding success as he led the Blues to wins in both the Pura Cup (their first trophy in the competition since 1993–94) and the ING Cup to bring up a hat-trick of victories. On a personal note, Waugh completed four centuries and 964 runs at 45.90 for the first-class season to place him second in the batting aggregates behind Martin Love's 1120 runs at 65.88. Stuart MacGill had an exceptional season with the ball to capture 60 wickets at 29.56 runs apiece. In an ironical twist, Test specialist Justin Langer was the ING Cup Player of the Series with 434 runs at 72.33. Finally, Waugh's availability for the West Indies resulted in his being named captain on his fourth tour of the Caribbean with Ponting as his deputy.

Australia's World Cup campaign, meanwhile, proceeded smoothly towards the finals with nine successive victories. Brilliant batting by Andrew Symonds in his undefeated 143 against Pakistan in the opening game was followed by an outstanding spell by Jason Gillespie in the win over India. In the fifth match at Potchefstroom, Australia were far too accomplished for Namibia whom they dismissed in just 14 overs for 45 with Glenn McGrath taking 7/15. The only times the side was tested were in two games at Port Elizabeth against England and in the Super Six contest against New Zealand. Each time they displayed great mettle in fighting their way out of trouble. In the first England had moved to 66 in the tenth over before slumping to 87 for five and then recovering to 204 with Andy Bichel taking the amazing figures of 7/20 from 10 overs. Australia started poorly and were in trouble at 48 for four and 135 for eight before Bichel joined Michael Bevan in a match-winning partnership. The second game saw the Australians slump against New Zealand pace man Shane Bond whose 6/23 reduced them to 84 for 7 before a 97-run stand by Bevan and Bichel gave them a target to defend. It proved beyond the Kiwis, especially when Brett Lee exploded through the lower order in a spell of 5/3. In the semi-final Sri Lanka did well to restrict Australia to 217 on a slow wicket but their batsmen were unable to overhaul that target. The final against India then saw Australia at their savage best.

Australia's 359 for two, after Sourav Ganguly offered them first use of the pitch, was simply amazing. Adam Gilchrist went full throttle from the outset and his 57 from 48 balls and century stand with Matthew Hayden paved the way for even more fireworks to follow. Ricky Ponting and Damien Martyn's smashing 234 run partnership in 30.1 overs, then batted India out of the match. Ponting's undefeated 140 from 121 balls, including an incredible eight sixes, capped a memorable tournament. The fact that Symonds, who led the World Cup averages with 163.00, and such fine players as Lehmann and Bevan didn't even get a hit, underlined Australia's quality.

While the World Cup was in progress came a media release on 6 March 2003 detailing the change of name of the Australian Cricket Board to Cricket Australia (CA) in the middle of the year. The release was couched in market-speak, the strategic plan, *From Backyard to Baggy Green* (2002), having successfully built on the 1999 plan, *Putting Runs on the Board*. Steve Waugh resumed the Test captaincy less than three weeks after the World Cup. His return to the Caribbean was an important marker on his personal calendar, a reminder of his and the Australian team's success at Kingston, Jamaica, in 1995, and his own desire to make up for the disappointment of a tied series when his leadership began there four years before. As he led his side out at the Bourda ground in Georgetown, Guyana, it was the first match without Warne (suspension) and McGrath, who stayed in Australia for the first two Tests due to his wife's illness. A broken finger also kept Martyn at home, with his number four position being taken by Lehmann.

To cover the bowling losses the Australians played a five-man attack – the pace of Gillespie, Lee and Bichel being supported by the wrist spin of MacGill and Hogg in the first two Tests, and McGrath replacing Hogg for the last two. It worked. The Australians were the first visiting side to win three consecutive Tests in the West Indies with easy margins of nine wickets at Guyana, 118 runs in Trinidad, and nine wickets in Barbados, before the home side broke through for a three-wicket win in achieving a world-record 418 run-chase in Antigua. There was heavy scoring with ten centuries registered by the Australians and seven by the West Indians, but the home pace attack were poor successors to Curtley Ambrose and Courtney Walsh. Most of the time, the Australians simply had more contributors with both bat and ball.

At Georgetown, the West Indies collapsed on the first morning, were revived by a blazing century by Shivnarine Chanderpaul (the third fastest in Test history – from 69 balls), but were then buried by an Australian second-wicket stand of 248 between Justin Langer (146) and Ricky Ponting (117). Centuries for Darren Ganga and skipper Brian Lara in an even-time third-wicket partnership of 185 established a lead, but after their departure Jason Gillespie (5/39) swept through the tail on the fourth morning for his seventh five-wicket haul in his last 19 Tests.

The Queen's Park Oval in Port-of-Spain was the flattest of flat tracks and the Australians set about bullying an attack comprising just three front-line bowlers, and lost only seven wickets during the course of the game. The designated number five batsman, Waugh, did not bother to bat in either innings. Ponting and Lehmann had little trouble amassing a third-wicket stand of 315 from 73 overs on the first day. Lehmann's 160 made him the oldest Australian, at 33 years and 73 days, to reach a maiden Test hundred since Lindsay Hassett in 1946, and produced a memorable phrase from Cricinfo reporter Christian Ryan, who described him as a "bulbous phenomenon". Ponting then continued to a double-hundred (206) and, with Gilchrist slamming a century (from 104 balls), reached 576 for four before Waugh declared. Ganga and Lara provided the backbone of the West Indies first innings of 408 but, after another Hayden century, only Lara's second-innings hundred provided resistance on the final day.

Steve Waugh broke Don Bradman's Australian record for most Test centuries by reaching his 30th in the following game at Bridgetown. The Australians also responded to Lara's invitation to bat by reaching 605 for nine declared, with Ponting (113) joining Waugh (115) as a century-maker and Lehmann, sandwiched between them, failing to do so by just four runs. The West Indies fought hard to avoid defeat, but MacGill's 5/75 in the second innings (9/182 for the match) proved decisive. The one bright spot for the home side was Jermaine Lawson's first-ball dismissal of Langer, and the completion of a hat-trick spread over four days, as Australia chased eight runs to win.

Although the series had already been decided, the last match turned out to be a remarkable affair. Lawson (7/78) fired out the Australians for 240, but the performance lost some of its gloss when he was reported for a suspect bowling action. The West Indies replied with an identical score before Langer (111) and Hayden (177), in their second-innings partnership of 242, became the first Test pair to record five double-century partnerships out of Australia's total of 417. It left the West Indies requiring an unlikely target in two days and a session. Despite an infamous altercation with McGrath, Ramnaresh Sarwan kept a cool head as he and Chanderpaul both brought up hundreds in a surprise win.

Overall the statistical superiority was with the Australians. In the batting averages Ponting missed the last Test with flu, but recorded 523 runs at 130.75 and five of his team-mates averaged more than 50. MacGill led the bowling aggregate with 20 wickets and Gillespie and Lee captured 17 apiece. Lara was outstanding for the losers, with 533 runs in four matches.

Seven one-day internationals followed and the Australians were plainly bored by the end of them. After winning the first four games comfortably, to make it 21 one-day victories in a row, they lost the last three – perhaps uncomfortably. A long season closed at Queen's Park, St. Georges on 1 June with a nine-wicket defeat.

The modern cricket clock doesn't stop for long. It started again when Bangladesh, the newest kids on the Test block, made their first Australian tour, with two Test matches scheduled in the tropical north in July at Darwin and Cairns. Both cities promoted the events as a tourist experience, but the respective match attendances of 13,862 and 13,279 were disappointing.

Waugh became the third Australian Test captain to lead his side in 50 Tests at the Marrara Cricket Ground where he achieved a world-record 37th win, surpassing Clive Lloyd, by an innings margin inside three days. Bangladesh were out for 97, after which Lehmann (110) and Waugh (100 not out) plundered easy centuries out of 407 for seven declared, before Stuart MacGill (5/65) wrapped up the game with his hard-spun leg-breaks.

Cazaly's Stadium in Cairns at least saw the Bangladeshi batsmen survive the first day, but from then on it was one-way traffic and a four-day innings victory. Lehmann (177) ran amok in the final session of day two, adding 105 runs from 32 overs, and with further unbeaten centuries by Waugh (156) and Martin Love (100) a declaration came at 556 for four. While the conditions were expected to favour seam bowlers, it was MacGill's spin that scattered the batsmen, as he claimed match figures of 10/133 (5/77 and 5/56) to give him 17 wickets at 12.88 in the series. Lehmann (287 at 143.50) and Waugh's 256 runs (without being dismissed) led the batting aggregates.

Three limited-over internationals at the same venues in August brought average crowds of 8,000, but the results were even more one-sided as Australia made a clean sweep. That the games held little significance was borne out by Damien Martyn's comment after his undefeated 92 off 51 balls in a nine-wicket win from 20 overs in the second Cairns match. When told that he could have recorded the fastest one-day hundred by an Australian, he replied that he "wouldn't have had a clue".

There are records and records. The 2003-04 Australian season opened with a short two-Test tour by Zimbabwe in early October, which was virtually completed before the first Pura Cup match began. Such programming suited ICC commitments, but made it difficult for Australian players outside the Test side to force their way in.

The Perth Test was dominated by Matthew Hayden's monumental world individual Test-record innings of 380 made from 438 balls in 622 minutes and including 38 fours and 11 sixes. Critics could argue about the quality of the bowling, but Zimbabwe captain Heath Streak remarked that Hayden mishit shots over the boundary; and a triple-century in any class of cricket is a tremendous feat. Worse for the visitors was finding Adam Gilchrist in his most destructive mood as he reached 113 from 95 balls and enjoyed a partnership of 233 in 140 minutes with Hayden, before Waugh's merciful declaration at 735 for six. The Australian bowlers shared the wickets around in their win by an innings and 175 runs, but a disturbing outcome were the torn-muscle injuries to Jason Gillespie and Stuart MacGill, and Achilles tendon damage suffered by Darren Lehmann; their replacements at Sydney the following week would be fast bowler Brad Williams, for his Test debut, and Brad Hogg and Simon Katich, who would be making their first home-Test appearances.

Spectators stayed away from a Sydney Test match, which was that in name only. Although the Zimbabweans shaped up better than in Perth, the match attracted a pathetic crowd of 18,363 over four days, including a mere 1,312 on the final day. Ricky Ponting's 169 dominated Australia's first-innings 403 and he along with another thumping hundred by Hayden (from 85 balls) was chiefly responsible for a nine-wicket win. The most interesting spectacle of the match was the rare "Chinaman" combination of Hogg and Katich bowling in the Zimbabwe second innings, the honours going to part-timer Katich with 6/65. Hayden's two-Test feast brought him 501 runs at an average of 250.50.

Ponting was back in charge of an Indian one-day sojourn in October-November, a tri-series involving New Zealand, for the TVS Cup. The Australian squad contained none of its main bowlers. McGrath, Gillespie, Lee and Warne were replaced by Andy Bichel, Williams, Michael Kasprowicz, Nathan Bracken and Hogg; all of which made their six wins out of seven games the more creditable. Left-armer Bracken moved the ball disconcertingly to capture 14 wickets at 13.93.

India's four-Test series beginning in December 2003 would serve as almost a sub-plot to Steve Waugh's farewell tour. Leading a side *sans* McGrath *sans* Warne against a powerful batting line-up was always going to be a challenge and so it proved, although the erratic rotation of third pace men Bichel, Williams and Bracken coupled with injuries to Lee and Gillespie further destabilized the side.

Rain ruined the opening match in Brisbane in which Australia, led by Justin Langer (121), batted into the third day for 323, and Sourav Ganguly led from the front for India in his 144 out of 409 that carried into the fifth day. Waugh was the subject of criticism for running out his partner, Martyn, and then treading on his wicket for a duck in the first innings. However, he made amends in the second when Hayden bashed a quickfire 99 (from 98 balls) and Waugh and Martyn added 128 runs without difficulty before a late declaration offered India a target of 199 in 23 overs. The visitors turned down the offer.

The second Test in Adelaide was one of the great turnaround games. After Australia had reached 556 on the back of a supreme double-hundred by Ponting (242), and removed the first four Indian batsmen for 85, an Australian victory seemed a foregone conclusion. Then came Dravid-Laxman Mark II, the famous follow-up to their huge stand in Kolkata in 2001. This time Rahul Dravid (233) recorded the highest score by a visiting player at Adelaide and, along with V.V.S. Laxman (148) added 303 runs for the fifth wicket out of India's total of 523. Surprisingly, the Australians fell apart on the fourth afternoon with batting described by coach John Buchanan as "immature"; one argument was that they knew how to attack but not to defend. While leg-spinner Anil Kumble provided the pressure from one end the inoffensive medium pace of Ajit Agarkar gained the glory with 6/41 to set up a four-wicket win. Australia found themselves in the rare position of trailing 0-1 in a home Test series.

If they had not been so aggressive, thoughts of slipping to a 0-2 series deficit might have entered the Australian players' heads on the first afternoon in Melbourne when opener Virender Sehwag was blazing to 195 and India reached 278 for one. Instead, they turned the match around, and started by claiming nine wickets for 88 runs. Hayden (136) and Ponting (257) then continued their summer of plenty with a second-wicket stand of 234 in a total of 558. It turned out to be a strong basis for a nine-wicket win.

Sydney's second Test of the summer was a statisticians delight. Steve Waugh's 168th and final Test drew a staggering 181,053 people, ten times that of the Zimbabwe match – and many of them were provided with red rags by a local newspaper to mop their faces (like Waugh himself) during the event. India's first innings raised plenty of sweat for the Australians as they batted into the third day for 705 for seven, the highest score ever by a visiting side. Tendulkar (241 not out) and Laxman (178) provided the core of the innings with a fourth-wicket partnership of 353, and while Brett Lee took four wickets, the 201 runs he conceded made him only the second Australian bowler to pass the 200-run milestone. Langer (117) and Katich (125) led a strong Australian reply of 474 against inspired bowling by Kumble (8/141), but India's swift second-innings declaration left Australia needing an unlikely 443 to win in just over a day. In the end it was a bridge too far. Waugh was caught off Kumble for the top score of 80 as his team battled to 357 for six. Bat dominated ball throughout the series with Dravid (619 runs at 123.80) and Ponting (706 runs at 100.86) leading the way. Only Kumble, with 24 wickets (including 12/279 at Sydney), gathered his wickets at less than 30 apiece. Waugh finished fourth in the Australian averages with 267 runs at 44.50.

It is ironic that Waugh's captaincy was bookended by two drawn series – the first 2-2 against the West Indies in 1999 and this last 1-1 with two draws – because no captain worked harder for wins. Of course, he achieved that: the incredible 16-win sequence from 1999 to 2001, and 41 victories in 57 Tests as captain made him the most successful leader in Test history. How did Waugh reach this position in the game? The hard way.

Waugh began his Test career at twenty-one on Boxing Day 1985 against India in the dark days of Australian cricket, and in his first four series experienced two draws (against India) and losses to New Zealand and England. The first series win (1-0) came against New Zealand in 1987-88 and then, following a draw and a win in one-off

Tests against England and Sri Lanka in 1988, came further losses to Pakistan and the West Indies. Waugh was selected and retained on promise because he took a long time to fulfil expectations. After his first five Tests, and nine innings, the future batting iron man had recorded scores of 13, 5, 8, 0, 11, 74, 1, 1 and 0 – 113 runs at a disappointing average of 12.55; at that stage his medium-pace bowling was of greater account. Waugh took 27 Tests and 42 innings to reach his first hundred, at Headingley, in 1989 but even though he enjoyed a brilliant series that summer he still had periods of struggle. Replaced by his twin brother Mark in the Adelaide Ashes Test of 1991, he was dropped again on the West Indies tour that followed shortly after, and was omitted from the home series against India in 1991-92 and the 1992 Sri Lankan tour.

At this point, after 44 Tests, Waugh might well have been stood down permanently, as happened to Dean Jones a year later after a similar number of games. Instead, partly at Jones' expense, he grabbed the lifeline thrown at the start of the 1992-93 series against the West Indies and re-established his career on his second England tour six months later. It was on that 1993 tour, and once again at Headingley, that Waugh might have recognized the value of playing hard. Partnering his skipper, Allan Border, in an unbeaten partnership of 321 as Australia's first innings dragged into a third day, he would have grasped the lesson of never giving a sucker (an opponent or a rival team-mate) a break. Early in his career Waugh had to fend off the rib-ticklers of the barrage of the West Indian pace bowlers and he observed the arrogance of their batsmen led by Vivian Richards. As captain, he applied hard bowling and hard fielding to bring about the "mental disintegration" in opponents, but he also added a third element – hard batting. Waugh revolutionized the game by making batting an intimidating force, setting such aggressive scoring rates that he gave his bowlers, and especially his gun spinner Shane Warne, time to bowl opponents out twice. His claim to greatness in Test cricket history was assured.

# Chapter 42

# Ponting at the Helm

With Steve Waugh's retirement Ricky Ponting was back as captain of the one-day team and ready to take over the Test captaincy. The VB series, which began in January 2004, was more pointless than ever as Zimbabwe were never competitive. The tired format saw Australia qualify for the finals with six wins from seven completed games, their only loss coming in their fourth match against India at Brisbane. They also beat India comprehensively in two finals in early February, the first by seven wickets with ten overs to spare in Melbourne, and the second by 208 runs in Sydney, where they equalled their World Cup final score in Johannesburg of 359. Adam Gilchrist and Matthew Hayden got Australia away to flying starts and Gilchrist's crunching 172 against Zimbabwe at the Bellerive Oval came from just 126 balls. Brad Williams put aside his Test disappointments with 15 wickets at 16.67, including career-best figures of 5/22 against Zimbabwe at Sydney.

Australia began their Sri Lankan tour with a 3-2 win in the one-day series, in which Ponting was the leading run scorer, and then went on to sweep the Test series 3-0, despite trailing on the first innings in each match. A remarkable statistical feature was that Darren Lehmann headed both the Test batting and bowling averages with 375 runs at 62.50 and 6 wickets at 16.83 after a frustrating summer in which he was sidelined by injury for the Indian Tests, passed over for the VB series, and won possibly the last tour spot with a brilliant, last-gasp 237 in a Pura Cup match against New South Wales in Sydney.

Andrew Symonds made his Test debut at Galle and thc Australians worked their way back into the match in their second innings with centuries by Matthew Hayden (130), Damien Martyn (110) and Lehmann (129) out of 512 for eight declared. Martyn and Lehmann's fourth-wicket partnership of 206 on the fourth day was crucial, not only for their mastery of Muttiah Muralitharan's trick spin, in match figures of 11/212 (6/59 and 5/153), but because it provided a sufficient target for leg-spinners Shane Warne and Stuart MacGill to work well in tandem, capturing nine of the ten wickets on the last day. Warne's return to Test cricket after a 12-month absence was triumphant as he claimed 10/159 (5/116 and 5/43) in the match.

The first day at Kandy in the second Test belonged to the bowlers with 17 wickets falling, but the Australians grabbed the initiative on the second afternoon when an out-of-form Adam Gilchrist, batting at number three, savaged 144 runs (from 185 balls) and played a significant role in a third-wicket stand of 200 with Martyn, whose 161 piloted his side to 442. Despite an aggressive hundred by Sanath Jayasuriya, the Sri Lankans fell 27 runs short of a target of 351. Warne was again the bowling hero with his second successive ten-wicket haul (5/65, 5/90).

Australia's 401 was matched by Sri Lanka's 407 in the first innings of the Colombo game, with Lehmann (153) and Marvan Atapattu each topping the three figures. Justin Langer's 166 provided the foundation of a second-innings 375 by the tourists, and Lehmann's orthodox spin was a valuable support to Warne in a 121-run victory. Warne picked up his 500th Test wicket at Galle and Muralitharan did so one match later on his home turf at Kandy. Throughout the series, the spinners had a great personal duel, with Warne gathering 26 wickets at 20.04 and Muralitharan 28 wickets at 23.18.

The Australian cricket season was punctured on 19 January 2004 when Victorian coach David Hookes died tragically as the result of a blow to the head he received outside a St Kilda hotel, where he and several Bushranger players had earlier celebrated a narrow win over South Australia in an ING Cup game with Redbacks coach Wayne Phillips and captain Lehmann.

A moving memorial service before a crowd of 10,000 people was held at Adelaide Oval eight days later and telecast nationally by Channel 9. Celebrities like the actor Russell Crowe and boxer Anthony Mundine attended the event, as well as a who's who of Australian cricket, past and present. Former Australian captains Ian Chappell (who read one of the eulogies), Greg Chappell, Richie Benaud, Allan Border, Mark Taylor and Kim Hughes were present, as were former international captains Tony Greig, Clive Lloyd and Martin Crowe. Many of Hookes' past club and state team-mates were present as were the current Australian, Victorian and South Australian sides. Especially poignant touches were the simple message on the historic scoreboard: DAVID HOOKES (1955–2004), REST IN PEACE; and on the centre square where three of the stumps used in his last game had Hookes' bright red South Australian cap hanging from one and one of his bats leaning gently against the others.

It was to the Victorians credit that they were able to salvage their first-class season under assistant coach Greg Shipperd to win the Pura Cup in convincing fashion, their first victory since the Sheffield Shield win in 1990-91. Undefeated, they annihilated Queensland by 321 runs in a home final after amassing 710 runs in the first innings spread over three days. In a first-class season in which 76 hundreds were scored, Victorian opening batsman Matthew Elliott reminded the national selectors that he was still around by leading the way with seven. Elliott also headed the aggregates with 1,429 runs at 79.39 as nine other players reached four figures. Of the bowlers, only Stuart MacGill (58 wickets at 35.95) topped 50 wickets, Andy Bichel took the one ten-wicket haul, but the Victorian attack was the most potent as pace men Brenton Wise, Andrew McDonald and Mick Lewis, and leg-spinner Cameron White each gathered 30 wickets.

Western Australia took the ING Cup, their 11th one-day crown, when they defeated Queensland with two balls to spare. The competition employed a couple of innovations. Batsmen were offered a free hit for a front-foot no-ball and umpires wore microphones – for little purpose. It was also a season for record-breaking: Queensland ran riot to reach 405 for four against Western Australia at the Gabba as Jimmy Maher belted 187 in an opening partnership of 194 with veteran leading run-getter Stuart Law from 22.4 overs; Law also smashed a 69-ball century against Tasmania at the Bellerive Oval; and South Australian express Shaun Tait made a strike for the bowlers with 8/43 against Tasmania at the Adelaide Oval.

The summer was also interesting because of a number of legal and quasi-legal issues that arrested the attention of Melbourne legal and cricket scholar, J. Neville Turner. Turner gave several examples. Steve Waugh's surprise announcement in November that the Sydney Test against India would be his last hinted that he was being nudged into retirement as a victim of ageism. Brad Williams' petulance after being replaced by Nathan Bracken for the Brisbane Test and comment that he bowled with the "wrong arm" was a breach of his contract with Cricket Australia, but could also be regarded as a denial of free speech. Radio and newspaper criticism of umpire Steve Bucknor's lbw decision against Sachin Tendulkar in Brisbane indicated that "it was the worst decision ever" and that he [Bucknor] was "over the hill" was actionable for defamation as well as ageism. Writing about media reaction after David Hookes' death, Turner noted: "The newspaper coverage of the Hookes death was so prejudicial as to make it virtually impossible for his accused killer to enjoy a fair trial anywhere in Australia. If, in fact, a charge has been laid, the matter is *sub judice*, and newspapers who published any detail of it would be guilty of contempt of court."

Australia's international players continued on cricket's less than merry-go-round in May with a two-Test series against Zimbabwe, which never should have been considered, abandoned. Stuart MacGill was the only Australian whose reputation was enhanced and that was because he withdrew from the tour to "maintain a clear conscience" after

Zimbabwe captain, Heath Streak, and 15 white players went on strike over players being selected on racial grounds. Three one-day international matches were brought forward and Australia won each of these at a canter. Before leaving Zimbabwe a couple of statements need to be recalled. Australian commentator Dean Jones said of brutish President Robert Mugabe: "I'm just here to watch cricket and I don't give a rat's arse what he does about his country." And Cricket Australia's public affairs manager, Peter Young, said of the tour: "We need to put it behind us, put a tick in that box." Morality, clearly, was not an issue.

Winter cricket was programmed for the second year running with Tests against Sri Lanka again in Darwin and Cairns. There was some criticism of Sri Lankan spin ace Muttiah Murilatharan skipping the tour as Australia won the first match and drew the second. Adam Gilchrist captained the home side in Darwin in Ricky Ponting's absence due to the death of an aunt. A low-scoring affair, it was dominated by the movement through the air and off the pitch by each side's pace attacks. Australia placed an unprecedented batting line-up of six left-hand batsman in its first seven – Langer, Hayden, Elliott (replacing Ponting), Martyn, Lehmann, Katich and Gilchrist – but barely topped 200 runs in each innings. However, Glenn McGrath took 5/37 out of Sri Lanka's first-innings total of 97, and Michael Kasprowicz (7/39) grabbed the third seven-wicket haul of his career for an easy 149-run win.

Each side made big scores in the first innings at Cairns. Australia's 517 was built on the 255-run partnership between opening batsmen Langer (162) and Hayden (117), the sixth double-century stand between the pair, to which Sri Lanka replied with 455, including a century from Marvan Atapattu. Then Hayden weighed in with a second ton (132), but Shane Warne, despite equalling Muralitharan's world record of 527 wickets, was unable to force a win in the last half hour.

It must have seemed as though life on the road, or in the air, would never end. Instead of resting weary bones, two more limited-over competitions were scheduled in August and September. One of the most meaningless, without a doubt, was the Videocon Cup in the Netherlands, where Australia made the final in Amstelveen against Pakistan without bowling a ball, and went on to win by 17 runs. They then won the first three games in the ICC Champions Trophy in England – including a ludicrous match against the United States where they passed the USA's score of 65 in 7.5 overs – before losing to the host nation (their first loss to England in 15 one-day matches over five years) in the semi-final.

The 2004-05 season began overseas and found fulfilment with a 2-1 series win over India in October and early November. Adam Gilchrist captained Australia in the first three Tests in the absence of Ricky Ponting, who remained at home with a broken thumb, but there was one unaccountable omission from the team. On pitches that usually favoured spin, Australia's selectors chose spin tyros, Victorian batsman/leg-spinner Craig White and Queensland off-spinner Nathan Hauritz, ahead of Stuart MacGill to support Shane Warne. Following his stand on Zimbabwe, had MacGill blotted his copybook? Either way, the selection criteria were curious. MacGill had been the leading wicket-taker the previous summer and was a proven Test campaigner. In 2003-04 White's 30 wickets at 36.83 together with his 581 runs at 36.31 were probably good enough to get him a third spinner's guernsey, but Hauritz's 16 wickets at 63.94 were undeserving of higher reward.

Australia got off to a grand start at the Chinnaswamy Stadium in the first game at Bangalore, and especially after debutant Michael Clarke, the man his team-mates christened "Pup", joined Simon Katich on the first afternoon with the score at 149 for four. Using dancing footwork against the wily spin of Anil Kumble and Harbhajan Singh, and driving with grace and power, Clarke first added 107 runs with Katich, and spreadeagled the field in a dynamic stand of 167 with Gilchrist to push Australia to a first-innings total of 474. Clarke's 151 from 249 balls made him a deserving man of the match winner, while Gilchrist's belligerent 104 came from just 109 balls. Harbhajan snared 11/224 (5/146, 6/78), but Glenn McGrath swung the game heavily in Australia's favour with the wickets of Aakash Chopra and Rahul Dravid for ducks in his first two overs, and fellow quicks Jason Gillespie and Michael Kasprowicz maintained the pressure in both innings. Warne gave a listless performance by his own high standards, but produced a humdinger delivery to bowl V.V.S. Laxman in the first innings.

Torrential rain washed out a great contest on the last day of the second Test at Chennai. After Justin Langer and Matthew Hayden got Australia off to a fantastic start with a century opening partnership, Kumble broke the innings apart on the first afternoon as eight wickets fell for 64. Virender Sehwag's dazzling hundred was chiefly responsible for India's solid lead of 141, and Kumble's vicious spin and bounce on the third afternoon suggested that the home team would have little trouble polishing off the Australian innings. Then came one of the most heroic partnerships in Test history with Gillespie (26 from 165 balls) supporting Damien Martyn (104) in a fifth-wicket stand of 140 in just over four hours. Kumble completed match figures of 13/181 (7/48, 6/133) and Australia's 369 meant India required 228 to win. Sehwag's three boundaries in three overs had locals hopeful, but then the skies opened.

Australia won the Border-Gavaskar Trophy when they beat India at home for the first time in 35 years following a 342-run win at Nagpur.

Martyn took the man of the match honours with a brilliant double of 114 and 97 and was well supported by his fellow middle-order batsmen: Lehmann (70) in the first innings; Clarke (91 and 73); and Katich (99). Apart from a sparkling opening by Sehwag, no Indian batsman attempted to take the attack to the disciplined Australians. After giving away 16 runs in his first over, Gillespie finished with match figures of 9/80 from 38.5 overs (5/56, 4/24) – the best of his Test career.

Ponting returned to captain Australia on a woeful pitch at the Wankhede Stadium in Mumbai, which saw India, with a better-armed spin attack, win by 13 runs as they bowled out Australia for 93 on the third day. Australia's troubles were magnified after Warne broke his right thumb during practice and Hauritz was pressed into service for his debut. After rain restricted play to just 11 overs on the first day, 18 wickets fell on the second and an even more incredible 20 on the third. The only sizeable partnership was a fourth-wicket stand of 148 between Laxman and Sachin Tendulkar in India's second innings before an amazing spell of 38 balls by part-time orthodox spinner Clarke saw him gather six wickets for nine runs. Australia's final demise lasted just 30.5 overs. It marked the end of an unpredictable series; one that could have ended 2-2, 3-1, or even 4-0 to Australia.

Mercifully, there were no one-day internationals tacked on to the Tests. It meant the Australians had at least a fortnight to prepare for the first of two Tests against New Zealand, at Brisbane and Adelaide, in November. They must have been grateful for the break.

The Kiwis opened well at the Gabba. Jacob Oram's hundred carried plenty of punch in the first innings of 353 and when Australia slumped to 128 for four they held the upper hand, but not for long. Australia's heroes from India, Martyn and Clarke, rebuilt the innings to 222; Clarke (141) and Gilchrist (126) then proceeded to tear the attack asunder in a sixth-wicket partnership of 216; and Gillespie and McGrath added to the Kiwis' humiliation with a last-wicket stand of 114 to take the score to 585. One batsman who missed out was Darren Lehmann, but he had enjoyed less than ideal preparation for the match, as three days before the game he was giving evidence at the manslaughter trial of Zdavko Micevic in Melbourne regarding David Hookes' death.

New Zealand buckled and broke in 36.2 overs for 76, nearly as quickly as Australia's Mumbai shambles, to lose by an innings and 156 runs, but the manner of Australia's win raised some contentious issues. New Zealand wicket-keeper Brendon McCullum was given out by umpire Steve Bucknor, caught behind off Gillespie from a ball he missed by a wide margin, and left without demur. Shortly after, Craig McMillan edged to Gilchrist, stood his ground, Bucknor rejected the appeal, and was sledged by the keeper. McMillan responded to Gilchrist that because he had once walked it did not mean everyone would do the same.

The official margin of Australia's win at Adelaide in the second Test was 213 runs, but should have read ten wickets and 213 runs as the home side declared twice. Australia's first innings stretched well into the second day for 575 for eight with Langer occupying the crease for 499 minutes to reach 215 and Hayden, Ponting, Lehmann, Gilchrist and Warne enjoying themselves with half-centuries. The one disappointment for local fans was Lehmann's dismissal for 81 when a century would have tied up his spot on the Ashes tour seven months away. It was appropriate that the tourist's only bowler, attacking or defensive, Daniel Vettori, captured five wickets. After dismissing the New Zealanders for 251, Ponting could easily have enforced the follow-on but batted again – sluggishly – before declaring four runs after the lunch break on the fourth day; it was an ugly decision, and one that showed contempt for the spectators. The visitors had no hope of surviving five sessions and succumbed on the final day with a neat symmetry for 250.

Nothing succeeds like excess and plugging a gap before the next Test against Pakistan in Perth in mid-December meant three more one-day international matches. The penchant for naming competitions also meant the creation of the Chappell-Hadlee Trophy and a 1-1 result followed. New Zealand achieved its only win in 12 matches of both forms of cricket during the summer with two balls to spare at Docklands Stadium in Melbourne; Australia won narrowly at Sydney; and the final game at Brisbane, on 10 December, was abandoned without a ball bowled.

The three-Test series against Pakistan opened at the WACA Ground five days later amid talk of a pace shoot-out between Rawalpindi Express Shoaib Akhtar and Brett Lee. Sadly, it failed to materialize. Australia stuck with their pace formula of the previous 12 months – McGrath, Gillespie and Kasprowicz – leaving Lee with the drink-waiting duties. Shoaib and Mohammad Sami struck early, reducing Australia to 78 for five but, thereafter, the home side assumed total control as Shoaib dissipated his energy with his 33-metre run-up. Local heroes Langer (191) and Gilchrist rebuilt the home side's innings of 381 with a sixth-wicket partnership of 152 and Kasprowicz vindicated the selector's continual trust in him with 5/30 to give the Australians a lead of 202. Ponting should have enforced the follow on but again batted for the accountants. He and Langer registered meaningless nineties and Martyn an even 100 before a declaration set Pakistan 564 to win with more than two full days to play. Pakistan's 72 from 31.3 overs said more about their psychological state than any demons in the pitch. It was the nagging McGrath, delivering the ball at 130kph with steepling bounce, who destroyed them. When he had taken the first seven wickets he fancied getting all ten, but Kasprowicz snatched a couple and McGrath had to settle for career-best figures of 8/24. No doubt he would have been dismayed that the man of the match award went not to himself but to Langer.

Pakistan competed for half of the match in the Boxing Day Test in Melbourne, but again fizzled out. Younis Khan and Yousuf Youhana put on 192 runs for the fourth wicket in the first innings, but that was the tourists' only sizeable stand of the match. Another century by Martyn (142) saw Australia to a narrow lead – 379 to 341 – when Shoaib grabbed a second five-wicket haul, but the collapse of the Pakistani top order at the end of the third day resulted in an easy nine-wicket win for the home side.

Australia monstered their opponents in Sydney in the New Year with another nine-wicket win with the leg-spinners playing a major role. Pakistan's modest totals of 304 and 325 were gobbled up by Australia's 568, led by Ponting's classic 207 – his first century as captain – and Gilchrist's 113, of which 86 runs came in boundaries. SCG specialist MacGill returned to the side and took 5/87 in the first innings and eight wickets in the match to Warne's five, while Danish Kaneria gathered eight wickets for the losers. Australian cricket was just too damned good or as *Wisden Australia* editor Greg Baum opined in the last edition of the almanack: 'Sad to say even in the finest of games, virtuosity, if it is sustained for too long, grows humdrum, even tedious.'

A hastily convened Tsunami Appeal Match was staged at the MCG on 10 January for victims of the Boxing Day tsunami, which had struck Aceh province in Indonesia and left a trail of destruction in Sri Lanka and on India's east coast. The match was played in a carnival spirit between an ICC World XI and an ACC Asian XI and resulted in a win to the former by 344 runs to 232. Ponting, McGrath, Gilchrist, Hayden and Warne appeared for the World XI and Ponting played the innings of the match with 115 from 102 balls. More importantly, 70,000 spectators attended and $14.6 million was raised for World Vision.

The way of the future was revealed on 13 January 2005 when Australia A defeated Pakistan by 56 runs in the first authorized Twenty20 match played in Australia at the Adelaide Oval. The most important statistic was undoubtedly the size of the crowd: 21,254. The marketeers would be leaping out of their skins.

They needed something new because the VB Series demanded reform. Although the number of preliminary matches was reduced from eight to six, the West Indies were poor third performers. Brian Lara may have ignited the Adelaide Oval crowd with a sublime innings of 156 in a substantial win over Pakistan but, that innings apart, spectator interest in the West Indies was scant. Australia won four of their five completed first-round matches, but had to struggle in their two finals wins over Pakistan. Brett Lee and McGrath were in outstanding form in both matches, as they were in the series as a whole.

Australia would have made a clean sweep on its nine-match tour of New Zealand had fog and drizzle not interrupted proceedings at Wellington's Basin Reserve. Starting with the first-ever Twenty20 International at Eden Park, Auckland, on 17 February, it ended at the same ground on the 29 March. Ricky Ponting came frustratingly close to recording the first Twenty20 century, when he reached 98 not out from just 55 balls, as Australia totalled 214 to the Kiwis 170. They then won all five of their one-day matches, four by large margins, with Ponting recording the highest individual score of the series with 141 not out (from 127 balls) at Napier.

Australia won the Test series 2-0. Batting first at Lancaster Park, Christchurch, Hamish Marshall posted a maiden Test century out of 433, in which McGrath laboured honestly for his figures of 6/115. New Zealand seemed to be in control of the match when Australia slumped to 201 for six in reply, but Simon Katich (118) and rescue-man Gilchrist (121) stunned the Black Caps with a seventh-wicket partnership of 212 in less than three hours as the Australians finished one run behind. What had the makings of becoming a great contest ended quickly, however, as the New Zealand batsmen crumbled against Warne's sharp-spinning leg-breaks out of the bowlers' footmarks. Australia's spin wizard ended the innings with 5/39.

Half the match was lost to rain at Wellington, but there was still time for two glorious innings by Martyn (165) and Gilchrist (162 from 146 balls) as well as a sixth-wicket partnership of 256 runs out of 570 for eight declared, to which the home side's ineffectual reply was 244 and 48 for three. To give extra credit to Gilchrist, he overlooked the early starting time on the third morning and was swimming in the team's hotel pool with his son when alerted to the fact. After being rushed to the ground he arrived just a quarter of an hour before the start of the game.

The third Test at Auckland brought another nine-wicket trouncing for the home side. Ponting's 110 in a first innings of 383 and 86 not out (from 84 balls) gave him the man of the match award after New Zealand had been dismissed for 292 and 254. Gilchrist made 343 runs at the colossal average of 171.50 and Ponting, Martyn, Langer and Katich all more than 60, while McGrath and Warne were in ominous form with 18 and 17 wickets respectively. The international players could now rest for a couple of months. England be warned.

Back in Australia the first-class season had run its course. Tasmania won the ING Cup by defeating Queensland by seven wickets with 17 balls to spare at the Gabba – their second one-day trophy and first piece of silverware for 26 years. Discarded international one-day player, Michael Bevan, headed the aggregates and averages with 590 runs at

86.50 and Shaun Tait led the wicket-takers with 21 wickets at 19.90. New South Wales won the Pura Cup – their 44th state title – in a thrilling final at the Gabba by one wicket, an enormous effort given that the three leading runscorers for the state had all left. Steve and Mark Waugh had retired and Bevan had transferred to Tasmania. In a topsy-turvy game the home side batted first and was bowled out on a green wicket for 102. New South Wales then made 188. Queensland's Martin Love (116) scored the only century of the game to give the northern state a lead of 182. At 158 for four New South Wales seemed home and hosed, but then lost five wickets for three runs before the unlikely pairing of Stuart MacGill and Nathan Bracken added 22 runs to bring home the goods. In a season dominated less by the bat, the Pura Cup Player of the Year award went to Bevan for 1,464 runs at an average of 97.60 with eight centuries, but three bowlers topped 60 wickets; MacGill with 70, Tait 65 and Andy Bichel 60, all at averages of 23 or better.

The 2005 Ashes series was eagerly anticipated. Australia were playing brilliantly and were the undisputed king-pin, but England were bound to be competitive. During the course of the previous year, England had won nine, lost one and drawn two of their 12 Test matches against New Zealand and the West Indies at home, and South Africa abroad. They added two further wins against Bangladesh at home at the start of their summer.

The Tests did not begin until late July, by which time previous series had sometimes been decided. Before that came the one-day fripperies. Beginning with a Twenty20 match at Arundel on 9 June, Australia played 14 matches for seven wins, five losses, one tie and one game without a result. There were some worrying signs early on the tour with four successive losses: against England in a Twenty20 international at Southampton; against Somerset at Taunton where the county, led by centuries by South African Graeme Smith and Sri Lankan Sanath Jayasuriya, chased down a score of 342; against Bangladesh in an international at Cardiff, where Mohammed Ashraful scored a brilliant hundred; and against England at Bristol. There was also a magnificent tied final of the Natwest Series against England at Lord's on 2 July.

That final would have made a superb lead-in to the main event. Instead, there was another one-day tournament, the Natwest Challenge, which began at Headingley on 7 July, the same day that terrorist bombs in the underground railway system rocked London. The Australians were off their game that day, but secured easy wins in the last two matches. The sole first-class warm-up game came against Leicestershire and although Langer, Ponting and Martyn scored centuries, the bowlers found it difficult to remove Western Australian

Chris Rogers who made 209 in the second innings and was intent on underlining his own intentions to wear a baggy green cap some time in the future.

Maybe the best series of all time finally began at Lord's on 21 July. England fast bowler Steve Harmison was hostile and drew blood on the first morning on the way to claiming five wickets and removing Australia for 190 in 40.2 overs. However, Glenn McGrath's fast off-breaks were equally devastating, and his figures of 5/53 (and 9/82 for the match) were chiefly responsible for Australia's win by 239 runs. Only England's extrovert South African debutant Kevin Pietersen with twin fifties showed any fight. It appeared to be business as usual.

Edgbaston was the venue for one of the greatest games ever played. If McGrath hadn't trodden on a cricket ball playing touch rugby an hour before play; if Ricky Ponting hadn't put England in to bat after winning the toss – so ran the Australian excuses. But England took advantage. Andrew Flintoff came of age as a high-quality all-rounder (scoring 141 runs and taking 7/131 in the game), withstood Warne, who took 10/162 (4/116, 6/46), and broke through the Australian top order in the second innings. Even so, the Australians almost snatched the game on the fourth morning, despite trailing by 107 runs with two wickets to fall. Aggressive batting by Warne and Brett Lee reduced the target to 62, and then, incredibly, Lee and Michael Kasprowicz kept reducing it until the Queensland pace man got an inside edge from Harmison to wicket-keeper Geraint Jones to lose by two runs.

Australia were lucky to avoid defeat in a draw at Old Trafford. England captain Michael Vaughan's return to form with 166 and Simon Jones' six wickets put the home team in control after two days but the loss of most of the third day to rain gave Australia the opportunity to bat through the last day. Ponting's superb defensive innings of 156 lasted 411 minutes, although his late dismissal left Lee and McGrath to see out the last nine minutes of the game. Their survival meant that the Australians experienced similar euphoria to that of the Englishman in the previous game.

Trent Bridge saw Australia slip 1-2 behind, but not before a nail-biting fightback. England dominated the first half of the game, with a Flintoff century and a sixth-wicket partnership stand of 177 with Geraint Jones seeing them to a first-innings score of 477, and Simon Jones' reverse swing ripping through Australia for 218 with another five-wicket haul. Australia were forced to follow on for the first time since early during Allan Border's reign as captain and batted solidly in their second innings for 387. Warne and Lee then made England wobble, before the home side went on to record a nervy three-wicket win.

Australia lost the Ashes for the first time since 1989 at Kennington Oval on 12 September 2005. Rain and bad light conspired to assist

England to a draw, although just before lunch on the last day, if Warne had caught Pietersen in the slips, the match might have been won and the series saved. Earlier in the game Andrew Strauss recorded his second century of the series, and Australia threatened a big first-innings lead when Langer (105) and Hayden (138) recorded an opening partnership of 185. However, the need to bat in bad light was a significant factor in the last nine wickets falling for 103 runs. Warne bowled his heart out in each innings for 12/246 (6/122, 6/124), while Pietersen, after being given a second life, went on to brandish 158 second-innings runs with 15 fours and seven sixes.

At the end Australia had no cause for complaint. England had won most sessions of most matches and their four-man pace attack bowled a disciplined line throughout, especially to the left-hand batsmen. For Australia, McGrath slipped away after the first Test and Lee was expensive. The glaring weakness, however, was the third pace bowler, where the rapid decline of Jason Gillespie was unexpected, and neither Kasprowicz nor newcomer Shaun Tait proved effective. The aggressive solution would have been to play MacGill in company with Warne, but this not tried. In some respects the series could almost have been decided as an arm-wrestle between Warne and Flintoff: both players were outstanding. Warne took 40 wickets at 19.93 and scored 249 runs at 27.67 with a top score of 90. For the victors, Flintoff made 402 runs at an average of 40.20 and took 24 wickets at 27.29.

The Australians wasted little time in re-establishing supremacy over their rivals and the touring West Indian side the first victims in a three-Test series in November 2005, with the home side winning all three matches by margins of 379 runs, nine wickets and seven wickets.

Michael Hussey made his debut at the Gabba and continued the left-handed opening combinations as a replacement for the injured Justin Langer. Ricky Ponting (149) was the batting rock of the first-innings 435 and after the West Indies collapsed to the old firm of McGrath and Warne (5/48) for 210, Matthew Hayden (118) and Ponting with a second century (104 not out) enjoyed themselves on the way to a declaration at 283 for two. Brett Lee (5/30) and Nathan Bracken made short work of the visitors second time around.

Victorian top-order batsman Brad Hodge was the newest addition to the Australian side in Hobart where the match was decided on the first day when the West Indies folded for 149. Hayden (110) and Hussey (137) then ground the visitors pace attack into the dust with an opening partnership of 231 and it was to the tourists credit that they dismissed the Australians for 406. With the West Indies reeling on 140 for six early on the fourth day the game appeared to be over, but a surprising seventh-wicket partnership of 182 by century-making all-rounder Dwayne Bravo and wicket-keeper Darren Ramdin at least forced the home side to bat again.

Adelaide experienced the glory, and Australia's attack the stick, of Brian Lara's 226, during which he surpassed Allan Border's world-record Test run aggregate. But only Bravo with six first-innings wickets and 98 runs for the game provided significant support. Hussey (133 not out) from number five and Langer, returning to his opening spot, with 99, led a solid batting performance, while Warne's 6/80 in the second innings set up an easy victory target.

Three one-day matches for the Chappell-Hadlee Trophy were played in New Zealand at the start of December with the Kiwis staging two remarkable fightbacks after being outclassed in the first match at Auckland, which they lost by 147 runs, and where Lee returned the niggardly analysis of 6/4/5/3. At Wellington's Westpac Stadium, Andrew Symonds blasted the ball to all points of the compass in his commanding innings of 156 from 127 balls that contained eight sixes. Symonds and Michael Clarke added 220 in a fifth-wicket stand that took Australia to 322 for five, but New Zealand threatened to steal the game until they were dismissed two runs short with one ball to spare. In contrast to his earlier effort in Auckland, Lee's figures this time round were 1/85 from ten overs. The final game, in Christchurch, saw the Black Caps amazingly overhaul Australia's even higher total of 331 for seven, with one over to spare.

By this time the South African tourists had arrived in Australia for a three-Test series that saw the visitors salvage a hard-fought draw in the opening game in Perth before Australia's second great 16-match winning sequence began in Melbourne.

Makhaya Ntini's five wickets gave the visitors the early advantage at the WACA as Australia was dismissed for 258, but Lee led the home attack with 5/93 to bring the Australians back into the game on the second day. In just his third Test match, Hodge then emulated his former state team-mate Dean Jones by making his first Test century a double (203 not out) before Ponting declared at 528 for eight, giving Warne more than four sessions to bowl out his opponents. He had rarely let his skippers down in the past, but although the leg-spinner delivered 47 teasing overs, he found Jacques Rudolph's obdurate defence in a seven-hour century too difficult to penetrate.

Phil Jacques became Hayden's third opening partner for the summer (again as a stand-in for Langer) in the Melbourne Test, which Australia won by 184 runs after a batting collapse on the first day. With the home side reaching 154 for one and Hayden and Ponting in control shortly before tea, it was a surprise that after Ponting left for 117, the side slumped to 239 for eight at stumps. An even more unlikely scene, however, unfolded the following morning, as McGrath (11) survived for two hours and supported Hussey (122) in a last-wicket stand of 107 out of 355. South Africa replied with 311 and a Hayden century (137) was the brick and mortar in Australia's second innings of 321 for seven declared. For the second time the Proteas had to bat for four sessions to avoid defeat, and when they lost six wickets before stumps the game seemed as good as over. Australia completed the win the following day.

South Africa made a strong attempt to win in Sydney. Centuries for Jacques Kallis and Ashwell Prince helped them to 451 in 11 hours in their first innings and a second-innings declaration set Australia a respectable target of 287 on the last afternoon. However, twin centuries for Ponting (120 and a murderous 143 not out from 159 balls) gave Australia an easy eight-wicket win. The six home Tests saw Ponting, newcomer Hussey, and Hayden in superlative form, with Ponting registering 844 runs at 93.77 with five centuries, and Hussey and Hayden each scoring three tons. Lee and Warne led the attack with 31 and 30 wickets respectively.

Damien Martyn's 96 from 56 balls dominated Australia's 95-run win in the first Twenty20 international match against South Africa in Brisbane on 9 January 2006, after which the VB Series was contested with Sri Lanka as the third team. The one-day international matches were even more one-sided than normal, with Australia winning six of its first-round matches compared to three each for their opponents. However, Sri Lanka produced an upset victory in the first final at Adelaide Oval before Australia came back with emphatic wins at Sydney and Brisbane. The home side was in trouble at 10 for three in the second final, but Ponting (127) and Andrew Symonds (151) then mugged the Sri Lankan attack with a fourth-wicket partnership of 237 out of an eventual total of 5-368 and a winning margin of 167. In the deciding match, Sri Lanka set a solid score of 266 only for Adam Gilchrist (122) to produce a St Valentine's Day massacre. He slayed the bowlers and reached his hundred off a mere 67 balls as he and fellow opener Simon Katich (107 not out) posted an opening stand of 196 in just 32.2 overs to set up a nine-wicket win. Gilchrist's 432 runs in the tournament came at the impressive strike rate of 113.08 per 100 balls.

Unfortunately the summer was spoilt by off-field racism. Cricket Australia was forced to review its security policy after problems in each of the three South African Tests continued in the one-day arena. A spectator was evicted from the Gabba for a verbal assault on Shaun Pollock; and former international player, and the ICC's regional security chief, Jonty Rhodes, was punched by a drunken spectator at Melbourne's Telstra Dome. In addition, five spectators were ejected from Adelaide Oval on Australia Day for calling the Sri Lankan players "black cunts", the same expression Darren Lehmann had used three years earlier during a VB Series match against Sri Lanka. Following the incidents, Cricket Australia's chief executive James Sutherland called for lifetime bans on supporters found guilty of racial abuse.

Australia's return series in South Africa began with a two-run loss in a Twenty20 match at the New Wanderers Stadium, Johannesburg on 24 February and continued with the home team gaining a 3-2 win in the one-day matches that followed. Australia lost the first two one-day games by margins of six wickets and a massive 196 runs, but returned to even the score following narrow wins at Port Elizabeth and Durban. The last limited-over game at Johannesburg on 12 March saw the South Africans in the greatest run chase of all. Australia posted a world record 434 for four with skipper Ponting's 164 from 105 balls, including nine sixes, coming from what Cricinfo reporter Andrew Miller termed "an innings of cultured clubbing". No one could imagine the Proteas getting anywhere near it, but galvanized by Graeme Smith's 90 from 55 balls and Herschelle Gibbs' exhilarating 175 from 111 balls at the top of the order, they did so with one ball to spare.

The South Africans had the momentum flowing their way but the absence of Shaun Pollock from their first Test team at Cape Town four days later was crucial on a bouncy, seaming pitch. Stuart Clark made his Test debut as a replacement for Glenn McGrath who stayed at home to care for his wife, Jane, who was undergoing her third bout of cancer treatment. Clark captured 5/55 out of 205 in the first innings and ended up with figures of 9/89 for the match. Hayden and Ponting's second-wicket partnership of 154 in the first innings was the only substantial stand in the game and Australia had little difficulty sweeping to a seven-wicket victory inside three days.

Ponting's third set of twin centuries (103 and 116) and his second innings second-wicket partnership of 201 with Hayden (102) were the core of Australia's 369 and 307 for four declared at the Kingsmead Ground, Durban. Although Kallis worked long and hard for a hundred in South Africa's first innings of 267 Lee's fire in his 5/69, and Warne's guile in his second-innings 6/86, decided the series by 112 runs.

Lee and Michael Kasprowicz overcame their Edgbaston nightmare by adding 19 runs to give Australia a two-wicket win in the final Test at Johannesburg in early April. The game was an even contest between bat and ball: South Africa's 303 and 258 against Australia's 270 left the visitors needing 292 to win in the final innings. After Australia became the leading Test nation in the mid-1990s they would occasionally lose dead-rubber matches. Not now. Modern wearers of the baggy green possess an insatiable desire for success. Although Ntini proved a wonderful go-to man with match figures of 10/178, such desire carried Damien Martyn to a valiant 101 on a difficult pitch, and Lee to the man of the match award for his six wickets and 88 runs. One man who didn't experience much of the final game was Justin Langer, who was appearing in his 100th Test match. Langer turned into a Ntini bouncer, was concussed before he had scored a run, and played no further part in proceedings, although he was padded up ready to enter the fight had either Lee or Kasprowicz fallen.

Back home, the domestic season had ended. South Australian captain Darren Lehmann's frustration at losing the ING Cup final by one wicket led to an outburst that saw him charged by Cricket Australia for his comments. Lehmann was annoyed by the early start (at 9.30am), believing that losing the toss on a moist pitch contributed to the Redbacks being dismissed for 154. As he told the Adelaide *Advertiser*: "Cricket Australia need to work out if they want a decent final. It ended up being a great final only because we bowled well."

In fact, it was speedster Shaun Tait who bowled brilliantly with 6/41, which led to the Blues squeezing home by one wicket after Stuart MacGill leg-glanced Lehmann for a single. In so doing, New South Wales grabbed their fourth one-day title in succession; on the other hand, South Australia's performance was their best result in the competition for ten years. For ING it marked the end of their 14-year association with the competition and they were on the receiving end of another Lehmann parting shot: "Thank God we might be changing sponsors. That might allow us to play at different times. I don't know whether I can say that, but I have." Blues opening batsman Phil Jaques was the outstanding batsman in the competition (with 683 runs at an average of 85.37 with four centuries), while Tait gathered 14 wickets (at 13.28) from five games.

The Pura Cup competition was a closely fought affair with all states having a chance of reaching the final as they entered the final round of games. As it turned out, Queensland played hosts to Victoria and the final was the most one-sided of all. After Victoria were dismissed on the second morning for 344, Queensland batted until late on the fourth day to reach a gigantic 900 for six declared, the third highest score in Australian first-class cricket, and the only occasion in which four batsmen – captain Jimmy Maher (223), Martin Love (169), Shane Watson (201 retired hurt) and Clinton Perren (173) – topped 150 runs in the same innings. The score was a payback to the Victorians for the final two years earlier, and the visitors were bowled out in their second innings for 202 to leave Queensland celebrating an innings-and-354-run victory. Left-arm pace bowler Mitchell Johnson took 10/106 (4/55, 6/51) in the game, but the stars of the competition were retired Test player Lehmann, who scored 1168 runs at an average of 89.84; Jason Gillespie, who kept his name under the notice of Test selectors with 40 wickets at 21.27; and Andy Bichel (who didn't) with 50 wickets at 26.68.

Gillespie was recalled to the Australian team for its short tour of Bangladesh in April as he and Johnson took the pace spots of Kasprowicz and Tait, who had both picked up injuries in South Africa. Jaques also returned to the side as a replacement for Langer.

Bangladesh had won one match against an understrength Zimbabwe in six years of Test cricket, but gave Australia several almighty frights in the first game at the Narayanganj Osmani Stadium in Fatullah. On the first day, with opening batsman Shahriah Nafees making his first Test century and captain Habibul Bashar in full flight, they reached 238 for one in the 51st over. Then, on the second day, after being out for 427, they reduced Australia to 93 for six late in the afternoon. Opening bowlers Lee and Clark, who had demonized the South Africans, were ineffective, but the bowler who was really put to the sword was Warne, whose figures of 0/112 from 20 overs brought back memories of his first appearance in Sri Lanka in 1992. Instead, Australia had to be thankful for his leg-spin partner MacGill, who captured his Test-best analysis of 8/108. Left-arm orthodox spinner Mohammad Rafique's five wickets were chiefly responsible for the Australian slip, but Adam Gilchrist came out of his own form slump with a brilliant 144, which pushed the total to 269. The Bangladeshis collapsed the second time around, but a victory target of 306 still left the Australians with plenty of work to do. Had Rafique had stronger spin support they might not have made it, but a masterly captain's innings by Ponting (118) saw Australia home by three wickets.

A swift look at the result of the second Test at Chittagong, with an Australian victory by an innings and 80 runs, might suggest a return to order. The numbers told a different story, however. After Gillespie swept away the first three batsmen with just 17 runs on the board, the Bangladeshis reached 197, to which Australia replied with 76 for one at stumps. The strangest statistic of the day was not Gillespie's 3/11 from five overs, but that he was 5 not out. Steve Waugh as captain had banned nightwatchmen as ignoble: Ponting had restored them. Gillespie would have been expected to be out early the next day. Instead, he was still there at the end of it with 102 runs to his name. And he was still there when the innings closed, having batted for 574 minutes, faced 425 balls, shared partnerships of 53 with Jaques, 90 with Ponting, 320 with Martyn (who scored a brilliant 182 from 203 balls), and 51 with Michael Clarke. When Ponting declared at 581 for four Gillespie had made not only his first century in first-class cricket, but in any class of cricket. He was also amused that his 201 not out topped the highest Test scores of team-mates like Martyn and former team-mates Steve and Mark Waugh. Warne (5/113) and MacGill then ran through Bangladesh's solid second innings of 304 to give Australia seven wins in a row. Three easy one-day wins followed. However, the question posed most often by buffs during the winter was whether the Australian selectors would drop a man who had made a double-century when they picked the side for the next Test against England in November.

Malaysia in September saw an early start to the 2006-07 season. The DLF Cup involved Australia, the West Indies and India in a tri-series format with all matches staged at the Kinrara Academy Oval, Kuala Lumpur. Australia won two of the four preliminary matches with one game against India ending with no result. They then trounced the West Indies in the final.

Next followed the ICC's Champions Cup, a ridiculous one-day competition in which all Test-playing countries took part, and which was held in India in October and November 2006 less than five months before the ICC World Cup. Australia won four out of five matches, including another anti-climactic final against the West Indies less than three weeks before the first Test against England in Brisbane.

The Ashes series of 2006-07 could never be expected to live up to the pre-tour hyperbole, but neither would anyone have imagined that it would fall so far short of expectations.

Just fourteen months had passed between Australia losing the Ashes at The Oval and tilting for them again at the Gabba. During that time each side had played four series, but whereas Australia had won ten and drawn one game, England had won five, lost four and drawn four matches. Australia had a stable side; England, on the other hand, did not. When they arrived in Australia the English team was a muddle. Captain in abeyance Michael Vaughan had not played a Test for nearly a year, but was on his way to Australia claiming that he would be available for the third Test; and spin bowler Ashley Giles, who had not made a single appearance during the English first-class summer, may have passed a fitness test, but where was his form?

The tour turned out to be a financial bonanza but, as a contest, the cricket itself was dismal. Wayward English bowling in the opening match saw the Australians seize the initiative and Ponting's 196 dominated a huge total of 602 for nine declared. Australia's line and length men, Glenn McGrath (6/50) and Stuart Clark, then took control so that Ponting's second declaration at 202 for one, including an easy Langer hundred, gave England the mere matter of 653 runs to chase for victory. They were never going to threaten that but a fourth-wicket partnership of 153 by Paul Collingwood and Kevin Pietersen and a fourth-innings total of 370 at least put some wind in their sails.

The wind certainly dropped on the last day of the second Test at Adelaide when England's timid batting allowed Shane Warne to gain psychological mastery and Australia stole a game they shouldn't have had a ghost's chance of winning to build a 2-0 series lead. Earlier Collingwood (206) and Pietersen's (158) dominant fourth-wicket partnership of 310 had pushed England to 551 for six declared and appeared to push McGrath (0/107) and Warne (1/167) into the has-been category. At 65 for three Australia were in trouble, but a muffed catch from Ponting allowed the home side to get back into the game. While Ponting (142) was scratchy in his first 50 runs his innings grew in authority in building a fourth-wicket stand of 192 with Hussey, before Michael Clarke (124) provided the spine for the rest of the innings of 513. Matthew Hoggard gave an outstanding performance of cut and swing bowling with figures of 7/108. At the end of the fourth day, England led by 97 with nine wickets remaining and a draw was a foregone conclusion. Except for the visitors' lamentable defensive batting, and except for Warne's remarkable form reversal with second-innings figures of 32/12/49/4, which enabled Australia to have a late dash and gain a comfortable six-wicket win. Damien Martyn's sudden retirement announcement after scores of 29, 11 and 5 shook his team-mates and he admitted that he might lose friends. However, he added: "But I also said to myself that if I stayed doing what I was doing I may lose respect for myself and the friendship of those around me." Six weeks later, Martyn said that he had "never been comfortable with the whole celebrity stuff that comes with the game" and found it hard to deal with. It was a reminder that sporting pressures can be great and few players go out in glory.

At Perth, the Ashes were regained in another turnaround game. On the first day, Harmison found his radar and Monty Panesar (5/92) provided aggressive spin to remove Australia for 244, but England failed to capitalize and were dismissed for 215. In their second innings, Australia were at their rampaging best in scoring 527 for five declared at 4.70 runs per over. Hayden, Ponting, Hussey (103) and Clarke (135 not out) all scored fast enough, but the dynamite was provided by Gilchrist, whose 102 not out (12 fours and four sixes) came from 59 balls, just three more than the fastest century in Test history by Vivian Richards. England were left with more than two days to make 557 and though Alistair Cook's hundred and second-wicket partnership of 170 with Ian Bell gave them a small sniff of hope, Australia triumphed by 206 runs.

The only sniff England gave in Melbourne was that of a stinking corpse. Australia's great heroes, Shane Warne and Glenn McGrath, had determined to call it a day regarding Test cricket at the end of the series and Justin Langer decided to throw in his kit as well. Melbourne provided a great send-off for favourite son Warne and he obliged on Boxing Day with 5/39 as England crumbled to be all out for 159. England's bowlers fought back to have Australia 84 for five on the second morning, but inept captaincy by Andrew Flintoff failed to support potential danger men Harmison and Panesar with anything like adequate field settings. The result was that good mates Matthew Hayden (153) and Andrew Symonds (156), who had thus far appeared out of his depth in Test cricket, were able to consolidate and then smash the attack in a sixth-wicket stand of 279 on the way to a total of 419. Australia had little trouble achieving a three-day win by an innings and 99 runs.

Sydney would provide the answer to whether Ricky Ponting's team would be able to emulate Warwick Armstrong's whitewash of England in the 1920-21 series. Yes. England made a modest 291 in the first innings, to which Australia replied with 393, but then fell apart in the second innings for 147 giving the home team an easy ten-wicket win on the fourth afternoon. While Sydney is usually a spinners' paradise, on this occasion it was the pace men who did the damage by taking 17 of the 20 wickets. McGrath finished with 6/105 from 50 overs in the match compared to Warne's two wickets, although the leg-spinner had the satisfaction of top scoring with 71 in his only innings. Hussey (458 runs at 91.60) and Ponting (576 runs at 82.28) led the batting averages while Clarke, Symonds and Hayden also topped 50. Each of Australia's four main bowlers – Clark, McGrath, Warne and Lee – topped 20 wickets, with Clark recording the outstanding figures of 26 wickets at 17.03. Only Pietersen, for England, averaged more than 50.

The three retirees – Warne, McGrath and Langer – led their teammates out on the last day and at the end they left mountainous career statistics behind them. Warne was the world's leading Test wicket-taker with 708 wickets at an average of 25.41 from 145 Tests; McGrath was the leading pace bowler with 563 wickets at 21.64 from 124 Tests; and Langer made 7,696 runs at an average of 45.27 and 23 centuries from 105 Tests. Not since Dennis Lillee, Greg Chappell and Rod Marsh made their exodus from the game at Sydney 23 years before had two giants and one player of stature left the side at the one time. They would then leave for different destinations: Langer for the Pura Cup and county cricket with Somerset; Warne to bide his time before two seasons with Hampshire; and McGrath for the coming one-day international series and the climax of the World Cup.

The Commonwealth Bank replaced Carlton & United Breweries as the sponsor of the one-day competition in January and February, which, its critics argued, had itself become a corpse, and there was a minimal change of name from VB to CB Series. Australia won seven of its eight qualifying games to three by England and two by New Zealand, but England then produced the shock of the summer by defeating Australia in both finals. Chasing 252 at Melbourne, Paul Collingwood's century saw England gain victory by four wickets with three balls to spare. Then, in a rain-affected game at Sydney, England posted 246 and Australia were left to score 187 from 27 overs under Duckworth-Lewis rules, but were only able to muster 152.

Two one-day losses in a row would not a summer break, but five successive losses on the advent of the World Cup was more disturbing. The Australians (and the Kiwis for that matter) probably needed yet another one-day competition like a hole in the head, but the Chappell-Hadlee Trophy had been scheduled in New Zealand in mid-February.

Ricky Ponting and Adam Gilchrist were rested for this event, but no one would have expected the change in the New Zealanders' performances. At Wellington, on a pitch providing steep bounce and movement, fast bowler Shane Bond continued his outstanding efforts against Australia with 5/23 and only acting captain Michael Hussey provided resistance as his side was put out for 148. Lou Vincent and Kiwi skipper Stephen Fleming had no trouble knocking off the runs in 27 overs for a ten-wicket win. If this win was unexpected the next two run chases were even more astonishing. At Eden Park, Auckland, Hussey's 105 (from 84 balls) and Brad Hodge's 97 (from 86 balls) led Australia to 336 for four, but remarkable hitting by century-maker Ross Taylor, Peter Fulton and Craig McMillan's 52 (from 30 balls) saw New Zealand to 340 for five with eight balls remaining. This was the second-highest run chase in one-day history and it held its place for two days. At Seddon Park, Hamilton, on 20 February, Matthew Hayden's 181 not out from 166 balls was the highest individual score by an Australia in one-day history, but the total of 346 for five was run down, even more fantastically after New Zealand had lost their first four wickets for 41 runs. Craig McMillan's 67-ball century, and Brendon McCullum's 86 at nearly a run a ball, were the mainstays for the Kiwis, who reached their target with three balls to spare. With Brett Lee resting an ankle injury, the bowlers had let Australia down in the last two matches and as a disappointed Hussey put it, the team "had work to do" before the World Cup began in the West Indies in five weeks time. Fortunately, Australia's international players were finally given a chance to rest.

The Australian domestic season had still to run its course. In the Ford Ranger One-Day Cup, a century in the final at the Melbourne Cricket Ground by Queensland captain Jimmy Maher earned the Bulls their first one-day title since 1997-98. The player of the series was South Australian opener Matthew Elliott with 465 runs at 51.66, who showed that he retained his quality in the short form of the game, while disappointing at first-class level since his transfer from Victoria. The leading wicket-taker was Queensland all-rounder James Hopes, with 20 wickets at 21.05. Western Australian reserve wicket-keeper Luke Ronchi played the fastest innings in one-day domestic history with a 56 ball hundred against New South Wales.

Tasmania finally achieved their cricket dream on 23 March 2007 when they defeated New South Wales to win the Pura Cup for the first time. The competition was closely contested by five states, with South Australia saving themselves from complete embarrassment by winning their final game of the year.

Hosting the final at Bellerive Oval, the Tigers achieved a comprehensive victory with scores of 340 and 460 against 230 and 149, a margin of 421 runs. While the overall win may have been a team effort the standout players in the final were young all-rounder Luke Butterworth, opening bowler Ben Hilfenhaus, wicket-keeper Sean Clingeleffer, and veteran pace man Damien Wright. Chris Rogers was the player of the season, with 1,202 runs at an average of 70.70, and fast-medium bowler Hilfenhaus led the bowling aggregates, with 60 wickets at 25.38.

At the close of the ninth World Cup, staged in the West Indies, Cricinfo editor Sambit Bal wrote: "In the end it will be remembered for the bad, ugly and terrible. A horrible death [of Pakistan coach Bob Woolmer], underperformances [by India and Pakistan], resignations, sackings and retirements kept us busy. The legacy of this vast and meaningless World Cup will be despair and emptiness. It couldn't have ended sooner."

It wasn't that bad for everyone, but even the Australians – who enjoyed unprecedented success – would have been happy had the end come sooner. Australia, attempting to win a World Cup treble (after previous successes in 1999 and 2003), were again led by Ricky Ponting (Tasmania) with New South Welshmen Nathan Bracken, Stuart Clark, Michael Clarke, Brad Haddin, Brett Lee and Glenn McGrath; Matthew Hayden, Mitchell Johnson, Andrew Symonds and Shane Watson from Queensland; Western Australians Adam Gilchrist, Brad Hogg and Michael Hussey; South Australian Shaun Tait; and Victorian Brad Hodge.

It was a powerful, well-balanced outfit that not only quickly disposed of the February one-day cobwebs against England and New Zealand, but did not come under threat in any of its 11 matches. When batting first, they posted 300-plus scores in five games, including a highest score of 377 for six against South Africa at Basseterre, St Kitts; and, when chasing generally small targets, they defeated Bangladesh in 13.5 overs, Ireland in 12.2 overs, and South Africa – in a semi-final – in 31.3 overs. The only scores over 200 they had to overcome were against England and Sri Lanka at the Super Eight stage, and they did so with a minimum of fuss. In the final against Sri Lanka, at Kensington Oval, Barbados, on 28 April, they reached 281 for four from 38 overs due to a glorious innings of 149 from 104 balls by Adam Gilchrist. The result was never in doubt and the official margin was 53 runs under Duckworth Lewis. Almost inevitably the match ended in farce, as Cricinfo's Andrew Miller reported:

> It was too dark for the fielders to see anything, let alone any of the fans in the stadium or the press in the gantry, and besides, the Australians had already celebrated their moment of victory. That came after the sixth ball of the 33rd over, when the Sri Lankans – to all intents and purposes – accepted the offer of bad light, and appeared to have conceded the game with an improbable requirement of 63 from 18 balls.
>
> What happened next will doubtless be the subject of blame-games, buck-passing and recriminations. Australia's celebratory huddle was broken up by a tap on the shoulder from the umpire Aleem Dar; the groundstaff who had been unpegging the onfield logos were told to nail them back down and reposition the pitch markers, and out trooped the players to block their way into the twilight. It was asinine, undignified, and entirely appropriate for a tournament that long since detached itself from the origins of sporting contests.

As an indicator of Australia's dominance during the tournament, Shane Watson led the batting averages with 145.00; Matthew Hayden had the highest aggregate runs total with 659 and three centuries; Glenn McGrath, in his last tournament, led the bowling aggregate and average stakes (26 wickets at 13.73); Shaun Tait was equal second in the bowling aggregates with 23 wickets; and Brad Hogg and Nathan Bracken were fourth and fifth in the bowling averages. Their cup win was well deserved, and they could now put their feet up for the winter.

# Chapter 43

## A New Game?

Ponting's captaincy continued, but now it was a new game. The 2007-08 season began with the first Twenty20 World Cup in South Africa in September. It proved successful for the ICC, partly because of its compact programming, but also because the monotony of Australian victories was broken in the hit-and-miss game. A surprising opening loss to Zimbabwe was followed by wins over England and Bangladesh, a loss against Pakistan, a win against Sri Lanka, and a loss to eventual winners India in the semi-final in Durban. Although caution was expressed about the amount of Twenty20 matches that should be slotted into the calendar, the fact that even seasoned observers were claiming it as the way of the future had an ominous ring.

India's narrow win over Pakistan in the final led some local TV channels to bill their one-day series against Australia, which began on 29 September in Bangalore, as a "battle of the champions" – a ludicrous suggestion given the overall dominance of the visitors. Australia provided a swift reality check by winning a sometimes-spiteful series, in which Andrew Symonds was the butt of crowd racial abuse, 4-2 with one game ending without a result. India's only consolation prize was its win in the single Twenty20 match at Mumbai on 20 October.

Sri Lanka began its short tour of Australia a week later with the first of two back-to-back Tests for the Warne-Muralitharan Trophy, another named event, beginning at Brisbane on 8 November. There was a good deal of interest in these matches, because for Australia they represented the first after Warne and McGrath's retirement, and with a new opening batsman having to be found for Langer. They also had added piquancy with Sri Lankan spinner Muttiah Muralitharan needing just nine wickets to surpass Warne's Test wicket aggregate. When the Australian selections were made, Queensland left-arm quick Mitchell Johnson won the nod over Shaun Tait as the new pace man, Phil Jaques came in for Langer, and Stuart MacGill came in for Warne.

Mahela Jayawardene won the toss at the Gabba, but immediately lost the initiative by sending Australia in to bat and watching them compile an imposing 551 for four declared and go on to record an easy win by an innings and 40 runs. Jacques (100), Michael Hussey (133) and Michael Clarke (145 not out) each cracked centuries, with Hussey and Clarke enjoying a fourth-wicket partnership of 245. Brett Lee bowled with purpose as leader of the attack to take 8/113 in the match (4/26, 4/87) as Sri Lanka was dismissed for 211 and 300. MacGill was steady, suffered from dropped catches, but brought up the significant milestone of 200 wickets in his 41st Test.

At Hobart, the Australian batsmen again mauled the visitors' attack with declared innings of 542 for five and 210 for two. Jaques (150) and Hussey (132) made their second centuries in successive matches and Muralitharan had to pay 100 runs for each of his four wickets in the series. It was as though the Australian batsmen were determined to protect Warne and were saying to Murali: 'You won't take the record on our patch." Jayawardene's hundred was the highlight of Sri Lanka's first-innings 246, but even this superb effort was surpassed when the visitors were set 507 runs to win in the second, as Kumar Sangakkara displayed masterly batsmanship in his blazing 192 out of a total of 410. Lee's second eight-wicket haul gave him 16 wickets and the award for player of the series.

This Australian season had an odd shape: no Test matches for five weeks until Boxing Day against India; a swag of Pura Cup matches; and plugging the international gap, the Chappell-Hadlee Trophy. New Zealand's tour saw Australia win a single Twenty20 match in Perth and two of three one-day internationals in Adelaide and Brisbane, with the Sydney game having no result. After just three years there were mutterings that this annual event had already run its course.

Anil Kumble gained India's Test captaincy at the age of thirty-seven and this fine cricket warrior had no shortage of leadership skills in his ranks with former captains Rahul Dravid, Sourav Ganguly and Sachin Tendulkar on hand, along with one-day international leader M.S. Dhoni. With Virender Sehwag and Irfan Pathan also returning to the side India had additional competitive spirit, but a grave error was made when neither of these two players were chosen in the first two Tests. Chinaman bowler and one-day specialist Brad Hogg came into the Australian Test side for his first match in four years in place of MacGill, who had undergone an operation for carpal tunnel syndrome following the Hobart Test.

Australia won the first Test at Melbourne by the convincing margin of 337 runs. Fine spin bowling by Kumble got the Indians off to a good start and 343 was only a modest total after an opening partnership of 135 and Hayden (124) had gone on to his sixth century at the MCG. However, the visitors reply was supine and Rahul Dravid had to take much of the blame with a strokeless innings of 6 from 66 balls at the top of the order; 196 was a poor effort. The Australians declared their second innings at 351 for seven and had no trouble completing a win on the fourth afternoon.

Ponting's team equalled the performance of Steve Waugh's Australian side of 16 successive wins following a controversial 122-run win in Sydney. The numbers showed that Australia made 463 in its first innings with Andrew Symonds top scoring with an undefeated 162 to which India replied with 523, with centuries for V.V.S. Laxman and Tendulkar, and Lee capturing 5/119. Hayden (123) and Hussey (145 not out) then led the way before Australia's second-innings declaration came with the score on 401 for seven, before India were dismissed for 210. Disputes raised during and after the match were twofold: they related first to poor decisions made by umpires Steve Bucknor and Mark Benson, which favoured the home side about seven to one and had a significant effect on the result; and second to the conviction (and suspension for three Tests) of Harbhajan Singh, on circumstantial evidence, for the racial abuse of Symonds – he called him a "big monkey".

The first issue brought to a head the persistent appealing by the Australians over several years and the resultant mental disintegration of the umpires. India protested against Australia's manner of winning. The second issue revealed the flaws in administrative law with match referee Mike Procter taking the word of three Australian players against three Indians. What no doubt rubbed salt into the Indian wounds was Symonds' admission during the match that he was out for 30 in the first innings – and his subsequent man of the match award.

The Indians bounced back with a strong win in Perth where the scoring was modest – 330 and 294 by the visitors and 212 and 340 by the home side – and a heavy scoring draw in Adelaide. Tendulkar played a special innings of 153 at Adelaide for his first century on the ground, but Ponting made little attempt to dismiss the lower order on the second afternoon as they totalled 526. Australia's reply was impressive, with 563 and three century-makers in the innings. Hayden (103) made his third hundred of the series, Ponting battled hard to regain form in his 140 and Clarke reached 118. The game petered to a draw, although without a scorching 151 by Sehwag out of 269 for seven Australia might have forced a win. The shock of the match was the sudden announcement of his retirement by Adam Gilchrist, prompted by dropping an easy catch in India's first innings. Australia's master-blaster brought down the curtain on a 96-Test career that yielded 5,570 runs at an average of 47.60 with 17 centuries and 416 dismissals (379 catches, 37 stumpings) to hold a unique place in his country's cricket history.

In the end Australia took the series 2-1, with one draw, when a drawn series would probably have been fairer. Hayden and Symonds topped the Australian run list with 410 at respective averages of 82.00 and 68.33, and Lee again led the wicket-takers with 24 at 22.58. For India, Sachin Tendulkar, feted at every ground on what was seen as a farewell tour, made 493 runs at 70.42, while Kumble took 20 wickets.

The Indians had a win with Harbhajan's appeal to the ICC Appeals Commissioner, Justice John Hansen the day after the end of the Adelaide Test. Harbhajan's charge was reduced from the more serious Level 3 to a Level 2 offence of abuse and insult and the ban was turned into a fine. In making his decision, Hansen pointed to the importance of context and of Harbhajan replying to a vulgar epithet ("fuck") from Symonds. What he did not comment on was historical context. Three months earlier, in the one-day series in India, Harbhajan had claimed the Australians had targeted him with "personal and vulgar words" and added: "They think you cannot fight back and they do not like it when you do."

What led to Symonds' epithet in Sydney was revealing. At the end of a Brett Lee over Harbhajan had patted Lee on his backside. The action was interpreted by some observers as friendly, even congratulatory, but not by Symonds. Under questioning from the advocate for Harbhajan and the Board for the Cricket Council of India (BCCI), Vasha Manohar, about whether he objected to that pat, Symonds replied: 'Did I have an objection to it – my objection was that a Test match is no place to be friendly with an opposition player, is my objection.' On that reply, Hansen observed: 'If that is his view, I hope it not one shared by all international cricketers. It would be a sad day for cricket if it is.'

The last CB Series followed in February and early March. Although Australia won five of their eight qualifying matches, they lost both finals to India and big guns Ponting and Symonds appeared to have their minds on other things – possibly the Indian Premier League (IPL) – as they compiled less than 400 runs between them in ten matches. Nathan Bracken captured the man of the series award with 21 wickets, but Australia's leading batsman was fifth-placed Gilchrist with 322 runs at a strike rate of 98.17, including a dazzling 118 against Sri Lanka in Perth. Unfortunately Gilchrist's international career ended with a whimper as he contributed just 2 runs from three balls in the second final in Brisbane to give him 9,619 runs at 35.89 and 16 centuries in 287 one-day internationals to go with 472 dismissals.

Unfortunately, the mud-slinging continued and Harbhajan was at the centre of much of it. When Matthew Hayden called him an "obnoxious weed" on radio on 26 February, the spirit of cricket was truly diluted. The antipathy between some Indian and Australian players was curious given that vast sums of money were being spent by Indian leagues for Twenty20 cricket. On 14 February, Cricket Australia confirmed its policy on player participation in unofficial cricket events. It stated that selectors would treat players who took part in ICC-approved matches more favourably than those who did not; and that players would not be offered contracts or permitted to continue to be a party to player contracts

On the domestic front, Tasmania crept to victory in the Ford Ranger Cup in a rain-interrupted match at the Bellerive Oval on 23 February. After dismissing Victoria for 158, the Tigers won by one wicket with five balls to spare as they reached the revised target of 131 under Duckworth-Lewis. Brenton Geeves won the man of the match award for his early breakthroughs in the Victorian innings. In his last season, Matthew Elliott, with 521 runs at an average of 74.42, won his second consecutive player of the series award, while four bowlers – Victorian Bryce McGain and three Tasmanians, Geeves, Xavier Doherty and Brendan Drew, each took 15 wickets.

The Pura Cup season was one of the most one-sided in recent years, with only New South Wales and Victoria deserving to make the final. However, the Blues' hosting of the event, combined with the return of Australian players Brett Lee, Michael Clarke, Stuart Clark and Nathan Bracken, enabled them to win their 45$^{th}$ title by the comfortable margin of 258 runs. NSW captain Simon Katich enjoyed a superlative first-class season to score 1,506 runs at 94.12, including a power-laden career top-score of 306, while Queensland's Ashley Noffke had a superb year with both bat and ball, scoring 741 runs at 46.31 and capturing 51 wickets at 19.03. Both players won places in Australia's Test squad for the tour to the West Indies in May.

The mass exodus of first-class players was startling. South Australian hero Darren Lehmann might argue that retirement was thrust upon him, but he went out in a blaze of glory with centuries against Western Australia in his final one-day and four-day games. Lehmann was joined by one of Australia's greatest performers, fast-bowler Jason Gillespie, after 71 Tests and 259 wickets. Gillespie made a quiet exit with the ball, but topped his state's batting averages. In Queensland, former captain Jimmy Maher and former Australian pace man Michael Kasprowicz pulled up stumps as did Michael Di Venuto in Tasmania, Mick Lewis in Victoria, Matthew Elliott in South Australia, and Justin Langer and Matthew Innes, as well as Brad Hogg and Gilchrist, in Western Australia. All but left-arm pace bowler Innes represented Australia in international matches. In addition the sands of time appear to be running out for former Queensland and Australian players Andy Bichel and Martin Love.

In most cases dark clouds have dark linings and the abrupt departures of grand servants to Australian cricket like Gillespie, Kasprowicz, Elliott and Maher before season's end caused dismay, particularly when they did so to front for the Ahmedabad Rockets, Mumbai Champs, Chandigahr Lions and Hyderabad Heroes respectively, playing a second Twenty20 tournament in the privately-owned rebel Indian Cricket League (ICL). Kasprowicz termed his decision a "no-brainer" and certainly the financial rewards are handsome for the short-term effort required. Only long-time cricket-watchers have their doubts about the rush to money in a form of the game that might be viewed as a no-brainer itself.

The jury on the impact of the Indian Twenty20 competitions must remain out, at least until the completion of the inaugural Indian Premier League (IPL) competition in April 2008 and probably not until well beyond that. Created by the Board of Control for Cricket in India (BCCI) and sanctioned by the International Cricket Council (ICC), the promise of the IPL's 44-day, 59-match multi-billion-dollar extravaganza caused Andrew Symonds, who brought the highest foreign player bid of $1.47 million from the Deccan Chargers at the auction on 20 February, to withdraw from Australia's projected Test and one-day tour of Pakistan originally scheduled at the same time. Security concerns causing the cancellation of that tour may have saved Symonds from potential embarrassment, but in the future other players with high price tags (and their agents) will possibly be assessing the value of their contracts with Cricket Australia and state associations with eagle eyes.

Australia's fantastic cricket success in the recent past has been based on a well-organized system. Central to the plans are the pathways that begin with Have-A-Go Cricket, a child's first organized cricket experience, which provides youngsters with structured sessions including skill-based activities and modified games. Have-A-Go cricket is the base of a cricket pyramid and is the initial stimulus for interest in playing school, club and community cricket at junior levels in both metropolitan and country areas. Talent identification begins early, and thus players may represent the various states from primary school level. Intrastate competitions operate in the early teenage years and there are national and international competitions at Under-17 and Under-19 level. Meanwhile, young players intent on reaching the optimum level will be affiliated with grade clubs in the capital cities and the most promising players (generally below first-class level) will be invited to attend the Centre of Excellence (formerly the Australian Cricket Academy) as a sort of finishing school. When the players leave the Centre of Excellence they usually return to their grade clubs on the way to winning higher honours at state and international level.

The current "brand focus" (as Cricket Australia terms it) is to make cricket *The soul of Australian summer life* and its five-fold strategy is to reinforce and celebrate cricket's place in the Australian community; to thrive at the elite level; to increase participation in cricket substantially; to increase the financial resources available to invest in the game; and to work efficiently in our federal system. For the most part, this is being achieved. Australia dominates both men's and women's cricket; participation rates increased 3.15 per cent across the nation to

560,000 players; Cricket Australia recorded an operating surplus of $47.9 million in 2006-07, and the administration of the game by one national body, six state and two territory associations works effectively. However, because of international forces outside their control, the future is not quite as assured as the good planners might hope.

Since the first recorded game of cricket 205 years ago society has undergone many changes. From initially being a depository for Britain's unwanted poorer classes and criminal elements, Australia had in turn been used as a major provider of food, fighting men and minerals. In recent decades the crimson threads of kinship appeared to be breaking with the constitutional monarchy viewed by the Keating Labor Government of the early 1990s as an outmoded political form for the new millennium and Australia's ethnic mix of population becoming even more varied.

Until the early 1950s, Australia's population was predominantly Anglo-Celtic, but from then on more immigrants began to arrive from eastern and southern Europe. After them came refugees from the Middle East and South America, and in the late 1970s fleeing Vietnamese were joined by others from South-East Asia. More recently economic migrants came from Hong Kong, and refugees from the Middle East and Africa.

Australia was able to offer much in the way of space, land, freedom and a culture not fully appreciated by those from outside. For its part, since the 1960s Australia had begun to trade with America, Japan and South-East Asian nations as that with old partners like Britain dwindled. In the 1990s, an even more powerful economic engagement with Asia began.

How has this background affected cricket? From 1996 to 2007, socially conservative Liberal prime minister John Howard had a radical economic agenda. While his early call for Australians to be "relaxed and comfortable" incorporated a white-flannel view of history and a self-contained "white picket fence" view of society, Australian cricket proved more internationalist in expanding the game in Asia and Oceania and more inclusive too at home. Strong ACB/ Cricket Australia policies in recent years have certainly aimed to develop the game further among ethnic groups, indigenous Australians and women.

One hundred and sixteen years ago, Lord Sheffield gave money for a competition that he hoped would unite the colonies in cricket, but that competition would not have succeeded had there not already been a strong federalist mood among the colonies for a united Australia. At a point when many Australians remain nervous about the state of the world, Australia's cricket success and, more importantly, its moderate progressive stance towards the game's international development, offers the chance of more happy times. The one cloud on the horizon is the challenge to world (and Australian cricket) posed by the success of the professional Indian club league or leagues playing Twenty20 cricket and the financial windfalls that flow from them. When announcing the new Australian contracts on 9 April 2008 chairman of selectors Andrew Hilditch commented that he believed nationally contracted players would put the baggy green caps ahead of the lure of lucrative paydays on the sub-continent. The contracts range from Ricky Ponting and Brett Lee at the top on $1 million a year down to those such as Doug Bollinger, Beau Casson, Ben Hilfenhaus, David Hussey, Shaun Marsh and Ashley Noffke at the base on $160,000. Doomsayers predicting the death of Test cricket may be going too far too fast but of major concern is a survey conducted for the Australian Cricketers Association which revealed that 47 per cent of its previously nationally contracted players, and 49 per cent of state contracted players, had signalled the possibility of prematurely ending their domestic careers to join either the IPL or ICL. If that was the case Australian cricket could find itself in a similar position to Australian soccer, developing star players for competitions hosted by other nations. Time will surely tell.

# Appendix A

# Australia Test Match Averages

| Batting | T | I | NO | HS | Runs | Av | 100 | 50 | Ct/St |
|---|---|---|---|---|---|---|---|---|---|
| EL A'Beckett<br>*b 11 Aug 1907* | 4 | 7 | 0 | 41 | 143 | 20.42 | – | – | 4 |
| TM Alderman<br>*b 12 Jun 1956* | 41 | 53 | 22 | 26* | 203 | 6.54 | – | – | 27 |
| G Alexander<br>*b 22 Apr 1851* | 2 | 4 | 0 | 33 | 52 | 13.00 | – | – | 2 |
| HH Alexander<br>*b 9 Jun 1905* | 1 | 2 | 1 | 17* | 17 | 17.00 | – | – | – |
| FE Allan<br>*b 2 Dec 1849* | 1 | 1 | 0 | 5 | 5 | 5.00 | – | – | – |
| PJ Allan<br>*b 31 Dec 1935* | 1 | – | | | | | – | – | – |
| RC Allen<br>*b 2 Jul 1858* | 1 | 2 | 0 | 30 | 44 | 22.00 | – | – | 2 |
| TJE Andrews<br>*b 26 Aug 1890* | 16 | 23 | 1 | 94 | 592 | 26.90 | – | 4 | 12 |
| J Angel<br>*b 22 Apr 1968* | 4 | 7 | 1 | 11 | 35 | 5.83 | – | – | 1 |
| KA Archer<br>*b 17 Jan 1928* | 5 | 9 | 0 | 48 | 234 | 26.00 | – | – | – |
| RG Archer<br>*b 25 Oct 1933* | 19 | 30 | 1 | 128 | 713 | 24.58 | 1 | 2 | 20 |
| WW Armstrong<br>*b 22 May 1879* | 50 | 84 | 10 | 159* | 2863 | 38.68 | 6 | 8 | 44 |
| CL Badcock<br>*b 10 Apr 1914* | 7 | 12 | 1 | 118 | 160 | 14.54 | 1 | – | 3 |
| AC Bannerman<br>*b 21 Mar 1854* | 28 | 50 | 2 | 94 | 1108 | 23.08 | – | 8 | 21 |
| C Bannerman<br>*b 23 Jul 1851* | 3 | 6 | 2 | 165* | 239 | 59.75 | 1 | – | – |
| W Bardsley<br>*b 6 Dec 1882* | 41 | 66 | 5 | 193* | 2469 | 40.47 | 6 | 14 | 12 |
| SG Barnes<br>*b 5 Jun 1916* | 13 | 19 | 2 | 234 | 1072 | 63.05 | 3 | 5 | 14 |

| Batting | T | I | NO | HS | Runs | Av | 100 | 50 | Ct/St |
|---|---|---|---|---|---|---|---|---|---|
| BA Barnett<br>*b 23 Mar 1908* | 4 | 8 | 1 | 57 | 195 | 27.85 | – | 1 | 3/2 |
| JE Barrett<br>*b 15 Oct 1866* | 2 | 4 | 1 | 67 | 80 | 26.66 | – | 1 | 1 |
| GR Beard<br>*b 19 Aug 1950* | 3 | 5 | 0 | 49 | 114 | 22.80 | – | – | – |
| J Benaud<br>*b 11 May 1944* | 3 | 5 | 0 | 142 | 223 | 44.60 | 1 | – | – |
| R Benaud<br>*b 6 Oct 1930* | 63 | 97 | 7 | 122 | 2201 | 24.45 | 3 | 9 | 65 |
| MJ Bennett<br>*b 6 Oct 1956* | 3 | 5 | 2 | 23 | 71 | 23.66 | – | – | 5 |
| MG Bevan<br>*b 8 May 1970* | 18 | 30 | 3 | 91 | 785 | 29.07 | – | 6 | 8 |
| AJ Bichel<br>*b 27 Aug 1970* | 19 | 22 | 1 | 71 | 355 | 16.90 | – | 1 | 16 |
| JMcC Blackham<br>*b 11 May 1854* | 35 | 62 | 11 | 74 | 800 | 15.68 | – | 4 | 37/24 |
| DD Blackie<br>*b 5 Apr 1882* | 3 | 6 | 3 | 11* | 24 | 8.00 | – | – | 2 |
| GS Blewett<br>*b 29 Oct 1971* | 46 | 79 | 4 | 214 | 2552 | 34.02 | 4 | 15 | 45 |
| GJ Bonnor<br>*b 25 Feb 1855* | 17 | 30 | 0 | 128 | 512 | 17.06 | 1 | 2 | 16 |
| DC Boon<br>*b 29 Dec 1960* | 107 | 190 | 20 | 200 | 7422 | 43.65 | 21 | 32 | 99 |
| BC Booth<br>*b 19 Oct 1933* | 29 | 48 | 6 | 169 | 1773 | 42.21 | 5 | 10 | 17 |
| AR Border<br>*b 27 Jul 1955* | 156 | 265 | 44 | 205 | 11174 | 50.56 | 27 | 63 | 156 |
| HF Boyle<br>*b 10 Dec 1847* | 12 | 16 | 4 | 36* | 153 | 12.75 | – | – | 10 |
| NW Bracken<br>*b 12 Sep 1977* | 5 | 6 | 2 | 37 | 70 | 17.50 | – | – | – |
| DG Bradman<br>*b 27 Aug 1908* | 52 | 80 | 10 | 334 | 6996 | 99.94 | 29 | 13 | 32 |
| RJ Bright<br>*b 13 Jul 1954* | 25 | 39 | 8 | 33 | 445 | 14.35 | – | – | 13 |
| EH Bromley<br>*b 2 Sep 1912* | 2 | 4 | 0 | 26 | 38 | 9.50 | – | – | 2 |
| WA Brown<br>*b 31 Jul 1912* | 22 | 35 | 1 | 206* | 1592 | 46.82 | 4 | 9 | 14 |

| Batting | T | I | NO | HS | Runs | Av | 100 | 50 | Ct/St |
|---|---|---|---|---|---|---|---|---|---|
| W Bruce<br>*b 22 May 1864* | 14 | 26 | 2 | 80 | 702 | 29.25 | – | 5 | 12 |
| PJP Burge<br>*b 17 May 1932* | 42 | 68 | 8 | 181 | 2290 | 38.16 | 4 | 12 | 23 |
| JW Burke<br>*b 12 Jun 1930* | 24 | 44 | 7 | 189 | 1280 | 34.59 | 3 | 5 | 18 |
| EJK Burn<br>*b 17 Sep 1862* | 2 | 4 | 0 | 19 | 41 | 10.25 | – | – | – |
| FJ Burton<br>*b 2 Nov 1865* | 2 | 4 | 2 | 2* | 4 | 2.00 | – | – | 1/1 |
| ST Callaway<br>*b 6 Feb 1868* | 3 | 6 | 1 | 41 | 87 | 17.40 | – | – | – |
| IW Callen<br>*b 2 May 1955* | 1 | 2 | 2 | 22* | 26 | – | – | – | 1 |
| GD Campbell<br>*b 10 Mar 1964* | 4 | 4 | 0 | 6 | 10 | 2.50 | – | – | 1 |
| W Carkeek<br>*b 17 Oct 1878* | 6 | 5 | 2 | 6* | 16 | 5.33 | – | – | 6 |
| PH Carlson<br>*b 8 Aug 1951* | 2 | 4 | 0 | 21 | 23 | 5.75 | – | – | 2 |
| H Carter<br>*b 15 Mar 1878* | 28 | 47 | 9 | 72 | 873 | 22.97 | – | 4 | 44/21 |
| GS Chappell<br>*b 7 Aug 1948* | 87 | 151 | 19 | 247* | 7110 | 53.86 | 24 | 31 | 122 |
| IM Chappell<br>*b 26 Sep 1943* | 75 | 136 | 10 | 196 | 5345 | 42.42 | 14 | 26 | 105 |
| TM Chappell<br>*b 21 Oct 1952* | 3 | 6 | 1 | 27 | 79 | 15.80 | – | – | 2 |
| PC Charlton<br>*b 9 Apr 1867* | 2 | 4 | 0 | 11 | 29 | 7.25 | – | – | – |
| AG Chipperfield<br>*b 17 Nov 1905* | 14 | 20 | 3 | 109 | 552 | 32.47 | 1 | 2 | 15 |
| SR Clark<br>*b 28 Sep 1975* | 15 | 15 | 2 | 39 | 172 | 13.23 | – | – | 2 |
| WM Clark<br>*b 19 Sep 1953* | 10 | 19 | 2 | 33 | 98 | 5.76 | – | – | 6 |
| MJ Clarke<br>*b 2 Apr 1981* | 33 | 50 | 6 | 151 | 2044 | 46.45 | 6 | 8 | 29 |
| DJ Colley<br>*b 15 Mar 1947* | 3 | 4 | 0 | 54 | 84 | 21.00 | – | 1 | 1 |
| HL Collins<br>*b 21 Jan 1888* | 19 | 31 | 1 | 203 | 1352 | 45.06 | 4 | 6 | 13 |

| Batting | T | I | NO | HS | Runs | Av | 100 | 50 | Ct/St |
|---|---|---|---|---|---|---|---|---|---|
| A Coningham<br>*b 14 Jul 1863* | 1 | 2 | 0 | 10 | 13 | 6.50 | – | – | – |
| AN Connolly<br>*b 29 Jun 1939* | 29 | 45 | 20 | 37 | 260 | 10.40 | – | – | 17 |
| SH Cook<br>*b 29 Jan 1972* | 2 | 2 | 2 | 3* | 3 | – | – | – | – |
| BB Cooper<br>*b 15 Mar 1844* | 1 | 2 | 0 | 15 | 18 | 9.00 | – | – | 2 |
| WH Cooper<br>*b 11 Sep 1849* | 2 | 3 | 1 | 7 | 13 | 6.50 | – | – | 1 |
| GE Corling<br>*b 13 Jul 1941* | 5 | 4 | 1 | 3 | 5 | 1.66 | – | – | – |
| GJ Cosier<br>*b 25 Apr 1953* | 18 | 32 | 1 | 168 | 897 | 28.93 | 2 | 3 | 14 |
| JT Cottam<br>*b 5 Sep 1867* | 1 | 2 | 0 | 3 | 4 | 2.00 | – | – | 1 |
| A Cotter<br>*b 3 Dec 1884* | 21 | 37 | 2 | 45 | 457 | 13.05 | – | – | 8 |
| G Coulthard<br>*b 1 Aug 1856* | 1 | 1 | 1 | 6* | 6 | – | – | – | – |
| RM Cowper<br>*b 5 Oct 1940* | 27 | 46 | 2 | 307 | 2061 | 46.84 | 5 | 10 | 21 |
| ID Craig<br>*b 12 Jun 1935* | 11 | 18 | 0 | 53 | 358 | 19.88 | – | 2 | 2 |
| WPA Crawford<br>*b 3 Aug 1933* | 4 | 5 | 2 | 34 | 53 | 17.66 | – | – | 1 |
| DJ Cullen<br>*b 10 Apr 1984* | 1 | – | | | | | | | – |
| AC Dale<br>*b 30 Dec 1968* | 2 | 3 | 0 | 5 | 6 | 2.00 | – | – | – |
| J Darling<br>*b 21 Nov 1870* | 34 | 60 | 2 | 178 | 1657 | 28.56 | 3 | 8 | 27 |
| LS Darling<br>*b 14 Aug 1909* | 12 | 18 | 1 | 85 | 474 | 27.88 | – | 3 | 8 |
| WM Darling<br>*b 1 May 1957* | 14 | 27 | 1 | 91 | 697 | 26.80 | – | 6 | 5 |
| AK Davidson<br>*b 14 Jun 1929* | 44 | 61 | 7 | 80 | 1328 | 24.59 | – | 5 | 42 |
| IC Davis<br>*b 25 Jun 1953* | 15 | 27 | 1 | 105 | 692 | 26.61 | 1 | 4 | 9 |
| SP Davis<br>*b 8 Nov 1959* | 1 | 1 | 0 | 0 | 0 | – | – | – | – |

| Batting | T | I | NO | HS | Runs | Av | 100 | 50 | Ct/St |
|---|---|---|---|---|---|---|---|---|---|
| JH de Courcy *b 18 Apr 1927* | 3 | 6 | 1 | 41 | 81 | 16.20 | – | – | 3 |
| AR Dell *b 6 Aug 1947* | 2 | 2 | 2 | 3* | 6 | – | – | – | – |
| AIC Dodemaide *b 5 Oct 1963* | 10 | 15 | 6 | 50 | 202 | 22.44 | – | 1 | 6 |
| H Donnan *b 12 Nov 1864* | 5 | 10 | 1 | 15 | 75 | 8.33 | – | – | 1 |
| B Dooland *b 1 Nov 1923* | 3 | 5 | 1 | 29 | 76 | 19.00 | – | – | 3 |
| RA Duff *b 17 Aug 1878* | 22 | 40 | 3 | 146 | 1317 | 35.59 | 2 | 6 | 14 |
| JRF Duncan *b 25 Mar 1944* | 1 | 1 | 0 | 3 | 3 | 3.00 | – | – | – |
| GC Dyer *b 16 Mar 1959* | 6 | 6 | 0 | 60 | 131 | 21.83 | – | 1 | 22/2 |
| G Dymock *b 21 Jul 1945* | 21 | 32 | 7 | 31* | 236 | 9.44 | – | – | 1 |
| J Dyson *b 11 Jun 1954* | 30 | 58 | 7 | 127* | 1359 | 26.64 | 2 | 5 | 10 |
| CJ Eady *b 29 Oct 1870* | 2 | 4 | 1 | 10* | 20 | 6.66 | – | – | 2 |
| KH Eastwood *b 23 Nov 1935* | 1 | 2 | 0 | 5 | 5 | 2.50 | – | – | – |
| HI Ebeling *b 1 Jan 1905* | 1 | 2 | 0 | 41 | 43 | 21.50 | – | – | – |
| JD Edwards *b 12 Jun 1862* | 3 | 6 | 1 | 26 | 48 | 9.60 | – | – | 1 |
| R Edwards *b 1 Dec 1942* | 20 | 32 | 3 | 170* | 1171 | 40.37 | 2 | 9 | 7 |
| WJ Edwards *b 23 Dec 1949* | 3 | 6 | 0 | 30 | 68 | 11.33 | – | – | – |
| MTG Elliott *b 28 Sep 1971* | 21 | 36 | 1 | 199 | 1172 | 33.48 | 3 | 4 | 14 |
| PA Emery *b 25 Jun 1964* | 1 | 1 | 1 | 8* | 8 | – | – | – | 5/1 |
| SH Emery *b 16 Oct 1885* | 4 | 2 | 0 | 5 | 6 | 3.00 | – | – | 2 |
| E Evans *b 26 Mar 1849* | 6 | 10 | 2 | 33 | 82 | 10.25 | – | – | 5 |
| AG Fairfax *b 16 Jun 1906* | 10 | 12 | 4 | 65 | 410 | 51.25 | – | 4 | 15 |

| Batting | T | I | NO | HS | Runs | Av | 100 | 50 | Ct/St |
|---|---|---|---|---|---|---|---|---|---|
| LE Favell<br>*b 6 Oct 1929* | 19 | 31 | 3 | 101 | 757 | 27.03 | 1 | 5 | 9 |
| JJ Ferris<br>*b 21 May 1867* | 8 | 16 | 4 | 20* | 98 | 8.16 | – | – | 4 |
| JHW Fingleton<br>*b 28 Apr 1908* | 18 | 29 | 1 | 136 | 1189 | 42.46 | 5 | 3 | 13 |
| LO'B Fleetwood-Smith<br>*b 30 Mar 1910* | 10 | 11 | 5 | 16* | 54 | 9.00 | – | – | – |
| DW Fleming<br>*b 24 Apr 1970* | 20 | 19 | 3 | 71* | 305 | 19.06 | – | 2 | 9 |
| BC Francis<br>*b 18 Feb 1948* | 3 | 5 | 0 | 27 | 52 | 10.40 | – | – | 1 |
| EW Freeman<br>*b 13 Jul 1944* | 11 | 18 | 0 | 76 | 345 | 19.16 | – | 2 | 5 |
| FAW Freer<br>*b 4 Dec 1915* | 1 | 1 | 1 | 28* | 28 | – | – | – | – |
| JB Gannon<br>*b 8 Feb 1947* | 3 | 5 | 4 | 3* | 3 | 3.00 | – | – | 3 |
| TW Garrett<br>*b 26 Jul 1858* | 19 | 33 | 6 | 51* | 339 | 12.55 | – | 1 | 7 |
| RA Gaunt<br>*b 26 Feb* 1934 | 3 | 4 | 2 | 3 | 6 | 3.00 | – | – | 1 |
| DRA Gehrs<br>*b 29 Nov 1880* | 6 | 11 | 0 | 67 | 221 | 20.09 | – | 2 | 6 |
| G Giffen<br>*b 27 Mar 1859* | 31 | 53 | 0 | 161 | 1238 | 23.35 | 1 | 6 | 24 |
| WF Giffen<br>*b 20 Sep 1861* | 3 | 6 | 0 | 3 | 11 | 1.83 | – | – | 1 |
| DR Gilbert<br>*b 29 Dec 1960* | 9 | 12 | 4 | 15 | 57 | 7.12 | – | – | – |
| AC Gilchrist<br>*b 14 Nov 1971* | 96 | 137 | 20 | 204* | 5570 | 47.60 | 17 | 26 | 379/37 |
| JN Gillespie<br>*b 19 Apr 1975* | 71 | 93 | 28 | 201* | 1218 | 18.73 | 1 | 2 | 27 |
| GJ Gilmour<br>*b 26 Jun 1951* | 15 | 22 | 1 | 101 | 483 | 23.00 | 1 | 3 | 8 |
| JW Gleeson<br>*b 14 Mar 1938* | 29 | 46 | 8 | 45 | 395 | 10.39 | – | – | 17 |
| H Graham<br>*b 22 Nov 1870* | 6 | 10 | 0 | 107 | 301 | 30.10 | 2 | – | 3 |
| DW Gregory<br>*b 15 Apr 1845* | 3 | 5 | 2 | 43 | 60 | 20.00 | – | – | – |

| Batting | T | I | NO | HS | Runs | Av | 100 | 50 | Ct/St |
|---|---|---|---|---|---|---|---|---|---|
| EJ Gregory<br>*b 29 May 1839* | 1 | 2 | 0 | 11 | 11 | 5.50 | – | – | 1 |
| JM Gregory<br>*b 14 Aug 1895* | 24 | 34 | 3 | 119 | 1146 | 36.96 | 2 | 7 | 37 |
| RG Gregory<br>*b 28 Feb 1916* | 2 | 3 | 0 | 80 | 153 | 51.00 | – | 2 | 1 |
| SE Gregory<br>*b 14 Apr 1870* | 58 | 100 | 7 | 201 | 2282 | 24.53 | 4 | 8 | 25 |
| CV Grimmett<br>*b 25 Dec 1891* | 37 | 50 | 10 | 50 | 557 | 13.92 | – | 1 | 17 |
| TU Groube<br>*b 2 Sep 1857* | 1 | 2 | 0 | 11 | 11 | 5.50 | – | – | – |
| ATW Grout<br>*b 30 Mar 1927* | 51 | 67 | 8 | 74 | 890 | 15.08 | – | 3 | 163/24 |
| CEJ Guest<br>*b 7 Oct 1937* | 1 | 1 | 0 | 11 | 11 | 11.00 | – | – | – |
| RA Hamence<br>*b 25 Nov 1915* | 3 | 4 | 1 | 30* | 81 | 27.00 | – | – | 1 |
| JR Hammond<br>*b 19 Apr 1950* | 5 | 5 | 2 | 19 | 28 | 9.33 | – | – | 2 |
| J Harry<br>*b 1 Aug 1857* | 1 | 2 | 0 | 6 | 8 | 4.00 | – | – | 1 |
| RJ Hartigan<br>*b 12 Dec 1879* | 2 | 4 | 0 | 116 | 170 | 42.50 | 1 | – | 1 |
| AEV Hartkopf<br>*b 28 Dec 1889* | 1 | 2 | 0 | 80 | 80 | 40.00 | – | 1 | – |
| MR Harvey<br>*b 29 Apr 1918* | 1 | 2 | 0 | 31 | 43 | 21.50 | – | – | – |
| RN Harvey<br>*b 8 Oct 1928* | 79 | 137 | 10 | 205 | 6149 | 48.41 | 21 | 24 | 64 |
| AL Hassett<br>*b 28 Aug 1913* | 43 | 69 | 3 | 198* | 3073 | 46.56 | 10 | 11 | 30 |
| NM Hauritz<br>*b 18 Oct 1981* | 1 | 2 | – | 15 | 15 | 7.50 | – | – | 1 |
| NJN Hawke<br>*b 27 Jun 1939* | 27 | 37 | 15 | 45* | 365 | 16.59 | – | – | 9 |
| ML Hayden<br>*b 29 Oct 1971* | 94 | 167 | 13 | 380 | 8242 | 53.51 | 30 | 27 | 121 |
| GR Hazlitt<br>*b 4 Sep 1888* | 9 | 12 | 4 | 34* | 89 | 11.12 | – | – | 4 |
| IA Healy<br>*b 30 Apr 1964* | 119 | 182 | 23 | 161* | 4356 | 27.39 | 4 | 22 | 366/29 |

| Batting | T | I | NO | HS | Runs | Av | 100 | 50 | Ct/St |
|---|---|---|---|---|---|---|---|---|---|
| HSTL Hendry<br>*b 24 May 1895* | 11 | 18 | 2 | 112 | 335 | 20.93 | 1 | – | 10 |
| PA Hibbert<br>*b 23 Jul 1952* | 1 | 2 | 0 | 13 | 15 | 7.50 | – | – | 1 |
| JD Higgs<br>*b 11 Jul 1950* | 22 | 36 | 16 | 16 | 111 | 5.55 | – | – | 3 |
| AMJ Hilditch<br>*b 20 May 1956* | 18 | 34 | 0 | 119 | 1073 | 31.55 | 2 | 6 | 13 |
| C Hill<br>*b 18 Mar 1877* | 49 | 89 | 2 | 191 | 3412 | 39.21 | 7 | 19 | 33 |
| JC Hill<br>*b 25 Jun 1923* | 3 | 6 | 3 | 8* | 21 | 7.00 | – | – | 2 |
| DE Hoare<br>*b 19 Oct 1934* | 1 | 2 | 0 | 35 | 35 | 17.50 | – | – | 2 |
| BJ Hodge<br>*b 29 Dec 1974* | 5 | 9 | 2 | 203* | 409 | 58.42 | 1 | 1 | 9 |
| JR Hodges<br>*b 11 Aug 1855* | 2 | 4 | 1 | 8 | 10 | 3.33 | – | – | – |
| TG Hogan<br>*b 23 Sep 1956* | 7 | 12 | 1 | 42* | 205 | 18.63 | – | – | 2 |
| GB Hogg<br>*b 6 Feb 1971* | 7 | 10 | 3 | 79 | 186 | 26.57 | – | 1 | 1 |
| RM Hogg<br>*b 5 Mar 1951* | 38 | 58 | 13 | 52 | 439 | 9.75 | – | 1 | 7 |
| TV Hohns<br>*b 23 Jan 1954* | 7 | 7 | 1 | 40 | 136 | 22.66 | – | – | 3 |
| GB Hole<br>*b 6 Jan 1931* | 18 | 33 | 2 | 66 | 789 | 25.45 | – | 6 | 21 |
| RG Holland<br>*b 19 Oct 1946* | 11 | 15 | 4 | 10 | 35 | 3.18 | – | – | 5 |
| DW Hookes<br>*b 3 May 1955* | 23 | 41 | 3 | 143* | 1306 | 34.36 | 1 | 8 | 12 |
| AJY Hopkins<br>*b 3 May 1874* | 20 | 33 | 2 | 43 | 509 | 16.41 | – | – | 11 |
| TP Horan<br>*b 8 Mar 1854* | 15 | 27 | 2 | 124 | 471 | 18.84 | 1 | 1 | 6 |
| HV Hordern<br>*b 10 Feb 1883* | 7 | 13 | 2 | 50 | 254 | 23.09 | – | 1 | 6 |
| PM Hornibrook<br>*b 27 Jul 1899* | 6 | 7 | 1 | 26 | 60 | 10.00 | – | – | 7 |
| WP Howell<br>*b 29 Dec 1869* | 18 | 27 | 6 | 35 | 158 | 7.52 | – | – | 12 |

| Batting | T | I | NO | HS | Runs | Av | 100 | 50 | Ct/St |
|---|---|---|---|---|---|---|---|---|---|
| KJ Hughes *b 26 Jan 1954* | 70 | 124 | 6 | 213 | 4415 | 37.41 | 9 | 22 | 50 |
| MG Hughes *b 23 Nov 1961* | 53 | 70 | 8 | 72* | 1032 | 16.64 | – | 2 | 23 |
| WA Hunt *b 26 Aug 1908* | 1 | 1 | 0 | 0 | 0 | – | – | – | 1 |
| AG Hurst *b 15 Jul 1950* | 12 | 20 | 3 | 26 | 102 | 6.00 | – | – | 3 |
| A Hurwood *b 17 Jun 1902* | 2 | 2 | 0 | 5 | 5 | 2.50 | – | – | 2 |
| MEK Hussey *b 27 May 1975* | 22 | 36 | 8 | 182 | 2188 | 78.14 | 8 | 8 | 20 |
| RJ Inverarity *b 31 Jan 1944* | 6 | 11 | 1 | 56 | 174 | 17.40 | – | 1 | 4 |
| FA Iredale *b 19 Jun 1867* | 14 | 23 | 1 | 140 | 807 | 36.68 | 2 | 4 | 16 |
| H Ironmonger *b 7 Apr 1882* | 14 | 21 | 5 | 12 | 42 | 2.62 | – | – | 3 |
| JB Iverson *b 27 Jul 1915* | 5 | 7 | 3 | 1* | 3 | 0.75 | – | – | 2 |
| AA Jackson *b 5 Sep 1909* | 8 | 11 | 1 | 164 | 474 | 47.40 | 1 | 2 | 7 |
| PA Jaques *b 3 May 1979* | 8 | 13 | – | 150 | 657 | 50.53 | 2 | 5 | 3 |
| BN Jarman *b 17 Feb 1936* | 19 | 30 | 3 | 78 | 400 | 14.81 | – | 2 | 50/4 |
| AH Jarvis *b 19 Oct 1860* | 11 | 21 | 3 | 82 | 303 | 16.83 | – | 1 | 9/9 |
| TJ Jenner *b 8 Sep 1944* | 9 | 14 | 5 | 74 | 208 | 23.11 | – | 1 | 5 |
| CB Jennings *b 5 Jun 1884* | 6 | 8 | 2 | 32 | 107 | 17.83 | – | – | 5 |
| IW Johnson *b 8 Dec 1917* | 45 | 66 | 12 | 77 | 1000 | 18.51 | – | 6 | 30 |
| LJ Johnson *b 18 Mar 1919* | 1 | 1 | 1 | 25* | 25 | – | – | – | 2 |
| MG Johnson *b 2 Nov 1981* | 6 | 5 | 3 | 50* | 112 | 56.00 | – | 1 | 2 |
| WA Johnston *b 26 Feb 1922* | 40 | 49 | 25 | 29 | 273 | 11.37 | – | – | 16 |
| DM Jones *b 24 Mar 1961* | 52 | 89 | 11 | 216 | 3631 | 46.55 | 11 | 14 | 34 |

| Batting | T | I | NO | HS | Runs | Av | 100 | 50 | Ct/St |
|---|---|---|---|---|---|---|---|---|---|
| E Jones<br>*b 30 Sep 1869* | 19 | 26 | 1 | 20 | 126 | 5.04 | – | – | 21 |
| SP Jones<br>*b 1 Aug 1861* | 12 | 24 | 4 | 87 | 428 | 21.40 | – | 1 | 12 |
| LR Joslin<br>*b 13 Dec 1947* | 1 | 2 | 0 | 7 | 9 | 4.50 | – | – | – |
| BP Julian<br>*b 10 Aug 1970* | 7 | 9 | 1 | 56* | 128 | 16.00 | – | 1 | 4 |
| MS Kasprowicz<br>*b 10 Feb 1972* | 38 | 54 | 12 | 25 | 445 | 10.59 | – | – | 16 |
| SM Katich<br>*b 21 Aug 1975* | 23 | 38 | 3 | 125 | 1260 | 36.00 | 2 | 8 | 15 |
| C Kelleway<br>*b 25 Apr 1886* | 26 | 42 | 4 | 147 | 1422 | 37.42 | 3 | 6 | 24 |
| JJ Kelly<br>*b 10 May 1867* | 36 | 56 | 17 | 46* | 664 | 17.02 | – | – | 43/20 |
| TJD Kelly<br>*b 3 May 1844* | 2 | 3 | 0 | 35 | 64 | 21.33 | – | – | 1 |
| TK Kendall<br>*b 24 Aug 1851* | 2 | 4 | 1 | 17* | 39 | 13.00 | – | – | 2 |
| MF Kent<br>*b 23 Nov 1953* | 3 | 6 | 0 | 54 | 171 | 28.50 | – | 2 | 6 |
| RB Kerr<br>*b 16 Jun 1961* | 2 | 4 | 0 | 17 | 31 | 7.75 | – | – | 1 |
| AF Kippax<br>*b 25 May 1897* | 22 | 34 | 1 | 146 | 1192 | 36.12 | 2 | 8 | 13 |
| LF Kline<br>*b 29 Sep 1934* | 13 | 16 | 9 | 15* | 58 | 8.28 | – | – | 9 |
| BM Laird<br>*b 21 Nov 1950* | 21 | 40 | 2 | 92 | 1341 | 35.28 | – | 11 | 16 |
| JL Langer<br>*b 21 Nov 1970* | 105 | 182 | 12 | 250 | 7696 | 45.27 | 23 | 30 | 73 |
| GRA Langley<br>*b 14 Sep 1919* | 26 | 37 | 12 | 53 | 374 | 14.96 | – | 1 | 83/15 |
| TJ Laughlin<br>*b 30 Jan 1951* | 3 | 5 | 0 | 35 | 87 | 17.40 | – | – | 3 |
| FJ Laver<br>*b 7 Dec 1869* | 15 | 23 | 6 | 45 | 196 | 11.52 | – | – | 8 |
| SG Law<br>*b 18 Oct 1968* | 1 | 1 | 1 | 54* | 54 | – | – | 1 | 1 |
| WM Lawry<br>*b 11 Feb 1937* | 67 | 123 | 12 | 210 | 5234 | 47.15 | 13 | 27 | 30 |

| Batting | T | I | NO | HS | Runs | Av | 100 | 50 | Ct/St |
|---|---|---|---|---|---|---|---|---|---|
| GF Lawson *b 7 Dec 1957* | 46 | 68 | 12 | 74 | 894 | 15.96 | – | 4 | 10 |
| B Lee *b 8 Nov 1976* | 65 | 72 | 15 | 64 | 1184 | 20.77 | – | 4 | 19 |
| PK Lee *b 15 Sep 1904* | 2 | 3 | 0 | 42 | 57 | 19.00 | – | – | 1 |
| DS Lehmann *b 5 Feb 1970* | 27 | 42 | 2 | 177 | 1798 | 44.95 | 5 | 10 | 11 |
| DK Lillee *b 18 Jul 1949* | 70 | 90 | 24 | 73* | 905 | 13.71 | – | 1 | 23 |
| RR Lindwall *b 3 Oct 1921* | 61 | 84 | 13 | 118 | 1502 | 21.15 | 2 | 5 | 26 |
| HSB Love *b 10 Aug 1895* | 1 | 2 | 0 | 5 | 8 | 4.00 | – | – | 3 |
| ML Love *b 30 Mar 1974* | 5 | 8 | 3 | 100* | 223 | 46.60 | 1 | 1 | 7 |
| SJE Loxton *b 29 Mar 1921* | 12 | 15 | 0 | 101 | 554 | 36.93 | 1 | 3 | 7 |
| JJ Lyons *b 21 May 1863* | 14 | 27 | 0 | 134 | 731 | 27.07 | 1 | 3 | 3 |
| SCG MacGill *b 25 Feb 1971* | 42 | 45 | 11 | 43 | 347 | 10.20 | – | – | 16 |
| PA McAlister *b 11 Jul 1869* | 8 | 16 | 1 | 41 | 252 | 16.80 | – | – | 10 |
| SJ McCabe *b 16 Jul 1910* | 39 | 62 | 5 | 232 | 2748 | 48.21 | 6 | 13 | 41 |
| CL McCool *b 9 Dec 1916* | 14 | 17 | 4 | 104* | 459 | 35.30 | 1 | 1 | 14 |
| EL McCormick *b 16 May 1906* | 12 | 14 | 5 | 17* | 54 | 6.00 | – | – | 8 |
| RB McCosker *b 11 Dec 1946* | 25 | 46 | 5 | 127 | 1622 | 39.56 | 4 | 9 | 21 |
| CJ McDermott *b 14 Apr 1965* | 71 | 90 | 13 | 42* | 940 | 12.20 | – | – | 19 |
| CC McDonald *b 17 Nov 1928* | 47 | 83 | 4 | 170 | 3107 | 39.32 | 5 | 17 | 14 |
| EA McDonald *b 6 Jan 1891* | 11 | 12 | 5 | 36 | 116 | 16.57 | – | – | 3 |
| PS McDonnell *b 13 Nov 1858* | 19 | 34 | 1 | 147 | 955 | 28.93 | 3 | 2 | 6 |
| GD McGrath *b 9 Feb 1970* | 124 | 138 | 51 | 61 | 641 | 7.36 | – | 1 | 38 |

| Batting | T | I | NO | HS | Runs | Av | 100 | 50 | Ct/St |
|---|---|---|---|---|---|---|---|---|---|
| J McIlwraith<br>*b 7 Sep 1857* | 1 | 2 | 0 | 7 | 9 | 4.50 | – | – | 1 |
| PE McIntyre<br>*b 27 Apr 1966* | 2 | 4 | 1 | 16 | 22 | 7.33 | – | – | – |
| GD McKenzie<br>*b 24 Jun 1941* | 60 | 89 | 12 | 76 | 945 | 12.27 | – | 2 | 34 |
| TR McKibbin<br>*b 10 Dec 1870* | 5 | 8 | 2 | 28* | 88 | 14.66 | – | – | 4 |
| JW McLaren<br>*b 22 Dec 1886* | 1 | 2 | 2 | 0* | 0 | – | – | – | – |
| CE McLeod<br>*b 24 Oct 1869* | 17 | 29 | 5 | 112 | 573 | 23.87 | 1 | 4 | 9 |
| RW McLeod<br>*b 19 Jan 1868* | 6 | 11 | 0 | 31 | 146 | 13.27 | – | – | 3 |
| PG McShane<br>*b 18 Apr 1858* | 3 | 6 | 1 | 12* | 26 | 5.20 | – | – | 2 |
| CG Macartney<br>*b 27 Jun 1886* | 35 | 55 | 4 | 170 | 2131 | 41.78 | 7 | 9 | 17 |
| KD Mackay<br>*b 24 Oct 1925* | 37 | 52 | 7 | 89 | 1507 | 33.48 | – | 13 | 16 |
| JA Maclean<br>*b 27 Apr 1946* | 4 | 8 | 1 | 33* | 79 | 11.28 | – | – | 18 |
| LV Maddocks<br>*b 24 May 1926* | 7 | 12 | 2 | 69 | 177 | 17.70 | – | 1 | 18/1 |
| JN Maguire<br>*b 15 Sep 1956* | 3 | 5 | 1 | 15* | 28 | 7.00 | – | – | 2 |
| AA Mailey<br>*b 3 Jan 1886* | 21 | 29 | 9 | 46* | 222 | 11.10 | – | – | 14 |
| AA Mallett<br>*b 13 Jul 1945* | 38 | 50 | 13 | 43* | 430 | 11.62 | – | – | 30 |
| MF Malone<br>*b 9 Oct 1950* | 1 | 1 | 0 | 46 | 46 | 46.00 | – | – | – |
| AL Mann<br>*b 8 Nov 1945* | 4 | 8 | 0 | 105 | 189 | 23.62 | 1 | – | 2 |
| AP Marr<br>*b 28 Mar 1862* | 1 | 2 | 0 | 5 | 5 | 2.50 | – | – | – |
| GR Marsh<br>*b 31 Dec 1958* | 50 | 93 | 7 | 138 | 2854 | 33.18 | 4 | 15 | 38 |
| RW Marsh<br>*b 11 Nov 1947* | 96 | 150 | 13 | 132 | 3633 | 26.51 | 3 | 16 | 343/12 |
| JW Martin<br>*b 28 Jul 1931* | 8 | 13 | 1 | 55 | 214 | 17.83 | – | 1 | 5 |

| Batting | T | I | NO | HS | Runs | Av | 100 | 50 | Ct/St |
|---|---|---|---|---|---|---|---|---|---|
| DR Martyn<br>*b 21 Oct 1971* | 67 | 109 | 14 | 165 | 4406 | 46.37 | 13 | 23 | 36 |
| HH Massie<br>*b 11 Apr 1854* | 9 | 16 | 0 | 55 | 249 | 15.56 | – | 1 | 5 |
| RAL Massie<br>*b 14 Apr 1947* | 6 | 8 | 1 | 42 | 78 | 11.14 | – | – | 1 |
| CD Matthews<br>*b 22 Sep 1962* | 3 | 5 | 0 | 32 | 54 | 10.80 | – | – | 1 |
| GRJ Matthews<br>*b 15 Dec 1959* | 33 | 53 | 8 | 130 | 1849 | 41.08 | 4 | 12 | 17 |
| TJ Matthews<br>*b 3 Apr 1884* | 8 | 10 | 1 | 53 | 153 | 17.00 | – | 1 | 7 |
| TBA May<br>*b 26 Jan 1962* | 24 | 28 | 12 | 42* | 225 | 14.06 | – | – | 6 |
| ER Mayne<br>*b 2 Jul 1882* | 4 | 4 | 1 | 25* | 64 | 21.33 | – | – | 2 |
| LC Mayne<br>*b 23 Jan 1942* | 6 | 11 | 3 | 13 | 76 | 9.50 | – | – | 3 |
| I Meckiff<br>*b 6 Jan 1935* | 18 | 20 | 7 | 45* | 154 | 11.84 | – | – | 9 |
| KD Meuleman<br>*b 5 Sep 1923* | 1 | 1 | 0 | 0 | 0 | – | – | – | 1 |
| WE Midwinter<br>*b 19 Jun 1851* | 8 | 14 | 1 | 37 | 174 | 13.38 | – | – | 5 |
| CR Miller<br>*b 6 Feb 1964* | 18 | 24 | 3 | 43 | 174 | 8.28 | – | – | 6 |
| KR Miller<br>*b 28 Nov 1919* | 55 | 87 | 7 | 147 | 2958 | 36.97 | 7 | 13 | 38 |
| RB Minnett<br>*b 13 Jun 1888* | 9 | 15 | 0 | 90 | 391 | 26.06 | – | 3 | – |
| FM Misson<br>*b 19 Nov 1938* | 5 | 5 | 3 | 25* | 38 | 19.00 | – | – | 6 |
| TM Moody<br>*b 2 Oct 1965* | 8 | 14 | 0 | 106 | 456 | 32.57 | 2 | 3 | 9 |
| J Moroney<br>*b 24 Jul 1917* | 7 | 12 | 1 | 118 | 383 | 34.81 | 2 | 1 | – |
| AR Morris<br>*b 19 Jan 1922* | 46 | 79 | 3 | 206 | 3533 | 46.48 | 12 | 12 | 15 |
| S Morris<br>*b 22 Jun 1855* | 1 | 2 | 1 | 10* | 14 | 14.00 | – | – | – |
| H Moses<br>*b 13 Feb 1858* | 6 | 10 | 0 | 33 | 198 | 19.80 | – | – | 1 |

| Batting | T | I | NO | HS | Runs | Av | 100 | 50 | Ct/St |
|---|---|---|---|---|---|---|---|---|---|
| JK Moss<br>*b 29 Jun 1947* | 1 | 2 | 1 | 38* | 60 | 60.00 | – | – | – |
| WH Moule<br>*b 31 Jan 1858* | 1 | 2 | 0 | 34 | 40 | 20.00 | – | – | 1 |
| SA Muller<br>*b 11 Jul 1971* | 2 | 2 | 2 | 6* | 6 | – | – | – | 2 |
| WL Murdoch<br>*b 18 Oct 1854* | 18 | 33 | 5 | 211 | 896 | 32.00 | 2 | 1 | 14/– |
| HA Musgrove<br>*b 27 Nov 1860* | 1 | 2 | 0 | 9 | 13 | 6.50 | – | – | – |
| LE Nagel<br>*b 6 Mar 1905* | 1 | 2 | 1 | 21* | 21 | 21.00 | – | – | – |
| LJ Nash<br>*b 2 May 1910* | 2 | 2 | 0 | 17 | 30 | 15.00 | – | – | 6 |
| MJ Nicholson<br>*b 2 Oct 1974* | 1 | 2 | 0 | 9 | 14 | 7.00 | – | – | – |
| HC Nitschke<br>*b 14 Apr 1905* | 2 | 2 | 0 | 43 | 53 | 26.50 | – | – | 3 |
| MA Noble<br>*b 28 Jan 1873* | 42 | 73 | 7 | 133 | 1997 | 30.25 | 1 | 16 | 26 |
| G Noblet<br>*b 14 Sep 1916* | 3 | 4 | 1 | 13* | 22 | 7.33 | – | – | 1 |
| OE Nothling<br>*b 1 Aug 1900* | 1 | 2 | 0 | 44 | 52 | 26.00 | – | – | – |
| LPJ O'Brien<br>*b 2 Jul 1907* | 5 | 8 | 0 | 61 | 211 | 26.37 | – | 2 | 3 |
| JDA O'Connor<br>*b 9 Sep 1875* | 4 | 8 | 1 | 20 | 86 | 12.28 | – | – | 3 |
| SP O'Donnell<br>*b 26 Jan 1963* | 6 | 10 | 3 | 48 | 206 | 29.42 | – | – | 4 |
| KJ O'Keeffe<br>*b 25 Nov 1949* | 24 | 34 | 9 | 85 | 644 | 25.76 | – | 1 | 15 |
| NC O'Neill<br>*b 19 Feb 1937* | 42 | 69 | 8 | 181 | 2779 | 45.55 | 6 | 15 | 21 |
| WJ O'Reilly<br>*b 20 Dec 1905* | 27 | 39 | 7 | 56* | 410 | 12.81 | – | 1 | 7 |
| AD Ogilvie<br>*b 3 Jun 1951* | 5 | 10 | 0 | 47 | 178 | 17.80 | – | – | 5 |
| WAS Oldfield<br>*b 9 Sep 1894* | 54 | 80 | 17 | 65* | 1427 | 22.65 | – | 4 | 78/52 |
| RK Oxenham<br>*b 28 Jul 1891* | 7 | 10 | 0 | 48 | 151 | 15.10 | – | – | 4 |

| Batting | T | I | NO | HS | Runs | Av | 100 | 50 | Ct/St |
|---|---|---|---|---|---|---|---|---|---|
| GE Palmer<br>*b 22 Feb 1859* | 17 | 25 | 4 | 48 | 296 | 14.09 | – | – | 13 |
| RL Park<br>*b 30 Jul 1892* | 1 | 1 | 0 | 0 | 0 | – | – | – | – |
| LS Pascoe<br>*b 13 Feb 1950* | 14 | 19 | 9 | 30* | 106 | 10.60 | – | – | 2 |
| CE Pellew<br>*b 21 Sep 1893* | 10 | 14 | 1 | 116 | 484 | 37.23 | 2 | 1 | 4 |
| WB Phillips<br>*b 1 Mar 1958* | 27 | 48 | 2 | 159 | 1485 | 32.28 | 2 | 7 | 52 |
| WN Phillips<br>*b 7 Nov 1962* | 1 | 2 | 0 | 14 | 22 | 11.00 | – | – | – |
| PI Philpott<br>*b 21 Nov 1934* | 8 | 10 | 1 | 22 | 93 | 10.33 | – | – | 5 |
| WH Ponsford<br>*b 19 Oct 1900* | 29 | 48 | 4 | 266 | 2122 | 48.22 | 7 | 6 | 21 |
| RT Ponting<br>*b 19 Dec 1974* | 116 | 193 | 26 | 257 | 9776 | 58.53 | 34 | 39 | 133 |
| RJ Pope<br>*b 18 Feb 1864* | 1 | 2 | 0 | 3 | 3 | 1.50 | – | – | – |
| CG Rackemann<br>*b 3 Jun 1960* | 12 | 14 | 4 | 15* | 53 | 5.30 | – | – | 2 |
| VS Ransford<br>*b 20 Mar 1885* | 20 | 38 | 6 | 143* | 1211 | 37.84 | 1 | 7 | 10 |
| IR Redpath<br>*b 11 May 1941* | 66 | 120 | 11 | 171 | 4737 | 43.45 | 8 | 31 | 83 |
| JC Reedman<br>*b 9 Oct 1865* | 1 | 2 | 0 | 17 | 21 | 10.50 | – | – | 1 |
| BA Reid<br>*b 14 Mar 1963* | 27 | 34 | 14 | 13 | 93 | 4.65 | – | – | 5 |
| PR Reiffel<br>*b 19 Apr 1966* | 35 | 50 | 14 | 79* | 955 | 26.52 | – | 6 | 15 |
| DA Renneberg<br>*b 23 Sep 1942* | 8 | 13 | 7 | 9 | 22 | 3.66 | – | – | 2 |
| AJ Richardson<br>*b 24 Jul 1888* | 9 | 13 | 0 | 100 | 403 | 31.00 | 1 | 2 | 1 |
| VY Richardson<br>*b 7 Sep 1894* | 19 | 30 | 0 | 138 | 706 | 23.53 | 1 | 1 | 24 |
| KE Rigg<br>*b 21 May 1906* | 8 | 12 | 0 | 127 | 401 | 33.41 | 1 | 1 | 5 |
| DT Ring<br>*b 14 Oct 1918* | 13 | 21 | 2 | 67 | 426 | 22.42 | – | 4 | 5 |

| Batting | T | I | NO | HS | Runs | Av | 100 | 50 | Ct/St |
|---|---|---|---|---|---|---|---|---|---|
| GM Ritchie *b 23 Jan 1960* | 30 | 53 | 5 | 146 | 1690 | 35.20 | 3 | 7 | 14 |
| SJ Rixon *b 25 Feb 1954* | 13 | 24 | 3 | 54 | 394 | 18.76 | – | 2 | 42/5 |
| GR Robertson *b 28 May 1966* | 4 | 7 | 0 | 57 | 140 | 20.00 | – | 1 | 1 |
| WR Robertson *b 6 Oct 1861* | 1 | 2 | 0 | 2 | 2 | 1.00 | – | – | – |
| RD Robinson *b 8 Jun 1946* | 3 | 6 | 0 | 34 | 100 | 16.66 | – | – | 4 |
| RH Robinson *b 26 Mar 1914* | 1 | 2 | 0 | 3 | 5 | 2.50 | – | – | 1 |
| CJL Rogers *b 31 Aug 1977* | 1 | 2 | – | 15 | 19 | 9.50 | – | – | 1 |
| GF Rorke *b 27 Jun 1938* | 4 | 4 | 2 | 7 | 9 | 4.50 | – | – | 1 |
| JW Rutherford *b 25 Sep 1929* | 1 | 1 | 0 | 30 | 30 | 30.00 | – | – | – |
| J Ryder *b 8 Aug 1889* | 20 | 32 | 5 | 201* | 1394 | 51.62 | 3 | 9 | 17 |
| RA Saggers *b 15 May 1917* | 6 | 5 | 2 | 14 | 30 | 10.00 | – | – | 16/8 |
| JV Saunders *b 3 Feb 1876* | 14 | 23 | 6 | 11* | 39 | 2.29 | – | – | 5 |
| HJH Scott *b 26 Dec 1858* | 8 | 14 | 1 | 102 | 359 | 27.61 | 1 | 1 | 8 |
| RHD Sellers *b 20 Aug 1940* | 1 | 1 | 0 | 0 | 0 | – | – | – | 1 |
| CS Serjeant *b 1 Nov 1951* | 12 | 23 | 1 | 124 | 522 | 23.72 | 1 | 2 | 13 |
| AP Sheahan *b 30 Sep 1946* | 31 | 53 | 6 | 127 | 1594 | 33.91 | 2 | 7 | 17 |
| BK Shepherd *b 23 Apr 1937* | 9 | 14 | 2 | 96 | 502 | 41.83 | – | 5 | 2 |
| MW Sievers *b 13 Apr 1912* | 3 | 6 | 1 | 25* | 67 | 13.40 | – | – | 4 |
| RB Simpson *b 3 Feb 1936* | 62 | 111 | 7 | 311 | 4869 | 46.81 | 10 | 27 | 110 |
| DJ Sincock *b 1 Feb 1942* | 3 | 4 | 1 | 29 | 80 | 26.66 | – | – | 2 |
| KN Slater *b 12 Mar 1935* | 1 | 1 | 1 | 1* | 1 | – | – | – | – |

| Batting | T | I | NO | HS | Runs | Av | 100 | 50 | Ct/St |
|---|---|---|---|---|---|---|---|---|---|
| MJ Slater<br>*b 21 Feb 1970* | 74 | 131 | 7 | 219 | 5312 | 42.83 | 14 | 21 | 33 |
| PR Sleep<br>*b 4 May 1957* | 14 | 21 | 1 | 90 | 483 | 24.15 | – | 3 | 4 |
| J Slight<br>*b 20 Oct 1855* | 1 | 2 | 0 | 11 | 11 | 5.50 | – | – | – |
| DBM Smith<br>*b 14 Sep 1884* | 2 | 3 | 1 | 24* | 30 | 15.00 | – | – | – |
| SB Smith<br>*b 18 Oct 1961* | 3 | 5 | 0 | 12 | 41 | 8.20 | – | – | 1 |
| FR Spofforth<br>*b 9 Sep 1853* | 18 | 29 | 6 | 50 | 217 | 9.43 | – | 1 | 11 |
| KR Stackpole<br>*b 10 Jul 1940* | 43 | 80 | 5 | 207 | 2807 | 37.42 | 7 | 14 | 47 |
| GB Stevens<br>*b 29 Feb 1932* | 4 | 7 | 0 | 28 | 112 | 16.00 | – | – | 2 |
| A Symonds<br>*b 9 Jun 1975* | 19 | 28 | 3 | 162* | 1031 | 41.24 | 2 | 6 | 14 |
| HB Taber<br>*b 29 Apr 1940* | 16 | 27 | 5 | 48 | 353 | 16.04 | – | – | 56/4 |
| SW Tait<br>*b 22 Feb 1983* | 3 | 5 | 2 | 8 | 20 | 6.66 | – | – | 1 |
| D Tallon<br>*b 17 Feb 1916* | 21 | 26 | 3 | 92 | 394 | 17.13 | – | 2 | 50/8 |
| JM Taylor<br>*b 10 Oct 1895* | 20 | 28 | 0 | 108 | 997 | 35.60 | 1 | 8 | 11 |
| MA Taylor<br>*b 27 Oct 1964* | 104 | 186 | 13 | 334* | 7525 | 43.49 | 19 | 40 | 157 |
| PL Taylor<br>*b 22 Aug 1956* | 13 | 19 | 3 | 87 | 431 | 26.93 | – | 2 | 10 |
| G Thomas<br>*b 21 Mar 1938* | 8 | 12 | 1 | 61 | 325 | 29.54 | – | 3 | 3 |
| GR Thoms<br>*b 22 Mar 1927* | 1 | 2 | 0 | 28 | 44 | 22.00 | – | – | – |
| AL Thomson<br>*b 2 Dec 1945* | 4 | 5 | 4 | 12* | 22 | 22.00 | – | – | – |
| JR Thomson<br>*b 16 Aug 1950* | 51 | 73 | 20 | 49 | 679 | 12.81 | – | – | 20 |
| NFD Thomson<br>*b 29 May 1839* | 2 | 4 | 0 | 41 | 67 | 16.75 | – | – | 3 |
| HM Thurlow<br>*b 10 Jan 1903* | 1 | 1 | 0 | 0 | 0 | – | – | – | – |

| Batting | T | I | NO | HS | Runs | Av | 100 | 50 | Ct/St |
|---|---|---|---|---|---|---|---|---|---|
| PM Toohey<br>*b 20 Apr 1954* | 15 | 29 | 1 | 122 | 893 | 31.89 | 1 | 7 | 9 |
| ERH Toshack<br>*b 15 Dec 1914* | 12 | 11 | 6 | 20* | 73 | 14.60 | – | – | 4 |
| JPF Travers<br>*b 10 Jan 1871* | 1 | 2 | 0 | 9 | 10 | 5.00 | – | – | 1 |
| GE Tribe<br>*b 4 Oct 1920* | 3 | 3 | 1 | 25* | 35 | 17.50 | – | – | – |
| AE Trott<br>*b 6 Feb 1873* | 3 | 5 | 3 | 85* | 205 | 102.50 | – | 2 | 4 |
| GHS Trott<br>*b 5 Aug 1866* | 24 | 42 | 0 | 143 | 921 | 21.92 | 1 | 4 | 21 |
| H Trumble<br>*b 12 May 1867* | 32 | 57 | 14 | 70 | 851 | 19.79 | – | 4 | 45 |
| JW Trumble<br>*b 16 Sep 1863* | 7 | 13 | 1 | 59 | 243 | 20.25 | – | 1 | 3 |
| VT Trumper<br>*b 2 Nov 1877* | 48 | 89 | 8 | 214* | 3163 | 39.04 | 8 | 13 | 31 |
| A Turner<br>*b 23 Jul 1950* | 14 | 27 | 1 | 136 | 768 | 29.53 | 1 | 3 | 15 |
| CTB Turner<br>*b 16 Nov 1862* | 17 | 32 | 4 | 29 | 323 | 11.53 | – | – | 8 |
| TR Veivers<br>*b 6 Apr 1937* | 21 | 30 | 4 | 88 | 813 | 31.26 | – | 7 | 7 |
| MRJ Veletta<br>*b 30 Oct 1963* | 8 | 11 | 0 | 39 | 207 | 18.81 | – | – | 12 |
| MG Waite<br>*b 7 Jan 1911* | 2 | 3 | 0 | 8 | 11 | 3.66 | – | – | 1 |
| MHN Walker<br>*b 12 Sep 1948* | 34 | 43 | 13 | 78* | 586 | 19.53 | – | 1 | 12 |
| TW Wall<br>*b 13 May 1904* | 18 | 24 | 5 | 20 | 121 | 6.36 | – | – | 11 |
| FH Walters<br>*b 9 Feb 1860* | 1 | 2 | 0 | 7 | 12 | 6.00 | – | – | 2 |
| KD Walters<br>*b 21 Dec 1945* | 74 | 125 | 14 | 250 | 5357 | 48.26 | 15 | 33 | 43 |
| FA Ward<br>*b 23 Feb 1906* | 4 | 8 | 2 | 18 | 36 | 6.00 | – | – | 1 |
| SK Warne<br>*b 13 Sep 1969* | 145 | 199 | 17 | 99 | 3154 | 17.32 | – | 12 | 125 |
| JR Watkins<br>*b 16 Apr 1943* | 1 | 2 | 1 | 36 | 39 | 39.00 | – | – | 1 |

| Batting | T | I | NO | HS | Runs | Av | 100 | 50 | Ct/St |
|---|---|---|---|---|---|---|---|---|---|
| GD Watson<br>*b 8 Mar 1945* | 5 | 9 | 0 | 50 | 97 | 10.77 | – | 1 | 1 |
| SR Watson<br>*b 17 Jun 1981* | 3 | 4 | – | 31 | 81 | 20.25 | – | – | – |
| WJ Watson<br>*b 31 Jan 1931* | 4 | 7 | 1 | 30 | 106 | 17.66 | – | – | 2 |
| ME Waugh<br>*b 2 Jun 1965* | 128 | 209 | 17 | 153* | 8029 | 41.81 | 20 | 47 | 181 |
| SR Waugh<br>*b 2 Jun 1965* | 168 | 260 | 46 | 200 | 10927 | 51.06 | 32 | 50 | 112 |
| DM Wellham<br>*b 13 Mar 1959* | 6 | 11 | 0 | 103 | 257 | 23.36 | 1 | – | 5 |
| KC Wessels<br>*b 14 Sep 1957* | 24 | 42 | 1 | 179 | 1761 | 42.95 | 4 | 9 | 18 |
| DF Whatmore<br>*b 16 Mar 1954* | 7 | 13 | 0 | 77 | 293 | 22.53 | – | 2 | 13 |
| MR Whitney<br>*b 24 Feb 1959* | 12 | 19 | 8 | 13 | 68 | 6.18 | – | – | 2 |
| WJ Whitty<br>*b 15 Aug 1886* | 14 | 19 | 7 | 39* | 161 | 13.41 | – | – | 4 |
| JM Wiener<br>*b 1 May 1955* | 6 | 11 | 0 | 93 | 281 | 25.54 | – | 2 | 4 |
| BA Williams<br>*b 20 Nov 1974* | 4 | 6 | 3 | 10* | 23 | 7.66 | – | – | 4 |
| JW Wilson<br>*b 20 Aug 1921* | 1 | – | | | | | – | – | – |
| P Wilson<br>*b 12 Jan 1972* | 1 | 2 | 2 | 0* | 0 | – | – | – | – |
| GM Wood<br>*b 6 Nov 1956* | 59 | 112 | 6 | 172 | 3374 | 31.83 | 9 | 13 | 41 |
| AJ Woodcock<br>*b 27 Feb 1947* | 1 | 1 | 0 | 27 | 27 | 27.00 | – | – | 1 |
| WM Woodfull<br>*b 22 Aug 1897* | 35 | 54 | 4 | 161 | 2300 | 46.00 | 7 | 13 | 7 |
| SMJ Woods<br>*b 13 Apr 1867* | 3 | 6 | 0 | 18 | 32 | 5.33 | – | – | 1 |
| RD Woolley<br>*b 16 Sep 1954* | 2 | 2 | 0 | 13 | 21 | 10.50 | – | – | 7 |
| J Worrall<br>*b 12 May 1860* | 11 | 22 | 3 | 76 | 478 | 25.15 | – | 5 | 13 |
| KJ Wright<br>*b 27 Dec 1953* | 10 | 18 | 5 | 55* | 219 | 16.84 | – | 1 | 31/4 |

| Batting | T | I | NO | HS | Runs | Av | 100 | 50 | Ct/St |
|---|---|---|---|---|---|---|---|---|---|
| GN Yallop<br>*b 7 Oct 1952* | 39 | 70 | 3 | 268 | 2756 | 41.13 | 8 | 9 | 23 |
| B Yardley<br>*b 5 Sep 1947* | 33 | 54 | 4 | 74 | 978 | 19.56 | – | 4 | 31 |
| S Young<br>*b 13 Jun 1970* | 1 | 2 | 1 | 4* | 4 | 4.00 | – | – | – |
| TJ Zoehrer<br>*b 25 Sep 1961* | 10 | 14 | 2 | 52* | 246 | 20.50 | – | 1 | 18/1 |

| Bowling | Balls | Runs | Wkts | Av | Best | 5w | 10w |
|---|---|---|---|---|---|---|---|
| EL a'Beckett | 1062 | 317 | 3 | 105.66 | 1–41 | – | – |
| TM Alderman | 10181 | 4616 | 170 | 27.15 | 6–47 | 14 | 1 |
| G Alexander | 168 | 93 | 2 | 46.50 | 2–69 | – | – |
| HH Alexander | 276 | 154 | 1 | 154.00 | 1–129 | – | – |
| FE Allan | 180 | 80 | 4 | 20.00 | 2–30 | – | – |
| PJ Allan | 192 | 83 | 2 | 41.50 | 2–58 | – | – |
| TJE Andrews | 156 | 116 | 1 | 116.00 | 1–23 | – | – |
| J Angel | 748 | 463 | 10 | 46.30 | 3–54 | – | – |
| RG Archer | 3576 | 1318 | 48 | 27.45 | 5–53 | 1 | – |
| WW Armstrong | 8022 | 2923 | 87 | 33.59 | 6–35 | 3 | – |
| AC Bannerman | 292 | 163 | 4 | 40.75 | 3–111 | – | – |
| SG Barnes | 594 | 218 | 4 | 54.50 | 2–25 | – | – |
| GR Beard | 259 | 109 | 1 | 109.00 | 1–26 | – | – |
| J Benaud | 24 | 12 | 2 | 6.00 | 2–12 | – | – |
| R Benaud | 19108 | 6704 | 248 | 27.03 | 7–72 | 16 | 1 |
| MJ Bennett | 665 | 325 | 6 | 54.16 | 3–79 | – | – |
| MG Bevan | 1285 | 703 | 29 | 24.24 | 6–82 | 1 | 1 |
| AJ Bichel | 3366 | 1870 | 58 | 32.24 | 5–60 | 1 | – |
| DD Blackie | 1260 | 444 | 14 | 31.71 | 6–94 | 1 | – |
| GS Blewett | 1436 | 720 | 14 | 51.42 | 2–9 | – | – |
| GJ Bonnor | 164 | 84 | 2 | 42.00 | 1–5 | – | – |
| DC Boon | 36 | 14 | 0 | | | | |
| BC Booth | 436 | 146 | 3 | 48.66 | 2–33 | – | – |
| AR Border | 4009 | 1525 | 39 | 39.10 | 7–46 | 2 | 1 |
| HF Boyle | 1743 | 641 | 32 | 20.03 | 6–42 | 1 | – |
| NW Bracken | 1110 | 505 | 12 | 42.08 | 4–48 | – | – |

APPENDIX A

| Bowling | Balls | Runs | Wkts | Av | Best | 5w | 10w |
|---|---|---|---|---|---|---|---|
| DG Bradman | 160 | 72 | 2 | 36.00 | 1–8 | – | – |
| RJ Bright | 5541 | 2180 | 53 | 41.13 | 7–87 | 4 | 1 |
| EH Bromley | 60 | 19 | 0 | | | | |
| W Bruce | 988 | 440 | 12 | 36.66 | 3–88 | – | – |
| JW Burke | 814 | 230 | 8 | 28.75 | 4–37 | – | – |
| ST Callaway | 471 | 142 | 6 | 23.66 | 5–37 | 1 | – |
| IW Callen | 440 | 191 | 6 | 31.83 | 3–83 | – | – |
| GD Campbell | 951 | 503 | 13 | 38.69 | 3–79 | – | – |
| PH Carlson | 368 | 99 | 2 | 49.50 | 2–41 | – | – |
| GS Chappell | 5327 | 1913 | 47 | 40.70 | 5–61 | 1 | – |
| IM Chappell | 2873 | 1316 | 20 | 65.80 | 2–21 | – | – |
| PC Charlton | 45 | 24 | 3 | 8.00 | 3–18 | – | – |
| AG Chipperfield | 924 | 437 | 5 | 87.40 | 3–91 | – | – |
| SR Clark | 3394 | 1488 | 68 | 21.88 | 5–55 | 1 | – |
| WM Clark | 2793 | 1265 | 44 | 28.75 | 4–46 | – | – |
| MJ Clarke | 529 | 264 | 12 | 22.00 | 6–9 | – | – |
| DJ Colley | 729 | 312 | 6 | 52.00 | 3–83 | – | – |
| HL Collins | 654 | 252 | 4 | 63.00 | 2–47 | – | – |
| A Coningham | 186 | 76 | 2 | 38.00 | 2–17 | – | – |
| AN Connolly | 7818 | 2981 | 102 | 29.22 | 6–47 | 4 | – |
| SH Cook | 224 | 142 | 7 | 20.28 | 5–39 | 1 | – |
| WH Cooper | 466 | 226 | 9 | 25.11 | 6–120 | 1 | – |
| GE Corling | 1159 | 447 | 12 | 37.25 | 4–60 | – | – |
| GJ Cosier | 899 | 341 | 5 | 68.20 | 2–26 | – | – |
| A Cotter | 4639 | 2549 | 89 | 28.64 | 7–148 | 7 | – |
| RM Cowper | 3005 | 1139 | 36 | 31.63 | 4–48 | – | – |
| WPA Crawford | 437 | 107 | 7 | 15.28 | 3–28 | – | – |
| DJ Cullen | 84 | 54 | 1 | 54.00 | 1–25 | – | – |
| AC Dale | 348 | 187 | 6 | 31.16 | 3–71 | – | – |
| LS Darling | 162 | 65 | 0 | | | | |
| AK Davidson | 11587 | 3819 | 186 | 20.53 | 7–93 | 14 | 2 |
| SP Davis | 150 | 70 | 0 | | | | |
| AR Dell | 559 | 160 | 6 | 26.66 | 3–65 | – | – |
| AIC Dodemaide | 2184 | 953 | 34 | 28.02 | 6–58 | 1 | – |
| H Donnan | 54 | 22 | 0 | | | | |
| B Dooland | 880 | 419 | 9 | 46.55 | 4–69 | – | – |
| RA Duff | 180 | 85 | 4 | 21.25 | 2–43 | – | – |
| JRF Duncan | 112 | 30 | 0 | | | | |
| G Dymock | 5545 | 2116 | 78 | 27.12 | 7–67 | 5 | 1 |

| Bowling | Balls | Runs | Wkts | Av | Best | 5w | 10w |
|---|---|---|---|---|---|---|---|
| CJ Eady | 223 | 112 | 7 | 16.00 | 3–30 | – | – |
| KH Eastwood | 40 | 21 | 1 | 21.00 | 1–21 | – | – |
| HI Ebeling | 186 | 89 | 3 | 29.66 | 3–74 | – | – |
| R Edwards | 12 | 20 | 0 | | | | |
| MTG Elliott | 12 | 4 | 0 | | | | |
| SH Emery | 462 | 249 | 5 | 49.80 | 2–46 | – | – |
| E Evans | 1237 | 332 | 7 | 47.42 | 3–64 | – | – |
| AG Fairfax | 1520 | 645 | 21 | 30.71 | 4–31 | – | – |
| JJ Ferris | 2030 | 684 | 48 | 14.25 | 5–26 | 4 | – |
| LO'B Fleetwood-Smith | 3093 | 1570 | 42 | 37.38 | 6–110 | 2 | 1 |
| DW Fleming | 4129 | 1942 | 75 | 25.89 | 5–30 | 3 | – |
| EW Freeman | 2183 | 1128 | 34 | 33.17 | 4–52 | – | – |
| FAW Freer | 160 | 74 | 3 | 24.66 | 2–49 | – | – |
| JB Gannon | 726 | 361 | 11 | 32.81 | 4–77 | – | – |
| TW Garrett | 2728 | 970 | 36 | 26.94 | 6–78 | 2 | – |
| RA Gaunt | 716 | 310 | 7 | 44.28 | 3–53 | – | – |
| DRA Gehrs | 6 | 4 | 0 | | | | |
| G Giffen | 6391 | 2791 | 103 | 27.09 | 7–117 | 7 | 1 |
| DR Gilbert | 1647 | 843 | 16 | 52.68 | 3–48 | – | – |
| JN Gillespie | 14234 | 6770 | 259 | 26.13 | 7–37 | 8 | – |
| GK Gilmour | 2661 | 1406 | 54 | 26.03 | 6–85 | 3 | – |
| JW Gleeson | 8857 | 3367 | 93 | 36.20 | 5–61 | 3 | – |
| DW Gregory | 20 | 9 | 0 | | | | |
| JM Gregory | 5582 | 2648 | 85 | 31.15 | 7–69 | 4 | – |
| RG Gregory | 24 | 14 | 0 | | | | |
| SE Gregory | 30 | 33 | 0 | | | | |
| CV Grimmett | 14513 | 5231 | 216 | 24.21 | 7–40 | 21 | 7 |
| CEJ Guest | 144 | 59 | 0 | | | | |
| JR Hammond | 1031 | 488 | 15 | 32.53 | 4–38 | – | – |
| MJ Hartigan | 12 | 7 | 0 | | | | |
| AEV Hartkopf | 240 | 134 | 1 | 134.00 | 1–120 | – | – |
| RN Harvey | 414 | 120 | 3 | 40.00 | 1–8 | – | – |
| AL Hassett | 111 | 78 | 0 | | | | |
| NM Hauritz | 162 | 103 | 5 | 20.60 | 3–16 | – | – |
| NJN Hawke | 6974 | 2677 | 91 | 29.41 | 7–105 | 6 | 1 |
| ML Hayden | 54 | 40 | 0 | | | | |
| GR Hazlitt | 1563 | 623 | 23 | 27.08 | 7–25 | 1 | – |
| HSTL Hendry | 1706 | 640 | 16 | 40.00 | 3–36 | – | – |

| Bowling | Balls | Runs | Wkts | Av | Best | 5w | 10w |
|---|---|---|---|---|---|---|---|
| JD Higgs | 4752 | 2057 | 66 | 31.16 | 7–143 | 2 | – |
| JC Hill | 606 | 273 | 8 | 34.12 | 3–35 | – | – |
| DE Hoare | 232 | 156 | 2 | 78.00 | 2–68 | – | – |
| BJ Hodge | 12 | 8 | 0 | | | | |
| JR Hodges | 136 | 84 | 6 | 14.00 | 2–7 | – | – |
| TG Hogan | 1436 | 706 | 15 | 47.06 | 5–66 | 1 | – |
| GB Hogg | 1524 | 933 | 17 | 54.88 | 2–40 | – | – |
| RM Hogg | 7633 | 3503 | 123 | 28.47 | 6–74 | 6 | 2 |
| TV Hohns | 1528 | 580 | 17 | 34.11 | 3–59 | – | – |
| GB Hole | 398 | 126 | 3 | 42.00 | 1–9 | – | – |
| RG Holland | 2889 | 1352 | 34 | 39.76 | 6–54 | 3 | 2 |
| DW Hookes | 96 | 41 | 1 | 41.00 | 1–4 | – | – |
| AJY Hopkins | 1327 | 696 | 26 | 26.76 | 4–81 | – | – |
| TP Horan | 373 | 143 | 11 | 13.00 | 6–40 | 1 | – |
| HV Hordern | 2148 | 1075 | 46 | 23.36 | 7–90 | 5 | 2 |
| PM Hornibrook | 1579 | 664 | 17 | 39.05 | 7–92 | 1 | – |
| WP Howell | 3892 | 1407 | 49 | 28.71 | 5–81 | 1 | – |
| KJ Hughes | 85 | 28 | 0 | | | | |
| MG Hughes | 12285 | 6017 | 212 | 28.38 | 8–87 | 7 | 1 |
| WA Hunt | 96 | 39 | 0 | | | | |
| AG Hurst | 3054 | 1200 | 43 | 27.90 | 5–28 | 2 | – |
| A Hurwood | 517 | 170 | 11 | 15.45 | 4–22 | – | – |
| MEK Hussey | 30 | 23 | 0 | | | | |
| RJ Inverarity | 372 | 93 | 4 | 23.25 | 3–26 | – | – |
| FA Iredale | 12 | 3 | 0 | | | | |
| H Ironmonger | 4695 | 1330 | 74 | 17.97 | 7–23 | 4 | 2 |
| JB Iverson | 1108 | 320 | 21 | 15.23 | 6–27 | 1 | – |
| TJ Jenner | 1881 | 749 | 24 | 31.20 | 5–90 | 1 | – |
| IWG Johnson | 8780 | 3182 | 109 | 29.19 | 7–44 | 3 | – |
| LJ Johnson | 282 | 74 | 6 | 12.33 | 3–8 | – | – |
| MG Johnson | 1501 | 771 | 24 | 32.12 | 4–86 | – | – |
| WA Johnston | 11048 | 3826 | 160 | 23.91 | 6–44 | 7 | – |
| DM Jones | 198 | 64 | 1 | 64.00 | 1–5 | – | – |
| E Jones | 3754 | 1857 | 64 | 29.01 | 7–88 | 3 | 1 |
| SP Jones | 262 | 112 | 6 | 18.66 | 4–47 | – | – |
| BP Julian | 1098 | 599 | 15 | 39.93 | 4–36 | – | – |
| MS Kasprowicz | 7140 | 3716 | 113 | 32.88 | 7–36 | 4 | – |
| SM Katich | 659 | 406 | 12 | 33.83 | 6–65 | 1 | – |

| Bowling | Balls | Runs | Wkts | Av | Best | 5w | 10w |
|---|---|---|---|---|---|---|---|
| C Kelleway | 4363 | 1683 | 52 | 32.36 | 5–33 | 1 | – |
| TK Kendall | 563 | 215 | 14 | 15.35 | 7–55 | 1 | – |
| AF Kippax | 72 | 19 | 0 | | | | |
| LF Kline | 2373 | 776 | 34 | 22.82 | 7–75 | 1 | – |
| BM Laird | 18 | 12 | 0 | | | | |
| JL Langer | 6 | 3 | 0 | | | | |
| TJ Laughlin | 516 | 262 | 6 | 43.66 | 5–101 | 1 | – |
| FJ Laver | 2361 | 964 | 37 | 26.05 | 8–31 | 2 | – |
| SG Law | 18 | 9 | 0 | | | | |
| WM Lawry | 14 | 6 | 0 | | | | |
| GF Lawson | 11118 | 5501 | 180 | 30.56 | 8–112 | 11 | 2 |
| B Lee | 13698 | 8123 | 271 | 29.97 | 5–30 | 8 | – |
| PK Lee | 436 | 212 | 5 | 42.40 | 4–111 | – | – |
| DS Lehmann | 974 | 412 | 15 | 27.46 | 3–42 | – | – |
| DK Lillee | 18467 | 8493 | 355 | 23.92 | 7–83 | 23 | 7 |
| RR Lindwall | 13650 | 5251 | 228 | 23.03 | 7–38 | 12 | – |
| SJE Loxton | 906 | 349 | 8 | 43.62 | 3–55 | – | – |
| JJ Lyons | 316 | 149 | 6 | 24.83 | 5–30 | 1 | – |
| SCG MacGill | 10781 | 5713 | 203 | 28.14 | 8–108 | 12 | 2 |
| SJ McCabe | 3746 | 1543 | 36 | 42.86 | 4–13 | – | – |
| CL McCool | 2504 | 958 | 36 | 26.61 | 5–41 | 3 | – |
| EL McCormick | 2107 | 1079 | 36 | 29.97 | 4–101 | – | – |
| CJ McDermott | 16586 | 8332 | 291 | 28.63 | 8–97 | 14 | 2 |
| CC McDonald | 8 | 3 | 0 | | | | |
| EA McDonald | 2885 | 1431 | 43 | 33.27 | 5–32 | 2 | – |
| PS McDonnell | 52 | 53 | 0 | | | | |
| GD McGrath | 29248 | 12186 | 563 | 21.64 | 8–24 | 29 | 3 |
| PE McIntyre | 393 | 194 | 5 | 38.80 | 3–103 | – | – |
| GD McKenzie | 17681 | 7328 | 246 | 29.78 | 8–71 | 16 | 3 |
| TR McKibbin | 1032 | 496 | 17 | 29.17 | 3–35 | – | – |
| JW McLaren | 144 | 70 | 1 | 70.00 | 1–23 | – | – |
| CE McLeod | 3374 | 1325 | 33 | 40.15 | 5–65 | 2 | – |
| RW McLeod | 1089 | 382 | 12 | 31.83 | 5–53 | 1 | – |
| PG McShane | 108 | 48 | 1 | 48.00 | 1–39 | – | – |
| CG Macartney | 3561 | 1240 | 45 | 27.55 | 7–58 | 2 | 1 |
| KD Mackay | 5792 | 1721 | 50 | 34.42 | 6–42 | 2 | – |
| JN Maguire | 616 | 323 | 10 | 32.30 | 4–57 | – | – |
| AA Mailey | 6119 | 3358 | 99 | 33.91 | 9–121 | 6 | 2 |
| AA Mallett | 9990 | 3940 | 132 | 29.84 | 8–59 | 6 | 1 |

| Bowling | Balls | Runs | Wkts | Av | Best | 5w | 10w |
|---|---|---|---|---|---|---|---|
| MF Malone | 342 | 77 | 6 | 12.83 | 5–63 | 1 | – |
| AL Mann | 552 | 316 | 4 | 79.00 | 3–12 | – | – |
| AP Marr | 48 | 14 | 0 | | | | |
| RW Marsh | 72 | 54 | 0 | | | | |
| JW Martin | 1846 | 832 | 17 | 48.94 | 3–56 | – | – |
| DR Martyn | 348 | 168 | 2 | 84.00 | 1–0 | – | – |
| RAL Massie | 1739 | 647 | 31 | 20.87 | 8–53 | 2 | 1 |
| CD Matthews | 570 | 313 | 6 | 52.16 | 3–95 | – | – |
| GRJ Matthews | 6271 | 2942 | 61 | 48.22 | 5–103 | 2 | 1 |
| TJ Matthews | 1081 | 419 | 16 | 26.18 | 4–29 | – | – |
| TBA May | 6577 | 2606 | 75 | 34.74 | 5–9 | 3 | – |
| ER Mayne | 6 | 1 | 0 | | | | |
| LC Mayne | 1251 | 628 | 19 | 33.05 | 4–43 | – | – |
| I Meckiff | 3734 | 1423 | 45 | 31.62 | 6–38 | 2 | – |
| WE Midwinter | 949 | 333 | 14 | 23.78 | 5–78 | 1 | – |
| CR Miller | 4091 | 1805 | 69 | 26.15 | 5–32 | 3 | 1 |
| KR Miller | 10461 | 3906 | 170 | 22.97 | 7–60 | 7 | 1 |
| RB Minnett | 589 | 290 | 11 | 26.36 | 4–34 | – | – |
| FM Misson | 1197 | 616 | 16 | 38.50 | 4–58 | – | – |
| TM Moody | 432 | 147 | 2 | 73.50 | 1–17 | – | – |
| AR Morris | 111 | 50 | 2 | 25.00 | 1–5 | – | – |
| S Morris | 136 | 73 | 2 | 36.50 | 2–73 | – | – |
| WH Moule | 51 | 23 | 3 | 7.66 | 3–23 | – | – |
| SA Muller | 348 | 258 | 7 | 36.85 | 3–68 | – | – |
| LE Nagel | 262 | 110 | 2 | 55.00 | 2–110 | – | – |
| LJ Nash | 311 | 126 | 10 | 12.60 | 4–18 | – | – |
| MJ Nicholson | 150 | 115 | 4 | 28.75 | 3–56 | – | – |
| MA Noble | 7159 | 3025 | 121 | 25.00 | 7–17 | 9 | 2 |
| G Noblet | 774 | 183 | 7 | 26.14 | 3–21 | – | – |
| OE Nothling | 276 | 72 | 0 | | | | |
| JDA O'Connor | 692 | 340 | 13 | 26.15 | 5–40 | 1 | – |
| SP O'Donnell | 940 | 504 | 6 | 84.00 | 3–37 | – | – |
| KJ O'Keeffe | 5384 | 2018 | 53 | 38.07 | 5–101 | 1 | – |
| NC O'Neill | 1392 | 667 | 17 | 39.23 | 4–41 | – | – |
| WJ O'Reilly | 10024 | 3254 | 144 | 22.59 | 7–54 | 11 | 3 |
| RK Oxenham | 1802 | 522 | 14 | 37.28 | 4–39 | – | – |
| GE Palmer | 4517 | 1678 | 78 | 21.51 | 7–65 | 6 | 2 |
| RL Park | 6 | 9 | 0 | | | | |
| LS Pascoe | 3403 | 1668 | 64 | 26.06 | 5–59 | 1 | – |

| Bowling | Balls | Runs | Wkts | Av | Best | 5w | 10w |
|---|---|---|---|---|---|---|---|
| CE Pellew | 78 | 34 | 0 | | | | |
| PI Philpott | 2262 | 1000 | 26 | 38.46 | 5–90 | 1 | – |
| RT Ponting | 527 | 231 | 5 | 46.20 | 1–0 | – | – |
| CG Rackemann | 2719 | 1137 | 39 | 29.15 | 6–86 | 3 | 1 |
| VS Ransford | 43 | 28 | 1 | 28.00 | 1–9 | – | – |
| IR Redpath | 64 | 41 | 0 | | | | |
| JC Reedman | 57 | 24 | 1 | 24.00 | 1–12 | – | – |
| BA Reid | 6244 | 2784 | 113 | 24.63 | 7–51 | 5 | 2 |
| PR Reiffel | 6403 | 2804 | 104 | 26.96 | 6–71 | 5 | – |
| DA Renneberg | 1598 | 830 | 23 | 36.08 | 5–39 | 2 | – |
| AJ Richardson | 1812 | 521 | 12 | 43.41 | 2–20 | – | – |
| DT Ring | 3024 | 1305 | 35 | 37.28 | 6–72 | 2 | – |
| GM Ritchie | 6 | 10 | 0 | | | | |
| GR Robertson | 898 | 515 | 13 | 39.61 | 4–72 | – | – |
| WR Robertson | 44 | 24 | 0 | | | | |
| GF Rorke | 703 | 203 | 10 | 20.30 | 3–23 | – | – |
| JW Rutherford | 36 | 15 | 1 | 15.00 | 1–11 | – | – |
| J Ryder | 1897 | 743 | 17 | 43.70 | 2–20 | – | – |
| JV Saunders | 3565 | 1796 | 79 | 22.73 | 7–34 | 6 | – |
| HJH Scott | 28 | 26 | 0 | | | | |
| RHD Sellers | 30 | 17 | 0 | | | | |
| BK Shepherd | 26 | 9 | 0 | | | | |
| MW Sievers | 602 | 161 | 9 | 17.88 | 5–21 | 1 | – |
| RB Simpson | 6881 | 3001 | 71 | 42.26 | 5–57 | 2 | – |
| DJ Sincock | 724 | 410 | 8 | 51.25 | 3–67 | – | – |
| KN Slater | 256 | 101 | 2 | 50.50 | 2–40 | – | – |
| MJ Slater | 25 | 10 | 1 | 10.00 | 1–4 | – | – |
| PR Sleep | 2982 | 1397 | 31 | 45.06 | 5–72 | 1 | – |
| FR Spofforth | 4185 | 1731 | 94 | 18.41 | 7–44 | 7 | 4 |
| KR Stackpole | 2321 | 1001 | 15 | 66.73 | 2–33 | – | – |
| A Symonds | 1692 | 766 | 22 | 34.81 | 3–50 | – | – |
| SW Tait | 414 | 302 | 5 | 60.40 | 3–97 | – | – |
| JM Taylor | 114 | 45 | 1 | 45.00 | 1–25 | – | – |
| MA Taylor | 42 | 26 | 1 | 26.00 | 1–11 | – | – |
| PL Taylor | 2227 | 1068 | 27 | 39.55 | 6–78 | 1 | – |
| AL Thomson | 1519 | 654 | 12 | 54.50 | 3–79 | – | – |
| JR Thomson | 10535 | 5601 | 200 | 28.00 | 6–46 | 8 | – |
| NFD Thomson | 112 | 31 | 1 | 31.00 | 1–14 | – | – |
| HM Thurlow | 234 | 86 | 0 | | | | |

| Bowling | Balls | Runs | Wkts | Av | Best | 5w | 10w |
|---|---|---|---|---|---|---|---|
| PM Toohey | 2 | 4 | 0 | | | | |
| ERH Toshack | 3140 | 989 | 47 | 21.04 | 6–29 | 4 | 1 |
| JPF Travers | 48 | 14 | 1 | 14.00 | 1–14 | – | – |
| GE Tribe | 760 | 330 | 2 | 165.00 | 2–48 | – | – |
| AE Trott | 474 | 192 | 9 | 21.33 | 8–43 | 1 | – |
| GHS Trott | 1890 | 1019 | 29 | 35.13 | 4–71 | – | – |
| H Trumble | 8099 | 3072 | 141 | 21.78 | 8–65 | 9 | 3 |
| JW Trumble | 600 | 222 | 10 | 22.20 | 3–29 | – | – |
| VT Trumper | 546 | 317 | 8 | 39.62 | 3–60 | – | – |
| CTB Turner | 5179 | 1670 | 101 | 16.53 | 7–43 | 11 | 2 |
| TR Veivers | 4191 | 1375 | 33 | 41.66 | 4–68 | – | – |
| MG Waite | 552 | 190 | 1 | 190.00 | 1–150 | – | – |
| MHN Walker | 10094 | 3792 | 138 | 27.47 | 8–143 | 6 | – |
| TW Wall | 4812 | 2010 | 56 | 35.89 | 5–14 | 3 | – |
| KD Walters | 3295 | 1425 | 49 | 29.08 | 5–66 | 1 | – |
| FA Ward | 1268 | 574 | 11 | 52.18 | 6–102 | 1 | – |
| SK Warne | 40705 | 17995 | 708 | 25.41 | 8–71 | 37 | 10 |
| JR Watkins | 48 | 21 | 0 | | | | |
| GD Watson | 552 | 254 | 6 | 42.33 | 2–67 | – | – |
| SR Watson | 186 | 123 | 2 | 61.50 | 1–25 | – | – |
| WJ Watson | 6 | 5 | 0 | | | | |
| ME Waugh | 4853 | 2429 | 59 | 41.16 | 5–40 | 1 | – |
| SR Waugh | 7805 | 3445 | 92 | 37.44 | 5–28 | 3 | – |
| KC Wessels | 90 | 42 | 0 | | | | |
| DF Whatmore | 30 | 11 | 0 | | | | |
| MR Whitney | 2672 | 1325 | 39 | 33.97 | 7–27 | 2 | 1 |
| WJ Whitty | 3357 | 1373 | 65 | 21.12 | 6–17 | 3 | – |
| JM Wiener | 78 | 41 | 0 | | | | |
| BA Williams | 852 | 406 | 9 | 45.11 | 4–53 | – | – |
| JW Wilson | 216 | 64 | 1 | 64.00 | 1–25 | – | – |
| P Wilson | 72 | 50 | 0 | | | | |
| SMJ Woods | 217 | 121 | 5 | 24.20 | 2–35 | – | – |
| J Worrall | 255 | 127 | 1 | 127.00 | 1–97 | – | – |
| GN Yallop | 192 | 116 | 1 | 116.00 | 1–21 | – | – |
| B Yardley | 8909 | 3986 | 126 | 31.63 | 7–98 | 6 | 1 |
| S Young | 48 | 13 | 0 | | | | |

# Appendix B

## Sheffield Shield & Pura Cup Winners

| | |
|---|---|
| 1892-93 | Victoria |
| 1893-94 | South Australia |
| 1894-95 | Victoria |
| 1895-96 | New South Wales |
| 1896-97 | New South Wales |
| 1897-98 | Victoria |
| 1898-99 | Victoria |
| 1899-00 | New South Wales |
| 1900-01 | Victoria |
| 1901-02 | New South Wales |
| 1902-03 | New South Wales |
| 1903-04 | New South Wales |
| 1904-05 | New South Wales |
| 1905-06 | New South Wales |
| 1906-07 | New South Wales |
| 1907-08 | Victoria |
| 1908-09 | New South Wales |
| 1909-10 | South Australia |
| 1910-11 | New South Wales |
| 1911-12 | New South Wales |
| 1912-13 | South Australia |
| 1913-14 | New South Wales |
| 1914-15 | South Australia |
| 1915-19 | No competition |
| 1919-20 | New South Wales |
| 1920-21 | New South Wales |
| 1921-22 | Victoria |
| 1922-23 | New South Wales |
| 1923-24 | Victoria |
| 1924-25 | Victoria |
| 1925-26 | New South Wales |
| 1926-27 | South Australia |
| 1927-28 | Victoria |
| 1928-29 | New South Wales |
| 1929-30 | Victoria |
| 1930-31 | Victoria |
| 1931-32 | New South Wales |
| 1932-33 | New South Wales |
| 1933-34 | Victoria |
| 1934-35 | Victoria |
| 1935-36 | South Australia |
| 1936-37 | Victoria |
| 1937-38 | New South Wales |
| 1938-39 | South Australia |
| 1939-40 | New South Wales |
| 1940-45 | No competition |
| 1945-46 | Victoria |
| 1946-47 | Western Australia |
| 1948-49 | New South Wales |
| 1949-50 | New South Wales |
| 1950-51 | Victoria |
| 1951-52 | New South Wales |
| 1952-53 | South Australia |
| 1953-54 | New South Wales |
| 1954-55 | New South Wales |
| 1955-56 | New South Wales |
| 1956-57 | New South Wales |
| 1957-58 | New South Wales |
| 1958-59 | New South Wales |
| 1959-60 | New South Wales |
| 1960-61 | New South Wales |
| 1961-62 | New South Wales |
| 1962-63 | Victoria |
| 1963-64 | South Australia |
| 1964-65 | New South Wales |
| 1965-66 | New South Wales |
| 1966-67 | Victoria |
| 1967-68 | Western Australia |
| 1968-69 | South Australia |
| 1969-70 | Victoria |
| 1970-71 | South Australia |
| 1971-72 | Western Australia |
| 1972-73 | Western Australia |
| 1973-74 | Victoria |
| 1974-75 | Western Australia |
| 1975-76 | South Australia |
| 1976-76 | Western Australia |
| 1977-78 | Western Australia |
| 1978-79 | Victoria |
| 1979-80 | Victoria |
| 1980-81 | Western Australia |
| 1981-82 | South Australia |
| 1982-83 | New South Wales |
| 1983-84 | Western Australia |
| 1984-85 | New South Wales |
| 1985-86 | New South Wales |
| 1986-87 | Western Australia |
| 1987-88 | Western Australia |
| 1988-89 | Western Australia |
| 1989-90 | New South Wales |
| 1990-91 | Victoria |
| 1991-92 | Western Australia |
| 1992-93 | New South Wales |
| 1993-94 | New South Wales |
| 1994-95 | Queensland |
| 1995-96 | South Australia |
| 1996-97 | Queensland |
| 1997-98 | Western Australia |
| 1998-99 | Western Australia |
| **Pura Cup starts 1999–2000** | |
| 1999-00 | Queensland |
| 2000-01 | Queensland |
| 2001-02 | Queensland |
| 2002-03 | New South Wales |
| 2003-04 | Victoria |
| 2004-05 | New South Wales |
| 2005-06 | Queensland |
| 2006-07 | Tasmania |
| 2007-08 | New South Wales |

# Appendix C

# Limited-Over International Averages

| Batting | M | I | NO | HS | Runs | Av | 100 | 50 | Ct/St |
|---|---|---|---|---|---|---|---|---|---|
| TM Alderman | 65 | 18 | 6 | 9* | 32 | 2.66 | – | – | 29 |
| J Angel | 3 | 1 | 0 | 0 | 0 | – | – | – | – |
| GR Beard | 2 | – | | | | | – | – | – |
| MJ Bennett | 8 | 4 | 1 | 6* | 9 | 3.00 | – | – | 1 |
| MG Bevan | 232 | 196 | 67 | 108* | 6912 | 53.58 | 6 | 46 | 69 |
| AJ Bichel | 67 | 36 | 13 | 64 | 471 | 20.47 | – | 1 | 19 |
| GA Bishop | 2 | 2 | 0 | 7 | 13 | 6.50 | – | – | 1 |
| GS Blewett | 32 | 30 | 3 | 57* | 551 | 20.40 | – | 2 | 7 |
| DC Boon | 181 | 177 | 16 | 122 | 5964 | 37.04 | 5 | 37 | 45 |
| AR Border | 273 | 252 | 39 | 127* | 6524 | 30.62 | 3 | 39 | 127 |
| NW Bracken | 84 | 25 | 12 | 21* | 164 | 12.61 | – | – | 17 |
| RJ Bright | 11 | 8 | 4 | 19* | 66 | 16.50 | – | – | 2 |
| IW Callen | 5 | 3 | 2 | 3* | 6 | 6.00 | – | – | 2 |
| GD Campbell | 12 | 3 | 1 | 4* | 6 | 3.00 | – | – | 4 |
| RJ Campbell | 2 | 2 | 0 | 38 | 54 | 27.00 | – | – | 4/1 |
| PH Carlson | 4 | 2 | 0 | 11 | 11 | 5.50 | – | – | – |
| GS Chappell | 74 | 72 | 14 | 138* | 2331 | 40.18 | 3 | 14 | 23 |
| IM Chappell | 16 | 16 | 2 | 86 | 673 | 48.07 | – | 8 | 5 |
| TM Chappell | 20 | 13 | 0 | 110 | 229 | 17.61 | 1 | – | 8 |
| SR Clark | 33 | 11 | 7 | 16* | 67 | 16.75 | – | – | 8 |
| WM Clark | 2 | – | | | | | – | – | – |
| MJ Clarke | 132 | 116 | 27 | 130 | 3920 | 44.04 | 3 | 29 | 49 |
| DJ Colley | 1 | – | | | | | – | – | – |
| AN Connolly | 1 | – | | | | | – | – | – |
| MJ Cosgrove | 3 | 3 | – | 74 | 112 | 37.33 | – | 1 | – |

| Batting | M | I | NO | HS | Runs | Av | 100 | 50 | Ct/St |
|---|---|---|---|---|---|---|---|---|---|
| GJ Cosier | 9 | 7 | 2 | 84 | 154 | 30.80 | – | 1 | 4 |
| DJ Cullen | 5 | 1 | 1 | 2* | 2 | – | – | – | 2 |
| AC Dale | 30 | 12 | 8 | 15* | 78 | 19.50 | – | – | 11 |
| WM Darling | 18 | 18 | 1 | 74 | 363 | 21.35 | – | 1 | 6 |
| IC Davis | 3 | 3 | 1 | 11* | 12 | 6.00 | – | – | – |
| SP Davis | 39 | 11 | 7 | 6 | 20 | 5.00 | – | – | 5 |
| MJ DiVenuto | 9 | 9 | 0 | 89 | 241 | 26.77 | – | 2 | 1 |
| AIC Dodemaide | 24 | 16 | 7 | 30 | 124 | 13.77 | – | – | 7 |
| BR Dorey | 4 | 1 | – | 2 | 2 | 2.00 | – | – | – |
| GC Dyer | 23 | 13 | 2 | 45* | 174 | 15.81 | – | – | 24/4 |
| G Dymock | 15 | 7 | 4 | 14* | 35 | 11.66 | – | – | 1 |
| J Dyson | 29 | 27 | 4 | 79 | 755 | 32.82 | – | 4 | 12 |
| R Edwards | 9 | 8 | 1 | 80* | 255 | 36.42 | – | 3 | – |
| WJ Edwards | 1 | 1 | 0 | 2 | 2 | 2.00 | – | – | – |
| MTG Elliott | 1 | 1 | 0 | 1 | 1 | 1.00 | – | – | – |
| PA Emery | 1 | 1 | 1 | 11* | 11 | – | – | – | 3/– |
| DW Fleming | 88 | 31 | 18 | 29 | 152 | 11.69 | – | – | 14 |
| DR Gilbert | 14 | 8 | 3 | 8 | 39 | 7.80 | – | – | 3 |
| AC Gilchrist | 287 | 279 | 11 | 172 | 9619 | 35.89 | 16 | 55 | 417/55 |
| JN Gillespie | 97 | 39 | 16 | 44* | 289 | 12.56 | – | – | 10 |
| GJ Gilmour | 5 | 2 | 1 | 28* | 42 | 42.00 | – | – | 2 |
| SF Graf | 11 | 6 | 0 | 8 | 24 | 4.00 | – | – | 1 |
| BJ Haddin | 29 | 26 | 2 | 87* | 705 | 29.37 | – | 3 | 31/4 |
| JR Hammond | 1 | 1 | 1 | 15* | 15 | – | – | – | – |
| IJ Harvey | 49 | 37 | 10 | 47* | 495 | 18.33 | – | – | 13 |
| NM Hauritz | 8 | 4 | 3 | 20* | 35 | 35.00 | – | – | 2 |
| ML Hayden | 161 | 155 | 15 | 181 | 6133 | 43.80 | 10 | 36 | 68 |
| IA Healy | 168 | 120 | 36 | 56 | 1764 | 21.00 | – | 4 | 195/39 |
| AMJ Hilditch | 8 | 8 | 0 | 72 | 226 | 28.25 | – | 1 | 1 |
| BW Hilfenhaus | 1 | – | | | | | – | – | 1 |
| BJ Hodge | 25 | 21 | 2 | 123 | 575 | 30.26 | 1 | 3 | 16 |

APPENDIX C

| Batting | M | I | NO | HS | Runs | Av | 100 | 50 | Ct/St |
|---|---|---|---|---|---|---|---|---|---|
| TG Hogan | 16 | 12 | 4 | 27 | 72 | 9.00 | – | – | 10 |
| GB Hogg | 123 | 65 | 26 | 71* | 790 | 20.25 | – | 2 | 36 |
| RM Hogg | 71 | 35 | 20 | 22 | 137 | 9.13 | – | – | 8 |
| RG Holland | 2 | – | | | | | – | – | – |
| DW Hookes | 39 | 36 | 2 | 76 | 826 | 24.29 | – | 5 | 11 |
| JR Hopes | 28 | 19 | 1 | 63 | 433 | 24.05 | – | 1 | 8 |
| KJ Hughes | 97 | 88 | 6 | 98 | 1968 | 24.00 | – | 17 | 27 |
| MG Hughes | 33 | 17 | 8 | 20 | 100 | 11.11 | – | – | 6 |
| AG Hurst | 8 | 4 | 4 | 3* | 7 | – | – | – | 1 |
| MEK Hussey | 85 | 64 | 26 | 109* | 2113 | 55.60 | 2 | 12 | 49 |
| PA Jaques | 6 | 6 | – | 94 | 125 | 20.83 | – | 1 | 3 |
| TJ Jenner | 1 | 1 | 0 | 12 | 12 | 12.00 | – | – | – |
| MG Johnson | 34 | 15 | 6 | 24* | 89 | 9.88 | – | – | 6 |
| DM Jones | 164 | 161 | 25 | 145 | 6068 | 44.61 | 7 | 46 | 54 |
| BP Julian | 25 | 17 | 0 | 35 | 224 | 13.17 | – | – | 8 |
| MS Kasprowicz | 43 | 13 | 9 | 28* | 74 | 18.50 | – | – | 13 |
| SM Katich | 45 | 42 | 5 | 107* | 1324 | 35.78 | 1 | 9 | 13 |
| MF Kent | 5 | 5 | 1 | 33 | 78 | 19.50 | – | – | 4 |
| RB Kerr | 4 | 4 | 1 | 87* | 97 | 32.33 | – | 1 | 1 |
| BM Laird | 23 | 23 | 3 | 117* | 594 | 29.70 | 1 | 2 | 5 |
| JL Langer | 8 | 7 | 2 | 36 | 160 | 32.00 | – | – | 2/1 |
| TJ Laughlin | 6 | 5 | 1 | 74 | 105 | 26.25 | – | 1 | – |
| SG Law | 54 | 51 | 5 | 110 | 1237 | 26.89 | 1 | 7 | 12 |
| WM Lawry | 1 | 1 | 0 | 27 | 27 | 27.00 | – | – | 1 |
| GF Lawson | 79 | 52 | 18 | 33* | 378 | 11.11 | – | – | 18 |
| B Lee | 168 | 82 | 33 | 57 | 836 | 17.06 | – | 2 | 39 |
| S Lee | 45 | 35 | 8 | 47 | 477 | 17.66 | – | – | 23 |
| DS Lehmann | 117 | 101 | 22 | 119 | 3078 | 38.96 | 4 | 17 | 26 |
| ML Lewis | 7 | 1 | 1 | 4* | 4 | – | – | – | 1 |
| DK Lillee | 63 | 34 | 8 | 42* | 240 | 9.23 | – | – | 10 |
| SCG MacGill | 3 | 2 | 1 | 1 | 1 | 1.00 | – | – | 2 |

| Batting | M | I | NO | HS | Runs | Av | 100 | 50 | Ct/St |
|---|---|---|---|---|---|---|---|---|---|
| KH MacLeay | 16 | 13 | 2 | 41 | 139 | 12.63 | – | – | 2 |
| RB McCosker | 14 | 14 | 0 | 95 | 320 | 22.85 | – | 2 | 3 |
| RJ McCurdy | 11 | 6 | 2 | 13* | 33 | 8.25 | – | – | 1 |
| CJ McDermott | 138 | 78 | 17 | 37 | 432 | 7.08 | – | – | 27 |
| GD McGrath | 250 | 68 | 38 | 11 | 115 | 3.83 | – | – | 37 |
| GD McKenzie | 1 | – | | | | | – | – | 1 |
| JA Maclean | 2 | 1 | 0 | 11 | 11 | 11.00 | – | – | – |
| JN Maguire | 23 | 11 | 5 | 14* | 42 | 7.00 | – | – | 2 |
| JP Maher | 26 | 20 | 3 | 95 | 438 | 25.76 | – | 1 | 18 |
| AA Mallett | 9 | 3 | 1 | 8 | 14 | 7.00 | – | – | 4 |
| MF Malone | 10 | 7 | 3 | 15* | 36 | 9.00 | – | – | 1 |
| GR Marsh | 117 | 115 | 6 | 126* | 4357 | 39.97 | 9 | 22 | 31 |
| RW Marsh | 92 | 76 | 15 | 66 | 1225 | 20.08 | – | 4 | 120/4 |
| DR Martyn | 208 | 182 | 51 | 144* | 5346 | 40.80 | 5 | 37 | 69 |
| RAL Massie | 3 | 1 | 1 | 16* | 16 | – | – | – | 1 |
| GRJ Matthews | 59 | 50 | 13 | 54 | 619 | 16.72 | – | 1 | 23 |
| TBA May | 47 | 12 | 8 | 15 | 39 | 9.75 | – | – | 3 |
| TM Moody | 76 | 64 | 12 | 89 | 1211 | 23.28 | – | 10 | 21 |
| JK Moss | 1 | 1 | 0 | 7 | 7 | 7.00 | – | – | 2 |
| AA Noffke | 1 | – | | | | | – | – | – |
| SP O'Donnell | 87 | 64 | 15 | 74* | 1242 | 25.34 | – | 9 | 22 |
| KJ O'Keeffe | 2 | 2 | 1 | 16* | 16 | 16.00 | – | – | – |
| LS Pascoe | 29 | 11 | 7 | 15* | 39 | 9.75 | – | – | 6 |
| WB Phillips | 48 | 41 | 6 | 75* | 852 | 24.34 | – | 6 | 42/7 |
| RT Ponting | 298 | 289 | 35 | 164 | 11026 | 43.40 | 26 | 63 | 134 |
| GD Porter | 2 | 1 | 0 | 3 | 3 | 3.00 | – | – | 1 |
| CG Rackemann | 52 | 18 | 6 | 9* | 34 | 2.83 | – | – | 6 |
| IR Redpath | 5 | 5 | 0 | 24 | 46 | 9.20 | – | – | 2 |
| BA Reid | 61 | 21 | 8 | 10 | 49 | 3.76 | – | – | 6 |
| PR Reiffel | 92 | 57 | 21 | 58 | 503 | 13.97 | – | 1 | 25 |
| GM Ritchie | 44 | 42 | 7 | 84 | 959 | 24.07 | – | 9 | 9 |

| Batting | M | I | NO | HS | Runs | Av | 100 | 50 | Ct/St |
|---|---|---|---|---|---|---|---|---|---|
| SB Smith | 28 | 24 | 2 | 117 | 861 | 39.13 | 2 | 8 | 8 |
| KR Stackpole | 6 | 6 | 0 | 61 | 224 | 37.33 | – | 3 | 1 |
| AM Stuart | 3 | 1 | 0 | 1 | 1 | 1.00 | – | – | 2 |
| A Symonds | 190 | 154 | 32 | 156 | 4845 | 39.71 | 6 | 27 | 79 |
| SW Tait | 18 | 1 | – | 11 | 11 | 11.00 | – | – | 2 |
| MA Taylor | 113 | 110 | 1 | 105 | 3514 | 32.23 | 1 | 28 | 56 |
| PL Taylor | 83 | 47 | 25 | 54* | 437 | 19.86 | – | 1 | 34 |
| AL Thomson | 1 | – | | | | | – | – | – |
| JR Thomson | 50 | 30 | 6 | 21 | 181 | 7.54 | – | – | 9 |
| PM Toohey | 5 | 4 | 2 | 54* | 105 | 52.50 | – | 1 | – |
| GS Trimble | 2 | 2 | 1 | 4 | 4 | 4.00 | – | – | – |
| A Turner | 6 | 6 | 0 | 101 | 247 | 41.16 | 1 | – | 3 |
| MRJ Veletta | 20 | 19 | 4 | 68* | 484 | 32.26 | – | 2 | 8 |
| AC Voges | 1 | 1 | 1 | 16* | 16 | – | – | – | 1 |
| MHN Walker | 17 | 11 | 3 | 20 | 79 | 9.87 | – | – | 6 |
| KD Walters | 28 | 24 | 6 | 59 | 513 | 28.50 | – | 2 | 10 |
| SK Warne | 193 | 106 | 28 | 55 | 1016 | 13.02 | – | 1 | 80 |
| GD Watson | 2 | 2 | 1 | 11* | 11 | 11.00 | – | – | – |
| SR Watson | 65 | 47 | 18 | 79 | 1001 | 34.51 | – | 7 | 15 |
| ME Waugh | 244 | 236 | 20 | 173 | 8500 | 39.35 | 18 | 50 | 108 |
| SR Waugh | 325 | 288 | 58 | 120* | 7569 | 32.90 | 3 | 45 | 111 |
| DM Wellham | 17 | 17 | 2 | 97 | 379 | 25.26 | – | 1 | 8 |
| KC Wessels | 54 | 51 | 3 | 107 | 1740 | 36.25 | 1 | 14 | 19 |
| DF Whatmore | 1 | 1 | 0 | 2 | 2 | 2.00 | – | – | – |
| CL White | 16 | 10 | 3 | 45 | 157 | 22.42 | – | – | 5 |
| MR Whitney | 38 | 13 | 7 | 9* | 40 | 6.66 | – | – | 11 |
| JM Wiener | 7 | 7 | 0 | 50 | 140 | 20.00 | – | 1 | 2 |
| BA Williams | 25 | 6 | 4 | 13* | 27 | 13.50 | – | – | 4 |
| P Wilson | 11 | 5 | 2 | 2 | 4 | 1.33 | – | – | 1 |
| GM Wood | 83 | 77 | 11 | 114* | 2219 | 33.62 | 3 | 11 | 17 |
| AJ Woodcock | 1 | 1 | 0 | 53 | 53 | 53.00 | – | 1 | – |

| Batting | M | I | NO | HS | Runs | Av | 100 | 50 | Ct/St |
|---|---|---|---|---|---|---|---|---|---|
| RD Woolley | 4 | 3 | 2 | 16 | 31 | 31.00 | – | – | 1/1 |
| KJ Wright | 5 | 2 | 0 | 23 | 29 | 14.50 | – | – | 8/– |
| GN Yallop | 30 | 27 | 6 | 66* | 823 | 39.19 | – | 7 | 5 |
| B Yardley | 7 | 4 | 0 | 28 | 58 | 14.50 | – | – | 1 |
| BE Young | 6 | 3 | 1 | 18 | 31 | 15.50 | – | – | 2 |
| AK Zesers | 2 | 2 | 2 | 8* | 10 | – | – | – | 1 |
| TJ Zoehrer | 22 | 15 | 3 | 50 | 130 | 10.83 | – | 1 | 21/2 |

| Bowling | Balls | Runs | Wkts | Av | Best | 4w | RPO |
|---|---|---|---|---|---|---|---|
| TM Alderman | 3371 | 2056 | 88 | 23.36 | 5–17 | 3 | 3.65 |
| J Angel | 162 | 113 | 4 | 28.25 | 2–47 | – | 4.18 |
| GR Beard | 112 | 70 | 4 | 17.50 | 2–20 | – | 3.75 |
| MJ Bennett | 408 | 275 | 4 | 68.75 | 2–27 | – | 4.04 |
| MG Bevan | 1966 | 1655 | 36 | 45.97 | 3–36 | – | 5.05 |
| AJ Bichel | 3257 | 2463 | 78 | 31.57 | 7–20 | 3 | 4.53 |
| GS Blewett | 749 | 646 | 14 | 46.14 | 2–6 | – | 5.17 |
| DC Boon | 82 | 86 | 0 | | | – | 6.29 |
| AR Border | 2661 | 2071 | 73 | 28.36 | 3–20 | – | 4.66 |
| NW Bracken | 4146 | 3022 | 138 | 21.89 | 5–47 | 6 | 4.37 |
| RJ Bright | 462 | 350 | 3 | 116.66 | 1–28 | – | 4.54 |
| IW Callen | 180 | 148 | 5 | 29.60 | 3–24 | – | 4.93 |
| GD Campbell | 613 | 404 | 18 | 22.44 | 3–17 | – | 3.95 |
| PH Carlson | 168 | 70 | 2 | 35.00 | 1–21 | – | 2.49 |
| GS Chappell | 3108 | 2097 | 72 | 29.12 | 5–15 | 2 | 4.04 |
| IM Chappell | 42 | 23 | 2 | 11.50 | 2–14 | – | 3.28 |
| TM Chappell | 736 | 538 | 19 | 28.31 | 3–31 | – | 4.38 |
| SR Clark | 1588 | 1345 | 45 | 29.88 | 4–54 | 2 | 5.08 |
| WM Clark | 100 | 61 | 3 | 20.33 | 2–39 | – | 3.66 |
| MJ Clarke | 1616 | 1402 | 38 | 36.89 | 5–35 | 1 | 5.20 |
| DJ Colley | 66 | 72 | 0 | | | – | 6.54 |
| AN Connolly | 64 | 62 | 0 | | | – | 5.81 |
| MJ Cosgrove | 30 | 13 | 1 | 13.00 | 1–1 | – | 2.60 |
| GJ Cosier | 409 | 248 | 14 | 17.71 | 5–18 | 1 | 3.63 |

| Bowling | Balls | Runs | Wkts | Av | Best | 4w | RPO |
|---|---|---|---|---|---|---|---|
| DJ Cullen | 213 | 147 | 2 | 73.50 | 2–25 | – | 4.14 |
| AC Dale | 1596 | 979 | 32 | 30.59 | 3–18 | – | 3.68 |
| SP Davis | 2016 | 1133 | 44 | 25.75 | 3–10 | – | 3.37 |
| AIC Dodemaide | 1327 | 753 | 36 | 20.91 | 5–21 | 2 | 3.40 |
| BR Dorey | 162 | 146 | 2 | 73.00 | 1–12 | – | 5.40 |
| G Dymock | 806 | 412 | 15 | 27.46 | 2–21 | – | 3.06 |
| WJ Edwards | 1 | 0 | 0 | | | – | – |
| DW Fleming | 4619 | 3402 | 134 | 25.38 | 5–36 | 5 | 4.41 |
| DR Gilbert | 684 | 552 | 18 | 30.66 | 5–46 | 1 | 4.84 |
| JN Gillespie | 5144 | 3611 | 142 | 25.42 | 5–22 | 6 | 4.21 |
| GK Gilmour | 320 | 165 | 16 | 10.31 | 6–14 | 2 | 3.09 |
| SF Graf | 522 | 345 | 8 | 43.12 | 2–23 | – | 3.96 |
| JR Hammond | 54 | 41 | 1 | 41.00 | 1–41 | – | 4.55 |
| IJ Harvey | 2290 | 1783 | 55 | 32.41 | 4–28 | 2 | 4.67 |
| NM Hauritz | 360 | 308 | 9 | 34.22 | 4–39 | 1 | 5.13 |
| ML Hayden | 6 | 18 | 0 | | | – | 18.00 |
| BW Hilfenhaus | 42 | 26 | 1 | 26.00 | 1–26 | – | 3.71 |
| BJ Hodge | 66 | 51 | 1 | 51.00 | 1–17 | – | 4.63 |
| TG Hogan | 917 | 574 | 23 | 24.95 | 4–33 | 1 | 3.75 |
| GB Hogg | 5564 | 4188 | 156 | 26.84 | 5–32 | 5 | 4.51 |
| RM Hogg | 3677 | 2418 | 85 | 28.44 | 4–29 | 5 | 3.94 |
| RG Holland | 126 | 99 | 2 | 49.50 | 2–49 | – | 4.71 |
| DW Hookes | 29 | 28 | 1 | 28.00 | 1–2 | – | 5.79 |
| JR Hopes | 1031 | 719 | 21 | 34.23 | 2–16 | – | 4.18 |
| KJ Hughes | 1 | 4 | 0 | | | – | – |
| MG Hughes | 1639 | 1115 | 38 | 29.34 | 4–44 | 1 | 4.08 |
| AG Hurst | 402 | 203 | 12 | 16.91 | 5–21 | 1 | 3.02 |
| MEK Hussey | 192 | 167 | 2 | 83.50 | 1–22 | – | 5.21 |
| TJ Jenner | 64 | 28 | 0 | | | – | 2.62 |
| MG Johnson | 1620 | 1296 | 51 | 25.41 | 5–26 | 3 | 4.80 |
| DM Jones | 106 | 81 | 3 | 27.00 | 2–34 | – | 4.58 |
| BP Julian | 1146 | 997 | 22 | 45.31 | 3–40 | – | 5.21 |
| MS Kasprowicz | 2225 | 1674 | 67 | 24.98 | 5–45 | 3 | 4.51 |
| TJ Laughlin | 308 | 224 | 8 | 28.00 | 3–54 | – | 4.36 |
| SG Law | 807 | 635 | 12 | 52.91 | 2–22 | – | 4.72 |

| Bowling | Balls | Runs | Wkts | Av | Best | 4w | RPO |
|---|---|---|---|---|---|---|---|
| GF Lawson | 4259 | 2592 | 88 | 29.45 | 4–26 | 1 | 3.65 |
| B Lee | 8589 | 6751 | 296 | 22.80 | 5–22 | 19 | 4.71 |
| S Lee | 1706 | 1245 | 48 | 25.93 | 5–33 | 2 | 4.37 |
| DS Lehmann | 1793 | 1445 | 52 | 27.78 | 4–7 | 1 | 4.83 |
| ML Lewis | 341 | 391 | 7 | 55.85 | 3–56 | – | 6.87 |
| DK Lillee | 3593 | 2145 | 103 | 20.82 | 5–34 | 6 | 3.58 |
| SCG MacGill | 180 | 105 | 6 | 17.50 | 4–19 | 1 | 3.50 |
| KH MacLeay | 857 | 626 | 15 | 41.73 | 6–39 | 1 | 4.38 |
| RJ McCurdy | 515 | 375 | 12 | 31.25 | 3–19 | – | 4.36 |
| CJ McDermott | 7461 | 5018 | 203 | 24.71 | 5–44 | 5 | 4.03 |
| GD McGrath | 12970 | 8391 | 381 | 22.02 | 7–15 | 16 | 3.88 |
| GD McKenzie | 60 | 22 | 2 | 11.00 | 2–22 | – | 2.20 |
| JN Maguire | 1009 | 769 | 19 | 40.47 | 3–61 | – | 4.57 |
| AA Mallett | 502 | 341 | 11 | 31.00 | 3–34 | – | 4.07 |
| MF Malone | 612 | 315 | 11 | 28.63 | 2–9 | – | 3.08 |
| GR Marsh | 6 | 4 | 0 | | | – | 6.00 |
| DR Martyn | 794 | 704 | 12 | 58.66 | 2–21 | – | 5.31 |
| RAL Massie | 183 | 129 | 3 | 43.00 | 2–35 | – | 4.22 |
| GRJ Matthews | 2808 | 2004 | 57 | 35.15 | 3–27 | – | 4.28 |
| TBA May | 2504 | 1772 | 39 | 45.43 | 3–19 | | 4.24 |
| TM Moody | 2797 | 2014 | 52 | 38.73 | 3–25 | – | 4.32 |
| AA Noffke | 54 | 46 | 1 | 46.00 | 1–46 | – | 5.11 |
| SP O'Donnell | 4350 | 3102 | 108 | 28.72 | 5–13 | 6 | 4.27 |
| KJ O'Keeffe | 132 | 79 | 2 | 39.50 | 1–36 | – | 3.59 |
| LS Pascoe | 1568 | 1066 | 53 | 20.11 | 5–30 | 5 | 4.07 |
| RT Ponting | 150 | 104 | 3 | 34.66 | 1–12 | – | 4.16 |
| GD Porter | 108 | 33 | 3 | 11.00 | 2–13 | – | 1.83 |
| CG Rackemann | 2791 | 1833 | 82 | 22.35 | 5–16 | 4 | 3.94 |
| BA Reid | 3250 | 2203 | 63 | 34.96 | 5–53 | 1 | 4.06 |
| PR Reiffel | 4732 | 3096 | 106 | 29.20 | 4–13 | 5 | 3.92 |
| GR Robertson | 597 | 430 | 8 | 53.75 | 3–29 | – | 4.32 |
| RB Simpson | 102 | 95 | 2 | 47.50 | 2–30 | – | 5.58 |
| MJ Slater | 12 | 11 | 0 | | | – | 5.50 |
| SB Smith | 7 | 5 | 0 | | | – | 4.28 |
| KR Stackpole | 77 | 54 | 3 | 18.00 | 3–40 | – | 4.20 |
| AM Stuart | 180 | 109 | 8 | 13.62 | 5–26 | 1 | 3.63 |

| Bowling | Balls | Runs | Wkts | Av | Best | 4w | RPO |
|---|---|---|---|---|---|---|---|
| A Symonds | 5743 | 4796 | 125 | 38.36 | 5–18 | 3 | 5.01 |
| SW Tait | 849 | 774 | 33 | 23.45 | 4–39 | 1 | 5.46 |
| PL Taylor | 3937 | 2740 | 97 | 28.24 | 4–38 | 1 | 4.17 |
| AL Thomson | 64 | 22 | 1 | 22.00 | 1–22 | – | 2.06 |
| JR Thomson | 2696 | 1942 | 55 | 35.30 | 4–67 | 1 | 4.32 |
| GS Trimble | 24 | 32 | 0 | | | – | 8.00 |
| AC Voges | 18 | 33 | 0 | | | – | 11.00 |
| MHN Walker | 1006 | 546 | 20 | 27.30 | 4–19 | 1 | 3.25 |
| KD Walters | 314 | 273 | 4 | 68.25 | 2–24 | – | 5.21 |
| SK Warne | 10600 | 7514 | 291 | 25.82 | 5–33 | 13 | 4.25 |
| GD Watson | 48 | 28 | 2 | 14.00 | 2–28 | – | 3.50 |
| SR Watson | 2593 | 2115 | 62 | 34.11 | 4–39 | 2 | 4.89 |
| ME Waugh | 3687 | 2938 | 85 | 34.56 | 5–24 | 2 | 4.78 |
| SR Waugh | 8883 | 6761 | 195 | 34.67 | 4–33 | 3 | 4.56 |
| KC Wessels | 737 | 655 | 18 | 36.38 | 2–16 | – | 5.33 |
| CL White | 174 | 201 | 4 | 50.25 | 1–5 | – | 6.93 |
| MR Whitney | 2106 | 1249 | 46 | 27.15 | 4–34 | 2 | 3.55 |
| JM Wiener | 24 | 34 | 0 | | | – | 8.50 |
| BA Williams | 1203 | 814 | 35 | 23.25 | 5–22 | 3 | 4.05 |
| P Wilson | 562 | 450 | 13 | 34.61 | 3–39 | – | 4.80 |
| GN Yallop | 138 | 119 | 3 | 39.66 | 2–28 | – | 5.17 |
| B Yardley | 198 | 130 | 7 | 18.57 | 3–28 | – | 3.93 |
| BE Young | 234 | 251 | 1 | 251.00 | 1–26 | – | 6.43 |
| AK Zesers | 90 | 74 | 1 | 74.00 | 1–37 | – | 4.93 |

# Appendix D

# Select Bibliography


Minutes of the Australasian Cricket Council 1892–1900
Minutes of the Australian Board of Control for International Cricket 1905–73
Minutes of the Australian Cricket Board 1973–92
Minutes of the Interstate Conference 1919–73
Minutes of the Melbourne Cricket Club 1875–1914
Minutes of the New South Wales Cricket Association 1891–1939
Minutes of the South Australian Cricket(ing) Association 1871–1990
Minutes of the Victorian Cricket(ers) Association 1875–1939
Melbourne Cricket Club Annual Reports 1875–1992
New South Wales Cricket Association Annual Reports 1888–1992
Queensland Cricket Association Annual Reports 1905–1992
South Australian Cricket(ing) Association Annual Reports 1872–1992
Tasmanian Cricket Association Annual Reports 1876–1992
Victorian Cricket(ers) Association Annual Reports 1875–1992
Western Australian Cricket(ing) Association Annual Reports 1895–1992


**NEWSPAPERS**


Adelaide – Advertiser, Argus, Gazette, Mail, News, Observer, Register, Sunday Mail
Auckland – Star
Australian
Australian (Colonial NSW)
Australian (NSW)
Australian Sketcher

Brisbane – Courier, Courier-Mail

Canterbury (NZ) – Times
Cape (South Africa) – Argus, Times
Casino – Kyogle Courier
Cornwall Chronicle

The Dominion (NZ)

Eastern Province Herald (South Africa)

The Hindu (India)
Hobart Town Gazette

The Islander (Ceylon)

Labour Daily
Launceston – Daily Telegraph, Examiner
London – Daily Express, Daily Mail, Daily News, Daily Star, Daily Telegraph, Evening Standard, News Chronicle, Observer, Star, Sunday Times, The Times

Manchester Guardian
Melbourne – Age, Argus, Express, Herald, Leader, Sun-Herald, Sun-News Pictorial, Truth
The Monitor
Moreton Bay Courier
Mount Alexander Mail

Natal Mercury (South Africa)
New Zealand Herald
North Australian

Pakistan Observer
Perth Gazette
Port Denison Times
Port Philip Gazette

Straits Times (Singapore)
Sydney – Daily Mirror, Gazette and NSW Advertiser, Globe, Mail, Morning Herald, Sun, Sun-Herald

Tasmanian Daily Post

Wellington Evening Post (NZ)
The West Australian

## PERIODICALS

Australian Cricket Journal
Australian Cricketer
Australian Cricketers' Annual

Bell's Life in Australia
Bell's Life in Victoria
Blackwood's Magazine
Bradshaw's Guide
Bulletin (The)
Bulletin of the British Fascists

Cabinet (The)
Calcutta Illustrated News
Cathedral End
Cricket: A Weekly Record

Home News

Illustrated Sporting and Dramatic News
Illustrated Sydney news

Labour History

New Statesman (India)

Pall Mall Gazette
Playfair Cricket Monthly
Punch

Referee (The)
Review of Reviews

Sporting Globe
Sporting Life
Sporting Times (India)
Sporting Times (London)
Sporting Traditions
Sportsman (The)
Strand Magazine

Town and Country Journal
Town Life in Australia

Victorian Cricketer's Guide
Victorian Review

World (The)

## BOOKS

BAILEY, Jack: *Conflicts in Cricket* (Kingswood Press, 1989)

CARY, Clif: *Cricket Controversy: Test matches in Australia 1946–57* (Werner Laurie, 1948)

CASHMAN, Richard: *Australian Cricket Crowds: The Attendance Cycle 1877–1984* (University of New South Wales, 1984)

CASHMAN, Richard: *'Ave A Go, Yer Mug!: Australian Cricket Crowds from Larrikin to Ocker* (Collins, 1984)

CASHMAN, Richard: *Players, Patrons and the Crowd* (Orient Longman, 1980)

CASHMAN, Richard: *The 'Demon' Spofforth* (New South Wales University Press, 1990)

CASHMAN, Richard *and* MCKERNAN, Michael: *Sport in History: The Making of Modern Sporting History* (University of Queensland Press, 1979)

CASHMAN, Richard *and* MCKERNAN, Michael: *Sport: Money, Morality and the Media* (New South Wales University Press, 1982)

CHAPPLE, Stewart: *50 Years of Cricket in Tasmania's North East* (Telegraph Printery, 1985)

COX, Richard: *Sport in Britain: A Blbliography of Historical Publications 1800–1988* (Manchester University Press, 1991)

DALY, John: *Elysian Fields: Sport, Class and Community in Colonial South Australia* (Kingswood Press, 1989)

DARLING, Douglas: *Test Tussles On and Off the Field* (Walch & Sons, 1970)

DERRIMAN, Philip: *True to the Blue: A History of the New South Wales Cricket Association* (Richard Smart Publishing, 1985)

DUNSTAN, Keith: *The Paddock That Grew: The Story of the Melbourne Cricket Club* (Hutchinson, 1988)

ELEY, Stephen: *Padwick's Bibliography of Cricket: Volume II* (Library Association, 1991)

GIFFEN, George: *With Bat and Ball* (Ward Lock, 1898)

GRACE, William Gilbert *and* PORRITT, Arthur: *'W.G.': Cricketing Reminiscences and Personal Recollections* (J. Bowden, 1899)

GRIFFIN, Edward: *Eight Shameful Years* (Highgate House, 1988)

HARRIS, John: *Bendigo District Cricket, 1853–1990* (Crown Castleton Publishers, 1991)

HARTE, Chris: *The History of the Sheffield Shield* (Allen & Unwin, 1987)

HARTE, Chris: *SACA: The History of, the South Australian Cricket Association* (Sports Marketing, 1990)

HAWKE, Martin: *Recollections and Reminiscences* (Williams & Norgate, 1924)

HAYGARTH, Arthur: *Cricket Scores and Biographies of Celebrated Cricketers* (Longmans, 1895)

HILL, Les: *Australian Cricketers on Tour 1868–1974* (Lynton Publications, 1974)

HOWELL, Max ET AL: *The Sporting Image: Queenslanders at Play* (University of Queensland Press, 1989)

HUTCHEON, Ernest: *A History of Queensland Cricket* (OCA, 1946)

INGLIS, Gordon: *Sport and Pastime in Australia* (Methuen, 1912)

KNIGHT, Albert E.: *The Complete Cricketer* (Methuen, 1906)

LAWRENCE, Geoffrey *and* ROWE, David. *Power Play: Essays in the Sociology of Australian Sport* (Hale & Iremonger, 1986)

LUCKIN, Maurice: *The History of South African Cricket* (Hortor, 1915)

MAHONEY, John: *Wide Bay and Burnett Cricket, 1864–1908* (Maryborough CA, 1908)

MALONEY, Bruce: *A History of Cricket in Hamilton* (Hamilton Spectator, 1985)

MANCINI, A. *and* HIBBINS, G. M.: *Running With The Ball* (Lynedoch Publications, 1987)

MANDLE, Bill: *Going it Alone: Australia's National Identity in the Twentieth Century* (Penguin, 1978)

MANGAN, Tony: *The Games Ethic and Imperialism* (Viking, 1986)

MANGAN, Tony: *Pleasure, Profit, Proselytism: British Culture and Sport at Home and Abroad, 1700–1914* (Frank Cass, 1988)

MEREDITH, Anthony: *Summers in Winter: Four England Tours of Australia* (Kingswood Press, 1990)

MOODY, Clarence: *South Australian Cricket: Reminiscences of Fifty Years* (W. K. Thomas, 1898)

MULLINS, Pat: *Cradle Days of Australian Cricket* (Macmillan, 1989)

NOBLE, Montague: *The Game's the Thing* (Cassell, 1926)

O'DOWD, Kevin: *Geelong's Blazing Century* (Geelong Advertiser, 1989)

PADWICK, E. W.: *A Bibliography of Cricket* (Library Association, 1977)

PAGE, Roger: *A History of Tasmanian Cricket* (Tasmanian Government Printer, 1957)

PALMER, Harry: *Athletic Sports in America, England and Australia* (Hubbard Bros, 1889)

PIGGFORD, George: *Runs, Wickets and Reminiscence: The Newcastle and District Cricket Association's First 100 Years* (Davies & Cannington, 1989)

REESE, Thomas: *New Zealand Cricket* (Simpson & Williams, 1927)

ROSENWATER, Irving: *Sir Donald Bradman: A Biography* (Batsford, 1978)

SCOTT, James: *Early Cricket in Sydney, 1803–56* (NSWCA, 1991)

SHARP, Martin: *Sporting Spectacles: Cricket and Football in Sydney, 1890–1912* (the author, 1986)

SINCLAIR, Ron: *A History of Cricket in Maryborough and District* (MKM, 1988)

SLOANE, Peter: *Sport in the Market? The Economic Causes and Consequences of the Packer Revolution* (Institute of Economic Affairs, 1980)

STODDART, Brian: *Saturday Afternoon Fever: Sport in the Australian Culture* (Angus & Robertson, 1986)

THOMSON, Maudi: *Between the Stumps: A History of Cricket in South Gippsland* (South Gippsland Publishing, 1990)

TORRENS, Warwick: *Queensland Cricket and Cricketers, 1862–1981* (Bayfield Printers, 1981)

TURNER, Noel: *The Cricket Crisis of 1884–85* (np, 1979)

VAMPLEW, Wray: *Pay Up and Play the Game: Professional Sport in Britain, 1875–1914* (Cambridge University Press, 1988)

VAMPLEW, Wray et al: *The Oxford Companion to Australian Sport* (Oxford University Press, 1992)

WARNER, Pelham and ASHLEY-COOPER, F. S.: *Imperial Cricket* (London and Counties, 1912)

WILLIAMS, Kenneth: *Guide to First-Class Cricket Matches Played in Australia* (Association of Cricket Statisticians, 1983)

WILLIAMS, Ron: *A Century of Northern Tasmanian Cricket* (Foot & Playsted, 1986)

WALMOT, R. W. E.: *The Victorian Sporting Record* (McCarron Bird, 1903)

## THESES

BLADES, G. C.: 'Australian aborigines: cricket and pedestrianism: culture and conflict 1890–1910.' University of Queensland, 1985

EGLINGTON, J.: 'The Sydney Cricket Ground.' University of New South Wales School of Architecture, 1988

MCINNES, S.: "Cricket and South Australian Society.' University of Adelaide, 1970

MILLBANK, S. L: 'South Australian Cricket Association, cricket and South Australia 1871–1914.'Flinders University of South Australia, 1981

MOFFATT, H.: 'Aspects of the organisation of the Melbourne Cricket Club at the MCG.' Chisholm Institute of Technology, 1984

MONTEFIORE, D.: 'Cricket in the doldrums: the struggle between private and public control of Australian cricket in the 1880s.' University of New South Wales, 1989

PIESSE, K.: 'A history of Australian cricket annuals and magazines 1856–1977.' Royal Melbourne Institute of Technology, 1977

POKLINGHORNE, R. T.: 'The history of development at the Sydney Cricket Ground.' University of New South Wales School of Architecture, 1987

QUICK, S. P.: 'World Series Cricket, television and Australian culture.' Ohio State University, USA, 1990

STOBO, R. M.: 'Australian nationalism and cricket in the nineteenth century.' Sydney University, 1989

WHITE, A.: 'Players versus officials: the administration and organisation of Australian cricket 1878–1913.' Monash University, 1988

## PAPERS IN PROFESSIONAL JOURNALS

BONNEY, W.: 'Packer and televised cricket', *New South Wales Institute of Technology Media Papers*, 2, 1980

CASHMAN, R. L: 'Cricket and colonialism: colonial hegemony and indigenous subversion?' *Australian Cricket Journal*, L2, 198

CASHMAN, R. L: 'The cycle of cricket heroes', *Australian Cricket Journal,* 1:3, 1986

CASHMAN, R. L: 'Sport, big business and the spectator', *Australian Cricket Journal,* 2:3. 1987

CASHMAN, R. L: 'The rise and fall of the Australian Cricket Club 1826–68', *Australian Cricket Journal*, 5:1, 1989

CASHMAN, R. L: 'Symbols of unity: Anglo–Australian Cricketers 1877–1900', *International Journal of the History of Sport,* 7:1, 1990

DABSCHECK, B.: 'The Professional Cricketers' Association of Australia', *Sporting Traditions,* 8:1, 1991

FINLAY, R.: 'Lord Sheffield, W.G., and the Bulletin', *Australian Cricket Journal,* 1:3, 1986

FORSTER, C.: 'Sport, Society and Space: The changing geography of country cricket in South Australia 1836–1914', *Sporting Traditions,* 2:2, 1986

GOOLD, W. N.: 'The Old Newcastle Cricket Ground', *Journal of the Historical Society of Northern New South Wales,* 16, 1961

GRACE, E. W. R.: 'The rise and fall of the Australasian Cricket Council 1892–1900', *Sporting Traditions*, 2:1, 1985

HARRISS, I.: 'Cricket and rational economic man', *Sporting Traditions*, 3:1, 1986

HARTE, C. J.: 'Australian Second Eleven competition', *Australian Cricket Journal,* 2:2, 1986

HARTE, C. J.: 'The.Victorian Cricket Association and the Sheffield Shield 1918–19', *Australian Cricket Journal,* 2:2, 1986

HARTE, C. J.: 'Mr Murdoch's speech of 1882', *Australian Cricket Journal,* 2:3, 1987

HARTE, C. J.: 'The rise and progress of cricket in Victoria', *Australian Cricket Journal,* 4:1, 1988

MANDLE, W. F.: 'The professional cricketer in England in the nineteenth century', *Labour History,* XXIII, 1972

MANDLE, W. F.: 'Games people played: cricket, and football in England and Victoria in the late nineteenth century', *Historical Studies,* XV, 1973

MANDLE, W. F.: 'Cricket and Australian nationalism in the nineteenth century', *Journal of the Royal Australian Historical Society* 59, 1973

MOORE, A.: 'The Fascist Cricket Tour of 1924–25', *Sporting Traditions,*7:2, 1991

SANDIFORD, K. A. P.: 'Cricket and the Victorians: A historiographical essay', *Historical Reflections,* IX, 1982

SANDIFORD, K. A. P.: 'Cricket and the Victorian society', *Journal of Social History,* XVII, 1983

SANDIFORD, K. A. P.: 'The Professionalisation of Modern Cricket', *British Journal of Sports History,* 2:3, 1985

TATZ, C.: 'The Corruption of Sport', *Current Affairs Bulletin,* 59:4, 1982

TURNER, J. N.: 'The Australian Cricket Board's player contract and the litigation resulting therefrom', *Australian Cricket Journal*, 1:2, 1985

## UNPUBLISHED PAPERS

ARMSTRONG, T.: 'The effect of transport development on the history of crickete in Queensland 1846–96.' (Brisbane, 1983)

HARTE, C. J.: 'A corporate strategy for the South Australian Cricket Association.' (Adelaide, 1983)

INNISS, E.: 'West Indies Test cricket and its social implications.' (Bridgetown, 1978)

MULLEN, C. C.: 'Victorian Cricket to 1964–65.' (Melbourne, 1965)

MULLINS, P. J.: 'Cricket tours to the tropics 1894–1977.' (Brisbane, 1977)

MULLINS, P. J. *and* OGDEN, T.: 'Early Cricket in the Brisbane and Darling Downs District 1846–59.' (Brisbane, 1979)

SHARP, M. P.: 'A degenerate race: cricket and rugby crowds in Sydney 1890–1912.' (Canberra, 1987)

SHAW, M. J. C.: 'Early Cricket in Victoria 1860–1914 (Melbourne, 1966)

# BERNARD WHIMPRESS'S BIBLIOGRAPHY


## ANNUAL REPORTS

Australian Cricket Board/Cricket Australia Annual Reports 1993-2007

## BOOKS

DAVIS, Charles: *Test Cricket in Australia 1877–2002* (Charles Davis, 2002)

HAIGH, Gideon: *The Border Years* (Text, 1994)

HAIGH, Gideon: *All Out: the Ashes 2006-07* (Black Inc., 2007)

HAIGH, Gideon: *A Fair Field and No Favour: the Ashes 2005* (Scribe, 2005)

PIESSE, Ken: *The Taylor Years* (Penguin, 1999)

RAY, Mark: *Border & Beyond* (ABC, 1995)

WHIMPRESS, Bernard and HART, Nigel: *Great Ashes Battles: From Melbourne 1877 to Trent Bridge 2005* (Andre Deutsch, 2005)

## PERIODICALS

Allan's Cricket Annuals

Baggy Green

Cricket Week

Wisden Australia Cricket Almanack

## WEBSITES

Crickinfo website, www.cricket.org

# Index


Abbotsford 16, 73
Abbott, Walter 208
a'Beckett, E.L. 314, 316
Abel, Bobby 170, 189
Abrams, Leslie 191
Absolom, Charles 114
Adams, Jimmy 740, 745-6
Adamson, Lawrence 758
Adelaide 16, 21-3, 45, 107, 128, 151, 156, 179, 235, 274, 291, 738, 746, 750, 763, 769, 770, 776, 781-2, 788
  City Council 44, 173, 372
  Cricket Club 16, 21, 22, 128, 168
  Oval 22, 25, 44, 52, 88, 96, 128, 179, 183, 215, 230, 235, 247, 251, 273, 288, 315, 346, 402, 485, 515, 668, 720, 725, 726, 729-30, 731, 743-4, 752-3, 766, 777, 781-2,
  Post & Telegraph CC 287, 292, 306
  University CC 348
Adler, Rodney 706
Agarkar, Ajit 762
Ahmed, Ghulam 451
Ahmed, Imtiaz 465
Ahmed, Mushtaq 728
Ahmedabad 365, 467, 611
Aird, Ronnie 437, 441, 477
Aitken, James 207, 220, 238
Ajmer 365
Akhtar, Shoaib 751, 752 770, 771
Akram, Wasim 687, 737
Albany 30, 31, 135
Albert CC (Sydney) 6, 8, 40, 42, 46, 52, 70, 86, 89, 91, 100, 115, 123, 148, 158
Albert Park 54
Albert Sports Ground (Brisbane) 56, 130
Alberton Oval (Adelaide) 52
Albury 6, 8
Alcock, Charles 116
Alcott, Errol 658
Alderman, T.M. 626, 637, 651, 664, 676, 691
Alexander, G. 53, 115, 118, 133, 135
Alexander, Gerry 473, 474
Alexander, H.H. 307, 364
Ali, Mushtaq 390
Alice Springs 679
Allan Border Field (Brisbane) 745
Allan, F.E. 84, 85, 92, 115, 139, 274
Allan, P.J. 505
Allee, Charles 47, 53, 54
Allen, G.V. 228
Allen, George 'Gubby' 324, 369, 396, 442, 464, 528, 536, 556, 706
Allen, James 238, 263
Allen, Joseph 221
Allen, R.C. 145
Alley, Bill 391, 400, 446
Allsop, Arthur 364
Amar Singh 366
Amarnath, 'Lala' 365, 390, 400
Ambrose, Curtley 726, 731, 732, 741, 758
Ames, Leslie 355, 386
Amos, Gordon 332
Amritsar 366
Amstelveen 767
Andrews, Charles 332, 359
Andrews, T.J.E. 178, 303, 304, 350
Andrews, Walter 22
Angel, J. 713, 717-18, 721
Anson, George 158
Antigua 726, 737, 740, 758
Apted, Walter 468
Ararat, 16, 59, 73, 94, 284
Archer, K.A. 410, 414, 419
Archer, R.G. 426, 441, 446, 580, 587
Argall, Philip 186
Arlott, John 405, 434
Armstrong, W.W. 178, 203, 208, 219, 224, 227, 231-2, 240, 242, 243-4, 247, 251, 260-1, 268, 275-81, 282, 291, 303, 435, 744
Armstrong, Warwick 783
Arthur, Governor 19
Arthur, John 46, 99
Arundel 773
Ashes, The 130, 189, 206, 212, 219, 224, 231, 242, 301, 327, 339, 436, 445, 462, 479, 558, 602, 670, 682, 715-18, 724-5, 733-4, 738-9, 748-9, 752-3, 756, 757, 762, 763, 767, 773-5, 781-4, 785, 787
Ashraful, Mohammed 773
Ashwin, Edward 51
Asif Iqbal 446, 574, 600
Associated-Rediffusion 442
Atapattu, Marvan 765, 767
Atherton, Michael 716, 724-5
Atkinson, Denis 440
Atkinson, George 195
Attlee, Clement 388
Auckland 157, 181, 191, 198, 203, 209, 223, 261, 277, 296, 307, 393, 510, 554, 703, 714, 744, 772, 776, 784
Austin, 181
Australasia Cup 689
Australasian Cricket Council 174-202
Australian Associated Press Agency 705
Australian Board of Control 222-77, 295-311, 328, 333, 351, 363, 392, 397, 415, 424, 432, 466, 476-92, 510, 536, 542, 549
Australian Broadcasting Commission 376, 429, 448, 460, 464, 472, 503, 504, 520, 526, 544, 572, 579, 580, 587, 601, 617, 627

Australian CC (ACC) (Sydney) 4, 5, 6, 8
Australian CC (Melbourne) 14
Australian Council of Trade Unions 561
Australian Cricket Academy 654, 666, 690, 694, 695, 721, 758
Australian Cricket Board (ACB), 548-62, 579-94, 606, 617, 640, 704, 709, 716, 757, 766, 767, 777, 779, 790, 793
Australian Cricket Society 306, 499, 675
Australian Cricketers' Association (ACA) 734, 741, 794
Australian Federation of Commercial Broadcasting Stations 396, 438
Australian Gallery of Sport 674, 684
Australian Imperial Forces 243, 268-72, 385-91
Australian Institute of Sport 654, 690
Australian Journalists Association 343, 402, 565
Australian Lawn Tennis Association 448, 713
Australian Sports Council 556
Australian Sports Drug Agency (ASDA) 756-7
Australian Sports Drug Agency 756
Ayub Khan 466
Azharuddin, Mohammad 702, 736

Bacchus Marsh 284
Bacher, 'Ali' 640, 647, 719
Badcock, C.L. 353, 367, 370, 384
Bagenal Harvey Organisation 515
Bagot, Robert 44
Baig, Abbas Ali 701
Bailey, Abe 270
Bailey, Bertram 'Dick' 192
Bailey, George 31, 99
Bailey, Henry 53
Bailey, Jack 414, 595, 605
Bailey, Trevor 430, 460
Bailhache, Robin 551, 624, 676, 687
Bairnsdale 284
Baker, Frederick 54
Baker, Thomas 23
Ballarat 10, 16, 48, 53, 70, 73, 74, 86, 94, 284, 289, 691
ball-tampering 727, 728
Balmain 115
Balmain CC (Sydney) 314, 520
Banerjee, Montu 390
Bangalore 467, 522, 748, 787; Chinnaswamy Stadium 611, 659, 684, 736, 768
Bangladesh 759-60, 773, 780, 785
Bankstown 505, 710
Bannerman, A.C. 6, 40, 91, 99, 104, 111, 123, 130, 145, 170, 184, 292
Bannerman, C. 6, 40, 48, 76, 83, 91, 93, 107, 145, 186, 198, 223, 257, 287, 320, 332
Baqa Jilani 366
Barbados 740, 759
Barbour, Eric 234, 345
Barbour, George 758
Bardsley, W. 178, 234, 238, 256, 266, 275, 298, 304, 313, 369
Barkly, Henry 15
Barlow, Andrew 427
Barlow, Eddie 488
Barlow, Richard 145, 199
Barnes, Alan 413, 469, 480, 481-8, 492, 504, 515, 523, 524, 526, 530-1, 536, 537, 543-4, 549, 551, 556, 561, 564, 566, 571, 576, 579, 580, 587, 591, 596, 598, 615-16, 619, 621, 640, 668, 678
Barnes, Billy 145
Barnes, S.G. 375, 379, 384, 391, 397, 403, 407, 422, 453, 531
Barnes, Sidney (S.F.) 206, 230, 253, 361
Barnett, B.A. 354, 379, 400, 428
Barnett, Charles 377
Barnett, J.E. 164, 274
Baroda 482, 660
Baroda, Maharajah of 482, 549
Barritt, Denis 679
Barrow, John 23
Barry, Redmond 16
Barton, Edmund 111
Barwon Heads 345
Bashar, Habibul 780
Basin Reserve (Wellington) 163, 223, 453, 469, 510, 633, 657, 689, 772
Basseterre, St Kitts 591, 695, 785
Bates, Billy 129, 153
Bath 279
Bathurst 6, 8, 53, 68, 86, 94, 143, 163, 285
Batsford, Rob 683
Beal, Charles 74, 126, 153, 154
Beames, Percy 381
Bean, Ernest 227-41, 250-313, 318
Beard, G.R. 622
Beaumont 318
Beaurepaire, Frank 233
Becher, William 442
Bedi, Bishan 521, 535, 588
Bedser, Alec 362, 406, 414, 430, 445, 483, 557
Beecher, Eric 579
Beechworth 16, 67, 131
Beersheba 266
Beeson, John 5
Bell, Ian 782
Bell, Sandy 336
Bellerive Oval (Hobart) 668, 674, 686, 691, 766, 785, 791
Bellon, Brian 566
Belmont Park (Philadelphia) 180
Benalla 16, 284, 491
Benaud, J. 535, 542, 612
Benaud, R. 362, 419, 421, 441-89, 539, 553, 560, 565, 570, 573, 582, 596, 663, 682, 765
Bendigo 10, 16, 48, 65, 70, 73, 87, 94, 100, 115, 238, 284
Benjamin, Richard 259, 263
Bennett, Frederick 520-5, 560-6, 591, 619, 626, 641-72
Bennett, George 66, 69
Bennett, M.J. 647, 651
Benoni 456
Benson & Hedges Company 550, 572, 587, 606, 616, 654, 703, 708

Benson, Mark 789
Berea Park (Pretoria) 213, 270, 456
Beresford, Marcus 199
Best, Robert 161, 175
Bevan, John 52
Bevan, Michael 717-18, 720, 724, 729, 730, 731-2, 741, 742, 755, 757, 772-3
Bhubaneswar 667
Bichel, Andy 733, 748, 752, 755, 757, 758, 761, 766, 773, 779, 791
Bill, Wendell 334, 364
Birch, William 52
Birmingham 61
Bishop, Glenn 655
Bishop, Reginald 577
Blackham, J.M. 93, 104, 137, 159, 164, 171, 173, 179, 345, 435
Blackheath 334
Blackie, D.D. 307, 313, 350
Blanckenberg, Jimmy 271
Blarney, General Thomas 386
Blashki, Philip 176
Blewett, Greg 717, 725, 732, 733, 738, 742
Bligh, Ivo 127, 128, 139
Blinman, Harry 238, 352, 381
Blizzard, Philip 640
Bloemfontein 361
Blunt, Roger 277
Boak, James 75
Board of Control for Cricket in India (BCCI) 310, 328, 363, 390, 424, 427, 447, 454, 466, 520, 549, 700, 792
Boer War 200, 201, 203, 208
Bohemians CC (Melbourne) 54
Bolger, James 27, 28, 41
Bollinger, Doug 794
Bolton, Keane 283
Bombay 306, 310, 363, 389, 404, 521, 600, 619, 769, 787
Bombay Quadrangular Committee 306, 363
Bombay *see* Brabourne Stadium; Wankhede Stadium
Bond, Shane 757, 784
Bonnor, G.J. 129, 144, 163, 227, 274, 661
Boon, D.C. 651, 653, 663, 686, 689, 716, 717, 719, 722, 724, 725, 728-9
Booth, B.C. 483, 489, 493
Borde, Chandra 511
Border Cricket Association (South Africa) 361, 410, 456, 508, 732
Border, A.R. 601, 608, 626, 631, 638, 645, 650-723 passim, 724, 727, 730, 753, 763, 765, 776
Border-Gavaskar Trophy 747, 768
Borwick, George 396
Botham, Ian 615, 627, 639, 661, 714
Bott, Leo 284
Botten, William 24
Bourda (Georgetown) 440, 500, 592, 604, 643, 696, 741, 758
Bourke, Richard 9
Bournemouth 211
Bowden, Joseph 18, 19
Bowden, Percy 186, 197, 206, 221, 225, 266
Bowen 28
Bowen Hills 56, 311
Bowen, George 41
Bowral 309, 684, 691
Boycott, Geoffrey 493, 504, 527, 564, 584
Boyle & Scott Ltd 167
Boyle, H.F. 46, 51, 53, 54, 83, 85, 101, 115, 134, 137, 146, 163, 167
Brabourne Stadium (Bombay) 389, 451, 496, 612, 660
Bracken, Nathan 761, 766, 773, 775, 785, 786, 790, 791
Bradford 406
Bradman Medal of Honour 739
Bradman Museum 684
Bradman Trust 684, 691
Bradman, D.G. 1, 119, 122, 289, 290, 309-10, 316, 318-38, 339, 343-4, 346-7, 350-3, 356-60, 367, 369-82, 392, 396-9, 400-8, 409-10, 422, 425, 432- 43, 462-4, 469-71, 476-9, 480-7, 502, 509, 510-11, 515, 518, 520-1, 524-5, 528-31, 532-3, 535-6, 548, 554, 556, 565-6, 570, 578, 587, 601-3, 605, 614, 649, 652, 658, 666-7, 684-5, 687, 690, 693, 704, 711, death 748, 759
Bradman, George 309
Bravo, Dwayne 776
Brayshaw, Ian 511, 568
Breakfast Creek 130
Brearley, Michael 581, 583, 599, 600, 612, 616, 627
Brereton, Harry 297, 374, 413
bribery 738, 745
Brice, Alfred 277
Bridgetown: Kensington Oval 500, 547, 696, 726, 741, 759
Bridgman, Hugh 432
Briggs, Johnny 173, 185
Bright, R.J. 600, 619, 660
Brighton 10, 180, 275
Brindle, Terry 681
Brisbane 25-56, 100, 143, 225, 231, 247, 318, 330, 391, 719, 720, 725, 727-8, 734, 738, 741, 742, 746, 750, 751, 752, 755, 761, 764, 769, 777, 781, 787, 788: *see also* Allan Border Field; Exhibition Ground; Woolloongabba
Brisbane Cricket Club 28, 40, 557
Brisbane School of Arts 49
Briscoe, Edward 186, 196
Bristol 773
British Broadcasting Corporation 373, 434, 442, 495, 506
British Colombia 256
British Colonial Cricket Conference 241
British Empire Films 396
Brodie, James 17, 40, 75
Broken Hill 289
Bromley, E.H. 354
Brondy 683
Brookes, Norman 233

Brooks, Reginald 125
Brooks, Tom 551
Broome, Frederick 149, 181
Brown, Freddie 413-16, 462-3, 705
Brown, Harry 197
Brown, John 654
Brown, John T. 185
Brown, W.A. 355, 369, 378, 392, 401, 412, 425
Bruce, Stanley 342
Bruce, W. 141, 153, 171, 173, 184
Bruxner, Michael 368
Bryant, Frank 364, 524, 540, 551, 554
Buchanan, John 742, 761
Bucknor, Steve 766, 769, 789
Budd, Harry 51, 153, 173
Bufton, John 201
Buggy, Hugh 345
Bulawayo 456, 508, 699, 756
Bull, George 200
Bull, William 304, 306
Bulli soil 183
Bunbury 30, 31, 472
Bundaberg 132, 143, 225
Bundy, William 24
Bunten, D. 25
Bunting, William 47
Burdett, Leslie 642, 667, 702
Burge, Jack 440
Burge, P.J.P. 437, 440, 452, 477, 484, 491, 493, 510
Burke, J.W. 414, 427, 443, 452, 460, 531
Burn, E.J.K. 164
Burn, James 164
Burns, Tommy 233
Burrell Creek 543
Burrup, William 61
Burt, Selby 400
Burton, F.J. 145
Burton, Francis 88
Burwood CC (Sydney) 243
Bushby, Harold 353
Busselton 30
Butcher, Basil 517
Butcher, Mark 749
Butt, Qamaruddin 465
Butterworth, Ben 65, 73
Butterworth, Luke 785

Caddick, Andy 716, 748, 753
Caffyn, William 6, 40, 42, 62, 66, 73, 75, 77
Cairns 249 759, 760, 767
Cairns, Lance 624, 625
Cairo 376, 385
Calcutta/Kolkata 306, 365, 389, 451, 466, 522, 667, 747, 761: *see also* Eden Gardens
Calcutta CC (India) 306
Caldwell, Timothy 548, 553, 556, 562, 567, 614, 615
Calgary 304
Callaway, S.T. 157, 163, 170, 223
Callen, I.W. 588, 633
Camberwell 17
Cambridge University CC 12, 17, 29, 37, 50, 59, 162, 209, 294, 323, 376
Cameron, Frank 480
Cameron, Horace Brackenridge 'Jock' 335, 336
Campbell, Donald 40, 53
Campbell, G.D. 681
Campbell, Gordon 264, 269
Campbell, Sherwin 731, 741, 746
Campbell, William 238
Campbelltown 3, 5
Camperdown 16
Canadian Cricket Association 481, 737
Canberra (ACT) 204, 374, 391, 548, 556, 593, 601, 616, 654, 685, 691, 694, 708
Canterbury 53-6, 163, 181, 183, 204, 223, 244, 249, 261, 289, 296, 307, 393, 510, 524, 554
Canterbury CA (New Zealand) 55, 181
Cape Town 166, 212, 214, 270, 281, 361, 437, 457, 508, 662, 721, 778
Cardiff 495, 773
Cardus, Neville 369, 372, 377
Carew, Joey 726
Carkeek, W. 238, 255, 256
Carlson, P.H. 574
Carlton & United Series (later Carlton Series, CB Series) 736, 740, 744, 746, 783, 790
Carlton 17, 48, 60
Carmody, Keith 385, 387, 388, 401
Caro, Andrew 598
Carr, Arthur 300
Carr, Donald 577, 713, 721
Carrara 692
Carter, H. 208, 223, 230, 251, 266, 280, 337
Cary, Clif 401
Casino 7
Casson, Beau 794
Castlemaine 16, 70, 73, 87
Cavenagh, George 11
Cazaly's Stadium (Cairns) 760
Centenary Cup 724
Centennial Park Cricket League 348, 433
Central Cumberland CC (Sydney) 285
Centre of Excellence *see* Australian Cricket Academy
Centurion 732-3
Ceylon/Sri Lanka 405, 408, 727, 728-9, 730, 740, 742, 752, 755, 757, 763, 764-5, 767, 777, 785, 787-8
Chadwick, Derek 518, 524
Champions Cup 748
Chanderpaul, Shivnarine 758, 759
Chandigarh 659, 667
Chapman, Percy 300, 311, 324, 326, 339
Chappell, G.S., 203, 486, 524, 527, 548, 567-94, 615-48 passim 651, 657, 672-3, 675, 765, 783
Chappell, I.M., 486, 491, 497, 516, 519, 528, 539-69 passim 594, 600, 609, 613, 615, 702, 729, 765
Chappell, T.M. 486, 612, 625, 627
Chappell-Hadlee Trophy 770, 776, 784, 788
Charlton, Michael 472
Charlton, P.C. 158, 164, 234

Charters Towers 225
Chatswood 285
Chauhan, Chetan 624
Checkett, Charley 183, 193, 194, 253
Cheetham, Albert 387
Cheetham, Jack 424, 523
Chegwyn, Jack 385, 386
Chelmsford 700
Cheltenham 278
Chennai, India 736, 747-8, 768
Chester, Frank 325
Chesterfield 378
Chilvers, Hugh 324
Chinnaswamy Stadium *see* Bangalore
Chipperfield, A.G. 354, 377
Chittagong 780
Chittleborough, James 24
Chopra, Aakash 768
Christchurch 56, 72, 188, 192, 197, 225, 289, 296, 510, 575, 772: Lancaster Park 55, 223, 244, 453, 469, 575, 633, 657, 772
Christian, Arthur 245
Christy, Frederick 69
City & Suburban CA (Sydney) 215
Clare 22, 25
Claremont CC (Perth) 284
Clarence 7
Clark, David 527-9
Clark, Stuart 778, 780, 781, 782, 783, 791
Clark, W.M. 588, 592
Clarke, Alfred 163
Clarke, Marcus 94
Clarke, Michael 768, 769, 776, 780, 782, 785, 787-8, 789, 791
Claxton, Norrie 267
Clayton, Joseph 35, 38
Clemow, Brian 710
Clifford, Hugh 304
Clingeleffer, Sean 785
Cobcroft, Thomas 188
Cobham, John 371
Coca-Cola Cup 737
Cochrane, Gilbert 289
Cocker, John 22, 23, 25
Code of Behaviour 632
Cohen, Lewis 159
Cohen, Victor 172-9
Coimbatore 684
Colac 16, 284
Cole, Tom 47, 90
Coleman, Frederick 11
Colledge, George 225, 232
College 234, 375, 526
Colley, D.J. 722
Collingwood 10, 73, 322
Collingwood CC (Melbourne) 10, 256, 550
Collingwood, Paul 781, 782, 783
Collins, H.L. 257, 260, 269-71, 275-6, 281-2, 287, 291-2, 298-301, 312, 313, 314, 350
Colombo 128, 242, 299, 323, 354, 364, 377, 405, 478, 521, 707, 729, 765: *see also* Khettarama Stadium; Saravanamuttu Stadium
Colonial Stadium (Melbourne) 745
Colton, John 129
Commonwealth Bank 783
Commonwealth Games 737
Compton, Denis 377, 399, 406, 430
Congdon, Bevan 550, 554, 575
Coningham, A. 177, 184
Connolly, A.N. 486, 493, 509, 519
Consolidated Press 573, 636
Constantine, Learie 329
Conway, John 39, 47-50, 65-76, 83-8, 92-101, 108, 133-4
Cooch Behar, Maharaja of 363
Cook 274
Cook, Alistair 782
Cooktown 50
Coolgardie 182
Cooma 491
Cooper, B.B. 46, 83, 85, 93, 133, 274
Cooper, W.H. 54
Coopers & Lybrand 704
Cootamundra 119, 120, 138
Copenhagen 683
Copley, 324
Coppin, George 17, 46, 61
Corling, G.E. 493
Cornell, John 572, 575
corruption 738, 745
Cosier, G.J. 567, 569, 582, 608
Cosstick, Samuel 46, 65, 72, 76, 83, 85, 88, 107
Cottam, J.T. 145
Cotter, A. 178, 219, 222-5, 236, 251, 266
Coulthard, G. 54, 110
Court, Charles 612
Cowdrey, Colin 70, 435, 461, 478, 483, 503, 514, 558, 666, 711
Cowper, R.M. 486, 493, 500, 505, 512, 526, 571, 668, 679
Cowra 8
Coy, Arthur 437
Craddock, Robert 726
Crafter, Tony 630, 669, 702
Craig, I.D. 426, 452, 456-62
Craig, Reg 391
Crane, Edward 158
Crawford, Jack 242, 261, 267
Crawford, Joan 338
Crawford, W. P. A. 444, 447
Creswell, John 129-42, 151, 153, 160-73, 188, 190, 196-235, 284
Cricinfo 758, 785, 786
Cricket Australia *see* Australian Cricket Board
Cricklewood 278
Cristofani, Bob 387, 388
Crockett, Bob 186, 291, 702
Crompton, Alan 672, 708, 721
Cronje, Hansie 721, 732, 735
Crooks, Alexander 115
Crouch, George 251, 255, 256
Crowe, Jeff 669, 694
Crowe, Martin 655, 669, 718
Crowe, Russell 765

Cuff, Len 181
Cumberbatch, Clyde 696
Cunderdin 491
Cunningham, James 34
Cunningham, William 296
Curry, Michael 7
Curtin, John 384, 386
Curtis, George 46
Cush, Frank 333, 438, 441, 448
Cussen, Leo 231, 266
Cuttack 611, 667

Dacca 465: Dacca Stadium 465
Dacre, Ces 277
Dalby 28, 41
Dale, Adam 733, 744
Dalkeith 318
Danish Cricket Association 683
Dar, Aleem 786
Darling Downs 25, 26
Darling, J. 46, 178, 184, 189, 198, 202, 208, 222-37, 287, 345, 375, 382, 393, 422, 672, 715
Darling, John 46
Darling, L.S. 354
Darling, W.M. 588, 592, 608
Darlinghurst 175
Darvall, John 38
Darwin 384, 707, 759, 760, 767
Davidson, A.K. 412, 429, 444, 467, 473, 483
Davies, George 169, 239, 429
Davis, Coleman 163, 181, 196
Davis, I.C. 574
Davis, John 190, 232
Davis, S.P. 724
Davison, Brian 672
Dawes, Joe 748
De Beers Stadium, Kimberley (S.Africa) 362
de Mello, Anthony 365
de Silva, Aravinda 686, 729
de Villiers, Farnie 719
Deane, Sidney 164
DeCourcy, J.H. 429
Delhi 366, 389, 466, 611, 660, 667, 66: Feroz Shah Kotla 466, 521, 611
Dell, A.R. 724
Dempster, Eric 554
Deniliquin 8
Denison, William 35, 38
Denness, Mike 557, 559, 638
Department of Foreign Affairs 439, 455, 600, 619, 620, 652
Department of Home Affairs 328, 602
Depeiza, Clairmonte 440
Derbyshire CCC 117, 356, 378, 407, 539, 680
Derwent CC (Hobart) 19, 42, 69
Desborough, Lord 252
Devonport 491, 497, 613, 616
Dexter, Ted 478, 483, 494
Dhoni, M.S. 788
Di Venuto, Michael 733, 791
Diamond, Austin 226, 259
Dickson, Thomas 90
Dight, Charley 16
Dight, Thomas 16
DLF Cup 781
Docker, Cyril 152, 268
Docklands Stadium (Melbourne) 770
Dodds, Norman 238
Dodemaide, A.I.C. 670, 710
Doherty, Xavier 791
D'Oliveira, Basil 514
Dolling, Charles 261, 313, 322, 353
Domain, The 35, 37, 70, 71
Donald, Allan 721
Donnan, H. 157, 170, 189, 710
Donnelly, Arthur 351
Donovan, P.F. 190
Dooland, B. 400, 446
Dotiwalla, Dara 660
Douglas, J.H. 274
Douglas, Johnny (J.W.H.T.) 252, 274, 280, 296
Dowlah, Moin-ud 366
Dowling, Graham 679, 728
Dowling, William 443, 447, 462, 470, 476, 518
Downs, George 186
Draper, Mr Justice 344
Dravid, Rahul 747, 761, 762, 768, 788
Drennan, John 453
Drew, Brendan 791
Driver, Richard 34, 38, 39, 107, 305
drug testing 756-7
Drummoyne Oval, Balmain (Sydney) 542
du Croz, Gervase 33
Dubbo 8
Duckmanton, Talbot 504, 579, 580
Dudley, Robert 234
Duff, R.A. 178, 205, 208, 224, 253
Duffus, Louis 490
Duffy, William 149, 182
Duleepsinhji, Kumar 324, 363
Dulwich 290, 386
Duncan, J.R.F. 725
Dundee 377
Dunedin 55, 72, 191, 261, 412, 510, 554, 744: Carisbrook 55, 307, 469, 555
Dunning, Jack 525
Dunningham, John 368
Dunstan, Keith 513
Durban 213, 247, 270, 281, 361, 410, 456, 508, 662, 692, 751, 778, 787: *see also* Kingsmead; Lord's
Durham CCC 700
Durrani, S.K. 624
Duval, Clarence 158
Dwyer, Edmund 353, 393, 399, 404, 422, 425
Dyer, G.C. 660-9
Dymock, G. 555, 582, 608, 611
Dyson, J. 622, 627, 632, 639, 652, 662

Eady, C.J. 162, 189, 207, 346, 382
Eagar, Desmond 462
East London 214, 361, 456, 508
East Melbourne CC 10, 16, 17, 32, 47- 54, 65, 80, 100, 116, 127, 157, 162, 167, 183, 188, 257, 275

East Perth CC 284
Eastbourne 280, 386, 387
Eastwood, K.H. 725
Ebeling, H.I. 303, 354, 360, 551, 576
Echuca 284
Echunga 22
Eden Gardens (Calcutta) 389, 451, 468, 496, 522, 611, 667, 736
Eden Park (Auckland) 261, 307, 393, 453, 469, 555, 575, 633, 772, 784
Edenhope 77
Edgbaston 61, 210, 240, 478, 514, 562, 681, 716, 733, 741-2, 748-9, 774
Edrich, Bill 378, 397, 406, 505, 514, 528, 562
Edrich, John 493
Edwards, J.D. 154
Edwards, R. 537, 558, 561, 581, 594
Edwards, W.J. 725
Egar, Colin 476, 488, 517, 634, 643, 673, 684, 690, 705
Eisenhower, Dwight 466
Ellicott, Bob 602
Elliott, Gideon 36, 37, 53, 65
Elliott, John 20
Elliott, Matthew 731, 733, 734, 745, 766, 767, 784, 791
Ellis Park (Jo'burg) 410, 411
Ellis, Jack 299, 302, 364
Ellis, Matthew 275
Ellis, Reg 387, 389
Eltham 16
Emerald Hill 11, 16, 33
Emerson, Ross 727, 729
Emery, S.H. 255
Emmett, Tom 89, 107, 119
Endean, Russell 424, 635
Engel, Matthew 663
England *see* Ashes
Essendon 227
Essex CCC 240, 255, 274, 299, 405, 514, 562, 683, 700
Euroa 284
Evan, Mostyn 173, 175, 179, 192, 238, 246, 250, 261, 274
Evans, E. 6, 91, 141
Evans, Godfrey 399, 436
Everett, Samuel 299, 304, 320
Exhibition Ground (Brisbane) 176, 260, 302, 311

Facey, Ashley 244
Facy, Philip 245, 257
FAI Insurance Group 700, 706
Fairbanks, Douglas, jr 338
Fairfax, A.G. 315, 337, 354
Fairfax, John 38
Faisalabad: Iqbal Stadium 620, 635
Fane, Frederick 230
Farnes, Kenneth 374
Farrer, Frank 234
Fatullah 780
Faulkner, Aubrey 248, 490
Faulkner, Peter 652, 663
Favell, L.E. 453, 468, 480, 509
Fawkner, John 11
Fazal Mahmood 450, 465
Ferguson, James 52
Ferguson, William 419, 443, 454
Fergusson, Adam 42, 45
Fergusson, James 42
Ferris, LL 144, 154, 166, 188
Fiji 404, 468
Findlay, William 223, 311
Fingleton, J.H.W. 190, 335, 344, 349
Fisher, Ian 152, 186
Fitzgerald, Reginald 247
Fitzroy 183, 275, 507
Fleetwood-Smith, L.O. 289, 338, 354, 359, 369, 531, 737
Fleming, Damien 724, 738
Fleming, Stephen 734-5, 750, 784
Fletcher, Annie 130
Flintoff, Andrew 774, 775, 783
Flockton, Ray 427, 468
Flood, Edward 5
Flynn, Thomas 159, 186
Foenander, S.P. 259
Folkestone 323
Foot, Hugh 441
Forbes 285
Ford Ranger One-Day Cup 784, 791
Ford, Doug 480
Forster, Lord 292
Forsythe, Harry 227
Foster, Reginald (R.E.) 218, 326
Four Corners 503
Foxton, George 226, 238
Frames, Algy 310, 424, 470
Francis, B.C. 538, 637, 649, 651
Francis, J.V. 56
Frank Worrell Trophy 474, 500, 608, 696, 726, 730, 740, 746
Franklin, Governor 20
Fraser, Angus 716
Fraser, Dawn 1
Fraser, Malcolm 569, 595, 601, 625, 629, 636
Freeman, E.W. 509, 517
Freer, F.W. 397, 400
Fremantle 30, 31, 82, 192, 274, 278, 290, 323, 335, 369, 371, 400, 413, 483, 662
Fremantle CC (Perth) 30
French, Dick 669
Frith, Charles 54, 55
Frith, William 54
Fry, Charles 210, 369, 370
Fullarton, William 23, 24
Fuller, Eddie 427, 457
Fulton, Peter 784

'Gabba' *see* Woolloongabba
Gaggin, William 46, 47, 53
Galle 764, 765
Galle Face CC (Colombo) 242, 478
Ganga, Darren 758, 759
Ganguly, Sourav 747, 757, 788

Gannon, J.B. 726
Gardiner, James 68, 261
Garnsey, George 190
Garrett, T.W. 48, 92, 107, 115, 133, 182, 345, 374, 382
Gatting, Mike 661, 715
Gatton 50
Gaul, John 49, 50
Gaunt, R.A. 453, 477
Gavaskar, Sunil 588, 594, 624, 660, 701, 709, 712, 714
Gawler 45
Gayndah 28
Geelong 11, 67, 284, 374, 491, 569, 621
Geeves, Brenton 791
Gehrs, D.R.A. 219, 222, 250
George, Shane 730
Georgetown 440, 500, 592, 604, 643, 696, 741, 758
Geraldton 30
Gibbs, Charles 52
Gibbs, Herschelle 778
Gibbs, Lance 474, 500, 516, 564, 631
Gibson, George 54, 60
Gibson, John 173, 202, 214, 238
Giffen, G. 51, 90, 115, 121, 123, 138-73, 185-92, 216, 222, 229, 250, 274, 284, 287, 292, 305, 350, 559
Giffen, W.F. 145, 152, 162
Gilbert, D.R. 651, 660
Gilbert, Eddie 330, 334
Gilbert, George 35, 36, 39, 42
Gilchrist, Adam 730, 733, 736, 742, 743, 745, 747, 749, 751, 756, 757, 758, 760 764, 765, 767-8, 769, 770, 771, 772, 777, 780, 782, 784, 785, 789, 790, 791
Giles, Ashley 781
Gillespie, Jason 729, 731, 734, 737, 738, 740, 742, 747, 749, 753, 755, 757, 758, 759, 760, 761, 768, 769, 770, 775, 779, 780, 791
Gillette (Aust) Pty Ltd 525, 570, 603
Gilligan, Arthur 290-5
Gilligan, Harold 319
Gilmour, G.J. 561, 562, 575
Glamorgan CCC 494, 513, 562, 653, 681
Gleeson, J.W. 509, 511, 521
Glen Innes 8
Glenelg 128, 436, 684
Glenelg CC (Adelaide) 348
Glenferrie 374
Gloucestershire CCC 100, 117, 166, 188, 278, 405, 444, 681
Goddard, John 418-24
Goddard, Trevor 457, 489
Godden, Archibald 51
Gomez, Gerry 418, 421, 477, 500
Gooch, Graham 562, 681, 691, 693, 715, 716, 737
Gooden, James 90
Gordon CC (Sydney) 285, 301
Gore Hill 114, 224
Gorry, Charles 226, 238
Gosein, Ralph 593
Gosford 694
Gough, Darren 739, 748, 752
Goulburn 285, 289
Gower, David 616, 661, 680, 691
Grace, Edward 72, 74, 117, 118
Grace, G.F. 'Fred' 82, 89, 118
Grace, William Gilbert ('W.G.') 80-8, 100-6, 117-24, 165-73, 180, 189, 199, 223, 266
Grafton 7
Graham, H. 180, 184, 223, 628
Grant, G.C. 'Jack' 329
Graveney, Tom 514
Gravesend 77
Gray, Malcolm 655, 659, 661, 665-84, 703
Gray, Tony 695
Greatbatch, Mark 685
Greaves, William 39, 73, 76
Green, Douglas 238, 345
Greenwood, Ivor 569
Gregory, Arthur 6, 158
Gregory, Charles 6, 226, 287
Gregory, D.W. 6, 40, 46, 83, 91, 99, 101, 107-14, 147, 156, 162, 168, 274, 358
Gregory, E.J. 6, 40, 46, 76, 83, 91, 93, 183, 197
Gregory, Edward (snr) 6
Gregory, Harry 304
Gregory, J.M. 270, 274-313, 369
Gregory, R.G. 374
Gregory, S.E. 164, 166, 189, 198, 205, 219, 241, 255, 266
Greig, Robert 153, 159, 160, 173
Greig, Tony 534, 562, 564, 582, 600, 661, 665
Grieve, Richard 266
Grieves, Ken 391, 400
Griffin, Geoff 470
Griffith, Charlie 499, 517
Griffith, George 62, 66
Griffith, S.C. 'Billy' 70, 503-10, 524, 536
Griffith, Samuel Walker 49
Grimmett, C.V. 289, 299, 307, 316, 323, 335-80, 430, 464
Griqualand West CA (S. Africa) 362, 523
Groube, T.U. 54
Grout, A.T.W. 427, 453, 456, 474, 493
Guest, C.E.J. 484, 486
Guha, Subroto 521
Guildford 29, 391, 400, 503
Gul Mahomed 390
Gunasekera, D.B. 242, 478
Gunn, George 230, 254
Gunn, William 144
Gupta, Pankaj 400
Guy, Dick 657, 672
Guyana 741, 758
Gwalior 659
Gympie 56, 143, 225, 473

Haddin, Brad 785
Hadlee, Richard 554, 655, 669
Hadlee, Walter 393, 412, 596
Hadlow, Peter 566

Hahndorf 22
Haines, William 40
Hair, Darrell 728
Halbish, Graham 721
Halfpenny, Thomas 10
Hall, Wesley 473, 481, 500, 517
Halliwell, Ernest 213
Hamence, R.A. 368
Hamilton 7, 16, 284, 554, 745, 776, 784
Hamilton, Scott 713
Hamilton, Thomas 33, 81
Hammersley, William 40, 67
Hammond, J.R. 547
Hammond, Walter 312-16, 345, 348, 370, 374, 377, 387, 394-401
Hampshire CCC 224, 279, 562, 608, 622, 681, 783
Handfield, William 45, 47
Hanif Mohammad 465, 496
Hansen, Justice John 789
Harare 456, 508, 658, 699, 742, 756
Harcourt, Dr Peter 756
Hardy, John 5
Hardy, William 5
Harlow, Jean 338
Harmison, Steve 774, 775, 782, 783
Harris, Bruce 369, 436
Harris, Lord George 107-16, 133, 139, 194, 198, 212, 285, 296
Harris, Vere 55
Harrison, Colden 17
Harry, J. 164, 184, 186, 274
Harte, Chris 636, 714
Hartigan, R.J. 230, 238, 298
Hartkopf, A.E.V. 290
Harvey, Ian 755-6
Harvey, M.R. 728
Harvey, R.N. 403, 406, 425, 439, 452- 87, 504, 512, 535, 582
Hassett, A.L. 375, 385-91, 393, 403, 405-8, 410-12, 414-16, 420, 426, 429-35, 758
Hastings 405
Hauritz, Nathan 768, 769
Have-A-Go Cricket 792
Hawke, Bob 561, 571, 654
Hawke, Martin (Lord) 150, 172, 176, 210, 212, 214, 258, 280, 342
Hawke, N.J.N. 493, 519
Hawker, Cyril 528
Hawkes Bay 181, 198, 249, 296
Hawkes, George 24
Hawkins, Brian 619, 620
Hawkins, Laurie 249
Hawthorn 17, 73, 146, 183
Hawthorn CC (Melbourne) 140, 329
Hayden, Bill 652
Hayden, Matthew 710, 717, 720-1, 731, 733, 746, 747, 749-53, 755, 757, 759, 760, 761, 762, 764, 767, 768, 770, 771, 775, 776, 777, 778, 782, 783, 784, 785, 786, 788, 789, 790
Haygarth, Arthur 142
Hayman, William 77
Haysman, Michael 652, 662, 663
Hazare, Vijay 390, 403
Hazlitt, G.R. 230, 266
Headingley 210, 224, 240, 280, 300, 356, 378, 430, 444, 479, 514, 539, 561, 584, 627, 653, 681, 716, 718, 734, 749, 763 773
Headley, Dean 738-9
Headley, George 329, 330
Healesville 284
Healy, I.A. 692, 710, 715, 717, 718, 720, 721-2, 724, 730, 731-2, 734, 736, 737, 742
Heather, Edward 132, 140, 146, 153, 156, 160, 182, 207, 220, 221
Hele, George 316
Helsham, Justice 583
Hendry, H.S.T.L. 289, 296, 302, 364
Hennessey, Harold 304
Henry, Albert 207
Henty, William 21, 33
Herford, Robert 328
Heydon, Harold 297, 305, 309, 332, 345, 381, 385, 413
Hibbert, P.A. 588
Hick, Graeme 725
Hide, Jesse 51, 107, 115, 130, 132
Higgins, James 231
Higgs, J.D. 532, 560, 608, 624, 657
Hilditch, A.M.J. 608, 635, 650, 794
Hilfenhaus, Ben 785, 794
Hill, C. 45, 178, 189, 202, 219, 222, 236-42, 247-51, 263, 274, 298-311, 350, 360, 368, 380, 392
Hill, David 3
Hill, J.C. 429, 440
Hill, John 45, 251
Hilliard, Harry 6
Hills, Dene 720, 737
Hill-Smith, Wyndham 559
Hindmarsh 24
Hirst, George 210, 240
Hoare, D.E. 474
Hobart 8, 15-69, 132, 197, 253, 318, 323, 354, 373, 391, 497, 719, 728, 735, 738, 743, 746, 750, 775, 788: *see also* Bellerive Oval
Hobbs, Jack 209, 230, 253, 267, 275, 291, 313, 326, 369
Hobgen, Arthur 89
Hodge, Brad 775, 776, 784, 785
Hodges, J.H. 93
Hodgetts, Harry 267, 284, 301, 352, 360, 368, 375, 380, 392, 408
Hodgson, Arthur 26
Hogan, James 119
Hogan, Paul 572
Hogan, T.G. 639, 643
Hogg, Brad 756, 758. 760, 761, 785, 786, 788, 791
Hogg, R.M. 599, 608, 643
Hogg, William 42
Hoggard, Matthew 782
Hohns, T.V. 652, 664, 676, 681
Holdsworth, Wayne 717

Hole, G.B. 426
Holford, David 517, 713
Holland, John 577
Holland, R.G. 647, 650
Hollies, Eric 407
Hollioake brothers 734
Holmes, Errol 359
Holroyd, Henry (Lord Sheffield) 133, 142, 167-9, 169-70, 172-3, 176, 180, 188, 195, 207, 716, 759, 793
Hong Kong 666, 673
Hooker, Halford 317
Hookes, D.W. 576, 594, 622, 632, 646, 664, 765, 766, 769
Hope, Adam 39
Hopes, James 784
Hopkins, A.J.Y. 208, 225
Horan, Michael 672
Horan, T.P. 46-54, 86, 93, 104, 117, 132-9, 153, 157, 161, 165, 173, 266
Hordern, H.V. 249, 252, 263
Hornby, Albert 102, 124, 127, 139
Hornibrook, P.M. 277, 315, 327
Houston 689
Hove 123, 199, 211, 357
Howard, Geoffrey 434
Howard, John 738, 759
Howard, Roy 427
Howard, Tom 326
Howarth, Geoffrey 623
Howe, George 2
Howell, Henry 276
Howell, W. P. 193, 198, 219, 227, 382
Howlett, H.G. 252
Hoy, Colin 482
Hoy, Greg 756
Huddlestone, John 39, 65
Hudson, Andrew 721
Hughes, E.S. 343
Hughes, K.J., 529, 568, 572-582, 600, 603, 608-664 passim 692, 765
Hughes, M.G. 656, 677, 700, 710, 714, 715, 717, 718, 721
Hume, Ernest 251
Humphreys, John 186
Hunt, W.A. 731
Hunter, John 22
Hunters Hill 318
Hurst, A.G. 560, 567, 588, 607
Hurwood, A. 302, 329
Hussain, Nasser 733, 752
Hussey, David 794
Hussey, Michael 775, 776, 777, 782, 783, 784, 785, 787-8, 789
Hutcheon, John 246, 298, 313, 370, 413, 454
Hutton, Eric 171
Hutton, Len 377, 379, 387, 399, 406, 414, 430, 434
Hyde Park (Sydney) 2, 3
Hyderabad 634
Hyderabad CA (India) 685
ICC Champions Cup 781
ICC Champions Trophy 767
Iddison, Roger 68
Illingworth, Frank 167
Illingworth, Ray 527, 538
Imperial Conference 333, 341
Imperial Cricket Conference 241, 280, 290, 324, 339, 393, 400, 418, 438, 442, 447, 454, 463, 470, 477, 492
Imperial Economic Conference 342
Imperial Patriotic Fund 203
India 725, 729, 730, 736, 737, 742, 743-4, 747-8, 757, 761-2, 764, 767-8, 781, 785, 787
Indian Cricket League 791-2, 794
Indian Premier League 790
indoor matches 745
Indore 667
ING Cup 751, 755, 756-7, 765, 766, 772, 779
Innes, Matthew 791
Insole, Doug 503, 536, 556, 599
Institute of British Launderers 494
International Cricket Conference 511, 536, 582-5, 595, 612, 623, 666, 675, 679
International Cricket Council 698, 711, 745, 792
International Cricketers Association 610
International Cricketers Trust Fund 375
International Management Group 675
Interstate Conference 222, 268, 320, 331, 349, 384, 394, 408, 423, 428, 438, 472, 488, 497, 518, 544, 548
Inverarity, R.J. 511, 514, 524, 537, 632, 690
Invercargill 55, 56, 191
Ipswich 25, 41, 56, 371, 491
Iredale, F.A. 6, 178, 184, 189, 205, 237, 250, 266, 273, 285, 292, 297
Ireland 785
Ironmonger, H. 264, 277, 312, 324, 329, 335, 345, 350, 364
Isaacs, Issac 341
Iverson, J.B. 409, 412, 415, 427, 531

Jackson, A. 289, 307, 314, 319, 327, 334, 348, 564
Jackson, Stanley 180, 210, 224
Jackson, Vic 427
Jacobs, Ken 621, 687
Jacobs, William 507, 534
Jaipur 521
James, John 77, 148, 149
James, Trefor 756
Jammu & Kashmir Liberation Front 611
Jamnagar 365
Jan Smuts Ground (East London) 214
Jantke, Jack 456
Jaques, Phil 776, 779, 780, 787, 788
Jardine, Douglas 314, 316, 342-54, 430, 706
Jarman, B.N. 453, 477, 493, 498, 509, 514
Jarvis, A.H. 116, 153, 284
Jath, Raja of 380
Javed Miandad 630, 653
Jayasuriya, Sanath 765, 773

Jayawardene, Mahela 787, 788
Jeanes, William 297, 306, 311, 316, 324, 328, 333-413, 419, 422-36
Jenner, T.J. 524, 540, 559, 565, 717
Jennings, C.B. 255
Jerilderie 112
Jessop, Gilbert 210, 212
Jillett, Max 525
Johannesburg 212, 246, 270, 281, 310, 360, 362, 424, 456, 480, 522, 647, 662, 721, 751, 764, 778: *see also* Ellis Park; New Wanderers; Old Wanderers
Johns, Alfred 189
Johnson, I.W. 367, 397, 405, 412, 433, 439-41, 443-7, 452, 474, 529, 568, 581, 617
Johnson, Jack 233
Johnson, Keith 386, 404, 422
Johnson, L.J. 732
Johnson, Mel 630, 639
Johnson, Mitchell 779, 780, 785, 787
Johnston, W.A. 405, 410, 412, 420, 429, 441, 749
Jones, Andrew 669
Jones, Arthur 230, 238
Jones, Clem 488, 506, 525, 533, 551, 557, 567
Jones, D.M. 655, 659, 666, 677, 696, 710, 717, 720, 727, 763, 767, 776
Jones, Dick 322
Jones, E. 178, 184, 189, 193, 245, 350, 382
Jones, Geraint 774
Jones, Richard 38
Jones, S.P. 124, 133, 154, 198
Jones, Simon (England) 774
Jones, 39
Jordan, Cortez 499, 500
Jordon, Ray 552
Joslin, L.R. 732
Julian, Brendon 716, 718, 733, 741
Jullundur 521
Junction Oval (St Kilda) 15, 450
Jupp, Henry 82, 89

Kadavuleva, Penaia 229
Kadina 25, 87
Kalgoorlie 182, 284, 289
Kallicharran, Alvin 592
Kallis, Jacques 735, 750, 777, 778
Kandy 639, 707, 765: Asgiriya Stadium 639, 742
Kaneria, Danish 771
Kanhai, Rohan 473, 480, 500, 534, 548, 561
Kanpur: Green Park 467, 521, 611
Kapil Dev 611, 656, 660, 702
Karachi 365, 450, 466, 496, 619, 634: *see also* National Stadium
Kardar, Abdul Hafeez 451
Karloff, Boris 338
Kasprowicz, Michael 717-18, 731, 737, 745, 751, 761, 767, 768, 770, 774, 778, 791
Katanning 284
Katich, Simon 760, 761, 762, 767,768, 769, 772, 777, 791
Katunayeke 521, 626
Kelaart, Edward 323
Kelaart, Thomas 166, 242
Kelleway, C. 178, 247, 253, 260, 268, 350, 382, 392
Kelly, J.J. 189, 225
Kelly, Ned 111, 120
Kelly, Ros 709
Kelly, T.J.D. 48, 54, 83, 85, 95
Kelly, William 322, 324, 326, 328
Kendall, T. 54, 55, 93
Kennington Oval 78, 100, 117, 134, 189, 211, 224, 280, 353, 356, 379, 407, 430, 480, 514, 540, 561, 681, 716, 734, 774-5, 781
Kensington 24
Kensington Oval, Barbados 785
Kent CCC 17, 61, 84, 323, 513, 561, 608, 683
Kent, M.F. 574
Kentish, Esmond 570
Kenya 745, 756
Kerr, R.B. 656
Kew 48, 146
Kew CC (Melbourne) 146
Khan Mohammad 450
Khan, Imran 574, 631, 642, 667, 687, 704
Khan, Younis 771
Khettarama Stadium (Colombo) 707
Killara Golf Club (NSW) 413
Kimberley 362, 523
Kinara Academy Oval, Kuala Lumpur 781
King, Frank 52
King, Governor Philip Gidley 2
Kingsmead (Durban) 457, 656, 664, 722, 778
Kingston, Jamaica 758: Sabina Park 439, 499, 547, 604, 695, 726, 740
Kinloch, John 38
Kippax, A.F. 277, 289, 298, 307, 317, 320, 334, 337, 373, 408
Kirsten, Peter 662
Kitwe 456
Klemzig 22
Kline, L.F. 453, 456, 467, 474
Knight, Albert E. 209
Knopwood, Robert 18
Kolkata *see* Calcutta
Kooyong 560
Kowloon 673
Kruger, Paul 201
Kuala Lumpur 304, 317, 404, 737, 781
Kuitpo 332
Kumble, Anil 736, 762, 768, 788, 789
Kyneton 682

La Trobe, Charles 11
Lacey, Francis 216, 264
Lacy, Howard 269
Lahore 366, 389, 635, 667, 673: Gaddafi Stadium 465, 620, 724, 729
Laidler, Ernest 332
Laidley 50, 231
Laird, B. M. 560, 573, 617
Lake Oval (South Melbourne) 82

Laker, Jim 406, 431, 444, 461
Lambton 7
Lampard, Allie 268
Lancashire CCC 145, 198, 249, 269, 299, 323, 584, 603, 681, 688
Lance, Arthur 436, 461
Langdon, Wally 427, 535
Langer, J.L. 713, 714, 717, 720-1, 731, 733, 738, 743, 744, 749, 750, 753, 755, 757, 758, 759, 762, 765, 767, 768, 770, 773, 774, 775, 779, 780, 782, 787, 791
Langley, G.R.A. 430, 444
Lara, Brian 712, 726, 732, 740-1, 746, 758, 759, 771, 776
Largs Bay 192
Larwood, Harold 313, 327, 344, 348, 354, 470, 501
Laughlin, T.J. 589, 607
Launceston 8, 18, 32-69, 81, 87, 99, 132, 176, 197, 204, 238, 253, 283, 314, 323, 353, 373, 491, 497
Launceston CC (Tasmania) 20, 21, 33, 36, 42
Laver, F. 178, 198, 236, 241, 250-75
Law, Stuart 694, 699, 728, 766
Lawrence, Charles 6, 38, 40, 62, 70, 77, 107, 177, 266
Lawry, W.M. 479, 485, 493, 501, 504, 512, 521-5, 597, 649, 747
Lawson, G.F. 608, 622, 626, 632, 719
Lawson, Jermaine 759
Laxman, V.V.S. 744, 747, 761, 762, 768, 769, 789
Le Roux, Garth 600, 657
Leader, Charles 51
League of Victorian Cricketers 220
Leather, Tom 364
Ledward, Jack 413, 434, 440-67, 566
Ledwidge, Reg 551
Lee, Brett 744, 755, 757, 758, 759, 761, 762, 770, 772, 774, 775, 776, 777, 778, 780, 783, 784, 785, 788, 789, 789, 790, 791, 794
Lee, P.K. 352
Lee, Richard Egan 171
Lehmann, Darren 689, 710, 717-18, 720, 741, 746, 748, 752, 755, 758, 759, 760, 764-5, 769, 770, 777-8, 779, 791
Leicestershire CCC 376, 405, 429, 444, 494, 515, 519, 539, 682, 691, 705, 773
Levin, William 163
Levy, Roy 332
Lewis, Mick 766, 791
Leyland, Maurice 315, 355
Leyton 240
Library of 168, 711, 715
Liddicut, Arthur 277
Lill, John 676
Lillee, D.K. 524, 534, 537, 548, 561, 573, 602, 615, 621, 630, 643, 731, 749, 783
Lillywhite, James 51, 82, 88, 100, 107, 119, 135, 144, 150
Lillywhite, John 17
Lilydale 16
Lindsay, Denis 508
Lindwall, R.R. 397, 403, 408, 412, 419, 444, 462, 512
Lipscomb, Jack 196
Lismore 7, 491, 700
Little, Ray 551
Liverpool 63, 100, 223
Livingston, 'Jock' 400, 446
Llewellyn, Charles 213
Lloyd, Charles 196
Lloyd, Clive 516, 561, 564, 567, 592, 632, 654, 675, 759
Lock, Tony 430, 445, 461, 508, 518
Locker, Tom 544
Lohmann, George 144, 156, 170, 189
London 9, 15, 71, 124, 138, 168, 278: *see also* Kennington Oval; Lord's
Lonergan, Roy 413
Long, Edward 243
Lord's (Durban) 213
Lord's (London) 1, 78, 100-4, 143, 189, 199, 224, 255, 299, 377, 387, 405, 444, 514, 538, 561, 622, 627, 653, 680, 716, 718, 733, 741, 749, 774
Los Angeles 690, 742
Love, H.S.B. 364
Love, Martin 748, 751, 757, 760, 773, 779, 791
Lovekin, Jack, 149ò
Loxton, S.J.E. 404, 406, 427, 467, 524, 535, 582
Lucas, Alfred 118
Luckhurst, Brian 527, 529, 539
Luckin, Maurice 213
Lungley, Alex 47
Lusk, Harold 249
Luttrell, Bert 286, 311
Luxton, Mayor 318
Lyon, Allan 446
Lyons, J.J. 145, 151, 154, 170, 292
Lyons, Joseph 341
Lyttelton, Alfred 124

Macartney, C.G. 178, 230, 238, 255- 68, 289, 302, 364, 694
McAlister, P.A. 198, 219, 237-55, 275, 376
McAllen, Charles 162
McArthur, Donald 10, 47, 80
McAuliffe, Ron 646
McBride, Philip 424
McCabe, S.J. 320, 323, 334, 337, 349, 354, 374, 377, 422, 452, 515
McConnell, Peter 709
McCool, C.L. 397, 412, 427, 446
McCormick, E.L. 370, 372, 378, 477
McCosker, R.B. 558, 561, 562, 571
McCullum, Brendon 769, 784
McCurdy, Rod 651, 652, 662, 663
McDermott, C.J. 561, 669, 693, 709, 713, 715-16, 717, 718, 720, 725-6, 727, 731
McDermott, Peter 703
McDonald, Andrew 766
McDonald, C.C. 421, 426, 457, 464, 473
McDonald, Dr lan 464
McDonald, E.A. 474-7

McDonald, Ian 654, 714
MacDonald, Robert 187
McDonalds Cup 609, 615, 617
MacDonnell, Lady 24
McDonnell, P.S. 54, 117, 132, 144, 152, 187
McDowell, Robert 33
McElhone, William 202, 220-38, 245, 250-305, 318
McEvoy, Frederick 54
McEwan, Ken 626
McFarline, Peter 648
McGain, Bryce 791
MacGill, Stuart 735, 738, 739, 750, 757, 758, 759, 760, 764, 766, 768, 771, 773, 775, 779, 780, 787, 788
McGirr, Billy 163
McGlew, Jackie 424, 456, 722
McGrath, Glenn 718, 721, 726, 731, 733, 738, 740-1, 742, 744, 746, 749, 751, 753, 755, 757, 758, 759, 761, 767, 768, 770-71, 772, 774, 775, 776-7, 778, 781, 782, 783, 785, 786, 787
McGrath, Jane 778
McIlwraith, J. 141
McInnes, Mel 461, 462, 525, 551
McIntyre, Martin 82
McIntyre, Peter 730, 735
McKay, Harry 284
Mackay, James 225
Mackay, K.D. 443, 457, 465, 468, 474, 484
McKenzie, G.D. 476, 479, 493, 508, 519, 529, 540
McKibbin, T.R. 184, 189, 192
McKone, John 6, 34
MacLaren, Archie 184, 193, 204, 210, 215, 280, 285, 287, 461
McLaren, J.W. 735
McLaughin, John 205
McLean, Bob 409
Maclean, J.A. 540, 542, 600
McLean, Roy 427
McLennan, A.D. 186
McLeod, C.E. 184, 198, 224, 274
McLeod, R.W. 170, 184
McMahon, Norman 512, 582, 645
McMillan, Craig 769, 784
Macmillan, Ewart 438, 495, 503
McMillan, Quintin 335
McShane, George 54
McShane, P.G. 736
Macclesfield 23
Mackerdhuj, Krish 698
Macquarie University (NSW) 488, 596
Macquarie, Lachlan 2
Maddern, David 153, 173
Maddocks, L.V. 444, 468, 549, 560, 571, 577, 582, 594
Madras 366, 390, 451, 467, 521, 611, 659, 667, 684:
  Chidambaram Stadium 522, 611, 659, 684;
  Corporation Stadium 451, 496
Magill 22
Maguire, J.N. 642, 651, 662
Maher, Jimmy 755, 766, 779, 784, 791
Mailer, Ramsay 248, 298
Mailey, A.A. 261, 275, 299, 303, 337, 442, 559
Mair, Frederick 364
Maitland 6, 107, 249
Majid Khan 496, 631
Malaysia 781
Malcolm, Wesley 593
Malcolm, Devon 716
Malik, Salim 724, 727
Mallam, William 61, 63, 64
Mallett, A.A. 521, 528, 558, 565, 622
Mallett, Richard 339
Malone, M.F. 576, 584, 588, 594, 622
Manawatu 250
Manchester 133
  Old Trafford 133, 142, 166, 189, 211, 224, 255, 280, 300, 388, 430, 445, 479, 494, 538, 583, 680, 715, 717, 733, 774
Mandela Trophy 750
Manheim 259
Mankad, Vinoo 390, 401
Manly 71, 183, 710
Mann, A.L. 540, 588
Mann, George 413, 612
Manning, Jack 400, 446
Manohar, Vasha 790
Mansion House 118, 200
Mant, Gilbert 369
Manuka Oval (Canberra) 625
Marks, Alex 400
Marks, Lynn 498
Marlar, Robin 662
Marr, A.P. 736
Marrara Cricket Ground (Darwin) 759-60
Marrayatville 22
Marsden, Eric 229
Marsh, G.R. 656, 659-63, 682, 689, 694, 730, 740, 742
Marsh, Jack 207
Marsh, R.W. 527, 537, 571, 594, 643, 690, 723, 737, 783
Marsh, Shaun 794
Marshall, George 37, 39, 65, 66, 73
Marshall, Hamish 772
Marshall, Howard 355
Marshall, John 19, 20, 33, 36
Martin, Frank 330
Martin, J.W. 453, 476, 493, 509, 543
Martyn, D.R. 710, 717, 720, 721, 744, 746, 749, 751, 752, 756, 757, 758, 760, 764, 765, 767, 768, 769, 770, 771, 772, 773, 777, 778, 780, 782
Maryborough 73, 143, 225, 281, 284
Marylebone CC (London) 1, 17, 75-84, 101, 138, 160, 186, 202, 219-25, 239, 264, 279, 293, 311-19, 332, 339-49, 369-76, 394, 434-58, 477, 503, 524, 536, 597, 692, 699
Marylebone CC (Sydney) 5, 6
Massie, H.H. 6, 124, 133, 138
Massie, R.A.L. 535, 537
Masterton 412

Matthews, C.D. 737
Matthews, Greg 642, 646, 657, 660, 692, 708, 748
Matthews, T.J. 255, 256, 382
May, Peter 434, 444, 458-63, 638
May, T.B.A. 666, 712, 713, 716, 717-18, 719
Mayne, E.R. 259, 292, 296, 304
Mayne, L.C. 535
Meckiff, I. 452, 456, 460, 473, 486, 488
Melbourne 11, 14, 34, 39, 42, 67, 71-86, 114, 128, 135, 151, 159, 178, 183, 194, 204, 231, 245, 318, 447, 745, 746, 750, 753, 762, 764, 770, 770, 771, 776, 777, 782-3, 788
  Cricket Club 8-64, 71-82, 90, 107-16, 127-39, 146, 150-8, 176-227, 241-58, 278, 285, 303-18, 372-95, 452, 474, 481, 492, 576, 581, 646, 674
  Cricket Ground 34, 93, 120, 158, 268, 278, 359, 450, 534, 550, 558, 568, 668, 691, 701, 704, 719, 725, 727, 731, 735, 744, 755, 784
  Grammar School 234
  University 16, 188, 227, 596
Melder, Eddie 405
Melle, Michael 425
Mendis, R.E.S. 242
Menzies, Robert 382, 385, 419, 428, 441, 455, 487, 502, 556, 576, 691
Mercantile Mutual Cup 720, 727, 733, 748
Merchant, Vijay 390
Merewether, Edward 7
Merredin 284
Merri Creek soil 143, 183, 311
Merriman, Bob 610, 621, 632, 649, 659
Merry, Cyril 419
Meuleman, K.D. 408, 427, 535
Micevic, Zdavko 769
Middlesex CCC 61, 70, 84, 100, 115, 166, 363, 406, 515, 519, 563, 608
Middleton, Roy 352, 368, 428, 437, 440, 463, 502
Midwinter, W.E. 85, 93, 100, 120,130, 133, 718
Milburn, Colin 518
Mildura 284
Millard, Hugh 502
Miller, Allan 739
Miller, Colin 737, 739, 740, 746
Miller, K.R. 385-91, 393, 397-8, 406-7, 410-11, 413-15, 420-1, 425, 426, 429-30, 432, 435, 439-41, 443-6, 451
Minnett, R.B. 253, 263
Minor Counties 733
Mirza, Iskander 455
Misson, F.M. 474, 477
Mitcham 188
Mitchell, Bruce 337
Mitchell, Edward 228
Mittagong 357
Modi, Rusi 390
Mohammad, Mushtaq 574
Mohsin Khan 635
Moir, Albert 408
Moir, George 196, 203
Monte Carlo 278, 526
Montreal 105
Moody, Clarence 24, 65
Moody, Frederick 16
Moody, John 16
Moody, T.M. 666, 680, 699, 710
Moody, Thomas 60
Moonta 25
Moora 284
Moore, 'Jemmy' 28, 41, 42, 69
Morago 8
Moratuwa 707, 710:
  Tyronne Fernando Stadium 707
Moree 8
Moreton Bay 25, 27, 59
Morkel, Denys 335
Morley, Fred 102, 128, 135
Moroney, J. 408, 410, 427
Morpeth 6
Morphett Vale 22, 23
Morphy, Florence 131
Morris, A.R. 384, 396, 408, 414, 419, 430
Morris, S. 123, 157, 186
Morrisby, Ronald 364
Morrison, Danny 718
Mortlock, William 62
Moses, H. 6, 152, 170
Mosman CC (Sydney) 285
Moss Vale 309
Moss, J.K. 573, 607
Motibogh Palace 367
Moulden, Frank 274
Moule, W.H. 118
Mount Morgan 225
Movietone Films 396
Moyes, 'Johnnie' 190, 268, 285, 425, 459, 462
Muhali 729
Muldoon, Robert 625
Mullen, L.M. 346
Muller, Scott 743
Mullett, Leonard 287
Multan 620
Mumbai *see* Bombay
Mundine, Anthony 765
Mundy, Alfred 9
Mundy, C.F.N. 9
Munn, Darby 566
Munno Para 23
Muralitharan, Mutthiah 728, 740, 764, 765, 767, 788
Murdoch, W.L. 40, 91, 95, 110, 115, 117-24, 163-6, 199, 248, 249, 317
Murphy, Michael 47
Murray Districts 422
Murray, Deryck 564
Murray, John 563
Musgrove, H. 53, 54, 187
Mushtaq, Saqlain 741, 752
Mutare (Umtali) 699

Nafees, Shahriah 780
Nagel, L.E. 344, 364, 661
Nagpur 365, 768-9
Nakai, Sandeep 663

Namibia 757
Nanago 28
Napier 772
Naples 142, 375
Narayanganj Osmani Stadium, Fatullah 780
Narine, David 644
Nash, L.J. 738
National Press Club 593
National Stadium (Karachi) 450, 496, 620, 724, 737-8
Natwest Challenge 773
Natwest Series 773
Neath 653
Nehru Cup 685
Nehru, Jawaharlal 685
Nelson 307
Nerang 50
Netherlands Cricket Association 537
Netherlands, The 767
New Plymouth 510
New South Wales 36-48, 107-22, 140-69, 178, 190, 202, 220-5, 257, 272, 285, 381, 385, 481, 543, 583, 670, 672, 711, 719, 720, 723, 734, 748, 751, 756, 764, 773, 779, 784, 785, 791
  Cricketers Club 452, 652
  Cricketers Fund 301
New South Wales Intercolonial Committee 39
  Rugby League 210, 583, 646, 709
  Sports Broadcasting Association 409
New Wanderers (Jo'burg) 457, 508, 509, 657, 721, 732, 778
New York 256, 499, 690
New Zealand 181, 197, 276, 311, 351, 375, 380, 393, 400, 412, 415, 454, 469, 526, 554, 596, 633, 689, 714, 718-19, 720, 734-5, 736, 737, 741, 744-5, 750, 756, 757, 761, 762, 769-70, 772, 773, 776, 783, 784
New Zealand Broadcasting Corporation 551, 555
Newcastle 6, 7, 71, 285, 289, 371, 413, 491, 585
Newcastle District Cricket Association 543, 544
Newcombe, John 560
Newland, Philip 222, 223
Newlands (Cape Town) 212, 214, 270, 410, 508, 656, 722, 751
Nice 278
night cricket 727
Nissar, Mahomed 366
Nitschke, H.C. 352
Noble, M.A. 181, 198, 205, 218, 236, 239, 247, 250, 254, 266, 285, 293, 368, 382
Noblet, G. 410, 420
Noel, John 116
Noffke, Ashley 791, 794
Norfolk, Duke of 483, 487
Norgard, John 618
North Adelaide 22, 24, 45
North America Cup 689
North Melbourne CC 16, 196, 227, 275, 570
North 183
North CC 243, 249, 274
North Oval 183, 234, 419, 667, 670, 694
North, Frederick 169, 182, 190
Northam 30, 192, 284, 424
Northamptonshire CCC 323, 376, 626, 681, 715
Northern Tasmanian Cricket Association 245
Norton, Jack 452, 455, 456
Norwood 24, 45
Norwood CC (Adelaide) 24, 43, 90, 123, 160, 188
Nothling, O.E. 313
Nottinghamshire CCC 100, 106, 117, 176, 230, 255, 279, 299, 324, 356, 378, 388, 495, 622, 682
Nourse, 'Dave' 72, 247
Nourse, Dudley 361, 411, 490
Nowra 8
Ntini, Makhaya 776, 777, 778, 779
Nupen, Eiulf 281

O'Brien, L.P.J. 372
O'Brien, M.E. 40
O'Connell, Maurice 49, 190
O'Connell, Max 530, 542, 551, 615
O'Connor, J.D.A. 230, 238
O'Connor, Leo 320
O'Donnell, S.P. 651, 666
O'Keeffe, K.J. 524, 547, 573
O'Neill, Mark 658
O'Neill, N.C. 453, 458, 465, 473, 493, 501
O'Reilly, W.J. 289, 309, 354, 360, 384, 452, 671, 709, 715
O'Sullivan, David 551
Oates, T.W. 325
Oatlands 21, 37
Ogilvie, A.D. 573, 588, 589
Old Wanderers (Jo'burg) 212, 270, 361, 410
Oldfield, W.A.S. 269, 304, 307, 347, 354, 408
Oliver, Neville 686
Ollivier, A.M. 181
Olympic Games 262, 450, 512, 601
Ontario 338
Onyons, Basil 303
Oram, Jacob 769
Orange 285
Orange Free State 362
Orange Free State CA 362, 508
Oscroft, William 82, 88
Otago 55, 56, 163, 181, 188, 204, 223, 289, 307, 393, 412, 510, 524, 554
Ottawa 342
Oval *see* Kennington Oval
Owen-Smith, Michael 663
Oxenham, R. K. 307, 314, 364
Oxford 123
Oxford University CC 12, 17, 29, 50, 53, 123, 142, 224, 323, 376, 538
Oxlade, Aubrey 293, 305-53, 364, 368, 413, 419, 422, 435, 443
Packer, Frank 343
Packer, Kerry 572, 579, 584, 592, 595, 604, 612, 651, 665, 727
Padang, The 304
Paddington 197

Paddington CC (Sydney) 130, 197, 214
Pakistan 498, 520, 526, 619, 680, 724, 727-8, 729, 732, 737, 741, 742-3, 751-2, 757, 763, 767, 770-72, 785, 787, 792
Palairet, Richard 339
Palmer, G.E. 117, 137
Pan, Shambu 521
Panesar, Monty 782, 783
Panmure 284
Paramount Films 396
Pardon, Sydney 125, 143, 240
Paris 278
Parish, Robert 464, 469, 488, 499-515, 525, 528, 532-623, 654, 690
Park, R.L. 264, 268
Parker, 'Ace' 490
Parker, Sidney 149
Parker, William 49
Parkes 491
Parkes, Henry 107
Parr, George 61, 71, 72
Parramatta 3, 6, 151
Pascoe, L.S. 229, 248, 264, 266, 471, 583, 622
Pataudi, Nawab of (jnr) 496, 511
Pataudi, Nawab of (snr) 345, 363
Patel, Jasubhai 467
Paterson, Barry 679
Pathan, Irfan 788
Patiala 363, 366
Patiala, Maharjahiraj 363, 364
Patrick, Billy 296
Payne, John 25
Paynter, Eddie 347, 377
Pearce, Senator 270
Peate, Edmund 119, 120
Peebles, Ian 327
Pellew, C.E. 268
Penn, Frank 118
Penrith 5, 459
Pentelow, John 83
Pepper, Cec 386, 391, 393, 400
Pepsi Cup 737
Perren, Clinton 779
Perry, Cecil 42
Perth 29, 149, 182, 230, 283, 311, 316, 318, 323, 370, 391, 447, 472, 489, 675, 718, 725, 726, 728, 732, 734-5, 738, 743, 746, 750, 753, 755, 760, 782, 788, 789 *see also* WACA Ground
Perth CC 29, 30, 148
Peshawar 673, 737
Peterborough 274
Petherbridge, John 620
Pettiford, Jack 387, 400
Pettigrew, Alan 690
Pfeffer, Fred 157
Philadelphia 180, 256
Phillip, Arthur 1
Phillips, Jim 186, 193, 200
Phillips, Joseph 46
Phillips, Ray 748
Phillips, W.B. 633, 642, 644, 651
Phillips, W.N. 702, 714
Philpott, P.I. 501, 504, 626, 716-18
Pickering, John 45
Pietermaritzburg 270, 457
Pietersen, Kevin 774, 775 781, 782, 783
Pilling, Richard 119
Players Retirement Benefit Fund 549, 634, 636, 667
Plymouth 133, 142, 151
Poidevin, Leslie 205, 241, 263
Pointe-à-Pierre, Trinidad 643
Pollard, Jack 190, 433, 446, 460, 546, 646
Pollock, Graeme 489, 508, 523, 535, 656, 664
Pollock, Peter 489, 534
Pollock, Shaun 735, 777, 778
Pollock, William 369
Pollocks, A.T. 242
Pond, Christopher 60, 64, 66
Ponsford, W.H. 283, 286-9, 291, 295, 299- 300, 302, 307, 308, 313, 319, 322-3, 325-7, 329, 347, 348, 354-7, 504, 682
Ponting, Ricky 717, 728, 731, 734, 740, 742-4, 747, 751-2, 755, 757, 758. 759, 761, 762, 764-91 passim, 794
Pooley, Ted 89, 93
Poona 365, 521
Pope, R.J. 165
Port Adelaide 52, 135, 151, 168, 179, 184, 216, 247, 364
Port Augusta 274
Port Elizabeth 214, 410, 457, 507, 757, 778: *see also* St. George's Park
Port Melbourne 11, 63, 73
Port Moresby 385
Port Pirie 274
Porter, Graham 608
Portsmouth 1, 387
Portus, John 168, 172, 173, 179, 197, 305
Potchefstroom 757
Potter, Jack 486, 493, 496, 499, 666, 690
Powlett, Frederick 9, 10
Prahran CC (Melbourne) 464
Pretoria 213, 270, 662, 730
Price, Charles 387, 542
Prince Alfred College (Adelaide) 198
Prince, Ashwell 777
Princes Park, Carlton (Melbourne) 17
Procter, Mike 789
Professional Cricketers Association of Australia 594, 609, 610, 621
Prospect 24, 315
Proust, Jimmy 234
Prudential Trophy 540
Prue, Terry 709, 727
Publishing & Broadcasting Ltd 573, 598-625, 641
Pukekura Park, NZ 510
Pura (Milk) Cup 743, 745, 748, 751, 756, 760, 764, 765, 772, 779, 783, 785, 788, 791

Queen & Albert CA (Adelaide) 51, 52
Queen's Park Oval (Port-of-Spain) 440, 500, 548, 592, 604, 696, 726, 758

Queen's Park, St Georges 759
Queensland 42-56, 130, 143, 182, 195, 221, 232, 298, 311, 330, 473, 480, 498, 548, 572, 586, 723, 726-7, 733, 734, 741, 742, 745, 748, 751, 755, 765, 766, 772, 773, 779, 784, 785, 791
  Cricketers Club 571
  International Match Committee 49
  Rugby League 646
Quetta 465, 504, 673
Quick, Ian 468, 477
Quinlan, Laurie 249
Quinn, Neville 336
Quorn 274

Rabone, Geoff 434
Rackemann, C.G. 637, 642, 651, 727
Radford, Bob 566
Radio Pakistan 465
Rafique, Mohammad 780
Raith, Jacob 422
Rajkot 365
Rajputana CC (India) 363
Ramadhin, Sonny 418, 420
Ramblers Club, Bloemfontein 361
Ramchand, Gulabrai 451, 466
Ramdin, Dinesh 776
Ramprakash, Mark 749
Ranatunga, Arjuna 686, 728, 729
Randell, Alf 320, 394
Randell, Steve 686, 711, 721
Randwick 382
Randwick CC (Sydney) 385
Ranji Trophy 647, 673, 674
Ranjitsinhji, Kumar 189, 192, 209, 212, 324, 363
Ransford, V.S. 230, 238, 240, 251, 261, 263, 277, 303, 380, 452
Rawalpindi 466, 619, 634, 724, 737
Raymond Terrace 6
Read, Maurice 125, 180
Read, Walter 134
Recreation Ground (St John's) 592, 604, 697
Reddall, Thomas 2
Redfern 8
Redfern Oval (Sydney) 8, 214
Redpath, I.R. 486, 489, 493, 540, 558, 567, 609
Reedman, J.C. 159, 184
Reese, Dan 244, 260, 261
Reese, Tom 261
Reeves, Thomas 186
Reid, Alexander 61
Reid, B.A. 656, 661, 691, 701, 710
Reid, George 173
Reiffel, P.R. 694, 702, 716, 717, 745
Renmark 599
Renneberg, D.A. 514, 519, 524
Reuter 683
Rhodes, Jonty 777
Rhodes, Joseph 14
Rhodes, Wilfred 210, 218, 254, 274, 300
Rice, Clive 657, 662
Richards, Alan 551
Richards, Barry 523, 527, 600
Richards, David 566-7, 572, 577-8, 590-1, 607, 609, 620-1, 628, 634, 644-5, 672, 679, 685, 688, 689, 698, 716
Richards, Vivian 763
Richardson, A.J. 285, 299, 310, 408
Richardson, Richie 712, 726
Richardson, Tom 189
Richardson, V.Y. 277, 290, 307, 322, 327, 337, 351, 360, 369, 423, 486, 521
Richmond 7, 10, 48, 73, 183
Richmond CC (Melbourne) 10-17, 46-75, 94, 123, 149, 182-8, 421
Rickards, John 5
Ridings, Philip 420, 425, 535, 582, 614, 623-41, 658, 661, 674, 684, 690
Rigg, K.E. 329, 336, 351, 372, 380
Riley, Joseph 252, 287, 297
Ring, D.T. 412, 420, 425
Ringwood 16
Ritchie, G.M. 633, 642, 657
Rixon, S.J. 588, 652
Roberts, Ronald 495
Robertson, Allen 304, 343-8, 371, 376, 417, 435
Robertson, Austin 573, 575
Robertson, George 84, 86
Robertson, W.R. 741
Robinson, Augustus 47, 51, 175, 190
Robinson, R.D. 560, 573, 583, 609
Robinson, R.H. 370
Robinson, Ray 190, 276, 410, 462
Rock, Claude 162
Rockhampton 28, 50, 132, 225
Rogers, Chris 773-4, 785
Rolandson, M.G. 310
Roma 56
Rome 293, 450, 496
Ronchi, Luke 784
Roper, A.W. 'Mick' 387
Rorke, G.F. 460-7
Roseworthy Agricultural College 198
Ross, William 7
Row, Samuel 173
Rowan, Eric 411
Rowe, Harold 360, 371
Rudolph, Jacques 776
Rundle, Desmond 659, 679, 684
Rush, Harry 238, 311
Rush, Leo 443
Rushcutters Bay 183
Rushton, John 267
Russell, Alan 275
Russell, Robert 9, 10
Rutherford, J.W. 443
Ruthven le Hunte, George 229
Ryall, William 168
Ryan, Kevin 709
Ryder, J. 256, 268, 283, 298, 312-30, 364, 393, 404, 422, 425, 438, 477, 524

Saeed Ahmed 466
Saggers, R.A. 742

Saker, David 741
Sale 16, 284, 685
Salve, N.K.P. 666
Sami, Mohammad 770
Samuels, Robert 731, 732
San Francisco 157, 499, 537
Sang Hue, Douglas 593
Sangakkara, Kumar 788
Saravanamuttu Stadium (Colombo) 707, 752
Sarwan, Ramnaresh 759
Saunders, J.V. 208, 292
Saunders, Stuart 640
Sawle, Lawrie 645, 651, 657, 680, 684
Scandrett, James 22
Scarborough 117, 280, 379, 388, 515, 537
Scheult, Joe 329
Schroeder, William 235
Schwartz, Reggie 247
Scone 143
Scotland 733, 741
Scott, Andrew 47
Scott, H.J.H. 132, 141
Scott, Jack 260
Scott, James 4
Scotton, William 119, 120, 134, 146
Scotts Hotel (Melbourne) 202
Scrymgour, Bernard 286, 298, 344, 352
Scullin, James 341
Searcy, George 186
Secunderabad 366, 685
Seddon Park, Hamilton 784
Seddon, Dudley 438, 477, 512
Sehwag, Virender 762, 768, 769, 788, 789
Selby, John 89, 119, 120
Sellers, R.H.D. 491, 493
Selvey, Michael 682, 692
Serjeant, C.S. 582, 591
Shand, Jack 422
Sharjah 651, 664, 675, 685, 689, 720, 736, 737, 752
Sharp, James 234
Sharpe, Duncan 465, 504
Shaw, Alfred 89, 102, 119, 135, 144, 150
Sheahan, A.P. 507, 510, 521, 526
Sheehy, Thomas 76
Sheffield 211, 323, 387
Sheffield Park 133, 142, 180, 188
Sheffield Shield 21, 32, 47, 174, 268, 497, 518, 603, 718, 720, 723, 726-7, 729-30, 733, 737, 741, 742 *see also* Pura (Milk) Cup
Sheffield, Lord *see* Holroyd, Henry
Sheffield: Bramall Lane 211, 387, 406
Shelton, Harry 48
Shepherd, B.K. 481, 484
Sheppard, David 483
Sheridan, Ned 6, 107, 130, 186
Sheridan, Philip 183, 184, 191, 243
Sherwell, Percy 247, 248
Sherwin, Mordecai 144
Sherwood, David 495, 513
Shield, R.J. 345
Shiell, Alan 663
Shipperd, Greg 652, 663, 765
Shore Grammar School 234
Shrewsbury, Arthur 89, 119, 135, 144-50, 180, 430
Shute, Richard 196
Shuter, John 264
Siddons, Jamie 714, 717-18
Sidebottom, William 81, 162
Sievers, M.W. 360, 370, 372
Simmons, Jack 565
Simmons, Mick 327
Simpson, R.B. 453, 456-517, 565, 586-600, 660, 666, 680, 691, 705, 720, 721,723, 724, 730
Simpson, Reg 414
Sims, Arthur 260
Sinclair, Colin 245, 246
Sinclair, Jimmy 214
Sincock, D.J. 743
Singapore 304, 404, 465, 611, 647
Singer Cup 730
Singh, Harbhajan 747-8, 768, 789, 790
Sismey, Stan 387
Slagelse 683
Slater, K.N. 743
Slater, Michael 715, 716, 717, 719, 721, 724-5, 728, 739, 742, 744, 745, 748
Slater, Ross 369
Sleep, P.R. 608, 633, 655, 670
Slight, Alick 116
Slight, Billy 116, 186
Slight, J. 743
Small, Steve 694
Smith, C. Aubrey 150, 152, 338
Smith, Cammie 474
Smith, Clyde 469
Smith, Collie 440
Smith, D.B.M. 244, 256
Smith, Edwin 23, 87, 194, 234, 235
Smith, Frank Grey 127, 146, 183
Smith, George 77
Smith, Graeme 773, 778
Smith, J.A. 39
Smith, Michael 503, 701
Smith, Mike 734
Smith, S.B. 652, 657, 663
Smith, Sydney 250-305, 311, 348, 413, 506, 537
Smyth, G.B. 9, 10
Snedden, Martin 625, 689
Snow, John 529, 539
Sobers, Gary 473, 481, 491, 516, 534, 565
Solomon, Joey 473, 500
Solway, William 136
Somers, Lord 367, 371
Somerset CCC 224, 279, 378, 405, 513, 653, 680, 681, 773, 783
Sorell 20
South Africa 239, 241, 246, 270, 310, 334, 359, 424, 437, 470, 507, 523, 533, 640, 647, 719-20, 721-2, 724, 725, 730, 732, 735-6, 737, 741-2, 745, 750-1, 773, 776-7, 778-9, 785, 785
South Australia 43, 51, 88, 90, 97, 129, 153, 160, 179, 234, 250, 261, 273, 310, 332, 352,

392-408, 613, 649, 687, 726, 729-30, 743, 755, 765, 766, 779, 785
South Australian Allied Forces Executive 297
South Australian Cricket Club 23, 25, 44, 45, 52
South Brisbane 25, 28, 50, 263, 311
South Melbourne CC 10, 11, 14, 47, 54, 65, 80, 94, 100, 140, 203, 260, 435, 452, 486
Southampton 279, 395, 608, 622, 773
Southern Television 513
Southerton, James 82, 84, 89, 90
Southland 204, 227, 307
Southport 56, 491
Spalding, Albert 74, 157, 158
Sparks, Yorke 43, 44, 168, 173, 684
Spence, Peter 666, 690
Spiers, Felix 60, 64, 66
Spofforth, F.R. 6, 8, 74, 86, 91, 95, 100, 115, 117, 124, 144, 154, 189, 292
Sportsplan Marketing 590, 597, 602
Sri Lanka *see* Ceylon/Sri Lanka
Srinagar 611
St Davids 697
St George C.A. (Sydney) 247
St George CC (Bermuda) 697
St George CC (Sydney) 323, 348
St George's Park (Port Elizabeth) 214, 412, 509, 664, 732, 757
St John, Justice 618
St John's *see* Recreation Ground
St Kilda 10, 15, 48, 73, 765
St Kilda CC (Melbourne) 10-15, 64, 112, 188, 196, 286
St Marks Church, Darling Point 239
St Peters College (Adelaide) 24, 243, 350
Stackpole, K.R. 508, 527, 538, 550
Stanford, Ross 387, 391
Staples, Peter 709
Starr, Cecil 370
Stawell 86
Steel, Allan (A.G.) 130, 133
Steele, Raymond 477, 494, 506, 518, 525, 536, 564, 571, 580, 585, 595, 602, 609, 641, 654, 674
Steele, Tommy 563
Stephen, Elmslie 15
Stephen, Francis 5
Stephens, George 15, 17
Stephens, Richard 298
Stephenson, Heathfield 38, 40, 61, 66, 259
Stephenson, John 699
Stevens, G.B. 464, 467
Stewart, Alec 738, 748
Still, Robert 5
Still, William 6
Stoddart, Andrew 166, 171, 173, 180, 183, 191
Stolmeyer, Jeff 418, 421, 592
Stonehaven, Lord 341
Strathalbyn 23
Strauss, Andrew 775
Streak, Heath 760, 767
Sturt CC (Adelaide) 435
Subba Row, Raman 459, 478, 711
Subiaco-Leederville CC (Perth) 284
Suez 119, 128
Sullivan, Jane 646
Super Six contest 757
Surrey CCC 61, 70, 100, 105, 117, 155, 242, 269, 323, 355, 359, 376, 388, 405, 444, 622
Sussex CCC 61, 117, 166, 199, 211, 224, 299, 357, 388, 405, 513
Sutcliffe, Bert 434
Sutcliffe, Herbert 291, 314, 326, 345
Sutherland, James 778
Suva 223, 404, 468
Swan Hill 284
Sydney 1, 3, 8, 15, 34-9, 67, 78, 86, 106, 114, 123, 136, 138, 151, 163, 178, 183, 204, 224, 249, 309, 325, 472, 760, 762, 764, 770, 771, 777, 783, 784, 788, 789
  Choral Society 239
  Cricket Ground 2, 107, 119, 145, 153, 183, 195, 250, 276, 309, 395, 561, 583, 599, 602, 668, 670, 688, 692, 719, 725, 728, 731, 735, 744, 746, 756
  Grammar School 234
  Reform Group 672
  University 9, 38, 115, 183, 221
  University Sports Union 297
Symcox, Pat 735
Symonds, Andrew 755, 757, 764, 776, 777, 783, 785, 787, 789, 790, 792

Tabart, John 37
Tabart, Tom 33
Taber, H.B. 743
Taberer, Henry 213
Tait, Shaun 766, 773, 775, 779, 785, 786, 787
Tallangatta 284
Tallon, D. 382, 398, 408, 412
Tamil Nadu CA (India) 673, 684
Tamworth 8, 285
Tancred, Louis 213
Taranaki 307
Tarcoola 274
Taree 543
Tarrant, George 72, 74
Tarrent, Frank 363, 367
Tasmania 755, 766, 772, 773, 785, 791
Tasmanian Cricket Association 42, 76, 153, 245, 321, 395, 699, 720, 737
Tasmanian Cricket Council 497
Tate, Maurice 291, 324
Tate, Michael 708
Taunton 378, 773
Tayfield, Hugh 424, 426, 457, 637
Taylor, J.M. 268, 382, 442
Taylor, Lynton 608, 612, 619, 625, 645, 712
Taylor, M.A. 676, 682, 691, 699, 710, 715, 716, 717, 718-19, 721-2, 724-39, 740, 765
Taylor, Michael 652, 656
Taylor, P.L. 666, 689, 756
Taylor, Ross 784
Teece, Richard 83, 173
Telstra Dome, Melbourne 777

Tendulkar, Sachin 701, 736, 737, 744, 747, 762, 766, 769, 788, 789
Tennent, John 54
Tennyson, Lionel 280
Terry, Ben 51
Tesland County Cricket Board 537, 577, 579, 612, 622
Texaco Trophy 715, 733
The Hague 496, 537, 683
Thebarton 22
Thicknesse, John 718
Thomas, G. 505
Thomas, James 342
Thompson, Cecil 331
Thoms, G.R. 421, 427
Thomson, A.L. 523, 524, 527
Thomson, J.R. 546, 557, 573, 588, 591, 602, 622, 638, 651, 655
Thomson, N. 6, 8, 39, 41, 42, 76, 83, 93, 111
Thornton, C.I. 127, 280
Thorpe, Graham 716, 733, 734
throwing controversy 728, 729, 740
Thurlow, H.M. 320
Tilbury 151, 184, 230, 357, 405, 478
Timaru 56
Tindall, Sidney 249
Titan Cup 730
Titmus, Fred 493, 558
Titus, Ray 644
Tobin, Bert 352
Toodyay 30
Tooher, Jack 182, 186
Toohey, P.M. 588, 593
Toombul 56
Toone, Frederick 274, 291-5, 311
Toorak 73, 318
Toowoomba 25, 41, 50, 56, 247, 289, 491
Toronto 561
Toshack, E.R.H 397, 401, 406
Townsville 225
Tozer, Claude 234
Trade Practices Commission 606, 613
Trans-Tasman Trophy 656, 658, 719, 735, 750
Transvaal Cricket Union 214, 247, 270, 281, 411, 456, 457, 508
Travers, J.P.F. 352
Trent Bridge 66, 100, 199, 224, 255, 279, 299, 307, 324, 355, 377, 430, 493, 539, 584, 627, 680, 716, 734, 749, 774
Tressider, Phil 469, 553
Tretheway, Peter 464
Trezise, Neil 705
Tribe, G.E. 393, 396, 400, 427, 446
Trim, John 420
Trimble, Sam 491, 501, 513, 524, 527
Trinidad 726, 740, 758
Trott, A.E. 178, 184, 198, 266
Trott, G.H.S. 154, 162, 166, 187, 189, 238, 260, 266, 435
Truman, Les 413, 513
Trumble, H. 159, 164, 184, 189, 196, 198-206, 219, 249, 303, 380
Trumble, J.W. 141
Trumble, John 576
Trumper, V.T. 143, 178, 197-201, 205, 209-14, 219, 223, 225-6, 231-2, 235, 247-8, 251-8, 266, 710
Tufnell, Phil 716
Tunks, William 6, 34, 35, 38
Turner, A. 524, 561, 569, 574
Turner, C.T.B. 144, 152, 154, 185, 243, 382, 392
Turner, Glenn 554
Turner, J. Neville 766
Turramurra 114
Tusnami Appeal Match 771
TV & radio stations:
2FC (Sydney) 210
2GB (Sydney) 472
2UE (Sydney) 351, 472
2UW (Sydney) 472
3AR (Melbourne) 288, 291, 292
3LO (Melbourne) 292
3XY (Melbourne) 526
41P (Ipswich) 570
6PM (Perth) 612
Channel 9 448, 572, 598, 599, 601, 605, 606, 615, 618, 627, 631, 675, 676, 688, 696, 702, 725, 729, 734, 743, 765
GTV9 (Melbourne) 464, 581
TVW6 (Perth) 525
TVS Cup 761
Tweeds Heads 501
Twentieth Century Fox Films 396
Twenty20 international 771, 772, 773, 777, 778, 787, 788
Twenty20 World Cup 787
Twopenny, Robert 119
Tyler, Edward 301
Tyson, Frank 434, 574

Ulyett, George 89, 92, 107, 119, 120
Umrigar, 'Polly' 451
Underwood, Derek 514, 539
United States Cricket Control Board 563
University of New South Wales 706
Unley 486
Unley Oval (Adelaide) 215
Upper North 422
USA, matches in 690, 742, 767

Valentine, Alf 418, 420, 474
van Ryneveld, Clive 456
Vanthoff, Bill 417
Vaughan, Michael 752, 753, 781
Vautin, George 162
VB Series 750, 753, 755, 764, 771, 777, 783
Vehicle & General Insurance Co. 518, 524, 526
Veivers, T.R. 493, 566
Veletta, M.R.L 471, 664, 666, 681, 689
Venkataraghavan, Srinivas 521
Verity, Hedley 345, 355
Vernon, George 150
Verwoerdburg 662
Vettori, Daniel 735, 744-5, 770

Victor Trumper Trust 506
Victoria 17, 40, 47, 94, 115, 127, 136-46, 153-60, 179, 196, 207, 220, 232, 254, 266, 284, 340, 343, 368, 374, 395, 477, 486, 501, 506, 566, 576, 607, 650, 699, 711, 719, 728, 734, 745, 748, 755, 765, 766, 779, 791
Victoria Park, St Lucia 592
Victorian Arts Centre 675
Victorian Intercolonial Match Committee 39
Videocon Cup 767
Viljoen, Ken 336, 424
Vincent, Arthur 400
Vincent, Cyril 335
Vincent, Lou 784
Viswanath, Gundappa 521
Vizianagram, Maharajkumar 363, 366
Voce, Bill 356, 370
von Bibra, B. 29
von Mueller, Baron 44, 82
Vorster, John 514

W.D. & H.O. Wills 516, 552
WACA Ground (Perth) 182, 558, 668, 693, 733, 770, 776
Waddy, Edgar 261, 380
Waddy, Ernest 259
Wade, Henry 20
Wade, Herbert 361
Wagga 285, 345
Waine, Jack 191
Wairarapa 412
Waite, M.G. 378
Walcott, Keith 418, 564, 570
Walker, Alan 410, 427
Walker, Isaac 107
Walker, M.H.N. 546, 584
Walker, William 52, 53
Walkerville 22
Wall, T.W. 315, 349, 354
Wallace, LT. 186
Wallaroo 25
Wallsend 7, 543
Wallsend CC (Newcastle) 543, 544
Walsh, Alan 596, 598
Walsh, Courtney 726, 730, 740-1, 758
Walsh, Jack 446
Walters, F.H. 164
Walters, K.D. 498, 504, 517, 527, 558, 574, 624
Wanganui 203, 250, 307
Wangaratta 16
Wankhede Stadium (Bombay) 619, 769
Ward, Captain 38
Ward, F.A. 332, 360, 369
Ward, Tom 271
Wardill, Ben 82, 128, 141, 167-230
Wardill, Richard 40, 65, 80, 81
Warne, Brigitte 756
Warne, Shane 699, 701, 707, 710, 714-22, 724-6, 727-8, 731, 733-4, 735, 736, 738, 739, 740, 742, 743, 744, 747, 749, 750-3, 755-6, 758, 761, 763, 764, 765, 768, 769, 770, 771, 772, 774, 775, 776, 777, 778, 780, 781, 782, 783, 787
Warne-Muralitharan Trophy 787-8
Warner, Pelham 214, 252, 254, 339-52, 385
Warracknabeal 284
Warrandyte 16
Warrnambool 16, 86, 93, 491
Warry, C.S. 27
Warwick 28, 48, 50
Warwick CC (Sydney) 40, 71, 76, 123
Warwickshire CCC 378, 494, 503, 513,680
Washbrook, Cyril 388, 406, 414, 445
Watkin, Steve, 716
Watkins, J.R. 746
Watson, G.D. 537, 542
Watson, Shane 779, 785, 786
Watson, W.J. 453
Waugh, M.E. 683, 688, 692, 694, 710, 714, 716-17, 719, 722, 725-6, 728, 729, 731, 734, 735, 736, 738, 740, 742, 746, 749, 752, 763, 773, 780
Waugh, S.R. 655, 666, 692, 694, 710, 716-17, 719-22, 726, 729, 732, 733, 734, 735, 737, 740-1, 742, 744, 745, 747, 749, 750-1, 753, 756–63 passim, 764, 766, 773, 780
Waverley 585, 600
Waverley CC (Sydney) 197, 285, 289, 300, 564
Wazir Ali 366
Wazir Mohammad 451
Webb, Sydney 305, 443, 477, 488, 501, 506, 515, 536
Wellham, D.M. 626, 628, 640, 663, 714
Wellington 163, 181, 188, 191, 197, 204, 223, 244, 277, 287, 296, 307, 393, 510, 714, 744, 772, 776, 784 *see also* Basin Reserve
Wells, Billy 400
Wells, George 61, 62
Wentworth 8
Wentworth Park 183
Weser, Don 615
Wesley College (Melbourne) 222, 234
Wessels, K.C. 610, 636, 640, 661, 719, 721-2
West Indies 311, 328, 400, 417, 492, 501, 564, 592, 725-7, 729, 730-2, 740-1, 745-6, 757, 758-9, 763, 771, 773, 775-6, 781, 785
West Lakes 585
Westbrook, Thomas 68
Western Australia 148, 170, 176, 182, 197, 208, 245, 261, 283, 310, 319, 322, 344, 394, 408, 502, 513, 527, 612, 657, 718, 720, 727, 729-30, 733, 737, 741, 748, 755, 756, 766, 784, 785, 791
Western Ontario CC (Canada) 338
Western Suburbs CC (Sydney) 328, 586
Westpac Stadium, Wellington 776
Whatmore, D.F. 607
Whinham College (Adelaide) 24
White, Cameron 766
White, Craig 768
White, Philip 695
Whitehead, Rex 624
Whitesides, Thomas 42, 69
Whitfield, Harry 303
Whitington, Richard 360, 387, 389, 401, 424

Whitlam, Gough 548, 556, 568, 618
Whitney, M.R. 626, 670, 677, 702
Whitridge, William 45, 51, 160, 163, 173, 187, 202
Whitty, W.J. 238, 244
Whyalla 491
Wickham 7
Wiener, J.M. 471, 622
Wilkie, Daniel 47, 48, 51, 81
Williams, Brad 760, 761, 766
Williams, Graham 387
Williams, Justice 139
Williams, Justice Glen 756
Williams, Norm 303
Williams, Owen 47
Williams, Stan 426
Williamson, J.C 225
Williamstown 10, 16, 48, 73, 227
Willis, Bob 529, 558, 638
Wills Cup 724
Wills, Horace 59
Wills, Tom 7, 17, 35-9, 59, 71-87, 107
Willunga 22
Wilson, J.W. 444
Wilson, Rockley 274
Wimmera 289
Windsor, Edward 162
Wingello 309
Winnipeg 256
Winsor, William 340
Wise, Brenton 766
Wonthaggi 284
Wood, G.M. 588, 601, 608, 622, 651, 674
Wood, Reg 145
Woodcock, A.J. 748
Woodcock, John 663, 705
Woodford, Bert 238
Woodfull, W.M. 283, 296, 299, 300, 302, 304, 307-8, 312-13, 322, 325, 327, 335-6, 344-8, 353-7, 358, 435, 501
Woods, S.M.J. 154
Woodville 23
Woolcott, W.S. 14
Woolley, Frank 253, 287
Woolley, R. D. 632, 639, 646
Woolloongabba ('Gabba', Brisbane) 311, 335, 370, 395, 414, 473, 686, 691, 701, 722, 730-1, 755, 769, 773, 775-6, 781, 787
Woolmer, Bob 785
Wootton, Roger 575
Worcestershire CCC 269, 323, 354, 376, 405, 429, 444, 478, 513, 677, 680
Workman, Jim 387, 388
World Championship of Cricket 650
World Cup 729, 741-2, 745, 755-7, 781, 785-6
World Series Cricket 573, 587, 598, 606, 617, 720, 729, 732, 747
Worrall, J. 154, 188, 196, 202, 345
Worrell, Frank 419, 472, 474
Worrell, Tom 590, 602
Wran, Neville 583
Wright, Albert 336
Wright, Damien 785
Wright, Doug 399, 406
Wright, John 669, 685, 689
Wright, K.J. 608
Wyatt, Bob 326, 344, 355, 500
Wylie, Russell 714

Yallop, G.N. 588, 591, 600, 607, 640, 642, 647, 652
Yardley, B. 588, 593, 608, 632
Yardley, Norman 405, 413
Yass 8
Yeomans, Eric 409
York 30
Yorke Peninsula 22, 25, 87
Yorke Peninsula CA 87
Yorkshire CCC 61, 105, 116, 166, 210, 274, 291, 323, 356, 387, 406
Youhana, Yousuf 771
Young & Jackson's Hotel 191, 196, 228
Young 285
Young, John 68
Young, Peter 767
Youth World Cup 599

Zaheer Abbas 535, 574, 642
Zesers, Andrew 471, 666
Zimbabwe 725, 736, 742, 746, 756, 760-61, 764, 766–7, 780, 787
Zoehrer, T.J. 471, 662, 717
Zulch, Billy 270, 271
Zululand 410